MARKETING
Thirteenth Edition

Roger A. Kerin
Southern Methodist University

Steven W. Hartley
University of Denver

MARKETING, THIRTEENTH EDITION

Published by McGraw-Hill Education, 2 Penn Plaza, New York, NY 10121. Copyright © 2017 by McGraw-Hill Education. All rights reserved. Printed in the United States of America. Previous editions © 2015, 2013, 2011, and 2009. No part of this publication may be reproduced or distributed in any form or by any means, or stored in a database or retrieval system, without the prior written consent of McGraw-Hill Education, including, but not limited to, in any network or other electronic storage or transmission, or broadcast for distance learning.

Some ancillaries, including electronic and print components, may not be available to customers outside the United States.

This book is printed on acid-free paper.

1 2 3 4 5 6 7 8 9 0 DOW/DOW 1 0 9 8 7 6

ISBN 978-1-259-57-3545
MHID 1-259-57-3540

Senior Vice President, Products & Markets: *Kurt L. Strand*
Vice President, General Manager, Products & Markets: *Michael Ryan*
Vice President, Content Design & Delivery: *Kimberly Meriwether David*
Managing Director: *Susan Gouijnstook*
Brand Manager: *Kim Leistner*
Director, Product Development: *Meghan Campbell*
Lead Product Developer: *Kelly Delso*
Product Developer: *Kelly Pekelder*
Marketing Manager: *Elizabeth Schonagen*
Director, Content Design & Delivery: *Terri Schiesl*
Program Manager: *Mary Conzachi*
Content Project Managers: *Christine Vaughan; Danielle Clement*
Buyer: *Susan K. Culbertson*
Design: *Matt Diamond*
Cover Image: *Francisco Diez Photography/Getty Images*
Content Licensing Specialists: *Michelle D. Whitaker; DeAnna Dausener*
Compositor: *Aptara®, Inc.*
Typeface: *10.5/12 STIXMathJax_Main*
Printer: *R.R. Donnelley*

All credits appearing on page or at the end of the book are considered to be an extension of the copyright page.

Library of Congress Cataloging-in-Publication Data

Names: Kerin, Roger A., author. | Hartley, Steven William, author.
Title: Marketing / Roger A. Kerin, Southern Methodist University,
    Steven W. Hartley, University of Denver.
Description: 13th edition. | New York, NY : McGraw-Hill Education, [2017]
Identifiers: LCCN 2015046552 | ISBN 9781259573545 (alk. paper)
Subjects: LCSH: Marketing.
Classification: LCC HF5415 .M29474 2017 | DDC 658.8—dc23 LC record available at
http://lccn.loc.gov/2015046552

The Internet addresses listed in the text were accurate at the time of publication.
The inclusion of a website does not indicate an endorsement by the authors or McGraw-Hill Education, and
McGraw-Hill Education does not guarantee the accuracy of the information presented at these sites.

WELCOME FROM THE AUTHORS!

Do words and phrases such as *social, mobile, digital, viral, gamification, big data, binge-watching, Internet of Things, wearable technology, brand storytelling, customer-centricity, value proposition, native advertising,* or *sustainability* sound familiar or interesting to you? If they do, you already have a great start to learning about some of the newest topics in the business world. These topics are just of few of the many new and emerging concepts and tools you'll learn about during the next several months as you undertake your study of marketing. It is our pleasure to provide a textbook to facilitate your introduction to this exciting discipline!

While this may be your first formal introduction to studying marketing we know you have important exposure to the world of marketing as a consumer, a volunteer, or possibly as an employee in a business. All of these experiences provide important perspectives on the role of marketing in our local, national, and global economies. We encourage you to use your past activities as reference points and build on your existing understanding of our marketplace and marketing practices. In addition, we hope that you will think about your future career aspirations as you navigate the many new marketing topics you will encounter.

The new aspects of marketing make this edition of our book particularly exciting. We believe our past experiences writing this book have given us many insights into the content, writing style, examples, exercises, and supporting materials that lead to effective learning. As the dramatic changes related to consumer values, global competition, digital technology, and regulation have taken place, we have integrated the new perspectives to give you the most up-to-date skills you will need as a marketing professional. Our approach to presenting the complexities of marketing is based on three important dimensions:

- **Engagement.** As professors we have benefited from interactions with many exceptional students, managers, and instructors. Their insights have contributed to our approach to teaching and learning and, subsequently, to our efforts as textbook authors. One of the essential elements of our approach is a commitment to active learning through engaging, integrated, and timely materials. In-class activities, an interactive blog, Building Your Marketing Plan exercises, and in-text links to online ads and web pages are just a few examples of the components of our engagement model.
- **Leadership.** Our approach is also based on a commitment to taking a leadership role in the development and presentation of new ideas, principles, theories, and practices in marketing. This is more important now than ever before, as the pace of change in our discipline accelerates and influences almost every aspect of traditional marketing. We are certain that exposure to leading-edge material related to topics such as ethics, social media, data analytics, and marketing metrics can help students become leaders in their jobs and careers.
- **Innovation.** New educational technologies and innovative teaching tools have magnified the engagement and leadership aspects of our approach. *Connect, LearnSmart,* and *SmartBook,* for example, provide a digital and interactive platform that embraces the "anytime and anywhere" styles of today's students. In addition, we have provided new videos and increased the visual impact of the text and PowerPoint materials to facilitate multimedia approaches to learning.

Through the previous 12 U.S. editions, and 19 international editions in 11 languages, we have been gratified by the enthusiastic feedback we have received from students and instructors. We are very excited to have this opportunity to share our passion for this exciting discipline with you today. Welcome to the 13th edition of *Marketing*!

Roger A. Kerin
Steven W. Hartley

PREFACE

Marketing utilizes a unique, innovative, and effective pedagogical approach developed by the authors through the integration of their combined classroom, college, and university experiences. The elements of this approach have been the foundation for each edition of *Marketing* and serve as the core of the text and its supplements as they evolve and adapt to changes in student learning styles, the growth of the marketing discipline, and the development of new instructional technologies. The distinctive features of the approach are illustrated below:

High-Engagement Style
Easy-to-read, high-involvement, interactive writing style that engages students through active learning techniques.

Rigorous Framework
A pedagogy based on the use of learning objectives, learning reviews, learning objectives reviews, and supportive student supplements.

Personalized Marketing
A vivid and accurate description of businesses, marketing professionals, and entrepreneurs—through cases, exercises, and testimonials—that allows students to personalize marketing and identify possible career interests.

Marketing, 13/e
Pedagogical Approach

Traditional and Contemporary Coverage
Comprehensive and integrated coverage of traditional and contemporary marketing concepts.

Integrated Technology
The use of powerful technical resources and learning solutions, such as Connect, LearnSmart, SmartBook, www.kerinmarketing.com, and in-text video links.

Marketing Decision Making
The use of extended examples, cases, and videos involving people making marketing decisions.

The goal of the 13th edition of *Marketing* is to create an exceptional experience for today's students and instructors of marketing. The development of *Marketing* was based on a rigorous process of assessment, and the outcome of the process is a text and package of learning tools that are based on *engagement, leadership,* and *innovation* in marketing education.

ENGAGEMENT

The members of this author team have benefited from extraordinary experiences as instructors, researchers, and consultants, as well as the feedback of users of previous editions of *Marketing*—now more than one million students! The authors believe that success in marketing education in the future will require the highest levels of engagement. They ensure engagement by facilitating interaction between students and four learning partners—the instructor, other students, businesses, and the publisher. Some examples of high-engagement elements of *Marketing* include:

In-Class Activities.   These activities are designed to engage students in discussions with the instructor and among themselves. They involve surveys, online resources, out-of-class assignments, and personal observations. Each activity illustrates a concept from the textbook and can be done individually or as a team. Examples include: Designing a Candy Bar, Marketing Yourself, Pepsi vs. Coke Taste Test, and What Makes a Memorable TV Commercial?

Interactive Web Page and Blog (www.kerinmarketing.com).   Students can access recent articles about marketing and post comments for other students. The site also provides access to a *Marketing* Twitter feed!

Building Your Marketing Plan.   The Building Your Marketing Plan guides at the end of each chapter are based on the format of the Marketing Plan presented in Appendix A. On the basis of self-study or as part of a course assignment, students can use the activities to organize interactions with businesses to build a marketing plan. Students and employers often suggest that a well-written plan in a student's portfolio is an asset in today's competitive job market.

LEADERSHIP

The popularity of *Marketing* in the United States and around the globe is the result, in part, of the leadership role of the authors in developing and presenting new marketing content and pedagogies. For example, *Marketing* was the first text to integrate ethics, technology, and interactive marketing. It was also the first text to develop custom-made videos to help illustrate marketing principles and practices and bring them to life for students as they read the text. The authors have also been leaders in developing new learning tools such as a three-step learning process that includes learning objectives, learning reviews, and learning objectives reviews; and new testing materials that are based on Bloom's learning taxonomy. Other elements that show how *Marketing* is a leader in the discipline include:

Chapter 19: Using Social Media and Mobile Marketing to Connect with Consumers. *Marketing* features a dedicated chapter for social media and mobile marketing. This new environment is rapidly changing and constantly growing. The authors cover the building blocks of social media and mobile marketing and provide thorough, relevant content and examples. The authors discuss major social media platforms like Twitter, Facebook, LinkedIn, and YouTube. They explain how managers and companies can use those outlets for marketing purposes. Also discussed in Chapter 19 are methods of measuring a company's success with social media and mobile marketing. This chapter is one of many ways *Marketing* is on the cutting edge of the field.

Applying Marketing Metrics. The *Applying Marketing Metrics* feature in the text delivers two of the newest elements of the business and marketing environment today—performance metrics and dashboards to visualize them. Some of the metrics included in the text are: Category Development Index (CDI), Brand Development Index (BDI), Load Factor (a capacity management metric), Price Premium, Sales per Square Foot, Same-Store Sales Growth, Promotion-to-Sales Ratio, and Cost per Thousand (CPM) impressions. The feature is designed to allow readers to learn, practice, and apply marketing metrics.

Color-Coded Graphs and Tables. The use of color in the graphs and tables enhances their readability and adds a visual level of learning to the textbook for readers. In addition, these color highlights increase student comprehension by linking the text discussion to colored elements in the graphs and tables.

New Video Cases. Each chapter ends with a case that is supported by a video to illustrate the issues in the chapter. New cases such as Amazon, Mall of America, and Taco Bell, and recent cases such as Chobani Greek Yogurt, X-1 Audio, Secret Deodorant, LA Galaxy, Carmex lip balm, and StuffDOT provide current and relevant examples that are familiar to students.

INNOVATION

In today's fast-paced and demanding educational environment, innovation is essential to effective learning. To maintain *Marketing*'s leadership position in the marketplace, the author team consistently creates innovative pedagogical tools that match contemporary students' learning styles and interests. The authors keep their fingers on the pulse of technology to bring real innovation to their text and package. Innovations such as in-text links, a Twitter feed, hyperlinked PowerPoint slides, and an online blog augment the McGraw-Hill Education online innovations such as Connect, LearnSmart, and SmartBook.

In-text Links.   You can see Internet links in magazine ads; on television programming; as part of catalogs, in-store displays, and product packaging; and throughout *Marketing,* 13/e! These links bring the text to life with ads and videos about products and companies that are discussed in the text. These videos also keep the text even more current. While each link in the text has a caption, the links are updated to reflect new campaigns and market changes. In addition, the links allow readers to stream the video cases at the end of each chapter. You can simply click on the links in the digital book or use your smartphone or computer to follow the links.

Twitter Feed and Online Blog.   Visit www.kerinmarketing.com to participate in *Marketing*'s online blog discussion and to see Twitter feed updates. You can also subscribe to the Twitter feed to receive the Marketing Question of the Day and respond with the #QotD hashtag.

Connect, LearnSmart, and SmartBook Integration.   These McGraw-Hill Education products provide a comprehensive package of online resources to enable students to learn faster, study more efficiently, and increase knowledge retention. The products represent the gold standard in online, interactive, and adaptive learning tools and have received accolades from industry experts for their Library and Study Center elements, filtering and reporting functions, and immediate student feedback capabilities. In addition, the authors have developed book-specific interactive assignments, including (a) auto-graded applications based on the marketing plan exercises, and (b) activities based on the Applying Marketing Metrics box and marketing metrics presented in the text.

Innovative Test Bank.   Containing almost 7,000 multiple-choice and essay questions, the *Marketing,* 13/e Test Bank reflects more than two decades of innovations. The Test Bank includes two Test Item Tables for each chapter that organize all the chapter's test items by Bloom's three levels of learning against both (1) the main sections in the chapter, and (2) the chapter's learning objectives. In addition, a number of "visual test questions" for each chapter reward students who have spent the effort to understand key graphs, tables, and images in the chapter.

Required=Results

McGraw-Hill Connect®
Learn Without Limits

Connect is a teaching and learning platform that is proven to deliver better results for students and instructors.

Connect empowers students by continually adapting to deliver precisely what they need, when they need it, and how they need it, so your class time is more engaging and effective.

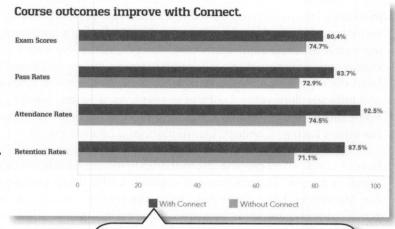

Course outcomes improve with Connect.

	With Connect	Without Connect
Exam Scores	80.4%	74.7%
Pass Rates	83.7%	72.9%
Attendance Rates	92.5%	74.5%
Retention Rates	87.5%	71.1%

Using **Connect** improves passing rates by **10.8%** and retention by **16.4%**.

88% of instructors who use **Connect** require it; instructor satisfaction **increases** by 38% when **Connect** is required.

Analytics

Connect helps students achieve better grades

| With Connect | A 36% | B 29.5% | C 22% | D 4.3% | F 8.2% |
| Without Connect | A 22.2% | B 22.3% | C 25.6% | D 9.8% | F 20% |

Based on McGraw-Hill Education Connect Effectiveness Study 2013

Connect Insight®

Connect Insight is Connect's new one-of-a-kind visual analytics dashboard—now available for both instructors and students—that provides at-a-glance information regarding student performance, which is immediately actionable. By presenting assignment, assessment, and topical performance results together with a time metric that is easily visible for aggregate or individual results, Connect Insight gives the user the ability to take a just-in-time approach to teaching and learning, which was never before available. Connect Insight presents data that empowers students and helps instructors improve class performance in a way that is efficient and effective.

Students can view their results for any **Connect** course.

Mobile

Connect's new, intuitive mobile interface gives students and instructors flexible and convenient, anytime–anywhere access to all components of the Connect platform.

Adaptive

THE FIRST AND ONLY ADAPTIVE READING EXPERIENCE DESIGNED TO TRANSFORM THE WAY STUDENTS READ

> More students earn **A's** and **B's** when they use McGraw-Hill Education **Adaptive** products.

SmartBook®

Proven to help students improve grades and study more efficiently, SmartBook contains the same content within the print book, but actively tailors that content to the needs of the individual. SmartBook's adaptive technology provides precise, personalized instruction on what the student should do next, guiding the student to master and remember key concepts, targeting gaps in knowledge and offering customized feedback, and driving the student toward comprehension and retention of the subject matter. Available on smartphones and tablets, SmartBook puts learning at the student's fingertips—anywhere, anytime.

> Over **4 billion questions** have been answered, making McGraw-Hill Education products more intelligent, reliable, and precise.

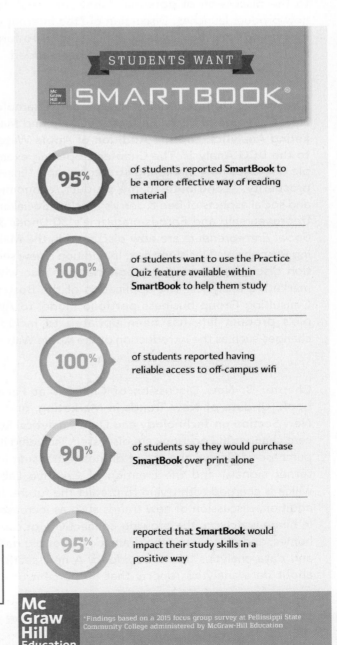

STUDENTS WANT

SMARTBOOK®

95% of students reported **SmartBook** to be a more effective way of reading material

100% of students want to use the Practice Quiz feature available within **SmartBook** to help them study

100% of students reported having reliable access to off-campus wifi

90% of students say they would purchase **SmartBook** over print alone

95% reported that **SmartBook** would impact their study skills in a positive way

Mc Graw Hill Education

*Findings based on a 2015 focus group survey at Pellissippi State Community College administered by McGraw-Hill Education

www.learnsmartadvantage.com

NEW AND REVISED CONTENT

Chapter 1: New Discussion of Marketing at Chobani, New Showstopper Analysis, and New Material on the Internet of Everything. Chapter 1 begins with an update of Chobani's saavy use of marketing to create a new food category. Examples include Chobani's use of a YouTube channel, its introduction of yogurt cafés, and its development of new products such as Chobani Flip. New product examples such as Apple Newton, StuffDOT, and Pepsi True have been added to the discussion of potential "showstoppers" for new-product launches. Discussion of "the Internet of everything" and how data analytics is used to form relationships with customers has also been added.

Chapter 2: Updated Chapter Opening Example, New Coverage of Social Entrepreneurship and Marketing Analytics, and the Addition of Apple Watch to the BCG Analysis. The Chapter 2 opening example discusses how marketing strategies, and "linked prosperity," contribute to the product, economic, and social aspects of Ben & Jerry's mission. Social entrepreneurship and *Forbes* magazine's *30 Under 30 Social Entrepreneurs* are now discussed in the Making Responsible Decisions box. In addition a new section discusses tracking strategic performance with marketing analytics. The application of the Boston Consulting Group business portfolio model to Apple's product line has been updated to include changes such as the introduction of the Apple Watch.

Chapter 3: New Discussion of Changes at Facebook, Update of New Trends in Marketing, and a New Section on Technology and Data Analytics. Recent changes at Facebook are discussed, including its purchase of Oculus, the use of drones to transmit Internet signals, and the creation of Creative Labs which is charged with trying to predict the future. In addition, discussion of new trends such as increases in binge-watching; the growing connectivity of cars, homes, and planes; and the dramatic rise of big data and data analytics has been added. A new section about data analytics reports that 50 percent of all

managers thought that improving information and analytics was a top priority.

Chapter 4: New Emphasis on Sustainable Marketing and the Ethics of Buying Counterfeit Products. New text explains how marketers have embraced societal responsibility through sustainable marketing, which seeks to meet economic, environmental, and social needs without compromising the opportunity for future generations to meet theirs. The financial impact of counterfeit products has been expanded and updated.

Chapter 5: New Evaluative Criteria Data and New Emphasis on Student Trial of VALS. The Alternative Evaluation discussion has been updated to show new data for Apple, HTC, Motorola Droid, and Samsung Galaxy phones. In addition, the Consumer Lifestyle section now includes additional discussion to increase student use of the VALS survey and self-assessment of their personal VALS profile.

Chapter 6: New Chapter Organization, New Marketing Insights About Me Box, and New Buying Function Section. The first section of the chapter has been reorganized to reflect the important distinction between organizational buyers and organizational markets. In addition, a new Marketing Insights About Me box has been added to allow students to assess the diversity practices of potential supplier organizations. A new section on the buying function in organizations has also been added.

Chapter 7: New Examples Related to World Trade, Countertrade, Exchange Rates, and Market Entry Strategies. The relative influence of the United States, China, and Germany in world trade has been updated. In addition, the countertrade discussion now includes an example of PepsiCo agreeing to purchase tomatoes in India for its Pizza

Hut division. Other new examples include Procter & Gamble's losses due to exchange rate fluctuations, and the significant cost of Target's entry and exit from Canada.

Chapter 8: Updated Chapter Opening Example, New Primary and Secondary Data Coverage, and New Section on Big Data and Data Analytics. The chapter opening example has been updated with new research methods such as "social listening" which uses Twitter, YouTube, Tumblr, and other social media to monitor movie campaigns. An update of secondary data sources is included in the Marketing Matters Box and a new discussion of the difficulties of obtaining an accurate assessment of television viewing behavior has been added. In addition, new examples of Procter & Gamble and IKEA using observational research techniques, an online version of the Wendy's survey, and a new section Big Data and Data Analytics have been added. New topics such as data visualization, the intelligent enterprise, and cloud computing are introduced.

Chapter 9: Update of Zappos Segmentation Approach and New Segmentation Examples. The discussion of Zappos.com's successful segmentation strategy has been updated. In addition, examples of segmentation for book series, movies, and theme parks have been added. Walmart's new strategy to compete for the discount chain (e.g., Dollar General) segment with Walmart Neighborhood Market stores is also discussed and the Wendy's product-market grid and discussion have been updated to reflect new products and digital marketing activities.

Chapter 10: Update of Apple's New-Product Development Successes and Failures and Greater Emphasis on Open Innovation. The chapter opening example has been updated to include a history of Apple's notable innovation successes and failures and the introduction of the Apple Watch. The concept of open innovation has been added and approaches to implementing open innovation are discussed in the

description of the new-product development process. A new Marketing Matters box discusses the introduction of Google Glass in 2012 and its withdrawal from the market in 2015. Other new examples include P&G's Swiffer WetJet, the Chevy Bolt, and Burger King's French fries.

Chapter 11: New Material on Brand Repositioning at Gatorade, and New Trademark Coverage. The Chapter 11 discussion of Gatorade now includes its efforts to reposition the brand and to develop different lines of Gatorade products for different types of athletes. New examples about Apple's iPhone 6, Gillette's Body line of shaving products for "manscaping," and American Express Green, Gold, Platinum, Optima Blue, and Centurion cards have been added. In addition, the Marketing Insights About Me box discusses how to check for a business name that features your name, and the text discusses how Kylie and Kendall Jenner have filed to have their first names trademarked.

Chapter 12: Updated Discussion of Airbnb, New Economic Impact Data, and New Advertisements. An update of Airbnb's success and its influence on the sharing economy has been added. In addition, global and U.S. services valuations have been updated. New advertisements from United Airline, Merrill Lynch, Outward Bound, United Way, American Red Cross, the United States Postal Service, Hertz, and Accenture have been added.

Chapter 13: New Chapter Opening Example about Vizio, and New Marketing Matters Boxes about Spirit Airlines and Big Data. The new chapter opening example describes VIZIO's approach to pricing smart televisions so that they are affordable for the average consumer. A new Marketing Matters box describes how Spirit Airlines offers fares that are 40 percent lower than other airlines and how customers assess the value of Spirit's offerings. In addition, another new Marketing Matters box describes the price elasticity of demand for cigarettes among different age groups.

Chapter 14: New Chapter Opening Example about the Pricing of E-books, New Discussion of Dynamic Pricing, and New Making Responsible Decisions Box about "Surge" Pricing. Chapter 14 now begins with a discussion of the pricing practices related to printed books and e-books, including the use of odd prices such as $19.99. The section on dynamic pricing includes the concept of "surge" pricing, when a company raises the price of its product if there is a spike in demand. The new Making Responsible Decisions box asks students to evaluate the economic and ethical perspectives of surge pricing.

Chapter 15: New Amazon Video Case, New Disintermediation Example, Updated Making Responsible Decisions Box. A description of a disagreement between Amazon and Hachette Book Group about how e-book revenue should be divided between the two companies has been added to the disintermediation section. The Making Responsible Decisions box has been updated to reflect Hewlett-Packard's use of recycled plastic in its ink and toner cartridges. The chapter ends with a new video case about Amazon, including coverage of its new drone initiative!

Chapter 16: New Chapter Opening Example about Wearable Technology, Updated Making Responsible Decisions Box, New Section on Data Analytics, and New Mall of America Video Case. Chapter 16 opens with a description of the potential impact of wearable technology on consumers and retailers. Products such as smartwatches, mobile apps, near field communication, and Apple Pay, and their use at retailers such as Target, Kohl's, and Marsh Supermarkets are discussed. The Making Responsible Decisions box now includes information about *Newsweek*'s annual "green rankings" and encourages students to review the rankings of their favorite retailers. In addition, a new section describing data analytics as the "new science of retailing" has been added. Finally, the end-of-chapter video case on Mall of America is completely new!

Chapter 17: New Video Case on Taco Bell, Updated Discussion of Marketing to College Students, New

Advertisements, and New Example of an IMC Program for a Movie. The Marketing Matters Box has been updated to include the most recent suggestions for successful use of mobile marketing to reach college students. New advertisements include examples from The North Face, Klondike, M&M's, Gulfstream, and Jurassic World. The IMC program used to promote the movie *Jurassic World* has been added to the Scheduling section. In addition, a new end-of-chapter video case about Taco Bell has been added.

Chapter 18: New Chapter Opening Example about Virtual Reality, New Advertisements and Sales Promotion Examples, and New Discussion of the Advertising Agency of the Year. The impact of virtual reality is the new topic of the chapter opening example. Current VR campaigns by Mountain Dew, Game of Thrones, and Marriott hotels, and future campaigns by Fox Sports and NASCAR are discussed. New advertising examples from Levi's, Samsung, American Red Cross, Whole Foods, Milk Life, the Air Force, the Meth Project, Bebe, and Old Spice, and new sales promotion examples from Ben & Jerry's, Plenti, and *The Tonight Show* have been added. In addition, the chapter includes new discussion of *Advertising Age*'s Agency of the Year—R/GA.

Chapter 19: New Chapter Opening Example, New Discussion of Web 3.0, New Section on Mobile Marketing at Facebook, and New Marketing Matters Box on Mobile Marketing. Chapter 19 opens with a discussion of the "ultimate marketing machine"—a smartphone. The discussion includes a summary of usage rates, current advertising revenue, and likely future developments. New discussion also includes the next-generation web, Web 3.0. A new section on mobile marketing has been added to the discussion of Facebook. Chapter 19 also includes a new Marketing Matters box about the importance of video in a mobile marketing campaign.

Chapter 20: Update of the Chapter Opening Example, New Discussion of the Importance of Personal Selling to Entrepreneurs, and New Photo Examples. The chapter opening example about GE's Lindsey

Smith has been updated to include a description of her new responsibilities and job title. A new discussion about the three reasons personal selling is critical to successful entrepreneurial efforts has been added. In addition, new photo examples of a Medtronic salesperson, team selling, and a trade show have also been added.

Chapter 21: Expanded Discussion about Marketing in Two Environments, New Marketing Insights About Me Box, and New Discussion about the Cross-Channel Consumer. The Marketing in Two Environments section now discusses how some retailers provide showrooms for consumers that purchase online, while some luxury fashion retailers don't have an online presence. A new Marketing Insights About Me box discusses Internet shopping addiction. In addition, the Cross-Channel Consumer section discusses showrooming and webrooming.

Chapter 22: Updated Chapter Opening Example, Expanded Discussion of Resource Allocation, and New Marketing Matters Box. The chapter opening example has been updated to describe how the strategic marketing process at General Mills has led to many new products such as Fiber One snack bars, Chex gluten-free mix, and Warm Delights. The resource allocation discussion now introduces the concept of the capitalist's dilemma. Finally, a new Marketing Matters box discusses how to create innovation in the "blue oceans" of uncontested marketspace.

INSTRUCTOR RESOURCES

Test Bank
We offer almost 7,000 test questions categorized by topic learning objectives, and level of learning.

Instructor's Manual
The IM includes lecture notes, video case teaching notes, Appendix D case teaching notes, and In-Class Activities.

Video Cases
A unique series of 22 marketing video cases includes new videos featuring Amazon, Mall of America, and Taco Bell.

Appendix D Cases
Alternate cases for each chapter for instructors who elect to assign additional cases.

In-Class Activities
Chapter-specific in-class activities for today's students who learn from active, participative experiences.

PowerPoint Slides
Media-enhanced and hyperlinked slides enable engaging and interesting classroom discussions.

Practice Marketing (Simulation)
Practice Marketing is a 3D, online, multiplayer game that enables students to gain practical experiences in an interactive environment.

Marketing, 13/e
Instructor Resources

Connect, LearnSmart, and SmartBook
The unique content platform delivering powerful technical resources and adaptive learning solutions.

Blog
www.kerinmarketing.com
A blog written specifically for use in the classroom! Throughout each term we post new examples of marketing campaigns, along with a classroom discussion and participation guide.

Practice Marketing

McGraw-Hill's Practice Marketing is a 3D, online, multiplayer game that enables students to gain practical experience by applying the skills they learn in a highly interactive and engaging environment. Using the knowledge built on their course, students become the marketing manager for a company entering the backpack market. By making decisions and seeing the results, players get feedback on their actions and learn by doing. Practice Marketing is the first in this series of new digital products from McGraw-Hill. Contact your local rep for more details.

Create

Instructors can now tailor their teaching resources to match the way they teach! With McGraw-Hill Create, www.mcgrawhillcreate.com, instructors can easily rearrange chapters, combine material from other content sources, and quickly upload and integrate their own content-like course syllabi or teaching notes. Find the right content in Create by searching through thousands of leading McGraw-Hill textbooks. Arrange the material to fit your teaching style. Order a Create book and receive a complimentary print review copy in 3–5 business days or a complimentary electronic review copy (echo) via e-mail within one hour. Go to www.mcgrawhillcreate.com today and register.

Tegrity Campus

Tegrity makes class time available 24/7 by automatically capturing every lecture in a searchable format for students to review when they study and complete assignments. With a simple one-click start-and-stop process, you capture all computer screens and corresponding audio. Students can replay any part of any class with easy-to-use browser-based viewing on a PC or Mac. Educators know that the more students can see, hear, and experience class resources, the better they learn. In fact, studies prove it. With patented Tegrity "search anything" technology, students instantly recall key class moments for replay online or on iPods and mobile devices. Instructors can help turn all their students' study time into learning moments immediately supported by their lecture. To learn more about Tegrity, watch a two-minute Flash demo at http://tegritycampus.mhhe.com.

Blackboard® Partnership

McGraw-Hill Education and Blackboard have teamed up to simplify your life. Now you and your students can access Connect and Create right from within your Blackboard course—all with one single sign-on. The grade books are seamless, so when a student completes an integrated Connect assignment, the grade for that assignment automatically (and instantly) feeds your Blackboard grade center. Learn more at www.domorenow.com.

McGraw-Hill Campus™

McGraw-Hill Campus is a new one-stop teaching and learning experience available to users of any learning management system. This institutional service allows faculty and students to enjoy single sign-on (SSO) access to all McGraw-Hill Higher Education materials, including the award-winning McGraw-Hill Connect platform, from directly within the institution's website. With McGraw-Hill Campus, faculty receive instant access to teaching materials (e.g., ebooks, test banks, PowerPoint slides, animations, learning objects, etc.), allowing them to browse, search, and use any instructor ancillary content in our vast library at no additional cost to instructor or students. In addition, students enjoy SSO access to a variety of free content (e.g., quizzes, flash cards, narrated presentations, etc.) and subscription-based products (e.g., McGraw-Hill Connect). With McGraw-Hill Campus enabled, faculty and students will never need to create another account to access McGraw-Hill products and services. Learn more at www.mhcampus.com.

Assurance of Learning Ready

Many educational institutions today focus on the notion of *assurance of learning,* an important element of some accreditation standards. *Marketing* is designed specifically to support instructors' assurance of learning initiatives with a simple yet powerful solution. Each test bank question for *Marketing* maps to a specific chapter learning objective listed in the text. Instructors can use our test bank software, EZ Test and EZ Test Online, to easily query for learning objectives that directly relate to the learning outcomes for their course. Instructors can then use the reporting features of EZ Test to aggregate student results in similar fashion, making the collection and presentation of assurance of learning data simple and easy.

AACSB Tagging

McGraw-Hill Education is a proud corporate member of AACSB International. Understanding the importance and value of AACSB accreditation, *Marketing*'s Test Bank recognizes the curricula guidelines detailed in the AACSB standards for business accreditation by connecting selected questions in the text and the test bank to six of the general knowledge and skill guidelines in the AACSB standards. The statements contained in *Marketing* are provided only as a guide for the users of this textbook. The AACSB leaves content coverage and assessment within the purview of individual schools, the mission of the school, and the faculty. While the *Marketing* teaching package makes no claim of any specific AACSB qualification or evaluation, we have within *Marketing* labeled selected questions according to the six general knowledge and skills areas.

McGraw-Hill Customer Experience
Group Contact Information

At McGraw-Hill, we understand that getting the most from new technology can be challenging. That's why our services don't stop after you purchase our products. You can e-mail our Product Specialists 24 hours a day to get product training online. Or you can search our knowledge bank of Frequently Asked Questions on our support website. For Customer Support, call 800-331-5094, e-mail mhsupport@mcgraw-hill.com, or visit www.mhhe.com/support. One of our Technical Support Analysts will be able to assist you in a timely fashion.

Acknowledgments

To ensure continuous improvement of our textbook and supplements we have utilized an extensive review and development process for each of our past editions. Building on that history, the *Marketing,* 13th edition development process included several phases of evaluation and a variety of stakeholder audiences (e.g., students, instructors, etc.).

Reviewers who were vital in the changes that were made to the 13th edition and its supplements include:

A. Diane Barlar
Abe Qastin
Abhay Shah
Abhi Biswas
Abhik Roy
Adrienne Hinds
Ahmed Maamoun
Al Holden
Alan Bush
Alexander Edsel
Alicia Revely
Allan Palmer
Allen Smith
Amy Frank
Anand Kumar
Andrei Strijnev
Andrew Dartt
Andrew Thacker
Andy Aylesworth
Angela Stanton
Anil Pandya
Ann Kuzma
Ann Little
Ann Lucht
Ann Veeck
Annette George
Anthony Koh
Anthony R. Fruzzetti
Aysen Bakir
Barbara Evans
Barbara Ribbens
Barnett Greenberg
Barry Bunn
Bashar Gammoh
Beibei Dong
Ben Oumlil
Beth Deinert
Bill Curtis
Bill Murphy
Bill Peterson
Blaise Waguespack Jr.

Bob Dahlstrom
Bob Dwyer
Bob E. Smiley
Bob McMillen
Bob Newberry
Brent Cunningham
Brian Kinard
Brian Murray
Bronis J. Verhage
Bruce Brown
Bruce Chadbourne
Bruce Ramsey
Bruce Robertson
Bryan Hayes
Carl Obermiller
Carmen Powers
Carmina Cavazos
Carol Bienstock
Carol M. Motley
Carolyn Massiah
Casey Donoho
Catherine Campbell
Cathie Rich-Duval
Cathleen H. Behan
Cathleen Hohner
Cecil Leonard
Cesar Maloles
Charla Mathwick
Charles Bodkin
Charles Ford
Charles Schewe
Cheryl Stansfield
Chiranjeev Kohli
Chris Anicich
Chris Ratcliffe
Christie Amato
Christine Lai
Christopher Blocker
Christopher Kondo
Christopher Ziemnowicz
Chuck Pickett

Cindy Leverenz
Clare Comm
Clark Compton
Clay Rasmussen
Clint Tankersley
Clyde Rupert
Connie Bateman
Corinne Asher
Craig Stacey
Cristanna Cook
Cydney Johnson
Dan Darrow
Dan Goebel
Dan Sherrel
Dan Toy
Daniel Butler
Daniel Rajaratnam
Darrell Goudge
Dave Olson
David Erickson
David Gerth
David J. Burns
David Jamison
David Kuhlmeier
David Smith
David Terry Paul
Deana Ray
Deb Jansky
Debbie Coleman
Debra Laverie
Deepa Pillai
Dennis Pappas
Dennis Rosen
Diana Joy Colarusso
Diane Dowdell
Diane T. McCrohan
Don Weinrauch
Donald Chang
Donald F. Mulvihill
Donald Fuller
Donald G. Norris

Donald Hoffer
Donald Larson
Donald R. Jackson
Donald V. Harper
Donna Wertalik
Doris M. Shaw
Dotty Harpool
Douglas Kornemann
Dr. Priscilla G. Aaltonen
Duncan G. LaBay
Eberhard Scheuling
Ed Gonsalves
Ed Laube
Ed McLaughlin
Eddie V. Easley
Edna Ragins
Edwin Nelson
Elaine Notarantonio
Eldon L. Little
Elena Martinez
Elizabeth R. Flynn
Ellen Benowitz
Eric Ecklund
Eric Newman
Eric Shaw
Erin Baca Blaugrund
Erin Cavusgil
Erin Wilkinson
Ernan Haruvy
Eugene Flynn
Farrokh Moshiri
Fekri Meziou
Frances Depaul
Francis DeFea
Francisco Coronel
Frank A. Chiaverini
Fred Honerkamp
Fred Hurvitz
Fred Morgan
Fred Trawick
Frederick J. Beier
Gail M. Zank
Gary Carson
Gary F. McKinnon
Gary Law
Gary Poorman
Gary Tucker
George Kelley
George Miaoulis
George Young
Gerald O. Cavallo

Gerard Athaide
Gerald Waddle
Glen Brodowsky
Glen Gelderloos
Godwin Ariguzo
Gonca Soysal
Gordon Mosley
Greg Kitzmiller
Guy Lochiatto
Harlan Wallingford
Harold Lucius
Harold S. Sekiguchi
Havva Jale Meric
Heidi Rottier
Heikki Rinne
Helen Koons
Herbert A. Miller
Herbert Katzenstein
Howard Combs
Hsin-Min Tong
Hugh Daubek
Imran Khan
Irene Dickey
Irene Lange
Ismet Anitsal
J. Ford Laumer
Jacqueline Karen
Jacqueline Williams
James A. Henley Jr.
James A. Muncy
James C. Johnson
James Cross
James Garry Smith
James Gaubert
James Ginther
James Gould
James H. Barnes
James H. Donnelly
James L. Grimm
James Lollar
James Marco
James McAlexander
James Meszaros
James Munch
James Olver
James P. Rakowski
James V. Spiers
James Wilkins
James Zemanek
Jane Cromartie
Jane Lang

Jane McKay-Nesbitt
Janet Ciccarelli
Janet Murray
Janice Karlen
Janice Taylor
Janice Williams
Jarrett Hudnal
Jason Little
Jay Lambe
Jean Murray
Jean Romeo
Jeanne Munger
Jeff Blodgett
Jeff Finley
Jeffrey W. von Freymann
Jefrey R. Woodall
Jennie Mitchell
Jennifer Nelson
Jerry Peerbolte
Jerry W. Wilson
Jianfeng Jiang
Jim McHugh
Jo Ann McManamy
Joan Williams
Joanne Orabone
Jobie Devinney-Walsh
Joe Cronin
Joe Kim
Joe M. Garza
Joe Puzi
Joe Ricks
Joe Stasio
John Benavidez
John Brandon
John C. Keyt
John Coppett
John Cox
John Finlayson
John Fitzpatrick
John Gaskins
John H. Cunningham
John Kuzma
John Penrose
John Striebich
Jonathan Hibbard
Joseph Belonax
Joseph Defilippe
Joseph Myslivec
Joseph Wisenblit
Juan (Gloria) Meng
Judy Bulin

Judy Foxman
Judy Wagner
Julie Haworth
Julie Sneath
Jun Ma
June E. Parr
Karen Becker-Olsen
Karen Berger
Karen Flaherty
Karen Gore
Karen LeMasters
Kasia Firlej
Katalin Eibel-Spanyi
Kathleen Krentler
Kathleen Stuenkel
Kathleen Williamson
Kathryn Schifferle
Kathy Meyer
Katie Kemp
Kay Chomic
Kaylene Williams
Keith B. Murray
Keith Jones
Keith Murray
Kellie Emrich
Ken Crocker
Ken Fairweather
Ken Herbst
Ken Murdock
Ken Shaw
Kenneth Goodenday
Kenneth Jameson
Kenneth Maricle
Kerri Acheson
Kevin Feldt
Kevin W. Bittle
Kim Montney
Kim Richmond
Kim Sebastiano
Kim Wong
Kimberly D. Smith
Kimberly Grantham
Kin Thompson
Kirti Celly
Koren Borges
Kristen Regine
Kristine Hovsepian
Kristy McManus
Kumar Sarangee
Kunal Sethi
Lan Wu

Larry Borgen
Larry Carter
Larry Feick
Larry Goldstein
Larry Marks
Larry Rottmeyer
Laura Dwyer
Lauren Wright
Lawrence Duke
Lawrence Marks
Lee Meadow
Leon Zurawicki
Leonard Lindenmuth
Leslie A. Goldgehn
Leta Beard
Linda Anglin
Linda M. Delene
Linda Morable
Linda Munilla
Linda N. LaMarca
Linda Rochford
Lindell Phillip Chew
Lisa M. Sciulli
Lisa Siegal
Lisa Simon
Lisa Troy
Lisa Zingaro
Lori Feldman
Lowell E. Crow
Lynn Harris
Lynn Loudenback
Marc Goldberg
Maria McConnell
Maria Randazzo-Nardin
Maria Sanella
Marilyn Lavin
Mark Collins
Mark Weber
Mark Young
Martin Bressler
Martin Decatur
Martin St. John
Marton L. Macchiete
Martyn Kingston
Marva Hunt
Mary Ann McGrath
Mary Beth DeConinck
Mary Conran
Mary Joyce
Mary Schramm
Mary Tripp

Matt Meuter
Max White
Mayukh Dass
Melissa Clark
Melissa Moore
Michael Callow
Michael Drafke
Michael Fowler
Michael Mayo
Michael Peters
Michael Pontikos
Michael R. Luthy
Michael Swenson
Michelle Kunz
Michelle Wetherbee
Mike Hagan
Mike Hyman
Mike Luckett
Milton Pressley
Miriam B. Stamps
Nadia J. Abgrab
Nancy Bloom
Nancy Boykin
Nancy Grassilli
Nanda Kumar
Nathan Himelstein
Neel Das
Nikolai Ostapenko
Norman Smothers
Notis Pagiavlas
Ottilia Voegtli
Pamela Grimm
Pamela Hulen
Parimal Bhagat
Pat Spirou
Patricia Baconride
Patricia Bernson
Patricia Manninen
Paul Dion
Paul Dowling
Paul Jackson
Paul Londrigan
Paul Myer
Peter J. McClure
Philip Kearney
Philip Parron
Philip Shum
Phyllis Fein
Phyllis McGinnis
Poh-Lin Yeoh
Pola B. Gupta

Priscilla LaBarbera
Priyali Rajagopal
Rae Caloura
Rajesh Iyer
Rajiv Kashyap
Ram Kesaran
Randall E. Wade
Randy Stuart
Ravi Shanmugam
Raymond Marzilli
Reid Claxton
Renee Foster
Renee Pfeifer-Luckett
Rex Moody
Rhonda Mack
Rhonda Taylor
Richard C. Leventhal
Richard D. Parker
Richard Hansen
Richard Hargrove
Richard J. Lutz
Richard Lapidus
Richard M. Hill
Richard Penn
Rick Sweeney
Rita Dynan
Robert C. Harris
Robert Jones
Robert Lawson
Robert Luke
Robert Morris
Robert S. Welsh
Robert Swerdlow
Robert W. Ruekert
Robert Williams
Robert Witherspoon
Roberta Schultz
Roger McIntyre
Roger W. Egerton
Ron Dougherty
Ron Hasty
Ron Larson
Ron Weston
Ronald A. Feinberg
Ronald Michaels
Rosemary Ramsey
Roy Adler
Roy Klages
Ruth Ann Smith
Ruth Rosales

Ruth Taylor
S. Choi Chan
S. Tamer Cavusgil
Sally Sledge
Samuel E. McNeely
Sanal Mazvancheryl
Sandipan Sen
Sandra Robertson
Sandra Smith
Sandra Young
Sang Choe
Sanjay S. Mehta
Santhi Harvey
Scott Cragin
Scott Swan
Scott Thorne
Shabnam Zanjani
Sheila Wexler
Sherry Cook
Siva Balasubramanian
Soon Hong Min
Srdan Zdravkovic
Stacia Gray
Stan Garfunkel
Stan Scott
Starr F. Schlobohm
Stephen Calcich
Stephen Garrott
Stephen Pirog
Stephen W. Miller
Steve Hertzenberg
Steve Taylor
Steven Engel
Steven Moff
Sudhir Karunakaran
Sue Lewis
Sue McGorry
Sue Umashankar
Suman Basuroy
Sundaram Dorai
Sunder Narayanan
Susan Godar
Susan Peterson
Susan Sieloff
Susan Stanix
Susie Pryor
Suzanne Murray
Sylvia Keyes
Tamara Masters
Teri Root

Terrance Kevin McNamara
Terry Kroeten
Theodore Mitchell
Theresa Flaherty
Thom J. Belich
Thomas Brashear
Thomas L. Trittipo
Thomas M. Bertsch
Thomas Passero
Tim Aurand
Tim Landry
Timothy Donahue
Timothy Reisenwitz
Tina L. Williams
Tino DeMarco
Tom Castle
Tom Deckelman
Tom Marshall
Tom Rossi
Tom Stevenson
Tom Thompson
Tracy Fulce
Vahwere Kavota
Van R. Wood
Vicki Rostedt
Victoria Miller
Vincent P. Taiani
Vladimir Pashkevich
Vonda Powell
Walter Kendall
Wendy Achey
Wendy Wood
Wesley Johnston
William B. Dodds
William Brown
William D. Ash
William Foxx
William G. Browne
William G. Mitchell
William J. Carner
William Motz
William Pertula
William R. Wynd
William Rodgers
William S. Piper
Wilton Lelund
Yi He
Yue Pan
Yunchuan Liu

This is the first edition of *Marketing* without William Rudelius as our coauthor. Our relationship with Bill began as his students at the University of Minnesota, but in addition to being an exceptional professor he also quickly became a mentor, colleague, and friend. It was Bill's idea to write a textbook and many of our innovations such as video cases, the social media chapter, and in-class activities were the direct result of his commitment to improving the marketing education experience for students. We will miss the day-to-day interaction with Bill as he now takes time to travel and continue his research on improving undergraduate education. We are certain, however, that he will continue to be an influence on the content, appearance, and rigor of this and future editions. For ourselves, and on behalf of the many students and instructors who have benefited from Bill's insights, skills, and professionalism, we cannot say "thank you" enough.

Thanks are also due to many people, including students, instructors, university staff, librarians and researchers, business periodical authors and editors, company representatives, and marketing professionals of every kind. Their assistance has been essential in our efforts to continue to provide the most comprehensive and up-to-date teaching and learning package available. We have been fortunate to have so many people be part of our team!

Nancy Harrower of Concordia University, St. Paul led our efforts on the Instructor's Manual, the PowerPoint slides, and the In-Class Activities. In addition, she provides the content for our blog (kerinmarketing.com). Antony Peloso of W. P. Carey School of Business at Arizona State University was responsible for the Test Bank and Quizzes. Tia Quinlan-Wilder of the University of Denver was responsible for the LearnSmart component of our interactive learning package. Erin Steffes of Towson University was responsible for the Connect interactives. All of these professors are exceptional educators and we are very fortunate that they are part of our team. Michael Vessey, our long-time collaborator who passed away last year, also provided assistance in the preparation of the text and supplements.

Thanks are also due to many other colleagues who contributed to the text, cases, and supplements. They include: Richard Lutz of the University of Florida; Linda Rochford of the University of Minnesota–Duluth; Kevin Upton of the University of Minnesota–Twin Cities; Nancy Nentl of Metropolitan State University; Leslie Kendrick of Johns Hopkins University; Lau Geok Theng of the National University of Singapore; and Leigh McAlister of the University of Texas at Austin. Rick Armstrong of Armstrong Photography, Dan Hundley and George Heck of Token Media, Nick Kaufman and Michelle Morgan of NKP Media, Bruce McLean of World Class Communication Technologies, Paul Fagan of Fagan Productions, Martin Walter of White Room Digital, Scott Bolin of Bolin Marketing, and Andrew Schones of Pure Imagination produced the videos.

Many businesspeople also provided substantial assistance by making available information that appears in the text, videos, and supplements—much of it for the first time in college materials. Thanks are due to Daniel Jasper, Jill Renslow, and Sarah Schmidt of Mall of America; Mike Pohl of ACES Flight Simulation; Chris Klein, Jaime Cardenas, Casey Leppanen, Heather Peace, and Lori Nevares of LA Galaxy; Carl Thomas, Peter Dirksing, and Dana Swanson of X-1 Audio, Inc.; Ian Wolfman and Jana Boone of meplusyou; David Ford and Don Rylander of Ford Consulting Group; Mark Rehborg of Tony's Pizza; Vivian Callaway, Sandy Proctor, and Anna Stoesz of General Mills; David Windorski, Tom Barnidge, and Erica Schiebel of 3M; Nicholas Skally, Jeremy Stonier, and Joe Olivas of Prince Sports; Ian Wolfman of imc[2]; Brian Niccol of Pizza Hut; Kim Nagele of JCPenney, Inc.; Charles Besio of the Sewell Automotive Group, Inc.; Lindsey Smith of GE Healthcare; Beverly Roberts of the U.S. Census Bureau; Sheryl Adkins-Green of Mary Kay, Inc.; Mattison Crowe of Seven Cycles, Inc.; Alisa Allen, Kirk Hodgdon, Patrick Hodgdon, and Nick Naumann of Altus Marketing and Business Development; and Nelson Ng from Dundas Data Visualization, Inc.

Those who provided the resources for use in both the *Marketing*, 13th edition textbook, Instructor's Manual, and/or PowerPoint presentations include: Todd Walker and Jean Golden of Million Dollar Idea; Karen Cohick of Susan G. Komen for the Cure; Liz

Stewart of Ben & Jerry's; John Formella and Patricia Lipari of Kodak; Apple, Inc.; Erica Schiebel of 3M; Karen Cohick of Susan G. Komen for the Cure; Joe Diliberti of *Consumer Reports*; Patricia Breman of Strategic Business Insights (VALS); Brian Nielsen of the Nielsen Company; David Walonick of StatPac; Mark Rehborg of Schwan's Consumer Brands (Tony's Pizza); Jennifer Olson of Experian Simmons; Kitty Munger and Mary Wykoff of Wendy's; Mark Heller of RetailSails; Nicky Hutcheon of ZenithOptimedia; Amy Thompson and Jennifer Allison of Dell, Inc.; Adriana Carlton of Walmart and Rick Hill of Bernstein-Rein Advertising (Walmart); Janine Bolin of Saks, Inc.; Dr. Yory Wurmser of the Direct Marketing Association; Elizabeth Clendenin of Unilever (Caress); Jennifer Katz, Kelsey Fisher, Jenny Caffoe, Lexi Diederich, and Malyn Mueller of StuffDOT, Inc.; and Eric Fleming of Segway.

We also want to thank the following people who generously provided assistance with our *Marketing,* 13th edition In-Class Activities (ICAs) and associated PowerPoint presentations: Mitch Forster and Carla Silveira of Ghirardelli Chocolate Company; Karolyn Warfel and Betsy Boyer of Woodstream Corp. (Victor Pest); Leonard Fuld of Fuld & Co.; Maggie Jantzen of Starbucks Coffee Company; Michelle Green and Victoria Glazier of the U.S. Census Bureau; Lisa Castaldo of Pepsi; Muffie Taggert of General Mills; Robert M. McMath, formerly of NewProductWorks; Greg Rodriguez; Jeremy Tucker, Julia Wells, and Lisa Cone of Frito-Lay (Doritos); Susan Carroll and Bob Robinson of Apple, Inc.; Willard Oberton of Fastenal Company; Scott Wosniak and Jennifer Arnold of Toro; Kim Eskro of Fallon Worldwide (Gold'n Plump); Robin Grayson of TBWA/Chiat/Day (Apple); Katie Kramer of Valassis Communications, Inc. (Nutella/Advil); Triestina Greco of Nutella/Ferrero; Tim Stauber of Wyeth Consumer Healthcare (Advil); Yvonne Pendleton and Lucille Storms of Mary Kay.

Staff support from the Southern Methodist University and the University of Denver was essential. We gratefully acknowledge the help of Jeanne Milazzo and Gloria Valdez for their many contributions.

Checking countless details related to layout, graphics, clear writing, and last-minute changes to ensure timely examples is essential for a sound and accurate textbook. This also involves coordinating activities of authors, designers, editors, compositors, and production specialists. Christine Vaughan, our lead content project manager, of McGraw-Hill Education's production staff and editorial consultant, Gina Huck Siegert of Imaginative Solutions, Inc., provided the necessary oversight and hand-holding for us, while retaining a refreshing sense of humor, often under tight deadlines. Thank you again!

Finally, we acknowledge the professional efforts of the McGraw-Hill Education staff. Completion of our book and its many supplements required the attention and commitment of many editorial, production, marketing, and research personnel. Our McGraw-Hill team included Kim Leistner, Kelly Pekelder, Matt Diamond, Michelle Whitaker, Danielle Clement, and many others. In addition, we relied on David Tietz for constant attention regarding photo elements of the text. Handling the countless details of our text, supplement, and support technologies has become an incredibly complex challenge. We thank all these people for their efforts!

Roger A. Kerin
Steven W. Hartley

BRIEF CONTENTS

Part 1 — Initiating the Marketing Process

1 Creating Customer Relationships and Value through Marketing 2
2 Developing Successful Organizational and Marketing Strategies 26
    Appendix A Building an Effective Marketing Plan 54
3 Scanning the Marketing Environment 70
4 Ethical and Social Responsibility for Sustainable Marketing 100

Part 2 — Understanding Buyers and Markets

5 Understanding Consumer Behavior 122
6 Understanding Organizations as Customers 152
7 Understanding and Reaching Global Consumers and Markets 174

Part 3 — Targeting Marketing Opportunities

8 Marketing Research: From Customer Insights to Actions 204
9 Market Segmentation, Targeting, and Positioning 236

Part 4 — Satisfying Marketing Opportunities

10 Developing New Products and Services 264
11 Managing Successful Products, Services, and Brands 290
12 Services Marketing 320
13 Building the Price Foundation 348
14 Arriving at the Final Price 370
    Appendix B Financial Aspects of Marketing 397
15 Managing Marketing Channels and Supply Chains 406
16 Retailing and Wholesaling 434
17 Integrated Marketing Communications and Direct Marketing 468
18 Advertising, Sales Promotion, and Public Relations 498
19 Using Social Media and Mobile Marketing to Connect with Consumers 538
20 Personal Selling and Sales Management 566

Part 5 — Managing the Marketing Process

21 Implementing Interactive and Multichannel Marketing 596
22 Pulling It All Together: The Strategic Marketing Process 620
    Appendix C Planning a Career in Marketing 652
    Appendix D Alternate Cases, available in SmartBook or Connect Instructor Resources

Glossary 673
Name Index 683
Company/Product Index 691
Subject Index 698

DETAILED CONTENTS

Part 1	Initiating the Marketing Process

1 CREATING CUSTOMER RELATIONSHIPS AND VALUE THROUGH MARKETING   2

At Chobani, Marketing Is "Nothing But Good"!   2
  Understanding Consumers' Food Values   2
  Reaching Customers   2
  Chobani Today   3
  Chobani, Marketing, and You   3
What Is Marketing?   4
  Marketing and Your Career   4
  Marketing: Delivering Value to Customers   5
  The Diverse Elements Influencing Marketing Actions   5
  What Is Needed for Marketing to Occur   6
How Marketing Discovers and Satisfies Consumer Needs   7
  Discovering Consumer Needs   7
  The Challenge: Meeting Consumer Needs with New Products   7
  Satisfying Consumer Needs   9
The Marketing Program: How Customer Relationships Are Built   10
  Relationship Marketing: Easy to Understand, Hard to Do   10
  The Marketing Program and Market Segments   12
  3M's Strategy and Marketing Program to Help Students Study   12
How Marketing Became So Important   14
  Evolution of the Market Orientation   14
  Focusing on Customer Relationship Management   15
  Ethics and Social Responsibility in Marketing: Balancing the Interests of Different Groups   16
  The Breadth and Depth of Marketing   17

Learning Objectives Review   19
Learning Review Answers   19
Focusing on Key Terms   20
Applying Marketing Knowledge   20
Building Your Marketing Plan   20

Video Case 1: Chobani®: Making Greek Yogurt a Household Name   21
Chapter Notes   24

2 DEVELOPING SUCCESSFUL ORGANIZATIONAL AND MARKETING STRATEGIES   26

Making the World a Better Place, One Scoop at a Time!   26

Today's Organizations   28
   Kinds of Organizations   28
   What Is Strategy?   28
   The Structure of Today's Organizations   28

   Making Responsible Decisions: Social Entrepreneurs Are Creating New Types of Organizations to Pursue Social Goals   29

Strategy in Visionary Organizations   30
   Organizational Foundation: Why Does It Exist?   30
   Organizational Direction: What Will It Do?   32
   Organizational Strategies: How Will It Do It?   33
   Tracking Strategic Performance with Marketing Analytics   33

   Applying Marketing Metrics: How Well Is Ben & Jerry's Doing?   35

Setting Strategic Directions   35
   A Look Around: Where Are We Now?   35
   Growth Strategies: Where Do We Want to Go?   36

   Marketing Matters: Filling the Shoes of Apple CEO Tim Cook: Where Will Apple's Projected Future Growth for Its Major SBUs Come From?   37

The Strategic Marketing Process   40
   The Planning Phase of the Strategic Marketing Process   40
   The Implementation Phase of the Strategic Marketing Process   43
   The Evaluation Phase of the Strategic Marketing Process   45

Learning Objectives Review   47
Learning Review Answers   48
Focusing on Key Terms   49
Applying Marketing Knowledge   49
Building Your Marketing Plan   49

Video Case 2: IBM: Using Strategy to Build a "Smarter Planet"   49
Chapter Notes   51
Appendix A   Building an Effective Marketing Plan 54

3   SCANNING THE MARKETING ENVIRONMENT   70

Is "Connecting the World" an Ambitious Vision? Not If You Are Facebook!   70
   Facebook in the Future   70
Environmental Scanning   72
   Tracking Environmental Trends   72
   An Environmental Scan of Today's Marketplace   73
Social Forces   74
   Demographics   74

Making Responsible Decisions: Millennials Are a Force
for Good   77

Culture   80
Economic Forces   82
Macroeconomic Conditions   82
Consumer Income   83

Marketing Insights About Me: American FactFinder: Your
Source for Economic Information   83

Technological Forces   84
Technology of Tomorrow   84
Technology's Impact on Customer Value   85
Technology Enables Data Analytics   86
Competitive Forces   86
Alternative Forms of Competition   87
Components of Competition   87
Small Businesses as Competitors   88
Regulatory Forces   88
Protecting Competition   88
Product-Related Legislation   89
Pricing-Related Legislation   90
Distribution-Related Legislation   91
Advertising- and Promotion-Related
Legislation   91

Marketing Matters: Online Tracking: Is Big Brother
Watching?   92

Control through Self-Regulation   92

Learning Objectives Review   93
Learning Review Answers   93
Focusing on Key Terms   94
Applying Marketing Knowledge   94
Building Your Marketing Plan   94

*Video Case 3: Geek Squad: A New Business for a New
Environment   95*
Chapter Notes   97

4   ETHICAL AND SOCIAL RESPONSIBILITY FOR
SUSTAINABLE MARKETING   100

Anheuser–Busch: Becoming the Best Beer Company in a
Better World   100
Alcohol Responsibility   100
Environmental Preservation   101
Nature and Significance of Marketing Ethics   102
An Ethical/Legal Framework for Marketing   102
Critical Perceptions of Ethical Behavior   103

Four Factors Affect Ethical Marketing Behavior   103
    Societal Culture and Norms   103
    Business Culture and Industry Practices   104

    Making Responsible Decisions: Corporate Conscience in the
    Cola War   106

    Corporate Culture and Expectations   106

    Marketing Insights About Me: Is Commercial Bribery More
    or Less Common in My Country?   107

    Your Personal Moral Philosophy and Ethical Behavior   107
Understanding Social Responsibility for Sustainable Marketing   110
    Three Concepts of Social Responsibility   110

    Marketing Matters: Will Consumers Switch Brands
    for a Cause? Yes, If . . .   112

    The Social Audit and Sustainable Development:
    Doing Well by Doing Good   113
    Turning the Table: Consumer Ethics and Social
    Responsibility   114

Learning Objectives Review   115
Learning Review Answers   116
Focusing on Key Terms   116
Applying Marketing Knowledge   116
Building Your Marketing Plan   117

Video Case 4: Toyota: Building Cleaner, Greener Cars   117
Chapter Notes   120

Part 2   Understanding Buyers and Markets

5   UNDERSTANDING CONSUMER BEHAVIOR   122

Enlightened Carmakers Know What Custom(h)ers and
   Influenc(h)ers Value   122
Consumer Purchase Decision Process and Experience   124
    Problem Recognition: Perceiving a Need   124
    Information Search: Seeking Value   124
    Alternative Evaluation: Assessing Value   124
    Purchase Decision: Buying Value   125
    Postpurchase Behavior: Realizing Value   126

    Marketing Matters: How Much Is a Satisfied Customer
    Worth?   127

    Consumer Involvement Affects Problem Solving   129
    Situational Influences That Affect Purchase
    Decisions   129
Psychological Influences on Consumer Behavior   130
    Consumer Motivation and Personality   130

Consumer Perception   131

Making Responsible Decisions: The Ethics of Subliminal
Messages   132

Consumer Learning   133
Consumer Values, Beliefs, and Attitudes   134
Consumer Lifestyle   135

Marketing Insights About Me: What Motivates You?
Identifying Your VALS Profile   136

Sociocultural Influences on Consumer Behavior   137
Personal Influence   137
Reference Group Influence   138

Marketing Matters: BzzAgent—The Buzz Experience   139

Family Influence   140
Social Class Influence   142
Culture and Subculture Influences   142

Learning Objectives Review   144
Learning Review Answers   145
Focusing on Key Terms   146
Applying Marketing Knowledge   146
Building Your Marketing Plan   146

*Video Case 5: Groupon: Helping Consumers with Purchase
Decisions   146*
Chapter Notes   149

6   UNDERSTANDING ORGANIZATIONS AS CUSTOMERS   152

Buying Is Marketing Too! Purchasing Publication Paper for
  JCPenney   152
Business-to-Business Marketing and Organizational Buyers   154
Organizational Buyers   154
Organizational Markets   154
Measuring Organizational Markets   155
Characteristics of Organizational Buying   156
Demand Characteristics   156
Size of the Order or Purchase   157
Number of Potential Buyers   157
Organizational Buying Objectives   157
Organizational Buying Criteria   158

Marketing Insights About Me: Do I Buy from Organizations
That Promote Diversity among Their Suppliers and in Their
Workplaces?   158

Buyer–Seller Relationships and Supply Partnerships   159

Marketing Matters: At Milsco Manufacturing, "Our Marketing
Philosophy Is Designed to Develop Partnerships" and Deliver
a Great Ride for Customers' Seats   160

Making Responsible Decisions: Sustainable Procurement for Sustainable Growth at Starbucks   161

The Organizational Buying Function and Process and the Buying Center   161
    The Buying Function in Organizations   161
    Stages in the Organizational Buying Process   161
    The Buying Center: A Cross-Functional Group   162
Online Buying in Business-to-Business Marketing   164
    Prominence of Online Buying in Organizational Markets   164
    E-Marketplaces: Virtual Organizational Markets   165

Marketing Matters: eBay Means Business for Entrepreneurs   165

    Online Auctions in Organizational Markets   166

Learning Objectives Review   *167*
Learning Review Answers   *168*
Focusing on Key Terms   *168*
Applying Marketing Knowledge   *168*
Building Your Marketing Plan   *169*

Video Case 6: Trek: Building Better Bikes through Organizational Buying   *169*
Chapter Notes   *172*

7   UNDERSTANDING AND REACHING GLOBAL CONSUMERS AND MARKETS   174

Building a Two Billion Dollar Business in India the Dell Inc. Way   174
Dynamics of World Trade   176
    Global Perspective on World Trade   176
    U.S. Perspective on World Trade   177
Marketing in a Borderless Economic World   177
    Decline of Economic Protectionism   178

Making Responsible Decisions: Global Ethics and Global Economics—The Case of Protectionism   178

    Rise of Economic Integration   179
    A New Reality: Global Competition among Global Companies for Global Consumers   181

Marketing Matters: The Global Teenager—A Market of 2 Billion Voracious Consumers   183

    Emergence of a Networked Global Marketspace   184
    Growing Prevalence of Economic Espionage   185
A Global Environmental Scan   185
    Cultural Diversity   185
    Economic Considerations   188

> Marketing Insights About Me: Checking My Country's Political Risk Rating—Are You Surprised? 191

Political-Regulatory Climate 191
Comparing Global Market-Entry Strategies 192
   Exporting 192

> Marketing Matters: Creative Cosmetics and Creative Export Marketing in Japan 193

   Licensing 193
   Joint Venture 194
   Direct Investment 194
Crafting a Worldwide Marketing Program 195
   Product and Promotion Strategies 195
   Distribution Strategy 196
   Pricing Strategy 197

Learning Objectives Review 198
Learning Review Answers 198
Focusing on Key Terms 199
Applying Marketing Knowledge 199
Building Your Marketing Plan 199

Video Case 7: Mary Kay, Inc.: Building a Brand in India 199
Chapter Notes 202

8   MARKETING RESEARCH: FROM CUSTOMER INSIGHTS TO ACTIONS 204

Marketing Research Goes to the Movies 204
   A Film Industry Secret 204
The Role of Marketing Research 206
   What Is Marketing Research? 206
   The Challenges in Doing Good Marketing Research 206
   Five-Step Marketing Research Approach 207
Step 1: Define the Problem 207
   Set the Research Objectives 207
   Identify Possible Marketing Actions 208
Step 2: Develop the Research Plan 208
   Specify Constraints 208
   Identify Data Needed for Marketing Actions 209
   Determine How to Collect Data 209
Step 3: Collect Relevant Information 210
   Secondary Data: Internal 210
   Secondary Data: External 211
   Advantages and Disadvantages of Secondary Data 211

> Marketing Matters: Online Databases and Internet Resources Useful to Marketers 212

Primary Data: Watching People 212
Primary Data: Asking People 214
Primary Data: Other Sources 218

Applying Marketing Metrics: Are the Carmex Social Media
Programs Working Well? 220

Advantages and Disadvantages of Primary Data 222
Analyzing Primary Data Using Cross Tabulations 222

Making Responsible Decisions: No More Personal Secrets:
The Downside of Data Mining 223

Step 4: Develop Findings 224
Analyze the Data 225
Present the Findings 225
Step 5: Take Marketing Actions 226
Make Action Recommendations 226
Implement the Action Recommendations 227
Evaluate the Results 227
Sales Forecasting Techniques 227
Judgments of the Decision Maker 228
Surveys of Knowledgeable Groups 228
Statistical Methods 228

Learning Objectives Review 229
Learning Review Answers 230
Focusing on Key Terms 231
Applying Marketing Knowledge 231
Building Your Marketing Plan 232

*Video Case 8: Carmex® (A): Leveraging Facebook for
Marketing Research 232*
Chapter Notes 235

9 MARKET SEGMENTATION, TARGETING, AND
POSITIONING 236

Zappos.com Is Powered by Service—and Segmentation! 236
Segmentation Is a Key to Success 236
Delivering WOW Customer Service 236
Why Segment Markets? 238
What Market Segmentation Means 238
When and How to Segment Markets 239
Steps in Segmenting and Targeting Markets 242
Step 1: Group Potential Buyers into Segments 242

Marketing Insights About Me: To Which "Flock" Do You
Belong? 245

Step 2: Group Products to Be Sold into Categories 248
Step 3: Develop a Market-Product Grid and Estimate
the Size of Markets 250

Step 4: Select Target Markets 251
Step 5: Take Marketing Actions to Reach Target Markets 252
Market-Product Synergies: A Balancing Act 254

Marketing Matters: Apple's Segmentation Strategy—Camp
Runamok No Longer 255

Positioning the Product 256
Two Approaches to Product Positioning 256
Writing a Positioning Statement 256
Product Positioning Using Perceptual Maps 256
A Perceptual Map to Reposition Chocolate Milk
for Adults 257

Learning Objectives Review 258
Learning Review Answers 258
Focusing on Key Terms 259
Applying Marketing Knowledge 259
Building Your Marketing Plan 259

*Video Case 9: Prince Sports, Inc.: Tennis Racquets
for Every Segment 260*
Chapter Notes 262

Part 4   Satisfying Marketing Opportunities

10   DEVELOPING NEW PRODUCTS AND SERVICES 264

Apple: The World-Class New-Product Machine 264
Apple's New-Product Development Successes . . . 264
. . . And New-Product Development Stumbles 264
The Next Chapter in Apple's Story: Apple Watch 265
What Are Products and Services? 266
A Look at Goods, Services, and Ideas 266
Classifying Products 266
Classifying Services 267
Product Classes, Forms, Items, Lines, and Mixes 268
New Products and Why They Succeed or Fail 268
What Is a New Product? 268

Marketing Matters: Feature Bloat: Geek Squad to the
Rescue! 269

Why Products and Services Succeed or Fail 271
How Applying Marketing Metrics Can Improve
New-Product Performance 273

Applying Marketing Metrics: Which States Are
Underperforming? 273

The New-Product Development Process 274
Stage 1: New-Product Strategy Development 274
Stage 2: Idea Generation 275

Stage 3: Screening and Evaluation   277

Marketing Matters: Was the Google Glass Half Full or Half Empty?   278

Stage 4: Business Analysis   279
Stage 5: Development   279
Stage 6: Market Testing   280
Stage 7: Commercialization   281

Learning Objectives Review   282
Learning Review Answers   283
Focusing on Key Terms   284
Applying Marketing Knowledge   284
Building Your Marketing Plan   285

Video Case 10: X-1: Breaking the Barriers of Sound with New-Product Development   285
Chapter Notes   288

11 MANAGING SUCCESSFUL PRODUCTS, SERVICES, AND BRANDS   290

Gatorade: Bringing Science to Sweat for 50 Years   290
    Creating the Gatorade Brand   290
    Building the Gatorade Brand   290
Charting the Product Life Cycle   292
    Introduction Stage   292
    Growth Stage   294
    Maturity Stage   295
    Decline Stage   295

Marketing Matters: Will E-mail Spell Extinction for Fax Machines?   296

Three Aspects of the Product Life Cycle   296
Managing the Product Life Cycle   300
    Role of a Product Manager   300
    Modifying the Product   300
    Modifying the Market   300

Applying Marketing Metrics: Knowing Your CDI and BDI   301

Repositioning the Product   303

Making Responsible Decisions: Consumer Economics of Downsizing—Get Less, Pay More   303

Branding and Brand Management   303

Marketing Insights About Me: Do You Want to Start a Business Using Your Own Name? Better Check First!   304

Brand Personality and Brand Equity   305
Picking a Good Brand Name   306
Branding Strategies   307

Packaging and Labeling Products   310
    Creating Customer Value and Competitive Advantage through
    Packaging and Labeling   311

    Marketing Matters: Creating Customer Value through
    Packaging—Pez Heads Dispense More Than Candy   311

    Packaging and Labeling Challenges and Responses   312
Product Warranty   312

Learning Objectives Review   313
Learning Review Answers   314
Focusing on Key Terms   314
Applying Marketing Knowledge   314
Building Your Marketing Plan   315

Video Case 11: P&G's Secret Deodorant: Finding
Inspiration in Perspiration   315
Chapter Notes   318

12 SERVICES MARKETING   320

Airbnb Redefines Services—and the Economy!   320
The Uniqueness of Services   322
    The Four I's of Services   323
    The Service Continuum   325
    Classifying Services   326

    Marketing Matters: Social Marketing Is a Must for
    Nonprofits   328

How Consumers Purchase Services   329
    The Purchase Process   329
    Assessing Service Quality   329
    Customer Contact and Relationship Marketing   330

    Marketing Matters: Managing Service Failures: The
    Importance of Monitoring and Guarantees   331

Managing the Marketing of Services   333
    Product (Service)   333
    Price   333
    Place (Distribution)   334
    Promotion   335
    People   335
    Physical Environment   336
    Process   336

    Applying Marketing Metrics: Are JetBlue's Flights
    Profitably Loaded?   337

Services in the Future   338

Learning Objectives Review   339
Learning Review Answers   339

Focusing on Key Terms 340
Applying Marketing Knowledge 340
Building Your Marketing Plan 340

Video Case 12: LA Galaxy: Where Sports Marketing Is a Kick! 341
Chapter Notes 344

13   BUILDING THE PRICE FOUNDATION   348

VIZIO, Inc.—Delivering Beautifully Simple Products at a Great Value   348

Nature and Importance of Price   350
    What Is a Price?   350
    Price as an Indicator of Value   351

    Marketing Matters: Does Spirit Airlines Engage in Value Pricing? For Some Yes, for Others No   352

    Price in the Marketing Mix   352
Step 1: Identify Pricing Objectives and Constraints   353
    Identifying Pricing Objectives   353
    Identifying Pricing Constraints   355
Step 2: Estimate Demand and Revenue   358
    Estimating Demand   358
    Price Elasticity of Demand   360

    Marketing Matters: Using Big Data to Curb Smoking: Uncovering the Price Elasticity of Demand for Cigarettes   361

    Fundamentals of Estimating Revenue   361
Step 3: Determine Cost, Volume, and Profit Relationships   362
    The Importance of Controlling Costs   362
    Break-Even Analysis   362

Learning Objectives Review 364
Learning Review Answers 365
Focusing on Key Terms 365
Applying Marketing Knowledge 366
Building Your Marketing Plan 366

Video Case 13: Washburn Guitars: Using Break-Even Points to Make Pricing Decisions 367
Chapter Notes 368

14   ARRIVING AT THE FINAL PRICE   370

E-books and E-conomics: A Twisted Tale of Pricing for Profit   370
    Setting the Stage with E-readers: Amazon's Kindle   370
    Printed Book Pricing Practices   370
    Enter E-books   370
    Pricing E-books . . . Profitably   371

Step 4: Select an Approximate Price Level   372

Demand-Oriented Pricing Approaches   372

Marketing Matters: Energizer's Lesson in Price Perception—
Value Lies in the Eye of the Beholder   374

Cost-Oriented Pricing Approaches   375

Profit-Oriented Pricing Approaches   377

Competition-Oriented Pricing Approaches   379

Applying Marketing Metrics: Are Red Bull Prices Above,
At, or Below the Market?   380

Step 5: Set the List or Quoted Price   381

Choose a Price Policy   381

Consider Company, Customer, and Competitive Effects on
Pricing   382

Making Responsible Decisions: The Ethics and Economics
of Surge Pricing   383

Balance Incremental Costs and Revenues   384

Step 6: Make Special Adjustments to the List or Quoted Price   385

Discounts   385

Allowances   387

Geographical Adjustments   388

Marketing Matters: Everyday Low Prices at the
Supermarket = Everyday Low Profits—Creating
Customer Value at a Cost   388

Legal and Regulatory Aspects of Pricing   389

Learning Objectives Review   391
Learning Review Answers   392
Focusing on Key Terms   393
Applying Marketing Knowledge   393
Building Your Marketing Plan   393

*Video Case 14: Carmex (B): Setting the Price of the Number
One Lip Balm*   394

Chapter Notes   396

Appendix B   Financial Aspects of Marketing   397

15   MANAGING MARKETING CHANNELS AND SUPPLY
CHAINS   406

Callaway Golf: Designing and Delivering the Goods for Great Golf   406

Nature and Importance of Marketing Channels   408

What Is a Marketing Channel of Distribution?   408

How Customer Value Is Created by Intermediaries   408

Marketing Channel Structure and Organization   410

Marketing Channels for Consumer Products and
Services   410

Marketing Channels for Business Products and Services   411
Internet Marketing Channels   412
Direct and Multichannel Marketing   413
Dual Distribution and Strategic Channel Alliances   413

Marketing Matters: Nestlé and General Mills—Cereal Partners Worldwide   414

Vertical Marketing Systems   414
Marketing Channel Choice and Management   416
Factors Affecting Channel Choice and Management   416

Applying Marketing Metrics: Channel Sales and Profit at Charlesburg Furniture   418

Managing Channel Relationships: Conflict and Cooperation   418
Logistics and Supply Chain Management   421
Supply Chains versus Marketing Channels   421
Sourcing, Assembling, and Delivering a New Car: The Automotive Supply Chain   422
Supply Chain Management and Marketing Strategy   423

Marketing Matters: IBM's Integrated Supply Chain— Delivering a Total Solution for Its Customers   424

Two Concepts of Logistics Management in a Supply Chain   425
Total Logistics Cost Concept   425
Customer Service Concept   425
Closing the Loop: Reverse Logistics   426

Making Responsible Decisions: Reverse Logistics and Green Marketing Go Together at Hewlett-Packard: Recycling e-Waste   427

Learning Objectives Review   428
Learning Review Answers   428
Focusing on Key Terms   429
Applying Marketing Knowledge   429
Building Your Marketing Plan   430

Video Case 15: Amazon: Delivering the Earth's Biggest Selection!   430
Chapter Notes   432

16   RETAILING AND WHOLESALING   434

Shoppers Are Wearing the Future of Retailing!   434
The Value of Retailing   436
Consumer Utilities Offered by Retailing   436
The Global Economic Impact of Retailing   437
Classifying Retail Outlets   438
Form of Ownership   438

**Making Responsible Decisions: How Green Is Your Retailer?
The Rankings Are Out!** 439

    Level of Service 440

    Type of Merchandise Line 441

Nonstore Retailing 443

    Automatic Vending 443

    Direct Mail and Catalogs 444

    Television Home Shopping 445

    Online Retailing 445

    Telemarketing 446

    Direct Selling 447

Retailing Strategy 447

    Positioning a Retail Store 447

    Retailing Mix 449

**Applying Marketing Metrics: Why Apple Stores May Be the
Best in the United States!** 452

The Changing Nature of Retailing 453

    The Wheel of Retailing 453

    The Retail Life Cycle 454

Future Changes in Retailing 455

    Multichannel Retailing 455

**Marketing Matters: The Multichannel Marketing
Multiplier** 456

    Data Analytics 456

Wholesaling 457

    Merchant Wholesalers 457

    Agents and Brokers 458

    Manufacturer's Branches and Offices 458

Learning Objectives Review 459

Learning Review Answers 459

Focusing on Key Terms 460

Applying Marketing Knowledge 460

Building Your Marketing Plan 461

*Video Case 16: Mall of America®: America's Biggest Mall
Knows the Secret to Successful Retailing!* 461

Chapter Notes 463

17   **INTEGRATED MARKETING COMMUNICATIONS AND
DIRECT MARKETING** 468

Taco Bell Loves Twitter! 468

The Communication Process 470

    Encoding and Decoding 471

    Feedback 471

    Noise 472

The Promotional Elements   472
    Advertising   472
    Personal Selling   473
    Public Relations   474
    Sales Promotion   475
    Direct Marketing   475
Integrated Marketing Communications—Developing the
  Promotional Mix   476
    The Target Audience   476

Marketing Matters: Tips for Targeting College Students   477

    The Product Life Cycle   477
    Product Characteristics   478
    Stages of the Buying Decision   479
    Channel Strategies   480
Developing an Integrated Marketing Communications Program   482
    Identifying the Target Audience   482
    Specifying Promotion Objectives   482
    Setting the Promotion Budget   483

Applying Marketing Metrics: How Much Should You
Spend on IMC?   484

    Selecting the Right Promotional Tools   485
    Designing the Promotion   485
    Scheduling the Promotion   485
Executing and Assessing the Promotion Program   486
Direct Marketing   487
    The Growth of Direct Marketing   488
    The Value of Direct Marketing   488
    Technological, Global, and Ethical Issues in Direct Marketing   489

Making Responsible Decisions: What Is the Future of
Your Privacy?   490

Learning Objectives Review   *491*
Learning Review Answers   *491*
Focusing on Key Terms   *492*
Applying Marketing Knowledge   *492*
Building Your Marketing Plan   *493*

*Video Case 17: Taco Bell: Using IMC to Help
Customers Live Más!*   *493*
Chapter Notes   *495*

18 ADVERTISING, SALES PROMOTION, AND PUBLIC
    RELATIONS   498

Virtual Reality Is the New Reality for Advertising!   498
Types of Advertisements   500
    Product Advertisements   500
    Institutional Advertisements   501

Developing the Advertising Program   502
  Identifying the Target Audience   502
  Specifying Advertising Objectives   502
  Setting the Advertising Budget   503

  Marketing Insights About Me: Are You an Expert at Picking the Best Super Bowl Ads?   504

  Designing the Advertisement   504
  Selecting the Right Media   507

  Applying Marketing Metrics: What Is the Best Way to Reach 1,000 Customers?   508

  Different Media Alternatives   509

  Making Responsible Decisions: Who Is Responsible for Preventing Click Fraud?   514

  Scheduling the Advertising   515
Executing the Advertising Program   516
  Pretesting the Advertising   516
  Carrying Out the Advertising Program   517
Assessing the Advertising Program   518
  Posttesting the Advertising   518
  Making Needed Changes   518
Sales Promotion   519
  Consumer-Oriented Sales Promotions   519
  Trade-Oriented Sales Promotions   524
Public Relations   526
  Publicity Tools   526
Increasing the Value of Promotion   526
  Building Long-Term Relationships   526
  Self-Regulation   527

Learning Objectives Review   528
Learning Review Answers   528
Focusing on Key Terms   529
Applying Marketing Knowledge   529
Building Your Marketing Plan   530

Video Case 18: Google, Inc.: The Right Ads at the Right Time   530
Chapter Notes   533

19 USING SOCIAL MEDIA AND MOBILE MARKETING TO CONNECT WITH CONSUMERS   538

The Ultimate Marketing Machine . . . Is in Your Pocket!   538
Understanding Social Media   540
  What Are Social Media?   540
  Comparing Social and Traditional Media   542

A Look at Four Important Social Media 543
   Comparing Four Social Media 543
   Facebook 543
   Twitter 546
   LinkedIn 547
   YouTube 548

   Marketing Matters: Mobile Marketing Discovers
   Video Bloggers! 549

Integrating Social Media into Today's Marketing Strategies 550
   Social Media and the Strategic Marketing Process 550
   Selecting Social Media 551
   How Social Media Produce Sales 551
   Measuring the Results of Social Media Programs 552
   Carmex Goes Viral with Luck and a LeBron James
   Bear Hug 554
The Future: Social Media + Smartphones + Exotic Apps 556
   The Convergence of Real and Digital Worlds 556
   Mobile Marketing: Tightening Links to Marketing
   Actions 557

Learning Objectives Review 559
Learning Review Answers 560
Focusing on Key Terms 561
Applying Marketing Knowledge 561
Building Your Marketing Plan 561

*Video Case 19: StuffDOT™, Inc.: Rewarding Users for
Actively Shopping and Sharing! 561*
Chapter Notes 564

20 PERSONAL SELLING AND SALES MANAGEMENT 566

Meet Today's Sales Professional 566
Scope and Significance of Personal Selling and Sales
  Management 568
   Nature of Personal Selling and Sales Management 568
   Selling Happens Almost Everywhere 568
   Personal Selling in Marketing and Entrepreneurship 569
   Creating Customer Solutions and Value through Salespeople:
   Relationship and Partnership Selling 569

   Marketing Matters: Science and Selling: Is Customer Value
   Creation in Your Genes? 571

The Many Forms of Personal Selling 571
   Order-Taking Salespeople 571
   Order-Getting Salespeople 572
   Customer Sales Support Personnel 572

   Marketing Matters: Creating and Sustaining Customer Value
   through Cross-Functional Team Selling 574

The Personal Selling Process: Building Relationships   574
    Prospecting: Identifying and Qualifying Prospective
    Customers   575
    Preapproach: Preparing for the Sales Call   576
    Approach: Making the First Impression   577
    Presentation: Tailoring a Solution for a Customer's Needs   577

    Marketing Matters: Imagine This . . . Putting the Customer into
    Customer Solutions!   579

    Close: Asking for the Customer's Order or Business   580
    Follow-up: Solidifying the Relationship   580
The Sales Management Process   580

    Making Responsible Decisions: The Ethics of Asking
    Customers about Competitors   581

    Sales Plan Formulation: Setting Direction   581
    Sales Plan Implementation: Putting the Plan into Action   585

    Marketing Insights About Me: What Is Your Emotional
    Intelligence? You Might Be Surprised   586

    Salesforce Evaluation: Measuring Results   587

    Applying Marketing Metrics: Tracking Salesperson Performance
    at Moore Chemical & Sanitation Supply, Inc.   588

    Salesforce Automation and Customer Relationship
    Management   589

Learning Objectives Review   590
Learning Review Answers   591
Focusing on Key Terms   591
Applying Marketing Knowledge   592
Building Your Marketing Plan   592

*Video Case 20: Xerox: Building Customer Relationships
through Personal Selling*   593
Chapter Notes   594

Part 5   **Managing the Marketing Process**

21   IMPLEMENTING INTERACTIVE AND MULTICHANNEL
    MARKETING   596

Seven Cycles Delivers Just One Bike. Yours.   596
Creating Customer Value, Relationships, and Experiences in
    Marketspace   598
    Marketing in Two Environments   598
    Creating Customer Value in Marketspace   598
    Interactivity, Individuality, and Customer Relationships in
    Marketspace   599
    Creating an Online Customer Experience   601

Applying Marketing Metrics: Sizing Up Site Stickiness at
Sewell Automotive Companies 604

Online Consumer Behavior and Marketing Practice in Marketspace 604
Who Is the Online Consumer? 604

Marketing Insights About Me: Am I Addicted to the Internet?
Answer 20 Questions to Find Out 605

What Online Consumers Buy 605
Why Consumers Shop and Buy Online 605
When and Where Online Consumers Shop and Buy 610

Making Responsible Decisions: Who Is Responsible for
Internet Privacy and Security? 610

Cross-Channel Consumers and Multichannel Marketing 611
Who Is the Cross-Channel Consumer? 611
Implementing Multichannel Marketing 612

Learning Objectives Review 613
Learning Review Answers 614
Focusing on Key Terms 614
Applying Marketing Knowledge 615
Building Your Marketing Plan 615

Video Case 21: Pizza Hut and imc²: Becoming a
Multichannel Marketer 615
Chapter Notes 619

22 PULLING IT ALL TOGETHER: THE STRATEGIC MARKETING
PROCESS 620

Strategic Marketing Helps General Mills Adapt to New Tastes! 620
Planning for Even More Change 620
Creative Initiatives at General Mills 621
Marketing Basics: Doing What Works and Allocating
Resources 622
Finding and Using What Really Works 622
Allocating Marketing Resources Using Sales Response
Functions 623
The Planning Phase of the Strategic Marketing Process 626
The Use of Marketing Metrics in Marketing Planning 626
The Variety of Marketing Plans 627
Marketing Planning Frameworks: The Search for
Growth 627

Marketing Matters: A Test of Your Skills: Where Are the
Synergies? 629

Some Marketing Planning and Strategy Lessons 639

Marketing Matters: Ask Disruptive Questions to Achieve
Disruptive Innovations 633

The Implementation Phase of the Strategic Marketing
Process   634

    Is Planning or Implementation the Problem?   634

    Increasing Emphasis on Marketing Implementation   634

    Improving Implementation of Marketing Programs   634

    Marketing Matters: Learning from Mistakes and Avoiding
    Traps on the Way to Blue Oceans   636

    Organizing for Marketing   638

The Evaluation Phase of the Strategic Marketing Process   640

    The Marketing Evaluation Process   640

    Marketing ROI, Metrics, and Dashboards   642

    Evaluation Using Marketing Metrics and Marketing
    Dashboards at General Mills   642

Learning Objectives Review   644

Learning Review Answers   645

Focusing on Key Terms   646

Applying Marketing Knowledge   647

Building Your Marketing Plan   647

*Video Case 22: General Mills Warm Delights: Indulgent,
Delicious, and Gooey!   647*

Chapter Notes   649

Appendix C   Planning a Career in Marketing   652

Appendix D   Alternate Cases, available in SmartBook or Connect
               Instructor Resources

Part 1

D-1   3M's Post-it Flag Highlighter: Extending the Concept!

D-2   Daktronics, Inc.: Global Displays in 68 Billion Colors

D-3   Jamba Juice: Scanning the Marketing Environment

D-4   BP's Deepwater Horizon: Ethics and Environmental Effects

Part 2

D-5   Decoding a Purchase Decision

D-6   Motetronix Technology: Marketing Smart Dust

D-7   Callaway Golf: The Global Challenge

Part 3

D-8   HOM Furniture: Where Keen Observation Pays

D-9   Lawn Mowers: Segmentation Challenges

Part 4

*D-10   Medtronic in China: Where "Simpler" Serves
       Patients Better*

D-11   Pampered Pooches Travel in Style

D-12   Philadelphia Phillies, Inc.: Sports Marketing 101

*D-13   Wellness Getaways, Inc.: The Challenge of Setting
       a Price*

D-14   Glitzz: Devising a Pricing Strategy

D-15   *Shiseido: Channeling Cosmetics in China*

D-16   *Trader Joe's: Upscale Value*

D-17   *Banyan Tree Holdings: Creating a Brand with IMC*

D-18   *Target Corporation: Award-Winning Advertising*

D-19   *AOI Marketing: Using Facebook to Launch Bitter Girls*

D-20   *Morgantown Furniture: Making Promotion Trade Offs*

Part 5

D-21   *Crate and Barrel: Multichannel Marketing*

D-22   *Naked® Juice: Strategy for Growth*

Glossary   673

Name Index   683

Company/Product Index   691

Subject Index   698

MARKETING

Creating Customer Relationships and Value through Marketing

LEARNING OBJECTIVES

After reading this chapter you should be able to:

LO 1-1 Define marketing and identify the diverse factors that influence marketing actions.

LO 1-2 Explain how marketing discovers and satisfies consumer needs.

LO 1-3 Distinguish between marketing mix factors and environmental forces.

LO 1-4 Explain how organizations build strong customer relationships and customer value through marketing.

LO 1-5 Describe how today's customer relationship era differs from prior eras.

At Chobani, Marketing Is "Nothing But Good"!

If you are like many consumers today, your food tastes have been changing. Interest in healthful, nutritious, organic products is growing dramatically, and companies like Chobani are creating new offerings to provide customer value!

It was Hamdi Ulukaya's marketing saavy that first helped him create Chobani. As an immigrant from Turkey, he observed that American-style yogurt "was full of sugar and preservatives," unlike the typical Greek-style yogurt he experienced growing up. The Greek yogurt was strained to remove the liquid whey and had more protein than the unstrained American yogurts marketed by Yoplait and Dannon. To meet the changing tastes of American consumers, Ulukaya bought a recently closed dairy in a small town in New York with a Small Business Administration loan and began developing a new yogurt recipe.[1]

Understanding Consumers' Food Values

"I was very picky. It took us 18 months to get the recipe right. I knew I had only one shot, and it had to be perfect," says Ulukaya. The result was Chobani Greek Yogurt, a product that is higher in protein, lower in sugar, and thicker and creamier than typical American yogurt. The timing fit perfectly with the shift in demand for healthier and simpler products. Food purchases by young adults, particularly millennials, were increasingly influenced by concern for wellness. Chobani's yogurt and its message "Nothing But Good" fit consumers' new values.[2]

Reaching Customers

Chobani had little money for traditional advertising, so the new company relied on positive word of mouth, with one happy customer telling another about the new style of yogurt. In 2010, Chobani's "CHOmobile" started to tour the country, handing out free samples to encourage consumers to try Chobani's Greek Yogurt for the first time. In addition, one of Chobani's biggest breakthroughs in gaining public awareness was its sponsorship of the 2012 U.S. Olympic and Paralympic Teams.

The company also created a YouTube channel that featured "Just Add Good" recipes to show customers how to use yogurt in meals and desserts. It also interacted with consumers through other social media sites such as Twitter and Instagram, and in just five years had 800,000 Facebook fans.

Chobani also pushed for distribution in major grocery chains rather than smaller niche stores, and encouraged placement of the product in the main dairy cases of the stores, not the specialty or health food sections. Ulukaya was convinced that Americans would really like Greek yogurt if they tried it, and that they

Chobani LLC

Video 1-1

Chobani 2014 Super Bowl Ad

kerin.tv/13e/v1-1

would try it if they had heard about it and could find it easily in their grocery store. By 2013 Chobani Greek Yogurt was sold nationwide in the United States, the United Kingdom, and Australia.[3]

Chobani Today

Chobani continues to monitor changing consumer tastes and offers new products to accommodate them. For example, the company recently introduced Chobani Kids and Chobani Tots Greek yogurt pouches, Chobani Greek Yogurt Oats—Ancient Grain Blend, and Chobani Flip Creations. The products are designed for new and existing consumers and for new eating occasions.

One way Chobani stays in touch with consumer interests is through its yogurt café in New York's SoHo neighborhood. New ideas are continually tested on the menu and the feedback has been so useful that Chobani plans to open similar outlets in Los Angeles, San Francisco, Chicago, and other U.S. cities. Chobani also recently announced a plan to open the Chobani Food Incubator, which is designed to invest in and cultivate ideas from emerging food entrepreneurs.

Today, Chobani boasts a 40 percent market share of the Greek Yogurt segment, which makes up almost half of the $8 billion yogurt market. The company's success has even led to a Super Bowl ad featuring a 1,400-pound bear in search of a healthy snack![4]

Located in New York City, Chobani SoHo is the brand's first-of-its-kind retail concept, serving yogurt creations with innovative toppings.

© Diane Bondareff/Invision for Chobani/AP Images

Chobani, Marketing, and You

Will Hamdi Ulukaya and his Chobani Greek Yogurt continue this fantastic success story—especially with the recent appearance of competing Greek yogurts from Yoplait, Dannon, and PepsiCo? For Ulukaya, one key factor will be how well Chobani understands and uses marketing—the subject of this book.

WHAT IS MARKETING?

The good news is that you are already a marketing expert! You perform many marketing activities and make marketing-related decisions every day. For example, would you sell more LG 77-inch 4K UltraHD OLED TVs at $24,999 or $2,499? You answered $2,499, right? So your experience in shopping gives you some expertise in marketing. As a consumer, you've been involved in thousands of marketing decisions, but mostly on the buying and not the selling side. But to test your expertise, answer the "marketing expert" questions posed in Figure 1–1. You'll find the answers within the next several pages.

The bad news is that good marketing isn't always easy. That's why every year thousands of new products fail in the marketplace and then quietly slide into oblivion.

Are you a marketing expert? If so, what would you pay for this cutting-edge TV?
© LG Electronics

Marketing and Your Career

Marketing affects all individuals, all organizations, all industries, and all countries. This book seeks to teach you marketing concepts, often by having you actually "do marketing"—by putting you in the shoes of a marketing manager facing actual marketing decisions. The book also shows marketing's many applications and how it affects our lives. This knowledge should make you a better consumer and enable you to be a more informed citizen, and it may even help you in your career planning.

Perhaps your future will involve doing sales and marketing for a large organization. Working for a well-known company—Apple, Ford, Facebook, or General Mills—can be personally satisfying and financially rewarding, and you may gain special respect from your friends.

Small businesses also offer marketing careers. Small businesses are the source of the majority of new U.S. jobs. So you might become your own boss by being an entrepreneur and starting your own business.

In February 2004, a 19-year-old college sophomore from Harvard University started his own small web service business from his dorm room. He billed it as "an online directory that connects people through social networks at colleges." That student, of course, was Mark Zuckerberg. The success of the Facebook launch defies comprehension. Zuckerberg's Thefacebook.com website signed up 900 Harvard students in the four days after it appeared in early 2004. By the second week there were almost 5,000 members, and today there are more than 1.4 billion members throughout the world. Perhaps your interest in marketing will lead to the next sensational new business success![5]

The chief executive officer of the world's largest social media company started it as a 19-year-old college sophomore.
© David Paul Morris/Bloomberg via Getty Images

FIGURE 1–1

The see-if-you're-really-a-marketing-expert test.

Answer the questions below. The correct answers are given later in the chapter.

1. What is the name of Pepsi's most recent entry into the mid-calorie market for cola flavored soft drinks? (a) Pepsi XL, (b) Pepsi Edge, (c) Pepsi Next, (d) Pepsi True.

2. True or False. The 60-year lifetime value of a loyal Kleenex customer is $994.

3. To be socially responsible, 3M puts what material into its very successful Scotch-Brite™ Greener Clean "non-scratch" pads? (a) aluminum, (b) plastic bottles, (c) Agave plant leaves.

MARKETING: DELIVERING VALUE TO CUSTOMERS

> **LO 1-1** Define marketing and identify the diverse factors that influence marketing actions.

The American Marketing Association represents individuals and organizations involved in the development and practice of marketing worldwide. It defines **marketing** as the activity, set of institutions, and processes for creating, communicating, delivering, and exchanging offerings that have value for customers, clients, partners, and society at large.[6] This definition shows that marketing is far more than simply advertising or personal selling. It stresses the need to deliver genuine value in the offerings of goods, services, and ideas marketed to customers. Also, notice that an organization's marketing activities should also create value for its partners and for society.

To serve both buyers and sellers, marketing seeks (1) to discover the needs and wants of prospective customers and (2) to satisfy them. These prospective customers include both individuals, buying for themselves and their households, and organizations, buying for their own use (such as manufacturers) or for resale (such as wholesalers and retailers). The key to achieving these two objectives is the idea of **exchange**, which is the trade of things of value between a buyer and a seller so that each is better off after the trade.[7]

The Diverse Elements Influencing Marketing Actions

Although an organization's marketing activity focuses on assessing and satisfying consumer needs, countless other people, groups, and forces interact to shape the nature of its actions (see Figure 1–2). Foremost is the organization itself, whose mission and objectives determine what business it is in and what goals it seeks. Within the organization, management is responsible for establishing these goals. The marketing department works closely with a network of other departments and employees to help provide the customer-satisfying products required for the organization to survive and prosper.

Figure 1–2 also shows the key people, groups, and forces outside the organization that influence its marketing activities. The marketing department is responsible for facilitating relationships, partnerships, and alliances with the organization's customers, its shareholders (or often representatives of nonprofit organizations), its suppliers, and other organizations. Environmental forces involving social, economic, technological, competitive, and regulatory considerations also shape an organization's marketing

FIGURE 1–2

A marketing department relates to many people, organizations, and forces. Note that the marketing department both *shapes* and *is shaped by* its relationship with these internal and external groups.

The Organization and Its Departments

actions. Finally, an organization's marketing decisions are affected by and, in turn, often have an important impact on society as a whole.

The organization must strike a balance among the sometimes differing interests of these groups. For example, it is not possible to simultaneously provide the lowest-priced and highest-quality products to customers and pay the highest prices to suppliers, the highest wages to employees, and the maximum dividends to shareholders.

What Is Needed for Marketing to Occur

For marketing to occur, at least four factors are required: (1) two or more parties (individuals or organizations) with unsatisfied needs, (2) a desire and ability on their part to have their needs satisfied, (3) a way for the parties to communicate, and (4) something to exchange.

Marketing doesn't happen in a vacuum. The text describes the four factors needed to buy a product like a Domino's Handmade Pan Pizza.
© Domino's Pizza

Two or More Parties with Unsatisfied Needs Suppose you've developed an unmet need—a desire for a late-night dinner after studying for an exam—but you don't yet know that Domino's Pizza has a location in your area. Also unknown to you is that Domino's has a special offer for its tasty Handmade Pan Pizza, just waiting to be ordered, handmade, and delivered. This is an example of two parties with unmet needs: you, desiring a meal, and your local Domino's Pizza owner, needing someone to buy a Handmade Pan Pizza.

Desire and Ability to Satisfy These Needs Both you and the Domino's Pizza owner want to satisfy these unmet needs. Furthermore, you have the money to buy the Domino's Handmade Pan Pizza and the time to order it online or over the telephone. The Domino's owner has not only the desire to sell its Handmade Pan Pizza but also the ability to do so since the pizza is easily made and delivered to (or picked up by) you.

A Way for the Parties to Communicate The marketing transaction of purchasing a Domino's Handmade Pan Pizza will never occur unless you know the product exists and its location (street/web address and/or phone number). Similarly, the Domino's Pizza owner won't sell the Handmade Pan Pizza unless there's a market of potential buyers nearby. When you receive a coupon on your phone or drive by the Domino's store location, this communication barrier between you (the buyer) and the Domino's Pizza owner (the seller) is overcome.

Something to Exchange Marketing occurs when the transaction takes place and both the buyer and seller exchange something of value. In this case, you exchange your money ($8.99) for the Domino's Handmade Pan Pizza. Both you and the Domino's Pizza owner have gained and also given up something, but you are both better off because each of you has satisfied the other's unmet needs. You have the opportunity to eat a Domino's Handmade Pan Pizza to satisfy your hunger, but you gave up some money to do so; the Domino's Pizza owner gave up the Handmade Pan Pizza but received money, which will help the owner remain in business. The ethical and legal foundations of this exchange process are central to marketing and are discussed in Chapter 4.

learning review »

1-1. What is marketing?

1-2. Marketing focuses on _____ and _____ consumer needs.

1-3. What four factors are needed for marketing to occur?

HOW MARKETING DISCOVERS AND SATISFIES CONSUMER NEEDS

LO 1-2 Explain how marketing discovers and satisfies consumer needs.

The importance of discovering and satisfying consumer needs in order to develop and offer successful products is so critical to understanding marketing that we look at each of these two steps in detail next. Let's start by asking you to analyze the three products below.

For these three products, identify (1) what benefits the product provides buyers and (2) what factors or "showstoppers" might doom the product in the marketplace. Answers are discussed in the text.
Left: © SSPL/Getty Images; Middle: Courtesy of StuffDOT, Inc.; Right: © Consumer Trends/Alamy

A message pad with handwriting recognition software.

An e-commerce site with financial benefits for users.

A mid-calorie cola.

Discovering Consumer Needs

The first objective in marketing is discovering the needs of prospective customers. Marketers often use customers surveys, concept tests, and other forms of marketing research (discussed in detail in Chapter 8) to better understand customer ideas. Many firms also use "crowdsourcing" websites to solicit and evaluate ideas from customers. At LEGO Group, for example, ideas that receive 10,000 votes from site visitors are considered for possible addition to the product line. LEGO Group products that were discovered through the website include its Ghostbuster ambulance, its Mars rover Curiosity, and a set based on the Minecraft video game! Sometimes, however, customers may not know or be able to describe what they need and want. Personal computers, smartphones, and electric cars are all examples of this, in which case an accurate long-term prediction of consumer needs is essential.[8]

The Challenge: Meeting Consumer Needs with New Products

While marketers are improving the ways they can generate new product ideas, experts estimate that it takes 3,000 raw ideas to generate one commercial success. Market intelligence agency Mintel estimates that 33,000 new products are introduced worldwide each month. In addition, studies of new-product launches indicates that about 40 percent of the products fail. Robert M. McMath, who has studied more than 110,000 of these new-product launches, has two key suggestions: (1) focus on what the customer benefit is, and (2) learn from past mistakes.[9]

The solution to preventing product failures seems embarrassingly obvious. First, find out what consumers need and want. Second, produce what they need and want, and don't produce what they don't need and want. The three products shown above illustrate just how difficult it is to achieve new-product success, a topic covered in more detail in Chapter 10.

Without reading further, think about the potential benefits to customers and possible "showstoppers"—factors that might doom the product—for each of the three products pictured. Some of the products may come out of your past, and others may be on your horizon. Here's a quick analysis of the three products:

- *Apple Newton.* In the 1990s Apple launched its Newton MessagePad, the first handheld device in a category that came to be known as personal digital assistants. Apple invested more than $1.5 billion in today's dollars but sold just a few hundred thousand units before Steve Jobs took the product off the market. In many ways the showstopper for this product was that it was before its time. It launched before the World Wide Web, before cellphones, and before the broad use of e-mail. As a result, while the product was revolutionary, the uses for consumers were limited![10]

- *StuffDOT®.* This recent start-up is a social e-commerce site that seeks to reward consumers for their online shopping and sharing activity. This is possible because Internet retailers like Amazon and Target.com make small payments to the owners of websites that refer shoppers to their products. These payments are a big and growing business, generating a projected $4.5 billion in 2016.[11] StuffDOT's founders believe that consumers deserve to share in those payments, so they have developed a platform that enables users to earn a portion of the revenue that they generate by sharing links and shopping online. A potential showstopper: Will consumers understand the benefits of StuffDOT well enough to change their shopping habits to take advantage of the opportunity?

- *Pepsi True.* At the 2014 Clinton Global Initiative, PepsiCo and Coca-Cola announced an agreement to reduce the calorie content of their products by 20 percent before 2025. As part of this agreement PepsiCo launched a new product—Pepsi True. The new cola is sweetened with a combination of sugar and stevia leaf extract, resulting in a soft drink with the same flavor of Pepsi-Cola but only 60 calories. Pepsi True is offered in the U.S. through Amazon. com and in grocery stores, and will be introduced in Great Britain where it will compete with Coca-Cola's Coca-Cola Life. A potential showstopper: In the past, mid-calorie soft drinks such as Pepsi Next (2012), Pepsi Edge (2004), and Pepsi XL (1995) have not been successful as "transition" sodas from regular to diet. Will Pepsi True be next? As always, as a consumer, you will be the judge![12]

Firms spend billions of dollars annually on marketing and technical research that significantly reduces, but doesn't eliminate, new-product failure. So meeting the changing needs of consumers is a continuing challenge for firms around the world.

Consumer Needs and Consumer Wants   Should marketing try to satisfy consumer needs or consumer wants? Marketing tries to do both. Heated debates rage over this question, fueled by the definitions of needs and wants and the amount of freedom given to prospective customers to make their own buying decisions.

A *need* occurs when a person feels deprived of basic necessities such as food, clothing, and shelter. A *want* is a need that is shaped by a person's knowledge, culture, and personality. So if you feel hungry, you have developed a basic need and desire to eat something. Let's say you then want to eat a Cool Mint Chocolate Clif Bar because, based on your past experience, you know it will satisfy your hunger need. Effective marketing, in the form of creating an awareness of good products at fair prices and convenient locations, can clearly shape a person's wants.

Certainly, marketing tries to influence what we buy. A question then arises: At what point do we want government and society to step in to protect consumers? Most

Studying late at night for an exam and being hungry, you decide to eat a Cool Mint Chocolate Clif Bar. Is this a need or want? The text discusses the role of marketing in influencing decisions like this.
© *McGraw-Hill Education/David A. Tietz, photographer*

FIGURE 1–3

Marketing seeks first to discover consumer needs through extensive research. It then seeks to satisfy those needs by successfully implementing a marketing program possessing the right combination of the marketing mix—the four Ps.

Organization's marketing department

Discover consumer needs by researching what consumers needs are

Concepts for products

Satisfy consumer needs by designing a marketing program having the right combination of:
• Product
• Price
• Promotion
• Place

Information about needs

Products, services, ideas

Potential consumers: The market

consumers would say they want government to protect us from harmful drugs and unsafe cars but not from candy bars and soft drinks. To protect college students, should government restrict their use of credit cards?[13] Such questions have no clear-cut answers, which is why legal and ethical issues are central to marketing. Because even psychologists and economists still debate the exact meanings of *need* and *want*, we shall use the terms interchangeably throughout the book.

As shown in the left side of Figure 1–3, discovering needs involves looking carefully at prospective customers, whether they are children buying M&M's candy, college students buying Chobani Greek Yogurt, or firms buying Xerox color copiers. A principal activity of a firm's marketing department is to scrutinize its consumers to understand what they need and want and the forces that shape those needs and wants.

What a Market Is   Potential consumers make up a **market**, which is people with both the desire and the ability to buy a specific offering. All markets ultimately are people. Even when we say a firm bought a Xerox copier, we mean one or several people in the firm decided to buy it. People who are aware of their unmet needs may have the desire to buy the product, but that alone isn't sufficient. People must also have the ability to buy, such as the authority, time, and money. People may even "buy" an idea that results in an action, such as having their blood pressure checked annually or turning down their thermostat to save energy.

Satisfying Consumer Needs

Marketing doesn't stop with the discovery of consumer needs. Because the organization obviously can't satisfy all consumer needs, it must concentrate its efforts on certain needs of a specific group of potential consumers. This is the **target market**—one or more specific groups of potential consumers toward which an organization directs its marketing program.

LO 1-3   Distinguish between marketing mix factors and environmental forces.

The Four Ps: Controllable Marketing Mix Factors   Having selected its target market consumers, the firm must take steps to satisfy their needs, as shown in the right side of Figure 1–3. Someone in the organization's marketing department, often the marketing manager, must develop a complete marketing program to reach consumers by using a combination of four elements, often called "the four Ps"—a useful shorthand reference to them first published by Professor E. Jerome McCarthy:[14]

- *Product.* A good, service, or idea to satisfy the consumer's needs.
- *Price.* What is exchanged for the product.
- *Promotion.* A means of communication between the seller and buyer.
- *Place.* A means of getting the product to the consumer.

We'll define each of the four Ps more carefully later in the book, but for now it's important to remember that they are the elements of the **marketing mix**. These four elements are the controllable factors—product, price, promotion, and place—that can be used by the marketing manager to solve a marketing problem. For example, when a company puts a product on sale, it is changing one element of the marketing mix—namely, the price. The marketing mix elements are called *controllable factors* because they are under the control of the marketing department in an organization.

Designing an effective marketing mix also conveys to potential buyers a clear **customer value proposition**, which is a cluster of benefits that an organization promises customers to satisfy their needs. For example, Walmart's customer value proposition can be described as "help people around the world save money and live better—anytime and anywhere." Michelin's customer value proposition can be summed up as "providing safety-conscious parents greater security in tires at a premium price."[15]

Firms can affect some environmental forces with breakthrough products such as the Apple Watch.

© *Chesnot/Getty Images*

The Uncontrollable, Environmental Forces While marketers can control their marketing mix factors, there are forces that are mostly beyond their control (see Figure 1–2). These are the **environmental forces** that affect a marketing decision, which consist of social, economic, technological, competitive, and regulatory forces. Examples are what consumers themselves want and need, changing technology, the state of the economy in terms of whether it is expanding or contracting, actions that competitors take, and government restrictions. Covered in detail in Chapter 3, these five forces may serve as accelerators or brakes on marketing, sometimes expanding an organization's marketing opportunities and at other times restricting them.

Traditionally, many marketing executives have treated these environmental forces as rigid, absolute constraints that are entirely outside their influence. However, recent studies and marketing successes have shown that a forward-looking, action-oriented firm can often affect some environmental forces by achieving technological or competitive breakthroughs, such as Apple's new Apple Watch.

THE MARKETING PROGRAM: HOW CUSTOMER RELATIONSHIPS ARE BUILT

LO 1-4 Explain how organizations build strong customer relationships and customer value through marketing.

An organization's marketing program connects it with its customers. To clarify this link, we will first discuss the critically important concepts of customer value, customer relationships, and relationship marketing. Then we will illustrate these concepts using 3M's marketing program for its Post-it® Flag Highlighter products.

Relationship Marketing: Easy to Understand, Hard to Do

Intense competition in today's fast-paced global markets has prompted many successful U.S. firms to focus on "customer value." Gaining loyal customers by providing unique value is the essence of successful marketing. What is new is a more careful attempt at

Target, Starbucks, and Nordstrom provide customer value using three very different approaches. For their strategies, see the text.

Left: © Target; Middle: © Starbucks; Right © Studio Works/Alamy

understanding how a firm's customers perceive value and then actually creating and delivering that value to them.[16] **Customer value** is the unique combination of benefits received by targeted buyers that includes quality, convenience, on-time delivery, and both before-sale and after-sale service at a specific price. Firms now actually try to place a dollar value on the purchases of loyal, satisfied customers during their lifetimes. For example, loyal Kleenex customers average 6.7 boxes a year, about $994 over 60 years in today's dollars (see question 2, Figure 1–1).[17]

Research suggests that firms cannot succeed by being all things to all people. Instead, firms seek to build long-term relationships with customers by providing unique value to them. Many successful firms deliver outstanding customer value with one of three value strategies: best price, best product, or best service.[18]

With the intense competition among U.S. businesses, being seen as "best" is admittedly difficult. Still, the three firms shown in the ads on the previous page have achieved great success as reflected in the mission, vision, and values statements they stress and live by:[19]

- Best price: Target. It uses the Target brand promise of "Expect More, Pay Less®" to "make Target the preferred shopping destination for our guests by delivering outstanding value."
- Best product: Starbucks. Starbucks seeks "to inspire and nurture the human spirit—one person, one cup and one neighborhood at a time," stressing "The best coffee for the best YOU," in the process.
- Best service: Nordstrom. As a leading fashion specialty retailer, Nordstrom works to "deliver the best possible shopping experience, helping customer possess style—not just buy fashion." Nordstrom is "committed to providing our customers with the best possible service—and improving it every day."

Remaining among the "best" is a continuing challenge for today's businesses.

A firm achieves meaningful customer relationships by creating connections with its customers through careful coordination of the product, its price, the way it's promoted, and how it's placed.

The hallmark of developing and maintaining effective customer relationships is today called **relationship marketing**, which links the organization to its individual customers, employees, suppliers, and other partners for their mutual long-term benefit. Relationship marketing involves a personal, ongoing relationship between the organization and its individual customers that begins before and continues after the sale.[20]

Information technology, along with cutting-edge manufacturing and marketing processes, better enables companies to form relationships with customers today. Smart, connected products, now elements of "the Internet of everything," help create detailed databases about product usage. Then, using data analytics, or the examination of data to discover relevant patterns, companies can gain insights into how products create value for customers. For example, BMW receives data transmitted by each new vehicle it sells and General Electric collects information sent in by the jet engines it builds to help them understand how customers use their products and when service may be

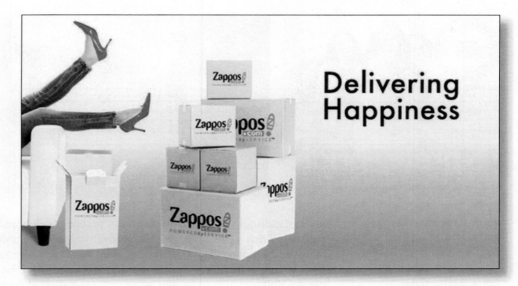

needed. Online shoe retailer Zappos observes and tracks its customers' purchases to provide personal connections and create customers for life.[21]

The Marketing Program and Market Segments

Effective relationship marketing strategies help marketing managers discover what prospective customers need and convert these ideas into marketable products (see Figure 1–3). These concepts must then be converted into a tangible **marketing program**—a plan that integrates the marketing mix to provide a good, service, or idea to prospective buyers. Ideally, they can be formed into **market segments**, which are relatively homogeneous groups of prospective buyers that (1) have common needs and (2) will respond similarly to a marketing action. This action might be a product feature, a promotion, or a price. As shown in Figure 1–3, in an effective organization this process is continuous: Consumer needs trigger product concepts that are translated into actual products that stimulate further discovery of consumer needs.

learning review »

1-4. An organization can't satisfy the needs of all consumers, so it must focus on one or more subgroups, which are its _____.

1-5. What are the four marketing mix elements that make up the organization's marketing program?

1-6. What are environmental forces?

3M's Strategy and Marketing Program to Help Students Study

"How do college students *really* study?" asked David Windorski, a 3M inventor of Post-it® brand products, when thinking about adding a new item to the Post-it® line.[22]

To answer this question, Windorski worked with a team of four college students. Their task was to observe and question dozens of students about their study behavior, such as how they used their textbooks, took notes, wrote term papers, and reviewed for exams. Often, they watched students highlight a passage and then mark the page with a Post-it® Note or the smaller Post-it® Flag. Windorski realized there was an opportunity to merge the functions of two products into one to help students study!

Moving from Ideas to a Marketable Highlighter Product After working on 15 or 20 models, Windorski concluded he had to build a highlighter product that

3M's initial product line of Post-it® Flag Highlighters and Post-it® Flag Pens includes variations in color and line widths.

© Mike Hruby

would dispense Post-it® Flags because the Post-it® Notes were simply too large to put inside the barrel of a highlighter.

Hundreds of the initial highlighter prototypes with Post-it® Flags inside were produced and given to students—and also office workers—to get their reactions. This research showed users wanted a convenient, reliable cover to protect the Post-it® Flags in the highlighter. So the Post-it® Flag Highlighter with a rotating cover was born.

Adding the Post-it® Flag Pen   Most of David Windorski's initial design energies had gone into his Post-it® Flag Highlighter research and development. But Windorski also considered other related products. Many people in offices need immediate access to Post-it® Flags while writing with pens. Students are a potential market for this product, too, but probably a smaller market segment than office workers.

A Marketing Program for the Post-it® Flag Highlighter and Pen   After several years of research, development, and production engineering, 3M introduced its new products. Figure 1–4 outlines the strategies for each of the four marketing mix elements in 3M's program to market its Post-it® Flag Highlighters and Post-it® Flag Pens. Although similar, we can compare the marketing program for each of the two products:

- *Post-it® Flag Highlighter.* The target market shown in the orange column in Figure 1–4 is mainly college students, so 3M's initial challenge was to build student awareness of a product that they didn't know existed. The company used a mix of print ads in college newspapers and a TV ad and then relied on word-of-mouth advertising—students telling their friends about how great the product is. Gaining distribution in college bookstores was also critical. Plus, 3M charged a price to distributors that it hoped would give a reasonable bookstore price to students and an acceptable profit to distributors and 3M.

FIGURE 1–4

Marketing programs for the launch of two Post-it® brand products targeted at two target market segments.

MARKETING PROGRAM ACTION TO REACH:

MARKETING MIX ELEMENT	COLLEGE STUDENT MARKET SEGMENT	OFFICE WORKER MARKET SEGMENT	RATIONALE FOR MARKETING PROGRAM ACTION
Product strategy	Offer Post-it® Flag Highlighter to help college students in their studying	Offer Post-it® Flag Pen to help office workers in their day-to-day work activities	Listen carefully to the needs and wants of potential customer segments to use 3M technology to introduce a useful, innovative product
Price strategy	Seek retail price of about $3.99 to $4.99 for a single Post-it® Flag Highlighter or $5.99 to $7.99 for a three-pack	Seek retail price of about $3.99 to $4.99 for a single Post-it® Flag Pen; wholesale prices are lower	Set prices that provide genuine value to the customer segment being targeted
Promotion strategy	Run limited promotion with a TV ad and some ads in college newspapers and then rely on student word-of-mouth messages	Run limited promotion among distributors to get them to stock the product	Increase awareness among potential users who have never heard of this new, innovative 3M product
Place strategy	Distribute Post-it® Flag Highlighters through college bookstores, office supply stores, and mass merchandisers	Distribute Post-it® Flag Pens through office wholesalers and retailers as well as mass merchandisers	Make it easy for prospective buyers to buy at convenient retail outlets (both products) or to get at work (Post-it® Flag Pens only)

Welcome to the third generation of Post-it® Flag Highlighters: the 3-in-1 Post-it® Flag Pen and Highlighter. The cap contains the Post-it® flags.
© Mike Hruby

- *Post-it® Flag Pen.* The primary target market shown in the green column in Figure 1–4 is people working in offices. The Post-it® Flag Pens are mainly business products—bought by the purchasing department in an organization and stocked as office supplies for employees to use. So the marketing program for Post-it® Flag Pens emphasizes gaining distribution in outlets used by an organization's purchasing department.

How well did these new 3M products do in the marketplace? They have done so well that 3M bestowed a prestigious award on David Windorski and his team. And in what must be considered any inventor's dream come true, Oprah Winfrey flew Windorski to Chicago to appear on her TV show and thank him in person. She told Windorski and her audience that the Post-it® Flag Highlighter is changing the way she does things at home and at work—especially in going through potential books she might recommend for her book club. "David, I know you never thought this would happen when you were in your 3M lab...but I want you to take a bow before America for the invention of this...(highlighter). It's the most incredible invention," she said.[23]

Extending the Product Line   Feedback about these two products led Windorski to design a second generation of Post-it® Flag Highlighters and Pens *without* the rotating cover to make it easier to insert replacement flags. The new tapered design is also easier for students to hold and use.

The success of the second generation of Post-it® Flag Highlighters, in turn, encouraged Windorski to continue to ask questions about how students study.

Is it too much trouble when you're studying to grab for a 3M Post-it® Flag, then a highlighter, and then your pen? You're in luck! New to the family of 3M products is the latest generation of Windorski's innovations: A 3-in-1 combination that has a highlighter on one end, a pen on the other, and 3M Post-it® Flags in the removable cap, as shown in the photo.

HOW MARKETING BECAME SO IMPORTANT

 LO 1-5 Describe how today's customer relationship era differs from prior eras.

To understand why marketing is a driving force in the modern global economy, let us look at (1) the evolution of the market orientation, (2) ethics and social responsibility in marketing, and (3) the breadth and depth of marketing activities.

Evolution of the Market Orientation

Many American manufacturers have experienced four distinct stages in the life of their firms.[24] The first stage, the *production era,* covers the early years of the United States up until the 1920s. Goods were scarce and buyers were willing to accept virtually any goods that were available and make do with them.[25] In the *sales era* from the 1920s to the 1960s, manufacturers found they could produce more goods than buyers could consume. Competition grew. Firms hired more salespeople to find new buyers. This sales era continued into the 1960s for many American firms.

Starting in the late 1950s, marketing became the motivating force among many American firms and the *marketing concept era* dawned. The **marketing concept** is the idea that an organization should (1) strive to satisfy the needs of consumers while also (2) trying to achieve the organization's goals. General Electric probably launched the marketing concept and its focus on consumers when its 1952 annual report stated: "The concept introduces . . . marketing . . . at the beginning rather than the end of the production cycle and integrates marketing into each phase of the business."[26]

FIGURE 1–5

Four different orientations in the history of American business. Today's customer relationship era focuses on satisfying the high expectations of customers.

Production era

Sales era

Marketing concept era

Customer relationship era

1840 1860 1880 1900 1920 1940 1960 1980 2000 2020 2040

Firms such as General Electric, Marriott, and Facebook have achieved great success by putting huge effort into implementing the marketing concept, giving their firms what has been called a *market orientation*. An organization that has a **market orientation** focuses its efforts on (1) continuously collecting information about customers' needs, (2) sharing this information across departments, and (3) using it to create customer value.[27] Today's *customer relationship era*, the brown bar in Figure 1–5, started in the 1980s and occurs as firms continuously seek to satisfy the high expectations of customers.

Focusing on Customer Relationship Management

A recent focus in the customer relationship era has been the advent of social networking, in which organizations and their customers develop relationships through social media websites such as Facebook, Twitter, and YouTube, among others. This focus has allowed organizations to understand and market to current and prospective customers in ways that are still evolving, such as in using social media.

An important outgrowth of this focus on the customer is the recent attention placed on **customer relationship management (CRM)**, the process of identifying prospective buyers, understanding them intimately, and developing favorable long-term perceptions of the organization and its offerings so that buyers will choose them in the marketplace.[28] This process requires the involvement and commitment of managers and employees throughout the organization[29] and a growing application of information, communication, and Internet technology, as will be described throughout this book.

The foundation of customer relationship management is really **customer experience**, which is the internal response that customers have to all aspects of an organization and its offering. This internal response includes both the direct and indirect contacts of the customer with the company. Direct contacts include the customer's contacts with the seller through buying, using, and obtaining service. Indirect contacts most often involve unplanned "touches" with the company through word-of-mouth comments from other customers, reviewers, and news reports.

In terms of outstanding customer experience, Trader Joe's is high on the list. It was

Trader Joe's has been ranked as America's favorite supermarket chain for two consecutive years. This reflects the company's focus on providing a great customer experience, as described in the text.

© David Paul Morris/Bloomberg via Getty Images

ranked as America's favorite supermarket chain by *Market Force Information* and called "America's hottest retailer" by *Fortune* magazine:

> But Trader Joe's is no ordinary grocery chain. It's an offbeat, fun discovery zone that elevates food shopping from a chore to a cultural experience. It stocks its shelves with a winning combination of low-cost, yuppie-friendly staples (cage-free eggs and organic blue agave sweetener) and exotic, affordable luxuries—Belgian butter waffle cookies or Thai lime-and-chili cashews—that you simply can't find anyplace else.[30]

Trader Joe's has about 415 stores in over 35 states. It started in California and then expanded on the West Coast before jumping to the East Coast in 1996 and the Midwest in 2000.

What makes the customer experience and loyalty of shoppers at Trader Joe's unique? The reasons include:

- Setting low prices, made possible by offering its own brands rather than well-known national ones.
- Offering unusual, affordable products, like Thai lime-and-chili cashews, not available from other retailers.
- Providing rare employee "engagement" to help customers, like actually walking them to where the roasted chestnuts are—rather than saying "aisle five."

This commitment to providing an exceptional customer experience is what gives Trader Joe's its high rankings. Recent studies support this approach, suggesting that companies must watch for differences between the experience they offer and what consumers expect at each interaction, and they must excel at managing the complete experience from start to finish.[31]

Ethics and Social Responsibility in Marketing: Balancing the Interests of Different Groups

As organizations have changed their orientation, society's expectations of marketers have also changed. Today, the standards of marketing practice have shifted from an emphasis on producers' interests to consumers' interests. Guidelines for ethical and socially responsible behavior can help managers balance consumer, organizational, and societal interests.

Ethics   Many marketing issues are not specifically addressed by existing laws and regulations. Should information about a firm's customers be sold to other organizations? Should advertising by professional service providers, such as accountants and attorneys, be restricted? Should consumers be on their own to assess the safety of a product? These questions raise difficult ethical issues. Many companies, industries, and professional associations have developed codes of ethics to assist managers.

Social Responsibility   While many ethical issues involve only the buyer and seller, others involve society as a whole. For example, suppose you have the oil in your car changed at a local oil change center. Is this just a transaction between you and the service center? Not quite! The used oil and oil filter have potential to contaminate the environment if they are not recycled, and contamination represents a cost to society in terms of lost use of landfill space or eventual cleanup of the discarded waste products. To reduce the social cost of individual purchases today, many organizations use a variety of strategies that range from pure philanthropy, to environmentally friendly and sustainable practices, to creating "shared" value.[32] These strategies illustrate the issue of *social responsibility*, the idea that organizations are accountable to a larger society.

The well-being of society at large should also be recognized in an organization's marketing decisions. In fact, some marketing experts stress the **societal marketing concept**, the view that organizations should satisfy the needs of consumers in a way that provides for society's well-being.[33] For example, 3M's Scotch-Brite® Greener Clean non-scratch scrub sponges are made from recycled agave plant fibers that remain after the plants are harvested for tequila production (see question 3, Figure 1-1). The sponges outlast 30 rolls of paper towels!

3M's Scotch-Brite® Greener Clean non-scratch scrub sponges—made from agave plants—reflect the increasing concern among today's organizations for society's well-being.

© McGraw-Hill Education/David A. Tietz, photographer

The Breadth and Depth of Marketing

Marketing today affects every person and organization. To understand this, let's analyze (1) who markets, (2) what is marketed, (3) who buys and uses what is marketed, (4) who benefits from these marketing activities, and (5) how consumers benefit.

Who Markets? Every organization markets. It's obvious that business firms involved in manufacturing (Heinz), retailing (Trader Joe's), and providing services (Marriott) market their offerings. And nonprofit organizations such as museums, your local hospital or college, places (cities, states, countries), and even special causes (Race for the Cure) also engage in marketing. Finally, individuals such as political candidates often use marketing to gain voter attention and preference.

What Is Marketed? Goods, services, and ideas are marketed. *Goods* are physical objects, such as toothpaste, cameras, or computers, that satisfy consumer needs. *Services* are intangible items such as airline trips, financial advice, or art museums. *Ideas* are thoughts about concepts, actions, or causes.

In this book, goods, services, and ideas are all considered "products" that are marketed. So a **product** is a good, service, or idea consisting of a bundle of tangible and intangible attributes that satisfies consumers' needs and is received in exchange for money or something else of value.

Services like those offered by art museums, hospitals, and sports teams are relying more heavily on effective marketing. For example, financial pressures have caused art museums to innovate to market their unique services—the viewing of works of art by visitors—to increase revenues. This often involves levels of rare creativity unthinkable several decades ago.

Strategies in marketing art museums include planning new "satellite" museums like this one for the Louvre in Abu Dhabi . . .

© AFP/Getty Images

This creativity ranges from establishing a global brand identity by launching overseas museums to offering sit-at-home video tours. France's Louvre, home to the *Mona Lisa* painting, is developing a new satellite museum in Abu Dhabi housed in an architecturally space-age building.[34] Russia's world-class 1,000-room State Hermitage Museum wanted to find a way to market itself to potential first-time visitors. So it partnered with IBM to let you take a "virtual tour" of its exhibits while watching on your iPad and relaxing.

Ideas are most often marketed by nonprofit organizations or the government. So the Nature Conservancy markets the cause of protecting the environment. Charities market the idea that

... or taking a "virtual tour" of Russia's State Hermitage Museum—courtesy of IBM.

© Izzet Keribar/Lonely Plant Images/Getty Images

Video 1-5
Hermitage Tour
kerin.tv/13e/v1-5

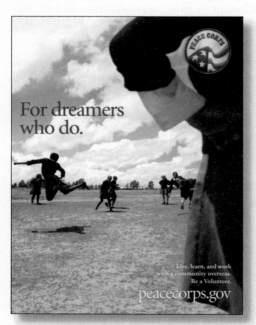

For dreamers who do.

Live, learn, and work with a community overseas. Be a Volunteer.

peacecorps.gov

Marketing the idea of volunteering for the Peace Corps can benefit society.

United States Peace Corps

it's worthwhile for you to donate your time or money. The Peace Corps markets to recruit qualified volunteers. And state governments in Arizona and Florida market taking a warm, sunny winter vacation in their states.

Who Buys and Uses What Is Marketed?

Both individuals and organizations buy and use products that are marketed. **Ultimate consumers** are the people—whether 80 years or eight months old—who use the products and services purchased for a household. In contrast, **organizational buyers** are those manufacturers, wholesalers, retailers, service companies, not-for-profit organizations and government agencies that buy products and services for theirown use or for resale. Although the terms *consumers, buyers,* and *customers* are sometimes used for both ultimate consumers and organizations, there is no consistency on this. In this book you will be able to tell from the example whether the buyers are ultimate consumers, organizations, or both.

Who Benefits?

In our free-enterprise society, there are three specific groups that benefit from effective marketing: consumers who buy, organizations that sell, and society as a whole. True competition between products and services in the marketplace ensures that consumers can find value from the best products, the lowest prices, or exceptional service. Providing choices leads to the consumer satisfaction and quality of life that we expect from our economic system.

Organizations that provide need-satisfying products with effective marketing programs—for example, Target, IBM, and Avon—have blossomed. But competition creates problems for ineffective competitors, including the hundreds of dot-com businesses, such as Pets.com, that failed over a decade ago.

Finally, effective marketing benefits society.[35] It enhances competition, which both improves the quality of products and services and lowers their prices. This makes countries more competitive in world markets and provides jobs and a higher standard of living for their citizens.

How Do Consumers Benefit?

Marketing creates **utility**, the benefits or customer value received by users of the product. This utility is the result of the marketing exchange process and the way society benefits from marketing. There are four different utilities: form, place, time, and possession. The production of the product or service constitutes *form utility*. *Place utility* means having the offering available where consumers need it, whereas *time utility* means having it available when needed. *Possession utility* is the value of making an item easy to purchase through the provision of credit cards or financial arrangements. Marketing creates its utilities by bridging space (place utility) and hours (time utility) to provide products (form utility) for consumers to own and use (possession utility).

learning review ≫

1-7. What are the two key characteristics of the marketing concept?

1-8. What is the difference between ultimate consumers and organizational buyers?

LEARNING OBJECTIVES REVIEW

LO 1-1 *Define marketing and identify the diverse factors that influence marketing actions.*

Marketing is an organizational function and a set of processes for creating, communicating, and delivering value to customers and for managing customer relationships in ways that benefit the organization and its stakeholders. This definition relates to two primary goals of marketing: (*a*) discovering the needs of prospective customers and (*b*) satisfying them. Achieving these two goals also involves the four marketing mix factors largely controlled by the organization and the five environmental forces that are generally outside its control.

LO 1-2 *Explain how marketing discovers and satisfies consumer needs.*

The first objective in marketing is discovering the needs and wants of consumers who are prospective buyers and customers. This is not easy because consumers may not always know or be able to describe what they need and want. A need occurs when a person feels deprived of basic necessities such as food, clothing, and shelter. A want is a need that is shaped by a person's knowledge, culture, and personality. Effective marketing can clearly shape a person's wants and tries to influence what he or she buys. The second objective in marketing is satisfying the needs of targeted consumers. Because an organization obviously can't satisfy all consumer needs, it must concentrate its efforts on certain needs of a specific group of potential consumers or target market—one or more specific groups of potential consumers toward which an organization directs its marketing program. It then selects its target market segment(s), which are relatively homogeneous groups of prospective buyers that (1) have common needs and (2) will respond similarly to a marketing action. Finally, the organization develops a set of marketing actions in the form of a unique marketing program to reach them.

LO 1-3 *Distinguish between marketing mix factors and environmental forces.*

Four elements in a marketing program designed to satisfy customer needs are product, price, promotion, and place. These elements are called the marketing mix, the four Ps, or the marketer's controllable variables. The marketing mix also provides a clear customer value proposition—a cluster of benefits that an offering satisfies. Environmental forces, also called uncontrollable variables, are largely beyond the organization's control. These include social, economic, technological, competitive, and regulatory forces.

LO 1-4 *Explain how organizations build strong customer relationships and customer value through marketing.*

The essence of successful marketing is to provide sufficient value to gain loyal, long-term customers. Customer value is the unique combination of benefits received by targeted buyers that usually includes quality, price, convenience, on-time delivery, and both before-sale and after-sale service. Marketers do this by using one of three value strategies: best price, best product, or best service.

LO 1-5 *Describe how today's customer relationship era differs from prior eras.*

U.S. business history is divided into four overlapping periods: the production era, the sales era, the marketing concept era, and the current customer relationship era. The production era covers the period up until the 1920s, when buyers were willing to accept virtually any goods that were available. The central notion was that products would sell themselves. The sales era lasted from the 1920s to the 1960s. Manufacturers found they could produce more goods than buyers could consume, and competition grew, so the solution was to hire more salespeople to find new buyers. In the late 1950s, the marketing concept era dawned when organizations adopted a strong market orientation and integrated marketing into each phase of their business. In today's customer relationship era, organizations continuously seek to satisfy the high expectations of customers—an aggressive extension of the marketing concept era. This is increasingly done through social media.

LEARNING REVIEW ANSWERS

1-1 **What is marketing?**
Answer: Marketing is the activity for creating, communicating, delivering, and exchanging offerings that benefit customers, the organization, its stakeholders, and society at large.

1-2 **Marketing focuses on _____ and _____ consumer needs.**
Answer: discovering; satisfying

1-3 **What four factors are needed for marketing to occur?**
Answer: The four factors are: (1) two or more parties (individuals or organizations) with unsatisfied needs; (2) a desire and ability on their part to have their needs satisfied; (3) a way for the parties to communicate; and (4) something to exchange.

1-4 **An organization can't satisfy the needs of all consumers, so it must focus on one or more subgroups, which are its _____.**
Answer: target market

1-5 **What are the four marketing mix elements that make up the organization's marketing program?**
Answer: product, price, promotion, place

1-6 **What are environmental forces?**
Answer: Environmental forces are the uncontrollable forces that affect a marketing decision. They consist of social, economic, technological, competitive, and regulatory forces.

1-7 **What are the two key characteristics of the marketing concept?**
Answer: An organization should (1) strive to satisfy the needs of consumers while also (2) trying to achieve the organization's goals.

1-8 **What is the difference between ultimate consumers and organizational buyers?**
Answer: Ultimate consumers are the people who use the products and services purchased for a household. Organizational buyers are those manufacturers, wholesalers, retailers, and government agencies that buy products and services for their own use or for resale.

customer experience p. 15
customer relationship management
  (CRM) p. 15
customer value p. 11
customer value proposition p. 10
environmental forces p. 10
exchange p. 5

market p. 9
market orientation p. 15
market segments p. 12
marketing p. 5
marketing concept p. 14
marketing mix p. 10
marketing program p. 12

organizational buyers p. 18
product p. 17
relationship marketing p. 12
societal marketing concept p. 17
target market p. 9
ultimate consumers p. 18
utility p. 18

APPLYING MARKETING KNOWLEDGE

1 What consumer wants (or benefits) are met by the following products or services? (*a*) 3M Post-it® Flag Highlighter, (*b*) Nike running shoes, (*c*) Hertz Rent-A-Car, and (*d*) television home shopping programs.

2 Each of the four products, services, or programs in question 1 has substitutes. Respective examples are (*a*) a Bic™ highlighter, (*b*) regular tennis shoes, (*c*) a bus ride, and (*d*) a department store. What consumer benefits might these substitutes have in each case that some consumers might value more highly than those mentioned in question 1?

3 What are the characteristics (e.g., age, income, education) of the target market customers for the following products or services? (*a*) *National Geographic* magazine, (*b*) Chobani Greek Yogurt, (*c*) New York Giants football team, and (*d*) Facebook.

4 A college in a metropolitan area wishes to increase its evening-school offerings of business-related courses such as marketing, accounting, finance, and management. Who are the target market customers (students) for these courses?

5 What actions involving the four marketing mix elements might be used to reach the target market in question 4?

6 What environmental forces (uncontrollable variables) must the college in question 4 consider in designing its marketing program?

7 Does a firm have the right to "create" wants and try to persuade consumers to buy goods and services they didn't know about earlier? What are examples of "good" and "bad" want creation? Who should decide what is good and what is bad?

BUILDING YOUR MARKETING PLAN

If your instructor assigns a marketing plan for your class, don't make a face and complain about the work—for two special reasons. First, you will get insights into trying to actually "do marketing" that often go beyond what you can get by simply reading the textbook. Second, thousands of graduating students every year get their first job by showing prospective employers a "portfolio" of samples of their written work from college—often a marketing plan if they have one. This can work for you.

This "Building Your Marketing Plan" section at the end of each chapter suggests ways to improve and focus your marketing plan. You will use the sample marketing plan in Appendix A (following Chapter 2) as a guide, and this section after each chapter will help you apply those Appendix A ideas to your own marketing plan.

The first step in writing a good marketing plan is to have a business or product that enthuses you and for which you can get detailed information, so you can avoid glittering generalities. We offer these additional bits of advice in selecting a topic:

- *Do* pick a topic that has personal interest for you—a family business; a business, product, or service you or a friend might want to launch; or a student organization that needs marketing help.
- *Do not* pick a topic that is so large it can't be covered adequately or so abstract it will lack specifics.

1 Now to get you started on your marketing plan, list four or five possible topics and compare these with the criteria your instructor suggests and those shown above. Think hard, because your decision will be with you all term and may influence the quality of the resulting marketing plan you show to a prospective employer.

2 When you have selected your marketing plan topic, whether the plan is for an actual business, a possible business, or a student organization, write the "company description" in your plan, as shown in Appendix A (following Chapter 2).

"Everybody should be able to enjoy a pure, simple cup of yogurt. And that's what Chobani is," says Hamdi Ulukaya, founder and chief executive officer of Chobani, LLC, in summarizing his vision for the company.

Video 1-6
Chobani
Video Case
kerin.tv/13e/v1-6

As the winner of the 2013 Ernst & Young World Entrepreneur of the Year award, his words and success story carry great credibility.

THE IDEA

Hamdi Ulukaya came to the United States in 1994 to learn English and study business. He started a feta cheese company, Euphrates, when his visiting father complained about the quality of American feta cheese. In 2005, Kraft Foods closed its New Berlin, New York, yogurt plant built in 1885. While tidying up his office, Ulukaya stumbled upon a postcard about the sale of the shuttered Kraft plant and threw it out. After sleeping on the decision, he fished it out of the wastebasket, visited the plant, and purchased it with the help of a U.S. Small Business Administration loan.

Ulukaya (center in photo) had no real experience in the yogurt business. He grew up milking sheep at his family's dairy in eastern Turkey and eating the thick, tangy yogurt of his homeland. Describing the regular yogurt he found on shelves in America, he has one comment: "Terrible!" In his view, it is too thin, too sweet, and too fake. So he decided to produce what is known as "Greek yogurt"—an authentic strained version that produces a thick texture, high protein content, and with little or no fat. With the help of four former Kraft employees and yogurt master Mustafa Dogan, Ulukaya worked 18 months to perfect the recipe for Chobani Greek Yogurt.

© Diane Bondareff/Invision for Chobani/AP Images

The very first cup for sale of Ulukaya's Greek yogurt appeared on shelves of a small grocer on Long Island, New York, in 2007. The new-product launch focused on the classic "4Ps" elements of marketing mix actions: product, price, place, and promotion.

PRODUCT STRATEGY

From the start Ulukaya's Greek yogurt carried the brand name "Chobani." There was no room for error, and the product strategy for the Chobani brand focused on the separate elements of (1) the product itself and (2) its packaging.

The Chobani product strategy stresses its authentic straining process that removes excess liquid whey. This results in a thicker, creamier yogurt that yields 13 to 18 grams of protein per single-serve cup, depending on the flavor. Chobani is free of ingredients like milk protein concentrate and animal-based thickeners, which some manufacturers add to make "Greek-style" yogurts.

Chobani uses three pounds of milk to make one pound of Chobani Greek Yogurt. Some other features that make Chobani Greek Yogurt *"nothing but good,"* to quote its tagline:

- Higher in protein than regular yogurt.
- Made with real fruit and only natural ingredients.
- Preservative-free.
- No artificial flavors or artificial sweeteners.
- Contains five live and active cultures, including three probiotics.

Then, and still today, Ulukaya obsesses about Chobani's packaging of the original cups. In 2007, Ulukaya concluded that *not any cup* would do. He insisted on a European-style cup with a circular opening *exactly* 95 millimeters across. This made for a shorter, wider cup that was more visible on retailer's shelves. Also, instead of painted-on labels, Ulukaya chose shrink-on plastic sleeves that adhere to the cup and offer eye-popping colors.

"With our packaging people would say, 'You're making it all look different and why are you doing that?'" says Kyle O'Brien, executive vice president of sales. "If people pay attention to our cups—bright colors and all—we know we have won them, because what's inside the cup is different from anything else on the shelf."

PRICE STRATEGY

To keep control of their product, Ulukaya and O'Brien approached retailers directly rather than going through

© Mike Hruby

distributors. Prices were set high enough to recover Chobani's costs and give reasonable margins to retailers but not so high that future rivals could undercut its price. Today, prices remain at about $1.29 for a single-serve cup.

PLACE STRATEGY

The decision of Ulukaya and O'Brien to get Chobani Greek Yogurt into the conventional yogurt aisle of traditional supermarkets—not on specialty shelves or in health food stores—proved to be sheer genius. Today Chobani sees its Greek Yogurt widely distributed in both conventional and mass supermarkets, club stores, and natural food stores. On the horizon: growing distribution in convenience and drugstores, as well as schools. Chobani is also focused on educating food service directors at schools across the United States about Greek yogurt's health benefits for schoolkids.

The Chobani growth staggers imagination. From the company's first order of 200 cases in 2007, its sales have grown to over 2 million cases per week. To increase capacity and bring new products to market faster, in 2012 Chobani opened a nearly one million square foot plant in Idaho. Built in just 326 days, it is the largest yogurt manufacturing facility in the world. Along the way Chobani faced a strange glitch: Demand for Chobani's Greek yogurt far surpassed supply, leading to unhappy retailers with no Chobani cups to sell. Kyle O'Brien launched Operation Bear Hug. "Instead of hiding behind letters to retailers, we decided to get on a plane and to communicate with them within 24 hours about the problem and what we

proposed to do about it," says O'Brien. "So we found it critical to be very transparent and open with our communication at times like that."

PROMOTION STRATEGY

In its early years Chobani had no money for traditional advertising, so it relied on word-of-mouth recommendation from enthusiastic customers. The brand harnessed consumer passion on social media channels early on and found that people loved the taste of Chobani once they tried it. So in 2010, Chobani kicked off its CHOmobile tour: a mobile vehicle sampling Chobani at events across the country, encouraging consumers to taste Greek yogurt for the first time. As Chobani grew, it began to launch new promotional activities tied to (1) traditional advertising, (2) social media, and (3) direct communication with customers.

In 2011, Chobani launched its first national advertising campaign, "Real Love Stories." The only problem: apparently it was *too* successful! The resulting additional consumer demand for Chobani Greek Yogurt exceeded its production capacity, leaving retailers unhappy because of complaining consumers. What did Chobani do then? It stopped the advertising campaign and sent in another Operation Bear Hug team to communicate with retailers. Since then it has run other successful national advertising campaigns, including sponsorship of the 2012 and 2014 U.S. Olympic Teams.

"Social media has been important to Chobani, which has embraced a high-touch model that emphasizes positive communication with its customers," says Sujean Lee, head of corporate affairs. Today, Chobani's Customer Loyalty Team receives about 7,000 inbound customer e-mails and phone calls a month and are able to make return phone calls to most of them. Consumers also get a handwritten note. Chobani launched its "Go Real Chobani" campaign in 2013 to highlight that they are a *real* company making *real* products and engaging consumers through *real* conversations.

Aside from Facebook (www.Facebook.com/Chobani), the company interacts with its consumers through Twitter, Pinterest, Instagram, Foursquare, and other social media platforms. Chobani Kitchen (www.chobanikitchen.com) is an online resource with recipes, videos, and tips on how to use its Greek yogurt in favorite recipes.

AGGRESSIVE INNOVATION AND POSITIVE SOCIAL CHANGE

Dannon, Yoplait, and PepsiCo were shocked by the success of Chobani Greek Yogurt. Each now offers its own competing Greek yogurt. With giant competitors

© John Minchillo/AP Images

like these, what can Chobani do? Chobani's focus: Innovate! And with creative, new Greek yogurt products!

"Today we offer our Chobani Greek Yogurt in single-serve and multi-serve sizes, while expanding our authentic strained Greek yogurt to new occasions and forms," says Joshua Dean, vice president of brand advertising. Its recent new-product offerings include:

- Chobani Simply 100™—a 5.3-ounce cup of yogurt made with only natural ingredients and 100 calories for the calorie conscious segment. Sample flavor: Tropical Citrus.
- Chobani Kids Pouches—made with 25 percent less sugar than other kids' yogurt products, in pouches with twist-off lids that are resealable. Sample flavor: Vanilla Chocolate Dust.
- Chobani Flip™—a 5.3-ounce, two-compartment package that lets consumers bend or "flip" mix-ins like granola or hazelnuts into the Chobani Greek Yogurt compartment. Sample flavor: Almond Coco Loco, a coconut low-fat yogurt paired with dark chocolate and sliced toasted almonds.

Chobani gives 10 percent of all profits to its Shepherd's Gift Foundation to support people and organizations working for positive, long-lasting change. The name comes from the "spirit of a shepherd," an expression in Turkey used to describe people who give without expecting anything in return. To date the foundation has supported over 50 projects—from local ones to international famine relief efforts.

WHERE TO NOW?

International operations and a unique test-market boutique in New York City give a peek at Chobani's future.

International markets provide a growth opportunity. Already sold internationally in Australia, Chobani opened its international headquarters office in 2013. Other countries have far greater annual per capita consumption than that for U.S. consumers. For example, some Europeans eat five or six times as much on average. So while entrenched competitors exist in many foreign countries, the markets are often huge, too.

How do you test ideas for new Greek yogurt flavors? In Chobani's case, it opened what it calls a "first-of-its-kind Mediterranean yogurt bar"—called Chobani SoHo—in a trendy New York City neighborhood. Here, customers can try new yogurt creations—from Strawberry + Granola to Toasted Coconut + Pineapple. The Chobani marketing team obtains consumer feedback at Chobani SoHo, leading to potential new flavors or products in the future.

Hmmm! Ready to schedule a visit to New York City and Chobani SoHo? And then sample a creation made with Pistachio + Chocolate (plain Chobani topped with pistachios, dark chocolate, honey, oranges, and fresh mint leaves), and perhaps influence what Chobani customers will be buying in the future?[36]

Questions

1 From the information about Chobani in the case and at the start of the chapter, (a) whom did Hamdi Ulukaya identify as the target for his first cups of Greek yogurt and (b) what was his initial "4Ps" marketing strategy?

2 (a) What marketing actions would you expect the companies selling Yoplait, Dannon, and PepsiCo yogurts to take in response to Chobani's appearance and (b) how might Chobani respond?

3 What are (a) the advantages and (b) the disadvantages of Chobani's Customer Loyalty Team that handles communication with customers—from phone calls and e-mails to Facebook and Twitter messages?

4 As Chobani seeks to build its brand, it opened a unique retail store in New York City: Chobani SoHo. Why did Chobani do this?

5 (a) What criteria might Chobani use when it seeks markets in new countries and (b) what three or four countries meet these criteria?

Chapter Notes

1. "Millennials' Hunger for Fresh Foods Eats into Food Giants' Profits," *Plus Media Solutions,* December 26, 2014; and Dave Fusaro, "Chobani Selected as *Food Processing* 2012 Processor of the Year," *Food Processing,* December 5, 2012.

2. Annie Gasparro, "Chobani Expands to Desserts, Dips," *The Wall Street Journal,* April 21, 2014, p. B7; and Meghan Walsh, "Chobani Takes Gold in the Yogurt Aisle," *Bloomberg Businessweek,* July 12, 2012.

3. Fusaro, "Chobani Selected as Food Processing 2012 Processor of the Year"; "Chobani Brings the Heart of Central New York to the London 2012 Olympic Games," Chobani press release, July 26, 2012; and Samuel Greengard, "How Chobani Yogurt Used Social Media to Boost Sales," *Entrepreneur,* September 16, 2012.

4. "Chobani Launches New Greek Yogurt Product Platforms," *Plus Media Solutions,* February 11, 2015; Lauren Coleman-Lochner, "Chobani's Boutique Test Kitchen," *Bloomberg Businessweek,* October 6, 2014, p. 30; "Chobani's New York Café Doubles as Test Kitchen," *Plus Media Solutions,* October 7, 2014; "U.S. Champions Innovators at 5th Global Entrepreneurship Summit," *Plus Media Solutions,* November 25, 2014; and Emily Steel, "Newcomers Buy Ad Time at Big Game," *The New York Times,* January 31, 2015, p. B1.

5. Garett Sloane, "How Facebook Targets Ads Globally Based on Users' Phones," *Adweek,* March 13, 2015, p. 1; Lev Grossman, "2010 Person of the Year: Mark Zuckerberg," *Time,* December 27, 2010–January 3, 2011, pp. 44–75; and Ben Mezrich, *The Accidental Billionaire* (New York: Anchor Books, 2009), pp. 92–150.

6. See http://www.marketing-dictionary.org/ama (definition approved by the American Marketing Association Board of Directors, July 2013).

7. Richard P. Bagozzi, "Marketing as Exchange," *Journal of Marketing,* October 1975, pp. 32–39; and Gregory T. Gundlach and Patrick E. Murphy, "Ethical and Legal Foundations of Relational Marketing Exchanges," *Journal of Marketing,* October 1993, pp. 35–46.

8. Gordon Wyner, "Looking for Innovation in All the Right Places," *Marketing News,* January 2015, pp. 20–21; Katarina Gustafsson, "Who Ya Gonna Call? Lego Dials Fans," *Bloomberg Businessweek,* April 7, 2014, pp. 27–28; J. J. McCorvey, "The Crowd Can Be Harnessed—Up To a Point," *Fast Company,* October, 2014, p. 72.

9. Mintel Global New Products Database, http://www.mintel.com/global-new-productsdatabase, accessed March 20, 2015; George Castellion and Stephen K Markham, "Perspective: New Product Failure Rates: Influence of Argumentum ad Populum and Self-Interest," *Journal of Product Innovation Management* 30, no. 5 (2013), pp. 976–79; Robert M. McMath and Thom Forbes, *What Were They Thinking?* (New York: Times Business, 1998), pp. 3–22.

10. Rich Karlgaard, "Ahead of Their Time Nobel Flops," *Forbes,* September 2, 2013, p. 1; Kate Rockwood, "When Bad Products Happen to Big Companies," *Fast Company,* April 2010, p. 22; and Yukari Iwatani Kane and Don Clark, "Apple Seeks to Avoid Previous Tablet Flops," *The Wall Street Journal,* January 27, 2010, p. B1.

11. "Affiliate Marketing—The Direct and Indirect Value That Affiliates Deliver to Advertisers," prepared by Forrester Consulting for Rakuten LinkShare, June 2012, p. 4. See http://m.www.linksynergy.com/share/pdf/2012_various/forrester_rakuten_linkShare_062612.pdf.

12. Bill Saporito, "Pepsi Pops Open a New Low-Calorie Soda," *Time.com,* October 3, 2014, p.1; and Thomas Hobbs, "Is Pepsi Readying a Coca-Cola Life Rival for UK Launch?" *Marketing Week,* January 22, 2015, p. 1.

13. "Washington: Marketing to College Student Appears to Have Declined," *Plus Media Solutions,* February 27, 2014.

14. Jerome McCarthy, *Basic Marketing: A Managerial Approach* (Homewood, IL: Richard D. Irwin, 1960); and Walter van Waterschool and Christophe Van den Bulte, "The 4P Classification of the Marketing Mix Revisited," *Journal of Marketing,* October 1992, pp. 83–93.

15. "Walmart CEO Oulines Growth Strategy at Annual Meeting for the Investment Community," *Walmart News Archive,* October 15, 2014, Walmart.com; David J. Collis and Michael G. Rukstad, "Can You Say What Your Strategy Is?" *Harvard Business Review,* April 2008, pp. 82–90; and Roger A. Kerin and Robert A. Peterson, *Strategic Marketing Problems: Cases and Comments,* 13th ed. (Upper Saddle River, NJ: Prentice-Hall, 2013), p. 12.

16. Ashish Kothari and Joseph Lackner, "A Value-Based Approach to Management," *Journal of Business and Industrial Marketing* 21, no. 4, pp. 243–49; and James C. Anderson, James A. Narius, and Wouter van Rossum, "Customer Value Propositions in Business Markets," *Harvard Business Review,* March 2006, pp. 91–99.

17. V. Kumar, *Managing Customers for Profit* (Upper Saddle River, NJ: Pearson Education, 2008); and "What's a Loyal Customer Worth?" *Fortune,* December 11, 1995, p. 182.

18. Michael Treacy and Fred D. Wiersema, *The Discipline of Market Leaders* (Reading, MA: Addison-Wesley, 1995); Michael Treacy and Fred Wiersema, "How Market Leaders Keep Their Edge," *Fortune,* February 6, 1995, pp. 88–89; and Michael Treacy, "You Need a Value Discipline—But Which One?" *Fortune,* April 17, 1995, p. 195.

19. Target, Starbucks, and Nordstrom corporate websites.

20. Robert W. Palmatier, Rajiv P. Dant, Dhruv Grewal, and Kenneth R. Evans, "Factors Influencing the Effectiveness of Relationship Marketing: A Meta-Analysis," *Journal of Relationship Marketing,* October 2006, pp. 136–53; and William Boulding, Richard Staelin, Michael Ehret, and Wesley J. Johnson, "A Customer Relationship Management Roadmap: What Is Known, Potential Pitfalls, and Where to Go," *Journal of Marketing,* October 2005, pp. 155–66.

21. Michael E. Porter and James E. Hepplemann, "How Smart, Connected Products Are Transforming Competition," *Harvard Business Review,* November 2014, pp. 65–88; Tony Hsieh, *Delivering Happiness* (New York: Business Plus, 2010); and Susan Foumier, Susan Dobscha, and David Glen Mick, "Preventing the Premature Death of Relationship Marketing," *Harvard Business Review,* January–February 1998, pp. 42–51.

22. The 3M Post-it® Flag Highlighter and 3M Post-it® Flag Pen examples are based on a series of interviews and meetings with 3M inventor and researcher David Windorski from 2004 to 2011.

23. See www.oprah.com for January 15, 2008; and "Post-it® Flags Co-Sponsors Oprah's Live Web Event," *3M Stemwinder,* March 4–17, 2008, p. 3.

24. Reservations about and elaborations of these simplified stages appear in D. G. Brian Jones and Eric H. Shaw, "A History of Marketing Thought," chapter 2 in *Handbook of Marketing,* ed. Barton Weitz and Robin Wensley (London: Sage Publications, 2006), pp. 39–65; Frederick E. Webster Jr., "The Role of Marketing and the Firm," chapter 3 in *Handbook of Marketing,* ed. Barton Weitz and Robin Wensley (London: Sage Publications, 2006), pp. 66–82; and Frederick E. Webster Jr., "Back to the Future: Integrating Marketing as Tactics, Strategy and Organizational Culture," *Journal of Marketing,* October 2005, pp. 4–8.

25. Robert F. Keith, "The Marketing Revolution," *Journal of Marketing,* January 1960, pp. 35–38.

26. *Annual Report* (New York: General Electric Company, 1952), p. 21.

27. John C. Narver, Stanley F. Slater, and Brian Tietje, "Creating a Market Orientation," *Journal of Market Focused Management,* no. 2 (1998), pp. 241–55; Stanley F. Slater and John C. Narver, "Market Orientation and the Learning Organization," *Journal of Marketing,* July 1995, pp. 63–74; and George S. Day, "The Capabilities of Market-Driven Organizations," *Journal of Marketing,* October 1994, pp. 37–52.

28. The definition of customer relationship management is adapted from Rajendra K. Srivastava, Tasadduq A. Shervani, and Liam Fahey, "Marketing, Business Processes, and Shareholder Value: An Embedded View of Marketing Activities and the Discipline of Marketing," *Journal of Marketing,* special issue (1999), pp. 168–79; Gary F. Gebhardt, Gregory S. Carpenter, and John F. Sherry Jr., "Creating a Market Orientation: A Longitudinal, Multifirm, Grounded Analysis of Cultural Transformation," *Journal of Marketing,* October 2006, pp. 37–55; and Christopher Meyer and Andre Schwager, "Understanding Customer Experience," *Harvard Business Review,* February 2007, pp. 117–26.

29. Gary F. Gebhardt, Gregory S. Carpenter, and John F. Sherry Jr., "Creating a Market Orientation: A Longitudinal, Multifirm, Grounded Analysis of Cultural Transformation," *Journal of Marketing,* October 2006, pp. 37–55.

30. "America's Favorite Super: Trader Joe's," *MMR,* June 9, 2014, p. 87; "Trader Joe's Tops Satisfaction Poll in US," *Europe News,* June 2014, p. 12; and Beth Kowitt, "Inside Trader Joe's," *Fortune,* September 6, 2010, p. 87.

31. Alex Rawson, Ewan Duncan, and Conor Jones, "The Truth about Customer Experience," *Harvard Business Review,* September 2013, pp. 90–98; and Meyer and Schwager, "Understanding Customer Experience."

32. Kasturi Rangan, Lisa Chase, and Sohel Karim, "The Truth about CSR," *Harvard Business Review,* January–February 2015, pp. 41–49.

33. Philip Kotler and Sidney J. Levy, "Broadening the Concept of Marketing," *Journal of Marketing,* January 1969, pp. 10–15; and Jim Rendon, "When Nations Need a Little Marketing," *The New York Times,* November 23, 2003, p. BU6.

34. Peter Gumbel, "Louvre, Inc." *Time,* August 11, 2008, pp. 51–52; and Stella Wai-Art Law, *A Branding Context: The Guggenheim and the Louvre,* M.A. Thesis, Columbus, OH: The Ohio State University, 2008.

35. William L. Wilkie and Elizabeth S. Moore, "Marketing's Relationship to Society," chapter 1 in *Handbook of Marketing,* ed. Barton Weitz and Robin Wensley (London: Sage Publications, 2006), pp. 9–38.

36. Chobani, LLC. : This case was written by William Rudelius, based on personal interviews with Chobani executives Joshua Dean, Sujean Lee, and Kyle O'Brien. Other sources include "The Chobani Story," MEDIA@CHOBANI.COM, 2013; Megan Durisin, "Chobani CEO: Our Success Has Nothing to Do with Yogurt," *Business Retail Insider,* May 3, 2013, p. 1; and Sarah E. Needleman, "Old Factory, Snap Decision Spawn Greek Yogurt Craze," *The Wall Street Journal,* June 21, 2012, pp. B1, B2.

Developing Successful Organizational and Marketing Strategies

LEARNING OBJECTIVES

After reading this chapter you should be able to:

LO 2-1 Describe three kinds of organizations and the three levels of strategy in them.

LO 2-2 Describe core values, mission, organizational culture, business, and goals.

LO 2-3 Explain why managers use marketing dashboards and marketing metrics.

LO 2-4 Discuss how an organization assesses where it is now and where it seeks to be.

LO 2-5 Explain the three steps of the planning phase of the strategic marketing process.

LO 2-6 Describe the four components of the implementation phase of the strategic marketing process.

LO 2-7 Discuss how managers identify and act on deviations from plans.

Making the World a Better Place, One Scoop at a Time!

Ben & Jerry's started in 1978 when longtime friends Ben Cohen and Jerry Greenfield headed north to Vermont to open an ice cream parlor in a renovated gas station. Buoyed with enthusiasm, $12,000 in borrowed and saved money, and ideas from a $5 correspondence course in ice cream making, Ben and Jerry were off and scooping. Their first flavor? Vanilla—because it's a universal best seller. Other flavors such as Chunky Monkey, Cherry Garcia, Peanut Butter Cup, and many others soon followed.

The ice cream flavors weren't the only extraordinary thing about the company though. Ben and Jerry embraced a concept they called "linked prosperity," which encouraged the success of all constituents including employees, suppliers, customers, and neighbors. They set out to achieve linked prosperity with a three-part mission statement:

- Product Mission: To make, distribute and sell the finest quality all-natural ice cream.

- Economic Mission: To operate the company for sustainable financial growth.

- Social Mission: To operate the company in ways that make the world a better place.

The mission statement guided the entrepreneurs' decisions related to many aspects of the business including purchasing practices, ingredient sourcing, manufacturing, and involvement in the community.[1]

Ben and Jerry's mission-driven approach led them to successfully implement many highly creative organizational and marketing strategies. Some examples include:

- *Fairtrade.* Ben & Jerry's believes that farmers who grow ingredients for their ice cream products (such as cocoa, coffee, and vanilla) should receive a fair price for their harvest. In return Fairtrade farmers agree to use sustainable farming practices, implement fair working standards, and invest in local communities.

- *B-Corp Certification.* Ben & Jerry's was one of the first companies involved in the Benefit Corporation movement, which has developed a rigorous set of principles and standards on which to evaluate companies in terms of social and environmental performance, accountability, and transparency. The certification, provided by the nonprofit organization B-Lab, indicates that Ben & Jerry's is using the power of business to solve social and environmental problems.

- *PartnerShop Program.* PartnerShops are Ben & Jerry scoop shops that are independently owned and operated by community-based nonprofit organizations. The shops employ youth and young adults who may face barriers to employment to help them build better lives.

As you can see, Ben & Jerry's has a strong link between its mission and its strategies. CEO Jostein Solheim explains that their purpose at Ben & Jerry's is "to be part of a global movement that makes changing the world seem fun and achievable."[2]

Today, Ben & Jerry's is owned by Unilever, which is the market leader in the global ice cream industry—one that is expected to reach $74 billion by 2018.[3] While customers love Ben & Jerry's rich premium ice cream, many buy its products to support its social mission. As a testament to its success, Ben & Jerry's has over 7.5 million fans on Facebook—the most of any premium ice cream marketer!

Chapter 2 describes how organizations set goals to provide an overall direction to their organizational and marketing strategies. The marketing department of an organization converts these strategies into plans that must be implemented and then evaluated so deviations can be exploited or corrected based on the marketing environment.

© Rafael Ben-Ari/Alamy

TODAY'S ORGANIZATIONS

LO 2-1 Describe three kinds of organizations and the three levels of strategy in them.

In studying today's organizations, it is important to recognize (1) the kinds of organizations that exist, (2) what strategy is, and (3) how this strategy relates to the three levels of structure found in many large organizations.

Kinds of Organizations

An *organization* is a legal entity that consists of people who share a common mission. This motivates them to develop *offerings* (goods, services, or ideas) that create value for both the organization and its customers by satisfying their needs and wants.[4] Today's organizations are of three types: (1) for-profit organizations, (2) nonprofit organizations, and (3) government agencies.

A *for-profit organization,* often called a *business firm,* is a privately owned organization such as Target, Nike, or Cree that serves its customers to earn a profit so that it can survive. **Profit** is the money left after a for-profit organization subtracts its total expenses from its total revenues and is the reward for the risk it undertakes in marketing its offerings.

In contrast, a *nonprofit organization* is a nongovernmental organization that serves its customers but does not have profit as an organizational goal. Instead, its goals may be operational efficiency or client satisfaction. Regardless, it also must receive sufficient funds above its expenses to continue operations. Organizations like SIRUM and Teach For America, described in the Making Responsible Decisions box, seek to solve the practical needs of society and are often structured as nonprofit organizations.[5] For simplicity in the rest of the book, the terms *firm, company*, and *organization* are used interchangeably to cover both for-profit and nonprofit organizations.

Last, a *government agency* is a federal, state, county, or city unit that provides a specific service to its constituents. For example, the Census Bureau, a unit of the U.S. Department of Commerce, is a federal government agency that provides population and economic data.

Organizations that develop similar offerings create an *industry*, such as the computer industry or the automobile industry.[6] As a result, organizations make strategic decisions that reflect the dynamics of the industry to create a compelling and sustainable advantage for their offerings relative to those of competitors to achieve a superior level of performance.[7] Much of an organization's marketing strategy is having a clear understanding of the industry within which it competes.

What Is Strategy?

An organization has limited human, financial, technological, and other resources available to produce and market its offerings—it can't be all things to all people! Every organization must develop strategies to help focus and direct its efforts to accomplish its goals. However, the definition of strategy has been the subject of debate among management and marketing theorists. For our purpose, **strategy** is an organization's long-term course of action designed to deliver a unique customer experience while achieving its goals.[8] All organizations set a strategic direction. And marketing helps to both set this direction and move the organization there.

The Structure of Today's Organizations

Large organizations are extremely complex. They usually consist of three organizational levels whose strategies are linked to marketing, as shown in Figure 2–1.

Corporate Level The *corporate level* is where top management directs overall strategy for the entire organization. "Top management" usually means the board of

Video 2-1
Cree® LED
Bulb Ad
kerin.tv/13e/v2-1

Cree is an example of a for-profit organization. Its Cree LED light bulb replaces traditional incandescent bulbs, consumes 85 percent less energy, and lasts 25,000 hours.

© H.S. Photos/Alamy

Making **Responsible Decisions**

Social Entrepreneurs Are Creating New Types of Organizations to Pursue Social Goals

Each year a growing number of "social entrepreneurs" start new ventures that address important social needs and issues. These new enterprises are often organized as non-profit organizations that combine traditional approaches for generating revenue with the pursuit of social goals. The issues they have focused on range from health care delivery, to increasing access to education, to improving agricultural efficiency. Some experts predict that these types of social ventures represent the new way of doing business.

One indication of the influence of these new types of organizations is *Forbes* magazine's annual list of *30 Under 30 Social Entrepreneurs*. Each year 30 of the most innovative new social ventures are featured in the article. For example, Kiah Williams left the Clinton Foundation to start SIRUM (Supporting Initiatives to Redistribute Unused Medicine). The organization works with health care systems to distribute unused prescription drugs (that would otherwise be destroyed) to patients who can't afford to pay for the drugs. "We're like the Match.com for unused drugs," explains Williams.

Teach For America is another example of a creative nonprofit organization. Launched by college senior Wendy Kopp, Teach For America is the national corps of outstanding recent college graduates who commit to teach for two years in urban and rural public schools and become lifelong leaders in expanding educational opportunity. Each year more than 10,000 corps members teach 750,000 students.

These examples illustrate how organizations are changing to create value for a broad range of constituents by addressing the needs and challenges of society.

© Forbes

directors and senior management officers with a variety of skills and experiences that are invaluable in establishing the organization's overall strategy.

The president or chief executive officer (CEO) is the highest ranking officer in the organization and is usually a member of its board of directors. This person must possess leadership skills ranging from overseeing the organization's daily operations to spearheading strategy planning efforts that may determine its very survival.

FIGURE 2–1

The board of directors oversees the three levels of strategy in organizations: corporate, strategic business unit, and functional.

Prada manages a portfolio or group of businesses—including perfume, leather goods, and luggage—each of which may be viewed as a strategic business unit (SBU).

© Imaginechina via AP Images

In recent years, many large firms have changed the title of the head of marketing from vice president of marketing to chief marketing officer (CMO). These CMOs have an increasingly important role in top management because of their ability to think strategically. Most bring multi-industry backgrounds, cross-functional management expertise, analytical skills, and intuitive marketing insights to their job. These CMOs are increasingly called upon to be their organizations' "visionaries for the future" by staying in touch with consumers' needs and wants.[9]

Strategic Business Unit Level   Some multimarket, multiproduct firms, such as Prada and Johnson & Johnson, manage a portfolio or group of businesses. Each group is a *strategic business unit (SBU)*, which is a subsidiary, division, or unit of an organization that markets a set of related offerings to a clearly defined target market. At the *strategic business unit level*, managers set a more specific strategic direction for their businesses to exploit value-creating opportunities. For less complex firms with a single business focus, such as Ben & Jerry's, the corporate and business unit levels may merge.

Functional Level   Each strategic business unit has a *functional level*, where groups of specialists actually create value for the organization. The term *department* generally refers to these specialized functions such as marketing and finance (see Figure 2–1). At the functional level, the organization's strategic direction becomes its most specific and focused. Just as there is a hierarchy of levels within an organization, there is a hierarchy of strategic directions set by managers at each level.

A key role of the marketing department is to look outward by listening to customers, developing offerings, implementing marketing program actions, and then evaluating whether those actions are achieving the organization's goals. When developing marketing programs for new or improved offerings, an organization's senior management may form *cross-functional teams*. These consist of a small number of people from different departments who are mutually accountable to accomplish a task or a common set of performance goals. Sometimes these teams will have representatives from outside the organization, such as suppliers or customers, to assist them.

learning review »

2-1. What is the difference between a for-profit and a nonprofit organization?

2-2. What are examples of a functional level in an organization?

STRATEGY IN VISIONARY ORGANIZATIONS

LO 2-2   Describe core values, mission, organizational culture, business, and goals.

To be successful, today's organizations must be forward-looking. They must anticipate future events and then respond quickly and effectively to those events. In addition, they must thrive in today's uncertain, chaotic, rapidly changing environment. A visionary organization must specify its foundation (why does it exist?), set a direction (what will it do?), and formulate strategies (how will it do it?), as shown in Figure 2–2.[10]

Organizational Foundation: Why Does It Exist?

An organization's foundation is its philosophical reason for being—why it exists. Successful visionary organizations use this foundation to guide and inspire their employees through three elements: core values, mission, and organizational culture.

Organizational foundation (why)		Organizational direction (what)		Organizational strategies (how)	

• Core values
• Mission (vision)
• Organizational culture
	+	• Business
		• Goals (objectives)
		  ○ Long-term
		  ○ Short-term
			=	• By level
				  ○ Corporate
				  ○ SBU
				  ○ Functional
					• By product
					  ○ Good
					  ○ Service
					  ○ Idea

FIGURE 2–2

Today's visionary organizations use key elements to (1) establish a foundation and (2) set a direction using (3) strategies that enable them to develop and market their products successfully.

Core Values   An organization's **core values** are the fundamental, passionate, and enduring principles that guide its conduct over time. A firm's founders or senior management develop these core values, which are consistent with their essential beliefs and character. They capture the firm's heart and soul and serve to inspire and motivate its *stakeholders*—employees, shareholders, board of directors, suppliers, distributors, creditors, unions, government, local communities, and customers. Core values also are timeless and guide the organization's conduct. To be effective, an organization's core values must be communicated to and supported by its top management and employees; if not, they are just hollow words.[11]

Mission   By understanding its core values, an organization can take steps to define its **mission**, a statement of the organization's function in society that often identifies its customers, markets, products, and technologies. Often used interchangeably with *vision*, a *mission statement* should be clear, concise, meaningful, inspirational, and long-term.[12]

Inspiration and focus appear in the mission statement of for-profit organizations, as well as nonprofit organizations and government agencies. For example:

Video 2-2

Southwest Airlines

kerin.tv/13e/v2-2

- Southwest Airlines: "To be dedicated to the highest quality of Customer Service delivered with a sense of warmth, friendliness, individual pride, and Company Spirit."[13]
- American Red Cross: "To prevent and alleviate human suffering in the face of emergencies by mobilizing the power of volunteers and the generosity of donors."[14]
- Federal Trade Commission: "To prevent business practices that are anticompetitive or deceptive or unfair to consumers; to enhance informed consumer choice and public understanding of the competitive process; and to accomplish this without unduly burdening legitimate business activity."

Each statement exhibits the qualities of a good mission: a clear, challenging, and compelling picture of an envisioned future.[15]

Recently, many organizations have added a social element to their mission statements to reflect an ideal that is morally right and worthwhile. This is what Ben & Jerry's social mission statement shows in the chapter opener. Stakeholders, particularly customers, employees, and now society, are asking organizations to be exceptional citizens by providing long-term value while solving society's problems.

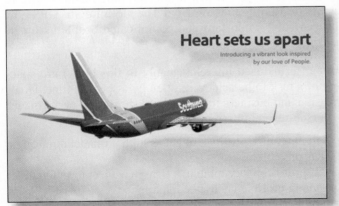

Providing a warm, friendly experience is part of Southwest Airlines' organizational strategy.

© Southwest

Organizational Culture   An organization must connect with all of its stakeholders. Thus, an important corporate-level marketing function is communicating its core values and mission to them. These activities send clear messages to employees and other stakeholders about **organizational culture**—the set of values, ideas, attitudes, and norms of behavior that is learned and shared among the members of an organization.

In the first half of the 20th century, what "business" did railroad executives believe they were in? The text reveals their disastrous error.

© Digital Vision

Organizational Direction: What Will It Do?

As shown in Figure 2–2, the organization's foundation enables it to set a direction in terms of (1) the "business" it is in and (2) its specific goals.

Business A **business** describes the clear, broad, underlying industry or market sector of an organization's offering. To help define its business, an organization looks at the set of organizations that sell similar offerings—those that are in direct competition with each other—such as "the ice cream business." The organization can then begin to answer the questions "What do we do?" or "What business are we in?"

Professor Theodore Levitt saw that 20th-century American railroads defined their business too narrowly, proclaiming, "We are in the railroad business!" This myopic focus caused them to lose sight of who their customers were and what they needed. So railroads failed to develop strategies to compete with airlines, barges, pipelines, and trucks. As a result, many railroads merged or went bankrupt. Railroads should have realized they were in "the transportation business."[16]

With today's increased global competition, many organizations are rethinking their *business model*, the strategies an organization develops to provide value to the customers it serves. Technological innovation is often the trigger for this business model change. American newspapers are looking for a new business model as former subscribers now get their news online.[17] Bookstore retailer Barnes & Noble, too, is rethinking its *business model* as e-book readers like Amazon's Kindle and Apple's iPad have gained widespread popularity.[18]

Why is UPS changing the definition of its business? See the text for the answer.

UPS

United Parcel Service (UPS), the company known for its brown delivery trucks, is redefining its business. The company recently launched a new campaign with the tagline "United Problem Solvers," which replaced its previous "We Love Logistics" campaign. Some of the language from the campaign explains the new perspective: "Bring us your problems. Your challenges. Your daydreams. Your scribbles. Your just about anything. Because we're not just in the shipping business. We're in the problem solving business." Taking a lesson from Theodore Levitt, UPS now sees itself as a service that can solve important and complicated problems for its customers, rather than a package delivery business.[19]

Goals **Goals** or **objectives** (terms used interchangeably in this book) are statements of an accomplishment of a task to be achieved, often by a specific time. Goals convert an organization's mission and business into long- and short-term performance targets. Business firms can pursue several different types of goals:

- *Profit.* Most firms seek to maximize profits—to get as high a financial return on their investments (ROI) as possible.
- *Sales* (dollars or units). If profits are acceptable, a firm may elect to maintain or increase its sales even though profits may not be maximized.
- *Market share.* **Market share** is the ratio of sales revenue of the firm to the total sales revenue of all firms in the industry, including the firm itself.
- *Quality.* A firm may seek to offer a level of quality that meets or exceeds the cost and performance expectations of its customers.
- *Customer satisfaction.* Customers are the reason the organization exists, so their perceptions and actions are of vital importance. Satisfaction can be measured with surveys or by the number of customer complaints.

- *Employee welfare.* A firm may recognize the critical importance of its employees by stating its goal of providing them with good employment opportunities and working conditions.
- *Social responsibility.* Firms may seek to balance the conflicting goals of stakeholders to promote their overall welfare, even at the expense of profits.

Nonprofit organizations (such as museums and hospitals) also have goals, such as to serve consumers as efficiently as possible. Similarly, government agencies set goals that seek to serve the public good.

Organizational Strategies: How Will It Do It?

As shown in Figure 2–2, the organizational foundation sets the "why" of organizations and the organizational direction sets the "what." To convert these into actual results, the organizational strategies are concerned with the "how." These organizational strategies vary in at least two ways, depending on (1) a strategy's level in the organization and (2) the offerings an organization provides to its customers.

Variation by Level   Moving down the levels in an organization involves creating increasingly specific, detailed strategies and plans. So, at the corporate level, top managers may struggle with writing a meaningful mission statement; while at the functional level, the issue is who makes tomorrow's sales call.

Variation by Product   Organizational strategies also vary by the organization's products. The strategy will be far different when marketing a very tangible physical good (Ben & Jerry's ice cream), a service (a Southwest Airlines flight), or an idea (a donation to the American Red Cross).

Most organizations develop a marketing plan as a part of their strategic marketing planning efforts. A **marketing plan** is a road map for the marketing actions of an organization for a specified future time period, such as one year or five years. The planning phase of the strategic marketing process (discussed later) usually results in a marketing plan that directs the marketing actions of an organization. Appendix A at the end of this chapter provides guidelines for writing a marketing plan.

learning review »

2-3. What is the meaning of an organization's mission?

2-4. What is the difference between an organization's business and its goals?

Tracking Strategic Performance with Marketing Analytics

LO 2-3 Explain why managers use marketing dashboards and marketing metrics.

Although marketing managers can set strategic direction for their organizations, how do they know if they are making progress in getting there? As several industry experts have observed, "You can't manage what you don't measure."[20] One answer to this problem is the growing field of data analytics, or big data, which enables data-driven decisions by collecting data and presenting them in a visual format such as a marketing dashboard.

Car Dashboards and Marketing Dashboards   A **marketing dashboard** is the visual display of the essential information related to achieving a marketing objective.[21] Often, active hyperlinks provide further detail. An example is when a chief marketing officer (CMO) wants to see daily what the effect of a new TV advertising campaign is on a product's sales.[22]

The idea of a marketing dashboard really comes from the display of information found on a car's dashboard. On a car's dashboard, we glance at the fuel gauge and take action when our gas is getting low. With a marketing dashboard, a marketing manager glances at a graph or table and makes a decision whether to take action or to analyze the problem further.[23]

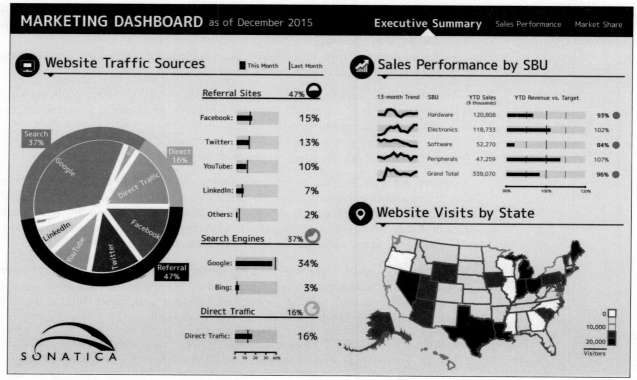

Dundas Data Visualization, Inc.

FIGURE 2–3

An effective marketing dashboard, like this one from Sonatica, a hypothetical hardware and software firm, helps managers assess a business situation at a glance.

Dashboards, Metrics, and Plans   The marketing dashboard of Sonatica, a hypothetical hardware and software firm, appears in Figure 2–3. It shows graphic displays of key performance indicators linked to its product lines.[24] Each display in a marketing dashboard shows a **marketing metric**, which is a measure of the quantitative value or trend of a marketing action or result.[25] Choosing which marketing metrics to display is critical for a busy manager, who can be overwhelmed with irrelevant data.[26]

Today's marketers use *data visualization,* which presents information about an organization's marketing metrics graphically so marketers can quickly (1) spot deviations from plans during the evaluation phase and (2) take corrective actions.[27] This book uses data visualization in many figures to highlight in color key points described in the text. The Sonatica marketing dashboard in Figure 2–3 uses data visualization tools like a pie chart, a line or bar chart, and a map to show how parts of its business are performing as of December 2015:

- *Website Traffic Sources.* The color-coded perimeter of the pie chart shows the three main sources of website traffic (referral sites at 47 percent, search engines at 37 percent, and direct traffic at 16 percent). These three colors link to those of the circles in the column of website traffic sources. Of the 47 percent of traffic coming from referral sites, the horizontal *bullet graphs* to the right show that Sonatica's Facebook visits comprise 15 percent of total website traffic, up from a month ago (as shown by the vertical line).
- *Sales Performance by SBU.* The *spark lines* (the wavy lines in the far left column) show the 13-month trends of Sonatica's strategic business units (SBUs). For example, the trends in electronics and peripherals are generally up, causing their sales to exceed their YTD (year to date) targets. Conversely, both software and hardware sales failed to meet YTD targets, a problem quickly noted by a marketing manager seeing the red "warning" circles in their rows at the far right. This suggests that immediate corrective actions are needed for the software and hardware SBUs.

Applying **Marketing Metrics**

How Well Is Ben & Jerry's Doing?

As the marketing manager for Ben & Jerry's, you need to assess how it is doing within the United States in the super-premium ice cream market in which it competes. For this, you choose two marketing metrics: dollar sales and dollar market share.

Your Challenge

Scanner data from checkout counters in supermarkets and other retailers show the total industry sales of super-premium ice cream were $1.25 billion in 2015. Internal company data show you that Ben & Jerry's sold 50 million units at an average price of $5.00 per unit in 2015. A "unit" in super-premium ice cream is one pint.

Your Findings

Dollar sales and dollar market share can be calculated for 2015 using simple formulas and displayed on the Ben & Jerry's marketing dashboard as follows:

$$\text{Dollar sales}(\$) = \text{Average price} \times \text{Quantity sold}$$
$$= \$5.00 \times 50 \text{ million units}$$
$$= \$250 \text{ million}$$

$$\text{Dollar market share}(\%) = \frac{\text{Ben \& Jerry's sales (\$)}}{\text{Total industry sales (\$)}}$$
$$= \frac{\$250 \text{ million}}{\$1.25 \text{ billion}}$$
$$= 0.20 \text{ or } 20\%$$

Ben & Jerry's Dollar Sales and Market Share

Your dashboard displays show that from 2014 to 2015 dollar sales increased from $240 million to $250 million and that dollar market share grew from 18.4 to 20.0 percent.

Your Action

The results need to be compared with the goals established for these metrics. In addition, they should be compared with previous years' results to see if the trends are increasing, flat, or decreasing. This will lead to marketing actions.

- *Website Visits by State.* The U.S. map shows that the darker the state, the greater the number of website visits for the current month. For example, Texas has close to 20,000 visits per month, while Illinois has none.

The Ben & Jerry's dashboard in the Applying Marketing Metrics box shows how the two widely used marketing metrics of dollar sales and dollar market share can help the company assess its growth performance from 2014 to 2015. The Applying Marketing Metrics boxes in later chapters highlight other key marketing metrics and how they can lead to marketing actions.

SETTING STRATEGIC DIRECTIONS

 LO 2-4 Discuss how an organization assesses where it is now and where it seeks to be.

To set a strategic direction, an organization needs to answer two difficult questions: (1) Where are we now? and (2) Where do we want to go?

A Look Around: Where Are We Now?

Asking an organization where it is at the present time involves identifying its competencies, customers, and competitors.

Competencies   Senior managers must ask the question: What do we do best? The answer involves an assessment of the organization's core *competencies*, which

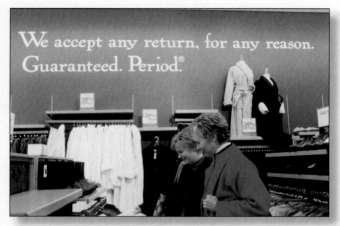

Lands' End's unconditional guarantee for its products highlights its focus on customers.

© Rick Armstrong

are its special capabilities—the skills, technologies, and resources—that distinguish it from other organizations and provide customer value. Exploiting these competencies can lead to success.[28] Competencies should be distinctive enough to provide a *competitive advantage*, a unique strength relative to competitors that provides superior returns, often based on quality, time, cost, or innovation.[29]

Customers   Ben & Jerry's customers are ice cream and frozen yogurt eaters who have different preferences (form, flavor, health, and convenience). Medtronic's pacemaker customers include cardiologists and heart surgeons who serve patients that need this type of device. Lands' End communicates a remarkable commitment to its customers and its product quality with these unconditional words:

Guaranteed. Period.®

The Lands' End website points out that this guarantee has always been an unconditional one. It reads: "If you're not satisfied with any item, simply return it to us at any time for an exchange or refund of its purchase price." But to get the message across more clearly to its customers, it created the two-word guarantee. The point is that Lands' End's strategy must provide genuine value to customers to ensure that they have a satisfying experience.[30]

Competitors   In today's global marketplace, the distinctions among competitors are increasingly blurred. Lands' End started as a catalog retailer. But today, Lands' End competes with not only other clothing catalog retailers but also traditional department stores, mass merchandisers, and specialty shops. Even well-known clothing brands such as Liz Claiborne now have their own chain stores. Although only some of the clothing in any of these stores directly competes with Lands' End offerings, all of these retailers have websites to sell their offerings over the Internet. This means there's a lot of competition out there.

Growth Strategies: Where Do We Want to Go?

Knowing where the organization is at the present time enables managers to set a direction for the firm and allocate resources to move in that direction. Two techniques to aid managers with these decisions are (1) business portfolio analysis and (2) diversification analysis.

Business Portfolio Analysis   Successful organizations have a portfolio or range of offerings (products and services) that possess different growth rates and market shares within the industry in which they operate. The Boston Consulting Group (BCG), an internationally known management consulting firm, has developed **business portfolio analysis**. It is a technique that managers use to quantify performance measures and growth targets to analyze their firms' SBUs as though they were a collection of separate investments.[31] The purpose of this tool is to determine which SBU or offering generates cash and which one requires cash to fund the organization's growth opportunities.

As described in the Marketing Matters box, let's assume you are filling the shoes of Apple CEO Tim Cook. Based on your knowledge of Apple products, you are currently conducting a quick analysis of four major Apple SBUs through 2018. Try to rank them from highest to lowest in terms of percentage growth in expected unit sales. We will

Marketing **Matters**

Filling the Shoes of Apple CEO Tim Cook: Where Will Apple's Projected Future Growth for Its Major SBUs Come From?

Every CEO of a for-profit organization faces one problem in common: trying to find ways to increase future sales and profits to keep it growing!

Put yourself in Tim Cook's shoes. One of his jobs is to search for new growth opportunities. Using your knowledge about Apple products, do a quick analysis of four SBUs shown below to determine where Apple should allocate its time and resources. Rate these growth opportunities from highest to lowest in terms of percentage growth in unit sales from 2015 to 2018:

1. _____ (Highest)

2. _____

3. _____

4. _____ (Lowest)

We'll walk you through possible answers. You then can evaluate your performance over the next two pages and decide whether you're really ready for Mr. Cook's job!

iPod

iPhone

iPad/iPad mini

Apple Watch

All product photos: © Apple

introduce you to business portfolio analysis as we look at the possible future of the four Apple SBUs.

The BCG business portfolio analysis requires an organization to locate the position of each of its SBUs on a growth-share matrix (see Figure 2–4). The vertical axis is the _market growth rate_, which is the annual rate of growth of the SBU's industry. The horizontal axis is the _relative market share_, defined as the sales of the SBU divided by the sales of the largest firm in the industry. A relative market share of 10× (at the left end of the scale) means that the SBU has 10 times the share of its largest competitor, whereas a share of 0.1× (at the right end of the scale) means it has only 10 percent of the share of its largest competitor.

The BCG has given specific names and descriptions to the four resulting quadrants in its growth-share matrix based on the amount of cash they generate for or require from the organization:

1. _Question marks_ are SBUs with a low share of high-growth markets. They require large injections of cash just to maintain their market share, much less increase it. The name implies management's dilemma for these SBUs: choosing the right ones to invest in and phasing out the rest.
2. _Stars_ are SBUs with a high share of high-growth markets that may need extra cash to finance their own rapid future growth. When their growth slows, they are likely to become cash cows.
3. _Cash cows_ are SBUs that generate large amounts of cash, far more than they can use. They have dominant shares of slow-growth markets and provide cash to cover the organization's overhead and to invest in other SBUs.

FIGURE 2–4

Boston Consulting Group (BCG) business portfolio analysis for four of Apple's consumer-related SBUs. The red arrow indicates typical movement of a product through the matrix.

All product photos: © Apple

What can Apple expect in future growth of sales revenues from its iPhone products . . .

© Apple

4. *Dogs* are SBUs with low shares of slow-growth markets. Although they may generate enough cash to sustain themselves, they may no longer be or may not become real winners for the organization. Dropping SBUs that are dogs may be required if they consume more cash than they generate, except when relationships with other SBUs, competitive considerations, or potential strategic alliances exist.[32]

An organization's SBUs often start as question marks and go counterclockwise around Figure 2–4 to become stars, then cash cows, and finally dogs. Because an organization has limited influence on the market growth rate, its main objective is to try to change its relative dollar or unit market share. To do this, management decides what strategic role each SBU should have in the future and either injects cash into or removes cash from it.

According to Interbrand, a leading brand management consulting firm, Apple has been consistently cited as one of the top global brands over the past decade in its annual Best Global Brands survey. What has made Apple so iconic is not only its revolutionary products but also its commitment to infusing the "human touch" with its technology such that its customers connect with the brand on both a cognitive *and* an emotional level. The late Steve Jobs was instrumental in creating Apple's organizational culture and core values that will continue to guide its future.[33]

Using the BCG business portfolio analysis framework, Figure 2–4 shows that the Apple picture might look this way from 2015 to 2018 for four of its SBUs:[34]

1. *Apple Watch* (wearable technology). Apple entered the wearable technology market in April 2015 with its version of a smart watch, the Apple Watch. The watch competes with Samsung, Pebble, and Motorola watches and a wide range of other wearable technologies such as Fitbit and Jawbone fitness trackers. The market grew at a rate of more than 100 percent in 2015, and Apple Watch sales were substantial despite a relatively high price and short battery life. The Apple watch enters the market as a *question mark* and awaits consumers' response.[35]

2. *iPhone* (smartphones). Apple launched its revolutionary iPhone smartphone in 2007. iPhone unit sales skyrocketed and Apple's U.S. market share has grown to

. . . or its iPod devices?

© Apple

47.7 percent, exceeding the market share of its largest competitor, Samsung. The smartphone market is expected to grow at an annual rate of 9.8 percent through 2018 due to growth in China and falling prices. High market share and high growth suggest that Apple's iPhone is a *star*.[36]

3. *iPad/iPad mini* (tablets). Launched in 2010, iPad unit sales reached 40 percent market share by 2013—leading both Samsung's Galaxy (18 percent) and Amazon's Kindle (4 percent). Tablet sales are increasing although the rate of growth is plummeting as consumers are substituting big-screen smartphones, or "phablets," for tablets. For Apple, its iPad SBU is a *cash cow* (high market share in a low-growth market).[37]

4. *iPod* (music players). Apple entered the music player market with its iPod device in 2001. The product became a cultural icon, selling more that 50 million units annually until 2010 when the iPhone integrated a music player. Since 2010 sales have been declining dramatically and in October 2014 Apple announced that it was discontinuing the iPod classic. Today Apple still sells three iPod product lines—the nano, the shuffle, and the touch—although declining sales and discontinued products suggest that this SBU is entering the *dog* category.[38]

So, how did you—as Tim Cook—rank the growth opportunity for each of the four SBUs? The Apple Watch represents the highest unit growth rate at more than 100 percent. The iphone SBU is likely to continue growing at almost 10 percent, while the iPad SBU is experiencing a declining growth rate. Despite the difference in growth rates, the iPhone and iPad product lines together accounted for 72 percent of Apple's revenues in 2014. These revenues are used to pursue growth opportunities such as the Apple Watch, a next generation phone, and a huge 13-inch iPad. Finally, no growth and the discontinuation of the iPod classic may signal the beginning of the end for Apple's iPod.[39]

The primary strength of business portfolio analysis lies in forcing a firm to place each of its SBUs in the growth-share matrix, which in turn suggests which SBUs will be cash producers and cash users in the future. Weaknesses of this analysis arise from the difficulty in (1) getting the needed information and (2) incorporating competitive data into business portfolio analysis.[40]

Diversification Analysis **Diversification analysis** is a technique that helps a firm search for growth opportunities from among current and new markets as well as current and new products.[41] For any market, there is both a current product (what the firm now sells) and a new product (what the firm might sell in the future). And for any product there is both a current market (the firm's existing customers) and a new market (the firm's potential customers). As Ben & Jerry's seeks to increase sales revenues, it considers all four market-product strategies shown in Figure 2–5:

Video 2-4
B&J's Bonnaroo Buzz Ad
kerin.tv/13e/v2-4

- *Market penetration* is a marketing strategy to increase sales of current products in current markets, such as selling more Ben & Jerry's Bonnaroo Buzz Fair Trade–sourced ice cream to U.S. consumers. There is no change in either the basic product line or the markets served. Increased sales are generated by selling either more ice cream (through better promotion or distribution) *or* the same amount of ice cream at a higher price to its current customers.
- *Market development* is a marketing strategy to sell current products to new markets. For Ben & Jerry's, Brazil is an attractive new market. There is good news and bad news for this strategy: As household incomes of Brazilians increase, consumers can buy more ice cream; however, the Ben & Jerry's brand may be unknown to Brazilian consumers.
- *Product development* is a marketing strategy of selling new products to current markets. Ben & Jerry's could leverage its brand by selling children's clothing in

FIGURE 2–5

Four market-product strategies: alternative ways to expand sales revenues for Ben & Jerry's using diversification analysis.

MARKETS	PRODUCTS	
	Current	**New**
Current	**Market penetration** Selling more Ben & Jerry's super-premium ice cream to Americans	**Product development** Selling a new product such as children's clothing under the Ben & Jerry's brand to Americans
New	**Market development** Selling Ben & Jerry's super-premium ice cream to Brazilians for the first time	**Diversification** Selling a new product such as children's clothing under the Ben & Jerry's brand to Brazilians for the first time

the United States. This strategy is risky because Americans may not see the company's expertise in ice cream as extending to children's clothing.

- *Diversification* is a marketing strategy of developing new products and selling them in new markets. This is a potentially high-risk strategy for Ben & Jerry's if it decides to try to sell Ben & Jerry's branded clothing in Brazil. Why? Because the firm has neither previous production nor marketing experience from which to draw in marketing clothing to Brazilian consumers.

learning review

2-5. What is the difference between a marketing dashboard and a marketing metric?

2-6. What is business portfolio analysis?

2-7. Explain the four market-product strategies in diversification analysis.

THE STRATEGIC MARKETING PROCESS

LO 2-5 Explain the three steps of the planning phase of the strategic marketing process.

After an organization assesses where it is and where it wants to go, other questions emerge, such as:

1. How do we allocate our resources to get where we want to go?
2. How do we convert our plans into actions?
3. How do our results compare with our plans, and do deviations require new plans?

To answer these questions, an organization uses the **strategic marketing process**, whereby an organization allocates its marketing mix resources to reach its target markets. This process is divided into three phases: planning, implementation, and evaluation, as shown in Figure 2–6.

The Planning Phase of the Strategic Marketing Process

Figure 2–6 shows the three steps in the planning phase of the strategic marketing process: (1) situation (SWOT) analysis, (2) market-product focus and goal setting, and (3) the marketing program.

Step 1: Situation (SWOT) Analysis The essence of **situation analysis** is taking stock of where the firm or product has been recently, where it is now, and where it

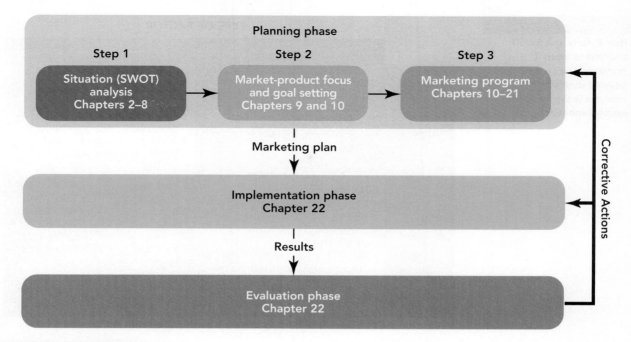

FIGURE 2–6

The strategic marketing process has three vital phases: planning, implementation, and evaluation. The figure also indicates the chapters in which these phases are discussed in the text.

How can Ben & Jerry's develop new products and social responsibility programs that contribute to its mission? The text describes how the strategic marketing process and its SWOT analysis can help.
© Mike Hruby

is headed in terms of the organization's marketing plans and the external forces and trends affecting it. An effective summary of a situation analysis is a **SWOT analysis**, an acronym describing an organization's appraisal of its internal **S**trengths and **W**eaknesses and its external **O**pportunities and **T**hreats.

The SWOT analysis is based on an exhaustive study of four areas that form the foundation upon which the firm builds its marketing program:

- Identify trends in the organization's industry.
- Analyze the organization's competitors.
- Assess the organization itself.
- Research the organization's present and prospective customers.

Assume you are responsible for doing the SWOT analysis for Ben & Jerry's shown in Figure 2–7. Note that the SWOT table has four cells formed by the combination of internal versus external factors (the rows) and favorable versus unfavorable factors (the columns) that identify Ben & Jerry's strengths, weaknesses, opportunities, and threats.

The task is to translate the results of the SWOT analysis into specific marketing actions that will help the firm grow. The ultimate goal is to identify the *critical* strategy-related factors that impact the firm and then build on vital strengths, correct glaring weaknesses, exploit significant opportunities, and avoid disaster-laden threats.

The Ben & Jerry's SWOT analysis in Figure 2–7 can be the basis for these kinds of specific marketing actions. An action in each of the four cells might be:

- *Build on a strength.* Find specific efficiencies in distribution with parent-company Unilever's existing ice cream brands.
- *Correct a weakness.* Recruit experienced managers from other consumer product firms to help stimulate growth.
- *Exploit an opportunity.* Develop new product lines of low-fat, low-carb frozen Greek-style yogurt flavors to respond to changes in consumer tastes.
- *Avoid a disaster-laden threat.* Focus on less risky international markets, such as Brazil and Argentina.

FIGURE 2–7

Ben & Jerry's: A SWOT analysis to keep it growing. The picture painted in this SWOT analysis is the basis for management actions.

LOCATION OF FACTOR	TYPE OF FACTOR	
	Favorable	Unfavorable
Internal	**Strengths** • Prestigious, well-known brand name among U.S. consumers • Complements Unilever's other ice cream brands • Recognized for its social mission, values, and actions	**Weaknesses** • B&J's social responsibility actions could reduce focus • Experienced managers needed to help growth • Modest sales growth and profits in recent years
External	**Opportunities** • Growing demand for quality ice cream in overseas markets • Increasing U.S. demand for Greek-style yogurt • Many U.S. firms successfully use product and brand extensions	**Threats** • B&J customers read nutritional labels and are concerned with sugary and fatty desserts • Competes with General Mills and Nestlé brands • Increasing competition in international markets

Step 2: Market-Product Focus and Goal Setting   Determining which products will be directed toward which customers (step 2 of the planning phase in Figure 2–6) is essential for developing an effective marketing program (step 3). This decision is often based on **market segmentation**, which involves aggregating prospective buyers into groups, or segments, that (1) have common needs and (2) will respond similarly to a marketing action. This enables an organization to focus specific marketing programs on its target market segments. The match between products and segments is often related to **points of difference**, or those characteristics of a product that make it superior to competitive substitutes. Goal setting involves specifying measurable marketing objectives to be achieved.

So step 2 in the planning phase of the strategic marketing process—deciding which products will be directed toward which customers—is the foundation for step 3, developing the marketing program.

Step 3: Marketing Program   Activities in step 2 tell the marketing manager which customers to target and which customer needs the firm's product offerings can satisfy—the *who* and *what* aspects of the strategic marketing process. The *how* aspect—step 3 in the planning phase—involves developing the program's marketing mix (the four Ps) and its budget. Figure 2–8 shows that each marketing mix element is combined to provide a cohesive marketing program.

Putting a marketing program into effect requires that the firm commit time and money to it in the form of a sales forecast (see Chapter 8) and budget that must be approved by top management.

learning review

2-8. What are the three steps of the planning phase of the strategic marketing process?

2-9. What are points of difference and why are they important?

FIGURE 2–8

The four Ps elements of the marketing mix must be blended to produce a cohesive marketing program.

The Implementation Phase of the Strategic Marketing Process

LO 2-6 Describe the four components of the implementation phase of the strategic marketing process.

As shown in Figure 2–6, the result of the hours spent in the planning phase of the strategic marketing process is the firm's marketing plan. Implementation, the second phase of the strategic marketing process, involves carrying out the marketing plan that emerges from the planning phase. If the firm cannot execute the marketing plan—in the implementation phase—the planning phase wasted time and resources.

There are four components of the implementation phase: (1) obtaining resources, (2) designing the marketing organization, (3) defining precise tasks, responsibilities, and deadlines, and (4) actually executing the marketing program designed in the planning phase.

Obtaining Resources   A key task in the implementation phase of the strategic marketing process is finding adequate human and financial resources to execute the marketing program successfully. Small business owners often obtain funds from savings, family, friends, and bank loans. Marketing managers in existing organizations obtain these resources by getting top management to divert profits from BCG stars or cash cows.

Designing the Marketing Organization   A marketing program needs a marketing organization to implement it. Figure 2–9 shows the organization chart of a typical manufacturing firm, giving some details of the marketing department's structure. Four managers of marketing activities are shown to report to the vice president of marketing or CMO. Several regional sales managers and an international sales manager may report to the manager of sales. The product or brand managers and their subordinates help plan, implement, and evaluate the marketing plans for their offerings. However, the entire marketing organization is responsible for converting these marketing plans into realistic marketing actions.

Defining Precise Tasks, Responsibilities, and Deadlines   Successful implementation requires that team members know the tasks for which they are responsible and the deadlines for completing them. To implement the thousands of tasks on a new aircraft design, Lockheed Martin typically holds weekly program meetings. The

President/Chief Executive Officer

Vice President Information Systems Department

Vice President Research and Development Department

Vice President Manufacturing Department

Vice President Marketing Department*

Vice President Accounting and Finance Department

Vice President Human Resources Department

Product or Brand Manager

Manager Marketing Research

Manager Sales

Manager Advertising and Promotion

Associate Product Managers

Marketing Assistants

Sales Regions and Representatives

*Called chief marketing officer (CMO) in many organizations.

FIGURE 2–9

Organization of a typical manufacturing firm, showing a breakdown of the marketing department.

outcome of each of these meetings is an *action item list*, an aid to implementing a marketing plan consisting of four columns: (1) the task, (2) the person responsible for completing that task, (3) the date to finish the task, and (4) what is to be delivered. Within hours of completing a program meeting, the action item list is circulated to those attending. This then serves as the starting agenda for the next meeting. Meeting minutes are viewed as secondary and backward-looking. Action item lists are forward-looking, clarify the targets, and put strong pressure on people to achieve their designated tasks by the deadline.

Suppose, for example, that you and two friends undertake a term project on the problem, "How can the college increase attendance at its performing arts concerts?" The instructor says the term project must involve a mail survey of a sample of students, and the written report with the survey results must be submitted by the end of the 11-week quarter. To begin, you identify all the project tasks and then estimate the time required to complete each one. To complete it in 11 weeks, your team must plan which activities can be done concurrently (at the same time) to save time.

Scheduling activities can be done efficiently with a *Gantt chart*, which is a graph of a program schedule. Figure 2–10 shows a Gantt chart—invented by Henry L. Gantt— used to schedule the class project, demonstrating how the concurrent work on several tasks enables the students to finish the project on time. Software applications such as Microsoft Project simplify the task of developing a program schedule or Gantt chart.

The key to all scheduling techniques is to distinguish tasks that *must* be done sequentially from those that *can* be done concurrently. For example, Tasks 1 and 2 that are shaded yellow in Figure 2–10 *must* be done sequentially. This is because in order to type and copy the final questionnaire before mailing (Task 2), the student *must* have a final draft of the questionnaire (Task 1). In contrast, Tasks 6 and 7 that are shaded blue *can* be done concurrently. So writing the final report (Task 7) *can* be started before tabulating the questions (Task 6) is completed. This overlap speeds up project completion.

Executing the Marketing Program Marketing plans are meaningless without effective execution of those plans. This requires attention to detail for both marketing strategies and marketing tactics. A **marketing strategy** is the means by which a marketing goal

FIGURE 2–10

This Gantt chart shows how three students (A, B, and C) can schedule tasks to complete a term project on time. Software applications, such as Microsoft Project, simplify the task of developing a program schedule or Gantt chart.

Task description	Students involved in task	Week of quarter 1 2 3 4 5 6 7 8 9 10 11
1. Construct, test on friends, and complete a final draft of a questionnaire	A	
2. Type the final questionnaire	C	
3. Randomly select the names of 200 students from the school directory	A	
4. E-mail questionnaires	C	
5. Monitor completed questionnaires	B	
6. Analyze data from completed questionnaires	B	
7. Write final report	A, B, C	
8. Type and submit final report	C	

KEY: ▲ Planned completion date ■ Planned period of work Current date
△ Actual completion date ■ Actual period of work

is to be achieved, usually characterized by a specified target market and a marketing program to reach it. The term implies both the end sought (target market) and the means or actions to achieve it (marketing program).

To implement a marketing program successfully, hundreds of detailed decisions are often required to develop the actions that comprise a marketing program for an offering. These actions, called **marketing tactics**, are detailed day-to-day operational marketing actions for each element of the marketing mix that contribute to the overall success of marketing strategies. Writing ads and setting prices for new product lines are examples of marketing tactics.

The Evaluation Phase of the Strategic Marketing Process

LO 2-7 Discuss how managers identify and act on deviations from plans.

The evaluation phase of the strategic marketing process seeks to keep the marketing program moving in the direction set for it (see Figure 2–6). Accomplishing this requires the marketing manager to (1) compare the results of the marketing program with the goals in the written plans to identify deviations and (2) act on these deviations—exploiting positive deviations and correcting negative ones.

Comparing Results with Plans to Identify Deviations At the end of its fiscal year, which is September 30, Apple begins the evaluation phase of its strategic marketing process. Suppose you are on an Apple task force in late 2005 that is responsible for making plans through 2014. You observe that extending the 2000–2005 trend of Apple's recent sales revenues (line AB in Figure 2–11) to 2014 along line BC shows an annual growth in sales revenue unacceptable to Apple's management.

Looking at potential new products in the Apple pipeline, your task force set an aggressive annual sales growth target of 25 percent per year—the line BD in Figure 2–11. This would give sales revenues of $42 billion in 2010 and $104 billion in 2014.

This reveals a gray wedge-shaped gap DBC in the figure. Planners call this the *planning gap,* the difference between the projection of the path to reach a new sales revenue goal (line BD) and the projection of the path of a plan already in place (line BC). The ultimate purpose of the firm's marketing program is to "fill in" this planning gap—in the case of your Apple task force, to move its future sales revenue line from the slow-growth line BC up to the more challenging target of line BD.

This is the essence of evaluation: comparing actual results with goals set. To reach aggressive growth targets in sales revenues, firms like Apple must continuously look for a new BCG SBU or product *cash cow* or *star.*

The evaluation phase of the strategic marketing process requires that the organization compare actual results with goals to identify and act on deviations to fill in its "planning gap." The text describes how Apple is working to fill in its planning gap.

Apple logos: Left: © Mickey Pfleger/LIFE Images/Getty Images; Right: © Jerome Favre/Bloomberg via Getty Images

Acting on Deviations

When evaluation shows that actual performance differs from expectations, managers need to take immediate marketing actions—exploiting positive deviations and correcting negative ones. Comparing the explosion in Apple's actual sales revenues from 2006 to 2014 (line BE in Figure 2–11) to its target sales revenues (line BD) shows Apple's rare, world-class ability to both generate and anticipate consumer demand and commercialize new technologies for its revolutionary offerings. Let's consider some of its marketing actions:

- *Exploiting a positive deviation.* Favorable customer reactions to Apple's iPhone (2007) and its iPad (2010) enable it to sell the products globally and to introduce improved versions and models, such as the iPad mini (2012) and the Apple Watch (2015).
- *Correcting a negative deviation.* As Apple's desktop PCs became dated, it moved aggressively to replace them with new iMacs and MacBooks. Also, Apple refreshed its MacBook Air and MacBook Pro lines of laptops (2013).

As we saw earlier in the BCG business portfolio analysis of the four Apple product lines, the firm has several *stars* and *cash cows* to fill in its planning gap. We shall explore Apple's market-product strategies in more detail later in Chapters 9 and 10.

learning review

2-10. What is the implementation phase of the strategic marketing process?

2-11. How do the goals set for a marketing program in the planning phase relate to the evaluation phase of the strategic marketing process?

LO 2-1 *Describe three kinds of organizations and the three levels of strategy in them.*

An organization is a legal entity that consists of people who share a common mission. It develops offerings (goods, services, or ideas) that create value for both the organization and its customers by satisfying their needs and wants. Today's organizations are of three types: for-profit organizations, nonprofit organizations, and government agencies. A for-profit organization serves its customers to earn a profit so that it can survive. Profit is the money left after a for-profit organization subtracts its expenses from its total revenues and is the reward for the risk it undertakes in marketing its offerings. A nonprofit organization is a nongovernmental organization that serves its customers but does not have profit as an organizational goal. Instead, its goals may be operational efficiency or client satisfaction. A government agency is a federal, state, county, or city unit that provides a specific service to its constituents. Most large for-profit and nonprofit organizations are divided into three levels of strategy: (*a*) the corporate level, where top management directs overall strategy for the entire organization; (*b*) the strategic business unit level, where managers set a more specific strategic direction for their businesses to exploit value-creating opportunities; and (*c*) the functional level, where groups of specialists actually create value for the organization.

LO 2-2 *Describe core values, mission, organizational culture, business, and goals.*

Organizations exist to accomplish something for someone. To give organizations direction and focus, they continuously assess their core values, mission, organizational culture, business, and goals. Today's organizations specify their foundation, set a direction, and formulate strategies—the "why," "what," and "how" factors, respectively. Core values are the organization's fundamental, passionate, and enduring principles that guide its conduct over time. The organization's mission is a statement of its function in society, often identifying its customers, markets, products, and technologies. Organizational culture is a set of values, ideas, attitudes, and norms of behavior that is learned and shared among the members of an organization. To answer the question, "What business are we in?" an organization defines its "business"—the clear, broad, underlying industry category or market sector of its offering. Finally, the organization's goals (or objectives) are statements of an accomplishment of a task to be achieved, often by a specific time.

LO 2-3 *Explain why managers use marketing dashboards and marketing metrics.*

Marketing managers use marketing dashboards to visually display on a single computer screen the essential information required to make a decision to take an action or further analyze a problem. This information consists of key performance measures of a product category, such as sales or market share, and is known as a marketing metric, which is a measure of the quantitative value or trend of a marketing activity or result. Most organizations tie their marketing metrics to the quantitative objectives established in their marketing plan, which is a road map for the marketing activities of an organization for a specified future time period, such as one year or five years.

LO 2-4 *Discuss how an organization assesses where it is now and where it seeks to be.*

Managers of an organization ask two key questions to set a strategic direction. The first question, "Where are we now?" requires an organization to (*a*) reevaluate its competencies to ensure that its special capabilities still provide a competitive advantage; (*b*) assess its present and prospective customers to ensure they have a satisfying customer experience—the central goal of marketing today; and (*c*) analyze its current and potential competitors from a global perspective to determine whether it needs to redefine its business.

The second question, "Where do we want to go?" requires an organization to set a specific direction and allocate resources to move it in that direction. Business portfolio and diversification analyses help an organization do this. Managers use business portfolio analysis to assess the organization's strategic business units (SBUs), product lines, or individual products as though they were a collection of separate investments (*cash cows*, *stars*, *question marks*, and *dogs*) to determine the amount of cash each should receive. Diversification analysis is a tool that helps managers use one or a combination of four strategies to increase revenues: market penetration (selling more of an existing product to existing markets); market development (selling an existing product to new markets); product development (selling a new product to existing markets); and diversification (selling new products to new markets).

LO 2-5 *Explain the three steps of the planning phase of the strategic marketing process.*

An organization uses the strategic marketing process to allocate its marketing mix resources to reach its target markets. This process is divided into three phases: planning, implementation, and evaluation. The planning phase consists of (*a*) a situation (SWOT) analysis, which involves taking stock of where the firm or product has been recently, where it is now, and where it is headed and focuses on the organization's internal factors (strengths and weaknesses) and the external forces and trends affecting it (opportunities and threats); (*b*) a market-product focus through market segmentation (grouping buyers into segments with common needs and similar responses to marketing programs) and goal setting, which in part requires creating points of difference (those characteristics of a product that make it superior to competitive substitutes); and (*c*) a marketing program that specifies the budget and actions (marketing strategies and tactics) for each marketing mix element.

LO 2-6 *Describe the four components of the implementation phase of the strategic marketing process.*

The implementation phase of the strategic marketing process carries out the marketing plan that emerges from the planning phase. It has four key components: (*a*) obtaining resources; (b) designing the marketing organization to perform product management, marketing research, sales, and advertising and promotion activities; (c) developing schedules to identify the tasks that need to be done, the time that is allocated to each one, the people responsible for each task, and the deadlines for each task—often with an action item list and Gantt chart; and (d) executing the marketing strategies, which are the means by which marketing goals are to be achieved, and their associated marketing tactics, which are the detailed day-to-day marketing actions for each element of the marketing mix that contribute to the overall success of a firm's marketing strategies. These are the marketing program actions a firm takes to achieve the goals set forth in its marketing plan.

LO 2-7 *Discuss how managers identify and act on deviations from plans.*

The evaluation phase of the strategic marketing process seeks to keep the marketing program moving in the direction that was established in the marketing plan. This requires the marketing manager to compare the results from the marketing program with the marketing plan's goals to (a) identify deviations or "planning gaps" and (b) take corrective actions to exploit positive deviations or correct negative ones.

LEARNING REVIEW ANSWERS

2-1 **What is the difference between a for-profit and a nonprofit organization?**

Answer: A for-profit organization is a privately owned organization that serves its customers to earn a profit so that it can survive. A nonprofit organization is a nongovernmental organization that serves its customers but does not have profit as an organizational goal. Instead, its goals may be operational efficiency or client satisfaction.

2-2 **What are examples of a functional level in an organization?**

Answer: The functional level in an organization is where groups of specialists from the marketing, finance, manufacturing/operations, accounting, information systems, research and development, and/or human resources departments focus on a specific strategic direction to create value for the organization.

2-3 **What is the meaning of an organization's mission?**

Answer: A mission is a clear, concise, meaningful, inspirational, and long-term statement of the organization's function in society, often identifying its customers, markets, products, and technologies. It is often used interchangeably with *vision*.

2-4 **What is the difference between an organization's business and its goals?**

Answer: An organization's business describes the clear, broad, underlying industry or market sector of an organization's offering. An organization's goals (or objectives) are statements of an accomplishment of a task to be achieved, often by a specific time. Goals convert an organization's mission and business into long- and short-term performance targets to measure how well it is doing.

2-5 **What is the difference between a marketing dashboard and a marketing metric?**

Answer: A marketing dashboard is the visual computer display of the essential information related to achieving a marketing objective. Each variable displayed in a marketing dashboard is a marketing metric, which is a measure of the quantitative value or trend of a marketing action or result.

2-6 **What is business portfolio analysis?**

Answer: Business portfolio analysis is a technique that managers use to quantify performance measures and growth targets to analyze their firms' SBUs as though they were a collection of separate investments. The purpose of this tool is to determine which SBU or offering generates cash and which one requires cash to fund the organization's growth opportunities.

2-7 **Explain the four market-product strategies in diversification analysis.**

Answer: The four market-product strategies in diversification analysis are: (1) Market penetration, which is a marketing strategy to increase sales of current products in current markets. There is no change in either the basic product line or the markets served. Rather, selling more of the product or selling the product at a higher price generates increased sales. (2) Market development, which is a marketing strategy to sell current products to new markets. (3) Product development, which is a marketing strategy of selling new products to current markets. (4) Diversification, which is a marketing strategy of developing new products and selling them in new markets. This is a potentially high-risk strategy because the firm has neither previous production nor marketing experience on which to draw in marketing a new product to a new market.

2-8 **What are the three steps of the planning phase of the strategic marketing process?**

Answer: The three steps of the planning phase of the strategic marketing process are: (1) Situation analysis, which involves taking stock of where the firm or product has been recently, where it is now, and where it is headed in terms of the organization's marketing plans and the external forces and trends affecting it. To do this, an organization uses a SWOT analysis, an acronym that describes an organization's appraisal of its internal **S**trengths and **W**eaknesses and its external **O**pportunities and **T**hreats. (2) Market-product focus and goal setting, which determine what products an organization will offer to which customers. This is often based on market segmentation—aggregating prospective buyers into groups or segments that have common needs and will respond similarly to a marketing action. (3) Marketing program, which is where an organization develops the marketing mix elements and budget for each offering.

2-9 **What are points of difference and why are they important?**

Answer: Points of difference are those characteristics of a product that make it superior to competitive substitutes—offerings the organization faces in the marketplace. They are important factors in the success or failure of a new product.

2-10 **What is the implementation phase of the strategic marketing process?**

Answer: The implementation phase carries out the marketing plan that emerges from the planning phase and consists of: (1) obtaining resources; (2) designing the marketing organization; (3) defining precise tasks, responsibilities, and deadlines; and (4) executing the marketing program designed in the planning phase.

2-11 **How do the goals set for a marketing program in the planning phase relate to the evaluation phase of the strategic marketing process?**

Answer: The planning phase goals or objectives are used as the benchmarks with which the actual performance results are compared in the evaluation phase to identify deviations from the written marketing plans and then exploit positive ones or correct negative ones.

FOCUSING ON KEY TERMS

business   p. 32
business portfolio analysis   p. 36
core values   p. 32
diversification analysis   p. 39
goals (objectives)   p. 32
market segmentation   p. 42
market share   p. 32

marketing dashboard   p. 33
marketing metric   p. 34
marketing plan   p. 33
marketing strategy   p. 44
marketing tactics   p. 45
mission   p. 31
objectives (goals)   p. 32

organizational culture   p. 31
points of difference   p. 42
profit   p. 28
situation analysis   p. 40
strategic marketing process   p. 40
strategy   p. 28
SWOT analysis   p. 41

APPLYING MARKETING KNOWLEDGE

1   *(a)* Using Medtronic as an example, explain how a mission statement gives it a strategic direction. *(b)* Create a mission statement for your own career.

2   What competencies best describe *(a)* your college or university and *(b)* your favorite restaurant?

3   Compare the advantages and disadvantages of Ben & Jerry's attempting to expand sales revenues by using *(a)* a product development strategy or *(b)* a market development strategy.

4   Select one strength, one weakness, one opportunity, and one threat from the Ben & Jerry's SWOT analysis shown in Figure 2–7. Suggest an action that a B&J marketing manager might take to address each factor.

5   What is the main result of each of the three phases of the strategic marketing process? *(a)* planning, *(b)* implementation, and *(c)* evaluation.

6   Parts of Tasks 5 and 6 in Figure 2–10 are done both concurrently and sequentially. *(a)* How can this be? *(b)* How does it help the students meet the term paper deadline? *(c)* What is the main advantage of scheduling tasks concurrently rather than sequentially?

7   The goal-setting step in the planning phase of the strategic marketing process sets quantified objectives for use in the evaluation phase. What does a manager do if measured results fail to meet objectives? Exceed objectives?

BUILDING YOUR MARKETING PLAN

1   Read Appendix A, "Building an Effective Marketing Plan." Then write a 600-word executive summary for the Paradise Kitchens marketing plan using the numbered headings shown in the plan. When you have completed the draft of your own marketing plan, write a 600-word executive summary to go in the front of your own marketing plan.

2   Using Chapter 2 and Appendix A as guides, focus your marketing plan by *(a)* writing your mission statement in 25 words or less, *(b)* listing three non-financial goals and three financial goals, *(c)* writing your competitive advantage in 35 words or less, and *(d)* creating a SWOT analysis table.

3   Draw a simple organization chart for your organization.

VIDEO CASE 2   IBM: Using Strategy to Build a "Smarter Planet"

"'Smarter Planet' is not an advertising campaign, it's not even a marketing campaign, it is a business strategy," explains Ann Rubin, vice president of advertising at IBM.

Video 2-5
IBM Video Case
kerin.tv/13e/v2-5

The "Smarter Planet" strategy is based on the idea that the next major revolution in the global marketplace will be the instrumentation and integration of the world's processes and infrastructures, generating unprecedented amounts of data. The data captured and analyzed in industries such as banking, energy, health care, and retailing will allow IBM to help businesses be more efficient, productive, and responsive.

THE COMPANY

Founded in 1911, IBM has a history of innovation and focus on customers. The blue covers on its computers, blue letters in the IBM logo, and dark blue suits worn by IBM salespeople led to the now popular company nickname, "Big Blue." Today, it has over 380,000 employees in more than 170 countries. *Forbes* magazine ranks IBM as the fifth most valuable brand in the world. The company is a leading developer of new business technologies, receiving more than 5,000 patents each year. Some of its well-known inventions include the automated teller machine (ATM), the hard disk drive, the magnetic stripe card, relational databases, and the Universal Product Code (UPC). In addition, IBM recently gained attention for its artificial intelligence program called Watson, which challenged two *Jeopardy!* game show champions and won! According to Virginia Rometty, the current CEO of IBM, "IBM is an innovation company."

© Peter Probst/Alamy

VALUES, MISSION, AND STRATEGY

Recently, IBM initiated a project to facilitate online discussions of key business issues among 50,000 employees to identify common themes and perspectives. According to Sam Palmisano, former CEO of IBM, "We needed to affirm IBM's reason for being, what sets the company apart, and what should drive our actions as individual IBMers." The results were three underlying values of IBM's business practices: (1) dedication to every client's success, (2) innovation that matters—for our company and for the world, and (3) trust and personal responsibility in all relationships. These values now come to life at IBM in its "policies, procedures, and daily operations," explains Palmisano.

IBM's core values also help to define its mission, or its general function in society. In clear, concise, inspirational language, IBM's mission statement is:

- At IBM, we strive to lead in the invention, development and manufacture of the industry's most advanced information technologies, including computer systems, software, storage systems, and microelectronics.
- We translate these advanced technologies into value for our customers through our professional solutions, services, and consulting businesses worldwide.

The mission, and the values it represents, helps define the organizational culture at IBM. Executives, managers, and all employees create the culture through the strategies they select and the detailed plans for accomplishing them.

IBM's strategies are based on its assessment of fundamental changes in the business environment. First, IBM sees global changes such as fewer trade barriers, the growth of developing economies, and increasing access to the World Wide Web. These changes necessitate a new type of corporation that IBM calls the "globally integrated enterprise." Second, IBM foresees a new model of computing that includes computational capability in phones, cameras, cars, and other appliances and allows economic, social, and physical systems to be connected. This connectivity creates a "smarter planet." Finally, IBM predicts a growing demand for technological solutions that help organizations measure and achieve specific outcomes.

As a result, IBM began to shift from commodity-based businesses such as PCs and hard disk drives, to "customizable" businesses such as software and services. The change in IBM was so substantial that it has described its plan in a document called the *2015 Road Map*. The Map describes four strategic opportunities: (1) growth markets such as China, India, Brazil, and Africa, (2) business analytics and optimization, (3) cloud and smarter computing, and (4) the connected, "smarter" planet. These opportunities suggest a strategy that delivers value through business and IT innovation to selected industries with an integrated enterprise. The overarching strategy that highlights IBM's capabilities is called "Building a Smarter Planet."

BUILDING A SMARTER PLANET

The Smarter Planet initiative is designed for clients who value IBM's industry and process expertise, systems integration capability, and research capacity. A smarter planet, while global by definition, happens on the industry level. It is driven by forward-thinking organizations that share a common outlook: They see change as an opportunity, and they act on possibilities, not just react to problems.

John Kennedy, vice president of marketing, explains, "'A Smarter Planet' actually surfaced from observing what was happening in our clients. They were looking to take the vast amount of data that was being generated inside their companies and looking to better understand it." To IBM "smart" solutions have three characteristics. They are instrumented, they are intelligent, and they are interconnected. Millions of digital devices, now connected through the Internet, produce data that can be turned into knowledge through advanced computational

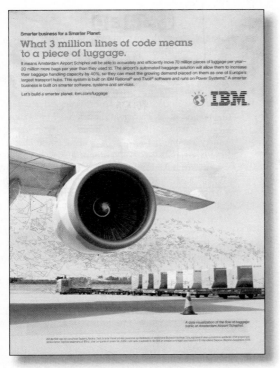

power. IBM believes that this knowledge can help reduce costs, cut waste, improve efficiency, and increase productivity for companies, industries, and cities.

Since introducing the Smarter Planet strategy, IBM has collaborated with more than 600 organizations around the globe. The success of the strategy is evident in the broad range of industries where "smart" solutions are being implemented. They include banking; communications; electronics, automotive and aerospace; energy and utilities; government; health care; insurance; oil and gas; retailing; and transportation. Each industry has reported a variety of applications.

In a study of 439 cities, for example, smart solutions such as ramp metering, signal coordination, and accident management reduced travel delays by more than 700,000 annually, saving each city $15 million. A study by the U.S. Department of Energy found that consumers with smart electric meters cut their power usage and saved 10 percent on their power bills. Retailers who implemented smart systems to analyze buying behavior, merchandise assortment, and demand were able to cut supply chain costs by 30 per-

cent, reduce inventory levels by 25 percent, and increase sales by 10 percent.

THE BUILDING A SMARTER PLANET MARKETING PLAN

Marketing and communications professionals at IBM have developed the marketing plan for IBM's Smarter Planet strategy. The general goal is to describe the company's view of the next era of information technology and its impact on business and society. The execution of the plan includes messaging from IBM leaders, an advertising campaign, an Internet presence, and public relations communications. In addition, IBM measures and tracks the performance of the marketing activities.

The importance of the Smarter Planet strategy was first communicated through a message from the top. Palmisano prepared a "Letter from the Chairman" for the annual report. His message was a powerful statement. Smarter Planet, according to Palmisano, "is not a metaphor. It describes the infusion of intelligence into the way the world actually works."

IBM also used a print and television advertising campaign to add detail to the general message. The ads focused on the ability to improve the world now, with IBM's help. "I think what's different about Smarter Planet," says Ann Rubin, "is that it was not inward facing, it was looking out at what the world needed. We felt like we could go out there and influence the world for the better."

IBM recently celebrated its 100th anniversary! Its record of success is testimony to the resilience of a business model that encourages long-term strategies that can say "Welcome to a Smarter Planet."[42]

Questions

1 What is IBM's Smarter Planet business strategy? How does this strategy relate to IBM's mission and values?

2 Conduct a SWOT analysis for IBM's Smarter Planet initiative. What are the relevant trends to consider for the next three to five years?

3 How can IBM communicate its strategy to companies, cities, and governments?

4 What are the benefits of the Smarter Planet initiative to (a) society and (b) IBM?

5 How should IBM measure the results of the Smarter Planet strategy?

CHAPTER 2 Developing Successful Organizational and Marketing Strategies

Chapter Notes

1. "Our Values," from Ben & Jerry's website, http://www.benjerry.com/values, April 3, 2015; and "Ice Cream History Revealed! What Was Ben & Jerry's First Ice Cream Flavor?" *BusinessWire,* November 15, 2011, http://www.businesswire.com/news/home/20111115007275/en/Ice-Cream-History-Revealed!-Ben-Jerry%E2%80%99s-Ice#.VR8B7J50yM8.

2. Nick Craig and Scott Snook, "From Purpose to Impact," *Harvard Business Review,* May 2014, pp. 105–11; Joe Van Brussel, "Ben & Jerry's Become B-Corp Certified, Adds Credibility to Impact Investing Movement," *Huffington Post: Business,* October 23, 2012, http://www.huffingtonpost.com/2012/10/23/ben-and-jerrys-b-corp-impactinvesting_n_2005315.html; and "What Are B-Corps?" B-Corporation website, see http://www.bcorporation.net/what-are-b-corps.

3. "Global Ice Cream," press release posted at www.market-research.com, October 10, 2014.

4. Roger Kerin and Robert Peterson, *Strategic Marketing Problems: Cases and Comments,* 13th ed. (Upper Saddle River, NJ: Prentice Hall, 2013), p. 140.

5. "Introducing Forbes' 30 Under 30 Social Entrepreneurs, Class of 2015," www.forbes.com, January 5, 2015; Richard Murphy and Denielle Sachs, "The Rise of Social Entrepreneurship Suggests a Possible Future for Global Capitalism," www.forbes.com, May 2, 2013; and http://www.teachforamerica.org.

6. For a discussion on how industries are defined and offerings are classified, see the Census Bureau's Economic Classification Policy Committee Issues Paper #1 (http://www.census.gov/eos/www/naics/history/docs/issue_paper_1.pdf), which aggregates industries in the NAICS from a "production-oriented" view; see also the American Marketing Association definition at https://www.ama.org/resources/Pages/Dictionary.aspx?dLetter=I.

7. W. Chan Kim and Reneé Mauborgne, "Blue Ocean Strategy: From Theory to Practice," *California Management Review* 47, no. 3 (Spring 2005), p. 105; and Michael E. Porter, "What Is Strategy?" *Harvard Business Review,* November–December 1996, p. 2.

8. The definition of *strategy* reflects thoughts appearing in Porter, "What Is Strategy?" pp. 4, 8; a condensed definition of strategy is found on the American Marketing Association website https://www.ama.org/resources/Pages/Dictionary.aspx?dLetter=S; Gerry Johnson, Kevan Scholes, and Richard Wittington, *Exploring Corporate Strategy* (Upper Saddle River, NJ: Prentice Hall, 2005), p. 10; and Costas Markides, "What Is Strategy and How Do You Know If You Have One?" *Business Strategy Review* 15, no. 2 (Summer 2004), p. 5.

9. Frank Holland, "Tomorrow's CMO Will Be Plugged into the Entire Marketing Cycle," *Adweek,* January 9, 2015, p. 1; George S. Day and Robert Malcolm, "The CMO and the Future of Marketing," *Marketing Management,* Spring 2012, pp. 34–43; Gordon Wyner, "Getting Engaged," *Marketing Management,* Fall, 2012, pp. 4–9; Christine Moorman, "Ten Trends from the CMO SurveyTM," *Marketing Management,* Fall 2012, pp. 15–17; John Kador, "The View from Marketing: How to Get the Most from Your CMO," *Chief Executive,* July–August 2011, pp. 60–61; Jessica Shambora, "Wanted: Fearless Marketing Execs," *Fortune,* April 15, 2011, p. 27; Roger A. Kerin, "Strategic Marketing and the CMO," *Journal of Marketing,* October 2005, pp. 12–13; *and The CMO Council: Biographies of Selected Advisory Board Members,* www.cmocouncil.org/advisory-board.php.

10. Taken in part from Jim Collins and Morten T. Hansen, *Great By Choice* (New York: HarperCollins Publishers, 2011); and Jim Collins and Jerry I. Porras, *Built to Last: Successful Habits of Visionary Companies* (New York: HarperCollins Publishers, 2002), p. 54.

11. Collins and Porras, *Built to Last: Successful Habits of Visionary Companies,* p. 73; Patrick M. Lencioni, "Make Your Values Mean Something," *Harvard Business Review,* July 2002, p. 6; Aubrey Malphurs, *Values-Driven Leadership: Discovering and Developing Your Core Values for Ministry,* 2nd ed. (Grand Rapids, MI: BakerBooks, 2004), p. 31; and Catherine M. Dalton, "When Organizational Values Are Mere Rhetoric," *Business Horizons* 49 (September–October 2006), p. 345.

12. Collins and Porras, *Built to Last,* pp. 94–95; and Tom Krattenmaker, "Write a Mission Statement That Your Company Is Willing to Live," *Harvard Management Communication Letter,* March 2002, pp. 3–4.

13. Courtesy of Southwest Airlines, https://www.southwest.com/html/about-southwest.

14. Courtesy of The American National Red Cross, http://www.redcross.org/about-us/mission.

15. See http://www.southwestonereport.com/2011/#!/thirty-thousand-foot-view/mission-andvision; http://www.redcross.org/about-us/mission; and https://www.ftc.gov/about-ftc.

16. Theodore Levitt, "Marketing Myopia," *Harvard Business Review,* July–August 1960, pp. 45–56.

17. Nu Yang and Rich Kane, "10 Newspapers That Do It Right," *Editor & Publisher,* March 2015, pp. 52–67; and Nu Yang, "Calling All Newspapers," *Editor & Publisher,* January 2015, pp. 34–40.

18. Jim Milliot, "E-books Gained, Online Retailers Slipped in 2014," *Publishers Weekly,* March 30, 2015, pp. 4–5; and Jeffrey A. Trachtenberg, "What's Barnes & Noble's Survival Plan?" *The Wall Street Journal,* April 18, 2014, p. B1.

19. Laura Stevens, "UPS Launched New Ad Campaign," *The Wall Street Journal,* March 8, 2015; and "UPS Abandons 'We Love Logistics' in Favor of 'United Problem Solvers,'" *Supply Chain 24/7,* March 10, 2015, www.supplychain247.com.

20. Andrew McAfee and Erik Brynjolfsson, "Big Data: The Management Revolution," *Harvard Business Review,* October 2012, pp. 61–68.

21. The definition is adapted from Stephen Few, *Information Dashboard Design: The Effective Visual Communication of Data* (Sebastopol, CA: O'Reilly Media, Inc., 2006), pp. 2–46.

22. Koen Pauwels et al., *Dashboards & Marketing: Why, What, How and What Research Is Needed?* (Hanover, NH: Tuck School, Dartmouth, May 2008).

23. 21 Few, *Information Dashboard Design;* Michael T. Krush, Raj Agnihotri, Kevin J. Trainor, and Edward L. Nowlin, "Enhancing Organizational Sensemaking: An Examination of the Interactive Effects of Sales Capabilities and Marketing Dashboards," *Industrial Marketing Management,* July 2013, pp. 824–35; Bruce H. Clark, Andrew V. Abela, and Tim Ambler, "Behind the Wheel," *Marketing Management,* May–June 2006, pp. 19–23; Spencer E. Ante, "Giving the Boss the Big Picture," *BusinessWeek,* February 13, 2006, pp. 48–49; and *Dashboard Tutorial* (Cupertino, CA: Apple Computer, Inc., 2006).

24. Few, *Information Dashboard Design,* p. 13.

25. Mark Jeffery, *Data-Driven Marketing: The 15 Metrics Everyone in Marketing Should Know* (Hoboken, NJ: John Wiley & Sons, 2010), chapter 1; Michael Krauss, "Balance Attention to Metrics with Intuition," *Marketing News,* June 1, 2007, pp. 6–8; John

Davis, *Measuring Marketing: 103 Key Metrics Every Marketer Needs* (Singapore: John Wiley & Sons [Asia], 2007); and Paul W. Farris, Neil T. Bendle, Phillip E. Pfeifer, and David J. Reibstein, *Marketing Metrics,* 2nd ed. (Upper Saddle River, NJ: Wharton School Publishing, 2010).

26. David Burrows, "Too Many Metrics: The Perils of Training Marketers to Calculate ROI," *Marketing Week,* September 11, 2014, p. 42; Art Weinstein and Shane Smith, "Game Plan," *Marketing Management,* Fall 2012, pp. 24–31; Alexander Chiang, "Special Interview with Stephen Few, Dashboard and Data Visualization Expert," *Dundas Dashboard,* July 14, 2011; Stephen Few, *Now You See It* (Oakland, CA: Analytics Press, 2009), chapters 1–3; and Jacques Bughin, Amy Guggenheim Shenkan, and Mark Singer, "How Poor Metrics Undermine Digital Marketing," *The McKinsey Quarterly,* October 2008.

27. The now-classic reference on effective graphic presentation is Edward R. Tufte, *The Visual Display of Quantitative Information,* 2nd ed. (Cheshire, CT: Graphics Press, 2001); see also Few, *Information Dashboard Design,* chapters 3–5.

28. George Stalk, Phillip Evans, and Lawrence E. Shulman, "Competing on Capabilities: The New Rules of Corporate Strategy," *Harvard Business Review,* March–April 1992, pp. 57–69; and Darrell K. Rigby, *Management Tools 2007: An Executive's Guide* (Boston: Bain & Company, 2007), p. 22.

29. Kerin and Peterson, *Strategic Marketing Problems,* pp. 2–3; and Derek F. *Abell, Defining the Business* (Englewood Cliffs, NJ: Prentice Hall, 1980), p. 18.

30. Robert D. Hof, "How to Hit a Moving Target," *BusinessWeek,* August 21, 2006, p. 3; and Peter Kim, *Reinventing the Marketing Organization* (Cambridge, MA: Forrester, July 13, 2006), pp. 7, 9, and 17.

31. Adapted from *The Experience Curve Reviewed, IV: The Growth Share Matrix of the Product Portfolio* (Boston: The Boston Consulting Group, 1973). See also https://www.bcgperspectives. com/content/classics/strategy_the_product_portfolio (registration and login required for access).

32. Roger A. Kerin, Vijay Mahajan, and P. Rajan Varadarajan, *Contemporary Perspectives on Strategic Marketing Planning* (Boston: Allyn & Bacon, 1990), p. 52.

33. "The Top 100 Brands: Best Global Brands 2014," *Interbrand,* http://bestglobalbrands.com/2014/ranking/.

34. See the Apple press release library at http://www.apple. com/pr/library/.

35. Joseph Palenchar, "Apple Watch the One to Watch," *The Week in Consumer Electronics,* March 16, 2015, www.twice.com.

36. Parmy Oson, "Apple's U.S. iPhone Sales Surpass Android for First Time in Years," *Forbes.com,* February 4, 2014, p. 2-2; and "Worldwide Smartphone Growth Forecast to Slow from a Boil

to a Simmer as Prices Drop and Markets Mature, According to IDC," press release, December 1, 2014, International Data Corporation (IDC), http://www.idc.com/getdoc. jsp?containerId=prUS25282214.

37. Jack Linshi, "5 Charts That Show Why the iPad's Fifth Birthday Is Bittersweet," www.time.com, April 6, 2015; "The State of the Tablet Market," *TabTimes Weekly,* April 10, 2015, http:// tabtimes.com/resources/the-state-of-the-tablet-market/; and Larry Magid, "Apple's Tablets Selling Well but Market Share Slips While Samsung Grows, *Forbes,* May 1, 2013, http://www.forbes.com/sites/larrymagid/2013/05/01/ apples-tablet-market-share-slips-and-samsunggrows.

38. Don Reisinger, "iPod History: 10 Milestones in the Wearable Music Player's Evolution," *eWeek,* October 31, 2014, p. 1-1; James Hall, "MP3 Players Are Dead," *Business Insider,* December 26, 2012, http://www.businessinsider.com/ mp3-players-are-dead-2012-12; Zak Islam, "Smartphones Heavily Decrease Sales of iPod, MP3 Players," *Tom's Hardware,* December 31, 2012, http://www.tomshardware.com/ news/SmartphonesiPod-MP3-Players-Sales,20062.html.

39. "Company Profile: Apple Inc." *MarketLine,* November 6, 2014, www.marketline.com.

40. Strengths and weaknesses of the BCG technique are based on Derek F. Abell and John S. Hammond, *Strategic Market Planning: Problem and Analytic Approaches* (Englewood Cliffs, NJ: Prentice Hall, 1979); Yoram Wind, Vijay Mahajan, and Donald Swire, "An Empirical Comparison of Standardized Portfolio Models," *Journal of Marketing,* Spring 1983, pp. 89–99; and J. Scott Armstrong and Roderick J. Brodie, "Effects of Portfolio Planning Methods on Decision Making: Experimental Results," *International Journal of Research in Marketing,* Winter 1994, pp. 73–84.

41. H. Igor Ansoff, "Strategies for Diversification," *Harvard Business Review,* September–October 1957, pp. 113–24.

42. IBM: This case was written by Steven Hartley. Sources: Jessi Hempel, "IBM's Super Second Act," *Fortune,* March 21, 2011, pp. 114–24; Bruce Upbin, "IBM Plays Jeopardy!" *Forbes,* January 17, 2011, pp. 36–37; Kurt Badenhausen, "The World's Most Valuable Brands," *Forbes,* May 13, 2015; Jeffrey M. O'Brien, "IBM's Grand Plan to Save the Planet," *Fortune,* May 4, 2009, pp. 84–91; *IBM 2009 Annual Report; IBM 2010 Annual Report;* Samuel J. Palmisano, "Our Values at Work on Being an IBMer," IBM website, see http://www.ibm.com/ibm/values/us; and "Welcome to the Decade of Smart," IBM website, http://www.ibm.com/smarterplanet/us/en/events/ sustainable_development/12jan2010/files/palmisano_ decadeofsmart-12jan2010.pdf.

BUILDING AN EFFECTIVE MARKETING PLAN

APPENDIX **A**

"If you have a real product with a distinctive point of difference that satisfies the needs of customers, you may have a winner," says Arthur R. Kydd, who has helped launch more than 60 start-up firms. "And you get a real feel for this in a well-written marketing or business plan," he explains.[1]

This appendix (1) describes what marketing and business plans are, including the purposes and guidelines in writing effective plans, and (2) provides a sample marketing plan.

MARKETING PLANS AND BUSINESS PLANS

After explaining the meanings, purposes, and audiences of marketing plans and business plans, this section describes some writing guidelines for them and what external funders often look for in successful plans.

Meanings, Purposes, and Audiences

A **marketing plan** is a road map for the marketing actions of an organization for a specified future time period, such as one year or five years.[2] No single "generic" marketing plan applies to all organizations and all situations. Rather, the specific format for a marketing plan for an organization depends on the following:

- *The target audience and purpose.* Elements included in a particular marketing plan depend heavily on (1) who the audience is and (2) what its purpose is. A marketing plan for an internal audience seeks to point the direction for future marketing activities and is sent to all individuals in the organization who must implement the plan or who will be affected by it. If the plan is directed to an external audience, such as friends, banks, venture capitalists, or crowdfunding sources like Kickstarter

for the purpose of raising capital, it has the additional function of being an important sales document. So it contains elements such as the strategic focus, organizational structure, and biographies of key personnel that would rarely appear in an internal marketing plan. The elements of a marketing plan for each of these two audiences are compared in Figure A–1.

- *The kind and complexity of the organization.* A neighborhood restaurant has a less detailed marketing plan than Apple, which serves international markets. The restaurant's plan would be relatively simple and directed at serving customers in a local market. In Apple's case, because there is a hierarchy of marketing plans, various levels of detail would be used—such as the entire organization, the strategic business unit, or the product/product line.

- *The industry.* Both the restaurant serving a local market and Apple, selling electronic devices globally, analyze elements of their industry. However, their geographic scopes are far different, as are the complexities of their offerings and, hence, the time periods likely to be covered by their plans. A one-year marketing plan may be adequate for the restaurant, but Apple may need a five-year planning horizon because product development cycles for complex, new electronic devices may be many years.

In contrast to a marketing plan, a **business plan** is a road map for the entire organization for a specified future period of time, such as one year or five years.[3] A key difference between a marketing plan and a business plan is that the business plan contains details on the research and development (R&D)/operations/manufacturing activities of the organization. Even for a manufacturing business, the marketing plan is probably 60 or 70 percent of the entire business plan. For firms like a small restaurant or an auto repair shop, their marketing and business plans are virtually identical. The elements of a business

54

Element of the plan	Marketing plan		Business plan	
	For internal audience (to direct the firm)	For external audience (to raise capital)	For internal audience (to direct the firm)	For external audience (to raise capital)
1. Executive summary	✓	✓	✓	✓
2. Description of company		✓		✓
3. Strategic plan/focus		✓		✓
4. Situation analysis	✓	✓	✓	✓
5. Market-product focus	✓	✓	✓	✓
6. Marketing program strategy and tactics	✓	✓	✓	✓
7. R&D and operations program			✓	✓
8. Financial projections	✓	✓	✓	✓
9. Organization structure		✓		✓
10. Implementation plan	✓	✓	✓	✓
11. Evaluation	✓		✓	
Appendix A: Biographies of key personnel		✓		✓
Appendix B, etc.: Details on other topics	✓	✓	✓	✓

FIGURE A–1

Elements in typical marketing and business plans targeted at different audiences.

plan typically targeted at internal and external audiences appear in the two right-hand columns in Figure A–1.

The Most-Asked Questions by Outside Audiences

Lenders and prospective investors reading a business plan or a marketing plan that is used to seek new capital are probably the toughest audiences to satisfy. Their most-asked questions include the following:

1. Is the business or marketing idea valid?
2. Is there something unique or distinctive about the product or service that separates it from substitutes and competitors?
3. Is there a clear market for the product or service?
4. Are the financial projections realistic and healthy?
5. Are the key management and technical personnel capable, and do they have a track record in the industry within which they must compete?
6. Does the plan clearly describe how those providing capital will get their money back and make a profit?

Rhonda Abrams, author of books on writing business plans, observes, "Although you may spend five months preparing your plan, the cold, hard fact is that an investor or lender can dismiss it in less than five minutes. If you don't make a positive impression in those critical first five minutes, your plan will be rejected."[4] While her comments apply to plans seeking to raise capital, the first five questions listed above apply equally well to plans prepared for internal audiences.

Writing and Style Suggestions

There are no magic one-size-fits-all guidelines for writing successful marketing and business plans. Still, the following writing and style guidelines generally apply:[5]

- Use a direct, professional writing style. Use appropriate business terms without jargon. Present and future tenses with active voice ("I will write an effective marketing plan") are generally better than past tense and passive voice ("An effective marketing plan was written by me").

- Be positive and specific to convey potential success. At the same time, avoid superlatives ("terrific," "wonderful"). Specifics are better than glittering generalities.
- Use numbers for impact, justifying projections with reasonable quantitative assumptions, where possible.
- Use bullet points for succinctness and emphasis. As with the list you are reading, bullets enable key points to be highlighted effectively.
- Use A-level (the first level) and B-level (the second level) headings under the numbered section headings to help readers make easy transitions from one topic to another. This also forces the writer to organize the plan more carefully.
- Use visuals where appropriate. Photos, illustrations, graphs, and charts enable massive amounts of information to be presented succinctly.
- Shoot for a plan 15 to 35 pages in length, not including financial projections and appendices. An uncomplicated small business may require only 15 pages, while a high-technology start-up may require more than 35 pages.
- Use care in layout, design, and presentation. Use 11- or 12-point type (you are now reading 10.5-point type) in the text. Use a serif type (with "feet," like that you are reading now) in the text because it is easier to read, and sans serif (without "feet") in graphs and charts like Figure A–1. A bound report with a nice cover and a clear title page adds professionalism.

These guidelines are used, where possible, in the sample marketing plan that follows.

SAMPLE FIVE-YEAR MARKETING PLAN FOR PARADISE KITCHENS, INC.

To help interpret the marketing plan for Paradise Kitchens, Inc. that follows, we will describe the company and suggest some guidelines for interpreting the plan.[6]

Background on Paradise Kitchens, Inc.

Randall and Leah Peters have over 40 years of food industry experience for General Foods and Pillsbury with a number of diverse responsibilities. With these backgrounds and their savings, they co-founded Paradise Kitchens, Inc. to produce and market a new line of high-quality frozen chili products.

Interpreting the Marketing Plan

The marketing plan on the next pages, based on an actual Paradise Kitchens plan, is directed at an external audience (see Figure A–1). For simplicity, let us assume it is early 2016, the Peters have company data through 2015, and they are developing a five-year marketing plan through 2020. Some details and dates have been altered, but the basic logic of the plan has been kept.

Notes in the margins next to the Paradise Kitchens plan fall into two categories:

1. *Substantive notes* are in blue boxes. These notes explain the significance of an element in the marketing plan and are keyed to chapter references in this textbook.
2. *Writing style, format, and layout notes* are in red boxes and explain the editorial or visual rationale for the element.

A word of encouragement: Writing an effective marketing plan is hard but also challenging and satisfying work. Dozens of the authors' students have used effective marketing plans they wrote for class in their interviewing portfolio to show prospective employers what they could do and to help them get their first job.

Color-Coding Legend

Blue boxes explain significance of marketing plan elements.

Red boxes give writing style, format, and layout guidelines.

The Table of Contents provides quick access to the topics in the plan, usually organized by section and subsection headings.

Seen by many experts as the single most important element in the plan, the two-page Executive Summary "sells" the plan to readers through its clarity and brevity. For space reasons, it is not shown here, but the Building Your Marketing Plan exercise at the end of Chapter 2 asks the reader to write an Executive Summary for this plan.

The Company Description highlights the recent history and recent successes of the organization.

The Strategic Focus and Plan sets the strategic direction for the entire organization, a direction with which proposed actions of the marketing plan must be consistent. This section is not included in all marketing plans. See Chapter 2.

The qualitative Mission statement focuses the activities of Paradise Kitchens for the stakeholder groups to be served. See Chapter 2.

FIVE-YEAR MARKETING PLAN
Paradise Kitchens,® Inc.

Table of Contents

1. Executive Summary

2. Company Description

Paradise Kitchens,® Inc. was started by co-founders Randall F. Peters and Leah E. Peters to develop and market Howlin' Coyote® Chili a, unique line of single serve and microwavable Southwestern/Mexican style frozen chili products. The Howlin' Coyote line of chili was first introduced into the Minneapolis–St. Paul market and expanded to Denver two years later and Phoenix two years after that.

To the Company's knowledge, Howlin' Coyote is the only premium-quality, authentic Southwestern/Mexican style frozen chili sold in U.S. grocery stores. Its high quality has gained fast, widespread acceptance in its targeted markets. In fact, same-store sales doubled in the last year for which data are available. The Company believes the Howlin' Coyote brand can be extended to other categories of Southwestern/Mexican food products, such as tacos, enchiladas, and burritos.

Paradise Kitchens believes its high-quality, high-price strategy has proven successful. This marketing plan outlines how the Company will extend its geographic coverage from 3 markets to 20 markets by the year 2020.

3. Strategic Focus and Plan

This section covers three aspects of corporate strategy that influence the marketing plan: (1) the mission, (2) goals, and (3) core competency/sustainable competitive advantage of Paradise Kitchens.

Mission

The mission of Paradise Kitchens is to market lines of high-quality Southwestern/ Mexican food products at premium prices that satisfy consumers in this fast-growing food segment while providing challenging career opportunities for employees and above-average returns to stockholders.

Goals

For the coming five years Paradise Kitchens seeks to achieve the following goals:

- Nonfinancial goals
  1. To retain its present image as the highest-quality line of Southwestern/Mexican products in the food categories in which it competes.
  2. To enter 17 new metropolitan markets.
  3. To achieve national distribution in two convenience store or supermarket chains by 2016 and five by 2017.
  4. To add a new product line every third year.
  5. To be among the top five chili lines—regardless of packaging (frozen or canned—in one-third of the metro markets in which it competes by 2017 and two-thirds by 2019.
- Financial goals
  1. To obtain a real (inflation-adjusted) growth in earnings per share of 8 percent per year over time.
  2. To obtain a return on equity of at least 20 percent.
  3. To have a public stock offering by the year 2017.

Core Competency and Sustainable Competitive Advantage

In terms of core competency. Paradise Kitchens seeks to achieve a unique ability to (1) provide distinctive, high-quality chilies and related products using Southwestern/Mexican recipes that appeal to and excite contemporary tastes for these products and (2) deliver these products to the customer's table using effective manufacturing and distribution systems that maintain the Company's quality standards.

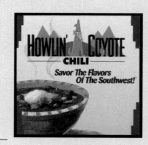

To help achieve national distribution through chains, Paradise Kitchens introduced this point-of-purchase ad that adheres statically to the glass door of the freezer case.

To translate these core competencies into a sustainable competitive advantage, the Company will work closely with key suppliers and distributors to build the relationships and alliances necessary to satisfy the high taste standards of our customers.

To improve readability, each numbered section usually starts on a new page. (This is not done in this plan to save space.)

The Situation Analysis is a snapshot to answer the question "Where are we now?" See Chapter 2.

The SWOT analysis identifies strengths, weaknesses, opportunities, and threats to provide a solid foundation, which is the springboard to identify subsequent actions in the marketing plan. See Chapter 2.

Each long table, graph, or photo is given a figure number and title. It then appears as soon as possible after the first reference in the text, accommodating necessary page breaks. This avoids breaking long tables like this one in the middle. Short tables or graphs are often inserted in the text without figure numbers because they don't cause serious problems with page breaks.

Effective tables seek to summarize a large amount of information in a short amount of space.

4. Situation Analysis

This situation analysis starts with a snapshot of the current environment in which Paradise Kitchens finds itself by providing a brief SWOT (strengths, weaknesses, opportunities, threats) analysis. After this overview, the analysis probes ever-finer levels of detail: industry, competitors, company, and consumers.

SWOT Analysis

Figure 1 shows the internal and external factors affecting the market opportunities for Paradise Kitchens. Stated briefly, this SWOT analysis highlights the great strides taken by the company since its products first appeared on grocers' shelves.

Figure 1.   SWOT Analysis for Paradise Kitchens

Internal Factors	Strengths	Weaknesses
Management	Experienced and entrepreneurial management and board	Small size can restrict options
Offerings	Unique, high-quality, high-price products	Many lower-quality, lower-price competitors
Marketing	Distribution in three markets with excellent consumer acceptance	No national awareness or distribution; restricted shelf space in the freezer section
Personnel	Good workforce, though small; little turnover	Big gap if key employee leaves
Finance	Excellent growth in sales revenues	Limited resources may restrict growth opportunities when compared to giant competitors
Manufacturing	Sole supplier ensures high quality	Lack economies of scale of huge competitors
R&D	Continuing efforts to ensure quality in delivered products	Lack of canning and microwavable food processing expertise

External Factors	Opportunities	Threats
Consumer/Social	Upscale market, likely to be stable; Southwestern/Mexican food category is fast-growing segment due to growth in Hispanic American population and desire for spicier foods	Premium price may limit access to mass markets; consumers value a strong brand name
Competitive	Distinctive name and packaging in its markets	Not patentable; competitors can attempt to duplicate product; others better able to pay slotting fees
Technological	Technical breakthroughs enable smaller food producers to achieve many economies available to large competitors	Competitors have gained economies in canning and microwavable food processing
Economic	Consumer income is high; convenience important to U.S. households	More households "eating out," and bringing prepared take-out into home
Legal/Regulatory	High U.S. Food & Drug Administration standards eliminate fly-by-night competitors	Mergers among large competitors being approved by government

The text discussion of Figure 1 (the SWOT Analysis table) elaborates on its more important elements. This "walks" the reader through the information from the vantage point of the plan's writer.

The Industry Analysis section provides the backdrop for the subsequent, more detailed analysis of competition, the company, and the company's customers. Without an in-depth understanding of the industry, the remaining analysis may be misdirected. See Chapter 2.

Sales of Mexican entrees are significant and provide a variety of future opportunities for Paradise Kitchens.

Even though relatively brief, this in-depth treatment of sales of Mexican foods in the U.S. demonstrates to the plan's readers the company's understanding of the industry within which it competes.

The Competitor Analysis section demonstrates that the company has a realistic understanding of its major chili competitors and their marketing strategies. Again, a realistic assessment gives confidence that subsequent marketing actions in the plan rest on a solid foundation. See Chapters 2, 3, 8, and 9.

In the Company's favor internally are its strengths: an experienced management team and board of directors, excellent acceptance of its product line in the three metropolitan markets within which it competes, and a strong manufacturing and distribution system to serve these limited markets. Favorable external factors include the increasing appeal of Southwestern/Mexican foods, the strength of the upscale market for the Company's products, and food-processing technological breakthroughs that make it easier for smaller food producers to compete.

Among unfavorable factors, the main weakness is the limited size of Paradise Kitchens relative to its competitors in terms of the depth of the management team, the available financial resources, and the national awareness and distribution of product lines. Threats include the danger that the Company's premium prices may limit access to mass markets and competition from the "eating-out" and "take-out" markets.

Industry Analysis: Trends in Frozen and Mexican Foods

Frozen Foods. According to *Grocery Headquarters*, consumers are flocking to the frozen food section of grocery retailers. The reasons: hectic lifestyles demanding increased convenience and an abundance of new, tastier, and nutritious products.[7] By 2014, total sales of frozen food in supermarkets, drugstores, and mass merchandisers reached $31 billion. Prepared frozen meals, which are defined as meals or entrees that are frozen and require minimal preparation, accounted for about one-quarter of the total frozen food market.[8]

Sales of Mexican entrees now exceed $500 million. Heavy consumers of frozen meals, those who eat five or more meals every two weeks, tend to be kids, teens, and adults 35–44 years old.[9]

Mexican Foods. Currently, Mexican foods such as burritos, enchiladas, and tacos are used in two-thirds of American households. These trends reflect a generally more favorable attitude on the part of all Americans toward spicy foods that include red chili peppers. The growing Hispanic population in the United States, over 51 million and about $1.3 trillion in purchasing power, partly explains the increasing demand for Mexican food. This Hispanic purchasing power is projected to be over $1.6 trillion in 2018.[10]

Competitor Analysis: The Chili Market

The chili market represents over $500 million in annual sales. On average, consumers buy five to six servings annually, according to the NPD Group. The products fall primarily into two groups: canned chili (75 percent of sales) and dry chili (25 percent of sales).

Bluntly put, the major disadvantage of the segment's dominant product, canned chili, is that it does not taste very good. A taste test described in an issue of *Consumer Reports* magazine ranked 26 canned chili products "poor" to "fair" in overall sensory quality. The study concluded, "Chili doesn't have to be hot to be good. But really good chili, hot or mild, doesn't come out of a can."

Company Analysis

The husband-and-wife team that co-founded Paradise Kitchens, Inc. has 44 years of experience between them in the food-processing business. Both have played key roles in the management of the Pillsbury Company. They are being advised by a highly seasoned group of business professionals, who have extensive understanding of the requirements for new-product development.

The Company now uses a single outside producer with which it works closely to maintain the consistently high quality required in its products. The greater volume has increased production efficiencies, resulting in a steady decrease in the cost of goods sold.

Customer Analysis

In terms of customer analysis, this section describes (1) the characteristics of customers expected to buy Howlin' Coyote products and (2) health and nutrition concerns of Americans today.

Customer Characteristics.   Demographically, chili products in general are purchased by consumers representing a broad range of socioeconomic backgrounds. Howlin' Coyote chili is purchased chiefly by consumers who have achieved higher levels of education and whose income is $50,000 and higher. These consumers represent 50 percent of canned and dry mix chili users.

The household buying Howlin' Coyote has one to three people in it. Among married couples, Howlin' Coyote is predominantly bought by households in which both spouses work. While women are a majority of the buyers, single men represent a significant segment.

Because the chili offers a quick way to make a tasty meal, the product's biggest users tend to be those most pressed for time. Howlin' Coyote's premium pricing also means that its purchasers are skewed toward the higher end of the income range. Buyers range in age from 25 to 54 years old and often live in the western United States where spicy foods are more readily eaten.

The five Howlin' Coyote entrees offer a quick, tasty meal with high-quality ingredients.

Margin annotations (left column):

This page uses a "block" style and does *not* indent each paragraph, although an extra space separates each paragraph. Compare this page with the opposite page, which has indented paragraphs. Most readers find that indented paragraphs in marketing plans and long reports are easier to follow.

The Company Analysis provides details of the company's strengths and marketing strategies that will enable it to achieve the mission and goals identified earlier. See Chapters 2 and 8.

The "A heading" for this section ("4. Situation Analysis") identifies the major section of the plan. The "B heading" of Customer Analysis has a more dominant typeface and position than the lower-level "C heading" of Customer Characteristics. These headings introduce the reader to the sequence and level of topics covered within each major "A level" section. The organization of this textbook uses this kind of structure and headings.

Satisfying customers and providing genuine value to them is why organizations exist in a market economy. This section addresses the question "Who are the customers for Paradise Kitchens's products?" See Chapters 5, 6, 7, 8, and 9.

Health and Nutrition Concerns. Coverage of food issues in the U.S. media is often erratic and occasionally alarmist. Because Americans are concerned about their diets, studies from organizations of widely varying credibility frequently receive significant attention from the main news organizations. For instance, a study of fat levels of movie popcorn was reported in all the major media. Similarly, studies on the healthfulness of Mexican food have received prominent play in print and broadcast reports. The high caloric levels of much Mexican and southwestern-style food have been widely reported and often exaggerated. Some Mexican frozen-food competitors, such as Don Miguel, Mission Foods, Ruiz Foods, and José Olé, plan to offer or have recently offered more "carb-friendly" and "fat-friendly" products in response to this concern.

Howlin' Coyote is already lower in calories, fat, and sodium than its competitors, and those qualities are not currently being stressed in its promotions. Instead, in the space and time available for promotions, Howlin' Coyote's taste, convenience, and flexibility are stressed.

5. Market-Product Focus

This section describes the five-year marketing and product objectives for Paradise Kitchens and the target markets, points of difference, and positioning of its lines of Howlin' Coyote chilies.

Marketing and Product Objectives

Howlin' Coyote's marketing intent is to take full advantage of its brand potential while building a base from which other revenue sources can be mined—both in and out of the retail grocery business. These are detailed in four areas below:

- *Current markets.* Current markets will be grown by expanding brand and flavor distribution at the retail level. In addition, same-store sales will be grown by increasing consumer awareness and repeat purchases, thereby leading to the more efficient broker/warehouse distribution channel.

- *New markets.* By the end of Year 5, the chili, salsa, burrito, and enchilada business will be expanded to a total of 20 metropolitan areas, which represent 53 percent of the 38 major U.S. metropolitan markets. This will represent 70 percent of U.S. food store sales.

- *Food service.* Food service sales will include chili products and smothering sauces. Sales are expected to reach $693,000 by the end of Year 3 and $1.5 million by the end of Year 5.

- *New products.* Howlin' Coyote's brand presence will be expanded at the retail level through the addition of new products in the frozen-foods section. This will be accomplished through new-product concept screening in Year 1 to identify new potential products. These products will be brought to market in Years 2 and 3.

Target Markets

The primary target market for Howlin' Coyote products is households with one to three people, where often both adults work, and with individual income typically above $50,000 per year. These households contain more experienced, adventurous consumers of Southwestern/Mexican food and want premium quality products.

To help buyers see the many different uses for Howlin' Coyote chili, recipes are even printed on the *inside* of the packages.

Points of Difference

The "points of difference"—characteristics that make Howlin' Coyote chilies unique relative to competitors—fall into three important areas:

- *Unique taste and convenience.* No known competitor offers a high-quality, "authentic" frozen chili in a range of flavors. And no existing chili has the same combination of quick preparation and home-style taste that Howlin' Coyote does.

- *Taste trends.* The American palate is increasingly intrigued by hot spices. In response to this trend, Howlin' Coyote brands offer more "kick" than most other prepared chilies.

- *Premium packaging.* Howlin' Coyote's packaging graphics convey the unique, high-quality product contained inside and the product's nontraditional positioning.

Positioning

In the past, chili products have been either convenient or tasty, but not both. Howlin' Coyote pairs these two desirable characteristics to obtain a positioning in consumers' minds as very high-quality "authentic Southwestern/Mexican tasting" chilies that can be prepared easily and quickly.

6. Marketing Program

The four marketing mix elements of the Howlin' Coyote chili marketing program are detailed below. Note that "chile" is the vegetable and "chili" is the dish.

Product Strategy

After first summarizing the product line, this section describes Howlin Coyote's approach to product quality and packaging.

Product Line. Howlin' Coyote chili, retailing for $3.99 for an 11-ounce serving, is available in five flavors: Green Chile Chili, Red Chile Chili, Beef and Black Bean Chili, Chicken Chunk Chili, and Mean Bean Chili.

Unique Product Quality. The flavoring systems of the Howlin' Coyote chilies are proprietary. The products' tastiness is due to extra care lavished upon the ingredients during production. The ingredients used are of unusually high quality. Meats are low-fat cuts and are fresh, not frozen, to preserve cell structure and moistness. Chilies are fire-roasted for fresher taste. Tomatoes and vegetables are of select quality. No preservatives or artificial flavors are used.

Packaging. Reflecting the "cutting edge" marketing strategy of its producers, Howlin' Coyote bucks conventional wisdom in its packaging. It specifically avoids placing predictable photographs of the product on its containers. Instead, Howlin' Coyote's package shows a Southwestern motif that communicates the product's out-of-the-ordinary positioning. As noted earlier, both women and men represent significant segments of actual purchasers of Howlin' Coyote Chili. The southwestern motif on the packaging is deliberately designed to appeal to both women and men.

The southwestern motif makes Howlin' Coyote's packages stand out in a supermarket's freezer case.

Price Strategy

At a $3.99 retail price for an 11-ounce package. Howlin' Coyote chili is priced comparably to the other frozen offerings but higher than the canned and dried chili varieties. However, the significant taste advantages it has over canned chilies and the convenience advantages over dried chilies justify this pricing strategy. This retail price also provides adequate margins for wholesalers and retailers in Howlin' Coyote's channel of distribution.

Promotion Strategy

Key promotion programs feature in-store demonstrations, recipes, and cents-off coupons.

Elements of the Promotion Strategy are highlighted in terms of the three key promotional activities the company is emphasizing: in-store demonstrations, recipes, and cents-off coupons. For space reasons, the company's online strategies are not shown in the plan. See Chapters 17, 18, and 19.

Another bulleted list adds many details for the reader, including methods of gaining customer awareness, trial, and repeat purchases as Howlin' Coyote enters new metropolitan areas.

The Place Strategy is described here in terms of both (1) the present method and (2) the new one to be used when the increased sales volume makes it feasible. See Chapters 15 and 16.

All the marketing mix decisions covered in the just-described marketing program have both revenue and expense effects. These are summarized in this section of the marketing plan.

Note that this section contains no introductory overview sentence. While the sentence is not essential, many readers prefer to see it to avoid the abrupt start with Past Sales Revenues.

In-Store Demonstrations. In-store demonstrations enable consumers to try Howlin' Coyote products and discover their unique qualities. Demos will be conducted regularly in all markets to increase awareness and trial purchases.

Recipes. Because the products' flexibility of use is a key selling point, recipes are offered to consumers to stimulate use. The recipes are given at all in-store demonstrations, on the back of packages, through a mail-in recipe book offer, and in coupons sent by direct-mail or freestanding inserts.

Cents-Off Coupons. To generate trial and repeat purchase of Howlin' Coyote products, coupons are distributed in four ways:

- *In Sunday newspaper inserts.* These inserts are widely read and help generate awareness.
- *In-pack coupons.* Each box of Howlin' Coyote chili will contain coupons for $1 off two more packages of the chili. These coupons will be included for the first three months the product is shipped to a new market. Doing so encourages repeat purchases by new users.
- *Direct-mail chili coupons.* Those households that fit the Howlin' Coyote demographics described previously will be mailed coupons.
- *In-store demonstrations.* Coupons will be passed out at in-store demonstrations to give an additional incentive to purchase.

Place (Distribution) Strategy

Howlin' Coyote is distributed in its present markets through a food distributor. The distributor buys the product, warehouses it, and then resells and delivers it to grocery retailers on a store-by-store basis. As sales grow, we will shift to a more efficient system using a broker who sells the products to retail chains and grocery wholesalers.

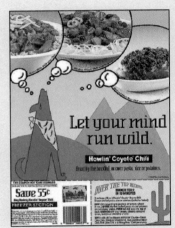

Sunday newspaper inserts encourage consumer trial and provide recipes to show how Howlin' Coyote chili can be used in summer meals.

7. Financial Data and Projections

Past Sales Revenues

Historically, Howlin' Coyote has had a steady increase in sales revenues since its introduction in 2007. In 2011, sales jumped spectacularly, due largely to new promotion strategies. Sales have continued to rise, but at a less dramatic rate. Sales revenues appear in Figure 2.

Five-Year Projections

Five-year financial projections for Paradise Kitchens appear below. These projections reflect the continuing growth in the number of cases sold (with eight packages of Howlin' Coyote chili per case).

Figure 2.   Sales Revenues for Paradise Kitchens, Inc.

	Projections (000s)					
Financial Element	Actual 2015	Year 1 2016	Year 2 2017	Year 3 2018	Year 4 2019	Year 5 2020
Cases sold (000s)	353	684	889	1,249	1,499	1,799
Net sales ($000s)	$5,123	$9,913	$12,884	$18,111	$21,733	$26,080
Gross profit ($000s)	$2,545	$4,820	$6,527	$8,831	$10,597	$12,717
Operating profit ($000s)	$339	$985	$2,906	$2,805	$3,366	$4,039

8. Organization

Paradise Kitchens's present organization appears in Figure 3. It shows the four people reporting to the President. Below this level are both the full-time and part-time employees of the Company.

Figure 3.   The Paradise Kitchens Organization

The Implementation Plan shows how the company will turn its plan into results. Charts are often used to set deadlines and assign responsibilities for the many tactical marketing decisions needed to enter a new market.

At present, Paradise Kitchens operates with full-time employees in only essential positions. It now augments its full-time staff with key advisors, consultants, and subcontractors. As the firm grows, people with special expertise will be added to the staff.

9. Implementation Plan

Introducing Howlin' Coyote chilies to 17 new metropolitan markets is a complex task and requires that creative promotional activities gain consumer awareness and initial trial. Counting the three existing metropolitan markets in which Paradise Kitchens competes, by 2020 it will be in 20 metropolitan markets or 53 percent of the top 38 U.S. metropolitan markets. The anticipated rollout schedule to enter these metropolitan markets appears in Figure 4.

Figure 4.   Rollout Schedule to Enter New U.S. Markets

Year	New Markets Added Each Year	Cumulative Markets	Cumulative Percentage of 38 Major U.S. Markets
Last (2015)	2	5	16
Year 1 (2016)	3	8	21
Year 2 (2017)	4	12	29
Year 3 (2018)	2	14	37
Year 4 (2019)	3	17	45
Year 5 (2020)	3	20	53

The essence of Evaluation is comparing actual sales with the targeted values set in the plan and taking appropriate actions. Note that the section briefly describes a contingency plan for alternative actions, depending on how successful the entry into a new market turns out to be.

The diverse regional tastes in chili will be monitored carefully to assess whether minor modifications may be required in the chili recipes. As the rollout to new metropolitan areas continues, Paradise Kitchens will assess manufacturing and distribution trade-offs. This is important in determining whether to start new production with selected high-quality regional contract packers.

10. Evaluation

Monthly sales targets in cases have been set for Howlin' Coyote chili for each metropolitan area. Actual case sales will be compared with these targets and tactical marketing programs modified to reflect the unique sets of factors in each metropolitan area.

Various appendices may appear at the end of the plan, depending on the plan's purpose and audience. For example, résumés of key personnel or detailed financial spreadsheets often appear in appendices. For space reasons these are not shown here.

Appendix A. Biographical Sketches of Key Personnel

Appendix B. Detailed Financial Projections

Appendix Notes

1. Personal interview with Arthur R. Kydd, St. Croix Management Group.

2. Examples of guides to writing marketing plans include William A. Cohen, *The Marketing Plan,* 5th ed. (New York: Wiley and Sons, 2006); and Roman G. Hiebing Jr., and Scott W. Cooper, *The Successful Business Plan: A Disciplined and Comprehensive Approach* (New York: McGraw-Hill, 2008).

3. Examples of guides to writing business plans include Rhonda Abrams, *Business Plan in a Day,* 2nd ed. (Palo Alto, CA: The Planning Shop, a Division of Rhonda, Inc., 2009); Rhonda Abrams, *The Successful Business Plan,* 5th ed. (Palo Alto, CA: The Planning Shop, a Division of Rhonda, Inc., 2010); Joseph A. Covello and Brian J. Hazelgren, *The Complete Book of Business Plans,* 2nd ed. (Naperville, IL: Sourcebooks, 2006); Joseph A. Covello and Brian J. Hazelgren, *Your First Business Plan,* 5th ed. (Naperville, IL: Sourcebooks, 2005); and Mike McKeever, *How to Write a Business Plan,* 8th ed. (Berkeley, CA: Nolo, 2007).

4. Abrams, *The Successful Business Plan,* p. 41.

5. Some of these points are adapted from Abrams, *The Successful Business Plan,* pp. 41–49; others were adapted from William Rudelius, *Guidelines for Technical Report Writing* (Minneapolis: University of Minnesota, undated). See also William Strunk Jr. and E. B. White, *The Elements of Style,* 4th ed. (Needham Heights, MA: Allyn & Bacon, 2000).

6. Personal interviews with Randall F. and Leah E. Peters, Paradise Kitchens, Inc.

7. Rebecca Zimoch, "The Dawn of the Frozen Age," Grocery Headquarters, December 2002; see www.groceryheadquarters.com.

8. "Frozen Food Production in the U.S.: Market Research Report," *IBISWorld,* March 2015; and Annie Gasparro, "Frozen Foods Grow Cold as Tastes Shift to Fresher Fare," *The Wall Street Journal,* wsj.com, June 26, 2014.

9. Chuck Van Hyning, *NPD's National Eating Trends;* see www.npdfoodworld.com.

10. Jeffrey M. Humphreys, "The Multicultural Economy 2009," *Georgia Business and Economic Conditions* 69, no. 3 (Third Quarter, 2009), pp. 1–13.

3 Scanning the Marketing Environment

LEARNING OBJECTIVES

After reading this chapter you should be able to:

LO 3-1 Explain how environmental scanning provides information about social, economic, technological, competitive, and regulatory forces.

LO 3-2 Describe how social forces such as demographics and culture can have an impact on marketing strategy.

LO 3-3 Discuss how economic forces such as macroeconomic conditions and consumer income affect marketing.

LO 3-4 Describe how technological changes can affect marketing.

LO 3-5 Discuss the forms of competition that exist in a market and the key components of competition.

LO 3-6 Explain the major legislation that ensures competition and regulates the elements of the marketing mix.

Is "Connecting the World" an Ambitious Vision? Not If You Are Facebook!

In 2004 Mark Zuckerberg started Facebook in his Harvard dorm room. His vision was not just to be a company, but to connect everyone in the world. Today, with 1.4 billion active users, or one-fifth of the world's population, Facebook is well on its way to accomplishing that vision!

Facebook's incredible success is the result of many things, including its ability to observe and adapt to a rapidly changing marketing environment. Let's take a look at the environmental forces that influence Facebook:

- *Social* forces are changing as people look for new ways to communicate, obtain information, and offer opinions. Simple online interactions that began on desktops have migrated to mobile devices and now include communication with photos, group and video chats, and instant messaging.

- *Economic* forces also influence the demand for Facebook as the cost of smartphones and wireless connectivity declines and Internet access expands throughout the globe, making social networking increasingly affordable to more and more people.

- *Technological* advances in software integration, server speed, and data storage are making Facebook increasingly fast and convenient. New enhancements such as photo editing and an app development kit also increase use of Facebook.

- *Competitive* forces such as the rivalry with Google, Twitter, and Snapchat, the ability of users to easily switch platforms, and the constant threat of new social networks targeted at specific interest groups, encourage rapid expansion.

- *Legal and regulatory* forces also influence the growth of Facebook. The company obtains trademark and patent rights to its name and many of its features, and it provides guidelines for a variety of topics such as privacy, data protection, protection of minors, and taxation.

Zuckerberg's rapid responses to changes in the environment and his willingness to try new things has resulted in the world's largest social network—one that is quickly connecting the world.

Facebook in the Future

Facebook's challenge now is to keep growing by continuing to respond to changes in the marketing environment. As Zuckerberg explains, Facebook

© dolphfyn/Alamy

needs to "think about the next big things that we want to do." For example, Zuckerberg wants Facebook to become more intuitive, and to help users answer questions and solve problems. Another change may be related to Facebook's requirement that users login with their own names. In some parts of the world where Facebook hopes to expand, anonymity encourages users to speak freely. In addition, Facebook is currently testing large drones that are powered by solar panels to hover above remote communities and transmit Internet signals. Facebook also purchased virtual reality headset company Oculus VR for $2 billion in anticipation of consumer interest in 3-D communication. Finally, Facebook created a new division of the company called Creative Labs, which is charged with trying to predict the future and developing Facebook's future products![1] Chapter 19 provides additional discussion on social networks and social media.

Many businesses operate in environments where important forces change. Anticipating and responding to changes often means the difference between marketing success and failure. This chapter describes how the marketing environment has changed in the past and how it is likely to change in the future.

ENVIRONMENTAL SCANNING

LO 3-1 Explain how environmental scanning provides information about social, economic, technological, competitive, and regulatory forces.

Video 3-1
Starbucks
kerin.tv/13e/v3-1

Changes in the marketing environment are a source of opportunities and threats to be managed. The process of continually acquiring information on events occurring outside the organization to identify and interpret potential trends is called **environmental scanning**.

Tracking Environmental Trends

Environmental trends typically arise from five sources: social, economic, technological, competitive, and regulatory forces. As shown in Figure 3–1 and described later in this chapter, these forces affect the marketing activities of a firm in numerous ways. To illustrate how environmental scanning is used, consider the following trends:[2]

Coffee industry marketers have observed that the percentage of adults who drink coffee declined from 64 percent in 2012 to 59 percent today. The percentage of households with single-cup brewers, however, has increased from 10 percent in 2012 to 27 percent today. In addition, tea sales have been increasing at an annual rate of approximately 5 percent.

What types of businesses are likely to be influenced by these trends? What future would you predict for coffee?

You may have concluded that these changes in coffee consumption are likely to influence coffee manufacturers, coffee shops, and supermarkets. If so, you are correct. Due to the recent decline in coffee consumption, manufacturers are offering new flavors and seasonal blends, coffee shops such as Starbucks are testing a delivery service and new flavors such as S'mores Frappuccino, and supermarkets are adding boutiques and gourmet brands. The increase in the percentage of households with single-cup brewers has also led to changes. Starbucks recently announced a five-year partnership with Keurig Green Mountain to sell K-Cup single-serving coffee packs. Predicting the future requires assumptions about the number of years the trends will continue and their rate of increase or decline. Do you believe the recent growth in tea consumption will continue?

The growth of single cup brewers is one of the trends in the coffee industry.

© McGraw-Hill Education/David A. Tietz, photographer

FIGURE 3–1

Environmental forces affect the organization, as well as its suppliers and customers.

Suppliers → **Organization**
• Marketing department
• Other departments
• Employees
→ Customers

Environmental forces

Social	Economic	Technological	Competitive	Regulatory
• Demographic shifts • Cultural changes	• Macroeconomic conditions • Consumer income	• Changing technology • Technology's impact on customer value • Technology enabled data analytics	• Alternative forms of competition • Small businesses	• Laws protecting competition • Laws affecting marketing mix actions • Self-regulation

ENVIRONMENTAL FORCE	TRENDS IDENTIFIED BY AN ENVIRONMENTAL SCAN
Social	• Binge-watching is becoming a common way for consumers to view television programming. • Video bloggers (vloggers) are growing in popularity and influence. • Consumers are placing a growing emphasis on personalized consideration lists (friend recommendations).
Economic	• Companies are increasing their focus on cost control as sales slow in emerging markets and competition increases in mature countries. • China and the U.S. are likely to account for a growing part of the world's economic growth. • The U.S. personal saving rate has increased to 5.8%, indicating reduced spending, although income has been growing at about 2%.
Technological	• Connectivity and mobility have combined to increase the use of mobile and wearable devices and to create connected cars, homes, and airplanes. • Addressable TV (IPTV) will soon allow advertising targeted to individual households based on their characteristics. • Social media such as Facebook and Twitter are adding new features such as a "Buy" button to allow marketers to sell directly to users.
Competitive	• Established industries such as banking, insurance, and retailing will be challenged by new competitors such as peer-to-peer lenders, self-insurance groups, and direct-to-consumer food producers. • Companies will increase their use of data and data analytics to compete with personalized products, promotion, and pricing. • Competitors are moving away from loyalty programs based only on points toward rewards, cash, and promotions.
Regulatory	• Privacy guidelines must find a balance to accommodate millennial consumers who do not mind their mobile devices being tracked if they receive timely and relevant advertising. • Net neutrality—that all Internet traffic should receive equal access and speed—is a growing issue for consumers, companies, content creators, and marketers. • The Federal Trade Commission is adding stricter requirements regarding promotions, disclosures, and substantiation studies.

FIGURE 3–2

An environmental scan of today's marketplace shows the many important trends that influence marketing.

Environmental scanning also involves explaining trends. Why is coffee consumption declining? One explanation is that consumers are switching from coffee to other beverages, such as tea, that are perceived to be healthier options. The decline might also be the result of increased use of single-cup coffee machines, which are much more efficient and result in less waste. Finally, the decline may be the result of economic forces that cause consumers to reduce discretionary expenditures. Identifying and interpreting trends, such as the changes in coffee consumption, and developing explanations (such as those offered in this paragraph) are essential to successful environmental scanning.[3]

An Environmental Scan of Today's Marketplace

What other trends might affect marketing in the future? A firm conducting an environmental scan of the marketplace might uncover key trends such as those listed in Figure 3–2 for each of the five environmental forces.[4] Although the list of trends in Figure 3–2 is far from complete, it reveals the breadth of an environmental scan—from the growing popularity of video bloggers, to the increasing mobility and connectivity of consumers, to the importance of issues such as net neutrality. These trends affect consumers and the organizations that serve them. Trends such as these are described in the following discussion of the five environmental forces.

SOCIAL FORCES

LO 3-2 Describe how social forces such as demographics and culture can have an impact on marketing strategy.

The **social forces** of the environment include the demographic characteristics of the population and its culture. Changes in these forces can have a dramatic impact on marketing strategy.

Demographics

Describing a population according to selected characteristics such as age, gender, ethnicity, income, and occupation is referred to as **demographics**. Several organizations such as the Population Reference Bureau and the United Nations monitor the world population profile, while many other organizations such as the U.S. Census Bureau provide information about the American population.

The World Population at a Glance The most recent estimates indicate there are 7.3 billion people in the world today, and the population is likely to grow to 9.6 billion by 2050. While this growth has led to the term *population explosion*, the increases have not occurred worldwide; they are primarily in the developing countries of Africa, Asia, and Latin America. In fact, India is predicted to have the world's largest population in 2050 with 1.66 billion people, and China will be a close second with 1.31 billion people. World population projections show that the populations of Japan, Russia, and Germany will be declining by more than 13 percent.[5]

Another important global trend is the shifting age structure of the world population. Worldwide, the number of people 65 years and older is expected to more than triple in the coming decades and reach 1.5 billion by 2050. Again, the magnitude of this trend varies by country as Japan, South Korea, Germany, China, Brazil and Mexico are all expected to have older populations than the United States. Global income levels and

What are the implications of the shifting age structure of the world population?

World population
By five-year age group, m

Source: UN   1950 2010 2050* —2100*   *Projection

living standards have also been increasing, although the averages across countries are very different. Per capita income, for example, ranges from $102,700 in Norway, to $52,210 in Canada, to $470 in Ethiopia.[6]

For marketers, global trends such as these have many implications. Obviously, the relative size of countries such as India and China will mean they represent huge markets for many product categories. Elderly populations in developed countries are likely to save less and begin spending their funds on health care, travel, and other retirement-related products and services. Economic progress in developing countries will lead to growth in entrepreneurship, new markets for infrastructure related to manufacturing, communication, and distribution, and the growth of exports.

The U.S. Population   Studies of the demographic characteristics of the U.S. population suggest several important trends. Generally, the population is becoming larger, older, and more diverse. The U.S. Census Bureau estimates that the current population of the United States is approximately 321 million people. If current trends in life expectancy, birthrates, and immigration continue, by 2030 the U.S. population will exceed 359 million people. This growth suggests that niche markets based on age, life stage, family structure, geographic location, and ethnicity will become increasingly important.

The global trend toward an older population is particularly true in the United States. Today, there are more than 46 million people 65 and older. By 2030, this age group will include more than 74 million people or 21 percent of the population. You may have noticed companies trying to attract older consumers by making typefaces larger, lowering store shelves, and avoiding colors that are difficult to read (yellow and blue). Finally, the term *minority* as it is currently used is likely to become obsolete as the total size of all ethnic groups will grow from 37 percent of the population to 50 percent of the population in 2044.[7]

Generational Cohorts   A major reason for the graying of America is that the 76 million **baby boomers**—the generation of children born between 1946 and 1964—are growing older. Baby boomers are retiring at a rate of 10,000 every 24 hours, and they will all be 65 or older by 2030. Their participation in the workforce has made them the wealthiest generation in U.S. history, accounting for an estimated 50 percent of all consumer spending.

Companies that target boomers will need to respond to their interests in health, fitness, retirement housing, financial planning, and appearance. Frito-Lay, for example, attracts baby boomers with its Lay's Kettle Cooked potato chips, which have 40 percent less fat than regular potato chips. Similarly, Prudential offers a retirement plan and Olay offers anti-aging and restoration products for this age group. Baby boomers are also called the "sandwich generation" because they often find themselves balancing obligations to their parents and their children.[8]

The baby boom cohort is followed by **Generation X**, which includes the 50 million people born between 1965 and 1976. This period is also known as the *baby bust*, because during this time the number of children born each year was declining. This is a generation of consumers who are self-reliant, supportive of racial and ethnic diversity, and better educated than any previous generation. They are not prone to extravagance and are likely to pursue lifestyles that are a blend of caution, pragmatism, and traditionalism.

In terms of net worth, Generation X is the first generation to have less than the previous generation. As baby boomers move toward retirement, however, Generation X is becoming a dominant force in many markets. Generation X, for example, spends more on food, housing, apparel, and entertainment than other generations. In addition, this generation is on the Internet more than any other generation and also leads in terms of online spending. Surveys of Generation X consumers indicate they want online customer support; websites that are comprehensive, professional, and interactive; and

Which generational cohorts are these three advertisers trying to reach?

Left: Transamerica; Middle: Singapore Airlines; Right: Samsung

advertising that is authentic, family-oriented, and unique. Generation X is also replacing baby boomers as the largest segment of business travelers. In response, American Airlines is offering travelers in-flight Wi-Fi, entertainment on demand, and personal powerports.[9]

The generational cohort labeled **Generation Y** includes the 72 million Americans born between 1977 and 1994. This was a period of increasing births, which resulted from baby boomers having children, and it is often referred to as the *echo-boom* or *baby boomlet*. Generation Y exerts influence on music, sports, computers, video games, and all forms of communication and networking. Generation Y members are interested in distinctive, memorable, and personal experiences and are very adept at managing their lives to create a work–life balance. They are strong-willed, passionate about the environment, and optimistic. This is also a group that is attracted to purposeful work where they have control. The Making Responsible Decisions box describes how millennials' interest in sustainability is influencing colleges, graduate schools, and employers. The term *millennials* is used, with inconsistent definitions, to refer to younger members of Generation Y and sometimes to Americans born since 1994. Immigration projections suggest that Generation Y will soon become larger than the boomer generation.[10]

Because the members of each generation are distinctive in their attitudes and consumer behavior, marketers have been studying the many groups or cohorts that make up the marketplace and have developed *generational marketing* programs for them.

The American Household As the population age profile has changed, so has the structure of the American household. In 1960, 75 percent of all households consisted of married couples. Today, that type of household is just 48 percent of the population. Only 20 percent of households are married couples with children, and only 10 percent are households with working fathers and stay-at-home moms. Some of the fastest-growing types of households are those with an adult child who has moved back home with his or her parents, those with unmarried partners, and those with same-sex partners. These three categories include 17 million households (21 million young adults), 7.8 million couples, and 605,000 couples, respectively.

Analysis by the U.S. Bureau of the Census indicates that young people are postponing marriage and parenthood and that the increase in households with unmarried partners reflects that "pooling resources by moving in together may be one method of coping with extended unemployment." Businesses are adjusting to the changes because they have implications for purchases related to weddings, homes, baby and child products, and many other industries.[11]

Making **Responsible Decisions**   Sustainability

Millennials Are a Force for Good

As the next generation of business leaders, millennials are determined to redefine the workplace as an outlet for creating both profit and meaning. They are idealistic, energetic, transparent, and eager to get started. In short, they are a force for good, particularly when it comes to social and environmental responsibility. The group includes students in college and graduate school and many early career employees, who are all driving change in different ways.

There are approximately 17 million undergraduate millennials who expect sustainable campus communities that include LEED (Leadership in Energy and Environmental Design)–certified housing, campus transit systems, and recycling programs. Graduate students are looking for programs with sustainability electives, case studies, and potential for involvement with organizations such as Net Impact (www.netimpact.org), a nonprofit for students who want to "use business to improve the world." Sara Hochman is a typical example. She was interested in environmental issues in college, and her first job was an environmental consultant. To make a bigger impact on her clients, she enrolled in graduate school at the University of Chicago where she could take an elective on renewable energy and join the Energy Club.

Early career employees want "green" jobs such as social responsibility officer, corporate philanthropy manager, and sustainability database specialist. In addition they want to work at companies that advocate good corporate citizenship, responsible capitalism, and "B-corp" status. They view themselves as part of a "positive business" movement that balances the interests of shareholders, employees, and society. Charlotte Moran, a mid-20s group marketing manager for Siemens Home Appliances, explains: "I'd find it very hard to work for a company that didn't understand its impact on the environment and didn't make an effort to change for the better."

NET IMPACT

Some companies are taking note of millennials' interests. Unilever has launched its Sustainable Living Plan to create "brands with purpose," Apple's new headquarters is described as "the greenest building on the planet," and Whole Foods Market makes decisions only after considering the needs of all stakeholders.

How will your interests in being a force for good influence your education and career decisions? The world will know soon!

© R Heyes Design/Alamy

The increase in cohabitation (households with unmarried partners) may be one reason the national divorce rate has declined during recent years. Even so, the likelihood that a couple will divorce exceeds 40 percent, and divorce among baby boomers—what is being called *gray divorce*—appears to be increasing. The majority of divorced people eventually remarry, which has created the **blended family**, one formed by merging two previously separated units into a single household. Today, one of every three Americans is a stepparent, stepchild, stepsibling, or some other member of a blended family. Hallmark Cards, Inc. now has specially designed cards and sentiments for blended families.[12]

Population Shifts   A major regional shift in the U.S. population toward southern and western states is under way. The most recent Census Bureau estimates indicate that the populations of North Dakota, Texas, Utah, and Wyoming grew at the fastest rates, while the population of Vermont declined in size. Nearly a century ago each of the top 10 most populous cities in the United States was within 500 miles of the Canadian border. Today, 7 of the top 10 are in states that border Mexico. Last year, Texas gained more people than any other state—its population increased by more than 450,000![13]

Populations are also shifting within states. In the early 1900s, the population shifted from rural areas to cities. From the 1930s through the 2000s, the population shifted from cities to suburbs and then from suburbs to more remote suburbs called *exurbs*. The recent recession, however, made it difficult for families to move, causing a reverse in the trend and growth in urban areas. Some demographers anticipate that as millennials start having children and forming households, suburban growth will increase. Today, 30 percent of all Americans live in central cities, 50 percent live in suburbs, and 20 percent live in rural locations.[14]

To assist marketers in gathering data on the population, the Census Bureau has developed a classification system to describe the varying locations of the population. The system consists of two types of *statistical areas*:

- A *metropolitan statistical area* has at least one urbanized area of 50,000 or more people and adjacent territory that has a high degree of social and economic integration.
- A *micropolitan statistical area* has at least one urban cluster of at least 10,000 but less than 50,000 people and adjacent territory that has a high degree of social and economic integration.

If a metropolitan statistical area contains a population of 2.5 million or more, it may be subdivided into smaller areas called *metropolitan divisions*. In addition, adjacent metropolitan statistical areas and micropolitan statistical areas may be grouped into *combined statistical areas*.[15]

There are currently 388 metropolitan statistical areas, which include 85 percent of the population, and 541 micropolitan statistical areas, which include 9 percent of the population.

Racial and Ethnic Diversity A notable trend is the changing racial and ethnic composition of the U.S. population. Approximately one in three U.S. residents belongs to the following racial or ethnic groups: African American, Native American or Alaska Native, Asian American, or Native Hawaiian or Pacific Islander. Diversity is further evident in the variety of peoples that make up these groups. For example, Asians consist of Asian Indians, Chinese, Filipinos, Japanese, Koreans, and Vietnamese.

The 2010 Census allowed respondents to choose more than one of the five race options, and more than 5 million people reported more than one race. Hispanics, who may be from any race, currently make up 16 percent of the U.S. population and are represented by Mexicans, Puerto Ricans, Cubans, and others of Central and South American ancestry. While the United States is becoming more diverse, Figure 3–3 suggests that the minority racial and ethnic groups tend to be concentrated in geographic regions.[16]

FIGURE 3–3

Racial and ethnic groups (excluding Caucasians) are concentrated in geographic regions of the United States.

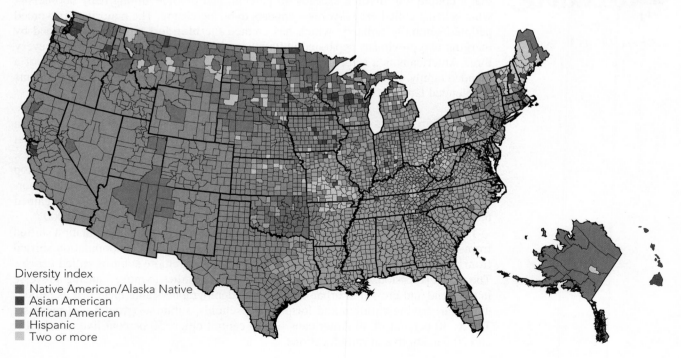

Diversity index
- Native American/Alaska Native
- Asian American
- African American
- Hispanic
- Two or more

The racial and ethnic composition of the United States is expected to change even more in the future. By 2030, the Hispanic population will grow from 51 million to more than 78 million, or 22 percent of the population. The number of Asians in the United States will almost double to 23 million, or 6 percent of the population, and the African American population will be approximately 49 million, or 14 percent of the population. The multiracial category currently makes up 1.7 percent of the population and is expected to grow to 3.6 percent. Overall, the trends in the composition of the population suggest that the U.S. market will no longer be dominated by one group and that non-Hispanic Caucasians will be a declining majority over the next 15 years.

While the growing size of these groups has been identified through new Census data, their economic impact on the marketplace is also very noticeable. Hispanics, African Americans, and Asian Americans spend more than $1.3 trillion, $1.1 trillion, and $770 billion each year, respectively. To adapt to this new marketplace, many companies are developing **multicultural marketing** programs, which are combinations of the marketing mix that reflect the unique attitudes, ancestry, communication preferences, and lifestyles of different races. Because businesses must now market their products to a consumer base with many racial and ethnic identities, in-depth marketing research that allows an accurate understanding of each culture is essential.[17]

Additional analysis of population demographic data, such as the information shown in Figure 3–3, suggests that racial and ethnic groups tend to be concentrated in geographic regions. This information allows companies to combine their multicultural marketing efforts with regional marketing activities. Consider, for example, that 48 percent of Asian Americans live in Los Angeles, New York City, and San Francisco and that two-thirds of Hispanics live in Florida, Texas, and California. *Advertising Age*'s Multicultural Agency of the Year, Alma, creates advertising by "focusing the work on a deeper cultural knowledge, elevating the work beyond the 'clichés.'" The agency creates Hispanic campaigns for McDonald's, Goodyear, Kraft Foods, Revlon, and many others. For example, Alma created the ad shown to appeal to McDonald's Hispanic audience.

Many other changes are facilitating multicultural marketing programs. Increasingly diverse television programming such as *Black-ish, Empire,* and *Fresh off the Boat,* for example, is available for advertisers. Sports such as soccer, baseball, and basketball are implementing programs such as the NBA's Latin Nights events, which display team names as spoken by bilingual fans (the Miami Heat is also El Heat). In addition, retailers often designate stores for bilingual signage and staff.

Video 3-2
McDonald's
kerin.tv/13e/v3-2

McDonald's combines ethnic and regional marketing by using Spanish-language promotions like this one in some states.

© *McDonald's®. Image courtesy of Alma Advertising. Actors Left: Christian Vázquez and Right: Vicente Torres.*

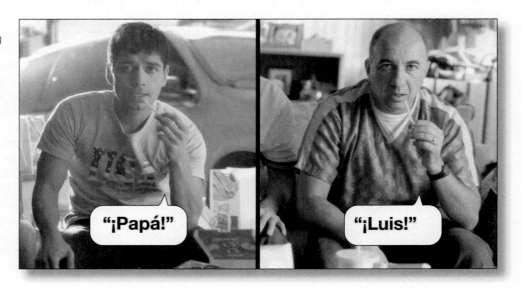

Finally, marketers have learned that mobile devices and social media are often the best way to reach multicultural audiences. Facebook recently began using online information to designate Hispanic, African American, and Asian American affinity groups for advertisers.[18]

Culture

A second social force, **culture**, incorporates the set of values, ideas, and attitudes that are learned and shared among the members of a group. Because many of the elements of culture influence consumer buying patterns, monitoring national and global cultural trends is important for marketing. Cross-cultural analysis needed for global marketing is discussed in Chapter 7.

The Changing Attitudes and Roles of Men and Women

One of the most notable cultural changes in the United States in the past 30 years has been in the attitudes and roles of men and women in the marketplace. Some experts predict that as this trend continues, the buying patterns of men and women will eventually be very similar.

Your mothers and grandmothers probably remember advertising targeted at them that focused on the characteristics of household products—like laundry detergent that got clothes "whiter than white." In the 1970s and 1980s, ads began to create a bridge between genders with messages such as Secret's "strong enough for a man, but made for a woman." In the 1990s, marketing to women focused on their challenge of balancing family and career interests. Since then, women and men have encouraged the slow movement toward equality in the marketplace. As a result, today's Generation Y represents the first generation of women who have no collective memory of the dramatic changes we have undergone. As one expert explains, "Feminism today is like fluoride; we scarcely notice that we have it."

Several factors have contributed to the shift in attitudes. First, many young women had career mothers who provided a reference point for lifestyle choices. Second, increased participation in organized sports eliminated one of the most visible inequalities in opportunities for women. And finally, the Internet has provided exposure to the marketplace through a mechanism that makes gender, race, and ethnicity invisible. Recent surveys, however, suggest that many of the 35 million Generation Y women believe that there is still a need for equal opportunities and treatment in the workplace and in politics.[19]

Many companies that had a consumer base that was primarily women or primarily men in the past are preparing for growth from the other gender. Grocery stores, car dealers, investment services, video game developers, and many others hope to appeal to both groups in the future. Under Armour, for example, is trying to attract women with clothing specifically designed for them, while Lululemon is trying to attract men by opening stand-alone men's yoga clothing stores. Similarly, social media site Pinterest hopes to attract more men to the site by subtly making its search results more gender-neutral. Such efforts often face resistance, though, as UGG learned when it signed football star Tom Brady to endorse its distinctive boots but still couldn't attract male consumers.

Some industries are trying to avoid creating separate products for men and women. Professional sports leagues are targeting women, and spas are targeting men. Moschino recently introduced a new fragrance called Toy, and Calvin Klein offers CK One, both for men and women. In general, the trend is toward fewer gender distinctions, particularly in marketing directed at young consumers. For example, Diesel's "Be Stupid" advertising campaign typically depicts men and women

Diesel is making changes to appeal to women as well as men.

Diesel

Growing interest in hybrid vehicles reflects new consumer values related to sustainability and the environment.

© Ellen Isaacs/Alamy

Video 3-3
Brita
kerin.tv/13e/v3-3

Save money. Live better.

© R Heyes Design/Alamy

in partnership roles rather than portraying either one in a dominant or subordinate role.[20]

Changing Values   Culture also includes values that may differ over time and between countries. During the 1970s, a list of values in the United States included achievement, work, efficiency, and material comfort. Today, commonly held values include personal control, continuous change, equality, individualism, self-help, competition, future orientation, and action. These values are useful in understanding most current behaviors of U.S. consumers, particularly when they are compared to values in other countries. Contrasting values outside the United States, for example, include belief in fate, the importance of tradition, the importance of rank and status, a focus on group welfare, and acceptance of birthright.

An increasingly important value for consumers in the United States and around the globe is sustainability and preserving the environment. Concern for the environment is one reason consumers are buying hybrid gas-electric automobiles, such as the Toyota Prius, the Chevy Volt, and the Ford C-MAX. Companies are also changing their business practices to respond to trends in consumer values. Coca-Cola has been working on alleviating global water scarcity, Facebook has committed to reducing the carbon footprint of its data centers and Wal-Mart Stores, Inc., has set ambitious goals to cut energy use by buying more local products, reducing packaging, and switching to renewable power. Recent research also indicates that consumers are committed to brands with a strong link to social action. For example, Brita's "Filter For Good" campaign asks consumers to take a pledge to reduce their plastic bottle waste.[21]

A change in consumption orientation is also apparent. In the past, consumers often used debt to make many of their purchases. High unemployment, lower real estate prices, and tax increases, however, have changed their perspective. Today, U.S. consumers have become cautious buyers. **Value consciousness**—or the concern for obtaining the best quality, features, and performance of a product or service for a given price—is driving consumption behavior for many products at all price levels. For example, the recent recession led consumers to cut back on brand-name products such as toothpaste, shampoo, and toilet paper so that they could still afford discretionary products such as high-definition televisions and smartphones. Likewise, the recent recession and slow economic recovery prompted consumers to reduce the distances they would drive to shop.

Innovative marketers have responded to this new value-conscious orientation in numerous ways. Dollar General, for example, opened new stores in convenient locations and installed taller shelves so that it could build up its stock of name-brand food, health, and beauty products. The store quickly saw sales increase by 6 percent. Similarly, Walmart and other retailers began providing special deals to customers who shop for bargains online.[22]

learning review »

3-1. Describe three generational cohorts.

3-2. Why are many companies developing multicultural marketing programs?

3-3. How are important values such as sustainability reflected in the marketplace today?

ECONOMIC FORCES

LO 3-3 Discuss how economic forces such as macroeconomic conditions and consumer income affect marketing.

The second component of the environmental scan, the **economy**, pertains to the income, expenditures, and resources that affect the cost of running a business and household. We'll consider two aspects of these economic forces: a macroeconomic view of the marketplace and a microeconomic perspective of consumer income.

Macroeconomic Conditions

Of particular concern at the macroeconomic level is the performance of the economy based on indicators such as GDP (gross domestic product), unemployment, and price changes (inflation or deflation). In an inflationary economy, the cost to produce and buy products and services escalates as prices increase. From a marketing standpoint, if prices rise faster than consumer incomes, the number of items consumers can buy decreases. This relationship is evident in the cost of a college education. The College Board reports that since 2000 college tuition and fees have increased 160 percent (from $3,508 to $9,139) while family incomes have declined by 7 percent. The share of family income required to pay for tuition at public four-year colleges has risen from 5 percent in 2000 to 14 percent today.[23]

Periods of declining economic activity are referred to as recessions. During recessions, businesses decrease production, unemployment rises, and many consumers have less money to spend. The U.S. economy experienced recessions from 1973–75, 1981–82, 1990–91, and in 2001. Most recently, a recessionary period began in 2007 and ended in 2009, becoming the longest in recent history.[24]

Consumer expectations about the economy are an important element of environmental scanning. Consumer spending, which accounts for two-thirds of U.S. economic activity, is affected by expectations of the future. The two most popular surveys of consumer expectations are the Consumer Confidence Index, conducted by a nonprofit business research organization called the Conference Board, and the Index of Consumer Sentiment (ICS), conducted by the Survey Research Center at the University of Michigan. The surveys track the responses of consumers to specific questions about their expectations, and the results are reported once each month. For example, the Index of Consumer Sentiment asks, "Looking ahead, do you think that a year from now you will be better off financially, worse off, or just about the same as now?" The answers to the questions are used to construct an index. The higher the index, the more favorable are consumer expectations. Figure 3–4 shows the fluctuation in the ICS and

FIGURE 3–4

The Index of Consumer Sentiment (ICS) is closely related to economic conditions.

green bands represent recessionary periods

Marketing **Insights About Me**

American FactFinder: Your Source for Economic Information

Marketers collect and use environmental information to better understand consumers. One way to begin an environmental scan is to compare economic and demographic data about a particular segment of the population to what is "typical" or "average" for the entire population. Do you think your hometown is typical? To find out, visit the American FactFinder at http://factfinder.census.gov and use the "Community Facts" tool to obtain information about your hometown. Just type in the zip code of your hometown and FactFinder will give you population size, median age, and median income information from the U.S. Census. You can also click on links listed under *American Community Survey* for more detailed information. Use the tool to look up information about your state or the United States to make comparisons.

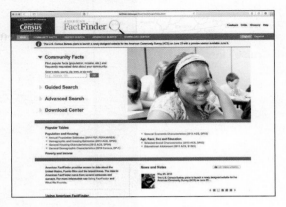

American Factfinder

its close relationship to economic conditions (green areas represent recessionary periods). The consumer expectations surveys are closely monitored by many companies, particularly manufacturers and retailers of cars, furniture, and major appliances.[25]

Consumer Income

The microeconomic trends in terms of consumer income are also important issues for marketers. Having a product that meets the needs of consumers may be of little value if they are unable to purchase it. A consumer's ability to buy is related to income, which consists of gross, disposable, and discretionary components.

Gross Income   The total amount of money made in one year by a person, household, or family unit is referred to as **gross income** (or "money income" at the Census Bureau). While the typical U.S. household earned only about $8,700 of income in 1970, it earned about $51,939 in 2013. When gross income is adjusted for inflation, however, income of that typical U.S. household was relatively stable. In fact, inflation-adjusted income has only varied between $46,425 and $56,895 since 1970. Approximately 54 percent of U.S. households have an annual income between $25,000 and $99,999.[26] Are you from a typical household? Read the Marketing Insights About Me box to learn how you can determine the median household income in your hometown.

Disposable Income   The second income component, **disposable income**, is the money a consumer has left after paying taxes to use for necessities such as food, housing, clothing, and transportation. Thus, if taxes rise or fall faster than income, consumers are likely to have more or less disposable income. Similarly, dramatic changes in the prices of products can lead to spending adjustments. The recent decline in the price of gasoline, for example, has led to increases in consumer spending in other categories. In addition, changes in home prices have a psychological impact on consumers, who tend to spend more when they feel their net worth is rising and postpone purchases when it declines. During a recessionary period, spending, debt, and the use of credit all decline. The recent recession led many middle-income consumers to switch from premium brands to lower-priced brands.[27]

Discretionary Income   The third component of income is **discretionary income**, the money that remains after paying for taxes and necessities. Discretionary income is

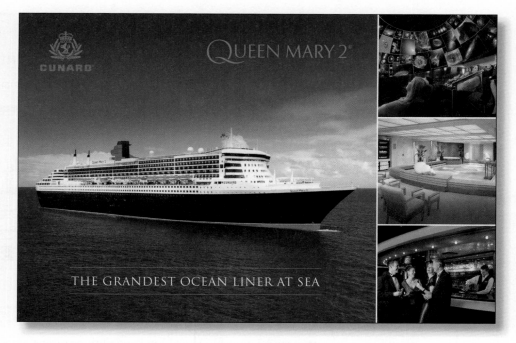

used for luxury items such as a Cunard cruise. An obvious problem in defining discretionary versus disposable income is determining what is a luxury and what is a necessity.

The Department of Labor monitors consumer expenditures through its annual Consumer Expenditure Survey. The most recent report indicates that consumers spend about 13 percent of their income on food, 33 percent on housing, and 3 percent on clothes. While an additional 24 percent is often spent on transportation and health care, the remainder is generally viewed as discretionary. The percentage of income spent on food and housing typically declines as income increases, which can provide an increase in discretionary income. Discretionary expenditures also can be increased by reducing savings. The Bureau of Labor Statistics observed that during the 1990s and early 2000s the savings rate declined to approximately 2 percent. That trend was reversed in 2008 when the government issued stimulus checks designed to improve the economy and, instead of spending the money, consumers saved it. Recent data on consumer expenditures indicate that the savings rate is now approximately 5.8 percent.[28]

TECHNOLOGICAL FORCES

LO 3-4 Describe how technological changes can affect marketing.

Our society is in a period of dramatic technological change. **Technology**, the third environmental force in Figure 3–2, refers to inventions or innovations from applied science or engineering research. Each new wave of technological innovation can replace existing products and companies. Do you recognize the items pictured on the next page and what they may replace?

Technology of Tomorrow

Technological change is the result of research, so it is difficult to predict. Some of the most dramatic technological changes occurring now, however, include the following:

- Connectivity will grow to include all customers, homes, vehicles, appliances, and mobile devices to create the "Internet of Things."

Technological change leads to new products. What products might be replaced by these innovations?

Left: © Rogers Communications Inc. - FRA/Newscom; Middle: Tesla Motors; Right: © Bryan Thomas/Getty Images

- Computers will develop all five senses to create intelligent data collection and personalized predictive capabilities.
- Green technologies such as smart grid electricity services, online energy management, and consumer-generated energy (e.g., home solar systems) will gain widespread acceptance among American consumers.
- 3D technologies will move from movie theaters and televisions to many new and useful applications.

Some of these trends in technology are already being realized in today's marketplace. Oral-B toothbrushes, for example, now connect to your smartphone to provide real-time feedback on your brushing. MindMeld uses speech recognition to listen to your phone calls and pull up search data related to your conversations. Amazon recently introduced its 3D Printing Store, which offers jewelry, home décor, and tech accessories in customizable 3D options. Other technologies such as the Next Issue App, Tesla's electric cars, and Apple Pay are likely to replace or become substitutes for existing products and services such as paper versions of magazines, gasoline-powered vehicles, and plastic credit cards and money.[29]

Technology's Impact on Customer Value

Advances in technology have important effects on marketing. First, the cost of technology is plummeting, causing the customer value assessment of technology-based products to focus on other dimensions such as quality, service, and relationships. *PC Magazine* (www.pcmag.com) publishes an article titled "The Best Free Software" each year to tell readers about companies that give their software away, with the expectation that advertising or upgrade purchases will generate revenue. A similar approach is used by many U.S. mobile phone vendors, who subsidize the purchase of a telephone if the purchase leads to a long-term telephone service contract.[30]

Technology also provides value through the development of new products. More than 3,600 companies recently unveiled 20,000 new products at the Consumer Electronics Show held in Las Vegas. New products included Telepresence Robots that allow you to attend a meeting remotely; Sling TV, which allows you to watch live TV on any device; and wireless charging pads! *Better Homes and Gardens* magazine announced 93 best new product award winners in four categories: beauty, food and beverage, health and personal care, and household. Some of the winners included Cheerios Protein Oats & Honey cereal, Gillette Fusion razor with FlexBall technology, and the Dyson Air Multiplier tower fan. Other new products likely to be available soon include injectable health monitors that will send biometric information to a mobile monitor such as a watch or a phone, and universal translators that allow people speaking different languages to communicate.[31]

Tomra offers recycling through its kiosks.

© Gero Breloer/picture-alliance/dpa/AP Images

Technology can also change existing products and the ways they are produced. Many companies are using technological developments to recycle products through the manufacturing cycle several times. The National Association for PET Container Resources, for example, estimates that 31 percent of all plastic bottles are now recycled, usually to make polyester fibers that are spun into everything from sweaters to upholstery. Tomra Systems has installed more than 70,000 reverse vending machines in North America, Europe, Japan, South America, and the Middle East, facilitating the collection of more than 35 billion cans and bottles annually. In California, there are more than 450 re-PLANET recycling centers where consumers can bring back their empty beverage containers and redeem them for the deposit paid when the products were purchased. Another approach is *precycling*, or efforts by manufacturers and consumers to avoid creating waste. For manufacturers, this includes decreasing the amount of packaging they use; and for consumers, it means buying products that last longer, avoiding products with excess packaging, and reusing as much as possible. According to marketing expert Melissa Lavigne, "It's about being conscious about products you buy in the first place. That's the idea behind precycling."[32]

Technology Enables Data Analytics

Technology has also had a dramatic impact on the operations of marketing organizations. First, the development of online capabilities created the **marketspace**, an information- and communication-based electronic exchange environment occupied by sophisticated computer and telecommunication technologies and digital offerings. Second, these capabilities led to **electronic commerce** (e-commerce), or the activities that use electronic communication in the inventory, promotion, distribution, purchase, and exchange of products and services. Internet-based technology also allows companies to create *intranets* to communicate within the organization, and *extranets* to communicate with suppliers, distributors, and other partners such as advertising agencies.

Today, technologies have advanced to allow computer chips to be placed in almost anything and to be connected to a network almost anywhere. This network of products embedded with connectivity-enabled electronics has come to be known as the **Internet of Things (IoT)**. The information generated by the Internet of Things has led to an explosion in interest in advanced analytics that can predict consumer preferences and behavior. A recent survey by IBM and MIT showed that 50 percent of managers around the globe thought that improving information and analytics was a top priority. Some experts suggest that the use of analytics is associated with success in the marketplace. Firms that have grown their revenues through analytical insights include Netflix, Google, Amazon, Dell, and eBay.[33]

The Internet of Things has contributed to the growth in data analytics.

© Askold Romanov/Getty Images

COMPETITIVE FORCES

The fourth component of the environmental scan, **competition**, refers to the alternative firms that could provide a product to satisfy a specific market's needs. There are various forms of competition, and each company must consider its present and potential competitors in designing its marketing strategy.

Alternative Forms of Competition

LO 3-5 Discuss the forms of competition that exist in a market and the key components of competition.

Four basic forms of competition create a continuum from pure competition to monopolistic competition to oligopoly to pure monopoly. Chapter 13 contains further discussions on pricing practices under these four forms of competition.

At one end of the continuum is *pure competition*, in which there are many sellers and they each have a similar product. Companies that deal in commodities common to agribusiness (for example, wheat, rice, and grain) often are in a pure competition position in which distribution (in the sense of shipping products) is important but other elements of marketing have little impact.

In the second point on the continuum, *monopolistic competition*, many sellers compete with substitutable products within a price range. For example, if the price of coffee rises too much, consumers may switch to tea. Coupons or sales are frequently used marketing tactics.

Oligopoly, a common industry structure, occurs when a few companies control the majority of industry sales. The wireless telephone industry, for example, is dominated by four carriers that serve more than 95 percent of the U.S. market. Verizon, AT&T, Sprint, and T-Mobile have 131, 120, 55, and 55 million subscribers, respectively. Similarly, the entertainment industry in the United States is dominated by Viacom, Disney, and Time Warner, and the major firms in the U.S. defense contractor industry are Boeing, Northrop Grumman, and Lockheed Martin. Critics of oligopolies suggest that because there are few sellers, price competition among firms is not desirable because it leads to reduced profits for all producers.[34]

The final point on the continuum, *pure monopoly*, occurs when only one firm sells the product. Monopolies are common for producers of products and services considered essential to a community: water, electricity, and cable service. Typically, marketing plays a small role in a monopolistic setting because it is regulated by the state or federal government. Government control usually seeks to ensure price protection for the buyer, although deregulation in recent years has encouraged price competition in the electricity market. Concern that Microsoft's 86 percent share of the PC operating system market was a monopoly that limited consumer access to competitors' Internet browsers led to lawsuits and consent decrees from the U.S. Justice Department and investigations and fines from the European Union. A recent Federal Trade Commission investigation of Google found that although the company's market share of the online search market exceeds 70 percent, it had not harmed competition in the marketplace. An investigation by the European Union, however, is still in progress.[35]

Components of Competition

In developing a marketing program, companies must consider the factors that drive competition: entry, the bargaining power of buyers and suppliers, existing rivalries, and substitution possibilities.[36] Scanning the environment requires a look at all of them. These factors relate to a firm's marketing mix decisions and may be used to create a barrier to entry, increase brand awareness, or intensify a fight for market share.

Entry In considering the competition, a firm must assess the likelihood of new entrants. Additional producers increase industry capacity and tend to lower prices. A company scanning its environment must consider the possible **barriers to entry** for other firms, which are business practices or conditions that make it difficult for new firms to enter the market. Barriers to entry can be in the form of capital requirements, advertising expenditures, product identity, distribution access, or the cost to customers of switching suppliers. The higher the expense of the barrier, the more likely it will deter new entrants. For example, Western Union and MoneyGram dominate the $529 billion money transfer market because of their huge distribution networks of branch offices and global pickup locations. Potential competitors find it difficult to enter the market because lack of distribution limits consumer access.[37]

© Jeffrey Blackler/Alamy

Power of Buyers and Suppliers A competitive analysis must consider the power of buyers and suppliers. Powerful buyers exist when they are few in number, there are low switching costs, or the product represents a significant share of the buyer's total costs. This last factor leads the buyer to exert significant pressure for price competition. A supplier gains power when the product is critical to the buyer and when it has built up the switching costs.

Existing Competitors and Substitutes Competitive pressures among existing firms depend on the rate of industry growth. In slow-growth settings, competition is more heated for any possible gains in market share. High fixed costs also create competitive pressures for firms to fill production capacity. For example, airlines offer discounts for making early reservations and charge penalties for changes or cancellations in an effort to fill seats, which represent a high fixed cost.

Small Businesses as Competitors

While large companies provide familiar examples of the forms and components of competition, small businesses make up the majority of the competitive landscape for most businesses. Consider that there are approximately 28.2 million small businesses in the United States, which employ 48 percent of all private sector employees. In addition, small businesses generate 63 percent of all new jobs and 46 percent of the GDP. Research has shown a strong correlation between national economic growth and the level of new small business activity in previous years.[38]

learning review »

3-4. What is the difference between a consumer's disposable and discretionary income?

3-5. How does technology impact customer value?

3-6. In pure competition there are a _____ number of sellers.

REGULATORY FORCES

LO 3-6 Explain the major legislation that ensures competition and regulates the elements of the marketing mix.

For any organization, the marketing and broader business decisions are constrained, directed, and influenced by regulatory forces. **Regulation** consists of restrictions state and federal laws place on business with regard to the conduct of its activities. Regulation exists to protect companies as well as consumers. Much of the regulation from the federal and state levels is the result of an active political process and has been passed to ensure competition and fair business practices. For consumers, the focus of legislation is to protect them from unfair trade practices and ensure their safety.

Protecting Competition

Major federal legislation has been passed to encourage competition, which is deemed desirable because it permits the consumer to determine which competitor will succeed and which will fail. The first such law was the *Sherman Antitrust Act* (1890). Lobbying by farmers in the Midwest against fixed railroad shipping prices led to the passage of this act, which forbids (1) contracts, combinations, or conspiracies in restraint of trade and (2) actual monopolies or attempts to monopolize any part of trade or commerce. Because of vague wording and government inactivity, however, there was only one successful case against a company in the nine years after the act became law, and the Sherman Act was supplemented with the *Clayton Act* (1914). This act forbids certain actions that are likely to lessen competition, although no actual harm has yet occurred.

In the 1930s, the federal government had to act again to ensure fair competition. During that time, large chain stores appeared, such as the Great Atlantic & Pacific Tea Company (A&P). Small businesses were threatened, and they lobbied for the *Robinson-Patman Act* (1936). This act makes it unlawful to discriminate in prices charged to different purchasers of the same product, where the effect may substantially lessen competition or help to create a monopoly.

Product-Related Legislation

Various federal laws in existence specifically address the product component of the marketing mix. Some are aimed at protecting the company, some at protecting the consumer, and at least one at protecting both.

A company can protect its competitive position in new and novel products under the patent law, which gives inventors the right to exclude others from making, using, or selling products that infringe the patented invention. The federal copyright law is another way for a company to protect its competitive position in a product. The copyright law gives the author of a literary, dramatic, musical, or artistic work the exclusive right to print, perform, or otherwise copy that work. Copyright is secured automatically when the work is created. However, the published work should bear an appropriate copyright notice, including the copyright symbol, the first year of publication, and the name of the copyright owner, and it must be registered under the federal copyright law.

Digital technology has necessitated additional copyright legislation, called the *Digital Millennium Copyright Act* (1998), to improve protection of copyrighted digital products. In addition, producers of DVD movies, music recordings, and software want protection from websites and devices designed to circumvent antipiracy elements of their products.[39]

There are many consumer-oriented federal laws regarding products. The various laws include more than 30 amendments and separate laws relating to food, drugs, and cosmetics, such as the *Infant Formula Act* (1980), the *Nutritional Labeling and Education Act* (1990), and new labeling requirements for dietary supplements (1997) and trans fats (2006). Recently, several states have proposed new legislation that would require the labeling of genetically modified food.[40] Various other consumer protection laws have a broader scope, such as the *Fair Packaging and Labeling Act* (1966), the *Child Protection Act* (1966), and the *Consumer Product Safety Act* (1972), which established the Consumer Product Safety Commission to monitor product safety and establish uniform product safety standards. Many of these laws came about because of **consumerism**, a grassroots movement started in the 1960s to increase the influence, power, and rights of consumers in dealing with institutions. This movement continues and is reflected in the growing consumer demand for ecologically safe products and ethical and socially responsible business practices. One hotly debated issue concerns liability for environmental abuse.

Trademarks are intended to protect both the firm selling a trademarked product and the consumer buying it. A Senate report states:

> The purposes underlying any trademark statute [are] twofold. One is to protect the public so that it may be confident that, in purchasing a product bearing a particular trademark which it favorably knows, it will get the product which it asks for and wants to get. Secondly, where the owner of a trademark has spent energy, time, and money in presenting to the public the product, he is protected in this investment from misappropriation in pirates and cheats.

This statement was made in connection with another product-related law, the *Lanham Act* (1946), which provides for registration of a company's trademarks.

Historically, the first user of a trademark in commerce had the exclusive right to use that particular word, name, or symbol in its business. Registration under the Lanham Act provides important advantages to a trademark owner that has used the trademark in interstate or foreign commerce, but it does not confer ownership. A company can lose its trademark if it becomes *generic*, which means that it has primarily come to be merely a common descriptive word for the product. Coca-Cola, Whopper, and Xerox are registered trademarks, and competitors cannot use these names. Aspirin and escalator are former trademarks that are now generic terms in the United States and can be used by anyone.

In 1988, the *Trademark Law Revision Act* resulted in a major change to the Lanham Act, allowing a company to secure rights to a name before actual use by declaring an intent to use the name.[41] In 2003, the United States agreed to participate in the *Madrid Protocol*, which is a treaty that facilitates the protection of U.S. trademark rights throughout the world. Currently, 95 nations are members of the Madrid Protocol, including the United States, Australia, China, the European Union, France, Germany, Japan, and the United Kingdom.[42]

One of the most recent changes in trademark law is the U.S. Supreme Court's ruling that companies may obtain trademarks for colors associated with their products. Over time, consumers may begin to associate a particular color with a specific brand. Examples of products that may benefit from the new law include NutraSweet's sugar substitute in pastel blue packages and Owens Corning Fiberglas Corporation's pink insulation.[43] Another recent addition to trademark law is the *Federal Trademark Dilution Act* (1995, 2006), which is used to prevent someone from using a trademark on a noncompeting product (e.g., "Cadillac" brushes).[44]

Pricing-Related Legislation

The pricing component of the marketing mix is the focus of regulation from two perspectives: price fixing and price discounting. Although the Sherman Act did not outlaw price fixing, the courts view this behavior as *per se illegal* (*per se* means "through or of itself"), which means the courts see price fixing itself as illegal.

Certain forms of price discounting are allowed. Quantity discounts are acceptable; that is, buyers can be charged different prices for a product provided there are differences in manufacturing or delivery costs. Promotional allowances or services may be given to buyers on an equal basis proportionate to volume purchased. Also, a firm can meet a competitor's price "in good faith." Legal and regulatory aspects of pricing are covered in more detail in Chapter 14.

CHAPTER 3   Scanning the Marketing Environment

Distribution-Related Legislation

The government has four concerns with regard to distribution—earlier referred to as "place" actions in the marketing mix—and the maintenance of competition. The first, *exclusive dealing*, is an arrangement a manufacturer makes with a reseller to handle only its products and not those of competitors. This practice is illegal under the Clayton Act only when it substantially lessens competition.

Requirement contracts require a buyer to purchase all or part of its needs for a product from one seller for a time period. These contracts are not always illegal but depend on the court's interpretation of their impact on distribution.

Exclusive territorial distributorships are a third distribution issue often under regulatory scrutiny. In this situation, a manufacturer grants a distributor the sole rights to sell a product in a specific geographical area. The courts have found few violations with these arrangements.

The fourth distribution strategy is a *tying arrangement*, whereby a seller requires the purchaser of one product to also buy another item in the line. These contracts may be illegal when the seller has such economic power in the tying product that the seller can restrain trade in the tied product. Legal aspects of distribution are reviewed in greater detail in Chapter 15.

Advertising- and Promotion-Related Legislation

Federal Trade Commission

Promotion and advertising are aspects of marketing closely monitored by the FTC, which was established by the *FTC Act of 1914*. The FTC is concerned with deceptive or misleading advertising and unfair business practices and has the power to (1) issue cease and desist orders and (2) order corrective advertising. In issuing a *cease and desist order,* the FTC orders a company to stop practices the commission considers unfair. With *corrective advertising,* the FTC can require a company to spend money on advertising to correct previous misleading ads. The enforcement powers of the FTC are so significant that often just an indication of concern from the commission can cause companies to revise their promotion.

A landmark legal battle regarding deceptive advertising involved the FTC and Campbell Soup Co. It had been Campbell's practice to insert clear glass marbles into the bottom of soup containers used in print advertisements to bring the soup ingredients (e.g., noodles or chicken) to the surface. The FTC ruled that the advertising was deceptive because it misrepresented the amount of solid ingredients in the soup, and it issued a cease and desist order. Campbell and its advertising agency agreed to discontinue the practice. Future ads used a ladle to show the ingredients.[45]

Other laws have been introduced to regulate promotion practices. The *Deceptive Mail Prevention and Enforcement Act* (1999), for example, provides specifications for direct-mail sweepstakes, such as the requirement that the statement "No purchase is necessary to enter" be displayed in the mailing, in the rules, and on the entry form. Similarly, the *Telephone Consumer Protection Act* (1991) provides requirements for telemarketing promotions, including fax promotions. Telemarketing is also subject to a law that created the *National Do Not Call Registry*, which is a list of consumer phone numbers of people who do not want to receive unsolicited telemarketing calls.

Finally, new laws such as the *Children's Online Privacy Protection Act* (1998), the *European Union Data Protection Act* (1998), and the *Controlling the Assault of Non-Solicited Pornography and Marketing (CAN-SPAM) Act* (2004) are designed to restrict information collection and unsolicited e-mail promotions and specify simple opt-out procedures on the Internet. See the Marketing Matters box to learn about the FTC's effort to create a "Do Not Track" system to ensure online privacy.[46] A related Internet issue, taxation, has generated an ongoing debate and temporary laws such as the *Internet Tax Freedom Act* (2007).[47]

Online Tracking: Is Big Brother Watching?

Have you ever wondered how your web browser determines which advertisements appear on your screen? The answer is that your actions are "tracked" to create a profile of your interests. Each of the major browser makers—Microsoft, Google, Mozilla, and Apple—can keep a record of the web pages you visit or the topics you discuss in your e-mail. The information allows advertisers to match their advertising specifically to you. So, ideally, you only see advertising that offers products or services of interest to you. You see dog food ads if you are a dog owner and cat food ads if you are a cat owner, for example.

The collection of this information, however, has also raised the issue of privacy. Privacy advocates suggest that many consumers do not realize that the information is being collected and used without their consent. They also argue that in extreme situations the information could lead to unintended outcomes for the consumers—being turned down for a mortgage or a health insurance policy because of online book or food purchases, for example.

To facilitate the debate, the FTC recently released a report calling for better self-regulation of online information collection. In its report, the FTC suggests that each browser should offer users a "Do Not Track" option to signal a computer user's desire not to be tracked. Advertisers would be asked to comply with the request. This opt-out system would be very similar to the current "Do Not Call" system. In Europe, the guidelines are more restrictive, requiring consumers to explicitly "opt-in."

The questions related to this issue are not simple. Consumers will need to decide if giving up some privacy by sharing data is a reasonable trade-off for targeted advertising, customized news sites, and online social networks. Organizations in the $24 billion advertising industry will need to evaluate their ability to self-regulate, and the FTC eventually will need to decide whether legislation is needed. The situation is likely to become even more complicated in the near future as consumers, and especially children, increase their use of smartphone mobile apps that generate tracking data. How do you think the debate will be resolved?

Control through Self-Regulation

Companies must meet certain requirements before they can display this logo on their websites.

Better Business Bureau logo. Used with permission

Better Business Bureau
www.bbb.org

The government has provided much legislation to create a competitive business climate and protect the consumer. An alternative to government control is **self-regulation**, where an industry attempts to police itself. The major television networks, for example, have used self-regulation to set their own guidelines for TV ads for children's toys. These guidelines have generally worked well. There are two problems with self-regulation, however: noncompliance by members and enforcement. In addition, if attempts at self-regulation are too strong, they may violate the Robinson-Patman Act.

The best-known self-regulatory group is the Better Business Bureau (BBB). This agency is a voluntary alliance of companies whose goal is to help maintain fair practices. The BBB is a nonprofit corporation that tries to use "moral suasion" to encourage members to comply with its standards. The BBB offers an Accredited Business Seal Program to provide consumers assurance that an organization is part of a community of trustworthy businesses. Before they display the BBB Accredited Business Seal, participating companies must, among other things, first agree to adhere to the BBB Code of Business Practices, have been in business for at least one year, respect the privacy and e-mail preference of its online visitors, and commit to work with its customers and BBB to resolve disputes that arise over products or services promoted or advertised on their site.[48]

3-7. The _____ Act was punitive toward monopolies, whereas the _____ Act was preventive.

3-8. Describe some of the recent changes in trademark law.

3-9. How does the Better Business Bureau encourage companies to follow its standards for commerce?

LEARNING OBJECTIVES REVIEW

LO 3-1   *Explain how environmental scanning provides information about social, economic, technological, competitive, and regulatory forces.*

Many businesses operate in environments where important forces change. Environmental scanning is the process of acquiring information about these changes to allow marketers to identify and interpret trends. There are five environmental forces businesses must monitor: social, economic, technological, competitive, and regulatory. By identifying trends related to each of these forces, businesses can develop and maintain successful marketing programs. Several trends that most businesses are monitoring include the growing popularity of video bloggers, the increasing mobility and connectivity of consumers, and the importance of issues such as net neutrality.

LO 3-2   *Describe how social forces such as demographics and culture can have an impact on marketing strategy.*

Demographic information describes the world population; the U.S. population; the generational cohorts such as baby boomers, Generation X, and Generation Y; the structure of the American household; the geographic shifts of the population; and the racial and ethnic diversity of the population, which has led to multicultural marketing programs. Cultural factors include the trend toward fewer differences in male and female consumer behavior and the impact of values such as sustainability on consumer preferences.

LO 3-3   *Discuss how economic forces such as macroeconomic conditions and consumer income affect marketing.*

Economic forces include the strong relationship between consumers' expectations about the economy and their spending. Gross income has remained stable for more than 40 years although the rate of saving has fluctuated, declining to 2 percent before rising to 5.8 percent recently.

LO 3-4   *Describe how technological changes can affect marketing.*

Technological innovations can replace existing products and services. Changes in technology can also have an impact on customer value by reducing the cost of products, improving the quality of products, and providing new products that were not previously feasible. Electronic commerce is transforming how companies do business.

LO 3-5   *Discuss the forms of competition that exist in a market and the key components of competition.*

There are four forms of competition: pure competition, monopolistic competition, oligopoly, and monopoly. The key components of competition include the likelihood of new competitors, the power of buyers and suppliers, and the presence of competitors and possible substitutes. While large companies are often used as examples of marketplace competitors, there are 28.2 million small businesses in the United States, which have a significant impact on the economy.

LO 3-6   *Explain the major legislation that ensures competition and regulates the elements of the marketing mix.*

Regulation exists to protect companies and consumers. Legislation that ensures a competitive marketplace includes the Sherman Antitrust Act. Product-related legislation includes copyright and trademark laws that protect companies and packaging and labeling laws that protect consumers. Pricing- and distribution-related laws are designed to create a competitive marketplace with fair prices and availability. Regulation related to promotion and advertising reduces deceptive practices and provides enforcement through the Federal Trade Commission. Self-regulation through organizations such as the Better Business Bureau provides an alternative to federal and state regulation.

LEARNING REVIEW ANSWERS

3-1   **Describe three generational cohorts.**

Answer: (1) Baby boomers are the generation of 76 million among the U.S. population born between 1946 and 1964. These Americans are growing older and will all be 65 or older by 2030. (2) Generation X are those among the 15 percent of the U.S. population born between 1965 and 1976. These well-educated Americans, also known as the baby bust cohort because of declining birthrates, are supportive of racial and ethic diversity. (3) Generation Y, or millennials, are the 72 million Americans among the U.S. population born between 1977 and 1994. The rising birthrates of this "baby boomlet" cohort is the result of baby boomers having children.

3-2   **Why are many companies developing multicultural marketing programs?**

Answer: Multicultural marketing programs consist of combinations of the marketing mix that reflect the unique attitudes, ancestry, communication preferences, and lifestyles of different races and ethnic groups. The reason for developing these programs is that the racial and ethnic diversity of the U.S. is changing rapidly due to the increases in the African American, Asian, and Hispanic populations, which increases their economic impact.

3-3   **How are important values such as sustainability reflected in the marketplace today?**

Answer: Many Americans desire and practice sustainability to preserve the environment. Specifically, these consumers buy products such as hybrid gas-electric cars. Consumers also prefer brands that have a strong link to social action (like Ben & Jerry's—see Chapter 2). Companies are responding to this consumer trend by producing products that use renewable energy and less packaging.

3-4   **What is the difference between a consumer's disposable and discretionary income?**

Answer: Disposable income is the money a consumer has left after paying taxes to use for necessities such as food, housing, clothing, and transportation. Discretionary income is the money that remains after paying for taxes and necessities and is usually spent on luxury items.

3-5   **How does technology impact customer value?**

Answer: (1) Because the cost of technology is plummeting, this allows consumers to assess the value of technology-based products on other dimensions, such as quality, service, and relationships. (2) Technology provides value through the development of new products. (3) Technology has changed the way existing products are produced through recycling and precycling. (4) Technology enables the collection of data used in the growing field of data analytics.

3-6   **In pure competition there are a _____ number of sellers.**

Answer: large

3-7   **The _____ Act was punitive toward monopolies, whereas the _____ Act was preventive.**

Answer: *Sherman Antitrust; Clayton*

3-8 Describe some of the recent changes in trademark law.

Answer: Trademarks are intended to protect both the firm selling a trademarked product and the consumer buying it. The *Lanham Act* (1946) provides for registration of a company's trademarks. The *Trademark Law Revision Act* (1988), which modified the *Lanham Act*, allows companies to secure rights to a name before its actual use by declaring an intent to use the name. In 2003, the United States agreed to participate in the *Madrid Protocol*, which is a treaty that facilitates the protection of U.S. trademark rights. Also, the U.S. Supreme Court recently ruled that a company may obtain trademarks for colors associated with their products. Finally, the *Federal Dilution Act* (1995, 2006) prevents someone from using a trademark on a noncompeting product (such as the "Cadillac" of brushes).

3-9 How does the Better Business Bureau encourage companies to follow its standards for commerce?

Answer: The Better Business Bureau (BBB) uses moral suasion to get members to comply with its standards. Companies, which join the BBB voluntarily, must agree to follow these standards before they are allowed to display the BBB Accredited Business logo.

FOCUSING ON KEY TERMS

baby boomers p. 75
barriers to entry p. 87
blended family p. 77
competition p. 86
consumerism p. 89
culture p. 80
demographics p. 74
discretionary income p. 83

disposable income p. 83
economy p. 82
electronic commerce p. 86
environmental scanning p. 72
Generation X p. 75
Generation Y p. 76
gross income p. 83

Internet of Things (IoT) p. 86
marketspace p. 86
multicultural marketing p. 79
regulation p. 88
self-regulation p. 92
social forces p. 74
technology p. 84
value consciousness p. 81

APPLYING MARKETING KNOWLEDGE

1 For many years Gerber has manufactured baby food in small, single-sized containers. In conducting an environmental scan, (*a*) identify three trends or factors that might significantly affect this company's future business, and (*b*) propose how Gerber might respond to these changes.

2 Describe the new features you would add to an automobile designed for consumers in the 55+ age group. In what magazines would you advertise to appeal to this target market?

3 The population shift from suburbs to exurbs and small towns was discussed in this chapter. What businesses and industries are likely to benefit from this trend? How will retailers need to change to accommodate these consumers?

4 New technologies are continuously improving and replacing existing products. Although technological change is often difficult to predict, suggest how the following companies and products might be affected by the Internet and digital technologies: (*a*) Kodak cameras and film, (*b*) American Airlines, and (*c*) the Metropolitan Museum of Art.

5 In recent years in the brewing industry, a couple of large firms that have historically had most of the beer sales (Anheuser-Busch and Miller) have faced competition from many small "micro" brands. In terms of the continuum of competition, how would you explain this change?

6 The Johnson Company manufactures buttons and pins with slogans and designs. These pins are inexpensive to produce and are sold in retail outlets such as discount stores, hobby shops, and bookstores. Little equipment is needed for a new competitor to enter the market. What strategies should Johnson consider to create effective barriers to entry?

7 Why would Xerox be concerned about its name becoming generic?

8 Develop a "Code of Business Practices" for a new online vitamin store. Does your code address advertising? Privacy? Use by children? Why is self-regulation important?

BUILDING YOUR MARKETING PLAN

Your marketing plan will include a situation analysis based on internal and external factors that are likely to affect your marketing program.

1 To summarize information about external factors, create a table similar to Figure 3–2 and identify three trends related to each of the five forces (social, economic, technological, competitive, and regulatory) that relate to your product or service.

2 When your table is completed, describe how each of the trends represents an opportunity or a threat for your business.

"As long as there's innovation there is going to be new kinds of chaos," explains Robert Stephens, founder of the technology support company Geek Squad. The chaos Stephens is referring to is the difficulty we have all experienced trying to keep up with the many changes in our environment, particularly those related to computers, technology, software, communication, and entertainment. Generally, consumers have found it difficult to install, operate, and use many of the electronic products available today. "It takes time to read the manuals," Stephens says. "I'm going to save you that time because I stay home on Saturday nights and read them for you!"

Video 3-5

Geek Squad

Video Case

kerin.tv/13e/v3-5

THE COMPANY

The Geek Squad story begins when Stephens, a native of Chicago, passed up an Art Institute scholarship to pursue a degree in computer science. While Stephens was a computer science student he took a job fixing computers for a research laboratory, and he also started consulting. He could repair televisions, computers, and a variety of other items, although he decided to focus on computers. His experiences as a consultant led him to realize that most people needed

© Tim Boyle/Getty Images

help with technology and that they saw value in a service whose employees would show up at a specified time, be friendly, use understandable language, and solve the problem. So, with just $200, Stephens formed Geek Squad in 1994.

Geek Squad set out to provide timely and effective help with all computing needs regardless of the make, model, or place of purchase. Geek Squad employees were called "agents" and wore uniforms consisting of black pants or skirts, black shoes, white shirts, black clip-on ties, a badge, and a black jacket with a Geek Squad logo to create a "humble" attitude that was not threatening to customers. Agents drove black-and-white Volkswagen Beetles, or Geekmobiles, with a

logo on the door, and charged fixed prices for services, regardless of how much time was required to provide the service. The "house call" services ranged from installing networks, to debugging a computer, to setting up an entertainment system, and cost from $100 to $300. "We're like 'Dragnet'; we show up at people's homes and help," Stephens says. "We're also like *Ghostbusters* and there's a pseudogovernment feel to it like *Men in Black*."

In 2002, Geek Squad was purchased by leading consumer electronics retailer Best Buy for about $3 million. Best Buy had observed very high return rates for most of its complex products. Shoppers would be excited about new products, purchase them and take them home, get frustrated trying to make them actually work, and then return them to the store demanding a refund. In fact, Best Buy research revealed that consumers were beginning to see service as a critical element of the purchase. The partnership was an excellent match. Best Buy consumers welcomed the help. Stephens became Geek Squad's chief inspector and a Best Buy vice president and began putting a Geek Squad "precinct" in every Best Buy store, creating some stand-alone Geek Squad Stores, and providing 24-hour telephone support. There are now more than 20,000 agents in the United States, Canada, the United Kingdom, and China, and return rates have declined by 25 to 35 percent. Geek Squad service plans are also being sold on eBay. The Geek Squad website proclaims that the company is "Serving the Public, Policing Technology and Protecting the World."

THE CHANGING ENVIRONMENT

Many changes in the environment occurred to create the need for Geek Squad's services. Future changes are also likely to change the way Geek Squad operates. An environmental scan helps illustrate the changes.

The most obvious changes may be related to technology. Wireless broadband technology, high-definition televisions, products with Internet interfaces, and a general trend toward computers, smartphones, entertainment systems, and even appliances being interconnected are just a few examples of new products and applications for consumers to learn about. There are also technology-related problems such as viruses, spyware, lost data, and "crashed" or inoperable computers. New technologies have also created a demand for new types of maintenance such as password management, operating system updates, disk cleanup, and "defragging."

Another environmental change that contributes to the popularity of Geek Squad is the change in social factors such as demographics and culture. In the past many electronics manufacturers and retailers focused primarily on men. Women, however, are becoming increasingly interested in personal computing and home entertainment and, according to the Consumer Electronics Association, are likely to outspend men in the near future. Best Buy's consumer research indicates that women expect personal service during the purchase as well as during the installation after the purchase—exactly the service Geek Squad is designed to provide. Our culture is also embracing the Geek Squad concept. For example, in the recently discontinued television series *Chuck*

© Tim Boyle/Getty Images

(2007–2012), one of the characters worked for the "Nerd Herd" at "Buy More" and drove a car like a Geekmobile on service calls!

Competition, economics, and the regulatory environment have also had a big influence on Geek Squad. As discount stores such as Walmart and PC makers such as Dell began to compete with Best Buy, new services such as in-home installation were needed to create value for customers. Now, just as change in competition created an opportunity for Geek Squad, it is also leading to another level of competition as Staples has introduced EasyTech services and Office Depot has introduced Tech Depot services. The economic situation for electronics continues to improve as prices decline and demand increases. Consumers purchased 2 million 3D TVs in 2010, and sales of all consumer electronics exceeded $180 billion. Finally, the regulatory environment continues to change with

respect to the electronic transfer of copyrighted materials such as music and movies and software. Geek Squad must monitor the changes to ensure that its services comply with relevant laws.

THE FUTURE FOR GEEK SQUAD

The combination of many positive environmental factors helps explain the extraordinary success of Geek Squad. Today, it repairs more than 3,000 PCs a day and generates more than $2 billion in revenue. Because Geek Squad services have a high profit margin they contribute to the overall performance of Best Buy, and they help generate traffic in the store and create store loyalty. To continue to grow, however, Geek Squad will need to continue to scan the environment and try new approaches to creating customer value.

One possible new approach is to create new partnerships. Geek Squad and Ford, for example, have developed a partnership to help consumers install in-car communication systems. In the future, Best Buy will offer 240-volt home charging stations for Ford's electric vehicle, the Focus. Geek Squad will offer electrical audits and residential installations for the car owners. Geek Squad is also using new technology to improve. Agents now use a smartphone to access updated schedules, log in their hours, and run diagnostics tests on clients' equipment. Best Buy is also testing a "Solutions Central" desk, similar to the Genius Bar concept in Apple stores, and staffing it with Geek Squad agents. Finally, to attract the best possible employees, Geek Squad and Best Buy are trying a "results-only work environment" that has no fixed schedules and no mandatory meetings. By encouraging employees to make their own work–life decisions, the Geek Squad hopes to keep morale and productivity high.

Other changes and opportunities are certain to appear soon. However, despite the success of the Geek Squad and the potential for additional growth, Robert Stephens is modest and claims, "Geeks may inherit the Earth, but they have no desire to rule it!"[49]

Questions

1 What are the key environmental forces that created an opportunity for Robert Stephens to start the Geek Squad?

2 What changes in the purchasing patterns of (*a*) all consumers and (*b*) women made the acquisition of Geek Squad particularly important for Best Buy?

3 Based on the case information and what you know about consumer electronics, conduct an environ-mental scan for Geek Squad to identify key trends. For each of the five environmental forces (social, economic, technological, competitive, and regulatory), identify trends likely to influence Geek Squad in the near future.

4 What promotional activities would you recommend to encourage consumers who currently use independent installers to switch to Geek Squad?

Chapter Notes

1. "Company Profile: Facebook, Inc.," *MarketLine,* February 6, 2015, www.marketline.com; Ben Geier, "Zuckerberg Says Facebook's Giant Internet Drones Are Already Flying," *Fortune.com,* April 1, 2015; Aaron Tilley, "Looking Beyond Mobile, Facebook Is Getting into The Internet of Things," *Forbes.com,* March 25, 2015; Jack Linshi, "Facebook Will Now Help Your Photos Look Way Better," *Time.com,* December 18, 2014; Michael L. Best, "Global Computing: The Internet That Facebook Built," *Communications of the ACM,* December 2014; Trefis Team, "Facebook Through the Lens of Porter's Five Forces," *Forbes.com,* November 28, 2014; Austin Carr, "Facebook Everywhere," *Fast Company,* July–August 2014, pp. 56–92; Brad Stone and Sarah Frier, "Facebook's Next Decade," *Bloomberg Businessweek,* February 3, 2014, pp. 44–49.

2. "U.S. Coffee Drinking Grinds Lower," *Fortune.com,* March 23, 2015; "Coffee Consumption," *2015 National Coffee Drinking Trends Study* (New York: National Coffee Association of U.S.A., Inc., 2015); Olivia Waxman, "Starbucks Introduces S'mores Frappuccino," *Time.com,* April 20, 2015; Alexandra Sifferlin, "This Is Where Starbucks Will Test Its Delivery Service," *Time.com,* March 25, 2015; Nicholas Upton, "State of the Coffee Industry," *specialty-coffee.com,* February 2014; Pat Pope, "Tea for Two and More," *Convenience Store Decision,* October 2014, pp. 44–46.

3. Dan Mitchell, "Love K-Cups? You're Killing the Coffee Business," *Time.com,* April 20, 2015; "This Is the Drink People Are Getting instead of Coffee," *Time.com,* March 18, 2015.

4. Peter Coy, Shobhana Chandra, and Rich Miller, "Go," *Bloomberg Businessweek,* April 13, 2015, pp. 11–12; Sarah Vizard, "The Marketing Year: Key Trends 2014," *Marketing Week,* December 4, 2014, p. 1; Matthew Idema, "Digital Market Trends in the New Year," *businesstoday.co.om,* May 4, 2015; "2015 Emerging Top 10 Trends," *management.co.nz,* April 2015; Linda A. Goldstein, "Current FTC Hot Buttons and Trends," *Response,* April 2015, p. 60; Jonathan Bacon, "The Marketing Year: Technology Trends 2014," *Marketing Week,* December 5, 2014, p. 1; Karen Nayler, "Trends and Issues," *Marketing Magazine,* 2014, pp. 10–12; Mindi Chahal, "Five Trends Marketers Need to Know for 2015," *Marketing Week,* December 3, 2014, p. 1; and Juan M. Sanchez, "Growth Around the World Is Still Below the Trend," *The Regional Economist,* January 2015, pp. 4–7.

5. *2014 World Population Data Sheet* (Washington, DC: Population Reference Bureau, 2014), pp. 2–5; and Rakesh Kochihar, "10 Projections for the Global Population in 2050," Pew Research Center, February 3, 2014.

6. "GNI per Capita, Atlas Method," *World Development Indicators Database* (Washington, DC: World Bank Group, 2015); and *World Population Prospects: The 2012 Revision,* Key Finding and Advance Tables (New York: United Nations, Department of Economic and Social Affairs, Population Division, 2013).

7. U.S. Population, United States Census Bureau, http://www.census.gov/topics/population.html, May 7, 2015; Sandra L. Colby and Jennifer M. Ortman, "Projections of the Size and Composition of the U.S. Population: 2014 to 2060, Current Population Reports," U.S. Department of Commerce, March 2015; Ellen Byron, "How to Market to an Aging Boomer: Flattery, Subterfuge and Euphemism," *The Wall Street Journal,* February 5, 2011, p. A1; and "U.S. Census Bureau Projections Show a Slower Growing, Older, More Diverse Nation a Half Century from Now," U.S. Census Bureau, December 12, 2012.

8. David Port, "Sandwiched," *Retirement Advisor,* May 2015, pp 34–38; Marilyn Alva, "Homebuilders Bet on Baby Boomer Wave," *Investors Business Daily,* January 9, 2015, p. A10; Tom Sightings, "How Baby Boomers Will Change the Economy," *USNews.com,* January 15, 2013; "Lay's Unveils 2 New Kettle Cooked Potato Chip Varieties," *Entertainment Close-Up,* July 11, 2012; and Byron, "How to Market to an Aging Boomer," p. A1.

9. Chris Matthews, "America's Most Indebted Generation, Gen X," *Fortune.com,* August 29, 2014; Leonard Klie, "Gen X: Stuck in the Middle," *destinationCRM.com,* February 1, 2012; Michele Hammond, "Gen X Pips Boomers to Lead Online Retail Spending," www.startupsmart.com.au, January 10, 2013; Chris Johns, "Hotels for Hipsters," *The Globe and Mail,* November 13, 2012, p. E1; and Piet Levy, "Segmentation by Generation," *Marketing News,* May 15, 2011, p. 20.

10. "Millennials Will Overtake Baby Boomers to Become America's Biggest Generation," *Time.com,* January 20, 2015; Suzy Bashford, "Marketing for Good," *Marketing,* May 2015, p. 1; Alison Davis-Blake, "Educators: Teach Millennials How to Be a Force for Good," *Businessweek.com,* March 6, 2014; p. 3; "The Unilever School of Marketing for Good," *Marketing,* May 2015, p. 1; Colleen Kane, "Will Apple's New Complex Really Be the 'Greenest Building on the Planet?'" *Fortune.com,* April 29, 2015; "Generations X, Y Adopt Smartphones as Media Hubs," *Business Wire,* July 31, 2012; "The Truth about Millennials— Are You Ready for These New Professionals?" *States News Service,* March 30, 2012; and Geoff Gloeckler, "Here Come the Millennials," *BusinessWeek,* November 24, 2008, pp. 46–50.

11. Jonathan Vespa, Jamie M. Lewis, and Rose M. Kreider, "America's Families and Living Arrangements: 2012," U.S. Census Bureau, August 2013; Richard Fry, "A Rising Share of Young Adults Live in Their Parents' Home," *pewsocialtrends.org,* Pew Research Centers, August 1, 2013; "American Housing Survey Reveals Rise in Doubled-Up Households during Recession," *PD&R Edge,* http://www.huduser.org/portal/pdredge/pdr_edge_research_012714.html; Rose M. Kreider, "Increase in Opposite-Sex Cohabiting Couples from 2009 to 2010," in the Annual Social and Economic Supplement (ASEC) to the Current Population Survey (CPS), U.S. Bureau of the Census, September 15, 2010; and "Young Careers Will Carry

Scars of Great Recession," *Chattanooga Times Free Press,* November 7, 2010, p. C1.

12. "National Marriage and Divorce Rate Trends," National Center for Health Statistics, National Vital Statistics System, January 10, 2012; "Births, Marriages, Divorces, and Deaths: Provisional Data for 2009," National Vital Statistics Reports, August 27, 2010, Table A; Gail Sheehy, "The Gray Divorce," *Harper's Bazaar,* November 1, 2010, p. 189; and Alexandra Montgomery, "U.S. Families 2025: In Search of Future Families," *Futures,* May 2008, p. 377.

13. "A Decade of State Population Change," http://www.census.gov/dataviz/visualizations/043/508.php, U.S. Census Bureau, Population Division, January 10, 2013; and "State and County QuickFacts," http://quickfacts.census.gov/qfd/states/48000.html, U.S. Census Bureau, March 31, 2015.

14. Stephane Fitch and Kristin Kloberdanz, "Back to the Future," *Forbes,* December 29, 2014, pp. 112–24; "Pulling Back from the Exurbs," *The New York Times,* April 10, 2012, p. 22; and David Peterson and Katie Humphrey, "Reverse Migration: Flight to the Exurbs Stops Cold," *StarTribune.com,* April 12, 2010.

15. "Revised Delineations of Metropolitan Statistical Areas, Micropolitan Statistical Areas, and Combined Statistical Areas," OMB Bulletin No. 13-01, Office of Management and Budget, February 28, 2013; "2010 Standards for Delineating Metropolitan and Micropolitan Statistical Areas," Office of Management and Budget, *Federal Register* 75, no. 123, June 28, 2010; and "About Metropolitan and Micropolitan Statistical Areas," U.S. Census Bureau, www.census.gov/population/www/estimates/aboutmetro.html.

16. "2010 Census Shows America's Diversity," U.S. Census Bureau, CB11–CN.125, March 24, 2011; "An Older and More Diverse Nation by Midcentury," Public Information Office, U.S. Census Bureau, Last Revised: February 2, 2011; Table 4: Projections of the Population by Sex, Race, and Hispanic Origin for the United States: 2010 to 2050 (NP2008-T4), Population Division, U.S. Census Bureau, August 14, 2008; and "Mapping Census 2000: The Geography of U.S. Diversity," Population Division, U.S. Census Bureau.

17. Matt Weeks, "Minorities Energize U.S. Consumer Market, According to UGA Multicultural Economy Report," press release, Public Affairs Division, The University of Georgia, September 30, 2014; "Research: Latino Purchasing Power Now Pegged at $1 Trillion," *Hispanically Speaking News,* May 3, 2011; "Black Buying Power to Reach $1.1 Trillion, Report Finds," *Huffington Post,* November 10, 2011; *State of the Asian American Consumer,* The Nielsen Company, Quarter 3, 2012, p. 14; and "The New Now: Defining the Future Together," *PR Newswire,* February 18, 2011.

18. Laurel Wentz, "Multicultural Agency of the Year: Alma," *Advertising Age,* January 26, 2015, p. 26; "About Us," Alma website, www.almaad.com, accessed May 9, 2015; Laurel Wentz, "Welcome to the Multicultural Mainstream," *Advertising Age,* April 6, 2015, p. 18; and Michael Sebastian, "Where's the Multicultural Mainstream? Looking at Their Phones," *Advertising Age,* April 6, 2015, p. 21.

19. Hannah Weinberger, "Where Are All the Millennial Feminists?" *CNN Wire,* November 9, 2012; "Salary Survey 2011: Taking a Lead on Gender Issues," *Marketing Week,* January 13, 2011, p. 17; "From 18 to 80: Women on Politics and Society," 2008 Women's Monitor Study, *PR Newswire,* August 20, 2008; and Rebecca Gardyn, "Granddaughters of Feminism," *American Demographics,* April 2001, p. 42.

20. Sam Frizell, "Here's How Pinterest Is Trying to Attract More Men," *Time.com,* January 23, 2015, p. 1; "Moschino Launches Scent in a Teddy," *Women's Wear Daily,* November 14, 2014, p. 8-1; "Gillian Rich, "Can Female-Focused Lululemon Sell Yoga Pants to Men?" *Investors Business Daily,* June 14, 2013, p. 1; Elizabeth Sweet, "Guys and Dolls No More?" *The New York Times,* December 23, 2012, p. 12; and Patricia Odell, "UGG VP Marketing on Tom Brady's Impact on the Brand," *Chief Marketer,* November 29, 2012.

21. Robin M. Williams Jr., *American Society: A Sociological Interpretation,* 3rd ed. (New York: Knopf, 1970); L. Robert Kohls, "Why Do Americans Act Like That?" International Programs, San Francisco State University; Eric Pooley, David Welch, and Alan Ohnsman, "Charged for Battle," *Bloomberg Businessweek,* January 3, 2011, pp. 48–56; Edwin R. Stafford and Cathy L. Hartman, "Promoting the Value of Sustainably Minded Purchase Behaviors," *Marketing News,* January 2013, p. 28; and Juan Rodriguez, "Selling the Righteous Life," *The Gazette,* September 18, 2010, p. B3.

22. "Consumers Cut Back on Toilet Paper, Pampers, Huggies," *Mish's Global Economic Trend Analysis,* January 14, 2013; Adam Davidson, "New Normal for Post-Recession Consumers," *The International Herald Tribune,* January 5, 2013, p. 8; Michelle Groenke, "Consumers Say 'Show Me the Bargains,'" *UPI,* November 22, 2012; Devin Leonard, "The New Abnormal," *Bloomberg Businessweek,* August 2, 2010, p. 50; and Chris Burritt, "Came for the Bargains, Stayed for the Brands," *Bloomberg Businessweek,* August 2, 2010, pp. 23–24.

23. "Tuition and Fees and Room and Board Charges over Time in Current Dollars and 2014 Dollars," College Board, http://trends.collegeboard.org/college-pricing/figures-tables/tuition-fees-room-board-time; and Carmen DeNavas-Walt and Bernadette D. Proctor, "Income, Poverty, and Health Insurance Coverage in the United States: 2013," *Current Population Reports* (Washington, DC: U.S. Census Bureau, September 16, 2014).

24. Azhar Iqbal and Mark Vitner, "The Deeper the Recession, the Stronger the Recovery: Is It Really That Simple?" *Business Economics,* 2011, pp. 22–31.

25. "Monthly Chart 1: The Index of Consumer Sentiment," data from Surveys of Consumers (Ann Arbor, MI: Survey Research Center, University of Michigan, June 2012). Copyright © 2015, The regents of the University of Michigan, www.sca.isr.umich.edu

26. Carmen DeNavas-Walt and Bernadette D. Proctor, "Income, Poverty, and Health Insurance Coverage in the United States: 2013," *Current Population Reports* (Washington, DC: U.S. Census Bureau, September 16, 2014).

27. Doug Handler and Nariman Behravesh, *U.S. Economic Environment,* IHS Economics, March 3, 2015; Nick Timiraos and Kris Hudson, "The Demand Divide: Two-Tier Economy Reshapes U.S. Marketplace," *The Wall Street Journal,* January 29, 2015; and Betsy Bohlen, Steve Carlotti, and Liz Mihas, "How the Recession Has Changed U.S. Consumer Behavior," *McKinsey Quarterly,* no. 1 (2010), pp. 17–20.

28. "Consumer Expenditures in 2012," U.S. Department of Labor, Bureau of Labor Statistics, March 2014, Table B; and "Personal Saving Rate Rises in February," *BEA News,* U.S. Department of Commerce, Bureau of Economic Analysis, March 30, 2015.

29. Clara Shih, "5 Tech Trends to Watch in 2015," *Fortune.com,* February 3, 2015; Emily Barone, "Power Struggle," *Time,* May 18, 2015, pp. 16–17; "Oral-B to Roll Out Interactive Brush," *MMR,* July 14, 2014, p. 15; Bruce Rogers, "3D Printing Goes Mainstream," *Forbes.com,* September 3, 2014; Kelli B. Grant, "4 Future Tech Trends," *MarketWatch,* January 15, 2013; and "The Biggest Tech Trends Coming in 2013," *First Digital Media,* January 22, 2013.

30. Eric Griffith, "The Best Free Software," *PCMag.com,* March 10, 2014; Daisuke Wakabayashi and Thomas Gryta, "For iPhone, Cutback in Subsidies Is a Risk," *The Wall Street Journal,* September 8, 2014, p. B1; and Koen Pauwels and Allen Weiss, "Moving

from Free to Fee: How Online Firms Market to Change Their Business Model Successfully," *Journal of Marketing,* May 2008, pp. 14–31.

31. John Falcone, "CES 2015: The Final Word," www.cnet.com, January 10, 2015; Roman H. Kepczyk, "CES 2015: It's All about the Gadgets!" www.CPAPracticeAdvisor.com, February 2015; CES website, http://www.cesweb.org/Why-CES-/CES-By-the-Numbers.aspx; "2015 Best New Product Awards," *Better Homes and Gardens,* www.bhg.com, January 2015; and Terri Briseno, "10 Futurist Predictions in the World of Technology," *howstuffworks,* http://electronics.howstuffworks.com/future-tech/10-futurist-predictions-in-the-world-of-technology.htm#page=9.

32. "Postconsumer PET Container Recycling Activity in 2013," National Association for PET Container Resources, October 8, 2014; Steve Richerson, "Sustainability: It Delivers Four Benefits," *Sales and Service Excellence,* September 2012, p. 16; and Becky Ebenkam, "'Precycling' Catches On with Consumers," *Brandweek.com,* August 12, 2008.

33. Marco Vriens and Patricia Kidd, "The Big Data Shift," *Marketing Insights,* November–December 2014, pp. 22–29; and Cliff Saran, "Big Data Technology Has Its Work Cut Out to Harness Web Analytics," *Computer Weekly,* May 13–19, 2014, p. 12.

34. "Grading the Top 8 U.S. Wireless Carriers in the Fourth Quarter of 2014," http://www.fiercewireless.com/special-reports/grading-top-us-wireless-carriers-fourth-quarter-2014, March 3, 2014; and "Economic Consequences of Armaments Production: Institutional Perspectives of J. K. Galbraith and T. B. Veblen," *Journal of Economic Issues,* March 1, 2008, p. 37.

35. Tom Huddelston Jr., "Google to Face Antitrust Charges in Europe," *Fortune.com,* April 29, 2015; James Kanter, "E.U. Accuses Microsoft of Violating Antitrust Deal," *The International Herald Tribune,* October 25, 2012, p. 17; and "Google Wins an Antitrust Battle," *The New York Times,* January 6, 2013, p. 10.

36. Michael Porter, *Competitive Advantage* (New York: Free Press, 1985); and Michael Porter, *Competitive Strategy* (New York: Free Press, 1980).

37. Jessica Silver-Greenberg, "New Rules for Money Transfers, but Few Limits," *The New York Times,* www.nytimes.com, June 1, 2012.

38. "Frequently Asked Questions," Small Business Administration, Office of Advocacy, www.sba.gov/advocacy, March 2014; "Small Business Trends," Small Business Administration, www.sba.gov/content/small-business-trends; and Kathryn Kobe, "Small Business GDP: Update 2002–2010," Small Business Administration, Office of Advocacy, January 2012.

39. "One Year Later, SOPA Activists Reignite Copyright Conversation," *CBS News,* January 18, 2013; and "Legal Roundup," *Billboard,* January 31, 2009.

40. Thomas A. Hemphill and Syagnik Banerjee, "Mandatory Food Labeling for GMOs," *Regulation,* Winter 2014–2105, p. 7; and Julie Ann Grimm, "Bill Would Require Labeling of Genetically Modified Food," *Las Cruces Sun-News,* January 19, 2013.

41. Dorothy Cohen, "Trademark Strategy Revisited," *Journal of Marketing,* July 1991, pp. 46–59.

42. Matthew Himich, "United States: Madrid Protocol: Is It for You?" *Mondaq Business Briefing,* February 10, 2012; and "Madrid System for the International Registration of Marks,"

World Intellectual Property Organization, http://www.wipo.int/madrid/en/, January 25, 2013.

43. Paul Barrett, "High Court Sees Color as Basis for Trademarks," *The Wall Street Journal,* March 29, 1995, p. A6; Paul Barrett, "Color in the Court," *The Wall Street Journal,* January 5, 1995, p. A1; and David Kelly, "Rainbow of Ideas to Trademark Color," *Advertising Age,* April 24, 1995, pp. 20, 22.

44. Vasilios Peros, "Famous Trademarks: Dilution versus Confusion," *Mondaq,* April 18, 2011; and Maxine L. Retsky, "Dilution of Trademarks Hard to Prove," *Marketing News,* May 12, 2003, p. 6.

45. Dick Mercer, "Tempest in a Soup Can," *Advertising Age,* October 17, 1994, pp. 25–29.

46. Cotton Delo, "You Are Big Brother (But That Isn't So Bad)," *Advertising Age,* April 23, 2012, p. 1; Ana Radelat, "Online Privacy, Postal Hikes Top List of DMA Concerns," *Advertising Age,* April 23, 2012, p. 3; Kate Kaye, "Capitol Hill Focuses on Mobile Privacy with Spate of Actions," *Advertising Age,* December 17, 2012, p. 9; "Twitter to Honor Do Not Track Requests," *Marketing News,* July 31, 2012, p. 7; "The Internet Browsing Cops," *The Wall Street Journal,* January 21, 2011, p. A12; Edmund Lee, "Government Says Self-Regulation of Online Privacy Is Coming Up Short," *Advertising Age,* December 6, 2010, p. 1; and Julia Angwin and Jennifer Valentino-DeVries, "Web Privacy 'Inadequate,'" *The Wall Street Journal,* December 2, 2010, p. B1.

47. "Internet Tax Reprieve," *The Wall Street Journal,* December 15, 2014, p. A12; "The New Internet Tax Freedom Act," *JD Supra,* May 16, 2008.

48. BBB Online Program Standards, http://us.bb.org, accessed January 25, 2013.

49. Geek Squad: This case was written by Steven Hartley. Sources: Thomas Lee, "Best Buy Stakes Big Share of Its Future on Geek Squad," *San Jose Mercury News,* August 7, 2012; Natalie Zmuda, "Best Buy Gets Back in the Game with New Tagline," *Advertising Age,* June 25, 2012, p. 4; "Best Buy Continues to Diversify by Selling Geek Squad Services," *Trefis,* October 9, 2012; Mike Snider and Edward C. Baig, "Companies Foresee Record Electronics Sales This Year," *USA Today,* January 10, 2011, p. 8A; "3D TV Surpasses HD Sales Success," *Broadcast,* February 25, 2011; "Ford Working with Best Buy to Offer Focus Electric Charging Station Sales and Support," *ENP Newswire,* January 10, 2011; Mary Ellen Lloyd, "Camp Teaches Power of Geekdom," *The Wall Street Journal,* July 11, 2007; Dean Foust, Michael Mandel, Frederick F. Jespersen, and David Henry, "The BusinessWeek 50—The Best Performers," *BusinessWeek,* March 26, 2007, p. 58; Jessica E. Vascellaro, "What's a Cellphone For? Businesses Are Finding All Sorts of New Uses for Mobile Devices," *The Wall Street Journal,* March 26, 2007, p. R5; Cade Metz, "Just How Stupid Are You? Geek Squad War Stories," *PC Magazine,* February 1, 2006; Brad Stone, "Lore of the Geek Squad," *Newsweek,* February 20, 2006, p. 44; Michelle Conlin, "Smashing the Clock," *BusinessWeek,* December 11, 2006, p. 60; "Best Buy: How to Break Out of Commodity Hell," *BusinessWeek,* March 27, 2006, p. 76; Pallavi Gogoi, "Meet Jane Geek," *BusinessWeek,* November 28, 2005, p. 94; Desiree J. Hanford, "Geek Squad Is Popular at Best Buy," *The Wall Street Journal,* December 14, 2005, p. 1; Michelle Higgins, "Getting Your Own IT Department," *The Wall Street Journal,* May 20, 2004, p. D1; and information contained on the Geek Squad website (www.geeksquad.com).

4

Ethical and Social Responsibility for Sustainable Marketing

Anheuser-Busch: Becoming the Best Beer Company in a Better World

Why would a company spend more than $980 million since 1982 trying to persuade people to use its products responsibly and tens of millions of dollars more to protect and preserve the environment? Ask Anheuser-Busch, the leading American brewer.

Alcohol Responsibility

Anheuser-Busch has been an advocate for responsible drinking for more than three decades. The company began an aggressive campaign to fight alcohol misuse and underage drinking with its landmark "Know When to Say When" campaign in 1982. In 1989, a Consumer Awareness and Education department was established within the company. This department, now called Corporate Social Responsibility (CSR), is charged with developing and implementing programs, advertising, and partnerships that promote responsible drinking; helping prevent drunk driving; and helping curb underage drinking before it starts. For example, millions of copies of the company's *Family Talk About Drinking* guidebook have been distributed free to parents and educators. The *Family Talk About Drinking* program helps parents and other adults talk with children about underage drinking; in 2011, it was extended to social media to include a dedicated Facebook Page (see www.facebook.com/ABFamilyTalk).

In 2004, the brewer began a new chapter in its awareness and education efforts with the launch of its "Responsibility Matters" campaign. This effort emphasized and implemented effective education and awareness programs that promoted responsibility and responsible behaviors. Anheuser-Busch believes these efforts have helped contribute—at least in part—to declines in drunk-driving fatalities, underage drinking, and other forms of alcohol misuse since 1982.

In 2012, Anheuser-Busch launched NationofResponsibleDrinkers.com, an online responsible drinking campaign with social media components to engage adult drinkers and raise awareness. The website asks adults to pledge their commitment to drink responsibly and then share it through Facebook to encourage friends to do the same. The pledge is threefold:

- Respect the legal drinking age.

- Enjoy responsibly and know when to say when.

- Be or use a designated driver.

Each pledge is then populated on an interactive map, showing those who have taken the pledge in their communities.

© Richard Ulreich/ZUMA Press/Newscom

In 2013, Budweiser launched its first-ever responsible drinking blimp. The airship, which carried the "Designate a Driver" message, embarked on a 17-week tour across much of the country. The blimp's flight plan coincided with major festivals, outdoor celebrations, and sporting events in tour cities. Adults could also log on to www.budblimp.com to pledge to drink responsibly and always designate a driver and then share their pledge through Facebook to encourage friends to do the same.

Anheuser-Busch also implements programs to help prevent underage drinking by providing retailers with tools to properly check IDs and help prevent sales to minors. The company also helps parents start and continue conversations about alcohol with their children; supports law enforcement in upholding the law; and, through a variety of community speakers, assists schools in building self-esteem among teens.

Environmental Preservation

Anheuser-Busch is committed to brewing the highest quality beers, improving its environmental performance, and making a positive impact in communities across the country. The company focuses environmental efforts both inside and outside its breweries on the key issues of water, energy, and recycling.

Water is a key ingredient in beer, and Anheuser-Busch strives to protect this natural resource. In 2013, the company reported that its breweries had reduced water use by 40 percent over the prior five years and had a 99.6 percent recycling rate. In fact, 130 of its operations worldwide are zero-waste. Anheuser-Busch has been a leading recycler of aluminum cans for more than 30 years, recycling nearly 15 billion cans annually. Other items, such as grain, beechwood chips, plastic, cardboard, glass, and metals, also are being reduced, reused, and recycled by the company. In fact, from 2009 to 2012, Anheuser-Busch reduced its packaging materials by nearly 73,000 tons.

Nearly one out of every six beers made by Anheuser-Busch is brewed with renewable fuels, including biogas and landfill gas. The company is one of the world's largest operators of the Bio-Energy Recovery System (BERS), a method of turning the nutrients in wastewater from the brewing process into renewable biogas.

Anheuser-Busch clearly acts on what it views as an ethical obligation to its customers and the general public with its alcohol awareness and education programs and community support. At the same time, the company's efforts to protect the natural environment and improve societal well-being reflect its broader social responsibility.[1]

NATURE AND SIGNIFICANCE OF MARKETING ETHICS

 LO 4-1 Explain the differences between legal and ethical behavior in marketing.

Ethics are the moral principles and values that govern the actions and decisions of an individual or group.[2] They serve as guidelines on how to act rightly and justly when faced with moral dilemmas.

An Ethical/Legal Framework for Marketing

A good starting point for understanding the nature and significance of ethics is the distinction between the legality and the ethicality of marketing decisions. Figure 4–1 helps visualize the relationship between laws and ethics.[3] Whereas ethics deal with personal moral principles and values, **laws** are society's values and standards that are enforceable in the courts. This distinction can sometimes lead to the rationalization that if a behavior is within reasonable ethical and legal limits, then it is not really illegal or unethical. When a recent survey asked the question, "Is it OK to get around the law if you don't actually break it?" about 61 percent of businesspeople who took part responded "yes."[4] How would you answer this question?

Judgment plays a large role in numerous situations in defining ethical and legal boundaries. Consider the following situations. After reading each, assign it to the cell in Figure 4–1 that you think best fits the situation along the ethical–legal continuum.[5]

1. More than 70 percent of the physicians in the Maricopa County (Arizona) Medical Society agreed to establish a maximum fee schedule for health services to curb rising medical costs. All physicians were required to adhere to this schedule as a condition for membership in the society. The U.S. Supreme Court ruled that this agreement to set prices violated the Sherman Act and represented price fixing, which is illegal. Was the society's action ethical?

2. A company in California sells a computer program to auto dealers showing that car buyers should finance their purchase rather than pay cash. The program omits the effect of income taxes and misstates the interest earned on savings over the loan period. The finance option always provides a net benefit over the cash option. Company employees agree that the program does mislead buyers, but they say the company will "provide what [car dealers] want as long as it is not against the law." Is this practice ethical?

3. China is the world's largest tobacco-producing country and has 300 million smokers. Approximately 1 million Chinese die annually from smoking-related

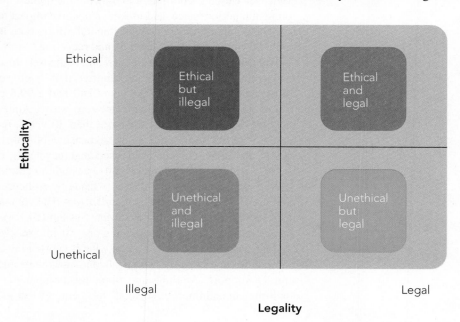

FIGURE 4–1

Four ways to classify marketing decisions according to ethical and legal relationships.

illnesses. This figure is expected to rise to more than 3 million by 2050. China legally restricts tobacco imports. U.S. trade negotiators advocate free trade, thus allowing U.S. tobacco companies to market their products in China. Is the Chinese trade position ethical?

4. A group of college students recorded movies at a local theater and then uploaded the movies to the Internet. Federal statutes state that the unauthorized reproduction, distribution, or exhibition of copyrighted motion pictures is illegal. The students then directed friends and family to a peer-to-peer Internet network that allowed them to download the movies for free, which they did. Is the students' behavior ethical? Is the behavior of their friends and family ethical?

Did these situations fit neatly into Figure 4–1 as clearly ethical and legal or unethical and illegal? Probably not. As you read further in this chapter, you will be asked to consider other ethical dilemmas faced by marketers and consumers.

Critical Perceptions of Ethical Behavior

There has been a public outcry about the ethical practices of businesspeople.[6] Public opinion surveys show that 17 percent of U.S. adults rate the ethical standards of business executives as "very high" or "high." Advertising practitioners, telemarketers, and car salespeople are thought to be among the least ethical occupations. Surveys of corporate employees generally confirm this public perception. When asked if they are aware of ethical misconduct in their companies, 41 percent say "yes."

There are at least four possible reasons the state of perceived ethical business conduct is at its present level. First, there is increased pressure on businesspeople to make decisions in a society characterized by diverse value systems. Second, there is a growing tendency for business decisions to be judged publicly by groups with different values and interests. Third, the public's expectations of ethical business behavior have increased. Finally, and most disturbing, ethical business conduct may have declined.

learning review >>

4-1. What are ethics?

4-2. What are four possible reasons for the present state of ethical conduct in the United States?

FOUR FACTORS AFFECT ETHICAL MARKETING BEHAVIOR

LO 4-2 Identify factors that influence ethical and unethical marketing decisions.

Researchers have identified four factors that influence ethical marketing behavior.[7] Figure 4–2 presents a framework that shows these factors and their relationships.

Societal Culture and Norms

As described in Chapter 3, *culture* refers to the set of values, ideas, and attitudes that are learned and shared among the members of a group. Culture also serves as a socializing force that dictates what is morally right and just. This means that moral standards are relative to particular societies.[8] These standards often reflect the laws and regulations that affect social and economic behavior, which can create ethical dilemmas. Companies that compete in the global marketplace recognize this fact. Consider UPS, the world's largest package delivery company operating in more than 200 countries and territories worldwide.[9] According to the company's global compliance and ethics coordinator, "Although languages and cultures around the world may be different, we do not change our ethical standards at UPS. Our ethics program is global in nature." Not surprisingly, UPS is consistently ranked among the world's most ethical companies.

FIGURE 4–2
A framework for
understanding ethical
behavior. Each of these
influences has an effect on
ethical marketing behavior,
as described in the text.

Societal values and attitudes also affect ethical and legal relationships among individuals, groups, and business institutions and organizations. Consider the copying of another's copyright, trademark, or patent. These are viewed as intellectual property. Unauthorized use, reproduction, or distribution of intellectual property is illegal in the United States and most countries and can result in fines and prison terms for perpetrators. The owners of intellectual property also lose. For example, annual worldwide lost sales from the theft of intellectual property amount to $7 billion in the music industry, $20.5 billion in the movie industry, and $63 billion in the software industry.[10] Lost sales, in turn, result in lost jobs, royalties, wages, and tax revenue.

But what about downloading copyrighted music, movies, and software over the Internet or from peer-to-peer file-sharing programs without paying the owner of this property? Is this an ethical or unethical act? It depends on who you ask. Surveys of the U.S. public indicate that the majority consider these acts unethical. However, only a third of U.S. college students say these acts are unethical.[11]

Business Culture and Industry Practices

Societal culture provides a foundation for understanding moral behavior in business activities. *Business cultures* "comprise the effective rules of the game, the boundaries between competitive and unethical behavior, [and] the codes of conduct in business dealings."[12] Consumers have witnessed instances where business cultures in the financial (insider trading), insurance (deceptive sales practices), and defense (bribery) industries went awry. Business culture affects ethical conduct both in the exchange relationship between sellers and buyers and in the competitive behavior among sellers.

Ethics of Exchange   The exchange process is central to the marketing concept. Ethical exchanges between sellers and buyers should result in both parties being better off after a transaction.

Before the 1960s, the legal concept of **caveat emptor**—let the buyer beware—was pervasive in the American business culture. In 1962, President John F. Kennedy outlined a **Consumer Bill of Rights** that codified the ethics of exchange between buyers and sellers. These were the right (1) to safety, (2) to be informed, (3) to choose, and (4) to be heard. Consumers expect and often demand that these rights be protected, as have American businesses.

The *right to safety* manifests itself in industry and federal safety standards for most products sold in the United States. In fact, the U.S. Consumer Product Safety Commission routinely monitors the safety of 15,000 consumer products. However, even the most vigilant efforts to ensure safe products cannot foresee every possibility. Personal claims and property damage from consumer product safety incidents cost companies

The Federal Trade Commission plays an active role in educating consumers and businesses about the importance of personal information privacy on the Internet. FTC initiatives, including proposals concerning children's online privacy, are detailed on its website.

© Lisa F. Young/iStock/Getty Images

Federal Trade Commission
www.ftc.gov

more than $700 billion annually. Consider the case of batteries used in laptop and notebook computers. Dell Inc. learned that the lithium-ion batteries in its notebook computers, made by Sony Energy Devices Corporation of Japan, posed a fire hazard to consumers. The company recalled 2.7 million batteries and gave consumers a replacement before any personal injuries resulted.[13]

The *right to be informed* means that marketers have an obligation to give consumers complete and accurate information about products and services. This right also applies to the solicitation of personal information over the Internet and its subsequent use by marketers.[14] An FTC survey of websites indicated that 92 percent collect personal information such as consumer e-mail addresses, telephone numbers, shopping habits, and financial data. Yet, only two-thirds of websites inform consumers of what is done with this information once obtained. The FTC wants more than posted privacy notices that merely inform consumers of a company's data-use policy, which critics say are often vague, confusing, or too legalistic to be understood. This view is shared by two-thirds of consumers who worry about protecting their personal information online. The consumer right to be informed has spawned much federal legislation, such as the *Children's Online Privacy Protection Act* (1998) and self-regulation initiatives restricting disclosure of personal information.

Relating to the *right to choose*, today many supermarket chains demand "slotting allowances" from manufacturers, in the form of cash or free goods, to stock new products.[15] This practice could limit the number of new products available to consumers and interfere with their right to choose. One critic of this practice remarked, "If we had had slotting allowances a few years ago, we might not have had granola, herbal tea, or yogurt."

Finally, the *right to be heard* means that consumers should have access to public-policy makers regarding complaints about products and services. This right is illustrated in limitations put on telemarketing practices. The FTC established the Do Not Call Registry in 2003 for consumers who do not want to receive unsolicited telemarketing calls. Today, over 220 million U.S. telephone numbers are listed in the registry, which is managed by the FTC. A telemarketer can be fined up to $16,000 for each call made to a telephone number posted on the registry.

Ethics of Competition   Business culture also affects ethical behavior in competition. Two kinds of unethical behavior are most common: (1) economic espionage and (2) bribery.

Economic espionage is the clandestine collection of trade secrets or proprietary information about a company's competitors. This practice is illegal and unethical and carries serious criminal penalties for the offending individual or business. Espionage activities include illegal trespassing, theft, fraud, misrepresentation, wiretapping, the search of a competitor's trash, and violations of written and implicit employment agreements with noncompete clauses. More than half of the largest firms in the United States have uncovered espionage in some form, costing them $300 billion annually in lost sales.[16]

Economic espionage is most prevalent in high-technology industries, such as electronics, specialty chemicals, industrial equipment, aerospace, and pharmaceuticals, where technical know-how and trade secrets separate industry leaders from followers. But espionage can occur anywhere—even in the soft drink industry! Read the Making Responsible Decisions box to learn how Pepsi-Cola responded to an offer to obtain confidential information about its archrival's marketing plans.[17]

The second form of unethical competitive behavior is giving and receiving bribes and kickbacks. Bribes and kickbacks are often disguised as gifts, consultant fees, and favors. This practice is more common in business-to-business and government marketing than in consumer marketing.

Making **Responsible Decisions**

Corporate Conscience in the Cola War

Suppose you are a senior executive at Pepsi-Cola and a Coca-Cola employee offers to sell you the marketing plan and sample for a new Coke product at a modest price. Would you buy it knowing Pepsi-Cola could gain a significant competitive edge in the cola war?

When this question was posed in an online survey of marketing and advertising executives, 67 percent said they would buy the plan and product sample if there were no repercussions. What did Pepsi-Cola do when this offer actually occurred? The company immediately contacted Coca-Cola, which contacted the FBI. An undercover FBI agent paid the employee $30,000 in cash stuffed in a Girl Scout cookie box as a down payment and later arrested the employee and accomplices. When asked about the

© Cliff Tew

incident, a Pepsi-Cola spokesperson said: "We only did what any responsible company would do. Competition must be tough, but must always be fair and legal."

Why did the 33 percent of respondents in the online survey say they would decline the offer? Most said they would prefer competing ethically so they could sleep at night. According to a senior advertising agency executive who would decline the offer: "Repercussions go beyond potential espionage charges. As long as we have a conscience, there are repercussions."

So what happened to the Coca-Cola employee and her accomplices? She was sentenced to eight years in prison and ordered to pay $40,000 in restitution. Her accomplices were each sentenced to five years in prison.

In general, bribery is most evident in industries experiencing intense competition and in countries in the earlier stages of economic development. According to a United Nations study, 15 percent of all companies in industrialized countries have to pay bribes to win or retain business. In Asia, this figure is 40 percent. In Eastern Europe, 60 percent of all companies must pay bribes to do business. A recent poll of senior executives engaged in global marketing revealed that Russia was the most likely country to engage in bribery to win or retain business. The Netherlands, Switzerland, and Belgium were the least likely.[18] Bribery on a worldwide scale is monitored by Transparency International. Visit its website described in the Marketing Insights About Me box to view the most recent country rankings on its Bribe Payers Index.

The prevalence of economic espionage and bribery in international marketing has prompted laws to curb these practices. Two significant laws, the *Economic Espionage Act* (1996) and the *Foreign Corrupt Practices Act* (1977), address these practices in the United States. Both are detailed in Chapter 7.

Corporate Culture and Expectations

A third influence on ethical practices is corporate culture. *Corporate culture* is the set of values, ideas, and attitudes that is learned and shared among the members of an organization. The culture of a company demonstrates itself in the dress ("We don't wear ties"), sayings ("The IBM Way"), and manner of work (team efforts) of employees. Culture is also apparent in the expectations for ethical behavior present in formal codes of ethics and the ethical actions of top management and co-workers.

Codes of Ethics   A **code of ethics** is a formal statement of ethical principles and rules of conduct. It is estimated that 86 percent of U.S. companies have some sort of ethics code and one of every four large companies has corporate ethics officers. Ethics

Marketing **Insights About Me**

Is Commercial Bribery More or Less Common in My Country?

Bribery as a means to win and retain business varies widely by country. Transparency International periodically polls employees of multinational firms and institutions and political analysts and ranks countries on the basis of their perceived level of bribery to win or retain business. To obtain the most recent ranking, visit the Transparency International website at www. transparency.org, click the "what we do" tab, and click "Bribe Payers Index."

Scroll the Bribe Payers Index to see where the United States stands in the worldwide rankings. How does the United States compare in relation to its neighbors, Canada and Mexico? Any surprises? Which country

listed in the index has the highest ranking and which has the lowest ranking?

© webphotographeer/E+/Getty Images

What does 3M's Scotchgard have to do with ethics, social responsibility, and a $200 million loss in annual sales? Read the text to find out.

© Mike Hruby

codes typically address contributions to government officials and political parties, customer and supplier relations, conflicts of interest, and accurate recordkeeping.

At United Technologies, for example, 500 business practices officers distribute the company's ethics code, translated into 37 languages, to about 210,000 employees who work for this defense and engineering giant in some 180 countries. United Technologies recently dismissed 330 employees for violations related to its code of ethics.[19]

However, an ethics code is rarely enough to ensure ethical behavior. Coca-Cola has an ethics code and emphasizes that its employees be ethical in their behavior. But that did not stop some Coca-Cola employees from rigging the results of a test market for a frozen soft drink to win Burger King's business. Coca-Cola subsequently agreed to pay Burger King and its operators more than $20 million to settle the matter.[20]

Lack of specificity is a major reason for the violation of ethics codes. Employees must often judge whether a specific behavior is unethical. The American Marketing Association has addressed this issue by providing a detailed statement of ethics, which all members agree to follow. This statement is shown in Figure 4–3.

Ethical Behavior of Top Management and Co-Workers A second reason for violating ethics codes rests in the perceived behavior of top management and co-workers.[21] Observing peers and top management and gauging responses to unethical behavior play an important role in individual actions. A study of business executives reported that 63 percent had witnessed ethically troubling behavior. About 21 percent of those who reported unethical behavior were penalized, through either outright punishment or a diminished status in the company.[22] Clearly, ethical dilemmas can bring personal and professional conflict. For this reason, states have enacted laws designed to protect **whistle-blowers**, employees who report unethical or illegal actions of their employers.

Your Personal Moral Philosophy and Ethical Behavior

Ultimately, ethical choices are based on the personal moral philosophy of the decision maker. Moral philosophy is learned through the process of socialization with friends and family and by formal education. It is also influenced by the societal, business, and corporate culture in which a person finds him- or herself. Two prominent personal moral philosophies have direct bearing on marketing practice: (1) moral idealism and (2) utilitarianism.

Moral Idealism **Moral idealism** is a personal moral philosophy that considers certain individual rights or duties as universal, regardless of the outcome. This philosophy exists in the Consumer Bill of Rights and is favored by moral philosophers

FIGURE 4–3

American Marketing Association Statement of Ethics

American Marketing Association

www.marketingpower.com

and consumer interest groups. For example, the right to know applies to probable defects in an automobile that relate to safety.

This philosophy also applies to ethical duties. A fundamental ethical duty is to do no harm. Adherence to this duty prompted the recent decision by 3M executives to phase out production of a chemical 3M had manufactured for nearly 40 years. The substance, used in far-ranging products from pet food bags, candy wrappers, carpeting, and 3M's popular Scotchgard fabric protector, had no known harmful health or environmental effect. However, the company discovered that the chemical appeared in minuscule amounts in humans and animals around the world and accumulated in tissue. Believing that the substance could be possibly harmful in large doses, 3M voluntarily stopped its production, resulting in a $200 million loss in annual sales.[23]

Utilitarianism   An alternative perspective on moral philosophy is **utilitarianism**, which is a personal moral philosophy that focuses on "the greatest good for the greatest number" by assessing the costs and benefits of the consequences of ethical behavior. If the benefits exceed the costs, then the behavior is ethical. If not, then the behavior is unethical. This philosophy underlies the economic tenets of capitalism and, not surprisingly, is embraced by many business executives and students.[24]

FIGURE 4–3
(Continued)

- We will recognize our special commitments to economically vulnerable segments of the market such as children, the elderly, and others who may be substantially disadvantaged.

Fairness—to try to balance justly the needs of the buyer with the interests of the seller.

- We will represent our products in a clear way in selling, advertising, and other forms of communication; this includes the avoidance of false, misleading, and deceptive promotion.
- We will reject manipulations and sales tactics that harm customer trust.
- We will not engage in price fixing, predatory pricing, price gouging, or "bait-and-switch" tactics.
- We will not knowingly participate in material conflicts of interest.

Respect—to acknowledge the basic human dignity of all stakeholders.

- We will value individual differences even as we avoid stereotyping customers or depicting demographic groups (e.g., gender, race, sexual orientation) in a negative or dehumanizing way in our promotions.
- We will listen to the needs of our customers and make all reasonable efforts to monitor and improve their satisfaction on an ongoing basis.
- We will make a special effort to understand suppliers, intermediaries, and distributors from other cultures.
- We will appropriately acknowledge the contributions of others, such as consultants, employees, and co-workers, to our marketing endeavors.

Openness—to create transparency in our marketing operations.

- We will strive to communicate clearly with all our constituencies.
- We will accept constructive criticism from our customers and other stakeholders.
- We will explain significant product or service risks, component substitutions, or other foreseeable eventualities that could affect customers or their perception of the purchase decision.
- We will fully disclose list prices and terms of financing as well as available price deals and adjustments.

Citizenship—to fulfill the economic, legal, philanthropic and societal responsibilities that serve stakeholders in a strategic manner.

- We will strive to protect the natural environment in the execution of marketing campaigns.
- We will give back to the community through volunteerism and charitable donations.
- We will work to contribute to the overall betterment of marketing and its reputation.
- We will encourage supply chain members to ensure that trade is fair for all participants, including producers in developing countries.

Implementation

Finally, we recognize that every industry sector and marketing subdiscipline (e.g., marketing research, e-commerce, direct selling, direct marketing, advertising) has its own specific ethical issues that require policies and commentary. An array of such codes can be accessed through links on the AMA website. We encourage all such groups to develop and/or refine their industry and discipline-specific codes of ethics to supplement these general norms and values.

Utilitarian reasoning was apparent in Nestlé Food Corporation's marketing of Good Start infant formula, sold by Nestlé's Carnation Company. The formula, promoted as hypoallergenic, was designed to prevent or reduce colic caused by an infant's allergic reaction to cow's milk, a condition suffered by 2 percent of babies. However, some severely milk-allergic infants experienced serious side effects after using Good Start, including convulsive vomiting. Physicians and parents charged that the hypoallergenic claim was misleading, and the Food and Drug Administration investigated the matter.

A Nestlé vice president defended the claim and product, saying, "I don't understand why our product should work in 100 percent of cases. If we wanted to say it was foolproof, we would have called it allergy-free. We call it hypo-, or less, allergenic."[25] Nestlé officials seemingly believed that most allergic infants would benefit from Good Start—"the greatest good for the greatest number." But, other views prevailed. The claim was dropped from the product label.

An appreciation for the nature of ethics, coupled with a basic understanding of why unethical behavior arises, alerts a person to when and how ethical issues arise in marketing decisions. Ultimately, ethical behavior rests with the individual, but the consequences affect many.

4-3. What rights are included in the Consumer Bill of Rights?

4-4. Economic espionage includes what kinds of activities?

4-5. What is meant by moral idealism?

UNDERSTANDING SOCIAL RESPONSIBILITY FOR SUSTAINABLE MARKETING

LO 4-3 Describe the different concepts of social responsibility.

As we saw in Chapter 1, the societal marketing concept stresses marketing's social responsibility by not only satisfying the needs of consumers but also providing for society's welfare. **Social responsibility** means that organizations are part of a larger society and are accountable to that society for their actions. Like ethics, agreement on the nature and scope of social responsibility is often difficult to come by, given the diversity of values present in different societal, business, and corporate cultures.

Three Concepts of Social Responsibility

Figure 4–4 shows three concepts of social responsibility: (1) profit responsibility, (2) stakeholder responsibility, and (3) societal responsibility.

Profit Responsibility *Profit responsibility* holds that companies have a simple duty: to maximize profits for their owners or stockholders. This view is expressed by Nobel Laureate Milton Friedman, who said, "There is one and only one social responsibility of business—to use its resources and engage in activities designed to increase

FIGURE 4–4

Three concepts of social responsibility. Each concept of social responsibility relates to particular constituencies. There is often conflict in satisfying all three constituencies at the same time.

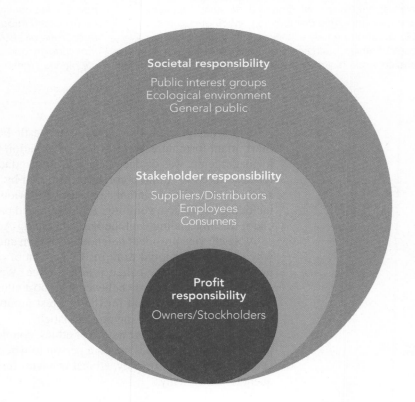

Video 4-2
Häagen-Dazs
kerin.tv/13e/v4-2

its profits so long as it stays within the rules of the game, which is to say, engages in open and free competition without deception or fraud."[26]

Genzyme, the maker of Cerdelga, a drug that treats a genetic illness called Gaucher's disease that affects 10,000 people worldwide, has been criticized for apparently adopting this view in its pricing practices. Genzyme charges up to $300,000 for a year's worth of Cerdelga. A Genzyme spokesperson responded saying the company spends millions of dollars annually to manufacture Cerdelga and freely gives the drug to patients without insurance. Also, the company invested considerable dollars in research over several years to develop Cerdelga, and the drug's profits are reinvested in ongoing R&D programs.[27]

Stakeholder Responsibility   Criticism of the profit view has led to a broader concept of social responsibility. *Stakeholder responsibility* focuses on the obligations an organization has to those who can affect achievement of its objectives. These constituencies include consumers, employees, suppliers, and distributors. Source Perrier S.A., the supplier of Perrier bottled water, exercised this responsibility when it recalled 160 million bottles of water in 120 countries after traces of a toxic chemical were found in 13 bottles. The recall cost the company $35 million, as well as the profit from $40 million in lost sales. Even though the chemical level was not harmful to humans, Source Perrier's president believed he acted in the best interests of the firm's consumers, distributors, and employees by removing "the least doubt, as minimal as it might be, to weigh on the image of the quality and purity of our product"—which it did.[28]

Failure to consider a company's broader constituencies can have negative consequences. For example, Toyota Motor Corporation executives were widely criticized for how they responded to complaints about the safety of selected Toyota brands. These cars had been linked to sticky gas pedals, which can lead to sudden acceleration problems. The company recalled over 9 million cars worldwide under pressure from the National Highway Traffic Safety Administration. After the recall, Toyota sales fell, which affected Toyota employees, suppliers, shareholders, and distributors.[29]

Societal Responsibility   An even broader concept of social responsibility has emerged in recent years. *Societal responsibility* refers to obligations that organizations have (1) to the preservation of the ecological environment and (2) to the general public. Emphasis is placed on the **triple-bottom line**—recognition of the need for organizations to improve the state of people, the planet, and profit simultaneously if they are to achieve sustainable, long-term growth.[30] Marketers have embraced societal responsibility through **sustainable marketing**, which seeks to meet today's (global) economic, environmental, and social needs without compromising the opportunity for future generations to meet theirs. Green marketing, cause marketing, social audits, and sustainable development reflect this recognition.

Green marketing—marketing efforts to produce, promote, and reclaim environmentally sensitive products—takes many forms.[31] At 3M, product development opportunities emanate both from consumer research and its "Pollution Prevention Pays" (3P) program. This program solicits employee suggestions on how to reduce pollution and recycle materials. Since 1975, this program has generated over 11,000 3P projects that have eliminated more than 4 billion pounds of air, water, and solid-waste pollutants from the environment. Levi Strauss & Co. uses 8 recycled plastic bottles in each pair of Waste<Less jeans, which are composed of at least 20 percent recycled plastic. This practice has eliminated millions of discarded plastic bottles from landfills and reduced the water consumed in the manufacturing process.

Walmart has instituted buying practices that encourage its suppliers to use containers and packaging made from corn, not oil-based, resins. The company expects this initiative will save 800,000 barrels of oil annually. These voluntary responses to environmental issues have been implemented with little or no additional cost to consumers and have resulted in cost savings to companies.

Will Consumers Switch Brands for a Cause? Yes, If . . .

American Express Company pioneered cause marketing when it sponsored the renovation of the Statue of Liberty. This effort raised $1.7 million for the renovation, increased card usage among cardholders, and attracted new cardholders. In 2001, U.S. companies raised more than $5 billion for causes they champion. It is estimated that cause marketing raised over $12 billion in 2013.

Cause marketing benefits companies as well as causes. Research indicates that 85 percent of U.S. consumers say they have a more favorable opinion of companies that support causes they care about. Also, 80 percent of consumers say they will switch to a brand or retailer that supports a good cause if the price and quality of brands or retailers are equal. In short, cause marketing may be a valued point of difference for brands and companies, all other things being equal.

For more information, including news, links, and case studies, visit the Cause Marketing Forum website at www.causemarketingforum.com.

© Joe Sohm/Visions of America/Photodisc/Getty Images

A cause marketing pioneer for more than three decades, Procter & Gamble focuses on supporting disadvantaged youth and disaster relief. A successful brand campaign in partnership with UNICEF includes the Pampers 1 Pack = 1 Vaccine initiative, protecting 300 million women and their babies against maternal and neonatal tetanus since 2006.

Courtesy of Procter & Gamble Babycare Western Europe and Unicef/United Nations Children's Fund

A global undertaking to further green marketing efforts is the *ISO 14000* initiative developed by the International Standards Organization (ISO) in Geneva, Switzerland. *ISO 14000* consists of worldwide standards for environmental quality and green marketing practices. These standards are embraced by 158 countries, including the United States. More than 260,000 companies have met *ISO 14000* standards for environmental quality and green marketing.[32]

Sustainable marketing efforts on behalf of the general public are becoming more common. A formal practice is **cause marketing**, which occurs when the charitable contributions of a firm are tied directly to the customer revenues produced through the promotion of one of its products.[33] This definition distinguishes cause marketing from a firm's standard charitable contributions, which are outright donations. For example, when consumers purchase selected company products, Procter & Gamble directs part of that revenue toward programs that support disadvantaged youth and provide disaster relief. MasterCard International links usage of its card with fund-raising for institutions that combat cancer, heart disease, child abuse, drug abuse, and muscular dystrophy. Häagen-Dazs supports the "help the honey bees" campaign, Barnes & Noble promotes literacy, and Coca-Cola sponsors local Boys and Girls Clubs. Avon Products, Inc. focuses on different issues in different countries, including breast cancer, domestic violence, and disaster relief, among many others.

Cause marketing programs incorporate all three concepts of social responsibility by addressing public concerns and satisfying customer needs. They can also enhance corporate sales and profits as described in the Marketing Matters box.[34]

The Social Audit and Sustainable Development: Doing Well by Doing Good

Converting socially responsible ideas into actions involves careful planning and monitoring of programs. Many companies develop, implement, and evaluate their social responsibility efforts by means of a **social audit**, which is a systematic assessment of a firm's objectives, strategies, and performance in terms of social responsibility. Frequently, marketing and social responsibility programs are integrated. Consider McDonald's. The company's concern for the needs of families with children who are chronically or terminally ill was converted into over 337 Ronald McDonald Houses around the world. These facilities, located near treatment centers, enable families to stay together during the child's care. In this case, McDonald's is contributing to the welfare of a portion of its target market.

A social audit consists of five steps:[35]

1. Recognition of a firm's social expectations and the rationale for engaging in social responsibility endeavors.
2. Identification of social responsibility causes or programs consistent with the company's mission.
3. Determination of organizational objectives and priorities for programs and activities it will undertake.
4. Specification of the type and amount of resources necessary to achieve social responsibility objectives.
5. Evaluation of social responsibility programs and activities undertaken and assessment of future involvement.

Corporate attention to social audits will increase as companies seek to achieve sustainable development and improve the quality of life in a global economy. **Sustainable development** involves conducting business in a way that protects the natural environment while making economic progress.

Ecologically responsible initiatives such as green marketing represent one such initiative. Recent initiatives related to working conditions at offshore manufacturing sites that produce goods for U.S. companies focus on quality-of-life issues. Public opinion surveys show that 90 percent of U.S. citizens are concerned about working conditions under which products are made in Asia and Latin America. Companies such as Reebok, Nike, Liz Claiborne, Levi Strauss, and Mattel have responded by

Marketing and social responsibility programs are often integrated, as is the case with McDonald's.

© Michael Holahan/ZUMA Press/ Newscom

imposing codes of conduct to reduce unsafe, harsh, or abusive working conditions at offshore manufacturing facilities.[36] Still, poor working conditions exist. For example, over 1,000 garment workers in Bangladesh died when their factory collapsed in 2013.

Companies that evidence sustainable marketing have been rewarded for their efforts. Research has shown that these companies (1) benefit from favorable word of mouth among consumers and (2) typically outperform less responsible companies in terms of financial performance.[37]

Turning the Table: Consumer Ethics and Social Responsibility

LO 4-4 Recognize unethical and socially irresponsible consumer behavior.

Consumers also have an obligation to act ethically and responsibly in the exchange process and in the use and disposition of products. Unfortunately, consumer behavior is spotty on both counts.

Unethical practices of consumers are a serious concern to marketers.[38] These practices include filing warranty claims after the claim period; misredeeming coupons; making fraudulent returns of merchandise; providing inaccurate information on credit applications; buying counterfeit products; pirating music, movies, and software from the Internet; and submitting phony insurance claims.

The cost to marketers of such unethical behavior in lost sales and prevention expenses is huge. For example, consumers who redeem coupons for unpurchased products or use coupons for other products cost manufacturers $1 billion each year. The willing purchase of counterfeit products by consumers—from phony designer watches, handbags, and sunglasses to automobile parts—costs companies $500 to $700 billion each year. Fraudulent automobile insurance claims cost insurance companies more than $10 billion annually. In addition, retailers lose about $112 billion yearly from shoplifting and $18 billion annually from fraudulent returns of merchandise. Consumers also act unethically toward each other. According to the FBI, consumer complaints about online auction fraud, in which consumers misrepresent their goods to others, outnumber all other reports of online crime.

Research on unethical consumer behavior indicates that these acts are rarely motivated by economic need. This behavior appears to be influenced by (1) a belief that a consumer can get away with the act and it is worth doing and (2) the rationalization that the act is justified or driven by forces outside the individual—"everybody does it." These reasons were vividly expressed by a 24-year-old who pirated a movie and was sentenced to six months of house arrest, three years of probation, and a $7,000 fine. He said, "I didn't like paying for movies," and added, "so many people do it, you never think you're going to get caught."[39]

Consumer purchase, use, and disposition of environmentally sensitive products relate to consumer social responsibility. Research indicates that consumers are sensitive to ecological issues.[40] For example, a recent survey of U.S. consumers indicated that 50 percent were personally willing to change their lifestyle to improve the environment. However, only 28 percent could identify personal changes in their own shopping or living habits over the past five years to illustrate their supposed commitment. Related research shows that consumers (1) may be unwilling to sacrifice convenience and pay higher prices to protect the environment and (2) lack the knowledge to make informed decisions dealing with the purchase, use, and disposition of products.

Consumer confusion over which products are environmentally safe is also apparent, given marketers' rush to offer "green products." For example, few consumers realize that nonaerosol "pump" hair sprays are the second-largest cause of air pollution, after drying paint. In California alone, 27 tons of noxious hair spray fumes are expelled every day. And some environmentally

Fake designer clothes and accessories are made by companies using trademarks stolen from legitimate companies. The purchase of counterfeit products is not illegal, but is it ethical?

National Intellectual Property Rights Coordination Center

safe claims made by marketers have been labeled *greenwashing*—the practice of making an unsubstantiated or misleading claim about the environmental benefits of a product, service, technology, or company practice.[41]

To address such claims, the FTC has drafted guidelines that describe the circumstances under which environmental claims can be made without constituting misleading information in regard to recyclable, biodegradable, and sustainable products and processes.[42] For example, an advertisement or product label touting a package as "50 percent more recycled content than before" could be misleading if the recycled content has increased from 2 percent to 3 percent.

Ultimately, marketers and consumers alike are accountable for ethical and socially responsible behavior. The 21st century will prove to be a testing period for both.

Video 4-3
**Corporate
Greenwashing**
kerin.tv/13e/v4-3

learning review »

4-6. What is meant by social responsibility?

4-7. Marketing efforts to produce, promote, and reclaim environmentally sensitive products are called _____.

4-8. What is a social audit?

LEARNING OBJECTIVES REVIEW

LO 4-1 *Explain the differences between legal and ethical behavior in marketing.*

A good starting point for understanding the nature and significance of ethics is the distinction between the legality and the ethicality of marketing decisions. Whereas ethics deal with personal moral principles and values, laws are society's values and standards that are enforceable in the courts. This distinction can lead to the rationalization that if a behavior is within reasonable ethical and legal limits, then it is not really illegal or unethical. Judgment plays a large role in defining ethical and legal boundaries in marketing. Ethical dilemmas arise when acts or situations are not clearly ethical and legal or unethical and illegal.

LO 4-2 *Identify factors that influence ethical and unethical marketing decisions.*

Four factors influence ethical marketing behavior. First, societal culture and norms serve as socializing forces that dictate what is morally right and just. Second, business culture and industry practices affect ethical conduct in both the exchange relationships between buyers and sellers and the competitive behavior among sellers. Third, corporate culture and expectations are often defined by corporate ethics codes and the ethical behavior of top management and coworkers. Finally, an individual's personal moral philosophy, such as moral idealism or utilitarianism, will dictate ethical choices. Ultimately, ethical behavior rests with the individual, but the consequences affect many.

LO 4-3 *Describe the different concepts of social responsibility.*

Social responsibility means that organizations are part of a larger society and are accountable to that society for their actions. There are three concepts of social responsibility. First,

profit responsibility holds that companies have a simple duty: to maximize profits for their owners or stockholders. Second, stakeholder responsibility focuses on the obligations an organization has to those who can affect achievement of its objectives. Those constituencies include consumers, employees, suppliers, and distributors. Finally, societal responsibility focuses on obligations that organizations have to the preservation of the ecological environment and the general public. Companies are placing greater emphasis on sustainable marketing today and are reaping the rewards of positive word of mouth from their consumers and favorable financial performance.

LO 4-4 *Recognize unethical and socially irresponsible consumer behavior.*

Consumers, like marketers, have an obligation to act ethically and responsibly in the exchange process and in the use and disposition of products. Unfortunately, consumer behavior is spotty on both counts. Unethical consumer behavior includes filing warranty claims after the claim period; buying counterfeit products; misredeeming coupons; pirating music, movies, and software from the Internet; and submitting phony insurance claims, among other behaviors. Unethical behavior is rarely motivated by economic need. Rather, research indicates that this behavior is influenced by (*a*) a belief that a consumer can get away with the act and it is worth doing and (*b*) the rationalization that such acts are justified or driven by forces outside the individual—"everybody does it." Consumer purchase, use, and disposition of environmentally sensitive products relate to consumer social responsibility. Even though consumers are sensitive to ecological issues they (*a*) may be unwilling to sacrifice convenience and pay potentially higher prices to protect the environment and (*b*) lack the knowledge to make informed decisions dealing with the purchase, use, and disposition of products.

4-1   What are ethics?

Answer: Ethics are the moral principles and values that govern the actions and decisions of an individual or group. They serve as guidelines on how to act rightly and justly when faced with moral dilemmas.

4-2   What are four possible reasons for the present state of ethical conduct in the United States?

Answer: (1) Increased pressure on businesspeople to make decisions in a society with diverse value systems. (2) A growing tendency for business decisions to be judged publicly by groups with different values and interests. (3) The public's expectations of ethical business behavior have increased. (4) Ethical business conduct may have actually declined.

4-3   What rights are included in the Consumer Bill of Rights?

Answer: The Consumer Bill of Rights (1962) codified the ethics of exchange between buyers and sellers. These are the rights to safety, to be informed, to choose, and to be heard.

4-4   Economic espionage includes what kinds of activities?

Answer: Economic espionage is the illegal and unethical clandestine collection of trade secrets or proprietary information about a company's competitors. This practice includes trespassing, theft, fraud, misrepresentation, wiretapping, searching of competitors' trash, and violations of written and implicit employment agreements with non-compete clauses.

4-5   What is meant by moral idealism?

Answer: Moral idealism is a personal moral philosophy that considers certain individual rights or duties as universal, regardless of the outcome; it is the philosophy embodied in the Consumer Bill of Rights and favored by consumer interest groups.

4-6   What is meant by social responsibility?

Answer: Social responsibility means that organizations are part of a larger society and are accountable to that society for their actions. It comprises three concepts: (1) profit responsibility—maximizing profits for the organization's owners or shareholders; (2) stakeholder responsibility—focusing on the obligations organizations have to those who can effect the achievement of its objectives; and (3) societal responsibility—focusing on the obligations organizations have to preserve the ecological environment and to the general public.

4-7   Marketing efforts to produce, promote, and reclaim environmentally sensitive products are called _____.

Answer: green marketing

4-8   What is a social audit?

Answer: A social audit is a systematic assessment of a firm's objectives, strategies, and performance in terms of social responsibility. It consists of five steps: (1) Recognition of a firm's social expectations and the rationale for engaging in social responsibility endeavors. (2) Identification of social responsibility causes or programs consistent with the company's mission. (3) Determination of organizational objectives and priorities for programs and activities it will undertake. (4) Specification of the type and amount of resources necessary to achieve social responsibility objectives. (5) Evaluation of social responsibility programs and activities undertaken and assessment of future involvement.

FOCUSING ON KEY TERMS

cause marketing p. 112
caveat emptor p. 104
code of ethics p. 106
Consumer Bill of
    Rights p. 104
economic espionage p. 105

ethics p. 102
green marketing p. 111
laws p. 102
moral idealism p. 107
social audit p. 113
social responsibility p. 110

sustainable
    development p. 113
sustainable marketing p. 111
triple-bottom line p. 111
utilitarianism p. 108
whistle-blowers p. 107

APPLYING MARKETING KNOWLEDGE

1   What concepts of moral philosophy and social responsibility are applicable to the practices of Anheuser-Busch described in the introduction to this chapter? Why?

2   Five ethical situations were presented in this chapter: (*a*) a medical society's decision to set fee schedules, (*b*) the use of a computer program by auto dealers to arrange financing, (*c*) smoking in China, (*d*) downloading movies, and (*e*) the pricing of Cerdelga for the treatment of a rare genetic illness. Where would each of these situations fit in Figure 4–1?

3   The American Marketing Association Statement of Ethics shown in Figure 4–3 details the rights and duties of parties in the marketing exchange process. How do these rights and duties compare with the Consumer Bill of Rights?

4   Compare and contrast moral idealism and utilitarianism as alternative personal moral philosophies.

5   How would you evaluate Milton Friedman's view of the social responsibility of a firm?

6   The text lists several unethical practices of consumers. Can you name others? Why do you think consumers engage in unethical conduct?

7   Cause marketing programs have become popular. Describe two such programs with which you are familiar.

BUILDING YOUR MARKETING PLAN

Consider these potential stakeholders that may be affected in some way by the marketing plan on which you are working: shareholders (if any), suppliers, employees, customers, and society in general. For each group of stakeholders:

1 Identify what, if any, ethical and social responsibility issues might arise.
2 Describe, in one or two sentences, how your marketing plan addresses each potential issue.

VIDEO CASE 4   Toyota: Building Cleaner, Greener Cars

"Toyota's mission is to become the most respected and admired car company in America," explains Jana Hartline, manager of environmental communications at Toyota. To accomplish this, Jana and her colleagues at Toyota are working toward a future where a wide range of innovative vehicles, fuel technologies, and partnerships converge to create an economically vibrant, mobile society in harmony with the environment. It's a challenge Jana finds exciting and the result is cleaner, greener cars!

Video 4-4
Toyota Video Case
kerin.tv/13e/v4-4

THE COMPANY

Kiichiro Toyoda began research on gasoline-powered engines in 1930. By 1935 he had developed passenger car prototypes, and in 1957 he introduced the "Toyopet" in the United States. The Toyopet was not successful and was discontinued. In 1965, however, the Corona was introduced, and it was followed by the Corolla in 1968. The Corolla went on to become the best-selling passenger car in the world, with 27 million purchased in more than 140 countries!

The popularity of Toyota's automobiles continued to grow in the United States and in 1975 it surpassed Volkswagen to become the number one import brand. In 1998 Toyota launched its first full-sized pickup, the Toyota Tundra. Toyota also expanded its product line by adding the Lexus brand, which became known for its exceptional quality and customer service. By 2000, Lexus was one of the best-selling luxury brands in the United States, competing with both Mercedes-Benz and BMW. Toyota also introduced the Scion brand of moderately priced vehicles for the youth market.

The company opened a national sales headquarters in Torrance, California, and also opened manufacturing facilities so it could produce cars in the United States. By 2012 Toyota had the capacity to build 2.2 million cars and trucks and 1.45 million engines in 15 plants across North America. Toyota's sales and distribution organization includes 1,500 Toyota, Lexus, and Scion dealers. Toyota's marketing organization has led to many memorable marketing campaigns. Some of its early taglines included "You Asked For It, You Got It!" and "Oh What a Feeling!" which included the "Toyota Jump." The Lexus tagline, "The Relentless Pursuit of Perfection," is still in use today, while Toyota's ads now exclaim, "Let's Go Places."

Today, Toyota is the world's largest automobile manufacturer. The company is ranked the tenth largest corporation by *Fortune* magazine. The company's core principle is "to contribute to society and the economy by producing high-quality products and services." Its success is often attributed to a business philosophy referred to as "The Toyota Way."

THE TOYOTA WAY

The Toyota Way is a business philosophy used to (1) improve processes and products, (2) build trust, and (3) empower individuals and teams. There are two values that act as pillars of The Toyota Way. They are continuous improvement and respect for people. These values are evident in five business practices:

- *Challenge*: To build a long-term vision and meet challenges with courage and creativity.
- *Kaizen*: To continuously improve business operations, always striving for innovation and evolution.
- *Genchi Genbutsu*: To always go to the source to find the facts and make correct decisions; to build consensus and expeditiously achieve goals.
- *Respect*: To respect others and the environment, to build trust and to take responsibility.
- *Teamwork*: To stimulate personal and professional growth, maximize individual and team performance.

In fact, according to Jana Hartline, the two values are "integrated into everything that we do on a daily basis," creating "a unique corporate environment."

As the company has grown it has also sought a larger role in society. For example, Toyota created the

© Toyota

Toyota USA Foundation with a $10 million endowment and a mission to make Toyota a leading corporate citizen. The foundation supports programs focused on the environment, education, and safety that help strengthen communities. Since 1991 Toyota has contributed over $500 million to philanthropic programs in the United States. Combining The Toyota Way with its corporate philanthropy has been very successful. Toyota believes that the foundation of its success involves a constant spirit of challenge and enthusiasm for new ideas. For example, Toyota's environmental vision includes the concept of sustainable mobility.

ENVIRONMENTAL VISION AND THE PRIUS

To make its environmental vision actionable, Toyota developed a five-year Environmental Action Plan. The plan is structured around five key areas:

- Energy and Climate Change
- Recycling and Resource Management
- Air Quality
- Environmental Management
- Cooperation with Society

For each area Toyota creates goals and measurable targets based on a life-cycle view of vehicles: from design, to manufacturing, to sales and distribution, to use, and finally to how the vehicle is recycled at end-of-life. One of its top goals has been to develop advanced vehicle technologies to complement traditional automobile technologies. Ed LaRocque, national manager of vehicle marketing, describes how Toyota started one of these initiatives:

> In the early 90s Toyota developed what we called the G21 vision. The goal of the G21 plan was to bring a vehicle to market that represented a great value, and had great environmental benefits, not just in Japan but globally.

The concept was eventually introduced as the Prius, a hybrid vehicle with a gasoline engine and an electric motor combination called the Hybrid Synergy Drive. The car received an EPA-estimated mileage rating of 50 mpg. Initially the Prius was attractive to very eco-conscious consumers but met with some resistance from the press and the general population. The cars were fuel efficient, but they were not attractive. Since the first introduction, Toyota has made changes and introduced two new generations of the Prius to help it become the world's most-popular hybrid, selling more than three million of the vehicles.

Toyota's development of new technologies such as the Hybrid Synergy Drive helped it recognize the implications for the entire mobility system. A strategy for sustainable mobility affects not only new technologies and vehicles, but also new energy sources, new transportation systems, and the many partnerships of involved stakeholders. Advertising for the Prius emphasizes this point, claiming the car provides "Harmony between man, nature, and machine." In the long-term, however, this strategy will not be successful if consumers are not aware of or knowledgeable about advanced technologies. To increase awareness and knowledge Toyota specified the development of partnerships as a goal.

STRATEGIC PARTNERSHIPS

Toyota believes that partnerships with relevant organizations help increase awareness of its technologies and products. These programs are designed to educate people so they can reduce their environmental footprint. One of these programs, for example, is *Together Green*—a $20 million, five-year alliance with Audubon to fund projects, train leaders, and offer volunteer opportunities. Similarly, Toyota has partnered with the World Wildlife Fund to establish hybrid energy systems, oil recycling programs, and renewable energy outreach campaigns. The exposure from these programs is often much more effective than other communication options. Mary Nickerson, National Manager of Advanced Technology, explains: "we [have] used partnerships with the American Lung Association, with the Electric Drive Transportation Association, Environmental Media Association, and the national parks to help touch many more millions of people than we ever could have done with a traditional advertising campaign."

Toyota recently announced a grant of $5 million and 25 Toyota vehicles in support of U.S. National Parks. Parks included in this grant and other Toyota partnerships are Yellowstone National Park, Great Smoky Mountains National Park, Everglades National Park, Yosemite National Park, the Grand Canyon, the Santa Monica National Recreation Area, and the Golden Gate Bridge Foundation. The national parks partnership offers an opportunity to enhance the experiences of visitors through education and hybrid vehicle use (park employees use the donated Toyota vehicles to reduce noise and emissions in the parks).

Generally, the goal of the national parks partnership program is to make a personal connection with park visitors about Toyota's hybrid vehicles when they are in a natural setting in which they are receptive to receiving a message about sustainable mobility. The message implies important links:

"Green" Vehicles > Cleaner Air > Preservation of Parks

In addition, Toyota believes that the programs have other benefits, including:

- Strengthening Toyota's image as an environmental leader among automakers.
- Communicating a message of environmental stewardship.
- Building awareness of the Prius and other Toyota hybrids.
- Educating park visitors on the benefits of advanced vehicle technology.

Research by Toyota indicates that the program is working. A recent corporate image study indicated that among four leading automakers (Toyota, Honda, Ford, and GM), Toyota was rated highest on dimensions such as "Leader in High MPG," "Leader in Technology Development," "Environmentally Friendly Vehicles," and "Wins Environmental Awards."

THE FUTURE

Figure 1 shows the results of a survey of consumer interests and their response to the question, "Who should take the lead in addressing environmental issues?" The results suggest that in the future consumers will expect businesses to be proactive about the environment and sustainability.

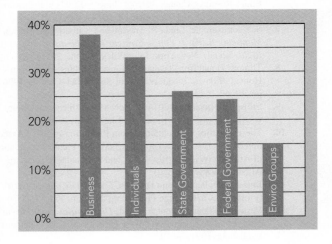

FIGURE 1

Who should take the lead in addressing environmental issues?

For Toyota, a focus on sustainability will mean considering the environmental, social, and economic consequences of the auto business and continuously working to reduce the negative and increase the positive impacts of its activities and decisions. The increasing importance of sustainability will challenge Toyota to look at these impacts from all stages of the vehicle life cycle. It will also encourage Toyota's managers to consider the opinions of many stakeholders such as consumers, regulators, local communities, and nongovernmental organizations.

The recent concerns about Toyota vehicle product quality, which led to the recall of 16 million vehicles, have hurt Toyota's reputation. In the future, all activities, including the partnership strategy and the national parks program, will determine if Toyota can become "the most respected car company in the world."[43]

Questions

1 How does Toyota's approach to social responsibility relate to the three concepts of social responsibility described in the text (profit responsibility, stakeholder responsibility, and societal responsibility)?

2 How does Toyota's view of sustainable mobility contribute to the company's overall mission?

3 Has Toyota's National Parks project been a success? What indicators suggest that the project has had an impact?

4 What future activities would you suggest for Toyota as it strives to improve its reputation?

Chapter Notes

1. www.anheuser-busch.com, downloaded March 15, 2015; "Anheuser-Busch 2014 Corporate Social Responsibility Report," www.anheuser-busch.com, downloaded March 15, 2015; and "America's Most Admired Companies," *Fortune,* March 1, 2015, p. 99.

2. For a discussion of the definition of ethics, see Patrick E. Murphy, Gene R. Laezniak, Norman E. Bowie, and Thomas A. Klein, *Ethical Marketing: Basic Ethics in Action* (Upper Saddle River, NJ: Prentice Hall, 2005).

3. Verne E. Henderson, "The Ethical Side of Enterprise," *Sloan Management Review,* Spring 1982, pp. 37–47. See also Joseph L. Badaracco Jr., *Defining Moments: When Managers Must Choose between Right and Right* (Boston: Harvard Business School Press, 1997).

4. "Honorable?" *Business 2.0,* February 2000, p. 92.

5. Andrew Martin, "The Chinese Government Is Getting Rich Selling Cigarettes," Bloombergbusinessweek.com, December 11, 2014; Roger O. Crockett, "Hauling in the Hollywood Hackers," *Businessweek,* May 15, 2006, pp. 80–82; Ray O. Werner, "Marketing and the Supreme Court in Transition, 1982–1984," *Journal of Marketing,* Summer 1985, pp. 97–105; and Jane Bryant Quinn, "Computer Program Deceives Consumers," *Dallas Morning News,* March 2, 1998, p. B3.

6. *The 2014 National Business Ethics Survey* (Washington, DC: Ethics Resource Center, 2015); "Honesty/Ethics in Professions," www.gallup.com, December 18, 2014.

7. See, for example, Linda K. Trevino and Katherine A. Nelson, *Managing Business Ethics: Straight Talk about How to Get It Right,* 5th ed. (New York: John Wiley & Sons, 2011).

8. Thomas Donaldson, "Values in Tension: Ethics Away from Home," *Harvard Business Review,* September–October 1996, pp. 48–62.

9. Ethisphere Institute, "2014 World's Most Ethical Companies," www.ethisphere.com, accessed January 3, 2015.

10. These statistics were obtained from Recording Industry Association of America (www.riaa.com), Motion Picture Association of America (www.mpaa.com), and the Business Software Alliance (www.bsa.org).

11. June Jamich Parsons and Dan Oja, *Computer Concepts 2010* (Florence, KY: Cengage Publishing, 2009), p. 171.

12. Vern Terpstra and Kenneth David, *The Cultural Environment of International Business,* 3rd ed. (Cincinnati: South-Western Publishing, 1991), p. 12.

13. Hukari Kane, "Recall Shows Battery Limits," *The Wall Street Journal,* August 18, 2006, p. A13; and "Dell Announces Recall of Notebook Computer Batteries Due to Fire Hazard," U.S. Consumer Product Safety Commission press release, August 15, 2006.

14. "Child Web Privacy Law Gets Updated," *The Wall Street Journal,* December 20, 2012, pp. B1, B2; and Timothy Muris, "Protecting Consumers' Privacy," www.ftc.gov, downloaded January 3, 2005.

15. For an extensive examination of slotting fees, see Paul N. Bloom, Gregory T. Gundlach, and Joseph P. Cannon, "Slotting Allowances and Fees: Schools of Thought and Views of Practicing Managers," *Journal of Marketing,* April 2000, pp. 92–109. Also see K. Sudhir and Vithala R. Rao, "Do Slotting Allowances Enhance Efficiency or Hinder Competition?" *Journal of Marketing Research* (May 2006), pp. 137–55.

16. Hedich Nasheri, *Economic Espionage and Industrial Spying* (Cambridge: Cambridge University Press, 2005).

17. "Coke Employee Faces Charges in Plot to Sell Secrets," *The Wall Street Journal,* July 6, 2006, p. B6; "Do the Right Thing? Not with a Rival's Inside Info," *Advertising Age,* July 17, 2006, p. 4; and "You Can't Beat the Real Thing," *Time,* July 17, 2006, pp. 10–11.

18. www.transparency.org, downloaded January 20, 2015.

19. "Interview with Michael A. Monts, UTC Vice President, Business Practices, on Ethics at UTC," United Technologies Corporation press release, July 26, 2011; and Trevino and Nelson, *Managing Business Ethics.*

20. "Coca-Cola Unit Head Resigns after Rigged Test," www.forbes.com, downloaded August 25, 2003.

21. *The 2014 National Business Ethics Survey.*

22. *The 2014 National Business Ethics Survey;* and "Critics Blow Whistle on Law," *The Wall Street Journal,* November 1, 2010, pp. B1, B11.

23. "Scotchgard Working Out Recent Stain on Its Business," www.mercurynews.com, downloaded June 22, 2003.

24. James Q. Wilson, "Adam Smith on Business Ethics," *California Management Review,* Fall 1989, pp. 57–72.

25. Alix M. Freedman, "Bad Reaction: Nestlé's Bid to Crash Baby-Formula Market in U.S. Stirs a Row," *The Wall Street Journal,* February 16, 1989, pp. A1, A6; and Alix Freedman, "Nestlé to Drop Claim on Label of Its Formula," *The Wall Street Journal,* March 13, 1989, p. B5.

26. Harvey S. James and Farhad Rassekh, "Smith, Friedman, and Self-Interest in Ethical Society," *Business Ethics Quarterly,* July 2000, pp. 659–74.

27. "FDA Approves Sanofi's Gaucher Disease Drug Cerdelga," *news.yahoo,* August 19, 2014.

28. "Perrier—Overresponding to a Crisis," in Robert F. Hartley, *Marketing Mistakes and Successes,* 10th ed. (New York: John Wiley & Sons, 2006), pp. 119–30.

29. Michael Connor, "Toyota Recall: Five Critical Lessons," www.business_ethics.com, January 31, 2010.

30. Andrew W. Savitz with Karl Weber, *The Triple Bottom Line: How Today's Best Run Companies Are Achieving Economic, Social and Environmental Success* (San Francisco, CA: Jossey-Bass, 2006).

31. "M 2012 Sustainability Report," downloaded May 25, 2015; "Levi's Has a New Color for Blue Jeans: Green," *Businessweek,* October 22–October 28, 2012, pp. 26, 28; and "Walmart 2012 Global Sustainability Report," www.walmart.com downloaded January 30, 2013.

32. *The ISO Survey of Management System Standard Classifications—2011* (Geneva, Switzerland: International Organization for Standardization, 2015).

33. For a seminal discussion on this topic, see P. Rajan Varadarajan and Anil Menon, "Cause-Related Marketing: A Coalignment of Marketing Strategy and Corporate Philanthropy," *Journal of Marketing,* July 1988, pp. 58–74.

34. "Even as Cause Marketing Grows, 83 Percent of Consumers Still Want to See More," press release, Cone LLC, September 15, 2010; and Larry Chiagouris and Ipshita Ray, "Saving the World with Cause-Related Marketing," *Marketing Management,* July–August 2007, pp. 48–51.

35. These steps are adapted from J. J. Corson and G. A. Steiner, *Measuring Business's Social Performance: The Corporate Social Audit* (New York: Committee for Economic Development, 1974). See also Risako Morinoto, John Ash, and Chris Hope, "Corporate Social Responsibility Audit: From Theory to Practice," *Journal of Business Ethics* (December 2005), pp. 315–25; and William B. Werther Jr. and David Chandler, *Strategic Corporate Social Responsibility* (Thousand Oaks, CA: Sage Publications, Inc., 2006).

36. Unmesh Kher, "Getting Smart at Being Good . . . Are Companies Better Off for It?" *Time,* January 2006, pp. A1–A37; and Pete Engardio, "Beyond the Green Corporation," *Businessweek,* January 29, 2007, pp. 50–64.

37. "Economics—Creating Environmental Capital," *The Wall Street Journal,* March 24, 2008, Section R; Remi Trudel and June Cotte, "Does Being Ethical Pay?" *The Wall Street Journal,* May 12, 2008, p. R4; and Pete Engardio, "Beyond the Green Corporation," *Businessweek,* January 29, 2007, pp. 50–64.

38. This discussion is based on Wayne D. Hoyer, Deborah J. MacInnis, and Rik Pieters, *Consumer Behavior,* 6th ed. (New York: Houghton Mifflin Company, 2013), pp. 535–37; "For Retailers, It's Many Unhappy Returns," *The Wall Street Journal,* December 27–28, 2014; "Crackdown on Counterfeiting," www.iso.org, January 8, 2014; and www.shopliftingprevention.org, downloaded January 7, 2015.

39. "A Pirate and His Penance," *Time,* January 26, 2004, p. 60; and Crockett, "Hauling in the Hollywood Hackers."

40. Jack Neff, "As More Marketers Go Green, Fewer Consumers Willing to Pay for It," *Advertising Age,* September 24, 2012, p. 6; and Jack Neff, "Has Green Stopped Giving?" *Advertising Age,* November 8, 2010, pp. 1, 19.

41. "Misleading Claims on 'Green' Labeling," *The Wall Street Journal,* October 26, 2010, p. D4.

42. Jack Neff, "FTC Green Guidelines May Leave Marketers Red-Faced," *Advertising Age,* August 23, 2010, pp. 1, 21.

43. Toyota Inc.: This case was written by Steven Hartley. Sources: "Global 500: The World's Largest Corporations," *Fortune,* July 23, 2012, p. F-1; "2010 North America Environmental Report," Toyota Motor North America, Inc., p. 1; "Toyota's Mobile Hybrid Tour and The Power of Partnership," Presentation by Mary Nickerson, National Marketing Manager, Toyota Motor sales, U.S.A., Inc.; Toyota website, http://www.toyota.com/sitemap.html, accessed July 6, 2013; "Lexus Seeks to Regain Luxury Crown with New Advertisement," *AutoShopper.com,* June 28, 2013; Tim Higgins, "Luxury Cars Are Neck and Neck in the U.S.," *Bloomberg Businessweek,* October 18, 2010, p. 26; Lucy Tobin, "Recall Tarnishes Toyota's Reputation," *The Evening Standard,* July 3, 2013, p. 45; and Mark Rechtin, "Toyota Reputation Starts to Recover," *Advertising Age,* January 24, 2011, p. 34.

Understanding Consumer Behavior

LEARNING OBJECTIVES

After reading this chapter you should be able to:

 LO 5-1 Describe the stages in the consumer purchase decision process.

 LO 5-2 Distinguish among three variations of the consumer purchase decision process: extended, limited, and routine problem solving.

 LO 5-3 Identify the major psychological influences on consumer behavior.

 LO 5-4 Identify the major sociocultural influences on consumer behavior.

Enlightened Carmakers Know What Custom(h)ers and Influenc(h)ers Value

Who makes 60 percent of new-car buying decisions? Who influences 80 percent of new-car buying decisions? Women. Yes, women.

Women are a driving force in the U.S. automobile industry. Enlightened carmakers have hired women designers, engineers, and marketing executives to better understand and satisfy this valuable car buyer and influencer. What have they learned? While car price and quality are important, women and men think and feel differently about car features and key elements of the new-car buying decision process and experience.

- *The sense of styling.* Women and men care about styling. For men, styling is more about a car's exterior lines and accents or "curb appeal." Women are more interested in interior design and finishes. Designs that fit their proportions, provide good visibility, offer ample storage space, and make for effortless parking are particularly important.

- *The need for speed.* Both sexes want speed, but for different reasons. Men think about how many seconds it takes to get from zero to 60 miles per hour. Women want to feel secure that the car has enough acceleration to outrun an 18-wheeler trying to pass them on a freeway entrance ramp.

- *The substance of safety.* Safety for men is about features that help avoid an accident, such as antilock brakes and responsive steering. For women, safety is about features that help to survive an accident. These features include passenger airbags and reinforced side panels.

- *The shopping experience.* The new-car-buying experience differs between men and women in important ways. Generally, men decide up front what car they want and set out alone to find it. By contrast, women approach it as an intelligence-gathering expedition. Referred to as *CROPing,* women shoppers look for *CR*edible *OP*inions. They actively seek information and postpone a purchase decision until all options have been evaluated. Women, more frequently than men, visit auto-buying websites, read car-comparison articles, and scan car advertisements. Still, recommendations of friends and relatives matter most to women. Women typically shop three dealerships before making a purchase decision—one more than men.

Carmakers have learned that women, more than men, dislike the car-buying experience—specifically, the experience of dealing with car salespeople. In contrast to many male car buyers, women do not typically revel in the gamesmanship of car buying. "Men get all excited about going out to buy a car and talk about how they're going to one-up the salesman and get a great deal," said Anne Fleming, president of <u>www.women-drivers.com</u>, a consumer ratings site. "I've never heard or seen any comments from women like that." In particular, women dread the price negotiations that are often involved in buying a new car. Not surprisingly, about half of women car buyers take a man with them to finalize the terms of sale.[1]

This chapter examines **consumer behavior**, the actions a person takes in purchasing and using products and services, including the mental and social processes that come before and after these actions. This chapter shows how the behavioral sciences help answer questions such as why people choose one product or brand over another, how they make these choices, and how companies use this knowledge to provide value to consumers.

© Blend Images/Getty Images

CONSUMER PURCHASE DECISION PROCESS AND EXPERIENCE

LO 5-1 Describe the stages in the consumer purchase decision process.

Behind the visible act of making a purchase lies an important decision process and consumer experience that must be investigated. The stages a buyer passes through in making choices about which products and services to buy is the **purchase decision process**. This process has the five stages shown in Figure 5–1: (1) problem recognition, (2) information search, (3) alternative evaluation, (4) purchase decision, and (5) postpurchase behavior.

Problem Recognition: Perceiving a Need

Problem recognition, the initial step in the purchase decision, is perceiving a difference between a person's ideal and actual situations big enough to trigger a decision.[2] This can be as simple as finding an empty milk carton in the refrigerator; noting, as a first-year college student, that your high school clothes are not in the style that other students are wearing; or realizing that your notebook computer may not be working properly.

In marketing, advertisements or salespeople can activate a consumer's decision process by showing the shortcomings of competing (or currently owned) products. For instance, an advertisement for a new generation smartphone could stimulate problem recognition because it emphasizes "maximum use from one device."

Information Search: Seeking Value

After recognizing a problem, a consumer begins to search for information, the next stage in the purchase decision process. First, you may scan your memory for previous experiences with products or brands.[3] This action is called *internal search.* For frequently purchased products such as shampoo and conditioner, this may be enough.

In other cases, a consumer may undertake an *external search* for information.[4] This is needed when past experience or knowledge is insufficient, the risk of making a wrong purchase decision is high, and the cost of gathering information is low. The primary sources of external information are (1) *personal sources,* such as relatives and friends whom the consumer trusts; (2) *public sources,* including various product-rating organizations such as *Consumer Reports*, government agencies, and TV "consumer programs"; and (3) *marketer-dominated sources,* such as information from sellers including advertising, company websites, salespeople, and point-of-purchase displays in stores.

Suppose you are considering buying a new smartphone. You will probably tap several of these information sources: friends and relatives, advertisements, brand and company websites, and stores carrying these phones (for demonstrations). You also might study the comparative evaluation of selected smartphones from independent rating agencies in Figure 5–2.[5]

Alternative Evaluation: Assessing Value

FIGURE 5–1

The purchase decision process consists of five stages.

The alternative evaluation stage clarifies the problem for the consumer by (1) suggesting criteria to use for the purchase, (2) yielding brand names that might meet the

Common Selection Criteria	Brand and Model Name				
	Apple iPhone 6	HTC One	LG G4	Motorola Dröid Turbo	Samsung Galaxy S6
Retail Price (with contract)	$250	$150	$200	$150	$250
Phone Display	★★★	★★★	★★★	★★★	★★★
Audio Quality	★★	★	★	★★	★★
Text Messaging	★★	★★★	★★★	★★★	★★★
Web Capability	★★★	★★★	★★★	★★★	★★★
Camera Quality	★★★	★	★★★	★★★	★★★
Battery	★★	★★★	★★★	★★★	★★★

Composite Smartphone Evaluations by Testing Organization

★★★	★★	★
Superior	Above Average	Average

FIGURE 5–2

Common consumer selection criteria for the evaluation of smartphones.

criteria, and (3) developing consumer value perceptions. Given only the information shown in Figure 5–2, which selection criteria would you use in buying a smartphone? Would you use price, phone display, audio quality, text messaging, web capability, camera image quality, battery life, or some other combination of these or other criteria?

For some of you, the information provided may be inadequate because it does not contain all the factors you might consider when evaluating smartphones. These factors are a consumer's *evaluative criteria,* which represent both the objective attributes of a brand (such as display) and the subjective ones (such as prestige) you use to compare different products and brands.[6] Firms try to identify and capitalize on both types of criteria to create the best value for the money paid by you and other consumers. These criteria are often displayed in advertisements.

Consumers often have several criteria for evaluating brands. Knowing this, companies seek to identify the most important evaluative criteria that consumers use when comparing brands. For example, among the seven criteria shown in Figure 5–2, suppose you use four in considering smartphones: (1) a retail price of $200 or less, (2) superior text messaging, and (3) superior battery life. These criteria establish the brands in your *consideration set*—the group of brands a consumer would consider acceptable from among all the brands in the product class of which he or she is aware.[7]

Your evaluative criteria result in three brands/models: the HTC One, LG G4, and the Motorola Dröid Turbo in your consideration set. If the brand alternatives are equally attractive based on your original criteria, you might expand your list of desirable features. For example, you might decide that camera and audio quality are also important and compare the alternatives based on those criteria as well.

Purchase Decision: Buying Value

Having examined the alternatives in the consideration set, you are almost ready to make a purchase decision. Two choices remain: (1) from whom to buy and (2) when to buy. For a product like a smartphone, the information search process probably involved visiting retail stores, seeing different brands advertised on television and newspapers, and

Shoppers routinely browse online and shop retail stores, often during the same shopping trip.

© Seb Oliver/Cultura/Getty Images

viewing a smartphone on a seller's website. The choice of which seller to buy from will depend on such considerations as the terms of sale, your past experience buying from the seller, and the return policy. Often a purchase decision involves a simultaneous evaluation of both product attributes and seller characteristics. For example, you might choose the second-most preferred smartphone brand at a store or website with a liberal refund and return policy versus the most preferred brand from a seller with more conservative policies.

Deciding when to buy is determined by a number of factors. For instance, you might buy sooner if one of your preferred brands is on sale or its manufacturer offers a rebate. Other factors such as the store atmosphere, pleasantness or ease of the shopping experience, salesperson assistance, time pressure, and financial circumstances could also affect whether a purchase decision is made now or postponed.[8]

Use of the Internet to gather information, evaluate alternatives, and make buying decisions adds a technological dimension to the consumer purchase decision process and buying experience. For example, 45 percent of consumers with price comparison smartphone apps routinely compare prices for identical products across different sellers at the point of purchase prior to making a purchase decision.[9]

Postpurchase Behavior: Realizing Value

After buying a product, the consumer compares it with his or her expectations and is either satisfied or dissatisfied. If the consumer is dissatisfied, marketers must determine whether the product was deficient or consumer expectations were too high. Product deficiency may require a design change. If expectations are too high, a company's advertising or the salesperson may have oversold the product's features and benefits.

Sensitivity to a customer's consumption or use experience is extremely important in a consumer's value perception. For example, research on telephone services provided by Sprint and AT&T indicates that satisfaction or dissatisfaction affects consumer value perceptions.[10] Studies show that satisfaction or dissatisfaction affects consumer communications and repeat-purchase behavior. Satisfied buyers tell three other people about their experience. In contrast, about 90 percent of dissatisfied buyers will not buy a product again and will complain to nine people.[11] Satisfied buyers also tend to buy from the same seller each time a purchase occasion arises. The financial impact of repeat-purchase behavior is significant, as described in the Marketing Matters box.[12]

Firms such as General Electric (GE), Johnson & Johnson, Coca-Cola, and British Airways focus attention on postpurchase behavior to maximize customer satisfaction and retention. These firms, among many others, now provide toll-free telephone numbers, offer liberalized return and refund policies, and engage in extensive staff training to handle complaints, answer questions, record suggestions, and solve consumer problems. For example, GE has a database that stores 750,000 answers regarding about 8,500 of its models in 120 product lines to handle 3 million calls annually. Such efforts produce positive postpurchase communications among consumers and foster relationship building between sellers and buyers.

Often a consumer is faced with two or more highly attractive alternatives, such as a LG G4 or Motorola Dröid Turbo. If you choose the LG G4, you might think, "Should I have purchased the Motorola Dröid Turbo?" This feeling of postpurchase psychological tension or anxiety is called *cognitive dissonance*. To alleviate it, consumers often attempt to applaud themselves for making the right choice. So after your purchase, you may seek information to confirm your choice by asking friends questions like, "Don't you like my new phone?" or by reading ads of the brand you chose. You might even look for negative features about the brands you didn't buy and decide that the Motorola

Marketing Matters

How Much Is a Satisfied Customer Worth?

Customer satisfaction and experience underlie the marketing concept. But how much is a satisfied customer worth?

This question has prompted firms to calculate the financial value of a satisfied customer over time. Frito-Lay, for example, estimates that the average loyal consumer in the southwestern United States eats 21 pounds of snack chips a year. At a price of $2.50 a pound, this customer spends $52.50 annually on the company's snacks such as Lay's and Ruffles potato chips, Doritos and Tostitos tortilla chips, and Fritos corn chips. Exxon estimates that a loyal customer will spend $500 annually for its branded gasoline, not including candy, snacks, oil, or repair services purchased at its gasoline stations. Kimberly-Clark reports that a loyal customer will buy 6.7 boxes of its Kleenex tissues each year and will spend $994 on facial tissues over 60 years, in today's dollars.

These calculations have focused marketer attention on the buying experience, customer satisfaction, and retention. Ford Motor Company set a target of increasing customer retention—the percentage of Ford owners whose next car is also a Ford—from 60 to 80 percent. Why? Ford executives say that each additional percentage point is worth a staggering $100 million in profits. In 2015, Ford's customer retention was 64 percent and the company remains the most profitable American automaker.

This calculation is not unique to Ford. Research shows that a 5 percent improvement in customer retention can increase a company's profits by 70 to 80 percent.

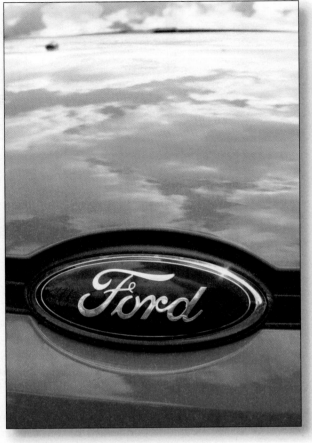

© DWImages Motoring/Alamy

Dröid Turbo smartphone did not feel right. Firms often use ads or follow-up calls from salespeople in this postpurchase behavior stage to comfort buyers that they made the right decision. For many years, Buick ran an advertising campaign with the message, "Aren't you really glad you bought a Buick?"

Consumer Involvement Affects Problem Solving

LO 5-2 Distinguish among three variations of the consumer purchase decision process: extended, limited, and routine problem solving.

Sometimes consumers don't engage in the five-stage purchase decision process. Instead, they skip or minimize one or more stages depending on the level of **involvement**, the personal, social, and economic significance of the purchase to the consumer.[13] High-involvement purchase occasions typically have at least one of three characteristics: The item to be purchased (1) is expensive, (2) can have serious personal consequences, or (3) could reflect on one's social image. For these occasions, consumers engage in extensive information searches, consider many product attributes and brands, form attitudes, and participate in word-of-mouth communication. Low-involvement purchases, such as toothpaste and soap, barely involve most of us, but audio and video systems and automobiles are very involving.

CHARACTERISTICS OF THE CONSUMER PURCHASE DECISION PROCESS	HIGH ◄ CONSUMER INVOLVEMENT ► LOW		
	EXTENDED PROBLEM SOLVING	LIMITED PROBLEM SOLVING	ROUTINE PROBLEM SOLVING
Number of brands examined	Many	Several	One
Number of sellers considered	Many	Several	Few
Number of product attributes evaluated	Many	Moderate	One
Number of external information sources used	Many	Few	None
Time spent searching	Considerable	Little	Minimal

FIGURE 5–3

Comparison of problem-solving variations: extended problem solving, limited problem solving, and routine problem solving.

There are three general variations in the consumer purchase decision process based on consumer involvement and product knowledge. Figure 5–3 shows some of the important differences between the three problem-solving variations.

Extended Problem Solving In extended problem solving, each of the five stages of the consumer purchase decision process is used and considerable time and effort are devoted to the search for external information and the identification and evaluation of alternatives. Several brands are in the consideration set, and these are evaluated on many attributes. Extended problem solving exists in high-involvement purchase situations for items such as automobiles and audio systems.

Limited Problem Solving In limited problem solving, consumers typically seek some information or rely on a friend to help them evaluate alternatives. Several brands might be evaluated using a moderate number of attributes. Limited problem solving is appropriate for purchase situations that do not merit a great deal of time or effort, such as choosing a toaster or a restaurant for lunch.

Routine Problem Solving For products such as table salt and milk, consumers recognize a problem, make a decision, and spend little effort seeking external information and evaluating alternatives. The purchase process for such items is virtually a habit and typifies low-involvement decision making. Routine problem solving is typically the case for low-priced, frequently purchased grocery products.

Consumer Involvement and Marketing Strategy Low and high consumer involvement have important implications for marketing strategy. If a company markets a low-involvement product and its brand is a market leader, attention is placed on (1) maintaining product quality, (2) avoiding stockout situations so that buyers don't substitute a competing brand, and (3) using repetitive advertising messages that reinforce a consumer's knowledge or assure buyers they made the right choice. Market challengers have a different task. They must break buying habits by using free samples, coupons, and rebates to encourage trial of their brand. Advertising messages will focus on

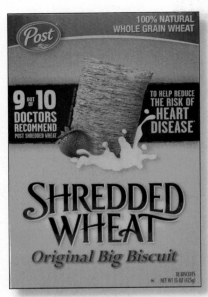

What is a behavioral explanation for why Post Cereals prominently displays heart-healthy claims on its packaging?

© Mike Hruby

getting their brand into a consumer's consideration set. For example, Campbell's V8 vegetable juice advertising message—"Could've Had a V8"—is targeted at consumers who routinely consider only fruit juices and soft drinks for purchase. Marketers can also link their brand attributes with high-involvement issues. Post Cereals does this by linking consumption of its whole grain cereals with improved heart health and protection against major diseases.

Marketers of high-involvement products know that their consumers constantly seek and process information about objective and subjective brand attributes, form evaluative criteria, rate product attributes of various brands, and combine these ratings for an overall brand evaluation—like that described in the smartphone purchase decision. Market leaders ply consumers with product information through advertising and personal selling and use social media to create online experiences for their company or brand. Market challengers capitalize on this behavior through comparative advertising that focuses on existing product attributes and often introduce novel evaluative criteria for judging competing brands. Challengers also benefit from Internet search engines such as Microsoft Bing and Google that assist buyers of high-involvement products.

Situational Influences That Affect Purchase Decisions

Often the purchase situation will affect the purchase decision process. Five *situational influences* have an impact on the purchase decision process: (1) the purchase task, (2) social surroundings, (3) physical surroundings, (4) temporal effects, and (5) antecedent states.[14]

The purchase task is the reason for engaging in the decision. The search for information and the evaluation of alternatives may differ depending on whether the purchase is a gift, which often involves social visibility, or for the buyer's own use. Social surroundings, including the other people present when a purchase decision is made, may also affect what is purchased. Consumers accompanied by children buy about 40 percent more items than consumers shopping by themselves. Physical surroundings such as decor, music, and crowding in retail stores may alter how purchase decisions are made. Temporal effects such as time of day or the amount of time available will influence where consumers have breakfast and lunch and what is ordered. Finally, antecedent states, which include the consumer's mood or the amount of cash on hand, can influence purchase behavior and choice. For example, consumers with credit cards purchase more than those with cash or debit cards.

Figure 5–4 shows the many influences that affect the consumer purchase decision process. In addition to situational influences, the decision to buy a product also involves and is affected by important psychological and sociocultural influences. These two influences are covered in the remainder of this chapter. Marketing mix influences are described later in Part 4 of the book. Chapter 21 elaborates on consumer behavior in the context of online information search and buying.

learning review

5-1. What is the first stage in the consumer purchase decision process?

5-2. The brands a consumer considers buying out of the set of brands in a product class of which the consumer is aware are collectively called the _____.

5-3. What is the term for postpurchase anxiety?

FIGURE 5–4

Influences on the consumer purchase decision process come from both internal and external sources.

PSYCHOLOGICAL INFLUENCES ON CONSUMER BEHAVIOR

LO 5-3 | Identify the major psychological influences on consumer behavior.

Psychology helps marketers understand why and how consumers behave as they do. In particular, psychological concepts such as motivation and personality; perception; learning; values, beliefs, and attitudes; and lifestyle are useful for interpreting buying processes and directing marketing efforts.

Consumer Motivation and Personality

Motivation and personality are two familiar psychological concepts that have specific meanings and marketing implications. These concepts are closely related and are used to explain why people do some things and not others.

Motivation   **Motivation** is the energizing force that stimulates behavior to satisfy a need. Because consumer needs are the focus of the marketing concept, marketers try to arouse these needs.

An individual's needs are boundless. People possess physiological needs for basics such as water, shelter, and food. They also have learned needs, including self-esteem, achievement, and affection. Psychologists point out that these needs may be hierarchical; that is, once physiological needs are met, people seek to satisfy their learned needs.

Figure 5–5 shows one need hierarchy and classification scheme that contains five need classes.[15] *Physiological needs* are basic to survival and must be satisfied first. A Red Lobster advertisement featuring a seafood salad attempts to activate the need for food. *Safety needs* involve self-preservation as well as physical and financial well-being.

FIGURE 5–5

The Maslow hierarchy of needs is based on the idea that motivation comes from a need. If a need is met, it's no longer a motivator, so a higher-level need becomes the motivator. Higher-level needs demand support of lower-level needs.

Video 5-1
Match.com
kerin.tv/13e/v5-1

Self-actualization needs:
Self-fulfillment

Personal needs:
Status, respect, prestige

Social needs:
Friendship, belonging, love

Safety needs:
Freedom from harm, financial security

Physiological needs:
Food, water, shelter, oxygen

Smoke detector and burglar alarm manufacturers focus on these needs, as do insurance companies and retirement plan advisors. *Social needs* are concerned with love and friendship. Dating services, such as Match.com and eHarmony, and fragrance companies try to arouse these needs. *Personal needs* include the need for achievement, status, prestige, and self-respect. The American Express Centurian Card and Brooks Brothers Clothiers appeal to these needs. Sometimes firms try to arouse multiple needs to stimulate problem recognition. Michelin has combined safety with parental love to promote tire replacement for automobiles. *Self-actualization needs* involve personal fulfillment. For example, a long-running U.S. Army recruiting program invited enlistees to "Be all you can be."

Personality   While motivation is the energizing force that makes consumer behavior purposeful, a consumer's personality guides and directs behavior. **Personality** refers to a person's consistent behaviors or responses to recurring situations. Although many personality theories exist, most identify *key traits*—enduring characteristics within a person or in his or her relationships with others. Such traits include assertiveness, extroversion, compliance, dominance, and aggression, among others. These traits are inherited or formed at an early age and change little over the years.

Research suggests that compliant people prefer known brand names and use more mouthwash and toilet soaps. Aggressive types use razors, not electric shavers, apply more cologne and aftershave lotions, and purchase signature goods such as Gucci and Yves St. Laurent as an indicator of status.[16]

These personality characteristics are often revealed in a person's *self-concept*, which is the way people see themselves and the way they believe others see them. Marketers recognize that people have an actual self-concept and an ideal self-concept. The actual self refers to how people actually see themselves. The ideal self describes how people would like to see themselves.

These two self-images—actual and ideal—are reflected in the products and brands a person buys, including automobiles, home appliances and furnishings, magazines, consumer electronics, clothing, grooming and leisure products, and frequently, the stores in which a person shops. The importance of self-concept is summed up by a senior marketing executive at Lenovo, a global supplier of notebook computers: "The notebook market is getting more like cars. The car you drive reflects you, and notebooks are becoming a form of self-expression as well."[17]

Consumer Perception

One person sees a Cadillac as a mark of achievement; another sees it as ostentatious. This is the result of **perception**—the process by which an individual selects, organizes, and interprets information to create a meaningful picture of the world.

Selective Perception   Because the average consumer operates in a complex environment, the human brain attempts to organize and interpret information with a process called *selective perception*, a filtering of exposure, comprehension, and retention. *Selective exposure* occurs when people pay attention to messages that are consistent with their attitudes and beliefs and ignore messages that are inconsistent with them.

The Ethics of Subliminal Messages

For over 50 years, the topic of subliminal perception and the presence of subliminal messages and images embedded in commercial communications have sparked heated debate.

The Federal Communications Commission has denounced subliminal messages as deceptive. Still, consumers spend $50 million a year for subliminal messages designed to help them raise their self-esteem, stop compulsive buying, quit smoking, or lose weight. Almost two-thirds of U.S. consumers think subliminal messages are present in commercial communications; about half are firmly convinced that this practice can cause them to buy things they don't want.

Subliminal messages are not illegal in the United States, however, and marketers are often criticized for pursuing opportunities to create these messages in both electronic and print media. A book by August Bullock, *The Secret Sales Pitch,* is devoted to this topic. Bullock identifies images and advertisements that he claims contain subliminal messages and describes techniques that can be used for conveying these messages. Do you "see" the subliminal message that is embedded in the book's cover?

Do you believe that a marketer's attempts to implant subliminal messages in electronic and print media are a deceptive practice and unethical, regardless of their intent?

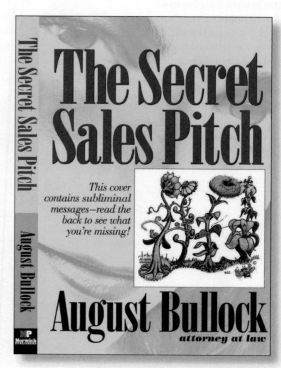

The Secret Sales Pitch: An Overview of Subliminal Advertising. Copyright © 2004 by August Bullock. All Rights Reserved. Used with permission. The SecretSalesPitch.com

Selective exposure often occurs in the postpurchase stage of the consumer decision process, when consumers read advertisements for the brand they just bought. It also occurs when a need exists—you are more likely to "see" a McDonald's advertisement when you are hungry rather than after you have eaten a pizza.

Selective comprehension involves interpreting information so that it is consistent with your attitudes and beliefs. A marketer's failure to understand this can have disastrous results. For example, Toro introduced a small, lightweight snowblower called the Snow Pup. Even though the product worked, sales failed to meet expectations. Why? Toro later found out that consumers perceived the name to mean that Snow Pup was a toy or too light to do any serious snow removal. When the product was renamed Snow Master, sales increased sharply.[18]

Selective retention means that consumers do not remember all the information they see, read, or hear, even minutes after exposure to it. This affects the internal and external information search stage of the purchase decision process. This is why furniture and automobile retailers often give consumers product brochures to take home with them when they leave the showroom.

Because perception plays an important role in consumer behavior, it is not surprising that the topic of subliminal perception is a popular item for discussion. *Subliminal perception* means that you see or hear messages without being aware of them. The presence and effect of subliminal perception on behavior is a hotly debated issue, with more popular appeal than scientific support. Indeed, evidence suggests that such messages have limited effects on behavior.[19] If these messages did influence behavior, would their use be an ethical practice? (See the Making Responsible Decisions box.)[20]

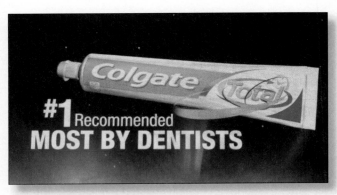

How did Colgate-Palmolive marketers allay consumers' perceived risk and change consumers' attitudes toward Colgate Total toothpaste to create a brand with over $1 billion in sales worldwide? The answers appear in the text.
© Richard Levine/Alamy

Colgate-Palmolive
www.colgate.com

How does this advertisement for Tylenol 8-Hour apply to cognitive learning? Read the text to find out.
© McNeil Consumer Healthcare Division of McNeil-PPC, Inc.

Tylenol
www.tylenol.com

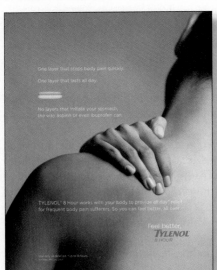

Perceived Risk   Perception plays a major role in the perceived risk in purchasing a product or service. **Perceived risk** represents the anxiety felt because the consumer cannot anticipate the outcomes of a purchase but believes there may be negative consequences. Examples of possible negative consequences are the size of the financial outlay required to buy the product (can I afford $900 for those skis?), the risk of physical harm (is bungee jumping safe?), and the performance of the product (will the whitening toothpaste work?). A more abstract form is psychosocial (what will my friends say about my tattoo?).

Perceived risk affects a consumer's information search. The greater the perceived risk, the more extensive the external search stage is likely to be. For example, the average car shopper spends about 14 hours online researching cars and almost 4 hours visiting car dealerships when choosing a car.[21]

Recognizing the importance of perceived risk, companies develop strategies to reduce the consumer's perceived risk and encourage purchases. These strategies and examples of firms using them include the following:

- *Obtaining seals of approval:* The Good Housekeeping Seal for Fresh Step cat litter.
- *Securing endorsements from influential people:* Colgate-Palmolive secured the endorsements of dentists to make the claim that Colgate Total toothpaste is the #1 recommended toothpaste by most dentists.
- *Providing free trials of the product:* Samples of Mary Kay's Velocity fragrance.
- *Giving extensive usage instructions:* Clairol hair coloring.
- *Providing warranties and guarantees:* Kia Motors's 10-year, 100,000-mile limited powertrain warranty.

Consumer Learning

Much consumer behavior is learned. Consumers learn which information sources to consult for information about products and services, which evaluative criteria to use when assessing alternatives, and, more generally, how to make purchase decisions. **Learning** refers to those behaviors that result from (1) repeated experience and (2) reasoning.

Behavioral Learning   *Behavioral learning* is the process of developing automatic responses to a situation built up through repeated exposure to it. Four variables are central to how consumers learn from repeated experience: drive, cue, response, and reinforcement. A *drive* is a need that moves an individual to action. Drives, such as hunger, might be represented by motives. A *cue* is a stimulus or symbol perceived by consumers. A *response* is the action taken by a consumer to satisfy the drive. *Reinforcement* is the reward. Being hungry (drive), a consumer sees a cue (a billboard), takes action (buys a sandwich), and receives a reward (it tastes great!).

Marketers use two concepts from behavioral learning theory. *Stimulus generalization* occurs when a response elicited by one stimulus (cue) is generalized to another stimulus. Using the same brand name for different products is an application of this concept, such as Tylenol Cold & Flu and Tylenol P.M. *Stimulus discrimination* refers to a person's ability to perceive differences in stimuli. Consumers' tendency to perceive all light beers as being alike led to Budweiser Light commercials that distinguished between many types of "light beers" and Bud Light.

Cognitive Learning Consumers also learn through thinking, reasoning, and mental problem solving without direct experience. This type of learning, called *cognitive learning*, involves making connections between two or more ideas or simply observing the outcomes of others' behaviors and adjusting your own accordingly. Firms also influence this type of learning. Through repetition in advertising, messages such as "Feel Better, Tylenol 8-Hour" link a brand (Tylenol 8-Hour) and an idea (pain reliever) by showing someone using the brand and finding relief.

Brand Loyalty Learning is also important to marketers because it relates to habit formation—the basis of routine problem solving. Furthermore, there is a close link between habits and **brand loyalty**, which is a favorable attitude toward and consistent purchase of a single brand over time. Brand loyalty results from the positive reinforcement of previous actions. A consumer reduces risk and saves time by consistently purchasing the same brand of shampoo and has favorable results—healthy, shining hair. There is evidence of brand loyalty in many commonly purchased products in the United States and the global marketplace. However, the incidence of brand loyalty appears to be declining in North America, Western Europe, and Japan.[22]

Consumer Values, Beliefs, and Attitudes

Values, beliefs, and attitudes play a central role in consumer decision making and related marketing actions.

Attitude Formation An **attitude** is a "learned predisposition to respond to an object or class of objects in a consistently favorable or unfavorable way."[23] Attitudes are shaped by our values and beliefs, which are learned. Values vary by level of specificity. We speak of American core values, including material well-being and humanitarianism. We also have personal values, such as thriftiness and ambition. Marketers are concerned with both but focus mostly on personal values. Personal values affect attitudes by influencing the importance assigned to specific product attributes. Suppose thriftiness is one of your personal values. When you evaluate cars, fuel economy (a product attribute) becomes important. If you believe a specific car brand has this attribute, you are likely to have a favorable attitude toward it.

Beliefs also play a part in attitude formation. **Beliefs** are a consumer's subjective perception of how a product or brand performs on different attributes. Beliefs are based on personal experience, advertising, and discussions with other people. Beliefs about product attributes are important because, along with personal values, they create the favorable or unfavorable attitude the consumer has toward certain products, services, and brands.

Attitude Change Marketers use three approaches to try to change consumer attitudes toward products and brands, as illustrated in the following examples.[24]

1. *Changing beliefs about the extent to which a brand has certain attributes.* To allay mothers' concerns about ingredients in its mayonnaise, Hellmann's successfully communicated the product's high Omega 3 content, which is essential to human health.
2. *Changing the perceived importance of attributes.* Pepsi-Cola made freshness an important product attribute when it stamped freshness dates on its cans. Before doing so, few consumers considered cola freshness an issue. After Pepsi spent about $25 million on advertising and promotion, a consumer survey found that 61 percent of cola drinkers believed freshness dating was an important attribute.
3. *Adding new attributes to the product.* Colgate-Palmolive included a new antibacterial ingredient, triclosan, in its Colgate Total toothpaste and spent $100 million marketing the brand. The result? Colgate Total toothpaste is now a billion-dollar-plus global brand.

Consumer Lifestyle

Lifestyle is a mode of living that is identified by how people spend their time and resources, what they consider important in their environments, and what they think of themselves and the world around them. The analysis of consumer lifestyles, called *psychographics,* provides insights into consumer needs and wants. Lifestyle analysis has proven useful in segmenting and targeting consumers for new and existing products and services (see Chapter 9).

Psychographics is a catchall label used to describe a variety of segmentations such as those based on behaviors, attitudes, activities, interests, opinions, and social values. The practice of combining psychology, lifestyle, and demographics can be used to uncover consumer motivations for buying and using products and services; they are time-consuming and expensive to construct accurately and reliably. VALS™, owned and operated by Strategic Business Insights (SBI), is more than a lifestyle segmentation because VALS examines the intersection of psychology, demographics, and lifestyles.[25] VALS measures the enduring differences between people that explain and predict lifestyles meaningfully. Eight primary segments—personalities—are identified on the basis of motivations and resources (see Figure 5–6).

According to SBI, consumers are motivated to buy products and services and seek life experiences that give shape, substance, and satisfaction to their lives. Consumers are driven by one of three motivations—ideals, achievement, and self-expression—that give

FIGURE 5–6

The VALS survey places individuals into one of the eight groups. The VALS framework is the visualization of the consumer groups. Consumers with abundant resources—psychological, emotional, and material means and capabilities—are near the top of the framework and those with minimal resources are at the bottom. Consumer groups within a motivation can be targeted together. For instance, a marketer may target Thinkers and Believers together.

www.strategicbusinessinsights.com/VALS © 2014 by Strategic Business Insights. All rights reserved. This version is for the United States only. Different frameworks are used for different countries. Used with permission.

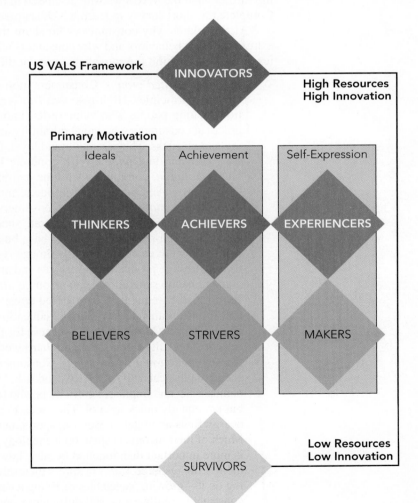

The figure labels: US VALS Framework, INNOVATORS, High Resources High Innovation, Primary Motivation, Ideals, Achievement, Self-Expression, THINKERS, ACHIEVERS, EXPERIENCERS, BELIEVERS, STRIVERS, MAKERS, Low Resources Low Innovation, SURVIVORS.

The VALS™ system run by Strategic Business Insights has identified eight unique consumer segments based on a person's primary motivation and resources. The text provides a brief description of each segment.

Do you wish to know your VALS profile? If you do, respond to the questions on the VALS survey at www. strategicbusinessinsights.com. Simply click "VALS." Next, click the "Take the VALS Survey" link. In addition to obtaining your profile in real time, you can examine the characteristics of your own and other profiles in greater detail.

meaning to their self and the world and govern their activities. The different levels of resources enhance or constrain a person's expression of his or her primary motivation.

A person's resources include psychological, emotional, demographic and material capacities such as self-confidence, curiosity, risk-taking, age, and income. Before reading further, visit the VALS website discussed in the Marketing Insights About Me box. Complete the short survey to learn which segment best describes you.

VALS explains why consumers who share the same demographics and lifestyles exhibit different behaviors and why consumers who do not share the same demographics or lifestyles exhibit the same behaviors for different reasons.

- *Ideals-motivated groups.* Consumers motivated by ideals are guided by knowledge and principles. High-resource *Thinkers* are mature, reflective, and information-seeking people who value order, knowledge, and responsibility. They are practical consumers who value durability and functionality in products over styling and newness. They are not brand loyal. Low-resource *Believers* are conservative, conventional people with concrete beliefs based on established codes: family, religion, community, and the nation. They choose familiar products and brands, favor American-made products, and are generally brand loyal.

- *Achievement-motivated groups.* Consumers motivated by achievement look for products and services that demonstrate success to their peers or to a group they aspire to. High-resource *Achievers* have busy, goal-directed lifestyles and a deep commitment to career and family. Image is important to them. They favor established, prestige products and services and are interested in time-saving devices to manage hectic schedules. Low-resource *Strivers* are trend followers. They seek fun to offset frequent, self-inflicted stress-producing situations. Many believe that life is unfair but they lack the education, skills, and tenacity to change their circumstances. Money defines success for them; however, they believe that success is the result of good luck, not hard work.

- *Self-expression-motivated groups.* Consumers motivated by self-expression desire social or physical activity, variety, and risk. High-resource *Experiencers* are young, enthusiastic, and impulsive consumers who become excited about new possibilities but are equally quick to cool. They seek to make an impact on their world. Their energy finds an outlet in exercise, sports, outdoor recreation, and social activities. Much of their income is spent on technology, entertainment, and socializing. Form is more important than function because how something looks is very important to them. Low-resource *Makers* express themselves and experience the world by working on it—growing vegetables or fixing a car. They are practical people who have constructive skills, value self-sufficiency and independence, and are unimpressed by material possessions except those with a practical or functional purpose.

- *High- and low-resource groups.* Two segments stand apart from primary motivation. High-resource *Innovators* are successful, sophisticated, take-charge people. Image is important to them, not as evidence of power or status, but as an expression of cultivated tastes, independent thinking, and character. They are early adopters and change leaders. Their lives are characterized by richness and variety. Low-resource *Survivors* focus on meeting basic needs—such as food, clothing and shelter, safety and security—rather than fulfilling desires. They represent a modest market for most products and services. They are loyal to favorite brands, especially if they can be purchased at a discount. Each segment receives and processes information differently and exhibits unique media preferences. For example, Experiencers are the most likely to visit Facebook and to read magazines. Makers and Achievers drive the most miles each week; therefore, they are the most likely segment to view outdoor advertising. Innovators and Thinkers are the most likely to read national newspapers. Survivors watch over 50 hours of television in an average week. GeoVALS™ estimates the percentage of each VALS group by zip code.

learning review »

5-4. The problem with the Toro Snow Pup was an example of selective
_____.

5-5. What three attitude-change approaches are most common?

5-6. What does *lifestyle* mean?

SOCIOCULTURAL INFLUENCES ON CONSUMER BEHAVIOR

LO 5-4 Identify the major sociocultural influences on consumer behavior.

Sociocultural influences, which evolve from a consumer's formal and informal relationships with other people, also exert a significant impact on consumer behavior. These involve personal influence, reference groups, family influence, social class, culture, and subculture.

Personal Influence

A consumer's purchases are often influenced by the views, opinions, or behaviors of others. Two aspects of personal influence are very important to marketing: opinion leadership and word-of-mouth activity.

Opinion Leadership   Individuals who exert direct or indirect social influence over others are called **opinion leaders**. Opinion leaders are considered to be knowledgeable about or users of particular products and services, so their opinions influence others' choices.[26] Opinion leadership is widespread in the purchase of cars and trucks, entertainment, clothing and accessories, club membership, consumer electronics, vacation destinations, food, and financial investments. A study by *Popular Mechanics* magazine identified 18 million opinion leaders who influence the purchases of some 85 million consumers for do-it-yourself products.

About 10 percent of U.S. adults are opinion leaders. Identifying, reaching, and influencing opinion leaders is a major challenge for companies. Some firms use actors or sports figures as spokespersons to represent their products. Others promote their products in media believed to reach opinion leaders. Still others use more direct approaches. For example, a carmaker recently invited influential community leaders and business executives to test-drive its new models. Some 6,000 accepted the offer, and

Companies use world-class athletes as spokespersons to represent their products, such as football player Eli Manning for Citizen watches.

© Citizen Watch Company of America, Inc.

98 percent said they would recommend their tested car. The company estimated that the number of favorable recommendations totaled 32,000.

Word of Mouth The influencing of people during conversations is called **word of mouth**. Word of mouth is the most powerful and authentic information source for consumers because it typically involves friends viewed as trustworthy. About 75 percent of all consumer conversations about brands happen face-to-face, 15 percent happen over the phone, and 10 percent happen online.[27] According to a recent study, 67 percent of U.S. consumer product sales are directly based on word-of-mouth activity among friends, family, and colleagues.[28]

The power of personal influence has prompted firms to promote positive and retard negative word of mouth. For instance, "teaser" advertising campaigns are run in advance of new-product introductions to stimulate conversations. Other techniques such as advertising slogans, music, and humor also heighten positive word of mouth. Many commercials shown during the Super Bowl are created expressly to initiate conversations about the advertisements and featured product or service the next day. Increasingly, companies recruit and deploy people to produce *buzz*—popularity created by consumer word of mouth. Read the Marketing Matters box to learn how this is done by BzzAgent.[29] Then go to the video link in the margin to see a video of BzzAgent's campaign for Dove hair care products.

Video 5-2
Dove
kerin.tv/13e/v5-2

Unfortunately, word of mouth can also be a source of negative information. For example, consider the damaging (and untrue) rumors that have plagued Kmart (snake eggs in clothing), Taco Bell (beef content in taco meat filling), Corona Extra beer (contamination), and Snickers candy bars in Russia (a cause of diabetes). Overcoming or neutralizing negative word of mouth is difficult and costly. However, supplying factual information, providing toll-free numbers for consumers to call the company, and giving appropriate product demonstrations have proven helpful.

The power of word of mouth is magnified by the Internet through online forums, blogs, social media, and websites. In fact, companies use special software to monitor online messages and find out what consumers are saying about their products, services, and brands. They have found that 30 percent of people spreading negative information have never owned or used the product, service, or brand![30]

Reference Group Influence

Reference groups are people to whom an individual looks as a basis for self-appraisal or as a source of personal standards. Reference groups affect consumer purchases because they influence the information, attitudes, and aspiration levels that help set a

BzzAgent—The Buzz Experience

Have you recently heard about a new product, movie, website, book, or restaurant from someone you know . . . or a complete stranger? If so, you may have had a word-of-mouth experience.

Marketers recognize the power of word of mouth. The challenge has been to harness that power. BzzAgent Inc. does just that. Its worldwide volunteer army of one million natural-born talkers channel their chatter toward products and services they deem authentically worth talking about, either online or in person. "Our goal is to capture honest word of mouth," says David Balter, BzzAgent's founder, "and to build a network that turns passionate customers into brand evangelists."

BzzAgent's method is simple. Once a client signs on with BzzAgent, the company searches its "agent" database for those who match the demographic and psychographic profile of the target market for a client's offering. Agents then can sign up for a buzz campaign and receive a sample product and a training manual for buzz-creating strategies. Each time an agent completes an activity, he or she is expected to file an online report describing the nature of the buzz and its effectiveness. BzzAgent coaches

respond with encouragement and feedback on additional techniques.

Agents keep the products they promote. They also earn points redeemable for books, CDs, and other items by filing detailed reports. Who are the agents? About 65 percent are older than 25 and 70 percent are women. All are gregarious and genuinely like the product or service, otherwise they wouldn't participate in the buzz campaign.

Estée Lauder, Monster.com, Anheuser-Busch, Penguin Books, Lee, Michelin, Wrigley, Arby's, Nestlé, Hershey Foods, Procter & Gamble, Danone, and Volkswagen have used BzzAgent. But BzzAgent's buzz isn't cheap, and not everything is buzz worthy. Deploying 1,000 agents on a 12-week campaign can cost a company $95,000, exclusive of product samples. BzzAgent researches a product or service before committing to a campaign and rejects about 80 percent of the companies that seek its service. It also refuses campaigns for politicians, religious groups, and certain products, such as firearms. Interested in BzzAgent? Visit its website at www.bzzagent.com or www.facebook.com/bzzagent.

consumer's standards. For example, one of the first questions one asks others when planning to attend a social occasion is, "What are you going to wear?" Reference groups influence the purchase of luxury products rather than necessities—particularly when the use or consumption of a chosen brand will be highly visible to others.

Consumers have many reference groups, but three groups have clear marketing implications.[31] An *associative group* is one to which a person actually belongs, including fraternities and sororities and alumni associations. Such groups are easily identifiable and are targeted by firms selling insurance, insignia products, and charter vacations.

Associative reference groups can also form around a brand, as is the case with clubs like the HOG (Harley Owners Group), which is made up of Harley-Davidson fans. A **brand community** is a specialized group of consumers with a structured set of relationships involving a particular brand, fellow customers of that brand, and the product in use. A consumer who is a member of a brand community thinks about brand names (e.g., Harley-Davidson), the product category (e.g., motorcycles), other customers who use the brand (e.g., HOG members), and the marketer that makes and promotes the brand.

The Harley Owners Group (HOG) has over 1 million members and is a prototypical brand community. Read the text to learn about the characteristics of a brand community.

© Joseph Eid/AFP/Getty Images

An *aspiration group* is one that a person wishes to be a member of or wishes to be identified with, such as a professional society or sports team. Firms frequently rely on spokespeople or settings associated with their target market's aspiration group in their advertising.

A *dissociative group* is one that a person wishes to maintain a distance from because of differences in values or behaviors. Firms often avoid dissociative reference groups in their marketing. For example, retailer Abercrombie & Fitch once offered to pay cast members of the controversial TV reality show *Jersey Shore* to *not* wear its clothing. "We understand that the show is for entertainment purposes, but believe this association is contrary to the aspirational nature of our brand, and may be distressing to many of our fans," the retailer stated.[32]

Family Influence

Family influences on consumer behavior result from three sources: consumer socialization, passage through the family life cycle, and decision making within the family or household.

Consumer Socialization The process by which people acquire the skills, knowledge, and attitudes necessary to function as consumers is called *consumer socialization*.[33] Children learn how to purchase (1) by interacting with adults in purchase situations and (2) through their own purchasing and product usage experiences. Research shows that children evidence brand preferences at age two, and these preferences often last a lifetime. This knowledge prompted the licensing of the well-known Craftsman brand name to MGA Entertainment for its children's line of My First Craftsman toys and power tools and Time Inc.'s *Sports Illustrated Kids*.

Family Life Cycle Consumers act and purchase differently as they go through life. The **family life cycle** concept describes the distinct phases that a family progresses through from formation to retirement, each phase bringing with it identifiable purchasing behaviors.[34] Figure 5–7 illustrates the traditional progression as well as contemporary variations of the family life cycle. Today, the *traditional family*—married couple with children younger than 18 years—constitutes just 21 percent of all U.S. households. The remaining 78 percent of U.S. households include single parents; unmarried couples; divorced, never-married, or widowed individuals; and older married couples whose children no longer live at home.

FIGURE 5–7

Modern family life cycle stages and flows. Can you identify people you know in different stages? Do they follow the purchase patterns described in the text?

Young singles' buying preferences are for nondurable items, including prepared foods, clothing, personal care products, and entertainment. They represent a target market for recreational travel, automobile, and consumer electronics firms. Young married couples without children are typically more affluent than young singles because usually both spouses are employed. These couples exhibit preferences for furniture, housewares, and gift items for each other. Young marrieds with children are driven by the needs of their children. They make up a sizable market for life insurance, various children's products, and home furnishings. Single parents with children are the least financially secure of households with children. Their buying preferences are often affected by a limited economic status and tend toward convenience foods, child care services, and personal care items.

Middle-aged married couples with children are typically better off financially than their younger counterparts. They are a significant market for leisure products and home improvement items. Middle-aged couples without children typically have a large amount of discretionary income. These couples buy better home furnishings, status automobiles, and financial services. Persons in the last two phases—older married and older unmarried—make up a sizable market for prescription drugs, medical services, vacation trips, and gifts for younger relatives.

Family Decision Making   A third source of family influence on consumer behavior involves the decision-making process that occurs within the family.[35] Two decision-making styles exist: spouse-dominant and joint decision making. With a joint decision-making style, most decisions are made by both husband and wife. Spouse-dominant decisions are those for which either the husband or the wife is mostly responsible. Research indicates that wives tend to have more say when purchasing groceries, children's toys, clothing, and medicines. Husbands tend to be more influential in home and car maintenance purchases. Joint decision making is common for cars, vacations, houses, home appliances and electronics, family finances, and medical care. As a rule, joint decision making increases with the education of the spouses.

Roles of individual family members in the purchase process are another element of family decision making. Five roles exist: (1) information gatherer, (2) influencer, (3) decision maker, (4) purchaser, and (5) user. Family members assume different roles for different products and services. This knowledge is important to firms. For example, 89 percent of wives either influence or make outright purchases of men's clothing. Even though women are often the grocery decision makers, they are not necessarily the purchasers. Today, 31 percent of men are the primary grocery shoppers in their households.

Increasingly, preteens and teenagers are the information gatherers, influencers, decision makers, and purchasers of products and services for the family, given the prevalence of working parents and single-parent households. The market for products bought by or for preteens and teenagers surpasses $208 billion annually. These figures help explain why, for example, Johnson & Johnson, Apple, Kellogg, P&G, Nike, Sony, and Oscar Mayer, among countless other companies, spend more than $70 billion annually in electronic and print media that reach preteens and teens.

Social Class Influence

A subtler influence on consumer behavior than direct contact with others is the social class to which people belong. **Social class** may be defined as the relatively permanent, homogeneous divisions in a society into which people sharing similar values, interests, and behavior can be grouped. A person's occupation, source of income (not level of income), and education determine his or her social class. Generally speaking, three major social class categories exist—upper, middle, and lower—with subcategories within each. This structure has been observed in the United States, Great Britain, Western Europe, and Latin America.

To some degree, persons within social classes exhibit common values, attitudes, beliefs, lifestyles, and buying behaviors. Compared with the middle classes, people in the lower classes have a more short-term time orientation, think in concrete rather than abstract terms, and see fewer personal opportunities. Members of the upper classes focus on achievements and the future and think in abstract or symbolic terms.

Companies use social class as a basis for identifying and reaching particularly good prospects for their products and services. For instance, JCPenney has historically appealed to the middle classes. *New Yorker* magazine reaches the upper classes. In general, people in the upper classes are targeted by companies for items such as financial investments, expensive cars, and formal evening wear. The middle classes represent a target market for home improvement centers, automobile parts stores, and personal hygiene products. Firms also recognize differences in media preferences among classes: lower and working classes prefer tabloid magazines; middle classes read fashion, romance, and celebrity (*People*) magazines; and upper classes tend to subscribe to literary, travel, and news magazines.

Culture and Subculture Influences

Video 5-3
Nissan Ad
kerin.tv/13e/v5-3

As described in Chapter 3, *culture* refers to the set of values, ideas, and attitudes that are learned and shared among the members of a group. Thus, we often refer to the American culture, the Latin American culture, or the Japanese culture. Cultural underpinnings of American buying patterns were described in Chapter 3; Chapter 7 will explore the role of culture in global marketing.

Subgroups within the larger, or national, culture with unique values, ideas, and attitudes are referred to as **subcultures**. Various subcultures exist within the American culture. The three largest racial/ethnic subcultures in the United States are Hispanics, African Americans, and Asian Americans. Collectively, they are expected to account for more than one in four U.S. consumers and to spend almost $4 trillion for goods and services in 2019, which will represent almost one-fifth percent of the United States' total buying power.[36] Each group exhibits sophisticated social and cultural behaviors that affect buying patterns, described next.

Why does ACH Food Companies, Inc. advertise its Mazola Corn Oil in Spanish? Read the text for the answer. Mazola Corn Oil, www.mazola.com

MAZOLA® is a registered trademark of ACH FOOD COMPANIES, Inc.

African American women represent a large market for health and beauty products. Cosmetics companies actively seek to serve this market.

The Advertising Archives

Hispanic Buying Patterns   Hispanics represent the largest racial/ethnic subculture in the United States in terms of population and spending power. About 36 percent of Hispanics in the United States are immigrants, and the majority are under the age of 29. One-half of Hispanics are younger than 18.

Research on Hispanic buying practices has uncovered several consistent patterns:[37]

1. Hispanics are quality and brand conscious. They are willing to pay a premium price for premium quality and are often brand loyal.
2. Hispanics prefer buying American-made products, especially those offered by firms that cater to Hispanic needs.
3. Hispanic buying preferences are strongly influenced by family and peers.
4. Hispanics consider advertising a credible product information source, and U.S. firms spend about $10 billion annually on advertising to Hispanics.
5. Convenience is not an important product attribute to Hispanic homemakers with respect to food preparation or consumption, nor is low caffeine in coffee and soft drinks, low fat in dairy products, or low cholesterol in packaged foods.

Despite some consistent buying patterns, marketing to Hispanics has proven to be a challenge for two reasons. First, the Hispanic subculture is diverse and composed of Mexicans, Puerto Ricans, Cubans, and others of Central and South American ancestry. Cultural differences among these nationalities often affect product preferences. For example, Campbell Soup Company sells its Casera line of soups, beans, and sauces using different recipes to appeal to Puerto Ricans on the East Coast and Mexicans in the Southwest. Second, a language barrier exists, and commercial messages are frequently misinterpreted when translated into Spanish. Volkswagen learned this lesson when the Spanish translation of its "Drivers Wanted" slogan suggested "chauffeurs wanted." The Spanish slogan was changed to "*Agarra Calle*," a slang expression that can be loosely translated as "let's hit the road."

Sensitivity to the unique needs of Hispanics by firms has paid huge dividends. For example, Metropolitan Life Insurance is the largest insurer of Hispanics. Goya Foods dominates the market for ethnic food products sold to Hispanics. Mazola Corn Oil captures two-thirds of the Hispanic market for this product category. Time, Inc. has more than 750,000 subscribers to its *People en Español*.

African American Buying Patterns   African Americans have the second-largest spending power of the three racial/ethnic subcultures in the United States. Consumer research on African American buying patterns has focused on similarities and differences with Caucasians. When socioeconomic status differences between African Americans and Caucasians are removed, there are more similarities than points of difference. Differences in buying patterns are greater within the African American subculture, due to levels of socioeconomic status, than between African Americans and Caucasians of similar status.

Even though similarities outweigh differences, there are consumption patterns that do differ between African Americans and Caucasians.[38] For example, African Americans spend far more than Caucasians on boys' clothing, rental goods smartphones, and audio equipment. African American women spend three times more on health and beauty products than Caucasian women. Furthermore, the typical African American family is five years younger than the typical Caucasian family. This factor alone accounts for some of the observed differences in preferences for clothing, music, shelter, cars, and many other products, services, and activities. Finally, it must be emphasized that, historically, African Americans have been deprived of employment and educational opportunities in the United States. Both factors have resulted in income disparities between African Americans and Caucasians, which influence purchase behavior.

Recent research indicates that while African Americans are price conscious, they are strongly motivated by quality and choice. They respond more to products and advertising that appeal to African American cultural images, as well as address their ethnic features and needs regardless of socioeconomic status. African Americans are much more likely to tell their friends about products and services they like than the general public as a whole.

Asian American Buying Patterns   Asian Americans are the fastest-growing racial/ethnic subculture in the United States. About 70 percent of Asian Americans are immigrants. Most are under the age of 30.

The Asian subculture is composed of Chinese, Japanese, Filipinos, Koreans, Asian Indians, people from Southeast Asia, and Pacific Islanders. The diversity of the Asian subculture is so great that generalizations about buying patterns of this group are difficult to make.[39] Consumer research on Asian Americans suggests that individuals and families can be divided into two groups. *Assimilated* Asian Americans are conversant in English, highly educated, hold professional and managerial positions, and exhibit buying patterns very much like the typical American consumer. *Nonassimilated* Asian Americans are recent immigrants who still cling to their native languages and customs.

The diversity of Asian Americans evident in language, customs, and tastes requires marketers to be sensitive to different Asian nationalities. For example, Anheuser-Busch's agricultural products division sells eight varieties of California-grown rice, each with a different Asian label to cover a range of nationalities and tastes. The company's advertising also addresses the preferences of Chinese, Japanese, and Koreans for different kinds of rice bowls. McDonald's actively markets to Asian Americans. According to a company executive, "We recognize diversity in this market. We try to make our messages in the language they prefer to see them."

Studies show that the Asian American subculture as a whole is characterized by hard work, strong family ties, appreciation for education, and median family incomes exceeding those of any other ethnic group. This subculture is also the most entrepreneurial in the United States, as evidenced by the number of Asian-owned businesses. These qualities led Metropolitan Life Insurance to identify Asian Americans as a target for insurance following the company's success in marketing to Hispanics.

learning review

5-7. What are the two primary forms of personal influence?

5-8. Marketers are concerned with which types of reference groups?

5-9. What two challenges must marketers overcome when marketing to Hispanic consumers?

LEARNING OBJECTIVES REVIEW

LO 5-1 *Describe the stages in the consumer purchase decision process.*
The consumer purchase decision process consists of five stages. They are problem recognition, information search, alternative evaluation, purchase decision, and postpurchase behavior. Problem recognition is perceiving a difference between a person's ideal and actual situation big enough to trigger a decision. Information search involves remembering previous purchase experiences (internal search) and external search behavior such as seeking information from other sources. Alternative evaluation clarifies the problem for the consumer by (*a*) suggesting the evaluative criteria to

use for the purchase, (*b*) yielding brand names that might meet the criteria, and (*c*) developing consumer value perceptions. The purchase decision involves the choice of an alternative, including from whom to buy and when to buy. Postpurchase behavior involves the comparison of the chosen alternative with a consumer's expectations, which leads to satisfaction or dissatisfaction and subsequent purchase behavior.

LO 5-2 *Distinguish among three variations of the consumer purchase decision process: extended, limited, and routine problem solving.*

Consumers don't always engage in the five-stage purchase decision process. Instead, they skip or minimize one or more stages depending on the level of involvement—the personal, social, and economic significance of the purchase. For high-involvement purchase occasions, each of the five stages of the consumer purchase decision process is used and considerable time and effort are devoted to the search for external information and the identification and evaluation of alternatives. With limited problem solving, consumers typically seek some information or rely on a friend to help them evaluate alternatives. For low-involvement purchase occasions, consumers engage in routine problem solving. They recognize a problem, make a decision, and spend little effort seeking external information and evaluating alternatives.

LO 5-3 *Identify the major psychological influences on consumer behavior.*

Psychology helps marketers understand why and how consumers behave as they do. In particular, psychological concepts such as motivation and personality, perception, learning, values, beliefs and attitudes, and lifestyle are useful for interpreting buying processes. Motivation is the energizing force that stimulates behavior to satisfy a need. Personality refers to a person's consistent behaviors or responses to recurring situations. Perception is the process by which an individual selects, organizes, and interprets information to create a meaningful picture of the world. Consumers filter information through selective exposure, comprehension, and retention.

Much consumer behavior is learned. Learning refers to those behaviors that result from (*a*) repeated experience and (*b*) reasoning. Brand loyalty results from learning. Values, beliefs, and attitudes are also learned and influence how consumers evaluate products, services, and brands. A more general concept is lifestyle. Lifestyle, also called psychographics, combines psychology and demographics and focuses on how people spend their time and resources, what they consider important in their environment, and what they think of themselves and the world around them.

LO 5-4 *Identify the major sociocultural influences on consumer behavior.*

Sociocultural influences, which evolve from a consumer's formal and informal relationships with other people, also affect consumer behavior. These involve personal influence, reference groups, the family, social class, culture, and subculture. Opinion leadership and word-of-mouth behavior are two major sources of personal influence on consumer behavior. Reference groups are people to whom an individual looks as a basis for self-approval or as a source of personal standards. Family influences on consumer behavior result from three sources: consumer socialization, passage through the family life cycle, and decision making within the family or household. Persons within social classes tend to exhibit common values, attitudes, beliefs, lifestyles, and buying behavior. Finally, a person's culture and subculture have been shown to influence product preferences and buying patterns.

LEARNING REVIEW ANSWERS

5-1 **What is the first stage in the consumer purchase decision process?**
Answer: problem recognition—perceiving a need

5-2 **The brands a consumer considers buying out of the set of brands in a product class of which the consumer is aware are collectively called the _____.**
Answer: consideration set

5-3 **What is the term for postpurchase anxiety?**
Answer: cognitive dissonance

5-4 **The problem with the Toro Snow Pup was an example of selective _____.**
Answer: comprehension—consumers perceived the name to mean that Snow Pup was a toy that was too light to do any serious snow removal.

5-5 **What three attitude-change approaches are most common?**
Answer: (1) Change beliefs about the extent to which a brand has certain attributes. (2) Change the perceived importance of these attributes. (3) Add new attributes to the product.

5-6 **What does *lifestyle* mean?**
Answer: Lifestyle is a mode of living that is identified by how people spend their time and resources, what they consider important in their environment, and what they think of themselves and the world around them.

5-7 **What are the two primary forms of personal influence?**
Answer: (1) Opinion leadership—persons considered to be knowledgeable about or users of particular products and services and (2) word of mouth—the influencing of people (friends, family, and colleagues) during conversations.

5-8 **Marketers are concerned with which types of reference groups?**
Answer: Three reference groups have clear marketing implications: (1) associative groups—ones to which a person actually belongs, such as a brand community that consists of a specialized group of consumers with a structured set of relationships involving a particular brand; (2) aspiration groups—ones that people wish to be a member of or identified with; and (3) dissociative groups—ones that people wish to maintain a distance from because of differences in values or behaviors.

5-9 **What two challenges must marketers overcome when marketing to Hispanic consumers?**
Answer: (1) The diversity of nationalities among this subculture that affect product preferences and (2) the language barrier that can lead to misinterpretation or mistranslation of commercial messages when translated into Spanish.

APPLYING MARKETING KNOWLEDGE

1 Review Figure 5–2, which shows common smartphone attributes. Which attributes are important to you? What other attributes might you consider? Which brand would you prefer?

2 Suppose research at Panasonic reveals that prospective buyers are anxious about buying high-definition television sets. What strategies might you recommend to the company to reduce consumer anxiety?

3 Assign one or more levels of the Maslow hierarchy of needs described in Figure 5–5 to the following products: (*a*) life insurance, (*b*) cosmetics, (*c*) *The Wall Street Journal,* and (*d*) hamburgers.

4 With which stage in the family life cycle would the purchase of the following products and services be most closely identified? (*a*) bedroom furniture, (*b*) life insurance, (*c*) a Caribbean cruise, (*d*) a house mortgage, and (*e*) children's toys.

BUILDING YOUR MARKETING PLAN

To conduct a consumer analysis for the product—the good, service, or idea—in your marketing plan:

1 Identify the consumers who are most likely to buy your product—the primary target market—in terms of (*a*) their demographic characteristics and (*b*) any other kind of characteristics you believe are important.

2 Describe (*a*) the main points of difference of your product for this group and (*b*) what problem they help solve for the consumer in terms of the first stage in the consumer purchase decision process in Figure 5–1.

3 For each of the four outside boxes in Figure 5–4 (marketing mix, psychological, sociocultural, and situational influences), identify the one or two key influences with respect to your product.

This consumer analysis will provide the foundation for the marketing mix actions you develop later in your plan.

connect

VIDEO CASE 5   Groupon: Helping Consumers with Purchase Decisions

University of Chicago graduate student Andrew Mason was in a rut. "There's so much to do in Chicago," he explains, "but I found myself going to the same movie theaters and restaurants."

Video 5-4
Groupon Video Case
kerin.tv/13e/v5-4

To help people like him try new places, Mason started a website that offered coupons to large groups. He reasoned that people would try something new if the price was low enough, and that businesses would offer low prices if they knew they could sell a large quantity. The result was Groupon, a company that offers "group coupons" in deal-of-the-day offerings for local or national businesses. Consumers love the concept, buying everything from restaurant certificates, to yoga lessons, to tickets to a museum exhibit. "We think the Internet has the potential to change the way people discover and buy from local businesses," says Mason.

THE COMPANY AND GROUPON CONCEPT

Mason started with a website called ThePoint.org, which was designed to organize campaigns, protests, boycotts, and fund-raising drives for important social issues. ThePoint was not successful but it provided the concept of making offers that are carried out only if enough people commit to participate in them. With that idea Mason launched Groupon in October 2008 with a two-pizzas-for-the-price-of-one offer at the Motel Bar, located in the same building where The-Point rented space. The concept quickly grew in Chicago and Groupon expanded into other U.S. cities and then into other countries. Today Groupon is available in 375 American cities and 48 countries, and its subscriber base has grown from 400 in 2008 to 200 million today. In its fourth full year of operation, Groupon generated $5.4 billion in gross billings.

Part of Groupon's success is the simplicity of its business model—offer subscribers at least one deal in their city each day. The unique aspect of the concept is that a certain number of people need to buy into the offer before the coupon discount is valid. Approximately 95 percent of Groupon offers "tip," or reach the number of buyers required by the merchant. Once the minimum number is met, Groupon and the merchant split the revenue. For example, a yoga studio might offer a $100 membership for $50 if 200 people participate in the offer. Once 200 consumers have indicated interest, the deal "tips" and Groupon and the yoga studio each receive 50 percent of the revenue.

Everyone wins. Consumers receive an exceptional value, the merchant obtains new customers without any advertising cost, and Groupon generates revenue for creating value in the marketplace.

Many of the deals have generated extraordinary demand. The Joffrey Ballet, for example, sold 2,338 season subscriptions, doubling its subscriber base in one day! Similarly, consumers purchased 445,000 Groupons offering $50 worth of merchandise for $25 at the Gap and 6,561 tickets to a King Tut exhibit in New York's Times Square for half price at $18 apiece. The most popular offering so far was a $25 ticket for an architectural boat tour in Chicago for $12. Groupon sold 19,822 tickets in eight hours! The company's attention to customer satisfaction ensures success stories like these. "We have a policy called 'The Groupon Promise' that any customer can return a Groupon, no questions asked—even if they used it—if they feel like Groupon has let them down," explains Mason. Groupon's success has attracted many more merchants than it can accommodate. In fact, only about 12 percent of all merchants that contact Groupon are selected to offer a deal.

In addition to the deal-of-the-day offerings, Groupon has several other services. GrouponLive offers deals to obtain tickets to sporting events, concerts, theatrical performances, and other forms of live entertainment. Groupon Getaways offers travel experiences in two forms—as a specific booking or as a voucher where consumers make a separate reservation. Groupon Goods features deals on new and innovative products. Finally, Groupon is testing a concept it calls

© Daniel Acker/Bloomberg via Getty Images

"Pull," which enables customers to search among thousands of deals that they can buy and use instantly. To use the service, consumers log on to the Groupon Mobile app on their smartphone and select "Nearby." The app then determines the location of the consumer and displays a map of nearby deals. More than 40 million people have downloaded the Groupon Mobile app, and approximately 45 percent of Groupon's transactions in the United States are completed from a mobile device.

Groupon's growth is evident in some amazing numbers. The company has offered more than 400 million deals, with over 500,000 merchant partners, and employs 11,000 people around the globe. In addition, Groupon has created a market of consumer deal hunters that includes its 41.7 million active customers and an industry of approximately 500 competitive deal services. The competitors include LivingSocial, Amazon Local, Google Offers, Plum District, Tippr, Bloomspot, Scoutmob, and many others. While the industry is large and growing, the competition has been intense, leading Facebook, Yahoo!, and others to test social-buying deal services but discontinue the offerings.

USING COUPONS TO INFLUENCE CONSUMERS' BUYING BEHAVIOR

"Part of the reason that Groupon has grown as quickly as it has is because we really understand consumer behavior," explains Julie Mossler, public relations & consumer marketing manager at Groupon. Generally, Groupon consumers follow the same purchase decision process common to many consumer purchases. The first stage, problem recognition, may be triggered by an e-mail or an appointment to have lunch with friends. Groupon deal-of-the-day e-mail messages, for example, often present consumers with an opportunity to do something they wouldn't ordinarily do—take sky-diving lessons or subscribe to the ballet. Groupon Nearby presents real-time offers on smartphone apps in response to an immediate need in a specific location. While the two types of offers generate different types of purchases, they both begin the purchase process.

The second stage, information search, may simply be a review of previous experiences with the merchant making the offer, online comparisons with competitors, or discussions with friends on Facebook or Twitter. In fact, the collective buying aspect of Groupon encourages subscribers to share promotions with family and friends to increase the chances of reaching the required number of buyers.

In the alternative evaluation stage many Groupon customers focus on price as the most important evaluative criteria, although other aspects such as quantity or time restrictions may be considered. The Groupon Nearby offers, for example, may be valid only on specific days or during short windows of time. Piece Brewery & Pizzeria in Chicago, for example, used Groupon to sell a $30 coupon for $20 valid only during its slow periods—11 A.M. to 3 P.M. Tuesday through Thursday.

The fourth stage, the purchase decision, is made online and then confirmed when the deals tip. Bo Hurd, national sales manager at Groupon, believes that the purchase stage is unique for Groupon users. He explains, "the fact that [consumers] have put money on the line . . . is driving them from the online piece, to the computers . . . to do something, to try something." Finally, after the purchase consumers compare their experience with their expectations to determine if they are satisfied or dissatisfied.

Psychological, sociocultural, and situational factors also influence Groupon users' purchase behavior. The recession has increased the importance of personal values such as thriftiness, so deal-prone people who were attracted to websites such as Gilt in fashion and Woot in consumer electronics are also attracted to Groupon. The typical Groupon user is an 18- to 34-year-old woman with an average income of about $70,000. This is significant because this group's affinity to social media enables the use of Groupon, which depends on e-mail and smartphone apps to reach its customers. Specific situations such as planning entertainment activities, finding a close restaurant for lunch, or buying a gift are also common to Groupon users. As Groupon has learned more about its subscribers, it has begun personalizing the deals they see. The company uses variables such as gender, location of residence or office, and buying history to match deals with the customers. This process provides offers that are more likely to be of interest to consumers and allows Groupon to serve more merchants.

GROUPON CHALLENGES

As popular as Groupon has become, it does face three challenges. The first challenge is related to the use of coupons. Some consumers buy the coupons but never use them, eventually leaving them dissatisfied and unlikely to use Groupon again. Some consumers use the coupons but do not become regular customers. Because of the deep discounts used to sell the Groupons, most of the deals are not profitable for the merchants, so they are dissatisfied if the Groupon users do not make repeat purchases. David Perlman, owner of the Essex restaurant in New York City, for example, offered deals on Groupon and Open Table, selling 1,500 and 1,000 coupons, respectively. Now he is comparing the diners each deal brought in to determine which group has generated more repeat customers. Some merchants are also concerned that frequent discounting could discourage customers from ever making purchases without a discount.

Another challenge facing Groupon is managing its growth. The company has expanded into Europe, Latin America, Asia, and Russia by acquiring local daily deal services. For example, in Europe it purchased CityDeal, in Russia it purchased Darberry, and in Japan it purchased Qpod. It also acquired sites with customer bases in Hong Kong, Singapore, Taiwan, and the Philippines. As a result, Groupon currently has more subscribers abroad than in the United States, although more deals are still sold in the United States. According to Groupon Co-CEO Eric Lefkofsky, "We're applying our North American playbook to our international business in order to standardize systems and processes." As Groupon continues to grow, it anticipates that it must also develop a comprehensive understanding of the differences in international buying behaviors.

Finally, Groupon faces an extraordinary level of competition. Part of the problem is that the daily deal technology is not very sophisticated and the model is easy to copy. Manufacturers, large retailers, and small businesses are all trying the concept. ConAgra has offered a group coupon deal for its Healthy Choice brand through a Facebook app, Walmart launched its own deal-of-the-day coupon service, and some businesses use recently developed plug-and-play software that helps build deals into their websites. Mason hopes that Groupon Nearby is one answer to this challenge because it is

© Iain Masterton/Alamy

much more difficult to replicate. "We have always been thinking about how to solve these fundamental problems of our model. We have known since very early on that some form of real-time deal optimization is where this had to go," he explains.

Groupon's success is the result of a simple and effective business model and an insightful understanding of consumer behavior. In the future Groupon's strategies will require continued attention to understanding consumers around the globe. Mossler explains: "Groupon has been heralded as the fastest-growing company of all time, and the reason for that is because we have solved this unsolvable problem, which is how do you engage with local customers. The model really works anywhere as long as you adapt for local communities."[40]

Questions

1 How has an understanding of consumer behavior helped Groupon grow from 400 subscribers in Chicago in 2008 to 200 million subscribers in 48 countries today?

2 What is the Groupon Promise? How does the Groupon Promise affect a consumer's perceived risk and cognitive dissonance?

3 Describe the five-stage purchase decision process for a typical Groupon user.

4 What are possible psychological and sociological influences on the Groupon consumer purchase decision process?

5 What challenges does Groupon face in the future? What actions would you recommend related to each challenge?

Chapter Notes

1. "Americans Rethinking How They Buy Cars," *money.msn.com*, April 4, 2014; "Car-Buying Tips Men Can Learn from Women," www.leasetrader.com, January 30, 2012; "New Efforts to Shorten the Car-Buying Process," *The Wall Street Journal*, February 27, 2013, p. D3; Jerry Hirsh, "Car Buying: How Men and Women Compare," www.latimes.com, April 7, 2011; "What Matters the Most When People Buy Cars," *BrandWeek*, October 11, 2010, p. 23; "Gender Wars and Car Shopping: Men Want Power, Women Want Cloth Seats," www.autos.aol.com, July 16, 2010; and Michael J. Silverstein and Kate Sayre, "The Female Economy," *Harvard Business Review*, September 2009, pp. 46–53.

2. Roger D. Blackwell, Paul W. Miniard, and James F. Engel, *Consumer Behavior*, 10th ed. (Mason, OH: South-Western Publishing, 2006).

3. For thorough descriptions of consumer expertise, see Joseph W. Alba and J. Wesley Hutchinson, "Knowledge Calibration: What Consumers Know and What They Think They Know," *Journal of Consumer Research*, September 2000, pp. 123–57.

4. For in-depth studies on external information search patterns, see Brian T. Ratchford, Debabrata Talukdar, and Myung-Soo Lee, "The Impact of the Internet on Consumers' Use of Information Sources for Automobiles: A Re-Inquiry," *Journal of Consumer*

Research, June 2007, pp. 111–19; Joel E. Urbany, Peter R. Dickson, and William L. Wilkie, "Buyer Uncertainty and Information Search," *Journal of Consumer Research,* March 1992, pp. 452–63; and Sharon E. Beatty and Scott M. Smith, "External Search Effort: An Investigation across Several Product Categories," *Journal of Consumer Research,* June 1987, pp. 83–95.

5. "The 10 Best Smartphones," www.pcmag.com, March 18, 2015; "Ten Best Smartphones in the U.S.," www.techradar.com, April 4, 2015.

6. For an extended discussion on evaluative criteria, see Delbert I. Hawkins, David L. Mothersbaugh, and Roger Best, *Consumer Behavior: Building Marketing Strategy,* 12th ed. (Burr Ridge, IL: McGraw-Hill/Irwin, 2013).

7. John A. Howard, *Buyer Behavior in Marketing Strategy,* 2nd ed. (Englewood Cliffs, NJ: Prentice Hall, 1994). For an extended discussion on consumer choice sets, see Allan D. Shocker, Moshe Ben-Akiva, Brun Boccara, and Prakesh Nedungadi, "Consideration Set Influences on Consumer Decision Making and Choice: Issues, Models, and Suggestions," *Marketing Letters,* August 1991, pp. 181–98.

8. Robert J. Donovan, John R. Rossiter, Gillian Marcoolyn, and Andrew Nesdale, "Store Atmosphere and Purchasing Behavior," *Journal of Retailing,* Fall 1994, pp. 283–94; and Eric A. Greenleaf and Donald R. Lehmann, "Reasons for Substantial Delay in Consumer Decision Making," *Journal of Consumer Research,* September 1995, pp. 186–99.

9. "Phone-Wielding Shoppers Strike Fear into Retailers," *The Wall Street Journal,* December 16, 2010, pp. A1, A9.

10. Sunil Gupta and Valarie Zeithaml, "Customer Metrics and Their Impact on Financial Performance," *Marketing Science,* November–December 2006, pp. 718–39.

11. These estimates are given in Jagdish N. Sheth and Banwari Mitral, *Consumer Behavior,* 2nd ed. (Mason, OH: South-Western Publishing, 2003), p. 32.

12. For an in-depth examination of this topic, see "Car Buyers Are Most Loyal to These Brands," *cnbc.com,* July 2, 2014; and Sunil Gupta and Donald R. Lehmann, *Managing Customers as Investments* (Upper Saddle River, NJ: Pearson Education, Inc., 2005).

13. For an overview of research on involvement, see Wayne D. Hoyer, Deborah J. MacInnis, and Rik Pieters, *Consumer Behavior,* 6th ed. (Florence, KY: South-Western Education Publishing, 2013).

14. Russell Belk, "Situational Variables and Consumer Behavior," *Journal of Consumer Research,* December 1975, pp. 157–63. The examples in this section are taken from Martin Lindstrom, *buy.ology: Truth and Lies about Why We Buy* (New York: Doubleday Publishing, 2008).

15. A. H. Maslow, *Motivation and Personality* (New York: Harper & Row, 1970). Also see Richard Yalch and Frederic Brunel, "Need Hierarchies in Consumer Judgments of Product Design: Is It Time to Reconsider Maslow's Hierarchy?" in Kim Corfman and John Lynch, eds., *Advances in Consumer Research* (Provo, UT: Association for Consumer Research, 1996), pp. 405–10.

16. Bernardo J. Carducci, *The Psychology of Personality,* 2nd ed. (Oxford, UK: John Wiley & Sons, 2009), pp. 182–84.

17. Jane Spencer, "Lenovo Puts Style in New Laptop," *The Wall Street Journal,* January 3, 2008, p. B5.

18. This example is provided in Michael R. Solomon, *Consumer Behavior,* 4th ed. (Upper Saddle River, NJ: Prentice Hall, 1999), p. 59.

19. For further reading on subliminal perception, see Lindstrom, *buy.ology;* B. Bahrami, N. Lavie, and G. Rees, "Attentional Load Modulates Responses of Human Primary Visual Cortex to Invisible Stimuli," *Current Biology,* March 2007, pp. 39–47; and J. Karremans, W. Stroebe, and J. Claus, "Beyond Vicary's Fantasies: The Impact of Subliminal Priming and Brand Choice," *Journal of Experimental Social Psychology* 42 (2006), pp. 792–98.

20. August Bullock, *The Secret Sales Pitch* (San Jose, CA: Norwich Publishers, 2004); and Dave Lakhani, *Subliminal Persuasion* (Hoboken, NJ: John Wiley & Sons, 2008).

21. "Say Goodbye to the Car Salesman," *The Wall Street Journal,* November 21, 2013, pp. B1, B6.

22. Steve Olenski, "Is Brand Loyalty Dying a Slow and Painful Death?" www.forbes.com, January 7, 2013; and Sholnn Freeman, "Brand Breakdown," *The Washington Post,* March 26, 2006, p. F1ff.

23. Martin Fishbein and I. Aizen, *Belief, Attitude, Intention and Behavior: An Introduction to Theory and Research* (Reading, MA: Addison-Wesley, 1975), p. 6.

24. Richard J. Lutz, "Changing Brand Attitudes through Modification of Cognitive Structure," *Journal of Consumer Research,* March 1975, pp. 49–59.

25. This discussion is based on "The VALS™ Types," www.strategicbusinessinsights.com, downloaded February 1, 2015.

26. This discussion is based on Ed Keller and Jon Berry, *The Influentials* (New York: Simon and Schuster, 2003).

27. Ed Keller and Brad Fay, "Word-of-Mouth Advocacy: A New Key to Advertising Effectiveness," *Journal of Advertising Research,* December 2012, pp. 459–64.

28. Emanuel Rosen, *The Anatomy of Buzz Revisited* (New York: Crown Business, 2009).

29. www.bzzAgent.com, downloaded January 10, 2015.

30. Emanuel Rosen, "Conversation Starter," *BrandWeek,* April 12, 2010, p. 16.

31. Hoyer, MacInnis, and Pieters, *Consumer Behavior.*

32. Elizabeth Holmes, "Abercrombie and Fitch Offers to Pay 'The Situation' to Stop Wearing Its Clothes," *The Wall Street Journal,* August 16, 2011, p. B2.

33. For an extensive review on consumer socialization of children, see Deborah Roedder John, "Consumer Socialization of Children: A Retrospective Look at Twenty-Five Years of Research," *Journal of Consumer Research,* December 1999, pp. 183–213. Also see Gwen Bachmann Achenreiner and Deborah Roedder John, "The Meaning of Brand Names to Children: A Developmental Investigation," *Journal of Consumer Psychology* 13, no. 3 (2003), pp. 205–19; and Elizabeth S. Moore, William L. Wilkie, and Richard J. Lutz, "Passing the Torch: Intergenerational Influences as a Source of Brand Equity," *Journal of Marketing,* April 2002, pp. 17–37.

34. J. Paul Peter and Jerry C. Olson, *Consumer Behavior and Marketing Strategy,* 9th ed. (Burr Ridge, IL: McGraw-Hill/Irwin, 2010); "Grocers Catering More to Men" *Dallas Morning News,* January 13, 2013, p. 3D; "Who Makes the Call at the Mall, Men or Women?" *The Wall Street Journal,* April 23–24, 2011, p. A1; and Rich Morin and D'Vera Cohn, "Women Call the Shots at Home: Public Mixed on Gender Roles in Jobs," www.pewresearch.org, downloaded February 4, 2011. Also see Rex Y. Du and Wagner A. Kamakura, "Household Life Cycles and Lifestyles in the United States," *Journal of Marketing Research,* February 2006, pp. 121–32.

35. This discussion is based on Hawkins, Mothersbaugh, and Best, *Consumer Behavior: Building Marketing Strategy;* "Groceries Become a Guy Thing," *The Wall Street Journal,* October 17, 2013, pp. D1, D2; *The Kids and Tweens Market in the U.S.,* 9th ed. (Rockville, MD: Packaged Facts, August 1, 2008); and "How Teens Use Media" (New York: Neilsen Company, June 2009).

36. Jeffrey M. Humphreys, "The Multicultural Economy in 2014," Selig Center for Economic Growth, Terry College of Business, The University of Georgia.

37. The remainder of this discussion is based on Hoyer, MacInnis, and Pieters, *Consumer Behavior;* "The Lust for Latino Lucre," *The Economist,* May 11, 2013, p. 71; *Engaging the Evolving*

Hispanic Consumer (New York: The Nielsen Company, 2014); and *10th Annual Hispanic Fact Pack* (New York: Advertising Age, 2014).

38. The remainder of this discussion is based on Peter and Olson, *Consumer Behavior and Marketing Strategy;* and *Powerful, Growing, Influencial: The African-American Consumer* (New York: The Nielsen Company, 2014).

39. The remainder of this discussion is based on *The State of the Asian American Consumer: Growing Market, Growing Impact* (New York: The Nielsen Company, 2012); Christine Birkner, "Asian-Americans in Focus," *Marketing News,* March 2013, p. 14; and Lee Siegel, "Rise of the Tiger Nation," *The Wall Street Journal,* October 27–28, 2012, pp. C1, C2.

40. Groupon: This case was written by Steven Hartley. Sources: Bari Weiss, "The Journal Interview with Andrew Mason: Groupon's $6 Billion Gambler," *The Wall Street Journal,* December 20, 2010, p. 12; Brad Stone and Douglas

MacMillan, "Are Four Words Worth $25 Billion?" *Bloomberg Businessweek*, March 21, 2011, pp. 70–75; Brendan Coffey, "What's the Deal?" *Forbes*, April 25, 2011, pp. 20–22; Brad Stone and Douglas MacMillan, "Groupon's $6 Billion Snub," *Bloomberg Businessweek*, December 13, 2010, pp. 6–7; Christopher Steiner, "Meet the Fastest Growing Company Ever," *Forbes*, August 30, 2010; Rupal Parekh, "Groupon," *Advertising Age*, November 15, 2010, p. 20; "10 Big Stories for the Week," *Advertising Age*, December 13, 2010, pp. 12–13; Jessi Hempel, "Social Media Meets Retailing," *Fortune*, March 22, 2010, p. 30; Kunur Patel, "Suddenly, Everyone Wants to Be Groupon," *Advertising Age*, November 1, 2010, p. 1; Brad Stone, "Coupon Deathmatch, Party of Two?" *Bloomberg Businessweek*, October 4, 2010, pp. 37–38; and "Q1 2013 Fact Sheet" and "2012 Letter to Shareholders," on Groupon website, http://investor.groupon.com/, accessed July 8, 2013.

6

Understanding Organizations as Customers

LEARNING OBJECTIVES

After reading this chapter you should be able to:

 LO 6-1 Distinguish among industrial, reseller, and government organizational markets.

 LO 6-2 Describe the key characteristics of organizational buying that make it different from consumer buying.

 LO 6-3 Explain how buying centers and buying situations influence organizational purchasing.

LO 6-4 Recognize the importance and nature of online buying in industrial, reseller, and government organizational markets.

Buying Is Marketing, Too! Purchasing Publication Paper for JCPenney

Kim Nagele views paper differently than most people do. As the senior purchasing manager at JCPMedia, Inc., he and a team of purchasing professionals annually buy about 150,000 tons of publication paper.

JCPMedia, Inc. is responsible for print and paper purchasing at JCPenney, one of the largest department store retailers in the United States. Paper purchasing is a serious marketing responsibility for JCPMedia, Inc., which buys publication paper for JCPenney newspaper inserts and direct-mail pieces. Some 10 companies from around the world—including Verso Paper in the United States, Catalyst Paper, Inc. in Canada, Norske Skog in Norway, and UPM-Kymmene, Inc. in Finland—supply paper to JCPenney.

"The choice of paper and suppliers is also a significant marketing decision given the sizable revenue and expense consequences," notes Tom Cassidy, Vice President–Marketing Production at JCPMedia, Inc. JCPMedia, Inc. paper buyers work closely with senior JCPenney marketing executives and within budget constraints to assure that the right appearance, quality, and quantity of publication paper is purchased at the right price point for merchandise featured in the millions of JCPenney newspaper inserts and direct-mail pieces distributed every year in the United States.

JCPMedia, Inc. paper buyers themselves are thoroughly trained in many facets of purchasing. For example, Kim Nagele is a Certified Professional in Supply Management (CPSM). The CPSM designation is awarded to those individuals who have demonstrated competence in such areas as contracting and negotiation, cost management, forecasting, and materials and inventory management through a rigorous examination process.

In addition to paper appearance, quality, quantity, and price, JCPMedia paper buyers formally evaluate paper supplier capabilities, often by extended visits to supplier facilities in the United States, Canada, and Europe. Supplier capabilities include the capacity to deliver on-time selected grades of paper from specialty items to magazine papers, the availability of specific types of paper to meet printing deadlines, and formal programs focused on the life cycle of paper products. For example, a supplier's forestry management and sustainability practices are considered in the paper buying process. In fact, paper bought by JCPMedia, Inc. is certified through the Sustainable Forestry Initiative, Forest Stewardship Council, or the Programme for the Endorsement of Forest Certification—three prominent certification programs for forest management.[1]

The next time you thumb through a JCPenney newspaper insert or direct-mail piece, take a moment to notice the paper. Considerable effort and attention was given to its selection and purchase decision by Tom Cassidy, Kim Nagele, and JCPMedia, Inc. paper buyers.

Purchasing paper for JCPMedia is one example of organizational buying. This chapter examines the different types of organizational buyers; key characteristics of organizational buying, including online buying; buying situations; unique aspects of the organizational buying process compared with the consumer purchase process; and some typical buying procedures and decisions in today's organizational markets.

BUSINESS-TO-BUSINESS MARKETING AND ORGANIZATIONAL BUYERS

LO 6-1 Distinguish among industrial, reseller, and government organizational markets.

Understanding organizational markets and buying behavior is a necessary prerequisite for effective business-to-business marketing. **Business-to-business marketing** is the marketing of products and services to companies, governments, or not-for-profit organizations for use in the creation of products and services that they can produce and market to others. Because over half of all U.S. business school graduates take jobs in firms that engage in business marketing, it is important to understand the characteristics of organizational buyers and their buying behavior.

Organizational Buyers

Organizational buyers are those manufacturers, wholesalers, retailers, service companies, not-for-profit organizations, and government agencies that buy products and services for their own use or for resale. For example, these organizations buy computers and telephone services for their own use. However, manufacturers buy raw materials and parts that they reprocess into the finished goods they sell. Wholesalers and retailers resell the goods they buy without reprocessing them.

Organizational buyers include all buyers in a nation except ultimate consumers. These organizational buyers purchase and lease large volumes of capital equipment, raw materials, manufactured parts, supplies, and business services. In fact, because they often buy raw materials and parts, process them, and sell the upgraded product several times before it is purchased by the final organizational buyer or ultimate consumer, the total annual purchases of organizational buyers are far greater than those of ultimate consumers. IBM alone buys over $50 billion in products and services each year for its own use or resale.[2]

Organizational Markets

Organizational buyers are divided into three markets: (1) industrial, (2) reseller, and (3) government.[3] Each market is described next.

Industrial Markets   There are about 7.5 million firms in the industrial, or business, market. These *industrial firms* in some way reprocess a product or service they buy before selling it again to the next buyer. This is certainly true of Corning, Inc., which transforms an exotic blend of materials to create optical fiber capable of carrying much of the telephone traffic in the United States on a single strand. It is also true (if you stretch your imagination) of a firm selling services, such as a bank that takes money from its depositors, reprocesses it, and "sells" it as loans to borrowers.

Companies that primarily sell physical goods (manufacturers; mining; construction; and farms, timber, and fisheries) represent 25 percent of all the industrial firms. The services market sells diverse services such as legal advice, auto repair, and dry cleaning. Service companies—finance, insurance, and real estate businesses; transportation, communication, and public utility firms; and not-for-profit organizations—represent 75 percent of all industrial firms. Because of the size and importance of service companies and not-for-profit organizations (such as the American Red Cross), services marketing is discussed in detail in Chapter 12.

Reseller Markets   Wholesalers and retailers that buy physical products and resell them again without any reprocessing are *resellers*. In the United States there are about 1.1 million retailers and 435,000 wholesalers. In Chapters 15 and 16 you will see how manufacturers use wholesalers and retailers in their distribution ("place") strategies as channels through which their products reach ultimate consumers. In this chapter, we look at these resellers mainly as organizational buyers in terms of (1) how they make their own buying decisions and (2) which products they choose to carry.

The Orion spacecraft to be designed, developed, tested, and evaluated by Lockheed Martin Corp. is an example of a purchase by a government unit, namely the National Aeronautics and Space Administration (NASA). Read the text to find out how much NASA will pay for Orion's development, test flights, and its first manned mission in 2021.

Courtesy Lockheed Martin Company

Video 6-1

NASA

kerin.tv/13e/v6-1

Government Markets   *Government units* are the federal, state, and local agencies that buy goods and services for the constituents they serve. There are about 89,500 of these government units in the United States. These purchases include the $11.4 billion the National Aeronautics and Space Administration (NASA) intends to pay Lockheed Martin to develop and launch the with its first manned mission in 2021.[4]

Measuring Organizational Markets

The measurement of industrial, reseller, and government markets is an important first step for a firm interested in gauging the size of one, two, or all three of these markets in the United States and around the world. This task has been made easier with the **North American Industry Classification System (NAICS)**. The NAICS provides common industry definitions for Canada, Mexico, and the United States, which makes it easier to measure economic activity in the three member countries of the North American Free Trade Agreement (NAFTA).

The NAICS groups economic activity to permit studies of market share, demand for products and services, import competition in domestic markets, and similar studies. It designates industries with a numerical code in a defined structure. A six-digit coding system is used. The first two digits designate a sector of the economy, the third digit designates a subsector, and the fourth digit represents an industry group. The fifth digit designates a specific industry and is the most detailed level at which comparable data are available for Canada, Mexico, and the United States. The sixth digit designates individual country-level national industries.

learning review

6-1.   Organizational buyers are _____.

6-2.   What are the three main types of organizational buyers?

CHARACTERISTICS OF ORGANIZATIONAL BUYING

 LO 6-2 Describe the key characteristics of organizational buying that make it different from consumer buying.

Organizations are different from individuals, so buying for an organization is different from buying for yourself or your family. In both cases the objective in making the purchase is to solve the buyer's problem—to satisfy a need or want. However, the unique objectives and policies of an organization put special constraints on how it makes buying decisions. Understanding the characteristics of organizational buying is essential in designing effective marketing programs to reach these buyers. Key characteristics of organizational buying are listed in Figure 6–1 and discussed next.[5]

Demand Characteristics

Consumer demand for products and services is affected by their price and availability and by consumers' personal tastes and discretionary income. By comparison, industrial demand is derived. **Derived demand** means that the demand for industrial products and services is driven by, or derived from, demand for consumer products and services. For example, the demand for Weyerhaeuser's pulp and paper products is based on consumer demand for newspapers, FedEx packages, and disposable diapers. Derived demand is based on expectations of future consumer demand. For instance, Whirlpool buys parts for its washers and dryers in anticipation of consumer demand, which is affected by the replacement cycle for these products and by consumer income.

FIGURE 6–1

Key characteristics and dimensions of organizational buying behavior.

CHARACTERISTICS	DIMENSIONS
Market characteristics	• Demand for industrial products and services is derived. • Few customers typically exist, and their purchase orders are large.
Product or service characteristics	• Products or services are technical in nature and purchased on the basis of specifications. • Many of the goods purchased are raw and semifinished. • Heavy emphasis is placed on delivery time, technical assistance, and postsale service.
Buying process characteristics	• Technically qualified and professional buyers follow established purchasing policies and procedures. • Buying objectives and criteria are typically spelled out, as are procedures for evaluating sellers and their products or services. • There are multiple buying influences, and multiple parties participate in purchase decisions. • There are reciprocal arrangements, and negotiation between buyers and sellers is commonplace. • Online buying over the Internet is widespread.
Marketing mix characteristics	• Direct selling to organizational buyers is the rule, and distribution is very important. • Advertising and other forms of promotion are technical in nature. • Price is often negotiated, evaluated as part of broader seller and product/service qualities, and frequently affected by quantity discounts.

Size of the Order or Purchase

The size of the purchase involved in organizational buying is typically much larger than that in consumer buying. The dollar value of a single purchase made by an organization often runs into thousands or millions of dollars. For example, Siemens was recently awarded a $300 million contract to build a natural-gas-fired power plant in Texas.[6] The Boeing Company, the world's largest aerospace company, charges about $96 million for its "average" Boeing 737 commercial jetliner, $327 million for its Boeing 777, and $257 million for the Boeing 787.[7]

With so much money at stake, most organizations place constraints on their buyers in the form of purchasing policies or procedures. Buyers must often get competitive bids from at least three prospective suppliers when the order is above a specific amount, such as $5,000. When the order is above an even higher amount, such as $50,000, it may require the review and approval of a vice president or even the president of the company. Knowing how order size affects buying practices is important in determining who will participate in the purchase decision, who will make the final decision, and the length of time that will be required to arrive at a purchase agreement.

Buying commercial aircraft is time-consuming, involved, and expensive. Read the text to find out how much a new Boeing airplane costs.

© Karie Hamilton/Bloomberg via Getty Images

Number of Potential Buyers

Firms marketing consumer products or services often try to reach thousands or millions of individuals or households. For example, your local supermarket or bank probably serves thousands of people. Kellogg tries to reach 80 million North American households with its breakfast cereals and probably succeeds in selling to a third or half of these in any given year. Firms marketing to organizations are often restricted to far fewer buyers. Gulfstream Aerospace Corporation can sell its business jets to a few thousand organizations throughout the world, and Goodyear sells its original equipment tires to fewer than 10 car manufacturers.

Organizational Buying Objectives

Organizations buy products and services for one main reason: to help them achieve their objectives. For business firms, the buying objective is usually to increase profits through reducing costs or increasing revenues. For example, 7-Eleven buys automated inventory systems to increase the number of products that can be sold through its convenience stores and to keep them fresh. Nissan Motor Company switched its advertising agency because it expects the new agency to devise a more effective ad campaign to help it sell more cars and increase revenues. To improve executive decision making, many firms buy advanced computer systems to process data. The objectives of nonprofit firms and government agencies are usually to meet the needs of the groups they serve.

Many companies today have broadened their buying objectives to include an emphasis on buying from minority- and women-owned suppliers and vendors. Companies such as Pitney Bowes, PepsiCo, AT&T, Coors, and JCPenney report that sales, profits, and customer satisfaction have increased because of their minority- and women-owned supplier and vendor initiatives. To learn more about companies that have successful supplier diversity programs, and corporate diversity overall, visit diversityinc.com described in the Marketing Insights About Me box.

Pitney Bowes is a leader in supplier diversity. The company has hundreds of diverse suppliers that account for millions of dollars in annual purchases.

© Pitney Bowes

Supplier Diversity Program

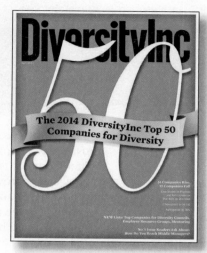
Other companies include environmental sustainability initiatives. For example, Lowe's and Home Depot no longer purchase lumber from companies that harvest timber from the world's endangered forests. Successful business marketers recognize that understanding a company's buying objectives is a necessary first step in marketing to organizations.

Organizational Buying Criteria

In making a purchase, the buying organization must weigh key buying criteria that apply to the potential supplier and what it wants to sell. *Organizational buying criteria* are the objective attributes of the supplier's products and services and the capabilities of the supplier itself. These criteria serve the same purpose as the evaluative criteria used by consumers and described in Chapter 5. The most commonly used criteria are (1) price, (2) ability to meet the quality specifications required for the item, (3) ability to meet required delivery schedules, (4) technical capability, (5) warranties and claim policies in the event of poor performance, (6) past performance on previous contracts, and (7) production facilities and capacity.[8] Suppliers that meet or exceed these criteria create customer value.

As a practical example, Figure 6–2 shows the actual buying criteria employed by organizational buyers when choosing among machine vision system products and suppliers, as well as the frequency with which these criteria are used. Interestingly, of the various selection criteria listed, a machine vision system's price is among the least frequently mentioned.[9]

Many organizational buyers today are transforming their buying criteria into specific requirements that are communicated to prospective suppliers. This practice, called *supplier development,* involves the deliberate effort by organizational buyers to build relationships that shape suppliers' products, services, and capabilities to fit a buyer's needs and those of its customers. Consider Deere & Company,

FIGURE 6–2

Product and supplier selection criteria for buying machine vision equipment emphasize factors other than price.

© Keyence Corporation of America

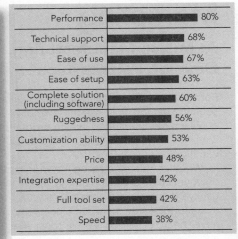

Performance	80%
Technical support	68%
Ease of use	67%
Ease of setup	63%
Complete solution (including software)	60%
Ruggedness	56%
Customization ability	53%
Price	48%
Integration expertise	42%
Full tool set	42%
Speed	38%

A machine vision inspection camera is used in the automotive industry to perform a gear inspection—in this case, to check if the notches are correctly angled and sized.

Percentage of machine vision buyers citing individual selection criteria as most important when making a product or supplier decision.

the maker of John Deere farm, construction, and lawn-care equipment. Deere employs supplier-development engineers who work full-time with the company's suppliers to improve their efficiency and quality and reduce their costs. According to a Deere senior executive, "Their quality, delivery, and costs are, after all, our quality, delivery, and costs."[10]

Buyer–Seller Relationships and Supply Partnerships

Another distinction between organizational and consumer buying behavior lies in the nature of the relationship between organizational buyers and suppliers. Specifically, organizational buying is more likely to involve complex negotiations concerning delivery schedules, price, technical specifications, warranties, and claim policies. These negotiations also can last for an extended period. This was the case when the Lawrence Livermore National Laboratory acquired an IBM Sequoia supercomputer at a cost of about $250 million. In terms of processing speed, the amount of data that the Sequoia can process in one hour is equivalent to what 6.7 billion people would be able to calculate (using calculators)—if they had 320 years to do their work![11]

Reciprocal arrangements also exist in organizational buying. *Reciprocity* is an industrial buying practice in which two organizations agree to purchase each other's products and services. The U.S. Justice Department disapproves of reciprocal buying because it restricts the normal operation of the free market. However, the practice exists and can limit the flexibility of organizational buyers in choosing alternative suppliers.

Long-term contracts are also prevalent. Hewlett-Packard has a 10-year, $3 billion contract to manage Procter & Gamble's information technology in 160 countries.[12]

In some cases, buyer–seller relationships evolve into supply partnerships. A *supply partnership* exists when a buyer and its supplier adopt mutually beneficial objectives, policies, and procedures for the purpose of lowering the cost or increasing the value of products and services delivered to the ultimate consumer. A classic example of a supply partnership is the one between Harley-Davidson and Milsco Manufacturing.

At Milsco Manufacturing, "Our Marketing Philosophy Is Designed to Develop Partnerships" and Deliver a Great Ride for Customers' Seats

Form, fit, and functionality are the hallmarks of a proper seating solution. Just ask the executives and engineers at Milsco Manufacturing, which produces more than 3 million seats annually in more than 200 unique variations.

Whether you are cruising the wide open spaces on your Harley-Davidson motorcycle or mowing your backyard on a John Deere lawn tractor, you're getting a comfortable ride thanks to a company you may have never heard of. Milsco is a Wisconsin-based designer and producer of seating solutions. Its customers include Harley-Davidson, John Deere, Yamaha, Caterpillar, Arctic Cat, Kubata, Toro, and Toyota, as well as numerous other well-known and respected household names in the motorcycle, power sports, agricultural, construction, marine recreation, turf care, industrial lift, golf cart, and mobility markets.

Milsco's marketing philosophy is designed to develop partnerships with its customers. The 82-year partnership between Harley-Davidson and Milsco is a case in point. Since 1934, Milsco has been the sole source of original equipment motorcycle seats and a major supplier of after-market parts and accessories, such as saddlebags, for Harley-Davidson. Milsco engineers and designers work closely with their Harley counterparts in the design of each year's new products.

In fact, Milsco partners with each of its customers to design and manufacture the most effective and functional seating solution. Every year, the company launches over 100 new products, many of which are crafted by hand, in response to new and changing customer requirements.

The next time you sit down on a Harley or a John Deere lawn tractor (or any other product involving a partnership with Milsco Manufacturing), notice the

© Lluis Gene/AFP/Getty Images

seat and remember that it was designed and manufactured for your form, fit, and functionality—and, of course, comfort.

Milsco has designed and manufactured Harley-Davidson motorcycle seats for 82 years. The importance of supply partnerships for Milsco is described in the Marketing Matters box.[13]

Retailers, too, have forged partnerships with their suppliers. Walmart has such a relationship with Procter & Gamble for ordering and replenishing P&G's products in its stores. By using computerized cash register scanning equipment and direct electronic linkages to P&G, Walmart can tell P&G what merchandise is needed, along with how much, when, and to which store to deliver it on a daily basis.

Supply partnerships often include provisions for what is called *sustainable procurement*. This buying practice is described in the Making Responsible Decisions box.[14]

Video 6-2
Starbucks
Sustainability
kerin.tv/13e/v6-2

Making **Responsible Decisions** |

Sustainable Procurement for Sustainable Growth at Starbucks

Manufacturers, retailers, wholesalers, and governmental agencies are increasingly sensitive to how their buying decisions affect the environment. Concerns about the depletion of natural resources; air, water, and soil pollution; and the social consequences of economic activity have given rise to the concept of sustainable procurement. Sustainable procurement aims to integrate environmental considerations into all stages of an organization's buying process with the goal of reducing the negative impact on human health and the physical environment.

Starbucks is a pioneer and worldwide leader in sustainable procurement. The company's attention to quality coffee extends to its coffee growers located in more than 20 countries. This means that Starbucks pays coffee farmers a fair price for the beans; that the coffee is grown in an ecologically sound manner; and that Starbucks

invests in the farming communities where its coffees are produced. In this way, Starbucks focuses on the sustainable growth of its suppliers.

© Jewel Samad/AFP/Getty Images

THE ORGANIZATIONAL BUYING FUNCTION AND PROCESS AND THE BUYING CENTER

Organizational buyers, like consumers, engage in a decision process when selecting products and services. **Organizational buying behavior** is the decision-making process that organizations use to establish the need for products and services and identify, evaluate, and choose among alternative brands and suppliers. There are important similarities and differences between the two decision-making processes. To better understand the nature of organizational buying behavior, we first describe the buying function in organizations. The organizational buying process itself is then detailed by comparing it with consumer buying behavior. We then describe a unique feature of organizational buying—the buying center.

The Buying Function in Organizations

The buying function in an organization is primarily responsible for facilitating the selection and purchase of products and services for the organization's own use or resale to consumers. The buying function involves gathering and screening information about products and services, prices, and suppliers, called *vendors*. The buying function is often responsible for the formal solicitation of bids from suppliers (vendors) and making awards of purchasing contracts.

Individuals responsible for the selection and purchase of goods and services are typically called purchasing managers or agents, procurement managers, or sourcing managers. Their role in the organizational buying process is described below.

Stages in the Organizational Buying Process

As shown in Figure 6–3, the five stages a student might use in buying a smartphone also apply to organizational purchases. However, comparing the two smartphone columns in Figure 6–3 reveals some key differences. For example, when a manufacturer

STAGE IN THE BUYING DECISION PROCESS	CONSUMER PURCHASE: SMARTPHONE FOR A STUDENT	ORGANIZATIONAL PURCHASE: EARBUD HEADSET FOR A SMARTPHONE
Problem recognition	Student doesn't like the features of the smartphone now owned and desires a new one.	Marketing research and sales departments observe that competitors are improving the earbud headsets for their smartphones. The firm decides to improve the earbud headsets on its own new models, which will be purchased from an outside supplier.
Information search	Student uses personal past experience and that of friends, ads, the Internet, and *Consumer Reports* to collect information and uncover alternatives.	Design and production engineers draft specifications for earbud headsets. The purchasing department identifies suppliers of earbud headsets.
Alternative evaluation	Alternative smartphones are evaluated on the basis of important attributes desired in a phone, and several stores are visited.	Purchasing and engineering personnel visit with suppliers and assess (1) facilities, (2) capacity, (3) quality control, and (4) financial status. They drop any suppliers not satisfactory on these attributes.
Purchase decision	A specific brand of smartphone is selected, the price is paid, and the student leaves the store.	They use (1) quality, (2) price, (3) delivery, and (4) technical capability as key buying criteria to select a supplier. Then they negotiate terms and award a contract.
Postpurchase behavior	Student reevaluates the purchase decision and may return the phone to the store if it is unsatisfactory.	They evaluate suppliers using a formal vendor rating system and notify a supplier if the earbud headsets do not meet their quality standard. If the problem is not corrected, they drop the firm as a future supplier.

FIGURE 6–3

Comparing the stages in a consumer and organizational purchase decision process.

buys an earbud headset for its units from a supplier, more individuals are involved, supplier capability becomes more important, and the postpurchase evaluation behavior is more formal. The earbud headset buying decision process is typical of the steps made by organizational buyers.

The Buying Center: A Cross-Functional Group

LO 6-3 — Explain how buying centers and buying situations influence organizational purchasing.

For routine purchases with a small dollar value, a single buyer or purchasing manager often makes the purchase decision alone. In many instances, however, several people in the organization participate in the buying process. The individuals in this group, called a **buying center**, share common goals, risks, and knowledge important to a purchase decision. For most large multistore chain resellers, such as Target, 7-Eleven convenience stores, or Safeway, the buying center is highly formalized and is called a *buying committee*. However, most industrial firms or government units use informal groups of people or call meetings to arrive at buying decisions.

The importance of the buying center requires that a firm marketing to many industrial firms and government units understand the structure, the technical and business functions represented, and the behavior of these groups.[15] Four questions provide guidance in understanding the buying center in these organizations:

1. Which individuals are in the buying center for the product or service?
2. What is the relative influence of each member of the group?

3. What are the buying criteria of each member?

4. How does each member of the group perceive our firm, our products and services, and our salespeople?

People in the Buying Center   The composition of the buying center in a given organization depends on the specific item being bought. Although a buyer or purchasing manager is almost always a member of the buying center, individuals from other functional areas are included, depending on what is to be purchased. In buying a million-dollar machine tool, the president (because of the size of the purchase) and the production vice president or manager would probably be members. For key components to be included in a final manufactured product, a cross-functional group of individuals from research and development (R&D), engineering, and quality control are likely to be added. For new word-processing equipment, experienced secretaries who will use the equipment would be members. Still, a major question in penetrating the buying center is finding and reaching the people who will initiate, influence, and actually make the buying decision.

Roles in the Buying Center   Researchers have identified five specific roles that an individual in a buying center can play.[16] In some purchases the same person may perform two or more of these roles.

Effective marketing to organizations requires an understanding of buying centers and their role in purchase decisions.
© Mark Adams/Media Bakery

- *Users* are the people in the organization who actually use the product or service, such as a secretary who will use a new word processor.
- *Influencers* affect the buying decision, usually by helping define the specifications for what is bought. The information technology manager would be a key influencer in the purchase of a new mainframe computer.
- *Buyers* have formal authority and responsibility to select the supplier and negotiate the terms of the contract. Kim Nagele performs this role as senior purchasing manager at JCPMedia, as described in the chapter opening example.
- *Deciders* have the formal or informal power to select or approve the supplier that receives the contract. In routine orders the decider is usually the buyer or purchasing manager; in important technical purchases it is more likely to be someone from R&D, engineering, or quality control. The decider for a key component being incorporated in a final manufactured product might be any of these three people.
- *Gatekeepers* control the flow of information in the buying center. Purchasing personnel, technical experts, and secretaries can all keep salespeople or information from reaching people performing the other four roles.

Buying Situations and the Buying Center   The number of people in the buying center largely depends on the specific buying situation. Researchers who have studied organizational buying identify three types of buying situations, called **buy classes**. These buy classes vary from the routine reorder, or *straight rebuy*, to the completely new purchase, termed *new buy*. In between these extremes is the *modified rebuy*. Figure 6–4 summarizes how buy classes affect buying center tendencies in different ways. Some examples will clarify the differences.[17]

- *New buy*. Here the organization is a first-time buyer of the product or service. This involves greater potential risks in the purchase, so the buying center is enlarged to include all those who have a stake in the new buy. Procter & Gamble's purchase of a multimillion-dollar fiber-optic network from Corning, Inc. for its corporate offices in Cincinnati, represented a new buy.

BUYING CENTER DIMENSION	BUY-CLASS SITUATION		
	NEW BUY	STRAIGHT REBUY	MODIFIED REBUY
People involved	Many	One	Two to three
Decision time	Long	Short	Moderate
Problem definition	Uncertain	Well-defined	Minor modifications
Buying objective	Good solution	Low-priced supplier	Low-priced supplier
Suppliers considered	New/present	Present	Present
Buying influence	Technical/operating personnel	Purchasing agent	Purchasing agent and others

FIGURE 6–4

The buying situation affects buying center behavior in different ways. Understanding these differences can pay huge dividends for companies that market to organizations.

- *Straight rebuy.* Here the buyer or purchasing manager reorders an existing product or service from the list of acceptable suppliers, probably without even checking with users or influencers from the engineering, production, or quality control departments. Office supplies and maintenance services are usually obtained as straight rebuys.
- *Modified rebuy.* In this buying situation the users, influencers, or deciders in the buying center want to change the product specifications, price, delivery schedule, or supplier. Although the item purchased is largely the same as with the straight rebuy, the changes usually necessitate enlarging the buying center to include people outside the purchasing department.

 learning review

6-3. What one department is almost always represented by a person in the buying center?

6-4. What are the three types of buying situations or buy classes?

ONLINE BUYING IN BUSINESS-TO-BUSINESS MARKETING

 LO 6-4 Recognize the importance and nature of online buying in industrial, reseller, and government organizational markets.

Organizational buying behavior and business-to-business marketing continues to evolve with the application of Internet technology. Organizations dwarf consumers in terms of online transactions made, average transaction size, and overall purchase volume. In fact, organizational buyers account for about 80 percent of the global dollar value of all online transactions.

Prominence of Online Buying in Organizational Markets

Online buying in organizational markets is prominent for three major reasons.[18] First, organizational buyers depend heavily on timely supplier information that describes product availability, technical specifications, application uses, price, and delivery schedules. This information can be conveyed quickly via Internet technology. Second, this technology has been shown to substantially reduce buyer order processing costs. At General Electric, online buying has cut the cost of a transaction from $50 to $100 per purchase to about $5. Third, business marketers have found that Internet technology can reduce marketing costs, particularly sales and advertising expense, and broaden their potential customer base for many types of products and services.

For these reasons, online buying is popular in all three kinds of organizational markets. For example, airlines electronically order over $400 million in spare parts from the Boeing Company each year. Customers of W. W. Grainger, a large U.S. wholesaler of maintenance, repair, and operating supplies, buy almost $4 billion worth of these products annually online. Supply and service purchases totaling over $650 million each year are made online by the Los Angeles County government.

E-Marketplaces: Virtual Organizational Markets

A significant development in organizational buying has been the creation of online trading communities, called **e-marketplaces**, that bring together buyers and supplier organizations. These online communities go by a variety of names, including *B2B exchanges* and *e-hubs,* and make possible the real-time exchange of information, money, products, and services.

E-marketplaces can be independent trading communities or private exchanges. Independent e-marketplaces act as a neutral third party and provide an Internet technology trading platform and a centralized market that enable exchanges between buyers and sellers. They charge a fee for their service and exist in settings that have one or more of the following features: (1) thousands of geographically dispersed buyers and sellers, (2) volatile prices caused by demand and supply fluctuations, (3) time sensitivity due to perishable offerings and changing technologies, and (4) easily comparable offerings between a variety of sellers.

Examples of independent e-marketplaces include PlasticsNet (plastics), Hospital Network.com (health care supplies and equipment), and TextileWeb (garment and apparel products). Small business buyers and sellers, in particular, benefit from independent e-marketplaces. These e-marketplaces offer them an economical way to expand their customer base and reduce the cost of products and services. For example, eBay provides an electronic platform for entrepreneurs and the small business market in the United States and other countries. Read the Marketing Matters box to learn more about how eBay promotes entrepreneurship.[19]

Large companies tend to favor private exchanges that link them with their network of qualified suppliers and customers. Private exchanges focus on streamlining a company's purchase transactions with its suppliers and customers. Like independent e-marketplaces, they provide a technology trading platform and central market for buyer–seller interactions. They are not a neutral third party, however, but represent the interests of their owners. For example, NeoGrid is an international business-to-business private exchange. It connects more than 250 retail customers with 80,000 suppliers. Its members include Best Buy, Campbell Soup, Costco, Safeway, Target, Tesco, and Walgreens. The Global Healthcare Exchange engages in the buying and selling of health care products for over 4,000 hospitals and more than 400 health care suppliers, such as Abbott Laboratories, GE Medical Systems, Johnson & Johnson, Medtronic USA, and McKesson Corporation in North America.

Online Auctions in Organizational Markets

FIGURE 6–5

Buyer and seller participants and price behavior differ by type of online auction. As an organizational buyer, would you prefer to participate in a traditional auction or a reverse auction?

Top left, bottom right: © Jim Esposito/blend Images/Getty Images; Top right, bottom left: © Comstock Images/Getty Images

Online auctions have grown in popularity among organizational buyers and business marketers. Many e-marketplaces offer this service. Two general types of auctions are common: (1) a traditional auction and (2) a reverse auction.[20] Figure 6–5 shows how buyer and seller participants and price behavior differ by type of auction. Let's look at each auction type more closely to understand the implications of each for buyers and sellers.

In a **traditional auction** a seller puts an item up for sale and would-be buyers are invited to bid in competition with each other. As more would-be buyers become involved, there is an upward pressure on bid prices. Why? Bidding is sequential. Prospective buyers observe the bids of others and decide whether or not to increase the bid price. The auction ends when a single bidder remains and "wins" the item with its highest price. Traditional auctions are often used to dispose of excess merchandise.

Traditional auction

One seller → Price / Number of buyers ← Many buyers

Reverse auction

Many sellers → Price / Number of sellers ← One buyer

For example, Dell Inc. sells surplus, refurbished, or closeout computer merchandise at its www.dellauction.com website.

A reverse auction works in the opposite direction from a traditional auction. In a **reverse auction**, a buyer communicates a need for a product or service and would-be suppliers are invited to bid in competition with each other. As more would-be suppliers become involved, there is a downward pressure on bid prices for the buyer's business. Why? Like traditional auctions, bidding is sequential and prospective suppliers observe the bids of others and decide whether or not to decrease the bid price. The auction ends when a single bidder remains and "wins" the business with its lowest price. Reverse auctions benefit organizational buyers by reducing the cost of their purchases. As an example, United Technologies Corp. estimates that it has saved $600 million on the purchase of $6 billion in supplies using online reverse auctions.[21]

Clearly, buyers welcome the lower prices generated by reverse auctions. Suppliers often favor reverse auctions because they give them a chance to capture business that they might not have otherwise had, perhaps because of a long-standing purchase relationship between the buyer and another supplier. On the other hand, suppliers say reverse auctions put too much emphasis on prices, discourage consideration of other important buying criteria, and may threaten supply partnership opportunities.[22]

learning review ≫

6-5. What are e-marketplaces?

6-6. In general, which type of online auction creates upward pressure on bid prices and which type creates downward pressure on bid prices?

LEARNING OBJECTIVES REVIEW

LO 6-1 *Distinguish among industrial, reseller, and government organizational markets.*
There are three different organizational markets: industrial, reseller, and government. Industrial firms in some way reprocess a product or service they buy before selling it to the next buyer. Resellers—wholesalers and retailers—buy physical products and resell them again without any reprocessing. Government agencies, at the federal, state, and local levels, buy goods and services for the constituents they serve. The North American Industry Classification System (NAICS) provides common industry definitions for Canada, Mexico, and the United States, which facilitates the measurement of economic activity for these three organizational markets.

LO 6-2 *Describe the key characteristics of organizational buying that make it different from consumer buying.*
Seven major characteristics of organizational buying make it different from consumer buying. These include demand characteristics, the size of the order or purchase, the number of potential buyers, buying objectives, buying criteria, buyer–seller relationships and supply partnerships, and multiple buying influences within organizations. The organizational buying process itself is more formalized, more

individuals are involved, supplier capability is more important, and the postpurchase evaluation behavior often includes performance of the supplier and the item purchased. Figure 6–3 details how the purchase decision process differs between a consumer and an organization.

LO 6-3 *Explain how buying centers and buying situations influence organizational purchasing.*
Buying centers and buying situations have an important influence on organizational purchasing. A buying center consists of a group of individuals who share common goals, risks, and knowledge important to a purchase decision. A buyer or purchasing manager is almost always a member of a buying center. However, other individuals may affect organizational purchasing due to their unique roles in a purchase decision. Five specific roles that a person may play in a buying center include users, influencers, buyers, deciders, and gatekeepers. The specific buying situation will influence the number of people and the different roles played in a buying center. For a routine reorder of an item—a straight rebuy situation—a purchasing manager or buyer will typically act alone in making a purchasing decision. When an organization is a first-time purchaser of

a product or service—a new buy situation—a buying center is enlarged and all five roles in a buying center often emerge. A modified rebuy situation lies between these two extremes. Figure 6–4 offers additional insights into how buying centers and buying situations influence organizational purchasing.

LO 6-4 *Recognize the importance and nature of online buying in industrial, reseller, and government organizational markets.*

Organizations dwarf consumers in terms of online transactions made and purchase volume. Online buying in organizational markets is popular for three reasons. First, organizational buyers depend on timely supplier information that describes product availability, technical specifications, application uses, price, and delivery schedules. This information can be conveyed quickly via Internet technology. Second, this technology substantially reduces buyer order processing costs. Third, business marketers have found that Internet technology can reduce marketing costs, particularly sales and advertising expense, and broaden their customer base. Two developments in online buying have been the creation of e-marketplaces and online auctions. E-marketplaces provide a technology trading platform and a centralized market for buyer–seller transactions and make possible the real-time exchange of information, money, products, and services. These e-marketplaces can be independent trading communities, such as Plastics-Net, or private exchanges, such as the Global Healthcare Exchange. Online traditional and reverse auctions represent a second major development. With traditional auctions, the highest-priced bidder "wins." Conversely, the lowest-priced bidder "wins" with reverse auctions.

LEARNING REVIEW ANSWERS

6-1 Organizational buyers are _____.
Answer: Those manufacturers, wholesalers, retailers, service companies, not-for-profit organizations, and government agencies that buy products and services for their own use or for resale.

6-2 What are the three main types of organizational buyers?
Answer: (1) industrial firms, which in some way reprocess a product or service they buy before selling it again to the next buyer; (2) resellers, which are wholesalers and retailers that buy physical products and resell them again without any reprocessing; and (3) government units, which are the federal, state, and local agencies that buy products and services for the constituents they serve.

6-3 What one department is almost always represented by a person in the buying center?
Answer: purchasing department

6-4 What are the three types of buying situations or buy classes?
Answer: (1) new buy—the organization is a first-time buyer of the product or service; (2) straight rebuy—the organization reorders an existing product or service from a list of acceptable suppliers; and (3) modified rebuy—an organization's buying center changes the product's specifications, price, delivery schedule, or supplier.

6-5 What are e-marketplaces?
Answer: E-marketplaces are online trading communities that bring together buyers and supplier organizations to make possible the real-time exchange of information, money, products, and services.

6-6 In general, which type of online auction creates upward pressure on bid prices and which type creates downward pressure on bid prices?
Answer: traditional auction; reverse auction

FOCUSING ON KEY TERMS

business-to-business marketing p. 154
buy classes p. 163
buying center p. 162
derived demand p. 156

e-marketplaces p. 165
North American Industry Classification System (NAICS) p. 155
organizational buyers p. 154

organizational buying behavior p. 161
reverse auction p. 167
traditional auction p. 166

APPLYING MARKETING KNOWLEDGE

1 Describe the major differences among industrial firms, resellers, and government units in the United States.

2 List and discuss the key characteristics of organizational buying that make it different from consumer buying.

3 What is a buying center? Describe the roles assumed by people in a buying center and what useful questions should be raised to guide any analysis of the structure and behavior of a buying center.

4   A firm that is marketing multimillion-dollar wastewater treatment systems to cities has been unable to sell a new type of system. This setback has occurred even though the firm's systems are cheaper than competitive systems and meet U.S. Environmental Protection Agency (EPA) specifications. To date, the firm's marketing efforts have been directed to city purchasing departments and the various state EPAs to get on approved bidders' lists. Talks with city-employed personnel have indicated that the new system is very different from current systems and therefore city sanitary and sewer department engineers, directors of these two departments, and city council members are unfamiliar with the workings of the system. Consulting engineers, hired by cities to work on the engineering and design features of these systems and paid on a percentage of system cost, are also reluctant to favor the new system. (*a*) What roles do the various individuals play in the purchase process for a wastewater treatment system? (*b*) How could the firm improve the marketing effort behind its new system?

BUILDING YOUR MARKETING PLAN

Your marketing plan may need an estimate of the size of the market potential or industry potential (see Chapter 8) for a particular product market in which you compete. Use these steps:

1   Define the product market precisely, such as ice cream.

2   Visit the NAICS website at www.census.gov.

3   Click "NAICS" and enter a keyword that describes your product market (e.g., ice cream).

4   Follow the instructions to find the specific NAICS code for your product market and the economic Census data that detail the dollar sales and provide the estimate of market or industry potential.

connect

VIDEO CASE 6   Trek: Building Better Bikes through Organizational Buying

"Let me tell you a little bit about the history of Trek," says Mark Joslyn, vice president of human resources at Trek Bicycle Corporation. "It's a fantastic story," he continues proudly. "It's a story about a business that started in response to a market opportunity." That opportunity was to build bicycles with the highest-quality frames. In fact, Trek's mission was simple: "Build the best bikes in the world." To do this Trek needed to find the best raw materials from the best vendors. Michael Leighton, a Trek product manager, explains, "Our relationship with our vendors is incredibly important, and one of our recipes for success!"

Video 6-3
Trek Video Case
kerin.tv/13e/v6-3

THE COMPANY

Trek Bicycle was founded in 1976 by Richard Burke and Bevill Hogg. With just five employees they began manufacturing bicycles in a Wisconsin barn. From the beginning they targeted the high-quality, prestige segment of the bicycle market, using only the best materials and components for their bicycles. The first year they manufactured 900 custom-made bicycles which sold quickly. Soon, Trek exceeded its manufacturing capacity. It built a new 26,000-square-foot factory and corporate headquarters to help meet growing demand.

Trek's focus on quality meant that it was very sensitive to the materials used to manufacture the bicycles. The first models, for example, used hand-brazed steel for the frames. Then, borrowing ideas from the aerospace industry, Trek soon began making frames out of bonded aluminum. Following on the success of its aluminum bicycles, Trek began manufacturing bicycles out of carbon fiber. The idea was to be "at the front of technology," explains Joslyn.

The company also expanded its product line. Its first bikes were designed to compete directly with Japanese and Italian bicycles and included road racing models. In 1983 Trek manufactured its first mountain bike. In 1990 Trek developed a new category of bicycle—called a multitrack—that combined the speed of road bikes with the ruggedness of mountain bikes. The company also began manufacturing children's bikes, tandem bikes, BMX bikes, and models used by police departments and the U.S. Secret Service. In addition, it added a line of cycling apparel called Trek Wear and cycling accessories such as helmets. Recently, Trek also undertook an Eco Design initiative to build bicycles and parts that are "green" in terms of the environmental impact of manufacturing them, how long they last, and how they can be recycled. To accommodate these production demands, Trek expanded its facilities two more times.

As Trek's popularity increased, it began to expand outside of the United States. For example, the company acquired a Swiss bicycle company called Villiger and the oldest bicycle company in Germany, Diamant. It also expanded into China, opening two stores and signing deals with 20 Chinese distributors.

Today, Trek is one of the leading manufacturers of bicycles and cycling products, with more than $800 million in sales and 2,000 employees. Trek's products are now marketed through 1,700 dealers in North America and wholly owned subsidiaries in seven countries and through distributors in 90 other countries. Its brands include Trek, Gary Fisher, and Bontrager. As a global company, Trek's mission has evolved also, and today the mission is to "help the world use the bicycle as a simple solution to complex problems." Trek employees believe that the bicycle is the most efficient form of human transportation and that it can combat climate change, ease urban congestion, and build human fitness. Their motto: "We believe in bikes." Mark Joslyn explains:

In the world today we are faced with a number of challenges. We are faced with congestion, issues with mobility, issues with the environment, and quite frankly, issues with health. We believe that the bicycle is a simple solution to all of those things. We are clearly an alternative to other forms of transportation and that's evident in the way that people are embracing cycling not just for recreation but also for transportation. And more and more, particularly in the United States, we are seeing people move to the bike as a way to get around and get to the places they need to ultimately get their life done.

ORGANIZATIONAL BUYING AT TREK

Trek's success at accomplishing its mission is the result of many important business practices, including its organizational buying process. The process begins when managers specify types of materials such as

© Jean Christophe Bott/Keystone/AP Images

carbon fiber, component parts such as wheels and shifters, and finishing materials such as paint and decals needed to produce a Trek product. In addition, they specify quality requirements, sizing standards, and likely delivery schedules. According to Leighton, once the requirements are known, the next step is to "go to our buying center and say 'can you help us find this piece?'"

The buying center is the group of individuals who are responsible for finding the best suppliers and vendors for the organization's purchases. At Trek the buying center consists of a purchasing manager, buyers who identify domestic and international sources of materials and components, and representatives from research and development, production, and quality control. The communication between the product managers and the buying center is important. "I work very closely with our buying centers to ensure that we're partnering with vendors who can supply reliable quality, and they are actually the ones who, with our quality control team, go in and say 'yes this vendor is building product to the quality that meets Trek's standards,' and they also negotiate the pricing. Our buying center domestically is a relatively small team of people and they are focused on specific components."

When potential suppliers are identified, they are evaluated on four criteria—quality, delivery capabilities, price, and environmental impact of their production process. This allows Trek to compare alternative suppliers and to select the best match for Trek and its customers. Once a business is selected as a Trek supplier, it is continuously evaluated on elements of the four criteria. For example, current suppliers might receive scores on the number of defects in a large quantity of supplies, whether just-in-time orders made their deadlines, if target prices were maintained, and if recycled packaging was used. At Trek the tool that is used to record information about potential and existing suppliers is called a "white paper." Michael Leighton describes how this works: "Our buying center is tasked with developing what we call white papers. It's a sheet that managers can look at that shows issues and benefits related to working with these people." Every effort is made to develop long-term relationships with suppliers so that they become partners with Trek. These partnerships mean that Trek's success also contributes to the partner's success.

Trek's product managers and the buying center are involved in three types of organizational purchases. First, new buys are purchases that are made for the first time. Second, modified rebuys involve changing some aspect of a previously ordered product. Finally, straight rebuys are reorders of existing products from the list of acceptable suppliers. Leighton offers examples of each type of purchase at Trek:

So, [for] a new buy, we work with our buying centers to find new products, something we've never done before whether it's a new saddle with a new material or a new technology that goes into the frame that damps vibration or gives a better ride. Another case might be electric bikes—maybe we are putting a motor in a bike, that's a new thing, so our buying center will help us go find those vendors. A modified rebuy is basically a saddle with a little bit different material but we are sharing some components of it, so the existing components of the saddle [are the same] but the cover is new, so it's a little bit different, but it's just the evolution of the product. A straight rebuy is looking at our strategic vision for the component further on down the line where we are just buying the same component and the volume goes up. We look at how can we make this a better business; can we save some money or can we make it more worth our while to keep buying the same product rather than buying something new.

While each of the types of purchases may occur frequently at Trek, the criteria that are used to select or evaluate a vendor may vary by the type of purchase and the type of product, making the buying process a dynamic challenge for managers.

ECO BUYING AND THE FUTURE AT TREK

One of Trek's criteria for evaluating existing and potential vendors is their environmental impact. Joslyn says it well: "We evaluate our vendors on many criteria including, increasingly, the elements that we would consider to be the 'green' part" of their offering. For example, Trek recently selected a supplier that (1) owned a quarry for extracting material, (2) used its own manufacturing facilities, and (3) used natural gas instead of coal in its production process. This was appealing to Trek because it suggested that the supplier had a "thorough understanding" of the impact of the product on the environment from start to finish.

Trek's organizational buying reflects the growing importance of its "Eco" perspective. Its bikes are becoming "smarter" as it adds electric-assist components to help them become a practical transportation alternative. Its bikes are also becoming "greener" as more low-impact materials and components are used and as packaging size and weight are reduced. Trek is also addressing the issue of recycling by building the bikes to last longer, using its dealers to help recycle tires and tubes, and funding a nonprofit organization called Dream Bikes to teach youth to fix and repair donated bikes.

In addition to changing bikes and the way it makes them, Trek faces several other challenges as it strives to improve its organizational buying process. For example, the growing number of suppliers and vendors necessitates constant, coordinated, and real-time communication to ensure that all components are available when they are needed. In addition, changes in consumer interests and economic conditions mean that Trek must anticipate fluctuations in demand and make appropriate changes in order sizes and delivery dates. As Mark Joslyn explains, "Everything we do all the time can and should be improved. So the search for ideas inside of our business and outside of our business, always looking for ways that we can improve and bring new technology and new solutions to the marketplace, is just a core of who we are."[23]

Questions

1 What is the role of the buying center at Trek? Who is likely to comprise the buying center in the decision to select a new supplier at Trek?

2 What selection criteria does Trek utilize when it selects a new supplier or evaluates an existing supplier?

3 How has Trek's interest in the environmental impact of its business influenced its organizational buying process?

4 Provide an example of each of the three buying situations—straight rebuy, modified rebuy, and new buy—at Trek.

Chapter Notes

1. Interview with Kim Nagele, JCPenney, February 1, 2015; "Catalog Makes a Comeback at Penney," *The Wall Street Journal*, January 20, 2015, pp. B1, B2.

2. *Transforming Big Blue's Procurement Operations* (Sumers, NY: IBM Corporation, June 2013).

3. Figures reported in this discussion are provided by the U.S. Department of Commerce at www.commerce.gov, April 10, 2015.

4. Personal correspondence with Lockheed Martin, April 15, 2014.

5. This list of characteristics and portions of the discussion in this section are based on F. Robert Dwyer and John F. Tanner Jr., *Business Marketing,* 4th ed. (Burr Ridge, IL: McGraw-Hill/ Irwin, 2009); and Michael D. Hutt and Thomas W. Speh, *Business Marketing Management: B2B,* 11th ed. (Mason, OH: South-Western, 2012).

6. "Siemens Receives Contract for High-Efficiency Power Plant in the United States," Siemens USA press release, July 18, 2012.

7. "Boeing Lands a Blockbuster Sale—That No One Has Heard About," www.money.msn.com, March 30, 2015.

8. Hutt and Speh, *Business Marketing Management: B2B.*

9. *Global Machine Vision Market 2012–2016* (Ann Arbor: Automated Imaging Association, September 2013).

10. This example is found in Sandy D. Jap and Jakki J. Mohr, "Leveraging Internet Technologies in B2B Relationships," *California Management Review,* Summer 2002, pp. 24–38.

11. "IBM's 'Sequoia' Unseats Fujitsu; Tops the List as Fastest Supercomputer," www.washingtonpost.com, June 6, 2012.

12. "HP Finalizes $3 Billion Outsourcing Agreement to Manage Procter & Gamble's IT Infrastructure," Hewlett-Packard news release, May 6, 2003.

13. "About Us," www.milsco.com, downloaded January 25, 2015; and "Milsco Manufacturing: Easy Rider," *Industry Today,* February 2010, pp. 86–87.

14. *Starbucks Global Responsibility Report: Goals and Progress 2013,* downloaded January 5, 2015; Helen Walker and Wendy Phillips, "Sustainable Procurement: Emerging Issues," *International Journal of Procurement Management* 2, no. 1 (2009), pp. 41–61.

15. Thomas V. Bonoma, "Major Sales: Who Really Does the Buying?" *Harvard Business Review,* May–June 1982, pp. 11–19. Also see Philip L. Dawes, Don Y. Lee, and Grahame R. Dowling, "Information Control and Influence in Emerging Buying Centers," *Journal of Marketing,* July 1998, pp. 55–68; and Thomas Tellefsen, "Antecedents and Consequences of Buying Center Leadership: An Emergent Perspective," *Journal of Business-to-Business Marketing* 13, no. 1 (2006), pp. 53–59.

16. These definitions are adapted from Frederick E. Webster Jr. and Yoram Wind, *Organizational Buying Behavior* (Englewood Cliffs, NJ: Prentice Hall, 1972), p. 6.

17. Jeffrey E. Lewin and Naveen Donthu, "The Influence of Purchase Situation on Buying Center Structure and Involvement: A Select Meta-Analysis of Organizational Buying Behavior Research," *Journal of Business Research,* October 2005, 1381–90. Representative studies on the buy-class framework that document its usefulness include Erin Anderson, Wujin Chu, and Barton Weitz, "Industrial Purchasing: An Empirical Exploration of the Buy-Class Framework," *Journal of Marketing,* July 1987, pp. 71–86; and Thomas W. Leigh and Arno J. Ethans, "A Script-Theoretic Analysis of Industrial Purchasing Behavior," *Journal of Marketing,* Fall 1984, pp. 22–32. Studies not supporting the buy-class framework include Donald W. Jackson, Janet E. Keith, and Richard K. Burdick, "Purchasing Agents' Perceptions of Industrial Buying Center Influences: A Situational Approach," *Journal of Marketing,* Fall 1984, pp. 75–83; R. Vekatesh, Ajay Kohli, and Gerald Zaltman, "Influence Strategies in Buying Centers," *Journal of Marketing,* October 1995, pp. 61–72; Gary L. Lilien and Anthony Wong, "An Exploratory Investigation of the Structure of the Buying Center in the Metal Working Industry," *Journal of Marketing Research,* February 1984, pp. 1–11; and Wesley J. Johnston and Thomas V. Bonoma, "The Buying Center: Structure and Interaction Patterns," *Journal of Marketing,* Summer 1981, pp. 143–56.

18. This discussion is based on "E-commerce Accounts for Nearly All of Grainger's Annual Sales Growth," www.internetretailer.com, January 27, 2015; "B2B, Take 2,"

Business Week Online, November 25, 2005; and Jennifer Reinhold, "What We Learned in the New Economy," Fast Company, March 4, 2004, pp. 56ff.

19. "Global McKinsey Institute Report Confirms eBay, Inc. Research on Small Business Cross Border Trade," www.ebaymainstreet.com, April 24, 2014; "Meet the eBay Millionaires," www.huffingtonpost.com, August 4, 2011; "Former eBay CEO Urges Action on Small Business," www.washingtonpost.com, June 11, 2008; "New Study Reveals 724,000 Americans Rely on eBay Sales for Income," eBay press release, July 21, 2005; Robyn Greenspan, "Net Drives Profits to Small Biz," www.clickz.com, downloaded March 25, 2006; and "eBay Realizes Success in Small-Biz Arena," Marketing News, May 1, 2004, p. 11.

20. This discussion is based on Robert J. Dolan and Youngme Moon, "Pricing and Market Making on the Internet," Journal of Interactive Marketing, Spring 2000, pp. 56–73; and Ajit Kambil and Eric van Heck, Making Markets: How Firms Can Benefit

from Online Auctions and Exchanges (Boston: Harvard Business School Press, 2002).

21. Susan Avery, "Supply Management Is Core of Success at UTC," Purchasing, September 7, 2006, pp. 36–39.

22. Shawn P. Daley and Prithwiraz Nath, "Reverse Auctions for Relationship Marketers," Industrial Marketing Management, February 2005, pp. 157–66; and Sandy Jap, "The Impact of Online Reverse Auction Design on Buyer–Seller Relationships," Journal of Marketing, January 2007, pp. 146–59.

23. Trek: This case was written by Steven Hartley. Sources: "Trek Bicycle Corporation" Hoovers, 2011; "Alliance Data Signs Long-Term Extension Agreement with Trek Bicycle Corporation," PR Newswire, November 22, 2010; Lou Massante, "Trek Bicycle Buys Villiger, a Leader in the Swiss Market," Bicycle Retailer & Industry News, January 1, 2003, p. 10; "Trek Bicycle Corporation," Wikipedia, accessed September 4, 2011; and Trek website, http://www.trekbikes.com/us/en/company/believe, accessed September 4, 2011.

7

Understanding and Reaching Global Consumers and Markets

LEARNING OBJECTIVES

After reading this chapter you should be able to:

LO 7-1 Describe the nature and scope of world trade from a global perspective.

LO 7-2 Identify the major trends that have influenced world trade and global marketing.

LO 7-3 Identify the environmental forces that shape global marketing efforts.

LO 7-4 Name and describe the alternative approaches companies use to enter global markets.

LO 7-5 Explain the distinction between standardization and customization when companies craft worldwide marketing programs.

Building a Two Billion Dollar Business in India the Dell Inc. Way

Why did Dell Inc. embark on a bold global growth initiative in 2007? In the words of Steve Felice, former president of Dell Asia-Pacific and Japan, "Our success was going to be largely dependent on our ability to expand globally."

Dell's global initiative focused on emerging economies in Asia, Africa, and Latin America. Compared with mature economies in North America and Western Europe, emerging economies offered significant growth potential, according to Michael Dell, Dell's founder and chief executive officer. And Dell's global strategy has proven successful. India is a major growth market for Dell Inc. and now posts annual sales of $2.5 billion. Dell employs some 25,000 people in India, which represents about one-fourth of its global workforce.

Dell's global initiative was bold in its departure from prior product development practices. Prior to its global initiative, Dell designed products for global requirements and distributed the same product globally. The company now routinely designs low-cost notebook, tablet, laptop, and desktop personal computers for customers in China, India, and other emerging economies.

Dell's global initiative also required many changes in its signature direct sales, service, and distribution strategy. The company built its U.S. business with telephone- and Internet-based sales—without retailers. However, in emerging economies and India, customers prefer to see, touch, and use a personal computer before they buy. In response, Dell uses individual sales affiliates who reach out to customers in person and give them a firsthand product experience at their doorstep.

At the same time, Dell joined hands with Indian chain retailers such as Croma and eZone for a shop-in-a-shop counter for its products. Dell backs this hybrid retail model by offering extended onsite service (technicians who visit individuals' homes) in over 650 cities to both retail and small business customers.

Dell also opened Dell exclusive stores in 2008. According to a company spokesperson, "The exclusive Dell store is a step towards enhancing the overall purchase experience for consumers in India. We have rapidly increased our presence in the consumer market here with new products and by expanding our reach. With the launch of Dell exclusive stores, we offer our customers the touch and feel for Dell branded products within a unique shopping experience."

Each Dell exclusive store offers the advantages of Dell's direct purchasing model with the additional benefit of retail availability—allowing customers to browse, touch, and feel the product. Dell's approach makes it possible for customers to see the products on the retail shelves and then place an order for the preferred model with the choice to customize the looks and configuration of the unit. By 2015, Dell had 400 exclusive stores in India.

Dell's global initiative also involved a new advertising campaign, with Dell opting for real-life successful entrepreneurs in India to endorse its products. The "Take Your Own Path" advertising campaign has proven to be highly effective. Dell's success in India illustrates the importance of understanding global customers and reaching them by adapting to their specific needs and preferences.[1]

This chapter describes today's complex and dynamic global marketing environment. It begins by describing the dynamics of world trade and major trends that have influenced the landscape of global marketing. Attention is then focused on prominent cultural, economic, and political-regulatory factors that present both an opportunity and a challenge for global marketers. Four major global market entry strategies are then detailed, including the advantages and disadvantages of each. Finally, the task of designing, implementing, and evaluating worldwide marketing programs for companies such as Dell Inc. is described.

© Indian Photo Agency

DYNAMICS OF WORLD TRADE

LO 7-1 Describe the nature and scope of world trade from a global perspective.

The dollar value of world trade has more than doubled in the past decade. Manufactured products and commodities account for 75 percent of world trade. Service industries, including telecommunications, transportation, insurance, education, banking, and tourism, represent the other 25 percent.

All nations and regions of the world do not participate equally in world trade. World trade flows reflect interdependencies among industries, countries, and regions. These flows manifest themselves in country, company, industry, and regional exports and imports. The dynamics of world trade are evolving. China replaced the United States as the biggest country measured by world trade in 2015. Asia surpassed Western Europe as the largest region measured by world trade in 2015.[2]

Global Perspective on World Trade

The United States, China, Japan, Western Europe, and Canada together account for more than two-thirds of world trade in manufactured products and commodities. China is the world's leading exporter, followed by the United States and Germany. The United States is the world's leading importer, followed by China and Germany. China, Germany, and the United States remain well ahead of other countries in terms of imports and exports, as shown in Figure 7–1.

A global perspective on world trade views exports and imports as complementary economic flows: A country's imports affect its exports and exports affect its imports. Every nation's imports arise from the exports of other nations. As the exports of one country increase, its national output and income rise, which in turn leads to an increase in the demand for imports. This nation's greater demand for imports stimulates the exports of other countries. Increased demand for exports of other nations energizes their economic activity, resulting in higher national income, which stimulates their demand for imports. In short, imports affect exports and vice versa. This phenomenon is called the *trade feedback effect* and is one argument for free trade among nations.

Not all trade involves the exchange of money for products or services. In a world where 70 percent of all countries do not have convertible currencies or where government-owned enterprises lack sufficient cash or credit for imports, other means of payment are used. An estimated 10 to 15 percent of world trade involves **countertrade**, the practice of using barter rather than money for making global sales.

FIGURE 7–1

The United States, China, and Germany are the leaders in global merchandise trade by a wide margin. China exports more manufactured products and commodities than it imports. The United States imports more manufactured products and commodities than it exports. Read the text to learn about trends in U.S. exports and imports.

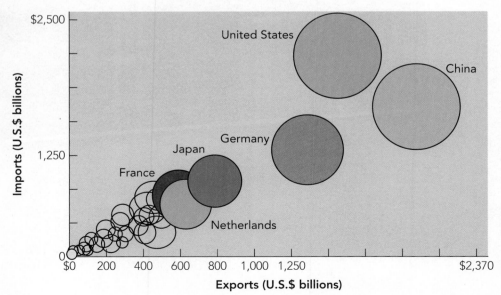

Countertrade is popular with many Eastern European nations, Russia, and Asian countries. For example, Daimler AG agreed to sell 30 trucks to Romania in exchange for 150 Romanian-made jeeps. Daimler then sold the jeeps in Ecuador in exchange for bananas, which it brought back to Germany and sold to a German supermarket chain in exchange for cash. When PepsiCo entered India, the Indian government stipulated that part of PepsiCo's local profits had to be to purchase tomatoes. This requirement worked for PepsiCo, which also owned Pizza Hut at the time.

United States Perspective on World Trade

The United States has been the world's perennial leader in terms of *gross domestic product (GDP),* which is the monetary value of all products and services produced in a country during one year. The United States is also among the world's leaders in exports due in large part to its global prominence in the aerospace, chemical, office equipment, information technology, pharmaceutical, telecommunications, and professional service industries. However, the U.S. percentage share of world exports has shifted downward over the past 30 years, whereas its percentage share of world imports has increased. Therefore, the relative position of the United States as a supplier to the world has diminished despite an absolute growth in exports. At the same time, its relative role as a marketplace for the world has increased, particularly for automobile, oil, textile, apparel, and consumer electronics products.

The difference between the monetary value of a nation's exports and imports is called the **balance of trade**. When a country's exports exceed its imports, it incurs a surplus in its balance of trade. When imports exceed exports, a deficit results. World trade trends in U.S. exports and imports are reflected in the U.S. balance of trade.

Two important things have happened in U.S. exports and imports over the past 30 years. First, imports have exceeded exports each year, indicating that the United States has a continuing balance of trade deficit. Second, the volume of both exports and imports has increased dramatically, showing why almost every American is significantly affected. The effect varies from the products they buy (Samsung smartphones from South Korea, Waterford crystal from Ireland, Louis Vuitton luggage from France) to those they sell (Cisco Systems's Internet technology to Europe, DuPont's chemicals to the Far East, Merck pharmaceuticals to Africa) and the jobs and improved standard of living that result.

World trade flows to and from the United States reflect demand and supply interdependencies for goods and services among nations and industries. The four largest importers of U.S. products and services are, in order: Canada, Mexico, China, and Japan. These individual countries purchase approximately two-thirds of U.S. exports. The four largest exporters to the United States are, in order: China, Canada, Mexico, and Japan.

learning review

7-1. What country is the biggest as measured by world trade?

7-2. What is the trade feedback effect?

MARKETING IN A BORDERLESS ECONOMIC WORLD

LO 7-2 | Identify the major trends that have influenced world trade and global marketing.

Global marketing has been and continues to be affected by a growing borderless economic world. Five trends have significantly influenced the landscape of global marketing:

Trend 1: Gradual decline of economic protectionism by individual countries.

Trend 2: Formal economic integration and free trade among nations.

Global Ethics and Global Economics—The Case of Protectionism

World trade benefits from free and fair trade among nations. Nevertheless, governments of many countries continue to use tariffs and quotas to protect their various domestic industries. Why? Protectionism earns profits for domestic producers and tariff revenue for the government. There is a cost, however. Protectionist policies cost Japanese consumers between $75 billion and $110 billion annually. U.S. consumers pay about $70 billion each year in higher prices because of tariffs and other protective restrictions.

Sugar and textile import quotas in the United States, automobile and banana import tariffs in European countries, shoe and

© Frans Lemmens/The Image Bank/Getty Images

automobile tire import tariffs in the United States, beer import tariffs in Canada, and rice import tariffs in Japan protect domestic industries but also interfere with world trade for these products. Regional trade agreements, such as those found in the provisions of the European Union and the North American Free Trade Agreement, may also pose a situation whereby member nations can obtain preferential treatment in quotas and tariffs but nonmember nations cannot.

Protectionism, in its many forms, raises an interesting global ethical question. Is protectionism, no matter how applied, an ethical practice?

Trend 3: Global competition among global companies for global customers.

Trend 4: Emergence of a networked global marketspace.

Trend 5: Growing prevalence of economic espionage.

Decline of Economic Protectionism

Protectionism is the practice of shielding one or more industries within a country's economy from foreign competition through the use of tariffs or quotas. The argument for protectionism is that it limits the outsourcing of jobs, protects a nation's political security, discourages economic dependency on other countries, and promotes development of domestic industries. Read the Making Responsible Decisions box and decide for yourself if protectionism has an ethical dimension.[3]

Tariffs and quotas discourage world trade, as depicted in Figure 7–2. **Tariffs**, which are a government tax on products or services entering a country, primarily serve to raise prices on imports. The average tariff on manufactured products in industrialized countries is 4 percent. However, wide differences exist across nations. For example, European Union countries have a 10 percent tariff on cars imported from Japan, which is about four times higher than the tariff imposed by the United States on Japanese cars.

The effect of tariffs on consumer prices is substantial. Consider U.S. rice exports to Japan. The U.S. Rice Millers' Association claims that if the Japanese rice market were opened to imports by lowering tariffs, lower prices would save Japanese consumers $6 billion annually, and the United States would gain a large share of the Japanese rice market. Tariffs imposed on bananas by European Union countries cost consumers $2 billion a year. U.S. consumers pay $5 billion annually for tariffs on imported shoes. Incidentally, 99 percent of shoes worn in the United States are imported.[4]

A **quota** is a restriction placed on the amount of a product allowed to enter or leave a country. Quotas can be mandated or voluntary and may be legislated or negotiated by governments. Import quotas seek to guarantee domestic industries access to a certain

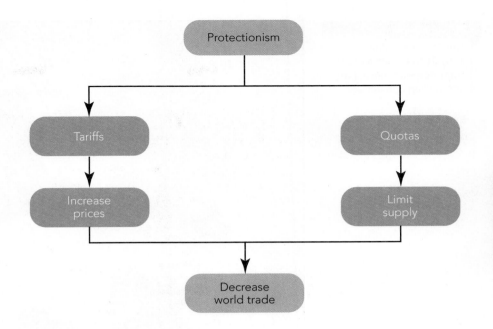

FIGURE 7–2

How does protectionism affect world trade? Protectionism hinders world trade through tariff and quota policies of individual countries. Tariffs increase prices and quotas limit supply.

Protectionism

Tariffs

Quotas

Increase prices

Limit supply

Decrease world trade

percentage of their domestic market. For example, there is a limit on Chinese dairy products sold in India, and in Italy there is a quota on Japanese motorcycles. China has import quotas on corn, cotton, rice, and wheat.

The United States also imposes quotas. For instance, U.S. sugar import quotas have existed for more than 70 years and preserve about half of the U.S. sugar market for domestic producers. American consumers pay $3 billion annually in extra food costs because of this quota. U.S. quotas on textiles are estimated to add 50 percent to the wholesale price of clothing for American consumers—which, in turn, raises retail prices.

The major industrialized nations of the world formed the **World Trade Organization (WTO)** in 1995 to address an array of world trade issues. There are 160 WTO member countries, including the United States, which account for more than 90 percent of world trade. The WTO is a permanent institution that sets rules governing trade between its members through panels of trade experts who decide on trade disputes between members and issue binding decisions. The WTO reviews more than 200 trade disputes annually.

Rise of Economic Integration

A number of countries with similar economic goals have formed transnational trade groups or signed trade agreements for the purpose of promoting free trade among member nations and enhancing their individual economies. Two of the best-known examples are the European Union (or simply EU) and the North American Free Trade Agreement (NAFTA). About 46 percent of all U.S. exports go to its free trade partners.

European Union   The European Union consists of 28 member countries that have eliminated most barriers to the free flow of products, services, capital, and labor across their borders (see Figure 7–3).[5] This single market houses more than 500 million consumers with a combined gross domestic product larger than that of the United States. In addition, 16 countries have adopted a common currency called the *euro*. Adoption of the euro has been a boon to electronic commerce in the EU by eliminating the need to continually monitor currency exchange rates.

The EU creates abundant marketing opportunities because firms do not need to market their products and services on a nation-by-nation basis. Rather, pan-European

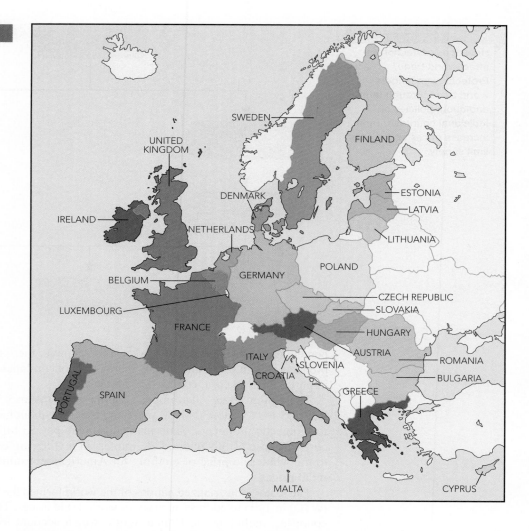

FIGURE 7–3
The European Union in early 2016 consists of 28 countries with more than 500 million consumers.

European Union
www.europa.eu.int

marketing strategies are possible due to greater uniformity in product and packaging standards; fewer regulatory restrictions on transportation, advertising, and promotion imposed by countries; and the removal of most tariffs that affect pricing practices. For example, Colgate-Palmolive Company now markets its Colgate toothpaste with one formula and package across EU countries at one price. Black & Decker—the maker of electrical hand tools, appliances, and other consumer products—now produces 8, not 20, motor sizes for the European market, resulting in production and marketing cost savings. These practices were previously impossible because of different government and trade regulations. Europeanwide distribution from fewer locations is also feasible given open borders. French tire maker Michelin closed 180 of its European distribution centers and now uses just 20 to serve all EU countries.

North American Free Trade Agreement The North American Free Trade Agreement (NAFTA) lifted many trade barriers between Canada, Mexico, and the United States and created a marketplace with more than 475 million consumers. NAFTA has stimulated trade flows among member nations as well as cross-border retailing, manufacturing, and investment. For example, NAFTA paved the way for Walmart to move to Mexico, and Mexican supermarket giant Gigante to move into the United States. Whirlpool Corporation's Canadian subsidiary stopped making washing machines in Canada and moved that operation to Ohio. Whirlpool then shifted the production of kitchen ranges and compact dryers to Canada. Ford invested $60 million in its Mexico City manufacturing plant to produce smaller cars and light trucks for global sales.[6]

A free trade agreement among Costa Rica, the Dominican Republic, El Salvador, Guatemala, Honduras, Nicaragua, and the United States extends many NAFTA benefits to Central American countries and the Dominican Republic. Called CAFTA-DR, this agreement is viewed as a step toward a 34-country Free Trade Area of the Americas for the Western Hemisphere.

A New Reality: Global Competition among Global Companies for Global Consumers

The emergence of a largely borderless economic world has created a new reality for marketers of all shapes and sizes. Today, world trade is driven by global competition among global companies for global consumers.

Global Competition **Global competition** exists when firms originate, produce, and market their products and services worldwide. The automobile, pharmaceutical, apparel, electronics, aerospace, and telecommunication fields represent well-known industries with sellers and buyers on every continent. Other industries that are increasingly global in scope include soft drinks, cosmetics, ready-to-eat cereals, snack chips, and retailing.

Global competition broadens the competitive landscape for marketers. The familiar "cola war" waged by Pepsi-Cola and Coca-Cola in the United States has been repeated around the world, including in India, China, Myanmar, and Argentina. Procter & Gamble's Pampers and Kimberly-Clark's Huggies have taken their disposable diaper rivalry from the United States to Western Europe. Boeing and Europe's Airbus vie for lucrative commercial aircraft contracts on virtually every continent.

Global Companies Three types of companies populate and compete in the global marketplace: (1) international firms, (2) multinational firms, and (3) transnational

Since opening its first international venture in Australia in 1971, Mary Kay, Inc. has expanded to more than 35 countries on five continents. This Korean ad features the company's CC Cream Sunscreen.

Courtesy Mary Kay, Inc.

Mary Kay, Inc.
marykay.com

CHAPTER 7 Understanding and Reaching Global Consumers and Markets

Mr. Clean has a different name in different countries and regions in the world. However, his image remains the same.

Source: Procter & Gamble

firms.[7] All three employ people in different countries, and many have administrative, marketing, and manufacturing operations (often called *divisions* or *subsidiaries*) around the world. However, a firm's orientation toward and strategy for global markets and marketing defines the type of company it is or attempts to be.

An *international firm* engages in trade and marketing in different countries as an extension of the marketing strategy in its home country. Generally, these firms market their existing products and services in other countries the same way they do in their home country. Avon, for example, successfully distributes its product line through direct selling in Asia, Europe, and South America, employing virtually the same marketing strategy used in the United States.

A *multinational firm* views the world as consisting of unique parts and markets to each part differently. Multinationals use a **multidomestic marketing strategy**, which means that they have as many different product variations, brand names, and advertising programs as countries in which they do business.

For example, Procter & Gamble markets Mr. Clean, its popular multipurpose cleaner, in North America and Asia. But you won't necessarily find the Mr. Clean brand name in other parts of the world. In Mexico and Puerto Rico, Mr. Clean is Maestro Limpio, and it is Don Limpio in Spain. Mr. Clean is Monsieur Propre in France and Belgium, Maestro Lindo in Italy, Pan Proper in Poland, and Mister Proper in Eastern Europe, the Middle East, and Russia.

A *transnational firm* views the world as one market and emphasizes cultural similarities across countries or universal consumer needs and wants rather than differences. Transnational marketers employ a **global marketing strategy**—the practice of standardizing marketing activities when there are cultural similarities and adapting them when cultures differ. This approach benefits marketers by allowing them to realize economies of scale from their production and marketing activities.

Global marketing strategies are popular among many business-to-business marketers such as Caterpillar and Komatsu (heavy construction equipment) and Texas Instruments, Intel, and Hitachi (semiconductors). Consumer product marketers such as Timex, Seiko, and Swatch (watches), Coca-Cola and Pepsi-Cola (cola soft drinks),

The Global Teenager—A Market of 2 Billion Voracious Consumers

The "global teenager" market consists of 2 billion 13- to 19-year-olds in Europe, North and South America, and industrialized nations of Asia and the Pacific Rim who have experienced intense exposure to television (MTV broadcasts in 169 countries in 28 languages), movies, travel, social media, and global advertising by companies such as Apple, Sony, Nike, and Coca-Cola. The similarities among teens across these countries are greater than their differences. For example, a global study of middle-class teenagers' rooms in 25 industrialized countries indicated it was difficult, if not impossible, to tell whether the rooms were in Los Angeles, Hong Kong, Mexico City, Tokyo, Rio de Janeiro, Sydney, or Paris. Why? Teens spend about $820 billion annually for a common gallery of products: Nintendo video games, Tommy Hilfiger apparel,

© Kim Petersen/Alamy

Levi's blue jeans, Nike and Adidas athletic shoes, Swatch watches, Apple iPhones, Benetton apparel, and Cover Girl cosmetics.

Teenagers around the world appreciate fashion and music, and they desire novelty and trendier designs and images. They also acknowledge an Americanization of fashion and culture based on another study of 6,500 teens in 26 countries. When asked what country had the most influence on their attitudes and purchase behavior, 54 percent of teens from the United States, 87 percent of those from Latin America, 80 percent of the Europeans, and 80 percent of those from Asia named the United States. This phenomenon has not gone unnoticed by parents. As one parent in India said, "Now the youngsters dress, talk, and eat like Americans."

Mattel and LEGO (children's toys), Nike and Adidas (athletic shoes), Gillette (personal care products), L'Oréal and Shiseido (cosmetics), and McDonald's (quick-service restaurants) successfully execute this strategy.

Each of these companies markets a **global brand**—a brand marketed under the same name in multiple countries with similar and centrally coordinated marketing programs.[8] Global brands have the same product formulation or service concept, deliver the same benefits to consumers, and use consistent advertising across multiple countries and cultures. This isn't to say that global brands are not sometimes tailored to specific cultures or countries. However, adaptation is used only when necessary to better connect the brand to consumers in different markets.

Consider McDonald's.[9] This global marketer has adapted its proven formula of "food, fun, and families" across 100 countries on six continents. Although the Golden Arches and Ronald McDonald appear worldwide, McDonald's tailors other aspects of its marketing program. It serves beer in Germany, wine in France, and coconut, mango, and tropical mint shakes in Hong Kong. Hamburgers are made with different meat and spices in Japan, Thailand, India, and the Philippines. But McDonald's world-famous french fry is standardized. Its french fry in Beijing, China, tastes like the one in Paris, France, which tastes like the one in your hometown.

Global Consumers Global competition among global companies often focuses on the identification and pursuit of global consumers, as described in the Marketing Matters box.[10] **Global consumers** consist of consumer groups living in many countries or regions of the world who have similar needs or seek similar features and benefits from products or services. Evidence suggests the presence of a global middle-income class, a youth market, and an elite segment, each consuming or using a common assortment of products and services, regardless of geographic location.

A variety of companies have capitalized on the global consumer. Whirlpool, Sony, and IKEA have benefited from the growing global middle-income class desire for kitchen appliances, consumer electronics, and home furnishings, respectively. Levi Strauss, Nike, Adidas, Coca-Cola, and Apple have tapped the global youth market. DeBeers, Rolex, Chanel, Gucci, Rolls-Royce, and Sotheby's and Christie's, the world's largest fine art and antique auction houses, cater to the elite segment for luxury products worldwide.

Emergence of a Networked Global Marketspace

The use of Internet technology as a tool for exchanging products, services, and information on a global scale is the fourth trend affecting world trade. Over 3 billion businesses, educational institutions, government agencies, and households worldwide are expected to have Internet access by 2017. The broad reach of this technology attests to its potential for promoting world trade.

A networked global marketspace enables the exchange of products, services, and information from sellers *anywhere* to buyers *anywhere* at *any time* and at a lower cost. In particular, companies engaged in business-to-business marketing have spurred the growth of global electronic commerce.[11] Ninety percent of global electronic commerce revenue arises from business-to-business transactions among a dozen countries in North America, Western Europe, and the Asia/Pacific Rim region.

Marketers recognize that the networked global marketspace offers unprecedented access to prospective buyers on every continent. Companies that have successfully capitalized on this access manage multiple country and language websites that customize content and communicate with consumers in their native tongue. Nestlé, the world's largest packaged food manufacturer, coffee roaster, and chocolate maker, is a case in point. The company operates 65 individual country websites in more than 20 languages that span five continents.

Video 7-1
Nestlé
Hungary Ad
kerin.tv/13e/v7-1

Sweden's IKEA is capitalizing on the home-improvement trend sweeping through China. The home-furnishings retailer is courting young Chinese consumers who are eagerly updating their housing with modern, colorful but inexpensive furniture. IKEA entered China in 1998. The company expects to have at least 18 stores open in China by 2016.

© Imaginechina/AP Images

IKEA
www.ikea.com

Growing Prevalence of Economic Espionage

The borderless economic world also has a dark side—economic espionage.[12] **Economic espionage** is the clandestine collection of trade secrets or proprietary information about a company's competitors. This practice is common in high-technology industries such as electronics, specialty chemicals, industrial equipment, aerospace, and pharmaceuticals, where technical know-how and trade secrets separate global industry leaders from followers.

It is estimated that economic espionage costs U.S. firms upwards of $250 billion a year in lost sales. The intelligence services of some 23 nations routinely target U.S. firms for information about research and development efforts, manufacturing and marketing plans, and customer lists. To counteract this threat, the *Economic Espionage Act (1996)* makes the theft of trade secrets by foreign entities a federal crime in the United States. This act prescribes prison sentences of up to 15 years and fines up to $500,000 for individuals. Agents of foreign governments found guilty of economic espionage face a 25-year prison sentence and a $10 million fine.

learning review »

7-3. What is protectionism?

7-4. The North American Free Trade Agreement was designed to promote free trade among which countries?

7-5. What is the difference between a multidomestic marketing strategy and a global marketing strategy?

A GLOBAL ENVIRONMENTAL SCAN

LO 7-3 Identify the environmental forces that shape global marketing efforts.

Global companies conduct continuing environmental scans of the five sets of environmental factors described earlier in Chapter 3 in Figure 3–1 (social, economic, technological, competitive, and regulatory forces). This section focuses on three kinds of uncontrollable environmental variables—cultural, economic, and political-regulatory—that affect global marketing practices in strikingly different ways than those in domestic markets.

Cultural Diversity

You will have to visit India to sample McDonald's Maharaja Mac or the McAloo Tikki burger described in the text.
Source: McDonald's

Marketers must be sensitive to the cultural underpinnings of different societies if they are to initiate and consummate mutually beneficial exchange relationships with global consumers. A necessary step in this process is **cross-cultural analysis**, which involves the study of similarities and differences among consumers in two or more nations or societies.[13] A thorough cross-cultural analysis involves an understanding of and an appreciation for the values, customs, symbols, and language of other societies.

Values   A society's **values** represent personally or socially preferable modes of conduct or states of existence that tend to persist over time. Understanding and working with these aspects of a society are important factors in global marketing. For example,

- McDonald's does not sell beef hamburgers in its restaurants in India because the cow is considered sacred by almost 85 percent of the population. Instead, McDonald's sells the Maharaja Mac: two all-chicken patties, special sauce,

Cultural symbols evoke deep feelings. What cultural lesson did Coca-Cola executives learn when they used the Eiffel Tower in Paris, France, and the Parthenon in Athens, Greece, in a global advertising campaign? Read the text to find the answer.

Left: © Sylvain Sonnet/ Photographer's Choice RF/Getty Images; Right: © Antonio M. Rosario/Getty Images

lettuce, cheese, pickles, onions on a sesame-seed bun. For the 40 percent of Indian consumers who eat no meat of any kind, McDonald's offers the McAloo Tikki burger, which features a spicy breaded potato patty, and the McPuff, a vegetable and cheese pastry.

- Germans have not been overly receptive to the use of credit cards such as Visa or MasterCard and installment debt to purchase products and services. Indeed, the German word for debt, *Schuld,* is the same as the German word for guilt.

Cultural values become apparent in the personal values of individuals that affect their attitudes and beliefs and the importance assigned to specific behaviors and attributes of products and services. These personal values affect consumption-specific values, such as the use of installment debt by Germans, and product-specific values, such as the importance assigned to credit card interest rates.

Customs   **Customs** are what is considered normal and expected about the way people do things in a specific country. Clearly customs can vary significantly from country to country. Consider, for example, that in France, men wear more than twice the number of cosmetics than women do and that Japanese women give Japanese men chocolates on Valentine's Day.

The custom of giving token business gifts is popular in many countries where they are expected and accepted. However, bribes, kickbacks, and payoffs offered to entice someone to commit an illegal or improper act on behalf of the giver for economic gain is considered corrupt in any culture.

The prevalence of bribery in global marketing has led to an agreement among the world's major exporting nations to make bribery of foreign government officials a criminal offense. This agreement is patterned after the **Foreign Corrupt Practices Act (1977)**, as amended by the *International Anti-Dumping and Fair Competition Act* (1998). These acts make it a crime for U.S. corporations to bribe an official of a foreign government or political party to obtain or retain business in a foreign country. For example, the German engineering company Siemens AG paid an $800 million fine for $1 billion in alleged bribes of government officials around the globe.[14]

Cultural Symbols   **Cultural symbols** are things that represent ideas and concepts in a specific culture. Symbols and symbolism play an important role in cross-cultural analysis because different cultures attach different meanings to things. So important is the role of symbols that a field of study, called *semiotics,* has emerged that examines the correspondence between symbols and their role in the assignment of meaning for people. By adroitly using cultural symbols, global marketers can tie positive symbolism to their products, services, and brands to enhance their attractiveness to consumers. However, improper use of symbols can spell disaster. A culturally sensitive global marketer will know that:

- North Americans are superstitious about the number 13, and Japanese feel the same way about the number 4. *Shi,* the Japanese word for four, is also the word for death. Knowing this, Tiffany & Company sells its fine glassware and china in sets of five, not four, in Japan.
- "Thumbs-up" is a positive sign in the United States. However, in Russia and Poland, this gesture has an offensive meaning when the palm of the hand is shown, as AT&T learned. The company reversed the gesture depicted in ads, showing the back of the hand, not the palm.

Cultural symbols evoke deep feelings. Consider how executives at Coca-Cola Company's Italian office learned this lesson. In a series of advertisements directed at Italian vacationers, the Eiffel Tower, the Empire State Building, and the Tower of Pisa were turned into the familiar Coca-Cola bottle. However, when the white marble columns in the Parthenon that crowns the Acropolis in Athens were turned into Coca-Cola bottles, the Greeks were outraged. Greeks refer to the Acropolis as the "holy rock," and a government official said the Parthenon is an "international symbol of excellence" and that "whoever insults the Parthenon insults international culture." Coca-Cola apologized for the ad.[15]

Language   Global marketers should know not only the native tongues of countries in which they market their products and services but also the nuances and idioms of a language. Even though about 100 official languages exist in the world, anthropologists estimate that at least 3,000 different languages are spoken. There are 24 official languages spoken in the European Union, and Canada has two official languages (English and French). Twenty major languages are spoken in India alone.

English, French, and Spanish are the principal languages used in global diplomacy and commerce. However, the best language to use to communicate with consumers is their own, as any seasoned global marketer will attest to. Unintended meanings of brand names and messages have ranged from the absurd to the obscene:

- When the advertising agency responsible for launching Pert shampoo in Canada realized that the name means "lost" in French, it substituted the brand name Pret, which means "ready."
- The Vicks brand name common in the United States is German slang for sexual intimacy; therefore, Vicks is called Wicks in Germany.

Experienced global marketers use **back translation**, where a translated word or phrase is retranslated into the original language by a different interpreter to catch errors. For example, IBM's first Japanese translation of its "Solution for a small planet" advertising message yielded "Answers that make people smaller." The error was corrected. Nevertheless, unintended translations can produce favorable results. Consider Kit Kat bars marketed by Nestlé worldwide. Kit Kat is pronounced "kitto katsu" in Japanese, which roughly translates to "Surely win." Japanese teens eat Kit Kat bars for good luck, particularly when taking crucial school exams.[16]

Cultural Ethnocentricity   The tendency for people to view their own values, customs, symbols, and language favorably is well known. However, the belief that aspects of one's culture are superior to another's is called *cultural ethnocentricity* and is a sure impediment to successful global marketing.

Video 7-2

Nestlé Japan Ad
kerin.tv/13e/v7-2

What does the Nestlé Kit Kat bar have to do with academic achievement in Japan? Read the text to find out.

© CB2/ZOB/WENN/Newscom

Nestlé Company
www.nestle.com

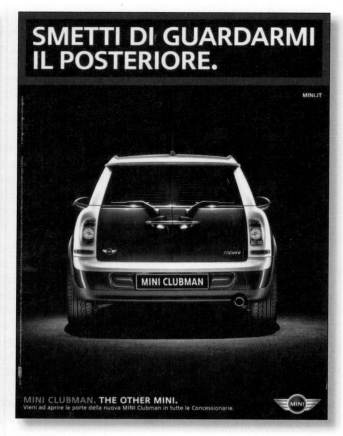

The Mini is marketed in many countries using many languages, such as English and Italian. The Italian translation is "Stop Looking at My Rear."
Source: MINI USA

An outgrowth of cultural ethnocentricity exists in the purchase and use of products and services produced outside of a country. Global marketers are acutely aware that certain groups within countries disfavor imported products, not on the basis of price, features, or performance, but purely because of their foreign origin.

Consumer ethnocentrism is the tendency to believe that it is inappropriate, indeed immoral, to purchase foreign-made products.[17] Ethnocentric consumers believe that buying imported products is wrong because such purchases are unpatriotic, harm domestic industries, and cause domestic unemployment. Consumer ethnocentrism has been observed among a segment of the population in the United States, France, Japan, Korea, and Germany as well as other parts of Europe and Asia. Consumer ethnocentrism makes the job of global marketers more difficult.

Economic Considerations

Global marketing is also affected by economic considerations. Therefore, a scan of the global marketplace should include (1) an assessment of the economic infrastructure in these countries, (2) measurement of consumer income in different countries, and (3) recognition of a country's currency exchange rates.

Consumer ethnocentrism is common in many countries. This bumper sticker is just one illustration of how ethnocentric consumers express themselves in the United States.
© R. Kerin

Economic Infrastructure The *economic infrastructure*—a country's communications, transportation, financial, and distribution systems—is a critical consideration in determining whether to try to market to a country's consumers and organizations. Parts of the infrastructure that North Americans or Western Europeans take for granted can be huge problems elsewhere—not

PepsiCo
pepsico.com

only in developing nations but even in Eastern Europe, the Indian subcontinent, and China, where such an infrastructure is assumed to be in place. For example, PepsiCo has invested $1.5 billion in transportation and manufacturing systems in China and India since 2010.

The communication infrastructures in these countries also differ. This infrastructure includes telecommunication systems and networks in use, such as telephones, cable television, broadcast radio and television, computer, satellite, and wireless telephone. In general, the communication infrastructure in many developing countries is limited or antiquated compared with that of developed countries.

Even the financial and legal system can cause problems. Formal operating procedures among financial institutions and the notion of private property are still limited. As a consequence, it is estimated that two-thirds of the commercial transactions in Russia involve nonmonetary forms of payment. The legal red tape involved in obtaining titles to buildings and land for manufacturing, wholesaling, and retailing operations also has been a huge problem. Still, the Coca-Cola Company planned to invest $1 billion by 2015 for bottling facilities in Russia. Frito-Lay spent $60 million to build a plant outside Moscow to make Lay's potato chips.

Consumer Income and Purchasing Power   A global marketer selling consumer products must also consider what the average per capita or household income is among a country's consumers and how the income is distributed to determine a nation's purchasing power. Per capita income varies greatly between nations. Average yearly per capita income in EU countries is about $35,500 and is less than $700 in some developing countries such as Liberia. A country's income distribution is important because it gives a more reliable picture of a country's purchasing power. Generally, as the proportion of middle-income households in a country increases, the greater that nation's purchasing capability tends to be.

Seasoned global marketers recognize that people in developing countries often have government subsidies for food, housing, and health care that supplement their income.

Levi Strauss & Co. launched its Denizen brand jeans in China. Created for teens and young adults in emerging markets who cannot afford Levi-branded jeans, Denizen is now sold in North America.

© *Eugene Hoshiko/AP Images*

Levi Strauss & Co.

www.levistrauss.com

Video 7-3
Denizen
kerin.tv/13e/v7-3

So people with seemingly low incomes are actually promising customers for a variety of products. For instance, a consumer in South Asia earning the equivalent of $250 per year can afford Gillette razors. When that consumer's income rises to $1,000, a Sony television becomes affordable, and a new Volkswagen or Nissan automobile can be bought with an annual income of $10,000. In developing countries of Eastern Europe, a $1,000 annual income makes a refrigerator affordable, and $2,000 brings an automatic washer within reach—good news for Whirlpool, the world's leading manufacturer and marketer of major home appliances.

Income growth in developing countries of Asia, Latin America, and Eastern Europe stimulates world trade. The number of consumers in these countries earning the equivalent of $10,000 per year surpassed the number of consumers in the United States, Japan, and Western Europe combined in 2015. By one estimate, half of the world's population has now achieved "middle-class" status.[18] For this reason, developing countries represent a prominent marketing opportunity for global companies.

Currency Exchange Rates Fluctuations in exchange rates among the world's currencies are of critical importance in global marketing. Such fluctuations affect everyone, from international tourists to global companies.

A **currency exchange rate** is the price of one country's currency expressed in terms of another country's currency, such as the U.S. dollar expressed in Japanese yen, euros, or Swiss francs. Failure to consider exchange rates when pricing products for global markets can have dire consequences. Mattel learned this lesson the hard way. The company was recently unable to sell its popular Holiday Barbie doll and accessories in some international markets because they were too expensive. Why? Barbie prices, expressed in U.S. dollars, were set without regard for how they would convert into foreign currencies and were too high for many buyers.[19]

Exchange rate fluctuations affect the sales and profits made by global companies. When foreign currencies can buy more U.S. dollars, for example, U.S. products are less expensive for the foreign customer. Short-term fluctuations, however, can have a significant effect on the profits of global companies.[20] Hewlett-Packard recently gained nearly a half million dollars of additional profit through exchange rate fluctuations in one year. On the other hand, Procter & Gamble lost $550 million on its operations in Russia due to devaluation of the Russian ruble in 2015.

Marketing **Insights About Me**

Checking My Country's Political Risk Rating—Are You Surprised?

The political climate in every country is regularly changing. Governments can make new laws or enforce existing policies differently. Numerous consulting firms prepare political risk analyses that incorporate a variety of variables such as the risk of internal turmoil, external conflict, government restrictions on company operations, and tariff and nontariff trade barriers.

Courtesy of The PRS Group

The PRS Group, Inc. maintains multiple databases of country-specific information and projections, including country political risk ratings for 100 countries. These ratings can be accessed at www.prsgroup.com. Click "Risk Index."

Which three countries have the highest rating (lowest risk), and which three have the lowest rating (highest risk)? Which countries have risk ratings closest to the United States?

Political-Regulatory Climate

Assessing the political and regulatory climate for marketing in a country or region of the world involves not only identifying the current climate but also determining how long a favorable or unfavorable climate will last. An assessment of a country or regional political-regulatory climate includes an analysis of its political stability and trade regulations.

Political Stability   Trade among nations or regions depends on political stability. Billions of dollars in trade have been lost in the Middle East and Africa as a result of internal political strife, terrorism, and war. Losses such as these encourage careful selection of politically stable countries and regions of the world for trade.

Political stability in a country is affected by numerous factors, including a government's orientation toward foreign companies and trade with other countries. These factors combine to create a political climate that is favorable or unfavorable for marketing and financial investment in a country or region of the world. Marketing managers monitor political stability using a variety of measures and often track country risk ratings supplied by agencies such as the PRS Group, Inc. Visit the PRS Group, Inc. website described in the Marketing Insights About Me box to see political risk ratings for 100 countries, including your own. Expect to be surprised by the ranking of countries, including the United States.

Trade Regulations   Countries have a variety of rules that govern business practices within their borders. These rules often serve as trade barriers. For example, Japan has some 11,000 trade regulations. Japanese car safety rules effectively require all automobile replacement parts to be Japanese and not American or European; public health rules make it illegal to sell aspirin or cold medicine without a pharmacist present. The Malaysian government has advertising regulations stating that "advertisements must not project or promote an excessively aspirational lifestyle," Sweden outlaws all advertisements to children, and Iran bans Mattel's Barbie dolls because they are a symbol of Western decadence.

learning review

7-6.   Cross-cultural analysis involves the study of _____.

7-7.   When foreign currencies can buy more U.S. dollars, are U.S. products more or less expensive for a foreign consumer?

COMPARING GLOBAL MARKET-ENTRY STRATEGIES

LO 7-4 | Name and describe the alternative approaches companies use to enter global markets.

Once a company has decided to enter the global marketplace, it must select a means of market entry. Four general options exist: (1) exporting, (2) licensing, (3) joint venture, and (4) direct investment.[21] As Figure 7–4 demonstrates, the amount of financial commitment, risk, marketing control, and profit potential increases as the firm moves from exporting to direct investment.

Exporting

Exporting is producing products in one country and selling them in another country. This entry option allows a company to make the least number of changes in terms of its product, its organization, and even its corporate goals. Host countries usually do not like this practice because it provides less local employment than under alternative means of entry.

Indirect exporting is when a firm sells its domestically produced products in a foreign country through an intermediary. It has the least amount of commitment and risk but will probably return the least profit. Indirect exporting is ideal for a company that has no overseas contacts but wants to market abroad. The intermediary is often a distributer that has the marketing know-how and resources necessary for the effort to succeed. Fran Wilson Creative Cosmetics uses an indirect exporting approach to sell its products in Japan. Read the Marketing Matters box to find out how this innovative marketer and its Japanese distributors sell 20 percent of the lipsticks exported to Japan by U.S. cosmetics companies.[22]

Direct exporting is when a firm sells its domestically produced products in a foreign country without intermediaries. Companies become involved in direct exporting when they believe their volume of sales will be sufficiently large and easy to obtain that they do not require intermediaries. For example, the exporter may be approached by foreign buyers that are willing to contract for a large volume of purchases. Direct exporting involves more risk than indirect exporting for the company but also opens the door to increased profits. The Boeing Company applies a direct exporting approach. Boeing is the world's largest aerospace company and the largest U.S. exporter.

Even though exporting is commonly employed by large firms, it is the prominent global market-entry strategy among small- and medium-sized companies. For example,

FIGURE 7–4

A firm's profit potential and control over marketing activities increase as it moves from exporting to direct investment as a global market-entry strategy. But so does a firm's financial commitment and risk. Firms often engage in exporting, licensing, and joint ventures before pursuing a direct investment strategy.

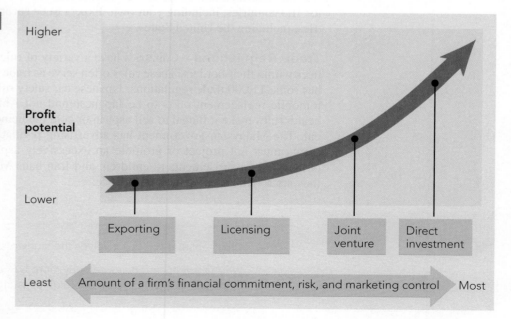

Marketing **Matters**

Creative Cosmetics and Creative Export Marketing in Japan

How does a medium-sized U.S. cosmetics firm sell 1.5 million tubes of lipstick in Japan annually? Fran Wilson Creative Cosmetics can attribute its success to a top-quality product, effective advertising, and a novel export marketing program. The firm's Mood-matcher lip coloring comes in green, orange, silver, black, and six other hues that change to a shade of pink, coral, or red, depending on a woman's chemistry when it's applied.

The company does not sell to department stores. According to a company spokesperson, "Shiseido and Kanebo (two large Japanese cosmetics firms) keep all the other Japanese or import brands out of the major department stores." Rather, the company sells its Moodmatcher lipstick through a network of Japanese distributors that reach Japan's 40,000 beauty salons.

The result? The company, with its savvy Japanese distributors, accounted for 20 percent of the lipsticks exported annually to Japan by U.S. cosmetics companies.

© Markus Sepperer/Anzenberger/Redux

McDonald's uses franchising as a market-entry strategy, and about two-thirds of the company's sales come from non–U.S. operations. Note that the golden arches appear prominently—one aspect of its global brand promise.
© China/Alamy

McDonald's
www.mcdonalds.com

about 97 percent of U.S. firms exporting products have fewer than 500 employees. These firms account for nearly 33 percent of total U.S. merchandise exports.[23]

Licensing

Under licensing, a company offers the right to a trademark, patent, trade secret, or other similarly valued item of intellectual property in return for a royalty or a fee. The advantages to the company granting the license are low risk and a capital-free entry into a foreign country. The licensee gains information that allows it to start with a competitive advantage, and the foreign country gains employment by having the product manufactured locally. For instance, Yoplait yogurt is licensed from Sodima, a French cooperative, by General Mills for sales in the United States.

There are some serious drawbacks to this mode of entry, however. The licensor forgoes control of its product and reduces the potential profits gained from it. In addition, while the relationship lasts, the licensor may be creating its own competition. Some licensees are able to modify the product somehow and enter the market with product and marketing knowledge gained at the expense of the company that got them started. To offset this disadvantage, many companies strive to stay innovative so that the licensee remains dependent on them for improvements and successful operation. Finally, should the licensee prove to be a poor choice, the name or reputation of the company may be harmed.

A variation of licensing is *franchising*. Franchising is one of the fastest-growing market-entry strategies. Over

75,000 franchises of U.S. firms are located in countries throughout the world. Franchises include soft-drink, motel, retailing, fast-food, and car rental operations and a variety of business services. McDonald's is a premier global franchiser, with some 14,000 franchised units outside the United States.

Joint Venture

When a foreign company and a local firm invest together to create a local business, it is called a **joint venture**. These two companies share the ownership, control, and profits of the new company. For example, the Strauss Group has a joint venture with PepsiCo to market Frito-Lay's Cheetos, Doritos, and other snacks in Israel.[24]

The advantages of this option are twofold. First, one company may not have the necessary financial, physical, or managerial resources to enter a foreign market alone. The joint venture between Ericsson, a Swedish telecommunications firm, and CGCT, a French switch maker, enabled them together to beat out AT&T for a $100 million French contract. Ericsson's money and technology combined with CGCT's knowledge of the French market helped them to win the contract. Second, a government may require or strongly encourage a joint venture before it allows a foreign company to enter its market. For example, in China, international giants such as Procter & Gamble, Starbucks, and General Motors operate wholly or in part through joint ventures.

The disadvantages arise when the two companies disagree about policies or courses of action for their joint venture or when governmental bureaucracy bogs down the effort. For example, U.S. firms often prefer to reinvest earnings gained, whereas some foreign companies may want to spend those earnings. Or a U.S. firm may want to return profits earned to the United States, while the local firm or its government may oppose this—a problem faced by many potential joint ventures. The collapse of the joint venture between France's Group Danone and a local company in China is a case in point. The joint venture partners could not agree on the distribution of profits.[25]

Direct Investment

The biggest commitment a company can make when entering the global market is *direct investment,* which entails a domestic firm actually investing in and owning a foreign subsidiary or division. Examples of direct investment are Nissan's Smyrna, Tennessee, plant that produces pickup trucks and the Mercedes-Benz factory in Vance, Alabama, that makes the M-class sports utility vehicle. Many U.S.-based global companies also use this mode of entry. Reebok entered Russia by creating a subsidiary known as Reebok Russia.

For many companies, direct investment often follows one of the other three market-entry strategies.[26] For example, both FedEx and UPS entered China through joint ventures with Chinese companies. Each subsequently purchased the interests of its partner and converted the Chinese operations into a division.

The advantages to direct investment include cost savings, a better understanding of local market conditions, and fewer local restrictions. Firms entering foreign markets using direct investment believe that these advantages outweigh the financial commitments and risks involved. However, sometimes they don't. U.S.-based Target Stores entered Canada in 2013 only to withdraw in 2015 after sizable operating losses and an investment of $5.7 billion.[27]

CRAFTING A WORLDWIDE MARKETING PROGRAM

> **LO 7-5** Explain the distinction between standardization and customization when companies craft worldwide marketing programs.

The choice of a market-entry strategy is a necessary first step for a marketer when joining the community of global companies. The next step involves the challenging task of planning, implementing, and evaluating marketing programs worldwide.

Successful global marketers standardize global marketing programs whenever possible and customize them wherever necessary. The extent of standardization and customization is often rooted in a careful global environment scan supplemented with judgment based on experience and marketing research.

Product and Promotion Strategies

Global companies have five strategies for matching products and their promotion efforts to global markets. As Figure 7–5 shows, the strategies focus on whether a company extends or adapts its product and promotion message for consumers in different countries and cultures.

A product may be sold globally in one of three ways: (1) in the same form as in its home market, (2) with some adaptations, or (3) as a totally new product:[28]

1. *Product extension.* Selling virtually the same product in other countries is a product extension strategy. It works well for products such as Coca-Cola, Gillette razors, Sony consumer electronics, Harley-Davidson motorcycles, Nike apparel and shoes, and Apple smartphones. As a general rule, product extension seems to work best when the consumer market target for the product is alike across countries and cultures—that is, consumers share the same desires, needs, and uses for the product.

2. *Product adaptation.* Changing a product in some way to make it more appropriate for consumer preferences or a country's climate is a product adaptation strategy. Wrigley's offers grapefruit, cucumber, and tea-flavored chewing gum in China. Frito-Lay produces and markets its potato chips in Russia, but don't expect them to taste like the chips eaten in North America. Russians prefer dairy, meat, and seafood-flavored potato chips. Gerber baby food comes in different varieties in different countries. Popular Gerber varieties outside the United States include vegetables and rabbit meat in Poland and freeze-dried sardines and rice in Japan. Maybelline's makeup is adapted to local skin types and weather across the globe, including an Asia-specific mascara that doesn't run during the rainy season.

3. *Product invention.* Alternatively, companies can invent totally new products designed to satisfy common needs across countries. Black & Decker did this with its Snake Light flexible flashlight. Created to address a global need for portable lighting, the product became a best seller in North America, Europe, Latin America, and Australia and is the most successful new product developed by

FIGURE 7–5

Five product and promotion strategies for global marketing exist based on whether a company extends or adapts its product and promotion message for consumers in different countries and cultures. Read the text to learn how different companies employ these strategies.

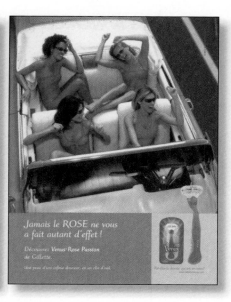

Gillette delivers the same global message whenever possible, as shown in the Gillette for Women Venus ads from the United States, Mexico, and France.

Source: Procter & Gamble

The Gillette Company
www.gillette.com

Video 7-4
Nescafé China
kerin.tv/13e/v7-4

Black & Decker. Similarly, Whirlpool developed a compact, automatic clothes washer specifically for households in developing countries with annual household incomes of $2,000. Called Ideale, the washer features bright colors because washers are often placed in home living areas, not hidden in laundry rooms (which don't exist in many homes in developing countries).

An identical promotion message is used for the product extension and product adaptation strategies around the world. Gillette uses the same global message for its men's toiletries: "Gillette, the Best a Man Can Get." Even though Exxon adapts its gasoline blends for different countries based on climate, the promotion message is unchanged: "Put a Tiger in Your Tank."

Global companies may also adapt their promotion message. For instance, the same product may be sold in many countries but advertised differently. As an example, L'Oréal, a French health and beauty products marketer, introduced its Golden Beauty brand of sun care products through its Helena Rubenstein subsidiary in Western Europe with a *communication adaptation strategy*. Recognizing that cultural and buying motive differences related to skin care and tanning exist, Golden Beauty advertising features dark tanning for northern Europeans, skin protection to avoid wrinkles among Latin Europeans, and beautiful skin for Europeans living along the Mediterranean Sea, even though the products are the same.

Other companies use a *dual adaptation strategy* by modifying both their products and promotion messages. Nestlé does this with Nescafé coffee. Nescafé is marketed using different coffee blends and promotional campaigns to match consumer preferences in different countries. For example, Nescafé, the world's largest brand of coffee, generally emphasizes the taste, aroma, and warmth of shared moments in its advertising around the world. However, Nescafé is advertised in Thailand as a way to relax from the pressures of daily life.

These examples illustrate the simple rule applied by global companies: Standardize product and promotion strategies whenever possible and customize them wherever necessary. This is the art of global marketing.[29]

Distribution Strategy

Distribution is of critical importance in global marketing. The availability and quality of retailers and wholesalers as well as transportation, communication, and warehousing facilities are often determined by a country's stage of economic development.

Seller → Seller's international marketing headquarters → Channels between nations → Channels within foreign nation → Final consumer

FIGURE 7–6

Channels of distribution in global marketing are often long and complex.

Figure 7–6 outlines the channel through which a product manufactured in one country must travel to reach its destination in another country. The first step involves the seller; its headquarters is the starting point and is responsible for the successful distribution to the ultimate consumer.

The next step is the channel between two nations, moving the product from one country to another. Intermediaries that can handle this responsibility include resident buyers in a foreign country, independent merchant wholesalers who buy and sell the product, or agents who bring buyers and sellers together.

Once the product is in the foreign nation, that country's distribution channels take over. These channels can be very long or surprisingly short, depending on the product line. In Japan, fresh fish go through three intermediaries before getting to a retail outlet. Conversely, shoes go through only one intermediary. Recall that Dell has had to revise its direct-marketing channel that originally featured online and phone buying in India, as described in the chapter-opening example.

Pricing Strategy

Global companies also face many challenges in determining a pricing strategy as part of their worldwide marketing effort. Individual countries, even those with free trade agreements, may impose considerable competitive, political, and legal constraints on the pricing latitude of global companies. For example, antitrust authorities in Germany limited Walmart from selling some items below cost to lure shoppers. Without this advantage, Walmart was unable to compete against German discount stores. This, and other factors, led Walmart to leave Germany following eight years without a profit.[30]

Pricing too low or too high can have dire consequences. When prices appear too low in one country, companies can be charged with dumping, a practice subject to severe penalties and fines. *Dumping* is when a firm sells a product in a foreign country below its domestic price or below its actual cost. This is often done to build a company's share of the market by pricing at a competitive level. Another reason is that the products being sold may be surplus or cannot be sold domestically and, therefore, are already a burden to the company. The firm may be glad to sell them at almost any price.

When companies price their products very high in some countries but competitively in others, they face a gray market problem. A *gray market,* also called *parallel importing,* is a situation where products are sold through unauthorized channels of distribution. A gray market comes about when individuals buy products in a lower-priced country from a manufacturer's authorized retailer, ship them to higher-priced countries, and then sell them below the manufacturer's suggested retail price through unauthorized retailers. Many well-known products have been sold through gray markets, including Seiko watches, Chanel perfume, and Mercedes-Benz cars. Parallel importing is legal in the United States. It is illegal in the European Union.

learning review

7-10. Products may be sold globally in three ways. What are they?

7-11. What is *dumping*?

LO 7-1 *Describe the nature and scope of world trade from a global perspective.*

A global perspective on world trade views exports and imports as complementary economic flows: A country's imports affect its exports and exports affects its imports. Trade flows reflect interdependencies among industries, countries, and regions.

LO 7-2 *Identify the major trends that have influenced world trade and global marketing.*

Five major trends have influenced the landscape of global marketing in the past decade. First, there has been a gradual decline of economic protectionism by individual countries, leading to a reduction in tariffs and quotas. Second, there is growing economic integration and free trade among nations, reflected in the creation of the European Union and the North American Free Trade Agreement. Third, there exists global competition among global companies for global consumers, resulting in firms adopting global marketing strategies and promoting global brands. Fourth, a networked global marketspace has emerged using Internet technology as a tool for exchanging products, services, and information on a global scale. And finally, economic espionage has grown among countries and companies because technical know-how and trade secrets separate global industry leaders from followers.

LO 7-3 *Identify the environmental forces that shape global marketing efforts.*

Three major environmental forces shape global marketing efforts. First, there are cultural forces, including values, customs, cultural symbols, and language. Economic forces also shape global marketing efforts. These include a country's stage of economic development and economic infrastructure, consumer income and purchasing power, and currency exchange rates. Finally, political-regulatory forces in a country or region of the world create a favorable or unfavorable climate for global marketing efforts.

LO 7-4 *Name and describe the alternative approaches companies use to enter global markets.*

Companies have four alternative approaches for entering global markets. These are exporting, licensing, joint venture, and direct investment. Exporting involves producing products in one country and selling them in another country. Under licensing, a company offers the right to a trademark, patent, trade secret, or similarly valued item of intellectual property in return for a royalty or fee. In a joint venture, a foreign company and a local firm invest together to create a local business. Direct investment entails a domestic firm actually investing in and owning a foreign subsidiary or division.

LO 7-5 *Explain the distinction between standardization and customization when companies craft worldwide marketing programs.*

Companies distinguish between standardization and customization when crafting worldwide marketing programs. Standardization means that all elements of the marketing program are the same across countries and cultures. Customization means that one or more elements of the marketing program are adapted to meet the needs or preferences of consumers in a particular country or culture. Global marketers apply a simple rule when crafting worldwide marketing programs: Standardize marketing programs whenever possible and customize them wherever necessary.

LEARNING REVIEW ANSWERS

7-1 What country is the biggest as measured by world trade?
Answer: China

7-2 What is the trade feedback effect?
Answer: The phenomenon in which one country's imports affect the exports of other countries and vice versa, thus stimulating trade among countries.

7-3 What is protectionism?
Answer: Protectionism is the practice of shielding one or more industries within a country's economy from foreign competition through the use of tariffs or quotas.

7-4 The North American Free Trade Agreement was designed to promote free trade among which countries?
Answer: the United States, Canada, and Mexico

7-5 What is the difference between a multidomestic marketing strategy and a global marketing strategy?
Answer: Multinational firms view the world as consisting of unique markets. As a result, they use a multidomestic marketing strategy because they have as many different product variations, brand names, and advertising programs as countries in which they do business. Transnational firms view the world as one market. As a result, they use a global marketing strategy, which involves standardizing marketing activities when there are cultural similarities and adapting them it when cultures differ.

7-6 Cross-cultural analysis involves the study of _____.
Answer: similarities and differences among consumers in two or more nations or societies.

7-7 When foreign currencies can buy more U.S. dollars, are U.S. products more or less expensive for a foreign consumer?
Answer: less expensive

7-8 What mode of entry could a company follow if it has no previous experience in global marketing?
Answer: indirect exporting through intermediaries

7-9 How does licensing differ from a joint venture?
Answer: Under licensing, a company offers the right to a trademark, patent, trade secret, or other similarly valued item of intellectual property in return for a fee or royalty. In a joint venture, a foreign company and a local firm invest together to create a local business to produce some product or service. The two companies share ownership, control, and profits of the new entity.

7-10 Products may be sold globally in three ways. What are they?
Answer: Products can be sold: (1) in the same form as in their home market (product extension); (2) with some adaptations (product adaptation); and (3) as totally new products (product invention).

7-11 What is *dumping*?
Answer: *Dumping* is when a firm sells a product in a foreign country below its domestic price or below its actual cost to produce.

back translation p. 187
balance of trade p. 177
consumer ethnocentrism p. 188
countertrade p. 176
cross-cultural
    analysis p. 185
cultural symbols p. 186
currency exchange rate p. 190
customs p. 186

economic espionage p. 185
exporting p. 192
Foreign Corrupt Practices
    Act (1977) p. 186
global brand p. 183
global competition p. 181
global consumers p. 183
global marketing strategy p. 182
joint venture p. 194

multidomestic marketing
    strategy p. 182
protectionism p. 178
quota p. 178
tariffs p. 178
values p. 185
World Trade Organization
    (WTO) p. 179

APPLYING MARKETING KNOWLEDGE

1   Explain what is meant by this statement: "Quotas are a hidden tax on consumers, whereas tariffs are a more obvious one."

2   How successful would a television commercial in Japan be if it featured a husband surprising his wife in her dressing area on Valentine's Day with a small box of chocolates containing four candies? Explain.

3   As a novice in global marketing, which global market-entry strategy would you be likely to start with? Why? What other alternatives do you have for a global market entry?

4   Coca-Cola is sold worldwide. In some countries, Coca-Cola owns the bottling facilities; in others, it has signed contracts with licensees or relies on joint ventures. When selecting a licensee in each country, what factors should Coca-Cola consider?

BUILDING YOUR MARKETING PLAN

Does your marketing plan involve reaching global customers outside the United States? If the answer is no, read no further and do not include a global element in your plan.

If the answer is yes, try to identify the following:

1   What features of your product are especially important to potential customers?

2   In which countries do these potential customers live?

3   What special marketing issues are involved in trying to reach them?

Answers to these questions will help in developing more detailed marketing mix strategies described in later chapters.

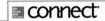

VIDEO CASE 7   Mary Kay, Inc.: Building a Brand in India

Sheryl Adkins-Green couldn't ask for a better assignment. As the newly appointed vice president of brand development at Mary Kay, Inc., she is responsible for development of the product portfolio around the world, including global initiatives and products specifically formulated for global markets. She is enthusiastic about her position, noting that "There is tremendous opportunity for growth. Even in these economic times, women still want to pamper themselves, and to look good is to feel good."

Video 7-5
Mary Kay
Video Case
kerin.tv/13e/v7-5

Getting up to speed on her new company and her new position topped her short-term agenda. She was specifically interested in the company's efforts to date to build the Mary Kay brand in India.

THE MARY KAY WAY

Mary Kay Ash founded Mary Kay Cosmetics in 1963 with her life savings of $5,000 and the support of her 20-year-old son, Richard Rogers, who currently serves as executive chair of Mary Kay, Inc. Mary Kay, Inc. is one of the largest direct sellers of skin care and color cosmetics in the world with more than

$2.5 billion in annual sales. Mary Kay brand products are sold in more than 35 markets on five continents. The United States, China, Russia, and Mexico are the top four markets served by the company. The company's global independent sales force exceeds 2 million. About 65 percent of the company's independent sales representatives reside outside the United States.

Mary Kay Ash's founding principles were simple, time-tested, and remain a fundamental company business philosophy. She adopted the Golden Rule as her guiding principle, determining the best course of action in virtually any situation could be easily discerned by "doing unto others as you would have them do unto you." She also steadfastly believed that life's priorities should be kept in their proper order, which to her meant "God first, family second, and career third." Her work ethic, approach to business, and success have resulted in numerous awards and recognitions including, but not limited to, the Horatio Alger American Citizen Award, recognition as one of "America's 25 Most Influential Women," and induction into the National Business Hall of Fame.

Mary Kay, Inc. engages in the development, manufacture, and packaging of skin care, makeup, spa and body, and fragrance products for men and women. It offers anti-aging, cleanser, moisturizer, lip and eye care, body care, and sun care products. Overall, the company produces more than 200 premium products in its state-of-the-art manufacturing facilities in Dallas, Texas, and Hangzhou, China. The company's approach to direct selling employs the "party plan," whereby independent sales representatives host parties to demonstrate or sell products to consumers.

GROWTH OPPORTUNITIES IN ASIA-PACIFIC MARKETS

Asia-Pacific markets represent major growth opportunities for Mary Kay, Inc. These markets for Mary Kay, Inc. include Australia, China, Hong Kong, India, Korea, Malaysia, New Zealand, the Philippines, Singapore, and Taiwan.

China accounts for the largest sales revenue outside the United States, representing about 25 percent of annual Mary Kay, Inc. worldwide sales. The company entered China in 1995 and currently has some 200,000 independent sales representatives or "beauty consultants" in that country.

Part of Mary Kay's success in China has been attributed to the company's message of female empowerment and femininity, which has resonated in China, a country where young women have few opportunities to start their own businesses. Speaking about the corporate philosophy at Mary Kay, Inc., KK Chua, president, Asia-Pacific, said, "Mary Kay's corporate objective is not only to create a market, selling skin care and cosmetics; it's all about enriching women's lives by helping women reach their full potential, find their inner beauty and discover how truly great they are." This view is echoed by Sheryl Adkins-Green, who notes that the Mary Kay brand has "transformational and aspirational" associations for users and beauty consultants alike.

Mary Kay, Inc. learned that adjustments to its product line and message for women were necessary in some Asia-Pacific markets. In China, for example, the order of life's priorities—"God first, family second, and career third"—has been modified to "Faith first, family second, and career third." Also, Chinese women aren't heavy users of makeup. Therefore, the featured products include skin cream, anti-aging cream, and whitening creams. As a generalization, whitening products are popular among women in China, India, Korea, and the Philippines, where lighter skin is associated with beauty, class, and privilege.

MARY KAY, INDIA

Mary Kay, Inc. senior management believed that India represented a growth opportunity for three reasons. First, the Indian upper and consuming classes were growing and were expected to total over 500 million individuals. Second, the population was overwhelmingly young and optimistic. This youthful population continues to push consumerism as the line between luxury and basic items continues to blur. Third, a growing number of working women have given a boost to sales of cosmetics, skin care, and fragrances in India's urban areas, where 70 percent of the country's middle-class women reside.

Senior management also believed that India's socioeconomic characteristics in 2007 were similar in many ways to China's in 1995, when the company entered that market (see Figure 1). The Mary Kay culture was viewed as a good fit with the Indian culture, which would benefit the company's venture into this market. For example, industry research has shown that continuing modernization of the country has led to changing aspirations. As a result, the need to be good looking, well-groomed, and stylish has taken on a newfound importance.

Mary Kay initiated operations in India in September 2007 with a full marketing launch in early 2008. The initial launch was in Delhi, the nation's capital and the second most populated metropolis in India, and Mumbai, the nation's most heavily populated metropolis. Delhi, with per capita income of U.S. $1,420, and Mumbai, with per capita income of $2,850, were among the wealthiest metropolitan areas in India.

FIGURE 1

Social and economic statistics for India in 2007 and China in 1995.

	India 2007	China 1995
Population (million)	1,136	1,198
Population age distribution (0–24; 25–49; 50+)	52%, 33%, 15%	43%, 39%, 18%
Urban population	29.2%	29.0%
Population/square mile	990	332
Gross domestic product (U.S.$ billion)	3,113	728
Per capita income (U.S.$)	$950	$399
Direct selling sales percent of total cosmetics/skin care sales	3.3%	3.0%

According to Rhonda Shasteen, chief marketing officer at Mary Kay, Inc., "For Mary Kay to be successful in India, the company had to build a brand, build a sales force, and build an effective supply chain to service the sales force."

Building a Brand

Mary Kay, Inc. executives believed that brand building in India needed to involve media advertising; literature describing the Mary Kay culture, the Mary Kay story, and the company's image; and educational material for Mary Kay independent sales representatives. In addition, Mary Kay, Inc. became the cosmetics partner of the Miss India Worldwide Pageant 2008. At this event, Mary Kay Miss Beautiful Skin 2008 was crowned.

Brand building in India also involved product mix and pricing. Four guidelines were followed:

1. Keep the offering simple and skin care focused for the new Indian sales force and for a new operation.
2. Open with accessibly priced basic skin care products in relation to the competition in order to establish Mary Kay product quality and value.
3. Avoid opening with products that would phase out shortly after launch.
4. Address the key product categories of Skin Care, Body Care, and Color based on current market information.

Brand pricing focused on offering accessibly priced basic skin care to the average middle-class Indian consumer between the ages of 25 and 54. This strategy, called "mass-tige pricing," resulted in product price points that were above mass but below prestige competitive product prices. Following an initial emphasis on offering high-quality, high-value products, Mary Kay introduced more technologically advanced products that commanded higher price points.

For example, the company introduced the Mary Kay MelaCEP Whitening System, consisting of seven products, which was specifically formulated for Asian skin in March 2009. This system was "priced on the lower price end of the prestige category with a great value for money equation," said Hina Nagarajan, country manager for Mary Kay India.

Building a Sales Force

According to Adkins-Green, "Mary Kay's most powerful marketing vehicle is the direct selling organization," which is a key component of the brand's marketing strategy. Mary Kay relied on its Global Leadership Development Program directors and National Sales directors and the Mary Kay Sales Education staff from the United States and Canada for the initial recruitment and training of independent sales representatives in India. New independent sales representatives received 2 to 3 days of intensive training and a starter kit that included not only products, but also information pertaining to product demonstrations, sales presentations, professional demeanor, the company's history and culture, and team building.

"Culture training is very important to Mary Kay (independent sales representatives) because they are going to be the messengers of Mary Kay," said Hina Nagarajan. "As a direct-selling company that offers products sold person-to-person, we recognize that there's a personal relationship between consultant and client with every sale," added Rhonda Shasteen. By late 2009, there were some 4,000 independent sales representatives in India present in some 200 cities mostly in the northern, western, and northeastern regions of the country.

Creating a Supply Chain

Mary Kay, India, imported products into India from China, Korea, and the United States. Products were shipped to regional distribution centers in Delhi and Mumbai, India, where Mary Kay Beauty Centers were located. Beauty Centers served as order pickup points for the independent sales representatives. Mary Kay beauty consultants purchased products from the company and, in turn, sold them to consumers.

LOOKING AHEAD

Mary Kay, Inc. plans to invest around $20 million in the next five years on product development, company infrastructure, and building its brand in India. "There is a tremendous opportunity for growth," says Sheryl Adkins-Green. India represents a particularly attractive opportunity. Developing the brand and brand portfolio and specifically formulating products for Indian consumers will require her attention to brand positioning and brand equity.[31]

Questions

1 Is Mary Kay an international firm, a multinational firm, or a transnational firm based on its marketing strategy? Why?
2 What global market-entry strategy did Mary Kay use when it entered India?
3 Is Mary Kay a global brand? Why or why not?

Chapter Notes

1. "Dell India regains Top Spot in Domestic PC Market," ibnlive.in.com, May 24, 2014; "Dell India Plans to Open More Exclusive Brand Outlets in India," www.business-standard.com, December 13, 2013; "Dell's Next Big Agenda," www.crn.in, February 21, 2012; Dell India Opens Its Exclusive Store in Hyderabad, www.greatandhra.com, September 12, 2012; and "How Dell Conquered India," www.CNNMoney.com, February and 10, 2011.

2. Unless otherwise indicated, all trade statistics and practices are provided by the World Trade Organization, www.wto.org, downloaded May 10, 2015.

3. Dennis R. Appleyard and Alfred J. Field, *International Economics,* 8th ed. (Burr Ridge, IL: McGraw-Hill, 2013), Chap. 15;

Tansa Mess, "Africa and Caribbean Fear EU Latam Banana Tariff Cuts," *International Herald Tribune,* August 26, 2008, p. 8; Yuri Kageyama, "Selling Rice to Japan? U.S. Plans to Try," www.msnbc.com, March 7, 2004; "A Shoe Tariff with a Big Footprint," *The Wall Street journal,* November 23, 2012, p. A13; and *Economic Report of the President* (Washington, DC: U.S. Government Printing Office, 2012).

4. "Time to Put Trade above Politics," *Time,* March 7, 2015, p. 24.

5. This discussion on the European Union is based on information provided at www.europa.eu, downloaded March 5, 2014.

6. These examples provided at ustr.gov.

7. For an overview of different types of global companies and marketing strategies, see, for example, Masaaki Kotabe and

Kristiaan Helsen, *Global Marketing Management,* 6th ed. (New York: Wiley, 2015); Warren J. Keegan and Mark C. Green, *Global Marketing,* 4th ed. (Upper Saddle River, NJ: Prentice Hall, 2005); and Michael Czinkota and Ilkka A. Ronkainen, *International Marketing,* 10th ed. (Mason, OH: South-Western, 2013).

8. Johnny K. Johansson and Ilkka A. Ronkainen, "The Brand Challenge," *Marketing Management,* March–April 2004, pp. 54–55.

9. Kevin Lane Keller, *Strategic Brand Management,* 4th ed. (Upper Saddle River, NJ: Prentice Hall, 2013).

10. "Purchase Power of Teens Tops $819 Billion," insights. mastercard.com, November 21, 2012; "Coca-Cola, Nike and Adidas Top Brands for Teens Globally, TRU Study Finds," www.teenresearch.com, March 2, 2009; "Global Habbo Youth Survey," marketinginsight@sulake.com, downloaded March 20, 2009; www.mtv.com/company, downloaded January 10, 2014; Bay Fong, "Spending Spree," *U.S. News & World Report,* May 1, 2006, pp. 42–50; and "Burgeoning Bourgeoisie," *The Economist,* February 14, 2009. Special report on the new middle classes.

11. "The Pocket World in Figures: 2015 Edition," *The Economist.*

12. "Industrial Espionage: Data Out the Door," *Financial Times,* February 1, 2011, p. 8; "FBI's New Campaign Targets Corporate Espionage," *The Wall Street Journal,* May 11, 2012, p. B4; and "The Staggering Cost of Economic Espionage Against the U.S.," www.thepochtimes, October 22, 2013.

13. For comprehensive references on cross-cultural aspects of marketing, see Paul A. Herbig, *Handbook of Cross-Cultural Marketing* (New York: Halworth Press, 1998); Jean Claude Usunier, *Marketing Across Cultures,* 4th ed. (London: Prentice Hall Europe, 2005); and Philip K. Cateora, Mary Gilly, and John L. Graham, *International Marketing,* 16th ed. (Burr Ridge, IL: McGraw-Hill/Irwin, 2013). Unless otherwise indicated, examples found in this section appear in these excellent sources.

14. "Bribery Law Dos and Don'ts," *The Wall Street Journal,* November 15, 2012, pp. B1, B2.

15. "Greeks Protest Coke's Use of Parthenon," *Dallas Morning News,* August 17, 1992, p. D4.

16. "How Did Kit Kat Become King of Candy in Japan?" www. cnnmoney.com, February 2, 2012.

17. "Terrence A. Shimp and Subhash Sharma, "Consumer Ethnocentrism: Construction and Validation of the CETSCALE," *Journal of Marketing Research*, August 1987, pp. 280–89. For a review of research on this topic, see A. Alsughayir, "Consumer Ethnocentrism: A Literature Review," *International Journal of Business and Management*, May 2013, pp. 50–54.

18. "Burgeoning Bourgeoisie," *The Economist.*

19. "Mattel Plans to Double Sales Abroad," *The Wall Street Journal,* February 11, 1998, pp. A3, A11.

20. "Strong Dollar Squeezes U.S. Firms," *The Wall Street Journal,* January 28, 2015, pp. A1, A2.

21. For an extensive and recent examination of these market-entry options, see for example, Johnny K. Johansson, *Global Marketing: Foreign Entry, Local Marketing, and Global Management,* 5th ed. (Burr Ridge, IL: McGraw Hill/Irwin, 2008); A. Coskun Samli, *Entering & Succeeding in Emerging Countries: Marketing to the Forgotten Majority* (Mason, OH: South-Western, 2004); and Keegan and Green, *Global Marketing.*

22. Based on an interview with Pamela Viglielmo, Director of International Marketing, Fran Wilson Creative Cosmetics; and "Foreign Firms Think Their Way into Japan," www.successstories. com/nikkei, downloaded March 24, 2003.

20. "Strong Dollar Squeezes U.S. Firms," *The Wall Street Journal,* January 28, 2015, pp. A1, A2.

23. *Small and Medium Sized Exporting Companies: Statistical Overview* (Washington, DC: International Trade Administration, April 16, 2012).

24. "About Us," www.strauss-group.com, downloaded March 15, 2015.

25. "Dannon Pulls Out of Disputed China Venture," *The Wall Street Journal,* October 1, 2009, p. B1.

26. "FedEx Expands Reach in China with Buyout of Joint Venture," *The Wall Street Journal,* January 25, 2006.

27. "Target's New CEO Makes a Bold Decision to Leave Canada," www.forbes.com, January 15, 2015.

28. This discussion is based on Keller, *Strategic Brand Management,* pp. 709–10; "Gum Makers Cater to Chinese Tastes," *The Wall Street Journal,* February 26, 2014, p. B9; "Global Sales of Lay's Chips Top $10 Billion in '11," *Dallas Morning News,* March 12, 2012, pp. D1, 10D; "Machines for the Masses," *The Wall Street Journal,* December 9, 2003, pp. A19, A20; "The Color of Beauty," *Forbes,* November 22, 2000, pp. 170–76; "It's Goo, Goo, Goo, Goo Vibrations at the Gerber Lab," *The Wall Street Journal,* December 4, 1996, pp. A1, A6; Donald R. Graber, "How to Manage a Global Product Development Process," *Industrial Marketing Management,* November 1996, pp. 483–98; and Herbig, *Handbook of Cross-Cultural Marketing.*

29. Jagdish N. Sheth and Atul Parvatiyar, "The Antecedents and Consequences of Integrated Global Marketing," *International Marketing Review* 18, no. 1 (2001), pp. 16–29. Also see D. Szymanski, S. Bharadwaj, and R. Varadarajan, "Standardization versus Adaptation of International Marketing Strategy: An Empirical Investigation," *Journal of Marketing,* October 1993, pp. 1–17.

30. "Where Wal-Mart Isn't: Four Countries the Retailer Can't Conquer," www.businessweek.com, October 10, 2013.

31. Mary Kay, India: This case was prepared by Roger A. Kerin based on company interviews.

8 Marketing Research: From Customer Insights to Actions

LEARNING OBJECTIVES

After reading this chapter you should be able to:

LO 8-1 Identify the reason for conducting marketing research.

LO 8-2 Describe the five-step marketing research approach that leads to marketing actions.

LO 8-3 Explain how marketing uses secondary and primary data.

LO 8-4 Discuss the uses of observations, questionnaires, panels, experiments, and newer data collection methods.

LO 8-5 Explain how information technology and data mining lead to marketing actions.

LO 8-6 Describe three approaches to developing a company's sales forecast.

Marketing Research Goes to the Movies

Avatar, Titanic, and *The Avengers* are blockbuster movies that have attracted millions of moviegoers worldwide. The revenues they generated each exceeded $1 billion, well above the $200+ million budgets needed to produce them.[1] Unfortunately, not every movie has such favorable results. So what can studios do to try to reduce the risk that a movie will be a box-office flop? Marketing research!

A Film Industry Secret

Bad titles, poor scripts, temperamental stars, costly special effects, competing movies, and everchanging consumers are just a few of the risks studio executives face. They try to reduce their risk through a largely secretive process of marketing research that involves small sample audiences selected to be representative of the larger population.

> **Video 8-1**
> ***Star Wars Episode VII Movie Trailer***
> Kerin.tv/13e/v8-1

Fixing bad movie names, for example, can turn potential disaster into successful blockbusters. Many studios use title testing—a form of marketing research—to choose a name. Here are a few examples:

- *3000* became *Pretty Woman* because the original title sounded too futuristic.

- *The Sessions,* which garnered Helen Hunt an Academy Award nomination, was originally titled *The Surrogate,* which was confusing, and then *Six Sessions,* which was difficult to say.

- *Rope Burns* became *Million Dollar Baby* because audiences didn't like the original name.

- *Shoeless Joe* became the baseball classic *Field of Dreams* to avoid suggesting that Kevin Costner was playing a homeless person.

Generally, filmmakers want movie titles that are short, memorable, appealing to consumers, and have no legal restrictions—the same factors that make a good brand name.[2] Studios also try to reduce their risks with additional forms of marketing research such as:

- *Concept testing and script assessment.* These techniques are used to assess early ideas for proposed new films. In addition, because many scripts and films today are part of a series such as *The Fast and The Furious, The Hunger*

GEORGE LUCAS AND WALT DISNEY PICTURES PRESENTS A J.J. ABRAMS FILM

STAR.WARS
EPISODE VII
IN THEATRES 2015

© Film Fanatique/Alamy

Games, and *Star Wars,* these forms of research can ensure that sequels are consistent with expectations created by the past movies.[3]

- *Test (or preview) screenings.* In test screenings, 300 to 400 prospective moviegoers are recruited to attend a "sneak preview" of a film before its release. After viewing the movie, the audience completes a survey to critique its title, plot, characters, music, and ending to identify improvements to make in the final edit. John Cameron, for example, used a test screening of a segment of *Avatar* to convince Twentieth Century Fox executives of the movie's potential appeal.[4]

- *Tracking studies.* Before an upcoming film's release studios will ask prospective moviegoers in the target audience three questions: (1) Are you aware of the film? (2) Are you interested in seeing the film? (3) Will you see the film? Studios also use "social listening" to understand what potential moviegoers are saying on Twitter, YouTube, Tumblr, Facebook, Instagram, and other social media sites. Studios use these data to monitor a promotional campaign, forecast the movie's opening weekend box-office sales and, if necessary, add additional marketing activities to promote the film.[5]

These examples show how marketing research leads to effective marketing actions, the main topic of this chapter. Also, marketing research is often used to help a firm develop its sales forecasts, the final topic of this chapter.

THE ROLE OF MARKETING RESEARCH

LO 8-1 Identify the reason for conducting marketing research.

Let's (1) look at what marketing research is, (2) identify some difficulties with it, and (3) describe the five steps marketers use to conduct it.

What Is Marketing Research?

Marketing research is the process of defining a marketing problem and opportunity, systematically collecting and analyzing information, and recommending actions.[6] Although imperfect, marketers conduct marketing research to reduce the risk of and thereby improve marketing decisions.

The Challenges in Doing Good Marketing Research

Whatever the marketing issue involved—whether discovering consumer tastes or setting the right price—good marketing research is challenging. For example:

- Suppose your firm is developing a product that is completely new to the marketplace, and you are charged with estimating demand for the product. How can marketing research determine if consumers will buy a product they have never seen, and never thought about, before?
- Understanding why consumers purchase some products often requires answers to personal questions. How can marketing research obtain answers that people know but are reluctant to reveal?
- Past purchase behaviors may help firms understand the influence of marketing actions. How can marketing research help people accurately remember and report their interests, intentions, and purchases?

Step 1	Step 2	Step 3	Step 4	Step 5
Define the problem • Set research objectives • Identify possible marketing actions	**Develop the research plan** • Specify constraints • Identify data needed for marketing actions • Determine how to collect data	**Collect relevant information** • Obtain secondary data • Obtain primary data	**Develop findings** • Analyze the data • Present the findings	**Take marketing actions** • Make action recommendations • Implement action recommendations • Evaluate results

Feedback to learn lessons for future research

FIGURE 8–1

Five-step marketing research approach leading to marketing actions. Lessons learned from past research mistakes are fed back to improve each of the steps.

Marketing research must overcome these difficulties and obtain the information needed so that marketers can assess what consumers want and will buy.

Five-Step Marketing Research Approach

A *decision* is a conscious choice from among two or more alternatives. All of us make many such decisions daily. At work we choose from alternative ways to accomplish an assigned task. At college we choose from alternative courses. As consumers we choose from alternative brands. No magic formula guarantees correct decisions.

Managers and researchers have tried to improve the outcomes of decisions by using more formal, structured approaches to *decision making,* the act of consciously choosing from among alternatives. The systematic marketing research approach used to collect information to improve marketing decisions and actions described in this chapter uses five steps and is shown in Figure 8–1. Although the five-step approach described here focuses on marketing decisions, it provides a systematic checklist for making both business and personal decisions.

LO 8-2 Describe the five-step marketing research approach that leads to marketing actions.

STEP 1: DEFINE THE PROBLEM

LEGO Group's MINDSTORMS® EV3 TRACK3R has an interchangeable bazooka and hammer—and can operate after only 20 minutes of assembly.

Source: LEGO Group

Every marketing problem faces its own research challenges. For example, the marketing strategy used by LEGO Group's toy researchers and designers in Denmark illustrates the wide variations possible in collecting marketing research data to build better toys.

LEGO Group's definition of "toy" has changed dramatically in the past 50 years— from interlocking plastic bricks to construction sets that create figures, vehicles, buildings, and even robots. One new version of a LEGO Group toy is the MINDSTORMS® kit, which integrates electronics, computers, and robots with traditional LEGO Group bricks. Developed with the help of the Media Lab at the Massachusetts Institute of Technology, the MINDSTORMS® kit appeals to a diverse market—from elementary school kids to world-class robotics experts. The kits can be found in homes, schools, universities, and industrial laboratories.[7]

A simplified look at the marketing research for the LEGO Group's MINDSTORMS® EV3 shows the two key elements in defining a problem: setting the research objectives and identifying possible marketing actions.

Set the Research Objectives

Research objectives are specific, measurable goals the decision maker seeks to achieve in conducting the marketing research. For

LEGO Group, let's assume the immediate research objective is to decide which of two new MINDSTORMS® designs should be selected for marketing.

In setting research objectives, marketers have to be clear on the purpose of the research that leads to marketing actions. The three main types of marketing research are as follows:

1. *Exploratory research* provides ideas about a vague problem. LEGO Group was concerned that middle school kids would be overwhelmed by the 500-plus pieces in MINDSTORMS® kits and quickly lose interest. LEGO Group's brainstorming—an example of exploratory research—revealed kids need to have a basic device up, running, and doing tricks in 20 minutes.

2. *Descriptive research* generally involves trying to find the frequency with which something occurs or the extent of a relationship between two factors. So if LEGO Group wants to know which of the two MINDSTORMS® kits is of greatest interest to middle school versus high school students, it might ask them. LEGO Group can then assess the relationship by doing a cross tabulation (discussed later in the chapter) of school level versus kit preference.

3. *Causal research* tries to determine the extent to which the change in one factor changes another one. Changing key pieces in a MINDSTORMS® kit affects how quickly the newly built device can do tricks—affecting acceptance by kit users. Test markets, discussed later, use causal research.

LEGO Group's MINDSTORMS® EV3RSTORM has infrared sensors that let it walk or skate.

Source: LEGO Group

Identify Possible Marketing Actions

Effective decision makers develop specific **measures of success**, which are criteria or standards used in evaluating proposed solutions to the problem. Different research outcomes, based on the measure of success, lead to different marketing actions. For LEGO Group, assume the measure of success is the total time spent with each of the two potential new MINDSTORMS® kits until a device that can do simple tricks is produced. This measure of success leads to a clear-cut marketing action: Market the kit that produces an acceptable device in the least amount of playing time.

Marketing researchers know that defining a problem is an incredibly difficult task. If the objectives are too broad, the problem may not be researchable. If they are too narrow, the value of the research results may be seriously lessened. This is why marketing researchers spend so much time defining a marketing problem precisely and writing a formal proposal that describes the research to be done.[8]

STEP 2: DEVELOP THE RESEARCH PLAN

The second step in the marketing research process requires that the researcher (1) specify the constraints on the marketing research activity, (2) identify the data needed for marketing actions, and (3) determine how to collect the data.

Specify Constraints

The **constraints** in a decision are the restrictions placed on potential solutions to a problem. Examples include the limitations on the time and money available to solve the problem.

What constraints might LEGO Group set in developing new LEGO Group MINDSTORMS® EV3 products? LEGO Group might establish the following constraints on its decision to select one of the two improved designs: The decision (1) must be made in five weeks (2) using 10 teams of middle schoolers playing with the two improved MINDSTORMS® kits.

Identify Data Needed for Marketing Actions

Effective marketing research studies focus on collecting data that will lead to effective marketing actions. In the MINDSTORMS® case, LEGO Group's marketers might want to know students' math skills, time spent playing video games, and so on. But that information, while nice to know, is largely irrelevant because the study should focus on collecting only those data that will help them make a clear choice between the two MINDSTORMS® designs.

Determine How to Collect Data

Determining how to collect useful marketing research data is often as important as actually collecting the data—step 3 in the process, which is discussed later. Two key elements to consider in deciding how to collect the data are (1) concepts and (2) methods.

Concepts In the world of marketing, *concepts* are ideas about products or services. To find out about consumer reactions to a potential new product, marketing researchers frequently develop a *new-product concept,* which is a picture or verbal description of a product or service the firm might offer for sale. For example, the LEGO Group designers might develop a new-product concept for a new MINDSTORMS® EV3 robot that uses a color sensor, responds to voice commands, or uses GPS navigation software.

Methods *Methods* are the approaches that can be used to collect data to solve all or part of a problem. To collect data, LEGO Group marketing researchers might use a combination of (1) observing the behavior of MINDSTORMS® users and (2) asking users questions about their opinions of the MINDSTORMS® kits. Observing people and asking them questions—the two main data collection methods—are discussed in the section that follows.

How successful is LEGO Group's marketing research and design strategy for its MINDSTORMS® products? Among younger users alone, tens of thousands of elementary and middle-school teams face off in competitions around the world each year.

How can you find and use the methods that other marketing researchers have found successful? Information on useful methods is available in tradebooks, textbooks, and handbooks that relate to marketing and marketing research. Some periodicals and technical journals, such as the *Journal of Marketing* and the *Journal of Marketing Research,* both published by the American Marketing Association, summarize methods and techniques valuable in addressing marketing problems.

Special methods vital to marketing are (1) sampling and (2) statistical inference. For example, marketing researchers often use *sampling* by selecting a group of distributors, customers, or prospects, asking them questions, and treating their answers as typical of all those in whom they are interested. They may then use *statistical inference* to generalize the results from the sample to much larger groups of distributors, customers, or prospects to help decide on marketing actions.

learning review »

8-1.   What is marketing research?

8-2.   What is the five-step marketing research approach?

8-3.   What are constraints as they apply to developing a research plan?

STEP 3: COLLECT RELEVANT INFORMATION

LO 8-3   Explain how marketing uses secondary and primary data.

Collecting enough relevant information to make a rational, informed marketing decision sometimes simply means using your knowledge to decide immediately. At other times it entails collecting an enormous amount of information at great expense.

Figure 8–2 shows how the different kinds of marketing information fit together. **Data**, the facts and figures related to the project, are divided into two main parts: secondary data and primary data. **Secondary data** are facts and figures that have already been recorded prior to the project at hand. As shown in Figure 8–2, secondary data are divided into two parts—internal and external secondary data—depending on whether the data come from inside or outside the organization needing the research. **Primary data** are facts and figures that are newly collected for the project. Figure 8–2 shows that primary data can be divided into observational data, questionnaire data, and other sources of data.

Secondary Data: Internal

The internal records of a company generally offer the most easily accessible marketing information. These internal sources of secondary data may be divided into two related parts: (1) marketing inputs and (2) marketing outcomes.

Marketing input data relate to the effort expended to make sales. These range from sales and advertising budgets and expenditures to salespeople's call reports, which describe the number of sales calls per day, who was visited, and what was discussed.

Marketing outcome data relate to the results of the marketing efforts. These involve accounting records on shipments and include sales and repeat sales, often broken down by sales representative, industry, and geographic region. In addition, e-mails, phone calls, and letters from customers can reveal both complaints and what is working well.[9]

FIGURE 8–2

Types of marketing information. Researchers must choose carefully among these to get the best results, considering time and cost constraints.

Scanner data at supermarket checkout counters provide valuable information for marketing decisions.

© Pixtal/AGE Fotostock

Video 8-2

Census

kerin.tv/13e/v8-2

Secondary Data: External

Published data from outside the organization are external secondary data. The U.S. Census Bureau publishes a variety of useful reports. Best known is the Census 2010, which is the most recent count of the U.S. population that occurs every 10 years. Recently, the Census Bureau began collecting data annually from a smaller number of people through the American Community Survey. Both surveys contain detailed information on American households, such as the number of people per household and the age, sex, race/ethnic background, income, occupation, and education of individuals within the household. Marketers use these data to identify characteristics and trends of ultimate consumers.

The Census Bureau also publishes the Economic Census, which is conducted every five years. These reports are vital to business firms selling products and services to organizations. The 2012 Economic Census contains data on the number and sales of establishments in the United States that produce a product or service based on each firm's geography (state, county, zip code, etc.), industry sector (manufacturing, retail trade, etc.), and North American Industry Classification System (NAICS) code. Data from the 2012 Economic Census are released from March 2014 through June 2016 and the next Economic Census takes place in October 2017.

Several market research companies pay households and businesses to record all their purchases using a paper or electronic diary. Such *syndicated panel* data economically answer questions that require consistent data collection over time, such as, "How many times did our customers buy our products this year compared to last year?" Examples of syndicated panels that provide a standard set of data on a regular basis are the Nielsen TV ratings and J.D. Power's automotive quality and customer satisfaction surveys.

Some data services provide comprehensive information on household demographics and lifestyle, product purchases, TV viewing behavior, responses to coupon and free-sample promotions, and social media use. Their advantage is that a single firm can collect, analyze, interrelate, and present all this information. For consumer product firms such as Procter & Gamble, sales data from various channels help them allocate scarce marketing resources. As a result, they use tracking services such as IRI's InfoScan to collect product sales and coupon/free-sample redemptions that have been scanned at the checkout counters of supermarket, drug, convenience, and mass merchandise retailers.

Finally, trade associations, universities, and business periodicals provide detailed data of value to market researchers and planners. These data are often available online and can be identified and located using a search engine such as Google or Bing. The Marketing Matters box provides examples.

Advantages and Disadvantages of Secondary Data

A general rule among marketing people is to obtain secondary data first and then collect primary data. Two important advantages of secondary data are (1) the tremendous time savings because the data have already been collected and published or exist internally and (2) the low cost, such as free or inexpensive Census reports. Furthermore, a greater level of detail is often available through secondary data, especially U.S. Census Bureau data.

However, these advantages must be weighed against some significant disadvantages. First, the secondary data may be out of date, especially if they are U.S. Census data collected only every 5 or 10 years. Second, the definitions or categories might not be quite right for a researcher's project. For example, the age groupings or product categories might be wrong for the project. Also, because the data have been collected for another purpose, they may not be specific enough for the project. In such cases, it may be necessary to collect primary data.

Marketing Matters

Online Databases and Internet Resources Useful to Marketers

Marketers in search of secondary data can utilize a wide variety of online databases and Internet resources. These resources provide access to articles in periodicals; statistical or financial data on markets, products, and organizations; and reports from commercial information companies.

Sources of news and articles include:

- LexisNexis Academic (www.lexisnexis.com) which provides comprehensive news and company information from domestic and foreign sources.
- *The Wall Street Journal* (www.wsj.com), *CNBC* (www.cnbc.com), and *Fox Business* (www.foxbusiness.com)), which provide up-to-the-minute business news and video clips about companies, industries, and trends.

Sources of statistical and financial data on markets, products, and organizations include:

- FedStats (www.fedstats.sites.usa.gov) and the Census Bureau (www.census.gov) of the U.S. Department of

Commerce, which provide information on U.S. business, economic, and trade activity collected by the federal government.

Portals and search engines include:

- USA.gov (www.usa.gov), the portal to all U.S. government websites. Users can click on links to browse by topic or enter keywords for specific searches.
- Google (www.google.com), the most popular portal to the entire Internet. Users enter keywords for specific searches and then click on results of interest.

Some of these websites are accessible only if you or your educational institution have paid a subscription fee. Check with your institution's website.

---

learning review

8-4. What is the difference between secondary and primary data?

8-5. What are some advantages and disadvantages of secondary data?

Primary Data: Watching People

LO 8-4 Discuss the uses of observations, questionnaires, panels, experiments, and newer data collection methods.

Observing people and asking them questions are the two principal ways to collect new or primary data for a marketing study. Facts and figures obtained by watching how people actually behave is the way marketing researchers collect **observational data**. Observational data can be collected by mechanical (including electronic), personal, or neuromarketing methods.

Mechanical Methods   National TV ratings, such as those of Nielsen shown in Figure 8–3, are an example of mechanical observational data collected by a "people meter." The device measures what channel and program are tuned in and who is watching. The people meter (1) is a box that is attached to a television, DVR, cable box, or satellite dish in about 30,000 households across the country;[10] (2) has a remote control unit that is used to indicate when a viewer begins and finishes watching a TV program; and (3) stores and then transmits the viewing information to Nielsen each night. Data about TV viewing are also collected using diaries (a paper-pencil recording system).

Obtaining an accurate picture of television viewing behavior is complicated, however, as audiences are increasingly delaying their viewing and watching on multiple devices. More than 40 percent of viewing of *The Blacklist,* for example, takes place on a delayed basis, while 37 percent of *Parks and Recreation* viewers watch on devices other than televisions. To address these issues, Nielsen introduced a "cross-platform television rating," which combines Nielsen's existing TV ratings with its new online ratings. These ratings include traditional consumer viewing of TV programs and

FIGURE 8–3

Nielsen Television Index Ranking Report for network TV prime-time households for the week ending May 11, 2015. The difference of a few share points in Nielsen TV ratings affects the cost of a TV ad on a show and even whether the show remains on the air.

Rank	Program	Network	Rating	Viewers (000)
1	*NCIS*	CBS	9.3	14,939
2	*Dancing with the Stars*	ABC	8.6	13,479
3	*NCIS: New Orleans*	CBS	8.5	13,610
4	*Dws: The Results Show(s)*	ABC	6.7	10,159
5	*Billboard Music Awards*	ABC	6.5	11,181
6	*The Voice*	NBC	6.2	10,051
7	*The Big Bang Theory*	CBS	6.1	9,567
8	*The Voice-Tues*	NBC	5.8	9,138
9	*60 Minutes*	CBS	5.7	8,989
10	*Grey's Anatomy*	ABC	5.7	8,332

Source: The Nielsen Company Broadcast Ranking Report for the week ending May 11, 2015. Viewing estimates include live viewing and DVR playback on the same day, defined as 3 A.M. to 3 A.M. Rank is based on the number of U.S. viewers (in millions) from Nielsen's National People Meter Sample. Nielsen © 2013.

What determines if *Dancing With The Stars* stays on the air? For the importance of the TV "ratings game," see the text.
© Adam Taylor/ABC via Getty Images

programming that is streamed on PCs, smartphones, tablets, and video game consoles.[11]

On the basis of all these observational data, Nielsen then calculates the rating of each TV program. With 116 million TV households in the United States, a single rating point equals 1 percent, or 1,160,000 TV households.[12] In some situations ratings are reported as share points, or the percentage of television households with a television in use that are tuned to the program. Because TV and cable networks sell over $67 billion annually in advertising and set advertising rates to advertisers on the basis of those data, precision in the Nielsen data is critical.[13]

A change of one percentage point in a rating can mean gaining or losing millions of dollars in advertising revenues because advertisers pay rates on the basis of the size of the audience for a TV program. So as shown by the green rows in Figure 8–3, we might expect to pay more for a 30-second TV ad on *NCIS* than one on *60 Minutes*. Broadcast and cable networks may change the time slot or even cancel a TV program if its ratings are consistently poor and advertisers are unwilling to pay a rate based on a higher rating.

Personal Methods   Watching consumers in person is another approach to collecting observational data. Procter and Gamble, for example, invests millions of dollars in observational research to identify new innovations. As several industry experts have observed, "Odds are that as you're reading this, P&G researchers are in a store somewhere observing shoppers, or even in a consumer's home." When observing consumers using its Tide laundry detergent in India, P&G noticed that because clothes were often washed by hand, the detergent sometimes caused skin irritation. As result, P&G introduced Tide Naturals, which cleaned well without causing irritation. Similarly, IKEA noticed that customers often stopped shopping when their baskets or carts were full, so additional shopping bags are now placed throughout IKEA stores.[14]

Another method of collecting observational data is through the use of mystery shoppers. Companies pay researchers to shop at their stores, outlets, or showrooms to obtain the point of view of actual customers. Mystery shoppers can check on the

Observational data led P&G to develop Tide Naturals.
© *Editorial Image, LLC*

availability and pricing of products and services and on the quality of the customer service provided by employees. Supermarkets such as Kroger, Publix, and H-E-B, for example, use this technique as part of their customer experience management efforts by evaluating customer service, store cleanliness, and staff appearance and conduct. This process provides unique marketing research information that can be obtained in no other way.[15]

Ethnographic research is a specialized observational approach in which trained observers seek to discover subtle behavioral and emotional reactions as consumers encounter products in their "natural use environment," such as in their home or car.[16] Recently, Kraft launched Deli Creations, which are sandwiches made with its Oscar Mayer meats, Kraft cheeses, and Grey Poupon mustard, after spending several months with consumers in their kitchens. Kraft discovered that consumers wanted complete, ready-to-serve meals that are easy to prepare—and it had the products to create them.[17]

Personal observation is both useful and flexible, but it can be costly and unreliable if different observers report different conclusions when watching the same event. And while observation can reveal *what* people do, it cannot easily determine *why* they do it.

"Neuromarketing" often uses a cap with dozens of sensors to measure brain waves to try to understand consumers better. For some changes made by Campbell Soup Company based on neuromarketing, see the text.

© *annedde/E+/Getty Images*

Neuromarketing Methods   Marketing researchers are also utilizing neuromarketing methods to observe responses to nonconscious stimuli. Neuromarketing is a relatively new field of study that merges technologies used to study the brain with marketing's interest in understanding consumers. Aradhna Krishna, one of the foremost experts in the field, suggests that "many companies are just starting to recognize how strongly the senses affect the deepest parts of our brains." Another expert, Martin Lindstrom, has used brain scanning to analyze the buying processes of more than 2,000 people. The findings of his research are summarized in his book *Buyology*.[18]

Based on the results of neuromarketing studies, Campbell Soup Company recently changed the labels of most of its soup cans. Some of the changes: Steam now rises from more vibrant images of soup; the "unemotional spoons" have disappeared; and the script logo is smaller and has been moved to the bottom of the can.[19]

Primary Data: Asking People

How many times have you responded to some kind of a questionnaire? Maybe a short survey at school or a telephone or e-mail survey to see if you are pleased with the

Focus groups of students and instructors were used in developing this textbook. To see the specific suggestion that may help you study, read the text.

© Spencer Grant/PhotoEdit

Wendy's spent over two years remaking its 42-year-old burger. The result: Dave's Hot 'N Juicy, named after Wendy's founder, Dave Thomas. See Figure 8–4 for some questions that Wendy's asked consumers in a survey to discover their fast-food preferences, behaviors, and demographics.

Source: Wendy's International, LLC

service you received. Asking consumers questions and recording their answers is the second principal way of gathering information.

We can divide this primary data collection task into (1) idea generation methods and (2) idea evaluation methods, although they sometimes overlap and each has a number of special techniques.[20] Each survey method results in valuable **questionnaire data**, which are facts and figures obtained by asking people about their attitudes, awareness, intentions, and behaviors.

Idea Generation Methods—Coming Up with Ideas

In the past, the most common way of collecting questionnaire data to generate ideas was through an *individual interview,* which involves a single researcher asking questions of one respondent. This approach has many advantages, such as being able to probe for additional ideas using follow-up questions to a respondent's initial answers. However, this method is very expensive. Later in the chapter we'll discuss some alternatives.

General Mills sought ideas about why Hamburger Helper didn't fare well when it was introduced. Initial instructions called for cooking a half-pound of hamburger separately from the noodles or potatoes, which were later mixed with the hamburger. So General Mills researchers used a special kind of individual interview, called a *depth interview,* in which researchers ask lengthy, free-flowing kinds of questions to probe for underlying ideas and feelings. These depth interviews discovered that consumers (1) didn't think it contained enough meat and (2) didn't want the hassle of cooking in two different pots. The Hamburger Helper product manager changed the recipe to call for a full pound of meat and to allow users to prepare it in one dish, leading to product success.

Focus groups are informal sessions of 6 to 10 past, present, or prospective customers in which a discussion leader, or moderator, asks for opinions about the firm's products and those of its competitors, including how they use these products and special needs they have that these products don't address. Often recorded and conducted in special interviewing rooms with a one-way mirror, these groups enable marketing researchers and managers to hear and watch consumer reactions.

The informality and peer support in an effective focus group help uncover ideas that are often difficult to obtain with individual interviews. For example, to improve understanding and learning by students using this textbook, focus groups were conducted among both marketing instructors and students. Both groups recommended providing answers to each chapter's set of Learning Review questions. This suggestion was followed, so you can see the answers by going to the section at the end of the chapter or by tapping your finger on the question in the SmartBook version.

Finding "the next big thing" for consumers has caused marketing researchers to turn to some less traditional techniques. For example, "fuzzy front end" methods attempt early identification of elusive consumer tastes or trends. Trend Hunter is a firm that seeks to anticipate and track "the evolution of cool." Trend hunting (or watching) is the practice of identifying "emerging shifts in social behavior," which are driven by changes in pop culture that can lead to new products. Trend Hunter has identified about 250,000 cutting edge ideas through its global network of 155,000 members, and features these new ideas on its daily Trend Hunter TV broadcast via its YouTube channel (trendhuntertv).[21]

Idea Evaluation Methods—Testing an Idea

In idea evaluation, the marketing researcher tries to test ideas discovered earlier to help the marketing manager recommend marketing actions. Idea evaluation methods often involve conventional questionnaires

1. What things are most important to you when you decide to eat out at a fast-food restaurant?

_____

_____

_____

2. Have you eaten at a fast-food restaurant in the past month?

◉ Yes   ◉ No

3. If you answered yes to question 2, how often do you eat at a fast-food restaurant?

◉ Once a week or more   ◉ 2 to 3 times a month   ◉ Once a month or less

4. How important is it to you that a fast-food restaurant satisfies you on the following characteristics?
[Check the response that describes your feelings for each characteristic listed.]

Characteristic	Very Important	Somewhat Important	Important	Unimportant	Somewhat Unimportant	Very Unimportant
• Taste of food	◉	◉	◉	◉	◉	◉
• Cleanliness	◉	◉	◉	◉	◉	◉
• Price	◉	◉	◉	◉	◉	◉
• Variety of menu	◉	◉	◉	◉	◉	◉

5. For each of the characteristics listed below check the space on the scale that describes how you feel about Wendy's. Mark an X on only one of the five spaces for each characteristic listed.

Characteristic		Check the space that describes the degree to which Wendy' is . . .					
• Taste of food	Tasty	____	____	____	____	____	Not Tasty
• Cleanliness	Clean	____	____	____	____	____	Dirty
• Price	Inexpensive	____	____	____	____	____	Expensive
• Variety of menu	Broad	____	____	____	____	____	Narrow

FIGURE 8–4

To obtain the most valuable information from consumers, this Wendy's survey utilizes four different kinds of questions discussed in the text.

using personal, mail, telephone, fax, and online (e-mail or Internet) surveys of a large sample of past, present, or prospective consumers. In choosing among them, the marketing researcher balances the cost of the particular method against the expected quality of the information and the speed with which it can be obtained.

Personal interview surveys enable the interviewer to be flexible in asking probing questions or getting reactions to visual materials but are very costly. _Mail surveys_ are usually biased because those most likely to respond have had especially positive or negative experiences with the product or brand. While _telephone interviews_ allow flexibility, unhappy respondents may hang up on the interviewer, even with the efficiency of computer-assisted telephone interviewing (CATI).

Increasingly, marketing researchers have begun to use _online surveys_ (e-mail and Internet) to collect primary data. The reason: Most consumers have an Internet connection and an e-mail account. Marketers can embed a survey in an e-mail sent to targeted respondents. When they open the e-mail, consumers can either see the survey or click on a link to access it from a website. Marketers can also ask consumers to complete a "pop-up" survey in a separate browser window when they access an organization's website. Many organizations use this method to have consumers assess their products and services or evaluate the design and usability of their websites.

6. Check the response that describes your agreement or disagreement with each statement listed below:

Statement	Strongly Agree	Agree	Don't Know	Disagree	Strongly Disagree
• Adults like to take their families to fast-food restaurants	○	○	○	○	○
• Our children have a say in where the family chooses to eat	○	○	○	○	○

7. How important are each of the following sources of information to you when selecting a fast-food restaurant at which to eat? [Check one response for each source listed.]

Source of Information	Very Important	Somewhat Important	Not at all Important
• Television	○	○	○
• Newspapers	○	○	○
• Radio	○	○	○
• Billboards	○	○	○
• Internet	○	○	○
• Social networks	○	○	○

8. How often do you eat out at each of the following fast-food restaurants? [Check one response for each restaurant listed.]

Restaurant	Once a week or more	2 to 3 Times a month	Once a month or less
• Burger King	○	○	○
• McDonald's	○	○	○
• Wendy's	○	○	○

9. As head of the household, please answer the following questions about you and your household. [Check only one response for each question.]

a. What is your gender?   ○ Male   ○ Female

b. What is your marital status?   ○ Single   ○ Married   ○ Other (widowed, divorced, etc.)

c. How many children under age 18 live in your home?   ○ 0   ○ 1   ○ 2   ○ 3 or more

d. What is your age?   ○ Under 25   ○ 25–44   ○ 45 or older

e. What is your total annual individual or household income?
  ○ Less than $15,000   ○ $15,000–$49,000   ○ Over $49,000

The advantages of online surveys are that the cost is relatively minimal and the turn-around time from data collection to report presentation is much quicker than the traditional methods discussed earlier. However, online surveys have serious drawbacks: Some consumers may view e-mail surveys as "junk" or "spam" and may either choose to not receive them (if they have a "spam blocker") or purposely or inadvertently delete them, unopened. For Internet surveys, some consumers have a "pop-up blocker" that prohibits a browser from opening a separate window that contains the survey; thus, they may not be able to participate in the research. For both e-mail and Internet surveys, consumers can complete the survey multiple times, creating a significant bias in the results. This is especially true for online panels. In response, research firms such as SurveyMonkey have developed sampling technology to prohibit this practice.[22]

The foundation of all research using questionnaires is developing precise questions that get clear, unambiguous answers from respondents.[23] Figure 8–4 shows a number of formats for questions taken from a Wendy's survey that assessed fast-food restaurant preferences among present and prospective consumers.

Question 1 is an example of an *open-ended question,* which allows respondents to express opinions, ideas, or behaviors in their own words without being forced to choose among alternatives that have been predetermined by a marketing researcher. This information is invaluable to marketers because it captures the "voice" of respondents, which is useful in understanding consumer behavior, identifying product benefits, or developing advertising messages.

In contrast, *closed-end* or *fixed alternative questions* require respondents to select one or more response options from a set of predetermined choices. Question 2 is an example of a *dichotomous question,* the simplest form of a fixed alternative question that allows only a "yes" or "no" response.

A fixed alternative question with three or more choices uses a *scale.* Question 5 is an example of a question that uses a *semantic differential scale,* a five-point scale in which the opposite ends have one- or two-word adjectives that have opposite meanings. For example, depending on the respondent's opinion regarding the cleanliness of Wendy's restaurants, he or she would check the left-hand space on the scale, the right-hand space, or one of the three other intervening points. Question 6 uses a *Likert scale,* in which the respondent indicates the extent to which he or she agrees or disagrees with a statement.

The questionnaire in Figure 8–4 provides valuable information to the marketing researcher at Wendy's. Questions 1 to 8 inform him or her about the respondent's likes and dislikes in eating out, frequency of eating out at fast-food restaurants generally and at Wendy's specifically, and sources of information used in making decisions about fast-food restaurants. Question 9 gives details about the respondent's personal or household characteristics, which can be used in trying to segment the fast-food market, a topic discussed in Chapter 9.

Marketing research questions must be worded precisely so that all respondents interpret the same question similarly. For example, in a question asking whether you eat at fast-food restaurants regularly, the word *regularly* is ambiguous. Two people might answer "yes" to the question, but one might mean "once a day" while the other means "once or twice a month." However, each of these interpretations suggests that dramatically different marketing actions be directed to these two prospective consumers.

The high cost of using personal interviews in homes has increased the use of *mall intercept interviews,* which are personal interviews of consumers visiting shopping centers. These face-to-face interviews reduce the cost of personal visits to consumers in their homes while providing the flexibility to show respondents visual cues such as ads or actual product samples. A disadvantage of mall intercept interviews is that the people interviewed may not be representative of the consumers targeted, giving a biased result.

Electronic technology has revolutionized traditional concepts of interviews or surveys. Today, respondents can walk up to a kiosk in a shopping center, read questions off a screen, and key their answers into a computer on a touch screen. Fully automated telephone interviews exist in which respondents key their replies on a touch-tone telephone.

Primary Data: Other Sources

Four other methods of collecting primary data exist that overlap somewhat with the methods just discussed. These involve using (1) social media, (2) panels and experiments, (3) information technology, and (4) data mining.

Social Media   Facebook, Twitter, and other social media are revolutionizing the way today's marketing research is done. In developing a new potato chip flavor, Frito-Lay substituted Facebook research for its usual focus groups. Visitors to its Facebook Page were polled, allowing them to suggest new flavors, three of which appeared in supermarkets. All they had to do was click a "Vote" button to show their preferences. And Estée Lauder asked social media users to vote on which discontinued shades to bring back.[24]

Visitors to Frito-Lay's Facebook Page voted on new potato chip flavors by clicking on the "Vote" button to show their preferences.

Source: Frito-Lay North America, Inc.

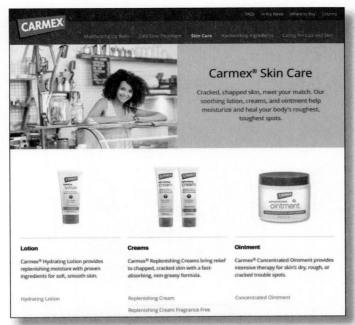

Carmex's home page topics range from its Twitter Giveaways to win Carmex products to its family history. For how it uses social media marketing research, see the Applying Marketing Metrics box.

Courtesy of Carma Laboratories, Inc.

Carma Laboratories, Inc., the maker of Carmex lip balm, is a third-generation, family-owned business with a history of accessibility to customers. In fact, founder Alfred Woelbing personally responded to every letter he received from customers. Today, Carma Labs relies on social media programs to help promote its products.[25]

Carmex lip balm is meant to reduce cold sore symptoms and soothe dry and chapped lips. It is packaged in jars, sticks, and squeezable tubes. The U.S. Carmex product line includes original, strawberry, lime twist, vanilla, pomegranate, and cherry flavors. Although Carmex lip balm sales trend behind ChapStick and Blistex, Carmex consumers tend to be loyalists—true zealots.

One opportunity for Carmex (www.mycarmex.com) is to conduct marketing research using social media listening tools to understand the nature of online lip balm conversations. Lip balm is a seasonal product, with both sales and online activity peaking during the cough–cold season of November through March.

The Applying Marketing Metrics box shows how Carmex uses marketing metrics to assess its social media programs for its line of products. Data have been modified to protect proprietary information.

Carmex uses several social media metrics, such as *conversation velocity, share of voice,* and *sentiment.*[26] These metrics are tracked by electronic search engines that comb the Internet for consumers' behaviors and "brand mentions" to calculate share of voice and determine whether these brand mentions appear to be "positive," "neutral," or "negative" in order to calculate "sentiment." A widely used Facebook metric measures the number of *likes,* which refers to the number of Facebook users opting in to a brand's messages and liking the brand.

Marketing researchers increasingly want to glean information from sites to "mine" their raw consumer-generated content in real time. However, when relying on this consumer-generated content, the sample of individuals from whom this content is gleaned may not be statistically representative of the marketplace.[27]

Panels and Experiments Two special ways that observations and questionnaires are sometimes used are panels and experiments.

Marketing researchers often want to know if consumers change their behavior over time, so they take successive measurements of the same people. A *panel* is a sample of consumers or stores from which researchers take a series of measurements. For example, the NPD Group collects data about consumer purchases such as apparel, food, and electronics from its Online Panel, which consists of nearly 2 million individuals worldwide. So a firm like General Mills can count the frequency of consumer purchases to measure switching behavior from one brand of its breakfast cereal (Wheaties) to another (Cheerios) or to a competitor's brand (Kellogg's Special K). A disadvantage of panels is that the marketing research firm needs to recruit new members continually to replace those who drop out. These new recruits must match the characteristics of those they replace to keep the panel representative of the marketplace.

An *experiment* involves obtaining data by manipulating factors under tightly controlled conditions to test cause and effect. The interest is in whether changing one of the

To discover how Walmart used test markets to help develop its internationally successful supercenters, such as this one in China, see the text.

© *Imaginechina/Corbis*

Applying **Marketing Metrics**

Are the Carmex Social Media Programs Working Well?

As a marketing consultant to Carmex, you've just been asked to assess its social media activities for its lip balm product line.

Carmex has recently launched new social media programs and promotions to tell U.S. consumers more about its line of lip balm products. These include Facebook and Twitter contests that allow Carmex fans and followers to win free samples by connecting with Carmex. A creative "Carmex Kiss" widget allows users to upload their photo and to send an animated kiss to a friend.

Your Challenge

To assess how the Carmex social media programs are doing, you choose these five metrics: (1) Carmex conversation velocity—total Carmex mentions on the Internet; (2) Facebook fans—the number of Facebook users in a time period who have liked Carmex's Facebook brand page; (3) Twitter followers—the number of Twitter users in a time period who follow Carmex's Twitter feed; (4) Carmex share of voice—Carmex mentions on the Internet as a percentage of mentions of all major lip balm brands; and (5) Carmex sentiment—the percentage of Internet Carmex share-of-voice mentions that are (a) positive, (b) neutral, or (c) negative.

Your Findings

Analyzing the marketing dashboard here, you reach these conclusions. First, the number of both Facebook fans and Twitter followers for Carmex is up significantly for 2015 compared to 2014 which is good news. Second, the Carmex share of voice of 35 percent is good, certainly relative to the 48 percent for the #1 brand ChapStick. But especially favorable is Carmex's 12 percent increase in share of voice compared to a year ago. Third, the Carmex sentiment dashboard shows 80 percent of the mentions are positive, and only 5 percent are negative. Even more

significant is that positive mentions are up 23 percent over last year.

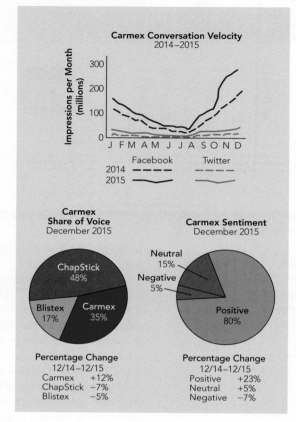

Carmex Conversation Velocity
2014–2015

Carmex Share of Voice
December 2015

Carmex Sentiment
December 2015

Percentage Change
12/14–12/15
Carmex   +12%
ChapStick −7%
Blistex   −5%

Percentage Change
12/14–12/15
Positive +23%
Neutral   +5%
Negative −7%

Your Actions

You conclude that Carmex's social media initiatives are doing well. Your next step is to probe deeper into the data to see which ones—such as free samples or the Carmex Kiss—have been especially effective in triggering the positive results and build on these successes in the future.

independent variables (a cause) will change the behavior of the dependent variable that is studied (the result). In marketing experiments, the independent variables of interest—sometimes called the marketing *drivers*—are often one or more of the marketing mix elements, such as a product's features, price, or promotion (like advertising messages or coupons). The ideal dependent variable usually is a change in the purchases (incremental unit or dollar sales) of individuals, households, or organizations. For example, food companies often use *test markets,* which offer a product for sale in a small geographic area to help evaluate potential marketing actions. In 1988, Walmart opened three experimental stand-alone supercenters to gauge consumer acceptance before deciding to open others. Today, Walmart operates over 4,000 supercenters around the world.

A potential difficulty with experiments is that outside factors (such as actions of competitors) can distort the results of an experiment and affect the dependent variable (such as sales). A researcher's task is to identify the effect of the marketing variable of interest on the dependent variable when the effects of outside factors in an experiment might hide it.

Big Data and Data Analytics   *Big data* is a vague term generally used to describe large amounts of data collected from a variety of sources and analyzed with an increasingly sophisticated set of technologies. **Information technology** includes all of the computing resources that collect, store, and analyze the data. Marketing researchers have observed that today we live in an era of data deluge. The challenge facing managers is not data collection or even storage but how to efficiently transform the huge amount of data into useful information. This transformation is accomplished through the use of data analytics. Products such as Yahoo's Hadoop and Google's Bigtables are examples of the analytical tools available for people often referred to as data scientists. Their work is also creating a new field of marketing research that focuses on *data visualization,* or the presentation of the results of the analysis.

Today, businesses can obtain data from many sources such as barcode scanners at checkout counters, online tracking software on computers and tablets, and usage histories on your telephone. In fact, the growth of the Internet of things now allows data collection from almost any device a consumer might use. Marketing managers must use the combination of data, technology, and analytics to convert the data into useful information that will answer marketing questions and lead to effective marketing actions. Organizations that accomplish this successfully are often referred to as an *intelligent enterprise.*[28]

As shown in Figure 8–5, the elements of an intelligent marketing enterprise platform interact to facilitate the work of the marketing researcher or data scientist. The top half of the figure shows how big data are created through a sophisticated communication network that collects data from internal and external sources. These data are stored, organized, and managed in databases. Collectively, these databases form a data warehouse. Data

FIGURE 8–5

How marketing researchers and managers use an intelligent enterprise platform to turn data into action.

Photo: © Todd Warnock/ Lifesize/Getty Images

Intelligent Marketing Enterprise Platform

Big data

Cloud environment
- Data storage
- Cloud computing capabilities

Internal data sources
- Customer orders
- Customer data
- Inventory
- Sales calls
- Promotions

Data warehouse
Databases
Internal
External

External data sources
- Global sources
- Trade associations
- U.S. Census data
- Internet of things
- Single-source services

Data analytics

Analytical tools to organize, manipulate, analyze, and present data

Buying queries
- Who buys...?
- How much...?
- Why...?

Results

Marketing researcher or data scientist

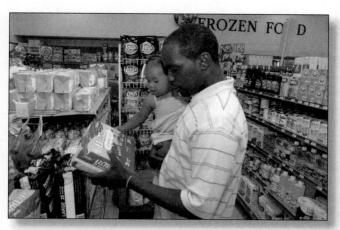

At 10 P.M., what is this man likely to buy besides these diapers? For the curious answer that data mining gives, see the text.

© Brent Jones

storage (and computing) may also take place in "the cloud," which is simply a collection of servers accessed through an Internet connection.

As shown at the bottom of Figure 8–5, data analytics consists of several elements. Marketers use computers to specify important marketing queries or questions and to access the databases in the warehouse (or the cloud). Analytical tools are used to organize and manipulate the data to identify any managerial insights that may exist. The results are then presented using tables and graphics for easier interpretation. When accessing a database, marketers can use sensitivity analysis to ask "what if" questions to determine how hypothetical changes in product or brand drivers—the factors that influence the buying decisions of a household or organization—can affect sales.

Traditional marketing research typically involves identifying possible drivers and then collecting data. For example, we might collect data to test the hypothesis that increasing couponing (the driver) during spring will increase trials by first-time buyers (the result).

Data Mining In contrast, *data mining* is the extraction of hidden predictive information from large databases to find statistical links between consumer purchasing patterns and marketing actions. Some of these are common sense: Since many consumers buy peanut butter and grape jelly together, why not run a joint promotion between Skippy peanut butter and Welch's grape jelly? But would you have expected that men buying diapers in the evening sometimes buy a six-pack of beer as well? Supermarkets discovered this when they mined checkout data from scanners. So they placed diapers and beer near each other, then placed potato chips between them—and increased sales on all three items! On the near horizon is RFID (radio frequency identification) technology using "smart tags" on the diapers and beer to tell whether they wind up in the same shopping bag. For how much online data mining can reveal about you personally and the ethical issues involved, see the Making Responsible Decisions box.[29]

Advantages and Disadvantages of Primary Data

Compared with secondary data, primary data have the advantages of being more flexible and more specific to the problem being studied. The main disadvantages are that primary data are usually far more costly and time-consuming to collect than secondary data.

Analyzing Primary Data Using Cross Tabulations

Wendy's Customer Satisfaction Survey allows customers to provide feedback on their meal experience. To take the survey, go to www.talktowendys.com. You'll need a receipt from a recent visit, which has an 8-digit code to start the survey. Your reward? A printable coupon that can be used on your next visit!

Courtesy of Wendy's

Suppose top management at Wendy's wants to use the questionnaire in Figure 8–4 to survey a sample of U.S. households to assess how often customers of different ages eat at fast-food restaurants. Management suspects that as the age of the head of the household increases, visits to fast-food restaurants decline. The data provided by the questionnaire confirm this, but the information is not in a format that suggests ideas for viable marketing actions. Using cross tabulations will provide answers leading to actions.

Developing Cross Tabulations A **cross tabulation**, or *cross tab*, is a method of presenting and analyzing data involving two or more variables to discover relationships in the data.

The Wendy's questionnaire in Figure 8–4 includes many questions that might be paired to understand the fast-food business better. For example, to try to answer

Making Responsible Decisions

No More Personal Secrets: The Downside of Data Mining

eXelate, Intellidyn, Rapleaf, Google Ad Preferences, Yahoo!, BlueKai, Alliance Data, reputation.com . . . yes . . . and Facebook and Twitter, too!

The common denominator for all these is their sophisticated data mining of the Internet and social media that reveals an incredible amount of personal information about any American. *Time* journalist Joel Stein, using both online and offline sources, discovered how easily outsiders could find his social security number and then found a number of other things about himself—some correct, some not.

For example, he likes hockey, rap, rock, parenting, recipes, clothes and beauty products, and movies. He makes most of his purchases online, averaging only $25 per purchase. He uses Facebook, Friendster, LinkedIn, MySpace, Pandora, and StumbleUpon. He bought his house in November, which is when his home insurance is up for renewal. His dad's wife has a traffic ticket.

And he uses an Apple iMac and is an 18- to 19-year-old woman???!!!

OK, OK, sometimes data mining errors occur!

These data are collected many ways from the Internet—from tracking devices (like cookies, discussed in Chapter 21) on websites to apps downloaded on a cell phone, PC, or tablet device that reveal a user's contact list and location.

These personal details have huge benefits for marketers. Data mining enables one-to-one personalization and now enables advertisers to target individual consumers. This involves using not only demographics such as age and sex but also "likes," past buying habits, social media used, brands bought, TV programs watched, and so on.

Want to do some sleuthing yourself? Download Ghostery at www.ghostery.com. It tells you all the companies grabbing your data when you visit a website.

the question in which Wendy's top management is interested, we can pair the question regarding the age of the head of the household in Figure 8–4 (question 9d) with the question that asks how often the respondent eats at a fast-food restaurant (question 3).

Using the answers to question 3 as the column headings and the answers to question 9d as the row headings gives the cross tabulation shown in Figure 8–6, based on answers from 586 respondents. The figure shows two forms of cross tabulations:

- The raw data or answers to the specific questions are shown in Figure 8–6A. For example, this cross tab shows that 144 households in the sample whose head was

FIGURE 8–6

Two forms of a cross tabulation relating age of head of household to frequency of fast-food restaurant patronage.

A. ABSOLUTE FREQUENCIES

Age of Head of Household (Years)	Frequency of Visiting Fast-Food Restaurants			
	Once a Week or More	2 to 3 Times a Month	Once a Month or Less	Total
Under 25	144	52	19	215
25 to 44	46	58	29	133
45 or Older	82	69	87	238
Total	272	179	135	586

B. ROW PERCENTAGES: RUN HORIZONTALLY

Age of Head of Household (Years)	Frequency of Visiting Fast-Food Restaurants			
	Once a Week or More	2 to 3 Times a Month	Once a Month or Less	Total
Under 25	67.0%	24.2%	8.8%	100.0%
25 to 44	34.6%	43.6%	21.8%	100.0%
45 or Older	34.5%	29.0%	36.5%	100.0%
Total	46.5%	30.5%	23.0%	100.0%

under 25 (shaded red) ate at fast-food restaurants once a week or more. It also shows the loyalty of many customers of fast-food restaurants; the number of customers who visit them once a week or more is more than double the number who visit them once a month or less, as indicated by the totals shaded brown in Figure 8–6A.

- Answers on a percentage basis, with the percentages running horizontally, are shown in Figure 8–6B. Of the 215 households headed by someone under 25, 67.0 percent ate at a fast-food restaurant at least once a week and only 8.8 percent ate there once a month or less. Also, across all age groups, 46.4 percent—almost half—ate in a fast-food restaurant once a week or more.

Two other forms of cross tabulation using the raw data shown in Figure 8–6A are described in problem 7 in Applying Marketing Knowledge at the end of the chapter.

Interpreting Cross Tabulations   A careful analysis of Figures 8–6A and 8–6B shows that patronage of fast-food restaurants is related to the age of the head of the household. The percentages on the diagonal (in orange) in Figure 8–6B reveal that younger households are far more likely than older households to visit fast-food restaurants once a week or more.

So if we want to reach frequent users of fast-food restaurants, we should target those whose head of household is under 25 years of age and who tend to visit these restaurants once a week or more, as shown in Figure 8–6B. Marketers often use special efforts to reach these loyal, frequent users. So Wendy's might advertise to the segment of households headed by a man or woman under 25 years old. But Figures 8–6A and 8–6B *do not* tell us what media to use to reach them—such as by television ads or social networks. For those answers, we need to relate the age of the head of household again to the answers given to question 7 in Figure 8–4—the source of information that households use.

Probably the most widely used technique for organizing and presenting marketing data, cross tabulations have some important advantages. The simple format permits direct interpretation and an easy means of communicating data to management. Cross tabs offer great flexibility and can be used to summarize questionnaire, observational, and experimental data.

Cross tabulations also have some disadvantages. For example, they can be misleading if the percentages are based on too few observations. Also, cross tabulations can hide some relationships because each cross tab typically shows only two or three variables. Balancing both advantages and disadvantages, more marketing decisions are probably made using cross tabulations than any other method of analyzing data.

STEP 4: DEVELOP FINDINGS

 LO 8-5 Explain how information technology and data mining lead to marketing actions.

Mark Twain once observed, "Collecting data is like collecting garbage. You've got to know what you're going to do with the stuff before you collect it." So, marketing data have little more value than garbage unless they are analyzed carefully and translated into information and findings, step 4 in the marketing research approach.[30]

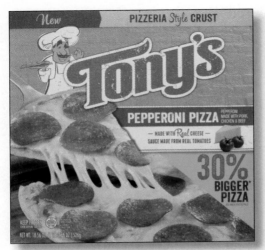

How are sales doing? To see how marketers at Tony's Pizza assessed this question and the results, read the text.

© Editorial Image, LLC

Analyze the Data

Schwan Food Company produces 3 million frozen pizzas a day under brand names that include Tony's and Red Baron. Let's see how Teré Carral, the marketing manager for the Tony's brand, might address a market segment question. We will use hypothetical data to protect Tony's proprietary information.

Teré is concerned about the limited growth in the Tony's brand over the past four years. She hires a consultant to collect and analyze data to explain what's going on with her brand and to recommend ways to improve its growth. Teré asks the consultant to put together a proposal that includes the answers to two key questions:

1. How are Tony's sales doing on a household basis? For example, are fewer households buying Tony's pizzas, or is each household buying fewer Tony's pizzas? Or both?
2. What factors might be contributing to Tony's very flat sales over the past four years?

Facts uncovered by the consultant are vital. For example, is the average household consuming more or less Tony's pizza than in previous years? Is Tony's flat sales performance related to a specific factor? With answers to these questions Teré can take actions to address the issues in the coming year.

Present the Findings

Findings should be clear and understandable from the way the data are presented. Managers are responsible for *actions*. Often it means delivering the results in clear pictures and, if possible, in a single page.

The consultant gives Teré the answers to her questions using the marketing dashboards in Figure 8–7, a creative way to present findings graphically. Let's look over Teré's shoulder as she interprets these findings:

- Figure 8–7A, *Annual Sales*—This shows the annual growth of Tony's Pizza is stable but virtually flat from 2012 through 2015.
- Figure 8–7B, *Average Annual Sales per Household*—Look closely at this graph. At first glance, it seems like sales in 2015 are *half* what they were in 2012, right? But be careful to read the numbers on the vertical axis. They show that household purchases of Tony's pizzas have been steadily declining over the past four years, from an average of 3.4 pizzas per household in 2012 to 3.1 pizzas per household in 2015. (Significant, but hardly a 50 percent drop.) Now the question is, if Tony's annual sales are stable, yet the average individual household is buying fewer Tony's pizzas, what's going on? The answer is, more households are buying pizzas—it's just that each household is buying fewer Tony's pizzas. That households aren't choosing Tony's is a genuine source of concern. But again, here's a classic example of a marketing problem representing a marketing opportunity. The number of households buying pizza is *growing,* and that's good news for Tony's.
- Figure 8–7C, *Average Annual Sales per Household, by Household Size*—This chart starts to show a source of the problem: Even though average sales of pizza to households with only one or two people are stable, households with three or four people and those with five or more are declining in average annual pizza consumption. Which households tend to have more than two people? Answer: Households *with children*. Therefore, we should look more closely at the pizza-buying behavior of households with children.

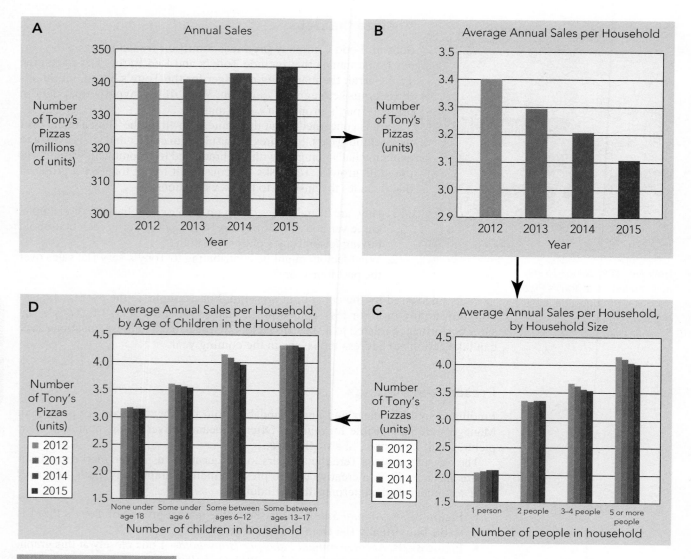

FIGURE 8–7

These marketing dashboards present findings to Tony's marketing manager that will lead to recommendations and actions.

Source: Teré Carral, Tony's Pizza.

- Figure 8–7D, *Average Annual Sales per Household, by Age of Children in the Household*—The real problem that emerges is the serious decline in average consumption in the households with younger children, especially in households with children in the 6-to-12-year-old age group.

Identifying a sales problem in households with children 6 to 12 years old is an important discovery, as Tony's sales are declining in a market segment that is known to be one of the heaviest in buying pizzas.

STEP 5: TAKE MARKETING ACTIONS

Effective marketing research doesn't stop with findings and recommendations—someone has to identify the marketing actions, put them into effect, and monitor how the decisions turn out, which is the essence of step 5.

Make Action Recommendations

Teré Carral, the marketing manager for Tony's Pizza, meets with her team to convert the market research findings into specific marketing recommendations with a

Marketing research at Tony's Pizza helped develop this colorful, friendly ad targeted at families with children in the 6-to-12-year-old age group.

Source: Schwan's Consumer Brands, Inc.

clear objective: Target households with children ages 6 to 12 to reverse the trend among this segment and gain strength in one of the most important segments in the frozen pizza category. Her recommendation is to develop:

- An advertising campaign that will target children 6 to 12 years old.
- A monthly promotion calendar with this age group target in mind.
- A special event program reaching children 6 to 12 years old.

Implement the Action Recommendations

As her first marketing action, Teré undertakes advertising research to develop ads that appeal to children in the 6-to-12-year-old age group and their families. The research shows that children like colorful ads with funny, friendly characters. She gives these research results to her advertising agency, which develops several sample ads for her review. Teré selects three that are tested on children to identify the most appealing one, which is then used in her next advertising campaign for Tony's Pizza. This is the ad shown to the left.

Evaluate the Results

Evaluating results is a continuing way of life for effective marketing managers. There are really two aspects of this evaluation process:

- *Evaluating the decision itself.* This involves monitoring the marketplace to determine if action is necessary in the future. For Teré, is her new ad successful in appealing to 6-to-12-year-old children and their families? Are sales increasing to this target segment? The success of this strategy suggests Teré should add more follow-up ads with colorful, funny, friendly characters.
- *Evaluating the decision process used.* Was the marketing research and analysis used to develop the recommendations effective? Was it flawed? Could it be improved for similar situations in the future? Teré and her marketing team must be vigilant in looking for ways to improve the analysis and results—to learn lessons that might apply to future marketing research efforts at Tony's.

Again, systematic analysis does not guarantee success. But, as in the case of Tony's Pizza, it can improve a firm's success rate for its marketing decisions.

learning review

8-9. In the marketing research for Tony's Pizza, what is an example of (*a*) a finding and (*b*) a marketing action?

8-10. In evaluating marketing actions, what are the two dimensions on which they should be evaluated?

SALES FORECASTING TECHNIQUES

 LO 8-6 | Describe three approaches to developing a company's sales forecast.

Forecasting or estimating potential sales is often a key goal in a marketing research study. Good sales forecasts are important for a firm as it schedules production. The term **sales forecast** refers to the total sales of a product that a firm expects to sell during a specified time period under specified environmental conditions and its own marketing efforts. For example, Betty Crocker might develop a sales forecast of 4 million cases of cake mix for U.S. consumers in 2016, assuming consumers' dessert preferences remain constant and competitors don't change prices.

Three main sales forecasting techniques are often used: (1) judgments of the decision maker, (2) surveys of knowledgeable groups, and (3) statistical methods.

Judgments of the Decision Maker

Probably 99 percent of all sales forecasts are simply the judgment of the person who must act on the results of the forecast—the individual decision maker. *A direct forecast* involves estimating the value to be forecast without any intervening steps. Examples appear daily: How many quarts of milk should I buy? How much money should I withdraw at the ATM?

A *lost-horse forecast* involves starting with the last known value of the item being forecast, listing the factors that could affect the forecast, assessing whether they have a positive or negative impact, and making the final forecast. The technique gets its name from how you'd find a lost horse: go to where it was last seen, put yourself in its shoes, consider those factors that could affect where you might go (to the pond if you're thirsty, the hayfield if you're hungry, and so on), and go there.

How might a marketing manager for the New Balance Zante running shoe create a sales forecast through 2018? Read the text to find out.

© Editorial Image, LLC

For example, New Balance recently introduced its Fresh Foam Zante, a shoe with an optimal balance between cushioning and stability. It is designed to be a lighter, better fitting, and functionally enhanced shoe. Suppose a New Balance marketing manager in early 2016 needs to make a sales forecast through 2018. She would take the known value of 2015 sales and list positive factors (Road Shoe of the Year Award, positive wear-tester comments) and the negative factors (increased competition, slow economic growth) to arrive at the final sales forecast.

Surveys of Knowledgeable Groups

If you wonder what your firm's sales will be next year, ask people who are likely to know something about future sales. Two common groups that are surveyed to develop sales forecasts are prospective buyers and the firm's salesforce.

A *survey of buyers' intentions forecast* involves asking prospective customers if they are likely to buy the product during some future time period. For industrial products with few prospective buyers, this can be effective. There are only a few hundred customers in the entire world for Boeing's large airplanes, so Boeing surveys them to develop its sales forecasts and production schedules.

A *salesforce survey forecast* involves asking the firm's salespeople to estimate sales during a forthcoming period. Because these people are in contact with customers and are likely to know what customers like and dislike, there is logic to this approach. However, salespeople can be unreliable forecasters—painting too rosy a picture if they are enthusiastic about a new product or too grim a forecast if their sales quota and future compensation are based on it.

Statistical Methods

The best-known statistical method of forecasting is *trend extrapolation,* which involves extending a pattern observed in past data into the future. When the pattern is described with a straight line, it is *linear trend extrapolation.* Suppose that in early 2000 you were a sales forecaster for the Xerox Corporation and had actual sales data running from 1988 to 1999 (see Figure 8–8). Using linear trend extrapolation, you draw a line to fit the past sales data and project it into the future to give the forecast values shown for 2000 through 2016.

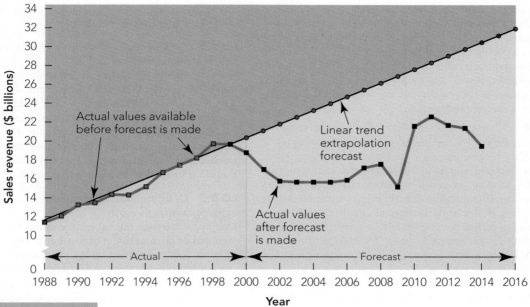

FIGURE 8–8

Linear trend extrapolation of sales revenues at Xerox, made at the start of 2000.

If in 2015 you want to compare your forecasts with actual results, you are in for a surprise—illustrating the strength and weakness of trend extrapolation. Trend extrapolation assumes that the underlying relationships in the past will continue into the future, which is the basis of the method's key strength: simplicity. If this assumption proves correct, you have an accurate forecast. However, if this proves wrong, the forecast is likely to be wrong. In this case, your forecasts from 2000 through 2014 were too high, as shown in Figure 8–8, largely because of fierce competition in the photocopying industry. The spike in 2010 sales revenues is mainly due to new acquisitions.

learning review

8-11. What are the three kinds of sales forecasting techniques?

8-12. How do you make a lost-horse forecast?

LEARNING OBJECTIVES REVIEW

LO 8-1 *Identify the reason for conducting marketing research.*

To be successful, products must meet the wants and needs of potential customers. So marketing research reduces risk by providing the vital information to help marketing managers understand those wants and needs and translate them into marketing actions.

LO 8-2 *Describe the five-step marketing research approach that leads to marketing actions.*

Marketing researchers engage in a five-step decision-making process to collect information that will improve marketing decisions. The first step is to define the problem, which requires setting the research objectives and identifying possible marketing actions. The second step is to develop the research plan, which involves specifying the constraints, identifying data needed for marketing decisions, and determining how to

collect the data. The third step is to collect the relevant information, which includes considering pertinent secondary data (both internal and external) and primary data (by observing and questioning consumers) as well as using information technology and data mining to trigger marketing actions. The fourth step is to develop findings from the marketing research data collected. This involves analyzing the data and presenting the findings of the research. The fifth and last step is to take marketing actions, which involves making and implementing the action recommendations and then evaluating the results.

LO 8-3 *Explain how marketing uses secondary and primary data.*

Secondary data have already been recorded prior to the start of the project and consist of two parts: (*a*) internal secondary data, which originate from within the organization, such as sales reports and customer comments, and (b) external secondary data, which are created by other organizations, such as the U.S. Census Bureau (which provides data on the country's population, manufacturers, retailers, and so on) or business and trade publications (which provide data on industry trends, market size, etc.). Primary data are collected specifically for the project and are obtained by either observing or questioning people.

LO 8-4   *Discuss the uses of observations, questionnaires, panels, experiments, and newer data collection methods.*
Marketing researchers observe people in various ways, such as electronically using Nielsen people meters to measure TV viewing behavior or personally using mystery shoppers or ethnographic techniques. A recent electronic innovation is neuromarketing—using high-tech brain scanning to record the responses of a consumer's brain to marketing stimuli like packages or TV ads. Questionnaires involve asking people questions (a) in person using interviews or focus groups or (b) via a questionnaire using a telephone, fax, print, e-mail, Internet, or social media survey. A cross tabulation is often used with questionnaire data to analyze the relationships among two or more variables to lead to marketing actions. Panels involve a sample of consumers or stores that are repeatedly measured through time to see if their behaviors change. Experiments, such as test markets, involve measuring the effect of marketing variables such as price or advertising on sales. Collecting data from social networks like Facebook or Twitter is increasingly important because users can share their opinions about products and services with countless "friends" around the globe.

LO 8-5   *Explain how information technology and data mining lead to marketing actions.*
Today's marketing managers are often overloaded with data—from internal sales and customer data to external data on TV viewing habits or grocery purchases from the scanner data at checkout counters. Information technology enables this massive amount of marketing data to be stored, accessed, and processed. The resulting databases can be queried using data mining to find statistical relationships useful for marketing decisions and actions.

LO 8-6   *Describe three approaches to developing a company's sales forecast.*
One approach uses the subjective judgments of the decision maker, such as direct or lost-horse forecasts. A direct forecast involves estimating the value to be forecast without any intervening steps. A lost-horse forecast starts with the last known value of the item being forecast and then lists the factors that could affect the forecast, assesses whether they have a positive or negative impact, and makes the final forecast. Surveys of knowledgeable groups, a second method, involve obtaining information such as the intentions of potential buyers or estimates provided by the salesforce. Statistical methods involving extending a pattern observed in past data into the future are a third approach. The best-known statistical method is linear trend extrapolation.

LEARNING REVIEW ANSWERS

8-1   What is marketing research?
Answer: Marketing research is the process of defining a marketing problem and opportunity, systematically collecting and analyzing information, and recommending actions to reduce the risk of and thereby improve marketing decisions.

8-2   What is the five-step marketing research approach?
Answer: The five-step marketing research approach provides a systematic checklist for making marketing decisions and actions. The five steps are: (1) define the problem; (2) develop the research plan; (3) collect relevant information (data); (4) develop findings; and (5) take marketing actions.

8-3   What are constraints, as they apply to developing a research plan?
Answer: Constraints in a decision are the restrictions placed on potential solutions to a problem, such as time and money. These set the parameters for the research plan—due dates, budget, etc.

8-4   What is the difference between secondary and primary data?
Answer: Secondary data are facts and figures that have already been recorded prior to the project at hand, whereas primary data are facts and figures that are newly collected for the project.

8-5   What are some advantages and disadvantages of secondary data?
Answer: Advantages of secondary data are the time savings, the low cost, and the greater level of detail that may be available.

Disadvantages of secondary data are that the data may be out of date, unspecific, or have definitions, categories, or age groupings that are wrong for the project.

8-6   What is the difference between observational data and questionnaire data?
Answer: Observational data are facts and figures obtained by watching, either mechanically or in person, how people actually behave. Questionnaire data are facts and figures obtained by asking people about their attitudes, awareness, intentions, and behaviors.

8-7   Which type of survey provides the greatest flexibility for asking probing questions: mail, telephone, or personal interview?
Answer: personal interview (or individual/depth interview)

8-8   What is cross tabulation?
Answer: Cross tabulation, or "cross tab," is a method of presenting and analyzing data involving two or more variables to discover relationships in the data. As the most widely used technique for organizing and presenting marketing data, the simple format and flexibility of cross tabulations permit the direct interpretation of and an easy means to communicate the data.

8-9   In the marketing research for Tony's Pizza, what is an example of (a) a finding and (b) a marketing action?
Answer: (a) Figure 8–7A depicts annual sales from 2012 to 2015; the finding is that annual sales are relatively flat, rising only 5 million units over the 4-year period. (b) Figure 8–7D shows a finding (the decline in pizza consumption) that leads to

a recommendation to develop an ad targeting children 6 to 12 years old (the marketing action).

8-10 In evaluating marketing actions, what are the two dimensions on which they should be evaluated?

Answer: There are two aspects marketers use to evaluate the results of marketing actions: (1) evaluate the decision itself, which involves monitoring the marketplace to determine if action is necessary in the future and (2) evaluate the decision process used to determine whether (*a*) the marketing research and analysis used to develop the recommendations was effective or flawed in some way and (*b*) the process could be improved for similar situations in the future.

8-11 What are the three kinds of sales forecasting techniques?

Answer: They are: (1) judgments of the decision maker who acts on the results of a sales forecast; (2) surveys of knowledgeable groups, those who are likely to know something about future sales; and (3) statistical methods such as trend extrapolation, which involves extending a pattern observed in past data into the future.

8-12 How do you make a lost-horse forecast?

Answer: To make a lost-horse forecast, begin with the last known value of the item being forecast, list the factors that could affect the forecast, assess whether they have a positive or negative impact, and then make the final forecast.

FOCUSING ON KEY TERMS

constraints p. 208
cross tabulation p. 222
data p. 210
information technology p. 221

marketing research p. 206
measures of success p. 208
observational data p. 212
primary data p. 210

questionnaire data p. 215
sales forecast p. 227
secondary data p. 210

APPLYING MARKETING KNOWLEDGE

1 Suppose your dean of admissions is considering surveying high school seniors about their perceptions of your school to design better informational brochures for them. What are the advantages and disadvantages of doing (*a*) telephone interviews and (*b*) an Internet survey of seniors requesting information about the school?

2 Wisk detergent decides to run a test market to see the effect of coupons and in-store advertising on sales. The index of sales is as follows:

Element in Test Market	Weeks before Coupon	Week of Coupon	Week after Coupon
Without in-store ads	100	144	108
With in-store ads	100	268	203

3 Nielsen obtains ratings of local TV stations in small markets by having households fill out diary questionnaires. These give information on (*a*) who is watching TV and (*b*) the program being watched. What are the limitations of this questionnaire method?

4 The format in which information is presented is often vital. (*a*) If you were a harried marketing manager and queried your information system, would you rather see the results in tables or charts and graphs? (*b*) What are one or two strengths and weaknesses of each format?

5 (*a*) Why might a marketing researcher prefer to use secondary data rather than primary data in a study? (*b*) Why might the reverse be true?

6 Look back at Figure 8–4. Which questions would you pair to form a cross tabulation to uncover the following relationships? (*a*) Frequency of fast-food restaurant patronage and restaurant characteristics important to the customer, (*b*) Age of the head of household and source of information used about fast-food restaurants, (*c*) Frequency of patronage of Wendy's and source of information used about fast-food restaurants, and (*d*) How much children have to say about where the family eats and number of children in the household.

7 Look back at Figure 8–6A. (*a*) Run the percentages vertically and explain what they mean. (*b*) Express all numbers in the table as a percentage of the total number of people sampled (586) and explain what the percentages mean.

8 Which of the following variables would linear trend extrapolation be more accurate for? (*a*) Annual population of the United States or (*b*) annual sales of cars produced in the United States by Ford. Why?

To help you collect the most useful data for your marketing plan, develop a three-column table:

1 In column 1, list the information you would ideally like to have to fill holes in your marketing plan.
2 In column 2, identify the source for each bit of information in column 1, such as doing an Internet

search, talking to prospective customers, looking at internal data, and so forth.

3 In column 3, set a priority on information you will have time to spend collecting by ranking each item: 1 = most important; 2 = next most important, and so forth.

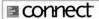

VIDEO CASE 8   Carmex® (A): Leveraging Facebook for Marketing Research

"What makes social media 'social' is its give and take," says Jeff Gerst of Bolin Marketing, who manages the Carmex® social media properties. By "give" Gerst is referring to the feedback consumers send on social media; "take" is what they receive— such as news and coupons. "For Carmex, Facebook isn't just a way to share coupons or the latest product news, but it is also a marketing research resource. We have instantaneous access to the opinions of our consumers."

Video 8-4
Carmex (A)
Video Case
kerin.tv/13e/v8-4

"While some people think of social media as 'free,' that is not true. However, almost everything in social media can be faster and cheaper than in the offline world," adds Dane Hartzell, general manager of Bolin Digital. "Many platforms have been prebuilt and we marketers only need to modify them slightly."

CARMEX AND ITS PRODUCT LINE

Although Carmex has been making lip balm since 1937, only in the last five years has it made serious efforts to stress growth and become more competitive. For example, Carmex has:

• Extended its lip balm products into new flavors and varieties.
• Expanded into nearly 30 international markets.

© Editorial Image, LLC

- Developed the Carmex Moisture Plus line of premium lip balms for women.
- Launched a line of skin care products, its first venture outside of lip care.

Carmex has used social media tools in developing all of these initiatives, but the focus of this case is how Carmex might use Facebook marketing research to grow its lip balm varieties in the United States.

FACEBOOK MARKETING RESEARCH: TREND SPOTTING

Brands can leverage Facebook and all social media platforms to test what topics and themes its audience engages with the most as well as validate concepts and ideas. In 2012 Carmex identified the growing trend of consumers seeking product customization. Carmex combined research with Facebook engagement data, which helped to validate consumer interest and led it to develop two new lines of limited-edition lip balm products that launched in 2013.

The first line was a set of three different Carmex "City Sticks" featuring New York, Chicago, and Las Vegas versions of the Carmex lip balm stick with recognizable landmarks from each city on them. The brand partnered with Walgreens to exclusively sell the "City Sticks" in each of the three cities. During this time Carmex leveraged its social media channels on Facebook and Instagram to solicit photos of fans holding up their favorite style of Carmex in front of a landmark in their own city. Carmex then used these photos to help it decide on new locations for future limited-edition "City Sticks."

Carmex's second line of new products was four fashion-forward "glamorous" designs of Carmex Moisture Plus. Carmex researched current design trends in the women's fashion industry to come up with the four different styles, and it had seen good engagement from its Facebook community on "fashion themed" posts, which helped validate the concept. The four styles were: "Chic," a black and white houndstooth; "Fab," with bright purple circles; "Adventurous," a leopard print; and "Whimsical," with blue, orange, green, and pink intertwined ribbons. Carmex first announced the line to its Facebook fans to generate interest and they were brought to market in the summer of 2013.

FACEBOOK MARKETING RESEARCH: TWO KEY METRICS

"We have three potential new flavors and we can only put two into quantitative testing," explains Jeff Gerst to his team. "So we have two goals in doing marketing research on this. One is to use Facebook to help us determine which two flavors we should move forward with. The second goal is to drive our Facebook metrics."

The two key Facebook metrics the Carmex marketing team has chosen to help narrow the flavor choices from three to two are "likes" and "engagement." "Likes" are the number of new "likers" to the brand's Facebook Page. This metric measures the size of the brand's Facebook audience. In contrast, "engagement" measures how active its Facebook audience is with Carmex. Anytime a liker posts a comment on the Carmex Wall, likes its status, or replies to one of its posts, the engagement level increases.

The easiest way for Carmex to grow the number of "likes" on its Facebook Page is through contests and promotions. If it gives away prizes, people will be drawn to its site and its likes will increase. However, these people may not actually be fans of the Carmex product so at the end of the promotion, they may "unlike" Carmex or they may remain fans but not engage with the Carmex Page at all.

"One of the biggest challenges facing Facebook Community Managers for brands is how to grow your likes without hurting the level of engagement," says Holly Matson, director of experience planning at Bolin Marketing.

"Depending on how we go about conducting the research," Gerst adds, "we can drive engagement with our existing Facebook community, we can use this as an opportunity to grow our Facebook community or, potentially, we could do both." The benefits of this Carmex Facebook strategy are twofold: (1) narrowing the number of flavors to be researched from three to two and (2) enhancing the connections with the Carmex Facebook community.

HOW THE METRICS MIGHT BE USED

Carmex's Facebook activity can benefit (1) by using a poll to increase engagement, (2) by launching a contest to increase the number of likers, and (3) by trying to increase both engagement and likers through combining a poll with a contest.

The "Engagement" Strategy: Use a Poll

Let's look at two ways to use the engagement strategy showing actual Facebook screens. First, Carmex can post a somewhat open-ended question on its Facebook Wall, such as, "Which Carmex lip balm flavor would you most like to see next: Watermelon, Green Apple, or Peach Mango?" (Figure 1). However, consumers are less likely to respond to a question if they have to type in a response and have their name attached to it.

Alternatively, Carmex can post the same question on its Wall as a fixed-alternative poll question (Figure 2). Then consumers need only click on a flavor to vote; this is quick, anonymous, and will drive more people to vote, where more votes means more engagement. Within five minutes Carmex will have several dozen votes and, by the end of a business day, Carmex can very easily have over 500 responses.

In this scenario, the consumers are content because they are able to engage with a brand they like and have their opinions heard. Carmex is content because it has engaged hundreds of its fans on its Facebook Page, and it gains results that are very helpful in deciding which flavors to put into testing. This scenario gets an answer quickly and drives fan engagement with existing fans but does not drive new likers to the Carmex Facebook Page.

The "Likes" Strategy: Use a Contest

If Carmex wants to grow the size of its Facebook community, which means the number of its brand page "likes," it can adopt a different strategy. Carmex can announce a contest where, if consumers "like" Carmex on Facebook and share a comment, they will be entered to win three limited-edition flavors. The chance to win limited-edition flavors is exciting to Carmex enthusiasts, and a contest like this will draw new consumers to the page. Carmex can ask the winners to review the limited-edition flavors and see if there is a consensus on which flavors should move on to quantitative testing. Setting up a contest, developing official rules, promoting the contest through Facebook ads, and fulfilling a contest can be costly and time-consuming.

FIGURE 1

Facebook Open-Ended Poll Question

Carmex
Which Carmex lip balm flavor would you most like to see next: Watermelon, Green Apple, or Peach Mango?

Like   Comment

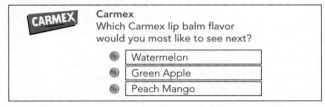

FIGURE 2

Facebook Fixed-Alternative Poll Question

Carmex
Which Carmex lip balm flavor would you most like to see next?

- Watermelon
- Green Apple
- Peach Mango

FIGURE 3

Potential Results from Three Possible Facebook Strategies

FACEBOOK STRATEGY	POTENTIAL IMPACT ON...		
	Increased "Engagement"	Increased "Likes"	Cost
Poll Only	High	Low	Low
Contest Only	Low	High	Moderate
Poll + Contest	High	High	Moderate to High

Favorable   Neutral   Unfavorable

The Combined Strategy: Use Poll and Contest

Carmex can also choose to layer these two strategies into a combined strategy where it runs the limited-edition flavor contest to promote new likes and meanwhile posts the poll question on its Facebook Wall to drive engagement.

REACHING A DECISION

Figure 3 shows the potential results from the three Facebook strategies being considered—the poll only, the contest only, or both strategies together. Assume the Carmex marketing team has sought your help in selecting a strategy and needs your answers to the questions below.[31]

Questions

1 What are the advantages and disadvantages for the Carmex marketing team in collecting data to narrow the flavor choices from three to two using (*a*) an online survey of a cross section of Internet households or (*b*) an online survey of Carmex Facebook likers?

2 (*a*) On a Facebook brand page, what are "engagement" and "likes" really measuring? (*b*) For Carmex, which is more important and why?

3 (*a*) What evokes consumers' "engagement" on a brand page on Facebook? (*b*) What attracts consumers to "like" a brand page on Facebook?

4 (*a*) What are the advantages of using a fixed-alternative poll question on Facebook? (*b*) When do you think it would be better to use an open-ended question?

5 (*a*) If you had a limited budget and two weeks to decide which two flavors to put into quantitative testing, would you choose a "poll only" or a "contest only" strategy? Why? (*b*) If you had a sizable budget and two months to make the same decision, which scenario would you choose? Why?

Chapter Notes

1. "Worldwide Grosses," Box Office Mojo, http://www.boxofficemojo.com/alltime/world/, accessed May 26, 2015.

2. Rachel Dodes, "Movies: What's in a Name?" *The Wall Street Journal*, October 19, 2012, p. D1; John Horn, "Studios Play Name Games," *Star Tribune*, August 10, 1997, p. F11; and "Flunking Chemistry," *Star Tribune*, April 11, 2003, p. E13.

3. Kathryn Lunte, "Screening Success: Marketing Research for Movies," *Film and Digital Media*, https://filmanddigitalmedia.wordpress.com/?s=screening+success, February 28, 2015.

4. Ronald Grover, Tom Lowry, and Michael White, "King of the World (Again)," *Bloomberg Businessweek*, February 1, 8, 2010, pp. 48–56; Richard Corliss, "Avatar Ascendant," *Time,* February 8, 2010, pp. 50–51; and Willow Bay, "Test Audiences Have Profound Effect on Movies," *CNN Newsstand & Entertainment Weekly*, September 28, 1998.

5. Brooks Barnes, "Hollywood Tracks Social Media Chatter to Target Hit Films," *The New York Times*, www.nytimes.com, December 7, 2014; Carl Diorio, "Tracking Projections: Box Office Calculations an Inexact Science," *Variety*, May 24, 2001.

6. A lengthier, expanded definition is found on the American Marketing Association's website. See http://www.marketingpower.com/AboutAMA/Pages/DefinitionofMarketing.aspx. For a researcher's comments on this and other definitions of marketing research, see Lawrence D. Gibson, "Quo Vadis, *Marketing Research?*" *Marketing Research*, Spring 2000, pp. 36–41.

7. Parmy Olson, "Gadgets We Love: LEGO Minstorms EV3," forbes.com, December 2, 2104, p. 1; and Harry McCracken, "Build-A-Bot," *Time*, January 21, 2013, pp. 52–53.

8. Lawrence D. Gibson, "Defining Marketing Problems," *Marketing Research*, Spring 1998, pp. 4–12.

9. David A. Aaker, V. Kumar, George S. Day, and Robert P. Leone, *Marketing Research*, 10th ed. (Hoboken, NJ: John Wiley & Sons, 2010), pp. 114–16.

10. Miriam Gottfried, "Nielsen Isn't Leaving the Living Room Soon," *The Wall Street Journal*, January 20, 2015, p. C8; and Meg James, "Nielsen 'People Meter' Changed the TV Ratings Game 25 Years Ago," *Los Angeles Times*, August 31, 2012.

11. George Winslow, "Researchers Tackle Cross-Platform Measurement," *Broadcasting & Cable*, September 15, 2014, p. 22; Jeanine Poggi, "The CMO's Guide to Fall TV Ratings," *Advertising Age*, September 29, 2014, p. 40; and Brian Stelter, "New Nielsen Ratings Measure TV and Online Ads Together," *The New York Times Media* Decoder, March 18, 2012.

12. "Nielsen Estimates More Than 116 Million TV Homes in the U.S.," The Nielsen Company website, August 29, 2014, http://www.nielsen.com/us/en/insights/news/2014/nielsenestimates-more-than-116-million-tv-homes-in-the-us.html.

13. "U.S. Ad Spending Forecast from ZenithOptimedia," *Advertising Age*, June 23, 2014, p. 32.

14. Bruce Brown and Scott Anthony, "How P&G Tripled Its Innovation Success Rate," *Harvard Business Review*, June 2011, p. 64–72; and "Observe and Learn From Consumers," *Managing People at Work*, April 2011, p. 4.

15. Jim Dudlicek, "Mystery Machine," *Progressive Grocer*, May 2015, p. 10; and Clive R. Boddy, "'Hanging Around with People': Ethnography in Marketing Research and Intelligence Gathering," *The Marketing Review* 11, no. 2 (2011), pp. 151–63.

16. Gavin Johnson and Melinda Rea-Holloway, "Ethnography: How to Know If It's Right for Your Study," *Alert! Magazine*, Marketing Research Association 47, no. 2 (February 2009), pp. 1–4.

17. Kenneth Chang, "Enlisting Science's Lessons to Entice More Shoppers to Spend More," *The New York Times*, September 19, 2006, p. D3; and Janet Adamy, "Cooking Up Changes at Kraft Foods," *The Wall Street Journal*, February 20, 2007, p. B1.

18. Kyle Hilton, "The Science of Sensory Marketing," *Harvard Business Review,* March 2015, pp. 28–29; Aradhna Krishna,

Customer Sense (New York: Palgrave Macmillan, 2013); Lluis Martinez-Ribes, "The Power of the Senses," http://www.martinez-ribes.com/the-power-ofthe-senses-sensory-applications-in-retail/, April 24, 2013; and Martin Lindstrom, *Buyology: Truth and Lies about Why We Buy* (New York: Doubleday, 2008), pp. 8–36.

19. Ilan Brat, "The Emotional Quotient of Soup Shopping," *The Wall Street Journal*, February 17, 2010, p. B6.

20. For a more complete discussion of questionnaire methods, see Joseph F. Hair Jr., Mary Wolfinbarger, Robert P. Bush, and David J. Ortinau, *Essentials of Marketing Research*, 3rd ed. (New York: McGraw-Hill/Irwin, 2013), Chapters 4 and 8.

21. See www.trendhunter.com/about-trend-hunter.

22. "What Is Online Research?" Marketing Research Association at http://www.marketingresearch.org/?q=node/221. See also www.surveymonkey.com.

23. For more discussion on wording questions effectively, see Gilbert A. Churchill Jr., Tom J. Brown, and Tracy A. Suter, *Basic Marketing Research*, 7th ed. (Mason, OH: South-Western, Cengage Learning, 2010), pp. 289–307.

24. Stephanie Clifford, "Social Media Act as a Guide for Marketers," *The New York Times*, July 31, 2012, pp. A1, A3; and Noam Cohen, "The Breakfast Meeting: Social Media as Focus Group," *The New York Times*, July 31, 2012, p. A3.

25. Jeff Gerst of Bolin Marketing provided the Carmex example, with the permission of Carma Laboratories, Inc.

26. Mark Jeffery, *Data-Driven Marketing: The 15 Metrics Everyone in Marketing Should Know* (Hoboken, NJ: John Wiley & Sons, Inc., 2010), pp. 156–86.

27. Douglas D. Bates, "The Future of Qualitative Research Is Online," *Alert! Magazine*, Marketing Research Association 47, no. 2 (February 2009); Jack Neff, "The End of Consumer Surveys?" *Advertising Age*, September 15, 2008; Jack Neff, "Marketing Execs: Researchers Could Use a Softer Touch," *Advertising Age*, January 27, 2009; Bruce Mendelsohn, "Social Networking: Interactive Marketing Lets Researchers Reach Consumers Where They Are," *Alert! Magazine*, Marketing Research Association 46, no. 4 (April 2008); Toby, "Social Media Research: Interview with Joel Rubinson of ARF: Part 1," *Diva Marketing Blog*, February 16, 2009; and Toby, "Social Media Research: Interview with Joel Rubinson of ARF: Part 2," *Diva Marketing Blog*, February 23, 2009.

28. Janakiraman Moorthy, Rangin Lahiri, Neelanjan Biswas, Dipyaman Sanyal, Jayanthi Ranjan, Krishnadas Nanath, and Pulak Ghosh, "Big Data: Prospects and Challenges," *Vikalpa*, January–March, 2015, pp. 74–96; Karthik Kambatla, Giorgos Kollias, Vipin Kumar, and Ananth Grama, "Trends in Big Data Analytics," *Journal of Parallel and Distributed Computing*," January 2014, pp. 2561–73; Steve LaValle, Eric Lesser, Rebecca Shockley, Michael S. Hopkins, and Nina Kruschwitz, "Big Data, Analytics and the Path From Insights to Value," *Sloan Management Review*, Winter 2011, pp. 21–31; and "Big Data: Before You Start Restricting It, Be Aware of All the Opportunities," *The Wall Street Journal,* November 19, 2012, p. R10.

29. Joel Stein, "Your Data, Yourself," *Time*, March 21, 2011, pp. 39–46; Ryan Flinn, "The Big Business of Sifting through Social Media Data," *Bloomberg Businessweek*, October 25–October 31, 2010, pp. 20–22; Michael Lev-Ram, "The Hot New Gig in Tech," *Fortune*, September 5, 2011, p. 29; and Geoffrey A. Fowler and Emily Steel, "Facebook Says User Data Sold to Broker," *The Wall Street Journal*, November 1, 2010, p. B3.

30. The step 4 discussion was written by David Ford and Don Rylander of Ford Consulting Group, Inc.; the Tony's Pizza example was provided by Teré Carral of Tony's Pizza.

31. Carmex: This case was written by Jeff Gerst of Bolin Marketing.

Market Segmentation, Targeting, and Positioning

LEARNING OBJECTIVES

After reading this chapter you should be able to:

 LO 9-1 Explain what market segmentation is and when to use it.

 LO 9-2 Identify the five steps involved in segmenting and targeting markets.

 LO 9-3 Recognize the bases used to segment consumer and organizational (business) markets.

 LO 9-4 Develop a market-product grid to identify a target market and recommend resulting marketing actions.

 LO 9-5 Explain how marketing managers position products in the marketplace.

Zappos.com Is Powered by Service—and Segmentation!

Tony Hsieh (opposite page) showed signs of being an entrepreneur early in life. In middle school he started a mail-order pin-on button-making business, in high school he developed software for filling out forms on a computer, and in college he sold pizzas out of his dorm room. Now he's running the extraordinarily entrepreneurial online shoe retailer Zappos.com![1]

Segmentation Is a Key to Success

Zappos was founded by Nick Swinmurn when he couldn't find a pair of Airwalk desert boots at a local mall. Tony invested in the company and as an advisor helped it develop its segmentation strategy: focus on people who will shop for and buy shoes online and like to use mobile technology. From a limited initial selection of shoes, Zappos grew to offer more than 1,000 brands, and eventually added lines of clothes, accessories, beauty aids, and housewares. This focus on the segment of online buyers generates more than $1 billion in sales annually.[2] Today, Tony is CEO of Zappos.com, which was acquired by Amazon.com for more than $1 billion.

In addition to a huge selection, Zappos provides extraordinary customer service and free shipping both ways. Pamela Leo, a New Jersey customer, says, "With Zappos I can try the shoes in the comfort of my own home . . . it's fabulous."[3]

Delivering WOW Customer Service

"We try to spend most of our time on stuff that will improve customer-service levels," Hsieh explains.[4] This customer-service obsession for its market segment of online customers means that all new Zappos.com employees—whether the chief financial officer or the children's footwear buyer—go through four weeks of customer-loyalty training. Hsieh offers $2,000 to anyone completing the training who wants to leave Zappos.com. The theory: If you take the money and run, you're not right for Zappos.com. Few take the money!

Ten "core values" are the foundation for the Zappos.com culture, brand, and business strategies. Some examples:[5]

#1. Deliver WOW through service. This focus on exemplary customer service encompasses all 10 core values.

#3. Create fun and a little weirdness. In a Zappos.com day, cowbells ring, parades appear, and modified-blaster gunfights arise.

#6. Build open and honest relationships with communication. Employees are told to say what they think.

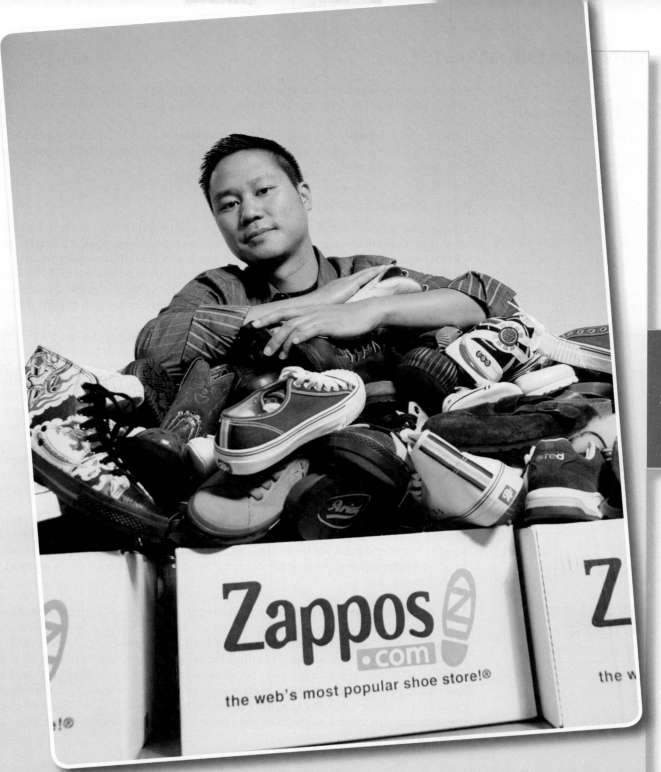

© Brad Swonetz/Redux

The other Zappos.com core values appear on its website: www.zappos.com.[6]

The Zappos.com strategy illustrates successful market segmentation and targeting, the first topics in Chapter 9. The chapter ends with the topic of positioning the organization, product, or brand.

WHY SEGMENT MARKETS?

LO 9-1 | Explain what market segmentation is and when to use it.

A business firm segments its markets so it can respond more effectively to the wants of groups of potential buyers and thus increase its sales and profits. Not-for-profit organizations also segment the clients they serve to satisfy client needs more effectively while achieving the organization's goals. Let's describe (1) what market segmentation is and (2) when to segment markets, sometimes using the Zappos.com segmentation strategy as an example.

What Market Segmentation Means

People have different needs and wants, even though it would be easier for marketers if they didn't. **Market segmentation** involves aggregating prospective buyers into groups, or segments, that (1) have common needs and (2) will respond similarly to a marketing action. As defined in Chapter 1, *market segments* are the relatively homogeneous groups of prospective buyers that result from the market segmentation process. Each market segment consists of people who are relatively similar to each other in terms of their consumption behavior.

The existence of different market segments has caused firms to use a marketing strategy of **product differentiation**. This strategy involves a firm using different marketing mix actions, such as product features and advertising, to help consumers perceive the product as being different and better than competing products. The perceived differences may involve physical features, such as size or color, or nonphysical ones, such as image or price.

Segmentation: Linking Needs to Actions The process of segmenting a market and selecting specific segments as targets is the link between the various buyers' needs and the organization's marketing program, as shown in Figure 9–1. Market segmentation is only a means to an end: It leads to tangible marketing actions that can increase sales and profitability.

Market segmentation first stresses the importance of grouping people or organizations in a market according to the similarity of their needs and the benefits they are looking for in making a purchase. Second, such needs and benefits must be related to specific marketing actions that the organization can take, such as a new product or special promotion.

The Zappos.com Segmentation Strategy The Zappos.com target customer segment originally consisted of people who wanted to (1) have a wide selection of shoes, (2) shop online in the convenience of their own homes, and (3) receive quick delivery and free returns. Zappos's actions include offering a huge inventory of shoes using an online selling strategy and providing overnight delivery. These actions have enabled Zappos.com to create a positive customer experience and generate repeat purchases. Zappos's success in selling footwear has enabled it to add lines of clothing, handbags, accessories (such as sunglasses), and housewares to reach new segments of buyers.

FIGURE 9–1

Market segmentation links market needs to an organization's marketing program—its specific marketing mix actions designed to satisfy those needs.

Identify market needs

Benefits in terms of:
- Product features
- Expense
- Quality
- Savings in time and convenience

Link needs to actions

Take steps to segment and target markets

Execute marketing program actions

A marketing mix of:
- Product
- Price
- Promotion
- Place (distribution)

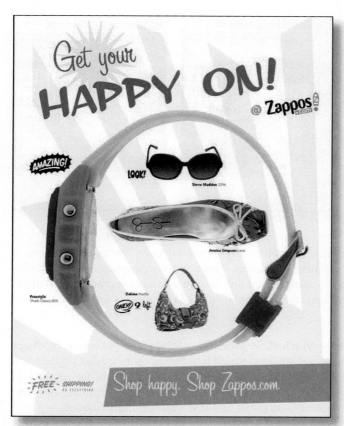

Zappos.com is reaching new market segments with new products and edgy, attention-getting ads.

Source: Zappos

With over 8 million customers and 5,000 calls daily to Zappos's service center, its executives believe the speed with which a customer receives an online purchase plays a big role in gaining repeat customers.[7] The company continues to stress this point of difference of providing the absolute best service among online sellers.

Using Market Product Grids How do you sleep—on your side, your back, or your stomach? These are really the key market segments of sleepers. Sleep researchers have discovered that you'll probably get a better night's sleep if you have the right firmness of pillow under your head. So we can develop the market-product grid shown in Figure 9–2.[8]

A **market-product grid** is a framework to relate the market segments of potential buyers to products offered or potential marketing actions. The market-product grid in Figure 9–2 shows the different market segments for bed pillows—the side, back, and stomach sleepers—in the horizontal rows. The product offerings—the pillows—appear in the vertical columns and are based on three different pillow firmnesses—firm, medium, and soft.

Market research reveals the size of each sleeper segment, as shown by both the percentages and circles in Figure 9–2. This tells pillow manufacturers the relative importance of each of the three market segments, which is critical information when scheduling production. It also emphasizes the importance of firm pillows, a product targeted at the side sleeper market segment. As Figure 9–2 shows, this segment is almost three times the size of the other two combined. Therefore, meeting the needs of this market segment with the right firmness of pillow is especially important.

When and How to Segment Markets

One-size-fits-all mass markets—like that for Tide laundry detergent 40 years ago—no longer exist. The marketing officer at Procter & Gamble, which markets Tide, says, "Every one of our brands is targeted." Due to the recent recession, the size of the middle-income market is shrinking. In response, P&G has begun implementing a new segmentation strategy: Offer different products to reach (1) high-income and (2) low-income families.[9]

A business goes to the trouble and expense of segmenting its markets when it expects that this extra effort will increase its sales, profit, and return on investment.

FIGURE 9–2

This market-product grid shows the kind of sleeper that is targeted for each of the bed pillow products. The percentages and sizes of the circles show that side sleepers are the dominant market segment and that they prefer firm pillows.

MARKET SEGMENTS	BED PILLOW PRODUCTS		
	Firm Pillows	Medium Pillows	Soft Pillows
Side sleepers	●=73%		
Back sleepers		●=22%	
Stomach sleepers			●=5%

These *different* covers for the *same* magazine issue show a very effective market segmentation strategy. For which strategy it is and why it works, see the text.

© Editorial Image, LLC

When expenses are greater than the potentially increased sales from segmentation, a firm should not attempt to segment its market. Three specific segmentation strategies that illustrate this point are (1) one product and multiple market segments, (2) multiple products and multiple market segments, and (3) segments of one, or mass customization.

One Product and Multiple Market Segments When an organization produces only a single product or service and attempts to sell it to two or more market segments, it avoids the extra costs of developing and producing additional versions of the product. In this case, the incremental costs of taking the product into new market segments are typically those of a separate promotional campaign or a new channel of distribution.

Magazines are single products frequently directed at two or more distinct market segments. The annual *Sporting News Baseball Yearbook* uses 17 different covers featuring a baseball star from each of its regions in the United States. Yet each regional issue has the same magazine content.

Other examples of a single offering for multiple segments include books, movies, and many services. Book series such as *Harry Potter, The Twilight Saga,* and *The Hunger Games* have phenomenal success in part due to the publishers' creativity in marketing to preteen, teen, and adult segments. Movies have a similar challenge, particularly since different segments are reached through different channels such as movie theaters, streaming services, and pay-per-view cable channels. Finally, services such as Disney's resorts offer the same basic experience to at least three distinct segments—children, parents, and grandparents. Although separate advertising, promotion, and distribution for these offerings can be expensive, these expenses are minor compared with the costs of producing a different version of the offerings for each segment.[10]

Multiple Products and Multiple Market Segments Ford's different lines of cars, SUVs, and pickup trucks are each targeted at a different type of customer—examples of multiple products aimed at multiple market segments. Producing these different vehicles is clearly more expensive than producing only a single vehicle. But this strategy is very effective *if* it meets customers' needs better, doesn't reduce quality or increase price, and adds to Ford's sales revenues and profits.

Unfortunately, this product differentiation strategy in the auto industry has a huge potential downside: The proliferation of different models and options can reduce quality and raise prices—especially in relation to foreign imports. Perhaps the extreme was in 1982, when the Ford Thunderbird had exactly 69,120 options compared with 32 (including colors) on the 1982 Honda Accord.[11]

More than three decades later Ford is relearning its models and options lessons. Its current successful turnaround is partly related to a reduction in the number of frames, engines, and brands offered. As a result, Ford has reduced its number of models from 97 to 36 and sold off the Jaguar, Land Rover, and Volvo brands, and discontinued the Mercury brand. Although there are fewer choices, Ford's simplified product line provides two benefits to consumers: (1) lower prices through producing a higher volume of fewer models and (2) higher quality because of the ability to debug fewer basic designs.[12]

Segments of One: Mass Customization

American marketers are rediscovering today what their ancestors running the corner general store knew a century ago: Each customer has unique needs and wants and desires special tender loving care. Economies of scale in manufacturing and marketing during the past century made mass-produced products so affordable that most customers were willing to compromise their individual tastes and settle for standardized products. Today's Internet ordering and flexible manufacturing and marketing processes have made *mass customization* possible, which means tailoring products or services to the tastes of individual customers on a high-volume scale.

Mass customization is the next step beyond *build-to-order (BTO)*, manufacturing a product only when there is an order from a customer. Apple uses BTO systems that trim work-in-progress inventories and shorten delivery times to customers. To do this, Apple restricts its computer manufacturing line to only a few basic models that can be assembled in four minutes. This gives customers a good choice with quick delivery. But even this system falls a bit short of total mass customization because customers do not have an unlimited number of features from which to choose.

ANN INC.'s LOFT chain tries to reach younger and value-conscious women with a casual lifestyle, while its Ann Taylor chain targets more sophisticated and relatively affluent women. For the potential dangers of this two-segment strategy, see the text.
© McGraw-Hill Education/Jill Braaten, photographer

The Segmentation Trade-Off: Synergies versus Cannibalization

The key to successful product differentiation and market segmentation strategies is finding the ideal balance between satisfying a customer's individual wants and achieving *organizational synergy*, the increased customer value achieved through performing organizational functions such as marketing or manufacturing more efficiently. The "increased customer value" can take many forms: more products, improved quality of existing products, lower prices, easier access to products through improved distribution, and so on. So the ultimate criterion for an organization's marketing success is that customers should be better off as a result of the increased synergies.

The organization should also achieve increased revenues and profits from the product differentiation and market segmentation strategies it uses. When the increased customer value involves adding new products or a new chain of stores, the product differentiation–market segmentation trade-off raises a critical issue: Are the new products or new chain simply stealing customers and sales from the older, existing ones? This is known as *cannibalization*.

Marketers increasingly emphasize a two-tier, "Tiffany/Walmart" strategy. Many firms now offer different variations of the same basic offering to high-end and low-end segments. Gap's Banana Republic chain sells blue jeans for $58, whereas Old Navy stores sell a slightly different version for $22.

Unfortunately, the lines between customer segments can often blur and lead to problems. For example, consider the competition within the ANN INC. organization between stores in its two chains—Ann Taylor and LOFT. The Ann Taylor chain targets "successful, relatively affluent, fashion-conscious women," while its sister Ann Taylor LOFT chain targets "value-conscious women who want a casual lifestyle at work and home." The LOFT stores wound up stealing sales from the Ann Taylor chain. The result: More than 100 stores from both chains were recently closed.[13] Both chains are now aggressively targeting their customers by stressing online sales and opening new factory outlet stores.

The smaller Walmart Neighborhood Market format offers convenient locations to discount shoppers.
© Scott Olson/Getty Images

Walmart has been opening Walmart Neighborhood Market stores that are about one-fifth the size of its supercenters. These smaller stores are intended to compete for the segments that shop at discount chains such as Dollar General. Walmart

Neighborhood Markets are designed to meet a range of needs by offering fresh produce, health and beauty supplies, household items, gasoline, and a pharmacy. Walmart plans to open between 180 and 200 of the new format stores this year. Will its own Tiffany/Walmart strategy—or perhaps "Walmart/Dollar General" strategy—prove successful or lead to cannibalization of the larger stores? Watch for new stores near you during the next few years to determine the answer.[14]

learning review »

9-1. Market segmentation involves aggregating prospective buyers into groups that have two key characteristics. What are they?

9-2. In terms of market segments and products, what are the three market segmentation strategies?

STEPS IN SEGMENTING AND TARGETING MARKETS

LO 9-2 Identify the five steps involved in segmenting and targeting markets.

Figure 9–3 identifies the five-step process used to segment a market and select the target segments on which an organization wants to focus. Segmenting a market requires both detailed analysis and large doses of common sense and managerial judgment. So market segmentation is both science and art!

For the purposes of our discussion, assume that you have just purchased a Wendy's restaurant. Your Wendy's is located next to a large urban university, one that offers both day and evening classes. Your restaurant offers the basic Wendy's fare: hamburgers, chicken and deli sandwiches, salads, french fries, and Frosty desserts. Even though you are part of a chain that has some restrictions on menu and decor, you are free to set your hours of business and to develop local advertising. How can market segmentation help? In the sections that follow, you will apply the five-step process for segmenting and targeting markets to arrive at marketing actions for your Wendy's restaurant.

A local Wendy's restaurant—like yours!

© Reed Saxon/AP Images

Step 1: Group Potential Buyers into Segments

It's not always a good idea to segment a market. Grouping potential buyers into meaningful segments involves meeting some specific criteria that answer the questions,

FIGURE 9–3

The five key steps in segmenting and targeting markets link the market needs of customers to the organization's marketing program.

Identify market needs →

Link needs to actions. The steps:
1 Group potential buyers into segments
2 Group products to be sold into categories
3 Develop a market-product grid and estimate size of markets
4 Select target markets
5 Take marketing actions to reach target markets

→ Execute marketing program actions

"Would segmentation be worth doing?" and "Is it possible?" If so, a marketer must find specific variables that can be used to create these various segments.

Criteria to Use in Forming the Segments A marketing manager should develop market segments that meet five essential criteria:[15]

- *Simplicity and cost-effectiveness of assigning potential buyers to segments.* A marketing manager must be able to put a market segmentation plan into effect. This means identifying the characteristics of potential buyers in a market and then cost-effectively assigning them to a segment.
- *Potential for increased profit.* The best segmentation approach is the one that maximizes the opportunity for future profit and return on investment (ROI). If this potential is maximized without segmentation, don't segment. For non-profit organizations, the criterion is the potential for serving clients more effectively.
- *Similarity of needs of potential buyers within a segment.* Potential buyers within a segment should be similar in terms of common needs that, in turn, lead to common marketing actions, such as product features sought or advertising media used.
- *Difference of needs of buyers among segments.* If the needs of the various segments aren't very different, combine them into fewer segments. A different segment usually requires a different marketing action that, in turn, means greater costs. If increased sales don't offset extra costs, combine segments and reduce the number of marketing actions.
- *Potential of a marketing action to reach a segment.* Reaching a segment requires a simple but effective marketing action. If no such action exists, don't segment.

This MicroFridge appliance includes everything from a small refrigerator, freezer, and microwave oven to a charging station for laptops and mobile phones. To which market segment might this appeal? The answer appears in the text.

Source: Intirion Corporation

Ways to Segment Consumer Markets Figure 9–4 shows four general bases of segmentation and the typical variables that can be used to segment U.S. consumer markets. These four segmentation bases are (1) *geographic segmentation,* which is based on where prospective customers live or work (region, city size); (2) *demographic segmentation,* which is based on some *objective* physical (gender, race), measurable (age, income), or other classification attribute (birth era, occupation) of prospective customers; (3) *psychographic segmentation,* which is based on some *subjective* mental or emotional attributes (personality), aspirations (lifestyle), or needs of prospective customers; and (4) *behavioral segmentation,* which is based on some observable actions or attitudes by prospective customers—such as where they buy, what benefits they seek, how frequently they buy, and why they buy. Some examples are:

- *Geographic segmentation: Region.* Campbell Soup Company found that its canned nacho cheese sauce, which could be heated and poured directly onto nacho chips, was too spicy for Americans in the East and not spicy enough for those in the West and Southwest. The result: Campbell's plants in Texas and California now produce a hotter nacho cheese sauce to serve their regions better.
- *Demographic segmentation: Household size.* More than half of all U.S. households are made up of only one or two persons, so Campbell packages meals with only one or two servings for this market segment.
- *Psychographic segmentation: Lifestyle.* Nielsen's lifestyle segmentation is based on the belief that "birds of a feather flock together." Thus, people of similar lifestyles tend to live near one another, have similar interests, and buy similar offerings. This is of great value to marketers. Nielsen PRIZM® classifies every household in the United States into

Basis of Segmentation	Segmentation Variables	Typical Breakdowns
Geographic	Region	Northeast; Midwest; South; West; etc.
	City size	Under 10,000; 10,000–24,999; 25,000–49,999; 50,000–99,999; etc.
	Statistical area	Metropolitan and micropolitan statistical areas; Census tract; etc.
	Media-television	210 designated market areas (DMA) in the U.S. (Nielsen)
	Density	Urban; suburban; small town; rural
Demographic	Gender	Male; female
	Age	Under 6 yrs; 6–11 yrs; 12–17 yrs; 18–24 yrs; 25–34 yrs; etc.
	Race/ethnicity	African American; Asian; Hispanic; White/Caucasian; etc.
	Life stage	Infant; preschool; child; youth; collegiate; adult; senior
	Birth era	Baby boomer (1946–1964); Generation X (1965–1976); etc.
	Household size	1; 2; 3–4; 5 or more
	Marital status	Never married; married; separated; divorced; widowed; domestic partner
	Income	Under $15,000; $15,000–$24,999; $25,000–$34,999; etc.
	Education	Some high school or less; high school graduate (or GED); etc.
	Occupation	Managerial & professional; technical, sales; farming; etc.
Psychographic	Personality	Gregarious; compulsive; extroverted; aggressive; ambitious; etc.
	Values (VALS2)	Innovators; Thinkers; Achievers; Experiencers; Believers; Strivers; etc.
	Lifestyle (Nielsen PRIZM)	Blue Blood Estates; Single City Blues; etc. (66 total neighborhood clusters)
	Needs	Quality; service; price/value; health; convenience; etc.
Behavioral	Retail store type	Department; specialty; outlet; convenience; mass merchandiser; etc.
	Direct marketing	Mail order/catalog; door-to-door; direct response; Internet
	Product features	Situation-specific; general
	Usage rate	Light user; medium user; heavy user
	User status	Nonuser; ex-user; prospect; first-time user; regular user
	Awareness/intentions	Unaware; aware; interested; intending to buy; purchaser; rejection

FIGURE 9–4

Segmentation bases, variables, and breakdowns for U.S. consumer markets. Marketing managers should select segmentation variables that lead to marketing actions.

one of 66 unique market segments. See the Marketing Insights About Me box for a profile of where you live.

- *Behavioral segmentation: Product features.* Understanding what features are important to different customers is a useful way to segment markets because it can lead directly to specific marketing actions, such as a new product, an ad campaign, or a distribution channel. For example, college dorm residents frequently want to keep and prepare their own food to save money or have a late-night snack. However, their dorm rooms are often woefully short of space. Micro-Fridge understands this and markets a combination microwave, refrigerator, freezer, and charging station appliance targeted to these students.
- *Behavioral segmentation: Usage rate.* **Usage rate** is the quantity consumed or patronage—store visits—during a specific period. It varies significantly among different customer groups. Airlines have developed frequent-flyer programs to encourage passengers to use the same airline repeatedly to create loyal customers. This technique, sometimes called *frequency marketing,* focuses on usage rate. One key conclusion emerges about usage: In market segmentation studies, some measurement of usage by, or sales obtained from, various segments is central to the analysis.

The Aberdeen Group recently analyzed which segmentation bases were used by the 20 percent most profitable organizations of the 220 surveyed. From highest to lowest, these were the segmentation bases they used:

- Geographic bases—88 percent.
- Demographic bases—53 percent.
- Behavioral bases—65 percent.
- Psychographic bases—43 percent.

Marketing **Insights About Me**

To Which "Flock" Do You Belong?

There is an old saying that "birds of a feather flock together." This also applies to the formation of market segments and gives rise to the following questions marketers must ask and answer: Who are your target customers? What are they like? Where do they live? How can you reach them?

These questions are answered in part by Nielsen, whose PRIZM® consumer segmentation system classifies every household into one of 66 demographically and behaviorally distinct neighborhood segments to identify lifestyles and purchase behavior within a defined geographic market area, such as zip code. Many organizations today use these neighborhood segments, especially with social media.

Want to know what your neighborhood is like? Go to www.claritas.com/MyBestSegments/Default.jsp and click the "ZIP Code Look-up" link or "Enter ZIP Code" button on the MyBestSegments home page. Then, type in your five-digit zip code and security code. Last, click the "Submit" button to find out what the most common segments are in your neighborhood.

For a description of these segments, click the "Segment Explorer" tab. Is this your "flock"? What specific product or service organizations might be interested in targeting these segments?

24 Up-and-Comers

Upper Mid Younger w/o Kids

Source: The Nielsen Company

The top 20 percent often use more than one of these bases in their market segmentation studies, plus measures such as purchase histories and usage rates of customers.[16]

Experian Simmons continuously surveys over 25,000 adults each year to obtain quarterly, projectable usage rate data from the U.S. national population for more than 500 consumer product categories and 8,000-plus brands. Its purpose is to discover how the products and services they buy and the media they use relate to their behavioral, psychographic, and demographic characteristics.

Patronage of Fast-Food Restaurants   Figure 9–5 shows the results of a question Experian Simmons asked about adult respondents' frequency of use (or patronage)

FIGURE 9–5

Patronage of fast-food restaurants by adults 18 years and older. The table shows the critical importance of attracting heavy users and medium users to a fast-food restaurant.

User or Nonuser	Specific Segment	Number (1,000s)	Percent	Actual Consumption Percent	Usage Index per Person	Importance of Segment
Users	Heavy users (14 + per month)	82,502	36.1%	63.6%	640	High
	Medium users (6–13 per month)	68,634	30.0%	31.4%	380	
	Light users (0–5 per month)	41,264	18.1%	5.0%	100	
Total Users		**192,400**	**84.2%**	**100.0%**	—	
Nonusers	Prospects	2,708	1.2%	—	—	
	Nonprospects	33,459	14.6%	—	—	
Total Nonusers		**36,167**	**15.8%**	—	—	Low
Total	Users + Nonusers	**228,567**	**100.0%**	—	—	

Source: Experian Marketing Services Simmons Winter 2013 NHCS Full-Year Adult Survey 12-Month OneView^{SM} Crosstabulation Report, Experian Marketing Services, 2013. See http://www.experian.com/marketing-services/consumer-insights.html.

245

CHAPTER 9   Market Segmentation, Targeting, and Positioning

of fast-food restaurants.[17] As shown by the arrow in the far right column of Figure 9–5, the importance of the segment increases as we move up the table. Among nonusers of these restaurants, prospects (who might become users) are more important than nonprospects (who are never likely to become users). Moving up the rows to users, it seems logical that light users of these restaurants (0 to 5 times per month) are important but less so than medium users (6 to 13 times per month), who, in turn, are a less important segment than the critical group: heavy users (14 or more times per month). The Actual Consumption column in Figure 9–5 shows how much of the total monthly usage of these restaurants is accounted for by heavy, medium, and light users.

Usage rate is sometimes referred to in terms of the **80/20 rule**, a concept that suggests 80 percent of a firm's sales are obtained from 20 percent of its customers. The percentages in the 80/20 rule are not really fixed at exactly 80 percent and 20 percent, but they suggest that a small fraction of customers provides most of a firm's sales. For example, the orange shading in Figure 9–5 shows that the 36.1 percent of the U.S. population who are heavy users of fast-food restaurants provide 63.6 percent of the actual consumption volume. This high percentage illustrates the situation where one group of customers is responsible for a disproportionately high percentage of sales.

The Usage Index per Person column in Figure 9–5 emphasizes the importance of the heavy-user segment even more. Giving the light users (0 to 5 restaurant visits per month) an index of 100, the heavy users have an index of 640. In other words, for every $1.00 spent by a light user in one of these restaurants in a month, each heavy user spends $6.40. This is the reason that as a Wendy's restaurant owner, you want to focus most of your marketing efforts on reaching the highly attractive heavy-user market segment.

As part of its survey, Experian Simmons asked adults which fast-food restaurant(s) was (were) (1) the sole or only restaurant, (2) the primary one, or (3) one of several secondary ones they patronized. As a Wendy's restaurant owner, the information depicted in Figure 9–6 should give you some ideas in developing a marketing

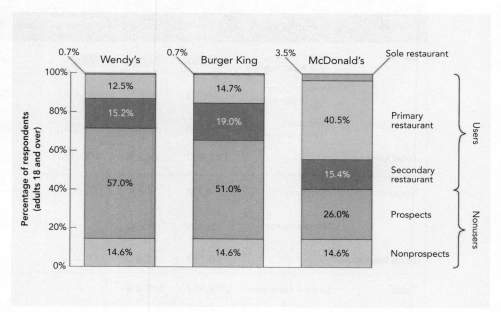

FIGURE 9–6

Comparison of various kinds of users and nonusers for Wendy's, Burger King, and McDonald's fast-food restaurants. This figure gives Wendy's restaurants a snapshot of its customers compared to those of its major competitors.

Source: Experian Marketing Services Simmons Winter 2013 NHCS Full-Year Adult Survey 12-Month OneView^SM Crosstabulation Report, Experian Marketing Services, 2013. See http://www.experian.com/marketing-services/consumer-insights.html.

program for your local market. For example, the Wendy's bar graph in Figure 9–6 shows that your sole (0.7 percent) and primary (12.5 percent) user segments are somewhat behind Burger King and far behind McDonald's. Thus, your challenge is to look at these two competitors and devise a marketing program to win customers from them.

The nonusers part of the Wendy's bar graph in Figure 9–6 shows that 14.6 percent of adult Americans don't go to fast-food restaurants in a typical month and are really nonprospects—unlikely to ever patronize any fast-food restaurant. However, 57.0 percent of nonusers are prospects who may be worth a targeted marketing program. These adults use the product category (fast food) but do not yet patronize Wendy's. New menu items or promotional strategies may succeed in converting these prospects into users that patronize Wendy's.

Variables to Use in Forming Segments for Wendy's   To analyze your Wendy's customers, you need to identify which variables to use to segment them. Because the restaurant is located near a large urban university, the most logical starting point for segmentation is really behavioral: Are the prospective customers students or nonstudents?

To segment the students, you could try a variety of (1) geographic variables, such as city or zip code; (2) demographic variables, such as gender, age, year in school, or college major; or (3) psychographic variables, such as personality or needs. But none of these variables really meets the five criteria listed previously—particularly, the fifth criterion about leading to a doable marketing action to reach the various segments. The behavioral basis of segmentation for the "students" segment really combines two variables: (1) where students live and (2) when they are on campus. This results in four "student" segments:

- Students living in dormitories (residence halls, sororities, fraternities).
- Students living near the university in apartments.
- Day commuter students living outside the area.
- Night commuter students living outside the area.

The three main segments of "nonstudents" include:

- Faculty and staff members who work at the university.
- People who live in the area but aren't connected with the university.
- People who work in the area but aren't connected with the university.

People in each of these nonstudent segments aren't quite as similar as those in the student segments, which makes them harder to reach with a marketing program or action. Think about (1) whether the needs of all these segments are different and (2) how various advertising media can be used to reach these groups effectively.

Ways to Segment Organizational (Business) Markets   A number of variables can be used to segment organizational (business) markets (see Figure 9–7). For example, a product manager at Xerox responsible for its new line of multifunction color printers (MFPs) might use these segmentation bases and corresponding variables:

- *Geographic segmentation: Statistical area.* Firms located in a metropolitan statistical area might receive a personal sales call, whereas those in a micropolitan statistical area might be contacted by telephone.
- *Demographic segmentation: NAICS code.* Firms categorized by the North American Industry Classification System code as manufacturers that deal with customers throughout the world might have different document printing needs than retailers or lawyers serving local customers.

What variables might Xerox use to segment organizational markets to respond to a firm's color copying problems? For the possible answer and related marketing actions, see the text.

Courtesy of Xerox

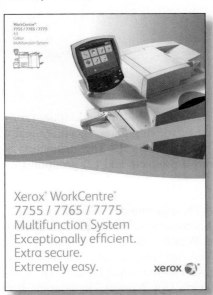

Basis of Segmentation	Segmentation Variables	Typical Breakdowns
Geographic	Global region or country Statistical area Density	European Union, South America, etc.; U.S., Japan, India, etc. Metropolitan and micropolitan statistical areas; Census tract; etc. Urban; suburban; small town; rural
Demographic	NAICS code NAICS sector Number of employees Annual sales	2 digit: sector; 3 digit: subsector; 4 digit: industry group; etc. Agriculture, forestry (11); mining (21); utilities (22); etc. 1–99; 100–499; 500–999; 1,000–4,999; 5,000+ Under $1 million; $1 million–$9.9 million; $10 million–$49.9 million; etc.
Behavioral	Number of locations Kind Where used Application Purchase location Who buys Type of buy	1–9; 10–49; 50–99; 100–499; 500–999; 1,000+ Product; service Installation; component; supplies; etc. Office; production; etc. Centralized; decentralized Individual buyer; industrial buying group New buy; modified rebuy; straight rebuy

FIGURE 9–7

Segmentation bases, variables, and breakdowns for U.S. organizational markets. These variables are used in business-to-business marketing.

- *Demographic segmentation: Number of employees.* The size of the firm is related to the volume of digital documents produced, so firms with varying numbers of employees might be specific target markets for different Xerox MFPs.
- *Behavioral segmentation: Usage rate.* Similar to this segmentation variable for consumer markets, features are often of major importance in organizational markets. So Xerox can target organizations needing fast printing, copying, faxing, and scanning in color—the benefits and features emphasized in the ad for its Xerox Color WorkCentre 7775/7765/7775 Multifunction System.

learning review

9-3. The process of segmenting and targeting markets is a bridge between which two marketing activities?

9-4. What is the difference between the demographic and behavioral bases of market segmentation?

Step 2: Group Products to Be Sold into Categories

Video 9-2

Dave's Hot 'N Juicy Ad

kerin.tv/13e/v9-2

What does your Wendy's restaurant sell? Of course you are selling individual products such as Frostys, hamburgers, and fries. But for marketing purposes you're really selling combinations of individual products that become a "meal." This distinction is critical, so let's discuss both (1) individual Wendy's products and (2) groupings of Wendy's products.

Individual Wendy's Products When Dave Thomas founded Wendy's in 1969, he offered only four basic items: "Hot 'N Juicy" hamburgers, Frosty Dairy Desserts (Frostys), french fries, and soft drinks. Since then, Wendy's has introduced many new products and innovations to compete for customers' fast-food dollars. Some of these are shown in Figure 9–8. New products include salads, low trans fat chicken sandwiches, natural-cut fries with sea salt, and the "Dave's Hot 'N Juicy" hamburger. But

MARKET SEGMENT		PRODUCT OR INNOVATION								
GENERAL	GROUP WITH NEED	HOT 'N JUICY HAMBURGER (1969)	DRIVE-THRU (1970)	99¢ SUPER VALUE MEALS (1989)	SALAD SENSATIONS (2002)	E-PAY (2003)	BREAKFAST SANDWICHES (2007)	NATURAL-CUT FRIES WITH SEA SALT (2010)	DAVE'S HOT 'N JUICY HAMBURGERS (2011)	MY WENDY'S MOBILE APP (2014)
GENDER	Male	P	P	P	S	P	P	P	P	P
	Female				P	P				P
NEEDS	Price/Value			P	S					
	Health-Conscious				P					
	Convenience	S	P		S	P	P		S	P
	Meat Lovers	P		S			S	S	P	
UNIVERSITY AFFILIATION	Affiliated (students, faculty, staff)	P	S	P	P	P	S		P	P
	Nonaffiliated (residents, workers)	S	P	S	S	S	P		S	S

Key: P = Primary market   S = Secondary market

Source: Wendy's International, LLC.

FIGURE 9–8

Wendy's new products and other innovations target specific market segments based on a customer's gender, needs, or university affiliation.

there are also nonproduct innovations to increase consumer convenience like drive-thru services and E-Pay to enable credit card purchases.

Figure 9–8 also shows that each product or innovation is not targeted equally to all market segments based on gender, needs, or university affiliation. The cells in Figure 9–8 labeled "P" represent Wendy's primary target market segments when it introduced each product or innovation. The boxes labeled "S" represent the secondary target market segments that also bought these products or used these innovations. In some cases, Wendy's discovered that large numbers of people in a segment not originally targeted for a particular product or innovation bought or used it anyway.

Groupings of Wendy's Products: Meals Finding a means of grouping the products a firm sells into meaningful categories is as important as grouping customers into segments. If the firm has only one product or service, this isn't a problem. But when it has many, these must be grouped in some way so buyers can relate to them. This is why department stores and supermarkets are organized into product groups, with the departments or aisles containing related merchandise. Likewise, manufacturers organize products into groupings in the catalogs they send to customers.

What are the product groupings for your Wendy's restaurant? It could be the item purchased, such as hamburgers, salads, Frostys, and french fries. This is where judgment—the qualitative aspect of marketing—comes in. Customers really buy an eating experience—a meal occasion that satisfies a need at a particular time of day. So the product groupings that make the most marketing sense are the five "meals" based on the time of day consumers buy them: breakfast, lunch, between-meal snack, dinner, and after-dinner snack. These groupings are more closely related to the way purchases are actually made and permit you to market the entire meal, not just your individual items such as french fries or hamburgers.

Step 3: Develop a Market-Product Grid and Estimate the Size of Markets

Develop a market-product grid to identify a target market and recommend resulting marketing actions.

As noted earlier in the chapter, a market-product grid is a framework to relate the market segments of potential buyers to products offered or potential marketing actions by an organization. In a complete market-product grid analysis, each cell in the grid can show the estimated market size of a given product sold to a specific market segment. Let's first look at forming a market-product grid for your Wendy's restaurant and then estimate market sizes.

Forming a Market-Product Grid for Wendy's   Developing a market-product grid means identifying and labeling the markets (or horizontal rows) and product groupings (or vertical columns), as shown in Figure 9–9. From our earlier discussion, we've chosen to divide the market segments into students versus nonstudents, with subdivisions of each. The columns—or "products"—are really the meals (or eating occasions) customers enjoy at the restaurant.

Estimating Market Sizes for Wendy's   Now the size of the market in each cell (the unique market-product combination) of the market-product grid must be estimated. For your Wendy's restaurant, this involves estimating the sales of each kind of meal expected to be sold to each student and nonstudent market segment.

The market size estimates in Figure 9–9 vary from a large market ("3") to no market at all ("0") for each cell in the market-product grid. These may be simple guesstimates if you don't have the time or money to conduct formal marketing research (as discussed in Chapter 8). But even such crude estimates of the size of specific markets using a market-product grid are helpful in determining which target market segments to select and which product groupings to offer.

FIGURE 9–9

A market-product grid for your Wendy's fast-food restaurant next to an urban university. The numbers in the grid show the estimated size of the market in each cell, which leads to selecting the shaded target market.

MARKET SEGMENTS		PRODUCT OR INNOVATION				
General	Where They Live	Break-fast	Lunch	Between-Meal Snack	Dinner	After-Dinner Snack
Student	Dormitory	0	1	3	0	3
	Apartment	1	3	3	1	1
	Day Commuter	0	3	2	1	0
	Night Commuter	0	0	1	3	2
Nonstudent	Faculty or Staff	0	3	1	1	0
	Live in Area	0	1	2	2	1
	Work in Area	1	3	0	1	0

Key: 3 = Large market; 2 = Medium market; 1 = Small market; and 0 = No market

Wendy's has been aggressive in introducing new menu items to appeal to customers—such as making its classic cheeseburger thicker and offering new premium toppings.

Source: Wendy's International, LLC

Step 4: Select Target Markets

A firm must take care to choose its target market segments carefully. If it picks too narrow a set of segments, it may fail to reach the volume of sales and profits it needs. If it selects too broad a set of segments, it may spread its marketing efforts so thin that the extra expense exceeds the increased sales and profits.

Criteria to Use in Selecting the Target Segments   Two kinds of criteria in the market segmentation process are those used to (1) divide the market into segments (discussed earlier) and (2) actually pick the target segments. Even experienced marketing executives often confuse them. Five criteria can be used to select the target segments for your Wendy's restaurant:

- *Market size.* The estimated size of the market in the segment is an important factor in deciding whether it's worth going after. There is really no market for breakfasts among dormitory students with meal plans, so you should not devote any marketing effort toward reaching this tiny segment. In your market-product grid (Figure 9–9), this market segment is given a "0" to indicate there is no market.
- *Expected growth.* Although the size of the market in the segment may be small now, perhaps it is growing significantly or is expected to grow in the future. Sales of fast-food meals eaten outside the restaurants are projected to exceed those eaten inside. And Wendy's has been shown to be the fast-food leader in average time to serve a drive-thru order—faster than McDonald's. This speed and convenience is potentially very important to night commuters in adult education programs.
- *Competitive position.* Is there a lot of competition in the segment now or is there likely to be in the future? The less the competition, the more attractive the segment is. For example, if the college dormitories announce a new policy of "no meals on weekends," this segment is suddenly more promising for your restaurant. Wendy's recently introduced its "My Wendy's" mobile app for ordering and payments at its restaurants to keep up with a similar service at Burger King.
- *Cost of reaching the segment.* A segment that is inaccessible to a firm's marketing actions should not be pursued. For example, the few nonstudents who live in the area may not be reachable with ads in newspapers or other media. As a result, you should not waste money trying to advertise to them.
- *Compatibility with the organization's objectives and resources.* If your Wendy's restaurant doesn't yet have the cooking equipment to make breakfasts and has a policy against spending more money on restaurant equipment, then don't try to reach the breakfast segment. As is often the case in marketing decisions, a particular segment may appear attractive according to some criteria and very unattractive according to others.

Choose the Wendy's Segments   Ultimately, a marketing executive has to use these criteria to choose the segments for special marketing efforts. As shown in Figure 9–9, let's assume you've written off the breakfast product grouping for two reasons: It's too small a market and it's incompatible with your objectives and resources. In terms of competitive position and cost of reaching the segment, you focus on the four student segments and *not* the three nonstudent segments (although you're certainly not going to turn their business away!). This combination of market-product segments—your target market—is shaded in Figure 9–9.

Step 5: Take Marketing Actions to Reach Target Markets

The purpose of developing a market-product grid is to trigger marketing actions to increase sales and profits. This means that someone must develop and execute an action plan in the form of a marketing program.

Your Immediate Wendy's Segmentation Strategy

With your Wendy's restaurant you've already reached one significant decision: There is a limited market for breakfast, so you won't open for business until 10:30 A.M. In fact, Wendy's first attempt at a breakfast menu was a disaster and was discontinued in 1986. However, that strategy has changed yet again, with its new "fresh made breakfast" menu now being offered in most locations.

Another essential decision is where and what meals to advertise to reach specific market segments. An ad in the student newspaper could reach all the student segments, but it might be too expensive. If you choose three segments for special attention (Figure 9–10), advertising actions to reach them might include:

- *Day commuters* (an entire market segment). Run ads inside commuter buses and put flyers under the windshield wipers of cars in parking lots used by day commuters. These ads and flyers promote all the meals at your restaurant to the day commuter segment of students, a horizontal orange row through the product groupings or "meals" in your market-product grid.
- *Between-meal snacks* (directed to all four student market segments). To promote eating during this downtime for your restaurant, offer "Ten percent off all purchases between 2:00 and 4:30 P.M. during spring semester." This ad promotes a single meal to all four student segments, a vertical blue column through the market-product grid.
- *Dinners to night commuters* (selecting a unique market-product combination). The most focused of all three campaigns, this strategy promotes a single meal to the single segment of night commuter students shaded green. The campaign uses flyers placed under the windshield wipers of cars in

FIGURE 9–10

Advertising actions to market various meals to a range of possible market segments of students.

MARKET SEGMENTS	PRODUCT GROUPINGS: MEAL OCCASION			
Behavioral: Where They Live	Lunch	Between-Meal Snack	Dinner	After-Dinner Snack
Dormitory Students	1	3	0	3
Apartment Students	3	3	1	1
Day Commuter Students	3	2	1	0
Night Commuter Students	0	1	3	2

Ads in buses; flyers under windshield wipers of cars in parking lots

Ad campaign: "10% off all purchases between 2:00 and 4:30 P.M. during spring semester"

Ad on flyer under windshield wipers of cars in night parking lots: "Free Frosty with this coupon when you buy a drive-thru meal between 5:00 and 8:00 P.M."

Key: 3 = Large market; 2 = Medium market; 1 = Small market; and 0 = No market

There's always plenty of competition in the hamburger business. Five Guys Burgers and Fries has grown to more than 1,000 outlets.

© ZUMA Press, Inc./Alamy

parking lots. To encourage eating dinner at Wendy's, offer a free Frosty with the coupon when the person buys a meal between 5 and 8 P.M. using the drive-thru window.

Depending on how your advertising actions work, you can repeat, modify, or drop them and design new campaigns for other segments you deem are worth the effort. This advertising example is just a small piece of a complete marketing program for your Wendy's restaurant.

Keeping an Eye on Competition Competitors will not be sitting still, so in running your Wendy's you must be aware of their strategies as well. McDonald's, for example, is testing a breakfast burrito bowl with kale as an offering for consumers seeking healthier foods. In addition, McDonald's is testing its new home delivery service called "McDelivery" in 88 locations, and it is also testing a hands-free payment app that requires customers simply to say their name. Meanwhile, Burger King tested and then added chicken fries to its year-round menu after a surge in demand for the product, and it stopped advertising soft drinks on its kids menu in response to concerns expressed by parents.[18]

Even new hamburger chains are popping up. In 1986, a Virginia husband-and-wife team started the Five Guys Burgers and Fries hamburger restaurant and 15 years later had only five restaurants in the Washington, D.C., area. But from 2003 to 2015, Five Guys exploded, with more than 1,000 locations nationwide and 1,500 new restaurants planned. Some of its points of difference: simple menu and decor, modest prices, only fresh ground beef (none frozen), and a trans-fat-free menu (cooking with peanut oil). But who's keeping track? The Big Three of McDonald's, Burger King, and Wendy's certainly are.[19]

In addition to competition from traditional hamburger chains like Five Guys, all three are responding aggressively to reach the new "fast-casual" market segment. These customers want healthier food and lower prices in sit-down restaurants—a market segment being successfully targeted by fast-casual restaurants like Chipotle Mexican Grill and Panera Bread.[20]

Finally, a new source of competition is emerging from a variety of chains that aren't necessarily classified as restaurants at all. These include convenience store chains like 7-Eleven, coffee shops like Starbucks, smoothie outlets like Jamba Juice, and gas stations with prepared and reheatable packaged food.[21] Many of these outlets are now selling food items and trying to gain market share from the Big Three.

Future Strategies for Your Wendy's Restaurant Changing customer tastes and competition mean you must alter your strategies when necessary. This involves looking at (1) what Wendy's headquarters is doing, (2) what competitors are doing, and (3) what might be changing in the area served by your restaurant.

Wendy's recently introduced aggressive new marketing programs that include:[22]

- Testing new menu items such as a veggie burger and organic tea for health-conscious consumers.
- Increasing its digital marketing activities through a partnership with Facebook's Global Marketing Services. Recent campaigns included the use of social media to develop lyrics for a song about its new pretzel bun and a script for a movie about the new Tuscan chicken sandwich.

- Offering a beacon-based mobile app in some locations. The free app can detect when a diner who placed an order via a smartphone has arrived at the restaurant.

The Wendy's strategy has been remarkably successful, replacing Burger King as the #2 burger chain in terms of sales behind McDonald's, and it has reported sales growth during a period when McDonald's has experienced declining demand. In addition, a recent *Consumer Reports* survey of the best and worst fast-food restaurants in America ranked Wendy's burgers higher than McDonald's, Burger King, and five other fast-food options.[23]

With these corporate Wendy's plans and new actions from competitors, maybe you'd better rethink your market segmentation decisions on hours of operation. Also, if new businesses have moved into your area, what about a new strategy to reach people that work in the area? Or you might consider a new promotion for the night owls and early birds—the 12 A.M. to 5 A.M. customers.

How has Apple moved from its 1977 Apple II to today's iMac? The Marketing Matters box provides insights.

© SSPL via Getty Images

Video 9-3
Apple's 1984 Super Bowl Ad
kerin.tv/13e/v9-3

What market-product synergies does Apple's iMac satisfy? Read the text to find out.

Source: Apple Inc.

Apple's Ever-Changing Segmentation Strategy

Steve Jobs and Steve Wozniak didn't realize they were developing today's multibillion-dollar PC industry when they invented the Apple I in a garage on April Fool's Day in 1976. However, when the Apple II was displayed at a computer trade show in 1977, consumers loved it and Apple Computer was born. Typical of young companies, Apple focused on its products and had little concern for its markets. Its creative, young engineers were often likened to "Boy Scouts without adult supervision."[24] Yet in 1984 the new Apple Macintosh revolutionized computers, and its 1984 Super Bowl TV ad is generally recognized as the best TV ad in history.

In 1997, Steve Jobs detailed his vision for a reincarnated Apple by describing a new market segmentation strategy that he called the "Apple Product Matrix." This strategy consisted of developing two general types of computer products (desktops and laptops) targeted at two market segments—the consumer and professional sectors.

In most segmentation situations, a single product does not fit into an exclusive market niche. Rather, product lines and market segments overlap. So Apple's market segmentation strategy enables it to offer different products to meet the needs of different market segments, as shown in the Marketing Matters box.

Market-Product Synergies: A Balancing Act

Recognizing opportunities for key synergies—that is, efficiencies—is vital to success in selecting target market segments and making marketing decisions. Market-product grids illustrate where such synergies can be found. How? Let's consider Apple's market-product grid in the Marketing Matters box and examine the difference between marketing synergies and product synergies shown there.

- *Marketing synergies.* Running horizontally across the grid, each row represents an opportunity for efficiency in terms of a market segment. Were Apple to focus on just one group of consumers, such as the medium/large business segment, its marketing efforts could be streamlined. Apple would not have to spend time learning about the buying habits of students or college faculty. So it could probably create a single ad to reach the medium/large business target segment

Apple's Segmentation Strategy—Camp Runamok No Longer

Camp Runamok was the nickname given to Apple in the early 1980s because the innovative company had no coherent series of product lines directed at identifiable market segments. Today, Apple has targeted its various lines of Macintosh computers at specific market segments, as shown in the accompanying market-product grid.

Because the market-product grid shifts as a firm's strategy changes, the one here is based on Apple's product lines in mid-2015. The grid suggests the market segmentation strategy Apple is using to compete in the digital age.

MARKETS		COMPUTER PRODUCTS					
SECTOR	SEGMENT	Mac Pro	MacBook Pro	iMac	MacBook Air	Mac Mini
CONSUMER	Individuals			✓	✓	✓
	Small/ home office		✓	✓	✓	
	Students			✓	✓	✓
	Teachers		✓	✓		
PROFESSIONAL	Medium/ large business	✓	✓	✓	✓	✓
	Creative	✓	✓	✓		
	College faculty		✓	✓	✓	
	College staff			✓	✓	

Source: Apple Inc.

(the yellow row), highlighting the only products it would need to worry about developing: the Mac Pro, the MacBook Pro, the iMac, the MacBook Air, and the Mac mini. Although clearly not Apple's strategy today, new firms often focus only on a single customer segment.

• *Product synergies.* Running vertically down the market-product grid, each column represents an opportunity for efficiency in research and development (R&D) and production. If Apple wanted to simplify its product line, reduce R&D and production expenses, and manufacture only one computer, which might it choose? Based on the market-product grid, Apple might do well to focus on the iMac (the orange column), because every segment purchases it.

Marketing synergies often come at the expense of product synergies because a single customer segment will likely require a variety of products, each of which will have to be designed and manufactured. The company saves money on marketing but spends more on production. Conversely, if product synergies are emphasized, marketing will have to address the concerns of a wide variety of consumers, which costs more time and money. Marketing managers responsible for developing a company's product line must balance both product and marketing synergies as they try to increase the company's profits.

learning review »

9-5. What factor is estimated or measured for each of the cells in a market-product grid?

9-6. What are some criteria used to decide which segments to choose for targets?

9-7. How are marketing and product synergies different in a market-product grid?

POSITIONING THE PRODUCT

LO 9-5 Explain how marketing managers position products in the marketplace.

When a company introduces a new product, a decision critical to its long-term success is how prospective buyers view it in relation to those products offered by its competitors. **Product positioning** refers to the place a product occupies in consumers' minds based on important attributes relative to competitive products. By understanding where consumers see a company's product or brand today, a marketing manager can seek to change its future position in their minds. This requires **product repositioning**, or *changing* the place a product occupies in a consumer's mind relative to competitive products.

Two Approaches to Product Positioning

Marketers follow two main approaches to positioning a new product in the market. *Head-to-head positioning* involves competing directly with competitors on similar product attributes in the same target market. Using this strategy, Dollar Rent A Car competes directly with Avis and Hertz.

Differentiation positioning involves seeking a less-competitive, smaller market niche in which to locate a brand. McDonald's tried to appeal to the health-conscious segment with its low-fat McLean Deluxe hamburger to avoid competing directly with Wendy's and Burger King. But this item was eventually dropped from the menu.

Writing a Positioning Statement

Marketing managers often convert their positioning ideas for the offering into a succinct written positioning statement. The positioning statement is used not only internally within the marketing department, but also for others outside it, such as research and development engineers or advertising agencies.[25] Here is the Volvo positioning statement for the North American market:

For upscale American families who desire a carefree driving experience, Volvo is a premium-priced automobile that offers the utmost in safety and dependability.

This focuses Volvo's North American marketing strategy, so Volvo advertising almost always mentions safety and dependability.

Product Positioning Using Perceptual Maps

A key to positioning a product or brand effectively is discovering the perceptions in the minds of potential customers by taking four steps:

1. Identify the important attributes for a product or brand class.
2. Discover how target customers rate competing products or brands with respect to these attributes.

More "zip" for chocolate milk? The text and Figure 9–11 describe how American dairies have successfully repositioned chocolate milk to appeal to adults.

© Mike Hruby

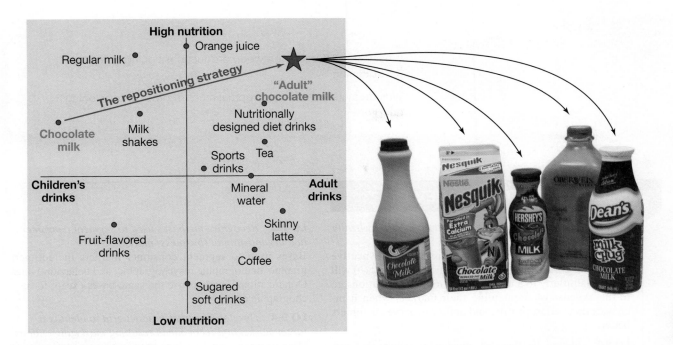

High nutrition

Orange juice

Regular milk

The repositioning strategy

"Adult" chocolate milk

Nutritionally designed diet drinks

Chocolate milk

Milk shakes

Sports drinks

Tea

Children's drinks

Adult drinks

Mineral water

Skinny latte

Fruit-flavored drinks

Coffee

Sugared soft drinks

Low nutrition

FIGURE 9–11

The strategy American dairies are using to reposition chocolate milk to reach adults: Have adults view chocolate milk as both more nutritional and more "adult."

© Mike Hruby

3. Discover where the company's product or brand is on these attributes in the minds of potential customers.
4. Reposition the company's product or brand in the minds of potential customers.

As shown in Figure 9–11, from these data it is possible to develop a **perceptual map**, a means of displaying in two dimensions the location of products or brands in the minds of consumers. This enables a manager to see how consumers perceive competing products or brands, as well as the firm's own product or brand.

A Perceptual Map to Reposition Chocolate Milk for Adults

Recently, U.S. dairies decided to reposition chocolate milk in the minds of American adults to increase its sales. This is how dairies repositioned chocolate milk for American adults using the four steps listed on the previous page:

1. *Identify the important attributes (or scales) for adult drinks.* Research reveals the key attributes adults use to judge various drinks are (*a*) low versus high nutrition and (*b*) children's drinks versus adult drinks, as shown by the two axes in Figure 9–11.
2. *Discover how adults see various competing drinks.* Locate various adult drinks on these axes, as shown in Figure 9–11.
3. *Discover how adults see chocolate milk.* Figure 9–11 shows adults see chocolate milk as moderately nutritious (on the vertical axis) but as mainly a child's drink (on the horizontal axis).
4. *Reposition chocolate milk to make it more appealing to adults.* What actions did U.S. dairies take to increase sales? They repositioned chocolate milk to the location of the red star shown in the perceptual map in Figure 9–11.

The dairies' arguments are nutritionally powerful. For women, chocolate milk provides calcium, critically important in female diets. And dieters get a more filling, nutritious beverage than with a soft drink for about the same calories. The result: Chocolate milk sales increased dramatically, much of it because of adult consumption.[26] Part of this is due to giving chocolate milk "nutritional respectability" for adults, but another part is due to the innovative packaging that enables many new chocolate milk containers to fit in a car's cup holders.

9-8. What is the difference between product positioning and product repositioning?

9-9. Why do marketers use perceptual maps in product positioning decisions?

LEARNING OBJECTIVES REVIEW

LO 9-1 *Explain what market segmentation is and when to use it.*
Market segmentation involves aggregating prospective buyers into groups that (*a*) have common needs and (*b*) will respond similarly to a marketing action. Organizations go to the expense of segmenting their markets when it increases their sales, profits, and ability to serve customers better.

LO 9-2 *Identify the five steps involved in segmenting and targeting markets.*
Step 1 is to group potential buyers into segments. Buyers within a segment should have similar characteristics to each other and respond similarly to marketing actions like a new product or a lower price. Step 2 involves putting related products to be sold into meaningful groups. In step 3, organizations develop a market-product grid with estimated sizes of markets in each of the market-product cells of the resulting table. Step 4 involves selecting the target market segments on which the organization should focus. Finally, step 5 involves taking marketing mix actions—often in the form of a marketing program—to reach the target market segments.

LO 9-3 *Recognize the bases used to segment consumer and organizational (business) markets.*
Bases used to segment consumer markets include geographic, demographic, psychographic, and behavioral ones. Organizational markets use the same bases except for psychographic ones.

LO 9-4 *Develop a market-product grid to identify a target market and recommend resulting marketing actions.*
Organizations use five key criteria to segment markets, whose groupings appear in the rows of the market-product grid. Groups of related products appear in the columns. After estimating the size of the market in each cell in the grid, they select the target market segments on which to focus. They then identify marketing mix actions—often in a marketing program—to reach the target market most efficiently.

LO 9-5 *Explain how marketing managers position products in the marketplace.*
Marketing managers often locate competing products on two-dimensional perceptual maps to visualize the products in the minds of consumers. They then try to position new products or reposition existing products in this space to attain maximum sales and profits.

LEARNING REVIEW ANSWERS

9-1 **Market segmentation involves aggregating prospective buyers into groups that have two key characteristics. What are they?**
Answer: The groups (1) should have common needs and (2) will respond similarly to a marketing action.

9-2 **In terms of market segments and products, what are the three market segmentation strategies?**
Answer: The three market segmentation strategies are: (1) one product and multiple market segments; (2) multiple products and multiple market segments; and (3) "segments of one," or mass customization—the next step beyond build-to-order.

9-3 **The process of segmenting and targeting markets is a bridge between which two marketing activities?**
Answer: identifying market needs and executing the marketing program

9-4 **What is the difference between the demographic and behavioral bases of market segmentation?**
Answer: Demographic segmentation is based on some objective physical (gender, race), measurable (age, income), or other classification attribute (birth era, occupation) of prospective customers.

Behavioral segmentation is based on some observable actions or attitudes by prospective customers—such as where they buy, what benefits they seek, how frequently they buy, and why they buy.

9-5 **What factor is estimated or measured for each of the cells in a market-product grid?**
Answer: Each cell in the grid can show the estimated market size of a given product sold to a specific market segment.

9-6 **What are some criteria used to decide which segments to choose for targets?**
Answer: Possible criteria include market size, expected growth, competitive position, cost of reaching the segment, and compatibility with the organization's objectives and resources.

9-7 **How are marketing and product synergies different in a market-product grid?**
Answer: Marketing synergies run horizontally across a market-product grid. Each row represents an opportunity for efficiency in the marketing efforts to a market segment. Product synergies run vertically down the market-product grid. Each column represents an opportunity for efficiency in

research and development (R&D) and production. Marketing synergies often come at the expense of product synergies because a single customer segment will likely require a variety of products, each of which will have to be designed and manufactured. The company saves money on marketing but spends more on production. Conversely, if product synergies are emphasized, marketing will have to address the concerns of a wide variety of consumers, which costs more time and money.

9-8 What is the difference between product positioning and product repositioning?

Answer: Product positioning refers to the place a product occupies in consumers' minds based on important attributes relative to competitive products. Product repositioning involves changing the place a product occupies in a consumer's mind relative to competitive products.

9-9 Why do marketers use perceptual maps in product positioning decisions?

Answer: Perceptual maps are a means of displaying in two dimensions the location of products or brands in the minds of consumers. Marketers use perceptual maps to see how consumers perceive competing products or brands as well as their own product or brand. Then they can develop marketing actions to move their product or brand to the ideal position.

FOCUSING ON KEY TERMS

80/20 rule p. 246
market segmentation p. 238
market-product grid p. 239
perceptual map p. 257
product differentiation p. 238
product positioning p. 256
product repositioning p. 256
usage rate p. 244

APPLYING MARKETING KNOWLEDGE

1 What variables might be used to segment these consumer markets? (*a*) lawn mowers, (*b*) frozen dinners, (*c*) dry breakfast cereals, and (*d*) soft drinks.

2 What variables might be used to segment these industrial markets? (*a*) industrial sweepers, (*b*) photocopiers, (*c*) computerized production control systems, and (*d*) car rental agencies.

3 In Figure 9–9, the dormitory market segment includes students living in college-owned residence halls, sororities, and fraternities. What market needs are common to these students that justify combining them into a single segment in studying the market for your Wendy's restaurant?

4 You may disagree with the estimates of market size given for the rows in the market-product grid in Figure 9–9. Estimate the market size, and give a brief justification for these market segments: (*a*) dormitory students, (*b*) day commuters, and (*c*) people who work in the area.

5 Suppose you want to increase revenues for your fast-food restaurant even further. Referring to Figure 9–10, what advertising actions might you take to increase revenues from (*a*) dormitory students, (*b*) dinners, and (*c*) after-dinner snacks consumed by night commuter students?

6 Locate these drinks on the perceptual map in Figure 9–11: (*a*) cappuccino, (*b*) beer, and (*c*) soy milk.

BUILDING YOUR MARKETING PLAN

Your marketing plan needs a market-product grid to (*a*) focus your marketing efforts and (*b*) help you create a forecast of sales for the company. Use these steps:

1 Define the market segments (the rows in your grid) using the bases of segmentation used to segment consumer and organizational markets.

2 Define the groupings of related products (the columns in your grid).

3 Form your grid and estimate the size of the market in each market-product cell.

4 Select the target market segments on which to focus your efforts with your marketing program.

5 Use the information and the lost-horse forecasting technique (discussed in Chapter 8) to make a sales forecast (company forecast).

6 Draft your positioning statement.

Video 9-4
Prince Sports
Video Case
kerin.tv/13e/v9-4

"Over the last decade we've seen a dramatic change in the media to reach consumers," says Linda Glassel, vice president of sports marketing and brand image of Prince Sports, Inc.

PRINCE SPORTS IN TODAY'S CHANGING WORLD

"Today—particularly in reaching younger consumers—we're now focusing so much more on social marketing and social networks, be it Facebook, Twitter, or internationally with Hi5, Bebo, and Orkut," she adds.

Linda Glassel's comments are a snapshot look at what Prince Sports faces in the changing world of tennis in the 21st century.

Prince Sports is a racquet sports company whose portfolio of brands includes Prince (tennis, squash, and badminton), Ektelon (racquetball), and Viking (platform/paddle tennis). Its complete line of tennis products alone is astounding: more than 150 racquet models; more than 50 tennis strings; over 50 footwear models; and countless types of bags, apparel, and other accessories.

Prince prides itself on its history of innovation in tennis—including inventing the first "oversize" and "longbody" racquets, the first "synthetic gut" tennis string, and the first "Natural Foot Shape" tennis shoe. Its challenge today is to continue to innovate to meet the needs of all levels of tennis players.

"One favorable thing for Prince these days is the dramatic growth in tennis participation—higher than it's been in many years," says Nick Skally, senior marketing manager. A recent study by the Sporting Goods Manufacturers Association confirms this point: Tennis participation in the United States was up 43 percent—the fastest-growing traditional individual sport in the country.

TAMING TECHNOLOGY TO MEET PLAYERS' NEEDS

Every tennis player wants the same thing: to play better. But they don't all have the same skills, or the same ability to swing a racquet fast. So adult tennis players fall very broadly into three groups, each with special needs:

- *Those with shorter, slower strokes.* They want maximum power in a lightweight frame.
- *Those with moderate to full strokes.* They want the perfect blend of power and control.
- *Those with longer, faster strokes.* They want greater control with less power.

To satisfy all these needs in one racquet is a big order.

"When we design tennis racquets, it involves an extensive amount of market research on players at all levels," explains Tyler Herring, global business director for performance tennis racquets. Prince's research led it to introduce its breakthrough O^3 technology. "Our O^3 technology solved an inherent contradiction between racquet speed and sweet spot," he says. Never before had a racquet been designed that simultaneously delivers faster racquet speed with a dramatically increased "sweet spot." The "sweet spot" in a racquet is the middle of the frame that gives the most power and consistency when hitting. Recently, Prince introduced its latest evolution of the O^3 platform called EXO^3. Its newly patented design suspends the string bed from the racquet frame—thereby increasing the sweet spot by up to 83 percent while reducing frame vibration up to 50 percent.

SEGMENTING THE TENNIS MARKET

"The three primary market segments for our tennis racquets are our performance line, our recreational line, and our junior line," says Herring. He explains that within each of these segments Prince makes difficult design trade-offs to balance (1) the price a player is willing to pay, (2) what playing features (speed versus spin, sweet spot versus control, and so on) they want, and (3) what technology can be built into the racquet for the price point.

Within each of these three primary market segments, there are at least two subsegments—sometimes overlapping! Figure 1 gives an overview of Prince's market segmentation strategy and identifies sample racquet models. The three right-hand columns show the design variations of length, unstrung weight, and head size. The figure shows the complexities Prince faces in converting its technology into a racquet with physical features that satisfy players' needs.

MARKET SEGMENTS				PRODUCT FEATURES IN RACQUET		
Main Segments	Subsegments	Segment Characteristics (Skill level, age)	Brand Name	Length (Inches)	Unstrung Weight (Ounces)	Head Size (Sq. in.)
Performance	Precision	For touring professional players wanting great feel, control, and spin	EXO³ Ignite 95	27.0	11.8	95
	Thunder	For competitive players wanting a bigger sweet spot and added power	EXO³ Red 95	27.25	9.9	105
Recreational	Small head size	For players looking for a forgiving racquet with added control	AirO Lightning MP	27.0	9.9	100
	Larger head size	For players looking for a larger sweet spot and added power	AirO Maria Lite OS	27.0	9.7	110
Junior	More experienced young players	For ages 8 to 15; somewhat shorter and lighter racquets than high school or adult players	AirO Team Maria 23	23.0	8.1	100
	Beginner	For ages 5 to 11; much shorter and lighter racquets; tennis balls with 50% to 75% less speed for young beginners	Air Team Maria 19	19.0	7.1	82

FIGURE 1

Prince targets racquets at specific market segments.

DISTRIBUTION AND PROMOTION STRATEGIES

"Prince has a number of different distribution channels—from mass merchants like Walmart and Target, to sporting goods chains, to smaller specialty tennis shops," says Nick Skally. For the large chains, Prince contributes co-op advertising for its in-store circulars, point-of-purchase displays, in-store signage, consumer brochures, and even "space planograms" to help the retailer plan the layout of Prince products in its tennis area. Prince aids for small tennis specialty shops include a supply of demo racquets, detailed catalogs, posters, racquet and string guides, merchandising fixtures, and hardware, such as racquet hooks and footwear

© Consumer Trends/Alamy

shelves, in addition to other items. Prince also provides these shops with "player standees," which are corregated life-size cutouts of professional tennis players.

Prince reaches tennis players directly through its website (www.princetennis.com), which gives product information, tennis tips, and the latest tennis news. Besides using social networks like Facebook and Twitter, Prince runs ads in regional and national tennis publications and develops advertising campaigns for online sites and broadcast outlets.

In addition to its in-store activities, advertising, and online marketing, Prince invests heavily in its Teaching Pro program. These sponsored teaching pros receive all the latest product information, demo racquets, and equipment from Prince, so they can truly be Prince ambassadors in their community. Aside from their regular lessons, instructors and teaching professionals hold local "Prince Demo events" around the country to give potential customers a hands-on opportunity to see and try various Prince racquets, strings, and grips.

Prince also sponsors over 100 professional tennis players who appear in marquee events such as the four Grand Slam tournaments (Wimbledon and the Australian, French, and U.S. Opens). TV viewers can watch Russia's Maria Sharapova walk onto a tennis court carrying a Prince racquet bag or France's Gael Monfils hit a service ace using his Prince racquet.

Where is Prince headed in the 21st century? "As a marketer, one of the biggest challenges is staying ahead of the curve," says Glassel. And she stresses, "It's learning, it's studying, it's talking to people who understand where the market is going."[27]

Questions

1 In the 21st century what trends in the environmental forces (social, economic, technological, competitive, and regulatory) (*a*) work for and (*b*) work against success for Prince Sports in the tennis industry?

2 Because sales of Prince Sports in tennis-related products depends heavily on growth of the tennis industry, what marketing activities might it use in the United States to promote tennis playing?

3 What promotional activities might Prince use to reach (*a*) recreational players and (*b*) junior players?

4 What might Prince do to gain distribution and sales in (*a*) mass merchandisers like Target and Walmart and (*b*) specialty tennis shops?

5 In reaching global markets outside the United States (*a*) what are some criteria that Prince should use to select countries in which to market aggressively, (*b*) what three or four countries meet these criteria best, and (*c*) what are some marketing actions Prince might use to reach these markets?

Chapter Notes

1. Tony Hsieh, *Delivering Happiness* (New York: Hatchette Book Group, 2010); Kimberly Weisal, "A Shine in Their Shoes," *BusinessWeek,* December 5, 2005, p. 84; and information from the "About Zappos" section of the Zappos.com website.

2. Deborah L. Cowles, Jan P. Owens, and Kristen L Walker, "Ensuring a Good Fit: Fortifying Zappos' Customer Service and User Experience," *International Journal of Integrated Marketing Communications,* Fall 2013, pp. 57–66; Dinah Eng, "Zappos's Silent Founder," *Fortune,* September 3, 2012, pp. 19–22; Jeffrey M. O'Brien, "Zappos Knows How to Kick It," *Fortune,* February 2, 2009, pp. 55–60; and Max Chafkin, Get Happy," *Inc.,* May 2009, pp. 66–71.

3. Chris Paradixo, "Improving Customer Experience with Digital Marketing," *Insurance Advocate,* December 22, 2014, p. 18; and Kimberly Weisal, "A Shine in Their Shoes."

4. Duff McDonald, "Zappos.com: Success through Simplicity," CIO-*Insight,* November 10, 2006.

5. Jon Wolske, "Ten Core Values Drive Zappos," *Credit Union Magazine,* July 2014, p. 12; Jena McGregor, "Zappos' Secret: It's an Open Book," *Bloomberg Businessweek,* March 23 and 30, 2009, p. 62; and Jeffrey M. O'Brien, "The 10 Commandments of Zappos," *Fortune,* January 22, 2009; see http:// money.cnn.com/2009/01/21/news/companies/ obrien_zappos10.fortune and Zappos.com.

6. Motoko Rich, "Why Is This Man Smiling?" *The New York Times,* April 10, 2011, pp. ST1, ST10; Christopher Palmeri, "Now for Sale, the Zappos Culture," *Bloomberg Businessweek,* January 11, 2010, p. 57.

7. Natalie Zmuda, "Marketer of the Year: Zappos," *Advertising Age,* October 20, 2008, p. 36.

8. Eric N. Berkowitz, Roger A. Kerin, and William Rudelius, *Marketing* (St. Louis, MO: Times Mirror/Mosby College Publishing, 1986), pp. 189–91; Sleep Research Institute, the National Sleep Foundation, and the International Sleep Products Association (March 20, 2007); and Frederick G. Crane, Roger A. Kerin, Steven W. Hartley, and William Rudelius, *Marketing,*

8th Canadian ed. (Toronto, Canada: McGraw-Hill Ryerson Ltd., 2011), pp. 229–32.

9. Ellen Byron, "As Middle Class Shrinks, P&G Aims High and Low," *The Wall Street Journal,* September 12, 2011, pp. A1, A16; Ellen Byron, "P&G Puts Spotlight on Newer Products," *The Wall Street Journal,* October 21, 2010, pp. B1, B2; Anthony Bianco, "The Vanishing Mass Market," *BusinessWeek,* July 12, 2004, pp. 61–65; and Geoff Colvin, "Selling P&G," *Fortune,* September 17, 2007, pp. 163–69.

10. John Patrick Pullen, "Hey, Millennials: Here's Where You Can Stream Your Favorite Movies," *Time.com,* April 29, 2015; John Stone, "Disney's Grand Adventure," *Travel Agent,* November 17, 2014, pp. 38, 40; and Jeffrey A. Trachtenberg and Ann Paul Sonne, "Rowling Casts E-Book Spell," *The Wall Street Journal,* June 24, 2011, pp. B1, B2.

11. James Cook, "Where's the Niche?" *Forbes,* September 24, 1984, p. 54.

12. "Company Timeline," Ford website, http://corporate.ford. com/company/history.html, accessed June 7, 2015; J. P. Donlon, "The Road Ahead," *Chief Executive,* July/August, 2011, pp. 31–37; "Epiphany in Dearborn," *The Economist,* December 11, 2010, pp. 72–74; and Bill Saporito, "How to Make Cars and Make Money Too," *Time,* August 9, 2010, pp. 36–39.

13. 2010 *Ann Taylor Annual Report* and selected press releases.

14. "Discounters Aim to Extend Reach with Small Formats," *Chain Drug Review,* April 27, 2105, p. 75; Jonathan Hipp, "The Strategy behind Walmart Neighborhood Market Stores," GlobeSt.com, http://www.globest.com/blogs/netleaseinsider/netlease/ The-Strategy-Behind-Walmart-Neighborhood-Market-Stores-358653-1.html, June 5, 2015; and Ann D'Innocenzio, "Wal-Mart to Accelerate Small Store Growth," *Associated Press,* October 10, 2012.

15. The relation of these criteria to implementation is discussed in Jacqueline Dawley, "Making Connections: Enhance the Implementation of Value of Attitude-Based Segmentation," *Marketing Research,* Summer 2006, pp. 16–22.

16. Ian Michiels, "Customer Analytics: Segmentation beyond Demographics," *The Aberdeen Group,* August 2008, p. 11.

17. The discussion of fast-food trends and market share is based on Experian Simmons Fall 2012 NCS/NHCS Full-Year Adult Survey 12 OneView^SM Crosstabulation Report © Experian Simmons 2013. See http://www.experian.com/simmons-research/consumer-study.html.

18. Phil Wahba, "McDonald's Testing Kale Months After Mocking It in Ad," *Fortune.com,* April 14, 2015; Leena Rao, "Google Is Testing Hands-free Payments with McDonald's and Papa Johns," *Time.com,* June 1, 2015; Patricia Odel, "McDonald's Tests McDelivery Home Delivery Service," *Promotional Marketing,* April 5, 2015, p. 1; and Benjamin Snyder, "Burger King Is Keeping This Popular Food on the Menu Year-round," *Fortune.com,* April 1, 2015.

19. Jack Dickey and Bill Saporito, "Beefed Up," *Time,* February 23, 2015, pp. 56–62; and "About Us," Five Guys Burger and Fries website, http://www.fiveguys.com/about-us.aspx, accessed June 8, 2015.

20. Justin Fox, "The Once but Not Future Burger," *Bloomberg Businessweek,* May 4, 2015, pp. 14–15; Julie Jargon, "Fast Food Aspires to Move Up the Food Chain," *The Wall Street Journal,* October 11, 2012, p. B11; Josh Sanburn, "Fast-Casual Nation," *Time,* April 23, 2012, pp. 60–61; Don Jacobson, "Fast-Casual Restaurants Are Just What Landlords Ordered," *Star Tribune,* January 20, 2012, p. D5; Tiffany Hsu, "Fast, Casual, Trendy," *Star Tribune,* January 5, 2012, pp. D1, D3; and Al Reis, "Viewpoint," *Advertising Age,* January 20, 2011, p. 16.

21. Keith O'Brien, "Supersize," *The New York Times Magazine,* May 6, 2012, pp. 44–48; and "A Look Ahead: 2011–Fast Food," *Advertising Age,* January 20, 2011, p. 4.

22. Victor Luckerson, "Wendy's Is Testing Out a Veggie Burger," *Time.com,* May 7, 2015; Maureen Morrison, "Wendy's Has No Beef with Its Latest Creative Consultant—Facebook," *Advertising Age,* October 13, 2014, p. 1; and "Wendy's Takes Ordering Next Level," *Restaurant Business,* March 2015, p. 18.

23. Dan Mitchell, "Here Is What's Going On with All Your Favorite Fast Food Chains," *Time.com,* May 7, 2015; "Best and Worst Fast-Food Restaurants in America," *ConsumerReports.org,* http://www.consumerreports.org/cro/magazine/2014/08/best-and-worst-fast-food-restaurants-inamerica/index.htm#, July 2014; and Trefis Team, "Key Trends Impacting Burger King's Business," *Forbes.com,* July 1, 2014.

24. The discussion of Apple's segmentation strategies through the years is based on information from its website, www.apple.com and www.apple-history.com/history.html.

25. Much of the discussion about positioning and perceptual maps is based on Roger A. Kerin and Robert A. Peterson, *Strategic Marketing Problems: Cases and Comments,* 13th ed. (Upper Saddle River, NJ: Prentice Hall, 2012), pp. 146–47; and John M. Mullins, Orville C. Walker Jr., and Harper W. Boyd Jr., *Marketing Management: A Strategic Decision-Marketing Approach,* 7th ed. (New York: McGraw-Hill/Irwin, 2010), p. 202.

26. Nicholas Zamiska, "How Milk Got a Major Boost by Food Panel," *The Wall Street Journal,* August 30, 2004, pp. B1, B5; and Rebecca Winter, "Chocolate Milk," *Time,* April 30, 2001, p. 20.

27. Prince Sports: This case was written by William Rudelius and is based on personal interviews with Linda Glassel, Tyler Herring, and Nick Skally.

10 Developing New Products and Services

LEARNING OBJECTIVES

After reading this chapter you should be able to:

LO 10-1 Recognize the various terms that pertain to products and services.

LO 10-2 Identify the ways in which consumer and business products and services can be classified.

LO 10-3 Explain the significance of "newness" in new products and services as it relates to the degree of consumer learning involved.

LO 10-4 Describe the factors contributing to the success or failure of a new product or service.

LO 10-5 Explain the purposes of each step of the new-product development process.

Apple: The World-Class New-Product Machine

How does a company become the most admired *and* financially valuable organization in the world? Just look to Apple Inc. and its legendary product innovations that have touched the lives of people on every continent for 40 years.

Apple's New-Product Development Successes . . .

Apple's new-product successes, orchestrated by its late co-founder, Steve Jobs, revolutionized five different industries: personal computing, music, smartphones, tablet computing, and digital publishing. A sampling of Apple's market-changing innovations includes:

- Apple II—the first commercial personal computer (1977).

- Macintosh—the first personal computer with a mouse and a graphical user interface (1984).

- iPod—the first and most successful MP3 music player (2001).

- iPhone—the world's best multi-touch smartphone and media player with almost 1 million apps (2007).

- iPad (2010) and iPad mini (2012)—the thin tablet devices that allow users to read books, newspapers, magazines, and even textbooks.

- CarPlay—a device that allows you to use your iPhone while driving your car to make calls, listen to music, and access messages by voice or touch (2014).

. . . and New-Product Development Stumbles

But Apple has stumbled at times too in its relentless pursuit of innovation. Examples of notable failures are:

- Apple III (1980) and Apple Lisa (1983)—two products intended for business users failed due to design flaws. Each product was discontinued four years after introduction.

- Apple Newton (1987)—a personal digital assistant (PDA) that featured handwriting recognition software. Newton was discontinued 10 years later because of its limited battery life and hard-to-read screen.

- Macintosh Portable (1989)—Apple's first attempt to create a battery-powered portable computer. Its high price coupled with an "un-portable" weight of 16 pounds led to its demise two years later.

- "Hockey Puck" Mouse (1998)—the first commercially released Apple Mouse to use a USB connection. The mouse's round shape made it difficult to hold and use. It was discontinued in 2000.

These examples illustrate that new-product development is a challenge, even for Apple. Apple learned from each stumble and applied valuable insights from failure to produce subsequent successes. In short, when a new-product development effort fails, Apple fails wisely. For example, the Macintosh was born from the failure of Apple Lisa. Apple's iPhone was a direct result of Apple's failed original music phone, produced in conjunction with Motorola.

The Next Chapter in Apple's Story: Apple Watch

In 2015, Apple introduced the Apple Watch, the most advanced piece of wearable technology in the marketplace. Apple Watch is the company's first all-new product since the iPad in 2010. According to Tim Cook, Apple's chief executive officer and hand-picked successor to Steve Jobs, "The Apple Watch is the next chapter in Apple's story," adding that it is "the most personal device we have ever created." The Apple Watch is positioned as a jack-of-all-trades, capable of tracking activity, delivering and receiving messages, reminding users of appointments, and creating a platform for new Apple software and services. And yes, an Apple Watch will also give its user the time of day across the country or around the globe. With prices starting at $349 and climbing to $17,000 for a gold-encased model, Apple Watch is viewed as a must-have smartwatch and a bona fide luxury item. Will Apple Watch achieve the success of so many earlier innovations? Only time will tell.

The life of an organization depends on how it conceives, produces, and markets *new* products and services. This chapter describes the nature of products and services, highlights why new products succeed or fail, and details the new-product development process. Chapter 11 will discuss how organizations manage *existing* products, services, and brands.[1]

WHAT ARE PRODUCTS AND SERVICES?

The essence of marketing is in developing products and services to meet buyer needs. A **product** is a good, service, or idea consisting of a bundle of tangible and intangible attributes that satisfies consumers' needs and is received in exchange for money or something else of value. Let's clarify the meanings of goods, services, and ideas.

A Look at Goods, Services, and Ideas

Nondurable goods like chewing gum are easily consumed and rely on consumer advertising.
© Mike Hruby

A *good* has tangible attributes that a consumer's five senses can perceive. For example, the Apple Watch can be touched and its features can be seen and heard. A good also may have intangible attributes consisting of its delivery or warranties and embody more abstract concepts, such as becoming healthier or wealthier. Goods also can be divided into nondurable goods and durable goods. A *nondurable* good is an item consumed in one or a few uses, such as food products and fuel. A *durable* good is one that usually lasts over many uses, such as appliances, cars, and smartphones. This classification method also provides direction for marketing actions. For example, nondurable goods, such as Wrigley's gum, rely heavily on consumer advertising. In contrast, costly durable goods, such as cars, generally emphasize personal selling.

Services are intangible activities or benefits that an organization provides to satisfy consumers' needs in exchange for money or something else of value. Services have become a significant part of the U.S. economy, and often augment products. For example, a product is Apple's iPhone 6 and iPhone 6 Plus, and Verizon is a wireless network.

Finally, in marketing, an *idea* is a thought that leads to a product or action, such as a concept for a new invention or getting people out to vote.

Throughout this book, *product* generally includes not only physical goods but services and ideas as well. When *product* is used in its narrower meaning of "goods," it should be clear from the example or sentence.

Classifying Products

Two broad categories of products widely used in marketing relate to the type of user. **Consumer products** are products purchased by the ultimate consumer, whereas **business products** (also called *B2B products* or *industrial products*) are products organizations buy that assist in providing other products for resale. Some products can be considered both consumer and business items. For example, an Apple iMac computer can be sold to consumers for personal use or to business firms for office use. Each classification results in different marketing actions. Viewed as a consumer product, the iMac would be sold through Apple's retail stores or directly from its online store. As a business product, an Apple salesperson might contact a firm's purchasing department directly and offer discounts for large volume purchases.

Consumer Products The four types of consumer products shown in Figure 10–1 differ in terms of (1) the effort the consumer spends on the decision, (2) the attributes used in making the purchase decision, and (3) the frequency of purchase. **Convenience products** are items that the consumer purchases frequently, conveniently, and with a minimum of shopping effort. **Shopping products** are items for which the consumer compares several alternatives on criteria such as price, quality, or style. **Specialty products** are items that the consumer makes a special effort to search out and buy. **Unsought products** are items that the consumer does not know about or knows about but does not initially want.

Figure 10–1 shows how each type of consumer product stresses different marketing mix actions, degrees of brand loyalty, and shopping effort. But how a consumer product is classified depends on the individual. One consumer may view a camera as a shopping

BASIS OF COMPARISON	CONVENIENCE PRODUCT	SHOPPING PRODUCT	SPECIALTY PRODUCT	UNSOUGHT PRODUCT
Product	Toothpaste, cake mix, hand soap, ATM cash withdrawal	Cameras, TVs, briefcases, airline tickets	Rolls-Royce cars, Rolex watches, heart surgery	Burial insurance, thesaurus
Price	Relatively inexpensive	Fairly expensive	Usually very expensive	Varies
Place (distribution)	Widespread; many outlets	Large number of selective outlets	Very limited	Often limited
Promotion	Price, availability, and awareness stressed	Differentiation from competitors stressed	Uniqueness of brand and status stressed	Awareness is essential
Brand loyalty of consumers	Aware of brand but will accept substitutes	Prefer specific brands but will accept substitutes	Very brand loyal; will not accept substitutes	Will accept substitutes
Purchase behavior of consumers	Frequent purchases; little time and effort spent shopping	Infrequent purchases; needs much comparison shopping time	Infrequent purchases; needs extensive search and decision time	Very infrequent purchases; some comparison shopping

FIGURE 10–1

How a consumer product is classified significantly affects which products consumers buy and the marketing strategies used.

product and visit several stores before deciding on a brand, whereas another consumer may view a camera as a specialty product and make a special effort to buy only a Nikon.

Business Products A major characteristic of business products is that their sales are often the result of *derived demand;* that is, sales of business products frequently result (or are derived) from the sale of consumer products. For example, as consumer demand for Ford cars (a consumer product) increases, the company may increase its demand for paint spraying equipment (a business product).

Business products may be classified as components or support products. *Components* are items that become part of the final product. These include raw materials such as lumber, as well as assemblies such as a Ford car engine. *Support products* are items used to assist in producing other products and services. These include:

- *Installations,* such as buildings and fixed equipment.
- *Accessory equipment,* such as tools and office equipment.
- *Supplies,* such as stationery, paper clips, and brooms.
- *Industrial services,* such as maintenance, repair, and legal services.

Strategies to market business products reflect both the complexities of the product involved (paper clips versus private jets) and the buy-class situations discussed in Chapter 6.

Classifying Services

Services can be classified according to whether they are delivered by (1) people or equipment, (2) business firms or nonprofit organizations, or (3) government agencies. These classifications are more thoroughly discussed in Chapter 12.

Product Classes, Forms, Items, Lines, and Mixes

What company cheerfully tells its customers to "Have a crappy day"? Read the text to find out about this "tasty" offering!
Source: Brainstorm Bakery

Most organizations offer a range of products and services to consumers. Each set of offerings can be categorized according to the *product class* or industry to which they belong, like the iPad, which is classified as a tablet device. Products can exist in various *product forms* within a product class (see Chapters 2 and 11). A **product item** is a specific product that has a unique brand, size, or price. For example, Ultra Downy softener for clothes comes in different forms (liquid for the washer and sheets for the dryer) and load sizes (40, 60, etc.). Each of the different product items represents a separate *stock keeping unit (SKU),* which is a unique identification number that defines an item for ordering or inventory purposes.

A **product line** is a group of product or service items that are closely related because they satisfy a class of needs, are used together, are sold to the same customer group, are distributed through the same outlets, or fall within a given price range. Nike's product lines include shoes and clothing, whereas the Mayo Clinic's service lines consist of inpatient hospital care and outpatient physician services. Each product line has its own marketing strategy.

The "Crapola Granola" product line started as an edgy party joke from Brian and Andrea Strom, owners of tiny Brainstorm Bakery.[2] The dried **CR**anberries and **AP**ples gran**OLA**—hence the "Crapola" name—also contains nuts and five organic grains sweetened with maple syrup and honey. Its package promises that Crapola "Makes Even Weird People Regular."

Crapola is sold in retail outlets in the Midwest, California, and Oregon as well as online at www.crapola.us. The Stroms have a strategy of developing Crapola into a broader product line. Currently, they offer three other recipes: "Number Two," Colonial Times, and Kissypoo. These product line extensions enable both consumers and retailers to simplify their buying decisions. So if a family has a good experience with Crapola, it might buy another product in the line. With a more extensive product line, the Stroms may manage to obtain distribution and shelf space in supermarket chains, which strive to increase efficiencies by dealing with fewer suppliers.

Many firms offer a **product mix**, which consists of all of the product lines offered by an organization. For example, Cray Inc. has a small product mix of three product lines (supercomputers, storage systems, and a "data appliance") that are sold mostly to governments and large businesses. Procter & Gamble, however, has a large product mix that includes product lines such as beauty and grooming (Crest toothpaste and Gillette razors) and household care (Downy fabric softener, Tide detergent, and Pampers diapers).

learning review »

10-1. What are the four main types of consumer products?

10-2. What is the difference between a product line and a product mix?

NEW PRODUCTS AND WHY THEY SUCCEED OR FAIL

LO 10-3 Explain the significance of "newness" in new products and services as it relates to the degree of consumer learning involved.

New products are the lifeblood of a company and keep it growing, but the financial risks can be large. Before discussing how new products reach the market, we'll begin by looking at *what* a new product is.

What Is a New Product?

The term *new* is difficult to define. Is Sony's PlayStation 4 *new* when there is already a PlayStation 3? Perhaps—because the PS4, Nintendo's Wii U, and Microsoft's new Xbox One will all position their consoles as entertainment "hubs" rather than just

Marketing **Matters**

Feature Bloat: Geek Squad to the Rescue!

Adding more features to a product to satisfy more consumers seems like a no-brainer strategy for success. Right?

Feature Bloat

In fact, most marketing research with potential buyers of a product shows that while they *say* they want more features, in actuality they are overwhelmed with the mind-boggling complexity—or "feature bloat"—of some new products.

Computers pose a special problem for home users because there's no in-house technical assistance like that existing in large organizations. Ever call the manufacturer's toll-free "help" line? One survey showed that 29 percent of the callers swore at the customer service representative and 21 percent just screamed.

© Dino Vournas/AP Images

Geek Squad to the Rescue

Computer feature bloat has given rise to what TV's *60 Minutes* says is "the multibillion-dollar service industry populated by the very people who used to be shunned in the high school cafeteria: Geeks like Robert Stephens!"

More than a decade ago he turned his geekiness into the Geek Squad—a group of technically savvy people who can fix almost any computer problem.

"The biggest complaint about tech support people is rude, egotistical behavior," says Stephens. So he launched the Geek Squad to show some friendly humility by having team members work their wizardry while:

1. Showing genuine concern to customers.
2. Dressing in geeky white shirts, black clip-on ties, and white socks, a "uniform" borrowed from NASA engineers.
3. Driving to customer homes or offices in black-and-white VW "geekmobiles."

Do customers appreciate the 20,000-person Geek Squad, now owned by Best Buy? Robert Stephens answers by explaining, "People will say, 'They saved me . . . they saved my data.'" These people include countless college students working on their papers or theses with data lost somewhere in their computers— "data they promised themselves they'd back up next week."

See the video case that concludes Chapter 3 for more on the Geek Squad.

game consoles. What does *new* mean for new-product marketing? Newness from several points of view are discussed next.

Newness Compared with Existing Products   If a product is functionally different from existing products, it can be defined as new. Sometimes this newness is revolutionary and creates a whole new industry, as in the case of the Apple II computer. At other times more features are added to an existing product to try to appeal to more customers. And as HDTVs, smartphones, and tablet devices become more sophisticated, consumers' lives get far more complicated. This proliferation of extra features—sometimes called "feature bloat"—overwhelms many consumers. The Marketing Matters box describes how founder Robert Stephens launched his Geek Squad to address the rise of feature bloat.[3]

Newness from the Consumer's Perspective   A second way to define new products is in terms of their effects on consumption. This approach classifies new products according to the degree of learning required by the consumer, as shown in Figure 10–2.

With a *continuous innovation*, consumers don't need to learn new behaviors. Toothpaste manufacturers can add new attributes or features like "whitens teeth" or "removes plaque" when they introduce a new or improved product, such as Colgate Total Advanced Gum Defense toothpaste. But the extra features in the new toothpaste do not require buyers to learn new tooth-brushing behaviors, so it is a continuous innovation.

BASIS OF COMPARISON	CONTINUOUS INNOVATION	DYNAMICALLY CONTINUOUS INNOVATION	DISCONTINUOUS INNOVATION
	LOW ← Degree of New Consumer Learning Needed → **HIGH**		
Definition	Requires no new learning by consumers	Disrupts consumer's normal routine but does not require totally new learning	Requires new learning and consumption patterns by consumers
Examples	New improved shaver, detergent, and toothpaste	Electric toothbrush, LED HDTVs, and smartphones	Wireless router, digital video recorder, and electric car
Marketing strategy	Gain consumer awareness and wide distribution	Advertise points of difference and benefits to consumers	Educate consumers through product trial and personal selling

FIGURE 10–2

The degree of "newness" in a new product affects the amount of learning effort consumers must exert to use the product and the resulting marketing strategy.

The text describes the potential benefits and dangers of an incremental innovation such as Purina's Elegant Medleys, its restaurant-inspired food for cats.
Source: Nestlé

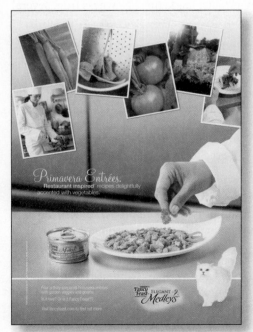

The benefit of this simple innovation is that effective marketing mainly depends on generating awareness, not re-educating customers.

With a *dynamically continuous innovation*, only minor changes in behavior are required. Procter & Gamble's Swiffer WetJet all-in-one mopping solution is a successful dynamically continuous innovation. Its novel design eliminates mess, elbow grease, and heavy lifting of floor cleaning materials without requiring any substantial behavioral change. So the marketing strategy here is to educate prospective buyers on the product's benefits, advantages, and proper use. Procter & Gamble did this with Swiffer. The result? A billion dollars in annual sales.

A *discontinuous innovation* involves making the consumer learn entirely new consumption patterns to use the product. Have you bought a wireless router for your computer? Congratulations if you installed it yourself! Recently, one-third of those bought at Best Buy were returned because they were too complicated to set up—the problem with a discontinuous innovation. Marketing efforts for discontinuous innovations usually involve not only gaining initial consumer awareness but also educating consumers on both the benefits and proper use of the innovative product, activities that can cost millions of dollars—and maybe require Geek Squad help.

Newness in Legal Terms   The U.S. Federal Trade Commission (FTC) advises that the term *new* be limited to use with a product up to six months after it enters regular distribution. The difficulty with this suggestion is in the interpretation of the term *regular distribution*.

Newness from the Organization's Perspective   Successful organizations view newness and innovation in their products at three levels. The lowest level, which usually involves the least risk, is a *product line extension*. This is an incremental improvement of an existing product line the company already sells. For example, Purina added its "new" line of Elegant Medleys, a "restaurant-inspired food for cats," to its existing line of 50 varieties of its Fancy Feast gourmet cat food. This has the potential benefit of adding new customers but the twin dangers of increasing expenses and cannibalizing products in its existing line.

At the next level is (1) a significant jump in innovation or technology or (2) a *brand extension* involving putting an established brand name on a new product in an unfamiliar market. In the first case, the significant jump in technology might be when a manufacturer offers new smartphones or digital cameras.

The second case—using an existing brand name to introduce a new product into an unfamiliar market—looks deceptively easy for companies with a powerful, national brand name. Colgate thought so. It puts its brand name on a line of frozen dinners called Colgate's Kitchen Entrees. The product line died quickly. A marketing expert calls this "one of the most bizarre brand extensions ever," observing that the Colgate brand name, which is strongly linked to toothpaste in people's minds, does not exactly get their "taste buds tingling."[4]

The third and highest level of innovation involves a radical invention, a truly revolutionary new product. Apple's Apple II, the first commercially successful "personal computer," and its iPad and iPod are examples of radical inventions. Effective new-product development in large firms exists at all three levels.

Why Products and Services Succeed or Fail

We all know the giant product and service successes—such as Apple's iPad, Netflix, and CNN. Yet the thousands of product failures every year that slide quietly into oblivion cost American businesses billions of dollars. Ideally, a new product or service needs a precise **protocol**, a statement that, before product development begins, identifies (1) a well-defined target market; (2) specific customers' needs, wants, and preferences; and (3) what the product will be and do to satisfy consumers.

Research reveals how difficult it is to produce a single commercially successful new product, especially among consumer packaged goods (CPG) that appear on supermarket shelves one month and are gone forever a few months later. Most American families buy the same 150 items over and over again—making it difficult to gain buyers for new products. So less than 3 percent of new consumer packaged goods exceed first-year sales of $50 million—the benchmark of a successful CPG launch.[5]

To learn marketing lessons and convert potential failures to successes, we can analyze why new products fail and then study several failures in detail. As we go through the new-product development process later in the chapter, we can identify ways such failures might have been avoided—admitting that hindsight is clearer than foresight.

Marketing Reasons for New-Product Failures Both marketing and nonmarketing factors contribute to new-product failures. Using the research results from several studies on new-product success and failure, we can identify critical marketing factors—which sometimes overlap—that often separate new-product winners and losers:[6]

> **LO 10-4** Describe the factors contributing to the success or failure of a new product or service.

1. *Insignificant point of difference.* Research shows that a distinctive point of difference is the single most important factor for a new product to defeat competing ones—having superior characteristics that deliver unique benefits to the user. Consider General Mills' launch of Fingos, a sweetened cereal flake about the size of a corn chip, with a $34 million promotional budget. Consumers were supposed to snack on them dry, but they didn't.[7] The point of difference was not important enough to get consumers to stop eating competing snacks such as popcorn and potato chips.
2. *Incomplete market and product protocol before product development starts.* Without this protocol, firms try to design a vague product for a phantom market. Developed by Kimberly-Clark, Avert Virucidal tissues contained vitamin C derivatives scientifically designed to kill cold and flu germs when users sneezed, coughed, or blew their noses into them. The product failed in test marketing. People didn't believe the claims and were frightened by the "cidal" in the brand name, which they connected to words like *suicidal*. A big part of Avert's failure was its lack of a product protocol that clearly defined how it would satisfy consumer wants and needs.[8]
3. *Not satisfying customer needs on critical factors.* Overlapping somewhat with point 1, this factor stresses that problems on one or two critical factors can kill the product, even though the general quality is high. For example, the Japanese,

Why was Microsoft's Zune MP3 Player a product failure? A poor product? No. Poor timing? Yes.

© Scott Olson/Getty Images

What dog or cat wouldn't want to drink vitamin-enriched, carbonated bottled water? As it happens, their human companions didn't think so and the product was short-lived on supermarket shelves due to lack of demand.

© Patrick Farrell/KRT/Newscom

like the British, drive on the left side of the road. Until 1996, U.S. carmakers sent Japan few right-hand-drive cars—unlike German carmakers, which exported right-hand-drive models in several of their brands.

4. *Bad timing.* This results when a product is introduced too soon, too late, or when consumer tastes are shifting dramatically. Bad timing gives new-product managers nightmares. Microsoft, for example, introduced its Zune player a few years after Apple launched its iPod and other competitors offered their new MP3 players. Microsoft discontinued Zune after failing to capture significant market share from the Apple iPod.

5. *No economical access to buyers.* Grocery products provide an example of this factor. Today's mega-supermarkets carry more than 60,000 different SKUs. With about 40,000 new consumer packaged goods (food, beverage, health and beauty aids, household, and pet items) introduced annually in the United States, the cost to gain access to retailer shelf space is huge. Because shelf space is judged in terms of sales per square foot, Thirsty Dog! (a zesty beef-flavored, vitamin-enriched, mineral-loaded, lightly carbonated bottled water for your dog) must displace an existing product on the supermarket shelves, a difficult task with the high sales-per-square-foot demands of these stores. Thirsty Dog! and its companion product Thirsty Cat! failed to generate enough sales to meet these requirements.

6. *Poor product quality.* This factor often results when a product is not thoroughly tested. The costs to an organization for poor quality can be staggering and include the labor, materials, and other expenses to fix the problem—not to mention the lost sales, profits, and market share that usually result. In early 2007, with a $500 million promotional budget, Microsoft launched its Windows Vista to replace its successful predecessor Windows XP. But the Vista software had so many quality problems with compatibility and performance, even Microsoft's most loyal users revolted.[9]

7. *Poor execution of the marketing mix: brand name, package, price, promotion, distribution.* Somewhere in the marketing mix there can be a showstopper that kills the product. Introduced by Gunderson & Rosario, Inc., Garlic Cake was supposed to be served as an hors d'oeuvre with sweet breads, spreads, and meats, but somehow the company forgot to tell this to potential consumers. Garlic Cake died because consumers were left to wonder just what a Garlic Cake is and when on earth a person would want to eat it.

8. *Too little market attractiveness.* The ideal is a large target market with high growth and real buyer need. But often the target market is too small or competitive to warrant the huge expenses necessary to reach it. OUT! International's Hey! There's A Monster In My Room spray was designed to rid scary creatures from a kid's bedroom and had a bubble-gum fragrance. While a creative and cute product, the brand name probably kept the kids awake at night more than their fear of the monsters because it implied the monster was still hiding in the bedroom. Also, was this a real market?

Simple marketing research should have revealed the problems in these new-product disasters. Developing successful new products may sometimes involve luck, but more often it involves having a product that really meets a need and has significant points of difference over competitive products.

Organizational Inertia in New-Product Failures Organizational problems and attitudes can also cause new-product disasters. Two key ones are:

- *Encountering "groupthink" in task force and committee meetings.*[10] Someone in the new-product planning meeting knows or suspects the product concept is a dumb idea. But that person is afraid to speak up for fear of being cast as a "negative

Applying **Marketing Metrics**

Which States Are Underperforming?

In 2012, you started your own company to sell a nutritious, high-energy snack you developed. It is now January 2016. As a marketer, you ask yourself, "How well is my business growing?"

Your Challenge

The snack is sold in all 50 states. Your goal is 10 percent annual growth. To begin 2016, you want to quickly solve any sales problems that occurred during 2015. You know that states whose sales are stagnant or in decline are offset by those with greater than 10 percent growth.

Studying a table of the sales and percentage change versus a year ago in each of the 50 states would work but be very time-consuming. A good graphic is better. You choose the following marketing metric, where "sales" are measured in units:

$$\text{Annual \% sales change} = \frac{(2015\ \text{Sales} - 2014\ \text{Sales}) \times 100}{2014\ \text{Sales}}$$

You want to act quickly to improve sales. In your map, growth that is greater than 10 percent is green, 0 to 10 percent growth is orange, and decline is red. Notice that you (1) picked a metric and (2) made your own rules that green is good, orange is bad, and red is very bad.

Your Findings

You see that sales growth in the northeastern states is weaker than the 10 percent target, and sales are actually declining in many of the states.

Annual Percentage Change in Unit Volume, by State

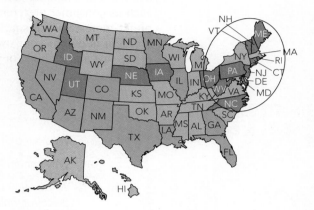

Your Action

Marketing is often about grappling with sales shortfalls. You'll need to start by trying to identify and correct the problems in the largest volume states that are underperforming—in this case in the northeastern United States.

You'll want to do marketing research to see if the problem starts with (1) an external factor involving consumer tastes or (2) an internal factor such as a breakdown in your distribution system.

thinker," "not a team player," and then being ostracized from real participation in the group. Do you think someone on the Life Savers new-product team suspected a Life Savers soda wasn't a good idea but was afraid to speak up? In the same way, a strong public commitment to a new product by its key advocate may make it difficult to kill the product even when new negative information comes to light. Groupthink can be minimized when group leaders encourage group members to challenge assumptions, express constructive dissent, and offer alternatives.

- *Avoiding the "NIH problem."* A great idea is a great idea, regardless of its source. Yet in the bureaucracy that can occur in large organizations, ideas from outside often get rejected simply because they come from outside—what has been termed the "not-invented-here (NIH) problem." Forward-looking companies attempt to deal with this problem by embracing the policy of open innovation. **Open innovation** consists of practices and processes that encourage the use of external as well as internal ideas as well as internal and external collaboration when conceiving, producing, and marketing new products and services. Approaches to open innovation are highlighted in the description of the new-product development process discussed shortly.

These organizational problems can contribute to the eight marketing reasons for new-product failures described above.

How Applying Marketing Metrics Can Monitor New-Product Performance

The Applying Marketing Metrics box shows how marketers measure actual market performance versus the goals set in new-product planning. It shows that you have set a goal of 10 percent annual growth for the new snack you developed. You have chosen a marketing metric of "annual % sales change" to measure the annual growth rate from 2014 and 2015 for each of the 50 states.

Your special concerns are the states shown in red, where sales have actually declined. As shown in the box, having identified the northeastern United States as a problem region, you can now conduct in-depth marketing research to lead to corrective actions. For example, is the decline in sales in this region due to an external factor, such as consumer preference? Perhaps consumers in the northeastern United States prefer more regional snack tastes or think your snack is too sweet. Or perhaps the problem is due to your own internal marketing strategy, such as poor distribution, prices that are too high, or ineffective advertising.

learning review

10-3. What kind of innovation would an improved electric toothbrush be?

10-4. Why can an "insignificant point of difference" lead to new-product failure?

10-5. What marketing metric might you use in a marketing dashboard to discover which states have weak sales?

THE NEW-PRODUCT DEVELOPMENT PROCESS

LO 10-5 Explain the purposes of each step of the new-product development process.

To develop new products efficiently, companies such as General Electric and 3M use a specific sequence of steps to make their products ready for market. Figure 10–3 shows the **new-product development process**, the seven stages an organization goes through to identify opportunities and convert them into salable products or services. Today many firms use a formal Stage-Gate® process to evaluate whether the results at each stage of the new-product development process are successful enough to warrant proceeding to the next stage. If problems in a stage can't be corrected, the project doesn't proceed to the next stage and product development is killed.[11]

Stage 1: New-Product Strategy Development

For companies, **new-product strategy development** is the stage of the new-product development process that defines the role for a new product in terms of the firm's

FIGURE 10–3

Carefully using the seven stages in the new-product development process increases the chances of new-product success.

1. New-product strategy development
2. Idea generation
3. Screening and evaluation
4. Business analysis
5. Development
6. Market testing
7. Commercialization

overall objectives. During this stage, the firm uses both a SWOT analysis (Chapter 2) and environmental scanning (Chapter 3) to assess its strengths and weaknesses relative to the trends it identifies as opportunities or threats. The outcome not only defines the vital "protocol" for each new-product idea but also identifies the strategic role it might serve in the firm's business portfolio.

Occasionally a firm's Stage 1 activities can be blindsided by a revolutionary new product or technology that completely disrupts its business, sometimes called a "disruptive innovation." For example:

- *Wikipedia*. This free and community-edited online encyclopedia caused Encyclopedia Britannica to cease print production after 244 years.
- *Digital photography*. Even though they were invented by Kodak, digital cameras made film and film cameras obsolete by the mid-2000s and drove Kodak into bankruptcy in 2012. Kodak did not actively market its digital cameras because it wanted to protect its film business, the firm's cash cow.

Clearly, a firm's new-product strategy development must be on the lookout for innovative products or technology that might disrupt its plans.

New-product development for services, such as buying a stock or airline ticket or watching a National Football League game, is often difficult. Why? Because services are intangible and performance-oriented. Nevertheless, service innovations can have a huge impact on our lives. For example, the online brokerage firm E*TRADE has revolutionized the financial services industry through its online investment trading.

Stage 2: Idea Generation

Idea generation, the second stage of the new-product development process, involves developing a pool of concepts to serve as candidates for new products, building upon the previous stage's results. Many forward-looking organizations have discovered that they are not generating enough useful new-product ideas. One internal approach for getting ideas within the firm is to train employees in the art and science of asking specific, probing questions. The goal in generating new-product ideas and strategies is to move from "what is" questions that describe the present situation to "what if" questions that focus on solutions and marketing actions.[12] The following discussion suggests methods of generating new-product ideas both internally and externally, the latter often using open innovation.

Suggestions from Employees and Friends Businesses often seek new-product ideas from employees through suggestion boxes placed around their workplace. The idea for Nature Valley granola bars from General Mills came when one of its marketing managers observed co-workers bringing granola to work in plastic bags.

The breakthrough for the Life Is Good T-shirt business (introduced earlier in Chapter 1) started with a 1994 keg party the company founders, brothers Bert and John Jacobs, had with friends. At their parties the brothers often posted drawings with sayings for possible T-shirt ideas on their living room wall and asked their friends to jot down their reactions on the drawings.[13] At one party the drawing of a smiling, beret-wearing stick figure with the phrase "Life is good" got the most favorable comments. They named the character "Jake," printed 48 T-shirts with a smiling Jake and the words "Life is good," and sold them out in less than an hour at a local street fair. Today Life Is Good with its positive, upbeat messages has $100 million in annual sales and sells Life Is Good T-shirts, hats, and other items for men and women in 4,500 retail stores nationwide.[14]

Brothers John and Bert Jacobs are constantly looking for positive, upbeat messages to print on their Life Is Good T-shirts.

© Michael Dwyer/AP Images

Video 10-3

P&G's Tide Pods Ad

kerin.tv/13e/v10-3

Customer and Supplier Suggestions Firms ask their salespeople to talk to customers and ask their purchasing personnel to talk to suppliers to discover new-product ideas. Whirlpool gets ideas from customers on ways to standardize components so that it can cut the number of different product platforms to reduce costs. Business researchers tell firms to actively involve customers and suppliers in the new-product development process. This means the focus should be on what the new product will actually do for them rather than simply what they want.

A. G. Lafley, CEO of Procter & Gamble (P&G), gave his executives a *revolutionary* thought: "Look outside the company for solutions to problems rather than insisting P&G knows best." When he ran P&G's laundry detergent business, he had to redesign the laundry boxes so they were easier to open. Why? While consumers *said* P&G's laundry boxes were "easy to open," cameras they agreed to have installed in their laundry rooms showed they opened the boxes with *screwdrivers*![15]

With a $150 million marketing budget, P&G launched Tide Pods, a revolutionary three-chamber liquid dose that cleans, fights stains, and brightens. P&G describes Tide Pods as "its biggest laundry innovation in more than a quarter century." P&G says Tide Pods has produced the highest consumer-satisfaction scores the company has ever seen for a new laundry product. Following its successful new-product launch, however, P&G redesigned its packaging after discovering that some children thought the pods were candy and tried to eat them. How successful has Tide Pods been for P&G? After its first year, the product garnered a 73 percent share of the "unit dose" segment of the detergent market on estimated sales of $500 million—making it one of the most successful product launches![16]

Procter & Gamble's new Tide Pods launch shows how it has improved both planning and implementation by involving consumers earlier in its innovation activities.

© Mike Hruby

"Crowdsourcing" is another creative idea-generation method if an R&D-marketing team wants ideas from 10,000 or 20,000 customers or suppliers. *Crowdsourcing* involves generating insights leading to actions based on ideas from massive numbers of people. This open innvotation practice requires a precise question to focus the idea-generation process. Dell used crowdsourcing to develop an online site to generate 13,464 ideas for new products as well as website and marketing improvements, of which 402 were implemented.[17]

Research and Development Laboratories Another source of new products is a firm's own research and development laboratories. Apple's sleek, cutting-edge designs for the iPad, iPhone, iMac, and Apple Watch came out of its Apple Industrial Design Group, guided by Senior Vice President of Design Jonathan Ive. What is the secret to Apple's world-class ability to convert vague concepts into tangible products? An action-item list from every meeting that focuses on *who* does *what* by *when*![18]

Professional R&D and innovation laboratories that are *outside* the walls of large corporations are also sources of open innovation and can provide new-product ideas. IDEO is a world-class new-product development firm that uses "design thinking," which involves incorporating human behavior as well as building upon the ideas of others in the innovation-design process. As the most prolific and influential design firm in the world, IDEO has created thousands of new products for its clients. Brainstorming sessions conducted at IDEO can generate 100 new ideas in an hour!

An IDEO innovation: A five-section, single-serve package for salads. Visit IDEO's website (www.ideo.com) to view its recent innovations.

Source: IDEO, www.ideo.com/work/gourmet-cafe-salad-packaging

IDEO designs include developing the standing Crest Neat Squeeze toothpaste dispenser and improving the original Apple mouse. Recently, Fresh Express asked IDEO to design an innovative single-serve package for salads. IDEO's solution: A five-section package—one large section for the salad greens and four smaller ones for proteins, dressings, and so on—with each section sealed in plastic (see the photo).[19]

Competitive Products Analyzing the competition can lead to new-product ideas. General Motors has targeted Tesla Motors as a reference for its new Chevrolet

Bolt—a $30,000 all-electric vehicle scheduled for introduction in 2017. The Bolt will be capable of driving 200 miles in a single charge and feature a hatchback design to look more like a cross-over vehicle. According to a General Motors executive, the Bolt will "completely shake up the status quo for electric vehicles as the first affordable long-range EV in the market." The Bolt is also designed to be a direct competitor to Tesla's coming Model 3, a $35,000 electric car scheduled to debut in 2017.[20]

Gary Schwartzberg partnered with Kraft Foods to get his cream cheese–filled bagels in stores across the United States.

Courtesy of Gary Schwartzberg

Smaller Firms, Universities, and Inventors   Many firms look for outside visionaries that have inventions or innovative ideas that can become products. Some sources of this open innovation strategy include:[21]

- *Smaller, nontraditional firms.* Small technology firms and even small, nontraditional firms in adjacent industries provide creative advances. General Mills partnered with Weight Watchers to develop Progresso Light soups, the first consumer packaged product in any grocery category to carry the Weight Watchers endorsement with a 0 points value per serving.
- *Universities.* Many universities have technology transfer centers that often partner with business firms to commercialize faculty inventions. The first-of-its-kind carbonated yogurt Go-Gurt Fizzix was launched as a result of General Mills partnering with Brigham Young University to license the university's patent to put the "fizz" into the yogurt.
- *Inventors.* Many lone inventors and entrepreneurs develop brilliant new-product ideas—like Gary Schwartzberg's tube-shaped bagel filled with cream cheese. A portable breakfast for the on-the-go person, the innovative bagel couldn't get widespread distribution. So Schwartzberg sold his idea to Kraft Foods, Inc., which now markets its Bagel-fuls filled with Kraft's best-selling Philadelphia cream cheese across the United States.

Crowdfunder Kickstarter.com enabled Pebble to market its customizable watch that runs a variety of apps.

© Neil Godwin/T3 Magazine via Getty Images

Early-stage financing is almost always a problem for inventors and those starting a new business. *Crowdfunding* is a way to gather an online community of supporters to financially rally around a specific project that is unlikely to get resources from traditional sources such as banks or venture capital firms. For example, Kickstarter.com raised $1.2 million for start-up SmartThings to introduce a product that allows users to monitor their homes by remote control. But its biggest crowdfunding project was for the Pebble digital smartwatch with iPhone and Android smartphone integration: Almost 70,000 backers contributed over $10 million to develop this amazing product, which initially sold for $150! If you want to donate to crowdfunding projects, that's fine, too: The average Kickstarter donor gives $25.[22]

Great ideas can come from almost anywhere—a central idea behind open innovation. The challenge is recognizing and implementing them.

Stage 3: Screening and Evaluation

Screening and evaluation is the stage of the new-product development process that internally and externally evaluates new-product ideas to eliminate those that warrant no further effort.

Internal Approach   In this approach to screening and evaluation, a firm's employees evaluate the technical feasibility of a proposed new-product idea to determine whether it meets the objectives defined in the new-product strategy development stage. For example, 3M scientists develop many world-class innovations in the company's

Was the Google Glass Half Full or Half Empty?

How did the Google Glass morph from being one of *Time* magazine's best inventions of the year in 2012 to an embarrassing flop in 2015? Perhaps, Google's product development team failed to ask three simple questions: How would consumers perceive Google Glass? Who would use it? and How would it be used?

Google Glass resembled a pair of eyeglasses with a small screen visible to the wearer (see the photo). Its notable features included a touchpad that allowed the wearer to "see" current and past events such as phone calls, photos and updates, and a camera to take pictures and record video. The sound video and graphics accessed through the screen created an *augmented reality* that overlaid the physical, real-world environment at the same time.

Google started selling a prototype (not the finished product) to 8,000 qualified "Glass Explorers" in April 2013, for $1,500. The intent was to collect feedback on the device and then quickly update and fix problems before a planned launch of the product in May 2014 for the same price. Unfortunately, by releasing Google Glass widely, and charging $1,500, the public believed the device to be a finished product, not a prototype. It quickly became apparent that the prototype suffered from a short battery life, poor sound quality, and distorted images.

The technical problems could be fixed. But Google Glass had more severe problems—all of which related to incomplete concept testing. For example, Google never really understood how consumers would perceive the

device. Was it simply a "cool" geeky gadget or wearable, chic eyeglass technology for a broader audience? How would wearers use the technology? As it happened, users immediately embraced the photo and video capabilities, and Google Glass wearers were thrown out of clubs and banned from theaters because of privacy and intellectual property concerns. More troubling, Google Glass wearers were derisively called "Glassholes."

The result? Google Glass was withdrawn from the market in January 2015. Google executives expect to introduce a new version of Google Glass that better meets the needs of consumers in 2016 or 2017.

© Rex Features/AP Images

labs. A recent innovation was its microreplication technology—one that has 3,000 tiny gripping "fingers" per square inch. An internal assessment showed 3M that this technology could be used to improve the gripping of both batting and work gloves.

Organizations that develop service-dominated offerings need to ensure that employees have the commitment and skills to meet customer expectations and sustain customer loyalty—an important criterion in screening a new-service idea. This is the essence of *customer experience management (CEM)*, which is the process of managing the entire customer experience within the company. Marketers must consider employees' interactions with customers so that the new services are consistently delivered and experienced, clearly differentiated from other service offerings, and relevant and valuable to the target market.

External Approach Firms that take an external approach to screening and evaluation use *concept tests*, external evaluations with consumers that consist of preliminary testing of a new-product idea rather than an actual finished product. Generally, these tests are more useful with minor modifications of existing products than with new, innovative products with which consumers are not familiar.

Concept tests rely on written descriptions of the product but may be augmented with sketches, mockups, or promotional literature. Key questions for concept testing include: How does the customer perceive the product? Who would use it? and How would it be used? Failure to address these questions can lead to disastrous results. Consumer response to Google Glass is a case in point as detailed in the Marketing Matters box.[23]

learning review »

10-6. What is the new-product strategy development stage in the new-product development process?

10-7. What are the main sources of new-product ideas?

10-8. How do internal and external screening and evaluation approaches differ?

Stage 4: Business Analysis

Business analysis specifies the features of the product or service and the marketing strategy needed to bring it to market and make financial projections. This is the last checkpoint before significant resources are invested to create a *prototype*—a full-scale operating model of the product or service. The business analysis stage assesses the total "business fit" of the proposed new product with the company's mission and objectives—from whether the product or service can be economically produced to the marketing strategy needed to have it succeed in the marketplace.

This process requires not only detailed financial projections but also assessments of the marketing and product synergies related to the company's existing operations. Will the new product require a lot of new equipment to produce it or can it be produced using the unused capacity of existing machines? Will the new product cannibalize sales of existing products or will it increase revenues by reaching new market segments? Can the new product be protected with a patent or copyright? Financial projections of expected profits require estimates of expected prices per unit and units sold, as well as detailed estimates of the costs of R&D, production, and marketing.

279

Stage 5: Development

Development is the stage of the new-product development process that turns the idea on paper into a prototype. This results in a demonstrable, producible product that involves not only manufacturing the product efficiently but also performing laboratory and consumer tests to ensure the product meets the standards established for it in the protocol.

Google's driverless car is an extreme example of the complexity of the Stage 5 development process for a durable consumer good. The Google team consists of 15 engineers and has a fleet of 10 vehicles as the test models, among them the Toyota Prius and the Lexus RX 450h. In early 2015, the Google team announced its cars had completed over 700,000 miles of accident-free, "autonomous driving." These miles were "driven" by a driver with an unblemished driving record behind the wheel and a Google engineer in the passenger seat. A spinning, roof-mounted laser range finder and sophisticated software negotiated the steep hairpin turns in San Francisco and trips both across the Golden Gate Bridge and along the curvy Pacific Coast Highway.

Where is Google's driverless car headed? Google has no plans to commercialize the vehicle itself but wants to market the technology to auto manufacturers. But it is clear

Is this what you'll be "driving" in 2020? Google's driverless cars have logged 700,000 miles without an accident!

© Rex Features/AP Images

Google will need to invest tens of millions of dollars into additional development and testing (see Stage 6 below) before anyone can buy a driverless car—typical of high-technology devices. Right now, only Nevada, California, and Florida have laws allowing driverless cars.

The good news for Google: safety. If its driverless car is perfected and allowed on U.S. highways, the highway fatalities and hospitalizations caused by car accidents annually should fall. This will surely be part of Google's marketing campaign!

Stage 6: Market Testing

Market testing is a stage of the new-product development process that involves exposing actual products to prospective consumers under realistic purchase conditions to see if they will buy. If the budget permits, consumer packaged goods firms do this by *test marketing*, which involves offering a product for sale on a limited basis in a defined area for a specific time period. The three main kinds of test markets are (1) standard, (2) controlled, and (3) simulated.[24] Because standard test markets are so time-consuming and expensive and can alert competitors to a firm's plans, some firms skip test markets entirely or use controlled or simulated test markets.

Standard Test Markets   In a *standard test market*, a company develops a product and then attempts to sell it through normal distribution channels in a number of test-market cities. Test-market cities must be demographically representative of markets targeted for the new product, have cable TV systems that can deliver different ads to different homes, and have retailers with checkout counter scanners to measure sales. A distinguishing feature of a standard test market is that the producer sells the product to distributors, wholesalers, and retailers, just as it would do for other products.

Controlled Test Markets   A *controlled test market* involves contracting the entire test program to an outside service. The service pays retailers for shelf space and can therefore guarantee a specified percentage of the test product's potential distribution volume. IRI is a leader in supplying controlled test markets to consumer packaged good firms like General Mills. Its BehaviorScan service uses five demographically representative cities to track sales made to a panel of households. In some cases the effectiveness of different TV commercials and other direct-to-consumer promotions can be measured.

Consumer products, such as those from General Mills, often use controlled test markets to assess the likely success of new-product, promotional, or pricing strategies.
Courtesy Bolin Marketing

Simulated Test Markets   To save time and money, companies often turn to *simulated (or laboratory) test markets (STMs)*, a technique that somewhat replicates a full-scale test market. STMs are often run in shopping malls, to find consumers who use the product class being tested. Next, qualified participants are shown the product or the product concept and are asked about usage, reasons for purchase, and important product attributes. They then see the company's and competitors' ads for the test product. Finally, participants are given money and allowed to choose between buying the firm's product or the products of competitors from a real or simulated store environment.

When Test Markets Don't Work   Not all products can use test markets. Test marketing a service is very difficult because consumers can't see what they are buying. For example, how do you test market a new building for an art museum? Similarly, test markets for expensive consumer products, such as cars or costly industrial products such as jet engines, are impractical. For these products, reactions of potential buyers to mockups or one-of-a-kind prototypes are all that is feasible.

Stage 7: Commercialization

Finally, the product is brought to the point of **commercialization**—the stage of the new-product development process that positions and launches a new product in full-scale production and sales. This is the most expensive stage for most new products. If competitors introduce a product that leapfrogs the firm's own new product or if cannibalization of its own existing products appears significant, the firm may halt the new-product launch. Companies can face disasters at the commercialization stage, regardless of whether they are selling business products or consumer products. Examples are Boeing's 787 Dreamliner and Burger King's french fries, which are discussed next.

Takeaway new-product lesson from the Boeing 787 Dreamliner: "Innovation . . . doesn't come easy." See the text for details.
© KiyoshiOta/Bloomberg via Getty Images

The Boeing 787 Dreamliner Experience   In 2004, Boeing announced the design for its Boeing 787 Dreamliner commercial airplane. Its technical advances would mean the plane would burn 20 percent less fuel and cost 30 percent less to maintain than present airliners. Boeing invested billions of dollars in the 787's development, and airlines had placed orders for almost 930 Dreamliners by mid-2013.

As the Dreamliner entered its commercialization stage, airlines around the world began taking deliveries. But with all the new technology in the Dreamliner, the new airplane was plagued by technical nightmares—even after extensive testing. Its wings, made with plastic-reinforced carbon fiber instead of aluminum, proved difficult to produce and attach to the fuselage. And with this new "high-tech skin," lightning doesn't dissipate like it did with the old aluminum skin. But an even more serious problem arose in early 2013: Lithium-ion batteries, which provide electrical power, caught fire on two Dreamliner aircraft, prompting regulators to ground all 50 Dreamliners in service around the world. Perhaps *The Wall Street Journal* gave the best new-product lesson from the Boeing 787 Dreamliner example: "Innovation—for all its value—doesn't come as easily as a catchphrase. It can get messy."[25]

Burger King's French Fries: The Complexities of Commercialization

McDonald's french fries are the gold standard against which all other fries in the fast-food industry are measured. In 1997, Burger King decided to take on McDonald's fries and spent millions of R&D dollars developing a whey/starch-coated fry designed to retain heat longer and add crispiness.

Burger King's thick-cut fries appeared in 2011 and had a new "coating" on the outside to create a "crispy, golden-brown deliciousness" while retaining the heat longer—for at least 10 minutes—because 75 percent of customers eat their fries "on the go" in their cars, offices, or homes. Burger King also launched the largest TV advertising campaign in its history to promote the new fries. The launch turned into a disaster. The reason: Except under ideal conditions, the new fry proved too complicated to get right day after day in Burger King restaurants.

To discover the downs and ups of commercializing a new product, see the text discussion of Burger King's 15-year search for a french fry recipe that can compete with McDonald's.
© Mike Hruby

Then in late 2013 Burger King introduced its "Satisfries" as the french fries in its kids meals. These were intended to help address concerns about nutrition for and obesity in children. Satisfries had about 20 percent fewer calories and 25 percent less fat than its regular fries. Burger King's latest commercialization problem: In mid-2014 Burger King discontinued its Satisfries at most of its restaurants because it couldn't communicate a meaningful point of difference to its customers and Satisfries cost more than its regular fries.[26]

The Special Risks in Commercializing Grocery Products   New grocery products pose special commercialization problems. Because shelf space is so limited, many supermarkets require a *slotting fee* for new products, a payment a manufacturer makes to place a new item on a retailer's shelf. This can run to several million dollars for a single product. But there's even another potential expense. If a new grocery product does not achieve a predetermined sales target, some retailers require a *failure fee*, a penalty payment a manufacturer makes to compensate a retailer for devoting valuable shelf space to a product that failed to sell.

These costly slotting fees and failure fees are further examples of why large grocery product manufacturers use regional rollouts. Companies selling consumer products using *regional rollouts* introduce a product sequentially into geographical areas of the United States to allow production levels and marketing activities to build up gradually, to minimize the risk of new-product failure. Grocery product manufacturers and telephone service providers use this strategy.

Speed as a Factor in New-Product Success   Companies have discovered that speed or *time to market (TtM)* is often vital in introducing a new product. Recent studies have shown that high-tech products coming to market on time are far more profitable than those arriving late. So companies like Sony, BMW, 3M, and Hewlett-Packard often overlap the sequence of stages described in this chapter.

With this approach, termed *parallel development*, cross-functional team members who conduct the simultaneous development of both the product and the production process stay with the product from conception to production. This approach enabled Hewlett-Packard to reduce the development time for notebook computers from 12 to 7 months. In software development, *fast prototyping* uses a "do it, try it, fix it" approach—encouraging continuing improvement even after the initial design. To speed up time to market, many firms insulate their new-product teams from routine administrative tasks to keep them from bogging down in red tape.

learning review

10-9. How does the development stage of the new-product development process involve testing the product inside and outside the firm?

10-10. What is a test market, and what are the three kinds?

10-11. What is the commercialization of a new product?

LEARNING OBJECTIVES REVIEW

LO 10-1   *Recognize the various terms that pertain to products and services.*
A product is a good, service, or idea consisting of a bundle of tangible and intangible attributes that satisfies consumers and is received in exchange for money or something else of value.

A good has tangible attributes that a consumer's five senses can perceive and intangible ones such as warranties; a laptop computer is an example. Goods also can be divided into nondurable goods, which are consumed in one or a few uses, and durable goods, which usually last over many uses.

Services are intangible activities or benefits that an organization provides to satisfy consumer needs in exchange for money or something else of value, such as an airline trip. An idea is a thought that leads to a product or action, such as eating healthier foods.

LO 10-2 *Identify the ways in which consumer and business products and services can be classified.*

By type of user, the major distinctions are consumer products, which are products purchased by the ultimate consumer, and business products, which are products that assist an organization in providing other products for resale.

Consumer products can be broken down based on the effort involved in the purchase decision process, marketing mix attributes used in the purchase, and the frequency of purchase: (*a*) convenience products are items that consumers purchase frequently and with a minimum of shopping effort; (*b*) shopping products are items for which consumers compare several alternatives on selected criteria; (*c*) specialty products are items that consumers make special efforts to seek out and buy; and (*d*) unsought products are items that consumers either do not know about or do not initially want.

Business products can be broken down into (*a*) components, which are items that become part of the final product, such as raw materials or parts, and (*b*) support products, which are items used to assist in producing other goods and services and include installations, accessory equipment, supplies, and industrial services.

Services can be classified in terms of whether they are delivered by (*a*) people or equipment, (*b*) business firms or nonprofit organizations, or (*c*) government agencies.

Firms can offer a range of products, which involve decisions regarding the product item, product line, and product mix.

LO 10-3 *Explain the significance of "newness" in new products and services as it relates to the degree of consumer learning involved.*

From the important perspective of the consumer, "newness" is often seen as the degree of learning that a consumer must engage in to use the product. With a continuous innovation, no new behaviors must be learned. With a dynamically continuous innovation, only minor behavioral changes are needed. With a discontinuous innovation, consumers must learn entirely new consumption patterns.

LO 10-4 *Describe the factors contributing to the success or failure of a new product or service.*

A new product or service often fails for these marketing reasons: (*a*) insignificant points of difference, (*b*) incomplete market and product protocol before product development starts, (*c*) a failure to satisfy customer needs on critical factors, (*d*) bad timing, (*e*) no economical access to buyers, (*f*) poor product quality, (*g*) poor execution of the marketing mix, and (*h*) too little market attractiveness.

LO 10-5 *Explain the purposes of each step of the new-product development process.*

The new-product development process consists of seven stages a firm uses to develop salable products or services: (1) *New-product strategy development* involves defining the role for the new product within the firm's overall objectives. (2) *Idea generation* involves developing a pool of concepts from consumers, employees, basic R&D, and competitors to serve as candidates for new products. (3) *Screening and evaluation* involves evaluating new-product ideas to eliminate those that are not feasible from a technical or consumer perspective. (4) *Business analysis* involves defining the features of the new product, developing the marketing strategy and marketing program to introduce it, and making a financial forecast. (5) *Development* involves not only producing a prototype product but also testing it in the lab and with consumers to see that it meets the standards set for it. (6) *Market testing* involves exposing actual products to prospective consumers under realistic purchasing conditions to see if they will buy the product. (7) *Commercialization* involves positioning and launching a product in full-scale production and sales with a specific marketing program.

LEARNING REVIEW ANSWERS

10-1 What are the four main types of consumer products?

Answer: They are: (1) convenience products—items that the consumer purchases frequently, conveniently, and with a minimum of shopping effort; (2) shopping products—items for which the consumer compares several alternatives on criteria such as price, quality, or style; (3) specialty products—items that the consumer makes a special effort to search out and buy; and (4) unsought products—items that the consumer does not know about or knows about but does not initially want.

10-2 What is the difference between a product line and a product mix?

Answer: A product line is a group of product or service items that are closely related because they satisfy a class of needs, are used together, are sold to the same customer group, are distributed through the same outlets, or fall within a given price range. The product mix consists of all the product lines offered by an organization.

10-3 What kind of innovation would an improved electric toothbrush be?

Answer: continuous innovation—no new learning is required by consumers

10-4 Why can an "insignificant point of difference" lead to new-product failure?

Answer: The product must have superior characteristics that deliver unique benefits to the user compared to those of competitors that must be sufficient enough to motivate a change in consumption behavior. Without these points of difference, the product will probably fail.

10-5 What marketing metric might you use in a marketing dashboard to discover which states have weak sales?

Answer: The marketing metric—annual percentage change in unit volume by state—will help identify those states that are underperforming.

10-6 What is the new-product strategy development stage in the new-product development process?

Answer: New-product strategy development is the first stage of the new-product development process that defines the role for a new product in terms of the firm's overall objectives. During this stage, the firm uses both a SWOT analysis and environmental scanning to assess its strengths and weaknesses relative to the trends it identifies as opportunities or threats. The outcome not only defines the vital "protocol" for each new-product idea but also identifies the strategic role it might serve in the firm's business portfolio.

10-7 What are the main sources of new-product ideas?

Answer: Many firms obtain ideas externally using open innovation, in which an organization finds and executes creative new-product ideas by developing strategic relationships with outside individuals and organizations. Some of these sources include employee and co-worker suggestions, customer and supplier suggestions (either directly, through the firm's salesforce or purchasing department or through crowd sourcing—soliciting ideas via the Internet from large numbers of people), R&D laboratories (both internal to the firm and professional innovation firms like IDEO), competitive products (analyzing their points of difference that lead to a competitive advantage for them), and smaller, nontraditional technology firms, university technology transfer centers that partner with business firms to commercialize faculty inventions, and lone inventors or entrepreneurs.

10-8 How do internal and external screening and evaluation approaches differ?

Answer: In internal screening, company employees evaluate the technical feasibility of new-product ideas to determine whether they meet the objectives defined in the new-product strategy development stage. For services, employees are assessed to determine whether they have the commitment and skills to meet customer expectations and sustain customer loyalty. In external screening, evaluation consists of preliminary concept testing of the new-product idea (not the actual product itself) using written descriptions, sketches, mockups, or promotional literature with consumers.

10-9 How does the development stage of the new-product development process involve testing the product inside and outside the firm?

Answer: Development is the stage of the new-product development process that turns the idea on paper into a prototype, which results in a demonstrable, producible product that can be efficiently manufactured. Internally, laboratory tests are done to see if the product achieves the physical, quality, and safety standards set for it. Externally, market testing is done to expose actual products to prospective consumers under realistic purchase conditions to see if they will buy.

10-10 What is a test market, and what are the three kinds?

Answer: Test marketing involves offering a product for sale on a limited basis in a defined area for a specific time period. The three main kinds of test markets are: (1) standard, (2) controlled, and (3) simulated. In a standard test market, a city (or cities) is selected that is viewed as being demographically representative of the markets targeted for the new product and has both cable TV systems that can deliver different ads to different homes and retailers with checkout counter scanners to measure sales results. In a controlled test market, the firm contracts the entire test program to an outside service, which pays retailers for shelf space to guarantee a specified percentage of the test product's potential distribution volume. In a simulated (or laboratory) test market (STM), the firm attempts to replicate a full-scale test market by creating a fictitious storefront in a shopping mall and exposing prospective customers to the product (or concept) and ads from both it and its competitors to see if they will buy.

10-11 What is the commercialization of a new product?

Answer: Commercialization, the most expensive stage for most new products, is the last stage of the new-product development process that involves positioning and launching a new product in full-scale production and sales.

FOCUSING ON KEY TERMS

business analysis p. 279
business products p. 266
commercialization p. 281
consumer products p. 266
convenience products p. 266
development p. 279
idea generation p. 275
market testing p. 280

new-product development
  process p. 274
new-product strategy
  development p. 274
open innovation p. 273
product p. 266
product item p. 268
product line p. 268

product mix p. 268
protocol p. 271
screening and evaluation p. 277
services p. 266
shopping products p. 266
specialty products p. 266
unsought products p. 266

APPLYING MARKETING KNOWLEDGE

1 Products can be classified as either consumer or business products. How would you classify the following products? (*a*) Johnson's baby shampoo, (*b*) a Black & Decker two-speed drill, and (*c*) an arc welder.

2 Are Nature Valley granola bars and Eddie Bauer hiking boots convenience, shopping, specialty, or unsought products?

3 Based on your answer to question 2, how would the marketing actions differ for each product and the classification to which you assigned it?

4 In terms of the behavioral effect on consumers, how would a computer, such as an Apple iMac, be classified? In light of this classification, what actions would you suggest to the manufacturers of these products to increase their sales in the market?

5 What methods would you suggest to assess the potential commercial success for the following new products? (*a*) a new, improved ketchup; (*b*) a three-dimensional television system that took the company 10 years to develop; and (*c*) a new children's toy on which the company holds a patent.

6 Concept testing is an important step in the new-product development process. Outline the concept tests for (*a*) an electrically powered car and (*b*) a new loan payment system for automobiles that is based on a variable interest rate. What are the differences in developing concept tests for products as opposed to services?

BUILDING YOUR MARKETING PLAN

In fine-tuning the product strategy for your marketing plan, do these two things:

1 Develop a simple three-column table in which (*a*) market segments of potential customers are in the first column and (*b*) the one or two key points of difference of the product to satisfy the segment's needs are in the second column.

2 In the third column of your table, write ideas for specific new products for your business in each of the rows in your table.

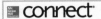

VIDEO CASE 10   X-1: Breaking the Barriers of Sound with New-Product Development

X-1 started as a simple idea for a business school project and has quickly grown to become the foremost leader in waterproof, sweatproof, and weatherproof audio equipment for athletes. Many factors contribute to the success of X-1, "but new product development is the engine that drives it all," explains CEO Carl Thomas.

Video 10-4
X-1 Video Case
kerin.tv/13e/v10-4

If you are a swimmer, runner, snowboarder, surfer, triathlete, climber, bicyclist, or any kind of sports enthusiast who enjoys music while you exercise, chances are you've seen X-1's products. The first product, a waterproof case for iPods, served as the starting point for a new-product development process that has added headphones, earbuds, cases, armbands, and accessories—an entire product line of audio solutions—to the company's offerings.

The commitment to new products has been so successful that the company now holds eight patents on its technology and was recognized by *Inc.* magazine as one of the top 500 fastest-growing companies in the United States. It is not surprising, then, to hear Thomas explain that marketing and new-product development "is a very key function for any company, but it's especially important for us."

THE COMPANY

X-1 has a fascinating history. Its founders were scuba divers who wanted to listen to music while they were diving, so they investigated how to use electronic devices and speakers underwater. The waterproof case they developed functioned to depths of 300 feet and led to a U.S. patent for a "waterproof enclosure for an audio device." At the same time, they were enrolled in a business school course that required the development of a business plan. They wrote the plan for their new technology, called their company Diver Entertainment, and began shipping products to other scuba divers.

It soon became obvious that the concept of waterproof audio equipment would appeal to many applications other than scuba diving. The company began developing waterproof headphones, changed its name to H2O Audio, and adopted the advertising tagline "Your Sport, Your Music." Swimmers, surfers, and triathletes were obvious potential customers, so Olympic swimmers Natalie Coughlin and Michael Phelps, professional surfer Laird Hamilton, and triathletes Greg and Laura Bennett were signed as official H2O Audio Ambassadors. The popularity of the brand grew rapidly as athletes in each of the sports learned about and tried the new products.

The success of H2O Audio products with aquatic athletes led the company to look for the next opportunity for growth. The obvious step was to expand to other sports and to attract athletes such as runners, kayakers, snowboarders, climbers, and weightlifters. In fact, H2O Audio soon came to realize that its market could be all athletes regardless of their sport.

The new strategy ran into an unexpected problem, however. While the H20 brand name was intuitive and descriptive and contributed to the initial success of

285

the products, it also limited the perception of the products' uses to water sports. Applications to sports where the athletes were not actually underwater were not immediately obvious to retail store managers. Bicycle retailers and shoe stores, for example, would often decline to carry the products saying, "You're just a swim company," explains Thomas. As a result, H2O Audio undertook a six-month review of its brand.

The review process included interviews with athletes, retailers, manufacturers, and current customers. A branding agency was hired to help assess the information and to identify possible changes in the products and brand. It asked, "What characteristics are important to enable all athletes to train and perform at their peak with music?" The answer was to expand the original "waterproof" product concept to "waterproof, weatherproof, and sweatproof technology that is durable and comfortable."

According to Thomas, "We learned that every single one of the athletes out there needed the headphone to be not only durable and stable in whatever environment they were in, but they wanted it to be comfortable, they wanted it to fit, and they wanted it to not fall out." The process also identified a new brand name, X-1, which was inspired by the first aircraft to break the sound barrier—the Bell X-1. The new name led to a new advertising tag line—"Breaking the Barriers of Sound"—and immediately changed the perception of the products.

The X-1 product line was expanded to reflect the new, broader appeal to all athletes. The line included:

- *Momentum.* An in-ear ultralight headphone that is rinsable, weatherproof, and sweatproof.
- *Surge.* An in-ear headphone that is waterproof, weatherproof, and sweatproof and has bass amplified sound and sportwrap options.
- *Women's Momentum and Surge.* Headphones that are designed for petite ears.
- *Amphibx.* Armbands and cases that hold most audio devices including iPod Shuffle, iPod Touch, iPod Classic, and iPhone.
- *Interval.* A solution designed specifically for swimmers to attach to goggle straps.

All of the headphones are customizable with 3 to 5 different sizes of ear tips, and the cases all allow full function of touchscreens and buttons. The entire product line is the result of and reflects the importance of the product development process.

THE PRODUCT DEVELOPMENT PROCESS AT X-1

"Here at X-1, new-product development is essential. We are constantly monitoring and speaking with our retail buyers to make sure that we have the best product

Courtesy of X-1 Audio, Inc.

mix for the marketplace," explains Peter Dirksing, director of product development at X-1. Generally, the company follows a rigorous sequence of steps or stages.

The first stage, new-product strategy development, reflects X-1's environmental scanning efforts. They observed that while the audio industry was mature, the advent of personal or mobile audio, created by products such as the Walkman, the Discman, the iPod, and now smartphones, represents an opportunity for new products.

The second stage is idea generation. X-1 uses many sources to help generate new ideas. Employees and co-workers, for example, can make suggestions at a "blue sky" meeting where, according to Dirksing, "No idea is a bad idea." The company also uses open innovation to generate new ideas by engaging retail buyers and soliciting ideas from a group of volunteer athletes called Team X-1.

The next stage, screening and evaluation, involves an evaluation of each idea to determine if it warrants further effort. X-1 assesses the feasibility of new technical requirements, synergy with existing technology, and the magnitude of resource requirements. All the factors "mix together to determine what is the greatest priority," explains Dirksing.

The fourth step, business analysis, involves creating a "business case" for the idea. The X-1 product development team works closely with sales and marketing to create a 12-month forecast that accounts for possible cannibalization of existing products and also estimates how long the product will be on the market before it reaches the break-even point.

In the development stage of the process, X-1 actually turns the idea into a prototype. The firm uses a 3D printer to check the aesthetics and the dimensions and to see how the product will actually fit on a person. Once the dimensions are determined, a functional prototype is needed. Dirksing explains, "After we've checked the outside dimensions on a 3D printed prototype, we'll actually send the final 3D drawings to a factory and get a functional prototype made."

The initial prototypes are used to conduct safety tests and the first functionality tests. "Part of my job is also making sure that the product functions as it's intended. So one of the really cool aspects of my job is that I'm taking prototypes out and hopping in the pool in the morning before work or getting in the water on my board and catching a wave or two before I get into the office just to make sure that these products we're developing are actually functioning in a real world environment," explains Dirksing.

Once production-quality prototypes are available, X-1 begins stage six, market testing. "We have a team of a few hundred amateur athletes that will get out and test the product and provide feedback," says Dirksing. X-1 also uses its website to connect with a cross-section of consumers and to get feedback as quickly as possible. Changes from this process lead to the final stage of the new-product development process, commercialization. X-1 develops a go-to-market plan, alerts the salesforce and retail buyers of the availability of new products, and begins production. Because X-1 is an international brand, this stage also includes developing the advertising and packaging for its customers in Europe, Asia, Australia, and around the world.

The new-product development process is an ongoing activity at X-1. At any given time the company may have 10 to 15 new-product ideas at various stages of the process. X-1's use of new technologies, such as 3D printers, as well as its fast-prototyping orientation has reduced product development time to about 12 months from start to commercialization. Once the new products are ready for consumers, the marketing department adds its expertise to ensure the success of the products.

MARKETING ADVANCED AUDIO SOLUTIONS

The marketing activities at X-1 are very comprehensive. "We do everything from print advertising, digital advertising, events, trade shows, social media, pretty much anything you can think of," says Dana Swanson, X-1 director of marketing. The many activities contribute to several different objectives, including changing the name of the company, rebranding the products, introducing new products, and communicating with different segments of consumers.

Changing the name from H2O Audio to X-1, for example, required marketing that helped get the product into people's hands so they could understand the value of the product. Swanson explains, "Something that is just going to splash our logo everywhere, like sponsoring a big race or an event, isn't as important to us as something like going to an event and having a booth where we can actually interact with people, talk about our product, and get our product into people's hands." This is also one of the reasons X-1 has product ambassadors. First, X-1 has contracts with selected professional and Olympic athletes who use X-1 products. Second, X-1 created a team of amateur athletes who receive product samples to use during amateur sporting events. In both cases, the ambassadors give X-1 products exposure to the marketplace and help demonstrate how they work.

X-1 also relies on social media, particularly to develop and introduce new products. "If it's out there, we've got a page, from Facebook to Twitter to Instagram," explains Swanson. "It's really all about just being where your people are and being there for them, interacting, talking, and answering questions," she goes on. Social media also allow X-1 to ask occasional questions about satisfaction with the products, color preferences, and even how the products are being used. Many of today's customers "love being involved," and their engagement is particularly helpful when X-1 introduces new products.

Communicating with different segments is also an important marketing objective. Currently, the three primary segments are:

- *Endurance Segment.* Includes athletes participating in all demanding athletic activities (e.g., marathons, triathalons, etc.) and training.
- *Outdoors Segment.* Includes all participants in activities that take place outside (e.g., hiking).
- *Club Segment.* Includes everyone who goes to a health club, fitness studio, or gymnasium.

One way X-1 ensures that it reaches these segments is through its sales channels. By offering its products through sporting goods stores (such as REI, Sports Chalet, and Eastern Mountain Sports), specialty retail stores, e-tailers (such as Amazon.com), and online through its own website, X-1 can reach the many potential consumers in each of the segments.

Public relations also helps provide a lot of exposure. X-1 is fortunate that it has many unique attributes such as reflective cables, customizable ear fit, ambient noise allowance, and special sizes for women to attract media interest. For example, *Fitness* magazine, *Women's Running* magazine, *MSN News, Fox News, The Wall Street Journal,* and *Travel Weekly* have all recently carried stories about X-1 products.

The combination of a great initial idea, a rigorous product development process, and excellent marketing actions all contribute to X-1's success. "I think X-1 products are successful because we actually are a solutions company," says Swanson, "We try to find a way that really works for athletes to bring their music with them while they're doing any activity."[27]

Questions

1 What are the points of difference, or unique attributes, for X-1 products?

2 What are X-1's primary target markets?

3 Describe the new-product development process used at X-1. What are the similarities and differences to the process described in Figure 10–3?

4 Which of the eight reasons for new-product failure did X-1 avoid to ensure the success of X-1's products?

5 Identify one new-product idea you would suggest that X-1 evaluate.

Chapter Notes

1. Adam Lashinsky, "Becoming Tim Cook," *Fortune,* April 1, 2015, pp. 60–72; "Apple's Goal for Smartwatch: Rolex Status," *The Wall Street Journal,* March 9, 2015, pp. B1, B3; "Lessons from Apple," www.economist.com, June 7, 2007.

2. www.crapola.us; and Todd Nelson, "On a Run with Crapola Granola," *Star Tribune,* January 14, 2013, p. D2.

3. www.geeksquad/about-us; interview with Geek Squad founder Robert Stephens on *60 Minutes,* January 28, 2007, www.geeksquad.com; Debora Viana Thompson, Rebecca W. Hamilton, and Roland Rust, "Feature Fatigue: When Product Capabilities Become Too Much of a Good Thing," *Journal of Marketing Research,* November 2005, pp. 431–42; and Ronald T. Rust, Debora Viana Thompson, and Rebecca W. Hamilton, "Defeating Feature Fatigue," *Harvard Business Review,* February 2006, pp. 98–107.

4. See "The 25 Biggest Product Flops of All Time," www.walletpop.com/photos/top-25-biggest-product-flops-of-all-time; and Zac Frank and Tania Khadder, "The 20 Worst Product Failures," www.saleshq.monster.com/news/articles/2655-the-20-worst-product-failures.

5. Joan Schneider and Julie Hall, "Why Most Product Launches Fail," *Harvard Business Review,* April 2011, pp. 21–23.

6. Robert G. Cooper, "New Products: What Separates the Winners from the Losers?" in *The PDMA Handbook of New Product Development,* Kenneth B. Kahn, ed. (New York: Wiley and Sons, 2013), pp. 3–34; and Merle Crawford and Anthony Di Benedetto, *New Products Management,* 11th ed. (New York: McGraw-Hill/Irwin, 2015).

7. Julie Fortser, "The Lucky Charm of Steve Sanger," *BusinessWeek,* March 26, 2001, pp. 75–76.

8. The Avert Virucidal tissues, Hey! There's A Monster In My Room spray, and Garlic Cake examples are adapted from Robert M. McMath and Thom Forbes, *What Were They Thinking?* (New York: Random House, 1998).

9. Schneider and Hall, "Why Most Product Launches Fail," p. 22.

10. "The 25 Biggest Product Flops of All Time"; Cass Sunstein and Reid Hastie, *Wiser: Getting Beyond Groupthink to Make Groups Smarter* (Boston: Harvard Business Review Press, 2015).

11. Robert G. Cooper, "What Leading Companies Are Doing to Reinvent Their NPD Process," *PDMA Visions Magazine,* September 2008, pp. 6–10; Robert G. Cooper, "The Stage-Gate Idea-to-Launch Process—Update: What's New and NexGen Systems," *Journal of Product Innovation Management,* May 2008, pp. 213–32; Leland D. Shaeffer and Michael Zirkle, "Beyond 'Phase Gate'—Why Not a Tailored Solution?" *PDMA*

Visions Magazine, June 2008, pp. 21–25; and Gloria Barczak, Abbie Griffin, and Kenneth B. Kahn, "Perspective: Trends and Drivers of Success in NPD Practices: Results of the 2003 PDMA Best Practices Study," *Journal of Product Innovation Management,* January 2009, pp. 3–23.

12. Hal B. Greyersen, Jeff Dyer, and Clayton M. Christensen, "Why Ask Why?" *ChiefExecutive.Net,* January/February 2012, pp. 40–43.

13. Dinah Eng, "Life Is Good in the T-shirt Business," *Fortune,* May 19, 2014, pp.39–42.

14. Ibid.

15. Sarah Ellison, "P&G Chief's Turnaround Recipe: Find Out What Women Want," *The Wall Street Journal,* June 1, 2005, pp. A1, A16.

16. Jack Neff, "Tide Pods Winning $7 Billion Detergent Wars by Defining Value," *Advertising Age,* December 18, 2012; Dale Buss, "P&G Awash in Success of Tide Pods Despite Wrinkles Along the Way," *Brandchannel,* December 18, 2012; Emily Glazer, "Tide Rides Convenience Wave," *The Wall Street Journal,* February 23, 2012, p. 138; and Emily Glazer, "P&G to Alter Tide Pods Packaging," *The Wall Street Journal,* May 26–27, 2012, p. B3.

17. Elisabeth A. Sullivan, "A Group Effort," *Marketing News,* February 28, 2010, pp. 22–29.

18. Adam Lashinsky, "Inside Apple," *Fortune,* May 23, 2011, p. 128; and Daniel Turner, "The Secret of Apple Design," *MIT Technology Review,* May/June 2007.

19. Charlie Rose, "How to Design Breakthrough Inventions," *CBS 60 Minutes,* air date January 6, 2013. See http://www.cbsnews.com/8301-18560_162-57562201/how-to-design-breakthrough-inventions.

20. "With Electric Cars, GM Targets Tesla," *The Wall Street Journal,* January 15, 2015, p. B2.

21. Peter Erickson, "One Food Company's Foray into Open Innovation," *PDMA Visions Magazine,* June 2008, pp. 12–14; and Simona Covel, "My Brain, Your Brawn," *The Wall Street Journal,* October 13, 2008, p. R12.

22. Kristin Tillotson, "Crowdfunding Gears Up for a Fresh Kick Start," *Star Tribune,* November 6, 2012, pp. A1, A10; and "Pebble Time Most Funded Kickstarter Ever," usatoday.com, March 3, 2015.

23. "Google Glass: What Went Wrong," cnn.com, January 20, 2015; "The Reason Why Google Glass, Amazon Fire Phone, and Segway All Failed," forbes.com, February 12, 2015; and "Google Glass Gets a New Direction," wsj.com, January 15, 2015.

24. Gilbert A. Churchill Jr., Tom J. Brown, and Tracy A. Suter, *Basic Marketing Research,* 7th ed. (Mason, OH: South-Western, Cengage Learning, 2010), pp. 122–30.

25. Daniel Michaels, "Innovation Is Messy Business," *The Wall Street Journal,* January 24, 2013, pp. B1, B2; Christopher Drew, "Dreamliner Troubles Put Boeing on Edge," *The New York Times,* January 20, 2013; Andy Pasztor and Jon Ostrower, "Probe of Boeing 787 Battery Fire Expands," *The Wall Street Journal,* January 24, 2013; and Brad Stone and Susanna Roy, "Don't Dream It's Over, "*Bloomberg Businessweek,* January 28–February 3, 2013, pp. 4–16.

26. Maureen Morrison, "Burger King Adds Satisfries Meals," adage.com, March 23, 2014; "Burger King Stores Discontinue Satisfries and Sales Sizzle," www.bloombergbusiness.com, August 13, 2014; "The French Fry Wars: Burger King Cooks Up a New Recipe," *The Miami Herald,* December 12, 2011; "New Fries at Burger King Restaurants," Burger King press release, November 30, 2011; "Burger King Introduces Hotter, Crispier, Better-Tasting French Fries," *PRNewswire,* December 10, 2011; and Jennifer Ordonez, "How Burger King Got Burned in Quest to Make the Perfect Fry," *The Wall Street Journal,* January 16, 2001, pp. A1, A8.

27. X-1: This case was written by Steven Hartley. Sources: "X-1 Breaks the Barriers of Sound with Innovative Rebranding and Website," PR.com, February 23, 2013; "US Patent Issued to H2O Audio on July 17 for 'Waterproof Enclosure for Audio Device,' *US Fed News,* July 23, 2012; "NetSuite Announces Outdoor Retail Customer Wins," *ENP Newswire,* August 6, 2012; X-1 website, www.x-1.com, accessed July 18, 2013; and personal interviews with X-1 personnel.

11

Managing Successful Products, Services, and Brands

LEARNING OBJECTIVES

After reading this chapter you should be able to:

 LO 11-1 Explain the product life-cycle concept.

 LO 11-2 Identify ways that marketing executives manage a product's life cycle.

 LO 11-3 Recognize the importance of branding and alternative branding strategies.

 LO 11-4 Describe the role of packaging, labeling, and warranties in the marketing of a product.

Gatorade: Bringing Science to Sweat for 50 Years

Why is the thirst for Gatorade unquenchable? Look no further than constant product improvement and masterful brand management.

Like Kleenex in the tissue market, Jell-O among gelatin desserts, and Scotch for cellophane tape, Gatorade is synonymous with sports drinks. Concocted in 1965 at the University of Florida as a rehydration beverage for the school's football team, the drink was coined "Gatorade" by an opposing team's coach after watching his team lose to the Florida Gators in the Orange Bowl. The name stuck, and a new beverage product class was born. Stokely-Van Camp, Inc. bought the Gatorade formula in 1967 and commercialized the product.

Creating the Gatorade Brand

The Quaker Oats Company acquired Stokely-Van Camp in 1983 and quickly increased Gatorade sales through a variety of means. More flavors were added. Multiple package sizes were offered using different containers. Distribution expanded from convenience stores and supermarkets to mass merchandisers such as Walmart. Consistent advertising and promotion effectively conveyed the product's unique performance benefits and links to athletic competition. International opportunities were vigorously pursued.

Today, Gatorade is a global brand and is sold in more than 80 countries. It is also the official sports drink of NASCAR, the National Football League, Major League Baseball, the National Basketball Association, the National Hockey League, Major League Soccer, and the Women's National Basketball Association.

Masterful brand management spurred Gatorade's success. Gatorade Frost was introduced in 1997 and aimed at expanding the brand's reach beyond organized sports to other usage occasions. Gatorade Fierce appeared in 1999. In the same year, Gatorade entered the bottled-water category with Propel Fitness Water, a lightly flavored water fortified with vitamins. The Gatorade Performance Series was introduced in 2001, featuring a Gatorade Energy Bar, Gatorade Energy Drink, and Gatorade Nutritional Shake.

Building the Gatorade Brand

Brand development accelerated after PepsiCo, Inc. purchased Quaker Oats and the Gatorade brand in 2001. Gatorade Xtremo, developed with a bilingual label for Latino consumers, was launched in 2002. Gatorade X-Factor followed in 2003. In 2005, Gatorade Endurance Formula was created for serious runners, construction

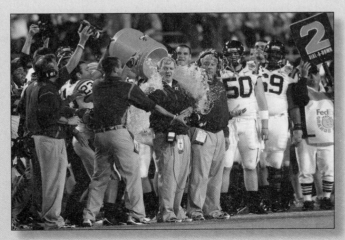

Gatorade's marketing performance is a direct result of continuous product improvement and masterful brand management as defined by the "Gatorade bath."

workers, and other people doing long, sweaty workouts. Gatorade Rain, a lighter-tasting version of regular Gatorade, arrived in 2006. A low-calorie Gatorade called G2 appeared in 2008.

In 2009, Gatorade executives unleashed a bevy of enhanced beverages in bold new packaging. "Just like any good athlete, Gatorade is taking it to the next level," said Gatorade's chief marketing officer. "Whether you're in it for the win, for the thrill or for better health, if your body is moving, Gatorade sees you as an athlete, and we're inviting you into the brand." According to a company announcement, "The new Gatorade attitude would be most visible through a total packaging redesign." For example, Gatorade Thirst Quencher now displays the letter G front and center along with the brand's iconic bolt. "For Gatorade, G represents the heart, hustle, and soul of athleticism and will become a badge of pride for anyone who sweats, no matter where they're active."

To differentiate the range of Gatorade offerings from the traditional Gatorade Thirst Quencher, newly enhanced beverages convey the attitude of a tough-love coach or personal trainer through in-your-face names on the label and nutrition benefits inside. For example, Gatorade Fierce is now Bring It and Gatorade X-Factor is now Be Tough. Continuing product development efforts guided the creation of the G Series of products in 2010 and 2011.

Beginning in 2011, Gatorade underwent a brand repositioning during which it developed different lines of Gatorade products targeted at different types of athletes. These lines included the traditional G Series for athletes and the G Series Endurance for extreme sports athletes. Product development within these lines continues today as evidenced by the launch of Gatorade Endurance Carb Energy chews.[1]

The marketing of Gatorade illustrates continuous product development and masterful brand management in a dynamic marketplace. Not surprisingly, Gatorade remains a vibrant multibillion-dollar brand 50 years after its creation. This chapter shows how the actions taken by Gatorade executives exemplify those made by successful marketers.

Video 11-1
Gatorade Ad
kerin.tv/13e/v11-1

CHARTING THE PRODUCT LIFE CYCLE

LO 11-1   Explain the product life-cycle concept.

Products, like people, are viewed as having a life cycle. The concept of the **product life cycle** describes the stages a new product goes through in the marketplace: introduction, growth, maturity, and decline (Figure 11–1).[2] The two curves shown in this figure, total industry sales revenue and total industry profit, represent the sum of sales revenue and profit of all firms producing the product. The reasons for the changes in each curve and the marketing decisions involved are detailed next.

Introduction Stage

The introduction stage of the product life cycle occurs when a product is introduced to its intended target market. During this period, sales grow slowly, and profit is minimal. The lack of profit is often the result of large investment costs in product development, such as the millions of dollars spent by Gillette to develop the Gillette Fusion razor shaving system. The marketing objective for the company at this stage is to create consumer awareness and stimulate *trial*—the initial purchase of a product by a consumer.

Companies often spend heavily on advertising and other promotion tools to build awareness and stimulate product trial among consumers in the introduction stage. For example, Gillette budgeted $200 million in advertising to introduce the Fusion shaving system to male shavers. The result? Over 60 percent of male shavers became aware of the new razor within six months and 26 percent tried the product.[3]

Advertising and promotion expenditures in the introduction stage are often made to stimulate *primary demand,* the desire for the product class rather than for a specific brand, since there are few competitors with the same product. As more competitors launch their own products and the product progresses along its life cycle, company attention is focused on creating *selective demand,* the preference for a specific brand.

Other marketing mix variables also are important at this stage. Gaining distribution can be a challenge because channel intermediaries may be hesitant to carry a new product. Also, a company often restricts the number of variations of the product to ensure control of product quality. As an example, the original Gatorade came in only one flavor—lemon-lime.

During introduction, pricing can be either high or low. A high initial price may be used as part of a *skimming* strategy to help the company recover the costs of development as well as capitalize on the price insensitivity of early buyers. A master of this strategy is 3M. According to a 3M manager, "We hit fast, price high, and get the heck out when the me-too products pour in."[4] High prices tend to attract competitors eager to enter the market because they see the opportunity for profit. To discourage competitive entry, a company can price low, referred to as *penetration pricing*. This pricing strategy helps build unit volume, but a company must closely monitor costs. These and other pricing techniques are covered in Chapter 14.

The success of the Gillette Fusion shaving system can be understood using product life-cycle concepts as discussed in the text.

© Mike Hruby

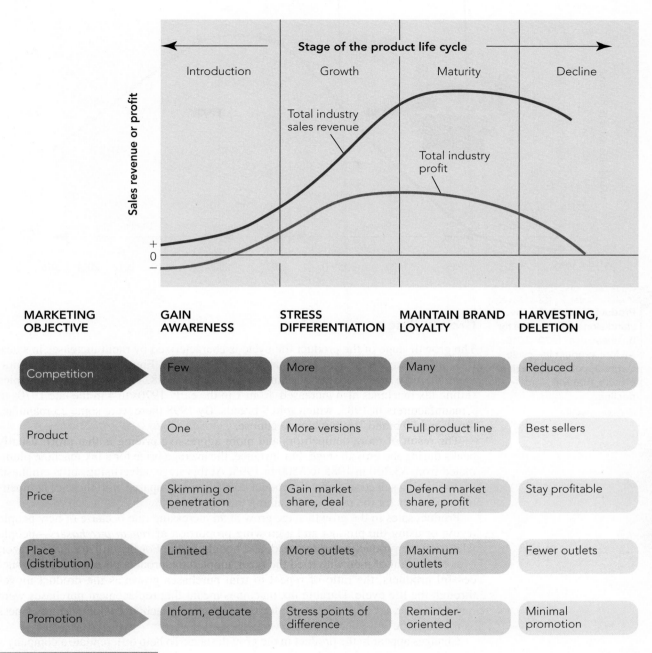

Stage of the product life cycle

	Introduction	Growth	Maturity	Decline
MARKETING OBJECTIVE	GAIN AWARENESS	STRESS DIFFERENTIATION	MAINTAIN BRAND LOYALTY	HARVESTING, DELETION
Competition	Few	More	Many	Reduced
Product	One	More versions	Full product line	Best sellers
Price	Skimming or penetration	Gain market share, deal	Defend market share, profit	Stay profitable
Place (distribution)	Limited	More outlets	Maximum outlets	Fewer outlets
Promotion	Inform, educate	Stress points of difference	Reminder-oriented	Minimal promotion

FIGURE 11–1

How stages of the product life cycle relate to a firm's marketing objectives and marketing mix actions.

Figure 11–2 charts the stand-alone fax machine product life cycle for business use in the United States from the early 1970s to 2016.[5] Sales grew slowly in the 1970s and early 1980s after Xerox pioneered the first portable fax machine. Fax machines were first sold direct to businesses by company salespeople and were premium priced. The average price for a fax machine in 1980 was a hefty $12,700, or almost $35,000 in today's dollars! Those fax machines were primitive by today's standards. They contained mechanical parts, not electronic circuitry, and offered few features seen in today's models.

Several product classes are in the introductory stage of the product life cycle today. These include smart TVs and all-electric-powered automobiles.

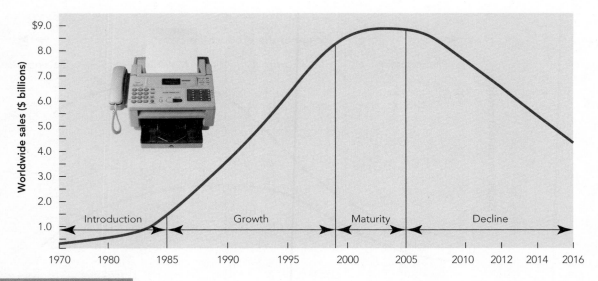

FIGURE 11–2

Product life cycle for the stand-alone fax machine for business use: 1970–2016. All four product life-cycle stages appear: introduction, growth, maturity, and decline.

© Getty Images

Growth Stage

The growth stage of the product life cycle is characterized by rapid increases in sales. It is in this stage that competitors appear. For example, Figure 11–2 shows the dramatic increase in sales of fax machines from 1986 to 1998. The number of companies selling fax machines also increased, from 1 in the early 1970s to 4 in the late 1970s to 7 manufacturers in 1983, which sold 9 brands. By 1998 there were some 25 manufacturers and 60 brands from which to choose.

The result of more competitors and more aggressive pricing is that profit usually peaks during the growth stage. For instance, the average price for a fax machine plummeted from $3,300 in 1985 to $500 in 1995. At this stage, advertising shifts emphasis to stimulating selective demand; product benefits are compared with those of competitors' offerings for the purpose of gaining market share.

Product sales in the growth stage grow at an increasing rate because of new people trying or using the product and a growing proportion of *repeat purchasers*—people who tried the product, were satisfied, and bought again. For the Gillette Fusion razor, over 60 percent of men who tried the razor adopted the product permanently. For successful products, the ratio of repeat to trial purchases grows as the product moves through the life cycle. Durable fax machines meant that replacement purchases were rare. However, it became common for more than one machine to populate a business as the machine's use became more widespread.

Changes appear in the product in the growth stage. To help differentiate a company's brand from competitors, an improved version or new features are added to the original design, and product proliferation occurs. Changes in fax machines included (1) models with built-in telephones; (2) models that used plain, rather than thermal, paper for copies; and (3) models that integrated electronic mail.

In the growth stage, it is important to broaden distribution for the product. In the retail store, for example, this often means that competing companies fight for display and shelf space. Expanded distribution in the fax industry is an example. Early in the growth stage, just 11 percent of office machine dealers carried this equipment. By the mid-1990s, over 70 percent of these dealers sold fax equipment, and distribution was expanded to other stores selling electronic equipment, such as Best Buy and Office Depot.

Numerous product classes or industries are in the growth stage of the product life cycle today. Examples include smartphones, e-book readers, and other tablet devices such as the iPad.

Electric automobiles like the Chevrolet Spark made by General Motors are in the introductory stage of the product life cycle. By comparison, smartphones such as the Apple iPhone 6 are in the growth stage of the product life cycle. Each product faces unique challenges based on its product life-cycle stage.

Left: © Kevork Djansezian/Getty Images; Right: Source: Apple

General Motors Company
www.gm.com

Apple
www.apple.com

Maturity Stage

The maturity stage is characterized by a slowing of total industry sales or product class revenue. Also, marginal competitors begin to leave the market. Most consumers who would buy the product are either repeat purchasers of the item or have tried and abandoned it. Sales increase at a decreasing rate in the maturity stage as fewer new buyers enter the market. Profit declines due to fierce price competition among many sellers, and the cost of gaining new buyers at this stage rises.

Marketing attention in the maturity stage is often directed toward holding market share through further product differentiation and finding new buyers and uses. For example, Gillette modified its Fusion shaving system with the addition of ProGlide, a five-blade shaver with an additional blade on the back for trimming. Fax machine manufacturers developed Internet-enabled multifunctional models with new features such as scanning, copying, and color reproduction. They also designed fax machines suitable for small and home businesses, which today represent a substantial portion of sales. Still, a major consideration in a company's strategy in this stage is to control overall marketing cost by improving promotional and distribution efficiency.

Fax machines entered the maturity stage in the late 1990s. At the time, about 90 percent of industry sales were captured by five producers (Hewlett-Packard, Brother, Sharp, Lexmark, and Samsung), reflecting the departure of marginal competitors. By 2004, 200 million stand-alone fax machines were installed throughout the world, sending more than 120 billion faxes annually.

Numerous product classes and industries are in the maturity stage of their product life cycle. These include carbonated soft drinks and presweetened breakfast cereals.

Decline Stage

The decline stage occurs when sales drop. Fax machines for business use moved to this stage in early 2005. By then, the average price for a fax machine had sunk below $100. Frequently, a product enters this stage not because of any wrong strategy on the part of companies, but because of environmental changes. For example, digital music pushed compact discs into decline in the recorded music industry. Will Internet technology and e-mail make fax machines extinct any time soon? The Marketing Matters box offers one perspective on this question that may surprise you.[6]

Numerous product classes or industries are in the decline stage of their product life cycle. Two prominent examples include analog TVs and desktop personal computers.

Products in the decline stage tend to consume a disproportionate share of management and financial resources relative to their future worth. A company will follow one of two strategies to handle a declining product: deletion or harvesting.

Will E-mail Spell Extinction for Fax Machines?

Technological substitution that creates value for customers often causes the decline stage in the product life cycle. Will e-mail replace fax machines?

This question has been debated for years. Even though e-mail continues to grow with broadening Internet access, millions of fax machines are still sold each year. Industry analysts estimated that the number of e-mail mailboxes worldwide would be 5.2 billion in 2018. However, the phenomenal popularity of e-mail has not brought fax machines to extinction. Why? The two technologies do not directly compete for the same messaging applications.

E-mail is used for text messages. Faxing is predominately used for communicating formatted documents by business users, notably doctors, concerned about Internet security. Fax usage is expected to increase through 2018, even though unit sales of fax machines have declined on a worldwide basis. Internet technology and e-mail may eventually replace facsimile technology and paper and make fax machines extinct, but not in the immediate future.

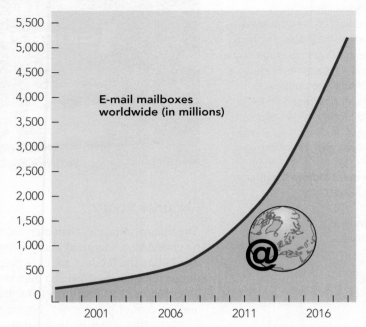

Deletion   Product *deletion,* or dropping the product from the company's product line, is the most drastic strategy. Because a residual core of consumers still consume or use a product even in the decline stage, product elimination decisions are not taken lightly. For example, Sanford Corporation continues to sell its Liquid Paper correction fluid for use with typewriters in the era of word-processing equipment.

Harvesting   A second strategy, *harvesting,* is when a company retains the product but reduces marketing costs. The product continues to be offered, but salespeople do not allocate time in selling nor are advertising dollars spent. The purpose of harvesting is to maintain the ability to meet customer requests. Coca-Cola, for instance, still sells Tab, its first diet cola, to a small group of die-hard fans. According to Coke's CEO, "It shows you care. We want to make sure those who want Tab, get Tab."[7]

Three Aspects of the Product Life Cycle

Some important aspects of product life cycles are (1) their length, (2) the shape of their sales curves, and (3) the rate at which consumers adopt products.

Length of the Product Life Cycle   There is no set time that it takes a product to move through its life cycle. As a rule, consumer products have shorter life cycles than business products. For example, many new consumer food products such as Frito-Lay's Baked Lay's potato chips move from the introduction stage to maturity in 18 months. The availability of mass communication vehicles informs consumers quickly and shortens life cycles. Technological change shortens product life cycles as new-product innovation replaces existing products. For instance, smartphones have largely replaced digital cameras in the amateur photography market.

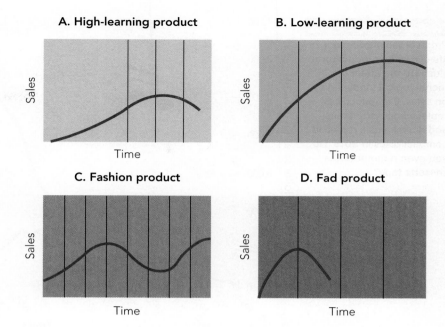

FIGURE 11–3

Alternative product life-cycle curves based on product types. Note the long introduction stage for a high-learning product compared with a low-learning product. Read the text for an explanation of the different product life-cycle curves.

A. High-learning product

Sales / Time

B. Low-learning product

Sales / Time

C. Fashion product

Sales / Time

D. Fad product

Sales / Time

Shape of the Life-Cycle Curve The product life-cycle sales curve shown in Figure 11–1 is the *generalized life cycle,* but not all products have the same shape to their curve. In fact, there are several life-cycle curves, each type suggesting different marketing strategies. Figure 11–3 shows the shape of life-cycle sales curves for four different types of products: high-learning, low-learning, fashion, and fad products.

A *high-learning product* is one for which significant customer education is required and there is an extended introductory period (Figure 11–3A). It may surprise you, but personal computers had this life-cycle curve. Consumers in the 1980s had to learn the benefits of owning the product or be educated in a new way of performing familiar tasks. Convection ovens for home use required consumers to learn a new way of cooking and alter familiar recipes used with conventional ovens. As a result, these ovens spent years in the introductory period.

In contrast, sales for a *low-learning product* begin immediately because little learning is required by the consumer and the benefits of purchase are readily understood (Figure 11–3B). This product often can be easily imitated by competitors, so the marketing strategy is to broaden distribution quickly. In this way, as competitors rapidly enter, most retail outlets already have the innovator's product. It is also important to have the manufacturing capacity to meet demand. A successful low-learning product is Gillette's Fusion razor. This product achieved $1 billion in worldwide sales in less than three years.

A *fashion product* (Figure 11–3C) is a style of the times. Life cycles for fashion products frequently appear in women's and men's apparel. Fashion products are introduced, decline, and then seem to return. The length of the cycles may be months, years, or decades. Consider women's hosiery. Product sales have been declining for years. Women consider it more fashionable to not wear hosiery—bad news for Hanes brands, the leading marketer of women's sheer hosiery. According to an authority on fashion, "Companies might as well let the fashion cycle take its course and wait for the inevitable return of pantyhose."[8]

A *fad product* experiences rapid sales on introduction and then an equally rapid decline (Figure 11–3D). These products are typically novelties and have a short life cycle. They include car tattoos, sold in Southern California and described as the first removable and reusable graphics for automobiles, and vinyl dresses and fleece bikinis made by a Minnesota clothing company.[9]

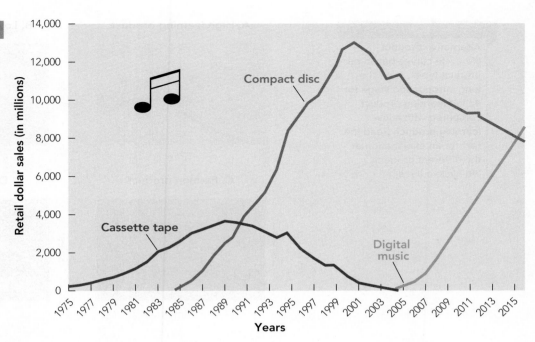

FIGURE 11–4

Prerecorded music product life cycles by product form illustrate the effect of technological innovation on sales. Compact discs replaced cassette tapes, and digital music replaced compact discs in 2015. Do you even remember the cassette tape?

The Product Level: Class and Form

The product life cycle shown in Figure 11–1 is a total industry or generalized product class sales curve. Yet, in managing a product it is often important to distinguish among the multiple life cycles (class and form) that may exist.

Product class refers to the entire product category or industry, such as prerecorded music. **Product form** pertains to variations of a product within the product class. For prerecorded music, product form exists in the technology used to provide the music such as cassette tapes, compact discs, and digital music downloading and streaming. Figure 11–4 shows the life cycles for these three product forms and demonstrates the impact of technological innovation on sales.[10]

The Product Life Cycle and Consumer Behavior

The life cycle of a product depends on sales to consumers. Not all consumers rush to buy a product in the introductory stage, and the shapes of the life-cycle curves indicate that most sales occur after the product has been on the market for some time. In essence, a product diffuses, or spreads, through the population, a concept called the *diffusion of innovation*.[11]

Some people are attracted to a product early. Others buy it only after they see their friends or opinion leaders with the item. Figure 11–5 shows the consumer population divided into five categories of product adopters based on when they adopt a new product. Brief profiles accompany each category. For any product to be successful, it must be purchased by innovators and early adopters. This is why manufacturers of new pharmaceuticals try to gain adoption by respected hospitals, clinics, and physicians. Once accepted by innovators and early adopters, successful new products move on to the early majority, late majority, and laggard categories.

Several factors affect whether a consumer will adopt a new product or not. Common reasons for resisting a product in the introduction stage are *usage barriers* (the product is not compatible with existing habits), *value barriers* (the product provides no incentive to change), *risk barriers* (physical, economic, or social), and *psychological barriers* (cultural differences or image).[12]

These factors help to explain the slow adoption of all-electric-powered automobiles in the United States. About one-third of 1 percent of cars sold in 2015

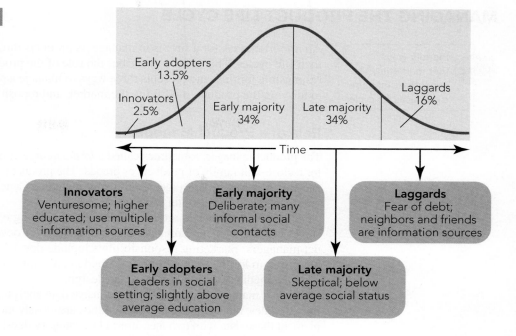

FIGURE 11–5

Five categories and profiles of product adopters. For a product to be successful, it must be purchased by innovators and early adopters.

were all-electric-powered vehicles. Industry analysts cite the usage barrier for disappointing sales. They note that prospective buyers believe these cars are not compatible with existing driving habits. Analysts also mention a value barrier. Consumers have not recognized the superiority of all-electric cars over vehicles with internal combustion engines. Third, a risk barrier exists in large measure to buyer uncertainty about the actual cost of all-electric-powered car ownership. According to one auto industry analyst, "The innovators and early adopters have purchased all-electric vehicles, but mainstream consumers have not followed." Not surprisingly, all-electric-powered automobiles remain in the introductory stage of the product life cycle.[13]

Companies attempt to overcome these barriers in numerous ways. For example, manufacturers of all-electric-powered automobiles provide low-cost leasing options to overcome usage, value, and risk barriers. Other companies provide warranties, money-back guarantees, extensive usage instructions, demonstrations, and free samples to stimulate initial trial of new products. For example, software developers offer demonstrations downloaded from the Internet. Cosmetics consumers can browse through the Embrace Your Face site at www.covergirl.com to find out how certain makeup products will look. Free samples are one of the most popular means to gain consumer trial. In fact, 71 percent of consumers consider a sample to be the best way to evaluate a new product.[14]

learning review »

11-1. Advertising plays a major role in the _____ stage of the product life cycle, and _____ plays a major role in maturity.

11-2. How do high-learning and low-learning products differ?

11-3. What are the five categories of product adopters in the diffusion of innovations?

MANAGING THE PRODUCT LIFE CYCLE

An important task for a firm is to manage its products through the successive stages of their life cycles. This section describes the role of the product manager, who is usually responsible for this, and presents three ways to manage a product through its life cycle: modifying the product, modifying the market, and repositioning the product.

Role of a Product Manager

The product manager, sometimes called a *brand manager,* manages the marketing efforts for a close-knit family of products or brands. The product manager style of marketing organization is used by consumer goods firms, including General Mills and PepsiCo, and by industrial firms such as Intel and Hewlett-Packard.

All product managers are responsible for managing existing products through the stages of the life cycle. Some are also responsible for developing new products. Product managers' marketing responsibilities include developing and executing a marketing program for the product line described in an annual marketing plan and approving ad copy, media selection, and package design.

Product managers also engage in extensive data analysis related to their products and brands. Sales, market share, and profit trends are closely monitored. Managers often supplement these data with two measures: (1) a category development index (CDI) and (2) a brand development index (BDI). These indexes help to identify strong and weak market segments (usually demographic or geographic segments) for specific consumer products and brands and provide direction for marketing efforts. The calculation, visual display, and interpretation of these two indexes for Hawaiian Punch are described in the Applying Marketing Metrics box.

Modifying the Product

Product modification involves altering one or more of a product's characteristics, such as its quality, performance, or appearance, to increase the product's value to customers and increase sales. Wrinkle-free and stain-resistant clothing made possible by nanotechnology revolutionized the men's and women's apparel business and stimulated industry sales of casual pants, shirts, and blouses. A common approach to product modification to increase a product's value to consumers is called *product bundling*—the sale of two or more separate products in one package. For example, Microsoft Office is sold as a bundle of computer software, including Word, Excel, and PowerPoint.

New features, packages, or scents can be used to change a product's characteristics and give the sense of a revised product. Procter & Gamble revamped Pantene shampoo and conditioner with a new vitamin formula and relaunched the brand with a multi-million-dollar advertising and promotion campaign. The result? Pantene, a brand first introduced in the 1940s, is now a top-selling shampoo and conditioner in the United States in an industry with more than 1,000 competitors.

Harley-Davidson redesigned some of its motorcycle models to feature smaller hand grips, a lower seat, and an easier-to-pull clutch lever to create a more comfortable ride for women. According to Genevieve Schmitt, founding editor of WomenRidersNow.com, "They realize that women are an up-and-coming segment and that they need to accommodate them."
© Gary Gardiner/Bloomberg via Getty Images

Harley-Davidson, Inc.
www.harley-davidson.com

Modifying the Market

With **market modification** strategies, a company tries to find new customers, increase a product's use among existing customers, or create new use situations.

Finding New Customers As part of its market modification strategy, LEGO Group is offering a new line of products to attract consumers outside of its traditional market. Known for its popular line of construction toys for young boys, LEGO Group has introduced a product line for young girls called LEGO Friends. Harley-Davidson

Applying **Marketing Metrics**

Knowing Your CDI and BDI

Where are sales for my product category and brand strongest and weakest? Data related to this question are displayed in a marketing dashboard using two indexes: (1) a category development index and (2) a brand development index.

Your Challenge

You have joined the marketing team for Hawaiian Punch, the top fruit punch drink sold in the United States. The brand has been marketed to mothers with children under 13 years old. The majority of Hawaiian Punch sales are in gallon and 2-liter bottles. Your assignment is to examine the brand's performance and identify growth opportunities for the Hawaiian Punch brand among households that consume prepared fruit drinks (the product category).

Your marketing dashboard displays a category development index and a brand development index provided by a syndicated marketing research firm. Each index is based on the calculations below:

Category Development Index (CDI) =

$$\frac{\text{Percent of a product category's total U.S. sales in a market segment}}{\text{Percent of the total U.S. population in a market segment}} \times 100$$

Brand Development Index (BDI) =

$$\frac{\text{Percent of a brand's total U.S. sales in a market segment}}{\text{Percent of the total U.S. population in a market segment}} \times 100$$

A CDI over 100 indicates above-average product category purchases by a market segment. A number under 100 indicates below-average purchases. A BDI over 100 indicates a strong brand position in a segment; a number under 100 indicates a weak brand position.

You are interested in CDI and BDI displays for four household segments that consume prepared fruit drinks: (1) households without children; (2) households with children 6 years old or under; (3) households with children aged 7 to 12; and (4) households with children aged 13 to 18.

Your Findings

The BDI and CDI metrics displayed below show that Hawaiian Punch is consumed by households with children, and particularly households with children under age 12. The Hawaiian Punch BDI is over 100 for both segments—not surprising since the brand is marketed to these segments. Households with children 13 to 18 years old evidence high fruit drink consumption with a CDI over 100. But Hawaiian Punch is relatively weak in this segment with a BDI under 100.

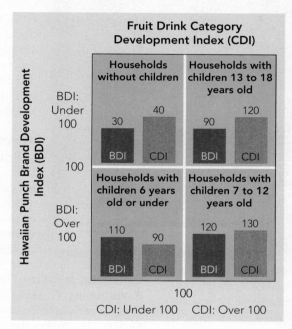

Your Action

An opportunity for Hawaiian Punch exists among households with children 13 to 18 years old—teenagers. You might propose that Hawaiian Punch be repositioned for teens. In addition, you might recommend that Hawaiian Punch be packaged in single-serve cans or bottles to attract this segment, much like soft drinks. Teens might also be targeted for advertising and promotions.

---

has tailored a marketing program to encourage women to take up biking, thus doubling the number of potential customers for its motorcycles.

Increasing a Product's Use   Promoting more frequent usage has been a strategy of Campbell Soup Company. Because soup consumption rises in the winter and declines during the summer, the company now advertises more heavily in warm months to encourage consumers to think of soup as more than a cold-weather food. Similarly, the Florida Orange Growers Association advocates drinking orange juice throughout the day rather than for breakfast only.

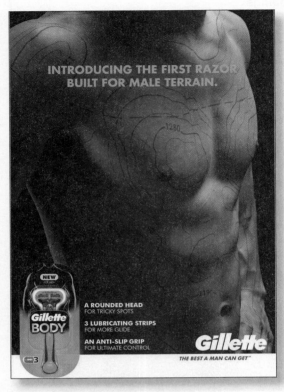

Video 11-2
Gillette Ad
kerin.tv/13e/v11-2

INTRODUCING THE FIRST RAZOR
BUILT FOR MALE TERRAIN.

1280

1190

NEW
FOR MEN

Gillette
BODY

A ROUNDED HEAD
FOR TRICKY SPOTS

3 LUBRICATING STRIPS
FOR MORE GLIDE

AN ANTI-SLIP GRIP
FOR ULTIMATE CONTROL

Gillette

THE BEST A MAN CAN GET™

Gillette razors, blades, and gels have been adapted for shaving men's body hair in areas below the neckline. This new use situation for its shaving products is called "manscaping."
Source: Procter & Gamble

Creating a New Use Situation   Finding new uses for an existing product has been the strategy behind Gillette, the world leader for men's shaving products. The company now markets its Gillette Body line of razors, blades, and shaving gels for "manscaping"—the art of shaving body hair in areas below the neckline—that represents a new use situation.

Repositioning the Product

Often a company decides to reposition its product or product line in an attempt to bolster sales. *Product repositioning* changes the place a product occupies in a consumer's mind relative to competitive products. A firm can reposition a product by changing one or more of the four marketing mix elements. Four factors that trigger the need for a repositioning action are discussed next.

Reacting to a Competitor's Position   One reason to reposition a product is because a competitor's entrenched position is adversely affecting sales and market share. New Balance, Inc. successfully repositioned its athletic shoes to focus on fit, durability, and comfort rather than competing head-on against Nike and Adidas on fashion and professional sports. The company offers an expansive range of shoes and networks with podiatrists, not sports celebrities.

Reaching a New Market   When Unilever introduced iced tea in Britain, sales were disappointing. British consumers viewed it as leftover hot tea, not suitable for drinking. The company made its tea carbonated and repositioned it as a cold soft drink to compete as a carbonated beverage and sales improved. Johnson & Johnson effectively repositioned its St. Joseph aspirin from a product for infants to an adult low-strength aspirin to reduce the risk of heart problems or strokes.

Catching a Rising Trend   Changing consumer trends can also lead to product repositioning. Growing consumer interest in foods that offer health and dietary benefits is an example. Many products have been repositioned to capitalize on this trend. Quaker Oats makes the FDA-approved claim that oatmeal, as part of a low-saturated-fat, low-cholesterol diet, may reduce the risk of heart disease. Calcium-enriched products, such as Kraft American cheese and Uncle Ben's Calcium Plus rice, emphasize healthy bone structure for children and adults. Weight-conscious consumers have embraced low-fat and low-calorie diets in growing numbers. Today, most food and beverage companies offer reduced-fat and low-calorie versions of their products.

Changing the Value Offered   In repositioning a product, a company can decide to change the value it offers buyers and trade up or down. **Trading up** involves adding value to the product (or line) through additional features or higher-quality materials. Michelin, Bridgestone, and Goodyear have done this with a "run-flat" tire that can travel up to 50 miles at 55 miles per hour after suffering total air loss. Dog food manufacturers, such as Ralston Purina, also have traded up by offering super-premium foods based on "life-stage nutrition." Mass merchandisers, such as Target and Walmart, can trade up by adding a designer clothes section to their stores.

Trading down involves reducing a product's number of features, quality, or price. For example, airlines have added more seats, thus reducing legroom, and limited meal service by offering snacks only on most domestic flights. Trading down also exists when companies engage in *downsizing*—reducing the package content without changing package size and maintaining or increasing the package price. Companies are criticized for this practice, as described in the Making Responsible Decisions box.[15]

Making **Responsible Decisions**

Consumer Economics of Downsizing—Get Less, Pay More

For more than 30 years, Starkist put 6.5 ounces of tuna into its regular-sized can. Today, Starkist puts 6.125 ounces of tuna into its can but charges the same price. Frito-Lay (Doritos and Lay's snack chips), PepsiCo (Tropicana orange juice), and Häagen-Dazs (ice cream) have whittled away at package contents 5 to 10 percent while maintaining their products' package size, dimensions, and prices.

Procter & Gamble recently kept its retail price on its jumbo pack of Pampers and Luvs diapers, but reduced the number of diapers per pack from 140 to 132. Similarly, Unilever reduced the number of Popsicles in each package from 24 to 20 without changing the package price. Georgia-Pacific reduced the content of its

© McGraw-Hill Education/Editorial Image, LLC, photographer

Brawny paper towel six-roll pack by 20 percent without lowering the price.

Consumer advocates charge that downsizing the content of packages while maintaining prices is a subtle and unannounced way of taking advantage of consumer buying habits. They also say downsizing is a price increase in disguise and a deceptive, but legal, practice. Some manufacturers argue that this practice is a way of keeping prices from rising beyond psychological barriers for their products. Other manufacturers say prices are set by individual stores, not by them.

Is downsizing an unethical practice if manufacturers do not inform consumers that the package contents are less than they were previously?

learning review

11-4. How does a product manager manage a product's life cycle?

11-5. What does "creating a new use situation" mean in managing a product's life cycle?

11-6. Explain the difference between trading up and trading down in product repositioning.

303

BRANDING AND BRAND MANAGEMENT

LO 11-3

Recognize the importance of branding and alternative branding strategies.

A basic decision in marketing products is **branding**, in which an organization uses a name, phrase, design, symbols, or combination of these to identify its products and distinguish them from those of competitors. A **brand name** is any word, device (design, sound, shape, or color), or combination of these used to distinguish a seller's products or services. Some brand names can be spoken, such as a Gatorade. Other brand names cannot be spoken, such as the white apple (the *logotype* or *logo*) that Apple puts on its machines and in its ads. A **trade name** is a commercial, legal name under which a company does business. The Coca-Cola Company is the trade name of that firm.

A **trademark** identifies that a firm has legally registered its brand name or trade name so the firm has its exclusive use, thereby preventing others from using it. In the United States, trademarks are registered with the U.S. Patent and Trademark Office and protected under the *Lanham Act*. A well-known trademark can help a company advertise its offerings to customers and develop their brand loyalty. For example, Kylie and Kendall Jenner, cast members of *Keeping Up with the Kardashians* reality television show, have filed to have their first names trademarked for use in "entertainment, fashion, and pop culture."[16]

Because a good trademark can help sell a product, *product counterfeiting,* which involves low-cost copies of popular brands not manufactured by the original producer, is a serious problem. Counterfeit products can steal sales from the original manufacturer or harm the company's reputation. U.S. companies lose about $250 billion each year to counterfeit products. The five most counterfeited branded products are, in order, handbags and wallets, watches and jewelry, clothing and accessories, consumer electronics, and shoes. To counteract counterfeiting, the U.S. government passed the *Stop Counterfeiting in Manufactured Goods Act* (2006), which makes counterfeiters subject to 20-year prison sentences and $15 million in fines.

Consumers may benefit most from branding. Recognizing competing products by distinct trademarks allows them to be more efficient shoppers. Consumers can recognize and avoid products with which they are dissatisfied, while becoming loyal to other, more satisfying brands. As discussed in Chapter 5, brand loyalty often eases consumers' decision making by eliminating the need for an external search.

Are you interested in creating a business using your name? If you are, you might first check to see if your name has been registered with the U.S. Patent and Trademark Office by visiting its website. See the Marketing Insights About Me box for details.

Brand Personality and Brand Equity

Product managers recognize that brands offer more than product identification and a means to distinguish their products from those of competitors.[17] Successful and established brands take on a **brand personality**, a set of human characteristics associated with a brand name. Research shows that consumers assign personality traits to products—traditional, romantic, rugged, sophisticated, rebellious—and choose brands that are consistent with their own or desired self-image.

Marketers can and do imbue a brand with a personality through advertising that depicts a certain user or usage situation and conveys emotions or feelings to be associated with the brand. For example, personality traits linked with Coca-Cola are all-American and real; with Pepsi, young and exciting; and with Dr Pepper, nonconforming and unique. The traits often linked to Harley-Davidson are masculinity, defiance, and rugged individualism.

Brand name importance to a company has led to a concept called **brand equity**, the added value a brand name gives to a product beyond the functional benefits provided. This added value has two distinct advantages. First, brand equity provides a competitive advantage. The Sunkist brand implies quality fruit. The Disney name defines children's entertainment. A second advantage is that consumers are often willing to pay a higher price for a product with brand equity. Brand equity, in this instance, is represented by the premium a

Video 11-3
Dr Pepper Ad
kerin.tv/13e/v11-3

The strong brand equity for the Louis Vuitton brand name permits the company to charge premium prices for its products.

The Advertising Archives

Louis Vuitton
www.louisvuitton.com

consumer will pay for one brand over another when the functional benefits provided are identical. Gillette razors and blades, Bose audio systems, Duracell batteries, Cartier jewelry, and Louis Vuitton luggage all enjoy a price premium arising from brand equity.

Creating Brand Equity Brand equity doesn't just happen. It is carefully crafted and nurtured by marketing programs that forge strong, favorable, and unique customer associations and experiences with a brand. Brand equity resides in the minds of consumers and results from what they have learned, felt, seen, and heard about a brand over time. Marketers recognize that brand equity is not easily or quickly achieved. Rather, it arises from a sequential building process consisting of four steps (see Figure 11–6).[18]

- The first step is to develop positive brand awareness and an association of the brand in consumers' minds with a product class or need to give the brand an identity. Gatorade and Kleenex have achieved this in the sports drink and facial tissue product classes, respectively.
- Next, a marketer must establish a brand's meaning in the minds of consumers. Meaning arises from what a brand stands for and has two dimensions—a functional, performance-related dimension and an abstract, imagery-related dimension. Nike has done this through continuous product development and improvement and its links to peak athletic performance in its integrated marketing communications program.
- The third step is to elicit the proper consumer responses to a brand's identity and meaning. Here attention is placed on how consumers think and feel about a brand. Thinking focuses on a brand's perceived quality, credibility, and superiority relative to other brands. Feeling relates to the consumer's emotional reaction to a brand. Michelin elicits both responses for its tires. Not only is Michelin thought of as a credible and superior-quality brand, but consumers also acknowledge a warm and secure feeling of safety, comfort, and self-assurance without worry or concern about the brand.

FIGURE 11–6

The customer-based brand equity pyramid shows the four-step building process that forges strong, favorable, and unique customer associations with a brand.

Consumer–brand connection

Consumer judgments | Consumer feelings

Brand performance | Brand imagery

Brand awareness

- The final, and most difficult, step is to create a consumer–brand connection evident in an intense, active loyalty relationship between consumers and the brand. A deep psychological bond characterizes a consumer–brand connection and the personal identification customers have with the brand. Brands that have achieved this status include Harley-Davidson, Apple, and eBay.

Valuing Brand Equity Brand equity also provides a financial advantage for the brand owner.[19] Successful, established brand names, such as Gillette, Louis Vuitton, Nike, Gatorade, and Apple, have an economic value in the sense that they are intangible assets. The recognition that brands are assets is apparent in the decision to buy and sell brands. For example, Triarc Companies bought the Snapple brand from Quaker Oats for $300 million and sold it three years later to Cadbury Schweppes for $900 million. This example illustrates that brands, unlike physical assets that depreciate with time and use, can appreciate in value when effectively marketed. However, brands can lose value when they are not managed properly. Consider the purchase and sale of Lender's Bagels. Kellogg bought the brand for $466 million only to sell it to Aurora Foods for $275 million three years later following deteriorating sales and profits.

Financially lucrative brand licensing opportunities arise from brand equity.[20] **Brand licensing** is a contractual agreement whereby one company (licensor) allows its brand name(s) or trademark(s) to be used with products or services offered by another company (licensee) for a royalty or fee. For example, Playboy earns more than $62 million licensing its name and logo for merchandise. Disney makes billions of dollars each year licensing its characters for children's toys, apparel, and games. Licensing fees for Winnie the Pooh alone exceed $3 billion annually.

Successful brand licensing requires careful marketing analysis to ensure a proper fit between the licensor's brand and the licensee's products. World-renowned designer Ralph Lauren earns over $140 million each year by licensing his Ralph Lauren, Polo, and Chaps brands for dozens of products, including paint by Glidden, furniture by Henredon, footwear by Rockport, eyewear by Luxottica, and fragrances by L'Oréal.[21] Kleenex diapers, Bic perfume, and Domino's fruit-flavored bubble gum are a few examples of poor matches and licensing failures.

Picking a Good Brand Name

We take brand names such as Red Bull, iPad, Android, and Axe for granted, but it is often a difficult and expensive process to pick a good name. Companies will spend

Ralph Lauren has a long-term licensing agreement with Luxottica Group, S.p.A. of Milan for the design, production, and worldwide distribution of prescription frames and sunglasses under the Ralph Lauren brand. The agreement is an ideal fit for both companies. Ralph Lauren is a leader in the design, marketing, and distribution of premium lifestyle products. Luxottica is the global leader in the premium and luxury eyewear sector.

© Rebecca Sapp/WireImage for Mediaplacement/Getty Images

Luxottica Group, S.p.A.
www.luxottica.com

Ralph Lauren Corporation
www.ralphlauren.com

between $25,000 and $100,000 to identify and test a new brand name. Six criteria are mentioned most often when selecting a good brand name.[22]

- *The name should suggest the product benefits.* For example, Accutron (watches), Easy Off (oven cleaner), Glass Plus (glass cleaner), Cling-Free (antistatic cloth for drying clothes), Chevrolet Spark (electric car), and Tidy Bowl (toilet bowl cleaner) all clearly describe the benefits of purchasing the product.
- *The name should be memorable, distinctive, and positive.* In the auto industry, when a competitor has a memorable name, others quickly imitate. When Ford named a car the Mustang, Pinto and Bronco soon followed. The Thunderbird name led to the Phoenix, Eagle, Sunbird, and Firebird from other car companies.
- *The name should fit the company or product image.* Sharp is a name that can apply to audio and video equipment. Bufferin, Excedrin, Anacin, and Nuprin are scientific-sounding names, good for analgesics. Eveready, Duracell, and DieHard suggest reliability and longevity—two qualities consumers want in a battery.
- *The name should have no legal or regulatory restrictions.* Legal restrictions produce trademark infringement suits, and regulatory restrictions arise through the improper use of words. For example, the U.S. Food and Drug Administration discourages the use of the word *heart* in food brand names. This restriction led to changing the name of Kellogg's Heartwise cereal to Fiberwise, and Clorox's Hidden Valley Ranch Take Heart Salad Dressing had to be modified to Hidden Valley Ranch Low-Fat Salad Dressing. Increasingly, brand names need a corresponding website address on the Internet. This further complicates name selection because over 250 million domain names are already registered globally.
- *The name should be simple* (such as Bold laundry detergent, Axe deodorant and body spray, and Bic pens) *and should be emotional* (such as Joy and Obsession perfumes and Caress soap, shower gel, and lotion).
- *The name should have favorable phonetic and semantic associations in other languages.* In the development of names for international use, having a non-meaningful brand name has been considered a benefit. A name such as Exxon does not have any prior impressions or undesirable images among a diverse world population of different languages and cultures. The 7UP name is another matter. In Shanghai, China, the phrase means "death through drinking" in the local dialect. Sales have suffered as a result.

Branding Strategies

Companies can choose from among several different branding strategies, including multiproduct branding, multibranding, private branding, and mixed branding (see Figure 11–7).

Figure 11–7).

FIGURE 11–7

Alternative branding strategies present both advantages and disadvantages to marketers. See the text for details.

Branding strategy			
Multiproduct branding strategy	**Multibranding strategy**	**Private branding strategy**	**Mixed branding strategy**
Toro makes:	Procter & Gamble makes:	Sears has:	Michelin makes:
• Toro snowblowers	• Tide	• Kenmore appliances	• Michelin tires
• Toro lawn mowers	• Cheer	• Craftsman tools	• Sears tires
• Toro garden hoses	• Ivory Snow	• DieHard batteries	Epson makes:
• Toro sprinkler systems	• Bold		• Epson printers
			• IBM printers

What branding concept is American Express using with its multicolored cards?

© Peter Jobst/Alamy

Multiproduct Branding Strategy With **multiproduct branding**, a company uses one name for all its products in a product class. This approach is sometimes called *family branding* or *corporate branding* when the company's trade name is used. For example, Microsoft, General Electric, Samsung, Gerber, and Sony engage in corporate branding—the company's trade name and brand name are identical. Church & Dwight uses the Arm & Hammer family brand name for all its products featuring baking soda as the primary ingredient.

There are several advantages to multiproduct branding. Capitalizing again on brand equity, consumers who have a good experience with the product will transfer this favorable attitude to other items in the product class with the same name. Therefore, this brand strategy makes possible *product line extensions,* the practice of using a current brand name to enter a new market segment in its product class.

Campbell Soup Company employs a multiproduct branding strategy with soup line extensions. It offers regular Campbell's soup, home-cooking style, and chunky varieties and more than 100 soup flavors. This strategy can result in lower advertising and promotion costs because the same name is used on all products, thus raising the level of brand awareness. A risk with line extension is that sales of an extension may come at the expense of other items in the company's product line. Line extensions work best when they provide incremental company revenue by taking sales away from competing brands or attracting new buyers.

Some multiproduct branding companies employ *subbranding,* which combines a corporate or family brand with a new brand, to distinguish a part of its product line from others. Consider American Express. It has applied subbranding with its American Express Green, Gold, Platinum, Optima Blue, and Centurion charge cards, with unique service offerings for each. Similarly, Porsche successfully markets its higher-end Porsche Carrera and its lower-end Porsche Boxster.

A strong brand equity also allows for *brand extension:* the practice of using a current brand name to enter a different product class. For instance, equity in the Huggies family brand name has allowed Kimberly-Clark to successfully extend its name to a full line of baby and toddler toiletries. This brand extension strategy generates $500 million in annual sales globally for the company. Honda's established name for motor vehicles has extended easily to snowblowers, lawn mowers, marine engines, and snowmobiles.

However, there is a risk with brand extensions. Too many uses for one brand name can dilute the meaning of a brand for consumers. Some marketing experts claim this has happened to the Arm & Hammer brand given its use for toothpaste, laundry detergent, gum, cat litter, air freshener, carpet deodorizer, and antiperspirant.[23]

For how Kimberly-Clark has used a brand extension strategy to leverage its Huggies brand equity among mothers, see the text.

© Mike Hruby

Kimberly-Clark Corporation
www.kimberly-clark.com

Multibranding Strategy Alternatively, a company can engage in **multibranding**, which involves giving each product a distinct name. Multibranding is a useful strategy when each brand is intended for a different market segment. Procter & Gamble makes Camay soap for those concerned with soft skin and Safeguard for those who want deodorant protection. Black & Decker markets its line of tools for the household do-it-yourselfer segment with the Black & Decker name but uses the DeWalt name for its professional tool line.

Multibranding is applied in a variety of ways. Some companies array their brands on the basis of price-quality segments. Marriott International offers 18 hotel and resort brands, each suited for a particular traveler experience and budget. To illustrate, Marriott

Black & Decker uses a multibranding strategy to reach different market segments. Black & Decker markets its tool line for the do-it-yourselfers with the Black & Decker name, but uses the DeWalt name for professionals.

Left: Source: The Black & Decker Corporation; Right: Source: DEWALT

Black & Decker

www.blackanddecker.com

EDITION hotels and Vacation Clubs offer luxury amenities at a premium price. Marriott and Renaissance hotels offer medium- to high-priced accommodations. Courtyard hotels and TownePlace Suites appeal to economy-minded travelers, whereas the Fairfield Inn is for those on a very low travel budget.

Other multibrand companies introduce new product brands as defensive moves to counteract competition. Called *fighting brands,* their chief purpose is to confront competitor brands.[24] For instance, Frito-Lay introduced Santitas brand tortilla chips to go head-to-head against regional tortilla chip brands that were biting into sales of its flagship Doritos and Tostitos brand tortilla chips. Ford launched its Fusion brand to halt the defection of Ford owners who were buying competitors' midsize cars. According to Ford's car group marketing manager, "Every year we were losing around 50,000 people from our products to competitors' midsize cars. We were losing Mustang, Focus, and Taurus owners. Fusion is our interceptor."[25]

Compared with the multiproduct strategy, advertising and promotion costs tend to be higher with multibranding. The company must generate awareness among consumers and retailers for each new brand name without the benefit of any previous impressions. The advantages of this strategy are that each brand is unique to each market segment and there is no risk that a product failure will affect other products in the line. Still, some large multibrand firms have found that the complexity and expense of implementing this strategy can outweigh the benefits. For example, Procter & Gamble recently announced that it would prune 100 of its brands through product deletion and sales to other companies.[26]

Private Branding Strategy   A company uses **private branding**, often called *private labeling* or *reseller branding,* when it manufactures products but sells them under the brand name of a wholesaler or retailer. Rayovac, Paragon Trade Brands, and ConAgra Foods are major suppliers of private-label alkaline batteries, diapers, and grocery products, respectively. Costco, Sears, Walmart, and Kroger are large retailers that have their own brand names. Private branding is popular because it typically produces high profits for manufacturers and resellers. Consumers also buy them. It is estimated that one of every five items purchased at U.S. supermarkets, drugstores, and mass merchandisers bears a private brand.[27]

Mixed Branding Strategy A fourth branding strategy is **mixed branding**, where a firm markets products under its own name(s) and that of a reseller because the segment attracted to the reseller is different from its own market. Companies such as Del Monte, Whirlpool, and Dial produce private brands of pet foods, home appliances, and soap, respectively.

PACKAGING AND LABELING PRODUCTS

LO 11-4 Describe the role of packaging, labeling, and warranties in the marketing of a product.

The **packaging** component of a product refers to any container in which it is offered for sale and on which label information is conveyed. A **label** is an integral part of the package and typically identifies the product or brand, who made it, where and when it was made, how it is to be used, and package contents and ingredients. To a great extent, the customer's first exposure to a product is the package and label, and both are an expensive and important part of marketing strategy. For Pez Candy, Inc., the central element of its marketing strategy is the character-head-on-a-stick plastic container that dispenses a miniature candy tablet. For more on how packaging creates customer value for Pez Candy, see the Marketing Matters box.[28]

Creating Customer Value and Competitive Advantage through Packaging and Labeling

Packaging and labeling cost U.S. companies about 15 cents of every dollar spent by consumers for products.[29] Despite their cost, packaging and labeling are essential because both provide important benefits for the manufacturer, retailer, and ultimate consumer. Packaging and labeling also can provide a competitive advantage.

Communication Benefits A major benefit of packaging is the label information it conveys to the consumer, such as directions on how, where, and when to use the product and the source and composition of the product, which is needed to satisfy legal requirements of product disclosure. For example, the labeling system for packaged and processed foods in the United States provides a uniform format for nutritional and dietary information. Many packaged foods contain informative recipes to promote usage of the product. Campbell Soup estimates that the green bean casserole recipe on its cream of mushroom soup can accounts for $20 million in soup sales each year![30] Other information consists of seals and symbols, either government-required or commercial seals of approval (such as the Good Housekeeping Seal).

Functional Benefits Packaging often plays a functional role—providing storage, convenience, or protection or ensuring product quality. Stackable food containers are one example of how packaging can provide functional benefits. For example, beverage companies have developed lighter and easier ways to stack products on shelves and in refrigerators. Examples include Coca-Cola beverage packs designed to fit neatly onto refrigerator shelves and Ocean Spray Cranberries's rectangular juice bottles that allow 10 units per package versus 8 of its former round bottles.

The convenience dimension of packaging is increasingly important. Kraft Miracle Whip salad dressing, Heinz ketchup, and Skippy Squeez'It peanut butter are sold in squeeze bottles; microwave popcorn has been a major market success; and Chicken of the Sea tuna and Folgers coffee are packaged in single-serving portions. Nabisco offers portion-control package sizes for the convenience of weight-conscious consumers. It offers 100-calorie packs of Oreos, Cheese Nips, and other products in individual pouches.

For the functional benefits provided by Pringles' cylindrical packaging, see the text.
© Mike Hruby

Marketing **Matters**

Creating Customer Value through Packaging— Pez Heads Dispense More Than Candy

Customer value can assume numerous forms. For Pez Candy, Inc. (www.pez.com), customer value manifests itself in some 450 Pez character candy dispensers. Each refillable dispenser ejects tasty candy tablets in a variety of flavors that delight preteens and teens alike in more than 60 countries.

Pez was formulated in 1927 by Austrian food mogul Edward Haas III and successfully sold in Europe as an adult breath mint. Pez, which comes from the German word for peppermint, *pfefferminz,* was originally packaged in a hygienic, headless plastic dispenser. Pez first appeared in the United States in 1953 with a headless dispenser, marketed to adults. After conducting extensive marketing research, Pez was repositioned with fruit flavors, repackaged with licensed character heads on top of the dispenser, and remarketed as a children's product in the mid-1950s. Since then, most top-level licensed characters and hundreds of other characters have become Pez heads. Consumers buy about 80 million Pez dispensers and 3 billion Pez tablets a year in the U.S. alone, and company sales growth exceeds that of the candy industry as a whole.

The unique Pez package dispenses a "use experience" for its customers beyond the candy itself, namely,

© Bob Eighmie/KRT/Newscom

fun. And fun translates into a 98 percent awareness level for Pez among teenagers and an 89 percent awareness level among mothers with children. Pez has not advertised its product for years. With that kind of awareness, who needs advertising?

Consumer protection is another important function of packaging, including the development of tamper-resistant containers. Today, companies commonly use safety seals or pop-tops that reveal previous opening. Consumer protection through labeling exists in "open dating," which states the expected shelf life of the product.

Functional features of packaging also can affect product quality. Pringles, with its cylindrical packaging, offers uniform chips, minimal breakage, and for some consumers, better value for the money than chips packaged in flex-bags.

Perceptual Benefits A third component of packaging and labeling is the perception created in the consumer's mind. Package and label shape, color, and graphics distinguish one brand from another, convey a brand's positioning, and build brand equity. According to the director of marketing for L'eggs hosiery, "Packaging is important to the positioning and equity of the L'eggs brand."[31] Why? Packaging and labeling have been shown to enhance brand recognition and facilitate the formation of strong, favorable, and unique brand associations.

Successful marketers recognize that changes in packages and labels can update and uphold a brand's image in the customer's mind. Pepsi-Cola embarked on a packaging change to uphold its image among teens and young adults. Beginning in 2013, Pepsi-Cola introduced new package graphics that change every few weeks to reflect different themes, such as sports, music, fashion, and cars.

Because labels list a product's source, brands competing in the global marketplace can benefit from "country of origin or manufacture" perceptions as described in Chapter 7. Consumers tend to hold stereotypes about country-product pairings that they judge "best"—English tea, French perfume, Italian leather, and Japanese electronics—which can affect a brand's image. Increasingly, Chinese firms are adopting

Packaging has been a major element of L'eggs hosiery positioning since its launch in 1969.

© Mike Hruby

Hanes Brands, Inc.

www.leggs.com

the English language and Roman letters for their brand labels sold in China. This is being done because of a common perception in many Asian countries that "things Western are good."[32]

Packaging and Labeling Challenges and Responses

Package and label designers face four challenges. They are (1) the continuing need to connect with customers; (2) environmental concerns; (3) health, safety, and security issues; and (4) cost reduction.

Connecting with Customers Packages and labels must be continually updated to connect with customers. The challenge lies in creating aesthetic and functional design features that attract customer attention and deliver customer value in their use. If done right, the rewards can be huge. For example, the marketing team responsible for Kleenex tissues converted its standard rectangular box into an oval shape with colorful seasonal graphics. Sales soared with this aesthetic change in packaging. After months of in-home research, Kraft product managers discovered that consumers often transferred Chips Ahoy! cookies to jars for easy access and to avoid staleness. The company solved both problems by creating a patented resealable opening on the top of the bag. The result? Sales of the new package doubled that of the old package.

Environmental Concerns Because of widespread global concern about the growth of solid waste and the shortage of viable landfill sites, the amount, composition, and disposal of packaging material continue to receive much attention. For example, PepsiCo, Coca-Cola, and Nestlé have decreased the amount of plastic in their beverage bottles to reduce solid waste. Recycling packaging material is another major thrust. Procter & Gamble now uses recycled cardboard in over 70 percent of its paper packaging. Its Spic and Span liquid cleaner is packaged in 100 percent recycled material. Other firms, such as Walmart, are emphasizing the use of less packaging material. Since 2008, the company has worked with its 600,000 global suppliers to reduce overall packaging and shipping material by 5 percent.

Health, Safety, and Security Issues A third challenge involves the growing health, safety, and security concerns of packaging materials. Today, most consumers believe companies should make sure products and their packages are safe and secure, regardless of the cost, and companies are responding in numerous ways. Most butane lighters sold today, like those made by Scripto, contain a child-resistant safety latch to prevent misuse and accidental fire. Childproof caps on pharmaceutical products and household cleaners and sealed lids on food packages are now common. New packaging technology and materials that extend a product's *shelf life* (the time a product can be stored) and prevent spoilage continue to be developed.

Cost Reduction About 80 percent of packaging material used in the world consists of paper, plastics, and glass. As the cost of these materials rises, companies are constantly challenged to find innovative ways to cut packaging costs while delivering value to their customers. Many food and personal care companies have replaced bottles and cans with sealed plastic or foil pouches. Pouches cut packaging costs by 10 to 15 percent.[33]

PRODUCT WARRANTY

A final component for product consideration is the **warranty**, which is a statement indicating the liability of the manufacturer for product deficiencies. There are various types of product warranties with different implications for manufacturers and customers.

America's Best Warranty®

10-Year/100,000-Mile
Powertrain Limited Warranty

Based on total package of warranty programs. See dealer for LIMITED WARRANTY details.

Hyundai has made a commitment to offer the best automobile warranty for buyers.

Hyundai Motor America
www.hyundaiusa.com

Some companies, like Hyundai, offer *express warranties,* which are written statements of liabilities. In recent years, the FTC has required greater disclosure on express warranties to indicate whether the warranty is a limited-coverage or full-coverage alternative. A *limited-coverage warranty* specifically states the bounds of coverage and, more important, areas of noncoverage. A *full warranty* has no limits of noncoverage. The *Magnuson-Moss Warranty/FTC Improvement Act* (1975) regulates the content of consumer warranties and so has strengthened consumer rights with regard to warranties. Increasingly, manufacturers are being held to *implied warranties,* which assign responsibility for product deficiencies to the manufacturer. Studies show that the type of warranty can affect a consumer's product evaluation. Brands with limited warranties tend to receive less positive evaluations compared with full-warranty items.

Warranties are also important in light of product liability claims. In the early part of the 20th century, the courts protected companies. The trend now is toward "strict liability" rulings, where a manufacturer is liable for any product defect, whether it followed reasonable research standards or not. This issue remains hotly contested between companies and consumer advocates.

learning review

11-7. What are the six criteria mentioned most often when selecting a good brand name?

11-8. What are the three major benefits of packaging and labeling?

11-9. What is the difference between an express and an implied warranty?

LEARNING OBJECTIVES REVIEW

LO 11-1 *Explain the product life-cycle concept.*
The product life cycle describes the stages a new product goes through in the marketplace: introduction, growth, maturity, and decline. Product sales growth and profitability differ at each stage, and marketing managers have marketing objectives and marketing mix strategies unique to each stage based on consumer behavior and competitive factors. In the introductory stage, the need is to establish primary demand, whereas the growth stage requires selective demand strategies. In the maturity stage, the need is to maintain market share; the decline stage necessitates a deletion or harvesting strategy. Some important aspects of product life cycles are (*a*) their length, (*b*) the shape of the sales curve, (*c*) how they vary by product classes and forms, and (*d*) the rate at which consumers adopt products.

LO 11-2 *Identify ways that marketing executives manage a product's life cycle.*
Marketing executives can manage a product's life cycle three ways. First, they can modify the product itself by altering its characteristics, such as product quality, performance, or appearance. Second, they can modify the market by finding new customers for the product, increasing a product's use among existing customers, or creating new use situations for the product. Finally, they can reposition the product using any one or a combination of marketing mix elements. Four factors trigger a repositioning action. They include reacting

to a competitor's position, reaching a new market, catching a rising trend, and changing the value offered to consumers.

LO 11-3 *Recognize the importance of branding and alternative branding strategies.*
A basic decision in marketing products is branding, in which an organization uses a name, phrase, design, symbols, or a combination of these to identify its products and distinguish them from those of its competitors. Product managers recognize that brands offer more than product identification and a means to distinguish their products from those of competitors. Successful and established brands take on a brand personality and acquire brand equity—the added value a given brand name gives to a product beyond the functional benefits provided—that is crafted and nurtured by marketing programs that forge strong, favorable, and unique consumer associations with a brand. A good brand name should suggest the product benefits, be memorable, fit the company or product image, be free of legal restrictions, be simple and emotional, and have favorable phonetic and semantic associations in other languages. Companies can and do employ several different branding strategies. With multiproduct branding, a company uses one name for all its products in a product class. A multibranding strategy involves giving each product a distinct name. A company uses private branding when it manufactures products but sells them under the brand name of a wholesaler or retailer. Finally, a company

can employ mixed branding, where it markets products under its own name(s) and that of a reseller.

LO 11-4 *Describe the role of packaging, labeling, and warranties in the marketing of a product.*

Packaging, labeling, and warranties play numerous roles in the marketing of a product. The packaging component of a product refers to any container in which it is offered for sale and on which label information is conveyed. Manufacturers, retailers, and consumers acknowledge that packaging and labeling provide communication, functional, and perceptual benefits. Contemporary packaging and labeling challenges include (*a*) the continuing need to connect with customers, (*b*) environmental concerns, (*c*) health, safety, and security issues, and (*d*) cost reduction. Warranties indicate the liability of the manufacturer for product deficiencies and are an important element of product and brand management.

LEARNING REVIEW ANSWERS

11-1 **Advertising plays a major role in the _____ stage of the product life cycle, and _____ plays a major role in maturity.**
Answer: introduction; product differentiation or finding new buyers

11-2 **How do high-learning and low-learning products differ?**
Answer: A high-learning product requires significant customer education and there is an extended introductory period. A low-learning product requires little customer education because the benefits of purchase are readily understood, resulting in immediate sales.

11-3 **What are the five categories of product adopters in the diffusion of innovations?**
Answer: The five categories of product adopters based on the diffusion of innovation are: (1) innovators—2.5 percent; (2) early adopters—13.5 percent; (3) early majority—34 percent; (4) late majority—34 percent; and (5) laggards—16 percent.

11-4 **How does a product manager help manage a product's life cycle?**
Answer: A product manager shepherds a product through its life cycle by (1) modifying the product, which involves altering one or more of its characteristics to increase its value to customers and thus increase sales; (2) modifying the market, which involves finding new customers, increasing a product's use among existing customers, or creating new use situations; and (3) repositioning the product, which involves changing the place it occupies in consumers' minds relative to competitive products.

11-5 **What does "creating a new use situation" mean in managing a product's life cycle?**
Answer: Creating a new use situation means finding new uses or applications for an existing product.

11-6 **Explain the difference between trading up and trading down in product repositioning.**
Answer: Trading up involves adding value to the product (or line) through additional features or higher-quality materials. Trading down involves reducing the number of features, quality, price, or downsizing—reducing the content of packages without changing package size and maintaining or increasing the package price.

11-7 **What are the six criteria mentioned most often when selecting a good brand name?**
Answer: A good brand name should: (1) suggest the product benefits; (2) be memorable, distinctive, and positive; (3) fit the company or product image; (4) have no legal or regulatory restrictions; (5) be simple and emotional; and (6) have favorable phonetic and semantic associations in other languages.

11-8 **What are the three major benefits of packaging and labeling?**
Answer: Packaging and labeling provide important benefits for the manufacturer, retailer, and ultimate consumer that can create a competitive advantage for the firm. The three benefits are: (1) communication benefits through label information; (2) functional benefits through storage, convenience, protection, or product quality; and (3) perceptual benefits such as package and label shape, color, and graphics that can both position a firm's brand relative to others and build brand equity.

11-9 **What is the difference between an express and an implied warranty?**
Answer: Express warranties are written statements of liabilities. Implied warranties assign responsibility for product deficiencies to the manufacturer even if the retailer sells the product.

FOCUSING ON KEY TERMS

brand equity p. 305
brand licensing p. 306
brand name p. 303
brand personality p. 305
branding p. 303
label p. 310
market modification p. 300

mixed branding p. 310
multibranding p. 308
multiproduct branding p. 308
packaging p. 310
private branding p. 309
product class p. 298
product form p. 298

product life cycle p. 292
product modification p. 300
trade name p. 303
trademark p. 303
trading down p. 302
trading up p. 302
warranty p. 312

APPLYING MARKETING KNOWLEDGE

1   Listed here are three different products in various stages of the product life cycle. What marketing strategies would you suggest to these companies? (*a*) Canon digital cameras—maturity stage, (*b*) Hewlett-Packard tablet computers—growth stage, and (*c*) handheld manual can openers—decline stage.

2   It has often been suggested that products are intentionally made to break down or wear out. Is this strategy a planned product modification approach?

3   The product manager of GE is reviewing the penetration of trash compactors in American homes. After more than two decades in existence, this product is in relatively few homes. What problems can account for this poor acceptance? What is the shape of the trash compactor life cycle?

4   For years, Ferrari has been known as a manufacturer of expensive luxury automobiles. The company plans to attract the major segment of the car-buying market that purchases medium-priced automobiles. As Ferrari considers this trading-down strategy, what branding strategy would you recommend? What are the trade-offs to consider with your strategy?

5   The nature of product warranties has changed as the federal court system reassesses the meaning of warranties. How does the regulatory trend toward warranties affect product development?

BUILDING YOUR MARKETING PLAN

For the product offering in your marketing plan,

1   Identify (*a*) its stage in the product life cycle and (*b*) key marketing mix actions that might be appropriate, as shown in Figure 11–1.

2   Develop (*a*) branding and (*b*) packaging strategies, if appropriate for your offering.

■ connect

VIDEO CASE 11   P&G's Secret Deodorant: Finding Inspiration in Perspiration

How do you revitalize a 50-plus-year-old brand? By focusing the brand's marketing efforts on its core purpose—a purpose that is both benefit-driven and inspirational—and using that purpose to build essential one-to-one personal connections with consumers.

Video 11-4

Secret Video Case

kerin.tv/13e/v11-4

Procter & Gamble's (P&G's) Secret brand, launched in 1956, has dominated the women's antiperspirant deodorant category for many years. Secret maintains its leadership position as one of many products in what is typically considered a low-involvement product category. Underarm deodorant isn't traditionally the type of product consumers think about engaging with in an ongoing, meaningful way. However, Secret has demonstrated that delivering the product benefit is important to establish trust and build engagement. This type of engagement often results in amplifying the brand's marketing investment, or paid media. Since 2009, Secret's purpose has been at the center of its marketing efforts, resulting in tremendous growth and brand advocacy among consumers.

PRODUCT BACKGROUND

Secret was the first deodorant marketed exclusively to women. In the 1960s and 1970s, Secret's growth was supported by a recurring series of ads featuring a husband and wife dealing with issues of the day, such as having children and returning to work afterward. "It was all about empowering women to make the right choices for themselves and to embrace those choices fearlessly," according to Kevin Hochman, marketing director for skin and personal care at P&G North America at the time.

However, in 2004–2005, brand executives felt the theme was getting dated, so Secret backed off from that positioning. "We walked away," Hochman says. "We thought, women are empowered, and maybe this isn't so relevant. That was a mistake. Of course the idea was still relevant; we just hadn't modernized it in a contemporary way." Secret made a deliberate decision to go back to its roots.

THE ROAD TO PURPOSE

Secret started to experience slower growth in 2008 due to a down economy. The launch of a super-premium line of antiperspirant, Secret Clinical Strength, helped increase sales and market share, but competitors soon followed suit with similar products. Meanwhile, top P&G management began infusing the idea of purpose-driven marketing throughout the organization. The companywide vision focused on building brands through lifelong, one-to-one personal connections that ultimately build relationships and fulfill the company's purpose to "touch and improve more lives of more consumers more completely."

With this in mind, Secret brand management realized it needed to get clear on defining who Secret was, why Secret existed, and what Secret's purpose was. The brand needed a reason for its consumers to care and wanted to give them a reason to share.

Through the leadership and efforts of its senior brand management and partner agencies, including MEplusYOU (formerly imc²), Leo Burnett Co., SMG, Marina Maher Communications, and consultancy group BrightHouse, the Secret brand team began to establish the brand's purpose and convey it

© Mike Hruby

across all marketing touch points in ways that resonated with target consumers' core values and beliefs. "It becomes about more than selling deodorant, or promoting functional benefits, and more about rallying around something higher-order," says Hochman.

The Secret team started by defining the brand's core beliefs: "We believe in the equality of the genders and that all people should be able to pursue their goals without fear. We believe that by acting courageously, supporting others, empathizing with their challenges and finding innovative solutions, we can help women be more fearless." Armed with Secret's core belief, the team developed a purpose statement that is grounded in the product benefit and allowed for fearlessness when you're not sweating: "Helping women of all ages to be more fearless."

"Just a few years ago, the majority of marketers' activities and expenditures occurred across unidirectional media channels that could only talk *at* consumers. This limited the role marketing could play in developing relationships between brands and people," says Ian Wolfman, principal and chief marketing officer of MEplusYOU. "Today, new media, in combination with mature media, allows marketers to play a more sophisticated role in facilitating deep, trusting relationships between brands and people as we simultaneously drive strong transactional activity. Brands like Secret realize that taking a stand on values it shares with consumers is the key to translating a brand's purpose into meaningful relationships and profit."

The brand carefully constructed an ecosystem of tactical marketing "ignitions." Each of these ignitions focused on sparking the interest of like-minded consumers and were designed to flex and surge with the needs of the brand. The brand's purpose served as the basis for each ignition in order to engage consumers across all channels (online and offline). With Facebook as the hub, Secret brand management used the Secret.com website, print advertising, public relations, creative and social media, and appropriate paid and organic search programs to complete each ignition.

DRIVING CONSUMER ENGAGEMENT AND SALES GROWTH THROUGH IGNITIONS

Secret brand management focused on activating brand purpose around the timeless idea of being more fearless and freshened it up with contemporary topics and pop culture. This effort included several ignitions. Two of these are Let Her Jump and Mean Stinks.

Let Her Jump

The first time Secret struck gold by focusing on purpose was through Let Her Jump, an effort to sanction women's ski jumping as an official Olympic sport. The Let Her Jump ignition was a companion piece to work P&G was already doing for the 2010 Winter Olympics.

Secret launched Let Her Jump with a small online media buy and a Facebook Page that included an inspirational video, petition, and Facebook Fan Page. The inspiring video encouraged viewers to visit LetHerJump.com (a custom fan page within Facebook), where they could lead the charge to get women's ski jumping included in the 2014 Winter Olympics. In 2011, the International Olympic Committee approved women's ski jumping for the 2014 Winter Games.

Let Her Jump was one of many elements that, in the spirit of a living brand purpose, helped fuel growth over the previous year. In addition to the video being viewed more than 700,000 times, 57 percent of visitors said this initiative improved brand perception, and

Secret saw a double-digit purchase intent increase among women and teens. "This [ignition] was the first time we could pinpoint that activating against purpose generated a huge sales lift," Hochman said. "We saw the Clinical Sport [stock keeping units] up 85 percent during the [2010] Olympics. We changed the world for the better. In a small way, yes, but a deodorant brand influencing pop culture is very exciting when you can then directly attribute it to business results." As an added bonus, the Let Her Jump program won the coveted Forrester Groundswell Award in 2010. The award recognizes excellence in achieving business and organizational goals with social technology applications and is awarded to some of the best social media programs in the world.

© Ace Pictures/Kristin Callahan/Newscom

The success of Let Her Jump helped pave the way for investment in another ignition. After proving that purpose-driven work leads to profitable growth for the brand, the team was ready to tackle one of the biggest fears young girls face—bullying. While Let Her Jump was tied to a distinct event in time, the team was excited at the prospect of rallying behind something that could live on and continue to do good in the world.

Mean Stinks

The Secret brand waged a battle for niceness through its Mean Stinks program, the next and biggest step in Secret's fearless movement. Through media monitoring and social listening, the Secret team determined that bullying was a critical issue facing many teen girls—which led to the creation of the Mean Stinks ignition. Mean Stinks, launched in early 2011, focused on ending girl-to-girl meanness, encouraging girls to grow up to be fearless, while providing a safe hub for conversation and creating brand affinity for Secret.

Through the Secret Mean Stinks movement, Secret brought a positive message to high school hallways, leading the charge to end the mean streak by showing teen girls that petty isn't pretty. Raising awareness of bullying is big, but "the need for education is tremendous—people aren't sure how to identify bullying, or what to do when it occurs," says Hochman.

"And what's so compelling about the Mean Stinks program is how true it is to the brand's original essence."

The Secret team launched a Facebook media buy for Secret Mean Stinks to create awareness of the program, asking fans (primarily teen girls aged 13–24 and role models aged 25+) to share their stories. The Mean Stinks Facebook Wall was flooded with thousands of public apologies and heartfelt messages of empathy and encouragement. And as Secret continued to make a difference, women celebrities joined to take a stand, offering "nice advice" to girls through the Mean Stinks Facebook app and iAd.

In a single day, Secret gained over 200,000 Facebook fans—bringing its total number of fans to over a million, while its Mean Stinks Page gained over 20,000 new fans. Within the first two weeks, visitors accessed the Mean Stinks Facebook app more than 250,000 times and Secret became the second-fastest-growing Facebook Page globally for one week. This ignition also helped contribute to 10 percent overall sales growth for the entire fiscal year, 11.5 percent in the six-month period during which Mean Stinks was launched.

In the summer of 2011, Secret and Apple joined forces to create an iAd experience that tackled the issue for girls on the device that's most personal—their iPhone. The ignition received unusually high engagement levels and led to many "firsts" for Secret:

- First brand to create and share customized wallpapers via iPhone and iPod touch devices, which led to an "average time spent" rate that was 16 percent higher than average.
- First brand to use transition banners on the iAd Network, which resulted in exceeding benchmarks for banner "Tap through Rates" (50 percent higher than average for iAd).
- First brand to drive donations for a cause through the iAd, which resulted in donations to PACER's National Bullying Prevention Center.

In the first 10 days after launch, 23,000 consumers engaged with the Secret iAd, with more than eight page views per visit and an average of 80 seconds spent on the ad.

WHAT'S NEXT FOR SECRET

Secret executives saw success behind the purpose activation the year after it was established, but they noticed it wasn't truly part of the brand's DNA or fully integrated into every marketing element. "[At first] we had a lot of grandiose ideas, but they added layers to our existing plan. Dollars were tight, and the purpose ideas started getting cut. Old Spice was ahead of us, and I wondered what they were doing differently," says Hochman. "By [working with our agency partners], we finally were able to ensure that [the ignitions] weren't just elements of our plans; they WERE our plan," Hochman says. "The way the Secret team operates now compared with four years ago—it's like day and night."

Hochman says the brand has more ideas that include educating, generating awareness, and empowering people to take meaningful action. Secret is recognized as being best in its class, something the brand is happy to tout. "But [success] isn't a Secret-only thing . . . it's a priority for all of our brands. And when people are living the brand, they're more excited to come to work. It's much more enabling and inspiring," Hochman says. And to continue in this success, Hochman suggests remembering that a brand's purpose is inextricably linked to the overall plan, it pervades everything about the business—including team culture—and it's in the company's roots.

Hochman emphasizes the importance of transparency, something he believes Secret will continue to win out on in the future. "Today, information is free and plentiful. If there's a lack of sincerity, consumers know it."[34]

Questions

1 What is "purpose-driven marketing" from a product and brand management perspective at Procter & Gamble?

2 How does "purpose-driven" marketing for Secret deodorant relate to the hierarchy of needs concept detailed in Chapter 4?

3 What dimensions of the consumer-based brand equity pyramid have the Secret brand team focused on with its "Let Her Jump" and "Mean Stinks" ignitions?

Chapter Notes

1. "Gatorade's New Selling Point: We're Necessary Performance Gear," www.adage.com, January 2, 2012; "The Best Goes On," *BrandWeek,* May 10, 2010, p. 22; "Gatorade: Before and After," *The Wall Street Journal,* April 23, 2010, p. B8; Darren Rovell, *First in Thirst: How Gatorade Turned the Science of Sweat into a Cultural Phenomenon* (New York: AMACOM, 2005); and www.Gatorade.com.

2. For an extended discussion of the generalized product life cycle, see Donald R. Lehmann and Russell S. Winer, *Product Management,* 5th ed. (Burr Ridge, IL: McGraw-Hill, 2008).

3. *Gillette Fusion Case Study* (New York: Datamonitor, June 6, 2008). All subsequent references to Gillette Fusion are based on this case study.

4. Orville C. Walker Jr. and John W. Mullins, *Marketing Management: A Strategic Decision-Making Approach,* 8th ed. (Burr Ridge, IL: McGraw-Hill/Irwin, 2014), p. 209.

5. Portions of this discussion on the fax machine product life cycle are based on Jonathan Coopersmith, *Faxed: The Rise and Fall of the Fax Machine* (Baltimore: Johns Hopkins University Press, 2015); Kurt Wagner, "Why the Fax Machine Refuses to Die," www.CNNMoney, May 15, 2013; and "Atlas Electronics Corporation," in Roger A. Kerin and Robert A. Peterson, *Strategic Marketing Problems: Cases and Comments,* 8th ed. (Upper Saddle River, NJ: Prentice Hall, 1998), pp. 494–506.

6. "Email Statistics Report, 2014–2018" (Palo Alto, CA: The Radicati Group, 2016); and "Why Fax Won't Die," www.fastcompany.com, February 10, 2015.

7. Kate MacArthur, "Coke Energizes Tab, Neville Isdell's Fave," *Advertising Age,* August 29, 2005, pp. 3, 21.

8. "Hosiery Sales Hit Major Snag," *Dallas Morning News,* December 18, 2006, p. 50.

9. Arthur Asa Berger, *Ads, Fads, and Consumer Culture: Advertising's Impact on American Character and Society,* 5th ed. (Lanham, MD: Rowman & Littlefield Publishing Group, 2015).

10. "Year-end Marketing Reports on U.S. Recorded Music Shipment" (New York Recording Industry Association of America); and "Digital Music Beats CDs," *The Wall Street Journal,* April 15, 2015, p. 6.

11. Everett M. Rogers, *Diffusion of Innovations,* 5th ed. (New York: Free Press, 2003).

12. Jagdish N. Sheth and Banwari Mittal, *Consumer Behavior: A Managerial Perspective,* 2nd ed. (Mason, OH: South-Western College Publishing, 2003).

13. "Demand Ebbs for Electric, Hybrid Cars," *wsj.com,* September 30, 2014.

14. "When Free Samples Become Saviors," *The Wall Street Journal,* August 14, 2001, pp. B1, B4.

15. "Shrinkflation: Consumer Goods That Got Downsized," *money.msn.com,* April 25, 2014; "Pop(sicle) Quiz," *Consumer Reports,* August 2012, p. 63; "Downsized: More and More Products Lose Weight," *Consumer Reports,* February 2011, p. 32ff; "P&G Lightens the Load on Diapers," *The Wall Street Journal,* September 9, 2013, p. B2; and Bruce Horovitz, "Shoppers Beware: Products Shrink but Prices Stay the Same," www.usatoday, June 11, 2008.

16. "Kylie and Kendall Jenner File to Trademark Their Names," www.huffington post.com, May 4, 2015.

17. This discussion is based on Kevin Lane Keller, *Strategic Brand Management,* 4th ed. (Upper Saddle River, NJ: Prentice Hall, 2013). Also see Susan Fornier, "Building Brand Community on the Harley-Davidson Posse Ride," Harvard Business School Note #5-501–502 (Boston: Harvard Business School, 2001).

18. Keller, *Strategic Brand Management.*

19. This discussion is based on John Deighton, "How Snapple Got Its Juice Back," *Harvard Business Review,* January 2002, pp. 47–53; and "Breakfast King Agrees to Sell Bagel Business," *The Wall Street Journal,* September 28, 1999, pp. B1, B6. Also see Vithala R. Rao, Manoj K. Agarwal, and Denise Dahlhoff,

"How Is Manifest Branding Strategy Related to the Value of a Corporation?" *Journal of Marketing,* October 2004, pp. 125–41.

20. Keach Hagey, "Rebuilding Playboy: Less Smut, More Money," *The Wall Street Journal,* February 20, 2013, pp. B1, B2; "Judge Pooh-poohs Lawsuit over Disney Licensing Fees," *USATODAY. com,* March 30, 2004; and Keller, *Strategic Brand Management.*

21. John Brodie, "The Many Faces of Ralph Lauren," www. Fortune.com, August 29, 2007; and "Polo Ralph Lauren Enters into Licensing Agreement with Luxottica Group, S.p.A., www.thebusinessedition.com, February 28, 2006.

22. Marc Fetscherin et al., "In China? Pick Your Brand Name Carefully," *Harvard Business Review,* September 2012, p. 26; Beth Snyder Bulik, "What's in a (Good) Product Name? Sales," *Advertising Age,* February 2, 2009, p. 10; and Keller, *Strategic Brand Management.*

23. Jack Neff, "The End of the Line for Line Extensions?" *Advertising Age,* July 7, 2008, pp. 3, 28; and "When Brand Extension Becomes Brand Abuse," *BrandWeek,* October 26, 1998, pp. 20, 22.

24. Mark Ritson, "Should You Launch a Fighter Brand?" *Harvard Business Review,* October 2009, pp. 87–94.

25. "Ribbons Roll Out on Rides," *Dallas Morning News* (September 30, 2005), p. 8D.

26. "P&G Brand Divestitures Will Be Bigger Than Original Targets, *adage.com,* February 19, 2015.

27. "Store Brand Share on the Rise," www.storebrandsdecisions. com, October 16, 2012.

28. www.pez.com, downloaded February 1, 2015; "So Sweet: William and Kate PEZ Dispensers," www.today.msnbc.com, March 30, 2012; David Welch, *Collecting Pez* (Murphysboro, IL: Bubba Scrubba Publications, 1995); and "Elements Design Adds Dimension to Perennial Favorite Pez Brand," *Package Design Magazine,* May 2006, pp. 37–38.

29. "Market Statistics," www.Packaging-Gateway.com, downloaded March 25, 2012.

30. "Green Bean Casserole Turns 50," *Dallas Morning News,* November 19, 2005, p. 10D.

31. "Iconic L'eggs Sheer Energy Egg Package Returns," *Package World,* March 6, 2014, pp. 16–17.

32. "Asian Brands Are Sprouting English Logos in Pursuit of Status, International Image," *The Wall Street Journal,* August 7, 2001, p. B7C.

33. "Packaging," www.hp.com, downloaded January 17, 2007.

34. P&G's Secret Deodorant: This case was prepared by Jana Boone. Used with permission.

12

Services Marketing

LEARNING OBJECTIVES

After reading this chapter you should be able to:

LO 12-1 Describe four unique elements of services.

LO 12-2 Recognize how services differ and how they can be classified.

LO 12-3 Explain how consumers purchase and evaluate services.

LO 12-4 Develop a customer contact audit to identify service advantages.

LO 12-5 Explain the role of the seven Ps in the services marketing mix.

LO 12-6 Discuss the important roles of internal marketing and customer experience management in service organizations.

Airbnb Redefines Services—and the Economy!

"We were just trying to solve our own problem," explains Brian Chesky, who started the first "sharing economy" business with co-founder Joe Gebbia.

Their problem was to make pocket cash as new residents in San Francisco. They didn't have anything except space in their apartment, so they created a website called Airbedandbreakfast.com to advertise floor space where people could temporarily sleep on air mattresses while attending a nearby conference. The idea was so successful they shortened the name to Airbnb.com and expanded the business to include many other kinds of spaces such as houses, villas, and even boats.

Initially, they focused on large events such as the Democratic and Republican national conventions where hotels were sold out. Airbnb offered to help visitors "Find a place to stay" by enabling them to rent from people who were willing to share their spaces. In exchange for providing the service, Airbnb charged the renter 3 percent and the traveler 6 to 12 percent. Demand for the service increased rapidly, and soon an average of 425,000 people were staying in an Airbnb listing each night. Today, Airbnb has 1,000,000 listings available in 34,000 cities and 190 countries. In addition, *Forbes* estimates that Chesky and Gebbia are now worth $1.5 billion each, and Airbnb was recently designated Company of the Year by *Inc.* magazine.

Airbnb was the genesis for what has come to be known as the sharing economy. It turns out that peer-to-peer sharing, or collaborative consumption, is a perfect match with the changes in consumer attitudes about ownership. Millennials typically don't buy newspapers, DVDs, or CDs; instead they find news on Facebook, stream movies from Hulu, and subscribe to music on Pandora. They are much more likely to borrow, rent, and share than previous generations of consumers.

As a result, many new services are being offered to accommodate these attitudes. Uber and Lyft now offer peer-to-peer ridesharing (similar to a taxi), while RelayRides and Getaround offer peer-to-peer car sharing (similar to a car rental). Parking Panda allows drivers to find homeowners who want to rent extra space in their driveway, and DogVacay helps pet owners find friendly places for canines to stay for a day. Rentoid and Spinlister help people rent products, tools, and bicycles rather than purchase them. Similarly, TaskRabbit allows users to outsource small jobs and tasks to people in their neighborhood. There are even sharing sites that encourage free exchanges, such as couchsurfing.org, which is a network of volunteers who offer free hospitality, advice, and accommodation to international travelers.

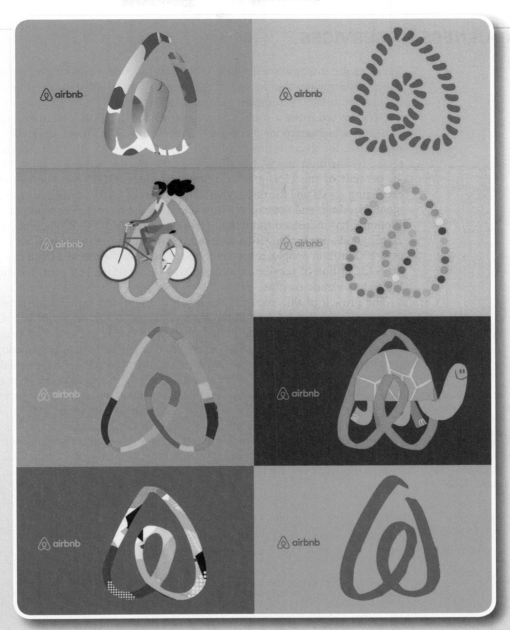

Source: Airbnb, Inc.

Video 12-1
Airbnb
kerin.tv/13e/v12-1

Experts estimate that hundreds of new peer-to-peer sharing services are now in operation and that the revenue generated by the sharing economy exceeds $15 billion annually. Neil Turner, the founder and CEO of adverCar, a service that allows drivers to rent advertising space on their cars, suggests that "this is the way of the future." As we move from a perspective based on ownership to this new approach based on sharing and renting, traditional businesses will need to make changes. Avis Budget Group, for example, recently paid $500 million for Zipcar, while General Motors invested in RelayRides. Home Depot has introduced product rental in about half of its stores.[1]

As these examples illustrate, services represent a dynamic and exciting component of our economy. In this chapter, we discuss how services differ from traditional products (goods), how service consumers make purchase decisions, and the ways in which the marketing mix is used for services.

THE UNIQUENESS OF SERVICES

Services are intangible activities or benefits (such as airline trips, financial advice, or automobile repair) that an organization provides to satisfy consumers' needs in exchange for money or something else of value.

Services today are a significant component of the global economy—and one of the most important components of the U.S. economy. The World Trade Organization estimates that, for all countries combined, exported merchandise and commercial services total $18.8 trillion and $4.6 trillion, respectively. As shown in Figure 12–1, more than 46 percent of the U.S. gross domestic product (GDP) now comes from services, exceeding goods and the three other components of GDP—business investment, government spending, and net exports (not shown in the figure). The value of services in the economy has increased more than 100 percent since 1990. Projections indicate that by 2022, goods-producing firms and service firms will employ 19.5 million people and over 130 million people, respectively. Services also represent a large export business— the $722 billion of service exports in 2014 is one of the few areas in which the United States has a trade surplus.[2]

The growth of this sector is the result of increased demand for services that have been available in the past and the increasing interest in new services. Concierge services, for example, have long been popular in hotels such as The Breakers in Palm Beach, Florida, which has a staff of 11 concierges, and the Ritz-Carlton, which offers concierges who specialize in technology support, shopping, and medical issues. Similar services are now being offered outside of the hotel industry. For example, One Concierge offers individuals and corporations travel on private jets, yacht charters, gift purchasing, and event planning services in 115 countries around the globe. Concierge services are even available for daily lifestyle needs. Ace Concierge, for example, will schedule car maintenance, pick up and deliver dry cleaning, walk your dog, or even shop for groceries! Other new services include: The Luggage Club, which offers door-to-door luggage delivery to and from 220 countries; Virgin Galactic, which offers

FIGURE 12–1

Services are now a larger part of the U.S. gross domestic product (GDP) than goods.

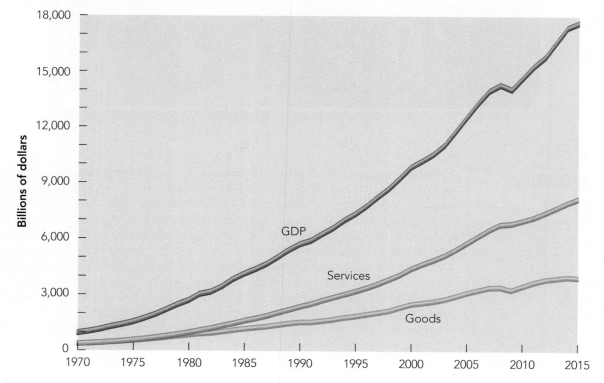

private space travel; and Ubitus GameCloud, which recently launched its cloud-based gaming service to stream games to smartphones, tablets, and televisions. These firms and many others like them are providing the types of imaginative services that will play a role in our economy in the future.[3]

The Four I's of Services

LO 12-1 Describe four unique elements of services.

There are four unique elements to services—*intangibility, inconsistency, inseparability,* and *inventory*—referred to as the **four I's of services.**

Intangibility   Services are intangible; that is, they can't be held, touched, or seen before the purchase decision. In contrast, before purchasing a traditional product, a consumer can touch a box of laundry detergent, kick the tire of an automobile, or sample a new breakfast cereal. Because services tend to be a performance rather than an object, they are much more difficult for consumers to evaluate. To help consumers assess and compare services, marketers try to make them tangible or show the benefits of using the service.

The American Airlines ad shows the airline's new seats and emphasizes their size and other tangible benefits. American Express also provides tangible benefits by allowing cardmembers to earn points for redemption of airline tickets, electronics, and gift cards through its Membership Rewards program.

Inconsistency   Developing, pricing, promoting, and delivering services is challenging because the quality of a service is often inconsistent. Because services depend on the people who provide them, their quality varies with each person's capabilities and day-to-day job performance. Inconsistency is much more of a problem in services than it is with tangible products. Tangible products can be good or bad in terms of quality, but with modern production lines the quality will at least be consistent. In contrast, the Philadelphia Phillies baseball team may have great hitting and pitching and look like a pennant winner one day—and the next day they may lose by 10 runs. Or a soprano at New York's Metropolitan Opera may have a bad cold and give a less-than-perfect performance on the night that you attend. Whether the service involves tax assistance at H&R Block or guest relations at the Ritz-Carlton, organizations attempt to reduce inconsistency through standardization and training.[4]

Inseparability   A third difference between services and products, and related to problems of consistency, is inseparability. In most cases, the consumer cannot (and

Why do many services emphasize their tangible benefits? The answer appears in the text.

Left: Source: United Airlines, Inc; Right: Source: American Express Company

United Airlines
www.united.com

American Express Co.
www.americanexpress.com

UNITED
A STAR ALLIANCE MEMBER

got your back . friendly

United BusinessFirst.
More flat-bed seats than any North American airline.
fly the friendly skies

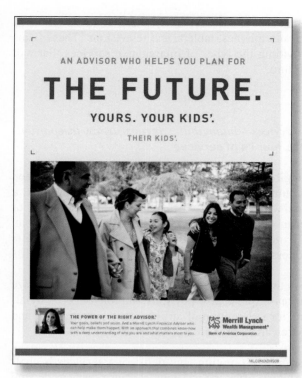

People play an important role in the delivery of many services. Many services ads emphasize the personal element of the offering.

Source: Bank of America Corporation

Merrill Lynch
www.wealthmanagement.ml.com

does not) separate the deliverer of the service from the service itself. For example, Allstate's reminder that "You're in good hands" emphasizes the importance of its agents. Similarly, to receive an education, a person may attend a university. The quality of the education may be high, but if the student has difficulty interacting with instructors, finds counseling services poor, or does not receive adequate library or computer assistance, he or she may not be satisfied with the educational experience. Students' evaluations of their education will be influenced primarily by their perceptions of instructors, counselors, librarians, and other people at the university. This interaction between the service provider and the consumer means that they often *co-create* value together.[5]

The amount of interaction between the consumer and the service provider depends on the extent to which the consumer must be physically present to receive the service. Some services, such as haircuts, golf lessons, medical diagnoses, and food service, require the customer to participate in the delivery of the services. Other services, such as car repair, dry cleaning, and waste disposal, process tangible objects with less involvement from the customer. Finally, services such as banking, consulting, and insurance are often delivered electronically, requiring no face-to-face customer interaction. Even pharmacies may soon be automated for shoppers who are willing to submit to a fingerprint scan. While this approach can create value for consumers, a disadvantage of some *self-service technologies* such as ATMs, grocery store scanning stations, and self-service gas station pumps is that they are perceived as being less personal.[6]

Inventory Inventory of services is different from that of products. Inventory problems exist with products because many items are perishable and because there are costs associated with handling inventory. With services, inventory carrying costs are more subjective and are related to **idle production capacity**, which is when the service provider is available but there is no demand for the service. The inventory cost of a service is the cost of paying the person used to provide the service along with any needed equipment. If a physician is paid to see patients but no one schedules an appointment, the fixed cost of the idle physician's salary is a high inventory carrying cost. In some service businesses, however, the provider of the service is on commission (a Merrill Lynch financial advisor) or is a part-time employee (a clerk at Macy's). In these businesses, inventory carrying costs can be significantly lower or nonexistent because the idle production capacity can be cut back by reducing hours or having no salary to pay because of the commission compensation system.

Figure 12–2 shows a scale of inventory carrying costs represented on the low end by real estate agencies and hair salons and on the high end by airlines and hospitals. The inventory carrying costs of airlines are high because of high-salaried pilots and very expensive equipment. In contrast, real estate agencies and hair salons have employees

FIGURE 12–2

Inventory carrying costs of services depend on the cost of employees and equipment.

LOW COST   Cost of inventory   HIGH COST

| Real estate agency / Hair salon | Insurance company | Dry cleaner | Auto repair center | Restaurant | Hotel | Amusement park | Airline / Hospital |

FIGURE 12–3

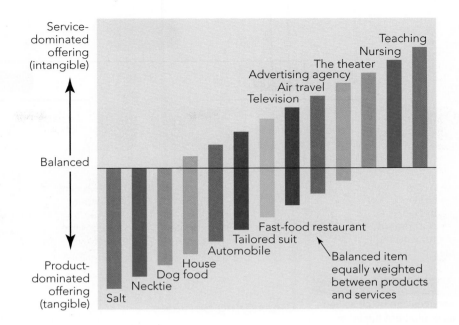

who work on commission and need little expensive equipment to conduct business. One reason service providers must maintain production capacity is because of the importance of time to today's customers.

The Service Continuum

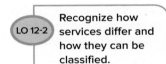

Recognize how services differ and how they can be classified.

The four I's differentiate services from products in most cases, but many companies are not clearly service-based or product-based organizations. Is Hewlett-Packard a manufacturer or a service provider? Although Hewlett-Packard manufactures printers and other products, many of the company's employees work in its services division providing systems integration, networking, consulting, education, and product support.[7] What companies bring to the market ranges from the tangible to the intangible. This range of product-dominant to service-dominant offerings is referred to as the **service continuum** (see Figure 12–3).

Teaching, nursing, and the theater are intangible, service-dominant activities, and intangibility, inconsistency, inseparability, and inventory are major concerns in their marketing. Salt, neckties, and dog food are tangible products, and the problems represented by the four I's are not relevant in their marketing. However, some businesses are a mix of intangible service and tangible product factors. A clothing tailor provides a service but also a product, the finished suit. How pleasant, courteous, and attentive the tailor is to the customer is an important component of the service, and how well the clothes fit is an important part of the product. As shown in Figure 12–3, a fast-food restaurant is about half tangible products (the food) and half intangible services (courtesy, cleanliness, speed, and convenience).

For many businesses today, it is useful to distinguish between their core offering—either a product or a service—and supplementary services. A core service offering such as a bank account, for example, also has supplementary services such as deposit assistance, parking or drive-thru availability, ATMs, and monthly statements. Supplementary services often allow service providers to differentiate their offering from competitors, and they may add value for consumers. While there are many potential supplementary services, key categories of supplementary services include consultation, finance, shipping, installation, maintenance, and upgrades. Innovation in core services today often relies on the creative efforts of the organization. Understanding the impact of supplementary services, however, may be best accomplished through input from customers.[8]

325

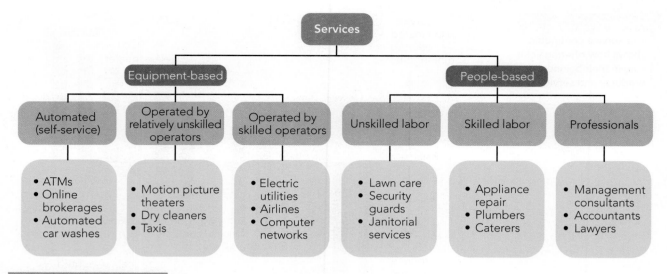

FIGURE 12–4

Services can be classified as equipment-based or people-based.

Classifying Services

Throughout this book, marketing organizations, techniques, and concepts are classified to show the differences and similarities in an organized framework. Services can also be classified in several ways, according to whether (1) they are delivered by people or equipment, (2) they are for-profit or nonprofit, or (3) they are government sponsored.

Delivery by People or Equipment As seen in Figure 12–4, many companies offer services. Professional services include management consulting firms such as Booz Allen Hamilton or Accenture. Skilled labor is required by Sears in order to offer services such as appliance repair and by Sheraton in order to offer its catering service. Unskilled labor such as that used by Brink's store-security forces is also a service provided by people.

Equipment-based services do not have the marketing concerns of inconsistency because people are removed from the provision of the service. Electric utilities, for example, can provide service without frequent personal contact with customers. Motion picture theaters have projector operators that consumers never see. A growing number of customers use self-service technologies such as Home Depot's self checkout, Southwest Airlines's self check-in, and Schwab's online stock trading without interacting with any service employees.[9]

For-Profit or Nonprofit Organizations Many organizations involved in services also distinguish themselves by their tax status as for-profit or nonprofit organizations. In contrast to *for-profit organizations, nonprofit organizations'* excesses in revenue over expenses are not taxed or distributed to shareholders. When excess revenue exists, the money goes back into the organization's treasury to allow continuation of the service. Based on the corporate structure of the nonprofit organization, it may pay tax on revenue-generating holdings not directly related to its core mission. Nonprofit organizations in the United States now have revenue of $1.77 trillion and account for 8 percent of all wages and salaries.[10]

United Way, Greenpeace, Outward Bound, The Salvation Army, and Girl Scouts are examples of nonprofit organizations. Historically, misconceptions have limited the use of marketing practices by such organizations.[11] In recent years, however, nonprofit organizations have turned to marketing to help achieve their goals. The American Red Cross is a good example. To increase blood donations and financial gifts, it hired creative agency BBDO to create its new Storytellers Campaign, which includes TV and print ads, direct marketing, public relations, and social media. In addition, to help its

Nonprofit service organizations often advertise to help achieve their goals.

Left: Courtesy of Outward Bound; Right: Courtesy of United Way Worldwide

Outward Bound
www.outwardbound.org

United Way
www.unitedway.org

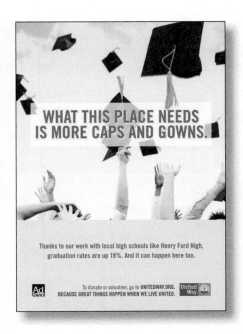

700 field offices integrate their messages, the American Red Cross hired another agency to create a web portal called Brand Central, which offers standardized templates for local communications materials. Other promotional activities include a campaign called Red Cross Racing, which is targeted at the 75 million NASCAR fans across the country, and the National Celebrity Cabinet, which currently includes Miley Cyrus, Pierce Brosnan, LL Cool J, Heidi Klum, Peyton Manning, and Patti LaBelle.

Other nonprofits have also been successful in using marketing to help achieve their goals. The American Marketing Association recently selected Kate Grant as the recipient of the Nonprofit Marketer of the Year award for her extraordinary leadership of the Fistula Foundation, which has provided support for more than 10,000 surgeries in Africa and Asia for women who have suffered from childbirth injuries.[12] See the Marketing Matters box to learn more about the social marketing activities of other nonprofit organizations, including Susan G. Komen for the Cure, the American Red Cross, and the March of Dimes.[13]

Government Sponsored   A third way to classify services is based on whether or not they are government sponsored. Although there is no direct ownership and they are nonprofit organizations, governments at the federal, state, and local levels provide a broad range of services. The United States Postal Service, for example, has adopted many marketing activities. First-class postage revenue has declined as postal service customers have increased their use of the Internet to send e-mail, pay bills, and file taxes. Rather than fight the trend, however, the U.S. Postal Service is embracing the Internet. Its website, www.usps.com, allows consumers to pay for postage, print shipping labels, and request a free package pickup. In addition, new post office boxes are being designed in sizes to better meet the needs of consumers who shop online, and greeting cards with a prepaid postage barcode are being offered through a partnership with Hallmark Cards. You may have noticed that many post offices are now also retail outlets that sell supplies, collector stamps, and even neckties. These marketing activities are designed to increase consumer use and to compete with UPS, FedEx, DHL, and foreign postal services for package delivery business. The U.S. Postal Service is also promoting online mailing list management and the use of direct mail.[14] The Peace Corps is another example of a government-sponsored service.

The United States Postal Service has adopted many marketing activities.

Source: United States Postal Service

Marketing Matters

Social Marketing Is a Must for Nonprofits

Video 12-2

American Red Cross

kerin.tv/13e/v12-2

"Make It Social" is the mantra for many nonprofit organizations today. The recent recession has reduced charitable donations substantially, so many of the 1.5 million public charities, private foundations, universities, religious congregations, and other nonprofit organizations have turned to social marketing and social media to engage potential contributors.

The Susan G. Komen for the Cure organization has been one of the most successful in using new approaches. In addition to its familiar walks and races, the Komen Foundation uses Facebook, Twitter, YouTube, and Flickr to promote its cause and fund-raising activities. Its fragrance, Promise Me, for example, is promoted on its website and social media sites. It also allows mobile giving by texting the word KOMEN from a mobile phone. The success of the Komen organization's marketing actions has allowed it to raise more than $2 billion for breast cancer research and community outreach programs.

The American Red Cross has also been quick to adopt social marketing tools. The organization recently opened a Social Media Digital Operations Center in Washington, D.C., to help it communicate with the general public, volunteers, and donors. In addition, the Red Cross has created tools such as its blood donation app, and crowdfunding websites on IndieGoGo and Crowdrise, which raised millions in contributions for Sandy victims. Social media tools such as

Source: The American National Red Cross

these are playing an increasingly important role in Red Cross operations as they become familiar to most people.

Nonprofit organizations should follow many of the same principles businesses use to engage people with social media. First, they should understand what motivates people to take up causes. One of the most important reasons is usually to feel like they are doing something, even if it is as simple as clicking the "like" button on Facebook. Second, nonprofit organizations need to be creative in their use of social media and incorporate digital photos, video, and gaming skills. As Jamie Henn, communications director for 350.org explains, "By using images and video we have been able to convey stories with emotional impact." The United Way, for example, partnered with CNN to deliver a live online panel discussion about its education goals. Finally, nonprofit campaigns should allow information sharing. The March of Dimes, for example, created on online forum where people can share stories, and it now has an average of 8,100 posts each month.

Social marketing campaigns and social media offer nonprofit organizations very effective tools for engaging their members, fans, friends, and the public. While the number of success stories is growing, it is important to remember to have a goal and measure progress toward that goal. Participation rates, donations, number of texts, posts on a blog, and other dimensions of effectiveness all contribute to the perception of the brand!

learning review

12-1. What are the four I's of services?

12-2. To eliminate service inconsistencies, companies rely on _____ and _____.

12-3. Would inventory carrying costs for an accounting firm with certified public accountants be (*a*) high, (*b*) low, or (*c*) nonexistent?

HOW CONSUMERS PURCHASE SERVICES

LO 12-3 Explain how consumers purchase and evaluate services.

Colleges, hospitals, hotels, and even charities are facing an increasingly competitive environment. Successful service organizations, like successful product-oriented firms, must (1) understand how the consumer makes a service purchase decision, (2) understand how the consumer evaluates quality, and (3) determine how to present a differential advantage relative to competing offerings.

The Purchase Process

Many aspects of services affect the consumer's evaluation of the purchase. Because services cannot be displayed, demonstrated, or illustrated, consumers cannot make a prepurchase evaluation of all the characteristics of services.[15] Similarly, because service providers may vary in their delivery of a service, an evaluation of a service may change with each purchase. Figure 12–5 on the next page portrays how different types of products and services are evaluated by consumers. Tangible products such as clothing, jewelry, and furniture have *search* properties, such as color, size, and style, which can be determined before purchase. Services such as restaurants and child care have *experience* properties, which can be discerned only after purchase or during consumption. Finally, services provided by specialized professionals such as medical diagnoses and legal services have *credence* properties, or characteristics that the consumer may find impossible to evaluate even after purchase and consumption.[16] To reduce the uncertainty created by these properties, service consumers turn to personal sources of information such as early adopters, opinion leaders, and reference group members during the purchase decision process. Research indicates that consumers search for much more information and they place an emphasis on trust, commitment, and expertise when trying to evaluate services with credence properties.[17] In response to this need for more information, the Mayo Clinic uses an organized, explicit approach called "evidence management" to present customers with concrete and convincing evidence of its strengths.[18]

Assessing Service Quality

Once a consumer tries a service, how is it evaluated? Primarily, a consumer assesses service quality by comparing expectations about a service offering to his or her

FIGURE 12–5

Consumers use search, experience, and credence properties to evaluate services.

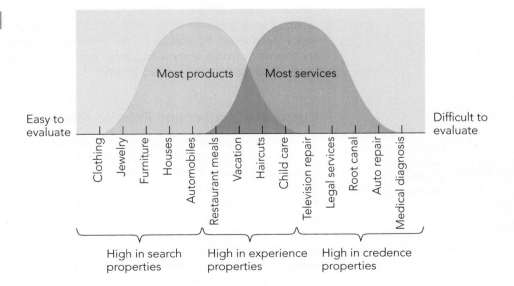

DIMENSION	DEFINITION	EXAMPLES OF QUESTIONS AIRLINE CUSTOMERS MIGHT ASK
Reliability	Ability to perform the promised service dependably and accurately	Is my flight on time?
Tangibility	Appearance of physical facilities, equipment, personnel, and communication materials	Are the gate, the plane, and the baggage area clean?
Responsiveness	Willingness to help customers and provide prompt service	Are the flight attendants willing to answer my questions?
Assurance	Knowledge and courtesy of employees and their ability to convey trust and confidence	Are the ticket counter attendants, flight attendants, and pilots knowledgeable about their jobs?
Empathy	Caring, individualized attention provided to customers	Do the employees determine if I have special seating, meal, baggage, transfer, or rebooking needs?

FIGURE 12–6

There are five dimensions of service quality.

actual experience with the service.[19] Differences between the consumer's expectations and experience are identified through **gap analysis**. This type of analysis asks consumers to assess their expectations and experiences on dimensions of service quality such as those described in Figure 12–6.[20] Expectations are influenced by word-of-mouth communications, personal needs, past experiences, and promotional activities, while actual experiences are determined by the way an organization delivers its service, particularly through interpersonal competencies.[21] The relative importance of the various dimensions of service quality varies by the type of service.[22] What if someone is dissatisfied and complains? Recent studies suggest that customers who experience a "service failure" will increase their satisfaction if the service provider makes a highly interactive service recovery effort, although they may not increase their intent to repurchase. In addition, service operators can increase customer satisfaction by explaining the cause of the service failure and letting customers choose between several recovery options.[23] See the Marketing Matters box for ideas about monitoring service failures.[24]

Customer Contact and Relationship Marketing

LO 12-4 | Develop a customer contact audit to identify service advantages.

Consumers judge services on the entire sequence of steps that make up the service process. To focus on these steps, or "service encounters," a firm can develop a **customer contact audit**—a flowchart of the points of interaction between consumers and service provider.[25] This is particularly important in high-contact services such as hotels, educational institutions, and automobile rental agencies. Figure 12–7 is a customer contact audit prepared for a car rental agency. The interactions identified in a customer contact audit often serve as the basis for developing relationships with customers. Recent research suggests that employees' competence and the authenticity and sincerity of their interactions affect the success of their customer relationships. Another version of a customer contact audit,

Marketing **Matters**

Managing Service Failures: The Importance of Monitoring and Guarantees

Only 5 to 10 percent of dissatisfied customers choose to complain—the rest switch companies or make negative comments to other people. Increasingly, the forum for personal comments is on the many social media now available to consumers. Companies can search for comments using search engines such as www.blogsearch.google.com, and they can search for images on Google and videos on YouTube. Domino's Pizza, for example, discovered that consumers were publishing comments that its pizza was "like cardboard." Web services such as www.technorati.com and www.reputationdefender.com are also available to monitor blogs, and media-monitoring firms will even watch for dissatisfied customers on Twitter.

© McGraw-Hill Education/Editorial Image, LLC, photographer

Most marketing experts agree that it is best to respond to service failures, particularly when the failure is viewed to be the result of a controllable factor. Regarding its product's comparison to cardboard, Domino's posted a response on YouTube, created a Twitter account, and then posted the real-time Twitter feed on a billboard in Times Square! Recent research also suggests that service providers should offer a service guarantee with two parts: a commitment to good service, and a promise to compensate the customer if good service is not provided.

To find out what consumers are saying about your favorite brands, try your own search now.

FIGURE 12–7

Customer contact audit for a car rental agency (green shaded boxes indicate customer activity).

Hertz manages its customer contacts.

Image courtesy of The Hertz Corporation. Production Company: Blacklist/Studio AKA. Design and Illustration: Christopher Gray.

The Hertz Corporation
www.hertz.com

called a *service blueprint,* includes all employee actions and acknowledges that services are designed to be "experiences."[26]

A Customer's Car Rental Activities   Let's look more closely at the customer contact audit illustrated in Figure 12–7. A customer decides to rent a car and (1) contacts the rental company. A customer service representative receives the information (2) and checks the availability of the car at the desired location. When the customer arrives at the rental site (3), the reservation system is again accessed, and the customer provides information regarding payment, address, and driver's license (4). A car is assigned to the customer (5), who proceeds by bus to the car pickup (6). On return to the rental location (7), the customer checks in (8), a customer service representative collects information on mileage, gas consumption, and damages (9), and a bill is printed (10).

Each of the steps numbered 1 to 10 is a customer contact point where the tangible aspects of the company's service are seen by the customer. Figure 12–7, however, also shows a series of steps lettered A to D that involve an inspection, maintenance, preparation for the next customer, and an update of the reservation system. These steps are essential in providing a clean, well-maintained car, but they are not points of customer interaction. To create a service advantage, a car rental agency—like any service company—must create a competitive advantage in the sequence of interactions with the customer. For example, Hertz has attempted to eliminate steps 4, 8, and 9 for some customers with its Gold Plus Rewards program. These customers simply pick up the car keys when they arrive and drop off the car when they return.

How many times will a Disney park visitor encounter a Disney employee? See the text for the answer.

© Katja Kreder/Inmagine

Relationship Marketing   The contact between a service provider and a customer represents a service encounter that is likely to influence the customer's assessment of the purchase. The number of encounters in a service experience may vary. Disney, for example, estimates that a park visitor will have 74 encounters with Disney employees in a single visit. These encounters represent opportunities to develop social bonds, or relationships, with customers. The relationship may also be developed through loyalty incentives such as airline frequent flyer programs. Relationship marketing provides several benefits for service customers, including the continuity of a single provider, customized service delivery, reduced stress due to a repetitive purchase process, and an absence of switching costs. Surveys of consumers have indicated that while customers of many services are interested in being "relationship customers," they require that the relationship be balanced in terms of loyalty, benefits, value, kinds of connections, and respect for privacy,[27] and their expectations of the future benefits of the service influence the likelihood that they continue the relationship.[28] Understanding the service characteristics that lead to repeat purchases can help services managers allocate their resources to appropriate relationship marketing activities.[29]

learning review »

12-4. What are the differences between search, experience, and credence properties?

12-5. Hertz created its differential advantage at the points of _____ in its customer contact audit.

MANAGING THE MARKETING OF SERVICES

LO 12-5 **Explain the role of the seven Ps in the services marketing mix.**

Logos and brand names help consumers identify services.

Top: © Agencja Fotograficzna Caro; Middle: DON EMMERT/ AFP/Getty Images; Bottom: © Ilene MacDonald/Alamy RF

Just as the unique aspects of services necessitate changes in the consumer's purchase process, the marketing management process also requires special adaptation.[30] As we have seen in earlier chapters, the traditional marketing mix is composed of the four Ps: product, price, place, and promotion. Careful management of the four Ps is important when marketing services. However, the distinctive nature of services requires that other variables also be effectively managed by service marketers. The concept of an expanded marketing mix for services has been adopted by many service-marketing organizations. In addition to the four Ps, the services marketing mix includes people, the physical environment, and the process, or the **seven Ps of services marketing**.[31]

Product (Service)

The concepts of the product component of the marketing mix discussed in Chapters 10 and 11 apply equally well to Cheerios (a product) and American Express (a service). Managers of products and services must design the product concept with the features and benefits desired by customers. An important aspect of the product concept is branding. Because services are intangible, and more difficult to describe, the brand name or identifying logo of the service organization is particularly important when a consumer makes a purchase decision.[32] Therefore, service organizations, such as banks, hotels, rental car companies, and restaurants, rely on branding strategies to distinguish themselves in the minds of consumers. Strong brand names and symbols are important for service marketers, not only as a means of differentiation, but also to convey an image of quality. A service firm with a well-established brand reputation will also find it easier to introduce new services than firms without a brand reputation.[33]

Many services have undertaken creative branding activities. Hotels, for example, have begun to extend their branding efforts to consumers' homes through services such as *Hotels at Home,* an in-room catalog that offers Westin's "Heavenly Bed," Hilton's bathrobes, and even artwork from Sheraton hotel rooms for consumers to buy and use at home. Similarly, Fairmont Hotels has formed co-branding partnerships with Adidas, which provides athletic gear to loyalty program members, and BMW, which offers BMW Cruise Bikes for guest use.[34] Look at the logos on this page to determine how successful some companies have been in branding their service with a name and symbol.

Price influences perceptions of the quality of services.

Courtesy of The Redirections Group

Price

In service businesses, price is referred to in many ways. Hospitals refer to *charges;* consultants, lawyers, physicians, and accountants to *fees;* airlines to *fares;* hotels to *rates;* and colleges and universities to *tuition.* Because of the intangible nature of services, price is often perceived by consumers as a possible indicator of the quality of the service. Do you expect higher quality from an expensive restaurant? Would you wonder about the quality of a $100 surgery? In many cases, there may be few other available cues for the customer to judge, so price becomes very important as a quality indicator.[35]

Pricing of services goes beyond the traditional tasks of setting the selling price. When customers buy a service, they also consider nonmonetary costs, such as the mental and physical efforts required to consume the service. Service marketers must try to minimize the effort required to purchase and use the service. Pricing also plays a role in balancing consumer demand for services. Many service businesses use **off-peak pricing**, which consists of charging different prices during different times of the day or during different days of the week to reflect variations in demand for the service. Airlines, for example, offer discounts for weekend travel, while movie theaters offer matinee prices.

Place (Distribution)

Place, or distribution, is a major factor in developing a service marketing strategy because of the inseparability of services from the producer. Rarely are intermediaries involved in the distribution of a service; the distribution site and the service deliverer are the tangible components of the service. Until recently, customers generally had to go to the service provider's physical location to purchase the service. Increased competition, however, has forced many service firms to consider the value of convenient distribution and to find new ways of distributing services to customers. Hairstyling chains such as Cost Cutters Family Hair Salon, tax preparation offices such as H&R Block, and accounting firms such as Ernst & Young all use multiple locations for the distribution of services. Technology is also being used to deliver services beyond the provider's physical locations. In the banking industry, for example, customers of participating banks using the Cirrus system can access any one of 1,000,000 automated teller machines in 93 countries. The availability of electronic distribution through the Internet also allows for global reach and coverage for a variety of services, including travel, education, entertainment, and insurance. With speed and convenience becoming increasingly important to customers when they select service providers, service firms can leverage the use of the Internet to deliver services on a 24/7 basis, in real time, on a global scale. This advantage varies by type of service, however: British grocery retailer Tesco has one million customers who shop online, while most health care services still rely on face-to-face interaction.[36]

Services use promotional programs to communicate benefits and provide a representation of the service encounter.

Left: Source: Accenture; Right: Courtesy of Space Adventures, Ltd

Accenture
www.accenture.com

Space Adventures
www.spaceadventures.com

Promotion

The value of promotion, especially advertising, for many services is to show consumers the benefits of purchasing the service. It is valuable to stress availability, location, consistent quality, and efficient, courteous service[37] and to provide a physical representation of the service or a service encounter.[38] The Accenture ad, for example, describes the benefits available to its customers—"High performance. Delivered." The Space Adventures ad describes the benefit of its service as being "the world's first civilian explorer to circumnavigate the moon," and it provides a photo of the service encounter—a close-up view of the moon! In most cases, promotional concerns of services are similar to those of products.

Another form of promotion, *publicity,* has played a major role in the promotional strategy of many service organizations. Nonprofit organizations such as public schools, religious organizations, and hospitals, for example, often use publicity to disseminate their messages. For many of these organizations, the most common form of publicity is the *public service announcement (PSA)* because it is free.[39] As discussed later in Chapter 18, however, using PSAs as the foundation of a promotion program is unlikely to be effective because the timing and location of the PSA are under the control of the medium, not the organization.

Personal selling, sales promotion, and direct marketing also can play an important role in services marketing. Service firm representatives, such as hotel employees handling check-in services or waitstaff in restaurants, are often responsible for selling their services. Similarly, sales promotions such as coupons, free trials, and contests are often effective tools for service firms. Finally, direct marketing activities are often used to reach specific audiences with interest in specific types of services. Increasingly, service firms are adopting an integrated marketing communications approach (see Chapter 17), similar to the approach used by many consumer packaged goods firms, to ensure that the many forms of promotion are providing a consistent message and contributing to a common objective.

Video 12-3

Space Adventures

kerin.tv/13e/v12-3

People

Many services depend on people for the creation and delivery of the customer service experience.[40] The nature of the interaction between employees and customers strongly influences the customer's perceptions of the service experience. Customers will often judge the quality of the service experience based on the performance of the people providing the service. This aspect of services marketing has led to a concept called internal marketing.[41]

Internal marketing is based on the notion that a service organization must focus on its employees, or internal market, before successful programs can be directed at customers.[42] Service firms need to ensure that employees have the attitude, skills, and commitment needed to meet customer expectations and to sustain customer loyalty. Employees with a commitment to mutually beneficial relationships with customers are most suitable for services today. This idea suggests that employee development through recruitment, training, communication, coaching, management, and leadership is critical to the success of service organizations.[43] Finally, many service organizations, such as educational institutions and athletic teams, must recognize that individual customer behavior may also influence the service outcome for other customers. These interactions suggest that the people element in services includes employees and all customers.

Once internal marketing programs have prepared employees for their interactions with customers, organizations can better manage the services they provide. **Customer experience management (CEM)**, introduced in Chapter 10, is the process of managing the entire customer experience with the company. CEM experts suggest that the process should be intentional and planned, consistent so that every experience is similar,

LO 12-6 Discuss the important roles of internal marketing and customer experience management in service organizations.

Applying **Marketing Metrics**

Are JetBlue's Flights Profitably Loaded?

Capacity management is critical in the marketing of many services. For example, having the right number of airline seats or hotel rooms available at the right time, price, and place can spell the difference between a profitable or unprofitable service operation.

Airlines feature *load factor* as a capacity management measure on their marketing dashboards, along with two other measures, namely, the *operating expense* per available seat flown one mile and the revenue generated by each seat flown one mile, called *yield*. Load factor is the percentage of available seats flown one mile occupied by a paying customer.

These three measures combine to show airline operating income or loss per available seat flown one mile:

Operating income (loss) per available seat flown one mile
$$= [\text{Yield} \times \text{Load factor}] - \text{Operating expense}$$

Your Challenge

As a marketing analyst for New York City–based JetBlue Airways, you have been asked to determine the operating income or loss per available seat flown one mile for the first six months of 2013. In addition, you have been asked to determine what load factor JetBlue must reach to break even assuming its current yield and operating expense will not change in the immediate future.

Your Findings

JetBlue's yield, load factor, and operating expense marketing dashboard displays are shown below.

You can conclude from these measures that JetBlue Airways posted about a 0.21¢ loss per available seat flown one mile in the first six months of 2013:

Operating loss per available seat flown one mile
$$= [9.83¢ \times 82.1\%] - 8.28¢ = -.2096¢$$

Assuming JetBlue's yield and operating expenses will not change and using a little algebra, the airline's load factor will have to increase from 82.1 percent to 84.23 percent to break even:

Operating income (loss) per available seat flown one mile
$$= [9.83¢ \times \text{Load factor}] - 8.28¢ = 0¢$$
$$\text{Load factor} = 84.23\%$$

Your Action

Assuming yield and operating expenses will not change, you should recommend that JetBlue consider revising its flight schedules to better accommodate traveler needs and advertise these changes. Consideration also might be given to how JetBlue utilizes its existing airplane fleet to serve its customers and produce a profit.

Yield (cents) — 9.83¢

Load Factor (%) — 82.1%

Operating Expense (cents) — 8.28¢

Courtesy of Zappos.com.

differentiated from other service offerings, and relevant and valuable to the target market. Companies such as Disney, Southwest Airlines, the Ritz-Carlton, and Starbucks all manage the experience they offer customers. They integrate their activities to connect with customers at each contact point to move beyond customer relationships to customer loyalty.[44] For example, Zappos.com, the online retailer profiled in the opener to Chapter 9, requires that all employees complete a four-week customer loyalty training program to help deliver one of the company's core concepts—"Deliver WOW through Service."[45]

Physical Environment

The appearance of the environment in which the service is delivered and where the firm and customer interact can influence the customer's perception of the service. The physical evidence of the service includes all the tangibles surrounding the service: the buildings, landscaping, vehicles, furnishings, signage, brochures, and equipment. Service firms need to manage physical evidence carefully and systematically to convey the proper impression of the service to the customer. This is sometimes referred to as impression, or evidence, management.[46] For many services, the physical environment provides an opportunity for the firm to send consistent and strong messages about the nature of the service to be delivered.

Process

Process refers to the actual procedures, mechanisms, and flow of activities by which the service is created and delivered. The actual creation and delivery steps that the customer experiences provide customers with evidence on which to judge the service. These steps involve not only "what" gets created but also "how" it is created. The customer contact audit discussed earlier in the chapter is relevant to understanding the service process discussed here. The customer contact audit can serve as a basis for ensuring better service creation and delivery processes. Grease Monkey believes that it has the right process in the vehicle oil change and fluid exchange service business. Customers do not need appointments, stores are open six days per week, the service is completed in 15–20 minutes, and a waiting room allows customers to read or work while the service is being completed.

Most services have a limited capacity due to the inseparability of the service from the service provider and the perishable nature of the service. For example, to "buy" an appendectomy, a patient must be in the hospital at the same time as the surgeon and only one patient can be helped at that time. Similarly, no additional surgery can be conducted tomorrow because of an unused operating room or an available surgeon today—the service capacity is lost if it is not used. So the service component of the marketing mix must be integrated with efforts to influence consumer demand.[47] This is referred to as **capacity management**.

Service organizations must manage the availability of the offering so that (1) demand matches capacity over the duration of the demand cycle (for example, one day, week, month, or year), and (2) the organization's assets are used in ways that will maximize the return on investment (ROI).[48] Figure 12–8 shows how a hotel tries to manage its capacity during the high and low seasons. Differing price structures are assigned to each segment of consumers to help moderate or adjust demand for the service. Airline contracts fill a fixed number of rooms throughout the year. In the low season, when more rooms are available, tour packages at appealing prices are used to attract groups or conventions, such as an offer for seven nights in Orlando at a reduced price. Weekend packages are also offered to vacationers. In the high-demand season, groups are less desirable because guests who will pay high prices travel to Florida on their own. The Applying Marketing Metrics box demonstrates how JetBlue Airways uses a capacity management measure called *load factor* to assess its profitability.

Different prices and packages help match hotel demand to capacity.

Week 7 (low season)   **Week 36 (high season)**

SERVICES IN THE FUTURE

What can we expect from the services industry in the future? New and better services, of course, and an unprecedented variety of choices. Many of the changes will be the result of three factors: technological development, improved understanding of service delivery and consumption, and the social imperative for sustainability.

Android TV is one example of how services are changing. Read the text to learn more.

© McGraw-Hill Education/Editorial Image, LLC, photographer

Video 12-4
Nexus Player and Android TV
kerin.tv/13e/v12-4

Technological advances are rapidly changing the services industry. The key elements of future services include mobility and personalization. AT&T, for example, recently introduced its mobile subscription service, Mobile TV, which allows consumers to view ESPN, Disney, Fox News, and other programs on their smartphones. Similarly, Google has introduced Nexus Player with Android TV, a smart TV platform that provides programming, app, and gaming options through voice recognition and app interfaces; the system makes recommendations based on viewing and usage behaviors.[49] Technology-mediated personalization can increase customers' perceptions of value; however, excessive attempts at personalization can also trigger privacy concerns.[50]

New data and information about service consumers and providers is also leading to changes in service delivery and consumption. Physicians at the University of Virginia Health System discovered that cardiac patients learned more and reported 98 percent satisfaction when they shared a 90-minute appointment with other patients, rather than meeting the doctor in the traditional, shorter, one-on-one format. Other studies of services have discovered that in some businesses, such as retailing, restaurants, and repair and installation, customer satisfaction levels are inflated because employees often engage in "service sweethearting"—giving unauthorized free products or services to customers. Many of these businesses are now changing employee recruiting and training activities to limit this type of behavior. Both examples emphasize how understanding the details of service transactions will lead to new forms of service in the future.[51]

Finally, a growing interest in sustainability and "green" businesses is also changing the services industry. This trend began when consumers became aware of the environmental impact of many products such as automobiles, appliances, and cleaning solutions. Today, this trend has expanded to include consumers' assessment of services. Recent surveys indicate that green practices influence many consumer purchase decisions for services, including those provided by dry cleaners, contractors, and hotels. In response, many service providers are developing new approaches to their offerings. Hilton has set conservation goals to help its hotels achieve environmental management certification from the International Organization for Standardization (ISO). Similarly, the U.S. Postal Service has introduced sustainability initiatives to reduce energy, water, and petroleum use and to increase its recycling activities.[52] These and other approaches are likely to expand globally as services strive to create a competitive advantage.[53]

learning review »

12-6. How does a movie theater use off-peak pricing?

12-7. Matching demand with capacity is the focus of _____ management.

12-8. What factors will influence future changes in services?

LEARNING OBJECTIVES REVIEW

LO 12-1   *Describe four unique elements of services.*
The four unique elements of services—the four I's—are intangibility, inconsistency, inseparability, and inventory. Intangibility refers to the tendency of services to be a performance that cannot be held or touched, rather than an object. Inconsistency is a characteristic of services because they depend on people to deliver them, and people vary in their capabilities and in their day-to-day performance. Inseparability refers to the difficulty of separating the deliverer of the service (hair stylist) from the service itself (hair salon). Inventory refers to the need to have service production capability when there is service demand.

LO 12-2   *Recognize how services differ and how they can be classified.*
Services differ in terms of the balance of the part of the offering that is based on products and the part of the offering that is based on service. Services can be delivered by people or equipment, they can be provided by for-profit or nonprofit organizations, and they can be government sponsored.

LO 12-3   *Explain how consumers purchase and evaluate services.*
Because services are intangible, prepurchase evaluation is difficult for consumers. To choose a service, consumers use search, experience, and credence qualities to evaluate the product and service elements of an offering. Once a consumer tries a service, it is evaluated by comparing expectations with the actual experience on five dimensions of quality—reliability, tangibility, responsiveness, assurance, and empathy. Differences between expectations and experience are identified through gap analysis.

LO 12-4   *Develop a customer contact audit to identify service advantages.*
A customer contact audit is a flowchart of the points of interaction between a consumer and a service provider.

The interactions identified in a customer contact audit often serve as the basis for developing relationships with customers.

LO 12-5   *Explain the role of the seven Ps in the services marketing mix.*
The services marketing mix includes seven Ps. An important aspect of the *product* element is branding—the use of a brand name or logo to help consumers identify a service. *Pricing* is reflected in charges, fees, fares, and rates and can be used to influence perceptions of the quality of a service and to balance demand for services. *Place* (or distribution) is used to provide access and convenience. *Promotional* tools such as advertising and publicity are a means of communicating the benefits of a service. *People* are responsible for the creation and delivery of the service. Internal marketing and customer experience management are concepts that result from a focus on people within the service organization and their interactions with customers. *Physical* environment refers to the appearance of the place where the services are delivered. *Process* refers to the actual procedures, mechanisms, and activities by which a service is created and delivered.

LO 12-6   *Discuss the important roles of internal marketing and customer experience management in service organizations.*
Because the employee plays a central role in creating the service experience and building and maintaining relationships with customers, services have adopted a concept called internal marketing. This concept suggests that services need to ensure that employees (the internal market) have the attitude, skills, and commitment needed to meet customer expectations. Customer experience management is the process of managing the entire customer experience with the company to ensure customer loyalty.

339

LEARNING REVIEW ANSWERS

12-1   What are the four I's of services?
Answer: The four I's of services are: (1) intangibility, which means that they can't be held, touched, or seen; (2) inconsistency, which means that their quality varies with each person's capabilities and day-to-day job performance; (3) inseparability, which means that the consumer cannot (and does not) separate the deliverer of the service from the service itself; and (4) inventory, which means that inventory carrying costs are more subjective and are related to idle production capacity—when the service provider is available but there is no demand for the service.

12-2   To eliminate service inconsistencies, companies rely on _____ and _____.
Answer: standardization; training

12-3   Would inventory carrying costs for an accounting firm with certified public accountants be (*a*) high, (*b*) low, or (*c*) nonexistent?
Answer: Inventory carrying costs are related to idle production capacity, which is when the service provider is available

but there is no demand. A CPA typically earns a high fixed cost salary. Therefore, if he/she is available but there is no demand for his/her service, the inventory cost of this service is (*a*) "high," because the cost of the accountant's salary must be paid regardless of whether or not the service is performed.

12-4   What are the differences between search, experience, and credence properties?
Answer: Search properties, such as color, size, and style, can be determined before purchase. Experience properties, such as with restaurants, can only be assessed during or after consumption. Credence properties, which are characteristics of services provided by specialized professionals such as legal advice or medical diagnostics, may be impossible to evaluate even after purchase and consumption.

12-5   Hertz created its differential advantage at the points of _____ in its customer contact audit.
Answer: interaction between consumer and service provider

12-6 How does a movie theater use off-peak pricing?
Answer: Off-peak pricing consists of charging different prices during different times of the day or during different days of the week to reflect variations in demand for the service. Movie theaters reduce prices for matinees and often for Monday through Thursday shows due to the lower demand for this service during this time of day or days of the week.

12-7 Matching demand with capacity is the focus of _____ management.
Answer: capacity

12-8 What factors will influence future changes in services?
Answer: Technology advances, improved understanding of service delivery and consumption, and the social imperative for sustainability are factors that will influence future changes in services.

FOCUSING ON KEY TERMS

capacity management p. 337
customer contact audit p. 330
customer experience management (CEM) p. 335

four I's of services p. 323
gap analysis p. 330
idle production capacity p. 324
internal marketing p. 335

off-peak pricing p. 334
service continuum p. 325
services p. 322
seven Ps of services marketing p. 333

APPLYING MARKETING KNOWLEDGE

1 Explain how the four I's of services would apply to a Marriott Hotel.

2 Idle production capacity may be related to inventory or capacity management. How would the pricing component of the marketing mix reduce idle production capacity for (a) a car wash, (b) a stage theater group, and (c) a university?

3 Look back at the service continuum in Figure 12–3. Explain how the following points in the continuum differ in terms of consistency: (a) salt, (b) automobile, (c) advertising agency, and (d) teaching.

4 What are the search, experience, and credence properties of an airline for (a) the business traveler and (b) the pleasure traveler? What properties are most important to each group?

5 Outline the customer contact audit for the typical deposit you make at your neighborhood bank.

6 How does off-peak pricing influence demand for services?

7 Draw the channel of distribution for the following services: (a) a restaurant, (b) a hospital, and (c) a hotel.

8 The text suggests that internal marketing is necessary before a successful marketing program can be directed at consumers. Why is this particularly true for service organizations?

9 Outline the capacity management strategies that an airline must consider.

10 In recent years, many service businesses have begun to provide their employees with uniforms. Explain the rationale behind this strategy in terms of the concepts discussed in this chapter.

BUILDING YOUR MARKETING PLAN

In this section of your marketing plan you should distinguish between your core product—a good or a service—and supplementary services.

1 Develop an internal marketing program that will ensure that employees are prepared to deliver the core and supplementary services.

2 Using the flowchart in Figure 12–7 as a guide, create a customer contact audit to identify specific points of interaction with customers.

3 Describe marketing activities that will (a) address each of the four I's as they relate to your service and (b) encourage the development of relationships with your customers.

Add this section as an appendix to your marketing plan and use the results to develop your marketing mix strategy.

connect

VIDEO CASE 12   LA Galaxy: Where Sports Marketing Is a Kick!

"We have a unique product for people," exclaims Chris Klein, president of the LA Galaxy soccer club.

> **Video 12-5**
> **LA Galaxy Video Case**
> kerin.tv/13e/v12-5

Soccer combines many elements of athleticism, teamwork, and competition to make it fast, exciting, engaging, fun, and increasingly popular. Klein goes on to explain, "This is a cool sport, and it's something that's growing." His enthusiasm is supported by a sophisticated strategy that Klein and his marketing team have designed to help people "experience the excitement" of their product!

THE LA GALAXY

The LA Galaxy is a professional soccer club competing in Major League Soccer (MLS). The club was one of ten charter clubs when the league began, and is now part of the league's Western Conference. "The LA Galaxy was founded in 1996," says Klein, and "through the course of the League's history, the Galaxy has been the most successful franchise in Major League Soccer." The team has been conference champions nine times, regular season champions four times, and the MLS championship winners five times.

The first Galaxy games were played at the Rose Bowl in Pasadena, California, until the team moved to its current location in the soccer-specific stadium StubHub Center in Carson, California. Players are primarily from the United States but also represent countries such as Brazil, Ireland, Italy, and Panama. "We have signed some of the biggest players, not only in our country, like Cobi Jones and Landon Donovan, but we've also signed some of the biggest players in the world," explains Klein. English soccer superstar David Beckham joined the LA Galaxy in 2007 and played through 2012, helping the team win two championships during that period.

Today, the LA Galaxy attracts an average of 23,000 fans to each of its games. While the hard-core fans tend to be 18- to 34-year-old men, the team also appeals to many other segments. For example, because soccer is the largest participant sport in the United States, many kids and youth soccer teams come to the games. In addition, many college students and families attend. According to Klein, it's a welcoming environment where "you can paint your face and yell" or you can bring your kids and just "have fun at the game." The team's mascot, Cozmo, is a frog-like extraterrestrial

© R Heyes Design/Alamy

who entertains fans at the games and throughout Southern California.

MAJOR LEAGUE SOCCER

As part of its negotiation to hold the 1994 FIFA (Federation Internationale de Football Association) World Cup in the United States, the U.S. Soccer Federation promised to establish a professional soccer league. The result was Major League Soccer. Since its beginning with 10 teams in 1996, Major League Soccer has expanded to 20 teams, including 3 teams in Canada. Each team plays 34 games during the regular season from March to October, and the top 12 teams participate in the playoffs, which end with the MLS Cup in December.

Even though soccer is popular around the world, introducing professional soccer in the United States presented some difficulties. Klein describes the problem:

> Soccer is the biggest sport in the world, but here in the U.S. we have a lot of competition. Major League Soccer is the equivalent to Major League Baseball, the NFL, the NBA, and the NHL. These are established leagues and MLS is the fifth major sport. In 1996, we started thinking that we had to get every baseball fan, basketball fan, and football fan to enjoy our sport.

To attempt to attract fans from other sports, MLS experimented with changes to traditional soccer rules. For example, MLS added shootouts to resolve tie games, used a countdown (to zero) clock rather than a progressive clock, allowed extra substitutions, and even considered making the goals bigger to increase the scoring. Eventually, the league concluded that the changes had alienated some traditional soccer fans without attracting new fans from other sports, so it went back to the traditional rules for MLS games.

As the league shifted from an "attract all sports fans" philosophy to a focus on people with some existing interest in soccer, it made several other changes. First, it began moving MLS games from large, rented, football facilities to new, smaller, more intimate soccer-specific stadiums. In addition, the league made efforts to internationalize the teams by allowing up to eight players per team from outside of the United States. Finally, MLS encouraged all teams to create youth development programs to help find talented local players. To complement these efforts, each team manages its own marketing program.

THE LA GALAXY MARKETING PROGRAM

"The primary marketing objective for the Galaxy is ticket sales," says Casey Leppanen, senior director of marketing and broadcasting. "Our product is soccer," he goes on to explain, "but we are more than that. We are an experience." So, to sell single-game tickets and season tickets, the Galaxy developed a comprehensive marketing program. According to Leppanen, "Our marketing mix is pretty similar to any other sports team or company you're going to find." The key difference in marketing a sport, or any service, is that every game offers a different experience to fans. The players, the opponents, the weather, and the outcomes of the games change constantly.

How does the Galaxy sell a product that is constantly changing? The first step is to understand that different segments may attend a soccer game for different types of experiences. For example:

- *Supporter clubs.* Attend to watch the strategy of a game and see the Galaxy score.
- *Families.* Want to have fun, see the mascot, and get a souvenir.
- *Latino community.* Enjoy watching soccer and forming connections with players from Central and South America.
- *Trendsetting youth.* Attend to meet friends, enjoy an event, and see star players.
- *Groups* (teams, corporations, religious groups, etc.). Want an opportunity for networking and teambuilding.

The different interests combined with the changing "product" create a special marketing challenge.

The experience the Galaxy provides to fans is much more than watching a soccer game. It includes the quality of play, the individual members of the team, the merchandise, food, facilities, activities, and interactions with staff, other fans, and players. Some of the specific elements of the Galaxy game experience include:

- *Star players.* Robbie Keane, Steven Gerrard, Sebastian Lletget, and Giovani dos Santos are all soccer stars that attract fans.
- *Team LA Store.* Offers LA Galaxy merchandise at StubHub Center and other locations.
- *Supporter clubs.* Three clubs—the Angel City Brigade, the Riot Squad, and the Galaxians—offer the opportunity to participate in an intense and festive fan experience, complete with songs and chants!
- *Promotional nights.* Special events include Family Nights, Bobblehead Nights, Jersey-Off-The-Back Auctions, and Student Nights.
- *"Name in Lights."* A donation gets your message on the home game scoreboard.
- *"Cozmo."* The team mascot who entertains all fans at every game.
- *StubHub Center.* The soccer-specific stadium offers a great atmosphere, amazing sight lines, event suites, terrace cabanas, restaurants, assigned seating, general admission seating, and an inclined lawn (also called the berm) for picnic-style seating.

Of course, there are many other elements that are all part of the experience the Galaxy marketing team manages and delivers at every game!

© Shaun Clark/Getty Images

Next, the Galaxy must deliver relevant messages to each segment. Leppanen explains that the Galaxy "want to make sure that we're delivering an authentic message, but speak[ing] to them with what they want to be spoken about." One way they accomplish this is through direct marketing, which consists of email messages and direct-mail literature. These messages are complemented with traditional media advertising, outdoor advertising, and digital advertising. The traditional media include radio, TV, and print. The outdoor advertising includes billboards and bus wraps. The digital platforms, which have a total of 1.3 million Galaxy fan users, include Facebook, Twitter, YouTube, Google+, Instagram, Pinterest, Flickr, and Foursquare. Digital is a very important part of the mix because "we can get really granular and sophisticated in who we're targeting and how we speak to them," explains Leppanen.

The Galaxy also use personal selling as part of their marketing program. A team of 25 people makes personal phone calls to help sell single-game tickets, family packs, group tickets, and season tickets. There are also two teams of brand ambassadors called the Star Squad and the Galaxy Street Team who are involved in about 500 events in the community each year. Lori Nevares, a marketing coordinator at Galaxy and former Street Team member, explains that "We got to go out and do all kinds of promotional events for different communities and see the fans and how much they were devoted to the Galaxy." A skills team called the Galaxy Futboleros provides high-energy performances throughout the community as well. Finally, Cozmo makes many appearances to deliver the Galaxy soccer message to current and potential fans.

© Carrie Jesenovec/Icon SMI/Corbis

One of the final steps in the ticket sales process is setting the price. According to Heather Pease, director of ticketing, "Every year we conduct a very in-depth analysis of our ticket sales. We go seat-by-seat, row-by-row, and category-by-category to see how many people have purchased seats and at what price." The analysis also includes a comparison of ticket prices at other sports teams in the area. Pease then uses the information to create a price and a package for every possible type of fan, ranging from Champions Lounge members, to season ticket holders, to groups or families, to single-game fans. She also offers discounted tickets for students and children.

There are a lot of marketing activities taking place at the Galaxy. In fact, Casey Leppanen says, "My role here at the Galaxy is to integrate all the pieces of our marketing department." The integration is paying off, as attendance at LA Galaxy games is well above the league average. In addition, the team currently has 8,500 season ticket holders and plans to reach 12,500 in three years!

THE BUSINESS OF SOCCER

While ticket sales represent a substantial source of revenue for the Galaxy, there are several other important elements of the soccer "business"—broadcast rights, sponsorships, and merchandise—that the team must manage. Early in the league's history, MLS had to pay television and cable networks to broadcast its games. As the number of viewers increased, however, the league was able to attract coverage from ESPN, ABC, NBC, and Fox. The Galaxy recently began a 10-year, $55 million deal with the Time Warner Cable Sports network. Currently, all games have television and radio coverage in English and Spanish, and there is play-by-play coverage and webchat on LAGalaxy.com.

Sponsorships are also essential to the financial success of MLS and the Galaxy. Pepsi is the official soft drink and Aquafina is the official water of MLS. Similarly, Herbalife is the official nutrition company of the LA Galaxy. In addition, Herbalife recently announced a 10-year agreement to be the official jersey sponsor of the Galaxy. Herbalife pays $4 million annually to sponsor the team and place its logo on the front of the team jerseys. Other team sponsors include Chevrolet, Nestlé, Alaska Airlines, Shasta, and Buffalo Wild Wings. The sponsors participate in many of the team's contests, promotions, and events to support the team and to gain exposure to customers with similar values and interests.

The marketing team at the LA Galaxy is always busy. "There is a business to run," says Pease. "It is about driving revenue at the end of the day," she continues, "but the best part about it is you get to walk out on a game day and see a sold-out stadium." Seeing the sold-out stadium is a thrill not only because it's a business, however, but also because the marketing team loves soccer. Galaxy president Chris Klein, who studied business and marketing in college, is a good example of the attitude at Galaxy. "I went to college on a soccer scholarship," says Klein, "then I played professionally in our league, and I'm now president of a major club." He is thrilled by "the challenge of marketing a sport that I love, a sport that I've played, and a sport that has so much potential."[54]

Questions

1 What is the LA Galaxy "product"?

2 Which of the seven elements of the service marketing mix are most important in the LA Galaxy marketing program?

3 How is promotion (advertising, personal selling, public relations, sales promotion, direct marketing) used by the LA Galaxy? Do these activities depend on the specific target markets?

4 How are social media integrated into the LA Galaxy's marketing strategy?

5 How does the LA Galaxy assess the impact of its marketing activities? Has its program been successful?

Chapter Notes

1. Burt Helm, "Airbnb: Company of the Year," *Inc.,* December 2014/January 2015, pp. 64–70, 130; Tx Zhuo, "Airbnb and Uber Are Just the Beginning," *Entrepreneur.com,* March 25, 2015; Tomio Geron, "The Share Economy," *Forbes,* February 11, 2013, pp. 58–66; "How Couchsurfing Epitomizes the 'Sharing Economy,'?" *The Huffington Post,* January 25, 2013; "adverCar Invites Drivers to Rent Car 'Real Estate' to Showcase Favorite Brands," *GlobeNewswire,* January 14, 2013; "Will You Leave Your Job to Join the Sharing Economy?" *VentureBeat,* January 22, 2013; "Airbnb's Brian Chesky: It's Only Day Two in the Sharing Economy," *PandoDaily,* January 11, 2013; and "A Step Forward for Ride-Sharing: California Suspends Fines against Lyft," *VentureBeat,* January 30, 2013.

2. "Gross Domestic Product: First Quarter 2015," news release, Bureau of Economic Analysis, U.S. Department of Commerce, May 29, 2015; *World Trade Report 2014,* World Trade Organization, p. 25; "Table 2.1 Employment by Major Industry Sector," Bureau of Labor Statistics, U.S. Department of Labor, December 19, 2013.

3. "One Concierge Makes Hard-to-Get Gift Ideas Easier with GiftVault.com," *PR.com,* October 6, 2012; "One Concierge Announces Partnership with Paramount Business Jets," *American Consumer News,* March 4, 2011; "Ubitus to Launch Cloud Gaming Services on Google TV," *PR Newswire,* January 7, 2013; and The Breakers Palm Beach website, www.thebreakers.com, accessed January 30, 2013.

4. Janet R. McColl-Kennedy and Tina White, "Service Provider Training Programs at Odds with Customer Requirements in Five Star Hotels," *Journal of Services Marketing* 11, no. 4 (1997), pp. 249–64; Ellyn A. McColgan, "How Fidelity Invests in Service Professionals," *Harvard Business Review,* January–February 1997, pp. 137–43; and Frederick F. Reichheld and W. Earl Sasser Jr., "Zero Defections: Quality Comes to Services," *Harvard Business Review,* September–October 1990, pp. 105–11.

5. Christian Gronroos, "Value Co-creation in Service Logic: A Critical Analysis," *Marketing Theory,* September 2011, pp. 279–301; and Stephen L. Vargo and Robert F. Lusch, "Evolving to a New Dominant Logic for Marketing," *Journal of Marketing,* January 2004, p. 1.

6. Alana Semuels, "Self-Service Machines Replacing Retail Workers," *The Star-Ledger,* March 13, 2011, p. 1; Zhen Zhu, Cheryl Nakata, and K. Sivakumar, "Self-Service Technology Effectiveness: The Role of Design Features and Individual Traits," *Journal of the Academy of Marketing Science,* Winter 2007, pp. 492–506; and Lawrence F. Cunningham, Clifford E. Young, and James Gerlach, "A Comparison of Consumer Views of Traditional Services and Self-Service Technologies," *Journal of Services Marketing* 1 (2009), pp. 11–23.

7. Ashlee Vance and Aaron Ricadela, "Hewlett-Packard's Free Fall," *Bloomberg Businessweek,* January 14–20, 2013, pp. 44–50; and "HP to Invest $1 Billion to Launch New Era of Enterprise Services," *Business Wire,* June 1, 2010.

8. Christopher Lovelock and Jochen Wirtz, *Services Marketing: People, Technology, Strategy,* 7th ed. (Upper Saddle River, NJ: Pearson Prentice-Hall, 2011); Lance A. Bettencourt, Stephen W. Brown, and Nancy J. Sirianni, "The Secret to True Service Innovation," *Business Horizons,* February 2013, pp. 13–22; and Thomas J. Delong and Vineeta Vijayaraghavan, "Should You Listen to the Customer?" *Harvard Business Review,* September 2012, pp. 129–33.

9. Suzanne C. Makarem, Susan M. Mudambi, and Jeffrey S. Podoshen, "Satisfaction in Technology-Enabled Service Encounters," *The Journal of Services Marketing* 3 (2009), p. 134; Peter C. Honebein and Roy F. Cammarano, "Customers at Work: Self-Service Customers Can Reduce Costs and Become Cocreators of Value," *Marketing Management,* January/February 2006, pp. 26–31; and Matthew L. Meuter, Amy L. Ostrom, Robert I. Roundtree, and Mary Jo Bitner, "Self-Service Technologies: Understanding Customer Satisfaction with Technology-Based Service Encounters," *Journal of Marketing,* July 2000, pp. 50–64.

10. Katie L. Roeger, Amy S. Blackwood, and Sarah L. Pettijohn, *The Nonprofit Almanac,* 2012; and "Quick Facts about Nonprofits," National Center for Charitable Statistics, http://nccsdataweb.urban.org, 2012.

11. Don Knapp, "Ten Nonprofit Myths—and How to Debunk Them," *Nonprofit World,* September/October 2010, pp. 12–14; and Jessi Hempl, "Selling a Cause? Better Make It Pop," *BusinessWeek,* February 13, 2006, p. 75.

12. "Apps for Donors," *Marketing Health Services,* Winter 2014, p. 4; Elyse Dupre, "The American Red Cross Braves the Campaign Storm," *DMNews,* January 2013; "American Red Cross Launches New Ad Campaign," *India Pharma News,* January 11, 2013; "Storytellers Campaign Shows Powerful Red Cross Moments," *States News Service,* December 13, 2012; Jane L. Levere, "To Tell Its Story, Red Cross Goes to Those It Helped," *The New York Times,* December 13, 2012, p. 3; "Corporate

Partners Support Red Cross Holiday Campaign," *PR Newswire,* December 12, 2012; Christine Birkner, "The American Red Cross Took a Centralized Approach to Protect Its Brand Message," *Marketing News,* July 30, 2011, p. 10; "National Celebrity Cabinet Members," American Red Cross website, http://www.redcross.org/supporters/celebrities, accessed June 9, 2015; and "Kate Grant Named 2014 Nonprofit Marketer of the Year," *Marketing News,* September 2014, p. 5.

13. Doug Donovan, "Fiscal Cliff Deal Could Hurt Charitable Giving," *The Chronicle of Philanthropy,* January 1, 2013; Michele Nichols, "U.S. Charitable Giving Approaches $300 Billion in 2011," *Reuters,* June 19, 2012; "The American Red Cross and Dell Launch First-of-Its-Kind Social Media Digital Operations Center," *Business Wire,* March 7, 2012; Alex Goldmark, "Everyone Chip In, Please; Crowdfunding Sandy," National Public Radio (transcript), December 10, 2012; "People Can Support Response by Giving to Red Cross Disaster Relief," American Red Cross, press release, October 29, 2012; Christine Birkner, "Give—and Give Again," *Marketing News,* May 31, 2012, p. 8; Pete Born, "Komen Foundation to Launch Fragrance," *Women's Wear Daily,* January 3, 2011, p. 4; "Telescope Inc. and Susan G. Komen for the Cure Los Angeles Join Forces to 'Text for the Cure,'" *PR Newswire,* December 15, 2010; Ann Marie Kerwin, "How to Get the Social-Media Generation Behind Your Cause," *Advertising Age,* June 28, 2010, p. 8; "American Red Cross Responds to Japan Earthquake and Pacific Tsunami," *PR Newswire,* March 11, 2011; Michael Bush, "Red Cross Delivers Real Mobile Results for a Real Emergency," *Advertising Age,* February 22, 2010, p. 38; and Maureen West, "How Nonprofits Can Use Social Media to Spark Change," *The Chronicle of Philanthropy,* February 20, 2011.

14. "U.S. Postal Service Details Free Package Pickup in New TV Ad," *Wireless News,* December 30, 2012; Joe Ryan, "The U.S. Postal Service Steps Up Its Mobile Game," *DMNews,* December 2012; "Hallmark and the U.S. Postal Service Launch Postage-Paid Greeting Cards," *PR Newswire,* February 17, 2011; "Postal Service Begins 2011 with Loss in First Quarter, Recession Eases, but First-Class Mail Volume Continues to Decline," *States News Service,* February 9, 2011; and Diane C. Lade, "Postal Service Learns to Love the Internet," *South Florida Sun-Sentinel,* March 15, 2007.

15. Keith B. Murray, "A Test of Services Marketing Theory: Consumer Information Acquisition Activities," *Journal of Marketing,* January 1991, pp. 10–25.

16. Dawn Iacobucci, "An Empirical Examination of Some Basic Tenets in Services: Goods-Services Continua," in *Advances in Services Marketing and Management,* vol. 1, eds. Teresa Swartz, David E. Bowen, and Stephen W. Brown (Greenwich, CT: JAI Press), pp. 23–52; and Valerie A. Zeithaml, "How Consumer Evaluation Processes Differ between Goods and Services," in *Marketing of Services,* eds. James H. Donnelly and William R. George (Chicago: American Marketing Association, 1981).

17. Jason Oliver, "The Consumer's Perspective on Evaluating Products: Service Is the Key" *Journal of Services Marketing,* 3 (2015), pp. 200–210; Ebrahim Mazaheri, Richard Marie-Odile, and Michel Laroche, "The Role of Emotions in Online Consumer Behavior: A Comparison of Search, Experience, and Credence Services," *Journal of Services Marketing* 7 (2012), pp. 535–50; Michael J. Dorsch, Stephen J. Grove, and William Darden, "Consumer Intentions to Use a Services Category," *Journal of Services Marketing* 2 (2000), pp. 92–117; and Murray, "A Test of Services Marketing Theory: Consumer Information Acquisition Activities."

18. Leonard L. Berry and Neeli Bendapudi, "Clueing in Customers," *Harvard Business Review,* February 2003, pp. 100–6.

19. John Ozment and Edward Morash, "The Augmented Service Offering for Perceived and Actual Service Quality," *Journal of the Academy of Marketing Science,* Fall 1994, pp. 352–63.

20. A. Parasuraman, Valerie A. Zeithaml, and Leonard L. Berry, "Reassessment of Expectations as a Comparison Standard in Measuring Service Quality: Implications for Further Research," *Journal of Marketing,* January 1994, pp. 111–24; and Leonard L. Berry, *On Great Service* (New York: Free Press, 1995).

21. Yu-Chi Wu, Chin-Shih Tsai, Hsiao-Wen Hsiung, and Kuan-Ying Chen, "Linkage Between Frontline Employee Service Competence Scale and Customer Perceptions of Service Quality," *Journal of Services Marketing* 3 (2015), pp. 224–34; Valerie A. Zeithaml, A. Parasuraman, and Leonard L. Berry, *Delivering Quality Service* (New York: Free Press, 1990); and Stephen W. Brown and Teresa Swartz, "A Gap Analysis of Professional Service Quality," *Journal of Marketing,* April 1989, pp. 92–98.

22. Amy Ostrom and Dawn Iacobucci, "Consumer Trade-Offs and the Evaluation of Services," *Journal of Marketing,* January 1995, pp. 17–28; and J. Joseph Cronin Jr., and Steven A. Taylor, "Measuring Service Quality: A Reexamination and Extension," *Journal of Marketing,* July 1992, pp. 55–68.

23. L. Jean Harrison-Walker, "The Role of Cause and Affect in Service Failure," *Journal of Services Marketing* 2 (2012), pp. 115–23; Kriengsin Prasongsukarn and Paul G. Patterson, "An Extended Service Recovery Model: The Moderating Impact of Temporal Sequence of Events," *Journal of Services Marketing* 7 (2012), pp. 510–20; Anna S. Mattila, "Do Women Like Options More Than Men? An Examination in the Context of Service Recovery," *Journal of Services Marketing* 7 (2012), pp. 499–508; Leslie M. Fine, "Service Marketing," *Business Horizons,* May–June 2008, pp. 163–68; and James G. Maxham III and Richard G. Netermeyer, "A Longitudinal Study of Complaining Customers' Evaluations of Multiple Service Failures and Recovery Efforts," *Journal of Marketing,* October 2002, pp. 57–71.

24. Barry Berman and Anil Mathur, "Planning and Implementing Effective Service Guarantee Programs," *Business Horizons* 57 (2014), pp. 107–116; K. Sivakumar, Mei Li, and Beibei Dong, "Service Quality: The Impact of Frequency, Timing, Proximity, and Sequence of Failures and Delights," *Journal of Marketing,* January 2014, pp. 41–58; "How to Earn Extreme Trust: The True Story of Domino's Pizza," *Fearless Competitor,* June 27, 2012; "Becoming Crystal Clear: The Hits and Misses of Brand Transparency," *Business 2 Community.com,* November 14, 2012; "Culture of Openness Gets the Thumbs Up," *Marketing Week,* August 4, 2011, p. 20; and Charles Enman, "Social Media Monitoring Firm Is Looking to Hire," *The Daily Gleaner,* March 8, 2011, p. D1.

25. Vicki Clift, "Everyone Needs Service Flow Charting," *Marketing News,* October 23, 1995, pp. 41, 43; Mary Jo Bitner, Bernard H. Booms, and Mary Stanfield Tetreault, "The Service Encounter: Diagnosing Favorable and Unfavorable Incidents," *Journal of Marketing,* January 1990, pp. 71–84; Eberhard Scheuing, "Conducting Customer Service Audits," *Journal of Consumer Marketing,* Summer 1989, pp. 35–41; and W. Earl Susser, R. Paul Olsen, and D. Daryl Wyckoff, *Management of Service Operations* (Boston: Allyn & Bacon, 1978).

26. Chi Kin (Bennett) Yim, Kimmy Wa Chan, and Simon S. K. Lam, "Do Customers and Employees Enjoy Service Participation? Synergistic Effect of Self- and Other-Efficacy," *Journal of Marketing,* November 2012, pp. 121–40; Joseph Pine and James H. Gilmore, *The Experience Economy,* Revised Edition (Boston: Harvard Business School Publishing, 2011); Mary Jo Bitner, Amy L. Ostrom, and Felicia N. Morgan, "Service Blueprinting: A Practical Technique for Service Innovation," *California Management Review,* Spring 2008, pp. 66–94; Thorsten Hennig-Thurau,

Markus Groth, Michael Paul, and Dwayne D. Gremler, "Are All Smiles Created Equal? How Emotional Contagion and Emotional Labor Affect Service Relationships," *Journal of Marketing,* July 2006, pp. 58–73.

27. Lance A. Bettencourt, Christopher P. Blocker, Mark B. Houston, and Daniel J. Flint, "Rethinking Customer Relationships," *Business Horizons* 58 (2015), pp. 99–108; Jill Avery, Susan Fournier, and John Wittenbraker, "Unlock The Mysteries of Your Customer Relationships," *Harvard Business Review,* July–August 2014, pp. 72–81; Leonard L. Berry, "Relationship Marketing of Services—Growing Interest, Emerging Perspectives," *Journal of the Academy of Marketing Science,* Fall 1995, pp. 236–45; Mary Jo Bitner, "Building Service Relationships: It's All about Promises," *Journal of the Academy of Marketing Science,* Fall 1995, pp. 246–51; Kevin P. Gwinner, Dwayne D. Gremler, and Mary Jo Bitner, "Relational Benefits in Services Industries: The Customer's Perspective," *Journal of the Academy of Marketing Science,* Spring 1998, pp. 101–14; Susan Fournier, Susan Dobscha, and David Glen Mick, "Preventing the Premature Death of Relationship Marketing," *Harvard Business Review,* January–February 1998, pp. 42–51; and John V. Petrof, "Relationship Marketing: The Wheel Reinvented?" *Business Horizons,* November–December 1997, pp. 26–31.

28. Katherine N. Lemon, Tiffany Barnett White, and Russell S. Winer, "Dynamic Customer Relationship Management: Incorporating Future Considerations into the Service Retention Decision," *Journal of Marketing,* January 2002, pp. 1–14.

29. Michael Paul, Thorsten Hennig-Thurau, Dwayne D. Gremler, Kevin P. Gwinner, and Caroline Wiertz, "Toward a Theory of Repeat Purchase Drivers for Consumer Services," *Journal of the Academy of Marketing Science,* Summer 2009, pp. 215–37.

30. Thomas S. Gruca, "Defending Service Markets," *Marketing Management* 1 (1994), pp. 31–38; and Leonard L. Berry, Jeffrey S. Conant, and A. Parasuraman. "A Framework for Conducting a Services Marketing Audit," *Journal of the Academy of Marketing Science,* Summer 1991, pp. 255–68.

31. Christopher Lovelock and Jochen Wirtz, *Service Marketing: People, Technology, Strategy,* 7th ed. (Upper Saddle River, NJ: Prentice Hall, 2011); Valerie A. Zeithaml, Mary Jo Bitner, and Dwayne D. Gremler, *Services Marketing,* 6th ed. (New York: McGraw-Hill, 2013), p. 26; and Brian Solis, "Exploring the Fifth and Sixth Ps of Marketing," *Marketing News,* January 2013, p. 7.

32. Dan R. E. Thomas, "Strategy Is Different in Service Businesses," *Harvard Business Review,* July–August 1978, pp. 158–65.

33. Sundar G. Bharedwaj, P. Rajan Varadarajan, and John Fahy, "Sustainable Competitive Advantage in Service Industries: A Conceptual Model and Research Propositions," *Journal of Marketing,* October 1993, pp. 83–99.

34. "Fairmont Hotels and Resorts to Offer Local Shuttle Service with BMW Vehicles," *Entertainment Close-Up,* January 30, 2013; "Westin Hotels Celebrates Anniversary of the Heavenly Bed with Limited-Time Sale," *Manufacturing Close-Up,* September 10, 2012; Abby Ellin, "No Place Like Home—Or a Hotel with the Gym You Use When You're There," *The International Herald Tribune,* November 2, 2011, p. 20; Elisabeth A. Sullivan, "Brand Power2: Fairmont Hotels Partners with Lifestyle Brands to Leverage Their Combined Reach and Add to Its Customer Experience," *Marketing News,* February 28, 2010, p. 11; and Daniel B. Honigman, "Hotels at Home: In-Room Catalog and E-Commerce Service Leverages Guest Experience While Increasing Brand Awareness," *Marketing News,* March 15, 2008, p. 12.

35. Kent B. Monroe, "Buyers' Subjective Perceptions of Price," *Journal of Marketing Research,* February 1973, pp. 70–80; and

Jerry Olson, "Price as an Informational Cue: Effects on Product Evaluation," in *Consumer and Industrial Buying Behavior,* eds. A. G. Woodside, J. N. Sheth, and P. D. Bennett (New York: Elsevier North-Holland, 1977), pp. 267–86.

36. Hean Tat Keh and Jun Pang, "Customer Reactions to Service Separation," *Journal of Marketing,* March 2010, pp. 55–70; Leonard L. Berry, Kathleen Seiders, and Dhruv Grewal, "Understanding Service Convenience," *Journal of Marketing* 66 (July 2002), pp. 1–17; and Charles L. Colby and A. Parasuraman, "Technology Still Matters: E-Services Are Alive and Well and Positioned for Growth," *Marketing Management* 12 (July–August 2003), pp. 28–33.

37. Robert E. Hite, Cynthia Fraser, and Joseph A. Bellizzi, "Professional Service Advertising: The Effects of Price Inclusion, Justification, and Level of Risk," *Journal of Advertising Research* 30 (August–September 1990), pp. 23–31; William R. George and Leonard L. Berry, "Guidelines for the Advertising of Services," *Business Horizons,* July–August 1981, pp. 52–56; and Eugene M. Johnson, Eberhard E. Scheuing, and Kathleen A. Gaida, *Profitable Service Marketing* (Homewood, IL: Dow Jones-Irwin, 1986).

38. Kathleen Mortimer, "Identifying the Components of Effective Service Advertisements," *Journal of Services Marketing* 22 (2008), pp. 104–13.

39. Joe Adams, "Why Public Service Advertising Doesn't Work," *Adweek,* November 17, 1980, p. 72.

40. Patriya Tansuhaj, Donna Randall, and Jim McCullough, "A Services Marketing Management Model: Integrating Internal and External Marketing Functions," *Journal of Sciences Marketing,* Winter 1998, pp. 31–38.

41. Christian Gronroos, "Internal Marketing Theory and Practice," in *Services Marketing in a Changing Environment,* eds. Thomas Bloch, G. D. Upah, and V. A. Zeithaml (Chicago: American Marketing Association, 1984).

42. Ibid.

43. Rita Di Mascio, "The Service Models of Frontline Employees," *Journal of Marketing,* July 2010, pp. 63–80; Yong-Ki Lee, Jung-Heon Nam, Dae-Hwan Park, and Kyung Ah Lee, "What Factors Influence Customer-Oriented Prosocial Behavior of Customer-Contact Employees?" *Journal of Services Marketing* 20, no. 4 (2006), pp. 251–64; Stephen W. Brown, "The Employee Experience," *Marketing Management* 12 (March–April 2003), pp. 12–13; Lawrence A. Crosby and Sheree L. Johnson, "Watch What I Do," *Marketing Management* 12 (November–December 2003), pp. 10–11; and March C. Gilly and Mary Wolfinbarger, "Advertising's Internal Audience," *Journal of Marketing,* January 1998, pp. 69–88.

44. Adrian Palmer, "Customer Experience Management: A Critical Review of an Emerging Idea," *Journal of Service Marketing* 3 (2010), pp. 196–208; Gabriel M. Gelb and John M. McKeever, "In Their Shoes," *Marketing Management,* July/August 2006, pp. 40–45; Lynette Ryals, "Making Customer Relationship Management Work: The Measurement and Profitable Management of Customer Relationships," *Journal of Marketing,* October 2005, pp. 252–61; Bernd H. Schmitt, *Customer Experience Management* (Hoboken, NJ: Wiley and Sons, 2003); and Shaun Smith and Joe Wheeler, *Managing the Customer Experience* (Englewood Cliffs, NJ: Prentice Hall, 2002).

45. Lance A. Bettencourt, "Fundamental Tenets of Service Excellence," *Marketing Management,* Fall 2012, pp. 19–23; "Zappos Family Core Values," Zappos website, http://about.zappos.com/our-unique-culture/zappos-core-values, accessed February 5, 2013; and Paula Andruss, "Delivering WOW Through Service," *Marketing News,* October 15, 2008, p. 10.

46. F. G. Crane, *Professional Services Marketing: Strategy and Tactics* (London: Haworth Press, 1993); and Leonard L. Berry

and Neeli Bendapudi, "Clueing in Customers," *Harvard Business Review,* February 2003, pp. 100–6.

47. Frederick H. deB. Harris and Peter Peacock, "Hold My Place, Please," *Marketing Management,* Fall 1995, pp. 34–46.

48. Christopher Lovelock and Jochen Wirtz, *Services Marketing* (Englewood Cliffs, NJ: Prentice Hall, 2007), pp. 260–84.

49. Dan Kedmey, "Google Unveils 'First-of-Its-Kind,' Android TV Streaming Device," *Time.com,* October 17, 2014; and Angel Moscaritolo, "AT&T Rebrands U-verse as Mobile TV," *PC Magazine,* February 4, 2013.

50. Anyuan Shen and A. Dwayne Ball, "Is Personalization of Services Always a Good Thing? Exploring the Role of Technology-Mediated Personalization (TMP) in Service Relationships," *Journal of Services Marketing* 23 (2009), pp. 80–92.

51. Kamalini Ramdas, Elizabeth Teisberg, and Amy L. Tucker, "4 Ways to Reinvent Service Delivery," *Harvard Business Review,* December 2012, pp. 99–106; Michael K. Brady, Clay M. Voorhees, and Michael J. Brusco, "Service Sweethearting: Its Antecedents and Customer Consequences," *Journal of Marketing,* March 2012, pp. 81–98.

52. "Washington: Green Teams Help U.S. Postal Service Save Millions," *Plus Media Solutions,* February 3, 2013; Hilton Worldwide website, Corporate Responsibility, http://www.hiltonworldwide.com/corporate-responsibility/sustainability/, February 10, 2013; Lawrence Crosby, "Sustainable Relationships," *Marketing Management,* Spring 2010, pp. 12–13; David A. Lubin and Daniel C. Esty, "The Sustainability Imperative," *Harvard Business Review,* May 2010, pp. 42–50; "Consumer Interest in 'Green' Service Doubled from 2008–2010,"

PR Newswire, March 8, 2011; "Choice Energy Services Enables Trump SoHo Hotel to Access 100 Percent Green Power through Innovative Energy Procurement and Management Program," *Business Wire,* March 16, 2011; E. Robinot and J. L. Giannelloni, "Do Hotels' 'Green' Attributes Contribute to Customer Satisfaction?" *Journal of Services Marketing* 2 (2010), pp. 157–69; and "Green Team Helps Postal Service Save Millions," *PR Newswire,* January 25, 2011.

53. Mary Jo Bitner and Stephen W. Brown, "The Service Imperative," *Business Horizons,* January–February 2008, pp. 39–46; and Valerie Zeithaml, Mary Jo Bitner, and Dwayne Gremler, "Services Marketing Strategy," *Marketing Strategy Encyclopedia* (Hoboken, NJ: Wiley and Sons, 2009).

54. LA Galaxy: This case was written by Steven Hartley. Sources: "Landon Donovan Retires a Champion as Galaxy Win MLS Cup," *Time.com,* December 8, 2014; "Galaxy's Home Has New Name," *The Daily News of Los Angeles,* March 5, 2013, p. A1; Kevin Baxter, "Beckham Will Hang Up His Boots: A Star in Europe, His Late Career Move to the Galaxy Brought U.S. Fans to Soccer and Put MLS on Map," *Los Angeles Times,* May 17, 2013, p. C2; "Galaxy, Tim Warner Strike 10-Year, $55 Million Deal," *The Daily News of Los Angeles,* November 16, 2011, p. C6; denz@rslsoapbox, "For Major League Soccer It Is All About the Numbers, TV, Attendance, and Season Tickets," *rslsoapbox.com,* May 18, 2012; Karl Greenberg, "Chevrolet Cleats Up for L.A. Galaxy Sponsorship," *Marketing Daily,* May 28, 2013; LA Galaxy website, www.lagalaxy.com, accessed July 26, 2013; and personal interviews with LA Galaxy personnel.

13

Building the Price Foundation

LEARNING OBJECTIVES

After reading this chapter you should be able to:

 LO 13-1 Identify the elements that make up a price.

 LO 13-2 Recognize the objectives a firm has in setting prices and the constraints that restrict the range of prices a firm can charge.

 LO 13-3 Explain what a demand curve is and the role of revenues in pricing decisions.

 LO 13-4 Describe what price elasticity of demand means to a manager facing a pricing decision.

LO 13-5 Explain the role of costs in pricing decisions and describe how various combinations of price, fixed cost, and unit variable cost affect a firm's break-even point.

Vizio, Inc.—Delivering Beautifully Smart Products at a Great Value

Can you name North America's #1 Smart TV company? Stumped? It's VIZIO, Inc., an entrepreneurial, Irvine, California–based company with a bold agenda. "Our goal is to be the next Sony in 20 to 30 years," says William Wang, VIZIO's co-founder and chief executive officer, who was born in Taiwan and immigrated to the United States at age 13.

In 2002, Wang was struck by an ad for a $10,000 flat-panel HDTV set and immediately saw an opportunity. Instead of marketing these sets as luxury items, Wang thought he could make and market an HDTV that would be affordable for the average customer.

Like many entrepreneurs, he borrowed money from friends and family and mortgaged his home. Within a year, he formed a company that is now known as VIZIO, Inc. and delivered the company's first VIZIO HDTV to Costco for distribution through that company's stores. VIZIO HDTVs are now sold through Costco, Walmart, BJ's Wholesale, Best Buy, Sam's Club, and Target stores nationwide, along with authorized online partners such as Amazon. The company has sold more than 38 million HDTV units shipped since 2002.

VIZIO's ability to deliver affordable HDTVs to the average customer is based on a novel strategy. VIZIO didn't invest in expensive manufacturing facilities but instead relied on contract manufacturers to build its products. Product development and marketing specialists in the United States handle product design and marketing. "The whole goal is to ensure that we have the right product at the right time and the right price and really drive a seamless end-to-end value chain," says a company spokesperson.

"VIZIO HDTVs are more popular and in greater demand than ever," adds Laynie Newsome, VIZIO's co-founder and chief sales officer. "Consumers want to save money without sacrificing quality or technology." Matt McRae, VIZIO's chief technology officer, adds that VIZIO's strategy is to make affordable products with innovative features, saying, "We're far from the cheapest brand on the market at present. Everybody deserves the latest technology, too."

VIZIO's visionary commitment to delivering high-quality technology at a great value to consumers is evident by its pioneering role in launching Smart TVs in 2010. Smart TV enables viewers to watch content from the Internet directly on their TV, for a more interactive TV watching experience. VIZIO has sold more than 3.2 million Smart TVs since 2010, making it North America's #1 Smart TV company.

YouTube: Second-Screen Experience

Full-Screen Apps Window

© RNewsFoto/VIZIO/AP Images

Video 13-1
VIZIO
kerin.tv/13e/v13-1

VIZIO's powerful and profitable price-value position clearly resonates with consumers. VIZIO is frequently ranked "Highest in Customer Satisfaction" with HDTVs by J.D. Power and Associates and listed among the largest privately held companies in the United States. Not bad for a company with about 400 employees and just 14 years old![1]

Welcome to the fascinating—and intense—world of pricing. This chapter describes the important factors organizations consider when they go about setting prices for their products and services.

NATURE AND IMPORTANCE OF PRICE

LO 13-1 Identify the elements that make up a price.

The price paid for products and services goes by many names. You pay *tuition* for your education, *rent* for an apartment, *interest* on a bank credit card, and a *premium* for car insurance. Your dentist or physician charges you a *fee,* a professional or social organization charges *dues,* and airlines charge a *fare.* In business, an executive is given a *salary,* a salesperson receives a *commission,* and a worker is paid a *wage.* And what you pay for clothes or a haircut is termed a *price.*

Among all marketing and operations factors in a business firm, price has a unique role. It is the place where all other business decisions come together. The price must be "right"—in the sense that customers must be willing to pay it; it must generate enough sales dollars to pay for the cost of developing, producing, and marketing the product; *and* it must earn a profit for the company. Small changes in price can have big effects on both the number of units sold and company profit.

What Is a Price?

From a marketing viewpoint, **price** is the money or other considerations (including other products and services) exchanged for the ownership or use of a product or service. For example, Wilkinson Sword has exchanged some of its knives for advertising used to promote its razor blades. This practice of exchanging products and services for other products and services rather than for money is called **barter**. Barter transactions account for billions of dollars annually in domestic and international trade. In the United States alone, $12 billion of products and services are traded every year without any money changing hands.[2]

The Price Equation   For most products, money is exchanged. However, the amount paid is not always the same as the list, or quoted, price because of discounts, allowances, and extra fees. One new 21st-century pricing tactic involves using "special fees" and "surcharges." This practice is driven by consumers' zeal for low prices combined with the ease of making price comparisons on the Internet. Buyers are more willing to pay extra fees than a higher list price, so sellers use add-on charges as a way of having the consumer pay more without raising the list price.

All the factors that increase or decrease the final price of an offering help construct a "price equation," which is shown for a few products in Figure 13–1. These are key considerations if you want to buy a 2017 Bugatti Chiron.[3] This all-wheel car accelerates from 0 to 60 mph in just 2.5 seconds. With its 1,500-horsepower engine, top speed is 288 mph! The aerodynamic body is made out of carbon fiber to safely handle the speed.

Are you interested in trading in your 2008 Mini-Cooper for a 2017 Bugatti Chiron, the world's most expensive car? Read the text to find out the true cost of purchasing a new car.

Credit: Left: Source: © Drive Images/Alamy; Right: Bugatti

ITEM PURCHASED	PRICE	= LIST PRICE	− INCENTIVES AND ALLOWANCES	+ EXTRA FEES
New car bought by an individual	Final price	= List price	− Rebate Cash discount Old car trade-in	+ Financing charges Special accessories Destination charges
Term in college bought by a student	Tuition	= Published tuition	− Scholarship Other financial aid Discounts for number of credits taken	+ Special activity fees Room and meals Books, computer Student loan interest (eventually)
Merchandise bought from a wholesaler by a retailer	Invoice price	= List price	− Quantity discount Cash discount Seasonal discount Functional or trade discount	+ Late payment penalty

FIGURE 13–1

The "price" a buyer pays can take different names depending on what is purchased, and it can change depending on the price equation.

Calculating a Final Price   The Bugatti Chiron U.S. list price is a cool $2.5 million, give or take. But the dealer has agreed to give you a trade-in allowance of $7,000 based on the *Kelley Blue Book* (www.kbb.com) trade-in value for your 2008 Mini-Cooper four-door sedan that is in good condition. And your great-uncle has offered to give you a 5-year interest-free loan. Other charges include: (1) an import duty of $50,000; (2) a gas-guzzler tax of $7,000; (3) a 7.5 percent sales tax of $229,125; (4) an auto registration fee of $5,000 to the state; and (5) a $50,000 destination charge to ship the car to you from France.

Applying the price equation shown in Figure 13–1 to your Bugatti Chiron purchase, your final price is:

$$
\begin{aligned}
\text{Final price} &= [\text{List price}] - [\text{Allowances}] + [\text{Extra fees}] \\
&= [\$2,500,000] - [\$7,000] + [\$50,000 + \$7,000 \\
&\quad + \$229,125 + \$5,000 + \$50,000] \\
&= \$2,500,000 - \$7,000 + \$341,125 \\
&= \$2,834,125
\end{aligned}
$$

Note that your final price is $334,125 more than the list price! Are you still interested in the 2017 Bugatti Chiron? If so, put yourself on the waiting list.

Price as an Indicator of Value

From a consumer's standpoint, price is often used to indicate value when it is compared with perceived benefits such as the quality or durability of a product or service. Specifically, **value** is the ratio of perceived benefits to price, or[4]

$$
\text{Value} = \frac{\text{Perceived benefits}}{\text{Price}}
$$

This relationship shows that for a given price, as perceived benefits increase, value increases. Not surprisingly, if you're used to paying $7.99 for a medium frozen cheese pizza, wouldn't a large one at the same price be more valuable? Conversely, for a given price, value decreases when perceived benefits decrease. The reduced contents in many consumer packaged products sold in supermarkets without a comparable drop in price decreases value to consumers.

Does Spirit Airlines Engage in Value Pricing? For Some Yes, for Others No

Does Spirit Airlines engage in value pricing? Well, it depends on what benefits certain passengers seek and the price they are willing to pay.

The U.S. Department of Transportation reports that Spirit Airlines fares are, on average, 40 percent lower than other airlines for the same trip. What benefit(s) do passengers get for this low fare? A seat that will not recline on an airplane that will get you to your intended destination faster than a car or bus. Do you want a boarding pass, a beverage, room in an overhead bin for luggage, or an assigned or aisle seat? You will pay separately for these benefits which increase your price to get to your destination.

So, does Spirit Airlines engage in value pricing? The answer is yes for

© Sam Pollitt/Alamy

those who wish to get to their destination as cheaply as currently possible. For others, no. They expect to get more (benefits) for what they give (fare). Not surprising, Spirit Airlines consistently ranks highest among U.S. airlines for complaints (e.g., on-time, performance, legroom), except fares. In response to passenger complaints, the company's CEO summed up his view on value pricing, saying Spirit Airlines won't "add cost for things that most customers don't value as much as our low fares just to reduce the complaints of a few customers. Doing that would raise prices for everyone, compromising our commitment to what our customers have continuously told us they truly value—the lowest possible price."

Using Value Pricing   Creative marketers engage in **value pricing**, the practice of simultaneously increasing product and service benefits while maintaining or decreasing price. For some products, price influences consumers' perception of overall quality and ultimately its value to them.[5] In a survey of home furnishing buyers, 84 percent agreed with the statement: "The higher the price, the higher the quality."[6] For example, Kohler introduced a walk-in bathtub that is safer for children and the elderly. Although priced higher than conventional step-in bathtubs, the product is successful because buyers are willing to pay a bit more for what they perceive as the value of extra safety.

In this context, "value" involves the judgment by a consumer of the worth of a product or service relative to substitutes that satisfy the same need. Through the process of comparing the costs and benefits of substitute items, a "reference value" emerges. For many consumers, the posted airfares of competing airlines serving the same cities become reference values. Based on airfare alone, Spirit Airlines usually offers the lowest price. But value assessments also include benefits received at a given price. Read the Marketing Matters box and decide whether or not Spirit Airlines offers value pricing.[7]

Price in the Marketing Mix

Pricing is a critical decision made by a marketing executive because price has a direct effect on a firm's profits. This is apparent from a firm's **profit equation**, where:

Profit = Total revenue − Total cost

= (Unit price × Quantity sold) − (Fixed cost + Variable cost)

What makes this relationship even more complicated is that price affects the quantity sold, as illustrated with demand curves later in this chapter. Furthermore, since the quantity sold usually affects a firm's costs because of efficiency of production, price also indirectly affects costs. Thus, pricing decisions influence both total revenue (sales) and total cost, which makes pricing one of the most important decisions marketing executives face.

FIGURE 13–2

The six steps in setting price. The first three steps are covered in this chapter, and the last three steps are covered in Chapter 14.

The importance of price in the marketing mix necessitates an understanding of six major steps in the process organizations go through in setting prices (see Figure 13–2):

1. Identify pricing objectives and constraints.
2. Estimate demand and revenue.
3. Determine cost, volume, and profit relationships.
4. Select an approximate price level.
5. Set list or quoted price.
6. Make special adjustments to list or quoted price.

The first three steps are covered in this chapter, and the last three are discussed in Chapter 14.

learning review »

13-1. What is price?

13-2. What factors impact the list price to determine the final price?

13-3. What is the profit equation?

STEP 1: IDENTIFY PRICING OBJECTIVES AND CONSTRAINTS

With such a variety of alternative pricing strategies available, a marketing manager must consider the pricing objectives and constraints that will narrow the range of choices. While pricing objectives frequently reflect corporate goals, pricing constraints often relate to conditions existing in the marketplace.

Identifying Pricing Objectives

Pricing objectives involve specifying the role of price in an organization's marketing and strategic plans. To the extent possible, these pricing objectives are carried to lower levels in the organization, such as in setting objectives for marketing managers

LO 13-2 Recognize the objectives a firm has in setting prices and the constraints that restrict the range of prices a firm can charge.

responsible for an individual brand. These objectives may change depending on the financial position of the company as a whole, the success of its products, or the segments in which it is doing business. Chapter 2 discussed broad objectives that an organization may pursue, which tie directly to the organization's pricing objectives covered next.

Profit   Three different objectives relate to a firm's profit, which is often measured in terms of return on investment (ROI) or return on assets (ROA). These objectives have different implications for pricing strategy. One objective is *managing for long-run profits,* in which companies—such as many Japanese car or HDTV manufacturers—give up immediate profit by developing quality products to penetrate competitive markets over the long term. Products are priced relatively low compared to their cost to develop, but the firm expects to make greater profits later because of its high market share.

A *maximizing current profit* objective, such as for a quarter or year, is common in many firms because the targets can be set and performance measured quickly. American firms are sometimes criticized for this short-run orientation. A *target return* objective occurs when a firm sets a profit goal (such as 20 percent for pretax ROI), usually determined by its board of directors.

Sales Revenue   Given that a firm's profit is high enough for it to remain in business, an objective may be to increase sales revenue, which can lead to increases in market share and profit. Objectives related to dollar sales revenue or unit sales have the advantage of being translated easily into meaningful targets for marketing managers responsible for a product line or brand. However, while cutting the price on one product in a firm's line may increase its sales revenue, it may also reduce the sales revenue of related products.

Market Share   *Market share* is the ratio of the firm's sales revenues or unit sales to those of the industry (competitors plus the firm itself). Companies often pursue a market share objective when industry sales are relatively flat or declining. In the late 1990s, Boeing cut prices drastically to try to maintain its 60 percent share of the commercial airline market to compete with Airbus. As a result, it encountered huge losses. Although increased market share is a primary goal of some firms, others see it as a means to other ends: increasing sales and profits.

Unit Volume   Many firms use *unit volume,* the quantity produced or sold, as a pricing objective. These firms often sell multiple products at very different prices and need to match the unit volume demanded by customers with price and production capacity. Using unit volume as an objective can be counterproductive if a volume objective is achieved, say, by drastic price cutting that drives down profit.

Companies in financial distress use pricing as a means to survival. Survival was the pricing objective for Radio-Shack when it faced bankruptcy.

© *Victor J. Blue/Bloomberg via Getty Images*

Survival   In some instances, profits, sales, and market share are less important objectives of the firm than mere survival. For example, RadioShack, an electronics retail chain, faced survival problems because it couldn't compete with the prices offered by other retailers. The company enacted price matching programs and promoted large discounts on its merchandise to raise cash and hopefully stave off bankruptcy. These efforts failed and RadioShack declared bankruptcy in 2015.

Social Responsibility   A firm may forgo higher profit on sales and follow a pricing objective that recognizes its obligations to customers and society in general. For example, Gerber supplies a specially formulated product free of charge to children who cannot tolerate foods containing cow's milk.

The price for a specific brand—like the Toyota Camry V6 here—is also affected by general demand for its product class (cars) and product group (family sedans), as discussed in the text.

© izmocars/Izmo/Corbis

Identifying Pricing Constraints

Factors that limit the range of prices a firm may set are referred to as **pricing constraints**. Consumer demand for the product clearly affects the price that can be charged. Other constraints on price vary from factors within the organization to competitive factors outside the organization. Legal and regulatory constraints on pricing are discussed in Chapter 14.

Demand for the Product Class, Product, and Brand

The number of potential buyers for the product class (cars), product group (family sedans), and specific brand (Toyota Camry V6) clearly affects the price a seller can charge. Likewise, whether the item is a luxury—like the Bugatti Chiron—or a necessity—like bread and a roof over your head—also affects the price that can be charged. Generally, the greater the demand for a product, the higher the price that can be set. For example, the New York Mets have set different ticket prices for their games based on the appeal of their opponent—prices are higher when they play the New York Yankees and lower when they play the Pittsburgh Pirates.[8]

Newness of the Product: Stage in the Product Life Cycle   The newer a product and the earlier it is in its life cycle, the higher the price that can usually be charged. Are you willing to spend $9,999 for an LG 55-inch 3D OLED HD Smart TV? The high initial price is possible because of patents and limited competition early in its product life cycle. By the time you read this, the price probably will be lower.

Sometimes—when nostalgia or fad factors come into play—prices may rise later in the product's life cycle. For example, collectibles can experience skyrocketing prices. Recently, consumers on eBay paid $250 for a Zip the Cat Beanie Baby (with black paws), $200 for a 2001 Ichiro Suzuki rookie bobble-head doll, and $29,500 for a 1963 copy of the first "Amazing Spiderman" issue. But these prices can nosedive, too, when the fad wears off or a recession appears. To play it safe—and perhaps finance your retirement—save your perfect-condition, in-the-box Barbies, Hot Wheels, and Star Wars lightsabers.[9]

Who makes how much on a pair of designer denim jeans? Read the text to find out.

© Amanda Edwards/WireImage/ Getty Images

Cost of Producing and Marketing the Product   Another profit consideration for marketers is to ensure that firms in their channels of distribution make an adequate profit. Without profits for channel members, a marketer is cut off from its customers. For example, of the $200 a customer spends for a pair of designer denim jeans, 50 percent of each dollar spent goes to a specialty retailer to cover its costs and profit. The other 50 percent goes to the marketer (34 percent) and manufacturers and suppliers (16 percent).[10] So, the next time you buy a $200 pair of designer denim jeans, remember that $100 goes to the specialty retailer that stocked, displayed, and sold the jeans to you.

Cost of Changing Prices and Time Period They Apply   If Scandinavian Airlines asks General Electric (GE) to provide spare jet engines to power the new Boeing 737 it just bought, GE can easily set a new price for the engines to reflect its latest information since only one buyer has to be informed. But if L.L.Bean decides that sweater prices in its catalog are too low after thousands of catalogs have been mailed to customers, it has a big problem. It must consider the cost of changing prices and which prices apply to which time periods, as well as the cost of revising its price list and reprinting and mailing another edition of its catalog. However, for many of today's consumer products, prices can change from minute to minute due to the transparency of prices afforded by the Internet.

What are the potential benefits and dangers of Apple's decision to offer a lower-priced iPhone mini? Read the text to find out.

© Joseph Branston/Apple Bookazine/Getty Images

Single Product versus a Product Line When Apple introduced its first iPhone, it was not only unique and in the introductory stage of its product life cycle, but it was also the first commercially successful smartphone sold. As a result, Apple had great latitude in setting and maintaining a premium price. However, there was soon an onslaught of lower-cost rival smartphones, many of which were powered by Google's Android operating system.

How should Apple respond to this competitive pressure? Apple's CEO Tim Cook has started to move away from the company's long-term strategy of having only a single model of a product that is targeted at high-end users. An example is Apple's iPad mini, which was introduced to broaden the iPad product line.

The question now facing Apple is whether to expand its iPhone product line with an iPhone mini—a 4-inch model—at a lower price. How Apple decides to price the mini model illustrates the unique challenge of pricing a single product versus multiple products in an expanding product line.[11] Product-line pricing is discussed further in Chapter 14.

Type of Competitive Market The seller's price is constrained by the type of market in which it competes. Economists generally delineate four types of competitive markets, as introduced in Chapter 3. From most competitive to least competitive, these are pure competition, monopolistic competition, oligopoly, and pure monopoly. Figure 13–3 shows that the type of competition dramatically influences the range of price competition and, in turn, the nature of product differentiation and the extent of advertising. A firm must recognize the general type of competitive market it is in to understand the range of both its price and nonprice strategies. Examples of how prices can be affected by the four competitive situations follow:

- *Pure competition.* Hundreds of local grain elevators sell corn whose price per bushel is set by the marketplace. Within strains, the corn is identical, so advertising only informs buyers that the seller's corn is available.

FIGURE 13–3

Pricing, product, and advertising strategies available to firms in four types of competitive markets.

TYPE OF COMPETITIVE MARKET

STRATEGIES AVAILABLE	PURE COMPETITION (Many sellers who follow the market price for identical, commodity products)	MONOPOLISTIC COMPETITION (Many sellers who compete on nonprice factors)	OLIGOPOLY (Few sellers who are sensitive to each other's prices)	PURE MONOPOLY (One seller who sets the price for a unique product)
Extent of price competition	Almost none: market sets price	Some: compete over range of prices	Some: price leader or follower of competitors	None: sole seller sets price
Extent of product differentiation	None: products are identical	Some: differentiate products from competitors	Various: depends on industry	None: no other producers
Extent of advertising	Little: purpose is to inform prospects that seller's products are available	Much: purpose is to differentiate firm's products from competitors	Some: purpose is to inform but avoid price competition	Little: purpose is to increase demand for product class

- *Monopolistic competition.* Dozens of regional, private brands of peanut butter compete with national brands like Skippy and Jif. Both price competition (regional, private brands being lower than national brands) and nonprice competition (product features and advertising) exist.
- *Oligopoly.* The few sellers of aluminum (Reynolds, Alcoa) or large jetliners (Boeing, Airbus) try to avoid price competition because it can lead to disastrous price wars in which they all lose money. Yet firms in such industries stay aware of a competitor's price cuts or increases and may follow suit. The products can be undifferentiated (aluminum) or differentiated (large jetliners), and informative advertising that avoids head-to-head price competition is used. In the early stages of the video game market, the Microsoft Xbox 360's oligopolistic competition with Sony and Nintendo was so severe that Microsoft lost $126 on every unit sold at its $399 introductory price.[12]
- *Pure monopoly.* Johnson & Johnson (J&J) revolutionized the treatment of coronary heart disease by introducing the stent—a tiny mesh tube "spring" that props open clogged arteries. Initially a monopoly, J&J stuck with its early $1,595 price and achieved $1 billion in sales and 91 percent market share in two years. But its reluctance to give price reductions to hospitals for large-volume purchases turned out to be a poor strategy. When competitors like Medtronic introduced an improved stent at lower prices, J&J's market share plummeted to 8 percent two years later.[13]

Competitors' Prices and Consumers' Awareness of Them   A company must know what specific prices its present and potential competitors are charging now as well as what they are likely to charge in the near future. The company then develops a marketing mix strategy—including setting prices—to respond to its competitors' prices. Today, the Internet has increased the number of "present and potential competitors" exponentially for many products.

Competitors' prices are important only if a prospective buyer both (1) knows about those prices and (2) can act to purchase them easily. Competitor changes and price transparency through the Internet and efficient distribution make possible (1) consumer-driven pricing actions and (2) seller/retailer-driven pricing actions.

- *Consumer-Driven Pricing Actions.* With consumers able to compare prices on the Internet, they can make more efficient buying decisions. This occurs, say, when a consumer visits the HDTV section of a store to actually examine a TV—and then goes home and orders it online at a lower price. RedLaser, an eBay-owned smartphone app, enables consumers to scan a product's barcode on a store's shelf and then compare that price to those both online and in nearby stores.[14]
- *Seller/Retailer-Driven Pricing Actions.* Aggressive price changes through the Internet started when airlines constantly changed ticket prices to fill the seats on their planes using their yield management systems. Today, many sellers are changing online prices even faster.

For example, the day before Thanksgiving 2012, online retailer Amazon.com sold the hugely popular Dance Central 3 (DC3) Xbox video game for $49.96—the same price as Walmart and 3 cents lower than Target. Then the pricing "dance moves" began. On Thanksgiving Day, Amazon lowered the game's price to $24.99, matching Best Buy. That same day, it dropped DC3's price to $15.00 to match Walmart. Then, over the next several days, Amazon raised and lowered the price *seven* times. If you were lucky, you paid a price that was two-thirds lower than those who were unlucky and bought DC3 at its highest price during that week![15]

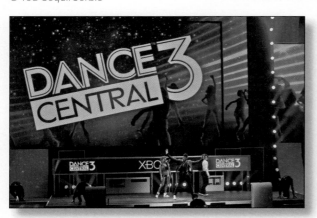

Read how Amazon priced the hot-selling Dance Central 3 video game, available for the Xbox.

© *Ted Soqui/Corbis*

Legal and Ethical Considerations Setting a final price is clearly a complex process. The task is further complicated by legal and ethical issues. Five pricing practices that have received special scrutiny are price fixing, price discrimination, deceptive pricing, geographical pricing, and predatory pricing, each of which is described more fully in Chapter 14.

learning review »

13-4. What is the difference between pricing objectives and pricing constraints?

13-5. How does the type of competitive market a firm is in affect its range in setting prices?

13-6. What are examples of (1) consumer-driven and (2) seller/retailer-driven actions made possible through price transparency on the Internet?

STEP 2: ESTIMATE DEMAND AND REVENUE

LO 13-3 Explain what a demand curve is and the role of revenues in pricing decisions.

What key factors affect the demand for Red Baron frozen cheese pizzas? Read the text to find out.

© Mike Hruby

Video 13-2
Red Baron
kerin.tv/13e/v13-2

Basic to setting a product's price is the extent of customer demand for it. Marketing executives must also translate this estimate of customer demand into estimates of revenues the firm expects to receive.

Estimating Demand

How much will you pay for a frozen cheese pizza you can pop in the oven for a quick dinner while you are studying for a marketing exam? $6? $8? $10? And what are some of the factors affecting this decision? Your preference for pizza compared to other quick-service food? The ease with which you can call Domino's or your local Chinese restaurant for an already-prepared meal delivered to your residence? How much money you have available in your credit card account while you're thinking about the tuition payment that's due next month? All these factors affect demand.

To illustrate the fundamentals of estimating demand, let's assume you are a consultant to the marketing manager at Red Baron® pizza and your job is to start analyzing the demand for its Red Baron frozen cheese pizzas. In the process, you'll have to consider what the demand curve for frozen cheese pizza might look like, how it affects Red Baron's sales revenues, and the price elasticity of demand.

The Demand Curve A **demand curve** is a graph that relates the quantity sold and price, showing the maximum number of units that will be sold at a given price. Based on secondary research you conducted regarding the annual demand for Red Baron frozen cheese pizza under circumstances that existed in 2014, you are able to construct the demand curve D_1 in Figure 13–4A, which you now need to update because market conditions have changed by 2015. Note the following relationship: As price falls, more people decide to buy Red Baron frozen cheese pizza, which increases its unit sales. But price is not the complete story when estimating demand. Economists emphasize three other key factors that influence demand for a product:

1. *Consumer tastes.* As we saw in Chapter 3, these depend on many forces such as demographics, culture, and technology. Because consumer tastes can

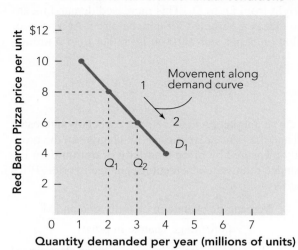

A: Demand curve under initial conditions

(vertical axis) Red Baron Pizza price per unit — $12, 10, 8, 6, 4, 2

Movement along demand curve — 1, 2

D_1

Q_1 Q_2

(horizontal axis) 0 1 2 3 4 5 6 7
Quantity demanded per year (millions of units)

B: Shift the demand curve with more favorable conditions

(vertical axis) Red Baron Pizza price per unit — $12, 10, 8, 6, 4, 2

New demand curve

Shift of demand curve

Initial demand curve

2 3

D_1 D_2

Q_2 Q_3

(horizontal axis) 0 1 2 3 4 5 6 7
Quantity demanded per year (millions of units)

FIGURE 13–4

Demand curves for Red Baron frozen cheese pizza showing the effect on annual sales (quantity demanded per year) by change in price caused by (A) a movement along the demand curve and (B) a shift of the demand curve.

change quickly, up-to-date marketing research is essential to estimate demand. For example, if research by nutritionists concludes that some pizzas are healthier (because they are now gluten-free or vegetarian), demand for them will probably increase.

2. *Price and availability of similar products.* If the price of a competitor's pizza that is a substitute for yours—like Tombstone® pizza—falls, more people will buy it; its demand will rise and the demand for yours will fall. Other low-priced dinners are also substitutes for pizza. For example, if you want something fast so you can study, you could call Domino's or a local Chinese restaurant and order a meal for home delivery. So, as the price of a substitute falls or its availability increases, the demand for your Red Baron frozen cheese pizza will fall.

3. *Consumer income.* In general, as real consumers' incomes increase (allowing for inflation), demand for a product will also increase. So, if you get a scholarship and have extra cash for discretionary spending, you might eat more Red Baron frozen cheese pizzas and fewer peanut butter and jelly sandwiches to satisfy your appetite.

The first two factors influence what consumers *want* to buy, and the third factor affects what they *can* buy. Along with price, these are often called **demand factors**, or factors that determine consumers' willingness and ability to pay for products and services. As discussed in Chapters 8 and 10, it can be challenging to estimate demand for new products, especially because consumer likes and dislikes are often so difficult to read clearly. For example, Campbell's (yes, the soup company) spent seven years and $55 million on a super secret project to produce a line of Intelligent Quisine (IQ) food products "scientifically proven to lower high levels of cholesterol, blood sugar, and blood pressure." After 15 months in an Ohio test market, Campbell's yanked the entire IQ line because customers found the line too pricey and lacking in variety.[16]

Movement Along versus Shift of a Demand Curve The 2014 demand curve D_1 for Red Baron frozen cheese pizzas in Figure 13–4A shows that as its price is lowered from $8 (point 1) to $6 (point 2), the quantity sold (demanded) increases from 2 million (Q_1) to 3 million (Q_2) units per year. This is an example of a *movement along a demand curve* and it assumes that other factors (consumer tastes, price and availability of substitutes, and consumers' incomes) remain unchanged.

What if some of these factors do change? For example, if advertising causes more people to want Red Baron frozen cheese pizzas, demand will increase. Now the initial demand curve, D_1 (the blue line in Figure 13–4B), no longer represents the demand. Instead, the new demand curve, D_2 (the red line in Figure 13–4B) represents the new demand for Red Baron frozen cheese pizzas. Economists call this a *shift in the demand curve*—in this case, a shift to the right from D_1 to D_2. This increased demand means that more Red Baron frozen cheese pizzas are wanted for a given price. At a price of $6 (point 3), the demand is 5 million units per year (Q_3) on D_2 rather than 3 million units per year (Q_2) on D_1.

Price Elasticity of Demand

LO 13-4 **Describe what price elasticity of demand means to a manager facing a pricing decision.**

With a downward-sloping demand curve, marketing managers are especially interested in how sensitive consumer demand and the firm's revenues are to changes in the product's price. This can be conveniently measured by **price elasticity of demand**, or the percentage change in quantity demanded relative to a percentage change in price. Price elasticity of demand (E) is expressed as follows:

$$\text{Price elasticity of demand}(E) = \frac{\text{Percentage change in quantity demanded}}{\text{Percentage change in price}}$$

Because quantity demanded usually decreases as price increases, price elasticity of demand is usually a negative number. However, for the sake of simplicity and by convention, elasticity figures are shown as positive numbers. Finally, price elasticity of demand assumes two forms discussed here: elastic demand and inelastic demand.

Elastic Demand and Inelastic Demand *Elastic demand* exists when a 1 percent decrease in price produces more than a 1 percent increase in quantity demanded, thereby actually increasing total revenue. This results in a price elasticity that is greater than 1 with elastic demand. In other words, a product with elastic demand is one in which a slight decrease in price results in a relatively large increase in demand or units sold. The reverse is also true; with elastic demand, a slight increase in price results in a relatively large decrease in demand. So marketers may cut price to increase consumer demand, the units sold, and total revenue for a product with elastic demand, depending on what competitors' prices are.

Inelastic demand exists when a 1 percent decrease in price produces less than a 1 percent increase in quantity demanded, thereby actually decreasing total revenue. This results in a price elasticity that is less than 1 with inelastic demand. So a product with inelastic demand means that slight increases or decreases in price will not significantly affect the demand, or units sold, for the product. The concern for marketers is that while lowering price will increase the quantity sold, total revenue will actually fall.

How Price Elasticity Affects Marketing and Public Policy Decisions

Price elasticity of demand is determined by a number of factors. The more substitutes a product or service has, the more likely it is to be price elastic. For example, a new sweater, shirt, or blouse has many possible substitutes and is price elastic, but gasoline has almost no substitutes and is price inelastic. In fact, given America's love affair with cars and driving, we are surprisingly insensitive to price increases in gasoline: One study showed a 10 percent increase in price results in only a 0.6 percent decrease in gasoline consumption.[17] This could change in the future as hybrid and all-electric cars become even more cost competitive.

Products and services considered to be necessities are price inelastic, so open-heart surgery is price inelastic, whereas airline tickets for a vacation are price elastic. Toothpaste is an example of a consumer product with inelastic demand. So even during recessions, Procter & Gamble's and Colgate's toothpastes often show price *increases* on the shelves of retailers.[18] Items that require a large cash outlay compared with a person's disposable income are price elastic. Accordingly, cars are price elastic; soft drinks tend to be price inelastic.

A consumer product that is a necessity, like toothpaste, has an inelastic demand, which can result in an *increased* price during a recession.

© *razorpix/Alamy*

Marketing **Matters**

Using Big Data to Curb Smoking: Uncovering the Price Elasticity of Demand for Cigarettes

Price elasticity of demand is often studied to gauge consumer response to taxes and fees imposed by federal, state, and local government agencies. Public concern about cigarette smoking and tobacco-related diseases has resulted in hundreds of studies dealing with changes in the price of cigarettes and the incidence of smoking. This research has shown that where consumers live, their education, income, and age can affect price elasticity of demand.

As an example, a recent large-scale study with some 34,000 consumers between the ages of 15 and 29 was conducted in the United States. The study demonstrated that the price elasticity of cigarettes was inelastic and varied inversely

$STOP $MOKING

with age: 0.83 for ages 15–17, 0.52 for ages 18–20, 0.37 for ages 21–23, 0.20 for ages 24–26, and 0.09 for ages 27–29. Thus, younger consumers (ages 15–17) were more likely to reduce the number of cigarettes smoked in response to increased prices than older consumers (ages 27–29).

To test these findings, New York City recently increased the combined taxes from federal, state, and local governments on a pack of Marlboro Light Kings cigarettes to $6.86. So the typical retail price in that city was more than $12 a pack. As a result of these inflated prices, the number of high school students smoking in New York City has hit a new low of 13.8 percent, far below the national average.

Price elasticity is not only a relevant concept for marketing managers, but also important for pricing practices involving public policy. The Marketing Matters box describes how price elasticity has been applied to curbing cigarette smoking.[19]

Fundamentals of Estimating Revenue

While economists may talk about "demand curves," marketing executives are more likely to speak in terms of "revenue generated." Demand curves lead directly to an essential revenue concept critical to pricing decisions: **total revenue**, or the total money received from the sale of a product. Total revenue (TR) equals the unit price (P) times the quantity sold (Q). Using this equation, let's recall our Red Baron pizza example and assume our annual demand has improved, our price is $6 per unit, and we sell 5 million per year. So,

$$TR = P \times Q$$
$$= \$6 \times 5,000,000$$
$$= \$30,000,000$$

This combination of price and quantity sold annually will give us a total revenue of $30,000,000 per year. Is that good? Are you making a profit? Alas, total revenue is only part of the profit equation that we saw earlier:

$$\text{Total profit} = \text{Total revenue} - \text{Total cost}$$

The next section covers the other part of the profit equation: cost.

learning review »

13-7. What is the difference between a movement along and a shift of a demand curve?

13-8. What is the difference between elastic demand and inelastic demand?

13-9. What is total revenue and how is it calculated?

STEP 3: DETERMINE COST, VOLUME, AND PROFIT RELATIONSHIPS

LO 13-5 | Explain the role of costs in pricing decisions and describe how various combinations of price, fixed cost, and unit variable cost affect a firm's break-even point.

While revenues are the moneys received by the firm from selling its products or services to customers, costs or expenses are the monies the firm pays out to its employees and suppliers. Marketing managers often use break-even analysis to relate revenues and costs, topics covered in this section.

The Importance of Controlling Costs

Understanding the role and behavior of costs is critical for all marketing decisions, particularly pricing decisions. Four cost concepts are important in pricing decisions: **total cost**, **fixed cost**, **variable cost**, and **unit variable cost** (see Figure 13–5).

Many firms go bankrupt because their costs get out of control, causing their total costs—the sum of their fixed costs and variable costs—to exceed their total revenues over an extended period of time. So firms constantly try to control their fixed costs, like insurance and executive salaries, and reduce the variable costs in their manufactured items by having production done outside the United States. This is why sophisticated marketing managers make pricing decisions that balance both revenues and costs.

Break-Even Analysis

Break-even analysis is a technique that analyzes the relationship between total revenue and total cost to determine profitability at various levels of output. Figure 13–6 provides the data needed to conduct a break-even analysis. The **break-even point (BEP)** is the quantity at which total revenue and total cost are equal. Profit then comes from all units sold beyond the BEP. In terms of the definitions in Figure 13–5:

$$BEP_{Quantity} = \frac{Fixed\ cost}{Unit\ price - Unit\ variable\ cost} = \frac{FC}{P - UVC}$$

Calculating a Break-Even Point   Suppose you are the owner of a picture frame shop and you wish to identify how many pictures you must sell to cover your fixed cost at a given price. Let's assume demand for your pictures is strong, so the average price customers are willing to pay for each picture is $120. Also, suppose your fixed cost

FIGURE 13–5

Fundamental concepts about "costs," which are the monies the firm pays out to its employees and suppliers.

Total cost (TC) is the total expense incurred by a firm in producing and marketing a product. Total cost is the sum of fixed cost and variable cost.

Fixed cost (FC) is the sum of the expenses of the firm that are stable and do not change with the quantity of a product that is produced and sold. Examples of fixed costs are rent on the building, executive salaries, and insurance.

Variable cost (VC) is the sum of the expenses of the firm that vary directly with the quantity of a product that is produced and sold. For example, as the quantity sold doubles, the variable cost doubles. Examples are the direct labor and direct materials used in producing the product and the sales commissions that are tied directly to the quantity sold. As mentioned above,

TC = FC + VC

Unit variable cost (UVC) is expressed on a per unit basis, or $UVC = \frac{VC}{Q}$

Quantity of Pictures Sold (Q)	Price per Picture (P)	Total Revenue (TR = P × Q)	Unit Variable Cost (UVC)	Total Variable Cost (VC = UVC × Q)	Fixed Cost (FC)	Total Cost (TC = FC + VC)	Profit (TR − TC)
0	$120	$0	$40	$0	$32,000	$32,000	($32,000)
400	$120	$48,000	$40	$16,000	$32,000	$48,000	$0
800	$120	$96,000	$40	$32,000	$32,000	$64,000	$32,000
1,200	$120	$144,000	$40	$48,000	$32,000	$80,000	$64,000
1,600	$120	$192,000	$40	$64,000	$32,000	$96,000	$96,000
2,000	$120	$240,000	$40	$80,000	$32,000	$112,000	$128,000

FIGURE 13–6

Calculating a break-even point for the picture frame shop in the text example shows that its profit starts at 400 pictures sold per year.

(FC) is $32,000 (real estate taxes, interest on a bank loan, etc.) and unit variable cost (UVC) for a picture is now $40 (labor, glass, frame, and matting). Your break-even quantity (BEP) is 400 pictures, as follows:

$$BEP_{Quantity} = \frac{\$32,000}{\$120 - \$40}$$

$$BEP_{Quantity} = 400 \text{ pictures}$$

Developing a Break-Even Chart   The row shaded in orange in Figure 13–6 shows that your break-even quantity at a price of $120 per picture is 400 pictures. At less than 400 pictures, your picture frame shop incurs a loss, and at more than 400 pictures, it makes a profit. Figure 13–7 depicts a graphic presentation of the break-even analysis, called a **break-even chart**. It shows that total revenue (line DE) and total cost (line AC) intersect and are equal at a quantity of 400 pictures

FIGURE 13–7

This break-even chart for a picture frame shop shows the break-even point at 400 pictures and the annual profit at 2,000 pictures.

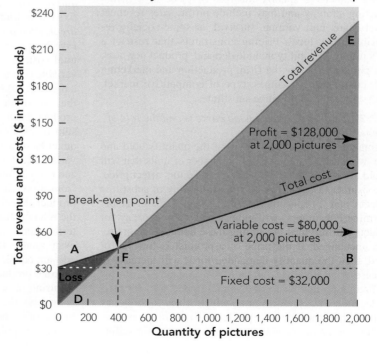

Break-Even Analysis Chart for the Picture Frame Shop

sold, which is the break-even point (F) at which profit is exactly $0. You want to do better? If your picture frame shop could increase the quantity sold annually to 2,000 pictures, the graph in Figure 13–7 shows you can earn an annual profit of $128,000 ($240,000 − $112,000 or line EC), shown by the row shaded in green in Figure 13–6.

learning review »

13-10. What is the difference between fixed costs and variable costs?

13-11. What is a break-even point?

LEARNING OBJECTIVES REVIEW

LO 13-1 *Identify the elements that make up a price.*
Price is the money or other considerations (such as barter) exchanged for the ownership or use of a product or service. Although price typically involves money, the amount exchanged is often different from the list or quoted price because of incentives (rebates, discounts, etc.), allowances (trade), and extra fees (finance charges, surcharges, etc.). The price of an offering is often used to indicate value, which is the ratio of perceived benefits to price. Pricing has a direct effect on a firm's profits, which is determined by the profit equation: Profit = Total revenue − Total cost.

LO 13-2 *Recognize the objectives a firm has in setting prices and the constraints that restrict the range of prices a firm can charge.*
Pricing objectives specify the role of price in a firm's marketing strategy and may include profit, sales revenue, market share, unit volume, survival, or some socially responsible price level. Pricing constraints that restrict a firm's pricing flexibility include demand, product newness, other products sold by the firm, production and marketing costs, cost of price changes, type of competitive market, and the prices of competitive substitutes.

LO 13-3 *Explain what a demand curve is and the role of revenues in pricing decisions.*
A demand curve is a graph relating the quantity sold and price, which shows the maximum number of units that will be sold at a given price. Three demand factors affect price: (*a*) consumer tastes, (*b*) price and availability of substitute products, and (*c*) consumer income. These demand factors determine consumers' willingness and ability to pay for products and services. Assuming these demand factors remain unchanged, if the price of a product is lowered or raised, then the quantity demanded for it will increase or decrease, respectively.

Three important forms of revenues impact a firm's pricing decisions: (*a*) total revenue, which is the total money received from the sale of a product; (*b*) average revenue, which is the average amount of money received for selling one unit of a product (which is simply the price of the unit); and (*c*) marginal revenue, which is the change in total revenue that results from producing and marketing one additional unit.

LO 13-4 *Describe what price elasticity of demand means to a manager facing a pricing decision.*
Price elasticity of demand measures the responsiveness of units of a product sold to a change in price, which is expressed as the percentage change in the quantity of a product demanded divided by the percentage change in price. Price elasticity is important to marketing managers because a change in price usually has an important effect on the number of units of the product sold and on total revenue.

LO 13-5 *Explain the role of costs in pricing decisions and describe how various combinations of price, fixed cost, and unit variable cost affect a firm's break-even point.*
Five important costs impact a firm's pricing decisions: (*a*) total cost, or total expenses, is the sum of fixed cost and variable cost incurred by a firm in producing and marketing a product; (*b*) fixed cost, is the sum of expenses of the firm that are stable and do not change with the quantity of a product that is produced and sold; (*c*) variable cost, is the sum of expenses of the firm that vary directly with the quantity of a product that is produced and sold; (*d*) unit variable cost, is variable cost expressed on a per unit basis; and (*e*) marginal cost, is the change in total cost that results from producing and marketing one additional unit of the product. Break-even analysis is a technique that analyzes the relationship between total revenue and total cost to determine profitability at various levels of output. The break-even point is the quantity at which total revenue and total cost are equal. Assuming no change in price, if the costs of a firm's product increase due to higher fixed costs (manufacturing or advertising) or variable costs (direct labor or materials), then its break-even point will be higher. And if total cost is unchanged, an increase in price will reduce the break-even point.

13-1 **What is price?**

Answer: Price is the money or other considerations (including other products and services) exchanged for the ownership or use of a product or service.

13-2 **What factors impact the list price to determine the final price?**

Answer: Several factors increase or decrease the final price of an offering that the consumer pays. These factors help construct the price equation, which includes incentives, such as cash discounts, allowances, and rebates, that decrease the final price and extra fees or surcharges that increase the final price.

13-3 **What is the profit equation?**

Answer: Price has a direct effect on a firm's profits, which can be expressed in the following profit equation: Profit = Total revenue − Total cost or [(Unit price × Quantity sold) − (Fixed cost + Variable cost)].

13-4 **What is the difference between pricing objectives and pricing constraints?**

Answer: Pricing objectives involve specifying the role of price in an organization's marketing and strategic plans whereas pricing constraints are factors that limit the range of prices a firm may set.

13-5 **How does the type of competitive market a firm is in affect its range in setting prices?**

Answer: The seller's price is constrained by the type of market in which it competes. Economists generally delineate four types of competitive markets: (1) With pure competition, there are many sellers who follow the market price for identical, commodity products. (2) With monopolistic competition, there are many sellers who compete on nonprice factors such as product features and advertising. (3) With an oligopoly, there are (*a*) a few sellers who are sensitive to each other's prices and (*b*) a firm that is a price leader that sets the market price that other firms follow. The firms that are price followers set a price based on the prices set by their competitors to avoid a price war. (4) With a pure monopoly, there is one seller in the market who can set any price it wants for its unique product.

13-6 **What are examples of (1) consumer-driven and (2) seller- or retailer-driven pricing actions made possible through price transparency on the Internet?**

Answer: Price transparency occurs as a result of a consumer's near-instantaneous access to competitors' prices for the same offering through the Internet. Two dimensions of price transparency are: (1) Consumer-driven pricing actions, in which consumers make more efficient buying decisions by comparing the price of an item first in the store and then on the Internet using a smartphone. If the price is lower on the Internet, they'll ask the store to match the price or go home and buy the item online. This behavior is called showrooming. (2) Seller- or retailer-driven pricing actions, in which sellers can quickly change their online prices. This is made possible by Internet-based dynamic pricing, in which the seller changes prices in response to its existing inventory and the prices of its competitors.

13-7 **What is the difference between a movement along and a shift of a demand curve?**

Answer: A demand curve is a graph that relates the quantity sold and price, showing the maximum number of units that will be sold at a given price. A movement along a demand curve (up or down) for a product occurs when its price is lowered or increased and the quantity demanded for it correspondingly increases or decreases, assuming that other factors such as consumer tastes, promotion (advertising and/or sales promotion), price and availability of substitute products, and/or consumer incomes remain unchanged. However, if one or more of these factors do change, then the demand curve for a product will shift to the right or left based on whether the change(s) was favorable or not. This means that there will be either an increase or decrease in demand for the product based on the change in the factor(s).

13-8 **What is the difference between elastic demand and inelastic demand?**

Answer: Price elasticity of demand is the percentage change in the quantity demanded relative to a percentage change in price and is expressed as follows: Price elasticity of demand (E) = Percentage change in quantity demanded (%Δ in Q) ÷ Percentage change in price (%Δ in P). Elastic demand exists when a 1 percent decrease in price produces more than a 1 percent increase in quantity demanded, thereby actually increasing total revenue. This results in a price elasticity that is greater than 1. Inelastic demand exists when a 1 percent decrease in price produces less than a 1 percent increase in quantity demanded, thereby actually decreasing total revenue. This results in a price elasticity that is less than 1.

13-9 **What is total revenue and how is it calculated?**

Answer: Total revenue (TR) is the total money received from the sale of a product. Total revenue (TR) equals the product's unit price (P) times the quantity sold (Q) or TR = P × Q.

13-10 **What is the difference between fixed costs and variable costs?**

Answer: Fixed cost (FC) is the sum of the expenses of the firm that are stable and do not change with the quantity of a product that is produced and sold. Examples of fixed costs are rent on the building, executive salaries, and insurance. Variable cost (VC) is the sum of the expenses of the firm that vary directly with the quantity of a product that is produced and sold. Examples are the direct labor and direct materials used in producing the product and the sales commissions that are tied directly to the quantity sold.

13-11 **What is a break-even point?**

Answer: Break-even analysis is a technique that analyzes the relationship between total revenue and total cost to determine profitability at various levels of output. The break-even point (BEP) is the quantity at which total revenue and total cost are equal. Profit then comes from all units sold beyond the BEP. Break-even point (BEP) = [Fixed cost ÷ (Unit price − Unit variable cost)].

FOCUSING ON KEY TERMS

barter p. 350
break-even analysis p. 362
break-even chart p. 363
break-even point (BEP) p. 362
demand curve p. 358
demand factors p. 359

fixed cost (FC) p. 362
price (P) p. 350
price elasticity of demand p. 360
pricing constraints p. 355
pricing objectives p. 353
profit equation p. 352

total cost (TC) p. 362
total revenue (TR) p. 361
unit variable cost (UVC) p. 362
value p. 351
value pricing p. 352
variable cost (VC) p. 362

1 How would the price equation apply to the purchase price of (a) gasoline, (b) an airline ticket, and (c) a checking account?

2 What would be your response to the statement, "Profit maximization is the only legitimate pricing objective for the firm"?

3 How is a downward-sloping demand curve related to total revenue and marginal revenue?

4 A marketing executive once said, "If the price elasticity of demand for your product is inelastic, then your price is probably too low." What is this executive saying in terms of the economic principles discussed in this chapter?

5 A marketing manager reduced the price on a brand of cereal by 10 percent and observed a 25 percent increase in quantity sold. The manager then thought that if the price were reduced by another 20 percent, a 50 percent increase in quantity sold would occur. What would be your response to the marketing manager's reasoning?

6 A student theater group at a university has developed a demand schedule that shows the relationship between ticket prices and demand based on a student survey (see the table that follows). (a) Graph the demand curve and the total revenue curve based on these data. What ticket price might be set based on this analysis? (b) What other factors should be considered before the final price is set?

Ticket Price	Number of Students Who Would Buy
$1	300
2	250
3	200
4	150
5	100

7 Touché Toiletries, Inc. has developed an addition to its Lizardman Cologne line tentatively branded Ode d'Toade Cologne. Unit variable costs are 45 cents for a three-ounce bottle, and heavy advertising expenditures in the first year would result in total fixed costs of $900,000. Ode d'Toade Cologne is priced at $7.50 for a three-ounce bottle. How many bottles of Ode d'Toade must be sold to break even?

8 Suppose that marketing executives for Touché Toiletries (see problem 7) reduced the price to $6.50 for a three-ounce bottle of Ode d'Toade and the fixed costs were $1,100,000. Suppose further that the unit variable cost remained at 45 cents for a three-ounce bottle. (a) How many bottles must be sold to break even? (b) What dollar profit level would Ode d'Toade achieve if 200,000 bottles were sold?

9 Executives of Random Recordings, Inc. produced a digital album titled *Sunshine/Moonshine* by the Starshine Sisters Band. (a) Using the price and cost information in the table, prepare a chart like that in Figure 13–10 showing total cost, fixed cost, and total revenue for album quantity sold levels starting at 10,000 through 100,000 digital albums at 10,000 intervals, that is, 10,000; 20,000; 30,000; and so on. (b) What is the break-even point for the digital album?

Selling price	$10.00 per album
Album cover	$1.00 per album
Songwriter's royalties	$0.30 per album
Recording artists' royalties	$0.70 per album
Direct material and labor costs to produce the album	$1.00 per album
Fixed cost of producing an album (advertising, studio fee, etc.)	$100,000

In starting to set a final price:

1 List two pricing objectives and three pricing constraints.

2 Think about your customers and competitors and set three possible prices.

3 Assume a fixed cost and unit variable cost and (a) calculate the break-even points and (b) plot a break-even chart for the three prices specified in step 2.

"We offer a guitar at every price point for every skill level," explains Kevin Lello, vice president of marketing at Washburn Guitars. Washburn is one of the most prestigious guitar manufacturers in the world, offering instruments that range from one-of-a-kind, custom-made acoustic and electric guitars and basses to less-expensive, mass-produced guitars. Lello has responsibility for marketing Washburn's products and ensuring that the price of each product matches the company's objectives related to sales, profit, and market share. "We do pay attention to break-even points," adds Lello. "We need to know exactly how much a guitar costs us, and how much the overhead is for each guitar."

© Paul Kane/Getty Images

THE COMPANY

The modern Washburn Guitars company started in 1977 when a small Chicago firm bought the century-old Washburn brand name and a small inventory of guitars, parts, and promotional supplies. At that time, annual company sales of about 2,500 guitars generated revenues of $300,000. Washburn's first catalog, appearing in 1978, told a frightening truth:

> Our designs are translated by Japan's most experienced craftsmen, assuring the consistent quality and craftsmanship for which they are known.

At that time, the American guitar-making craft was at an all-time low. Guitars made by Japanese firms, such as Ibanez and Yamaha, were in use by an increasing number of professionals.

Times have changed for Washburn. Today, the company sells about 50,000 guitars each year and annual revenues exceed $40 million. All this resulted from Washburn's aggressive marketing strategies to develop product lines with different price points targeted at musicians in distinctly different market segments.

THE PRODUCTS AND MARKET SEGMENTS

One of Washburn's early successes was the trendsetting Festival Series of cutaway, thin-bodied flattops,

with built-in bridge pickups and controls. This guitar became the standard for live performances as its popularity with rock and country stars increased. Over the years, several generations of musicians have used Washburn guitars. Early artists included Bob Dylan, Dolly Parton, Greg Allman, and the late George Harrison of the Beatles. In recent years, Mike Kennerty of The All-American Rejects, Rick Savage of Def Leppard, and Hugh McDonald of Bon Jovi have been among the many musicians who use Washburn products.

Until 1991, all Washburn guitars were manufactured in Asia. That year Washburn started building its high-end guitars in the United States. Today, Washburn marketing executives divide its product line into four categories to appeal to different market segments. From high-end guitars to low-end ones, these product groupings are:

- One-of-a-kind, custom instruments.
- Batch-custom instruments.
- Mass-customized instruments.
- Mass-produced instruments.

The one-of-a-kind custom products appeal to the many stars who use Washburn instruments as well as collectors. The batch-custom products appeal to professional musicians. The mass-customized products appeal to musicians with intermediate skill levels who may not yet be professionals. Finally, the mass-produced units are targeted at first-time buyers and are still manufactured in Asian factories.

PRICING ISSUES

Setting prices for its various lines presents a continuing challenge for Washburn. Not only do the prices have to reflect the changing tastes of its various segments of musicians, but the prices must also be competitive with the prices of other guitars manufactured and marketed globally. The price elasticity of demand, or price sensitivity, for Washburn's products varies between its segments. To reduce the price sensitivity for some of its products, Washburn uses endorsements by internationally known musicians who play its instruments and lend their names to lines of Washburn signature guitars. Stars playing Washburn guitars, such as Nuno Bettencourt of

Extreme, Paul Stanley of KISS, Scott Ian of Anthrax, and Dan Donegan of Disturbed, have their own lines of signature guitars—the "batch-custom" units mentioned earlier. These guitars receive excellent reviews. *Total Guitar* magazine, for example, recently said, "If you want a truly original axe that has been built with great attention to detail . . . then the Washburn Maya Pro DD75 could be the one."

Bill Abel, Washburn's vice president of sales, is responsible for reviewing and approving prices for the company's lines of guitars. Setting a sales target of 2,000 units for a new line of guitars, he is considering a suggested retail price of $349 per unit for customers at one of the hundreds of retail outlets carrying the Washburn line. For planning purposes, Abel estimates half of the final retail price will be the price Washburn nets when it sells its guitar to the wholesalers and dealers in its channel of distribution.

Source: Washburn Guitars

Looking at Washburn's financial data for its present plant, Abel estimates that this line of guitars must bear these fixed costs:

Rent and taxes	= $14,000
Depreciation of equipment	= $ 4,000
Management and quality control program	= $20,000

In addition, he estimates the variable costs for each unit to be:

Direct materials = $25/unit
Direct labor = 15 hours/unit @ $8/hour

Carefully kept production records at Washburn's plant make Abel believe that these are reasonable estimates. He explains, "Before we begin a production run, we have a good feel for what our costs will be. The U.S.–built N-4, for example, simply costs more than one of our foreign-produced electrics."

Caught in the global competition for guitar sales, Washburn continually searches for ways to reduce and control costs. For example, Washburn recently purchased Parker Guitar, another guitar manufacturer that designed products for professionals and collectors, and will combine the two production facilities in a new location. Washburn expects the acquisition to lower its fixed and variable costs. Specifically, Washburn projects that its new factory location will reduce its rent and taxes expense by 40 percent, and the new skilled employees will reduce the hours of work needed for each unit by 15 percent.

By managing the prices of its products, Washburn also helps its dealers and retailers. In fact, Abel believes it is another reason for Washburn's success: "We have excellent relationships with the independent retailers. They're our lifeblood, and our outlet to sell our product. We sell through chains and online dealers, but it's the independent dealer that sells the guitars. So we take a smaller margin from them because they have to do more work. They appreciate it, and they go the extra mile for us."[20]

Questions

1 What factors are most likely to affect the demand for the lines of Washburn guitars (*a*) bought by a first-time guitar buyer and (*b*) bought by a sophisticated musician who wants a signature model?

2 For Washburn, what are examples of (*a*) shifting the demand curve to the right to get a higher price for a guitar line (movement of the demand curve) and (*b*) pricing decisions involving moving along a demand curve?

3 In Washburn's factory, what is the break-even point for the new line of guitars if the retail price is (*a*) $349, (*b*) $389, and (*c*) $309? Also, (*d*) if Washburn achieves the sales target of 2,000 units at the $349 retail price, what will its profit be?

4 Assume that the merger with Parker leads to the cost reductions projected in the case. What will be the (*a*) new break-even point at a $349 retail price for this line of guitars and (*b*) new profit if it sells 2,000 units?

5 If, for competitive reasons, Washburn eventually has to move all its production back to Asia, (*a*) which specific fixed and variable costs might be lowered and (*b*) what additional fixed and variable costs might it expect to incur?

Chapter Notes

1. "The Vizio Story," *vizio.com,* downloaded May 15, 2015; "America's Largest Private Companies," *forbes.com,* November 5, 2014; "How Vizio Conquered TV," *fortune.com,* July 25, 2012; and "Vizio Extends Battle Plan," *The Wall Street Journal,* January 3, 2011, p. B3.

2. "Rise of the Barter Economy," *bloomberg.com,* April 26, 2012.

3. "2017 Bugatti Chiron," *Car and Driver,* May 15, 2015, p. 54.

4. Adapted from Kent B. Monroe, *Pricing: Making Profitable Decisions,* 3rd ed. (New York: McGraw-Hill, 2003).

5. Numerous studies have examined the price-quality-value relationship. See, for example, Jacob Jacoby and Jerry C. Olsen, eds., *Perceived Quality* (Lexington, MA: Lexington Books, 1985); William D. Dodds, Kent B. Monroe, and Dhruv Grewal, "Effects of Price, Brand, and Store Information on Buyers' Product Evaluations," *Journal of Marketing Research,* August 1991, pp. 307–19; and Roger A. Kerin, Ambuj Jain, and Daniel Howard, "Store Shopping Experience and Consumer Price-Quality-Value Perceptions," *Journal of Retailing,* Winter 1992, pp. 235–45. For a thorough review of the price-quality-value relationship, see Valerie A. Zeithaml, "Consumer Perceptions of Price, Quality, and Value," *Journal of Marketing,* July 1998, pp. 2–22.

6. Roger A. Kerin and Robert A. Peterson, "Haverwood Furniture, Inc. (A)," *Strategic Marketing Problems: Cases and Comments,* 11th ed. (Upper Saddle River, NJ: Prentice Hall, 2013), pp. 294–305.

7. "Spirit Named 2015 Value Airline of the Year," *airtransportworld. com,* February 25, 2015; "At Spirit Airlines, Airfares Come with Asterisks," *wsj.com,* February 15, 2015; and "Spirit Airlines Sees All Those Passenger Complaints as Mere Misunderstandings," *bloombergbusiness.com,* April 18, 2014.

8. Ken Belson, "Mets Going for the Gold on Tickets for More Games," *The New York Times,* April 8, 2009, p. B13.

9. Ann Zimmerman, "How Toy Crazes Are Born," *The Wall Street Journal,* December 15, 2010, pp. D1–D2; Mike Dodd, "Cards Hold 50 Years of Memories," *USA Today,* March 27, 2001, pp. 1A, 2A; and J. C. Conklin, "Don't Throw Out Those Old Sneakers, They're a Gold Mine," *The Wall Street Journal,* September 21, 1998, pp. A1, A20. Prices quoted on eBay.com on February 17, 2013.

10. Christina Binkley, "How Can Jeans Cost $300?" *The Wall Street Journal,* July 7, 2011, pp. D1–D2.

11. "4-inch iPhone 6 Photos Expose Apple's Bad Decision," *forbes.com,* March 30, 2015.

12. Arik Hesseldahl, "For Every Xbox, a Big Fat Loss," *BusinessWeek,* December 5, 2005, p. 13; and Akshay R. Rao, Mark E. Bergen, and Scott Davis, "How to Fight a Price War," *Harvard Business Review,* March–April 2000, pp. 107–16.

13. Ron Winslow, "How a Breakthrough Quickly Broke Down for Johnson & Johnson," *The Wall Street Journal,* September 18, 1988, pp. A1, A5.

14. Rob Veres, "Find the Lowest Price for Anything in a Store," *Time,* October 15, 2012, p. 40.

15. Jennifer Valentino-DeVries, Jeremy Singer-Vine, and Ashkan Soltani, "Websites Vary Prices, Deals Based on Users' Information," *The Wall Street Journal,* December 24, 2012, p. B1; and Stephanie Clifford, "Retail Frenzy: Prices on the Web Change Hourly," *The New York Times,* November 30, 2012, p. A3.

16. Vanessa O'Connell, "How Campbell Saw a Breakthrough Menu Turn into Leftovers," *The Wall Street Journal,* October 6, 1998, pp. A1, A12.

17. Peter Coy, "Can't Stop Guzzling," *BusinessWeek,* July 31, 2006, pp. 26–29.

18. Ellen Byron and Anjali Cordeiro, "P&G, Others Are Confident Higher Prices Will Stick," *The Wall Street Journal,* February 20, 2009, pp. B1, B2; and Jeff D. Opdyke, "In Colgate's Profit, a Breath of Fresh Air," *The Wall Street Journal,* January 29, 2009, p. C1.

19. "Cigarette Smoking Price Elasticity of Demand," in Irvin Tucker, *Microeconomics for Today,* 7th ed. (Boston, MA: Cengage, 2014), p. 141; "Big Tobacco Takes Its Last Drag as Economic Change Looms," *forbes.com,* September 6, 2013; and "Message Is Clear: Higher Prices Deter Smoking," *USA Today,* April 9, 2009, p. 10A.

20. Washburn Guitar: This case was edited by Steven Hartley. Sources: Burkhard Bilger, "String Theory, Building a Better Guitar," *The New Yorker,* May 14, 2007, p. 79; and the Washburn Guitar website (www.washburn.com).

LEARNING OBJECTIVES

After reading this chapter you should be able to:

 LO 14-1 Describe how to establish the "approximate price level" using demand-oriented, cost-oriented, profit-oriented, and competition-oriented approaches.

 LO 14-2 Recognize the major factors considered in deriving a final list or quoted price from the approximate price level.

 LO 14-3 Identify the adjustments made to the approximate price level on the basis of discounts, allowances, and geography.

 LO 14-4 Name the principal laws and regulations affecting specific pricing practices.

E-books and E-conomics: A Twisted Tale of Pricing for Profit

Have you ever wondered why e-book prices are set a few dollars or cents under an even number, such as $19.99? Or, from a business standpoint, does a publisher make less profit on an e-book than a printed book given the price difference? These questions may not keep you awake at night, but the answers may surprise you.

Setting the Stage with E-readers: Amazon's Kindle

One of the most disruptive changes in the book publishing industry has been the transition from print to electronic books, or e-books. The change wasn't initiated by book publishers, but by Amazon in 2007 with the introduction of its Kindle e-reader. Its innovation was quickly followed by Barnes & Noble with its Nook e-reader in 2009. Apple entered the e-book market in 2010 when it introduced the iPad.

Amazon executives knew that for Kindle e-readers to be successful, printed books had to be converted to e-books quickly. This conversion would supply content for Kindle e-readers, thus increasing their value to consumers. One way to do this was to make e-books cheaper than printed books through advances in digital technology. However, the traditional approach to print book pricing stood in the way. The solution? Change the approach to book pricing, of course! This is when the twisted tale of e-book pricing for profit begins.

Printed Book Pricing Practices

The approach for pricing printed books was steeped in tradition. Based on forecasted demand, a publisher would set a price to a distributor like Amazon (usually 50 percent of the publisher's suggested retail price). The distributor would sell the book to consumers at whatever price the distributor chose. A publisher would then subtract its unit variable costs, such as unit manufacturing (paper and ink), freight and handling cost, and author royalties (about 15 percent of the price) to arrive at its unit contribution per printed book. At a $20.00 suggested retail price ($10.00 to the distributor), the publisher would typically record a $4.40 unit contribution. This amount would be used to pay the total fixed costs assigned to the printed book and produce a profit.

Enter E-books

The dynamics in the e-book market proved to be quite different from the printed book market. For example, traditional distributors, such as bookstores, had an incentive to set a printed book's retail price from the publisher higher. In contrast,

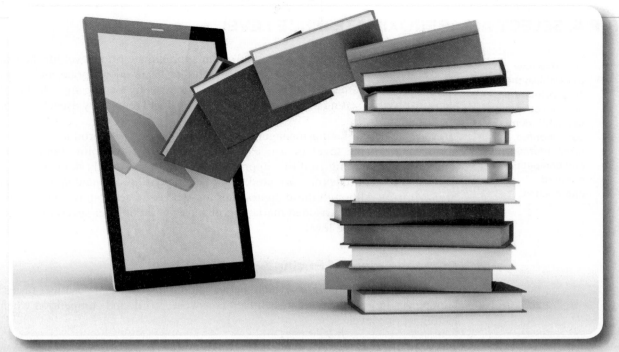

e-reader suppliers, such as Amazon, wanted lower retail prices for e-books to build the e-reader business. Therefore, Amazon initially decided to set a retail price for e-books at $9.99—a common decision based on belief that this act would stimulate e-book volume. This meant that Amazon would lose money on many e-book transactions: paying $10.00 for an item and then selling it for $9.99 presented a problem. At the same time, publishers believed that low e-book prices promoted by Amazon and other distributors would erode consumers' perception of the value of books, cannibalize printed book sales, and eventually result in lower prices charged to distributors. In short, neither party benefited.

Pricing E-books . . . Profitably

In 2010, book publishers changed their pricing approach. Publishers would set e-book list retail prices, and distributors, like Amazon, Barnes & Noble, or Apple, would get a commission on every e-book sold. The commission was usually 30 percent. Distributors could still set their own retail prices, but with a restriction. Distributors could set prices below a publisher's retail list price so long as they did not exceed the commission received from a publisher. Therefore, the most a publisher's retail list price of $20.00 could be discounted was $14.00. But consumers didn't see that retail price. Amazon and Apple usually set a price with an odd-ending number like 5, 7, or 9 as a matter of policy. The zeros in $14.00 would be replaced by one or more of these numbers, or $14.99.

So how do publishers and distributors make a profit using this approach to pricing? Suppose a publisher's retail list price for an e-book is $20.00. The distributor's e-book retail price is set at $14.99. The publisher would get 70 percent of $14.99, or $10.49, and the distributor would get $4.50. The publisher has no unit manufacturing, freight, or handling cost, just an author royalty, which drops to about $2.62. Therefore, the publisher's unit contribution per e-book is $7.87 ($10.49 − $2.62) to pay the total fixed costs assigned to the e-book and record a profit. Remember that a publisher's unit contribution for a printed book was $4.40. In short, both e-book distributors and publishers benefit from this pricing approach because both parties make a profit. Now you know a little bit more about e-book economics and the twisted tale of profitable pricing.[1]

STEP 4: SELECT AN APPROXIMATE PRICE LEVEL

LO 14-1 | Describe how to establish the "approximate price level" using demand-oriented, cost-oriented, profit-oriented, and competition-oriented approaches.

This chapter describes how companies set an approximate price level for their offerings, highlights important considerations in setting a list or quoted price, and identifies various price adjustments that can be made to prices set by a company—the last three steps involved in setting prices (Figure 14–1). Legal and regulatory aspects of pricing are also described.

A key for a marketing manager setting a final price for a product is to find an approximate price level to use as a reasonable starting point. Four common approaches to helping find this approximate price level are (1) demand-oriented, (2) cost-oriented, (3) profit-oriented, and (4) competition-oriented approaches (see Figure 14–2). Although these approaches are discussed separately below, some of them overlap, and a seasoned marketing manager will consider several in selecting an approximate price level.

Demand-Oriented Pricing Approaches

Demand-oriented approaches weigh factors underlying expected customer tastes and preferences more heavily than such factors as cost, profit, and competition when selecting a price level.

Skimming Pricing A firm introducing a new or innovative product can use **skimming pricing**, setting the highest initial price that customers who really desire the product are willing to pay. These customers are not very price sensitive because they weigh the new product's price, quality, and ability to satisfy their needs against the same characteristics of substitutes. As the demand of these customers is satisfied, the firm lowers the price to attract another, more price-sensitive segment. Thus, skimming pricing gets its name from skimming successive layers of "cream," or customer segments, as prices are lowered in a series of steps.

Skimming pricing is an effective strategy when (1) enough prospective customers are willing to buy the product immediately at the high initial price to make these sales profitable, (2) the high initial price will not attract competitors, (3) lowering price has only a minor effect on increasing the sales volume and reducing the unit costs, and (4) customers interpret the high price as signifying high quality. These four conditions are most likely to exist when the new product is protected by patents or copyrights or its uniqueness is understood and valued by consumers. Gillette, for example, adopted a skimming strategy for its five-blade Fusion brand shaving system since many of these

FIGURE 14–1

The six steps in setting price. The first three steps were covered in Chapter 13, and the last three steps are covered in this chapter.

Select an approximate price level

Demand-oriented approaches
- Skimming
- Penetration
- Prestige
- Price lining
- Odd-even
- Target
- Bundle
- Yield management

Cost-oriented approaches
- Standard markup
- Cost-plus
- Experience curve

Profit-oriented approaches
- Target profit
- Target return on sales
- Target return on investment

Competition-oriented approaches
- Customary
- Above, at, or below market
- Loss leader

FIGURE 14–2

Four approaches for selecting an approximate price level.

conditions applied. The Gillette Fusion shaving system has 70 patents that protect its product technology.

Penetration Pricing   Setting a low initial price on a new product to appeal immediately to the mass market is **penetration pricing**, the exact opposite of skimming pricing. Amazon consciously chose a penetration strategy when it introduced its Amazon Kindle Fire tablet computer at $199 when competitive models were priced at $499.[2]

The conditions favoring penetration pricing are the reverse of those supporting skimming pricing: (1) many segments of the market are price sensitive, (2) a low initial price discourages competitors from entering the market, and (3) unit production and marketing costs fall dramatically as production volumes increase. A firm using penetration pricing may (1) maintain the initial price for a time to gain profit lost from its low introductory level or (2) lower the price further, counting on the new volume to generate the necessary profit.

In some situations, penetration pricing may follow skimming pricing. A company might initially price a product high to attract price-insensitive consumers and recoup initial research and development costs and introductory promotional expenditures. Once this is done, penetration pricing is used to appeal to a broader segment of the population and increase market share.[3]

FIGURE 14–3

For prestige pricing, the demand curve for high-quality products bought by status-conscious consumers is backward sloping.

Prestige pricing demand curve

Prestige Pricing   As noted in Chapter 13, consumers may use price as a measure of the quality or prestige of an item so that as price is lowered beyond some point, demand for the item actually falls. **Prestige pricing** involves setting a high price so that quality- or status-conscious consumers will be attracted to the product and buy it (see Figure 14–3). The demand curve slopes downward and to the right between points *A* and *B* but turns back to the left between points *B* and *C* because demand is actually reduced between points *B* and *C*. From *A* to *B*, buyers see the lowering of price as a bargain and buy more; from *B* to *C*, they become dubious about the quality and prestige and buy less. A marketing manager's pricing strategy here is to stay above price P_0 (the initial price).

Rolls-Royce cars, Chanel perfume, Cartier jewelry, Lalique crystal, and Swiss watches, such as Rolex, have an element of prestige pricing in them and may sell worse at lower prices than at higher ones.[4] The recent success of Swiss watchmaker TAG Heuer is an example. The company raised the average price of its watches from $250 to $1,000, and its sales volume jumped sevenfold.[5] Recently, Energizer learned that buyers of high-performance alkaline batteries tend to link a lower price with lower quality. The Marketing Matters box on the next page describes the pricing lesson learned by Energizer.[6]

Energizer's Lesson in Price Perception—
Value Lies in the Eye of the Beholder

Battery manufacturers are as tireless as a certain drum-thumping bunny in their efforts to create products that perform better, last longer, and, not incidentally, outsell the competition. The commercialization of new alkaline battery technology at a price that creates value for consumers is not always obvious or easy. Just ask the marketing executives at Energizer about their experience with pricing Energizer Advanced Formula and Energizer e^2 AA alkaline batteries.

When Duracell launched its high-performance Ultra brand AA alkaline battery with a 25 percent price premium over standard Duracell batteries, Energizer quickly countered with its own high-performance battery—Energizer Advanced Formula. Believing that

© Scott Boehm/AP Images

consumers would not pay the premium price, Energizer priced its Advanced Formula brand at the same price as its standard AA alkaline battery, expecting to gain market share from Duracell. It did not happen. Why? According to industry analysts, consumers associated Energizer's low price with inferior quality in the high-performance segment. Instead of gaining market share, Energizer lost market share to Duracell and Rayovac, the number three battery manufacturer.

Having learned its lesson, Energizer subsequently released its e^2 high-performance battery, this time priced 4 percent higher than Duracell Ultra and about 50 percent higher than Advanced Formula. The result? Energizer recovered lost sales and market share. The lesson learned? Value lies in the eye of the beholder.

Price Lining Often a firm that is selling not just a single product but a line of products may price them at a number of different specific pricing points, which is called **price lining**. For example, a department store manager may price a line of women's casual slacks at $59, $79, and $99. As shown in Figure 14–4, this assumes that demand is elastic at each of these price points but inelastic between these price points. In some instances, all the items might be purchased for the same cost and then marked up at different percentages to achieve these price points based on color, style, and expected demand. In other instances, manufacturers design products for different price points, and retailers apply approximately the same markup percentages to achieve the three or four different price points offered to consumers. Sellers often feel that a limited number of price points (such as 3 or 4) are preferable to 8 or 10, which may only confuse prospective buyers.[7]

Odd-Even Pricing Sears offers a Craftsman radial saw for $499.99, the suggested retail price for the Gillette Fusion shaving system is $11.99, and Amazon sold a recent U2 CD for $3.99. Why not simply price these items at $500, $12, and $4, respectively? These firms are using **odd-even pricing**, which involves setting prices a few dollars or cents under an even number. The presumption is that consumers see the Craftsman radial saw as priced at "something over $400" rather than "about $500." In theory, demand increases if the price drops from $500 to $499.99. There is some evidence to suggest this does happen. However, research suggests that overuse of odd-ending prices tends to mute its effect on demand.[8]

Target Pricing Manufacturers will sometimes estimate the price that the ultimate consumer would be willing to pay for a product. They then work backward through markups taken by retailers and wholesalers to determine what price they can charge wholesalers for the product. This practice, called

FIGURE 14–4

For price lining, the demand curve is elastic at each price point but inelastic between price points.

Price lining demand curve

Which pricing strategy is used by DIRECTV? Read the text to find out which one and why.

Source: DIRECTV

target pricing, results in the manufacturer deliberately adjusting the composition and features of a product to achieve the target price to consumers.

Bundle Pricing A frequently used demand-oriented pricing practice is **bundle pricing**—the marketing of two or more products in a single package price. For example, Delta Air Lines offers vacation packages that include airfare, car rental, and lodging. Bundle pricing is based on the idea that consumers value the package more than the individual items. This is due to benefits received from not having to make separate purchases and enhanced satisfaction from one item given the presence of another. This is the idea behind McDonald's Extra Value Meal and DIRECTV's TV, phone, and Internet bundles. Moreover, bundle pricing often provides a lower total cost to buyers and lower marketing costs to sellers.[9]

Yield Management Pricing Have you noticed seats on airline flights are priced differently within coach class? This is **yield management pricing**—the charging of different prices to maximize revenue for a set amount of capacity at any given time. As described in Chapter 12, service businesses engage in capacity management, and an effective way to do this is by varying prices by time, day, week, or season. Yield management pricing is a complex approach that continually matches demand and supply to customize the price for a service. Airlines, hotels, cruise ships, and car rental companies frequently use it. American Airlines estimates that yield management pricing produces an annual revenue that exceeds $500 million.[10]

learning review

14-1. In pricing a new product, what circumstances might support skimming or penetration pricing?

14-2. What is odd-even pricing?

Cost-Oriented Pricing Approaches

With cost-oriented approaches, a price setter stresses the cost side of the pricing problem, not the demand side. Price is set by looking at the production and marketing costs and then adding enough to cover direct expenses, overhead, and profit.

What are the markups for soft drinks, candy, and popcorn at your movie theater? Read the text to learn what the markup is on these items.

© andresr/E+/Getty Images

Standard Markup Pricing Managers of supermarkets and other retail stores have such a large number of products that estimating the demand for each product as a means of setting price is impossible. Therefore, they use **standard markup pricing**, which entails adding a fixed percentage to the cost of all items in a specific product class. This percentage markup varies depending on the type of retail store (such as furniture, clothing, or grocery) and the product involved. High-volume products usually have smaller markups than low-volume products.

Supermarkets such as Kroger and Safeway have different markups for staple items and discretionary items. The markup on staple items such as sugar, flour, and dairy products varies from 10 percent to 23 percent. Markups on discretionary items like snack foods and candy range from 27 percent to 47 percent. These markups must cover all of the expenses of the store, pay for overhead costs, and contribute something to profits. Although these

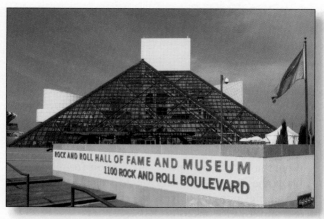

How was the price of the Rock and Roll Hall of Fame and Museum determined? Read the text to find out.

© Stan Rohrer/Alamy

Rock and Roll Hall of Fame and Museum

www.rockhall.com

markups may appear very large, they result in only a 1 percent profit on sales revenue, assuming the supermarket is operating efficiently.

By comparison, consider the markups on snacks and beverages purchased at your local movie theater. The markup is 87 percent on soft drinks, 65 percent on candy bars, and 90 percent on popcorn. These markups might sound high, but consider the consequences. "If we didn't charge as much for concessions as we did, a movie ticket would cost $20," says the CEO of Regal Entertainment, the largest U.S. theater chain.[11]

Cost-Plus Pricing Many manufacturing, professional services, and construction firms use a variation of standard markup pricing. **Cost-plus pricing** involves summing the total unit cost of providing a product or service and adding a specific amount to the cost to arrive at a price. Cost-plus pricing generally assumes two forms. With *cost-plus percentage-of-cost pricing,* a fixed percentage is added to the total unit cost. This is often used to price one- or few-of-a-kind items, as when an architectural firm charges a percentage of the construction costs of, say, the $92 million Rock and Roll Hall of Fame and Museum in Cleveland, Ohio.

In buying highly technical, few-of-a-kind products such as hydroelectric power plants or space satellites, governments have found that general contractors are reluctant to specify a formal, fixed price for the procurement. Therefore, they use *cost-plus fixed-fee pricing,* which means that a supplier is reimbursed for all costs, regardless of what they turn out to be, but is allowed only a fixed fee as profit that is independent of the final cost of the project. For example, suppose the National Aeronautics and Space Administration agreed to pay Lockheed Martin $4 billion as the cost for its Orion lunar spacecraft and agreed to a $6.5 billion fee for providing the lunar spacecraft in 2016. Even if Lockheed Martin's cost increased to $5 billion for the lunar spacecraft, its fee would remain at $6.5 billion.

Cost-plus pricing is the most commonly used method to set prices for business products. Increasingly, however, this method is finding favor among business-to-business marketers in the service sector. For example, the rising cost of legal fees has prompted some law firms to adopt a cost-plus pricing approach. Rather than billing business clients on an hourly basis, lawyers and their clients agree on a fixed fee based on expected costs plus a profit for the law firm. Many advertising agencies now use this approach. Here, the client agrees to pay the agency a fee based on the cost of its work plus some agreed-on profit, which is often a percentage of total cost.

Experience Curve Pricing The method of **experience curve pricing** is based on the learning effect, which holds that the unit cost of many products and services declines by 10 percent to 30 percent each time a firm's experience at producing and selling them doubles. This reduction is regular or predictable enough that the average cost per unit can be mathematically estimated. For example, if the firm estimates that costs will fall by 15 percent each time volume doubles, then the cost of the 100th unit produced and sold will be about 85 percent of the cost of the 50th unit, and the 200th unit will be 85 percent of the 100th unit. Therefore, if the cost of the 50th unit is $100, the 100th unit would cost $85, the 200th unit would be $72.25, and so on. Because prices often follow costs with experience curve pricing, a rapid decline in price is possible.

Japanese, Korean, and U.S. firms in the electronics industry often adopt this pricing approach. This cost-based pricing approach complements the demand-based pricing strategy of skimming followed by penetration pricing. For example,

Sony, Samsung, LG, VIZIO, and other television manufacturers use experience curve pricing for HDTV sets. Consumers benefit because prices decline as cumulative sales volume grows. In fact, HDTV prices have fallen by 40 percent in the past decade.[12]

Profit-Oriented Pricing Approaches

A price setter may choose to balance both revenues and costs to set price using profit-oriented approaches. These might either involve setting a target of a specific dollar volume of profit or expressing this target profit as a percentage of sales or investment.

Target Profit Pricing A firm that sets an annual target of a specific dollar volume of profit is using a **target profit pricing** approach. As the owner of a picture framing store, suppose you decide to use target profit pricing to establish a price for a typical framed picture. First, you need to make some assumptions, such as:

- Variable cost is a constant $22 per unit.
- Fixed cost is a constant $26,000.
- Demand is insensitive to price up to $60 per unit.
- A target profit of $7,000, at an annual volume of 1,000 units (framed pictures).

You can then calculate price as follows:

$$\text{Profit} = \text{Total revenue} - \text{Total cost}$$

$$\text{Profit} = (P \times Q) - [FC + (UVC \times Q)]$$

$$\$7{,}000 = (P \times 1{,}000) - [\$26{,}000 + (\$22 \times 1{,}000)]$$

$$\$7{,}000 = 1{,}000P - (\$26{,}000 + \$22{,}000)$$

$$1{,}000P = \$7{,}000 + \$48{,}000$$

$$P = \$55$$

Note that a critical assumption is that this higher average price for a framed picture will not cause the demand to fall.

Target Return-on-Sales Pricing A shortcoming with target profit pricing is that although it is simple and the target involves only a specific dollar volume, there is no benchmark of sales or investment used to show how much of the firm's effort is needed to achieve the target. Firms such as supermarket chains often use **target return-on-sales pricing** to set typical prices that will give them a profit that is a specified percentage, say, 1 percent, of the sales volume. Suppose you decide to use target return-on-sales pricing in your shop. To establish a price for a typical framed picture, you begin by making the same first three assumptions shown previously. However, for the fourth assumption, your target is now a 20 percent return on sales at an annual volume of 1,250 units. This results in the following price:

$$\text{Target return on sales} = \frac{\text{Target profit}}{\text{Total revenue}}$$

$$20\% = \frac{TR - TC}{TR}$$

$$0.20 = \frac{P \times Q - [FC + (UVC \times Q)]}{TR}$$

$$0.20 = \frac{P \times 1{,}250 - [\$26{,}000 + (\$22 \times 1{,}250)]}{P \times 1{,}250}$$

$$P = \$53.50$$

So at a price of $53.50 per unit and an annual quantity of 1,250 frames,

$$TR = P \times Q = \$53.50 \times 1,250 = \$66,875$$

$$TC = FC + (UVC \times Q) = \$26,000 + (\$22 \times 1,250) = \$53,500$$

$$Profit = TR - TC = \$66,875 - \$53,500 = \$13,375$$

As a check,

$$\text{Target return on sales} = \frac{\text{Target profit}}{\text{Total revenue}} = \frac{\$13,375}{\$66,875} = 20\%$$

Target Return-on-Investment Pricing   Large, publicly owned corporations and many public utilities set annual return-on-investment (ROI) targets such as an ROI of 20 percent. **Target return-on-investment pricing** is a method of setting prices to achieve this target.

As the owner of the picture frame shop, suppose you decide to set a target ROI of 10 percent, which is twice that achieved the previous year. You consider raising the average price of a framed picture to $54 or $58—up from last year's average of $50. To do this, you might improve product quality by offering better frames and higher-quality matting. This is likely to increase the cost, but higher prices will probably offset the decreased revenue from the lower number of units you are likely to sell next year.

To handle this wide variety of assumptions, managers use spreadsheets to project operating statements based on a set of assumptions. Figure 14–5 shows the results of a spreadsheet simulation, with assumptions shown at the top and the projected results at

FIGURE 14–5

Results of a spreadsheet simulation used to select a price that will achieve a target return on investment.

		SPREADSHEET SIMULATION				
Assumptions or Results	Financial Element	Last Year	A	B	C	D
ASSUMPTIONS	Price per unit (P)	$50	$54	$54	$58	$58
	Units sold (Q)	1,000	1,200	1,100	1,100	1,000
	Change in unit variable cost (UVC)	0%	+10%	+10%	+20%	+20%
	Unit variable cost	$22.00	$24.20	$24.20	$26.20	$26.40
	Total expenses	$8,000	Same	Same	Same	Same
	Owner's salary	$18,000	Same	Same	Same	Same
	Investment	$20,000	Same	Same	Same	Same
	State and federal taxes	50%	Same	Same	Same	Same
SPREADSHEET RESULTS	Net sales (P × Q)	$50,000	$64,800	$59,400	$63,800	$58,000
	Less: COGS (Q × UVC)	22,000	29,040	26,620	29,040	26,400
	Gross margin	$28,000	$35,760	$32,780	$34,760	$31,600
	Less: Total expenses	$26,000	$26,000	$26,000	$26,000	$26,000
	Net profit before taxes	$2,000	$9,760	$6,780	$8,760	$5,600
	Less: Taxes	1,000	4,880	3,390	4,380	2,800
	Net profit after taxes	$1,000	$4,880	$3,390	$4,380	$2,800
	Investment	$20,000	$20,000	$20,000	$20,000	$20,000
	Return on investment	5.0%	24.4%	17.0%	21.9%	14.0%

the bottom. A previous year's operating statement results are shown in the column headed "Last Year." The assumptions and spreadsheet results for four different sets of assumptions are shown in columns A, B, C, and D.

In choosing a price or another action using spreadsheet results, the manager must (1) study the results of the simulation projections and (2) assess the realism of the assumptions underlying each set of projections. For example, as the owner of the picture frame shop, you would look at the bottom row of Figure 14–5 and see that all four spreadsheet simulations exceed the after-tax target ROI of 10 percent. But after more thought, you might decide that it would be more realistic to set an average price of $58 per unit, allow the unit variable cost to increase by 20 percent to account for more expensive framing and matting, and settle for the same unit sales as the 1,000 units sold last year. Therefore, you would select simulation D in this spreadsheet approach to target ROI pricing, settling on a goal of 14 percent after-tax ROI.

Competition-Oriented Pricing Approaches

Rather than emphasize demand, cost, or profit factors, a price setter can stress what competitors or "the market" are doing.

Customary Pricing   For some products where tradition, a standardized channel of distribution, or other competitive factors dictate the price, **customary pricing** is used. For example, tradition prevails in the pricing of Swatch watches. The $50 customary price for the basic model has changed little in 10 years. Candy bars offered through standard vending machines have a customary price of $1.00. A significant departure from this price may result in a loss of sales for the manufacturer. Hershey changes the amount of chocolate in its candy bars depending on the price of raw chocolate rather than varying its customary retail price so that it can continue selling through vending machines.

Above-, At-, or Below-Market Pricing   For most products, it is difficult to identify a specific market price for a product or product class. Still, marketing managers often have a subjective feel for the competitors' price or market price. Using this benchmark, they then may deliberately choose a strategy of **above-, at-, or below-market pricing**.

Among watch manufacturers, Rolex takes pride in emphasizing that it makes one of the most expensive watches you can buy, a clear example of above-market pricing. Manufacturers of national brands of clothing such as Hart Schaffner & Marx and Christian Dior and retailers such as Neiman Marcus deliberately set premium prices for their products.

Revlon cosmetics and Arrow brand shirts are generally priced "at market." As such, they also provide a reference price for competitors that use above- and below-market pricing.

A number of firms use below-market pricing. Manufacturers and retailers that offer private brands of products ranging from peanut butter to shampoo deliberately set prices for these products about 8 to 10 percent below the prices of nationally branded competitive products such as Skippy peanut butter and Vidal Sassoon shampoo. Below-market pricing also exists in business-to-business marketing. Hewlett-Packard, for instance, initially priced its office personal computers below those of competitors to promote a value image among corporate buyers.[13]

Companies use a "price premium" to assess whether their products and brands are above, at, or below the market. An illustration of how the price premium measure is calculated, displayed, and interpreted appears in the Applying Marketing Metrics box.[14]

Has Red Bull's price premium among energy-drink brands sold in convenience stores increased or decreased? The Applying Marketing Metrics box answers this question.

© Mike Hruby

Applying **Marketing Metrics**

Are Red Bull Prices Above, At, or Below the Market?

How would you determine whether a firm's retail prices are above, at, or below the market? You might visit retail stores and record what prices retailers are charging for products or brands. However, this laborious activity can be simplified by combining dollar market share and unit volume market share measures to create a "price premium" display on your marketing dashboard.

Your Challenge

Red Bull is the leading energy-drink brand in the United States in terms of dollar market share and unit market share (see the table below). Company marketing executives have research showing that Red Bull has a strong brand equity. What they want to know is whether the brand's price premium resulting from its brand equity has eroded due to heavy price discounting in the convenience store channel. This channel accounts for 60 percent of energy-drink sales.

A price premium is the percentage by which the actual price charged for a specific brand exceeds (or falls short of) a benchmark established for a similar product or basket of products. As such, a price premium shows whether a brand is priced above, at, or below the market. This premium is calculated as follows:

Price premium (%)

$$= \frac{\text{Dollar sales market share for a brand}}{\text{Unit volume market share for a brand}} - 1$$

Your Findings

Using 2010 energy-drink brand market share data for U.S. convenience stores, the Red Bull price premium is 1.152, or 15.2 percent, calculated as follows: (38 percent ÷ 33 percent) −1 = .152. Red Bull's average price is 15.2 percent

higher than the average price for energy-drink brands sold in convenience stores. Red Bull's price premium based on 2009 brand market share data was 1.121, or 12.1 percent, calculated as follows: (37 percent ÷ 33 percent) −1 = 12.1. Red Bull's price premium has increased relative to its competitors, notably Monster Energy and Rockstar. The price premiums for Red Bull and these two competitive brands for 2009 and 2010 are displayed in the marketing dashboard shown below.

Your Action

Red Bull has increased its price premium while retaining its unit volume share, which is not only favorable news for the brand but also evidence of price discounting by other brands. Clearly, the company's brand-building effort, reflected in sponsorships and a singular focus on brand attributes valued by consumers, should be continued.

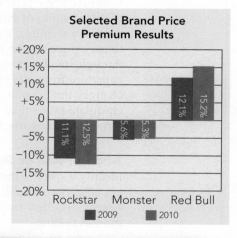

Selected Brand Price Premium Results

(Rockstar 2009: −11.1%, 2010: −12.5%; Monster 2009: −5.6%, 2010: −5.3%; Red Bull 2009: 12.1%, 2010: 15.2%) Legend: 2009, 2010

Brand	Dollar Sales Market Share		Unit Volume Market Share	
	2010	**2009**	**2010**	**2009**
Red Bull	38%	37%	33%	33%
Monster	18	17	19	18
Rockstar	7	8	8	9
Other brands	37	38	40	40
	100%	100%	100%	100%

Loss-Leader Pricing   For a special promotion, retail stores deliberately sell a product below its customary price to attract attention to it. The purpose of this **loss-leader pricing** is not to increase sales but to attract customers in hopes they will buy other products as well, particularly the discretionary items with large markups. For example, supermarkets often use milk as a loss leader.

learning review »

14-3. What is standard markup pricing?

14-4. What profit-based pricing approach should a manager use if he or she wants to reflect the percentage of the firm's resources used in obtaining the profit?

14-5. What is the purpose of loss-leader pricing when used by a retail firm?

STEP 5: SET THE LIST OR QUOTED PRICE

LO 14-2 | Recognize the major factors considered in deriving a final list or quoted price from the approximate price level.

So far, we have covered four of the six steps involved in setting a price—steps 1–3, covered in Chapter 13, and step 4, covered in the preceding section. The result of these four steps is an approximate price level for the product that appears reasonable. But it still remains for the manager to set a specific list or quoted price in light of all relevant factors. In deciding upon the specific price for a product, the manager must choose a price policy; consider company, customer, and competitive effects on pricing; and balance incremental costs and revenues.

Choose a Price Policy

Choosing a price policy is important in setting a list or quoted price. Two options are common—a fixed-price policy or a dynamic pricing policy.

Online retailers adjust prices several times a day. This chart shows how the price for a GE microwave oven changed one day on the Amazon, Best Buy, and Sears websites.

Fixed-Price Policy   Most companies use a fixed-price policy. A **fixed-price policy**, also called a *one-price policy,* is setting one price for all buyers of a product or service. For example, when you buy a Wilson Cirrus One BLX tennis racquet from a sporting goods store, you are offered the product at a single price. You can buy it or not, but there is no variation in the price under the seller's fixed-price policy. CarMax uses this approach in its stores and features a "no haggle, one price" price for cars. Some retailers have married this policy with a below-market approach. Dollar Value Stores and 99¢ Only Stores sell everything in their stores for $1 or less. Family Dollar Stores sell everything for $2.

Dynamic Pricing Policy   In contrast, a **dynamic pricing policy**, also called a *flexible-price policy,* involves setting different prices for products and services in real time in response to supply and demand conditions. A dynamic pricing policy gives sellers considerable discretion in setting the final price in light of demand, cost, and competitive factors. Yield management pricing is a form of dynamic pricing because prices vary by an individual buyer's purchase situation, company cost considerations, and competitive conditions. Dell Inc. uses dynamic pricing. It continually adjusts prices in response to changes in its own costs, competitive pressures, and demand from customers, from one segment of the personal computer market to another. "Our flexibility allows us to be [priced] different even within a day," says a Dell spokesperson.[15]

Dynamic pricing has grown in popularity because of increasingly sophisticated information technology. Today, many marketers have the ability to customize a price for an individual on the basis of his or her purchasing patterns, product preferences, and price sensitivity, all of which are stored in company data warehouses.[16] For example, online marketers, like Amazon, described in Chapter 13, routinely adjust prices in response to purchase situations and past purchase behaviors of online buyers. Some online marketers monitor an online shopper's *clickstream*—the way that person navigates through the website. If the visitor behaves like a price-sensitive shopper—perhaps by comparing many different products and prices—that person may be offered a lower price.

Dynamic pricing means that some customers pay more and others pay less for the same product or service. Dynamic pricing is not without its critics. One frequent criticism of dynamic pricing lies in the realm of "surge" pricing, which occurs when a company raises the price of its product or service if there is a spike in demand. Read the Making Responsible Decisions box to learn about the ethics and economics of surge pricing used by Uber and Lyft and decide where you stand on this practice.[17]

Consider Company, Customer, and Competitive Effects on Pricing

In determining a final list or quoted price, the manager must next assess company, customer, and competitive effects on pricing.

Company Effects   For a firm with more than one product, a decision on the price of a single product must consider the price of other items in its product line or related product lines in its product mix. Within a product line or mix there are usually some products that are substitutes for one another and some that complement each other. Frito-Lay recognizes that its Baked Tostitos, Tostitos, and Doritos brands are partial substitutes for one another and its bean and cheese dips and salsas complement the products in its tortilla chip line.

A manager's challenge when marketing multiple products is **product-line pricing**, the setting of prices for all items in a product line. When setting prices, the manager seeks to cover the total cost and produce a profit for the complete line, not necessarily for each item. For example, a penetration price for Sony's PlayStation 4 video game console was probably at or below its cost, but the prices of its video games (complementary products) were set high enough to cover any loss and deliver a handsome profit for the product line.

Product-line pricing involves determining (1) the lowest-priced product and price, (2) the highest-priced product and price, and (3) price differentials for all other products in the line.[18] The lowest- and highest-priced items in the product line play important roles. The highest-priced item is typically positioned as the premium item in quality and features. The lowest-priced item is the traffic builder designed to capture the attention

Making **Responsible Decisions**

The Ethics and Economics of Surge Pricing

Uber and Lyft have changed the way local taxi service operates. Using independent drivers and driver-owned vehicles, both companies serve as middlemen using digital technology to provide on-demand transportation services to consumers. Nevertheless, Uber and Lyft customers often complain about the practice of "surge" or "prime-time" pricing used by these companies during periods of peak demand. From a classical economics perspective, this form of dynamic pricing makes sense based on supply and demand relationships. Fare increases in periods of high demand—a shift in the demand curve to the right—in turn increase the supply of drivers available for passengers.

© Imaginechina/AP Images

From an ethical perspective, supporters of surge or prime-time pricing argue from a utilitarian view that this type of pricing increases the supply of drivers and more people get a ride. Remember from Chapter 4 that utilitarianism focuses on "the greatest good for the greatest number" by assessing the costs and benefits of the behavior, in this case, dynamic pricing.

Critics of surge or prime-time pricing argue that this practice is flagrant price gouging by Uber and Lyft. Where do you stand on the economics vs. ethics debate related to surge or prime-time pricing?

of the hesitant or first-time buyer. Price differentials between items in the line should make sense to customers and reflect differences in the perceived value of the products offered. Behavioral research also suggests that the price differentials should get larger as one moves up the product line.

Customer Effects   In setting a price, marketers pay close attention to factors that satisfy the perceptions or expectations of ultimate consumers, such as the customary prices for a variety of consumer products. For example, retailers have found that they should not price their store brands 20 to 25 percent below manufacturers' brands.[19] When they do, consumers often view the lower price as a signal of lower quality and don't buy.

Manufacturers and wholesalers must choose prices that result in profit for resellers in the channel to gain their cooperation and support. Toro learned this lesson the hard way when it decided to augment its traditional hardware outlet distribution by also selling its lawn mower and snow thrower product lines through mass merchandisers. To do so, it set mass merchandiser prices far below those for its traditional hardware

Frito-Lay recognizes that its tortilla chip products are partial substitutes for one another. Its bean and cheese dips and salsas complement tortilla chips. This knowledge is used by Frito-Lay in its product-line pricing.

Source: Frito-Lay North America, Inc.

Frito-Lay, Inc.
www.frito-lay.com

outlets. Unhappy hardware stores abandoned Toro products in favor of mowers and snow throwers from competitors.

Competitive Effects   A manager's pricing decision is immediately apparent to most competitors, who may retaliate with price changes of their own. Therefore, a manager who sets a final list or quoted price must anticipate potential price responses from competitors. Regardless of whether a firm is a price leader or follower, it wants to avoid cutthroat price wars in which no firm in the industry makes a profit.

A **price war** involves successive price cutting by competitors to increase or maintain their unit sales or market share. Price wars erupt in a variety of industries, from consumer electronics to disposable diapers, from soft drinks to airlines, and from grocery retailing to smartphone services. Managers who engage in price wars do so expecting that a lower price will result in a larger market share, higher unit sales, and greater profit for their company. These results may occur. But, if competitors match the lower price, other things being equal, the expected market share, sales, and profit gain are lost. According to an analysis of large U.S. companies, a 1 percent price cut—assuming no change in unit volume or costs—lowers a company's net profit by an average of 8 percent.[20]

Marketers are advised to consider price cutting only when one or more conditions exist: (1) the company has a cost or technological advantage over its competitors, (2) primary demand for a product class will grow if prices are lowered, and (3) the price cut is confined to specific products or customers (as with airline tickets) and is not across the board.

Balance Incremental Costs and Revenues

When a price is changed or new advertising or personal selling programs are planned, their effect on the quantity sold must be considered. This assessment involves a continuing, concise trade-off of incremental costs incurred against incremental revenues received.

Think about these managerial questions:

- How many extra units do we have to sell to pay for that $1,000 advertisement?
- Should we hire three more salespeople or not?

Figure 14–6 uses an example of a picture frame store owner to illustrate the advantages and disadvantages of using incremental analysis to make marketing decisions.

Suppose the owner of a picture framing store is considering buying a series of magazine ads to reach her upscale target market. The cost of the ads is $1,000, the average price of a framed picture is $50, and the unit variable cost (materials plus labor) is $30.

This is a direct application of marginal analysis that an astute manager uses to estimate the incremental revenue or incremental number of units that must be obtained to at least cover the incremental cost. In this example, the number of extra picture frames that must be sold is obtained as follows:

$$\text{Incremental number of frames} = \frac{\text{Extra fixed cost}}{\text{Price} - \text{Unit variable cost}}$$

$$= \frac{\$1,000 \text{ of advertising}}{\$50 - \$30}$$

$$= 50 \text{ frames}$$

So unless there are other benefits of the ads, such as long-term goodwill, she should buy the ads only if she expects they will increase picture frame sales by at least 50 units.

Note that the owner in this example must either conclude that a simple advertising campaign will more than pay for itself in additional sales or not undertake the campaign. The decision could also have been made to increase the average price of a framed picture to cover the cost of the campaign, but the principle still applies: Expected incremental revenues from pricing and other marketing actions must more than offset incremental costs.

The example in Figure 14–6 shows both the main advantage and the difficulty of incremental analysis. The advantage is its commonsense usefulness, and the difficulty is obtaining the necessary data to make decisions. The owner can measure the cost quite easily, but the incremental revenue generated by the ads is difficult to measure. To get a general idea, she might offer $2 off the purchase price with use of a coupon printed in the ad to see which sales resulted from the ad.

STEP 6: MAKE SPECIAL ADJUSTMENTS TO THE LIST OR QUOTED PRICE

> **LO 14-3** Identify the adjustments made to the approximate price level on the basis of discounts, allowances, and geography.

When you pay $1.00 for a bag of M&M's in a vending machine or receive a quoted price of $10,000 from a contractor to renovate a kitchen, the pricing sequence ends with the last step just described: setting the list or quoted price. But when you are a manufacturer of M&M's candies or Wolf gas ranges and you sell your product to dozens or hundreds of wholesalers and retailers in your marketing channel, you may need to make special adjustments to the list or quoted price. Wholesalers adjust the list or quoted prices they set for retailers. Retailers, in turn, do the same for consumers. Three special adjustments to the list or quoted price are (1) discounts, (2) allowances, and (3) geographical adjustments (see Figure 14–7).

Discounts

Discounts are reductions from the list price that a seller gives a buyer as a reward for some activity of the buyer that is favorable to the seller. Four kinds of discounts are especially important in marketing strategy: (1) quantity, (2) seasonal, (3) trade (functional), and (4) cash.[21]

Quantity Discounts To encourage customers to buy larger quantities of a product, firms at all levels in the marketing channel offer **quantity discounts**, which are reductions in unit costs for a larger order. For example, a photocopying service such as AlphaGraphics might set a price of 10 cents a copy for 1 to 25 copies, 9 cents a copy for 26 to 100, and 8 cents a copy for 101 or more. Because the photocopying service gets more of the buyer's business and has longer production runs that reduce its order-handling costs, it is willing to pass on some of the cost savings in the form of quantity discounts to the buyer.

FIGURE 14–7

Three special adjustments to the list or quoted price include discounts, allowances, and geographical adjustments. Each can substantially change the final price.

Quantity discounts are of two general kinds: noncumulative and cumulative. *Noncumulative quantity discounts* are based on the size of an individual purchase order. They encourage large individual purchase orders, not a series of orders. This discount is used by FedEx to encourage companies to ship a large number of packages at one time. *Cumulative quantity discounts* apply to the accumulation of purchases of a product over a given time period, typically a year. Cumulative quantity discounts encourage repeat buying by a single customer to a far greater degree than do noncumulative quantity discounts.

Seasonal Discounts

To encourage buyers to stock inventory earlier than their normal demand would require, manufacturers often use *seasonal discounts*. A firm such as Toro that manufactures lawn mowers and snow throwers offers seasonal discounts to encourage wholesalers and retailers to stock up on lawn mowers in January and February and on snow throwers in July and August—five or six months before the seasonal demand by ultimate consumers. This enables Toro to smooth out seasonal manufacturing peaks and troughs, thereby contributing to more efficient production. It also rewards wholesalers and retailers for the risk they accept in assuming increased inventory carrying costs and having supplies in stock at the time they are wanted by customers.

Trade (Functional) Discounts

To reward wholesalers and retailers for marketing functions they will perform in the future, a manufacturer often gives *trade,* or *functional, discounts*. These reductions off the list or base price are offered to resellers in the marketing channel on the basis of (1) where they are in the channel and (2) the marketing activities they are expected to perform in the future.

Suppose a manufacturer quotes price in the following form: list price—$100 less 30/10/5. The first number in the percentage sequence always refers to the retail end of the channel. The last number always refers to the wholesaler or jobber closest to the manufacturer in the channel. The trade discounts are simply subtracted one at a time. This price quote shows $100 is the manufacturer's suggested retail price; 30 percent of the suggested retail price is available to the retailer to cover costs and provide a profit of $30 ($100 × 0.3 = $30); wholesalers closest to the retailer in the channel get 10 percent of their selling price ($70 × 0.1 = $7); and the final group of wholesalers in the channel (probably jobbers) that are closest to the manufacturer get 5 percent of their selling price ($63 × 0.05 = $3.15). Thus, starting with the manufacturer's suggested retail price and subtracting the three trade discounts shows that the manufacturer's selling price to the wholesaler or jobber closest to it is $59.85 (see Figure 14–8).

Traditional trade discounts have been established in various product lines such as hardware, food, and pharmaceutical items. Although the manufacturer may suggest the trade discounts shown in the example just cited, the sellers are free to alter the discount schedule depending on their competitive situation.

FIGURE 14–8

The structure of trade discounts affects the manufacturer's selling price and the margins made by resellers in a marketing channel.

Cash Discounts   To encourage retailers to pay their bills quickly, manufacturers offer them *cash discounts*. Suppose a retailer receives a bill quoted at $1,000, 2/10 net 30. This means that the bill for the product is $1,000, but the retailer can take a 2 percent discount ($1,000 × 0.02 = $20) if payment is made within 10 days and send a check for $980. If the payment cannot be made within 10 days, the total amount of $1,000 is due within 30 days. It is usually understood by the buyer that an interest charge will be added after the first 30 days of free credit.

Retailers provide cash discounts to consumers as well to eliminate the cost of credit granted to consumers. These discounts take the form of discount-for-cash policies.

Allowances

Allowances, like discounts, are reductions from list or quoted prices to buyers for performing some activity. They include trade-in and promotional allowances.

Trade-in Allowances   A new-car dealer can offer a substantial reduction in the list price of that new Toyota Camry by offering you a trade-in allowance of $1,000 for your Honda Civic. A *trade-in allowance* is a price reduction given when a used product is accepted as part of the payment on a new product. Trade-ins are an effective way to lower the price a buyer has to pay without formally reducing the list price.

Promotional Allowances   Sellers in the marketing channel can qualify for **promotional allowances** by undertaking certain advertising or selling activities to promote a product. Various types of allowances include an actual cash payment or an extra amount of "free goods" (as with a free case of Red Baron frozen cheese pizzas to a retailer for every dozen cases purchased). Frequently, a portion of these savings is passed on to the consumer by retailers.

Some companies, such as Procter & Gamble, have chosen to reduce promotional allowances for retailers by using everyday low pricing. **Everyday low pricing (EDLP)** is the practice of replacing promotional allowances with lower manufacturer list prices. EDLP promises to reduce the average price to consumers while minimizing promotional allowances that cost manufacturers billions of dollars every year. However, EDLP does not necessarily benefit supermarkets, as described in the Marketing Matters box.[22]

Geographical Adjustments

Geographical adjustments to list or quoted prices are made by manufacturers or even wholesalers to reflect the cost of transportation of the products from seller to buyer. The two general methods for quoting prices related to transportation costs are (1) FOB origin pricing and (2) uniform delivered pricing.

387

Marketing Matters

Everyday Low Prices at the Supermarket = Everyday Low Profits—Creating Customer Value at a Cost

Who wouldn't welcome low retail prices every day? The answer is supermarket chains—76 percent of U.S. grocery stores have not adopted this practice. Supermarkets prefer Hi-Lo pricing based on frequent specials where prices are temporarily lowered and then raised again. Hi-Lo pricing reflects allowances that manufacturers give supermarkets to push their products. Consider a supermarket that sells Bumble Bee white tuna. It regularly pays $1.15 for a can of Bumble Bee white tuna ($55.43 ÷ 48 = $1.15), but the allowances reduce the cost to 96 cents. A price special of 99 cents still provides a 3 cent retail markup ($0.99 retail price in ad – $0.96 cost). When the price on tuna returns to its regular level, the store's gross margin on tuna increases substantially on those cans that were bought with the allowance but not sold during the special price promotion.

Everyday low pricing (EDLP) eliminates manufacturer allowances and can reduce average retail prices by up to 10 percent. While EDLP provides lower average prices than Hi-Lo pricing, EDLP does not allow for deeply discounted price specials. EDLP can create everyday customer value and modestly increase supermarket sales—but at a cost. Already slim supermarket chain profits can slip by 18 percent with EDLP without the benefit of allowances as described earlier. Also, some argue that EDLP without price specials is boring for many grocery shoppers who welcome price specials.

EDLP has been hailed as "value pricing" by manufacturers, but supermarkets view it differently. For them, EDLP means "Everyday Low Profits!"

FOB Origin Pricing   FOB means "free on board" some vehicle at some location, which means the seller pays the cost of loading the product onto the vehicle that is used (such as a barge, railroad car, or truck). **FOB origin pricing** usually involves the seller's naming the location of this loading as the seller's factory or warehouse (such as "FOB Detroit" or "FOB factory"). The title to the goods passes to the buyer at the point of loading, so the buyer becomes responsible for picking the specific mode of transportation, for all the transportation costs, and for subsequent handling of the product. Buyers farthest from the seller face the big disadvantage of paying higher transportation costs.

Uniform Delivered Pricing   When a **uniform delivered pricing** method is used, the price the seller quotes includes all transportation costs. It is quoted in a contract as "FOB buyer's location," and the seller selects the mode of transportation, pays the freight charges, and is responsible for any damage that may occur because the seller retains title to the goods until they are delivered to the buyer. Although they go by various names, there are four kinds of delivered pricing methods: (1) single-zone pricing, (2) multiple-zone pricing, (3) FOB with freight-allowed pricing, and (4) basing-point pricing.

In *single-zone pricing,* all buyers pay the same delivered price for the products, regardless of their distance from the seller. So, although a retail store offering free delivery in a metropolitan area incurs varying transportation costs depending on a customer's location in relation to the store, all customers pay the same delivered price.

In *multiple-zone pricing,* a firm divides its selling territory into geographic areas or zones. The delivered price to all buyers within any one zone is the same, but prices across zones vary depending on the transportation cost to each particular zone and the level of competition and demand within each zone.

With *FOB with freight-allowed pricing,* also called *freight absorption pricing,* the price is quoted by the seller as "FOB plant—freight allowed." The buyer is allowed to deduct freight expenses from the list price of the goods, so the seller agrees to pay, or "absorb," the transportation costs.

Basing-point pricing involves selecting one or more geographical locations (basing point) from which the list price for products plus freight expenses are charged to the buyer. For example, a company might designate St. Louis as the basing point and charge all buyers a list price of $100 plus freight from St. Louis to their location. Basing-point pricing methods have been used in the steel, cement, and lumber industries where freight expenses are a significant part of the total cost to the buyer and products are largely undifferentiated.

Legal and Regulatory Aspects of Pricing

LO 14-4 Name the principal laws and regulations affecting specific pricing practices.

Arriving at a final price is clearly a complex process. The task is further complicated by legal and regulatory restrictions. Five pricing practices have received the most scrutiny: (1) price fixing, (2) price discrimination, (3) deceptive pricing, (4) geographical pricing, and (5) predatory pricing (see Figure 14–9).

Price Fixing   A conspiracy among firms to set prices for a product is termed **price fixing**. Price fixing is illegal per se under the Sherman Act (*per se* means in and of itself). When two or more competitors explicitly or implicitly set prices, this practice is called *horizontal price fixing.* For example, in 2000, six foreign vitamin companies pled guilty to price fixing in the human and animal vitamin industry and paid the largest fine in U.S. history, a hefty $335 million.[23]

Vertical price fixing involves controlling agreements between independent buyers and sellers (a manufacturer and a retailer) whereby sellers are required to not sell products below a minimum retail price. This practice, called *resale price maintenance,* was declared illegal per se in 1975 under provisions of the *Consumer Goods Pricing Act.* Nevertheless, this practice is not uncommon. For example, shoe supplier Nine West was charged with restricting competition by coercing retailers to adhere to its resale prices. As part of its settlement, Nine West agreed to pay $34 million.[24] Although this type of coercive price fixing is illegal per se, manufacturers and wholesalers can set

FIGURE 14–9

Several pricing practices are affected by legal and regulatory restrictions. These restrictions seek to benefit both consumers and companies.

the maximum retail price for their products provided the price agreement does not create an "unreasonable restraint of trade" or is anticompetitive.

It is important to recognize that a "manufacturer's suggested retail price," or MSRP, is not illegal per se. The issue of legality only arises when manufacturers enforce such a practice by coercion. Furthermore, there appears to be a movement toward a *"rule of reason"* in horizontal and vertical price fixing cases.[25] This rule holds that circumstances surrounding a practice must be considered before making a judgment about its legality. The rule of reason perspective is the direct opposite of the per se rule.

Price Discrimination   The Clayton Act as amended by the Robinson-Patman Act prohibits **price discrimination**—the practice of charging different prices to different buyers for goods of like grade and quality. However, not all price differences are illegal; only those that substantially lessen competition or create a monopoly are deemed unlawful. Moreover, "goods" is narrowly defined and does not include discrimination in services.

A unique feature of the Robinson-Patman Act is that it allows for price differentials to different customers under the following conditions:

1. When price differences charged to different customers do not exceed the differences in the cost of manufacture, sale, or delivery resulting from differing methods or quantities in which such goods are sold or delivered to buyers. This condition is called the *cost justification defense*.
2. When price differences result from changing market conditions, avoiding obsolescence of seasonal merchandise, including perishables, or closing out sales.
3. When price differences are quoted to selected buyers in good faith to meet competitors' prices and are not intended to injure competition. This condition is called the *meet-the-competition defense*.

Buy one, get one free promotions are common. However, these promotions can be viewed as deceptive by the Federal Trade Commission. Read the text to learn when these promotions may be deceptive.

© DBurke/Alamy

The Robinson-Patman Act also covers promotional allowances. To legally offer promotional allowances to buyers, the seller must do so on a proportionally equal basis to all buyers distributing the seller's products. In general, the rule of reason applies frequently in price discrimination disputes and is often applied to cases involving firms that use dynamic pricing policies.

Deceptive Pricing   Price deals that mislead consumers fall into the category of *deceptive pricing*. Deceptive pricing is outlawed by the Federal Trade Commission Act. The FTC monitors such practices and has published a regulation titled "Guides against Deceptive Pricing" to help businesspeople avoid a charge of deception. The five most common deceptive pricing practices are described in Figure 14–10. As you read about these practices it should be clear that laws cannot be passed and enforced to protect consumers and competitors against all of these practices. So it is essential to rely on the ethical standards of those making and publicizing pricing decisions.

Geographical Pricing   FOB origin pricing is legal, as are FOB freight-allowed pricing practices, providing no conspiracy to set prices exists. Basing-point pricing can be viewed as illegal under the Robinson-Patman Act and the Federal Trade Commission Act if there is clear-cut evidence of a conspiracy to set prices. In general, geographical pricing practices have been immune from legal and regulatory restrictions, except in those instances in which a conspiracy to lessen competition exists under the Sherman Act or price discrimination exists under the Robinson-Patman Act.

DECEPTIVE PRICING PRACTICE	DESCRIPTION
Bait and switch	This deceptive practice exists when a firm offers a very low price on a product (the bait) to attract customers to a store. Once in the store, the customer is persuaded to purchase a higher priced item (the switch) using a variety of tricks, including (1) downgrading the promoted item, (2) not having the item in stock, or (3) refusing to take orders for the item.
Bargains conditional on other purchases	This practice may exist when a buyer is offered "1-Cent Sales," "Buy 1, Get 1 Free," and "Get 2 for the Price of 1." Such pricing is legal only if the first items are sold at the regular price, not a price inflated for the offer. Substituting lower quality items on either the first or second purchase is also considered deceptive.
Comparable value comparisons	Advertising such as "Retail Value $100.00, Our Price $85.00" is deceptive if a verified and substantial number of stores in the market area do not price the item at $100.
Comparisons with suggested prices	A claim that a price is below a manufacturer's suggested or list price may be deceptive if few or no sales occur at that price in a retailer's market area.
Former price comparisons	When a seller represents a price as reduced, the item must have been offered in good faith at a higher price for a substantial previous period. Setting a high price for the purpose of establishing a reference for a price reduction is considered deceptive.

FIGURE 14–10

Five most common deceptive pricing practices used by businesses. Have you ever witnessed or experienced one or more of these practices?

Predatory Pricing   **Predatory pricing** is the practice of charging a very low price for a product with the intent of driving competitors out of business. Once competitors have been driven out, the firm raises its prices. This practice is illegal under the Sherman Act and the Federal Trade Commission Act. Proving the practice of predatory pricing is difficult and expensive, because it must be shown that the predator explicitly attempted to destroy a competitor and the predatory price was below the defendant's average cost.

391

learning review

14-6.   Why would a seller choose a dynamic pricing policy over a fixed-price policy?

14-7.   If a firm wished to encourage repeat purchases by a buyer throughout a year, would a cumulative or a noncumulative quantity discount be a better strategy?

14-8.   Which pricing practices are covered by the Sherman Act?

LEARNING OBJECTIVES REVIEW

LO 14-1 *Describe how to establish the "approximate price level" using demand-oriented, cost-oriented, profit-oriented, and competition-oriented approaches.*
Demand, cost, profit, and competition influence the initial consideration of the approximate price level for a product or service. Demand-oriented pricing approaches stress consumer demand and revenue implications of pricing and include eight types: skimming, penetration, prestige, price

lining, odd-even, target, bundle, and yield management. Cost-oriented pricing approaches emphasize the cost aspects of pricing and include three types: standard markup, cost-plus, and experience curve pricing. Profit-oriented pricing approaches focus on a balance between revenues and costs to set a price and include three types: target profit, target return-on-sales, and target return-on-investment pricing. And finally, competition-oriented pricing approaches stress what competitors or the market-place are doing and include three types: customary; above-, at-, or below-market; and loss-leader pricing. Although these approaches are described separately, some of them overlap, and an effective marketing manager will consider several in searching for an approximate price level.

LO 14-2 *Recognize the major factors considered in deriving a final list or quoted price from the approximate price level.*
Given an approximate price level for a product or service, a manager sets a list or quoted price by considering three additional factors. First, a manager must decide whether to follow a fixed-price versus a dynamic pricing policy. Second, the manager should consider the effects of the proposed price on the company, customer, and competitors. Finally, consideration should be given to balancing incremental costs and revenues, particularly when price and cost changes are planned.

LO 14-3 *Identify the adjustments made to the approximate price level on the basis of discounts, allowances, and geography.*
Numerous adjustments can be made to the approximate price level. Discounts are reductions from the list or quoted price that a seller gives a buyer as a reward for some activ-ity of the buyer that is favorable to the seller. These include quantity, seasonal, trade (functional), and cash discounts. Allowances offered to buyers also reduce list or quoted prices. Trade-in allowances and promotional allowances are most common. Finally, geographical adjustments are made to list or quoted prices to reflect transportation costs from sellers to buyers. The two general methods for quoting prices related to transportation costs are FOB origin pricing and uniform delivered pricing.

LO 14-4 *Name the principal laws and regulations affecting specific pricing practices.*
There are four principal laws that affect six major pricing practices. The Sherman Act specifically prohibits horizontal price fixing and predatory pricing. The Consumer Goods Pricing Act makes it illegal for companies to engage in verti-cal price fixing (also called resale price maintenance agree-ments). The Federal Trade Commission Act outlaws deceptive pricing. Provisions in this act also address aspects of preda-tory pricing and geographical pricing. Finally, the Robinson-Patman Act prohibits price discrimination for goods of like grade and quality, covers the use of promotional allowances, and addresses certain aspects of geographical pricing.

LEARNING REVIEW ANSWERS

14-1 **In pricing a new product, what circumstances might sup-port skimming or penetration pricing?**
Answer: Skimming pricing is an effective strategy when: (1) the firm may want to recoup the initial R&D and promotion costs in developing and promoting the product; (2) enough prospective customers are willing to buy the product immediately at the high initial price to make these sales profitable because they are not very price sensitive; (3) the high initial price will not attract competitors; (4) lowering the price has only a minor effect on increasing the sales volume and reducing the unit costs; and (5) customers interpret the high price as signifying high quality. These conditions are most likely to exist when the new product is protected by patents or copyrights or its uniqueness is under-stood and valued by consumers. Penetration pricing is an effec-tive strategy when: (1) used after a skimming strategy to appeal to a broader segment of the population and increase market share; (2) many segments of the market are price sensitive; (3) a low initial price discourages competitors from entering the mar-ket; (4) unit production and marketing costs fall dramatically as production volumes increase; (5) a firm wants to maintain the initial price for a time to gain profit lost from its low introduc-tory level; and (6) a firm wants to lower the price further, count-ing on the new volume to generate the necessary profit.

14-2 **What is odd-even pricing?**
Answer: Odd-even pricing involves setting prices a few dollars or cents under an even number. Psychologically, a $499.99 price feels lower than $500.00, even though the difference is just 1 cent.

14-3 **What is standard markup pricing?**
Answer: Standard markup pricing entails adding a fixed per-centage to the cost of all items in a specific product class. The price varies based on the type of product and the retail store within which it is sold.

14-4 **What profit-based pricing approach should a manager use if he or she wants to reflect the percentage of the firm's resources used in obtaining the profit?**
Answer: target return-on-investment pricing

14-5 **What is the purpose of loss-leader pricing when used by a retail firm?**
Answer: Loss-leader pricing involves deliberately selling a product below its customary price not to increase sales but to attract customers in hopes they will buy other products as well, such as discretionary items with large markups.

14-6 **Why would a seller choose a dynamic pricing policy over a fixed-price policy?**
Answer: A dynamic pricing policy sets different prices for products and services in real time in response to supply and demand conditions. Sellers have considerable discretion in setting the final price in light of demand, cost, and competi-tive factors. Moreover, sellers can continually adjust prices due to the implementation of sophisticated information technology that gives them the ability to customize a price on the basis of customer purchasing patterns, product pref-erences, and price sensitivity. A fixed-price policy sets one price for all buyers of a product or service. Consumers can choose to buy or not buy, but there is no variation in the price from the seller.

14-7 **If a firm wished to encourage repeat purchases by a buyer throughout a year, would a cumulative or a noncumulative quantity discount be a better strategy?**
Answer: Cumulative quantity discounts apply to the accumula-tion of purchases of a product over a given time period (typically a year) and encourage repeat buying by a single customer to a far greater degree than do noncumulative quantity discounts.

14-8 **Which pricing practices are covered by the Sherman Act?**
Answer: The Sherman Act prohibits (1) horizontal price fixing, which is when two or more competitors ex-plicitly or implicitly set prices and (2) predatory pricing, which is the practice of charging a very low price for a product with the intent of driving competitors out of busi-ness. Once competitors have been driven out, the firm raises its prices.

FOCUSING ON KEY TERMS

above-, at-, or below-market pricing p. 379
basing-point pricing p. 389
bundle pricing p. 375
cost-plus pricing p. 376
customary pricing p. 379
dynamic pricing policy p. 382
everyday low pricing (EDLP) p. 387
experience curve pricing p. 376
fixed-price policy p. 381
FOB origin pricing p. 388

loss-leader pricing p. 380
odd-even pricing p. 374
penetration pricing p. 373
predatory pricing p. 391
prestige pricing p. 373
price discrimination p. 390
price fixing p. 389
price lining p. 374
price war p. 384
product-line pricing p. 382
promotional allowances p. 387

quantity discounts p. 385
skimming pricing p. 372
standard markup pricing p. 375
target pricing p. 375
target profit pricing p. 377
target return-on-investment pricing p. 378
target return-on-sales pricing p. 377
uniform delivered pricing p. 388
yield management pricing p. 375

APPLYING MARKETING KNOWLEDGE

1   Under what conditions would a digital camera manufacturer adopt a skimming price approach for a new product? A penetration approach?

2   What are some similarities and differences between skimming pricing, prestige pricing, and above-market pricing?

3   A producer of microwave ovens has adopted an experience curve pricing approach for its new model. The firm believes it can reduce the cost of producing the model by 20 percent each time volume doubles. The cost to produce the first unit was $1,000. What would be the approximate cost of the 4,096th unit?

4   The Hesper Corporation is a leading manufacturer of high-quality upholstered sofas. Current plans call for an increase of $600,000 in the advertising budget. If the firm sells its sofas for an average price of $850 and the unit variable costs are $550, then what dollar sales increase will be necessary to cover the additional advertising?

5   Suppose executives estimate that the unit variable cost for their DVD recorder is $100, the fixed cost related to the product is $10 million annually, and the target volume for next year is 100,000 recorders. What sales price will be necessary to achieve a target profit of $1 million?

6   A manufacturer of motor oil has a trade discount policy whereby the manufacturer's suggested retail price is $30 per case with the terms of 40/20/10. The manufacturer sells its products through jobbers, who sell to wholesalers, who sell to gasoline stations. What will the manufacturer's sale price be?

7   Suppose a manufacturer of exercise equipment sets a suggested price to the consumer of $395 for a particular piece of equipment to be competitive with similar equipment. The manufacturer sells its equipment to a sporting goods wholesaler who receives 25 percent of the selling price and a retailer who receives 50 percent of the selling price. What demand-oriented pricing approach is being used, and at what price will the manufacturer sell the equipment to the wholesaler?

8   Is there any truth in the statement, "Geographical pricing schemes will always be unfair to some buyers"? Why or why not?

393

BUILDING YOUR MARKETING PLAN

To arrive at the final price(s) for your offering(s):

1   In Chapter 13, you considered your customers and competitors and set three possible prices. Now, modify those three prices in light of (a) pricing considerations for demand-, cost-, profit-, and competition-oriented approaches described in this chapter and (b) possibilities for discounts, allowances, and geographic adjustments.

2   Do a break-even analysis for each of these three new prices.

3   Choose the final price(s).

VIDEO CASE 14   Carmex (B): Setting the Price of the Number One Lip Balm

Video 14-3
Carmex (B) Video Case
kerin.tv/13e/v14-3

"Carmex is dedicated to providing consumers with superior lip balm formulas—that heal, sooth and protect—while ensuring lips remain healthy and hydrated" exclaims Paul Woelbing, president of Carma Laboratories, Inc.

It's an ambitious mission, but the company has been extraordinarily successful with its 75-year-old product. Woelbing and his management team at Carma Laboratories can attribute their success to a strong brand, a loyal customer base, a growing product line, financial strength, and an exceptional talent for setting prices that achieve company objectives and still provide value to customers. Even during the recession and periods of slow growth the company has been successful. "In a rough economy, shopping habits change," Woelbing says. "People buy smaller quantities more frequently, but they still need personal care products."

THE COMPANY

Carmex was created by Paul's grandfather, Alfred Woelbing, in his kitchen in Wauwatosa, Wisconsin, in 1937. Alfred had an entrepreneurial spirit and experimented with ingredients such as camphor, menthol, phenol, lanolin, salicylic acid, and cocoa seed butter to make the new product. The name didn't have any meaning other than Alfred liked the sound of "Carma" and "ex" was a popular suffix for many brands at the time. He packaged the balm in small glass jars and sold the product for 25 cents from the trunk of his car by making personal sales calls to pharmacies in Wisconsin, Illinois, and Indiana. From the beginning, price and value were important to the product's success. If pharmacies weren't initially interested in Carmex, Alfred would leave a dozen jars for free. The samples would sell quickly and soon the pharmacies would place orders for more!

As the company grew, Alfred's son, Don, joined the business and helped add new products to the company's offerings. For example, in the 1980s Carmex made its first significant packaging change by also offering the balm in squeezable tubes. In the 1990s Carmex became available in stick form, which had been used by two of Carma's major competitors—

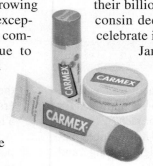

© McGraw-Hill Education/ Editorial Image, LLC, photographer

© McGraw-Hill Education/ Mark Dierker, photographer

ChapStick and Blistex. In the 2000s Carmex became available in mint, cherry, and strawberry flavors (see Chapter 8 for a description of the research techniques used to identify new flavors). The company also expanded into larger manufacturing facilities, added a new distribution center, and hired its first marketing experts.

Today, the company is led by Alfred's grandsons, Paul and Eric Woelbing, who continue to manage the company to new levels of success. They appeared on *The Oprah Winfrey Show* to announce the sale of their billionth jar of Carmex. The governor of Wisconsin declared a Carmex commemoration day to celebrate its 75th anniversary. NBA all-star LeBron James became a promotional partner. In addition, *Pharmacy Times* magazine recently named Carmex the number one pharmacist-recommended brand of lip balm for the 15th consecutive year. "We are honored to receive this unprecedented acknowledgement," said Woelbing.

Industry observers estimate that Carma Labs holds approximately 10 percent of the lip balm market. The company distributes its products through major drug, food, and mass merchant retailers, convenience stores, and online in more than 25 countries around the world. The company's most recent products—Carmex Healing Cream and Carmex Hydrating Lotion—represent a significant step from lip care to skin care. The expanded product line, multichannel distribution, growing volume, international trade, and direct competition make pricing decisions even more important today than when Alfred started the business many years ago.

SETTING PRICES OF CARMEX PRODUCTS

"There are many factors that go into what results in the retail price in the store," explains Kirk Hodgdon of Bolin Marketing. As one of the marketing experts who helps Carma Labs with advertising, marketing research, and pricing decisions, Hodgdon uses information about consumer demand, production and material costs, profit goals, and competition to help Woelbing and Carmex retailers arrive at specific prices. The many factors often overlap and lead to different prices for different products, channels, and target markets. "It's a challenge!" says Hodgdon.

Consumers' tastes and preferences, for example, influence the price of Carmex products. Bolin director of marketing, Alisa Allen, explains: "Consumers will tell you that they love Carmex because it's a great value. That doesn't necessarily mean that it's the absolute lowest price. It means that it does so much; they pay a dollar and they get all kinds of benefits from the product above and beyond what they would expect." A single jar of original formula Carmex may sell for $0.99 at mass retailers such as Walmart and Target, and between $1.59 and $1.79 in drug and food retailers such as Walgreens and Kroger. These prices are a good indication of how important it is to understand consumers when setting prices. "There are magic price points for consumers," says Allen, "Any time you can drop a penny off, the consumer responds to that price."

Carmex has also introduced a premium lip balm product, Carmex Moisture Plus, at a retail price between $2.49 and $2.99. Moisture Plus is a lip balm that is packaged in a sleek silver tube, offers a slant tip like lipstick, and is targeted toward women. The formula offers women a satin gloss shine and includes vitamin E and aloe for richer moisturization. The upscale package and additional product benefits help Carmex Moisture Plus command a higher price than the traditional Carmex jar and tube.

The cost of the ingredients that make up the Carmex lip balm formulas, the packaging, the manufacturing equipment, and the staffing are also factored into the price of the products. Volumes are a key driver of the cost of packaging and ingredients. For example, Carmex purchases up to 12 million yellow tubes each year for the traditional product, and 2 million sticks each year for the newer Moisture Plus product. The difference in quantities leads to a lower price for the traditional yellow tubes. Similarly, ingredient suppliers, label suppliers, and box suppliers all provide discounts for larger quantities. It is also more efficient for Carmex's manufacturing facility to make a large batch of traditional formula than it is to make a small batch of Moisture Plus. Carmex has also reduced its costs with efforts such as its new environmentally friendly Carmex jar which holds the same amount of lip balm but uses 20 percent less plastic, eliminating 35 tons of raw material costs and the related shipping costs!

Source: Carma Labs Inc.

Carmex also considers retailer margins when it sets it prices. According to Allen, "We typically sell our product to two types of retailers." There are everyday low pricing (EDLP) retailers such as Walmart, and high-low retailers such as Walgreens. EDLP retailers offer consumers the lowest price every day without discounting through promotions. High-low retailers charge consumers a higher price, but they occasionally discount the product through special promotions which Carmex often supports with "marketing discretionary funds." Carmex typically offers its products at different prices to EDLP and high-low retailers to allow each retailer to achieve its profit margin goals and to account for Carmex's promotion expenditures. When the additional expenditures are considered, however, the cost to both types of retailer is similar.

Finally, Carmex considers competitors' prices when setting its prices. Burt's Bees, ChapStick, Blistex, and many other brands offer lip balm products and consumers often compare their prices to the price of Carmex. "We have found through research that it is extremely important that the price gap is not too great," explains Allen. "If that gap becomes too wide consumers will leave the Carmex brand and purchase a competitor's product." When Carmex was preparing to launch its premium Moisture Plus product it conducted a thorough analysis of similar products to ensure that Moisture Plus was in an acceptable price range.

CARMEX IN THE FUTURE

The original, and now legendary, Carmex formula and packaging will continue into the future with occasional changes to its pricing practices. New products, however, are on the horizon and likely to challenge the perceptions of the traditional products and prices in the Carmex line. Carmex Moisture Plus products, for example, will be offered in limited edition designs that ask consumers "Which personality are you?" Paul Woelbing explains the new approach:

Lip care is an important component of a daily beauty regimen and consumers need a product they can rely on that protects and serves as an important foundation. The goal of the new Carmex Moisture Plus line is to offer our consumers a hard-working lip balm line that represent and reflects their unique style.

Some of the new styles include: *Chic* in houndstooth, *Fab* in a groovy retro look, *Adventurous* in a leopard print, *Whimsical* in an art deco design.

"We are so excited about the future of Carmex," says Hodgdon. "We are planning new products, we have new plans for retailers, and the future is nothing but bright!"[26]

Questions

1 Which of the four approaches to setting a price does Carmex use for its products? Should one approach be used exclusively?

2 Why do many Carmex product prices end in 9? What type of pricing is this called? What should happen to demand when this approach is used?

3 Should cost be a factor in Carmex's prices? What do you think is a reasonable markup for Carmex and for its retailers?

4 What is the difference between an EDLP retailer and a high-low retailer? Why does Carmex charge them different prices?

5 Conduct an online search of lip balm products and compare the price of a Carmex product with three similar products from competitors. How do you think the competitors are setting their prices?

Chapter Notes

1. This example is based on information and data contained in "What Amazon's E-book Numbers Are and Aren't Telling You," *latimes.com*, August 4, 2014; "HarperCollins and Amazon in Multiyear Publishing Deal," *nytimes.com*, April 13, 2015; and Lin Hao and Ming Fan, "An Analysis of Pricing Models in the Electronic Book Market," *MIS Quarterly* 38, no. 4 (2014), pp. 1017–32; www.vizio.com, downloaded March 10, 2013.

2. "Amazon Fights the iPad with 'Fire,'" *The Wall Street Journal*, September 29, 2011, pp. B1, 10.

3. The conditions favoring skimming versus penetration pricing are described in Kent B. Monroe, *Pricing: Making Profitable Decisions*, 3rd ed. (Burr Ridge, IL: McGraw-Hill/Irwin, 2003).

4. Jean-Noel Kapferer, *The New Strategic Brand Management: Advanced Insights and Strategic Thinking*, 5th ed. (London: Kogan Page Ltd, 2012).

5. Stacy Meichtry, "What Your Time Is Really Worth," *The Wall Street Journal*, April 7–8, 2007, pp. P1, P4.

6. "Premium AA Alkaline Batteries," *Consumer Reports*, March 21, 2002, p. 54; Kemp Powers, "Assault and Batteries," *Forbes*, September 4, 2000, pp. 54, 56; and "Razor Burn at Gillette," *BusinessWeek*, June 18, 2001, p. 37.

7. Michael Levy and Barton A. Weitz, *Retailing Management*, 7th ed. (Burr Ridge, IL: McGraw-Hill/Irwin, 2010), pp. 501–2.

8. "The Psychological Difference Between $12.00 and $11.67," www.theatlantic.com, January 30, 2015. For further reading on odd-even pricing, see Mark Stiving and Russell S. Winer, "An Empirical Analysis of Price Endings with Scanner Data," *Journal of Consumer Research*, June 1997, pp. 57–67; and Robert M. Schindler, "Patterns of Rightmost Digits Used in Advertised Prices: Implications for Nine-Ending Effects," *Journal of Consumer Research*, September 1997, pp. 192–201.

9. Thomas T. Nagle, John E. Hogan, and Joseph Zate, *The Strategy and Tactics of Pricing*, 5th ed. (Englewood Cliffs, NJ: Prentice Hall, 2011), pp. 243–49.

10. Scott McCartney, "You Paid What for That Flight?" *The Wall Street Journal*, August 26, 2010, pp. D1, D2.

11. "What Popcorn Prices Mean for Movies," *Advertising Age*, May 19, 2008, p. 4.

12. Ann Zimmerman, "Can Electronics Stores Survive?" *The Wall Street Journal*, August 31, 2012, pp. B1, B2.

13. "In Lean Times, Big Companies Make a Grab for Market Share," *The Wall Street Journal*, September 5, 2003, pp. A1, A6.

14. "A New Beverage Attitude," *Convenience Store/Petroleum News*, May 2010, pp. 110–12

15. "Dell Fine-Tunes Its PC Pricing to Gain an Edge in Slow Market," *The Wall Street Journal*, June 8, 2001, pp. A1, A8.

16. Bill Saporito, "This Offer Won't Last," *Time*, January 21, 2013, p. 56; "Don't Like This Price? Wait a Minute," *The Wall Street Journal*, September 5, 2012, pp. A1, A2; and "Online Retailers Vary Prices Based on a User's Location," *The Wall Street Journal*, December 24, 2012, pp. A1, A10.

17. "Pricing the Surge," www.economist.com, May 29, 2014; "The Price Is Right, or Uber Will Raise It," www.bloombergview.com, May 19, 2015.

18. Monroe, *Pricing*, pp. 396–97.

19. Jagmohan S. Raju, Raj Sethuraman, and Sanjay K. Dhar, "National Brand-Store Brand Price Differential and Store Brand Market Share," *Pricing Strategy & Practice* 3, no. 2 (1995), pp. 17–24; and Akshay R. Rao, "The Quality of Price as a Quality Cue," *Journal of Marketing Research*, November 2005, pp. 401–5.

20. Tim J. Smith, *Pricing Strategy* (Mason, OH: South-West Cengage Learning 2012). Also see Kevin P. Coyne and John Horn, "Predicting Your Competitor's Reaction," *Harvard Business Review*, April 2009, pp. 90–97.

21. Monroe, *Pricing*, Chapters 16 and 17.

22. "Everyday Low Prices in Spotlight," *insiderrretail.com*, April 29, 2015. Also see Barbara E. Kahn and Leigh McAlister, *The Grocery Revolution: The New Focus on the Consumer* (Reading, MA: Addison-Wesley Educational Publishers, 1996).

23. "Six Vitamin Firms Agree to Settle Price-Fixing Suit," *The Wall Street Journal*, October 11, 2000, p. B10.

24. "Price Fixing," *USA Today*, March 7, 2000, p. C1.

25. Ronald A. Cass, "When Price 'Fixing' Makes Sense," *The Wall Street Journal*, March 24–25, 2007, p. A10; and Joseph Pereira, "Discounters, Monitors Face Battle on Minimum Pricing," *The Wall Street Journal*, December 4, 2008, pp. A1, A8.

26. Carmex (B): This case was written by Steven Hartley and Alisa Allen. Sources: Kristen Scheuing, "The Man Behind Carmex," *Wisconsin Trails*, March/April 2011; "Carmex and Carma Laboratories: *Pharmacy Times* Names Carmex Number One Recommended Lip Balm," *IndiaPharma News*, June 21, 2013; "New Lip Balm Offers Sun Protection While Drenching Lips in Moisture," *Postmedia Breaking News*, May 21, 2013; Carma Laboratories website, www.mycarmex.com, accessed September 2, 2013; and interviews with Bolin Media personnel.

APPENDIX B

FINANCIAL ASPECTS OF MARKETING

Basic concepts from accounting and finance provide valuable tools for marketing executives. This appendix describes an actual company's use of accounting and financial concepts and illustrates how they assist the owner in making marketing decisions.

THE CAPLOW COMPANY

An accomplished artist and calligrapher, Jane Westerlund decided to apply some of her experience to the picture framing business in Minneapolis. She bought an existing retail frame store, The Caplow Company, from a friend who owned the business and wanted to retire. She avoided the do-it-yourself end of the framing business and chose three kinds of business activities: (1) cutting the frame, mats, and glass for customers who brought in their own pictures or prints to be framed; (2) selling prints and posters that she had purchased from wholesalers; and (3) restoring high-quality frames and paintings.

To understand how accounting, finance, and marketing relate to each other, let's analyze (1) the operating statement for her frame shop, (2) some general ratios of interest that are derived from the operating statement, and (3) some ratios that pertain specifically to her pricing decisions.

The Operating Statement

The *operating statement* (also called an *income statement* or *profit-and-loss statement*) summarizes the profitability of a business firm for a specific time period, usually a month, quarter, or year. The title of the operating statement for The Caplow Company shows it is for a one-year period (Figure B–1). The purpose of an operating statement is to show the profit of the firm and the revenues and expenses that led to that profit. This information tells the owner or manager what has happened in the past and suggests actions to improve future profitability.

The left side of Figure B–1 shows that there are three key elements to all operating statements: (1) sales of the firm's products and services, (2) costs incurred in making and selling these products and services, and (3) profit or loss, which is the difference between sales and costs.

Sales Elements   The sales elements of Figure B–1 have four terms that need explanation:

- *Gross sales* represent the total amount billed to customers. Dissatisfied customers or errors may reduce the gross sales through returns or allowances.
- *Returns* occur when a customer gives the item purchased back to the seller, who either refunds the purchase price or allows the customer a credit on subsequent purchases. In any event, the seller now owns the item again.
- *Allowances* are given when a customer is dissatisfied with the item purchased and the seller reduces the original purchase price. Unlike returns, in the case of allowances the buyer owns the item.
- *Net sales* are simply gross sales minus returns and allowances.

The operating statement for The Caplow Company shows that:

Gross sales	$80,500
Less: Returns and allowances	500
Net sales	$80,000

The low level of returns and allowances shows the shop generally has done a good job in satisfying customers, which is essential in building the repeat business necessary for success.

397

THE CAPLOW COMPANY

Operating Statement

For the Year Ending December 31, 2015

Sales	Gross sales			$80,500
	Less: Returns and allowances			500
	Net sales			$80,000
Costs	Cost of goods sold:			
	Beginning inventory at cost		$ 6,000	
	Purchases at billed cost	$21,000		
	Less: Purchase discounts	300		
	Purchases at net cost	20,700		
	Plus: freight-in	100		
	Net cost of delivered purchases		20,800	
	Direct labor (framing)		14,200	
	Cost of goods available for sale		41,000	
	Less: Ending inventory at cost		5,000	
	Cost of goods sold			36,000
	Gross margin (gross profit)			$44,000
	Expenses:			
	Selling expenses:			
	Sales salaries	2,000		
	Advertising expense	3,000		
	Total selling expense		5,000	
	Administrative expenses:			
	Owner's salary	18,000		
	Bookkeeper's salary	1,200		
	Office supplies	300		
	Total administrative expense		19,500	
	General expenses:			
	Depreciation expense	1,000		
	Interest expense	500		
	Rent expense	2,100		
	Utility expenses (heat, electricity)	3,000		
	Repairs and maintenance	2,300		
	Insurance	2,000		
	Social security taxes	2,200		
	Total general expense		13,100	
	Total expenses			37,600
Profit or loss	Profit before taxes			$ 6,400

Cost Elements   The *cost of goods sold (COGS)* is the total cost of the products sold during the period. This item varies according to the kind of business. A retail store purchases finished products and resells them to customers without reworking them in any way. In contrast, a manufacturing firm combines raw and semifinished materials and parts, uses labor and overhead to rework these into finished products, and then sells them to customers. All these activities are reflected in the cost of goods sold item on a manufacturer's operating statement. Note that The Caplow Company has features of both a pure retailer (prints and posters it buys that are resold without alteration) and a pure manufacturer (assembling the raw materials of molding, matting, and glass to form a completed frame).

Some terms that relate to cost of goods sold need clarification:

- *Inventory* is the physical material that is purchased from suppliers, may or may not be reworked, and is available for sale to customers. In the frame shop, inventory includes molding, matting, glass, prints, and posters.
- *Purchase discounts* are reductions in the original billed price for reasons such as prompt payment of the bill or the quantity bought.
- *Direct labor* is the cost of the labor used in producing the finished product. For Caplow, this is the cost of producing the completed frames from the molding, matting, and glass.
- *Gross margin (gross profit)* is the money remaining to manage the business, sell the products or services, and provide some profit. Gross margin is net sales minus cost of goods sold.

The two right-hand columns in Figure B–1 between "Net sales" and "Gross margin" calculate the cost of goods sold:

Net sales		$80,000
Cost of goods sold		
Beginning inventory at cost	$ 6,000	
Net cost of delivered purchases	20,800	
Direct labor (framing)	14,200	
Cost of goods available for sale	41,000	
Less: Ending inventory at cost	5,000	
Cost of goods sold		36,000
Gross margin (gross profit)		$44,000

Jane Westerlund (left) and an assistant assess the restoration of a gold frame for regilding.
© Bill Rudelius

This section considers the beginning and ending inventories, the net cost of purchases delivered during the year, and the cost of the direct labor going into making the frames. Subtracting the $36,000 cost of goods sold from the $80,000 net sales gives the $44,000 gross margin.

Three major categories of expenses are shown in Figure B–1 below the gross margin:

- *Selling expenses* are the costs of selling the product or service produced by the firm. For The Caplow Company there are two such selling expenses: sales salaries of part-time employees waiting on customers and the advertising expense of simple newspaper ads and direct-mail ads sent to customers.
- *Administrative expenses* are the costs of managing the business, which for The Caplow Company include three expenses: the owner's salary, a part-time bookkeeper's salary, and office supplies expense.
- *General expenses* are miscellaneous costs not covered elsewhere; for the frame shop these include seven items: depreciation expense (on equipment), interest expense, rent expense, utility expenses, repairs and maintenance expense, insurance expense, and social security taxes.

As shown in Figure B–1, selling, administrative, and general expenses total $37,600 for The Caplow Company.

Profit Element   What the company has earned, the *profit before taxes,* is found by subtracting cost of goods sold and expenses from net sales. For The Caplow Company, Figure B–1 shows that profit before taxes is $6,400.

General Operating Ratios to Analyze Operations

Looking only at the elements of Caplow's operating statement that extend to the right-hand column highlights the firm's performance on some important dimensions. Using operating ratios such as *expense-to-sales ratios* for expressing basic expense or profit elements as a percentage of net sales gives further insights:

Element in Operating Statement	Dollar Value	Percentage of Net Sales
Gross sales	$80,500	
Less: Returns and allowances	500	
Net sales	80,000	100%
Less: Cost of goods sold	36,000	45
Gross margin	44,000	55
Less: Total expenses	37,600	47
Profit (or loss) before taxes	$ 6,400	8%

Westerlund can use this information to compare her firm's performance from one time period to the next. To do so, it is especially important that she keep the same definitions for each element of her operating statement, also a significant factor in using the electronic spreadsheets discussed in Chapter 14. Performance comparisons between periods will be more difficult if she changes definitions for the accounting elements in the operating statement.

Westerlund can use either the dollar values or the operating ratios (the value of the element of the operating statement divided by net sales) to analyze the firm's performance. However, the operating ratios are more valuable than the dollar values for two reasons: (1) the simplicity of working with percentages rather than dollars and (2) the availability of operating ratios of typical firms in the same industry, which are published by Dun & Bradstreet and trade associations. Thus, Westerlund can compare her firm's performance not only with that of *other* frame shops but also with that of *small* frame shops that have annual net sales, for example, under $100,000. In this way, she can identify where her operations are better or worse than other similar firms. For example, if trade association data showed a typical frame shop of her size had a ratio of cost of goods sold to net sales of 37 percent, compared with her 45 percent, she might consider steps to reduce this cost through purchase discounts, reducing inbound freight charges, finding lower-cost suppliers, and so on.

Ratios to Use in Setting and Evaluating Price

Using The Caplow Company as an example, we can study four ratios that relate closely to setting a price: (1) markup, (2) markdown, (3) stockturns, and (4) return on investment. These terms are defined in Figure B–2 and explained below.

Markup   Both *markup* and gross margin refer to the amount added to the cost of goods sold to arrive at the selling price, and they may be expressed in either dollar or percentage terms. However, the term *markup* is more commonly used in setting retail prices. Suppose the average price Westerlund charges for a framed picture is $80. Then in terms of the first two definitions in Figure B–2 and the earlier information from the operating statement,

Element of Price	Dollar Value
Selling price	$80
Cost of goods sold	$36
Markup (or gross margin)	$44

FIGURE B–2

How to calculate selling price, markups, markdown, stockturn rate, and return on investment.

Name of Financial Element or Ratio	What It Measures	Equation
Selling price ($)	Price customer sees	Cost of goods sold (COGS) + Markup
Markup ($)	Dollars added to COGS to arrive at selling price	Selling price − COGS
Markup on selling price (%)	Relates markup to selling price	$\dfrac{\text{Markup}}{\text{Selling price}} \times 100 = \dfrac{\text{Selling price} - \text{COGS}}{\text{Selling price}} \times 100$
Markup on cost (%)	Relates markup to cost	$\dfrac{\text{Markup}}{\text{COGS}} \times 100 = \dfrac{\text{Selling price} - \text{COGS}}{\text{Selling price}} \times 100$
Markdown (%)	Ability of firm to sell its products at initial selling price	$\dfrac{\text{Markdowns}}{\text{Net sales}} \times 100$
Stockturn rate	Ability of firm to move its inventory quickly	$\dfrac{\text{COGS}}{\text{Average inventory at cost}}$ or $\dfrac{\text{Net sales}}{\text{Average inventory at selling price}}$
Return on investment (%)	Profit performance of firm compared with money invested in it	$\dfrac{\text{Net income}}{\text{Investment}} \times 100$

The third definition in Figure B–2 gives the percentage markup on selling price:

$$\text{Markup on selling price } (\%) = \frac{\text{Markup}}{\text{Selling price}} \times 100$$

$$= \frac{44}{80} \times 100 = 55\%$$

And the percentage markup on cost is obtained as follows:

$$\text{Markup on cost } (\%) = \frac{\text{Markup}}{\text{Cost of goods sold}} \times 100$$

$$= \frac{44}{36} \times 100 = 122.2\%$$

Inexperienced retail clerks sometimes fail to distinguish between the two definitions of markup, which (as the preceding calculations show) can represent a tremendous difference, so it is essential to know whether the base is cost or selling price. Marketers generally use selling price as the base for talking about markups unless they specifically state that they are using cost as a base.

Retailers and wholesalers that rely heavily on markup pricing (discussed in Chapter 14) often use standardized tables that convert markup on selling price to markup on cost, and vice versa. The two equations below show how to convert one to the other:

$$\text{Markup on selling price } (\%) = \frac{\text{Markup on cost } (\%)}{100\% + \text{Markup on cost } (\%)} \times 100$$

$$\text{Markup on cost } (\%) = \frac{\text{Markup on selling price } (\%)}{100\% - \text{Markup on selling price } (\%)}$$

Using the data from The Caplow Company gives:

$$\text{Markup on selling price } (\%) = \frac{\text{Markup on cost } (\%)}{100\% + \text{Markup on cost } (\%)} \times 100$$

$$= \frac{122.2}{100 + 122.2} \times 100 = 55\%$$

$$\text{Markup on cost } (\%) = \frac{\text{Markup on selling price } (\%)}{100\% - \text{Markup on selling price } (\%)} \times 100$$

$$= \frac{55}{100 - 55} \times 100 = 122.2\%$$

Consider the use of an incorrect markup base in Westerlund's business. A markup of 122.2 percent on her cost of goods sold for a typical frame she sells gives 122.2% × $36 = $44 of markup. Added to the $36 cost of goods sold, this gives her a selling price of $80 for the framed picture. However, a new clerk working for her who erroneously prices the framed picture at 55 percent of cost of goods sold sets the final price at $55.80 ($36 of cost of goods sold plus 55% × $36 = $19.80). The error, if repeated, could be disastrous: frames would be accidentally sold at $55.80, or $24.20 below the intended selling price of $80.

Markdown A *markdown* is a reduction in a retail price that is necessary if the item will not sell at the full selling price to which it has been marked up. The item

Jane Westerlund discusses framing and matting choices with a customer.
© Bill Rudelius

might not sell for a variety of reasons; perhaps the selling price was set too high or the item is out of style or has become soiled or damaged. The seller "takes a markdown" by lowering the price to sell it, thereby converting it to cash to buy future inventory that will sell faster.

The markdown percentage cannot be calculated directly from the operating statement. As shown in the fifth item of Figure B–2, the numerator of the markdown percentage is the total dollar markdowns. Markdowns are reductions in the prices of products that are purchased by customers. The denominator is net sales.

Suppose The Caplow Company had a total of $700 in markdowns on the prints and posters that are stocked and available for sale. Since the frames are custom made for individual customers, there is little reason for a markdown there. Caplow's markdown percent is then:

$$\text{Markdown}\,(\%) = \frac{\text{Markdowns}}{\text{Net sales}} \times 100$$

$$= \frac{\$700}{\$80,000} \times 100$$

$$= 0.875\%$$

Other kinds of retailers often have markdown ratios several times this amount. For example, women's dress stores have markdowns of about 25 percent, and menswear stores have markdowns of about 2 percent.

Stockturn Rate   A business firm is eager to have its inventory move quickly, or "turn over." *Stockturn rate,* or simply *stockturns,* measures this inventory movement. For a retailer, a slow stockturn rate may show it is buying merchandise customers don't want, so this is a critical measure of performance. When a firm sells only a single product, one convenient way to measure stockturn rate is simply to divide its cost of goods sold by average inventory at cost. The sixth item in Figure B–2 shows how to calculate stockturn rate using information in the operating statement:

$$\text{Stockturn rate} = \frac{\text{Cost of goods sold}}{\text{Average inventory at cost}}$$

The dollar amount of average inventory at cost is calculated by adding the beginning and ending inventories for the year and dividing by 2 to get the average. From Caplow's operating statement, we have:

$$\text{Stockturn rate} = \frac{\text{Cost of goods sold}}{\text{Average inventory at cost}}$$

$$= \frac{\text{Cost of goods sold}}{\dfrac{\text{Beginning inventory} + \text{Ending inventory}}{2}}$$

$$= \frac{\$36,000}{\dfrac{\$6,000 + \$5,000}{2}}$$

$$= \frac{\$36,000}{\$5,500}$$

$$= 6.5 \text{ stockturns per year}$$

What is considered a "good stockturn" varies by industry. For example, supermarkets have limited shelf space for thousands of new products from manufacturers each year, so they watch stockturn carefully by product line. The stockturn rate in supermarkets for breakfast foods is about 17 times per year, for pet food about 22 times per year, and for paper products about 25 times per year.

Return on Investment   A better measure of the performance of a firm than the amount of profit it makes in a year is its *return on investment (ROI),* which is the ratio of net income to the investment used to earn that net income. To calculate ROI, it is necessary to subtract income taxes from profit before taxes to obtain net income, then divide this figure by the investment that can be found on a firm's balance sheet (which is another accounting statement that shows the firm's assets, liabilities, and net worth). While financial and accounting experts have many definitions for *investment,* an often-used definition is "total assets."

For our purposes, let's assume that Westerlund has total assets (investment) of $20,000 in The Caplow Company, which covers inventory, store fixtures, and framing equipment. If she pays $1,000 in income taxes, her store's net income is $5,400. Therefore, using the return on investment ratio illustrated in the last item in Figure B–2, The Caplow Company's ROI is:

$$\text{Return on investment} = \text{Net income/Investment} \times 100$$

$$= \$5,400/\$20,000 \times 100$$

$$= 27\%$$

If Westerlund wants to improve her store's ROI next year, the strategies she might take are found in this alternative equation for ROI:

ROI = Net sales/Investment × Net income/Net sales

= Investment turnover × Profit margin

This equation suggests that The Caplow Company's ROI can be improved by raising investment turnover or increasing profit margin. Increasing stockturns will accomplish the former, whereas lowering cost of goods sold to net sales will cause the latter.

15 Managing Marketing Channels and Supply Chains

LEARNING OBJECTIVES

After reading this chapter you should be able to:

 LO 15-1 Explain what is meant by a marketing channel of distribution and why intermediaries are needed.

 LO 15-2 Distinguish among traditional marketing channels, electronic marketing channels, and different types of vertical marketing systems.

 LO 15-3 Describe factors that marketing executives consider when selecting and managing a marketing channel, including legal restrictions.

 LO 15-4 Explain what supply chain and logistics management are and how they relate to marketing strategy.

Callaway Golf: Designing and Delivering the Goods for Great Golf

What do Morgan Pressel and Phil Mickelson, two world-class golf professionals, have in common? Both use Callaway Golf equipment, accessories, and apparel when playing their favorite sport.

With annual sales approaching $900 million, Callaway Golf is one of the most recognized and highly regarded companies in the golf industry. With its commitment to continuous product innovation and broad distribution in the United States and more than 100 countries worldwide, Callaway Golf has built a strong reputation for designing and delivering the goods for golfers of all skill levels, both amateur and professional.

Callaway Golf primarily markets its products through more than 15,000 on- and off-course authorized golf retailers and sporting goods retailers, such as Golf Galaxy, Inc., Dick's Sporting Goods, Inc., and PGA Tour Superstores, which sell quality golf products and provide a level of customer service appropriate for the sale of such products. Callaway Golf considers its retailers a valuable marketing asset.

The company also has its own online store (CallawayGolf.com), which makes it a full-fledged multichannel marketer, and a successful one as well. Soon after CallawayGolf.com was launched, the chief executive of PGA of America called the store "innovative in that it combines that old legacy relationship with the retail channel with the new innovation of the Web." According to a Marketing Group spokesperson, "Callaway produces in-house a wide-ranging, high volume of original content from instructional videos to interviews with R&D leads and Tour Pros, blog posts and even live streams of Callaway events. This commitment to creating original content helps to give consumers a better feel for the Company and its products when they go to purchase equipment online and at retail."

Today, CallawayGolf.com is a dynamic, engaging and interactive website that constantly delivers new in-depth product information and media, original social content, user-generated content, and e-commerce capabilities. All of this helps consumers become better informed during the purchasing process. Not surprisingly, CallawayGolf.com is listed among the top Internet retailers in the United States.

Providing Callaway's authorized golf retailers and sporting goods retailers with the right products, at the right place, at the right time, and in the right quantity and condition is the responsibility of the company's supply chain. Callaway sources raw materials for its golf equipment, accessories, and all apparel from around the world. At the same time, Callaway delivers its finished products to company retailers through external shipping companies, such as United Parcel Service (UPS).[1]

This chapter first focuses on marketing channels of distribution and why they are an important component in the marketing mix. It then shows how such channels benefit consumers and the sequence of firms that make up a marketing channel. Finally, it describes factors that influence the choice and management of marketing channels, including channel conflict and cooperation.

The discussion then turns to the significance of supply chains and logistics management. In particular, attention is placed on the necessary alignment between supply chain management and marketing strategy and the trade-offs managers make between total distribution costs and customer service.

NATURE AND IMPORTANCE OF MARKETING CHANNELS

LO 15-1 Explain what is meant by a marketing channel of distribution and why intermediaries are needed.

Reaching prospective buyers, either directly or indirectly, is a prerequisite for successful marketing. At the same time, buyers benefit from distribution systems used by companies.

What Is a Marketing Channel of Distribution?

You see the results of distribution every day. You may have purchased Lay's potato chips at a 7-Eleven convenience store, a book online through Amazon.com, and Levi's jeans at a Kohl's department store. Each of these items was brought to you by a marketing channel of distribution, or simply a **marketing channel**, which consists of individuals and firms involved in the process of making a product or service available for use or consumption by consumers or industrial users.

Marketing channels can be compared to a pipeline through which water flows from a source to a terminus. Marketing channels make possible the flow of products and services from a producer, through intermediaries, to a buyer. Intermediaries go by various names (see Figure 15–1) and perform various functions. Some intermediaries purchase items from the seller, store them, and resell them to buyers. For example, Celestial Seasonings produces specialty teas and sells them to food wholesalers. The wholesalers then sell these teas to supermarkets and grocery stores, which, in turn, sell them to consumers. Other intermediaries such as brokers and agents represent sellers but do not actually take title to products—their role is to bring a seller and buyer together. Century 21 real estate agents are examples of this type of intermediary.

How Customer Value Is Created by Intermediaries

The importance of intermediaries is made even clearer when we consider the functions they perform and the value they create for buyers.

Important Functions Performed by Intermediaries Intermediaries make possible the flow of products from producers to ultimate consumers by performing three basic functions (see Figure 15–2). Intermediaries perform a *transactional function* when they buy and sell products or services. But an intermediary such as a wholesaler

FIGURE 15–1

Terms used for marketing intermediaries vary in specificity and use in consumer and business markets.

TERM	DESCRIPTION
Middleman	Any intermediary between the manufacturer and end-user markets
Agent or broker	Any intermediary with legal authority to act on behalf of the manufacturer
Wholesaler	An intermediary who sells to other intermediaries, usually to retailers; term usually applies to consumer markets
Retailer	An intermediary who sells to consumers
Distributor	An imprecise term, usually used to describe intermediaries who perform a variety of distribution functions, including selling, maintaining inventories, extending credit, and so on; a more common term in business markets but may also be used to refer to wholesalers
Dealer	A more imprecise term than *distributor* that can mean the same as distributor, retailer, wholesaler, and so forth

TYPE OF FUNCTION	ACTIVITIES RELATED TO FUNCTION
Transactional function	• *Buying*: Purchasing products for resale or as an agent for supply of a product • *Selling*: Contacting potential customers, promoting products, and seeking orders • *Risk taking*: Assuming business risks in the ownership of inventory that can become obsolete or deteriorate
Logistical function	• *Assorting*: Creating product assortments from several sources to serve customers • *Storing*: Assembling and protecting products at a convenient location to offer better customer service • *Sorting*: Purchasing in large quantities and breaking into smaller amounts desired by customers • *Transporting*: Physically moving a product to customers
Facilitating function	• *Financing*: Extending credit to customers • *Grading*: Inspecting, testing, or judging products and assigning them quality grades • *Marketing information and research*: Providing information to customers and suppliers, including competitive conditions and trends

FIGURE 15–2

Marketing channel intermediaries perform these fundamental functions, each of which consists of different activities.

also performs the function of sharing risk with the producer when it stocks merchandise in anticipation of sales. If the stock is unsold for any reason, the intermediary—not the producer—suffers the loss.

The logistics of a transaction (described at length later in this chapter) involve the details of preparing and getting a product to buyers. Gathering, sorting, and dispersing products are some of the *logistical functions* of the intermediary—imagine the several books required for a literature course sitting together on one shelf at your college bookstore! Finally, intermediaries perform *facilitating functions* that, by definition, make a transaction easier for buyers. For example, Macy's issues credit cards to consumers so they can buy now and pay later.

All three functions must be performed in a marketing channel, even though each channel member may not participate in all three. Channel members often negotiate which specific functions they will perform and for what price.

Consumer Benefits Consumers also benefit from intermediaries. Having the products and services you want, when you want them, where you want them, and in the form you want them is the ideal result of marketing channels.

In more specific terms, marketing channels help create value for consumers through the four utilities described in Chapter 1: time, place, form, and possession. *Time utility* refers to having a product or service when you want it. For example, FedEx provides next-morning delivery. *Place utility* means having a product or service available where consumers want it, such as having a Chevron gas station located on a long stretch of lonely highway. *Form utility* involves enhancing a product or service to make it more appealing to buyers. Consider the importance of bottlers in the soft-drink industry. Coca-Cola and Pepsi-Cola manufacture the flavor concentrate (cola, lemon-lime) and sell it to bottlers—intermediaries—which then add sweetener and the concentrate to carbonated water and package the beverage in bottles and cans, which are then sold to retailers. *Possession utility* entails efforts by intermediaries to help buyers take possession of a product or service, such as having airline tickets delivered by a travel agency.

learning review

15-1. What is meant by a marketing channel?

15-2. What are the three basic functions performed by intermediaries?

MARKETING CHANNEL STRUCTURE AND ORGANIZATION

LO 15-2 Distinguish among traditional marketing channels, electronic marketing channels, and different types of vertical marketing systems.

A product can take many routes on its journey from a producer to buyers. Marketers continually search for the most efficient route from the many alternatives available. As you'll see, there are some important differences between the marketing channels used for consumer products and business products.

Marketing Channels for Consumer Products and Services

Figure 15–3 shows the four most common marketing channels for consumer products and services. It also shows the number of levels in each marketing channel, as evidenced by the number of intermediaries between a producer and ultimate buyers. As the number of intermediaries between a producer and buyer increases, the channel is viewed as increasing in length. Thus, the producer → wholesaler → retailer → consumer channel is longer than the producer → consumer channel.

Direct Channel   Channel A represents a *direct channel* because the producer and the ultimate consumers deal directly with each other. Many products and services are distributed this way. Many insurance companies sell their services using a direct channel and branch sales offices. The Schwan's Food Company of Marshall, Minnesota, the largest direct-to-home provider of frozen foods in the United States, uses route sales representatives who sell from refrigerated trucks. Because there are no intermediaries with a direct channel, the producer performs all channel functions.

Indirect Channel   The remaining three channel forms in Figure 15–3 are *indirect channels* because intermediaries are inserted between the producer and consumers and perform numerous channel functions. Channel B, with a retailer added, is most common when a retailer is large and can buy in large quantities from a producer or when the cost of inventory makes it too expensive to use a wholesaler. Automobile manufacturers such as Toyota use this channel, and a local car dealer acts as a retailer. Why is there no wholesaler? So many variations exist in the product that it would be impossible for a wholesaler to stock all the models required to satisfy buyers; in addition, the cost of maintaining an inventory would be too high. However, large retailers such as Target, 7-Eleven, Staples, Safeway, and Home Depot buy in sufficient quantities to make it cost effective for a producer to deal with only a retail intermediary.

FIGURE 15–3

Common marketing channels for consumer products and services differ by the kind and number of intermediaries involved.

What kind of marketing channel does IBM use for its Watson computer—an artificially intelligent computer system capable of answering questions in natural language? Read the text to find out.

© Ben Hider/Getty Images

Adding a wholesaler in Channel C is most common for low-cost, low-unit value items that are frequently purchased by consumers, such as candy, confectionary items, and magazines. For example, Mars sells case quantities of its line of candies to wholesalers, who then break down (sort) the cases so that individual retailers can order in boxes or much smaller quantities.

Channel D, the most indirect channel, is employed when there are many small manufacturers and many small retailers; in this type of channel, an agent is used to help coordinate a large supply of the product. Mansar Products, Ltd. is a Belgian producer of specialty jewelry that uses agents to sell to wholesalers in the United States, who then sell to many small independent jewelry retailers.

Marketing Channels for Business Products and Services

The four most common channels for business products and services are shown in Figure 15–4. In contrast with channels used for consumer products, business channels typically are shorter and rely on one intermediary or none at all because business users are fewer in number, tend to be more concentrated geographically, and buy in larger quantities.

Direct Channel   Channel A in Figure 15–4, represented by IBM's large, mainframe computer business, is a direct channel. Firms using this channel maintain their own salesforce and perform all channel functions. This channel is employed when buyers are large and well defined, the sales effort requires extensive negotiations, and the products are of high unit value and require hands-on expertise in terms of installation or use. Not surprisingly, IBM's Watson supercomputer, priced at $3 million, is sold and delivered directly to buyers.

Indirect Channel   Channels B, C, and D in Figure 15–4 are indirect channels with one or more intermediaries between the producer and the industrial user. In Channel B, an industrial distributor performs a variety of marketing channel functions, including selling, stocking, delivering a full product assortment, and financing. In many

---

FIGURE 15–4

Common marketing channels for business products and services differ by the kind and number of intermediaries involved.

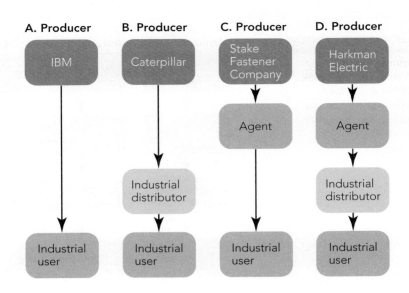

ways, industrial distributors are like wholesalers in consumer channels. Caterpillar uses industrial distributors to sell its construction and mining equipment in over 180 countries. In addition to selling, Caterpillar distributors stock 40,000 to 50,000 parts and service equipment using highly trained technicians.

Channel C introduces a second intermediary, an agent, who serves primarily as the independent selling arm of producers and represents a producer to industrial users. For example, Stake Fastener Company, a producer of industrial fasteners, has an agent call on industrial users rather than employing its own salesforce.

Channel D is the longest channel and includes both agents and industrial distributors. For instance, Harkman Electric, a producer of electric products, uses agents to call on electrical distributors who sell to industrial users.

Internet Marketing Channels

These common marketing channels for consumer and business products and services are not the only routes to the marketplace. *Internet marketing channels* also make products and services available for consumption or use by consumers or organizational buyers. A unique feature of these channels is that they combine electronic and traditional intermediaries to create time, place, form, and possession utility for buyers.

Figure 15–5 shows the Internet marketing channels for books (Amazon.com), automobiles (Autobytel.com), reservation services (Orbitz.com), and personal computers (Dell.com). Are you surprised that they look a lot like common consumer product marketing channels? An important reason for the similarity resides in the channel functions detailed in Figure 15–2. Electronic intermediaries can and do perform transactional and facilitating functions effectively and at a relatively lower cost than traditional intermediaries because of efficiencies made possible by Internet technology. But electronic intermediaries are incapable of performing elements of the logistical function, particularly for products such as books and automobiles. This function remains with traditional intermediaries or with the producer, as is evident with Dell Inc. and its direct channel.

Many services can be distributed through electronic marketing channels, such as car rental reservations marketed by Alamo.com, financial securities by Schwab.com, and insurance by MetLife.com. However, many other services, such as health care and auto repair, still involve traditional intermediaries.

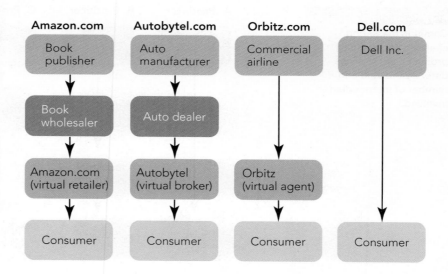

FIGURE 15–5

Consumer Internet marketing channels look much like those for consumer products and services. Read the text to learn why.

Eddie Bauer successfully engages in multichannel marketing through its 370 retail and outlet stores, its website, and its catalog.

Left: © Bonnie Kamin/PhotoEdit, Inc.; Middle: Source: Eddie Bauer, LLC; Right: © Mike Hruby

Eddie Bauer
www.eddiebauer.com

Direct and Multichannel Marketing

Many firms also use direct and multichannel marketing to reach buyers. *Direct marketing channels* allow consumers to buy products by interacting with various advertising media without a face-to-face meeting with a salesperson. Direct marketing channels include mail-order selling, direct-mail sales, catalog sales, telemarketing, interactive media, and televised home shopping (the Home Shopping Network). Some firms sell products almost entirely through direct marketing. These firms include L.L.Bean (apparel) and Newegg.com (consumer electronics). Marketers such as Nestlé, in addition to using traditional channels composed of wholesalers and retailers, also employ direct marketing through catalogs and telemarketing to reach more buyers.

Multichannel marketing, sometimes called *omnichannel marketing,* is the *blending* of different communication and delivery channels that are *mutually reinforcing* in attracting, retaining, and building relationships with consumers who shop and buy in traditional intermediaries and online. Multichannel marketing seeks to integrate a firm's electronic marketing and delivery channels. At Eddie Bauer, for example, every effort is made to make the apparel shopping and purchase experience for its customers the same across its retail store, catalog, and website channels. According to an Eddie Bauer marketing manager, "We don't distinguish between channels because it's all Eddie Bauer to our customers."[2]

Multichannel marketing also can leverage the value-adding capabilities of different channels. For example, retail stores leverage their physical presence by allowing customers to pick up their online orders at a nearby store or return or exchange nonstore purchases if they wish. Catalogs can serve as shopping tools for online purchasing, as they do for store purchasing. Websites can help consumers do their homework before visiting a store. Staples has leveraged its store, catalog, and website channels with impressive results. Staples is the third largest Internet retailer in the United States behind Amazon and Apple.[3]

Dual Distribution and Strategic Channel Alliances

In some situations, producers use **dual distribution**, an arrangement whereby a firm reaches different buyers by employing two or more different types of channels for the same basic product. For example, GE sells its large appliances directly to home and apartment builders but uses retail stores, including Lowe's home centers, to sell to consumers. In some instances, firms pair multiple channels with a multibrand strategy (see Chapter 10). This is done to minimize cannibalization of the firm's family brand and differentiate the channels. For example, Hallmark sells its Hallmark greeting cards through Hallmark stores and select department stores and its Ambassador brand of cards through discount and drugstore chains.

Nestlé and General Mills—Cereal Partners Worldwide

Can you say Nestlé Cheerios *miel aman-des*? Millions in France start their day with this European equivalent of General Mills's Honey Nut Cheerios, made possible by Cereal Partners Worldwide (CPW). CPW is a strategic alliance designed from the start to be a global business. It combines the cereal manufacturing and marketing capability of U.S.-based General Mills with the world-wide distribution clout of Swiss-based Nestlé. The photo shows Nestlé's Trix cereal (not General Mills) sold in China.

From its headquarters in Switzerland, CPW first launched General Mills cereals under the Nestlé label in France, the United Kingdom, Spain, and Portugal in 1991. Today, CPW competes in more than 140 international markets.

The General Mills–Nestlé strategic channel alliance also increased the ready-to-eat cereal worldwide market share of these companies, which are already rated as the two best-managed firms in the world. CPW currently accounts for more than 10 percent of the nearly $30 billion worldwide hot- and cold-cereal market, with more than $4 billion in annual revenue.

© picture alliance/Daniel Kalker/Newscom

An innovation in marketing channels is the use of *strategic channel alliances,* whereby one firm's marketing channel is used to sell another firm's products. Strategic alliances are popular in global marketing, where the creation of marketing channel relationships is expensive and time-consuming. For example, General Mills and Nestlé have an extensive alliance that spans about 140 international markets from Mexico to China. Read the Marketing Matters box so you won't be surprised when you are served Nestlé (not General Mills) Cheerios when traveling outside North America.[4]

Vertical Marketing Systems

The traditional marketing channels described so far represent a loosely knit network of independent producers and intermediaries brought together to distribute products and services. However, other channel arrangements exist for the purpose of improving efficiency in performing channel functions and achieving greater marketing effectiveness. These arrangements are called vertical marketing systems. **Vertical marketing systems** are professionally managed and centrally coordinated marketing channels designed to achieve channel economies and maximum marketing impact.[5] Figure 15–6 depicts the three major types of vertical marketing systems: corporate, contractual, and administered.

Corporate Systems   The combination of successive stages of production and distribution under a single ownership is a *corporate vertical marketing system*. For example, a producer might own the intermediary at the next level down in the channel. This practice, called *forward integration,* is exemplified by Ralph Lauren, which manufactures clothing and also owns apparel shops. Other examples of forward integration include Goodyear, Apple, and Sherwin-Williams. Alternatively, a retailer might own a manufacturing operation, a practice called *backward integration.* For example, Kroger supermarkets operate manufacturing facilities that produce everything from aspirin to cottage cheese for sale under the Kroger label. Tiffany & Co., the exclusive jewelry retailer, manufactures about half of the fine jewelry items for sale through its over 250 specialty stores and boutiques worldwide.

FIGURE 15–6

There are three major types of vertical marketing systems—corporate, contractual, and administered. Contractual systems are the most popular for reasons described in the text.

Companies seeking to reduce distribution costs and gain greater control over supply sources or resale of their products pursue forward and backward integration. However, both types of integration increase a company's capital investment and fixed costs. For this reason, many companies favor contractual vertical marketing systems to achieve channel efficiencies and marketing effectiveness.

Contractual Systems   Under a *contractual vertical marketing system,* independent production and distribution firms integrate their efforts on a contractual basis to obtain greater functional economies and marketing impact than they could achieve alone. Contractual systems are the most popular among the three types of vertical marketing systems.

Three variations of contractual systems exist. *Wholesaler-sponsored voluntary chains* involve a wholesaler that develops a contractual relationship with small, independent retailers to standardize and coordinate buying practices, merchandising programs, and inventory management efforts. With the organization of a large number of independent retailers, economies of scale and volume discounts can be achieved to compete with chain stores. IGA and Ben Franklin variety and craft stores represent wholesaler-sponsored voluntary chains. *Retailer-sponsored cooperatives* exist when small, independent retailers form an organization that operates a wholesale facility cooperatively. Member retailers then concentrate their buying power through the wholesaler and plan collaborative promotional and pricing activities. Examples of retailer-sponsored cooperatives include Associated Grocers and Ace Hardware.

The most visible variation of contractual systems is franchising. *Franchising* is a contractual arrangement between a parent company (a franchisor) and an individual or firm (a franchisee) that allows the franchisee to operate a certain type of business under an established name and according to specific rules.

Four types of franchise arrangements are most popular. *Manufacturer-sponsored retail franchise systems* are prominent in the automobile industry, where a manufacturer such as Ford licenses dealers to sell its cars subject to various sales and service conditions. *Manufacturer-sponsored wholesale franchise systems* exist in the soft-drink industry. For example, Pepsi-Cola licenses wholesalers (bottlers) that purchase concentrate from Pepsi-Cola and then carbonate, bottle, promote, and distribute its products to retailers and restaurants. *Service-sponsored retail franchise systems* are used by firms that have designed a unique approach for performing a service and wish to profit by selling the franchise to others. Holiday Inn, Avis, and McDonald's represent this type of franchising approach. *Service-sponsored franchise systems* exist when franchisors license individuals or firms to dispense a service under a trade name and according to specific guidelines. Examples include Snelling and Snelling, Inc. employment services and H&R Block tax services.

Administered Systems   In comparison, *administered vertical marketing systems* achieve coordination at successive stages of production and distribution by the size and influence of one channel member rather than through ownership. Procter & Gamble, given its broad product assortment ranging from disposable diapers to detergents, is able to obtain cooperation from supermarkets in displaying, promoting, and pricing its products. Walmart obtains cooperation from manufacturers in terms of product specifications, price levels, and promotional support due to its position as the world's largest retailer.

learning review

15-3.   What is the difference between a direct and an indirect channel?

15-4.   Why are channels for business products typically shorter than channels for consumer products?

15-5.   What is the principal distinction between a corporate vertical marketing system and an administered vertical marketing system?

MARKETING CHANNEL CHOICE AND MANAGEMENT

LO 15-3   Describe factors that marketing executives consider when selecting and managing a marketing channel, including legal restrictions.

Marketing channels not only link a producer to its buyers but also provide the means through which a firm implements various elements of its marketing strategy. Therefore, choosing a marketing channel is a critical decision.

Factors Affecting Channel Choice and Management

Marketing executives consider three questions when choosing a marketing channel and intermediaries:

1. Which channel and intermediaries will provide the best coverage of the target market?
2. Which channel and intermediaries will best satisfy the buying requirements of the target market?
3. Which channel and intermediaries will be the most profitable?

Target Market Coverage   Achieving the best coverage of the target market requires attention to the *density*—that is, the number of stores in a geographical area—and type of intermediaries to be used at the retail level of distribution. Three degrees of distribution density exist: intensive, exclusive, and selective.

Intensive distribution means that a firm tries to place its products and services in as many outlets as possible. Intensive distribution is usually chosen for convenience products or services such as candy, fast food, newspapers, and soft drinks. For example, Coca-Cola's retail distribution objective is to place its products "within an arm's reach of desire." Cash, yes cash, is distributed intensively by Visa. It operates over 1.4 million automated teller machines in more than 200 countries.

Exclusive distribution is the extreme opposite of intensive distribution because only one retailer in a specific geographical area carries the firm's products. Exclusive distribution is typically chosen for specialty products or services, such as some women's fragrances and men's and women's apparel and accessories. Gucci, one of the world's leading luxury products companies, uses exclusive distribution in the marketing of its Yves Saint Laurent, Sergio Rossi, Boucheron, Opium, and Gucci brands.

Retailers and industrial distributors prefer exclusive distribution for two reasons. First, it limits head-to-head competition for an identical product. Second, it provides a point of difference for a retailer or distributor. For instance, luxury retailer Saks Inc. seeks exclusive product lines for its stores. According to the company CEO, "It's incumbent on us not to be just a place where you can buy the big brands. Those brands are still critical—the Chanels, the Pradas, the Guccis—but even with those brands, we need to find things unique to us."[6]

Selective distribution lies between these two extremes and means that a firm selects a few retailers in a specific geographical area to carry its products. Selective distribution weds some of the market coverage benefits of intensive distribution to the control over resale evident with exclusive distribution. For example, Dell Inc. chose selective distribution when it decided to sell its products through U.S. retailers along with its direct channel.[7] According to Michael Dell, the company CEO, "There were plenty of retailers who said, 'sell through us,' but we didn't want to show up everywhere." The company now sells a limited range of its products through Walmart, Sam's Club, Best Buy, and Staples. Dell's decision was consistent with current trends. Today, selective distribution is the most common form of distribution intensity.

Buyer Requirements   A second consideration in channel choice is gaining access to channels and intermediaries that satisfy at least some of the interests buyers might want fulfilled when they purchase a firm's products or services. These interests fall into four broad categories: (1) information, (2) convenience, (3) variety, and (4) pre- or postsale services. Each relates to customer experience.

Information is an important requirement when buyers have limited knowledge or desire specific data about a product or service. Properly chosen intermediaries communicate with buyers through in-store displays, demonstrations, and personal selling. Apple has opened over 400 retail outlets staffed with highly trained personnel to communicate how its products can better satisfy each customer's needs.

Which buying requirements are satisfied by Jiffy Lube? Read the text to find out.

© David McNew/Getty Images

Convenience has multiple meanings for buyers, such as proximity or driving time to a retail outlet. For example, 7-Eleven stores, with more than 50,000 outlets worldwide, many of which are open 24 hours a day, satisfy this interest for buyers. Candy and snack-food firms benefit by gaining display space in these stores. For other consumers, convenience means a minimum of time and hassle. Jiffy Lube, which promises to change engine oil and filters quickly, appeals to this aspect of convenience. For those who shop on the Internet, convenience means that websites must be easy to locate and navigate, and image downloads must be fast. A commonly held view among website developers is the "eight second rule": Consumers will abandon their efforts to enter or navigate a website if download time exceeds eight seconds.[8]

Variety reflects buyers' interest in having numerous competing and complementary items from which to choose. Variety is evident in the breadth and depth of products and brands carried by intermediaries, which enhances their attraction to buyers. Thus, manufacturers of pet food and supplies seek distribution through pet superstores such as Petco and PetSmart, which offer a wide array of pet products and services.

Pre- or postsale services provided by intermediaries are an important buying requirement for products such as large household appliances that require delivery, installation, and credit. Therefore, Whirlpool seeks dealers that provide such services.

Profitability   The third consideration in choosing a channel is profitability, which is determined by the margins earned (revenue minus cost) for each channel member and for the channel as a whole. Channel cost is the critical dimension of profitability.

Applying **Marketing Metrics**

Channel Sales and Profit at Charlesburg Furniture

Charlesburg Furniture is one of 1,000 wood furniture manufacturers in the United States. The company sells its furniture through furniture store chains, independent furniture stores, and department store chains, mostly in the southern United States. The company has traditionally allocated its marketing funds for cooperative advertising, in-store displays, and retail sales support on the basis of dollar sales by channel.

Your Challenge

As the vice president of sales and marketing at Charlesburg Furniture, you have been asked to review the company's sales and profit in its three channels and recommend a course of action. The question: Should Charlesburg Furniture continue to allocate its marketing funds on the basis of channel dollar sales or profit?

Your Findings

Charlesburg Furniture tracks the sales and profit from each channel (and individual customer) and the three-year trend of sales by channel on its marketing dashboard. This information is displayed in the marketing dashboards below.

Several findings stand out. Furniture store chains and independent furniture stores account for 85.2 percent of Charlesburg Furniture sales and 93 percent of company profit. These two channels also evidence growth as measured by annual percentage change in sales. By comparison, the annual percentage sales growth of department store chains has declined, recording negative growth in 2015. This channel accounts for 14.8 percent of company sales and 7 percent of company profit.

Your Action

Charlesburg Furniture should consider abandoning the practice of allocating marketing funds solely on the basis of channel sales volume. The importance of independent furniture stores to Charlesburg's profitability warrants further spending, particularly given this channel's favorable sales trend. Doubling the percentage allocation for marketing funds for this channel may be too extreme, however. Charlesburg Furniture might also consider the longer term role of department store chains as a marketing channel.

These costs include distribution, advertising, and selling expenses associated with different types of marketing channels. The extent to which channel members share these costs determines the margins received by each member and by the channel as a whole.

Companies routinely monitor the performance of their marketing channels. Read the Applying Marketing Metrics box to see how Charlesburg Furniture views the sales and profit performance of its marketing channels.

Managing Channel Relationships: Conflict and Cooperation

Unfortunately, because channels consist of independent individuals and firms, there is always the potential for disagreements concerning who performs which channel

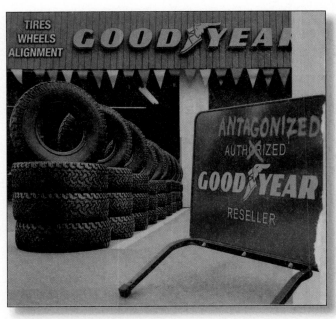

Channel conflict is sometimes visible to consumers. Read the text to learn what type of channel conflict has antagonized this independent Goodyear tire dealer.

© Joe & Kathy Heiner/Lindgren & Smith, Inc.

functions, how profits are allocated, which products and services will be provided by whom, and who makes critical channel-related decisions. These channel conflicts necessitate measures for dealing with them.

Sources of Conflict in Marketing Channels

Channel conflict arises when one channel member believes another channel member is engaged in behavior that prevents it from achieving its goals. Two types of conflict occur in marketing channels: vertical conflict and horizontal conflict.

Vertical conflict occurs between different levels in a marketing channel—for example, between a manufacturer and a wholesaler or retailer or between a wholesaler and a retailer. Three sources of vertical conflict are most common.[9] First, conflict arises when a channel member bypasses another member and sells or buys products direct, a practice called **disintermediation**. For example, conflict occurred when American Airlines decided to terminate its relationship with Orbitz and Expedia, two online ticketing and travel sites, and sell directly through AA Direct Connect. Second, conflict occurs due to disagreements over how profit margins are distributed among channel members. This happened when Amazon and the Hachette Book Group, the third-largest trade book and educational publisher, engaged in a seven-month dispute about how e-book revenue should be divided between the two companies. A third conflict situation arises when manufacturers believe wholesalers or retailers are not giving their products adequate attention. For example, Nike stopped shipping popular sneakers such as Nike Shox NZ to Foot Locker in retaliation for the retailer's decision to give more shelf space to shoes costing under $120.

Horizontal conflict occurs between intermediaries at the same level in a marketing channel, such as between two or more retailers (Target and Kmart) or two or more wholesalers that handle the same manufacturer's brands. Two sources of horizontal conflict are common.[10] First, horizontal conflict arises when a manufacturer increases its distribution coverage in a geographical area. For example, a franchised Cadillac dealer in Chicago might complain to General Motors that another franchised Cadillac dealer has located too close to its dealership. Second, dual distribution causes conflict when different types of retailers carry the same brands. For instance, independent Goodyear tire dealers became irate when Goodyear Tire Company decided to sell its brands through Sears, Walmart, and Sam's Club. Many switched to competing tire makers.

Securing Cooperation in Marketing Channels

Conflict can have destructive effects on the workings of a marketing channel so it is necessary to secure cooperation among channel members. One means is through a *channel captain,* a channel member that coordinates, directs, and supports other channel members. Channel captains can be producers, wholesalers, or retailers. P&G assumes this role because it has a strong consumer following in brands such as Crest, Tide, and Pampers. Therefore, it can set policies or terms that supermarkets will follow. McKesson, a pharmaceutical drug wholesaler, is a channel captain because it coordinates and supports the product flow from numerous small drug manufacturers to drugstores and hospitals nationwide. Walmart is a retail channel captain because of its strong consumer image, number of outlets, and purchasing volume.

A firm becomes a channel captain because it is the channel member with the ability to influence the behavior of other members. Influence can take four forms.

First, economic influence arises from the ability of a firm to *reward* other members given its strong financial position or customer franchise. Microsoft Corporation and Walmart have such influence. *Expertise* is a second source of influence. For example, American Hospital Supply helps its customers (hospitals) manage inventory and streamline order processing for hundreds of medical supplies. Third, *identification* with a particular channel member can create influence for that channel member. For instance, retailers may compete to carry the Ralph Lauren line, or clothing manufacturers may compete to be carried by Neiman Marcus, Nordstrom, or Bloomingdale's. In both instances, the desire to be identified with a channel member gives that firm influence over others. Finally, influence can arise from the *legitimate right* of one channel member to direct the behavior of other members. This situation is likely to occur in contractual vertical marketing systems where a franchisor can legitimately direct how a franchisee behaves.

Legal Considerations Conflict in marketing channels is typically resolved through negotiation or the exercise of influence by channel members. Sometimes conflict produces legal action. Therefore, knowledge of legal restrictions affecting channel strategies and practices is important. Some restrictions were described in Chapter 14, namely vertical price fixing and price discrimination. However, other legal considerations are unique to marketing channels.

In general, suppliers can select whomever they want as channel intermediaries and may refuse to deal with whomever they choose. However, the Federal Trade Commission and the Justice Department monitor channel practices that restrain competition, create monopolies, or otherwise represent unfair methods of competition under the Sherman Act (1890) and the Clayton Act (1914). Six channel practices have received the most attention (see Figure 15–7).

Dual distribution, although not illegal, can be viewed as anticompetitive in some situations. The most common situation arises when a manufacturer distributes through its own vertically integrated channel in competition with independent wholesalers and retailers that also sell its products. If the manufacturer's behavior is viewed as an attempt to lessen competition by eliminating wholesalers or retailers, then such action would violate both the Sherman and Clayton Acts.

Vertical integration is viewed in a similar light. Although not illegal, this practice is sometimes subject to legal action under the Clayton Act if it has the potential to lessen competition or foster monopoly.

The Clayton Act specifically prohibits exclusive dealing and tying arrangements when they lessen competition or create monopolies. *Exclusive dealing* exists when a supplier requires channel members to sell only its products or restricts distributors from selling directly competitive products. *Tying arrangements* occur when a supplier requires a distributor purchasing some products to buy others from the supplier. These arrangements often arise in franchising. They are illegal if the tied products could be purchased at fair market values from other suppliers at desired quality standards of the

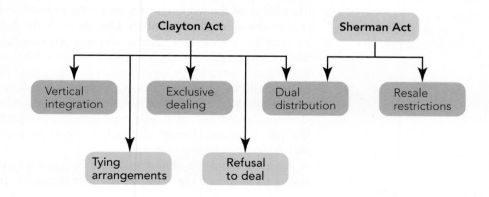

FIGURE 15–7

Channel strategies and practices are affected by legal restrictions. The Clayton Act and the Sherman Act restrict specific channel strategies and practices.

franchiser. *Full-line forcing* is a special kind of tying arrangement. This practice involves a supplier requiring that a channel member carry its full line of products in order to sell a specific item in the supplier's line.

Even though a supplier has a legal right to choose intermediaries to carry and represent its products, a *refusal to deal* with existing channel members may be illegal under the Clayton Act. *Resale restrictions* refer to a supplier's attempt to stipulate to whom distributors may resell the supplier's products and in what specific geographical areas or territories they may be sold. These practices have been prosecuted under the Sherman Act. Today, however, the courts apply the "rule of reason" in such cases and consider whether such restrictions have a "demonstrable economic effect."

learning review

15-6. What are the three questions marketing executives consider when choosing a marketing channel and intermediaries?

15-7. What are the three degrees of distribution density?

15-8. What is meant by exclusive dealing?

LOGISTICS AND SUPPLY CHAIN MANAGEMENT

> **LO 15-4** Explain what supply chain and logistics management are and how they relate to marketing strategy.

A marketing channel relies on logistics to make products available to consumers and industrial users. **Logistics** involves those activities that focus on getting the right amount of the right products to the right place at the right time at the lowest possible cost. The performance of these activities is *logistics management,* the practice of organizing the cost-effective flow of raw materials, in-process inventory, finished goods, and related information from point of origin to point of consumption to satisfy *customer requirements.*

Three elements of this definition deserve emphasis. First, logistics deals with decisions needed to move a product from the source of raw materials to consumption—that is, the *flow* of the product. Second, those decisions have to be *cost effective.* Third, while it is important to drive down logistics costs, there is a limit: A firm needs to drive down logistics costs as long as it can deliver expected *customer service,* which means satisfying customer requirements. The role of management is to see that customer needs are satisfied in the most cost-effective manner. When properly done, the results can be spectacular. Consider Procter & Gamble. The company set out to meet consumer needs more effectively by collaborating and partnering with its suppliers and retailers to ensure that the right products reached store shelves at the right time and at a lower cost. The effort was judged a success when, during an 18-month period, P&G's retail customers posted a $65 million savings in logistics costs and customer service increased.[11]

The P&G experience is not an isolated incident. Companies now recognize that getting the right items needed for consumption or production to the right place at the right time in the right condition at the right cost is often beyond their individual capabilities and control. Instead, collaboration, coordination, and information sharing among manufacturers, suppliers, and distributors are necessary to create a seamless flow of products and services to customers. This perspective is represented in the concept of a supply chain and the practice of supply chain management.

Supply Chains versus Marketing Channels

A **supply chain** refers to the various firms involved in performing the activities required to create and deliver a product or service to consumers or industrial users. It

421

differs from a marketing channel in terms of the firms involved. A supply chain includes suppliers that provide raw material inputs to a manufacturer as well as the wholesalers and retailers that deliver finished products to consumers. The management process is also different.

Supply chain management is the integration and organization of information and logistics activities *across firms* in a supply chain for the purpose of creating and delivering products and services that provide value to consumers. The relation among marketing channels, logistics management, and supply chain management is shown in Figure 15–8. An important feature of supply chain management is its application of sophisticated information technology that allows companies to share and operate systems for order processing, transportation scheduling, and inventory and facility management.

Sourcing, Assembling, and Delivering a New Car: The Automotive Supply Chain

All companies are members of one or more supply chains. A supply chain is essentially a series of linked suppliers and customers in which every customer is, in turn, a supplier to another customer until a finished product reaches the ultimate consumer. Even the simplified supply chain diagram for carmakers shown in Figure 15–9 illustrates how complex a supply chain can be.[12] A carmaker's supplier network includes thousands of firms that provide the 2,000 functional components, 30,000 parts, and 10 million lines of software code in a typical automobile. They provide items ranging from raw materials, such as steel and rubber, to components, including transmissions, tires, brakes, and seats, to complex subassemblies such as chassis and suspension systems that make for a smooth, stable ride. The process of coordinating and scheduling the flow of materials and components for their assembly into actual automobiles by carmakers is heavily dependent on logistical activities, including transportation, order processing, inventory control, materials handling, and information technology. A central link is the carmaker's supply chain manager, who is responsible for translating customer requirements into actual orders and arranging for delivery dates and financial arrangements for automobile dealers.

Logistical aspects of the automobile marketing channel are also an important part of the supply chain. Major responsibilities include transportation (which involves the selection and oversight of external carriers—trucking, airline, railroad, and shipping companies—for cars and parts to dealers), the operation of distribution centers, the management of finished goods inventories, and order processing for sales. Supply chain managers also play an important role in the marketing channel. They work with car dealer networks to ensure that the right mix of automobiles is delivered to each location. In addition, they make sure that spare and service parts are available so that dealers can meet the car maintenance and repair needs of consumers. All of this is done with the help of information technology that links the entire automotive supply chain. What does all of this cost? It is estimated that logistics costs represent 25 to 30 percent of the retail price that you pay for a new car.

Supply Chain Management and Marketing Strategy

The automotive supply chain illustration shows how information and logistics activities are integrated and organized across firms to create and deliver a car to you, the consumer. What's missing from this illustration is the linkage between a specific company's supply chain and its marketing strategy. Just as companies have different marketing strategies, they also design and manage supply chains differently. The goals to be achieved by a firm's marketing strategy determine whether its supply chain needs to be more responsive or efficient in meeting customer requirements.

Aligning a Supply Chain with Marketing Strategy   There are a variety of supply chain configurations, each of which is designed to perform different tasks well. Marketers today recognize that the choice of a supply chain follows from a clearly defined marketing strategy and involves three steps:[13]

1. *Understand the customer.* To understand the customer, a company must identify the needs of the customer segment being served. These needs, such as a desire for a low price or convenience of purchase, help a company define the relative importance of efficiency and responsiveness in meeting customer requirements.
2. *Understand the supply chain.* Second, a company must understand what a supply chain is designed to do well. Supply chains range from those that emphasize being responsive to customer requirements and demand to those that emphasize efficiency with a goal of supplying products at the lowest possible delivered cost.
3. *Harmonize the supply chain with the marketing strategy.* Finally, a company needs to ensure that what the supply chain is capable of doing well is consistent with the targeted customer's needs and its marketing strategy. If a mismatch exists between what the supply chain does particularly well and a company's marketing strategy, the company will need to either redesign the supply chain to support the marketing strategy or change the marketing strategy. Read the Marketing Matters box to learn how IBM overhauled its complete supply chain to support its marketing strategy.[14]

How are these steps applied and how are efficiency and responsiveness considerations built into a supply chain? Let's look at how two well-known companies—Dell and Walmart—have harmonized their supply chain and marketing strategy.[15]

Video 15-2
IBM
kerin.tv/13e/v15-2

IBM's Integrated Supply Chain—Delivering a Total Solution for Its Customers

IBM is one of the world's great business success stories because of its ability to reinvent itself to satisfy shifting customer needs in a dynamic global marketplace. The company's transformation of its supply chain is a case in point.

IBM has built a single integrated supply chain that can handle raw material procurement, manufacturing, logistics, customer support, order entry, and customer fulfillment across all of IBM—something that has never been done before. Why would IBM undertake this task? According to IBM's former CEO, Samuel J. Palmisano, "You cannot hope to thrive in the IT industry if you are a high-cost, slow-moving company. Supply chain is one of the new

© Peter Probst/Alamy

competitive battlegrounds. We are committed to being the most efficient and productive player in our industry."

The task is not easy. IBM's supply chain management organization works out of 360 locations in 64 countries, tracking more than 1.5 million assets for both IBM and its clients. The organization also deals with about 23,000 suppliers in nearly 100 countries. Yet with surprising efficiency, IBM's supply chain is linked from raw material sourcing to postsales support.

Today, IBM is uniquely poised to configure and deliver a tailored mix of hardware, software, and service to provide a total solution for its customers. Not surprisingly, IBM's integrated supply chain is heralded as one of the best in the world!

© Kristoffer Tripplaar/Alamy

Dell: A Responsive Supply Chain   The Dell marketing strategy primarily targets customers who desire having the most up-to-date computer systems customized to their needs. These customers are also willing to (1) wait to have their customized computer system delivered in a few days, rather than picking out a model at a retail store, and (2) pay a reasonable, though not the lowest, price in the marketplace. Given Dell's customer segment, the company has the option of adopting an efficient or responsive supply chain.

An efficient supply chain may use inexpensive, but slower, modes of transportation, emphasize economies of scale in its production process by reducing the variety of system configurations offered, and limit its assembly and inventory storage facilities to a single location. If Dell opted only for efficiency in its supply chain, it would be difficult to satisfy its target customers' desire for rapid delivery and a wide variety of customizable products with its assembly and storage facilities confined to its headquarters in Austin, Texas.

Dell instead has opted for a responsive supply chain. It relies on more expensive express transportation for receipt of components from suppliers and delivery of finished products to customers. The company achieves product variety and manufacturing efficiency by designing common platforms across several products and using common components. Also, Dell has invested heavily in information technology to link itself with suppliers and customers.

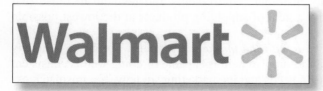

© R Heyes Design/Alamy

Walmart: An Efficient Supply Chain   Now let's consider Walmart. Walmart's marketing strategy is to be a reliable, lower-price retailer for a wide variety of mass consumption consumer goods. This strategy favors an efficient supply chain designed to deliver products to 245 million consumers each week at the lowest possible cost. Efficiency is achieved in a variety of ways. For instance, Walmart keeps relatively low inventory levels, and most of it is stocked in stores available for sale, not in warehouses gathering dust. The low inventory arises from Walmart's use of *cross-docking*—a practice that involves unloading products from suppliers, sorting products for individual stores, and quickly reloading products onto its trucks for a particular store. No warehousing or storing of products occurs, except for a few hours or, at most, a day. Cross-docking allows Walmart to operate only a small number of distribution centers to service its vast network of Walmart stores, Supercenters, Neighborhood Markets, Marketside stores, and Sam's Clubs, which contributes to efficiency.

Walmart has invested much more than its competitors in information technology to operate its supply chain. The company feeds information about customer requirements and demand from its stores back to its suppliers, which manufacture only what is being demanded. This large investment has improved the efficiency of Walmart's supply chain and made it responsive to customer needs.

Three lessons can be learned from these two examples. First, there is no one best supply chain for every company. Second, the best supply chain is the one that is consistent with the needs of the customer segment being served and complements a company's marketing strategy. And finally, supply chain managers are often called upon to make trade-offs between efficiency and responsiveness on various elements of a company's supply chain.

TWO CONCEPTS OF LOGISTICS MANAGEMENT IN A SUPPLY CHAIN

The objective of logistics management in a supply chain is to minimize total logistics costs while delivering the appropriate level of customer service.

Total Logistics Cost Concept

For our purposes, **total logistics cost** includes expenses associated with transportation, materials handling and warehousing, inventory, stockouts (being out of inventory), order processing, and return products handling. Note that many of these costs are interrelated so that changes in one will impact the others. For example, if a firm attempts to reduce its transportation costs by shipping in larger quantities, it will increase its inventory levels. While larger inventory levels will increase inventory costs, they should also reduce stockouts. It is important, therefore, to study the impact on all of the logistics decision areas when considering a change.

Customer Service Concept

Because a supply chain is a *flow,* the end of it—or *output*—is the service delivered to customers. Within the context of a supply chain, **customer service** is the ability of logistics management to satisfy users in terms of time, dependability, communication, and convenience. As suggested by Figure 15–10, a supply chain manager's key task is to balance these four customer service factors against total logistics cost factors.

FIGURE 15–10

Supply chain managers balance total logistics cost factors against customer service factors.

425

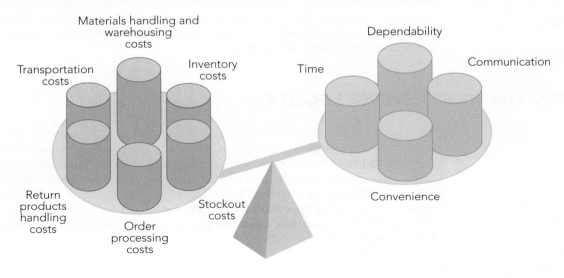

Time In a supply chain setting, time refers to *order cycle* or *replenishment* time for an item, which means the time between the ordering of an item and when it is received and ready for use or sale. The various elements that make up the typical order cycle include recognition of the need to order, order transmittal, order processing, documentation, and transportation. A current emphasis in supply chain management is to reduce order cycle time so that the inventory levels of customers may be minimized. Another emphasis is to make the process of reordering and receiving products as simple as possible, often through inventory systems called *quick response* and *efficient consumer response* delivery systems. For example, at Saks Fifth Avenue, point-of-sale scanner technology records each day's sales. When stock falls below a minimum level, a replenishment order is automatically produced. Vendors such as Donna Karan (DKNY) receive the order, which is processed and delivered within 48 hours.[16]

Dependability Dependability is the consistency of replenishment. This is important to all firms in a supply chain—and to consumers. How often do you return to a store if it fails to have in stock the item you want to purchase? Dependability can be broken into three elements: consistent lead time, safe delivery, and complete delivery. Consistent service allows planning (such as appropriate inventory levels), whereas inconsistencies create surprises. Intermediaries may be willing to accept longer lead times if they know about them in advance and can thus make plans.

Communication Communication is a two-way link between the buyer and supplier that helps in monitoring service and anticipating future needs. Status reports on orders are a typical example of communication between the buyer and seller.

Convenience The concept of convenience for a supply chain manager means that there should be a minimum of effort on the part of the buyer in doing business with the seller. Is it easy for the customer to order? Are the products available from many outlets? Will the seller arrange all necessary details, such as transportation? This customer service factor has promoted the use of **vendor-managed inventory (VMI)**, whereby the *supplier* determines the product amount and assortment a customer (such as a retailer) needs and automatically delivers the appropriate items.

Campbell Soup's system illustrates how VMI works.[17] Every morning, retailers electronically inform the company of their demand for all Campbell products and the inventory levels in their distribution centers. Campbell uses that information to forecast future demand and determine which products need replenishment based on upper and lower inventory limits established with each retailer. Trucks leave the Campbell shipping plant that afternoon and arrive at the retailer's distribution centers with the required replenishments the same day.

CLOSING THE LOOP: REVERSE LOGISTICS

The flow of products in a supply chain does not end with the ultimate consumer or industrial user. Companies today recognize that a supply chain can work in reverse. **Reverse logistics** is a process of reclaiming recyclable and reusable materials, returns, and reworks from the point of consumption or use for repair, remanufacturing, redistribution, or disposal. The effect of reverse logistics can be seen in the reduced waste in landfills and lowered operating costs for companies. The Making Responsible Decisions box describes the successful reverse logistics initiative at Hewlett-Packard.[18]

Making **Responsible Decisions**

Reverse Logistics and Green Marketing Go Together at Hewlett-Packard: Recycling e-Waste

About 53 million tons of electronics and electronic equipment find their way to landfills around the world annually. Americans alone discarded over 400 million analog TV sets and computer monitors and Japanese consumers trashed more than 610 million cell phones in 2014. The result? Landfills are seeping lead, chromium, mercury, and other toxins prevalent in digital debris into the environment.

Fortunately, Hewlett-Packard has taken it upon itself to act responsibly and address this issue through its highly regarded reverse logistics program. Hewlett-Packard has recycled computer and printer hardware since 1987 and is an industry leader in this practice. The company's recycling service is available today in more than 73 countries, regions, and territories. By early 2015, Hewlett-Packard will have recycled over 2 billion pounds of used electronic products and supplies to be refurbished for resale or donation or for recovery of materials.

The recycling effort at Hewlett-Packard is also part of the company's Design for Supply Chain program. Among other initiatives in this program, emphasis is placed on product and packaging changes to reduce reverse supply

Source: Hewlett-Packard Development Company, L.P.

chain and environmental costs. For example, more than 75 percent of the company's ink cartridges and 24 percent of its LaserJet toner cartridges are now manufactured with recycled plastic.

Video 15-3
UPS
kerin.tv/13e/v15-3

Companies such as Motorola and Nokia (return and reuse of mobile phones) and Caterpillar, Xerox, and IBM (remanufacturing and recycling) have implemented acclaimed reverse logistics programs. Other firms have enlisted third-party logistics providers such as UPS, FedEx, and Penske Logistics to handle this process along with other supply chain functions. GNB Technologies, Inc., a manufacturer of lead-acid batteries for automobiles and boats, has outsourced much of its supply chain activity to UPS Supply Chain Services.[19] The company contracts with UPS to manage its shipments between plants, distribution centers, recycling centers, and retailers. This includes movement of both new batteries and used products destined for recycling and covers both truck and railroad shipments. This partnership, along with the initiatives of other battery makers, has paid economic and ecological dividends. By recycling 90 percent of the lead from used batteries, manufacturers have kept the demand for new lead in check, thereby holding down costs to consumers. Also, solid waste management costs and the environmental impact of lead in landfills are reduced.

427

learning review »

15-9. What is the principal difference between a marketing channel and a supply chain?

15-10. The choice of a supply chain involves what three steps?

15-11. A manager's key task is to balance which four customer service factors against which six logistics cost factors?

LO 15-1 *Explain what is meant by a marketing channel of distribution and why intermediaries are needed.*

A marketing channel of distribution, or simply a marketing channel, consists of individuals and firms involved in the process of making a product or service available for use or consumption by consumers or industrial users. Intermediaries make possible the flow of products from producers to buyers by performing three basic functions. The transactional function involves buying, selling, and risk taking because intermediaries stock merchandise in anticipation of sales. The logistical function involves the gathering, storing, and dispensing of products. The facilitating function assists producers in making products and services more attractive to buyers. The performance of these functions by intermediaries creates time, place, form, and possession utility for consumers.

LO 15-2 *Distinguish among traditional marketing channels, electronic marketing channels, and different types of vertical marketing systems.*

Traditional marketing channels describe the route taken by products and services from producers to buyers. This route can range from a direct channel with no intermediaries, because a producer and the ultimate consumer deal directly with each other, to indirect channels where intermediaries (agents, wholesalers, distributors, or retailers) are inserted between a producer and consumer and perform numerous channel functions. Electronic marketing channels employ the Internet to make products and services available for consumption or use by consumer or business buyers. Vertical marketing systems are professionally managed and centrally coordinated marketing channels designed to achieve channel economies and maximum marketing impact. There are three major types of vertical marketing systems (VMSs). A corporate VMS combines successive stages of production and distribution under a single ownership. A contractual VMS exists when independent production and distribution firms integrate their efforts on a contractual basis to obtain greater functional economies and marketing impact than they could achieve alone. An administered VMS achieves coordination at successive stages of production and distribution by the size and influence of one channel member rather than through ownership.

LO 15-3 *Describe factors that marketing executives consider when selecting and managing a marketing channel, including legal restrictions.*

Marketing executives consider three questions when selecting and managing a marketing channel and intermediaries. (1) Which channel and intermediaries will provide the best coverage of the target market? Marketers typically choose one of three levels of market coverage: intensive, selective, or exclusive distribution. (2) Which channel and intermediaries will best satisfy the buying requirements of the target market? These buying requirements fall into four categories: information, convenience, variety, and pre- or postsale services. (3) Which channel and intermediaries will be the most profitable? Here marketers look at the margins earned (revenues minus cost) for each channel member and for the channel as a whole.

LO 15-4 *Explain what supply chain and logistics management are and how they relate to marketing strategy.*

A supply chain refers to the various firms involved in performing the various activities required to create and deliver a product or service to consumers or industrial users. Supply chain management is the integration and organization of information and logistics across firms for the purpose of creating value for consumers. Logistics involves those activities that focus on getting the right amount of the right products to the right place at the right time at the lowest possible cost. Logistics management includes the coordination of the flows of both inbound and outbound products, an emphasis on making these flows cost effective, and customer service. A company's supply chain follows from a clearly defined marketing strategy. The alignment of a company's supply chain with its marketing strategy involves three steps. First, a supply chain must reflect the needs of the customer segment being served. Second, a company must understand what a supply chain is designed to do well. Supply chains range from those that emphasize being responsive to customer requirements and demands to those that emphasize efficiency with the goal of supplying products at the lowest possible delivered cost. Finally, a supply chain must be consistent with the targeted customer's needs and the company's marketing strategy. The Dell and Walmart examples in the chapter illustrate how this alignment is achieved by two market leaders.

LEARNING REVIEW ANSWERS

15-1 What is meant by a marketing channel?
Answer: A marketing channel consists of individuals and firms involved in the process of making a product or service available for use or consumption by consumers or industrial users.

15-2 What are the three basic functions performed by intermediaries?
Answer: Intermediaries perform transactional, logistical, and facilitating functions.

15-3 What is the difference between a direct and an indirect channel?
Answer: A direct channel is one in which a producer of consumer or business products and services and ultimate consumers or industrial users deal directly with each other. An indirect channel has intermediaries that are inserted between the producer and ultimate consumers or industrial users and perform numerous channel functions.

15-4 **Why are channels for business products typically shorter than channels for consumer products?**

Answer: Business channels are typically shorter than consumer channels because business users are fewer in number, tend to be more concentrated geographically, and buy in larger quantities.

15-5 **What is the principal distinction between a corporate vertical marketing system and an administered vertical marketing system?**

Answer: A corporate vertical marketing system combines successive stages of production and distribution under a single ownership. An administered vertical marketing system achieves coordination by the size and influence of one channel member rather than through ownership.

15-6 **What are the three questions marketing executives consider when choosing a marketing channel and intermediaries?**

Answer: The three questions to consider when choosing a marketing channel and intermediaries are: (1) Which will provide the best coverage of the target market? (2) Which will best satisfy the buying requirements of the target market? (3) Which will be the most profitable?

15-7 **What are the three degrees of distribution density?**

Answer: intensive; exclusive; selective

15-8 **What is meant by exclusive dealing?**

Answer: Exclusive dealing exists when a supplier requires channel members to sell only its products or restricts distributors from selling directly competitive products. It is strictly prohibited under the Clayton Act when it lessens competition or creates monopolies.

15-9 **What is the principal difference between a marketing channel and a supply chain?**

Answer: A marketing channel consists of individuals and firms involved in the process of making a product or service available for use or consumption by consumers or industrial users. A supply chain differs from a marketing channel in terms of membership. It includes suppliers who provide raw materials to a manufacturer as well as the wholesalers and retailers—the marketing channel—that deliver the finished goods to ultimate consumers.

15-10 **The choice of a supply chain involves what three steps?**

Answer: (1) Understand the customer. (2) Understand the supply chain. (3) Harmonize the supply chain with the marketing strategy.

15-11 **A manager's key task is to balance which four customer service factors against which six logistics cost factors?**

Answer: The four customer service factors are time, dependability, communication, and convenience. The logistics cost factors are transportation costs, materials handling and warehousing costs, inventory costs, stockout costs (being out of inventory), order processing costs, and return products handling costs.

FOCUSING ON KEY TERMS

channel conflict p. 419	logistics p. 421	supply chain p. 421
customer service p. 425	marketing channel p. 408	total logistics cost p. 425
disintermediation p. 419	multichannel marketing p. 413	vendor-managed inventory
dual distribution p. 413	reverse logistics p. 426	(VMI) p. 426
exclusive distribution p. 416	selective distribution p. 417	vertical marketing systems p. 414
intensive distribution p. 416		

APPLYING MARKETING KNOWLEDGE

1 A distributor for Celanese Chemical Company stores large quantities of chemicals, blends these chemicals to satisfy the requests of customers, and delivers the blends to a customer's warehouse within 24 hours of receiving an order. What utilities does this distributor provide?

2 Suppose the president of a carpet manufacturing firm has asked you to look into the possibility of bypassing the firm's wholesalers (who sell to carpet, department, and furniture stores) and selling direct to these stores. What caution would you voice on this matter, and what type of information would you gather before making this decision?

3 What type of channel conflict is likely to be caused by dual distribution, and what type of conflict can be reduced by direct distribution? Why?

4 How does the channel captain idea differ among corporate, administered, and contractual vertical marketing systems with particular reference to the use of the different forms of influence available to firms?

5 List the customer service factors that would be vital to buyers in the following types of companies: (a) manufacturing, (b) retailing, (c) hospitals, and (d) construction.

Does your marketing plan involve selecting channels and intermediaries? If the answer is "no," read no further and do not include this element in your plan. If the answer is "yes":

1 Identify which channel and intermediaries will provide the best coverage of the target market for your product or service.

2 Specify which channel and intermediaries will best satisfy the important buying requirements of the target market.

3 Determine which channel and intermediaries will be the most profitable.

4 Select your channel(s) and intermediary(ies).

5 If inventory is involved, (*a*) identify the three or four major kinds of inventory needed for your organization (retail stock, finished products, raw materials, supplies, and so on), and (*b*) suggest ways to reduce their costs.

6 (*a*) Rank the four customer service factors (time, dependability, communication, and convenience) from most important to least important from your customers' point of view, and (*b*) identify actions for the one or two factors that are the most important in regard to your product or service.

▣ connect

VIDEO CASE 15   Amazon: Delivering the Earth's Biggest Selection!

"The secret is we are on our seventh generation of fulfillment centers and we have gotten better every time," explains Jeff Bezos, CEO of Amazon.com, Inc. The global online retailer is a pioneer of fast, convenient, low-cost shopping that has attracted millions of consumers. Of course, while Amazon has changed the way many people shop, the company still faces the traditional and daunting task of creating a seamless flow of deliveries to its customers—often millions of times each day.

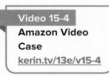

Video 15-4
Amazon Video Case
kerin.tv/13e/v15-4

THE COMPANY

Bezos started Amazon.com with a simple idea: use the Internet to transform book buying into the fastest, easiest, and most enjoyable shopping experience possible. The company was incorporated in 1994 and launched its website in July 1995. At the forefront of a huge growth of dot-com businesses, Amazon pursued a get-big-fast business strategy. Sales grew rapidly and Amazon began adding products and services other than books. In fact, Amazon soon set its goal on being "Earth's most customer-centric company, where customers can find and discover virtually anything they might want to buy online."

Today Amazon.com continues to grow by providing low prices, vast selection, and convenience. Its selection of products covers a broad range of categories including: Books; Movies, Music & Games; Electronics & Computers; Home, Garden & Tools; Beauty, Health & Grocery; Toys; Clothing, Shoes & Jewelry; Sports & Outdoors; and Automotive &

Industrial. In addition, Amazon offers digital music, an appstore for Android, Amazon Cloud Drive, Kindle e-readers, Kindle Fire tablets, Amazon Fire TV, and the Amazon Fire phone. Other services allow customers to:

- Search for a product or brand using all or part of its name.
- Place orders with one click using the "Buy Now with 1-Click" button on the website, and the "Mobile 1-Click" button for phones.
- Receive personalized recommendations based on past purchases through opt-in e-mails.

These products and services have attracted millions of people around the globe. Further, the company's growth has made Amazon.com, along with its international sites in Australia, Brazil, Canada, China, France, Germany, India, Italy, Japan, Mexico, Spain, and the United Kingdom, the world's largest online retailer.

Amazon's e-commerce platform is also used by more than 2 million small businesses, retail brands, and individual sellers. For example, programs such as Selling on Amazon, Fulfillment by Amazon, Amazon Webstore, and Checkout by Amazon allow small businesses to use Amazon's e-commerce platform to facilitate sales. Online retailers store their products at Amazon's fulfillment centers and when they sell a product, Amazon ships it! Amazon.com also operates retail websites for brands such as bebe, Marks & Spencer, Lacoste, and AOL's Shop@AOL. Individual sellers use the Amazon network to reach millions of potential customers. These business partnerships all contribute to Amazon's sales, which now exceed $75 billion.

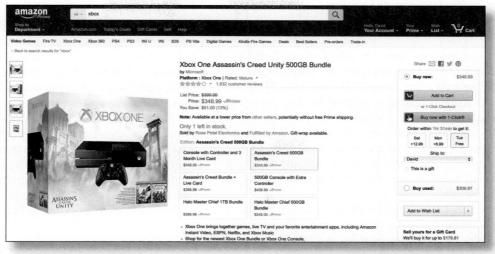

Source: Amazon.com, Inc.

Bezos defines Amazon by its "big ideas, which are customer centricity, putting the customer at the center of everything we do, and invention—we like to pioneer, we like to explore." Amazon's success is also the result of an intense focus on cost and efficiency that leads to lower prices. More specifically, Amazon is exceptional at managing the elements of its supply chain, which make up one of the most complex and expensive aspects of the company's business.

SUPPLY CHAIN AND LOGISTICS MANAGEMENT AT AMAZON.COM

What happens after an order is submitted on Amazon's website but before it arrives at the customer's door? A lot. Amazon.com maintains huge distribution, or "fulfillment," centers where it keeps inventory of millions of products. This is one of the key differences between Amazon.com and some of its competitors—it actually stocks products. Bezos describes how they have improved: "Years ago, I drove the Amazon packages to the post office every evening in the back of my Chevy Blazer. My vision extended so far that I dreamed we might one day get a forklift. Fast-forward to today and we have 96 fulfillment centers." So Amazon must manage the flow of products from its 15 million-plus suppliers to its U.S. and international fulfillment centers with the flow of customer orders from the fulfillment centers to individuals' homes or offices.

The process begins with the suppliers. Amazon collaborates with its suppliers to increase efficiencies and improve inventory turnover. For example, Amazon uses software to forecast purchasing patterns by region, which allows it to give its suppliers better information about delivery dates and volumes. After the products arrive at the fulfillment center they are scanned and placed on shelves in what often appear to be haphazard locations. That is, books may be on the same shelf next to toys and kitchen utensils. Dave Clark, vice president of worldwide operations and customer service at Amazon, explains: "If you look at how these items fit in the bin, they are optimized to utilize the available space, we have computers and algorithms that tell people the areas of the building that have the most space to put the product that's coming in at that time." Clark observes that one of its 1-million-square-foot fulfillment centers (the size of more than 20 football fields) represents a "physical manifestation of earth's biggest selection."

At the same time, Amazon has been improving the part of the process that sorts the products into the individual orders. Once an order is placed in the computer system, sophisticated software generates a map of the location of each product and a "pick ambassador" walks the aisles to select the products. Each item is scanned as it is selected so that inventory levels and locations are always up-to-date. Packers ensure that all items are included in the box before it is taped and labeled. The boxes then travel along a conveyor belt and are diverted into groups based on the delivery location. A network of trucks and regional postal hubs then conclude the process with delivery of the order. Amazon actually uses more trucks than planes!

The success of Amazon's logistics and supply chain management activities may be most evident during the year-end holiday shopping season. Amazon received orders for 36.8 million items on Cyber Monday (the Monday following Thanksgiving), including orders for Xbox and PlayStation gaming consoles that reached more than 1,000 units per minute. During the entire holiday season Amazon shipped orders to 185 countries. Well over 99 percent of the orders were shipped and delivered on time.

CONTINUOUS IMPROVEMENT AT AMAZON

In a recent letter to Amazon shareholders Bezos reported that Amazon employees are "always asking how do we make this better?" He also described the Amazon Kaizen program (named for the Japanese term meaning "change for the better") and how it is used to streamline processes and reduce defects and waste. As a result there are many new changes and improvements under way at Amazon, many of which are related to its supply chain and logistics management approach.

One example of a new service at Amazon is Amazon Fresh, its online, same-day-delivery service for groceries. The service has been in trial stage in Seattle for several years and recently expanded to Los Angeles and San Francisco. The success of the service in these cities is likely to influence how quickly Amazon expands into other cities. Another new service at Amazon is based on its agreement with the United States Postal Service to offer Sunday delivery to select cities. The demand for this service in the trial cities will also influence how quickly it is rolled out to other cities. Finally Amazon received a lot of attention when it revealed that it is developing unmanned aerial drones that could fly small shipments to customers within 30 minutes. "We can carry objects up to 5 pounds which covers 86 percent of the items that we deliver," explains Bezos. The Federal Aviation Administration granted Amazon permission to fly drones experimentally in early 2015.

Amazon.com has come a long way since 1995. Its logistics and supply chain management activities have provided Amazon with a cost-effective and efficient distribution system that combines automation and communication technology with superior customer service. To continue its drive to increase future sales, profits, and customer service, Amazon continues to use its inventive spirit to encourage innovation. According to Bezos, "what we are doing is challenging and fun—we get to work in the future."[20]

Questions

1 How do Amazon.com's logistics and supply chain management activities help the company create value for its customers?

2 What systems did Amazon develop to improve the flow of products from suppliers to Amazon fulfillment centers? What systems improved the flow of orders from the fulfillment centers to customers?

3 Why will logistics and supply chain management play an important role in the future success of Amazon.com?

Chapter Notes

1. Interview with Jeff Newton, Callaway Golf, July 3, 2014; "CallawayGolf.com: The Social Sport," *Internetretailer.com,* December 5, 2013; www.callawaygolf.com, downloaded April 15, 2015; and Stephanie Kang, "Callaway Will Use Retailers to Sell Goods Directly to Consumers Online," *The Wall Street Journal,* November 6, 2006, p. B5.

2. "Eddie Bauer's Banner Time of Year," *Advertising Age,* October 1, 2001, p. 55.

3. *Internet Retailer Top 500 Guide,* 2015 Edition. www.internetretailer.com, downloaded February 10, 2015.

4. "General Mills with Nestlé Is Trying to Make Cereal More Popular Overseas," www.startribune, May 15, 2015; "Cereal Marketers Race for Global Bowl Domination," *Advertising Age,* August 20, 2012, pp. 12–13; "General Mills Reports Fiscal 2014 Third-Quarter Results," General Mills press release, March 19, 2014; "Second-Largest Cereal Producer Turns 20, with Style," General Mills press release, September 13, 2010.

5. For an overview of vertical marketing systems, see Lou Pelton, Martha Cooper, David Strutton, and James R. Lumpkin, *Marketing Channels,* 3rd ed. (Burr Ridge, IL: McGraw-Hill/Irwin, 2005).

6. "Saks to Add Exclusive Lines," *The Wall Street Journal,* February 25, 2010, p. B2.

7. "Dell Treads Carefully into Selling PCs in Stores," *The Wall Street Journal,* January 3, 2008, p. B1.

8. Rafi A. Mohammed, Robert J. Fisher, Bernard J. Jaworski, and Gordon J. Paddison, *Internet Marketing: Building Advantage in a Networked Economy,* 2nd ed. (Burr Ridge, IL: McGraw-Hill/Irwin, 2004).

9. "American Airlines Yanks Its Flights off Travel Sites," www.USAtoday.com, December 23, 2010; "Amazon, Hachette Reach a Truce," *The Wall Street Journal,* November 14, 2014, pp. B1, B2; and "Feud with Seller Hurts Nike Sales, Shares," *Dallas Morning News,* June 28, 2003, p. 30.

10. For an extensive discussion on channel influence and power, see Robert W. Palmatier, Louis W. Stern, and Adel I. El-Ansary, *Marketing Channel Strategy,* 8th ed. (Upper Saddle River, NJ: Prentice Hall, 2015), Chapters 10 and 11.

11. David Simchi-Levi, Philip Kaminsky, and Edith Simchi-Levi, *Designing and Managing the Supply Chain,* 4th ed. (Burr Ridge, IL: McGraw-Hill/Irwin, 2011).

12. *The Smarter Supply Chain of the Future: Industry Edition* (Somer, NY: IBM Corporation, 2009); and John Paul MacDuffie and Takahiro Fujimoto, "Why Dinosaurs Will Keep Ruling the Automobile Industry," *Harvard Business Review,* June 2010, pp. 23–25.

13. Major portions of this discussion are based on Sunil Chopra and Peter Meindl, *Supply Chain Management: Strategy, Planning, and Operations,* 6th ed. (Upper Saddle River, NJ: Prentice Hall, 2016), Chapters 1–3; and Hau L. Lee, "The Triple-A Supply Chain," *Harvard Business Review* (October 2004), pp. 102–12.

14. Jessi Hempel, "IBM's Super Second Act," *Fortune,* March 21, 2011, pp. 115ff; Kevin O'Marah, "The AMR Supply Chain Top 25 for 2015," *Gartner, Inc.,* June 2015; and Thomas A. Foster, "World's Best-Run Supply Chains Stay on Top Regardless of the Competition," *Global Logistics & Supply Chain Strategies,* February 2006, pp. 27–41.

15. This discussion is based on Dave Blanchard, "Top 25 Supply Chains of 2015," www.industryweek.com, June 1, 2015; "The 2014 Supply Chain Top 25: Leading the Decade," *Supply Chain Management Review,* September–October, 2014, pp. 8–17; "*Harvard Business Review,* on Managing Supply Chains," *Harvard Business Review,* June 2011; "The Lessons from Dell's Supply Chain Transformation," www.supplychaindigest.com, March 18, 2011; Brett Booen, "Walmart's Supply Chain Acts as If Every Day Is Black Friday," *Supply Chain Digital,* November 19, 2010; and Chopra and Meindl, *Supply Chain Management.*

16. "Retailers Aim to Turn Minutes into Millions," *The Wall Street Journal,* December 19, 2012, pp. B1, B2; and Christina Passariello, "Logistics Are in Vogue with Designers," *The Wall Street Journal,* June 27, 2008, p. B1.

17. Jean Murphy, "Better Forecasting, S&OP Support Transformation at Campbell's Soup Co.," *Global Logistics & Supply Chain Strategies,* June 2004, pp. 28–30.

18. "Product Return and Recycling," *hp.com,* May 10, 2015; *Second Annual Report of the eCycling Leadership Initiative* (Consumer Electronics Association, April 2013); "Rewriting the Rules for E-Cycling," *Fortune,* March 22, 2010, Special Section; Steve Miller, "Recycling Becomes Electric for CE Brands," *BrandWeek,* May 13, 2008, p. 4; "Don't Toss Out That Old Gadget," *Newsweek,* November 3, 2008, p. E8; and Lorraine Woellert, "HP Wants Your Old PCs Back," *BusinessWeek,* April 10, 2006, pp. 82–83.

19. Doug Bartholomew, "IT Delivers for UPS," *Industry Week,* August 2002, pp. 35–36.

20. Amazon: This case was written by Steven Hartley. Sources: Tim Worstall, "Both Amazon and WalMart Are Really Logistics Companies, Not Retailers," *Forbes.com,* April 11, 2014; Dan Mitchell, "Next Up for Disruption: The Grocery Business," *Fortune.com,* April 4, 2014; Mae Anderson, "Amazon's Bezos Outlines Grocery, Drone Plans," *Businessweek.com,* April 10, 2014; Jeff Bercovici, "The Same-Day War: Amazon, Google and Walmart Race to Bring Your Groceries," *Forbes,* May 5, 2014; Brad Stone, "Why Amazon's Going Up In the Air," *Bloomberg Businessweek,* December 9–15, 2013, pp.12–13; "Record-Setting Holiday Season for Amazon Prime," Amazon press release, December 26, 2013; "Company Info: Overview," http://phx.corporate-ir.net/phoenix.zhtml?c=176060&p=irol-mediaKit; Jeff Bezos, "2013 Letter to Shareholders," http://phx.corporate-ir.net/phoenix.zhtml?c=97664&p=irol-reportsannual; "Amazon's Jeff Bezos Looks to the Future," *60 Minutes* episode, December 1, 2013; and Mark Veverka, "The World's Best Retailer," *Barron's,* March 30, 2009.

16 Retailing and Wholesaling

LEARNING OBJECTIVES

After reading this chapter you should be able to:

LO 16-1 Identify retailers in terms of the utilities they provide.

LO 16-2 Explain the alternative ways to classify retail outlets.

LO 16-3 Describe the many methods of nonstore retailing.

LO 16-4 Classify retailers in terms of the retail positioning matrix, and specify retailing mix actions.

LO 16-5 Explain changes in retailing with the wheel of retailing and the retail life-cycle concepts.

LO 16-6 Describe the types of firms that perform wholesaling activities and their functions.

Shoppers Are Wearing the Future of Retailing!

What will retailing look like in the future? What may be the most influential change taking place for retailers today? Don't look now but the answer is: you are wearing it!

Wearable technology has the potential to completely change the way we shop, and just as importantly, the way retailers sell. You may already own some of the early forms of wearable technology, such as the wristbands that track your activity. More recently, new products such as smartwatches and connected glasses have added many new capabilities. How will these technologies change retailing?

For consumers, wearable technology has the potential to create an enhanced customer experience. Smartwatches can provide information about deals, locations of products, and faster checkout. Target and Kohl's, for example, send messages about special offers to Apple Watch wearers who are near their stores. Once shoppers are in the store their smartphone app will direct them toward sale items and alert them when they are near a selected product. Marsh Supermarkets use the List Ease shopping app developed by mobile marketing company InMarket to guide shoppers to groceries on their list. "Think of it as a list on your wrist," explains InMarket's Dave Heinzinger. Similarly, Apple Watch users who "like" a recipe on cooking app Epicurious will be directed to the ingredients needed to make the meal!

Smartphones will also change the checkout experience for shoppers. Valpak has created an app to provide Apple Watch wearers access to coupons for stores within a 25-mile radius of their location. Similarly, loyalty card apps will eliminate the need to carry, and find, the cards as they will store the barcodes and provide them for display when needed. Even more dramatic is the growing use of near field communication (NFC) products such as Apple Pay and Google Wallet, which permit consumers to pay by holding a device near a payment terminal. In the case of an Apple Watch wearer, simply moving the watch near the scanner will initiate a payment from the shopper's credit card.

Retailers will benefit also. Connected glasses, such as Google Glass, resemble a pair of eyeglasses with a small display screen visible to the wearer. Image and voice recognition capabilities allow relevant information to be displayed on the screen. While consumers have been slow to adopt the glasses because of their appearance, enterprise applications have been much more successful. Retail clerks, salespeople, and technicians use the glasses to check manuals for technical information, verify stock inventories, place orders, or even check out customers from anywhere in the store.

© Marcio Jose Sanchez/AP Images   © Consumer Trends/Alamy

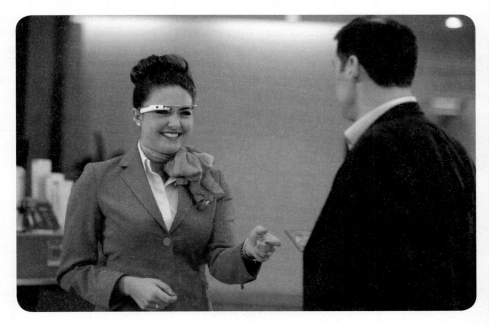

Source: Virgin Airlines

Video 16-1
Apple Watch
kerin.tv/13e/v16-1

In the near future smart contact lenses will be available to consumers and retailers. The lenses will have the potential to create an *augmented* reality that overlays the physical, real-world environment with stored images or graphics. For example, customers could see how a new piece of furniture would look in their apartment or if the color of a pair of shoes matches clothes at home in their closet.[1]

These are just a few examples of the many exciting changes occurring in retailing today. This chapter examines the critical role of retailing in the marketplace and the challenging decisions retailers face as they strive to create value for customers.

What types of products will consumers buy through catalogs, television, the Internet, or by telephone? In what type of store will consumers look for products they don't buy directly? How important is the location of the store? Will customers expect services such as alterations, delivery, installation, or repair? What price should be charged for each product? These are difficult and important questions that are an integral part of retailing. In the channel of distribution, retailing is where the customer meets the product. It is through retailing that exchange (a central aspect of marketing) occurs. **Retailing** includes all activities involved in selling, renting, and providing products and services to ultimate consumers for personal, family, or household use.

THE VALUE OF RETAILING

Identify retailers in terms of the utilities they provide.

Retailing is an important marketing activity. Not only do producers and consumers meet through retailing actions, but retailing also creates customer value and has a significant impact on the economy. To consumers, the value of retailing is in the form of utilities provided (see Figure 16–1). Retailing's economic value is represented by the people employed in retailing as well as by the total amount of money exchanged in retail sales (see Figure 16–2).

Consumer Utilities Offered by Retailing

The utilities provided by retailers create value for consumers. Time, place, form, and possession utilities are offered by most retailers in varying degrees, but one utility is often emphasized more than others. Look at Figure 16–1 to see how well you can match the retailer with the utility being emphasized in the description.

Providing mini banks in supermarkets, as Wells Fargo does, puts the bank's products and services close to the consumer, providing place utility. By providing financ-

FIGURE 16–1

Which retailer best provides which utilities?

Wells Fargo
www.wellsfargo.com

One of the largest and best-run consumer banks in the United States, Wells Fargo reaches 70 million retail customers through 8,700 stores and a worldwide network of 12,500 ATMs.

CarMax
www.carmax.com

CarMax is the nation's largest retailer of used cars, operating 140 superstores. Its "no-haggle" sales policy, test drives, financing, trade-ins, and electronic "walk-arounds" are all offered to encourage customers to purchase from CarMax.

Ralph Lauren
www.ralphlauren.com

Ralph Lauren's *Create Your Own* collection (at www.ralphlauren.com) allows customers to create their own custom shirts by selecting from among 15 styles, 13 colors, 2 logo locations, 12 font styles, 9 logo colors, and 5 sizes. The shirts are delivered in 1–3 business days.

Sports Authority
www.sportsauthority.com

Sports Authority is a sporting goods superstore that provides year-round inventory of equipment for just about any sport you can name. Even during the off-season of seasonal sports, equipment is available at more than 450 Sports Authority stores.

Can you match them?

Time utility

Place utility

Form utility

Possession utility

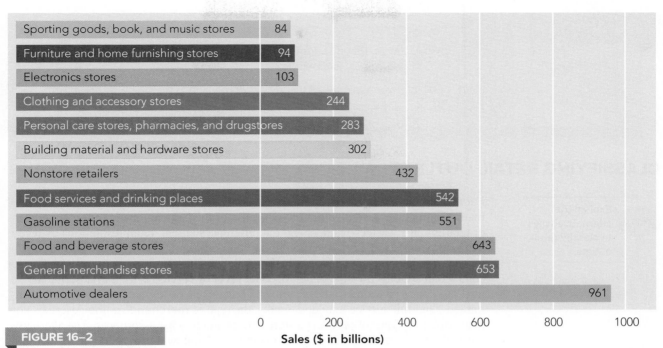

Store type	Sales ($ in billions)
Sporting goods, book, and music stores	84
Furniture and home furnishing stores	94
Electronics stores	103
Clothing and accessory stores	244
Personal care stores, pharmacies, and drugstores	283
Building material and hardware stores	302
Nonstore retailers	432
Food services and drinking places	542
Gasoline stations	551
Food and beverage stores	643
General merchandise stores	653
Automotive dealers	961

Sales ($ in billions)

FIGURE 16–2

Are you surprised by the relative sales of different types of retailers?

Video 16-2
CarMax
kerin.tv/13e/v16-2

ing or leasing and taking used cars as trade-ins, CarMax makes the purchase easier and provides possession utility. Form utility—production or alteration of a product—is offered by Ralph Lauren through its online *Create Your Own* program, which offers shirts that meet each customer's specifications. Finding the right sporting equipment during the off-season is the time utility provided by Sports Authority. Many retailers offer a combination of the four basic utilities. Some supermarkets, for example, offer convenient locations (place utility); are open 24 hours a day (time utility); customize purchases in the bakery, deli, and florist (form utility); and allow several payment and credit options (possession utility).

The Global Economic Impact of Retailing

Retailing is important to the U.S. and global economies. Four of the 40 largest businesses in the United States are retailers (Walmart, Costco, Home Depot, and Target). Walmart's $485 billion in annual sales in 2014 surpassed the gross domestic product of all but 38 countries for that same year. Walmart, Costco, Home Depot, and Target together have more than 3 million employees—more than the combined populations of Jacksonville, Florida; Austin, Texas; and San Jose, California.[2] Figure 16–2 shows that many types of retailers, including food stores, automobile dealers, and general merchandise outlets, are also significant contributors to the U.S. economy.[3]

Outside the United States large retailers include Aeon in Japan, Carrefour in France, Metro Group in Germany, and Tesco in Britain.[4] In emerging economies such as China and Mexico, a combination of local and global retailers is evolving. Walmart, for example, has more than 6,300 stores outside the United States, including stores in Argentina, Brazil, China, India, Japan, Mexico, and the United Kingdom. Despite the presence of these large retailers, however, most international markets are dominated by local retailers.[5]

Tesco is one of the largest retailers outside the United States.

© Keenretail/Alamy

437

CLASSIFYING RETAIL OUTLETS

LO 16-2 Explain the alternative ways to classify retail outlets.

For manufacturers, consumers, and the economy, retailing is an important component of marketing that has several variations. Because of the large number of alternative forms of retailing, it is easier to understand the differences among retail institutions by recognizing that outlets can be classified in several ways. First, **form of ownership** distinguishes retail outlets based on whether independent retailers, corporate chains, or contractual systems own the outlet. Second, **level of service** is used to describe the degree of service provided to the customer. Three levels of service are provided by self-, limited-, and full-service retailers. Finally, the type of **merchandise line** describes how many different types of products a store carries and in what assortment. The alternative types of outlets are discussed in greater detail in the following pages. For many consumers today, retail outlets are also evaluated in terms of their environmentally friendly, or green, activities, in addition to their level of service and merchandise line. The Making Responsible Decisions box gives examples of the green activities of several retailers.[6]

Form of Ownership

There are three general forms of retail ownership—independent retailer, corporate chain, and contractual systems.

Independent Retailer   One of the most common forms of retail ownership is the independent business owned by an individual. Independent retailers account for most of the 1.1 million retail establishments in the United States and include hardware stores, convenience stores, clothing stores, and computer and software stores. In addition, there are 26,700 jewelry stores, 18,500 florists, and 22,100 sporting goods and hobby stores. For the independent retailer, the advantage of this form of ownership is simple: The owner is the boss. For customers, the independent store can offer convenience, personal service, and lifestyle compatibility.[7]

© R Heyes Design/Alamy

Corporate Chain   A second form of ownership, the corporate chain, involves multiple outlets under common ownership. Macy's, Inc., for example, operates 773 Macy's department stores in 45 states. Macy's also owns 37 Bloomingdale's, which compete with other chain stores such as Saks Fifth Avenue and Neiman Marcus. Finally, Macy's recently acquired Bluemercury, which includes 62 specialty beauty and spa services stores.

In a chain operation, centralization in decision making and purchasing is common. Chain stores have advantages in dealing with manufacturers, particularly as the size of the chain grows. A large chain can bargain with a manufacturer to obtain good service or volume discounts on orders. Target's large volume makes it a strong negotiator with manufacturers of most products. For consumers, the buying power of chains translates into lower prices compared with other types of stores. Consumers also benefit in dealing with chains because there are multiple outlets with similar merchandise and consistent management policies.

Retailing has become a high-tech business for many large chains. Walmart, for example, has developed a sophisticated inventory management and cost control system

Making **Responsible Decisions**   Sustainability

How Green Is Your Retailer? The Rankings Are Out!

In a recent Nielsen survey of consumers from 60 countries, 55 percent of the respondents said they are willing to pay more for products and services provided by companies that are committed to positive social and environmental impact. In response, many retailers are "going green" and developing comprehensive and sophisticated business practices that reflect a new focus on social and environmental responsibility. The trend has become so important that *Newsweek* evaluates eight indicators of environmental performance to provide annual "green rankings" of large companies.

The U.S. Green Retail Association offers guidance for retailers who are getting started at implementing new practices, and also provides a third-party certification that recognizes a commitment to "green" values. Some practices are intuitive and simple, such as encouraging the use of reusable shopping bags, installing LED lighting, and using nontoxic cleaning products. Many retailers are even using recyclable materials for credit and gift cards, rather than plastic. Other practices, such as reducing CO_2 emissions with economical delivery vehicles, using rainwater for landscape maintenance, or

Source: Newsweek, LLC

finding alternative uses for landfill waste require a larger effort. Very often, however, these environmental initiatives also have financial benefits. When Home Depot switched light displays to CFL and LED light bulbs, painted the roofs of stores white, and installed solar panels, it reduced its energy use by 20 percent.

Shopping malls are adopting the practices also. In Syracuse, New York, for example, Destiny USA mall implemented water harvesting, air quality protection, landfill reclamation, and energy conservation practices to become the largest LEED (Leadership in Energy and Environmental Design) certified retail building in the world. Similarly, Walgreens became the first retailer to construct a Net Zero Energy store by using solar panels, wind turbines, daylight harvesting, and energy efficient building materials.

Do sustainability practices such as these influence your purchase decisions? If the answer is yes, you may want to review the green rankings at http://www. newsweek.com/search/site/green. Are your favorite retailers "green"?

that allows rapid price changes for each product in every store. In addition, stores such as Walmart and Target are implementing pioneering new technologies such as radio frequency identification (RFID) tags to improve the quality of information available about products.

Contractual Systems   Contractual systems involve independently owned stores that band together to act like a chain. Recall that in Chapter 15, we discussed three kinds of contractual vertical marketing systems: retailer-sponsored cooperatives, wholesaler-sponsored voluntary chains, and franchises (see Figure 15–6). One retailer-sponsored cooperative is Associated Grocers, which consists of neighborhood grocers that all agree with several other independent grocers to buy their goods directly from food manufacturers. In this way, members can take advantage of volume discounts commonly available to chains and also give the impression of being a large chain, which may be viewed more favorably by some consumers. Wholesaler-sponsored voluntary chains such as Independent Grocers Alliance (IGA) try to achieve similar benefits.

In a franchise system, an individual or firm (the franchisee) contracts with a parent company (the franchisor) to set up a business or retail outlet. The franchisor usually assists in selecting the location, setting up the store or facility, advertising, and training personnel. The franchisee usually pays a one-time franchise fee and an annual royalty, usually tied to the franchise's sales. There are two general types of franchises: *business-format franchises,* such as McDonald's, 7-Eleven, Subway, and Anytime Fitness and *product-distribution franchises,* such as a Ford dealership or a Coca-Cola distributor. In business-format franchising, the franchisor provides step-by-step procedures for most aspects of the business and guidelines for the most likely decisions

Franchise	Type of Business	Total Start-up Cost	Number of Franchises
Hampton Hotels	Hotels	$4,000,000–$14,000,000	1,964
Anytime Fitness	Fitness centers	$79,000–$371,000	2,839
Subway	Sandwiches	$117,000–$263,000	42,227
Jack in the Box	Hamburgers	$1,000,000–$2,000,000	2,251
Supercuts	Hair salons	$114,000–$243,000	2,469

a franchisee will face. In product-distribution franchising, the franchisor provides a few general guidelines and the franchisee is much more independent.

Franchising is attractive because it offers an opportunity for people to enter a well-known, established business for which managerial advice is provided. Also, the franchise fee may be less than the cost of setting up an independent business. The International Franchise Association recently estimated that there are 769,782 franchised businesses in the United States, which generate $845 billion in annual sales and employ more than 8.5 million people. Franchising is popular in international markets also: More than half of all U.S. franchisors have operations in other countries. What is one of the fastest-growing franchises? Subway now has 42,227 locations, including 15,610 stores outside the United States.[8]

Franchise fees paid to the franchisor can range from $15,000 for a Subway franchise to $45,000 for a McDonald's restaurant franchise. When the fees are combined with other costs such as real estate and equipment, however, the total investment can be much higher. Franchisees also pay an ongoing royalty fee that ranges from 5 percent for a Papa John's pizza franchise to 30 percent for an H&R Block tax preparation franchise. Figure 16–3 shows the top five franchises, as rated by *Entrepreneur* magazine, based on factors such as size, financial strength, stability, years in business, and costs. By selling franchises, an organization reduces the cost of expansion but loses some control. A good franchisor, however, will maintain strong control of the outlets in terms of delivery and presentation of merchandise and try to enhance recognition of the franchise name.[9]

Anytime Fitness is a popular business-format franchisor.

© Roberto Herrett/Alamy

Redbox provides a service without clerks.

© Ross Dettman/AP Images

Level of Service

Although most customers have little reason to notice form of ownership differences among retailers, they are typically aware of differences in terms of level of service. In some department stores, such as Loehmann's, very few services are provided. Some grocery stores, such as the Cub Foods chain, encourage customers to bag their groceries themselves. In contrast, outlets such as Neiman Marcus provide a wide range of customer services, from gift wrapping to wardrobe consultation.

Self-Service   Self-service requires that customers perform many functions during the purchase process. Warehouse clubs such as Costco, for example, are usually self-service, with all nonessential customer services eliminated. Many gas stations, supermarkets, and airlines today also have self-service lanes and terminals. Video retailer Redbox has 35,000 kiosks throughout the United States—and operates without a single clerk. New forms of self-service are being developed at convenience stores, fast-food restaurants, and even coffee shops! Shop24 offers self-service, automated convenience stores in more than 200 international locations and is expanding into the college and university market. At Zipcar you sign up, receive a Zipcard, book online, walk to a car, scan your card across a reader on the windshield to open the doors, and drive away! In general, the trend is toward retailing experiences that make customers co-creators of the value they receive. A recent survey showed that airline terminals with automated kiosks reduce the wait time for travelers by 22 percent.[10]

Limited Service   Limited-service outlets provide some services, such as credit and merchandise return, but not others, such as clothing alterations. General merchandise stores such as Walmart, Kmart, and Target are usually considered limited service outlets. Customers are responsible for most shopping activities, although salespeople are available in departments such as consumer electronics, jewelry, and lawn and garden.

Full Service   Full-service retailers, which include most specialty stores and department stores, provide many services to their customers. Neiman Marcus, Nordstrom, and Saks Fifth Avenue, for example, all rely on better service to sell more distinctive, higher-margin goods and to retain their customers. Nordstrom offers a wide variety of services, including on-site alterations and tailoring; free exchanges and easy returns; gift cards; credit cards through Nordstrom Bank; a 7-days-a-week customer service line; a live chat line with beauty, design, and wedding specialists; online shopping with in-store pickup; catalogs; and a four-level loyalty program called Nordstrom Rewards. During the next few years the company plans to spend $4.3 billion on additional services and improvements such as an in-store return capability for online purchases, personalized offers to rewards program members, and "smart" fitting rooms.[11]

Type of Merchandise Line

Retail outlets also vary by their merchandise lines, the key distinction being the breadth and depth of the items offered to customers (see Figure 16–4). **Depth of product line** means the store carries a large assortment of each item, such as a shoe store that offers running shoes, dress shoes, and children's shoes. **Breadth of product line** refers to the variety of different items a store carries, such as appliances and books.

Depth of Line   Stores that carry a considerable assortment (depth) of a related line of items are limited-line stores. Sports Authority sporting goods stores carry considerable depth in sports equipment ranging from weight-lifting accessories to running shoes. Stores that carry tremendous depth in one primary line of merchandise are single-line stores. Victoria's Secret, a nationwide chain, carries great depth in women's lingerie. Both limited- and single-line stores are often referred to as *specialty outlets.*

Specialty discount outlets focus on one type of product, such as electronics (Best Buy), office supplies (Staples), or books (Barnes & Noble), at very competitive prices. These outlets are referred to in the trade as *category killers* because they often dominate the market. Best Buy, for example, is the largest consumer electronics retailer

Staples is the category killer in office supplies because it dominates the market in that category.

© McGraw-Hill Education/Editorial Image, LLC, photographer

FIGURE 16–4

Stores vary in terms of the breadth and depth of their merchandise lines.

Breadth: Number of different product lines

	Shoes	Appliances	Books	Men's clothing
Depth: Number of items within each product line	• Nike running shoes • Florsheim dress shoes • Sperry boat shoes • Adidas tennis shoes • Vans skate shoes • Converse sneakers	• General Electric dishwashers • Panasonic microwave ovens • Whirlpool washers • Frigidaire refrigerators	• Mystery • Romance • Science fiction • History • Poetry • Entertainment	• Suits • Ties • Jackets • Overcoats • Socks • Shirts

with more than 1,650 stores, Staples operates more than 1,900 office supply stores, and Barnes & Noble is the largest book retailer. Interesting trends in this form of retailing include a shift to smaller stores, such as Best Buy Mobile stores, and the use of price matching to compete with online retailers.[12]

Breadth of Line Stores that carry a broad product line, with limited depth, are referred to as *general merchandise stores*. For example, large department stores such as Dillard's, Macy's, and Neiman Marcus carry a wide range of different types of products but not unusual sizes. The breadth and depth of merchandise lines are important decisions for a retailer. Traditionally, outlets carried related lines of goods. Today, however, **scrambled merchandising**, offering several unrelated product lines in a single store, is common. For example, the modern drugstore carries food, camera equipment, magazines, paper products, toys, small hardware items, and pharmaceuticals. Supermarkets sell flowers and videos and print photos, in addition to selling groceries.

A form of scrambled merchandising, the **hypermarket**, has been successful in Europe. Hypermarkets are large stores (often more than 200,000 square feet) based on a simple concept: Offer "everything under one roof," thus eliminating the need to stop at more than one location. These stores provide variety, quality, and low prices for groceries and general merchandise items. Carrefour, one of the largest retailers in this category, has 1,459 hypermarkets, including 237 in France, 489 in the rest of Europe, 291 in Latin America, and 375 in Asia. The growth of hypermarkets may be slowing in Europe, however, as consumers' interest in smaller stores and convenient locations has increased. In response, retailers have been cutting prices on food to attract customers and lure them away from competitors. Despite its declining popularity in some parts of the world, the original hypermarket concept is still growing in popularity in many countries; in China, for example, Carrefour, Tesco, and Walmart are expanding the number of stores they operate.[13]

Video 16-3
Walmart
kerin.tv/13e/v16-3

In the United States, retailers have discovered that shoppers are uncomfortable with the huge size of hypermarkets. In response, they have developed a variation of the hypermarket called the *supercenter,* which combines a typical merchandise store with a full-size grocery store. Walmart, Kmart, and Target now use this concept at 3,427 Walmart Supercenters, 11 Kmart Supercenters, and more than 249 SuperTarget stores. Due to the increasing popularity of online retailers, however, the large size of these supercenters is no longer a certain advantage; Amazon.com, for example, is able to offer an even larger selection than these huge stores. Also, due to modern supply chain management techniques, smaller retailers are now able to keep shelves stocked without a lot of inventory. As customer interest shifts, retailers are modifying the supercenter concept to accommodate consumers' interest in smaller, more convenient stores. Walmart, for example, is expanding the number of its grocery stores, Walmart Neighborhood Markets. Figure 16–5 shows the differences between the supercenter and hypermarket concepts.[14]

Scrambled merchandising is convenient for consumers because it eliminates the number of stops required in a shopping trip. However, for the retailer this merchandising policy means there is competition between very dissimilar types of retail outlets, or **intertype competition**. A local bakery may compete with a department store, discount outlet, or even a local gas station. Scrambled merchandising and intertype competition make it more difficult to be a retailer.

FIGURE 16–5

Hypermarkets are popular in Europe, and supercenters are popular in the United States.

	Hypermarket	Supercenter
Region of Popularity	Europe	United States
Average size	90,000–300,000 sq. ft.	100,000–215,000 sq. ft.
Number of products	20,000–80,000	35,000
Annual revenue	$100,000,000 per store	$60,000,000 per store

16-3. Centralized decision making and purchasing are an advantage of _____ ownership.

16-4. What are some examples of new forms of self-service retailers?

16-5. A shop for big men's clothes carries pants in sizes 40 to 60. Would this be considered a broad or a deep product line?

NONSTORE RETAILING

Describe the many methods of nonstore retailing.

Most of the retailing examples discussed thus far in the chapter, such as corporate chains, department stores, and limited- and single-line specialty stores, involve store retailing. Many retailing activities today, however, are not limited to sales in a store. Nonstore retailing occurs outside a retail outlet through activities that involve varying levels of customer and retailer involvement. Figure 16–6 shows six forms of nonstore retailing: automatic vending, direct mail and catalogs, television home shopping, online retailing, telemarketing, and direct selling.

Automatic Vending

Nonstore retailing includes vending machines, or *v-commerce,* which make it possible to serve customers when and where stores cannot. Machine maintenance, operating costs, and location leases can add to the cost of the products, so prices in vending machines are often higher than those in stores. About 34 percent of the products sold from vending machines are cold beverages, another 28 percent are candy and snacks, and 7 percent are food. Many new types of products are quickly becoming available in vending machines. Best Buy now uses vending machines to sell mobile phone and computer accessories, digital cameras, flash drives, and other consumer electronics products in airports, hospitals, and businesses. Similarly, HealthyYou Vending manufactures machines designed to distribute healthy drinks, snacks, and entrées in offices,

443

FIGURE 16–6

Many retailing activities do not involve a store. How many forms of nonstore retailing have you used?

health clubs, hospitals, schools, and colleges. The 4.8 million vending machines currently in use in the United States generate more than $19.5 billion in annual sales.[15]

Improved technology is making vending easier to use. Many vending machines now have touchscreens and credit card readers. In addition, some vending machine companies are testing wireless technology to allow consumers to make vending machine purchases using their mobile phones. Wireless technology is also being used by companies to monitor sales; this information is used to schedule trips to restock machines when items are sold out. Another improvement in vending machines is the trend toward "green" machines, which consume less energy by using more efficient compressors, more efficient lighting, and better insulation. Vending machines are popular with consumers; recent consumer satisfaction research indicates that 82 percent of consumers believe purchasing from a vending machine is equal to or superior to a store purchase. For today's consumers, vending machines represent an extension of brands that are already available in stores, through catalogs, and online.[16]

Vending machines offer a variety of products. Which types of products are most common in a vending machine? For the answer, see the text.
Source: HealthyYOU® Vending

Video 16-4
IKEA
kerin.tv/13e/v16-4

Specialty catalogs appeal to market niches. They create value by providing a fast and convenient way to shop.
Sources: Left: Inter IKEA Systems B.V.; Middle: Crate and Barrel; Right: L.L.Bean Inc.

Direct Mail and Catalogs

Direct-mail and catalog retailing has been called "the store that comes to the door." It is attractive for several reasons. First, it can eliminate the cost of a store and clerks. Dell, for example, is one of the largest computer and information technology retailers, and it does not have any stores. Second, direct mail and catalogs improve marketing efficiency through segmentation and targeting, and they create customer value by providing a fast and convenient means of making a purchase. Finally, many catalogs now serve as a tool to encourage consumers to visit a website, a social media page, or even a store. Online retailers such as Zappos, Amazon, and eBay, for example, now offer catalogs. The average U.S. household today receives 24 direct-mail items or catalogs each week. The Direct Marketing Association estimates that direct-mail and catalog retailing creates $642 billion in sales. Direct-mail and catalog retailing is popular outside the United States, also. Furniture retailer IKEA delivered 217 million copies of its catalog in 32 languages last year.[17]

Several factors have had an impact on direct-mail and catalog retailing in recent years. The influence of large retailers such as IKEA, Crate and Barrel, L.L.Bean, and others has been positive as their marketing activities have increased the number and variety of products consumers purchase through direct mail and catalogs. Higher paper costs and increases in postage rates, the growing interest in do-not-mail legislation, the concern for "green" mailings and catalogs, and the possibility of the U.S. Postal Service reducing delivery to five days, however, have caused direct-mail and catalog retailers to

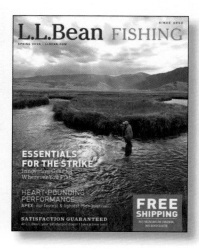

search for ways to provide additional customer value. One approach has been to focus on proven customers rather than prospective customers. Some merchants, such as Williams-Sonoma, reduce mailings to zip codes that have not been profitable. Another successful approach used by many catalog retailers is to send specialty catalogs to market niches identified in their databases. L.L.Bean, for example, has developed an individual catalog for fly-fishing enthusiasts.[18]

New, creative forms of direct-mail and catalog retailing are also being developed. For example, retailers are creating digital versions of catalogs, which can be accessed through catalog-aggregating apps such as Google Catalogs. In the future, you will also see merchants using direct mail and catalogs to direct customers to personalized URLs (PURLs), such as www.JohnSmith.offer.com, which are web pages preloaded with information and offerings specific to an individual.[19]

Television Home Shopping

Television home shopping is possible when consumers watch a shopping channel on which products are displayed; orders are then placed over the telephone or the Internet. Currently, the three largest programs are QVC, HSN, and ShopNBC. QVC ("quality, value, convenience") broadcasts live 24 hours each day, 364 days a year, and reaches 198 million cable and satellite homes in the United States, United Kingdom, Germany, Japan, and Italy. The company generates sales of $8.8 billion from its 60 million customers by offering more than 1,000 products each week. The television home shopping channels offer apparel, jewelry, cooking, home improvement products, electronics, toys, and even food. Of all these products, the best-selling item ever was a Dell personal computer.[20]

In the past, television home shopping programs attracted mostly 40- to 60-year-old women. To attract a younger audience, QVC has invited celebrities onto the show. For example, Heidi Klum has been on the show promoting her jewelry collection, and Kim, Khloe, and Kourtney Kardashian have been hosts selling their apparel line. Singer Dolly Parton recently appeared on the show to sell her newest album. Broadcasting events such as the Red Carpet Style show at the Four Seasons Hotel in Beverly Hills also helps attract new customers. In addition, QVC supports its television program with retail stores, a website, mobile apps, text alerts, and online chats during programming. Similarly, Home Shopping Network now offers a multiplatform shopping experience. Some experts suggest that television shopping programs are becoming a modern version of door-to-door retailing by combining elements of reality TV programs, talk shows, and infomercials.[21]

Television home shopping programs serve millions of customers each year. See the text to learn how they are attracting new customers.

© Rick Diamond/Getty Images for Webster PR

Online Retailing

Online retailing allows consumers to search for, evaluate, and order products through the Internet. For many consumers, the advantages of this form of retailing are the 24-hour access, the ability to comparison shop, in-home privacy, and variety. Early studies of online shoppers indicated that men were initially more likely than women to buy something online. As the number of online households has increased, however, the profile of online shoppers has changed to include all shoppers.

Today, traditional and online retailers—"bricks and clicks"—are melding, using experiences from both approaches to create better value and experiences for customers. For example, Walmart (www.walmart.com) offers its Site-to-Store service that allows customers to place an order online and pick it up at a Walmart store. In addition, Walmart now offers its HomeFree option, which provides free shipping to customers' homes when they order $50 or more of selected items. The Walmart Mobile app allows shoppers to order products using their smartphones

Shopping "bots" like mysimon.com find the best prices for products specified by consumers. Read the text to learn more!

Source: CBS Interactive Inc.

and tablets. Two of the biggest days for online retailing are the Friday after Thanksgiving—Black Friday—and the Monday after Thanksgiving—Cyber Monday—which generated $2.4 billion and $2.6 billion in online sales, respectively. Online sales account for approximately 6.5 percent of all retail sales and are expected to reach $500 billion in 2018.[22]

Online retail purchases can be the result of several very different approaches. First, consumers can pay dues to become a member of an online discount service such as www.netmarket.com. The service offers thousands of products and hundreds of brand names at very low prices to its subscribers. Another approach to online retailing is to use a shopping "bot" such as www.mysimon.com. This site searches the Internet for a product specified by the consumer and provides a report listing retailers with the best prices. Consumers can also use the Internet to go directly to online malls (www.fashionmall.com), apparel retailers (www.gap.com), bookstores (www.amazon.com), computer manufacturers (www.dell.com), grocery stores (www.peapod.com), music and video stores (www.tower.com), and travel agencies (www.travelocity.com). Another approach is the online auction such as www.ebay.com, where 157 million buyers and 25 million sellers trade "practically anything."[23] A final approach to online retailing is "flash sales" at sites such as www.gilt.com and www.hautelook.com which will send you text messages announcing limited-time offers at big discounts.[24]

One of the biggest problems online retailers face is that nearly two-thirds of online shoppers make it to "checkout" and then leave the website to compare shipping costs and prices on other sites. Of the shoppers who leave, 70 percent do not return. One way online retailers are addressing this issue is to offer consumers a comparison of competitors' offerings. At Allbookstores.com, for example, consumers can use a "comparison engine" to compare prices with Amazon.com, Barnesandnoble.com, and as many as 25 other bookstores. Experts suggest that online retailers should think of their websites as dynamic billboards if they are to attract and retain customers, and they should be easy to use, customizable, and facilitate interaction to enhance the online customer experience.[25] For example, BMW, Mercedes, and Jaguar encourage website visitors to "build" a vehicle by selecting interior and exterior colors, packages, and options; view the customized virtual car; and then use Facebook, Twitter, or e-mail to share the configuration.

Online retailing is also evolving to include social shopping options, including: *intermediaries,* such as Groupon and LivingSocial, that match consumers with merchants; *marketplaces,* such as Google Offer and Storenvy, that provide a self-service advertising site; and *aggregators,* such as Yipit, that crawl the Web to find deals to list on their own site. Many consumers also use online resources as price comparison sites that influence their offline shopping at local stores.[26]

Telemarketing

Another form of nonstore retailing, called **telemarketing**, involves using the telephone to interact with and sell directly to consumers. Compared with direct mail, telemarketing is often viewed as a more efficient means of targeting consumers. Insurance companies, brokerage firms, and newspapers have often used this form of retailing as a way to cut costs but still maintain access to their customers. According to the Direct Marketing Association, annual telemarketing sales exceed $332 billion.[27]

The telemarketing industry has recently gone through dramatic changes as a result of new legislation related to telephone solicitations. Issues such as consumer privacy, industry standards, and ethical guidelines have encouraged discussion among consumers, Congress, the Federal Trade Commission, and businesses. As a result, legislation created the National

Do Not Call Registry (www.donotcall.gov) for consumers who do not want to receive telephone calls related to company sales efforts. Currently, there are more than 221 million phone numbers on the registry. Companies that use telemarketing have already adapted by adding compliance software to ensure that numbers on the list are not called.[28]

Direct Selling

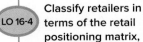

Direct selling, sometimes called door-to-door retailing, involves direct sales of products and services to consumers through personal interactions and demonstrations in their home or office. A variety of companies, including familiar names such as Avon, Fuller Brush, Mary Kay Cosmetics, and World Book, have created an industry with more than $31 billion in U.S. sales by providing consumers with personalized service and convenience. In the United States, there are more than 15 million direct salespeople working full time and part time in a variety of product categories, including wellness, home durables, and personal care.[29]

Growth in the direct-selling industry is the result of two trends. First, many direct-selling retailers are expanding into markets outside the United States. Avon, for example, has 6 million sales representatives in 80 countries. More than one-third of Amway's $11.8 billion in sales now comes from China and 90 percent comes from outside the United States. Similarly, other retailers such as Herbalife and Electrolux are rapidly expanding into new markets.[30] Direct selling is likely to continue to grow in markets where the lack of effective distribution channels increases the importance of door-to-door convenience and where the lack of consumer knowledge about products and brands increases the need for a person-to-person approach.

The second trend is the growing number of companies that are using direct selling to reach consumers who prefer one-on-one customer service and a social shopping experience rather than online shopping or big discount stores. The Direct Selling Association reports that the number of companies using direct selling is increasing. Pampered Chef, for example, has 60,000 independent sales reps who sell the company's products at in-home "Cooking Shows." Interest among potential sales representatives grew during the recent economic downturn as people sought independence and control of their work activities.[31]

learning review »

16-6. Successful catalog retailers often send _____ catalogs to _____ markets identified in their databases.

16-7. How are retailers increasing consumer interest and involvement in online retailing?

16-8. Where are direct-selling retail sales growing? Why?

RETAILING STRATEGY

This section describes how a retailer develops and implements a retailing strategy. Research suggests that factors related to market and competitor characteristics may influence strategic choices and that the combination of choices is an important consideration for retailers.[32] Figure 16–7 identifies the relationship between strategy, positioning, and the retailing mix.

Positioning a Retail Store

LO 16-4 Classify retailers in terms of the retail positioning matrix, and specify retailing mix actions.

The classification alternatives presented in the previous sections help determine one store's position relative to its competitors. The **retail positioning matrix** is a matrix

FIGURE 16–7

Retailing strategy

Retail store positioning

Retailing mix

Merchandise management

Store management

Retail pricing

Store location

Retail communication

Merchandise

developed by the MAC Group, Inc., a management consulting firm.[33] This matrix positions retail outlets on two dimensions: breadth of product line and value added. As defined previously, *breadth of product line* is the range of products sold through each outlet. The second dimension, *value added,* includes elements such as location (as with 7-Eleven stores), product reliability (as with Holiday Inn or McDonald's), or prestige (as with Saks Fifth Avenue or Brooks Brothers).

The retail positioning matrix in Figure 16–8 shows four possible positions. An organization can be successful in any position, but unique strategies are required within each quadrant. Consider the four retailers shown in the matrix:

1. Bloomingdale's has high value added and a broad product line. Retailers in this quadrant pay great attention to store design and product lines. Merchandise often has a high margin of profit and is of high quality. The stores in this position typically provide high levels of service.

FIGURE 16–8

Positioning strategies for retailers are based on breadth of product line and value added.

Walmart: © Frederic J. Brown/AFP/Getty Images; Bloomingdale's: © Richard Levine/Alamy; Tiffany & Co: © Ethan Miller/Getty Images; Payless ShoeSource: © Philip Scalia/Alamy

2. Walmart has low value added and a broad line. Walmart and similar firms typically trade a lower price for increased volume in sales. Retailers in this position focus on price with low service levels and an image of being a place for bargains.

3. Tiffany & Co. has high value added and a narrow line. Retailers of this type typically sell a very restricted range of products that are high in status and quality. Customers are also provided with high levels of service.

4. Payless ShoeSource has low value added and a narrow line. For example, it carries athletic shoes at a discount. Economies of scale are achieved through centralized advertising, merchandising, buying, and distribution. Stores are usually the same in design, layout, and merchandise; hence they are often referred to as "cookie-cutter" stores.

Retailing Mix

In developing a retailing strategy, managers work with the **retailing mix**, which includes activities related to managing the store and the merchandise in the store. The retailing mix is similar to the marketing mix and includes retail pricing, store location, retail communication, and merchandise (see Figure 16–7).

Retail Pricing   In setting prices for merchandise, retailers must decide on the markup, markdown, and timing for markdowns. As mentioned in Appendix B (following Chapter 14), the *markup* refers to how much should be added to the cost the retailer paid for a product to reach the final selling price. Retailers decide on the *original markup,* but by the time the product is sold, they end up with a *maintained markup.* The original markup is the difference between retailer cost and initial selling price. When products do not sell as quickly as anticipated, their price is reduced. The difference between the final selling price and retailer cost is the maintained markup, which is also called the *gross margin.*

Discounting a product, or taking a *markdown,* occurs when the product does not sell at the original price and an adjustment is necessary. Often new models or styles force the price of existing models to be marked down. Discounts may also be used to increase demand for complementary products.[34] For example, retailers might take a markdown on the price of cake mix to generate frosting purchases.

The *timing* of a markdown can be important. Many retailers take a markdown as soon as sales fall off to free up valuable selling space and cash. However, other stores delay markdowns to discourage bargain hunters and maintain an image of quality. There is no clear answer, but retailers must consider how the timing might affect future sales. Research indicates that frequent promotions increase consumers' ability to remember regular prices.[35]

Although most retailers plan markdowns, many retailers use price discounts as part of their regular merchandising policy. Walmart and Home Depot, for example, emphasize consistently low prices and eliminate most markdowns with a strategy often called *everyday low pricing* (EDLP).[36] Because consumers often use price as an indicator of product quality, however, the brand name of the product and the image of the store become important decision factors in these situations.[37] Another strategy, *everyday fair pricing,* is advocated by retailers that may not offer the lowest price but try to create value for customers through service and the total buying experience.[38] Consumers often use the prices of *benchmark* or *signpost* items, such as a can of Coke, to form an overall impression of a store's prices.[39] In addition, price is the most likely factor to influence consumers' assessment of merchandise value.[40] When store prices are based on rebates, retailers must be careful to avoid negative consumer perceptions if the rebate processing time is long (e.g., six weeks).[41]

A special issue for retailers trying to keep prices low is *shrinkage,* or breakage, theft, and fraud by customers and employees. The National Retail Federation estimates that the average retailer loses 1.4 percent of sales to shrinkage each year, totaling

At off-price retail stores like T.J. Maxx, prices are low but selection may be unpredictable.

© Tim Boyle/Bloomberg via Getty Images

approximately $34 billion. Fraudulent returns alone account for close to $9 billion. About 44 percent of retail shrinkage is due to employee theft. Some retailers have noticed an increase in theft and fraud as economic conditions have declined. In general, the issue has increased retailers' interest in new technical and surveillance techniques designed to detect and reduce shrinkage.[42]

Off-price retailing is a retail pricing practice that is used by retailers such as T.J. Maxx, Burlington Coat Factory, and Ross Stores. **Off-price retailing** involves selling brand-name merchandise at lower than regular prices. The difference between the off-price retailer and a discount store is that off-price merchandise is bought by the retailer from manufacturers with excess inventory at prices below wholesale prices. The discounter, however, buys at full wholesale prices but takes less of a markup than traditional department stores. Because of this difference in the way merchandise is purchased by the retailer, selection at an off-price retailer is unpredictable, and searching for bargains has become a popular activity for many consumers. "It's more like a sport than it is like ordinary shopping," says Christopher Boring of Columbus, Ohio's Retail Planning Associates.[43] Savings to the consumer at off-price retailers are reportedly as high as 70 percent off the prices of a traditional department store.

There are several variations of off-price retailing. One is the *warehouse club*. These large stores (100,000 to 140,000 square feet) are rather stark outlets that typically lack elaborate displays, customer service, or home delivery. Warehouse clubs require an annual membership fee (ranging from $30 to $100) for the privilege of shopping there. While a typical Walmart stocks 30,000 to 60,000 items, warehouse clubs carry 4,000 to 8,000 items and usually stock just one brand of appliance or food product. Service is minimal, and customers usually pay by cash or check. Customers are attracted by the ultra-low prices and surprise deals on selected merchandise, although several of the clubs have recently started to add ancillary services such as optical shops and pharmacies to differentiate themselves from competitors. The major warehouse clubs in the United States include Walmart's Sam's Club, BJ's Wholesale Club, and Costco's Warehouse Club. Sales of these off-price retailers have grown to approximately $410 billion annually.[44]

Off 5th provides an outlet for excess merchandise from Saks Fifth Avenue.

© Paul Sakuma/AP Images

A second variation is the *outlet store*. Factory outlets, such as Van Heusen Factory Store, Bass Shoe Outlet, and Gap Factory Store, offer products for 25 to 75 percent off the suggested retail price. Manufacturers use the stores to clear excess merchandise and to reach consumers who focus on value shopping. Retail outlets such as Nordstrom Rack and Off 5th (an outlet for Saks Fifth Avenue) allow retailers to sell excess merchandise and still maintain an image of offering merchandise at full price in their primary store. Increasingly, retailers are offering merchandise made expressly for the outlet division. The recessionary economic climate has increased demand for this type of off-price retailing, and many retailers have responded by opening more outlet stores. For example, Bloomingdale's recently opened its first outlets. According to Michael Gould, Bloomingdale's CEO, "Outlets deliver a compelling combination of fashion, quality, and value."[45]

A third variation of off-price retailing is offered by *single-price,* or *extreme value, retailers* such as Family Dollar, Dollar General, and Dollar Tree. These stores average about 6,000 square feet in size and attract customers who want value and a "corner store" environment rather than a large supercenter experience. Some experts predict extraordinary growth of these types of retailers. Dollar General, for example, already has 11,800 stores in 43 states and plans to open more.[46]

Store Location A second aspect of the retailing mix involves choosing a location and deciding how many stores to operate. Department stores, which started downtown in most cities, have followed customers to the suburbs, and in recent years more stores have been opened in large regional malls. Most stores today are near several others in one of five settings: the central business district, the regional center, the community shopping center, the strip mall, or the power center.

The **central business district** is the oldest retail setting, the community's downtown area. Until the regional outflow to suburbs, it was the major shopping area, but the suburban population has grown at the expense of the downtown shopping area. Consumers often view central business district shopping as less convenient because of lack of parking, higher crime rates, and exposure to the weather. Many cities such as Louisville, Denver, and San Antonio have implemented plans to revitalize shopping in central business districts by attracting new offices, entertainment, and residents to downtown locations.

Regional shopping centers consist of 50 to 150 stores that typically attract customers who live or work within a 5- to 10-mile range. These large shopping areas often contain two or three *anchor stores,* which are well-known national or regional stores such as Sears, Saks Fifth Avenue, and Bloomingdale's. The largest variation of a regional center in North America is the West Edmonton Mall in Alberta, Canada. This shopping center is a conglomerate of more than 800 stores, the world's largest indoor amusement park, more than 100 restaurants, a movie complex, and two hotels, all of which attract 30 million visitors each year.[47]

A more limited approach to retail location is the **community shopping center**, which typically has one primary store (usually a department store branch) and often about 20 to 40 smaller outlets. Generally, these centers serve a population of consumers who are within a 10- to 20-minute drive.

Not every suburban store is located in a shopping mall. Many neighborhoods have clusters of stores, referred to as a **strip mall**, to serve people who are within a 5- to 10-minute drive. Gas station, hardware, laundry, grocery, and pharmacy outlets are commonly found in a strip mall. Unlike the larger shopping centers, the composition of these stores is usually unplanned. A variation of the strip mall is called the **power center**, which is a huge shopping strip with multiple anchor (or national) stores such as Home Depot, Best Buy, or JCPenney. Power centers combine the convenience of location provided by strip malls with the power of national stores. These large strip malls often have two to five anchor stores and contain a supermarket, which brings the shopper to the power center on a weekly basis.[48]

Retail Communication A retailer's communication activities can play an important role in positioning a store and creating its image. While the typical elements of communication and promotion are discussed in Chapter 18 on advertising, sales promotion, and public relations, Chapter 19 on social media, and Chapter 20 on personal selling, the message communicated by the many other elements of the retailing mix is also important.

Deciding on the image of a retail outlet is an important retailing mix factor that has been widely recognized and studied since the late 1950s. Pierre Martineau described image as "the way in which the store is defined in the shopper's mind," partly by its functional qualities and partly by an aura of psychological attributes.[49] In this definition, *functional* refers to mix elements such as price ranges, store layouts, and breadth and depth of merchandise lines. The psychological attributes are the intangibles such as a sense of belonging, excitement, style, or warmth. Image has been found to include impressions of the corporation that operates the store, the category or type of store, the product categories in the store, the brands in each category, merchandise and service quality, and the marketing activities of the store.[50]

Closely related to the concept of image is the store's atmosphere, or ambience. Many retailers believe that sales are affected by layout, color, lighting, music, scent,[51] and other elements of the retail environment. This concept leads many retailers to use **shopper marketing**—the use of displays, coupons, product samples, and

© Stars and Stripes/Alamy

Applying **Marketing Metrics**

Why Apple Stores May Be the Best in the United States!

How effective is my retail format compared to other stores? How are my stores performing this year compared to last year? Information related to these questions is often displayed in a marketing dashboard using two measures: (1) sales per square foot and (2) same-store sales growth.

Your Challenge

You have been assigned to evaluate the Apple Store retail format. The store's simple, inviting, and open atmosphere has been the topic of discussion among many retailers. To allow an assessment of Apple Stores, use *sales per square foot* as an indicator of how effectively retail space is used to generate revenue and *same-store sales growth* to compare the increase in sales of stores that have been open for the same period of time. The calculations for these two indicators are:

$$\text{Sales per square foot} = \frac{\text{Total sales}}{\text{Selling area in square feet}}$$

Same-store sales growth

$$= \frac{\text{Store sales in year 2} - \text{Store sales in year 1}}{\text{Store sales in year 1}}$$

Your Findings

You decide to collect sales information for Target, Neiman Marcus, Best Buy, Tiffany, and Apple Stores to allow comparisons with other successful retailers. The information you collect allows the calculation of *sales per square foot* and *same-store growth* for each store. The results are then easy to compare in the graphs below.

Your Action

The results of your investigation indicate that Apple Stores' sales per square foot are higher than any of the comparison stores at $4,798. In addition, Apple's same-store growth rate of 22 percent is higher than all of the other retailers. You conclude that the elements of Apple's format are very effective and even indicate that Apple may currently be the best retailer in the United States.

other brand communications to influence shopping behavior in a store. Shopper marketing can also influence behavior in an online shopping environment and when shoppers use smartphone apps to identify shopping needs or make purchase decisions.[52] In creating the right image and atmosphere, a retail store tries to attract a target audience and fortify beliefs about the store, its products, and the shopping experience in the store. While store image perceptions can exist independently of shopping experiences, consumers' shopping experiences influence their perceptions of a store.[53] In addition, the physical surroundings of the retail environment influence a store's employees.[54]

Merchandise The final element of the retailing mix is the merchandise offering. Managing the breadth and depth of the product line requires retail buyers who are familiar with both the needs of the target market and the alternative products available from the many manufacturers that might be interested in having a product available in the store. A popular approach to managing the assortment of merchandise today is called **category management**. This approach assigns a manager the responsibility for selecting all products that consumers in a market segment might view as substitutes for each other, with the objective of maximizing sales and profits in the category. For example, a category manager might be responsible for shoes in a department store or paper products in a grocery store. As such, he or she would consider trade deals, order costs, and the between-brand effects of price range changes to determine brand assortment, order quantities, and prices.[55]

Retailers have a variety of marketing metrics that can be used to assess the effectiveness of a store or retail format. First, there are measures related to customers such as the number of transactions per customer, the average transaction size per customer, the number of customers per day or per hour, and the average length of a store visit. Second, there are measures related to the stores and the products such as level of inventory, number of returns, inventory turnover, inventory carrying cost, and average number of items per transaction. Finally, there are financial measures, such as gross margin, sales per employee, return on sales, and markdown percentage.[56] The two most popular measures for retailers are *sales per square foot* and *same-store sales growth*. The Applying Marketing Metrics box describes the calculation of these measures for Apple Stores.[57]

learning review »

16-9. What are the two dimensions of the retail positioning matrix?

16-10. How does original markup differ from maintained markup?

16-11. A huge shopping strip mall with multiple anchor stores is a(n) _____ center.

THE CHANGING NATURE OF RETAILING

LO 16-5 Explain changes in retailing with the wheel of retailing and the retail life-cycle concepts.

Retailing is the most dynamic aspect of a channel of distribution. New types of retailers are always entering the market, searching for a new position that will attract customers. The reason for this continual change is explained by two concepts: the wheel of retailing and the retail life cycle.

The Wheel of Retailing

Video 16-5
McDonald's
kerin.tv/13e/v16-5

The **wheel of retailing** describes how new forms of retail outlets enter the market.[58] Usually they enter as low-status, low-margin stores such as a drive-in hamburger stand with no indoor seating and a limited menu (Figure 16–9, box 1). Gradually these outlets add fixtures and more embellishments to their stores (in-store seating, plants, and chicken sandwiches as well as hamburgers) to increase the attractiveness for customers. With these additions, prices and status rise (box 2). As time passes, these outlets add still more services and their prices and status increase even further (box 3). These retail outlets now face some new form of retail outlet that again appears as a low-status, low-margin operator (box 4), and the wheel of retailing turns as the cycle starts to repeat itself.

When Ray Kroc bought McDonald's in 1955, it opened shortly before lunch and closed just after dinner, and it offered a limited menu for the two meals without any inside seating for customers. Over time, the wheel of retailing has led to new products

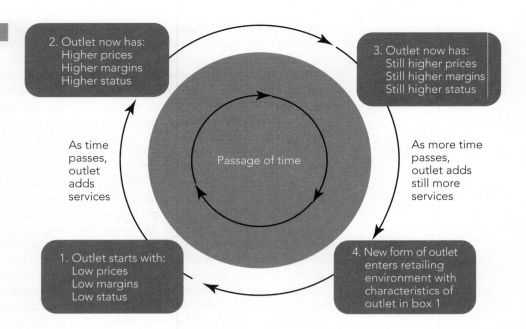

FIGURE 16–9

The wheel of retailing describes how retail outlets change over time. Read the text to find out the position of McDonald's and Checkers on the wheel of retailing.

2. Outlet now has:
Higher prices
Higher margins
Higher status

3. Outlet now has:
Still higher prices
Still higher margins
Still higher status

As time passes, outlet adds services

Passage of time

As more time passes, outlet adds still more services

1. Outlet starts with:
Low prices
Low margins
Low status

4. New form of outlet enters retailing environment with characteristics of outlet in box 1

Outlets such as Checkers enter the wheel of retailing as low-status, low-margin stores.

© McGraw-Hill Education/Mark Dierker, photographer

and services. In 1975, McDonald's introduced the Egg McMuffin and turned breakfast into a fast-food meal. Today, McDonald's offers an extensive menu, including oatmeal and premium coffee, and it provides seating and services such as wireless Internet connections and kid-friendly PlayPlaces. For the future, McDonald's is testing new food products including cakes and pastries, all-day breakfast, antibiotic-free chicken, and a "Create Your Taste" option, which allows consumers to select their own toppings for a gourmet burger, and new services such as touchscreen kiosks and even a bicycle drive-thru.[59]

These changes are leaving room for new forms of outlets such as Checkers Drive-In Restaurants. The Checkers chain opened fast-food stores that offered only basics—burgers, fries, and cola, a drive-thru window, and no inside seating—and now has more than 800 stores. The wheel is turning for other outlets, too—Boston Market has added pickup, delivery, and full-service catering to its original restaurant format, and it also provides Boston Market meal solutions through supermarket delis and Boston Market frozen meals in the frozen food sections of groceries. For still others, the wheel has come full circle. Taco Bell is now opening small, limited-offering outlets in gas stations, discount stores, or "wherever a burrito and a mouth might possibly intersect."[60]

The wheel of retailing is also evident in retail outlets outside the restaurant industry. Discount stores were a major new retailing form in the 1960s and priced their products below those of department stores. As prices in discount stores rose in the 1980s, they found themselves overpriced compared with a new form of retail outlet—the warehouse club. Today, off-price retailers and factory outlets are offering prices even lower than warehouse clubs.

The Retail Life Cycle

The process of growth and decline that retail outlets, like products, experience is described by the **retail life cycle**.[61] Figure 16–10 below shows the stages of the retail life cycle and where various forms of retail outlets are currently positioned along its spectrum. *Early growth* is the stage of emergence of a retail outlet, with a sharp departure from existing competition. Market share rises gradually, although profits may be low

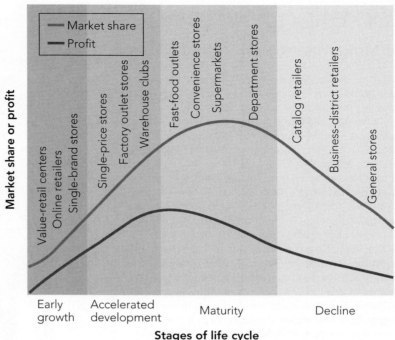

FIGURE 16–10
The retail life cycle describes stages of growth and decline for retail outlets.

because of start-up costs. In the next stage, *accelerated development*, both market share and profit achieve their greatest growth rates. Usually multiple outlets are established as companies focus on the distribution element of the retailing mix. In this stage, some later competitors may enter. Wendy's, for example, appeared on the hamburger chain scene almost 20 years after McDonald's had begun operation. The key goal for the retailer in this stage is to establish a dominant position in the fight for market share.

The battle for market share is usually fought before the *maturity stage*, and some competitors drop out of the market. In the war among hamburger chains, Jack in the Box, Gino's Hamburgers, and Burger Chef used to be more dominant outlets. In the maturity stage, new retail forms enter the market (such as Fatburger and In-N-Out Burger in the hamburger chain industry), stores try to maintain their market share, and price discounting occurs.

The challenge facing retailers is to delay entering the *decline stage*, in which market share and profit fall rapidly. Specialty apparel retailers, such as the Gap, Limited, Benetton, and Ann Taylor, have noticed a decline in market share after years of growth. To prevent further decline, these retailers will need to find ways of discouraging their customers from moving to low-margin, mass-volume outlets or high-price, high-service boutiques.[62]

FUTURE CHANGES IN RETAILING

Two exciting trends in retailing—the growth of multichannel retailing and the increasing use of data analytics—are likely to lead to many changes for retailers and consumers in the future.

Multichannel Retailing

The retailing formats described previously in this chapter represent an exciting menu of choices for creating customer value in the marketplace. Each format allows retailers

The Multichannel Marketing Multiplier

Multichannel marketing is the blending of different communication and delivery channels that are mutually reinforcing in attracting, retaining, and building relationships with consumers who shop and buy in the traditional marketplace and marketspace. Industry analysts refer to the complementary role of different communication and delivery channels as an *influence effect*.

Retailers that integrate and leverage their stores, catalogs, and websites have seen a sizable lift in yearly sales recorded from individual customers. Eddie Bauer is a good example. Customers who shop only one of its channels spend $100 to $200 per year. Those who shop in two channels spend $300 to $500 annually. Customers who shop all three channels—store, catalog, and website—spend $800 to $1,000 per year. Moreover, multichannel customers have been found to be *three times* as profitable as single-channel customers.

JCPenney has seen similar results. The company is a leading multichannel retailer and reports that a JCPenney customer who shops in all three channels—store, catalog, and website—spends *four to eight times* as much as a customer who shops in only one channel, as shown in the chart.

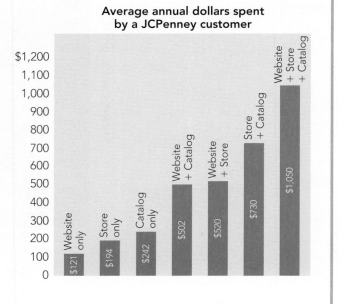

Average annual dollars spent by a JCPenney customer

Channel	Amount
Website only	$121
Store only	$194
Catalog only	$242
Website + Catalog	$502
Website + Store	$520
Store + Catalog	$730
Website + Store + Catalog	$1,050

Amazon is opening physical stores where consumers can shop and pick up orders.

© Joseph Paul

to offer unique benefits and meet the particular needs of various customer groups. While each format has many successful applications, retailers in the future are likely to combine many of the formats to offer a broader spectrum of benefits and experiences and to appeal to different segments of consumers.[63] These **multichannel retailers** will utilize and integrate a combination of traditional store formats and nonstore formats such as catalogs, television, home shopping, and online retailing. Barnes & Noble, for example, created Barnesandnoble.com to compete with Amazon.com. Similarly, Office Depot has integrated its store, catalog, and Internet operations, and Amazon has recently opened its first physical stores on college campuses.[64]

Multiple retail channels have often been viewed as alternatives that might cannibalize each other. When the channels are integrated, however, they can offer many opportunities to interact with and create value for a consumer. The various channels become a series of touch points. For example, a consumer might use a mobile app to scan a QR (quick response) code from a catalog, place an order online, pick up the product from the nearest store, call customer service for installation, and provide feedback on the retailer's social media page. In this way, the channels become complementary. Experts suggest this integration of various retail channels should be described with a new term—*omnichannel retailing*.

Multichannel retailers also benefit from the synergy of sharing information among the different channel operations. Online retailers have recognized that the Internet often serves as a source of information and a transactional tool rather than a relationship-building medium, and they are working to find ways to complement traditional customer interactions.[65] The benefits of multichannel marketing are also apparent in the spending behavior of consumers, as described in the Marketing Matters box.[66]

Data Analytics

Data analytics has been described as the "new science of retailing." Data now available from the use of wearable technology (described earlier in this chapter) and the growth of multichannel marketing complement the substantial amounts of data already collected through scanner and loyalty card systems. The combination of these data sources has the potential to enable a new, comprehensive, and integrated analytical tool for retailers. In fact, a survey of 418 managers in eight industries indicated that firms in the retail industry have the most to gain from deploying customer analytics.

The use of data analytics can benefit retailers in at least three ways. First, understanding how consumers use multiple channels, information sources, and payment options can help retailers predict shopping behavior. Second, detailed customer-specific data will allow merchants to provide personalized, real-time messaging and promotions. Finally, tracking customer needs allows retailers to offer innovative products, maintain optimal inventory levels, and manage prices to remain competitive and profitable. As one retailing expert explains, "this information is invaluable."[67]

learning review »

16-12. Using the wheel of retailing, describe the characteristics of a new retail form that has just entered the market.

16-13. Market share is usually fought out before the _____ stage of the retail life cycle.

16-14. What is an influence effect?

WHOLESALING

LO 16-6 Describe the types of firms that perform wholesaling activities and their functions.

Many retailers depend on intermediaries that engage in wholesaling activities—selling products and services for the purposes of resale or business use. There are several types of intermediaries, including wholesalers and agents (described briefly in Chapter 15), as well as manufacturers' sales offices, which are important to understand as part of the retailing process.

Merchant Wholesalers

Merchant wholesalers are independently owned firms that take title to the merchandise they handle. They go by various names, including *industrial distributor.* Most firms engaged in wholesaling activities are merchant wholesalers.

Merchant wholesalers are classified as either full-service or limited-service wholesalers, depending on the number of functions performed. Two major types of full-service wholesalers exist. *General merchandise* (or *full-line*) *wholesalers* carry a broad assortment of merchandise and perform all channel functions. This type of wholesaler is most prevalent in the hardware, drug, and clothing industries. However, these wholesalers do not maintain much depth of assortment within specific product lines. *Specialty merchandise* (or *limited-line*) *wholesalers* offer a relatively narrow range of products but have an extensive assortment within the product lines carried. They perform all channel functions and are found in the health foods, automotive parts, and seafood industries.

Four major types of limited-service wholesalers exist. *Rack jobbers* furnish the racks or shelves that display merchandise in retail stores, perform all channel functions, and sell on consignment to retailers, which means they retain the title to the products displayed and bill retailers only for the merchandise sold. Familiar products such as hosiery, toys, housewares, and health and beauty items are sold by rack jobbers. *Cash and carry wholesalers* take title to merchandise but sell only to buyers who call on them, pay cash for merchandise, and furnish their own transportation for merchandise. They carry a limited product assortment and do not make deliveries, extend credit, or supply market information. This type of wholesaler is common in electric supplies, office supplies, hardware products, and groceries.

Drop shippers, or *desk jobbers,* are wholesalers that own the merchandise they sell but do not physically handle, stock, or deliver it. They simply solicit orders from retailers and other wholesalers and have the merchandise shipped directly from a producer to a buyer. Drop shippers are used for bulky products such as coal, lumber, and chemicals, which are sold in extremely large quantities. *Truck jobbers* are small wholesalers that have a small warehouse from which they stock their trucks for distribution to retailers. They usually handle limited assortments of fast-moving or perishable items that are sold for cash directly from trucks in their original packages. Truck jobbers handle products such as bakery items, dairy products, and meat.

Agents and Brokers

Unlike merchant wholesalers, agents and brokers do not take title to merchandise and typically perform fewer channel functions. They make their profit from commissions or fees paid for their services, whereas merchant wholesalers make their profit from the sale of the merchandise they own.

Used with permission of Manufacturers' Agents National Association.

Manufacturers' agents and selling agents are the two major types of agents used by producers. **Manufacturers' agents**, or *manufacturers' representatives,* work for several producers and carry noncompetitive, complementary merchandise in an exclusive territory. Manufacturers' agents act as a producer's sales arm in a territory and are principally responsible for the transactional channel functions, primarily selling. They are used extensively in the automotive supply, footwear, and fabricated steel industries. The Manufacturers' Agents National Association (MANA) facilitates the process of matching manufacturers' representatives with logical products and companies.

By comparison, *selling agents* represent a single producer and are responsible for the entire marketing function of that producer. They design promotional plans, set prices, determine distribution policies, and make recommendations on product strategy. Selling agents are used by small producers in the textile, apparel, food, and home furnishing industries.

Brokers are independent firms or individuals whose principal function is to bring buyers and sellers together to make sales. Brokers, unlike agents, usually have no continuous relationship with the buyer or seller but negotiate a contract between two parties and then move on to another task. Brokers are used extensively by producers of seasonal products (such as fruits and vegetables) and in the real estate industry.

A unique broker that acts in many ways like a manufacturer's agent is a food broker, representing buyers and sellers in the grocery industry. Food brokers differ from conventional brokers because they act on behalf of producers on a permanent basis and receive a commission for their services. For example, Nabisco uses food brokers to sell its candies, margarine, and Planters peanuts, but it sells its line of cookies and crackers directly to retail stores.

Manufacturer's Branches and Offices

Unlike merchant wholesalers, agents, and brokers, manufacturer's branches and sales offices are wholly owned extensions of the producer that perform wholesaling activities. Producers assume wholesaling functions when there are no intermediaries to perform these activities, customers are few in number and geographically concentrated, or orders are large or require significant attention. A *manufacturer's branch office* carries a producer's inventory and performs the functions of a full-service wholesaler. A *manufacturer's sales office* does not carry inventory, typically performs only a sales function, and serves as an alternative to agents and brokers.

16-15. What is the difference between merchant wholesalers and agents?

16-16. Under what circumstances do producers assume wholesaling functions?

LEARNING OBJECTIVES REVIEW

LO 16-1 *Identify retailers in terms of the utilities they provide.*
Retailers provide time, place, form, and possession utilities. Time utility is provided by stores with convenient time-of-day (e.g., open 24 hours) or time-of-year (e.g., seasonal sports equipment available all year) availability. Place utility is provided by the number and location of the stores. Possession utility is provided by making a purchase possible (e.g., financing) or easier (e.g., delivery). Form utility is provided by producing or altering a product to meet the customer's specifications (e.g., custom-made shirts).

LO 16-2 *Explain the alternative ways to classify retail outlets.*
Retail outlets can be classified by their form of ownership, level of service, and type of merchandise line. The forms of ownership include independent retailers, corporate chains, and contractual systems that include retailer-sponsored cooperatives, wholesaler-sponsored voluntary chains, and franchises. The levels of service include self-service, limited-service, and full-service outlets. Stores classified by their merchandise line include stores with depth, such as sporting goods specialty stores, and stores with breadth, such as large department stores.

LO 16-3 *Describe the many methods of nonstore retailing.*
Nonstore retailing includes automatic vending, direct mail and catalogs, television home shopping, online retailing, telemarketing, and direct selling. The methods of nonstore retailing vary by the level of involvement of the retailer and the level of involvement of the customer. Vending, for example, has low involvement, whereas both the consumer and the retailer have high involvement in direct selling.

LO 16-4 *Classify retailers in terms of the retail positioning matrix, and specify retailing mix actions.*
The retail positioning matrix positions retail outlets on two dimensions: breadth of product line and value added. There

are four possible positions in the matrix—broad product line/low value added (Walmart), narrow product line/low value added (Payless ShoeSource), broad product line/high value added (Bloomingdale's), and narrow product line/high value added (Tiffany & Co.). Retailing mix actions are used to manage a retail store and the merchandise in a store. The mix variables include pricing, store location, communication activities, and merchandise. Two common forms of assessment for retailers are sales per square foot and same-store growth.

LO 16-5 *Explain changes in retailing with the wheel of retailing and the retail life-cycle concepts.*
The wheel of retailing concept explains how retail outlets typically enter the market as low-status, low-margin stores. Over time, stores gradually add new products and services, increasing their prices, status, and margins, and leaving an opening for new low-status, low-margin stores. The retail life cycle describes the process of growth and decline for retail outlets through four stages: early growth, accelerated development, maturity, and decline.

LO 16-6 *Describe the types of firms that perform wholesaling activities and their functions.*
There are three types of firms that perform wholesaling functions. First, merchant wholesalers are independently owned and take title to merchandise. They include general merchandise wholesalers, specialty merchandise wholesalers, rack jobbers, cash and carry wholesalers, drop shippers, and truck jobbers. Merchant wholesalers can perform a variety of channel functions. Second, agents and brokers do not take title to merchandise and primarily perform marketing functions. Finally, manufacturer's branches, which may carry inventory, and sales offices, which perform sales functions, are wholly owned by the producer.

LEARNING REVIEW ANSWERS

16-1 **When Ralph Lauren makes shirts to a customer's exact preferences, what utility is provided?**
Answer: form utility—involves the production or alteration of a product

16-2 **Two measures of the impact of retailing in the global economy are _____ and _____.**
Answer: the total annual sales—four of the 40 largest businesses in the United States are retailers; the number of employees working at large retailers

16-3 **Centralized decision making and purchasing are an advantage of _____ ownership.**
Answer: corporate chain

16-4 **What are some examples of new forms of self-service retailers?**
Answer: New forms of self-service are being developed at warehouse clubs, gas stations, supermarkets, airlines, convenience stores, fast-food restaurants, and even coffee shops.

16-5 **A shop for big men's clothes carries pants in sizes 40 to 60. Would this be considered a broad or deep product line?**

Answer: deep product line; the range of sizes relates to the assortment of a product item (pants) rather than the variety of product lines (pants, shirts, shoes, etc.)

16-6 **Successful catalog retailers often send _____ catalogs to _____ markets identified in their databases.**

Answer: specialty; niche

16-7 **How are retailers increasing consumer interest and involvement in online retailing?**

Answer: Retailers have improved the online retailing experience by adding experiential or interactive activities to their websites, allowing customers to "build" virtual products by customizing their purchases. And to minimize consumers leaving a website to compare prices and shipping costs on other sites, some firms now offer them the ability to compare competitors' offerings.

16-8 **Where are direct-selling retail sales growing? Why?**

Answer: Direct-selling retailers are (1) expanding into global markets outside the United States and (2) reaching consumers who prefer one-on-one customer service and a social shopping experience rather than shopping online or at big discount stores.

16-9 **What are the two dimensions of the retail positioning matrix?**

Answer: The two dimensions of the retail positioning matrix are: (1) breadth of product line, which is the range of products sold through each outlet; and (2) value added, which includes elements such as location, product reliability, or prestige.

16-10 **How does original markup differ from maintained markup?**

Answer: The original markup is the difference between retailer cost and initial selling price, whereas maintained markup is the difference between the final selling price and retailer cost, which is also called the gross margin.

16-11 **A huge shopping strip mall with multiple anchor stores is a(n) _____ center.**

Answer: power

16-12 **Using the wheel of retailing, describe the characteristics of a new retail form that has just entered the market.**

Answer: a low-status, low-margin, low-price outlet

16-13 **Market share is usually fought out before the _____ stage of the retail life cycle.**

Answer: maturity

16-14 **What is an influence effect?**

Answer: An influence effect is the complementary role that different communication and delivery channels have on sales.

16-15 **What is the difference between merchant wholesalers and agents?**

Answer: Merchant wholesalers are independently owned firms that take title to the merchandise they handle and make their profit from the sale of merchandise they own. Agents do not take title to merchandise, typically perform fewer channel functions, and make their profit from commissions or fees paid for their services.

16-16 **Under what circumstances do producers assume wholesaling functions?**

Answer: Producers assume wholesaling functions when there are no intermediaries to perform these activities, customers are few in number and geographically concentrated, or orders are large or require significant attention.

FOCUSING ON KEY TERMS

breadth of product line p. 441
brokers p. 458
category management p. 453
central business district p. 451
community shopping
    center p. 451
depth of product line p. 441
form of ownership p. 438
hypermarket p. 442

intertype competition p. 442
level of service p. 438
manufacturers' agents p. 458
merchandise line p. 438
merchant wholesalers p. 457
multichannel retailers p. 456
off-price retailing p. 450
power center p. 451
regional shopping centers p. 451

retail life cycle p. 454
retail positioning matrix p. 447
retailing p. 436
retailing mix p. 449
scrambled merchandising p. 442
shopper marketing p. 451
strip mall p. 451
telemarketing p. 446
wheel of retailing p. 453

APPLYING MARKETING KNOWLEDGE

1 Discuss the impact of the growing number of dual-income households on (*a*) nonstore retailing and (*b*) the retail mix.

2 How does value added affect a store's competitive position?

3 In retail pricing, retailers often have a maintained markup. Explain how this maintained markup differs from original markup and why it is so important.

4 What are the similarities and differences between the product and retail life cycles?

5 How would you classify Walmart in terms of its position on the wheel of retailing versus that of an off-price retailer?

6 Develop a chart to highlight the role of each of the four main elements of the retailing mix across the four stages of the retail life cycle.

7 Refer to Figure 16–8 and review the position of Payless ShoeSource on the retail positioning matrix. What strategies should Payless ShoeSource follow to move itself into the same position as Tiffany & Co.?

8 Breadth and depth are two important components in distinguishing among types of retailers. Discuss the breadth and depth implications of the following retailers discussed in this chapter: (*a*) Nordstrom, (*b*) Walmart, (*c*) L.L.Bean, and (*d*) Best Buy.

9 According to the wheel of retailing and the retail life cycle, what will happen to factory outlet stores?

10 The text discusses the development of online retailing in the United States. How does the development of this retailing form agree with the implications of the retail life cycle?

11 Comment on this statement: "The only distinction among merchant wholesalers and agents and brokers is that merchant wholesalers take title to the products they sell."

BUILDING YOUR MARKETING PLAN

Does your marketing plan involve using retailers? If the answer is "no," read no further and do not include a retailing element in your plan. If the answer is "yes":

1 Use Figure 16–8 to develop your retailing strategy by (*a*) selecting a position in the retail positioning matrix and (*b*) specifying the details of the retailing mix.

2 Develop a positioning statement describing the breadth of the product line (broad versus narrow) and value added (low versus high).

3 Describe an appropriate combination of retail pricing, store location, retail communication, and merchandise assortment.

4 Confirm that the wholesalers needed to support your retailing strategy are consistent with the channels and intermediaries you selected in Chapter 15.

■ connect

VIDEO CASE 16

Mall of America®: America's Biggest Mall Knows the Secret to Successful Retailing!

The secret to success at Mall of America is continually creating "new experiences for our guests," explains Jill Renslow, senior vice president of business development and marketing. "We want to make not only our locals, but also our tourists have a unique experience every time they come and visit," she adds.

Video 16-6
Mall of America Video Case
kerin.tv/13e/v16-6

That's an ambitious undertaking for any retailer, but it is particularly challenging for Mall of America because it attracts more than 40 million guests each year. To create new experiences the mall uses a combination of constantly changing retail offerings, entertainment options, and special attractions. From new stores, to musical acts, to celebrity book signings, to fashion shows, and even two appearances by Taylor Swift, Mall of America has become the "Hollywood of the Midwest." "The key truly is being fresh and exciting," says Renslow.

THE BIG IDEA FOR A BIG MALL

The concept of a huge mall was the result of several trends. First, covered shopping centers began to replace downtown main-street shopping areas in the United States. Second, retail developers observed that casinos were adding non-gambling activities to attract entire families. Taking their cue from Las Vegas, a Canadian family, the Ghermezians, built the West Edmonton Mall as a destination venue with shopping, restaurants, hotels, and a theme park. The success of the West Edmonton Mall led to the search for another location for the destination mall concept, and soon Mall of America was under construction in Minneapolis, Minnesota!

According to Dan Jasper, vice president of communications at Mall of America, the Ghermezians are a "wonder family that are visionaries." "They dream really big dreams, and they bring them to reality; they did that in Edmonton with the West Edmonton Mall, and they did that here in Minnesota with Mall of America," he explains. Today Mall of America is the largest mall in the United States with 4.8 million square feet of shopping and entertainment space. And it's getting bigger! "We're opening our new grand front entrance and that will bring us to 5.5 million square feet, making us by far not only the busiest, not only the most successful, but the largest, most massive mall in the nation," says Jasper.

Executives at Mall of America face several important challenges. First, they must keep a huge and diverse portfolio of retailers and attractions in the Mall. Second, they must attract millions of visitors each year. Finally, they must increase its marketing and social media presence in the marketplace. The combination of these three activities is essential to the mall's continued success. This is particularly true at a time when e-commerce and online shopping are growing in popularity.

MANAGING THE MALL

The size of Mall of America is difficult to comprehend. There are more than four miles of store front in an area the size of 88 football fields. Three anchor stores—Macy's, Nordstrom, and Sears—are complemented by more than 500 specialty stores. The diversity of the retail offerings is equally amazing. The types of stores range from familiar names such as Banana Republic, Apple, and True Religion to unique stores such as Brickmania, which offers custom LEGO® building kits, and Games by James, which offers thousands of board games and puzzles. According to Renslow, "That's what's special about Mall of America, that's what attracts people from around the world."

To encourage entrepreneurs to come to the mall there is a specialty leasing program that offers the new retailers an affordable entry-level lease in exchange for flexibility related to their location. Mike Pohl, owner of the ACES Flight Simulation store, is one example of the unique businesses the program attracts. "I decided to locate at Mall of America because it's the single biggest retail location in the country," Mike explains. "There are 40 million people

© Steve Skjold/Alamy

who come here every year, and it's primarily an entertainment mall compared to a traditional mall, so it was a wonderful match for ACES," he adds.

Mall of America also includes more than 20 restaurants, the House of Comedy for touring comedians, and an American Girl store with a doll hair salon and party facilities. The 14 Theaters at Mall of America include a 200-seat 3D theater equipped with D-Box motion seating, and a 148-seat theater for guests 21 and older.

Additional unique features of Mall of America include:

- Nickelodeon Universe®, a seven-acre theme park with more than 20 attractions and rides, including a roller coaster, Ferris wheel, and a water chute in a skylighted area with more than 400 trees.
- Sea Life® Minnesota aquarium, where visitors can see jellyfish, stingrays, and sea turtles, snorkel with tropical fish, or even SCUBA with sharks!
- Two connected-access hotels including a 342-room JW Marriott and a 500-room Radisson Blu.
- The Chapel of Love, which offers custom weddings and wedding packages and has performed more than 5,000 weddings in the mall!

Regular events and activities include the Art + Style Series, Toddler Tuesdays, the Mall Stars program for people who want to walk and exercise in the Mall, and the Mall of America Music Series. Mall of America also hosts corporate events for organizations with large groups. There are more than 12,000 free parking spaces available to accommodate any size group!

THE MARKET

From its opening day, visitors have been going to Mall of America at the extraordinary rate of 10,000 visitors per day. This is possible because the mall attracts shoppers from more than 18 states including Minnesota, Wisconsin, Kentucky, Michigan, Ohio, and Pennsylvania and from more than 11 countries including Canada, Great Britain, France, Mexico, Germany, Scandinavia, Italy, Netherlands, Japan, China, and Spain. The mall has worked closely with airlines

© Alvis Upitis/Alamy

and other partners to offer "Shop Till You Drop" packages that bring shoppers from around the world.

As Renslow explains: "Mall of America shoppers are literally from ages 3 to 83, which is a great opportunity for us but also a challenge. We need to be able to make sure that we communicate with each one of our guests. So we focus on the local market, which makes up 60 percent of our shoppers, and we also focus on our tourists who are 40 percent of our shoppers, and we have different messages to those different audiences." Another key target audience for the mall includes young women. Unmarried women have disposable income and like to travel, and married women are the primary purchase decision makers in their households and often bring their spouses, children, and girlfriends to the Mall.

MARKETING, SOCIAL MEDIA, AND MALL OF AMERICA

Another key to Mall of America's success has been its ability to manage its presence in the marketplace. According to Sarah Schmidt, public relations manager for Mall of America, "A typical campaign for Mall of America includes TV, radio, and print and we also include social media campaigns." A recent campaign called "The Scream Collector," for example, started with a TV ad and then followed up with progress re-

ports on billboards. Another campaign created a blizzard in the mall. The "blizzard was a tweet-powered blizzard where guests had to tweet #twizzard, and once it hit a certain number of tweets it started snowing in the mall," Schmidt says.

Social media are important elements of Mall of America campaigns. Dan Jasper explains, "Mall of America is at the forefront of social media and digital technology within the retail industry; for shopping malls nobody has us beat." The mall has created a communication hub that integrates social media, texting, phone, and security all in a single system. "What that allows us to do is to speak with one voice, and to give real-time answers, suggestions, and advice to consumers," he says.

What is in the future for Mall of America? According to Jasper the answer is an even bigger mall. "In the coming years we're going to double the size of Mall of America" he says. So, prepare yourself for an even more extraordinary retailing experience![68]

Questions

1 What is the key to success at Mall of America?
2 What trends contributed to the idea for the Mall of America? How did it get started?
3 What challenges does Mall of America face as it strives to continue its success?
4 What specific actions has Mall of America taken to address each challenge?

Chapter Notes

1. Clare O'Connor, "Here's What Shopping with Apple Watch Will Look Like," *Forbes.com,* March 13, 2015; Samuel Mueller, "Wearable Technology and Its Impact on Retail," *wearabletechworld.com,* April 14, 2015; Lisa Johnson, "First Look: Apple Watch Tech & Retail Apps," *twice.com,* May 4, 2015; "Retailers in Sync with Latest Developments in Technology," MMR, May 25, 2015, p. 42; "Study: Wearable Technology Will Upend Retail," *chainstoreage.com,* November 2014; "Valpak at Forefront of Technology," Valpak press release, www.valpak.com, April 22, 2015; and "Augmented Reality's Real Implications for Hardware, Software and Advertising: A Roadmap for Success," *PR Newswire,* February 5, 2013.

2. "The Fortune 500," *Fortune,* June 15, 2015, p. F-1; *The World Factbook* (Washington, DC: Central Intelligence Agency), www.cia.gov, accessed June 11, 2015; "Population Estimates: City and Town Totals Vintage 2014," Washington, DC: U.S. Department of Commerce, Bureau of the Census, May 2015.

3. "Estimated Annual Sales of U.S. Retail and Food Service Firms," 2013 Annual Retail Trade Report, Washington, DC: U.S. Department of Commerce, Bureau of the Census, March 9, 2015.

4. "The Global 2000," *Forbes,* May 25, 2015, p. 84; and http://www.forbes.com/global2000.

5. "Where in the World Is Walmart?" Walmart website, http://corporate.walmart.com/ourstory/our-business/locations/, accessed June 11, 2015; and Marcel Corstjens and Rajiv Lal, "Retail Doesn't Cross Borders," *Harvard Business Review,* April 2012, pp. 104–11.

6. Derrick Teal, "Retailers Going Green," *EDC,* November 2014, pp. 28–33; Leslie Eaton, "Wal-Mart and the Green Consumer," *The Wall Street Journal,* March 31, 2015, p. R6; "Global Consumers Are Willing to Put Their Money Where Their Heart Is," press release, Nielsen, June 17, 2014; "From One Generation to the Next," *Home Depot 2014 Sustainability Report*; Edwin R. Stafford and Cathy L. Hartman, "Promoting the Value of Sustainably Minded Purchase Behaviors," *Marketing News,* January 2013, p. 28.

7. "Retail Trade—Establishments, Employees, and Payroll," *County Business Patterns,* U.S. Census Bureau, July 2010, Table 1048.

8. "Franchise Business Economic Outlook for 2015," International Franchise Association, IHS Economics, March, 2015.

9. "2015 Franchise 500," *Entrepreneur,* http://www.entrepreneur.com/franchise500/index.html.

10. "Automated Kiosks Reduce Time Waiting at Airport," *Travel Agent,* April 20, 2015, p. 5; "When Customer Service Become Self-Service," *Consumer Reports,* September 2014, pp. 33–35; "The Next Generation of Retailing Driven by Automated, Self-Service Solutions," Market *News Publishing,*" February 4, 2013; and "Apartment Complex Readies for Automated C-Store," *States News Service,* September 10, 2012.

11. Phil Wahba, "Nordstrom's Multi-Billion dollar Plan for e-commerce Domination," *Fortune.com,* March 3, 2015; "Wealthy Customers Sing Praises of Shopping Experiences at Bergdorf, Nordstrom and Barneys," *Marketwire,* February 5, 2013; Megan Conniff, "Customer Service Is Changing, and So Is Nordstrom," www.Shop.org, September 12, 2012; and Michael A. Wiles, "The Effect of Customer Service on Retailers' Shareholder Wealth: The Role of Availability and Reputation Cues," *Journal of Retailing,* 2007, pp. 19–31.

12. "Best Buy Adopts Price-Matching in U.S., Big Box Retailer Takes on Amazon, Apple," *The Toronto Star,* February 20, 2013, p. B2; John Ewoldt, "Big-Box Retailers Take on Internet," *StarTribune,* November 18, 2012, p. 1A; and Michael Shedlock, "Big-Box Retailers Reconsider Size," *Mish's Global Economic Trend Analysis,* March 5, 2011.

13. "Store Network Under Banners," Carrefour website, http://www.carrefour.com/sites/default/files/PARCEN311214.pdf; Nadya Masidlover, "Corporate News: Carrefour Stems a Slide in Its Domestic Market," *The Wall Street Journal,* January 18, 2013, p. B7; "Mass Grocery Retail-Q3 2012," *BMI Food & Drink Report,* July 2012; and Tom Orlik and Bob David, "Relief on China Growth Comes with Caveats," *The Wall Street Journal,* January 19, 2013, p. A10.

14. Dana Mattioli, "Déjà vu for Sears CEO: Fix Kmart," *The Wall Street Journal,* January 24, 2013, p. B1; Andria Cheng, "Corporate News: Wal-Mart Lays Out Strategy," *The Wall Street Journal,* October 11, 2012, p. B8; Miguel Bustillo, "As Big Boxes Shrink, They Also Rethink," *The Wall Street Journal,* March 3, 2011, B1; and Miguel Bustillo, "Boss Talk: With Sales Flabby, Wal-Mart Turns to Its Core," *The Wall Street Journal,* March 21, 2011, p. B1; Walmart website, http://corporate.walmart.com/our-story/locations#/united-states, accessed February 25, 2013; and Kmart website, http://searsmedia.com/kmart/kmart.htm, accessed February 25, 2013.

15. Emily Refermat, "State of the Vending Industry Vending Special Report," *Automatic Merchandiser,* June 2014; "No Time to Shop for Your Valentine? From Flowers to Caviar, a Vending Machine Can Save the Day," *Targeted News Service,* February 11, 2013; Jill Becker, "Vending Machines for All Your Needs," www.CNN.com, August 15, 2012; Jackie Crosby, "Vending Machine Variety Goes beyond Snack Food Offerings," *Los Angeles Times,* January 18, 2011, p. B2; and Carlie Kollath, "Veggies in Vending Machines?" *Biz Buzz,* April 6, 2011.

16. Yukihiro Omoto, "Coca-Cola Setting Up More Green Vending Machines," *The Nikkei Weekly,* February 18, 2013; Ilan Brat, "Business Technology: Restocking the Snack Machine–Sales Pinched, Vending-Machine Operators Add Touch Screen, Card Readers," *The Wall Street Journal,* August 3, 2010, p. B5.

17. "Sustainability Report," IKEA Group, 2014; *Statistical Fact Book* (New York: Direct Marketing Association, 2010), pp. 4, 33; David Kaplan, "Catalogs Thinner but Still Carry Weight, Retailers Use Them to Draw Consumers to Stores, Web or Social Media Sites," *The Houston Chronicle,* November 28, 2010, p. 1; Mercedes Cardona, "Catalog Role Is Communications, Not Sales," *DM News,* November 1, 2010.

18. "How Much Will Postal Cuts Hurt?" *Advertising Age,* February 11, 2013, p. 3; Ira Teinowitz and Nat Ives, "No Day Is a Good Day for No Mail," *Advertising Age,* February 9, 2009, p. 8; "A Zip-Code Screen for Catalog Customers," *The Wall Street Journal,* June 24, 2008, p. B1; and Richard H. Levey, "It's All about Me," *Direct,* November 1, 2008.

19. Katherine Boehret, "The Digital Solution: Is Browsing a Catalog More Fun on a Tablet?" *The Wall Street Journal,* March 28, 2012, p. D2; Dianna Dilworth, "Print Stages a Comeback," *DM News,* March 1, 2011; and Chris Daniels, "Retailers Testing Out e-Catalog Versions, *DM News,* January 1, 2011.

20. "Fact Sheet" from the QVC website, http://www.qvc.com/AboutQVCFacts.content.html, accessed June 12, 2015.

21. Bianca Carneiro, "Mum Camila McConaughey Outshines Supermodels Miranda Kerr and Heidi Klum at QVC's Red

Carpet Style Event," *Mail Online,* February 23, 2013; Jordan Zakarin, "Inside QVC: The Semi-Scripted Reality of the $8 Billion Business Next Door," *The Hollywood Reporter,* December 17, 2012; and Elizabeth Holmes, "The Golden Age of TV Shopping," *The Wall Street Journal,* November 11, 2010, p. D1.

22. Paul Bucchioni, Xijian Liu, and Deanna Weidenhamer, "Quarterly Retail e-Commerce Sales," *U.S. Census Bureau News,* May 15, 2015; "Record Cyber Monday Might Be the Last One," *WWD,* December 3, 2014, p. 1; Thad Rueter, "Global e-Commerce Will Increase 22% This Year," *internetretailer.com,* December 23, 2014; and "Picking Up Orders with Site to Store," Walmart website, http://help.walmart.com/app/answers/detail/a_id/281, accessed June 12, 2015.

23. "eBay Marketplaces Fast Facts At-a-Glance," eBay website, http://www.ebayinc.com/sites/default/files/eBay%20 Marketplaces%20Fast%20Facts%20%20Q1%202015.pdf, accessed June 12, 2015.

24. Jacqueline Curtis, "How to Use the Best Flash Sale Sites to Score Deals," *Money Crashers,* February 20, 2013.

25. Susan Rose, Moira Clark, Phillip Samouel, and Neil Hair, "Online Customer Experience in e-Retailing: An Empirical Model of Antecedents and Outcomes," *Journal of Retailing* 2 (2012), pp. 308–22; and Feng Zhu and Xiaoquan (Michael) Zhang, "Impact of Online Consumer Reviews on Sales: The Moderating Role of Product and Consumer Characteristics," *Journal of Marketing* 74 (March 2010), pp. 133–48.

26. Onur H. Bodur, Noreen M. Klein, and Neeraj Arora, "Online Price Search: Impact of Price Comparison Sites on Offline Price Evaluations," *Journal of Retailing,* March 2015, pp. 125–139; and Lee and Kyoochun Lee, "Social Shopping Promotions from a Social Merchant's Perspective," *Business Horizons,* October 2012, pp. 441–51.

27. "DM-Driven Sales by Medium and Market," *Statistical Fact Book* (New York: Direct Marketing Association, 2010), p. 5.

28. "FTC Issues FY 2012 National Do Not Call Registry Data Book," *Federal Trade Commission Documents and Publications,* October 16, 2012; and Nate Anderson, "Do Not Call List Tops 200 Million, Some Scammers Still Ignore It," www.Wired.com, July 31, 2010.

29. "Direct Selling USA—Pinpoint Growth Sectors and Identify Factors Driving Change," *M2 Presswire,* April 12, 2011; and *Industry Statistics,* Direct Selling Association, http://www.dsa.org/research/2012-industry-statistics, accessed June 12, 2015.

30. Phil Wahba, "Amway Boss Defends Direct Selling, Touts 'Made in the USA'," *Fortune.com,* December 11, 2014; "Herbalife Plans Expansion of Manufacturing Capabilities in China," *Asia Pacific Biotech News,*" September 2014, p. 22; "Amway Says China Sales Increase to 27.1b Yuan," *China Daily,* February 21, 2013; "Avon Announces Management Realignments," *PR Newswire,* February 24, 2011; and "Herbalife Ltd. Receives Approval of Additional Direct-Selling Licenses in China," *Business Wire,* July 19, 2010.

31. Virginia Bridges, "In a Slow Economy, Some Try the Direct Approach," *The Virginian-Pilot,* February 17, 2013, p. K1; Maria Croce, "Recession Sparks a Massive Boom in Direct Selling Parties but Gone Are the Days of Selling Tupperware," *Daily Record,* June 2, 2012, pp. 34–35; Olivera Perkins, "Direct Sales Proves Attractive to Long-Term Jobless Workers; Companies Selling Retail Goods at Home Parties See Profits Climbing," *Plain Dealer,* February 6, 2011, p. D1; Carol Lewis, "Calling All Avon Ladies—Direct Selling Is Back," *The Times,* December 28, 2010, p. 40; and "Company Facts," The Pampered Chef

website, http://www.pamperedchef.com/company-facts.jsp, accessed February 27, 2013.

32. Dinesh Kumar Gauri, Minakshi Trivedi, and Dhruv Grewal, "Understanding the Determinants of Retail Strategy: An Empirical Analysis," *Journal of Retailing,* September 2008, p. 256.

33. The following discussion is adapted from William T. Gregor and Eileen M. Friars, *Money Merchandizing: Retail Revolution in Consumer Financial Services* (Cambridge, MA: Management Analysis Center, Inc., 1982).

34. Francis J. Mulhern and Robert P. Leon, "Implicit Price Bundling of Retail Products: A Multiproduct Approach to Maximizing Store Profitability," *Journal of Marketing,* October 1991, pp. 63–76.

35. Marc Vanhuele and Xavier Dreze, "Measuring the Price Knowledge Shoppers Bring to the Store," *Journal of Marketing,* October 2002, pp. 72–85.

36. "Are Sales a Thing of the Past?" *Newstex,* www.jennstrathman.com, January 10, 2013; and Gwen Ortmeyer, John A. Quelch, and Walter Salmon, "Restoring Credibility to Retail Pricing," *Sloan Management Review,* Fall 1991, pp. 55–66.

37. "On Sale! But Does Inexpensive Mean Cheap?" www.Futurity.org, November 27, 2012; Rajneesh Suri, Jane Zhen Cai, Kent B. Monroe, and Mrugank V. Thakor, "Retailers' Merchandise Organization and Price Perceptions," *Journal of Retailing* 1 (2012), pp. 168–79; and William Dodds, "In Search of Value: How Price and Store Name Information Influence Buyers' Product Perceptions," *Journal of Consumer Marketing,* Spring 1991, pp. 15–24.

38. Stephanie Clifford, "Stores Bend to Cost-Savvy Shoppers: Experiments in Pricing Move Away from Usual Markups and Discounts," *The International Herald Tribune,* March 29, 2012, p. 18; and Leonard L. Berry, "Old Pillars of New Retailing," *Harvard Business Review,* April 2001, pp. 131–37.

39. Eric Anderson and Duncan Simester, "Mind Your Pricing Cues," *Harvard Business Review,* September 2003, pp. 96–103.

40. Julie Baker, A. Parasuraman, Dhruv Grewal, and Glenn B. Voss, "The Influence of Multiple Store Environment Cues on Perceived Merchandise Value and Patronage Intentions," *Journal of Marketing,* April 2002, pp. 120–41.

41. Hyeong Min Kim, "Consumers' Responses to Price Presentation Formats in Rebate Advertisements," *Journal of Retailing* 4 (2006), pp. 309–17.

42. Kathy Grannis, "Retail Theft Decreased in 2011, According to Preliminary National Retail Security Survey Findings," press release, National Retail Federation, June 22, 2012; Shari Brown and Kathy Grannis, "Return Fraud to Cost Retailers $2.9 Billion This Holiday Season, According to NRF Survey," press release, National Retail Federation, December 4, 2012; Lloyd C. Harris, "Fraudulent Return Proclivity: An Empirical Analysis," *Journal of Retailing,* December 2008, p. 461; Sharna Johnson, "Businesses See Shoplifting Spike," *Clovis News Journal,* February 1, 2009; and "Nedap Retail Introduces New 'Invisible' Anti-Theft Tags in Partnership with Kovio," *PR Newswire,* November 13, 2012.

43. Rita Koselka, "The Schottenstein Factor," *Forbes,* September 28, 1992, pp. 104, 106.

44. "Industry Snapshot: Warehouse Clubs and Superstores," *Hoover's,* www.hoovers.com, June 10, 2015; and "Research and Markets: 2012 Report on the $390 Billion U.S. Warehouse Clubs & Superstores Industry Featuring Wal-Mart, Costco, BJs and Meijer," *M2 Presswire,* September 28, 2012.

45. "The Deal on Outlet Store Deals," *WalletPop,* March 22, 2011; and "Macy's to Launch 3 New Bloomingdale's Outlet Stores," *Entertainment Close-Up,* April 28, 2011.

46. "About Dollar General," Dollar General website, http://www2.dollargeneral.com/About-Us/pages/store-locations-map.aspx, accessed June 12, 2015.

47. "About WEM," West Edmonton Mall website, http://www.wem.ca/about-wem/overview, accessed June 12, 2015.

48. Ernesto Portillo, "Home Depot Part of Center Plan," *McClatchy-Tribune Business News,* November 20, 2008; and Lisa A. Bernard, "Anchor ID'd for 'Big Box' Power Center," *Dayton Daily News,* July 19, 2007.

49. Pierre Martineau, "The Personality of the Retail Store," *Harvard Business Review,* January–February 1958, p. 47.

50. Julie Baker, Dhruv Grewal, and A. Parasuraman, "Theories Influence of Store Environment on Quality Inferences and Store Image," *Journal of the Academy of Marketing Science,* Fall 1994, pp. 328–39; Howard Barich and Philip Kotler, "A Framework for Marketing Image Management," *Sloan Management Review,* Winter 1991, pp. 94–104; Susan M. Keaveney and Kenneth A. Hunt, "Conceptualization and Operationalization of Retail Store Image: A Case of Rival Middle-Level Theories," *Journal of the Academy of Marketing Science,* Spring 1992, pp. 165–75; James C. Ward, Mary Jo Bitner, and John Barnes, "Measuring the Prototypicality and Meaning of Retail Environments," *Journal of Retailing,* Summer 1992, p. 194; and Dhruv Grewal, R. Krishnan, Julie Baker, and Norm Burin, "The Effect of Store Name, Brand Name and Price Discounts on Consumers' Evaluations and Purchase Intentions," *Journal of Retailing,* Fall 1998, pp. 331–52. For a review of the store image literature, see Mary R. Zimmer and Linda L. Golden, "Impressions of Retail Stores: A Content Analysis of Consumer Images," *Journal of Retailing,* Fall 1988, pp. 265–93.

51. Andreas Herrmann, Manja Zidansek, David E. Sprott, and Eric R. Spangenberg, "The Power of Simplicity: Processing Fluency and the Effects of Olfactory Cues on Retail Sales," *Journal of Retailing* 1 (2013), pp. 30–43.

52. Jack Neff, "Shopper Marketing's New Frontier: e-Commerce," *Advertising Age,* March 14, 2011, p. 14; Andrew Adam Newman, "Taking Pickles Out of the Afterthought Aisle," *The New York Times,* April 26, 2011, p. 3: Piet Levy, "Snack Attack," *Marketing News,* February 28, 2011, p. 12; Yong Jian Wang, Michael S. Minor, and Jie Wei, "Aesthetics and the Online Shopping Environment: Understanding Consumer Responses," *Journal of Retailing* 87, no. 1 (2011), pp. 46–58; and Els Breugelmans and Katia Campo, "Effectiveness of In-Store Displays in a Virtual Store Environment," *Journal of Retailing* 87, no. 1 (2011), pp. 75–89.

53. Jans-Benedict Steenkamp and Michel Wedel, "Segmenting Retail Markets on Store Image Using a Consumer-Based Methodology," *Journal of Retailing,* Fall 1991, p. 300; Philip Kotler, "Atmospherics as a Marketing Tool," *Journal of Retailing* 49 (Winter 1973–74), p. 61; and Roger A. Kerin, Ambuj Jain, and Daniel L. Howard, "Store Shopping Experience and Consumer Price-Quality-Value Perceptions," *Journal of Retailing,* Winter 1992, pp. 376–97.

54. Mary Jo Bitner, "Servicescapes: The Impact of Physical Surroundings on Customers and Employees," *Journal of Marketing,* April 1992, pp. 57–71.

55. Joseph M. Hall, Praveen K. Kopale, and Aradhna Krishna, "Retailer Dynamic Pricing and Ordering Decisions: Category Management versus Brand-by-Brand Approaches," *Journal of Retailing* 86, no. 2 (2010), pp. 172–83; and "Category Management Professionals Can Benefit from Integration of Leading Category and Space Management Suite with Comprehensive and Accurate Product Information," *Business Wire,* April 28, 2011.

56. Kevin Peters, "How I Did It: Office Depot's President on How 'Mystery Shopping' Helped Spark a Turnaround," *Harvard Business Review,* November 2011, pp. 47–50; and John Davis, *Measuring Marketing* (Singapore: Wiley and Sons, 2007), p. 46.

57. Phil Wahba, "Apple Extends Its Lead in the Nation's Top 10 Retailers by Sales," *Fortune.com,* March 23, 2105; Tom Webb, "Retail Ramifications: Best Buy and Apple Seem a Perfect Pair—Except for Apple's Store Ambitions," *St. Paul Pioneer Press,* February 19, 2011; Paul W. Farris, Neil T. Bendle, Phillip E. Pfeifer, and David J. Reibstein, *Marketing Metrics* (Philadelphia: Wharton School Publishing, 2006), p. 106; Jerry Useem, "Simply Irresistible," *Fortune,* March 19, 2007, pp. 107–12; "Apple 2.0," blogs.business2.com/apple/the_evil_empire/index.html; Steve Lohr, "Apple, a Success at Stores, Bets Big on Fifth Avenue," *The New York Times,* May 19, 2006; Jim Dalrymple, "Inside the Apple Stores," *MacWorld,* June 2007, pp. 16–17; John Davis, *Measuring Marketing,* pp. 280–81; and Retailsails 2011 Chain Store Productivity Report, September 23, 2011, http://www.retailsails.com/, accessed October 7, 2011.

58. The wheel of retailing theory was originally proposed by Malcolm P. McNair, "Significant Trends and Developments in the Postwar Period," in *Competitive Distribution in a Free, High-Level Economy and Its Implications for the University,* ed. A. B. Smith, (Pittsburgh: University of Pittsburgh Press, 1958), pp. 1–25; also see Stephen Brown, "The Wheel of Retailing—Past and Future," *Journal of Retailing,* Summer 1990, pp. 143–49; and Malcolm P. McNair and Eleanor May, "The Next Revolution of the Retailing Wheel," *Harvard Business Review,* September–October 1978, pp. 81–91.

59. Kaltrina Bylykbashi, "McDonald's to Push 'Create Your Taste' to Recover Sales Decline," *Marketing Week,* January 26, 2015, p. 1; and Marilyn Geewax, "The Latest Item on McDonald's Shifting Menu: A $5 Burger," *npr.org,* April 8, 2015.

60. "Our Story," Checkers website, http://checkerscompany.com/our_story, accessed June 12, 2015; "Story," Boston Market website, http://www.bostonmarket.com/ourStory/index.jsp?page=story, accessed June 12, 2015; and Bill Saporito and Ronald B Lieber, "What's for Dinner?" *Fortune,* April 15, 1995, pp. 50–64.

61. William R. Davidson, Albert D. Bates, and Stephen J. Bass, "Retail Life Cycle," *Harvard Business Review,* November–December 1976, pp. 89–96.

62. Anne Marie Doherty, "Who Will Weather Economic Storms on the High Street?" *The Western Mail,* January 1, 2009, p. 29.

63. "A Business Survival Guide to Multi-Channel Retail," www.Business2Community.com, December 3, 2012; Umut Konus, Peter C. Verhoef, and Scott A. Neslin, "Multichannel Shopper Segments and Their Covariates," *Journal of Retailing,* December 2008, p. 398; and Robert A. Peterson and Sridhar Balasubramanian, "Retailing in the 21st Century: Reflections and Prologue to Research," *Journal of Retailing,* Spring 2002, pp. 9–16.

64. Tom Banks, "Amazon Launches First Physical Store," *Design Week,* February 4, 2015, p. 4; Judith Rosen, "Amazon at Your Campus: The Next-Generation Campus Store," *publishersweekly.com,* May 25, 2015, pp. 5–6; Koen Pauwels and Scott A. Neslin, "Building with Bricks and Mortar: The Revenue Impact of Opening Physical Stores in a Multichannel Environment," *Journal of Retailing,* June 2015, pp. 182–197; "PWC's Annual Survey of Online Shoppers Debunks 10 Myths of Multichannel Retailing," *PR Newswire,* February 6, 2013; Lawrence A. Crosby, "Multi-Channel Relationships," *Marketing Management,* Summer 2011, pp. 12–13; and Jim Carter and Norman Sheehan, "From Competition to Cooperation: E-Tailing's Integration with Retailing," *Business Horizons,* March–April 2004, pp. 71–78.

65. Darrel Rigby "The Future of Shopping," *Harvard Business Review,* December 2011, pp. 65–76; "Multi-Channel Retailing:

The Way Forward," *Images Retail,* November 12, 2012; Ranjay Gulati and Jason Garino, "Getting the Right Mix of Bricks and Clicks," *Harvard Business Review,* May–June 2000, pp. 107–14; Marshal L. Fisher, Ananth Raman, and Anna Sheen McClelland, "Rocket Science Retailing Is Almost Here: Are You Ready?" *Harvard Business Review,* July–August 2000, pp. 115–24; Charla Mathwick, Naresh Malhotra, and Edward Rigdon, "Experiential Value: Conceptualization, Measurement and Application in the Catalog and Internet Shopping Environment," *Journal of Retailing,* Spring 2001, pp. 39–56; Lawrence M. Bellman, "Bricks and Mortar: 21st Century Survival," *Business Horizons,* May–June 2001, pp. 21–28; Zhan G. Li and Nurit Gery, "E–Tailing—for All Products?" *Business Horizons,* November–December 2000, pp. 49–54; and Bill Hanifin, "Go Forth and Multichannel: Loyalty Programs Need Knowledge Base," *Marketing News,* August 27, 2001, p. 23.

66. Robert Berner, "J.C. Penney Gets the Net," *BusinessWeek,* May 7, 2007, p. 70; *Multi-Channel Integration: The New Retail Battleground* (Columbus, OH: PricewaterhouseCoopers, March 2001); and Richard Last, "JC Penney Internet Commerce," presentation at Southern Methodist University, February 12, 2001.

67. Frank Germann, Gary L. Lilien, Lars Fiedler, and Matthias Kraus, "Do Retailers Benefit from Deploying Customer Analytics?" *Journal of Retailing,* December 2014, pp. 587–93; "New Analytics Technology Puts Hong Kong's Fashion Retailers in the Fast Lane," *Network World Asia,* June/July 2014, p. 36; Murali Nadarajah, "Deck the Halls with Analytics," *Retail-Merchandiser.com,* November/December 2014, p. 17; and Marshall Fisher and Ananth Raman, "The New Science of Retailing: How Analytics Are Transforming the Supply Chain and Improving Performance," *Retail Merchandiser,* May/June 2010, p. 6.

68. Mall of America: This case was written by Steven Hartley. Sources: Jennifer Latson, "Why America's Biggest Mall Is Getting Bigger," *Time.com,* August 12, 2015; Samuel Greengard, "Mall of America Increases Its Social Presence," *CIO Insight,* July 28, 2015, p. 2; "This Is How You Resurrect America's Dying Malls," *Time.com,* April 15, 2014, p. 1; "JW Mall of America Hotel Set to Open in November," *Travel Weekly,* April 9, 2015, p. 17; Erika Fry, "Why Mall of America Is Expanding as Many Retailers Implode," *Fortune.com,* March 10, 2014; "Mall of America Marks 20 Years," *Women's Wear Daily,* November 5, 2012, p. 8; Jerry Gerlach and James Janke, "The Mall of America as a Tourist Attraction," *Focus,* Summer 2001, p. 32; and the Mall of America website http://www.mallofamerica.com/.

Integrated Marketing Communications and Direct Marketing

Taco Bell Loves Twitter!

More than 1.5 million people follow Taco Bell on Twitter. Many more are reached by other elements of its engaging integrated marketing campaign. If you've ever had a late-night snack at Taco Bell, you may be one of them!

Taco Bell has been wildly successful with its Cool Ranch Doritos Locos Tacos campaign. It began three weeks before the new taco was launched with password-only social media events. Taco Bell listened to real-time conversations on Twitter (@TacoBell) and rewarded fans with "epic deliveries." A woman who asked Taco Bell to be her Valentine, a student who promised to gather enough friends to eat 1,000 tacos, and a fan who posted a message about tacos on YouTube all received early tastes of the new product.

The campaign then used television, radio, outdoor, and cinema ads, as well as public relations support. The television ads included two 15-second spots titled "Wow" and "Duh" that were supported by a contest (printed on taco wrappers) inviting customers to post photos to Instagram or Twitter using the #wow and #duh hashtags for a chance to have their entry appear on a billboard in Times Square. The most unique element of the campaign was a 3D ad showing a Dorito chip exploding and then morphing into a Cool Ranch Doritos Locos Taco chip. The ad appeared in more than 8,000 movie theaters nationwide, and the new product quickly became the company's most liked, shared, retweeted, and talked-about product on Facebook, Twitter, and Vine.

One reason for Taco Bell's success is that all of the elements of its Doritos Locos Tacos campaign are integrated to have the same message and tone, and they focus on engaging consumers. Some marketers have observed that our marketplace is in the midst of a shift from traditional branding to an "age of engagement" and that social media promotions are the best way to accommodate this shift. In addition, they suggest several aspects of social media promotions are essential to engage today's customers. They are:

1. Post relevant content about the benefits and uses of the product.

2. Supplement text with photos and videos.

3. Create sweepstakes, contests, and deals that reward current and new customers.

4. Encourage and respond to comments and feedback, both positive and negative.

5. Be current and timely with all interactions.

In addition to a presence on Twitter, many brands are using other new forms of engagement, such as Facebook Pages, RSS (rich site summary) feeds, mobile apps, blogs, websites, and QR (quick response) codes. Even traditional

© Mike Hruby

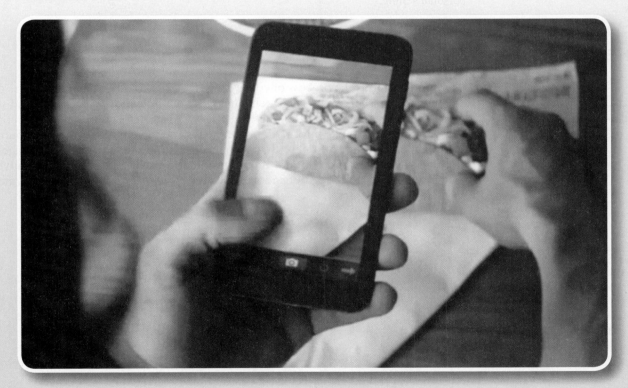

© Mike Hruby

media are engaging customers—for example, TV reality shows like *Dancing with the Stars* and *America's Got Talent* encourage online and telephone voting. In the future, successful integrated marketing communications campaigns will certainly be engaging you![1]

Taco Bell's successful Doritos Locos Tacos campaign demonstrates the opportunity for engaging potential customers and the importance of integrating the various elements of a marketing communication program. Promotion represents the fourth element in the marketing mix. The promotional element consists of five communication tools, including advertising, personal selling, sales promotion, public relations, and direct marketing. The combination of one or more of these communication tools is called the **promotional mix**. All of these tools can be used to (1) inform prospective buyers about the benefits of the product, (2) persuade them to try it, and (3) remind them later about the benefits they enjoyed by using the product. In the past, marketers often viewed these communication tools as separate and independent. The advertising department, for example, often designed and managed its activities without consulting departments or agencies that had responsibility for sales promotion or public relations. The result was often an overall communication effort that was uncoordinated and, in some cases, inconsistent. Today, the concept of designing marketing communications programs that coordinate all promotional activities—advertising, personal selling, sales promotion, public relations, and direct marketing—to provide a consistent message across all audiences is referred to as **integrated marketing communications (IMC)**. By taking consumer expectations into consideration, IMC is a key element in a company's customer experience management strategy.[2]

This chapter provides an overview of the communication process, a description of the promotional mix elements, several tools for integrating the promotional mix, and a process for developing a comprehensive promotion program. One of the promotional mix elements, direct marketing, is also discussed in this chapter. Chapter 18 covers advertising, sales promotion, and public relations, Chapter 19 covers social media, and Chapter 20 discusses personal selling.

THE COMMUNICATION PROCESS

| LO 17-1 | Discuss integrated marketing communications and the communication process. |

Communication is the process of conveying a message to others, and it requires six elements: a source, a message, a channel of communication, a receiver, and the processes of encoding and decoding[3] (see Figure 17–1). The **source** may be a company or person who has information to convey. The information sent by a source, such as a description of a new smartphone, forms the **message**. The message is conveyed by means of a **channel of communication** such as a salesperson, advertising media, or public relations tools. Consumers who read, hear, or see the message are the **receivers**.

FIGURE 17–1

The communication process consists of six key elements. See the text to learn about factors that influence the effectiveness of the process.

How would you decode this ad? What message is The North Face trying to send?

Source: The North Face

The North Face

www.thenorthface.com

Video 17-1

The North Face

kerin.tv/13e/v17-1

Encoding and Decoding

Encoding and decoding are essential to communication. **Encoding** is the process of having the sender transform an idea into a set of symbols. **Decoding** is the reverse, or the process of having the receiver take a set of symbols, the message, and transform the symbols into an idea. Look at the advertisement above: Who is the source, and what is the message?

Decoding is performed by the receivers according to their own frame of reference: their attitudes, values, and beliefs.[4] The North Face is the source and the advertisement is the message, which appeared in *Wired* magazine (the channel). How would you interpret (decode) this advertisement? The picture and text in the advertisement show that the source's intention is to generate interest in its product with the headline "Never Stop Exploring"—a statement the source believes will appeal to the readers of the magazine.

The process of communication is not always a successful one. Errors in communication can happen in several ways. The source may not adequately transform the abstract idea into an effective set of symbols, a properly encoded message may be sent through the wrong channel and never make it to the intended receiver, the receiver may not properly transform the set of symbols into the correct abstract idea, or finally, feedback may be so delayed or distorted that it is of no use to the sender. Although communication appears easy to perform, truly effective communication can be very difficult.

For the message to be communicated effectively, the sender and receiver must have a mutually shared **field of experience**—a similar understanding and knowledge they apply to the message. Figure 17–1 shows two circles representing the fields of experience of the sender and receiver, which overlap in the message. Some of the better-known message problems have occurred when U.S. companies have taken their messages to cultures with different fields of experience. Many misinterpretations are merely the result of bad translations. For example, KFC made a mistake when its "finger-lickin' good" slogan was translated into Mandarin Chinese as "eat your fingers off"![5]

Feedback

Figure 17–1 shows a line labeled *feedback loop,* which consists of a response and feedback. A **response** is the impact the message had on the receiver's knowledge, attitudes, or behaviors. **Feedback** is the sender's interpretation of the response and indicates whether the message was decoded and understood as intended. Chapter 18 reviews approaches called *pretesting,* which ensure that messages are decoded properly.

Noise

Noise includes extraneous factors that can work against effective communication by distorting a message or the feedback received (Figure 17–1). Noise can be a simple error, such as a printing mistake that affects the meaning of a newspaper advertisement or the use of words or pictures that fail to communicate the message clearly. Noise can also occur when a salesperson's message is misunderstood by a prospective buyer, such as when a salesperson's accent, use of slang terms, or communication style make hearing and understanding the message difficult.

learning review »

17-1. What six elements are required for communication to occur?

17-2. A difficulty for U.S. companies advertising in international markets is that the audience does not share the same _____.

17-3. A misprint in a newspaper ad is an example of _____.

THE PROMOTIONAL ELEMENTS

LO 17-2 Describe the promotional mix and the uniqueness of each component.

Magazines are a mass media outlet for advertising.

© H. S. Photos/Alamy

To communicate with consumers, a company can use one or more of five promotional alternatives: advertising, personal selling, public relations, sales promotion, and direct marketing. Figure 17–2 summarizes the distinctions among these five elements. Three of these elements—advertising, sales promotion, and public relations—are often said to use *mass selling* because they are used with groups of prospective buyers. In contrast, personal selling uses *customized interaction* between a seller and a prospective buyer. Personal selling activities include face-to-face, telephone, and interactive electronic communication. Direct marketing also uses messages customized for specific customers.

Advertising

Advertising is any paid form of nonpersonal communication about an organization, product, service, or idea by an identified sponsor. The *paid* aspect of this definition is important because the space for the advertising message normally must be bought. An occasional exception is the public service announcement, where the advertising time or space is donated. A full-page, four-color ad in *Time* magazine, for example, costs $338,900. The *nonpersonal* component of advertising is also important. Advertising involves mass media (such as TV, radio, and magazines), which are nonpersonal and do not have an immediate feedback loop as does personal selling. So before the message is sent, marketing research plays a valuable role; for example, it determines that the target market will actually see the medium chosen and that the message will be understood.

There are several advantages to a firm using advertising in its promotional mix. It can be attention-getting—as with the Klondike ad shown in

PROMOTIONAL ELEMENT	MASS OR CUSTOMIZED	COST	STRENGTHS	WEAKNESSES
Advertising	Mass	Fees paid for space or time	• Efficient means for reaching large numbers of people	• High absolute costs • Difficult to receive good feedback
Personal selling	Customized	Fees paid to salespeople as either salaries or commissions	• Immediate feedback • Very persuasive • Can select audience • Can give complex information	• Extremely expensive per exposure • Messages may differ between salespeople
Public relations	Mass	No direct payment to media	• Often most credible source in the consumer's mind	• Difficult to get media cooperation
Sales promotion	Mass	Wide range of fees paid, depending on promotion selected	• Effective at changing behavior in short run • Very flexible	• Easily abused • Can lead to promotion wars • Easily duplicated
Direct marketing	Customized	Cost of communication through mail, telephone, or computer	• Messages can be prepared quickly • Facilitates relationship with customer	• Declining customer response • Database management is expensive

FIGURE 17–2

Each of the five elements of the promotional mix has strengths and weaknesses.

this chapter—and also communicate specific product benefits to prospective buyers. By paying for the advertising space, a company can control *what* it wants to say and, to some extent, to *whom* the message is sent. Advertising also allows the company to decide *when* to send its message (which includes how often). The nonpersonal aspect of advertising also has its advantages. Once the message is created, the same message is sent to all receivers in a market segment. If the pictorial, text, and brand elements of an advertisement are properly pretested, an advertiser can ensure the ad's ability to capture consumers' attention and trust that the same message will be decoded by all receivers in the market segment.[6]

Advertising has some disadvantages. As shown in Figure 17–2 and discussed in depth in Chapter 18, the costs to produce and place a message are significant, and the lack of direct feedback makes it difficult to know how well the message was received.

Personal Selling

The second major promotional alternative is **personal selling**, which is the two-way flow of communication between a buyer and seller designed to influence a person's or group's purchase decision. Unlike advertising, personal selling is usually face-to-face communication between the sender and receiver. Why do companies use personal selling?

There are important advantages to personal selling, as summarized in Figure 17–2. A salesperson can control to *whom* the presentation is made, reducing the amount of *wasted coverage,* or communication with consumers who are not in the target audience. The personal component of selling has another advantage in that the seller can see or hear the potential buyer's reaction to the message. If the feedback is unfavorable, the salesperson can modify the message.

The flexibility of personal selling can also be a disadvantage. Different salespeople can change the message so that no consistent communication is given to all customers. The high cost of personal selling is probably its major disadvantage. On a cost-per-contact basis, it is generally the most expensive of the five promotional elements.

Public Relations

Public relations is a form of communication management that seeks to influence the feelings, opinions, or beliefs held by customers, prospective customers, stockholders, suppliers, employees, and other publics about a company and its products or services.[7] Many tools such as special events, lobbying efforts, annual reports, press conferences, social media (including Facebook and Twitter), and image management may be used by a public relations department, although publicity often plays the most important role.[8] **Publicity** is a nonpersonal, indirectly paid presentation of an organization, product, or service. It can take the form of a news story, editorial, or product announcement. A difference between publicity and both advertising and personal selling is the "indirectly paid" dimension. With publicity a company does not pay for space in a mass medium (such as television or radio) but attempts to get the medium to run a favorable story on the company. In this sense, there is an indirect payment for publicity in that a company must support a public relations staff.

An advantage of publicity is credibility. When you read a favorable story about a company's product (such as a glowing restaurant review), there is a tendency to believe it. Travelers throughout the world have relied on Fodor's guides such as *Essential Italy.* These books describe out-of-the-way, inexpensive restaurants and hotels, giving invaluable publicity to these establishments. Such businesses do not (nor can they) buy a mention in the guide. Publicity is particularly effective when consumers lack prior knowledge of the product or service.[9]

The disadvantage of publicity relates to the lack of the user's control over it. A company can invite media to cover an interesting event such as a store opening or a

The Klondike ad, Fodor's travel guide, and M&M's sweepstakes are examples of three elements of the promotional mix—advertising, public relations, and sales promotion.

Sources: Left: Unilever; Middle: © McGraw-Hill Education/ Editorial Image, LLC, photographer; Right: Mars, Incorporated

McDonald's facilitates online discussions with Twitter.

Source: McDonald's

new-product release, but there is no guarantee that a story will result, that it will be positive, or that the target audience will receive the message. Social media such as Facebook, Twitter, and topic-specific blogs have grown dramatically and allow public discussions of almost any company activity. Many public relations departments now focus on facilitating and responding to online discussions. McDonald's, for example, recently announced a one-hour Twitter chat with Bob Langert, vice president of corporate social responsibility and sustainability. Generally, publicity is an important element of most promotional campaigns, although the lack of control means that it is rarely the primary element. Research related to the sequence of IMC elements, however, indicates that publicity followed by advertising with the same message increases the positive response to the message.[10]

Sales Promotion

A fourth promotional element is **sales promotion**, a short-term inducement of value offered to arouse interest in buying a product or service. Used in conjunction with advertising or personal selling, sales promotions are offered to intermediaries as well as to ultimate consumers. Coupons, rebates, samples, contests, and sweepstakes such as the M&M's promotion are just a few examples of sales promotions discussed later in this chapter.

The advantage of sales promotion is that the short-term nature of these programs (such as a coupon or sweepstakes with an expiration date) often stimulates sales for their duration. Offering value to the consumer in terms of a cents-off coupon or rebate may increase store traffic from consumers who are not store-loyal.[11]

Sales promotions cannot be the sole basis for a campaign because gains are often temporary and sales drop off when the deal ends. Advertising support is needed to convert the customer who tried the product because of a sales promotion into a long-term buyer. If sales promotions are conducted continuously, they lose their effectiveness. Customers begin to delay purchase until a coupon is offered, or they question the product's value. Some aspects of sales promotions also are regulated by the federal government.[12] These issues are reviewed in detail in Chapter 18.

Direct Marketing

© Fotosearch, LLC

Another promotional alternative, **direct marketing**, uses direct communication with consumers to generate a response in the form of an order, a request for further information, or a visit to a retail outlet. The communication can take many forms, including face-to-face selling, direct mail, catalogs, telephone solicitations, direct response advertising (on television and radio and in print), and online marketing.[13] Like personal selling, direct marketing often consists of interactive communication. It also has the advantage of being customized to match the needs of specific target markets. Messages can be developed and adapted quickly to facilitate one-to-one relationships with customers.

While direct marketing has been one of the fastest-growing forms of promotion, it has several disadvantages. First, most forms of direct marketing require a comprehensive and up-to-date database with information about the target market. Developing and maintaining the database can be expensive and time-consuming. In addition, growing concern about privacy has led to a decline in response rates among some customer groups. Companies with successful direct marketing programs are sensitive to these issues and often use a combination of direct marketing alternatives together, or direct marketing combined with other promotional tools, to increase value for customers.

INTEGRATED MARKETING COMMUNICATIONS—DEVELOPING THE PROMOTIONAL MIX

LO 17-3 Select the promotional approach appropriate to a product's target audience, life-cycle stage, and characteristics, as well as stages of the buying decision and channel strategies.

A firm's promotional mix is the combination of one or more of the promotional tools it chooses to use. In putting together the promotional mix, a marketer must consider two issues. First, the balance of the elements must be determined. Should advertising be emphasized more than personal selling? Should a promotional rebate be offered? Would public relations activities be effective? Several factors affect such decisions: the target audience for the promotion, the stage of the product's life cycle, the characteristics of the product, the decision stage of the buyer, and even the channel of distribution. Second, because the various promotional elements are often the responsibility of different departments, coordinating a consistent promotional effort is necessary. A promotional planning process designed to ensure integrated marketing communications (IMC) can facilitate this goal.

The Target Audience

Promotional programs are directed to the ultimate consumer, to an intermediary (retailer, wholesaler, or industrial distributor), or to both. Promotional programs directed to buyers of consumer products often use mass media because the number of potential buyers is large. Personal selling is used at the place of purchase, generally the retail store. Direct marketing may be used to encourage first-time or repeat purchases. Combinations of many media alternatives are a necessity for some target audiences today. The Marketing Matters box describes how today's college students can be reached through mobile marketing programs.[14]

Advertising directed to business buyers is used selectively in trade publications such as *Restaurant Business* magazine for buyers of restaurant equipment and supplies. Because business buyers often have specialized needs or technical questions, personal selling is particularly important. The salesperson can provide information and the necessary support after the sale.

Intermediaries are often the focus of promotional efforts. As with business buyers, personal selling is the major promotional ingredient. The salespeople assist intermediaries in making a profit by coordinating promotional campaigns sponsored by the manufacturer and by providing marketing advice and expertise. Intermediaries' questions often pertain to the allowed markup, merchandising support, and return policies.

Publications such as *Restaurant Business* reach business buyers.
Source: CSP Business Media, LLC

Marketing **Matters**

Tips for Targeting College Students

College students represent an attractive target market for many businesses today for several reasons. First, they are early adopters shaping spending habits that could lead them to become lifelong customers. Second, experts estimate that their annual spending power is $417 billion. The challenge for marketers is that students are tech-savvy, hyper-connected, and demanding. In an effort to reach students with their offerings, marketers are tailoring their activities to match the segment's unique combination of characteristics.

College students consist of "digital natives" who have grown up with technology. They have and use laptop computers, high definition televisions, game consoles, tablet PCs, and smartphones. In fact, a recent study of university and college students found that 82 percent of new college students own a smartphone. They access Facebook, Twitter, YouTube, and Instagram; they download apps, coupons, and information 24/7; and they communicate with e-mail, text messages, and blogs. For many businesses, these facts suggest that marketing through cell phones, or mobile marketing will be an essential element in integrated marketing communications campaigns in the future.

Source: Volkswagen of America, Inc.

Several guidelines help ensure the success of mobile marketing. First, it is important to create a mobile-ready app that is flashy, fun, and has the potential to "go viral." In addition, successful mobile apps should help shoppers make price comparisons, and match product characteristics to their needs, preferences, and lifestyles. Communication must be short (140 characters on Twitter!), honest, authentic, and transparent about the purpose and value of the brand. Finally, mobile marketing campaigns should facilitate multitasking. According to one expert, marketers "should picture students looking at text and images while traveling on a bus, rushing to a lecture, or out socializing."

Examples of successful mobile marketing campaigns include MTV's use of a Twitter jockey to provide messages to its viewers, Starbuck's mobile app to make payments easier, and Volkswagen's Smileage app that measures fun on the road.

Watch for other brands that use mobile marketing as part of their campaigns to reach college students in the future.

477

The Product Life Cycle

All products have a product life cycle (see Chapter 11), and the composition of the promotional mix changes over the four life-cycle stages, as shown in Figure 17–3.

Advertising in *Dogster* can build awareness of a new dog food.

Source: I-5 Publishing, LLC

Introduction Stage Informing consumers in an effort to increase their level of awareness is the primary promotional objective in the introduction stage of the product life cycle. In general, all the promotional mix elements are used at this time, although the use of specific mix elements during any stage depends on the product and situation. News releases about a new dog food, for example, are sent to veterinary magazines, trial samples are sent to registered dog owners, advertisements are placed in *Dogster* magazine, and the salesforce begins to approach supermarkets and pet stores to get orders. Advertising is particularly important as a means of reaching as many people as possible to build awareness and interest. Publicity may even begin slightly before the product is commercially available.

Growth Stage The primary promotional objective of the growth stage is to persuade the consumer to buy the product rather than substitutes, so the marketing manager seeks to gain brand preference and solidify distribution. Sales promotion assumes less importance in this stage, and publicity is not a factor because it depends on novelty of the product. The primary promotional element is advertising, which stresses brand differences. Personal selling is used to solidify the channel of distribution. For consumer products such as

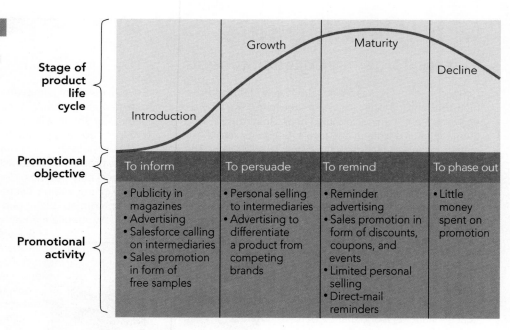

FIGURE 17–3

The product life cycle illustrates how promotional objectives and activities change over the four stages.

Stage of product life cycle	Introduction	Growth	Maturity	Decline
Promotional objective	To inform	To persuade	To remind	To phase out
Promotional activity	• Publicity in magazines • Advertising • Salesforce calling on intermediaries • Sales promotion in form of free samples	• Personal selling to intermediaries • Advertising to differentiate a product from competing brands	• Reminder advertising • Sales promotion in form of discounts, coupons, and events • Limited personal selling • Direct-mail reminders	• Little money spent on promotion

dog food, the salesforce calls on the wholesalers and retailers in hopes of increasing inventory levels and gaining shelf space. For business products, the salesforce often tries to get contractual arrangements to be the sole source of supply for the buyer.

Maturity Stage   In the maturity stage, the need is to maintain existing buyers, and advertising's role is to remind buyers of the product's existence. Sales promotion, in the form of discounts and coupons offered to both ultimate consumers and intermediaries, is important in maintaining loyal buyers. In a test of one mature consumer product, it was found that 80 percent of the product's sales at this stage resulted from sales promotions.[15] Sponsoring events can also help maintain loyalty. For the past 18 years, Purina has sponsored the Purina Pro Plan Incredible Dog Challenge, which is covered by a live stream for online viewers. In addition, Purina has developed an iPhone app called P5 to teach viewers how to train their dogs in the events they see performed during the Challenge.[16] Direct marketing actions such as direct mail are used to maintain involvement with existing customers and to encourage repeat purchases. Price cuts and discounts can also significantly increase a mature brand's sales. The salesforce at this stage seeks to satisfy intermediaries. An unsatisfied customer who switches brands is hard to replace.

Decline Stage   The decline stage of the product life cycle is usually a period of phaseout for the product, and little money is spent in the promotional mix. The rate of decline can be rapid, as is the case when a product is replaced by an improved or lower-cost product, for example, or slow, as often happens when there is a loyal group of customers.

Product Characteristics

The proper blend of elements in the promotional mix also depends on the type of product. Three specific characteristics should be considered: complexity, risk, and ancillary services. *Complexity* refers to the technical sophistication of the product and hence the amount of understanding required to use it. It's hard to provide much information in a one-page magazine ad or a 30-second television ad, so the more complex the product, the greater the emphasis on personal selling. Gulfstream asks potential

How do Gulfstream aircraft and Pepperidge Farm cookies differ on complexity, risk, and ancillary services?

Credit: (left) Source: General Dynamics; (right) Source: Pepperidge Farm, Incorporated

Gulfstream

www.gulfstream.com

Pepperidge Farm

www.pepperidgefarm.com

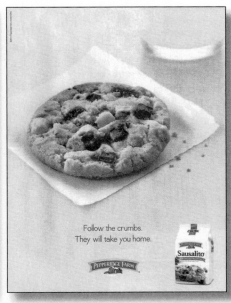

479

customers to call a representative identified in its ads. On the other hand, very little information is provided for simple products such as Pepperidge Farm cookies.

A second element is the degree of risk represented by the product's purchase. *Risk* for the buyer can be assessed in terms of financial risk, social risk, and physical risk. A private jet, for example, might represent all three risks—it is expensive, employees and customers may see and evaluate the purchase, and safety and reliability are important. Although advertising helps, the greater the risk, the greater the need for personal selling. Consumers are unlikely to associate any of these risks with a candy bar.

The level of ancillary services required by a product also affects the promotional strategy. *Ancillary services* pertain to the degree of service or support required after the sale. This characteristic is common to many industrial products and consumer purchases. Who will provide maintenance for the plane? Advertising's role is to establish the seller's reputation. Direct marketing can be used to describe how a product or service can be customized to meet individual needs. However, personal selling is essential to build buyer confidence and provide evidence of customer service.

Stages of the Buying Decision

Knowing the customer's stage of decision making can also affect the promotional mix. Figure 17–4 on the next page shows how the importance of the promotional elements varies with the three stages in the consumer purchase decision process.

Prepurchase Stage   In the prepurchase stage, advertising is more helpful than personal selling because advertising informs the potential customer of the existence of the product and the seller. Sales promotion in the form of free samples also can play an important role to gain low-risk trial. When the salesperson calls on the customer after heavy advertising, there is some recognition of what the salesperson represents. This is particularly important in industrial settings in which sampling of the product is usually not possible.

Purchase Stage   At the purchase stage, the importance of personal selling is highest, whereas the impact of advertising is lowest. Sales promotion in the form of coupons, deals, point-of-purchase displays, and rebates can be very helpful in

FIGURE 17–4

The importance of promotional elements varies during the stages of the consumer purchase decision process.

Stage of the consumer purchase decision process

encouraging demand. In this stage, social media can play an important role in the final decision by delivering promotions and giving consumers control of the process. Research indicates that direct marketing activities shorten the time consumers take to adopt a product or service.[17]

Postpurchase Stage   In the postpurchase stage, the salesperson is still important. In fact, the more personal contact after the sale, the more the buyer is satisfied. Advertising is also important to assure the buyer that the right purchase was made. Advertising and personal selling help reduce the buyer's postpurchase anxiety. Sales promotion in the form of coupons and direct marketing reminders can help encourage repeat purchases from satisfied first-time triers. Public relations plays a small role in the postpurchase stage.[18]

Channel Strategies

Chapter 15 discussed the channel flow from a producer to intermediaries to consumers. Achieving control of the channel is often difficult for the manufacturer, and promotional strategies can assist in moving a product through the channel of distribution. This is where a manufacturer has to make an important decision about whether to use a push strategy, pull strategy, or both in its channel of distribution.[19]

Push Strategy   Figure 17–5A shows how a manufacturer uses a **push strategy**, directing the promotional mix to channel members to gain their cooperation in ordering and stocking the product. In this approach, personal selling and sales promotions play major roles. Salespeople call on wholesalers to encourage orders and provide sales assistance. Sales promotions, such as case discount allowances (20 percent off the regular case price), are offered to stimulate demand. By pushing the product through the channel, the goal is to get channel members to push it to their customers.

Ford Motor Company, for example, provides support and incentives for its 3,263 Ford dealers. Through a multilevel program, Ford provides incentives to reward dealers for meeting sales goals. Dealers receive an incentive when they are

FIGURE 17–5

Push and pull strategies direct the promotional mix to different points in the channel of distribution.

A.   Push strategy

Manufacturer

Flow of demand stimulation

Flow of promotion; mainly personal selling directed to intermediaries

Wholesaler

Retailer

Consumer

B.   Pull strategy

Manufacturer

Flow of demand stimulation

Flow of promotion; mainly advertising directed to consumers

Wholesaler

Retailer

Consumer

Why does this ad for a drug that offers migraine pain relief suggest readers should "Ask your doctor about RELPAX today"? For the answer, see the text.

Source: Pfizer Inc.

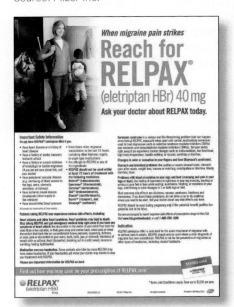

near a goal, another when they reach a goal, and an even larger one if they exceed sales projections. Ford also offers some dealers special incentives for maintaining superior facilities or improving customer service. All of these actions are intended to encourage Ford dealers to "push" the Ford products through the channel to consumers.[20]

Pull Strategy   In some instances, manufacturers face resistance from channel members who do not want to order a new product or increase inventory levels of an existing brand. As shown in Figure 17–5B, a manufacturer may then elect to implement a **pull strategy** by directing its promotional mix at ultimate consumers to encourage them to ask the retailer for a product. Seeing demand from ultimate consumers, retailers order the product from wholesalers and thus the item is pulled through the intermediaries. Pharmaceutical companies, for example, now spend more than $3.8 billion annually on *direct-to-consumer* prescription drug advertising, to complement traditional personal selling and free samples directed only at doctors.[21] The strategy is designed to encourage consumers to ask their doctor for a specific drug by name—pulling it through the channel. Successful campaigns such as the print ad, which says, "Ask your doctor about RELPAX today," can have dramatic effects on the sales of a product.

learning review ≫

17-7. Describe the promotional objective for each stage of the product life cycle.

17-8. At what stage of the consumer purchase decision process is the importance of personal selling highest? Why?

17-9. Explain the differences between a push strategy and a pull strategy.

DEVELOPING AN INTEGRATED MARKETING COMMUNICATIONS PROGRAM

LO 17-4 Describe the elements of the promotion decision process.

Because media costs are high, promotion decisions must be made carefully, using a systematic approach. Paralleling the planning, implementation, and evaluation steps described in the strategic marketing process (Chapter 2), the promotion decision process is divided into (1) developing, (2) executing, and (3) assessing the promotion program (see Figure 17–6). Development of the promotion program focuses on the four *W*s:

- *Who* is the target audience?
- *What* are (1) the promotion objectives, (2) the amounts of money that can be budgeted for the promotion program, and (3) the kinds of promotion to be used?
- *Where* should the promotion be run?
- *When* should the promotion be run?

Identifying the Target Audience

The first step in developing the promotion program involves identifying the *target audience,* the group of prospective buyers toward which a promotion program will be directed. To the extent that time and money permit, the target audience for the promotion program is the target market for the firm's product, which is identified from primary and secondary sources of marketing information. The more a firm knows about its target audience—including demographics, interests, preferences, media use, and purchase behaviors—the easier it is to develop a promotional program. A firm might use a profile based on gender, age, and income, for example, to place ads during specific TV programs or in particular magazines. Similarly, a firm might use *behavioral targeting*—collecting information about your web-browsing behavior to determine the banner and display ads that you will see as you surf the Web. Behavioral targeting is discussed in more detail in Chapter 21.[22]

Specifying Promotion Objectives

After the target audience has been identified, a decision must be reached on what the promotion should accomplish. Consumers can be said to respond in terms of a **hierarchy of effects**, which is the sequence of stages a prospective buyer goes through from initial awareness of a product to eventual action.[23] The five stages are:

- *Awareness*—the consumer's ability to recognize and remember the product or brand name.
- *Interest*—an increase in the consumer's desire to learn about some of the features of the product or brand.
- *Evaluation*—the consumer's appraisal of the product or brand on important attributes.

FIGURE 17–6

The promotion decision process includes planning, implementation, and evaluation.

| Planning
Developing the promotion program
• Identify the target audience
• Specify the objectives
• Set the budget
• Select the right promotional tools
• Design the promotion
• Schedule the promotion | Implementation
Executing the promotion program
• Pretest the promotion
• Carry out the promotion | Evaluation
Assessing the promotion program
• Posttest the promotion
• Make needed changes |

Corrective actions   Corrective actions

Rank	Company	Advertising ($ in millions)	+	All Other Promotion ($ in millions)	=	Total ($ in millions)
1	Procter & Gamble	$2,919		$1,688		$4,607
2	AT&T	$1,636		$1,636		$3,272
3	General Motors	$1,660		$1,460		$3,120
4	Comcast	$1,557		$1,472		$3,029
5	Verizon	$1,292		$1,234		$2,526
6	Ford	$842		$1,625		$2,467
7	American Express	$372		$1,992		$2,364
8	Fiat Chrysler	$1,128		$1,121		$2,249
9	L'Oréal	$1,474		$684		$2,158
10	Walt Disney	$869		$1,240		$2,109

FIGURE 17–7

U.S. promotion expenditures of the top 10 companies. Note that Ford, American Express, and Walt Disney spend more on promotion than on advertising.

© Peter Probst/Alamy

© PSL Images/Alamy

- *Trial*—the consumer's actual first purchase and use of the product or brand.
- *Adoption*—through a favorable experience on the first trial, the consumer's repeated purchase and use of the product or brand.

For a totally new product, the sequence applies to the entire product category, but for a new brand competing in an established product category, it applies to the brand itself. These steps can serve as guidelines for developing promotion objectives.

Although sometimes an objective for a promotion program involves several steps in the hierarchy of effects, it often focuses on a single stage. Regardless of what the specific objective might be, from building awareness to increasing repeat purchases, promotion objectives should possess three important qualities. They should (1) be designed for a well-defined target audience, (2) be measurable, and (3) cover a specified time period.

Setting the Promotion Budget

From Figure 17–7, it is clear that the promotion expenditures needed to reach U.S. households are enormous. Note that each of the companies spends a total of more than $2 billion annually on promotion.[24]

After setting the promotion objectives, a company must decide how much to spend. Determining the ideal amount for the budget is difficult because there is no precise way to measure the exact results of spending promotion dollars. However, several methods can be used to set the promotion budget.[25]

Percentage of Sales In the **percentage of sales budgeting** approach, funds are allocated to promotion as a percentage of past or anticipated sales, in terms of either dollars or units sold. A common budgeting method, this approach is often stated in terms such as, "Our promotion budget for this year is 3 percent of last year's gross sales."[26] The advantage of this approach is obvious: It is simple and provides a financial safeguard by tying the promotion budget to sales. However, there is a major fallacy in this approach, which implies that sales cause promotion. Using this method, a company may reduce its promotion budget because of a downturn in past sales or an anticipated downturn in future sales—situations in which it may need promotion the most. See the Applying Marketing Metrics box for an application of the promotion-to-sales ratio to the soft-drink industry.[27]

Competitive Parity A second common approach, **competitive parity budgeting**, is matching the competitor's absolute level of spending or the proportion per point of

Applying Marketing Metrics

How Much Should You Spend on IMC?

Integrated marketing communications (IMC) programs coordinate a variety of promotion alternatives to provide a consistent message across audiences. The amount spent on the various promotional elements, or on the total campaign, may vary depending on the target audience, the type of product, where the product is in the product life cycle, and the channel strategy selected. Managers often use the promotion-to-sales ratio on their marketing dashboard to assess how effective the IMC program expenditures are at generating sales.

Your Challenge

As a manager at PepsiCo, you've been asked to assess the effectiveness of all promotion expenditures during the past year. The promotion-to-sales ratio can be used to make year-to-year comparisons of a company's promotional programs, to compare the effectiveness of a company's program with competitors' programs, or to make comparisons with industry averages. You decide to calculate the promotion-to-sales ratio for PepsiCo. In addition, to allow a comparison, you decide to make the same calculation for one of your competitors, Coca-Cola, and for the entire nonalcoholic beverage industry. The ratio is calculated as follows:

Promotion-to-sales ratio =
Total promotion expenditures ÷ Total sales

Your Findings

The information needed for these calculations is readily available from trade publications and annual reports. The following graph shows the promotion-to-sales ratio for PepsiCo, Coca-Cola, and the entire nonalcoholic beverage industry. PepsiCo spent $196 million on its promotion program to generate $2.3 billion in sales for a ratio of 8.5 (percent). In comparison, Coca-Cola's ratio was 5.3, and the industry average was 5.5.

Your Action

PepsiCo's promotion-to-sales ratio is higher than Coca-Cola's and higher than the industry average. This suggests that the current mix of promotional activities and the level of expenditures may not be creating an effective IMC program. In the future, you will want to monitor the factors that may influence the ratio.

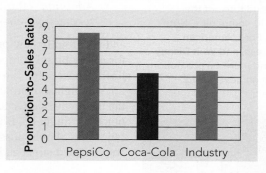

---

market share. This approach has also been referred to as *matching competitors* or *share of market*. It is important to consider the competition in budgeting. Consumer responses to promotion are affected by competing promotional activities, so if a competitor runs 30 radio ads each week, it may be difficult for a firm to get its message across with only 5 ads. The competitor's budget level, however, should not be the only determinant in setting a company's budget. The competition might have very different promotional objectives, which require a different level of promotion expenditures.[28]

All You Can Afford   Common to many small businesses is **all-you-can-afford budgeting**, in which money is allocated to promotion only after all other budget items are covered. As one company executive said in reference to this budgeting process, "Why, it's simple. First, I go upstairs to the controller and ask how much they can afford to give us this year. She says a million and a half. Later, the boss comes to me and asks how much we should spend, and I say, 'Oh, about a million and a half.' Then we have our promotion appropriation."[29]

Fiscally conservative, this approach has little else to offer. Using this budgeting philosophy, a company acts as though it doesn't know anything about a promotion-sales relationship or what its promotion objectives are.

Objective and Task   The best approach to budgeting is **objective and task budgeting**, whereby the company (1) determines its promotion objectives, (2) outlines the tasks it will undertake to accomplish those objectives, and (3) determines the promotion cost of performing those tasks.[30] This method takes into account what the company wants to accomplish and requires that the objectives be specified.[31] Strengths of the other budgeting methods are integrated into this approach because each previous method's strength is tied to the objectives. For example, if the costs are beyond what the company can afford, objectives are reworked and the tasks revised. The difficulty with this method is the judgment required to determine the tasks needed to accomplish objectives.

Selecting the Right Promotional Tools

Once a budget has been determined, the combination of the five basic IMC tools—advertising, personal selling, sales promotion, public relations, and direct marketing—can be specified. While many factors provide direction for selection of the appropriate mix, the large number of possible combinations of the promotional tools means that many combinations can achieve the same objective. Therefore, an analytical approach and experience are particularly important in this step of the promotion decision process. The specific mix can vary from a simple program using a single tool to a comprehensive program using all forms of promotion.

The Olympics have become a very visible example of a comprehensive integrated communications program. Because the Games are repeated every two years, the promotion is continuous during "on" and "off" years. Included in the program are advertising campaigns, personal selling efforts by the Olympic committee and organizers, sales promotion activities such as product tie-ins and sponsorships, public relations programs managed by the host cities, online and social media communication, and direct marketing efforts targeted at a variety of audiences, including governments, organizations, firms, athletes, and individuals.[32] At this stage, it is also important to assess the relative importance of the various tools. While it may be desirable to utilize and integrate several forms of promotion, one may deserve emphasis. The Olympics, for example, place primary importance on public relations and publicity.

Designing the Promotion

The central element of a promotion program is the promotion itself. Advertising consists of advertising copy and the artwork that the target audience is intended to see or hear. Personal selling efforts depend on the characteristics and skills of the salesperson. Sales promotion activities consist of the specific details of inducements such as coupons, samples, and sweepstakes. Public relations efforts are readily seen in tangible elements such as news releases, and direct marketing actions depend on written, verbal, and electronic forms of delivery. The design of the promotion will play a primary role in determining the message that is communicated to the audience. This design activity is frequently viewed as the step requiring the most creativity. In addition, successful designs are often the result of insight regarding consumers' interests and purchasing behavior. All of the promotion tools have many design alternatives. Advertising, for example, can utilize fear, humor, attractiveness, or other themes in its appeal. Similarly, direct marketing can be designed for varying levels of personal or customized appeals. One of the challenges of IMC is to design each promotional activity to communicate the same message.[33]

Scheduling the Promotion

Once the design of each of the promotional program elements is complete, it is important to determine the most effective timing of their use. The promotion schedule describes the order in which each promotional tool is introduced and the frequency of its use during the campaign.

PyeongChang 2018

This logo for the 2018 Winter Olympics in PyeongChang, South Korea, is part of a comprehensive IMC program.

© grzegorz knec/Alamy

Video 17-3
Olympics
kerin.tv/13e/v17-3

485

What promotional tools did Disney use to support the release of *Jurassic World*?
© Film Fanatique/Alamy

Universal Pictures movie studio, for example, uses a schedule of several promotional tools for movies. To generate interest in *Jurassic World,* the studio aired a "Jurassic Park" special on the SciFi Channel and also created "Jurassic Thursday" for Univision and Telemundo. The trailer for the movie was then aired just before kickoff at the Super Bowl, and the studio created a reality-based web experience, which presented Jurassic World as an actual vacation resort. In addition, the director of the original *Jurassic Park,* Steven Spielberg, did magazine, online, and TV interviews recalling his original film. Actors from the new film, including lead actor Chris Pratt, also made promotional appearances and Chris was highlighted in *Entertainment Weekly*'s movie double issue and on the cover of *GQ* magazine. The campaign culminated with a premiere event in Hollywood featuring Jimmy Buffett. The results were spectacular as the movie broke all records to become the number one movie for U.S. and overseas ticket sales![34]

Overall, the scheduling of the various promotions was designed to generate interest, bring consumers into theaters, and then encourage additional purchases after seeing the movie. Several factors such as seasonality and competitive promotion activity can also influence the promotion schedule. Businesses such as ski resorts, airlines, and professional sports teams are likely to reduce their promotional activity during the off-season. Similarly, restaurants, retail stores, and health clubs are likely to increase their promotional activity when new competitors enter the market.

EXECUTING AND ASSESSING THE PROMOTION PROGRAM

Carrying out the promotion program can be expensive and time-consuming. One researcher estimates that "an organization with sales less than $10 million can successfully implement an IMC program in one year, one with sales between $200 million and $500 million will need about three years, and one with sales between $2 billion and $5 billion will need five years." In addition, firms with a market orientation are more likely to implement an IMC program, and firms with support from top management have more effective IMC programs.[35] To facilitate the transition, approximately 200 integrated marketing communications agencies are in operation. In addition, some of the largest agencies are adopting approaches that embrace "total communications solutions."

Media agency MediaCom, which recently won *Advertising Age* magazine's Media Agency of the Year award, for example, is part of a global network of 5,000 people in 113 offices in 89 countries who "work on behalf of our clients to leverage their brands' entire system of communications." In fact, the agency website proclaims that "we optimize content and connections to fuel business success." MediaCom's clients include Volkswagen, Dell, Subway, Revlon, Shell, and many others. One of its integrated campaigns for Canon, called Project Imagin8ion, included a user-generated photo contest, a partnership with filmmaker Ron Howard, community participation through YouTube and Flickr, online and TV advertising, and an interactive billboard in Times Square. The campaign resulted in Canon becoming the detachable lens camera market share leader. While many agencies may still be specialists, the trend today is clearly toward an integrated perspective that includes all forms of promotion. Agencies can accomplish this by including account managers, channel experts, media specialists, and planning personnel in their campaign design efforts.[36]

Read the text to learn how an integrated campaign helped Canon become a market share leader.
Source: Canon

An important factor in developing successful IMC programs is to create a process that facilitates their design and use. A tool used to evaluate a company's current process is the IMC audit. The audit analyzes the internal communication network of the company; identifies key audiences; evaluates customer databases; assesses messages in recent advertising, public relations releases, packaging, websites, e-mail and social media communication, signage, sales promotions, and direct mail; and determines the IMC expertise of company and agency personnel.[37] This process is becoming increasingly important as consumer-generated media such as blogs, RSS, podcasts, and social networks become more popular and as the use of search engines increases. Now, in addition to ensuring that traditional forms of communication are integrated, companies must be able to monitor consumer content, respond to inconsistent messages, and even answer questions from individual customers. According to Professor Judy Franks, marketers should also be cognizant of consumers she calls "accelerators." These individuals easily move content from medium to medium—from TV to YouTube to a mobile phone text message, for example—without any influence or control from the message source.[38]

As shown earlier in Figure 17–6, the ideal execution of a promotion program involves pretesting each design before it is actually used to allow for changes and modifications that improve its effectiveness. Similarly, posttests are recommended to evaluate the impact of each promotion and the contribution of the promotion toward achieving the program objectives. The most sophisticated pretest and posttest procedures have been developed for advertising and are discussed in Chapter 18. Testing procedures for sales promotion and direct marketing efforts currently focus on comparisons of different designs or responses of different segments. To fully benefit from IMC programs, companies must create and maintain a test-result database that allows comparisons of the relative impact of the promotional tools and their execution options in varying situations. Information from the database will allow informed design and execution decisions and provide support for IMC activities during internal reviews by financial or administrative personnel. The San Diego Padres baseball team, for example, developed a database of information relating attendance to its integrated campaign, which included a new logo, special events, merchandise sales, and a loyalty program.

As many as three-fourths of businesses may individually test new communication elements such as digital advertising, while one-fourth of all businesses may assess "most of their communication tactics" using new and traditional measures of effectiveness.[39] For most organizations, the assessment focuses on trying to determine which element of promotion works better. In an integrated program, however, media advertising might be used to build awareness, sales promotion to generate an inquiry, direct mail to provide additional information to individual prospects, and a personal sales call to complete the transaction. The tools are used for different reasons, and their combined use creates a synergy that should be the focus of the assessment. In addition, the effectiveness of IMC programs is strongly related to overall company performance.[40] Another level of assessment is necessary when firms have international promotion programs.

© PSL Images/Alamy

learning review »

17-10. What are the characteristics of good promotion objectives?

17-11. What is the weakness of the percentage of sales budgeting approach?

17-12. How have advertising agencies changed to facilitate the use of IMC programs?

DIRECT MARKETING

LO 17-5   Explain the value of direct marketing for consumers and sellers.

Direct marketing takes many forms and utilizes a variety of media. Several forms of direct marketing—direct mail and catalogs, television home shopping, telemarketing, and direct selling—were discussed as methods of nonstore retailing in Chapter 16. In addition, although advertising is discussed in Chapter 18, a form of advertising—direct response advertising—is an important form of direct marketing. Finally, interactive marketing is discussed in detail in Chapter 21. In this section, the growth of direct marketing, its value for consumers and sellers, and key global, technological, and ethical issues are discussed.

Business expenditures and response rates of four popular forms of direct marketing. Read the text to learn why the use of direct marketing is increasing.

McGraw-Hill Education, Mark A. Dierker, photographer

The Growth of Direct Marketing

The increasing interest in customer relationship management is reflected in the dramatic growth of direct marketing. The ability to customize communication efforts and create one-to-one interactions is appealing to most marketers, particularly those with IMC programs, because it leads to more favorable attitudes from the recipients. While many direct marketing methods are not new, the ability to design and use them has increased with the availability of customer information databases and new printing technologies. In recent years, direct marketing growth has outpaced total economic growth. Direct marketing expenditures exceed $146 billion and are growing at a rate of 9 percent. Similarly, revenues are expected to grow to $2.4 trillion next year. Direct marketing currently accounts for 8.7 percent of the total U.S. gross domestic product. Figure 17–8 shows the annual expenditures on four popular forms of direct marketing and their typical response rates. For example, marketers spend over $33 billion on direct mail each year, and direct mail generates a 3.4 percent response rate.[41]

While telemarketing receives the highest level of expenditures, most campaigns use several methods. jcpenney is one company that has integrated its direct marketing activities. The company begins a campaign by sending coupons to customers through e-mail and text messages. Consumers also receive direct-mail postcards and "Look Books" that invite them to visit the company's e-commerce website www.jcpenney.com or mobile commerce site www.m.jcpenney.com. A special social commerce app is also available for purchases on jcpenney's Facebook "Fan" Page. Many companies also integrate their direct marketing with other forms of promotion. Porsche, for example, recently launched television ads to change consumer perceptions of its cars and supported the campaign with direct-mail brochures, a mobile application, and an online video contest. As part of its campaign, Porsche parked its cars in the driveways of selected homes, took photos, and then created customized cards for delivery to each of the homes! Mobile direct marketing sales and social network direct marketing sales are growing at 33 percent and 20 percent, respectively—the fastest of all direct marketing tools.[42]

The Value of Direct Marketing

One of the most visible indicators of the value of direct marketing for consumers is its increasing level of use in its various forms. For example, in the past year, 45 percent of the U.S. population ordered merchandise or services by mail; more than 114 million people made purchases online; and consumers spent more than $76 billion on products available through mobile (smartphone, smartwatch, tablet) offers. In addition, 57 percent of social media users say that they are more likely to purchase a product after seeing a positive post.

For consumers, direct marketing offers a variety of benefits, including: They don't have to go to a store; they can usually shop 24 hours a day; buying direct saves time; they avoid hassles with salespeople; they can save money; it's fun and entertaining; and it offers more privacy than in-store shopping. Many consumers also believe that direct marketing provides excellent customer service. Toll-free telephone numbers, customer service representatives with access to information regarding purchasing preferences, overnight delivery services, and unconditional guarantees all help create value for direct marketing customers. At Landsend.com, when customers need assistance they can click the "Live Help" icon to receive help from a sales representative on the phone or through online chat or online video until the correct product is found. "It's like we were walking down the aisle in a store!" says one Lands' End customer.[43]

The value of direct marketing for sellers can be described in terms of the responses it generates. **Direct orders** are the result of offers that contain all the information necessary for a prospective buyer to make a decision to purchase and complete the transaction. Priceline.com, for example, will send *PriceBreaker* alerts to people in its database. The messages offer discounted fares and rates to customers who can travel on very short notice. **Lead generation** is the result of an offer designed to generate interest in a product or service and a request for additional information. Four Seasons Hotels now sell private residences in several of their properties and send direct mail to prospective residents asking them to request additional information on the telephone or through a website. Finally, **traffic generation** is the outcome of an offer designed to motivate people to visit a business. Home Depot, for example, uses an opt-in e-mail alert to announce special sales that attract consumers to the store. Similarly, Mazda uses direct mail to generate traffic in its dealerships.[44]

Video 17-5

Priceline Ad

kerin.tv/13e/v17-5

Mazda uses direct mail to motivate people to visit its dealerships.

Source: Minacs Marketing Solutions

Technological, Global, and Ethical Issues in Direct Marketing

The information technology and databases described in Chapter 8 are key elements in any direct marketing program. Databases are the result of organizations' efforts to create profiles of customers so that direct marketing tools, such as e-mail and catalogs, can be directed at specific customers. While most companies try to keep records of their customers' past purchases, many other types of data are needed to use direct marketing to develop one-to-one relationships with customers. Some data, such as lifestyles, media use, and demographics, are best collected from the consumer. Other types of data, such as price, quantity, and brand, are best collected from the businesses where purchases are made. New integrated marketing databases match consumers' postal addresses, telephone numbers, and e-mail addresses. In addition, many businesses are beginning to match their customer records with Facebook profiles, Twitter following behavior, and Google search activity.[45]

Increases in postage rates and the decline in the economy have also increased the importance of information related to the cost of direct marketing activities. For example, the Direct Marketing Association estimates that e-mail advertising expenditures outperform social media advertising by a ratio of 3-to-1. Similarly, catalog businesses have found they can reduce the cost of printing by using innovations such as soy-based ink and recycled paper, and they can reduce postage fees through database list analysis. Related to postage fees, many direct marketers are assessing the potential impact of the USPS plan for a five-day mail delivery cycle.[46]

Direct marketing faces several challenges and opportunities in global markets today. Many countries, including the United Kingdom, Australia, the European

Making **Responsible Decisions**

What Is the Future of Your Privacy?

In 2003, the Federal Trade Commission opened the National Do Not Call Registry to give Americans a tool for maintaining their privacy on home and cellular telephone lines. More than 70 percent of all Americans registered. Since then, several state legislatures have also passed laws to create do-not-call lists for automated (robo) telephone calls. In addition, new discussions about privacy related to mail and computer use are now taking place.

Generally, the question being debated is, "What information is private?" Are telephone numbers, addresses of residences, and online activities private or public information? Proponents of a do-not-mail registry argue that, like telephone calls, citizens should be able to stop unsolicited mail. Proponents of do-not-track regulations suggest that website owners who use cookies to collect information about consumers' shopping habits should do so only with a consumer's consent. Marketers counter that consumers who share this information are more likely to receive messages and advertising that better match their interests.

The Direct Marketing Association currently advocates several solutions. First, it has created DMAchoice, an online tool to help consumers manage the types of mail and e-mail they receive. Second, the organization endorses a self-regulatory program for online behavioral advertising (OBA) that encourages advertisers to include an "Ad Choices" icon in the corner of online ads to allow consumers to opt out of having data collected about their online activities. The program is part of an advertising coalition called the Digital Advertising Alliance. Moving beyond self-regulation, the European Union recently passed the *E-Privacy Directive* to provide explicit laws for website owners. And in the United States, the Senate is evaluating the "Do Not Track Online Act." These guidelines and regulations, of course, have huge implications for advertisers, portals such as Facebook and Google, and consumers.

What is your opinion? What types of information should be private? Can we find a balance between self-regulation and legislation?

Used with permission of Digital Advertising Alliance.

Union, and Japan, have requirements for a mandatory "opt-in"—that is, potential customers must give permission to be included on a list for direct marketing solicitations. In addition, the mail, telephone, and Internet systems in many countries are not as well developed as they are in the United States. The need for improved reliability and security in these countries has slowed the growth of direct mail, while the dramatic growth of mobile phone penetration has created an opportunity for direct mobile marketing campaigns. Another issue for global direct marketers is payment. The availability of credit and credit cards varies throughout the world, creating the need for alternatives such as C.O.D. (cash on delivery), bank deposits, and online payment accounts.[47]

Global and domestic direct marketers both face challenging ethical issues today. Concerns about privacy, for example, have led to various attempts to provide guidelines that balance consumer and business interests. The European Union passed a consumer privacy law, called the *Data Protection Directive,* after several years of discussion with the Federation of European Direct Marketing and the UK's Direct Marketing Association. A new version of the law, called the *General Data Protection Regulation,* will address new developments such as social networks and cloud computing and is scheduled to take effect in 2016.

In the United States, the Federal Trade Commission and many state legislatures have also been concerned about privacy. Several bills that call for a do-not-mail registry similar to the Do Not Call Registry are being discussed. Similarly, there are growing concerns about the web "tracking" tools used by direct marketers to segment consumers and match them with advertising. The Making Responsible Decisions box describes some of the issues under consideration.[48]

Video 17-6
Ad Choices
kerin.tv/13e/v17-6

17-13. The ability to design and use direct marketing programs has increased with the availability of _____ and _____.

17-14. What are the three types of responses generated by direct marketing activities?

LEARNING OBJECTIVES REVIEW

LO 17-1 *Discuss integrated marketing communications and the communication process.*

Integrated marketing communications is the concept of designing marketing communications programs that coordinate all promotional activities—advertising, personal selling, sales promotion, public relations, and direct marketing—to provide a consistent message across all audiences. The communication process conveys messages with six elements: a source, a message, a channel of communication, a receiver, and encoding and decoding. The communication process also includes a feedback loop and can be distorted by noise.

LO 17-2 *Describe the promotional mix and the uniqueness of each component.*

There are five promotional alternatives. Advertising, sales promotion, and public relations are mass selling approaches, whereas personal selling and direct marketing use customized messages. Advertising can have high absolute costs but reaches large numbers of people. Personal selling has a high cost per contact but provides immediate feedback. Public relations is often difficult to obtain but is very credible. Sales promotion influences short-term consumer behavior. Direct marketing can help develop customer relationships, although maintaining a database can be very expensive.

LO 17-3 *Select the promotional approach appropriate to a product's target audience, life-cycle stage, and characteristics, as well as stages of the buying decision and channel strategies.*

The promotional mix depends on the target audience. Programs for consumers, business buyers, and intermediaries might emphasize advertising, personal selling, and sales promotion, respectively. The promotional mix also changes over the product life-cycle stages. During the introduction stage, all promotional mix elements are used. During the

growth stage advertising is emphasized, while the maturity stage utilizes sales promotion and direct marketing. Little promotion is used during the decline stage. Product characteristics also help determine the promotion mix. The level of complexity, risk, and ancillary services required will determine which element is needed. Knowing the customer's stage in the buying process can help marketers select appropriate promotions. Advertising and public relations can create awareness in the prepurchase stage, personal selling and sales promotion can facilitate the purchase, and advertising can help reduce anxiety in the postpurchase stage. Finally, the promotional mix can depend on the channel strategy. Push strategies require personal selling and sales promotions directed at channel members, while pull strategies depend on advertising and sales promotion directed at consumers.

LO 17-4 *Describe the elements of the promotion decision process.*

The promotional decision process consists of three steps: planning, implementation, and evaluation. The planning step consists of six elements: identify the target audience, specify the objectives, set the budget, select the right promotional elements, design the promotion, and schedule the promotion. The implementation step includes pretesting. The evaluation step includes posttesting.

LO 17-5 *Explain the value of direct marketing for consumers and sellers.*

The value of direct marketing for consumers is indicated by its increasing level of use. For example, during the past year, 52 percent of the U.S. population made a purchase by mail and more than 110 million people shopped online. The value of direct marketing for sellers can be measured in terms of three types of responses: direct orders, lead generation, and traffic generation.

LEARNING REVIEW ANSWERS

17-1 **What six elements are required for communication to occur?**

Answer: The six elements required for communication to occur are: (1) a source, which is a company or person who has information to convey; (2) a message, which is the information sent; (3) a channel of communication, which is how the information is conveyed; (4) a receiver, which is the consumer who reads, hears, or sees the message; and the processes of (5) encoding,

in which the sender transforms the idea into a set of symbols; and (6) decoding, in which the receiver takes the symbols, or the message, and transforms it back into an idea.

17-2 **A difficulty for U.S. companies advertising in international markets is that the audience does not share the same _____.**

Answer: field of experience, which is a similar understanding and knowledge that is applied to a message

17-3 A misprint in a newspaper ad is an example of _____.

Answer: noise, the extraneous factors that distort a message

17-4 Explain the difference between advertising and publicity when both appear on television.

Answer: Since advertising space on TV is paid for, a firm can control what it wants to say and to whom and how often the message is sent over a broadcast, cable, satellite, or local TV network. Since publicity is an indirectly paid presentation of a message about a firm or its products or services, the firm has little control over what is said to whom or when. Instead, it can only suggest to the TV medium that it run a favorable story about the firm or its offerings.

17-5 Cost per contact is high with the _____ element of the promotional mix.

Answer: personal selling

17-6 Which promotional element should be offered only on a short-term basis?

Answer: sales promotion

17-7 Describe the promotional objective for each stage of the product life cycle.

Answer: Introduction—to inform consumers of the product's existence; growth—to persuade consumers to buy the product; maturity—to remind consumers that the product still exists; and decline—to phase out the product.

17-8 At what stage of the consumer purchase decision process is the importance of personal selling highest? Why?

Answer: Personal selling is most important at the purchase stage of the consumer purchase decision process because salespeople can provide sales assistance to prospective customers and negotiate terms of the sale.

17-9 Explain the differences between a push strategy and a pull strategy.

Answer: In a push strategy, a firm directs the promotional mix to channel members to gain their cooperation in ordering and stocking the product. In a pull strategy, a firm directs the promotional mix at ultimate consumers to encourage them to ask retailers for the product, who then order it from wholesalers or the firm itself.

17-10 What are the characteristics of good promotion objectives?

Answer: Promotion objectives should possess three important qualities. They should (1) be designed for a well-defined target audience, (2) be measurable, and (3) cover a specified time period.

17-11 What is the weakness of the percentage of sales budgeting approach?

Answer: In the percentage of sales budgeting approach, funds are allocated to promotion based on a percentage of past or anticipated dollar or unit sales. The major fallacy of this method is that sales cause promotion. By using this method, a company may reduce its promotion budget because of actual or projected downturns in past or future sales—situations where promotion may be needed the most.

17-12 How have advertising agencies changed to facilitate the use of IMC programs?

Answer: Some agencies have adopted: (1) a total communications solutions approach; (2) an integrated perspective that includes all forms of promotion; (3) an IMC audit to analyze the internal communication network of the company to identify key audiences, evaluate customer databases, assess messages contained in recent advertising, press releases, packaging, websites, social media, direct marketing, etc., and determine the IMC expertise of company and agency personnel; and (4) strategies to monitor consumer content, respond to inconsistent messages, and answer questions from individual customers.

17-13 The ability to design and use direct marketing programs has increased with the availability of _____ and _____.

Answer: customer information databases; new printing technologies

17-14 What are the three types of responses generated by direct marketing activities?

Answer: They are: (1) direct orders, the result of offers that contain all the information necessary for a prospective buyer to make a decision to purchase and complete the transaction; (2) lead generation, the result of an offer designed to generate interest in a product or service and a request for additional information; and (3) traffic generation, the outcome of an offer designed to motivate people to visit a business.

FOCUSING ON KEY TERMS

advertising p. 472
all-you-can-afford budgeting p. 484
channel of communication p. 470
communication p. 470
competitive parity budgeting p. 483
decoding p. 471
direct marketing p. 475
direct orders p. 489
encoding p. 471
feedback p. 472

field of experience p. 471
hierarchy of effects p. 482
integrated marketing communications (IMC) p. 470
lead generation p. 489
message p. 470
noise p. 472
objective and task budgeting p. 484
percentage of sales budgeting p. 483
personal selling p. 473

promotional mix p. 470
public relations p. 474
publicity p. 474
pull strategy p. 481
push strategy p. 480
receivers p. 470
response p. 471
sales promotion p. 475
source p. 470
traffic generation p. 489

APPLYING MARKETING KNOWLEDGE

1   After listening to a recent sales presentation, Mary Smith signed up for membership at the local health club. On arriving at the facility, she learned there was an additional fee for racquetball court rentals. "I don't remember that in the sales talk; I thought they said all facilities were included with the membership fee," complained Mary. Describe the problem in terms of the communication process.

2 Develop a matrix to compare the five elements of the promotional mix on three criteria—to *whom* you deliver the message, *what* you say, and *when* you say it.

3 Explain how the promotional tools used by an airline would differ if the target audience were (*a*) consumers who travel for pleasure and (*b*) corporate travel departments that select the airlines to be used by company employees.

4 Suppose you introduced a new consumer food product and invested heavily both in national advertising (pull strategy) and in training and motivating your field salesforce to sell the product to food stores (push strategy). What kinds of feedback would you receive from both the advertising and your salesforce? How could you increase both the quality and quantity of each?

5 Fisher-Price Company, long known as a manufacturer of children's toys, has introduced a line of clothing for children. Outline a promotional plan to get this product introduced in the marketplace.

6 Many insurance companies sell health insurance plans to companies. In these companies the employees pick the plan, but the set of offered plans is determined by the company. Recently, Blue Cross–Blue Shield, a health insurance company, ran a television ad stating, "If your employer doesn't offer you Blue Cross–Blue Shield coverage, ask why." Explain the promotional strategy behind the advertisement.

7 Identify the sales promotion tools that might be useful for (*a*) Tastee Yogurt, a new brand introduction, (*b*) 3M self-sticking Post-it® Notes, and (*c*) Wrigley's Spearmint gum.

8 Design an integrated marketing communications program—using each of the five promotional elements—for Rhapsody, the online music service.

9 BMW recently introduced its first sports activity vehicle, the X6, to compete with other popular crossover vehicles such as the Mercedes-Benz R-Class. Design a direct marketing program to generate (*a*) leads, (*b*) traffic in dealerships, and (*c*) direct orders.

10 Develop a privacy policy for database managers that provides a balance of consumer and seller perspectives. How would you encourage voluntary compliance with your policy? What methods of enforcement would you recommend?

BUILDING YOUR MARKETING PLAN

To develop the promotion strategy for your marketing plan, follow the steps suggested in the planning phase of the promotion decision process described in Figure 17–6.

1 You should (*a*) identify the target audience, (*b*) specify the promotion objectives, (*c*) set the promotion budget, (*d*) select the right promotion tools, (*e*) design the promotion, and (*f*) schedule the promotion.

2 Also specify the pretesting and posttesting procedures needed in the implementation and evaluation phases.

3 Finally, describe how each of your promotion tools is integrated to provide a consistent message.

VIDEO CASE 17 Taco Bell: Using IMC to Help Customers Live Más!

"Every touch point is considered," explains Stephanie Perdue, Taco Bell's senior director of marketing, "from the posters in the restaurants down to the packaging, and all of the different media channels." Stephanie is describing the integrated marketing communications (IMC) approach used by Taco Bell, the nation's leading Mexican-style quick service restaurant. IMC is one of the key factors that has contributed to the extraordinary success of the food chain, which serves more than 36 million customers each week!

Video 17-7
Taco Bell Video Case
kerin.tv/13e/v17-7

THE COMPANY

The story behind Taco Bell and its success is fascinating. After World War II, a young marine named Glen Bell returned to his home state of California with an entrepreneurial spirit and an observation that people were hungry for fast, good food. He opened his first restaurant, Bell's Burgers, based on the simple concept that customers might want to walk up and get their food from a service window. Not far away, two brothers named McDonald were operating their new restaurant using a "drive-in" concept. For several years, Bell and the McDonald brothers enjoyed friendly competition as pioneers of the growing fast-food industry. However, when the burger restaurant market became crowded with competitors, Bell decided to try something new—tacos!

Tacos were new to most Americans so Bell experimented with many concepts. First he developed a crunchy taco shell and opened a restaurant called Taco Tia. His marketing activities consisted of handing out sombreros and having Mariachis play outside the restaurant. Next, Bell started another restaurant, El Taco, with a group of celebrity partners. Finally, after a friend suggested that Glen should use his name in his business, the first Taco Bell was opened in Downey, California.

© David Paul Morris/Bloomberg via Getty Images

Taco Bell grew quickly and as Bell began opening additional locations he decided that the restaurants should resemble the appearance of California's historic missions. With the help of an architect he created an inviting design based on an adobe-like exterior with a red clay-tile roof. The name and logo utilized a mission-style bell, a version of which is still in use today. Through franchises and additional corporate locations Taco Bell soon reached from coast to coast.

Today Taco Bell is a subsidiary of Yum! Brands, which also owns and operates KFC, Pizza Hut, and WingStreet. Taco Bell now has more than 6,500 locations and $7 billion in sales. Many locations are co-branded with KFC, Pizza Hut, and Long John Silver stores. Taco Bell also operates Taco Bell Express locations in convenience stores, truck stops, shopping malls, and airports.

INTEGRATED MARKETING COMMUNICATIONS AT TACO BELL

From its beginning, Taco Bell has used very creative promotional activities. For example, when the Mir space station was about to reenter the Earth's atmosphere, Taco Bell placed a target in the Pacific Ocean and announced that every person in the United States would receive a free taco if any piece of the falling space station hit the target. Similarly, in its "Steal a Base, Steal a Taco" promotion, Taco Bell promised to give everyone a free taco if any player steals a base in the World Series. While the space station did not hit the target, several players have stolen bases in the World Series, leading to free tacos for everyone! Taco Bell has also offered special promotions with Mountain Dew, partnered with the NBA as its official fast food, and created videos for movie-theater advertising.

You might remember some of Taco Bell's advertising campaigns such as "Yo quiero Taco Bell," "Grand Taste. Loco Value," or "Get it at The Bell." The more recent "Think Outside the Bun" campaign was designed for Millennials. Then as that group changed, Taco Bell executives recognized that they had an opportunity to reposition the chain. Tracee Larocca, brand creative director at Taco Bell, explains, "We realized there was a big opportunity as the culture shifted from 'food as fuel' to 'food as experience.'" Taco Bell considered many new taglines, such as "Keep Life Spicy" and "Hunger for Más," and eventually developed the "Live Más" campaign. As campaigns and positioning changes, integrated marketing becomes increasingly important. According to Larocca, "as the brand's creative director, my job is to make sure that all of our communications have the same look, tone, and feel across all platforms, making sure we maintain consistency in our brand voice no matter what we're doing internally or externally."

Advertising Age magazine recently named Taco Bell the winner of its Marketer of the Year award for its extraordinary use of integrated marketing in the launch of its Doritos Locos Tacos. The new product went through three years of development and 45 prototypes before its launch, which led to sales of 100 million units in its first 10 weeks. Taco Bell allocates approximately 70 percent of its budget to traditional media, 20 percent to digital media, and 10 percent to new media where it can "explore." The traditional media budget included a Super Bowl ad utilizing the "Live Más" theme. "It was all about a mindset and not necessarily an age range or a demographic," explains Larocca. The ad, called "Forever Young," showed "a group of old people breaking out of a retirement home and having a great night on the town," she adds.

The social media component of the campaign included Facebook, Twitter, Vine, Snapchat, and Instagram. The Twitter campaign, for example, included a Hometown Tweet-off where anyone could send a tweet saying why a Taco Bell truck should visit their hometown. Similarly, Taco Bell posted pictures to Facebook and watched the responses in the comments and the "likes." Some of the new media budget was used to try things such as Taco Bell's own video channels for Web and mobile, and a live stream to a billboard in Times Square. As Rob Poetsch, director of public affairs and engagement, observed about the Doritos Locos Tacos launch, "for the first time, we had a fully integrated plan that engaged all of our constituents."

THE FUTURE AT TACO BELL

Taco Bell continues to develop new products, brand concepts, and promotions. For example, waffle tacos, Cinnabon Delights, and the A.M. Crunchwrap are new additions to the menu. In addition, a new brand concept called Taco Bell Cantina, which is testing its first locations in Chicago and San Francisco, will offer "tapas-style" appetizers for customers to share, and beer and wine, in an urban setting. Finally, a new breakfast menu campaign used 25 men named Ronald McDonald to help suggest that a new generation of fast-food breakfast items is now available at Taco Bell. All of these activities are contributing to the company's continued growth. Yum! Brands expects Taco Bell's domestic sales to double by 2021![49]

Questions

1   What factors contributed to Taco Bell's early success?

2   Which of the promotional elements described in Figure 17–2 were used by Taco Bell in its Doritos Locos Tacos campaign?

3   How does Taco Bell ensure the continued success of the food chain?

Chapter Notes

1.   Sara Boboltz, "Whoever Runs Taco Bell's Twitter Account Deserves a Raise," *The Huffington Post,* February 28, 2014; Jenni Romaniuk, "Are You Ready for the Next Big Thing?" *Journal of Advertising Research,* December 2012, pp. 397–99; "Taco Bell Implements Its Largest Marketing Campaign Ever," *QSRweb,* March 7, 2013; "Highly Anticipated, Most Socially Requested Taco Bell Product Launch to Be Largest Marketing Campaign in Brand's History," *Business Wire,* March 7, 2013; "Yo Quiero Engagement? Taco Bell Charms the Twittersphere," www.Business2Community.com, February 4, 2013; Lynne D. Johnson, "Customer Engagement Is the New Marketing," *Journal of Advertising Research,* June 2010, pp. 118–19; Natalie Zmuda, "QR Codes Gaining Prominence Thanks to a Few Big Players," *Advertising Age,* March 21, 2011, p. 8; Alyssa S. Groom, "Integrated Marketing Communication Anticipating the 'Age of Engage,'" *Communication Research Trends,* December 1, 2008, p. 3; "How to Get More Followers on Twitter: Engage with Social Promotions," www.Business2Community.com, March 16, 2013; and "How to Engage Your Audience on Social Media," www.Business2Community.com, March 28, 2013.

2.   Sita Mishra and Sushma Muralie, "Managing Dynamism of IMC—Anarchy to Order," *Journal of Marketing and Communication,* September 2010, pp. 29–37; Philip J. Kitchen, Ilchul Kim, and Don E. Schultz, "Integrated Marketing Communications: Practice Leads Theory," *Journal of Advertising Research,* December 2008, pp. 531–46; Bob Liodice, "Essentials for Integrated Marketing," *Advertising Age,* June 9, 2008, p. 26; and Shu-pei Tsai, *Journal of Advertising* 34 (Winter 2005), pp. 11–23.

3.   Wilbur Schramm, "How Communication Works," in *The Process and Effects of Mass Communication,* Wilbur Schramm, ed. (Urbana: University of Illinois Press, 1955), pp. 3–26.

4.   E. Cooper and M. Jahoda, "The Evasion of Propaganda," *Journal of Psychology* 22 (1947), pp. 15–25; H. Hyman and P. Sheatsley, "Some Reasons Why Information Campaigns Fail," *Public Opinion Quarterly* 11 (1947), pp. 412–23; and J. T. Klapper, *The Effects of Mass Communication* (New York: Free Press, 1960), Chapter VII.

5.   "Mistakes in Advertising," on the Learn English website, http://www.learnenglish.de/mistakes/HorrorMistakes.htm, accessed March 18, 2013; and Bianca Bartz, "International Ads Lost in Translation," TrendHunter Marketing website, http://www.trendhunter.com/trends/advertising-bloopers-international-ads-lost-in-translation, accessed March 18, 2013.

6.   Rik Pieters and Michel Wedel, "Attention Capture and Transfer in Advertising: Brand, Pictorial, and Text-Size Effects," *Journal of Marketing,* April 2004, pp. 36–50.

7.   Adapted from American Marketing Association, Resource Library Dictionary, http://www.marketingpower.com/layouts/Dictionary.aspx?dLetter=P, accessed March 18, 2013.

8.   Dave Folkens, "3 Ways Social Media Is Changing Public Relations," *Online Marketing Blog,* February 17, 2011; Michael Bush, "How Social Media Is Helping the Public-Relations Sector Not Just Survive, but Thrive," *Advertising Age,* August 23, 2010, p. 1; David Robinson, "Public Relations Comes of Age," *Business Horizons* 49 (2006), pp. 247–56; and Dick Martin, "Gilded and Gelded: Hard-Won Lessons from the PR Wars," *Harvard Business Review,* October 2003, pp. 44–54.

9.   Martin Eisend and Franziska Kuster, "The Effectiveness of Publicity versus Advertising: A Meta-Analytic Investigation of Its Moderators," *Journal of the Academy of Marketing Science,* December 2011, pp. 906–21; and Joan Stewart, "Pros and Cons of Free Publicity in Newspapers, Magazines," www.Business2Community.com, January 30, 2013.

10.   "The Public Relations Metamorphosis: Social Media Is Here to Stay," www.Business2Community.com, December 21, 2012; Piet Levy, "CSR Take Responsibility," *Marketing News,* May 30, 2010, p. 20; Jooyoung Kim, Hye Jin Yoon, and Sun Young Lee, "Integrating Advertising and Publicity: A Theoretical Examination of the Effects of Exposure Sequence, Publicity Valence, and Product Attribute Consistency," *Journal of Advertising,* Spring 2010, p. 97; and Marsha D. Loda and Barbara Carrick Coleman, "Sequence Matters: A More Effective Way to Use Advertising and Publicity," *Journal of Advertising Research* 45 (December 2005), pp. 362–71.

11.   Kusum L. Ailawadi, Scott A. Neslin, and Karen Gedenk, "Pursuing the Value-Conscious Consumer: Store Brands versus National Brand Promotions," *Journal of Marketing,* January 2001, pp. 71–89.

12.   Nikki Hopewell, "The Rules of Engagement: A Bevy of Rules and Best Practices Govern Promotions and Contests," *Marketing News,* June 1, 2008, p. 6; and Gerard Prendergast, Yi- Zheng Shi, and Ka-Man Cheung, "Behavioural Response to Sales Promotion Tools," *International Journal of Advertising* 24 (2005), pp. 467–86.

13.   Adapted from American Marketing Association, Resource Library Dictionary, http://www.marketingpower.com/layouts/Dictionary.aspx?dLetter=D, accessed March 18, 2013.

14. Paul Jacobs, "3 Tips for Marketing to College Students," *Promotional Marketing,* May 26, 2015, p. 1; "Top 5 Brands Using Mobile Marketing Successfully," www.Business2Community.com, March 11, 2013; "Eight Out of Ten Freshers Have Smartphones, According to New UCAS Media Survey," *M2 Presswire,* March 13, 2013; "Mysteries and Myths of Millennials in Social Media," www.Business2Community.com, July 21, 2012; Stuart Elliott, "In an Upgrade, Google Adds to Its Model for Mobile Marketing," *The New York Times,* March 7, 2013, p. 3; "Tailoring Your Mobile Strategy to the New Millennials," *VentureBeat,* July 18, 2012; Nationwide Bank website, http://www.nationwide.com/cps/collegestudent-spending-habits-infographic.htm, accessed March 19, 2013; Antje Cockrill, Mark M. Goode, and Amy White, "The Bluetooth Enigma: Practicalities Impair Potential," *Journal of Advertising Research,* March 2011, pp. 298–312; and Thomas Pardee, "Media-Savvy Gen Y Finds Smart and Funny Is 'New Rock-N-Roll,'" *Advertising Age,* October 11, 2010, p. 17.

15. Dunn Sunnoo and Lynn Y. S. Lin, "Sales Effects of Promotion and Advertising," *Journal of Advertising Research* 18 (October 1978), pp. 37–42.

16. Lori Corbin, "Purina Po Plan Incredible Dog Challenge Returns to Huntington Beach for Western Regionals," *abc7.com,* May 29, 2015; and Don Kaplan, "Every Dog Has Its Day at Purina Challenge," *Daily News,* January 12, 2013, p. 1.

17. Todd Powers, Dorothy Advincula, Manila S. Austin, Stacy Graiko, and Jasper Snyder, "Digital and Social Media in the Purchase Decision Process," *Journal of Advertising Research,* December 2012, pp. 479–89; and Remco Prins and Peter C. Verhoef, "Marketing Communication Drivers of Adoption Timing of a New E-Service among Existing Customers," *Journal of Marketing* 71 (April 2007), pp. 169–83.

18. Anders Parment, "Distribution Strategies for Volume and Premium Brands in Highly Competitive Consumer Markets," *Journal of Retailing and Consumer Services,* July 2008, p. 250; and R. Srinivasan and Archana K. Murthy, "Integrated Brand Building Process: A Special Case," *International Journal of Business Research,* June 1, 2008, p. 174.

19. "Push vs. Pull Strategies," *Daily News,* May 3, 2011; "Question: Should B2B Be Focusing All Its Efforts on 'Pull' Marketing Therefore Turning Its Back on 'Push' Marketing Techniques?" *B2B Marketing Magazine,* September 2009; and Michael Levy, John Webster, and Roger Kerin, "Formulating Push Marketing Strategies: A Method and Application," *Journal of Marketing,* Winter 1983, pp. 25–34.

20. Bradford Wernle, "Quality, Market Share, Leasing Top Ford Dealers' Agenda," *Automotive News,* February 10, 2013; Jamie LaReau, "Ford Dealers Revamp Pay Plans; Some Efforts Resemble Stair-Step Programs," *Automotive News,* February 14, 2011, p. 10; and *Ford Motor Company Annual Report,* 2012, p. 14.

21. "Is Online Pharm DTC Ad Spend Continuing Its Downward Slide?" *Pharma Marketing Blog,* April 2, 2014, www.pharmamkting.blogspot.com; Beth Snyder Bulik, "Ad Spending: 15 Years of DTC," *Advertising Age Insights White Paper,* October 17, 2011; Sheng Yuan, "Public Response to Direct-to-Consumer Advertising of Prescription Drugs," *Journal of Advertising Research,* March 2008, pp. 30–41; and Fusun F. Gonul, Franklin Carter, Elina Petrova, and Kannan Srinivasan, "Promotion of Prescription Drugs and Its Impact on Physicians' Choice Behavior," *Journal of Marketing,* July 2001, pp. 79–90.

22. Don E. Shultz, Martin P. Block, and Kaylan Raman, "Understanding Consumer-Created Media Synergy," *Journal of Marketing Communications,* July 2012, pp. 173–87; "Why Behavioral Targeting Is Effective," www.Business2Community.com, January 15, 2013; Lauren Drell, "4 Ways Behavioral Targeting Is Changing the Web," *Mashable,* April 26, 2011; and

adapted from American Marketing Association, Resource Library Dictionary, http://www.marketingpower.com/_layouts/Dictionary.aspx?dLetter=B, accessed April 2, 2013.

23. Robert J. Lavidge and Gary A. Steiner, "A Model for Predictive Measurement of Advertising Effectiveness," *Journal of Marketing,* October 1961, p. 61.

24. "Leading National Advertisers," *Advertising Age,* June 13, 2015, p. 14.

25. George S. Low and Jakki J. Mohr, "Setting Advertising and Promotion Budgets in Multi-Brand Companies," *Journal of Advertising Research,* January/February 1999, pp. 67–78; Don E. Schultz and Anders Gronstedt, "Making Marcom an Investment," *Marketing Management,* Fall 1997, pp. 41–49; and J. Enrique Bigne, "Advertising Budget Practices: A Review," *Journal of Current Issues and Research in Advertising,* Fall 1995, pp. 17–31.

26. John Philip Jones, "Ad Spending: Maintaining Market Share," *Harvard Business Review,* January–February 1990, pp. 38–42; and Charles H. Patti and Vincent Blasko, "Budgeting Practices of Big Advertisers," *Journal of Advertising Research* 21 (December 1981), pp. 23–30.

27. "U.S. Market Leaders," *Advertising Age,* June 25, 2012, pp. 24–25.

28. Brenda Marlin, "Adding It Up: You Can Save Time by Trying One of Three Short-Cut Approaches to an Annual Budget," *ABA Banking,* October 1, 2007, p. 36; James A. Shroer, "Ad Spending: Growing Market Share," *Harvard Business Review,* January–February 1990, pp. 44–48; and Jeffrey A. Lowenhar and John L. Stanton, "Forecasting Competitive Advertising Expenditures," *Journal of Advertising Research* 16, no. 2 (April 1976), pp. 37–44.

29. Daniel Seligman, "How Much for Advertising?" *Fortune,* December 1956, p. 123.

30. James E. Lynch and Graham J. Hooley, "Increasing Sophistication in Advertising Budget Setting," *Journal of Advertising Research* 30 (February–March 1990), pp. 67–75.

31. Jimmy D. Barnes, Brenda J. Muscove, and Javad Rassouli, "An Objective and Task Media Selection Decision Model and Advertising Cost Formula to Determine International Advertising Budgets," *Journal of Advertising* 11, no. 4 (1982), pp. 68–75.

32. "The Olympic Brand Maintains Its Global Strength and Recognition," *States News Service,* February 12, 2013; Graham Ruddock, "London Olympics Sponsors Are Already into Their Stride," *The Daily Telegraph,* May 6, 2011, p. 8; "The Olympics Come But Once Every Two Years," *Marketing News,* November 1, 2008, p. 12; "Olympics Will Bring Online Opportunities for Many Brands," *Revolution,* July 14, 2008, p. 13; and Don E. Schultz, "Olympics Get the Gold Medal in Integrating Marketing Event," *Marketing News,* April 27, 1998, pp. 5, 10.

33. "It's Time to Take an Integrated Marketing Approach," www.Business2Community.com, January 22, 2013; "Integrated Marketing: One Message, Many Media," *Marketing Week,* September 18, 2008, p. 31; and Cornelia Pechman, Guangzhi Zhao, Marvin E. Goldberg, and Ellen Thomas Reibling, "What to Convey in Antismoking Advertisements for Adolescents: The Use of Protection Motivation Theory to Identify Effective Message Themes," *Journal of Marketing,* April 2003, pp. 1–18.

34. Todd Cunningham, "Inside 'Jurassic World's' T-Rex-Sized Marketing Triumph," *The Wrap,* June 15, 2015; Brent Lang, "'Jurassic World' Scores Biggest Opening Weekend in History, Beats 'Avengers' Record," *Variety,* June 15, 2015; and Helen Regan, "Catch a Glimpse of the Terrifying New Dinosaur in this Jurassic World Trailer," *Time.com,* February 2, 2015.

35. Sabine A. Einwiller and Michael Boenigk, "Examining the Link between Integrated Communication Management and Communication Effectiveness in Medium-Sized Enterprises," *Journal*

of *Marketing Communications,* December 2012, pp. 335–61; and Mike Reid, "Performance Auditing of Integrated Marketing Communication (IMC) Actions and Outcomes," *Journal of Advertising* 34 (Winter 2005), p. 41.

36. Alexandra Bruell, "Media Agency of the Year: MediaCom," *Advertising Age,* January 26, 2015, p. 24; and MediaCom website, http://www.mediacomusa.com/en/home.aspx, accessed June 15, 2015.

37. "Integrated Marketing: The Benefits of Integrated Marketing," *Marketing Week,* September 18, 2008, p. 33; and Tom Duncan, "Is Your Marketing Communications Integrated?" *Advertising Age,* January 24, 1994, p. 26.

38. Don E. Schultz, "The Media Circuits Evolution," *Marketing News,* March 30, 2011, p. 11; "Integrated Marketing: Digital Fuels Integration Boom," *Marketing Week,* December 11, 2008, p. 27; Don E. Schultz, "IMC Is Do or Die in New Pull Marketplace," *Marketing News,* August 15, 2006, p. 7; and Don E. Schultz, "Integration's New Role Focuses on Customers," *Marketing News,* September 15, 2006, p. 8.

39. Yunjae Cheong, John D. Leckenby, and Tim Eakin, "Evaluating the Multivariate Beta Binomial Distribution for Estimating Magazine and Internet Exposure Frequency Distributions," *Journal of Advertising,* Spring 2011, p. 7; Jack Neff, "Copy Testing Coming to Digital Marketing," *Advertising Age,* February 28, 2011, p.18; and "Measure for Measure," *Marketing Management,* January–February 2004, p. 7.

40. T. Reinold and J. Tropp, "Integrated Marketing Communications: How Can We Measure Its Effectiveness?" *Journal of Marketing Communications,* April 2012, pp. 113–32; Maria Angeles Navarro-Bailon, "Strategic Consistent Messages in Cross-Tool Campaigns: Effects on Brand Image and Brand Attitude," *Journal of Marketing Communications,* July 2012, pp. 189–202; and Don E. Shultz, "Measure IMC's Whole—Not Just Each Part," *Marketing News,* February 15, 2006, p. 8.

41. *Statistical Fact Book 2015* (New York: Direct Marketing Association, 2015); Tae Hyun Baek and Mariko Morimoto, "Stay Away from Me," *Journal of Advertising,* Spring 2012, pp. 59–76; and *Statistical Fact Book 2012* (New York: Direct Marketing Association, 2012), pp. 5, 16.

42. "Direct Mail Strategy: JCPenney's New Postcard Campaign," www.Business2Community.com, April 18, 2012; Cindy Waxer, "Automotive Brands Are Test-Driving New Marketing Strategies," *DMNews,* October 2012; "JCPenney America's Shopping Destination This Christmas," *Business Wire,* November 10, 2010; "JCPenney Kicks Off Christmas Gift Program," *Wireless News,* November 16, 2010; Alex Palmer, "JCPenney Launches Facebook e-Commerce Store," *DMNews,* December 15, 2010; Tim Peterson, "Porsche Launches Integrated Campaign to Shift Consumer Perception," *DMNews,* March 25, 2011; and *Statistical Fact Book 2012* (New York: Direct Marketing Association, 2012), p. 5.

43. *Statistical Fact Book 2015; Statistical Fact Book 2012,* pp. 24, 67; and "Six Ways Lands' End Makes Online Shopping a Joy," *PR Newswire,* November 21, 2007.

44. Theresa Howard, "E-mail Grows as Direct-Marketing Tool: They're Quicker to Make, Cheap to Send," *USA Today,* November 28, 2008, p. 5B.

45. Cotton Delo, "Facebook Testing Effort to Match Offline Purchases to Online Profiles," *Advertising Age,* February 25, 2013, p. 6; Michael Learmonth, "Facebook Goes the Route of Direct Marketing, While Twitter Plays It Safe with Focus on User Interests," *Advertising Age,* September 10, 2012, p. 20; and "Infogroup Targeting Solution Launches Sapphire™, a New Integrated Marketing Database," *GlobeNewswire,* August 7, 2012.

46. Sapna Maheshwari and Matt Townsend, "BC-E-MAIL-MARKETING-RETA," *Postmedia Breaking News,* March 14, 2013; "A-Catalog-Printer.com Uses Revolutionary Soy Ink Technology to Help the Environment and Reduce Costs of Printing," *SBWire,* March 22, 2013; Charley Howard, "Help USPS Help You: 3 Ways to Cut Mail Costs through Workshare Discounts," http://www.targetmarketingmag.com/article/3-ways-cut-mail-costs-throughworkshare-discounts-417119/1#, February 2011; and "How Much Will Postal Cuts Hurt?" *Advertising Age,* February 11, 2013, p. 3.

47 "Companies Opposing Anti-Spam Laws," *The Toronto Star,* February 9, 2013, p. B5; Beth Negus Viveiros, "New Bill Takes Permission Beyond Opt-In in EU," *Chief Marketer,* April 19, 2011; "China: New Media Blossoming as Business Models Revamp," *BBC Monitoring World Media,* December 9, 2008; "The Data Dilemma," *Marketing Direct,* February 6, 2007, p. 37; and Marc Nohr, "South Africa—A Worthy Contender," *Marketing Direct,* March 5, 2007, p. 20.

48. "Protecting Your Identity and Your Privacy," *Targeted News Service,* March 1, 2013; "The Do Not Track Online Act Was Reintroduced in Congress," *The Business Insider,* March 1, 2013; "Online Behavioral Advertising," in the DMA OBA Guidelines, Direct Marketing Association website, http://thedma.org/issues/dma-oba-guidelines, accessed April 6, 2013; Don E. Schultz, "The Bugaboo of Behaviors," *Marketing Management,* Summer 2011, pp. 10–11; "Cell Phones Now Protected by the Do Not Call List," *States News Service,* May 16, 2011; Jonathan Brunt, "'Do Not Mail' Can't Gain Traction," *Spokesman Review,* May 5, 2010, p. 7; "DMA: 'Do Not Track Online Act' Is Unnecessary," *States News Service,* May 9, 2011; "DMA Updates Its 'Guidelines for Ethical Business Practice,'" *States News Service,* May 25, 2011; Martin Courtney and Tony Lock, "Keep It Safe, Keep It Legal," *Computing,* May 26, 2011; Siobhain Butterworth, "Cookie Law Shambles Really Takes the Biscuit," *Guardian Unlimited,* May 27, 2011; and Lara O'Reilly, "New Cookie Law: What You Need to Know," *Marketing Week,* May 26, 2011.

49. Taco Bell: This case was written by Steven Hartley. Sources: Maureen Morrison, "In Breakfast Wars, Taco Bell's Bold Marketing Pays Off with Big Sales," *Advertising Age,* July 28, 2014, p. 6; "Taco Bell Serving Alcohol in Wicker Park Officially Opens Tuesday," WLS-TV, September 22, 2015; Maureen Morrison, "Taco Bell's New Concept: Designer Tacos in California," *Advertising Age,* April 28, 2014, p. 4; Vanessa Wong, "Taco Bell's Secret Recipe for New Products," *Bloomberg Businessweek,* June 2–8, 2014, pp. 18–20; Maureen Morrison, "Marketer of the Year 2013," *Advertising Age,* September 2, 2013, p. 15; Mark Brandau, "Yum Plans to Double U.S. Taco Bell Sales," *Restaurant News,* May 22, 2013; "The Glen Bell Legacy," www.tacobell.com/static_files/TacoBell/Static Assets/documents/GlenBellLegacy.pdf; "Taco Bell," http://www.yum.com/brands/tb.asp; and interviews with Taco Bell executives.

18 Advertising, Sales Promotion, and Public Relations

Virtual Reality Is the New Reality for Advertising!

You may remember when Facebook announced that it had paid $2 billion for a small company called Oculus Rift, and you wondered what could that company be doing that was so important. The answer is: virtual reality.

Oculus Rift manufactures wearable virtual reality (VR) headsets that look a little like ski goggles but when worn create a 360-degree immersive experience through high-quality video and audio. Many marketers believe VR will soon become an important way for advertisers to reach consumers. As Terry Block, a former Skype executive, explains, "When Facebook is involved, you know advertising is going to be a big piece of the picture."

So how will virtual reality work for businesses? According to Alex Lirtsman, cofounder of digital marketing agency ReadySetRocket, "It's the ultimate way a car company can showcase their latest car, a retailer can provide a view of their Fashion Week event, a travel destination can showcase activities, or any advertiser can truly take a 30-second spot to the next level." Virtual reality could also allow consumers to shop and browse at stores such as Nordstrom, IKEA, or Safeway at any time and without crowds.

Oculus Rift won't be the only company with a VR product on the market. Microsoft describes its HoloLens as a VR product that can be used for gaming, video-conferencing, and 3D modeling. Sony's Project Morpheus headset will potentially augment the gaming experience of the 10 million households that already own Sony PlayStation game systems. And Samsung's Gear VR is compatible with its Galaxy line of phones. Other entrants include HTC, Valve, and MergeVR. While current sales of VR products are approximately $60 million, experts suggest that sales will reach $150 billion in just five years.

Several companies have already implemented virtual reality campaigns. Mountain Dew, for example, created the VR Skate experience, which simulates a ride through the streets of Las Vegas with Dew Tour pro-skaters. Mountain Dew then followed up with another campaign for snowboarders. The TV series *Game of Thrones* created a VR experience where users ascend a 700-foot ice wall, and Marriott hotels created an experience that "teleported" people to London or Maui. In the future VR products will also link to your phone, watch, and other devices to add other sensory elements to the experience.

While some of this sounds like enthusiasm for a new gadget, advertisers are preparing for a substantial new medium. According to film director Chris Milk, "From an advertising perspective, it's a very powerful tool. Advertisers

Video 18-1
Virtual Reality
kerin.tv/13e/v18-1

are looking for two main things: penetrating people's consciousness and getting their undivided attention. With virtual reality, you have their undivided attention because they can't see or hear anything else." VR headsets also have the potential to be addressable like a computer or a phone so that advertisers can target specific market segments.

Watch for exciting new VR experiences in the near future. Fox Sports, for example, is testing VR offerings of NASCAR races in 180-degree and 360-degree viewing options. To participate in these and other virtual reality immersion experiences consumers are predicted to purchase 12 million VR headsets next year![1]

The growth of virtual reality is just one of the many exciting changes occurring in the field of advertising today. They illustrate the importance of advertising as one of the five promotional mix elements in marketing communications programs. This chapter describes three of the promotional mix elements—advertising, sales promotion, and public relations. Direct marketing was covered in Chapter 17, and personal selling is covered in Chapter 20.

© Rex Features via AP Images

TYPES OF ADVERTISEMENTS

Chapter 17 described **advertising** as any paid form of nonpersonal communication about an organization, a product, a service, or an idea by an identified sponsor. As you look through any magazine, watch television, listen to the radio, or browse the Internet, the variety of advertisements you see or hear may give you the impression that they have few similarities. Advertisements are prepared for different purposes, but they basically consist of two types: product advertisements and institutional advertisements.

Product Advertisements

Focused on selling a product or service, **product advertisements** take three forms: (1) pioneering (or informational), (2) competitive (or persuasive), and (3) reminder. Look at the ads for Levi's, Samsung, and Shaw's to determine the type and objective of each ad.

Used in the introductory stage of the product life cycle, *pioneering* advertisements tell people what a product is, what it can do, and where it can be found. The key objective of a pioneering advertisement (such as the ad for Levi's 501 CT jeans) is to inform the target market. Informational ads, particularly those with specific message content, have been found to be interesting, convincing, and effective.[2]

Advertising that promotes a specific brand's features and benefits is *competitive*. The objective of these messages is to persuade the target market to select the firm's brand rather than that of a competitor. An increasingly common form of competitive advertising is *comparative* advertising, which shows one brand's strengths relative to those of competitors.[3] The Samsung ad, for example, highlights the competitive advantages of Samsung's Galaxy smartphone compared to Apple's iPhone. Studies indicate that comparative ads attract more attention and increase the perceived quality of the advertiser's brand although their impact may vary by product type, message content, and audience gender.[4] Firms that use comparative advertising need market research to provide legal support for their claims.[5]

Reminder advertising is used to reinforce previous knowledge of a product. The Shaw's flower ad reminds consumers about a special event, in this case, Valentine's Day. Reminder advertising is good for products that have achieved a well-recognized position and are in the mature phase of their product life cycle. Another type of reminder ad, *reinforcement*, is used to assure current users they made the right choice. For example, consider the tag line used in Dial soap advertisements: "Aren't you glad you use Dial? Don't you wish everybody did?"

Product advertisements take three forms—pioneering, competitive, or reminder—depending on their objective. See if you can correctly identify the ads shown here.

Sources: Left: Levi Strauss & Co.; Middle: Samsung; Right: Shaw's

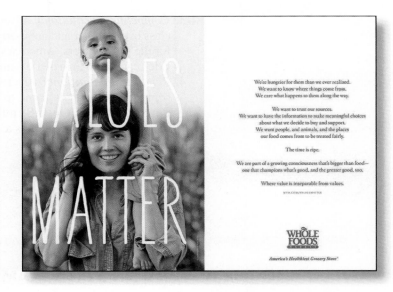

American Red Cross uses advocacy to make a request for donations. Whole Foods uses a pioneering ad to inform readers about its approach to business.

Sources: Left: American Red Cross; Right: Whole Foods Market

Video 18-2
Chevron
kerin.tv/13e/v18-2

Institutional Advertisements

The objective of **institutional advertisements** is to build goodwill or an image for an organization rather than promote a specific product or service. Institutional advertising has been used by companies such as Texaco, Pfizer, and IBM to build confidence in the company name.[6] Often this form of advertising is used to support the public relations plan or counter adverse publicity. Four alternative forms of institutional advertisements are often used:

1. *Advocacy* advertisements state the position of a company on an issue. Chevron's "We Agree" campaign places ads stating its position on issues such as renewable energy, protecting the planet, and community development. Another form of advocacy advertisement is used when organizations make a request related to a particular action or behavior, such as a request by the American Red Cross for donations.

2. *Pioneering institutional* advertisements, like the pioneering ads for products discussed earlier, are used for announcements about what a company is, what it can do, or where it is located. Recent Bayer ads stating, "We cure more headaches than you think," are intended to inform consumers that the company produces many products in addition to aspirin. Whole Foods uses pioneering institutional ads in its "Values Matter" campaign to inform people about its role as a champion for the greater good.

A competitive institutional ad by dairy farmers tries to increase demand for milk, and a reminder institutional ad by the U.S. Air Force tries to keep the attention of the target market.

Sources: Left: America's Milk Companies; Right: United States Air Force

3. *Competitive institutional* advertisements promote the advantages of one product class over another and are used in markets where different product classes compete for the same buyers. America's milk processors and dairy farmers use their "Milk Life" campaign to increase demand for milk as it competes against other beverages.

4. *Reminder institutional* advertisements, like reminder ads for products, simply bring the company's name to the attention of the target market again. The Air Force branch of the U.S. military sponsors a campaign to remind potential recruits of the opportunities available in the Air Force.

learning review »

18-1. What is the difference between pioneering and competitive ads?

18-2. What is the purpose of an institutional advertisement?

DEVELOPING THE ADVERTISING PROGRAM

 LO 18-2 Describe the steps used to develop, execute, and evaluate an advertising program.

The promotion decision process described in Chapter 17 can be applied to each of the promotional elements. Advertising, for example, can be managed by following the three steps (developing, executing, and evaluating) of the process.

Identifying the Target Audience

To develop an effective advertising program, advertisers must identify the target audience. All aspects of an advertising program are likely to be influenced by the characteristics of the prospective consumer. Understanding the lifestyles, attitudes, and demographics of the target market is essential. Diet Mountain Dew, for example, is targeted at Generation X males, while Kraft's Crystal Light Liquid is targeted at calorie-conscious women. Both campaigns emphasize advertising techniques that match their target audiences. To appeal to Generation X males, Diet Mountain Dew became the sponsor of Dale Earnhardt Jr.'s NASCAR team. Meanwhile, to attract calorie-conscious women, Crystal Light began providing nutritional information on a dedicated Facebook Page and on Twitter.

Similarly, the placement of the advertising depends on the audience. When Under Armour introduced its "I Will What I Want" campaign featuring women's apparel it created a website IWillWhatIWant.com, sponsored a segment on *Good Morning America,* made deals with flash-sale website Gilt, and posted a video on its YouTube channel that has been viewed 8,000,000 times, in addition to traditional print, digital, and outdoor advertising to reach competitive women. Even scheduling can depend on the audience. Nike schedules advertising, sponsorships, deals, and endorsements to correspond with the Olympics to appeal to amateur, college, and professional athletes.[7]

Under Armour places its ads to reach competitive women.
Source: Under Armour, Inc.

I WILL WHAT I WANT

To eliminate possible bias that might result from subjective judgments about some population segments, the Federal Communications Commission suggests that advertising program decisions be based on market research about the target audience.[8]

Specifying Advertising Objectives

The guidelines for setting promotion objectives described in Chapter 17 also apply to setting advertising objectives. This step helps advertisers with other choices in the promotion decision process, such as selecting media and evaluating a campaign. Advertising with an objective of creating awareness, for example, would be better matched with a magazine than a directory such as the Yellow Pages. The Association of Magazine Media believes objectives are so important that it is developing an awards program to recognize magazine advertising campaigns that demonstrate both creative excellence and effectiveness in meeting campaign objectives. Similarly, the Advertising Research Foundation sponsors research forums to advance the practice of measuring and evaluating the effectiveness of advertising and marketing communication.[9]

Experts believe that factors such as product category, brand, and consumer involvement in the purchase decision may change the importance—and, possibly, the sequence—of the stages of the hierarchy of effects (see Chapter 17). Snickers, for example, knew that its consumers were unlikely to engage in elaborate information processing when it designed a recent campaign. The result was ads with simple humorous messages rather than extensive factual information. New managerial perspectives also consider that advertising can have a long-term impact on the financial value of the organization.[10]

Setting the Advertising Budget

In 1990, advertisers paid $700,000 to place a 30-second ad during the Super Bowl. By 2015, the cost of placing a 30-second ad during Super Bowl 49 was $4.5 million (see Figure 18–1). The escalating cost is related to the growing number of viewers: 114 million

FIGURE 18–1

The Super Bowl delivers a huge audience, if you can afford the cost of placing an ad.

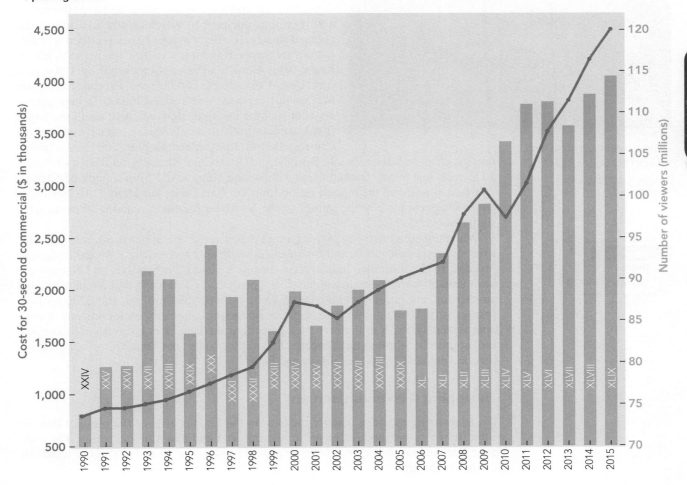

503

Marketing **Insights About Me**

Are You an Expert at Picking the Best Super Bowl Ads?

Let's compare your selection of the best Super Bowl ads with the experts. First go to www.superbowl-commercials. org to view the advertisements that appeared during the last Super Bowl. As you watch each ad evaluate the elements that you think create good advertising and then select your top 10 ads. Now visit *USA Today*'s Ad Meter at http://admeter.usatoday.com/. Ad Meter ranks the Super Bowl ads each year based on the votes from 7,000 panelists. For example, some of the top recent ads included Budweiser's "Lost Dog," Doritos' "Middle Seat," and Coca-Cola's "Make It Happy." So how did you do? Did you pick the same ads as Ad Meter? If you matched on five or more ads consider yourself an expert! To really test yourself, look at the winning commercials since 1989 and see if you agree!

Source: GeoClicks

Do you remember this Doritos ad from the Super Bowl?

Source: Frito-Lay North America, Inc.

Video 18-3
Doritos
kerin.tv/13e/v18-3

---

people watch the game. In addition, the audience is attractive to advertisers because research indicates it is equally split between men and women, who are likely to engage brands on social media before and after the game, and they look forward to watching the ads during the game. The ads are effective too: Lexus reported that following its Super Bowl ad, searches for its vehicles on Kelley Blue Book's website skyrocketed by 1,800 percent; Coca-Cola attracted 66,000 new Facebook fans; and McDonald's reported that it added 16,000 Twitter followers after running its Super Bowl ad. As a result the Super Bowl attracts both new advertisers, such as Carnival Cruises, Skittles, Loctite, and Mophie, and regular advertisers such as Anheuser-Busch, Doritos, and Coca-Cola. Recently, an Anheuser-Busch ad about a lost puppy finding its way home and being saved from trouble by Clydesdale horses received the highest rating from the *USA Today* Ad Meter.[11] To learn how your ratings compare to the ratings of the Ad Meter panelists, read the Marketing Insights About Me box.[12]

While not all advertising options are as expensive as the Super Bowl, most alternatives still represent substantial financial commitments and require a formal budgeting process. In the insurance industry, for example, Geico, Progressive, and Nationwide have market shares of approximately 19.2 percent, 11.1 percent, and 5.6 percent, and advertising and promotion budgets of $1.01 billion, $587 million, and $296 million, respectively. Using a competitive parity budgeting approach, each company spends approximately $52.8 million for each percent of market share. Using an objective and task approach, SlimFast has allocated $50 million to its "It's Your Thing" campaign to increase demand for its diet shakes and bars.[13]

Designing the Advertisement

An advertising message usually focuses on the key benefits of the product that are important to a prospective buyer in making trial and adoption decisions. The message depends on the general form or appeal used in the ad and the actual words included in the ad.

Message Content Most advertising messages are made up of both informational and persuasive elements. These two elements are so intertwined that it is sometimes difficult to tell them apart. For example, basic information such as the product name, benefits, features, and price can be presented in a way that tries to attract attention and encourage purchase. On the other hand, even the most persuasive advertisements have to contain at least some basic information to be successful.

Information and persuasive content can be combined in the form of an appeal to provide a basic reason for the consumer to act. Although the marketer can use many different types of appeals, common advertising appeals include fear, sex, and humor.

Fear appeals suggest to the consumer that he or she can avoid some negative experience through the purchase and use of a product or service, a change in behavior, or a reduction in the use of a product. Examples with which you may be familiar include automobile safety ads that depict an accident or injury; political candidate endorsements that warn against the rise of other, unpopular ideologies; or social cause ads warning of the serious consequences of drug and alcohol use. Insurance companies often try to show the negative effects on the relatives of those who die prematurely without carrying enough life or mortgage insurance. Food producers encourage the purchase of low-carb, low-fat, and high-fiber products as a means of reducing weight, lowering cholesterol levels, and preventing a heart attack. The Meth Project has run a series of ads that use fear appeals in headlines such as: "Beating An Old Man For Money Isn't Normal. But On Meth It Is." The image shows an unconscious man lying on the floor while attackers take his money.

When using fear appeals, the advertiser must be sure that the appeal is strong enough to get the audience's attention and concern but not so strong that it will lead them to tune out the message. Research suggests that overly threatening messages have a negative effect on the intention to adapt behavior. In fact, research on antismoking ads indicates that stressing the severity of long-term health risks may actually enhance smoking's allure among youth.[14]

In contrast, *sex appeals* suggest to the audience that the product will increase the attractiveness of the user. Sex appeals can be found in almost any product category, from automobiles to toothpaste. The contemporary women's clothing store bebe, for example, designs its advertising to "attract customers who are intrigued by the playfully sensual and evocative imagery of the bebe lifestyle." Studies indicate that sex appeals increase attention by helping advertising stand out in today's cluttered media environment. Unfortunately, sexual content does not always lead to changes in recall, recognition, or purchase intent. Experts suggest that sexual content is most effective when there is a strong fit between the use of a sex appeal in the ad and the image and positioning of the brand, as seen in the bebe ad.[15]

Read the text to learn why The Meth Project, bebe, and Old Spice use fear, sex, and humor appeals.

Sources: Left: Meth Project Foundation, Inc.; Middle: Bebe Studio, Inc.; Right: Procter & Gamble

Humorous appeals imply either directly or subtly that the product is more fun or exciting than competitors' offerings. As with fear and sex appeals, the use of humor is widespread in advertising and can be found in many product categories. You may have smiled at the popular Geico ads that use a talking pig, cavemen, and a gecko. These ads use humor to differentiate the company from its competitors. Geico has also created viral videos and posted them on video-sharing websites such as YouTube, where millions of viewers watch them within days.[16] You may have a favorite humorous ad character, such as the Energizer battery bunny, the Old Spice man, the AFLAC duck, or Travelocity's gnome. Advertisers believe that humor improves the effectiveness of their ads, although some studies suggest that humor wears out quickly, losing the interest of consumers. Another problem with humorous appeals is that their effectiveness may vary across cultures if used in a global campaign.[17]

Creating the Actual Message Advertising agency R/GA was recently designated *Advertising Age* magazine's Agency of the Year for its exceptional ability to meld technology and creativity. Examples of the agency's approach include its "The Game Before The Game" campaign for Beats by Dre, the "One Nike" campaign describing Nike's integrated website and platform of products and services, and "Google Outside," a digital outdoor billboard campaign in London. R/GA was also recognized by *Ad Week* as the Digital Agency of the Year for its use of mobile, social, and digital elements in its work. In fact, the tag line on its website is "R/GA for the connected age."[18]

R/GA and other agencies use many forms of advertising to create their messages. A very popular form of advertising today is the use of a celebrity spokesperson. R/GA's use of well-known celebrities, such as soccer player Neymar da Silva Santos, NFL quarterback Colin Kaepernick, and NBA star LeBron James in Beats by Dre ads, are examples. Many companies use athletes, film and television stars, musicians, and other celebrities to talk to consumers through their ads.

Advertisers who use a celebrity spokesperson believe that the ads are more likely to influence brand equity and sales. These ads feature a wide variety of celebrities, among them singer Beyoncé (Pepsi), actor Samuel L. Jackson (the Capital One Quicksilver card), and athlete Michael Jordan (Nike). L'Oréal Paris recently signed actress Naomi Watts as a spokeswoman for the company and its brands. Cyril Chapuy, brand global president, explains that Naomi was selected because "Her timeless beauty has made her the perfect woman to endorse our ultimate skincare innovation, Revitalift Filler." Who is the most effective spokesperson? A recent report by Nielsen indicates that Liam Neeson and Pierce Brosnan are tied for first. Other highly ranked celebrities include Matthew McConaughey, Jennifer Garner, and Sofia Vergara.[19]

One potential shortcoming of this form of advertising is that the spokesperson's image may change over time, becoming inconsistent with the image of the company or brand. For example, Tour de France cyclist Lance Armstrong lost endorsement contracts with Nike and golf pro Tiger Woods lost contracts with AT&T and Accenture after the athletes received negative public attention. Many companies now probe the backgrounds of potential endorsers and consider retired athletes and legacy (deceased) athletes who are low risk and still have lasting appeal in the marketplace. Some companies are also using licensing agreements where the spokesperson's compensation is directly related to the success of the product they endorse.[20]

Another issue involved in creating the message is the complex process of translating the copywriter's ideas into an actual advertisement. Designing quality artwork, layout, and production for advertisements is costly and time-consuming. The American Association of Advertising Agencies reports

The Game Before The Game campaign helped R/GA win *Advertising Age*'s Agency of the Year award.
Source: Beats Electronics LLC

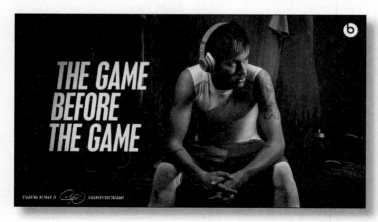

that a high-quality, 30-second TV commercial typically costs about $354,000 to produce. One reason for the high cost is that as companies have developed global campaigns, the need to shoot commercials in several locations has increased. Actors are also expensive: Compensation for a typical TV ad is $19,000.[21]

learning review ≫

18-3. What other decisions can advertising objectives influence?

18-4. What is a potential shortcoming of using a celebrity spokesperson?

Selecting the Right Media

Every advertiser must decide where to place its advertisements. The alternatives are the *advertising media*, the means by which the message is communicated to the target audience. Newspapers, magazines, radio, and TV are examples of advertising media. Media selection is related to the target audience, type of product, nature of the message, campaign objectives, available budget, and the costs of the alternative media. Figure 18–2 shows the distribution of the $224 billion spent on advertising by medium.[22]

Choosing a Medium and a Vehicle within That Medium   In deciding where to place advertisements, a company has several media to choose from and a number of alternatives, or vehicles, within each medium. Often advertisers use a mix of media forms and vehicles to maximize the exposure of the message to the target audience while at the same time minimizing costs. These two conflicting goals are of central importance to media planning.

Basic Terms   Media buyers speak a language of their own, so all advertisers involved in selecting the right media for their campaigns must be familiar with some common terms used in the advertising industry.

Because advertisers try to maximize the number of individuals in the target market exposed to the message, they must be concerned with reach. **Reach** is the number of different people or households exposed to an advertisement. The exact definition of reach

507

FIGURE 18–2

Television, direct mail, and newspapers account for more than 60 percent of all advertising expenditures ($ in millions).

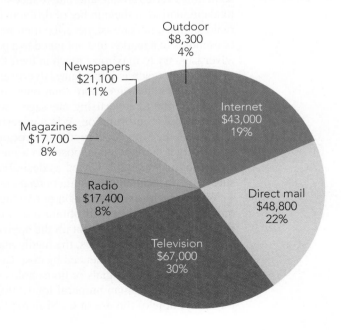

Outdoor
$8,300
4%

Newspapers
$21,100
11%

Magazines
$17,700
8%

Radio
$17,400
8%

Television
$67,000
30%

Internet
$43,000
19%

Direct mail
$48,800
22%

sometimes varies among alternative media. Newspapers often use reach to describe their total circulation or the number of different households that buy the paper. Television and radio stations, in contrast, describe their reach using the term **rating**—the percentage of households in a market that are tuned to a particular TV show or radio station. In general, advertisers try to maximize reach in their target market at the lowest cost.

Although reach is important, advertisers are also interested in exposing their target audience to a message more than once. This is because consumers often do not pay close attention to advertising messages, some of which contain large amounts of relatively complex information. When advertisers want to reach the same audience more than once, they are concerned with **frequency**, the average number of times a person in the target audience is exposed to a message or advertisement. Like reach, greater frequency is generally viewed as desirable. Studies indicate that with repeated exposure to advertisements consumers respond more favorably to brand extensions.[23]

When reach (expressed as a percentage of the total market) is multiplied by frequency, an advertiser will obtain a commonly used reference number called **gross rating points (GRPs)**. To obtain the appropriate number of GRPs to achieve an advertising campaign's objectives, the media planner must balance reach and frequency. The balance will also be influenced by cost. **Cost per thousand (CPM)** refers to the cost of reaching 1,000 individuals or households with the advertising message in a given medium (*M* is the Roman numeral for 1,000). See the Applying Marketing Metrics box for an example of the use of CPM in media selection.

Different Media Alternatives

Figure 18–3 summarizes the advantages and disadvantages of the major advertising media, which are described in more detail below. For detailed coverage of direct mail, refer to Chapter 17.

Television   Television is a valuable medium because it communicates with sight, sound, and motion. Print advertisements alone could never give you the sense of a sports car accelerating from a stop or cornering at high speed. In addition, television reaches more than 96 percent of all households—116.4 million, including households that get video delivered over the Internet to a TV. About 5 million "Zero TV" households receive programming on devices other than televisions. There are also many opportunities for out-of-home TV viewing, as televisions are present in many bars, hotels, offices, airports, and college campuses.[24]

Several aspects of traditional television viewing are changing. First, research at the Nielsen Company indicates that the amount of time allocated to television viewing is increasing. American viewers now spend 41 hours each week watching television programming on multiple screens, including traditional TVs, computers, tablets, and

FIGURE 18–3

Advertisers must consider the advantages and disadvantages of the many media alternatives.

MEDIUM	ADVANTAGES	DISADVANTAGES
Television	Reaches extremely large audience; uses picture, print, sound, and motion for effect; can target specific audiences	High cost to prepare and run ads; short exposure time and perishable message; difficult to convey complex information
Radio	Low cost; can target specific local audiences; ads can be placed quickly; can use sound, humor, and intimacy effectively	No visual element; short exposure time and perishable message; difficult to convey complex information
Magazines	Can target specific audiences; high-quality color; long life of ad; ads can be clipped and saved; can convey complex information	Long time needed to place ad; relatively high cost; competes for attention with other magazine features
Newspapers	Excellent coverage of local markets; ads can be placed and changed quickly; ads can be saved; quick consumer response; low cost	Ads compete for attention with other newspaper features; short life span; poor color
Yellow Pages	Excellent coverage of geographic segments; long use period; available 24 hours/365 days	Proliferation of competitive directories in many markets; difficult to keep up to date
Internet	Video and audio capabilities; animation can capture attention; ads can be interactive and link to advertiser	Animation and interactivity require large files and more time to load; effectiveness is still uncertain
Outdoor	Low cost; local market focus; high visibility; opportunity for repeat exposures	Message must be short and simple; low selectivity of audience; criticized as a traffic hazard
Direct mail	High selectivity of audience; can contain complex information and personalized messages; high-quality graphics	High cost per contact; poor image (junk mail)

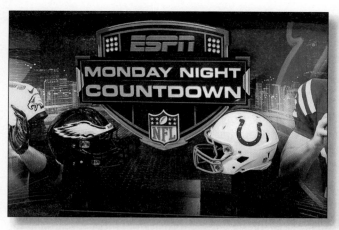

ESPN is one of many specialized channels available to advertisers on cable networks.

© Scott Boehm/AP Images

smartphones. In addition, viewers are increasingly time shifting their viewing with DVRs, DVDs, subscription services such as Netflix, and Internet options such as Hulu and Apple TV. Technologies are changing, too. In recent years, many consumers have purchased high-definition televisions. The future, however, will include 4K, 8K, OLED, and glass-less 3D televisions, which are four and eight times as sharp as high definition television, can convert ordinary television into 3D, offer voice-activated and motion controls, and allow two programs to be watched simultaneously.[25]

Television's major disadvantage is cost: The price of a prime-time, 30-second ad can range from $627,300 to run on *Sunday Night Football,* to $170,948 to run on *NCIS,* to $49,839 to run on *America's Funniest Home Videos.* Because of these high charges, many advertisers choose less expensive "spot" ads, which run between programs, or 15-second ads, rather than investing in ads that run the more traditional length of 30 or 60 seconds. In fact, approximately 34 percent of all TV ads are now 15 seconds long. Recent studies suggest that the placement of an ad within a program and relative to other ads in a sequence of ads may influence the ad's effectiveness. In addition, there is some indication that advertisers are shifting their interest to live events rather than programs that might be watched on a DVR days later.[26]

Another problem with television advertising is the likelihood of *wasted coverage*—having people outside the target market for the product see the advertisement. The cost and wasted coverage problems of TV advertising can be reduced through the specialized cable and satellite channels. Advertising time is often less expensive on cable and satellite channels than on the broadcast networks. According to the National Cable and Telecommunication Association, there are more than 900 cable channels such as Disney, ESPN, History, MTV, Oxygen, and Lifetime. Cable channels are also "tagging" their programs to allow advertisers to place ads in scenes with particular themes. Advertisements for golf equipment, for example, might be placed after a program scene that shows characters playing golf.[27]

Another popular form of television advertising is the infomercial. **Infomercials** are program-length (30-minute) advertisements that take an educational approach to communication with potential customers. You may remember seeing infomercials for the Magic Bullet, ThighMaster, and OxiClean products, using Ron Popeil, Suzanne Somers, and Anthony Sullivan, respectively, as the spokesperson.

Infomercials are increasingly popular because they can be both informative and entertaining, and because the average cost of a 30-minute block of television time is only $425. Each year, *Response Magazine* and Infomercial Monitoring Service Inc. publish a list of the top 50 infomercials from the past 12 months. Recent popular infomercials included the Insanity body fitness DVDs, Total Gym exercise equipment, NutriBullet high-speed blenders, and LifeLock identity theft protection products. The industry generates more than $150 billion in annual sales and has facilitated the long-term success of many products. The Total Gym infomercials featuring Chuck Norris and Christie Brinkley, for example, have led to more than $1 billion in sales![28]

Radio The United States has more than 27,800 radio stations. These stations consist of approximately 4,700 AM, 10,600 FM, and 12,500 HD (digital) and Internet stations. The major advantage of radio is that it is a segmented medium. For example, the Farm Radio Network, the Family Life Network, Business Talk Radio, and the Performance Racing Network are all listened to by different market segments. Satellite radio service SiriusXM offers more than 175 commercial-free, digital, coast-to-coast channels to consumers for a monthly fee, and Internet radio service Pandora offers up to 100 personalized channels to each listener. The large number of media options today has reduced the amount of time spent listening to radio, although radio still reaches 91 percent of all adults weekly. Millennials listen to radio an average of 9.8 hours each week, making radio an important medium for businesses with college students and recent graduates as a target market.[29]

A disadvantage of radio is that it has limited use for products that must be seen. Another problem is the ease with which consumers can tune out a commercial by switching stations. Radio is also a medium that competes for people's attention as they do other activities, such as driving, working, or relaxing. Radio listening time reaches its peak during the morning drive time (7 to 8 A.M.), remains high during the day, and then begins to decline in the afternoon (after 4 P.M.) as people return home and start evening activities.[30]

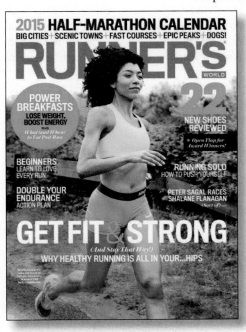

Magazines such as *Runner's World* appeal to narrowly defined segments such as athletes who are interested in running.

Magazines Magazines have become a very specialized medium. In fact, there are currently more than 7,289 consumer magazines. Some 231 new magazines were introduced last year, including *Raw Bike,* a magazine for home-built motorcycle enthusiasts; *Sneaker News,* a source of relevant news for the "sneakerhead" community; and *NO TOFU,* a magazine celebrating cutting-edge talent in film, fashion, music, and art. Many publishers are also adding digital versions of existing magazines. *Skateboarder,* for example, can now also be read on the magazine's website, an iPad, or a smartphone. Some magazines, such as *Auto Trader* and *Computer Weekly,* are dropping their print format to offer only an online version. Finally, several digital businesses have launched print magazines including Airbnb, which launched *Pineapple,* and Uber, which launched *Momentum.*[31]

The marketing advantage of this medium is the great number of special-interest publications that appeal to narrowly defined segments. Runners read *Runner's World,* sailors buy *Yachting,* gardeners subscribe to *Garden Design,* and children peruse *Sports Illustrated for Kids.* More than 675 publications focus on travel, 146 are dedicated to interior design and decoration, and 98 are related to golf. Each magazine's readers often represent a unique profile. Take the *Rolling Stone* reader, who tends to listen to music more than most people. SiriusXM Satellite Radio knows an ad in *Rolling Stone* is reaching the desired target audience. In addition, recent studies comparing advertising in different media suggest that magazine advertising is perceived to be more "inspirational" than other media.[32]

The cost of advertising in national magazines is a disadvantage, but many national publications publish regional and even metro editions, which reduces the absolute cost and wasted coverage. *Time* publishes well over 400 editions, including Latin American, Canadian, Asian, South Pacific, European, and U.S. editions. The U.S. editions include geographic and demographic options. In addition to cost, another limitation to magazines is their infrequency. At best, magazines are printed on a weekly basis, with many specialized publications appearing only monthly or less often. Although specialization can be an advantage of this medium, consumer interests can be difficult to translate into a magazine theme—a fact made clear by the hundreds of magazine failures during the past decade. *U.S. News and World Report, GamePro, CosmoGirl, Teen People, Business 2.0, PC Magazine, Men's Vogue, Gourmet,* and *Esquire Sportsman,* for example, all failed to attract and keep a substantial number of readers or advertisers. Which magazine has the highest circulation? It's *AARP The Magazine,* with a circulation of 22 million![33]

Newspapers Newspapers are an important local medium with excellent reach potential. Daily publication allows advertisements to focus on specific current events, such as a 24-hour sale. Local retailers often use newspapers as their sole advertising medium. Newspapers are rarely saved by the purchaser, however, so companies are generally limited to ads that call for an immediate customer response (although customers can clip

Metro offers a global audience of daily readers.

© Henrik Montgomery/AFP/Getty Images

and save ads they select). Companies also cannot expect newspapers to offer the same quality color reproduction available in most magazines.

National advertising campaigns rarely include this medium except in conjunction with local distributors of their products. In these instances, both parties often share the advertising costs using a cooperative advertising program, which is described later in this chapter. Another exception is the use of newspapers such as *The Wall Street Journal* and *USA Today,* which have national distribution of more than 2.3 and 1.6 million readers, respectively. One newspaper, *Metro,* offers a global audience of 18 million daily readers in Boston, New York, Philadelphia, and 100 cities in Europe, North and South America, and Asia.[34]

Several important trends are influencing newspapers today. First is the decline in circulation and advertising revenue. A recent report by the Alliance for Audited Media showed that circulation declined at 8 of the 25 largest newspapers during the past year. The shift is attributed to readers' growing preference for free websites and mobile services, as half of all Americans now get some form of local news on a mobile device. In addition, classified advertising revenue has declined as Craigslist and similar sites have become more popular with consumers.

The second trend is the growth in online newspapers. Today, hundreds of newspapers, including *The New York Times, The Wall Street Journal, Chicago Sun-Times,* and the *San Francisco Chronicle,* offer online versions of their printed newspapers. In fact, online subscriptions now account for 19 percent of all newspaper subscriptions. *The New York Times* now has more digital subscribers than print subscribers. Many newspapers also have online readers who are not subscribers. *USA Today,* for example, reports that it has 32 million readers on the free portion of its website. A final trend is the growth in new types of news organizations such as *The Huffington Post,* which covers entertainment, media, living, business, and politics and has more than 5 million Twitter followers, and *Examiner.com,* which utilizes a large group of freelance reporters.[35]

Yellow Pages   Yellow pages represent an advertising media alternative comparable to outdoor advertising in terms of expenditures—about $8 billion in the United States. According to the Local Search Association, consumers turn to print yellow pages approximately 11 billion times annually and online yellow pages (desktop, tablet, and mobile) an additional 5.6 billion times per year. One reason for this high level of use is that the 6,500 yellow pages directories reach almost all households. Yellow pages are a "directional" medium because they direct consumers to where purchases can be made after other media have created awareness and demand.

The yellow pages face several disadvantages today. First is the proliferation of directories. AT&T (*Real Yellow Pages*), Dex Media (*Dex One* and *Superpages*), and Hibu (*Yellowbook*) now produce competing directories for many cities, neighborhoods, and ethnic groups. Second, relative to other advertising options, the yellow pages have limited accountability and ROI metrics. Many advertisers believe that yellow pages need to improve their audience measurement research and circulation auditing practices. Finally, yellow pages publishers are facing increasing public concern about the environmental impact of the directories. One response from the industry is a website, www.yellowpagesoptout.com, that allows consumers to have an opt out option if they prefer not to receive print directories.[36]

Print yellow pages are used more than 11 billion times each year. See the text for advantages and disadvantages of this media alternative.

© Mike Hruby

Internet   The Internet represents a relatively new medium for many advertisers, although it has already attracted a wide variety of industries. Online advertising is similar to print advertising in that it offers a visual message. It has additional advantages, however, because it can also use the audio and video capabilities of the Internet. Sound and movement may simply attract more attention from viewers, or they

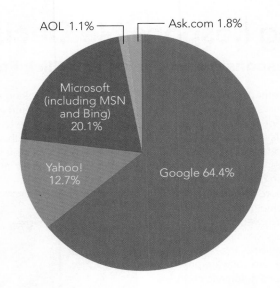

FIGURE 18–4

Google, Microsoft, and Yahoo! have the largest shares of Internet searches and offer opportunities for online advertising.

may provide an element of entertainment to the message. Online advertising also has the unique feature of being interactive. Called *rich media,* these interactive ads have drop-down menus, built-in games, or search engines to engage viewers. Online advertising also offers an opportunity to reach younger consumers who have developed a preference for online communication.

There are a variety of online advertising options. The most popular options are paid search, display (banner) ads, classified ads, and video. Paid search is one of the fastest-growing forms of Internet advertising, as approximately 80 percent of all Internet traffic begins at a search engine such as Google or Yahoo! (see Figure 18–4). Experts estimate that consumers conduct 20 billion searches each month. Now search engine agencies help firms add tags, wikis, and RSS (rich site summary) to the content of a site to increase search rankings. While the use of banner ads is growing also, there is some concern that consumers are developing "banner blindness" because the click-through rate has been declining to its current level of 0.1 percent. The effectiveness of the ads can be improved with targeted advertising, and research indicates that online visitors are more likely to consent to provide information needed for targeting if the websites suggest it is a form of reciprocity or exchange for the use of free websites.

Classified ads, such as those on Craigslist, and video ads also contribute to the growth of online advertising by providing many of the advantages and characteristics of other media such as yellow pages, magazines, newspaper, and television. Video ads also have the benefit of "going viral" when people share the ads with friends. The increasing availability of Internet access and the growing popularity of smartphones means that online advertising also provides the unique characteristic of being mobile. In fact, **mobile marketing** now includes the broad set of interactive messaging options that enable organizations to communicate and engage with consumers through any mobile device.[37]

One disadvantage of online advertising is that because the medium is relatively new, technical and administrative standards for the various formats are still evolving. This situation makes it difficult for advertisers to run national online campaigns across multiple sites. The Interactive Advertising Bureau provides "Guidelines, Standards & Best Practices" and creative guidelines to facilitate the use and growth of online advertising.

Another disadvantage to online advertising is the difficulty of measuring impact. Several companies are testing methods of tracking where viewers go on their computer in the days and weeks after seeing an ad. Nielsen's online rating service, for example, measures actual Internet use through meters installed on the computers of 500,000 individuals in

Making **Responsible Decisions**

Who Is Responsible for Preventing Click Fraud?

Spending on Internet advertising now exceeds $40 billion as many advertisers shift their budgets from print and TV to the Internet. For most advertisers one advantage of on-line advertising is that they pay only when someone clicks on their ad. Unfortunately, the growth of the medium has led to "click fraud," which is the deceptive clicking of ads solely to increase the amount advertisers must pay. There are several forms of click fraud. One method is the result of Paid-to-Read (PTR) websites that recruit and pay members to simply click on ads. Another method is the result of "clickbots," which are software programs that produce automatic clicks on ads, sometimes through mobile devices. The activity is difficult to detect and stop. Experts estimate that up to 20 percent of clicks may be the result of fraud and may be costing advertisers as much as $800 million each year!

Investigations of the online advertising industry have discovered a related form of click fraud that occurs when legitimate website visitors click on ads without any intention of

© BananaStock/PictureQuests

looking at the site. As one consumer explains, "I always try and remember to click on the ad banners once in a while to try and keep the sites free." Stephen Dubner calls this "webtipping"!

As the Internet advertising industry grows, it will become increasingly important to resolve the issue of click fraud. Consumers, advertisers, websites that carry paid advertising, and the large web portals are all involved in a complicated technical, legal, and social situation. The advertising industry's Media Ratings Council has suggested a possible solution: that 50 percent of a display ad must be in view for one second to be an impression that brands pay for. Similarly, some advertisers are now requesting "smart-pricing," which means that they pay less if the click does not lead to a consumer action such as a purchase or an information request.

Who should lead the way in the effort to find a solution to click fraud? What actions do you suggest for the advertising industry, websites, and consumers?

comScore's service can provide an assessment of the effectiveness of a website by measuring its impact on the digital audience.

Courtesy of comScore, Inc.

20 countries. Measuring the relationship between online and offline behavior is also important. Research by comScore, which studied 139 online ad campaigns, revealed that online ads didn't always result in a "click," but they increased the likelihood of a purchase by 17 percent and they increased visits to the advertiser's website by 40 percent.[38] The Making Responsible Decisions box describes how click fraud is increasing the necessity of assessing online advertising effectiveness.[39]

Outdoor A very effective medium for reminding consumers about your product is outdoor advertising, such as the scoreboard at San Diego's Qualcomm Stadium. The most common form of outdoor advertising, called *billboards,* often results in good reach and frequency and has been shown to increase purchase rates.[40] The visibility of this medium is good supplemental reinforcement for well-known products, and it is a relatively low-cost, flexible alternative. Also, a company can buy space in a specific, targeted geographical market. A disadvantage to billboards, however, is that no opportunity exists for lengthy advertising copy. Also, a good billboard site depends on traffic patterns and sight lines.

If you have ever lived in a metropolitan area, chances are you might have seen another form of outdoor advertising, *transit advertising.* This medium includes messages on the interior and exterior of buses, subway and light-rail cars, and taxis. As the use of mass transit grows, transit advertising may become increasingly important. Selectivity is available to advertisers, who can buy space by neighborhood or bus route. One disadvantage to this medium is that the heavy travel times, when the audiences are the largest, are not conducive to reading advertising copy. People are standing shoulder to shoulder on the subway, hoping not to miss their stop, and little attention is paid to the advertising.

Outdoor advertising can be an effective medium for reminding consumers about a product.

© Jim McIsaac/Getty Images

The outdoor advertising industry has experienced a growth surge recently. According to the Outdoor Advertising Association of America, outdoor advertising expenditures have grown to $7 billion annually. Much of the growth is the result of creative forms of outdoor advertising and the conversion to digital billboards, which allow advertisers to quickly present *conditional content*. Conditional content ads are based on current events, weather, business conditions, and even sports scores. Radio stations, for example, can display the title of the song currently playing on their station, newspapers can display current headlines, and retailers can advertise umbrellas or sunscreen based on the weather forecast.

Digital billboard companies have also donated billboard time to display public service announcements. For example, in Minnesota digital billboards display National Weather Service tornado warnings, and in Houston messages from the police department are displayed to help apprehend fugitives. A recent study found that 80 percent of U.S. residents can be reached daily through outdoor advertising and that many commuters think that digital billboards make the commute more interesting. While these are positive trends, the outdoor advertising industry also faces important environmental concerns. For example, several states have banned billboards, and a judge recently ordered two billboard companies in Los Angeles to turn off about 80 digital signs.[41]

Other Media As traditional media have become more expensive and cluttered, advertisers have been attracted to a variety of nontraditional advertising options called out-of-home advertising, or *place-based media*. Messages are placed in locations that attract a specific target audience such as airports, doctors' offices, health clubs, theaters (where ads are played on the screen before the movies are shown), grocery stores, storefronts, and even the bathrooms of bars, restaurants, and nightclubs. Soon there will be advertising on video screens on gas pumps, ATMs, and in elevators, and increasingly it will be interactive.

The $2.5 billion industry has attracted advertisers such as AT&T and JCPenney, which use in-store campaigns, and Geico, Sprint, and FedEx, which use out-of-home advertising to reach mobile professionals in health clubs, airports, and hotels. Research suggests that creative use of out-of-home advertising, such as preshow theater ads, enhances consumer recall of the ads.[42]

Out-of-home advertising such as this outdoor display is becoming interactive to engage consumers.

© Brent Jones

Selection Criteria Choosing between these alternative media is difficult and depends on several factors. First, knowing the media habits of the target audience is essential to deciding among the alternatives. Second, occasionally product attributes necessitate that certain media be used. For example, if color is a major aspect of product appeal, radio is excluded. Newspapers allow advertising for quick actions to confront competitors, and magazines are more appropriate for complicated messages because the reader can spend more time reading the message. The final factor in selecting a medium is cost. When possible, alternative media are compared using a common denominator that reflects both reach and cost—a measure such as CPM.

Scheduling the Advertising

There is no correct schedule to advertise a product, but three factors must be considered. First is the issue of *buyer turnover,* which is how often new buyers enter the market to buy the product. The higher the buyer turnover, the greater the amount of advertising required. A second issue in scheduling is the *purchase frequency;* the more frequently the product is purchased, the less repetition is required. Finally, companies must consider the *forgetting rate,* the speed with which buyers forget the brand if advertising is not seen.

Setting schedules requires an understanding of how the market behaves. Most companies tend to follow one of three basic approaches:

1. *Continuous (steady) schedule.* When seasonal factors are unimportant, advertising is run at a continuous or steady schedule throughout the year.
2. *Flighting (intermittent) schedule.* Periods of advertising are scheduled between periods of no advertising to reflect seasonal demand.
3. *Pulse (burst) schedule.* A flighting schedule is combined with a continuous schedule because of increases in demand, heavy periods of promotion, or introduction of a new product.

For example, products such as breakfast cereals have a stable demand throughout the year and would typically use a continuous schedule of advertising. In contrast, products such as snow skis and suntan lotions have seasonal demands and receive flighting-schedule advertising during the seasonal demand period. Some products such as toys or automobiles require pulse-schedule advertising to facilitate sales throughout the year and during special periods of increased demand (such as holidays or new car introductions). Some evidence suggests that pulsing schedules are superior to other advertising strategies.[43] In addition, research indicates the effectiveness of a particular ad wears out quickly and, therefore, many alternative forms of a commercial may be more effective.[44]

learning review »

18-5. You see the same ad in *Time* and *Fortune* magazines and on billboards and TV. Is this an example of reach or frequency?

18-6. Why has the Internet become a popular advertising medium?

18-7. What factors must be considered when choosing among alternative media?

EXECUTING THE ADVERTISING PROGRAM

Executing the advertising program involves pretesting the advertising copy and actually carrying out the advertising program. John Wanamaker, the founder of Wanamaker's Department Store in Philadelphia, remarked, "I know half my advertising is wasted, but I don't know what half." By evaluating advertising efforts, marketers can try to ensure that their advertising expenditures are not wasted.[45] Evaluation is done usually at two separate times: before and after the advertisements are run in the actual campaign. Several methods used in the evaluation process at the stages of idea formulation and copy development are discussed below.

Pretesting the Advertising

To determine whether the advertisement communicates the intended message or to select among alternative versions of the advertisement, **pretests** are conducted before the advertisements are placed in any medium.

Portfolio Tests   Portfolio tests are used to test copy alternatives. The test ad is placed in a portfolio with several other ads and stories, and consumers are asked to read through the portfolio. Afterward, subjects are asked for their impressions of the ads on several evaluative scales, such as from "very informative" to "not very informative."

Jury Tests   Jury tests involve showing the ad copy to a panel of consumers and having them rate how they liked it, how much it drew their attention, and how attractive they thought it was. This approach is similar to the portfolio test in that consumer reactions are obtained. However, unlike the portfolio test, a test advertisement is not hidden within other ads.

Theater Tests   Theater testing is the most sophisticated form of pretesting. Consumers are invited to view new television shows or movies in which test commercials are also shown. Viewers register their feelings about the advertisements either on handheld electronic recording devices used during the viewing or on questionnaires afterward.

Carrying Out the Advertising Program

The responsibility for actually carrying out the advertising program can be handled in one of three ways, as shown in Figure 18–5. The **full-service agency** provides the most complete range of services, including market research, media selection, copy development, artwork, and production. In the past, agencies that assisted a client by both developing and placing advertisements often charged a commission of 15 percent of the media costs. As corporations introduced integrated marketing communication approaches, however, many advertisers switched from paying commissions to incentive plans based on performance. These plans typically pay for agency costs and a 5 to 10 percent profit, plus bonuses if specific performance goals related to brand preference, lead generation, sales, and market share are met. The Association of National Advertisers estimates that 61 percent of all agency clients currently use this approach.

Anheuser-Busch recently introduced a new version of the full-service agency approach when it announced it would begin to compensate agencies for their costs based on rigid scope-of-work agreements. Vice President of Marketing Keith Levy explains, "We want partner agencies really tied to the strategy of the brand." In the future, clients may move to a value-based approach where compensation is dependent on sales of the advertised product or brand. This approach will add additional emphasis on agency contributions beyond advertising. In some instances, such as specialized direct-response agencies, compensation is already a percentage of revenue generated.[46]

Limited-service agencies specialize in one aspect of the advertising process, such as providing creative services to develop the advertising copy, buying previously unpurchased media (media agencies), or providing Internet services (Internet agencies).

FIGURE 18–5

Alternative structures of advertising agencies used to carry out the advertising program.

TYPE OF AGENCY	SERVICES PROVIDED
Full-service agency	Does research, selects media, develops copy, and produces artwork; also coordinates integrated campaigns with all marketing efforts
Limited-service (specialty) agency	Specializes in one aspect of creative process; usually provides creative production work; buys previously unpurchased media space
In-house agency	Provides range of services, depending on company needs

Limited-service agencies that deal in creative work are compensated by a contractual agreement for the services performed. Finally, **in-house agencies** made up of the company's own advertising staff may provide full services or a limited range of services.

ASSESSING THE ADVERTISING PROGRAM

The advertising decision process does not stop with executing the advertising program. The advertisements must be evaluated to determine whether they are achieving their intended objectives, and results may indicate that changes must be made in the advertising program.

Posttesting the Advertising

An advertisement may go through **posttests** after it has been shown to the target audience to determine whether it accomplished its intended purpose. Five approaches common in posttesting are discussed here.[47]

Aided Recall   After being shown an ad, respondents are asked whether their previous exposure to it was through reading, viewing, or listening. The Starch test shown in the accompanying photo uses aided recall to determine the percentage of those who (1) remember seeing a specific ad (*noted*), (2) saw or read any part of the ad identifying the product or brand (*associated*), (3) read any part of the ad's copy (*read any*), and (4) read at least half of the ad (*read most*). Elements of the ad are then tagged with the results, as shown in the photo.[48]

Unaided Recall   The unaided recall approach involves asking respondents a question such as, "What ads do you remember seeing yesterday?" without any prompting to determine whether they saw or heard advertising messages.

Attitude Tests   Attitude tests involve asking respondents questions to measure changes in their attitudes after an advertising campaign. For example, they might be asked whether they now have a more favorable attitude toward the product advertised. Recent research suggests that attitudes can be influenced by many factors, including the increasingly popular use of co-creation to develop consumer-generated ads.[49]

Inquiry Tests   Inquiry tests involve offering additional product information, product samples, or premiums to an ad's readers or viewers. Ads generating the most inquiries are presumed to be the most effective.

The Starch test uses aided recall to evaluate an ad on four dimensions. See the text to learn more.

Courtesy of GfK North America

Sales Tests   Sales tests involve studies such as controlled experiments (e.g., using radio ads in one market and newspaper ads in another and comparing the results) and consumer purchase tests (measuring retail sales that result from a given advertising campaign). The most sophisticated experimental methods today allow a manufacturer, a distributor, or an advertising agency to manipulate an advertising variable (such as schedule or copy) through cable systems and observe subsequent sales effects by monitoring data collected from checkout scanners in supermarkets.[50]

Making Needed Changes

Results of posttesting the advertising copy are used to reach decisions about changes in the advertising program.

If the posttest results show that an advertisement is doing poorly in terms of awareness, cost efficiency, or sales, it may be dropped and other ads run in its place in the future. On the other hand, sometimes an advertisement may be so successful it is run repeatedly or used as the basis of a larger advertising program.

learning review

18-8. Explain the difference between pretesting and posttesting advertising copy.

18-9. What is the difference between aided and unaided recall posttests?

SALES PROMOTION

LO 18-4 Discuss the strengths and weaknesses of consumer-oriented and trade-oriented sales promotions.

Sales promotion is a key element of the promotional mix today; it now accounts for more than $74 billion in annual expenditures. In a recent forecast by ZenithOptimedia, sales promotion expenditures accounted for 18 percent of all promotional spending.[51] The large allocation of marketing expenditures to sales promotion reflects the trend toward integrated marketing communications programs, which often include a variety of sales promotion elements. Selection and integration of the many promotion techniques require a good understanding of the advantages and disadvantages of each kind of sales promotion.[52] The two major kinds of sales promotions, consumer-oriented and trade-oriented, are discussed below.

Consumer-Oriented Sales Promotions

Coupons encourage trial by offering a discounted price. See the text to learn if coupons increase sales.

© Mike Hruby

Directed to ultimate consumers, **consumer-oriented sales promotions**, or simply *consumer promotions,* are sales tools used to support a company's advertising and personal selling. A variety of consumer-oriented sales promotion tools may be used, including coupons, deals, premiums, contests, sweepstakes, samples, loyalty programs, point-of-purchase displays, rebates, and product placements (see Figure 18–6).

Coupons   Coupons are sales promotions that usually offer a discounted price to the consumer, which encourages trial. Approximately 310 billion coupons worth $533 billion are distributed in the United States each year. More than 92 percent of all coupons are distributed as freestanding inserts in newspapers. Research indicates that consumer use of coupons rose during the recession and has remained at 77 percent in subsequent years. Consumers redeemed 2.75 billion of the coupons last year, for a savings of approximately $3.6 billion.

Companies that have increased their use of coupons include Procter & Gamble, Nestlé, and Kraft, while the top retailers for coupon redemption were Walmart, Kroger, and Target. The number of coupons generated at Internet sites (e.g., www.valpak.com and www.coupon.com) and on mobile phones has been increasing as well, although they account for less than 2 percent of all coupons. The redemption rate for online coupons—approximately 14 percent—however, is substantially higher than other forms of coupons. Daily deal sites like Groupon and Living-Social have helped fuel the growth in couponing. Today, coupons are available in almost every product category and they are used by men and women of all ages.[53]

519

KIND OF SALES PROMOTION	OBJECTIVES	ADVANTAGES	DISADVANTAGES
Coupons	Stimulate demand	Encourage retailer support	Consumers delay purchases
Deals	Increase trial; retaliate against competitor's actions	Reduce consumer risk	Consumers delay purchases; reduce perceived product value
Premiums	Build goodwill	Consumers like free or reduced-price merchandise	Consumers buy for premium, not product
Contests	Increase consumer purchases; build business inventory	Encourage consumer involvement with product	Require creative or analytical thinking
Sweepstakes	Encourage present customers to buy more; minimize brand switching	Get customer to use product and store more often	Sales drop after sweepstakes
Samples	Encourage new-product trial	Low risk for consumer	High cost for company
Loyalty programs	Encourage repeat purchases	Help create loyalty	High cost for company
Point-of-purchase displays	Increase product trial; provide in-store support for other promotions	Provide good product visibility	Hard to get retailer to allocate high-traffic space
Rebates	Encourage customers to purchase; stop sales decline	Effective at stimulating demand	Easily copied; steal sales from future; reduce perceived product value
Product placements	Introduce new products; demonstrate product use	Positive message in a noncommercial setting	Little control over presentation of product

FIGURE 18–6

Consumer-oriented sales promotion makes use of many different tools to achieve a variety of objectives.

Do coupons help increase sales? Studies suggest that market share does increase during the period immediately after coupons are distributed.[54] There are also indications, however, that couponing can reduce gross revenues by lowering the price paid by already-loyal consumers.[55] Therefore, the 9,000 manufacturers that currently use coupons are particularly interested in coupon programs directed at potential first-time buyers. One means of focusing on these potential buyers is through electronic in-store coupon machines that match coupons to your most recent purchases.

Coupons are often far more expensive than the face value of the coupon; a 25-cent coupon can cost three times that after paying for the advertisement to deliver it, dealer handling, clearinghouse costs, and redemption. In addition, misredemption, or attempting to redeem a counterfeit coupon or a valid coupon when the product was not purchased, should be added to the cost of the coupon. The Coupon Information Corporation estimates that companies pay out refunds worth hundreds of millions of dollars each year as a result of coupon fraud. Recent growth in coupon fraud has marketers considering adding holograms and visual aids to help cashiers identify valid coupons.[56]

Deals   Deals are short-term price reductions, commonly used to increase trial among potential customers or to retaliate against a competitor's actions. For example, if a rival manufacturer introduces a new cake mix, the company responds with a "two packages for the price of one" deal. This short-term price reduction builds up the stock on the kitchen shelves of cake mix buyers and makes the competitor's introduction more difficult.

Premiums   A promotion tool often used with consumers is the premium, which consists of merchandise offered free or at a significant savings over its retail price. This latter type of premium is called self-liquidating because the cost charged to the consumer covers the cost of the item. McDonald's, for example, used a free premium in a promotional partnership with Illumination Entertainment during the release of the movie *Minions*. Collectible toys that portrayed movie characters were given away free with the purchase of a Happy Meal. What are the most popular premiums? According to the Promotional Products Association International, the top premiums are apparel, writing instruments, shopping bags, cups and mugs, and desk accessories. By offering a premium, companies encourage customers to return frequently or to use more of the product. Research suggests that deal-prone consumers and value seekers are attracted to premiums.[57]

Contests   As shown in Figure 18–6, contests are another sales promotion tool used with consumers. Contests encourage consumers to apply their skill or analytical or creative thinking to try to win a prize. This form of promotion has been growing as requests for videos, photos, and essays are a good match with the trend toward consumer-generated content. For example, Doritos sponsors the "Crash the Super Bowl" ad contest, asking people to create their own 30-second ad about Doritos. A panel of judges then selects the finalists, posts the submissions on the Doritos Facebook Page, and opens up voting by the public. The winner is aired during the Super Bowl and is awarded a $1 million prize! If you like contests, you can enter online now at websites such as www.contests.about.com.[58]

McDonald's Monopoly sweepstakes offers a grand prize of $1 million.

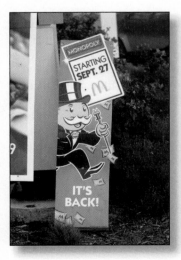

Sweepstakes   Sweepstakes are sales promotions that require participants to submit some kind of entry but are purely games of chance requiring no analytical or creative effort by the consumer. Popular sweepstakes include the HGTV "Dream Home Giveaway," which receives more than 90 million entries each year, and McDonald's Monopoly, which offers a grand prize of $1 million.[59]

Two variations of sweepstakes are popular now. First are sweepstakes that offer products that consumers value as prizes. Mars Chocolate, for example, created a sweepstakes where consumers enter a UPC code from M&M's products for a chance to win one of five Toyota automobiles. Coca-Cola has a similar sweepstakes called "My Coke Rewards" that allows consumers to use codes from bottle caps to enter to win prizes or to collect points to be redeemed for rewards.

The second type of sweepstakes offers an "experience" as the prize. For example, one of television's most popular series, *The Voice,* and Nissan sponsored a sweepstakes for a chance to win a trip for two to the season finale of *The Voice* in Los Angeles. Similarly, StumbleUpon and the Academy of Motion Picture Arts and Sciences created a sweepstakes where consumers entered for a chance to win a trip to the Oscars in Hollywood.

Federal laws, the Federal Trade Commission, and state legislatures have issued rules covering sweepstakes, contests, and games to regulate fairness, ensure that the chance for winning is represented honestly, and guarantee that the prizes are actually

Ben & Jerry's free samples encourage customers to try new flavors, while the Plenti loyalty program rewards frequent customers at participating businesses.

Sources: Left: Ben & Jerry's Homemade Inc.; Right: Plenti

awarded. Several well-known sweepstakes created by Publishers Clearing House and *Reader's Digest* have paid fines and agreed to new sweepstakes guidelines in response to regulatory scrutiny.[60]

Samples   Another common consumer sales promotion is sampling, which is offering the product free or at a greatly reduced price. Often used for new products, sampling puts the product in the consumer's hands. A trial size is generally offered that is smaller than the regular package size. If consumers like the sample, it is hoped they will remember and buy the product. Taco Bell has offered free tacos nationwide several times in the past to encourage customers to try new products. Recently, Taco Bell gave away 1,000,000 free Doritos Locos tacos to guests who placed orders on its mobile ordering app. The taco has become the company's most successful new product. Similarly, Ben & Jerry's offers a complimentary scoop of ice cream on "Free Cone Day." Some consumers watch for free samples online at sites such as www. startsampling.com. According to Stacy Fisher, who started trying free samples in college and now blogs about them, free samples are "a great way to try new things and save money."[61]

Loyalty Programs   Loyalty programs are a sales promotion tool used to encourage and reward repeat purchases by acknowledging each purchase made by a consumer and offering a premium as purchases accumulate. The most popular loyalty programs today are credit card reward programs. More than 75 percent of all cards offer incentives for use of their card. Citibank, for example, offers "Thank You" points for using Citi credit or debit cards. The points can be redeemed for books, music, gift cards, cash, travel, and special limited time rewards. Airlines, retailers, hotels, and grocery stores also offer popular loyalty programs. Specialty retailers such as Toys 'Я' Us and Best Buy have enhanced their reward programs to add value to their offerings as they compete with low-cost merchandise. A new rewards program, called Plenti, lets you earn points with several stores and businesses such as Macy's, Mobile, and Rite Aid. There are now more than 3.3 billion loyalty program memberships, for an average of 29 for each household in the United States, with point balances exceeding $50 billion.[62]

One trend in loyalty programs today is to customize the rewards and benefits for different segments of program members. This approach leads to promotions targeted at

Point-of-purchase displays help increase consumers' attention in a store.

© *McGraw-Hill Education/Mark Dierker, photographer*

new members, members with unique purchase histories, or members who have self-selected into "elite" status groups. American Airlines, for example, has offered bonus points for new members, an additional 50 percent of award points for members who fly first class, and special benefits for members who join the American Airlines Admirals Club. Another trend is the shift from programs where points and rewards can be earned from only one operator to an "open economy" for loyalty where points and rewards can be earned from many interchangeable programs. An example of a program moving in this direction is the Chase Ultimate Rewards program, which was recently rated highest in terms of overall customer satisfaction.[63]

Point-of-Purchase Displays   In a store aisle, you often encounter a sales promotion called a point-of-purchase display. These product displays take the form of advertising signs, which sometimes actually hold or display the product, and are often located in high-traffic areas near the cash register or the end of an aisle. The point-of-purchase display for the movie *Insurgent* is designed to maximize the consumer's attention to a DVD release and provide storage for the products. Annual expenditures on point-of-purchase promotions now exceed $20.3 billion and are expected to grow as point-of-purchase becomes integrated with all forms of promotion.

Some studies estimate that one-third of a consumer's buying decisions are made in the store. Grocery product manufacturers want to get their message to you at the instant you are next to their brand in your supermarket aisle, perhaps through a point-of-purchase display. At a growing number of supermarkets, this may be done with digital signage. Walmart, for example, is replacing its satellite-based in-store TV network with an Internet protocol system called Walmart Smart Network, which includes welcome screens, category screens, and "endcap" screens that display information about product categories, brands, and new products, respectively. The advantage of these methods of promotion is that they do not rely on the consumers' ability to remember the message for long periods. Other in-store promotions such as interactive kiosks are also becoming popular.[64]

Rebates   Another consumer sales promotion tool in Figure 18–6, the cash rebate, offers the return of money based on proof of purchase. For example, Virgin Mobile recently offered a $100 rebate to T-Mobile subscribers who switched their service during a seven-week period. When a rebate is offered on lower-priced items, the time and trouble of mailing in a proof of purchase to get the rebate check often means that many buyers never take advantage of it. However, this "slippage" is less likely to occur with frequent users of rebate promotions. In addition, online consumers are more likely to take advantage of rebates.[65]

Product Placements   A final consumer promotion tool, **product placement**, involves the use of a brand-name product in a movie, television show, video game, or commercial for another product. It was Steven Spielberg's placement of Hershey's Reese's Pieces in *E.T. the Extra Terrestrial* that first brought a lot of interest to the candy. Similarly, when Tom Cruise wore Bausch and Lomb's Ray-Ban sunglasses in *Risky Business* and its Aviator glasses in *Top Gun,* sales skyrocketed from 100,000 pairs to 7,000,000 pairs in five years. After *Toy Story,* Etch-A-Sketch sales increased 4,500 percent and Mr. Potato Head sales increased 800 percent.

More recently you might remember seeing products from Beats by Dre, Coca-Cola, Mercedes-Benz, and Starbuck in *Jurassic World;* N. Peal (sweaters), Range Rover, and Aston Martin in the James Bond movie *Spectre;* and Levis, Audi, and Under Armour in *Avengers: Age of Ultron.* Which brand has the highest level of product placement in film? It's Apple with placement in 9 of 35 top films, beating out Sony and Coca-Cola.

Product placement can take many forms today. Are you familiar with these examples?

Sources: Left: © AF archive/ Alamy; Middle: © Film Fanatique/ Alamy; Right: © Staples/ Newscom

The annual value of all product placements is estimated to be $6 billion. Complaints that product placement has become excessive have led the Federal Communications Commission to begin developing guidelines for TV product placements. Meanwhile, the British government recently passed a law allowing product placement only if a bold "P" logo is shown before and after the program. Research suggests that a product placement disclosure such as this may lead to less favorable attitudes toward the products.[66]

New forms of product placement may appear to be integrated into the program. An episode of *Modern Family,* for example, includes a scene in an Apple store. Some programs have recently begun digital product placement in programs after they have been filmed. Similarly, some companies such as Amway are creating partnerships with game developers in order to be included in video games, which can be effective if competing products are not also in the game. A variation of product placement, called *reverse product placement,* brings fictional products to the marketplace. Bertie Bott's Every Flavour Beans, for example, began as an imaginary brand in Harry Potter books. Similarly, the movie *Forrest Gump* led to the Bubba Gump Shrimp Company restaurant chain. And fans of *The Office* can purchase Dunder Mifflin office supplies from www.quill.com![67]

Trade-Oriented Sales Promotions

Trade-oriented sales promotions, or simply *trade promotions,* are sales tools used to support a company's advertising and personal selling directed to wholesalers, retailers, or distributors. Some of the sales promotions just reviewed are used for this purpose, but three other common approaches are targeted uniquely to these intermediaries: (1) allowances and discounts, (2) cooperative advertising, and (3) training of distributors' salesforces.

Allowances and Discounts   Trade promotions often focus on maintaining or increasing inventory levels in the channel of distribution. An effective method for encouraging such increased purchases by intermediaries is the use of allowances and discounts. However, overuse of these price reductions can lead to retailers changing their ordering patterns in the expectation of such offerings. Although there are many variations that manufacturers can use with discounts and allowances, three common approaches are the merchandise allowance, the case allowance, and the finance allowance.[68]

Reimbursing a retailer for extra in-store support or special featuring of the brand is a *merchandise allowance*. Performance contracts between the manufacturer and trade member usually specify the activity to be performed, such as a picture of the product in a newspaper with a coupon good at only one store. The merchandise allowance then consists of a percentage deduction from the list case price ordered during the promotional period. Allowances are not paid by the manufacturer until it sees proof of performance (such as a copy of the ad placed by the retailer in the local newspaper).

A second common trade promotion, a *case allowance,* is a discount on each case ordered during a specific time period. These allowances are usually deducted from the invoice. A variation of the case allowance is the "free goods" approach, whereby retailers receive some amount of the product free based on the amount ordered, such as 1 case free for every 10 cases ordered.[69]

A final trade promotion, the *finance allowance,* involves paying retailers for financing costs or financial losses associated with consumer sales promotions. This trade promotion is regularly used and has several variations. One type is the floor stock protection program—manufacturers give retailers a case allowance price for products in their warehouse, which prevents shelf stock from running down during the promotional period. Also common are freight allowances, which compensate retailers that transport orders from the manufacturer's warehouse.

Cooperative Advertising Resellers often perform the important function of promoting the manufacturer's products at the local level. One common sales promotional activity is to encourage both better quality and greater quantity in the local advertising efforts of resellers through **cooperative advertising**. These are programs by which a manufacturer pays a percentage of the retailer's local advertising expense for advertising the manufacturer's products.

Usually, the manufacturer pays a percentage, often 50 percent, of the cost of advertising up to a certain dollar limit, which is based on the amount of the manufacturer's products purchased by the retailer. In addition to paying for the advertising, the manufacturer often furnishes the retailer with a selection of different ad executions, sometimes suited for several different media. A manufacturer may provide, for example, several different print layouts as well as a few broadcast ads for the retailer to adapt and use.[70]

Training of Distributors' Salesforces One of the many functions the intermediaries perform is customer contact and selling for the producers they represent. Both retailers and wholesalers employ and manage their own sales personnel. A manufacturer's success often rests on the ability of the reseller's salesforce to represent its products. Thus, it is in the best interest of the manufacturer to help train the reseller's salesforce.

Because the reseller's salesforce is often less sophisticated and knowledgeable about the products than the manufacturer might like, training can increase their sales performance. Training activities include producing manuals and brochures to educate the reseller's salesforce. The salesforce then uses these aids in selling situations. Other activities include national sales meetings sponsored by the manufacturer and field visits to the reseller's location to inform and motivate the salesperson to sell the products. Manufacturers also develop incentive and recognition programs to motivate a reseller's salespeople to sell their products.

learning review »

18-10. What is the difference between a coupon and a deal?

18-11. Which sales promotion tool is most common for new products?

18-12. Which trade promotion approach focuses on maintaining or increasing inventory levels?

PUBLIC RELATIONS

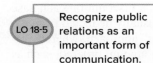

LO 18-5 Recognize public relations as an important form of communication.

As noted in Chapter 17, public relations is a form of communications management that seeks to influence the image of an organization and its products and services. Public relations efforts may utilize a variety of tools and may be directed at many distinct audiences. While public relations personnel usually focus on communicating positive aspects of the business, they may also be called on to minimize the negative impact of a problem or crisis. Carnival Cruises, BP, and Goldman Sachs, for example, faced substantial negative publicity for passengers stranded on disabled ships, the worst oil spill in U.S. history, and securities fraud charges, respectively.[71] The most frequently used public relations tool is publicity.

Publicity Tools

In developing a public relations campaign, several methods of obtaining nonpersonal presentation of an organization, product, or service without direct cost—**publicity tools**—are available to the public relations director. Many companies frequently use the *news release,* consisting of an announcement regarding changes in the company or the product line. The objective of a news release is to inform a newspaper, radio station, or other medium of an idea for a story.

Cameron Diaz receives publicity for her movies by visiting programs such as *The Tonight Show Starring Jimmy Fallon.*
© Mike Coppola/NBC/Getty Images

A second common publicity tool is the *news conference.* Representatives of the media are all invited to an informational meeting, and advance materials regarding the content are sent. This tool is often used when new products are introduced or significant changes in corporate structure and leadership are being made.

Nonprofit organizations rely heavily on *public service announcements (PSAs),* which are free space or time donated by the media. For example, the charter of the American Red Cross prohibits any local chapter from advertising, so to solicit blood donations local chapters often depend on PSAs on radio or television to announce their needs.

Finally, today many high-visibility individuals are used as publicity tools to create visibility for their companies, their products, and themselves. Richard Branson uses visibility to promote the Virgin Group, Cameron Diaz uses it to promote her movies, and U.S. senators use it to promote themselves as political candidates. These publicity efforts are coordinated with news releases, conferences, advertising, donations to charities, volunteer activities, endorsements, and any other activities that may have an impact on public perceptions.[72]

INCREASING THE VALUE OF PROMOTION

Today's customers seek value from companies that provide leading-edge products, hassle-free transactions at competitive prices, and customer intimacy.[73] Promotion practices have changed dramatically to improve transactions and increase customer intimacy by (1) emphasizing long-term relationships and (2) increasing self-regulation.

Building Long-Term Relationships

Many changes in promotional techniques have been driven by marketers' interest in developing long-term relationships with their customers. Promotion can contribute to brand and store loyalty by improving a company's ability to target individual preferences and by engaging customers in valuable and entertaining communication. New social and mobile media have provided immediate opportunities for personalized promotion activities. In addition, technological developments have helped traditional media such as TV and radio focus on individual preferences through services such as Android TV and SiriusXM Satellite Radio. Although the future holds extraordinary promise for the personalization of promotion, the industry will need to manage and balance consumers' concerns about privacy as it proceeds.

Changes that help engage consumers have also been numerous. Marketers have attempted to utilize interactive technologies and to integrate new media and technologies into the overall creative process. Ad agencies are increasingly integrating public relations, direct marketing, advertising, and sales promotion into comprehensive IMC campaigns. In fact, some experts predict that advertising agencies will soon become "communications consulting firms." Further, increasingly diverse and global audiences necessitate multimedia approaches and sensitivity communication techniques that engage the varied groups.[74] Overall, companies hope that these changes will build customer relationships for the long term—emphasizing a lifetime of purchases rather than a single transaction.

Self-Regulation

Unfortunately, over the years, many consumers have been misled, or even deceived, by some promotions. Examples include sweepstakes in which the gifts were not awarded, rebate offers that were a terrible hassle, and advertisements whose promises were great, until the buyer read the small print. In one of the worst scandals in promotion history, McDonald's assisted an FBI investigation of the firm responsible for the fast-food chain's sweepstakes because the promotion agency security director was suspected of stealing winning game pieces.[75]

Promotions targeted at special groups such as children and the elderly also raise ethical concerns. For example, providing free samples to children in elementary schools or linking product lines to TV programs and movies has led to questions about the need for restrictions on promotions.[76] Although the Federal Trade Commission (FTC) does provide some guidelines to protect consumers and special groups from misleading promotions, some observers believe more government regulation is needed.

Formal regulation of all promotional activities by federal, state, and local governments would be very expensive. As a result, advertising agencies, trade associations, and marketing organizations are increasing their efforts toward *self-regulation*.[77] By imposing standards that reflect the values of society on their promotional activities, marketers can (1) facilitate the development of new promotional methods, (2) minimize regulatory constraints and restrictions, and (3) help consumers gain confidence in the communication efforts used to influence their purchases. As organizations strive for effective self-regulation, marketing executives will need to make sound ethical judgments about the use of existing and new promotional practices.

learning review »

18-13. What is a news release?

18-14. What is the difference between government regulation and self-regulation?

LO 18-1 *Explain the differences between product advertising and institutional advertising and the variations within each type.*

Product advertisements focus on selling a good or service and take three forms: Pioneering advertisements tell people what a product is, what it can do, and where it can be found; competitive advertisements persuade the target market to select the firm's brand rather than a competitor's; and reminder advertisements reinforce previous knowledge of a product. Institutional advertisements are used to build goodwill or an image for an organization. They include advocacy advertisements, which state the position of a company on an issue, and pioneering, competitive, and reminder advertisements, which are similar to the product ads but focused on the institution.

LO 18-2 *Describe the steps used to develop, execute, and evaluate an advertising program.*

The promotion decision process can be applied to each of the promotional elements. The steps to develop an advertising program include the following: identify the target audience, specify the advertising objectives, set the advertising budget, design the advertisement, create the message, select the media, and schedule the advertising. Executing the program requires pretesting, and evaluating the program requires posttesting.

LO 18-3 *Explain the advantages and disadvantages of alternative advertising media.*

Television advertising reaches large audiences and uses picture, print, sound, and motion; its disadvantages, however, are that it is expensive and perishable. Radio advertising is inexpensive and can be placed quickly, but it has no visual element and is perishable. Magazine advertising can target specific audiences and can convey complex information, but it takes a long time to place the ad and is relatively expensive. Newspapers provide excellent coverage of local markets and can be changed quickly, but they have a short life span and poor color.

Yellow pages advertising has a long use period and is available 24 hours per day; its disadvantages, however, are that there is a proliferation of directories and they cannot be updated frequently. Internet advertising can be interactive, but its effectiveness is difficult to measure. Outdoor advertising provides repeat exposures, but its message must be very short and simple. Direct mail can be targeted at very selective audiences, but its cost per contact is high.

LO 18-4 *Discuss the strengths and weaknesses of consumer-oriented and trade-oriented sales promotions.*

Coupons encourage retailer support but may delay consumer purchases. Deals reduce consumer risk but also reduce perceived value. Premiums offer consumers additional merchandise they want, but they may be purchasing only for the premium. Contests create involvement but require creative thinking. Sweepstakes encourage repeat purchases, but sales drop after the sweepstakes. Samples encourage product trial but are expensive. Loyalty programs help create loyalty but are expensive to run. Displays provide visibility but are difficult to place in retail space. Rebates stimulate demand but are easily copied. Product placements provide a positive message in a noncommercial setting that is difficult to control. Trade-oriented sales promotions include (*a*) allowances and discounts, which increase purchases but may change retailer ordering patterns, (*b*) cooperative advertising, which encourages local advertising, and (*c*) salesforce training, which helps increase sales by providing the salespeople with product information and selling skills.

LO 18-5 *Recognize public relations as an important form of communication.*

Public relations activities usually focus on communicating positive aspects of the business. A frequently used public relations tool is publicity. Publicity tools include news releases and news conferences. Nonprofit organizations often use public service announcements.

18-1 **What is the difference between pioneering and competitive ads?**

Answer: Pioneering (or informational) ads, used in the introductory stage of the product life cycle, tell people what a product is, what it can do, and where it can be found. The key objective of a pioneering ad is to inform the target market. Competitive (or persuasive) ads promote a specific brand's features and benefits to persuade the target market to select the firm's brand rather than that of a competitor. A form of a competitive ad is the comparative ad that shows one brand's strengths relative to those of competitors.

18-2 **What is the purpose of an institutional advertisement?**

Answer: The purpose of an institutional advertisement is to build goodwill or an image for an organization rather than a specific offering. This form of advertising is often used to support the public relations plan or counter adverse publicity.

18-3 **What other decisions can advertising objectives influence?**

Answer: Advertising objectives can influence decisions such as selecting media and evaluating an advertising campaign.

18-4 **What is a potential shortcoming of using a celebrity spokesperson?**

Answer: The spokesperson's image may change to be inconsistent with the image of the company or brand.

18-5 **You see the same ad in *Time* and *Fortune* magazines and on billboards and TV. Is this an example of reach or frequency?**

Answer: This is an example of frequency—reaching the same audience more than once.

18-6   Why has the Internet become a popular advertising medium?

Answer: The Internet offers a visual message, can use both audio and video, is interactive through rich media, and tends to reach younger consumers.

18-7   What factors must be considered when choosing among alternative media?

Answer: Choosing among alternative media depends on: knowing the media habits of the target audience; understanding the product's attributes (such as color), the competitive situation, and the need for a complicated message; and the cost, as measured by CPM.

18-8   Explain the difference between pretesting and posttesting advertising copy.

Answer: Pretests are conducted before ads are placed in any medium to determine whether they communicate the intended message or to select among alternative versions of the ad. Posttests are conducted after the ads are shown to the target audience to determine whether they accomplished their intended purpose.

18-9   What is the difference between aided and unaided recall posttests?

Answer: Aided and unaided recall posttests are conducted after the ads are shown to the target audience. Aided recall involves showing an ad to respondents who then are asked if their previous exposure to it was through reading, viewing, or listening. Aided recall is used to determine the percentage of those (1) who remember seeing a specific magazine ad (noted), (2) who saw or read any part of the ad identifying the product or brand (seen-associated), (3) who read any part of the ad's copy (read some), and (4) who read at least half of the ad (read most). Unaided recall involves specifically asking respondents if they remember an ad without any prompting to determine if they saw or heard its message.

18-10   What is the difference between a coupon and a deal?

Answer: Coupons and deals are consumer-oriented sales promotion tools used to support a company's advertising and personal selling. A coupon usually offers a discounted price to encourage trial. A deal is a short-term price reduction used to increase trial among potential customers or to retaliate against a competitor's actions.

18-11   Which sales promotion tool is most common for new products?

Answer: A product sample (or sampling) is a consumer-oriented sales promotion tool that is given to consumers through the use of a trial-size package, which is generally smaller than the regular size.

18-12   Which trade promotion approach focuses on maintaining or increasing inventory levels?

Answer: Allowances and discounts encourage increased purchases by intermediaries to maintain or increase inventory levels in the channel of distribution.

18-13   What is a news release?

Answer: A news release is a publicity tool that consists of an announcement regarding changes in the company or the product line to inform the media of an idea for a story.

18-14   What is the difference between government regulation and self-regulation?

Answer: Government regulation involves laws or other controls that are set by an agency of local, state, or federal government and restrict some promotion activities. The Federal Trade Commission (FTC) issues guidelines to protect consumers from misleading promotions. Self-regulation involves imposing standards and ethical guidelines for the promotional activities of advertising agencies, trade associations, and marketing organizations that reflect the values of society.

FOCUSING ON KEY TERMS

advertising p. 500
consumer-oriented sales
    promotions p. 519
cooperative advertising p. 525
cost per thousand (CPM) p. 508
frequency p. 508
full-service agency p. 517

gross rating points (GRPs) p. 508
infomercials p. 510
in-house agencies p. 518
institutional advertisements p. 501
limited-service agencies p. 517
mobile marketing p. 513
posttests p. 518

pretests p. 516
product advertisements p. 500
product placement p. 523
publicity tools p. 526
rating p. 508
reach p. 507
trade-oriented sales promotions p. 524

APPLYING MARKETING KNOWLEDGE

1   How does competitive product advertising differ from competitive institutional advertising?

2   Suppose you are the advertising manager for a new line of children's fragrances. Which form of media would you use for this new product?

3   You have recently been promoted to be director of advertising for the Timkin Tool Company. In your first meeting with Mr. Timkin, he says, "Advertising is a waste! We've been advertising for six months now and sales haven't increased. Tell me why we should continue." Give your answer to Mr. Timkin.

4   A large life insurance company has decided to switch from using a strong fear appeal to a humorous approach. What are the strengths and weaknesses of such a change in message strategy?

5   Some national advertisers have found that they can have more impact with their advertising by running a large number of ads for a period and then running no ads at all for a period. Why might such a flighting schedule be more effective than a continuous schedule?

6 Which medium has the lowest cost per thousand (CPM)?

Medium	Cost of Ad	Audience Size
TV show	$5,000	25,000
Magazine	2,200	6,000
Newspaper	4,800	7,200
FM radio	420	1,600

7 Each year, managers at Bausch and Lomb evaluate the many advertising media alternatives available to them as they develop their advertising program for contact lenses. What advantages and disadvantages of each alternative should they consider? Which media would you recommend to them?

8 What are two advantages and two disadvantages of the advertising posttests described in the chapter?

9 Federated Banks is interested in consumer-oriented sales promotions that would encourage senior citizens to direct deposit their Social Security checks with the bank. Evaluate the sales promotion options, and recommend two of them to the bank.

10 How can public relations be used by Firestone and Ford following investigations into complaints about tire failures?

11 Describe a self-regulation guideline you believe would improve the value of (*a*) an existing form of promotion and (*b*) a new promotional practice.

BUILDING YOUR MARKETING PLAN

To augment your promotion strategy from Chapter 17:
1 Use Figure 18–3 to select the advertising media you will include in your plan by analyzing how combinations of media (e.g., television and Internet advertising, radio and yellow pages advertising) can complement each other.

2 Use Figure 18–6 to select your consumer-oriented sales promotion activities.
3 Specify which trade-oriented sales promotions and public relations tools you will use.

🔲 connect·

VIDEO CASE 18   Google, Inc.: The Right Ads at the Right Time

"So what we did, in essence, is we said advertising should be useful to a consumer just as much as the organic search results, and we don't want people just to buy advertising and be able to show an ad if it's irrelevant to the consumer's need," says Richard Holden, director of product management at Google. To accomplish this, Google developed a "Quality Score" model to predict how effective an ad will be. The model uses many factors such as click-through rates, advertiser history, and keyword performance to develop a score for each advertisement. "Essentially, what we're trying to do is predict ahead, before we actually show an ad, how a consumer will react to that ad, and our interest is in showing fewer ads, not more ads; just the right ads at the right time," Holden continues. The Google advertising model has revolutionized the advertising industry, and it continues to improve every day!

Video 18-6

Google Video Case

kerin.tv/13e/v18-6

© Justin Sullivan/Getty Images

THE COMPANY

Google began in 1996 as a research project for Stanford computer science students Larry Page and Sergey Brin. They started with a simple idea—that a search engine based on the relationships between websites would provide a better ranking than a search engine based only on the number of times a key term appeared on a website. The success of their model led to rapid growth, and the founders moved the company from their dorm room, to a friend's garage, to offices in Palo Alto,

California, and eventually to its current location, known as the Googleplex, in Mountain View, California. In 2000, Google began selling advertising as a means of generating revenue. Its advertising model allowed advertisers to bid on search words and pay for each "click" by a search-engine user. The ads were required to be simple and text-based so that the search result pages remained uncluttered and the search time was as fast as possible.

Page and Brin's first search engine was called "Back-Rub" because their technique was based on relationships, or backlinks, between websites. The name quickly changed, however. The name "Google" is a misspelling of the word "googol," which is a mathematical term for a 1 followed by 100 zeros. Page and Brin used the name in the original domain, www.google.stanford.edu, to reflect their interest in organizing the immense amount of information available on the Web. The domain name, of course, became www.google.com and eventually Webster's dictionary added the verb "google" with the definition "to use the Google search engine to obtain information on the Internet." The name has become so familiar that *Advertising Age* recently reported that Google is "the world's most powerful brand"!

Today, Google receives several hundred million inquiries each day as it pursues its mission: to organize the world's information and make it universally accessible and useful. The company generates more than $21 billion in annual revenue and has more than 20,000 employees. As Google has grown, it has developed 10 guidelines that represent the corporate philosophy. They are:

1. Focus on the user and all else will follow.
2. It's best to do one thing really, really well.
3. Fast is better than slow.
4. Democracy on the Web works.
5. You don't need to be at your desk to need an answer.
6. You can make money without doing evil.
7. There's always more information out there.
8. The need for information crosses all borders.
9. You can be serious without a suit.
10. Great just isn't good enough.

Using these guidelines, Google strives to continually improve its search engine. "The perfect search engine," explains Google cofounder Larry Page, "would understand exactly what you mean and give back exactly what you want."

ONLINE ADVERTISING

Google generates revenue by offering online advertising opportunities—next to search results or on specific web pages. The company always distinguishes ads from the search results or the content of a web page and it never sells placement in the search results. This approach ensures that Google website visitors always know when someone has paid to put a message in front of them. The advantage of online advertising is that it is measurable and allows immediate assessment of its effectiveness. As Gopi Kallayil, product marketing manager, explains: "There is a very high degree of measurability and trackability that you get through online advertising." In addition, he says, "With online advertising you can actually track the value of every single dollar that you spend, understand which particular customers the ad reached, and what they did after they received the advertising message."

The online advertising market has grown from its initial focus on simple text ads to a much larger set of options. There are five key categories of online advertising. They are:

- Search: 47%
- Display: 35%
- Classified: 10%
- Referral: 7%
- E-mail: 1%

Google is the dominant provider of online search requests and receives more than 60 percent of the search advertising revenue. The fastest-growing advertising category, however, is display advertising, where Yahoo! and Microsoft are established providers. Google believes that there is an opportunity to grow its display advertising sales by making the ads useful information instead of visual clutter. According to Google cofounder Sergey Brin, "It's like search-matching people with information they want. It just happens to be promotional."

Several improvements in technology and business practice tools contributed to Google's success. First, Google developed its patented PageRank™ algorithm, which evaluates the entire link structure of the Web and uses the link structure to determine which pages are most important. Then the process uses hypertext-matching analysis to determine which pages are relevant to a specific search. A combination of the importance and the relevance of web pages provides the search results—in just a fraction of a second. Second, Google developed two business practice tools—AdWords and AdSense—to help (1) advertisers create ads, and (2) content providers generate advertising revenue. Both tools have become essential elements of Google's advertising model.

AdWords

To help advertisers place ads on their search-engine results, Google developed an online tool called

AdWords. Advertisers can use AdWords to create ad text, select target keywords, and manage their account. The process allows advertisers to reach targeted audiences. Frederick Vallaeys, AdWords evangelist, explains: "One of my favorite things about AdWords is the fact that it really helps you find the right customer at the right time and show them the right message. With AdWords you can very specifically target your market because you're targeting them at a time when they do a search on Google. At that time they've told you a keyword, you know exactly what they're looking for, and here is your opportunity as a marketer to give them the exact answer to what they've just told you they wanted to find." Google has found that text ads that are relevant to the person reading them have much higher response ("click-through") rates than ads that are not targeted.

AdWords is also easy for any advertiser to use. Large or small businesses can simply open an account with a credit card and have ads appear within minutes. "When AdWords rolled out their self-service product, it really was one of the first times when it was very easy for a small business to put their ad up on the Internet on a search engine and compete on a level playing field alongside *Fortune* 1000 companies," says Vallaeys. Google has an experienced sales and service team available to help any advertiser select appropriate keywords, generate ad copy, and monitor campaign performance. The team is dedicated to helping its advertisers improve click-through rates because high click-through rates are an indication that ads are relevant to a user's interests. Methods of improving advertising performance include changing the keywords and rewriting copy. Because there is no limit to the number of keywords that an advertiser can select and each keyword can be matched with different ad copy, the potential for many very customer-specific options is high.

Another advantage of Google's AdWords program is that it allows advertisers to easily control costs. The ads appear as a "Sponsored Link" next to search results each time the Google search engine matches the search request with the ad's keywords and Quality Score, although the advertiser is not charged unless someone "clicks" on the link. In a traditional advertising model, advertisers were charged using a CPM (cost-per-thousand) approach, which charged for the impressions made by an ad. According to Holden, the Google model "transformed that to what we call a CPC, or a cost-per-click model, and this is a model that an advertiser, instead of paying for an impression, only pays when somebody actually clicks on that ad and is delivered to their website. So, in effect, they may be getting the benefit from impressions being shown, but we're not actually charging them anything unless there's a definite lead being delivered to their website." Google also offers advertisers real-time analytical services to allow assessment of and changes to any component of an advertising campaign.

AdSense

The AdSense program was designed for website owners as a tool for placing ads next to their web page content rather than next to search results. Currently, thousands of website managers use AdSense to place ads on their sites and generate revenue. Google applies the same general philosophy to matching ads with websites as it does to matching ads to search requests. By delivering ads that precisely target the content on the site's pages, Google believes the advertising enhances the experience for visitors to the website. In this way advertisers, website publishers, and information seekers all benefit.

AdSense is one of the tools Google is using to pursue its goal of increasing its display advertising business. Yahoo! and Microsoft's Bing are leaders in display advertising because they can put ads on their own websites such as Yahoo! Finance and MSN Money. To provide additional outlets for display ads, Google recently purchased YouTube. In addition, Google purchased DoubleClick, an advertising exchange where websites put space up for auction and ad agencies bid to place ads for their clients. Google is also trying to make it easy for anyone to create a display ad by introducing a new tool called Display Ad Builder. Some experts observe that because Google is so dominant at search advertising, its future growth will depend on success in display advertising.

GOOGLE'S FUTURE STRATEGY

How will Google continue its success? One possibility is that it will begin to try to win advertising away from the U.S. TV industry. While this is a new type of advertising requiring creative capabilities and relationships with large advertising agencies, Google has dedicated many of its resources to becoming competitive for television advertising expenditures. For example, Google recently helped Volvo develop a campaign that included a YouTube ad and Twitter updates. Google is also likely to develop new websites, establish blogs, and build relationships with existing sites.

Another opportunity for Google will be mobile telephone advertising. There are currently more than 5.4 billion mobile phones in use, and 1.9 billion of those are Internet-capable. Just as Google's search engine provides a means to match relevant information with consumers, phones offer a chance to provide real-time and location-specific information. Some of the challenges in mobile advertising will be that the networks are not fast and that the ad formats are not standardized. Google believes its new phone and its Android operating system will also help.

Finally, as Google pursues its mission it will continue to expand throughout the world. Search results are already available in more than 40 languages, and volunteers are helping with many others. It is obvious that Google is determined to "organize the world's information" and make it "accessible and useful."[78]

Questions

1 Describe several unique characteristics about Google and its business practices.
2 What is Google's philosophy about advertising? How can less advertising be preferred to more advertising?
3 Describe the types of online advertising available today. Which type of advertising does Google currently dominate? Why?
4 How can Google be successful in the display advertising business? What other areas of growth are likely to be pursued by Google in the future?

Chapter Notes

1. Dan Kedmey, "Virtually Real," *Time,* February 9, 2015, p. 12; Maria Minsker, "Facebook Gets Real about Virtual Reality," *Customer Relationship Management,* March 2015, p. 16; Michelle Castillo, "How Virtual Reality Could Revolutionize Ads in the Sports Industry," *Adweek,* May 22, 2015, p. 1; Rae Ann Fera, "Get the Most Out of VR," *Marketing Magazine,* January 2015, p. 18; Ann-Christine Diaz, "Grab Your Headset: Producer Plunge into Virtual Reality," *Advertising Age,* February 9, 2015, p. 26; Madeline Berg, "From HDR to Virtual Reality: Inside the Future of Entertainment," *Forbes.com,* June 10, 2015; and John Gaudiosi, "How Augmented Reality and Virtual Reality Will Generate $150 Billion in Revenue by 2020," *Fortune.com,* April 29, 2015.

2. Karen V. Fernandez and Dennis L. Rosen, "The Effectiveness of Information and Color in Yellow Pages Advertising," *Journal of Advertising,* Summer 2000, p. 61; David A. Aaker and Donald Norris, "Characteristics of TV Commercials Perceived as Informative," *Journal of Advertising Research* 22, no. 2 (April–May 1982), pp. 61–70.

3. Larry D. Compeau and Dhruv Grewal, "Comparative Price Advertising: An Integrative Review," *Journal of Public Policy & Marketing,* Fall 1998, pp. 257–73; and William Wilkie and Paul W. Farris, "Comparison Advertising: Problems and Potentials," *Journal of Marketing,* October 1975, pp. 7–15.

4. Chingching Chang, "The Relative Effectiveness of Comparative and Noncomparative Advertising: Evidence for Gender Differences in Information-Processing Strategies," *Journal of Advertising,* Spring 2007, p. 21; Jerry Gotlieb and Dan Sarel, "The Influence of Type of Advertisement, Price, and Source Credibility on Perceived Quality," *Journal of the Academy of Marketing Science,* Summer 1992, pp. 253–60; and Cornelia Pechmann and David Stewart, "The Effects of Comparative Advertising on Attention, Memory, and Purchase Intentions," *Journal of Consumer Research,* September 1990, pp. 180–92.

5. Kathy L. O'Malley, Jeffrey J. Bailey, Chong Leng Tan, and Carl S. Bozman, "Effects of Varying Web-Based Advertising-Substantiation Information on Attribute Beliefs and Perceived Product Quality," *Academy of Marketing Studies Journal,* 2007, p. 19; Bruce Buchanan and Doron Goldman, "Us vs. Them: The Minefield of Comparative Ads," *Harvard Business Review,* May–June 1989, pp. 38–50; Dorothy Cohen, "The FTC's Advertising Substantiation Program," *Journal of Marketing,* Winter 1980, pp. 26–35; and Michael Etgar and Stephen A. Goodwin, "Planning for Comparative Advertising Requires Special Attention," *Journal of Advertising* 8, no. 1 (Winter 1979), pp. 26–32.

6. David W. Schumann, Jan M. Hathcote, and Susan West, "Corporate Advertising in America: A Review of Published Studies on Use, Measurement, and Effectiveness," *Journal of Advertising,* September 1991, p. 35; Lewis C. Winters, "Does It Pay to Advertise in Hostile Audiences with Corporate Advertising?" *Journal of Advertising Research,* June–July 1988, pp. 11–18; and Robert Selwitz, "The Selling of an Image," *Madison Avenue,* February 1985, pp. 61–69.

7. Ashley Ross, "Why Models Are Addicted to This Fitness Trend," *Time.com,* May 7, 2015; Andrew Adam Newman, "Under Armour Heads Off the Sidelines for a Campaign Aimed at Women," *The New York Times,* July 31, 2014, p. 3; Jeanine Poggi, "'GMA' Blurs Line with Under Armour Segment," *Advertising Age,* September 15, 2014, p. 8; Eliana Dockterman, "Under Armour's Stunning Ballerina Ad Aims to Lure Women from Lululemon," *Time.com,* August 6, 2014; "New Crystal Light Liquid Drink Mix Frees You from the Choice between Taste or Calories," *PR Newswire,* February 11, 2013; Natalie Zmuda, "Diet Mtn Dew Steps Out from Shadow of Flagship Brand," *Advertising Age,* March 5, 2012, p. 4; E. J. Schultz and Natalie Zmuda, "No Solo Mio: Kraft's Smash Product Attracts Rival in Coke's Dasani," *Advertising Age,* November 5, 2012, p. 10; Katie Smith, "US: Nike in Uniform Deal with International Olympic Committee," *Just-Style Global News,* October 17, 2012; and Shareen Pthak, "How Nike Ambushed the Olympics with This Neon Shoe," *Advertising Age,* August 20, 2012, p. 1.

8. Ira Teinowitz, "Self-Regulation Urged to Prevent Bias in Ad Buying," *Advertising Age,* January 18, 1999, p. 4.

9. See the Advertising Research Foundation website, http://thearf.org/advancing-marketingforum.php, accessed May 4, 2013.

10. Demetrios Vakratsas and Tim Ambler, "How Advertising Works: What Do We Really Know?" *Journal of Marketing,* January 1999, pp. 26–43; and Amit Joshi and Dominique M. Hanssens, "The Direct and Indirect Effects of Advertising Spending on Firm Value," *Journal of Marketing,* January 2010, pp. 20–33.

11. Jeanine Poggi, "Is the Super Bowl Worth the Price? For These Advertisers, It Might Be," *Advertising Age,* February 9, 2015, p. 8; Christopher Heine, "Lexus' Super Bowl Ad Boosted Kelley Blue Book Searches for One Car by 1,800%," *Adweek,* February 6, 2015, p. 1; Mae Anderson, "First-Time Advertisers Gamble Big on Super Bowl Ads," *Associated Press,* January 28, 2015; Harlan E. Spotts, Scott C. Purvis and Sandeep Patnaik, "How Digital Conversations Reinforce Super Bowl Advertising,"

Journal of Advertising Research, December 2014, pp. 454–68; and Rama Ylkur, Chuck Tomkovick, and Patty Traczyk, "Super Bowl Effectiveness: Hollywood Finds the Games Golden," *Journal of Advertising Research,* March 2004, pp. 143–59.

12. See the Super Bowl Commercials website at www.superbowl-commercials.org and the *USA Today* Ad Meter website at http://admeter.usatoday.com/.

13. E. J. Schultz, "SlimFast Ditches Sex Vanity Play," *Advertising Age,* May 18, 2015; p. 8; and "100 Leading National Advertisers," *Advertising Age,* June 23, 2014, p. 30.

14. Sarah De Meulenaer, Patrick De Pelsmacker, and Nathalie Dens, "Have No Fear: How Individuals Differing in Uncertainty Avoidance, Anxiety, and Chance Belief Process Health Risk Messages, *Journal of Advertising* 44, no. 2 (2015), pp. 114–25; Ioni Lewis, Barry Watson, Richard Tay, and Katherine M. White, "The Role of Fear Appeals in Improving Driver Safety," *The International Journal of Behavioral Consultation and Therapy,* June 22, 2007, p. 203; Cornelia Pechmann, Guangzhi Zhao, Marvin E. Goldberg, and Ellen Thomas Reibling, "What to Convey in Antismoking Advertisements for Adolescents: The Use of Protection Motivation Theory to Identify Effective Message Themes," *Journal of Marketing,* April 2003, pp. 1–18; and John F. Tanner Jr., James B. Hunt, and David R. Eppright, "The Protection Motivation Model: A Normative Model of Fear Appeals," *Journal of Marketing,* July 1991, pp. 36–45.

15. "About Bebe," Bebe website, www.bebe.com, accessed June 16, 2011; and Sanjay Putrevu, "Consumer Responses toward Sexual and Nonsexual Appeals: The Influence of Involvement, Need for Cognition (NFC), and Gender," *Journal of Advertising,* Summer 2008, p. 57.

16. Rupal Parekh, "With Strong Work for Walmart and Geico, Martin Agency Is Creating a New Specialty: Making Marketers Recession-Proof," *Advertising Age,* January 19, 2009, p. 30; and Louis Llovio, "Geico Gecko's Viral Videos," *Richmond Times Dispatch,* March 28, 2009, p. B-9.

17. Thomas W. Cline and James J. Kellaris, "The Influence of Humor Strength and Humor-Message Relatedness on Ad Memorability: A Dual Process Model," *Journal of Advertising,* Spring 2007, p. 55; Yong Zhang and George M. Zinkham, "Responses to Humorous Ads," *Journal of Advertising,* Winter 2006, p. 113; and Yih Hwai Lee and Elison Ai Ching Lim, "What's Funny and What's Not: The Moderating Role of Cultural Orientation in Ad Humor," *Journal of Advertising,* Summer 2008, p. 71.

18. Mark Bergen, "Agency of the Year," *Advertising Age,* January 28, 2015, p. 14; Gabrie Beltron, "Agency of the Year: How R/GA Dominated Digital by Finding Its TV Groove," *Adweek,* December 15, 2014; and R/GA website, www.rga.com, accessed June 19, 2015.

19. Blake Powers, "Who Is the Most Effective Celebrity Spokesperson?" *kluv.cbslocal.com,* May 27, 2015; Katy Young, "Naomi Watts Is L'Oreal Paris' Latest Ambassador," *telegraph.co.uk,* October 23, 2104; and Judith Anne Garretson Folse, Richard G. Netemeyer, and Scot Burton, "Spokescharacters," *Journal of Advertising,* Spring 2012, pp. 17–32.

20. "Celebrities and the Art of High-Risk Marketing," *Postmedia Breaking News,* April 25, 2013; Chris Isidore, "Lance Armstrong: How He'll Make Money Now," *CNN Wire,* January 16, 2013; Francois A. Carrillat, Alain D'Astous, and Josianne Lazure, "For Better, for Worse? What to Do When Celebrity Endorsements Go Bad," *Journal of Advertising Research,* March 2013, pp. 15–30; and Chris Isidore, "Tiger Woods No Longer Top-Paid Athlete," *CNNMoney.com,* July 17, 2012.

21. "Results of 4A's 2011 Television Production Cost Survey," *4A's Bulletin,* January 22, 2013 (New York: American Association of Advertising Agencies); and "Washington: Results of 4A's

2011 Television Production Cost Survey," *Plus Media Solutions,* January 23, 2013.

22. "U.S. Ad Spending Forecast," *Advertising Age,* June 23, 2014, p. 32.

23. Vicki R. Lane, "The Impact of Ad Repetition and Ad Content on Consumer Perceptions of Incongruent Extensions," *Journal of Marketing,* April 2000, pp. 80–91.

24. "Rise of the 'Zero TV' Home: Ratings Altered to Take into Account the People Who Only Watch Online," *Mail Online,* April 8, 2013; and "Nielsen Estimates More Than 116 Million TV Homes in the U.S.," Nielsen website, http://www.nielsen.com/us/en/insights/news/2014/nielsen-estimates-more-than-116-million-tv-homes-in-the-us.html, August 29, 2014.

25. Mark Bergen and Tim Peterson, "CES Takeaways for Marketers," *Advertising Age,* January 12, 2015, p. 6; "Free to Move between Screens: The Cross-Platform Report," The Nielsen Company (New York), March 2013; and Ryan Kisiel, "Forget HD or 3D, 4K Television Is the Next Big Thing," *Daily Mail,* January 28, 2013.

26. "Cost for a 30-Second Commercial," *Marketing Fact Pack: 2015 Edition,* December 29, 2014, pp. 24–25; Emily Fredrix, "TV Commercials Shrink to Match Attention Spans," *USA Today,* October 30, 2010; Kate Newstead and Jenni Romaniuk, "Cost per Second: The Relative Effectiveness of 15- and 30-Second Television Advertisements," *Journal of Advertising Research,* 2009, pp. 68–76; and Srinivasan Swaminathan and Robert Kent, "Second-by-Second Analysis of Advertising Exposure in TV Pods," *Journal of Advertising Research,* March 2013, pp. 91–100.

27. "Industry Data," National Cable & Telecommunications Association, www.ncta.com, June 25, 2012; and Brian Steinberg, "Turner Experiments with Building a Smarter Ad for Its Cable Networks," *Advertising Age,* April 11, 2011, p. 3.

28. "IMS Top 50 Infomercials and Spots of 2013," *Response Magazine,* December 2013, pp. 34–35; "10 Best-Selling Infomercial Products," *Gizmodo,* May 1, 2013; "All the Info on Infomercials," www.Backstage.com, November 18, 2010; and Herb Weisbaum, "ConsumerMan: Busting Infomercial Myths," www.MSNBC.com, December 16, 2010.

29. "Average Weekly Reach" and "Radio's Weekly Reach Among Millennials," *Why Radio Fact Sheet,* Radio Advertising Bureau, June 2015; "National Radio Format Shares and Station Counts," *Radio Today 2013: How America Listens to Radio,* Arbitron, 2013; "Radio Today by the Numbers," Arbitron, Spring 2013; and Anthony Ha, "Pandora Resurrects Its 40-Hour Limit on Free Music," www.techcrunch.com, February 27, 2013.

30. "Hour-by-Hour Listening," in *Radio Today,* 2010 edition, Arbitron, p. 89.

31. *Magazine Media Factbook 2015* (New York: The Association of Magazine Media), pp. 68–71; "Divine December—59 New Magazine Titles—24 with Frequency," *mr.magazine* website, www.mrmagazine.com, December 31, 2014; "Skateboarder Magazine Changes the Game with Innovative Digital-First Platform," *States News Service,* April 16, 2013; and Rebecca Clancy, "*Auto Trader* Print Edition to Stop as Focus Shifts to Digital," *The Telegraph,* May 7, 2013.

32. "Number of Magazines by Category," The Association of Magazine Media, http://www.magazine.org/insights-resources/research-publications/trends-data/magazineindustry-facts-data/1998-2010-number, accessed May 13, 2013; and "Magazines Mean Engagement," *Magazine Media Factbook 2012/13* (New York: The Association of Magazine Media), p. 14.

33. "Top 25 U.S. Consumer Magazines by Paid and Verified Circulation," Research and Data, Alliance for Audited Media, http://auditedmedia.com/news/research-and-data/top-25-usconsumer-magazines-for-june-2014/, June 2014;

"Defunct or Suspended Magazines," The Association of Magazine Media, http://www.magazine.org/insights-resources/researchpublications/trends-data/magazine-industry-facts-data/publishing-trends.

34. "Average Circulation at the Top 25 U.S. Daily Newspapers," Research and Data, Alliance for Audited Media, http://auditedmedia.com/news/research-and-data/top-25-usnewspapers-for-march-2013/, March 2013; "About Us," *Metro* website, http://www.metro.us/about-us/; and "Metro Newspaper Is the #1 Free Daily Newspaper in Boston," *Business Wire,* June 13, 2011.

35. Tom Baxter, "Big News: Newspapers, Long Mourned, Aren't Really Dead," *SaportaReport,* May 13, 2013; "Average Circulation at the Top 25 U.S. Daily Newspapers," Research and Data, Alliance for Audited Media, http://auditedmedia.com/news/research-anddata/top-25-us-newspapers-for-march-2013/, March 2013; Christine Haughney, "Newspapers Post Gains in Digital Circulation," *The New York Times,* May 1, 2013, p. 5; "Digital Fees Pay Off for 2 Top-Selling Newspapers," Associated Press, April 30, 2013; and "Huffington Post Twitter: 3 Million Follower Giveaway," *The Huffington Post,* May 10, 2013.

36. "U.S. Ad Spending Forecast from ZenithOptimedia," *Marketing Fact Pack,* December 29, 2014, p. 14; "Can Yellow Pages Make a Come Back?" *Zacks Investment Research,* March 21, 2013; Chris Silver Smith, "Are Yellow Pages Toast?" www.searchengineland.com, March 26, 2012; "Mobile Searches for Local Business Info Replacing Desktop and Yellow Pages," *SBWire,* April 10, 2013; "As Media Habits Evolve, Yellow Pages and Search Engines Firmly Established as Go-To Sources for Consumer Shopping Locally," *PR Newswire,* June 13, 2011; and see National Yellow Pages Consumer Choice & Opt-Out Site, https://www.yellowpagesoptout.com/homepage.

37. "comScore Releases March 2015 U.S. Desktop Search Engine Rankings," press release, comScore website, http://www.comscore.com/Insights/Market-Rankings/comScore-Releases-March-2015-US-Desktop-Search-Engine-Rankings, April 15, 2015; Jan H. Schumann, Florian von Wangenheim, and Nicole Groene, "Targeted Online Advertising: Using Reciprocity Appeals to Increase Acceptance among Users of Free Web Services," *Journal of Marketing,* January 2014, pp. 59–75; "10 Ways to Improve the Banner Ad Design and Enhance the Click Through Rate," *Tech and Techie,* May 6, 2013; "'Banner Blindness' Now a Major Marketing Concern," *Bulldog Reporter's Daily Dog,* March 29, 2013; Thales Teixeira, "The New Science of Viral Ads," *Harvard Business Review,* March 2012, pp. 25–27; and the definition of mobile marketing is adapted from the Mobile Marketing Association definition, see http://www.mmaglobal.com/news/mma-updates-definition-mobile-marketing, November 17, 2009.

38. See "Guidelines, Standards & Best Practices," at the Interactive Advertising Bureau website, http://www.iab.net/guidelines; "IAB Releases New Standard Ad Unit Portfolio," press release, International Advertising Bureau, February 26, 2012; "Online Measurement," Nielsen website, http://www.nielsen.com/us/en/nielsen-solutions/nielsen-measurement/nielsen-onlinemeasurement.html; and Abbey Klaassen, "Why the Click Is the Wrong Metric for Online Ads," *Advertising Age,* February 23, 2009, p. 4.

39. Christopher Heine, "What Counts as an Online Ad View? A Standard Is Nearing, but the Fight's Not Over," *Adweek,* February 27, 2015, p. 1; Robert Lemos, "Ad Networks a Digital Paradise for Cyber-Criminals, Researchers Find," *eWeek,* November 11, 2014, p. 1; "Why We Need to Pivot in the Fight against Ad Fraud," *VentureBeat,* April 18, 2013; "Three Ways Advertisers Can Avoid Click Fraud," *ReadWriteWeb,*

September 6, 2012; "Click Fraud Rate Drops to 19.1 Percent in Q4 2010," *Business Wire,* January 26, 2011; Sara Yin, "Click Fraud Skyrockets," *PC Magazine,* October 21, 2010; Alex Mindlin, "Click Fraud Climbs with Mobile Gear," *The New York Times,* November 1, 2010, p. 2; Gareth Jones, "Briefing—Paid Search—Advertisers Stung by Rising Click Fraud," *Revolution,* May 1, 2009, p. 18; and Benjamin Edelman, "Pitfalls and Fraud in Online Advertising Metrics," *Journal of Advertising Research,* July 2014, pp. 127–32.

40. Arch G. Woodside, "Outdoor Advertising as Experiments," *Journal of the Academy of Marketing Science* 18 (Summer 1990), pp. 229–37.

41. "OOH Ad Spend 2009–2014," Outdoor Advertising Association of America website, http://www.oaaa.org/ResourceCenter/MarketingSales/Factsamp;Figures/Revenue/HistoricalRevenue.aspx; "New Report Evaluates Consumer Lifestyles to Determine Value of Out of Home Advertising," press release, Outdoor Advertising Association of America, May 2, 2012; "Clear Channel Outdoor Digital Billboards Help Houston Crime Stoppers Take a Bite Out of Crime," www.DigitalSignageToday.com, April 25, 2013; "Clear Channel Digital Billboards Will Carry Twin Cities Weather Warnings," www.DigitalSignageToday.com, April 26, 2013; "Judge Hits 'Off' Switch on Digital Billboards," *Plus Media Solutions,* April 26, 2013; "Beer, Donuts and Digital Billboard Advertising," www.DigitalSignageToday.com, March 19, 2013; and "Council Limits Supergraphics in Hollywood, Signs: Action Comes as Judge Upholds City's Billboard Ban," *The Daily News of Los Angeles,* September 29, 2010, p. A3.

42. "Clear Channel Outdoor Holdings Releases 'Out-of-Home Advertising and the Retail Industry' Report," *Professional Services Close-Up,* January 25, 2011; Andrew Hampp, "What's New with Outdoor Ads, and What's This Digital Out-of-Home I Keep Hearing About?" *Advertising Age,* September 27, 2010, p. 48; "The Year Ahead for . . . Outdoor," *Campaign,* January 9, 2009, p. 28; Andrew Hampp, "Digital Out of Home, That's Those Pixilated Billboards, Right?" *Advertising Age,* March 30, 2009; Andrew Hampp, "Out of Home That Stood Out," *Advertising Age,* December 15, 2008, p. 22; and Daniel W. Baack, Rick T. Wilson, and Brian D. Till, "Creativity and Memory Effects," *Journal of Advertising,* Winter 2008, p. 85.

43. Sehoon Park and Minhi Hahn, "Pulsing in a Discrete Model of Advertising Competition," *Journal of Marketing Research,* November 1991, pp. 397–405.

44. Peggy Masterson, "The Wearout Phenomenon," *Marketing Research,* Fall 1999, pp. 27–31; and Lawrence D. Gibson, "What Can One TV Exposure Do?" *Journal of Advertising Research,* March–April 1996, pp. 9–18.

45. Rik Pieters, Michel Wedel, and Rajeev Batra, "The Stopping Power of Advertising: Measure and Effects of Visual Complexity," *Journal of Marketing,* September 2010, pp. 48–60; Rob Norton, "How Uninformative Advertising Tells Consumers Quite a Bit," *Fortune,* December 26, 1994, p. 37; and "Professor Claims Corporations Waste Billions on Advertising," *Marketing News,* July 6, 1992, p. 5.

46. Rupal Parekh and Alexandra Bruell, "Over Half of Agency Compensation Deals Involve Pay-for-Performance," *Advertising Age,* May 13, 2013, p. 1; Rance Crain, "Why Agencies—and the Media—Are Reluctant to Bet It All on Value-Compensation Systems," *Advertising Age,* June 7, 2010, p. 31; Stephen Fajen, "The Agency Model Is Bent but Not Broken," *Advertising Age,* July 7, 2008, p. 17; Jeremy Mullman, "Anheuser-Busch Whacks Retainers for Its Agencies," *Advertising Age,* February 16, 2009, p. 1; and Jack Neff, "No One-Size-Fits-All Snuggie Model Exists for DRTV Shops," *Advertising Age,* March 23, 2009.

47. The discussion of posttesting is based on William F. Arens, Michael F. Weigold, and Christian Arens, *Contemporary Advertising*, 12th ed. (New York: McGraw-Hill Irwin, 2009), pp. 228–30.

48. "ROI Metric Available in MRI Starch Syndicated," Mediamark Research & Intelligence, www.mediamark.com, accessed April 23, 2009.

49. Debora V. Thompson and Prashant Malaviya, "Consumer-Generated Ads: Does Awareness of Advertising Co-Creation Help or Hurt Persuasion?" *Journal of Marketing,* May 2013, pp. 33–47; David A. Aaker and Douglas M. Stayman, "Measuring Audience Perceptions of Commercials and Relating Them to Ad Impact," *Journal of Advertising Research* 30 (August–September 1990), pp. 7–17; and Ernest Dichter, "A Psychological View of Advertising Effectiveness," *Marketing Management* 1, no. 3 (1992), pp. 60–62.

50. David Krugel, "Television Advertising Effectiveness and Research Innovation," *Journal of Consumer Marketing,* Summer 1988, pp. 43–51; and Laurence N. Gold, "The Evolution of Television Advertising Sales Measurement: Past, Present, and Future," *Journal of Advertising Research,* June–July 1988, pp. 19–24.

51. "U.S. Ad Spending Forecast from ZenithOptimedia," *Marketing Fact Pack: 2015 Edition,* December 29, 2014, p. 14.

52. Magid M. Abraham and Leonard M. Lodish, "Getting the Most Out of Advertising and Promotion," *Harvard Business Review,* May–June 1990, pp. 50–60; Steven W. Hartley and James Cross, "How Sales Promotion Can Work For and Against You," *Journal of Consumer Marketing,* Summer 1988, pp. 35–42; and Robert D. Buzzell, John A. Quelch, and Walter J. Salmon, "The Costly Bargain of Trade Promotion," *Harvard Business Review,* March–April 1990, pp. 141–49.

53. Charlie Brown, "Marketers' Coupon Strategies Deliver Increased Consumer Savings in 2014 While Staying within Budgets," *Annual Topline View CPG Coupon Facts,* NCH Marketing Services, 2015; Erin Aydelott, "Consumers Get Serious About Coupon Savings" Coupon Facts and Insigs, NCH website, https://www2.nchmarketing.com/ResourceCenter/couponknowledgestream4_ektid6221.aspx; "2012 NCH Consumer Survey: Demographic Profile of Coupon Users," NCH Marketing Services, 2012; Claudia Buck, "Coupon Industry: No Scissors Required," *The State Journal-Register,* February 24, 2013, p. 40; "Coupons.com Report Shows Upward Trend among Digital Coupon Users," *Wireless News,* May 19, 2013; and "How Mobile Coupons Are Driving an Explosion in Mobile Commerce," *The Business Insider,* May 22, 2013.

54. Kapil Bawa and Robert W. Shoemaker, "Analyzing Incremental Sales from a Direct-Mail Coupon Promotion," *Journal of Marketing,* July 1998, pp. 66–78.

55. Robert A. Strang, "Sales Promotion—Fast Growth, Faulty Management," *Harvard Business Review* 54 (July–August 1976), pp. 115–24; and Ronald W. Ward and James E. Davis, "Coupon Redemption," *Journal of Advertising Research* 18 (August 1978), pp. 51–58. Similar results on favorable mail-distributed coupons were reported by Alvin Schwartz, "The Influence of Media Characteristics on Coupon Redemption," *Journal of Marketing* 30 (January 1966), pp. 41–46.

56. "What Is Coupon Fraud?" The Coupon Information Corporation, http://www.couponinformationcenter.com, accessed May 26, 2013; Josh Elledge, "Coupon Fraud Hurts Us All," *Grand Rapids Press,* April 19, 2011, p. B1; and Amy Johannes, "Flying the Coup," *Promo,* July 1, 2008, p. 28.

57. "Next Happy Meal," McDonald's website, http://www.happymeal.com/en_US/; "The Influence of Promotional Products on Consumer Behavior," Promotional Product Association International, November 2012; Amy Johannes, "Premium Connections," *Promo,* October 2008, p. 34; and

58. Gerard P. Prendergast, Alex S. L. Tsang, and Derek T. Y. Poon, "Predicting Premium Proneness," *Journal of Advertising Research,* June 2008, p. 287.

58. Michele Castillo, "Doritos Reveals 10 'Crash the Super Bowl' Ad Finalists," *Adweek,* January 5, 2015; "2015 Doritos 'Crash the Super Bowl' Video Contest," *Online Video Contests,* https://www.onlinevideocontests.com/contest/6895; and "User Content Offers a New Perspective," *PR Week,* February 23, 2009, p. 21.

59. "Congratulations to Kathy of Alabama," HGTV Dream Home 2015, HGTV website, www.hgtv.com; "The Monopoly Game at McDonald's Returns Sept. 30," McDonald's website, http://news.mcdonalds.com/US/releases/The-MONOPOLY-Game-at-McDonald%E2%80%99s-Returns-Sept-30, September 14, 2014.

60. "Nissan Voice Sweepstakes 2015," *The Daily Jackpot,* http://sweeps.thedailyjackpot.com/?p=2330, December 18, 2014; "Mars Chocolate North America Launches 5 Characters, 5 Cars Promotion," *Travel & Leisure Close-Up,* June 20, 2011; "Buy a Large Coke at Carl's Jr. and Win—Guaranteed; Guests Can Win Big with My Coke Rewards Point and Food Prizes," *Business Wire,* May 27, 2011; and "StumbleUpon Partners with the Academy of Motion Picture Arts and Sciences for Sweepstakes," *Marketwire,* January 17, 2013.

61. Alison Spiegel, "Taco Bell Is Giving Away Free Doritos Locos Tacos for a Month, Starting Tomorrow," *The Huffington Post,* December 31, 2014; "Free Doritos Locos Tacos Available at Taco Bell If Bases Stolen in World Series," *Huff Post,* October 19, 2012; Elana Ashanti Jefferson, "Sample Hunters Offer Advice for Trying—Before You Buy," *Denver Post,* July 16, 2012, p. 3C; and Schuyler Velasco, "Ben & Jerry's Free Cone Day," *The Christian Science Monitor,* April 9, 2013.

62. Tom Hoffman, "How Valuable Is a Loyalty Program?," *Customer Strategist,* Peppers & Rogers Group, April 1, 2015; David Moin, "Macy's in New Plenti Program," *Women's Wear Daily,* March 18, 2015, p. 2-1; Jeff Berry, "The 2015 Colloquy Loyalty Census," *Colloquy,* February 2015; Kara McGuire, "Retailers Work to Make Shopping Its Own Reward," *Star Tribune,* December 19, 2010, p. 1A.

63. Richard Postrel and Kelly Hlavinka, "An Open Economy: The Evolution of Loyalty in the United States," *Colloquy,* September 2012, http://colloquy.com/white-view.asp?uid=38; and "Maritz Loyalty Marketing Survey Updates on Consumers' Top-Rated Loyalty Programs," *Entertainment Close-Up,* May 19, 2013.

64. Walmart Smart Network website, http://www.walmartsmartnetwork.com/default.aspx, accessed May 27, 2013; and Amy Johannes, "Watching the Carts," *Promo,* October 2008, p. 36.

65. "Virgin Mobile Offers $100 Rebate to T-Mobile Turncoats," *Engadget HD,* April 9, 2013; Nathalia Dens, Patrick De Pelsmacker, Marijke Wouters, and Nathalia Purnawirawan, "Do You Like What You Recognize?" *Journal of Advertising,* Fall 2012, pp. 35–53; "The Case for Rebates," *Chief Marketer,* July 1, 2011; and Marvin A. Jolson, Joshua L. Wiener, and Richard B. Rosecky, "Correlates of Rebate Proneness," *Journal of Advertising Research,* February–March 1987, pp. 33–43.

66. Abe Sauer, "Announcing the 2015 Brandcameo Product Placement Awards," *brandchannel,* February 20, 2015; Angie Han, "'Transformers: Age of Extinction' Tops 2015 Product Placement Awards," www.slashfilm.com, March 4, 2015; "PQ Media Update: US Product Placement Up 13% in 1H15": www.wdrb.com, June 15, 2015; Ekaterina V. Karniouchina, Can Uslay, and Grigori Erenburg, "Do Marketing Media Have Life Cycles? The Case of Product Placement in Movies," *Journal of Marketing,* May 2011, pp. 27–49; and Sophie C. Boerman, Eva A van Reijmersdal, and Peter C. Neijens, "Using Eye Tracking

to Understand the Effect of Brand Placement Disclosure Types in Television Programs," *Journal of Advertising,* 44, no. 3 (2015), pp. 196–7.

67. Haiming Hang, "Brand-Placement Effectiveness and Competitive Interference in Entertainment Media," *Journal of Advertising Research,* July 2014, pp. 192–99; "Direct Selling Leader Amway Leverages Product Placement in the Video Gaming World," *India Retail News,* April 5, 2013; Stuart Elliott, "Expanding Line of Dunder Mifflin Products Shows Success in Reverse Product Placement," *The New York Times Blogs,* November 23, 2012; Karen Idelson, "Product Placements Don't Derail Nom Hopes," *Daily Variety,* June 1, 2011, p. A8; Andrew Hampp, "Why Viewers and Marketers Are Loving 'Modern Family,'" *Advertising Age,* April 18, 2011, p. 4; "Sky and Discovery Launch Digital Product Placement," *Broadcast,* May 17, 2011; and Amy Johannes, "Simpson Mania," *Promo,* November 1, 2008, p. 8.

68. This discussion is drawn particularly from John A. Quelch, *Trade Promotions by Grocery Manufacturers: A Management Perspective* (Cambridge, MA: Marketing Science Institute, August 1982).

69. Michael Chevalier and Ronald C. Curhan, "Retail Promotions as a Function of Trade Promotions: A Descriptive Analysis," *Sloan Management Review* 18 (Fall 1976), pp. 19–32.

70. G. A. Marken, "Firms Can Maintain Control over Creative Co-op Programs," *Marketing News,* September 28, 1992, pp. 7, 9.

71. Kathleen Cleeren, Harald J. van Heerde, and Marnik G. Dekimpe, "Rising from the Ashes: How Brands and Categories Can Overcome Product-Harm Crises," *Journal of Marketing,* March 2013, pp. 58–77; "Carnival Cruises Tries to Dig Themselves Out of Another PR Crisis," *Bulldog Reporter's Daily Dog,* February 22, 2013; and Peter S. Goodman, "From Corporate Crises, a Handbook on Lost Love and Publicity: Missteps by Toyota, BP, and Goldman Show Trust Is Tough to Win Back," *The International Herald Tribune,* August 23, 2010, p. 1.

72. Irving Rein, Philip Kotler, and Martin Stoller, *High Visibility* (New York: Dodd, Mead, 1987); and Steven Colford, "Ross

Perot: A Winner after All," *Advertising Age,* December 21, 1992, pp. 4, 18.

73. Michael Treacy and Fred Wiersema, "Customer Intimacy and Other Value Disciplines," *Harvard Business Review,* January–February 1993, pp. 84–93.

74. Gerry Khermouch and Tom Lowry, "The Future of Advertising," *BusinessWeek,* March 26, 2001, p. 139; and "Outlook 2001: Advertising," *Marketing News,* January 1, 2001, p. 10.

75. Betsy Spethmann, "McFallout," *Promo,* October 2001, pp. 31–38.

76. "Kid Stuff," *Promo,* January 1991, pp. 25, 42; Steven W. Colford, "Fine-Tuning Kids' TV," *Advertising Age,* February 11, 1991, p. 35; and Kate Fitzgerald, "Toys Star-Struck for Movie Tie-Ins," *Advertising Age,* February 18, 1991, pp. 3, 45.

77. Herbert J. Rotfeld, Avery M. Abernathy, and Patrick R. Parsons, "Self-Regulation and Television Advertising," *Journal of Advertising* 19, no. 4 (1990), pp. 18–26.

78. Google, Inc.: This case was written by Steven Hartley. Sources: "2 Billion Consumers Worldwide to Get Smart(phones) by 2016," *emarketer,* December 11, 2014; Jessica E. Vascellaro, "Google Decides to Find Its Creative Side," *The Wall Street Journal,* October 7, 2009; Robert D. Hof, "Google's New Ad Weapon," *BusinessWeek,* June 22, 2009, p. 52; Maria Bartiromo, "Eric Schmidt on Where Google Is Headed," *BusinessWeek,* August 17, 2009, p. 11; "Why Microsoft–Yahoo Deal Could Be Good for Google," *Advertising Age,* August 10, 2009, p. 10; Peter Burrow, "Apple and Google: Another Step Apart," *BusinessWeek,* August 17, 2009, p. 24; Jeff Jarvis, "How the Google Model Could Help," *BusinessWeek,* February 9, 2009, p. 32; Abbey Klaasen, "Google Says Print Ads Isn't the Answer for Newspapers," *Advertising Age,* January 26, 2009, p. 17; Matthew Creamer, "Recession Doesn't Dent Total Value of Top 100 Brands," *Advertising Age,* April 27, 2009; "The 500 Largest U.S. Corporations," *Fortune,* May 4, 2009, p. F-1; "ComScore Releases August 2009 U.S. Search Engine Rankings," www.comscore.com, October 10, 2009; interviews with Google personnel; and information contained on the Google website (www.google.com).

19

Using Social Media and Mobile Marketing to Connect with Consumers

LEARNING OBJECTIVES

After reading this chapter you should be able to:

 LO 19-1 Define social media and describe how they differ from traditional advertising media.

LO 19-2 Identify the four major social media and how brand managers integrate them into marketing actions.

LO 19-3 Describe the differing roles of those receiving messages through traditional versus social media and how brand managers select social media.

 LO 19-4 Compare the performance measures of social media linked to costs (inputs) versus revenues (outputs).

 LO 19-5 Identify the cause of the convergence of the real and digital worlds and how this will affect the future of social media.

The Ultimate Marketing Machine . . . Is in Your Pocket!

Few aspects of business have changed as quickly as the marketing discipline during the past five years. And more change is inevitable. To see the future, however, you need look no further than your pocket. Social media and mobile marketing will soon make your phone the ultimate marketing machine!

Consumers regularly engage the marketplace with many forms of media. In fact, Nielsen estimates that each month more than 280 million people watch television, 250 million people listen to radio, and 190 million people access the Internet on a computer. While these are astounding numbers, it is the growth in the use of smartphones that is getting marketers' attention. Currently, each month more than 160 million people use their phone to access an app, while more than 120 million use social media on their phones. Smartphones and tablets are quickly replacing computers as the way most people access the Internet, apps, and social media. The always-on and always-connected aspects of these devices are adding mobility as an important dimension of marketing and creating mobile marketing as an essential tool for the future.

As the use of smartphones has grown, businesses have created a wide variety of mobile experiences for consumers. In a recent survey the most popular smartphone apps were Facebook, Google Search, YouTube, Google Play, Google Maps, Gmail, Facebook Messenger, Google+, and Instagram. These and other mobile experiences have attracted $32 billion in annual advertising revenue, and experts predict that they will soon account for 40 percent of all online display ad budgets.

Mobile marketing is continuing to evolve though. The current apps and social media experiences are designed for the small screen of a mobile phone but they do not necessarily take advantage of the user's location or mobility. The future of mobile marketing will focus on the ability to interact with a world of connected devices. As author Tina Desai explains, "In this connected world, it is the mobile device that becomes the digital remote control for the real world."

Shopping is one example of this interaction. When a customer walks into a store, a Bluetooth Low Energy (BLE) beacon will sense that the customer has arrived, then it will access customer loyalty data, create a personalized promotion, and send it to the shopper's smartphone. The shopper can select products from the ad and then follow in-store navigation to the selected products. Other areas where mobile marketing will have immediate

Courtesy of Estimote

applications is in health monitoring and fitness, home security and comfort, and automobile safety.

What are some other new elements of this dynamic environment? Watch for sponsored videos on Instagram, a buy button on Twitter, mobile payments with Apple Pay, self-destructing ads on Snapchat, and even virtual reality experiences![1]

This chapter defines social media, describes four widely used social media, explains how organizations use them in developing marketing strategies, and considers where social media are headed in the future.

UNDERSTANDING SOCIAL MEDIA

LO 19-1 Define social media and describe how they differ from traditional advertising media.

Defining *social media* is challenging, but it's necessary to help a brand or marketing manager select the right one. This section defines social media, positions a number of social media, and compares social and traditional media. As you read this, consider how you might choose from the social media alternatives if *you*—like college students around the globe—were using one to launch a start-up business or expand a small business.

What Are Social Media?

This section describes how social media came about, defines social media, and provides a means of classifying the countless social media available to assist marketing managers in choosing among them.

Defining Social Media   Social media represent a unique blending of technology and social interaction to create personal value for users. **Social media** are online media where users submit comments, photos, and videos—often accompanied by a feedback process to identify "popular" topics.[2] Most social media involve a genuine online conversation among people about a subject of mutual interest, one built on their personal thoughts and experiences. However, other social media sites involve games and virtual worlds in which the online interaction includes playing a game, completing a quest, controlling an avatar, and so on. Business firms also refer to social media as "consumer-generated media." A single social media site with millions of users interacting with each other, like Facebook, Twitter, and LinkedIn, is referred to as a *social network*.

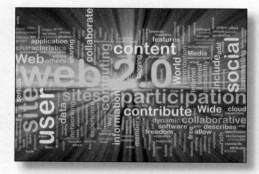

The text describes how Web 2.0 and user-generated content are the foundations of today's social media.

© Equinox Imagery/Alamy

How Social Media Came About   The term "social media" is sometimes used interchangeably with the terms "Web 2.0" and "user-generated content"—two concepts that are the foundations of today's social media.[3] Web 2.0 does not refer to any technical update of the World Wide Web, but identifies functionalities that make possible today's high degree of interactivity among users. So with Web 2.0, content is no longer seen as being created and published in final form exclusively by one author. Instead, the content can be modified continuously by all users in a participatory fashion, such as with blogs and wikis. The next-generation web, Web 3.0, will include new functionalities that are customized to each individual and his or her location, activity, interests, and needs.[4]

A **blog**—a contraction of "web log"—is a web page that serves as a publicly accessible personal journal and online forum for an individual or organization. Companies like Hewlett-Packard and Frito-Lay routinely monitor blogs to gain insights into customer complaints and suggestions. A *wiki* is a website whose content is created and edited by the ongoing collaboration of end users—such as generating and improving new-product ideas. They differ in that a blog is a diary that shows a sequential journey while a wiki shows the end result as a single entry.[5]

User-generated content (UGC) refers to the various forms of online media content that are publicly available and created by end users. The term "user-generated content" (also referred to as *consumer-generated content*) was in common use by 2005 and covers all the ways people can use social media. UGC satisfies three basic criteria:[6]

1. It is published either on a publicly accessible website or on a social media site, so it is not simply an e-mail.
2. It shows a significant degree of creative effort, so it is more than simply posting a newspaper article on a personal blog without editing or comments.
3. It is consumer-generated by an individual outside of a professional organization, without a commercial market in mind.

How do marketing managers choose the best social media sites to reach their target markets? As a first step, the text describes how social media can be classified and how they differ from traditional media.

© Anatolii Babii/Alamy

Classifying Social Media

Most of us would probably say that Facebook, Twitter, LinkedIn, and YouTube are well-known social media. But marketing managers trying to reach potential customers need a system to classify the more than 400 specialized and diverse social media to select the best among them. Kaplan and Haenlein have proposed a classification system for marketers based on two factors:[7]

1. *Media richness.* This involves the degree of acoustic, visual, and personal contact between two communication partners—face-to-face communications, say, being higher in media richness than telephone or e-mail communications. The higher the media richness and quality of presentation, the greater the social influence that communication partners have on each other's behavior.

2. *Self-disclosure.* In any type of social interaction, individuals want to make a positive impression to achieve a favorable image with others. This favorable image is affected by the degree of self-disclosure about a person's thoughts, feelings, likes, and dislikes—where greater self-disclosure is likely to increase one's influence on those reached.

Figure 19–1 uses these two factors of media richness and self-disclosure to position a number of social media sites in two-dimensional space. For example, Wikipedia is a collaborative project that is low on both self-disclosure and media richness.[8] LinkedIn, on the other hand, contains detailed career and résumé information for business networking and is high in self-disclosure but only moderate in media richness.

Marketing managers look carefully at the positioning of the social media shown in Figure 19–1 when selecting those to use in their plans. For example, LinkedIn, positioned in the Social Networking Sites segment in Figure 19–1, is a professional networking service with 360 million members in 200 countries. LinkedIn recently generated $454 million in annual advertising revenue from companies such as Citigroup, Microsoft, Chevron, HP, and Volkswagen, which promote their companies' career opportunities to people with specific job titles.[9]

FIGURE 19–1

A sample of social media, classified by media richness and self-disclosure. Note that in moving from words to photos, videos, and animation, media richness increases. Also, in moving from very impersonal messages to highly personal ones, self-disclosure increases.

See the text to learn why marketing managers advertise on LinkedIn.

© Piotr Malczyk/Alamy

Comparing Social and Traditional Media

Consumers receive information, news, and education from print (newspapers, magazines) and electronic (radio, television) media. But marketing managers know that social media are very different from traditional media like newspapers or even radio or television. Social media and traditional media have both similarities and differences that impact marketing strategies, as described below:[10]

- *Ability to reach both large and niche audiences.* Both kinds of media can be designed to reach either a mass market or specialized segments; however, good execution is critical, and audience size is not guaranteed.
- *Expense and access.* Messages and ads in traditional media like newspapers or television generally are expensive to produce and have restricted access by individuals. Also, traditional media are typically owned privately or by the government. In contrast, messages on social media are generally accessible everywhere to those with smartphones, computers, and tablet devices and can be produced cheaply.
- *Training and number of people involved.* Producing traditional media typically requires specialized skills and training and often involves teams of people. In contrast, sending messages on social media requires only limited skills, so practically anyone can post a message that includes words and images.
- *Time to delivery.* Traditional media can involve days or even months of continuing effort to deliver the communication, and time lags can be extensive. In contrast, individuals using social media can post virtually instantaneous content.
- *Permanence.* Traditional media, once created, cannot be altered. For example, once a magazine article is printed and distributed, it cannot be changed. But social media message content can be altered almost instantaneously by comments or editing.
- *Credibility and social authority.* Individuals and organizations can establish themselves as "experts" in their given field, thereby becoming "influencers" in that field. For example, *The New York Times* has immense credibility among newspaper media. But with social media, a sender often simply begins to participate in the "conversation," hoping that the quality of the message will establish credibility with the receivers, thereby enhancing the sender's influence.

In terms of privacy, with minor exceptions, recipients of traditional media like TV or radio ads are completely anonymous. Subscribers to newspapers or magazines are somewhat less so because publishers can sell subscription lists to advertisers. Social media users have much less privacy and anonymity. When social media sites breach expectations for privacy, unethical outsiders can access users' names.

learning review

19-1. What are social media?

19-2. In classifying social media, what do we mean by (*a*) media richness and (*b*) self-disclosure?

19-3. Compare traditional media and social media in terms of time required to deliver the communication.

A LOOK AT FOUR IMPORTANT SOCIAL MEDIA

LO 19-2 Identify the four major social media and how brand managers integrate them into marketing actions.

Facebook, Twitter, LinkedIn, and YouTube are four widely used options in the world of social media. So marketing managers need a special understanding of these four platforms as they integrate social media into their marketing strategies to supplement the traditional media they already use. This section briefly compares, defines, and explains each of these four major social media and shows how brand managers can use them. Because of its importance, Facebook merits more detailed coverage.

Comparing Four Social Media

Figure 19–2 compares four major social media (Facebook, Twitter, LinkedIn, and YouTube) from the point of view of a brand manager.[11] Facebook can increase brand exposure by enabling convenient user posting of links, photos, and videos. Twitter makes it easy to place brand messages and gain online customer support. While primarily a powerful network in helping users find jobs, LinkedIn has also found a niche in helping small businesses network to reach potential customers, as well as filling its traditional role of connecting job seekers and jobs. YouTube's videos make it especially useful in explaining a complex product.

Facebook

FIGURE 19–2

How brand managers can use four social media in developing their marketing strategies.

Facebook is the first choice among people seeking to create and maintain online connections with others by using photos, videos, and short text entries. Facebook

BASIS OF COMPARISON	SOCIAL MEDIA facebook	twitter	Linked in	You Tube
Male-Female Breakdown (U.S.)	42% male, 58% female	50% male, 50% female	56% male, 44% female	58% male, 42% female
Brand Exposure	Powerful for gaining brand exposure through convenient user posting of links, photos, and videos.	Consistent placement of brand messages is easy with applications like HootSuite and TweetCastor. Sponsored tweets promote brands.	Free opportunities exist, like Business Pages and LinkedIn Influencer posts. Paid Sponsored Updates provide added reach.	Powerful in gaining attention and explaining a complex product, and branding. Channels unite users on content and heighten viewership.
Customer Communication	Great for people who like your brand and want to share their opinions. Leads all social networks for this.	Twitter is powerful for gaining online customer support. Engaging one-on-one is simple and easy to track.	Half of those using social media for customer service use a LinkedIn Company Page while 40% do so with LinkedIn Groups.	YouTube gains user's ready attention in attracting customer support. Easy to allow responses to user comments and ratings.
Traffic to Website	Is the traffic leader through rewording engaging content with better news feed placement. But its share of referred visits is falling.	Referral traffic from Twitter is growing faster than any other social network. Photos and videos make tweets even more clickable.	LinkedIn generates referrals—though less than many other social networks—but can be valuable for B2B and business development.	YouTube is an important source of traffic. Get traffic back to user's site by adding a hyperlink in the video description.

Sources: The 2014 Male-Female Breakdowns are provided by Compete, Inc.; and DMR Directory of Social Network, App and Digital Stats; the other information is adapted from "The CMO's Guide to the 2014 Social Landscape."

Facebook logo: © AP Photo/Craig Ruttle; Twitter logo: © Ingvar Björk/Alamy; LinkedIn logo: Kristoffer Tripplaar/Alamy; YouTube logo: © TP/Alamy

enhanced its photo-sharing capability with its recent acquisition of Instagram. With over 1.4 billion active users—1 in every 5 people on the planet—Facebook is truly the 900-pound gorilla among all social media.

Mark Zuckerberg and Sheryl Sandberg are CEO and COO of Facebook, a social network that connects over 1.4 billion users.

© Zef Nikolla/Facebook via Bloomberg/Getty Images

Facebook: An Overview   **Facebook** is a website where users may create a personal profile, add other users as friends, and exchange comments, photos, videos, and "likes" with them. Facebook users today can keep friends and family updated on what they are thinking, doing, and feeling. In addition, users may chat with friends and create and join common-interest groups, and businesses can create Facebook Pages as a means of advertising and building relationships with customers. Facebook is open to anyone age 13 and older.

CEO Mark Zuckerberg and COO Sheryl Sandberg have managed Facebook through incredible growth. To understand the magnitude of the company consider that Facebook:

- Has 936 million daily active users.
- Processes 350 million photos, 4.5 billion likes, and 10 billion messages each day.
- Has 82 percent of its users living outside the United States
- Generates revenue from more than 2 million advertisers.

Half of all Facebook users have more than 200 friends in their network, and 18- to 29-year-olds have 300![12]

Facebook in a Brand Manager's Strategy   Facebook Pages were created as a method for brand managers to generate awareness for their product, service, or brand within Facebook. They allow brand managers to promote their business on Facebook, separate from their private and personal profiles. Done well, these are magnets for feedback. Additionally, Facebook Page information is generally public and cataloged by search engines so brand managers can identify influencers within their customer base.

To generate new customers and increase traffic to their Facebook Pages, brand managers can use paid ads and sponsored stories within the Facebook advertising platform. An advantage of these Facebook ads is that the content can migrate into Facebook conversations among friends—to the delight of advertisers.

The marketing challenge for an organization's Facebook Page is to post content that will generate the best response. Brand managers using Facebook seek to maintain a conversation with their fans. Research suggests the following guidelines to engage fans on Facebook:[13]

- *Be creative* in using links, photos, and videos.
- *Make it familiar, but with a twist.* Focus content strategy on imagery and messaging that is familiar to fans—punctuated with something unique. Aflac uses its Aflac Duck—the well-known "spokes-duck"—to treat fans to Aflac Duck commercials, virtual Duck gifts, and supplemental insurance offers.
- *Keep it fresh.* Redbox uses frequent posts to keep fans informed about its latest film releases.
- *Learn users' passions and let them guide content.* Taco Bell polls users to see which menu item they'd like featured in the following week's menu profile photo.

Gaining meaningful user loyalty enables a company to target promotional offers to its best customers. A recent study found that "Likes" or "Followers" on a brand's Facebook Page are worth an astounding $174 in terms of product spending, brand loyalty, and "propensity to recommend" the site to others.[14]

Launching a New Social Network Using Facebook Want to launch your own social network? For example, StuffDOT is a place for people to post the things they like and earn rewards for their recommendations and online purchases. It differs from other social-sharing websites because users "dot" their favorite things to StuffDOT and receive financial rewards or *commissions* when someone purchases that item. Commissions can be redeemed for gift cards with many major retailers, such as Amazon and Target.[15]

Figure 19–3 shows the Facebook Page for StuffDOT, a new start-up that targets college-aged women. The notes in the margins in Figure 19–3 show how elements on the StuffDOT Facebook Page seek to connect with fans, generate conversations, and help measure the success of the Facebook Page:

- *Profile and Cover Image.* Show StuffDOT's attention-getting logo.
- *People Like This Page.* Tells the number of people clicking the "Like" button.
- *Facebook Page Posts.* Pictures items like clothes and travel information shared with users.

FIGURE 19–3

StuffDOT's Facebook Page shows elements of interest to both its marketing team and potential users.

Courtesy of StuffDOT, Inc.

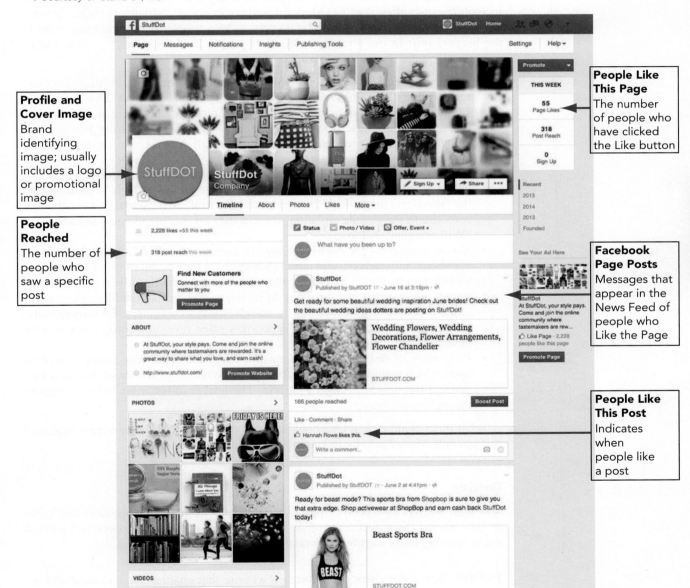

Profile and Cover Image
Brand identifying image; usually includes a logo or promotional image

People Reached
The number of people who saw a specific post

People Like This Page
The number of people who have clicked the Like button

Facebook Page Posts
Messages that appear in the News Feed of people who Like the Page

People Like This Post
Indicates when people like a post

545

Facebook offers its business customers a variety of ad templates that help measure the results of an ad, such as "Page Likes" (chosen by StuffDOT) or "Clicks to Website." StuffDOT also uses Facebook's "App Install" template to inform and encourage people to download the StuffDOT app.

StuffDOT's challenge is to break through the social media clutter and attract loyal users. So the StuffDOT marketing team works continuously to present an attention-getting, user-friendly Facebook Page.

As a start-up, StuffDOT finds new users and website testers by recruiting college Campus Ambassadors. StuffDOT Campus Ambassadors actively promote the site nationally through workshops, social media marketing, word-of-mouth, and promotional partnerships with events and businesses on college campuses. To learn more about what StuffDOT is up to now, go to http://www.stuffdot.com/.

Mobile Marketing at Facebook Keeping 1.4 billion users happy is a tall order—even for Facebook. As the most common method of accessing Facebook shifts from computers to mobile smartphones, the company is continually making changes to its mobile capabilities. As CEO Mark Zuckerberg explains: "Moving from just being a single service to a family of world-class apps to help people share in different ways is the biggest shift in our strategy to connect people in many years."[16] Some recent examples include:

- *Faster news publishing.* A new initiative called Instant Articles provides content, rather than links, from media organizations such as *The New York Times, National Geographic,* and *Buzzfeed* directly to Newsfeed. This makes access 10 times faster, prevents the Facebook experience from being interrupted, and acknowledges that two-thirds of all American adults now own a smartphone.[17]
- *Photo-sharing and facial recognition.* Facebook recently introduced a new app called Moments, which uses facial recognition to identify which "friends" are in the photos and then asks if the user would like to share the photo. It's Facebook's response to the mobile situation where a user takes a photo and someone asks, "Will you send that to me?"[18]
- *E-mail marketing for Facebook app.* In a program called Custom Audiences, Facebook helps advertisers target customers as they scroll through Facebook's mobile app by matching e-mail addresses provided by the advertisers with the e-mail addresses it has for many of its users. Facebook also identifies "look-alikes," people who are similar to an advertiser's customers, for targeted ads. Currently, more than half of Facebook's sales revenues come from mobile devices![19]
- *Integration of mobile app enhancements.* Facebook is building a suite of mobile apps, which includes Messenger, Instagram, WhatsApp, and about 40 others that connect through Messenger Platform. The goal is to better enable e-commerce through smartphones.[20]

What other changes will Facebook make as part of its mobile marketing strategy? Perhaps only Mark Zuckerberg knows!

Twitter

Now that "tweets" have become part of our everyday language, it's apparent that Twitter has entered the mainstream of American life. Twitter now has over 302 million active monthly users worldwide, who post 500 million tweets per day.[21]

Twitter: An Overview **Twitter** is a website that enables users to send and receive *tweets,* messages up to 140 characters long. Twitter is based on the principle of

Carmex (@Carmex) used Twitter to partner with members of TeamLeBron to give away a jar of Carmex lip balm with a 14-karat-gold cap.

Source: Carma Labs Inc.

"followers." So when you choose to follow another Twitter user, that user's tweets appear in reverse chronological order on your Twitter page.

Because of its short message length, the ease of posting and receiving tweets, and its convenience on a smartphone, Twitter can be a good source of information about a brand or product. Carma Laboratories, the maker of Carmex lip balm and skin care products, uses Twitter as an important tool in its social media program to communicate brand messages to its followers. As part of Carmex's social media outreach, the brand is active on Twitter with daily messages, retweets, and replies.

The immediacy of Twitter messaging allows brands like Carmex to operate promotions in real time. For example, Carmex partnered with LeBronJames.com to conduct a scavenger hunt on Twitter where members of TeamLeBron tweeted clues to their location. The first person to arrive at the destination won a jar of Carmex with a 14-karat-gold cap.

Beyond sending out messages, Carmex relies on Twitter as a listening device. Carmex's social media team monitors mentions of Carmex on Twitter to see what people are saying. If there are product concerns, Carmex can reach out to consumers to make sure their concerns are quickly addressed. For more on Carmex and how it uses social media to conduct marketing research, see Chapter 8.

Twitter in a Brand Manager's Strategy   With the 140-character limit on tweets, brand managers cannot expect extensive comments on their brands. But they can use social media management tools like TweetDeck or HootSuite to see what Twitter users are saying—good and bad—about both their own brands and competitive ones. They can then respond to the negative comments and retweet the positive ones.

Brand managers have various other strategies for listening to and interacting with current and potential consumers using Twitter. For example, they can:[22]

- Generate brand buzz by developing an official Twitter profile, recruiting followers, and showing photos of their products.
- Follow the Twitter profiles that mention their product and monitor what is being said, responding to user criticisms to develop happier customers.
- Tweet on topics that provide information of value to their consumers.

As with Facebook, Twitter can actively engage customers if done creatively. To further enhance this engagement, Twitter recently introduced new features to make the site more appealing and acquired Grip to analyze tweets for businesses hungry for user insights.[23]

LinkedIn

Unlike Facebook and Twitter, the LinkedIn site's main purpose is professional networking and job searching.

LinkedIn: An Overview   **LinkedIn** is a business-oriented website that lets users post their professional profiles to connect to a network of businesspeople. These businesspeople are also called *connections*. This social network has over 350 million registered members who conduct 6 billion professionally oriented searches annually. Because of its popularity, over 3 million companies have LinkedIn Company Pages to post news and job openings. LinkedIn's international presence, too, is staggering, used in over 200 countries and 24 languages.[24]

College students—like the one shown here—use LinkedIn to search for summer internships and permanent jobs after graduation.

Courtesy of StuffDOT, Inc.

LinkedIn in a Brand Manager's Strategy   Marketing managers can use LinkedIn to promote their brand in subtle ways. This is done mainly for business-to-business (B2B) image building and networking with industry-related groups. Using LinkedIn, brand managers can demonstrate the organization's expertise and create and moderate discussion groups.

According to a recent survey of small business owners, 41 percent see LinkedIn as potentially beneficial to their company—more than twice that for Facebook, Twitter, or YouTube.[25] LinkedIn recently streamlined its research process for finding qualified employees so that an employer can type its needs into the LinkedIn "search box," which results in a summary that includes people, jobs, groups, and companies. Brand managers also use LinkedIn for business development to identify sales leads and locate vendors.[26] Sales representatives often use LinkedIn to see the profiles of purchasing personnel or managers with whom they are meeting.

LinkedIn in a College Senior's Job Search   Of growing importance, LinkedIn has over 39 million students and recent college graduates as members. College career centers and the LinkedIn student link (http://university.linkedin.com/linkedin-for-students) give key ideas for building an attention-getting LinkedIn profile for students looking for jobs:[27]

- Write an informative short, memorable profile headline.
- Include an appropriate photo of you, nicely dressed, with a plain background that isn't a goofy Instagram "selfie." And smile.
- Create a professional summary—concisely giving your education, qualifications, goals, relevant work experience, and extracurriculars.
- Fill the Skills & Expertise section with keywords and phrases the recruiters use in their searches.
- Include recommendations from people who know you well—supervisors, colleagues, instructors, advisors.
- Set your LinkedIn profile to "public" and create a unique URL (www.linkedin.com/in/JohnSmith) that you also include in your résumé.

Finally, in your LinkedIn profile avoid these 10 most overused buzzwords: responsible, strategic, creative, effective, patient, expert, organizational, driven, innovative, analytical.[28]

YouTube

The ability of YouTube to reach its audience stretches the imagination. Think about this: YouTube's one billion users (1) make four billion views per day, (2) upload 300 hours of video each minute, and (3) generate 40 percent of YouTube's traffic from mobile devices.[29]

YouTube: An Overview   **YouTube** is a video-sharing website in which users can upload, view, and comment on videos. YouTube uses streaming video technology to display user-generated video content that includes movie and TV clips, music videos, and original videos developed by amateurs. While most of the content is uploaded by amateurs, many companies offer material on the site through a YouTube channel.

YouTube redesigns its home page periodically to provide a more organized structure to steer users to "channels," rather than simply encourage them to browse like in the past. Recently, YouTube also redesigned the format for its YouTube channels. These channels serve as home pages for organizations and individuals

Marketing **Matters**

Mobile Marketing Discovers Video Bloggers!

Fifty percent of all YouTube views now take place on a smartphone or a tablet. This incredible shift from just a few years ago signals a new era of consumer behavior and the essential role online video must have in mobile marketing strategies.

Research suggests that when Millennials watch a video on their phones they are twice as engaged as they are when watching on a television. They are also more likely to (1) change their opinion about the brands represented in the ads or the content, (2) discuss the brands with someone else, (3) visit a store carrying the brand, and (4) make a purchase. So getting video messages online is of growing importance to marketers.

Of course placing ads or posting branded content on YouTube is the first level of a mobile marketing strategy. Some marketers, however, have observed that video

> **Video 19-1**
> **Ultimate**
> **Handyman**
> kerin.tv/13e/v19-1

bloggers, or vloggers, are becoming the online versions of traditional celebrities. Snickers, for example, created an online version of its popular "You're Not You When You're Hungry" campaign by having vloggers from F2Freestyles and Ultimate Handyman create videos for their YouTube channels. As Dan Burdett, Snickers global brand director, explains, "Between them the international vloggers in this campaign have over 7.5 million subscribers, giving the brand campaign huge global reach."

How will mobile marketing utilize online video in the future? Experts think 360-degree videos, 4K videos, virtual reality videos, and augmented reality videos are not far into the future!

and allow them to upload their own videos, as well as post and share videos created by others.

What are the most watched videos on YouTube? They are Psy's "Gangnam Style," Justin Bieber's "Baby," and Taylor Swift's "Blank Space" with 2.3 billion, 1.1 billion, and 1.0 billion views, respectively. Each of these artists has YouTube channels that aggregate their music and other videos they have uploaded for fans and other users to view.[30]

YouTube in a Brand Manager's Strategy   YouTube offers great opportunity for a brand manager to produce and show a video that explains the benefits of a complex product. Since YouTube is owned by Google, it incorporates a search engine, so users interested in a specific topic can find it easily. In terms of cost advantages, while a brand manager must pay the cost of creating a video, launching a new channel on YouTube is free. YouTube also offers a program to help small businesses create video ads and buy and manage key words for their video ads on the website. For insight regarding new ways online video is becoming part of mobile marketing strategies see the Marketing Matters box.[31]

OK Go, a music group, watched downloaded songs from the Internet cause a meltdown in its CD sales and experienced difficulty in getting its own record label. So it used YouTube to win fans, licensees, and sponsors for its *very* offbeat music creations. OK Go's YouTube music videos—what it calls "treadmill videos"—are the foundation for its success. Examples include: an animation with 2,300 pieces of toast, the first-ever Rube Goldberg machine that operates in time to music, and paintball guns. OK Go is an example of unknown musicians using YouTube to achieve music success, a route far different than trying to attract attention from a music label company.[32]

Guidelines for marketing and promoting a brand using YouTube videos include:[33]

- Exploit visual aspects of your message, perhaps sacrificing product messages to tell a more entertaining story.

For how OK Go has used "This Too Shall Pass" (49 million views) on YouTube to gain fans, licensees, live shows, and sponsors, see the text.
© OK GO Partnership

- Create a branded channel rich in key words to improve the odds of the video showing up in user searches.
- Target viewers by using YouTube's insights and analytics research to reveal the number of views, the number of visits to your website, and what key words are driving user visits.

Of special interest to brand managers: YouTube recently started guaranteeing its audience size to advertisers—airing additional ads across its channels until they reach a specified percentage of the target audience.[34]

INTEGRATING SOCIAL MEDIA INTO TODAY'S MARKETING STRATEGIES

 LO 19-3 Describe the differing roles of those receiving messages through traditional versus social media and how brand managers select social media.

Thousands of marketing managers around the globe understand how to use traditional media to generate sales for their brand. Some are successful, and others are not. But many of these same managers will admit that social media are so complex they are not sure how best to use them.

This section looks at (1) how social media tie to the strategic marketing process, (2) how to select social media, (3) how social media can be used to generate sales, and (4) how to measure the results of social media programs. The section closes by describing Carmex's "Shot Seen 'Round the World" promotion. The ultimate dream for a brand manager, this Carmex–LeBronJames.com promotion went viral on YouTube!

Social Media and the Strategic Marketing Process

The strategic marketing process described in Chapter 2 and the communication process from sender to receiver in Chapter 17 apply to both traditional and social media. But note these important differences in the communication process:

- Traditional media like magazine or TV ads generally use one-way communication from sender to receiver, those whom the marketer hopes will buy the product advertised. A little word-of-mouth chatting may occur among the "passive receivers," but communications generally end with the receiver.
- Social media deliberately seek to ensure that the message *does not end* with an individual receiver. Instead, the goal is to reach "active receivers," those who will become "influentials" and be "delighted" with the brand advertised. These customers will then become "evangelists," who will send messages to their online friends and then back to the advertiser about the joys of using the brand.

Success in social media marketing relies heavily on the ability of a marketing program to convert "passive receivers" of the message to active "evangelists" who will spread favorable messages about the brand.

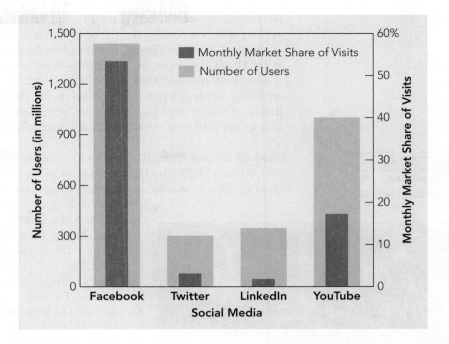

FIGURE 19–4

The number of users and monthly market share of visits for four social media sites: Facebook, Twitter, LinkedIn, and YouTube.

Selecting Social Media

In using social media, a brand manager tries to select and use one or more of the options from the hundreds that exist. This often entails assessing (1) the characteristics of the website's visitors and (2) the number of users or unique visitors to the website.

Audience Data Available for Social Media   Both marketing research organizations and the social media themselves provide user profile data for the social media to help brand managers choose among them. As presented earlier, the top row of Figure 19–2 shows a recent profile of the U.S. male–female audience breakdown for four major social media. As shown in the figure, Facebook users are 58 percent female and 42 percent male, while YouTube users are the reverse, important differences to brand managers allocating promotion budgets.

Recent Activity on the Four Social Media   Figure 19–4 compares the number of users and the monthly market share of visits for Facebook, Twitter, LinkedIn, and YouTube websites. Number of users is a measure of size of the audience. Market share is an indication of the use of the website relative to the other sites. In terms of the number of users, Facebook and YouTube have 1 billion or more users, although Facebook's market share is three times larger. Similarly, Twitter and LinkedIn have between 300 and 350 million users but Twitter has a higher market share indicating more frequent use.[35]

How Social Media Produce Sales

An example shows how a PepsiCo brand manager can use social media to produce sales and profits for her product or brand. Consider the roles of both the PepsiCo brand manager and social media in the following example.[36]

Role of the PepsiCo Brand Manager   The PepsiCo brand manager composes title, copy, and images or photos for the social media ad. She often specifies the web address to which its ad should link based on the brand's social media marketing goals.

To increase awareness and build up a fan base, she might link the ad to the PepsiCo website or its Facebook, Twitter, or Pinterest sites. Ideally, to encourage and produce new sales that can be tracked, she must link the ad to a coupon code, a specific product on the PepsiCo website, or other promotional offer.

The brand manager then defines the characteristics of the one or more market segments she wants to reach on the social media she has selected. This starts with demographic characteristics like geographic region, sex, age range, and education. She then adds factors like relationship status and user interests.

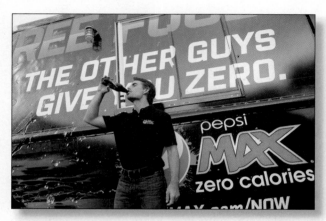

Video 19-2
Pepsi MAX
kerin.tv/13e/v19-2

In choosing to run a social media ad campaign like this Pepsi MAX video on YouTube, brand managers must assess the potential sales likely to result compared to a campaign using traditional media.

© Brian Blanco/Invision for Pepsi/ AP Images

Role of Social Media   Ads and videos on social media like YouTube and Facebook are less likely than traditional print ads to have a marketing objective of immediate sales. This is because social media images are often on the screen for only seconds. A more likely goal is to have viewers go to the advertiser's website and post it on their Facebook Pages or forward it to friends. The key for a brand manager using social media is to gain viewers' attention for a few extra seconds.

PepsiCo's "Test Drive" YouTube video is an example of this strategy. Building on its highly successful "Uncle Drew" videos and TV ads, PepsiCo used its entertaining "Test Drive" video to promote its Pepsi MAX beverages—a zero-calorie cola. In the video, NASCAR driver Jeff Gordon is disguised as "Mike," an average guy taking a test drive at a local dealership. The unsuspecting car salesman riding along will never forget it!

"Test Drive" was a huge hit for Pepsi MAX, with over 35 million views in its first two months. Even better, the video reinforces the product's tag line of "a great-tasting, zero-calorie cola in disguise." As a product in the mature stage of its product life cycle, Pepsi MAX uses an entertaining message to make its diet beverages relevant to a younger target audience. The video captures the viewer's attention by replacing some product messaging with entertainment.[37]

Measuring the Results of Social Media Programs

Performance measures for social media can be divided into (1) those linked to inputs or costs (Figure 19–5) and (2) those tied to the outputs or revenues resulting from social media. Clearly, the ideal performance measure for both conventional and social media is one that ties actual sales revenues to the cost of the ad or other promotion. With the explosion in the growth of social media, marketing and brand managers are being challenged to connect the cost of these new social media promotions to the sales they generate. The result has been an emergence of many new performance measures, often requiring a whole new language.

LO 19-4 Compare the performance measures of social media linked to costs (inputs) versus revenues (outputs).

Performance Measures Linked to Inputs or Costs   Figure 19–5 shows three performance measures for social media linked mainly to inputs or costs. Moving down the list of measures shown in Figure 19–5, one starts with a measure tied only to costs (cost per thousand, or CPM), then moves to a measure of interest in a product (cost per click, or CPC), and finally moves to a measure linked more closely to the sales revenues generated from the social media ad or action (cost per action, or CPA).

The cost per thousand (CPM) measure ties to the number of times the ad loads and a user might see it—but not whether the user has actually reacted to it. This measure is roughly equivalent to the CPM for traditional media discussed in Chapter 18. The cost per click (CPC) measure gives the rate the advertiser pays, say to Facebook, every time a visitor clicks on the ad and jumps from that page to the advertiser's website. Finally,

Performance Measure	Costs to Advertisers	Who Provides It	Who Uses It	An Assessment	
				Advantages	Disadvantages
Cost per thousand (CPM)	"I will pay $0.50 for every 1,000 times this ad loads, up to $100 per month."	Small websites that sell ads directly (may be using a third-party service)	Advertisers who simply want to build "awareness"	Simple to use	Impressions don't always lead to sales
Cost per click (CPC)	"I will pay $1.00 for every visitor who clicks on this ad and goes from your website to mine."	Most websites use this method—executed by a third party like Google/AdWords	Advertisers who want to pay for success, but may not be able to track sales from advertisement to purchase	I only pay for a visitor who has expressed an interest in my ad.	Ads may not display if they are a poor fit for the viewing audience
Cost per action (CPA)	"I will pay $5 for every purchase that originates from an ad on your site."	Usually executed through third parties; Google AdSense offers this feature	Sophisticated advertisers who want to pay for success	I only pay for what works.	Similar to CPC but harder to track and more expensive per action

FIGURE 19–5

Performance measures for social media linked mainly to inputs or costs, as seen by a brand manager.

the cost per action (CPA) measure ties loosely to actual sales—for example, paying $5 for every purchase that originates from an ad, say, on the Facebook site. By summing up the revenues from all these purchases, a difficult task, this CPA measure most closely ties the cost of the social media ad to the sales revenues the ad generates.

Performance Measures Linked to Outputs or Revenues Many of the measures for evaluating how a brand manager's social media promotion is doing reflect the two-way communications present in social media. These measures often tie to output results in terms of "fans," "friends," "followers," or "visitors" to a social media site, which can be a first step to estimating the sales revenue generated. From a brand manager's viewpoint, here are some of the frequently used Facebook measures, moving from the more general to the more specific:

- *Users/members.* Individuals who have registered on a social networking site by completing the process involved, such as providing their name, user ID (usually an e-mail address), and password, as well as answering a few questions (date of birth, gender, etc.).
- *Fans.* The number of people who have opted in to a brand's messages through a social media platform at a given time.
- *Share of voice.* The brand's share or percentage of all the online social media chatter related to, say, its product category or a topic.
- *Page views.* The number of times a Facebook Page is loaded in a given time period.
- *Visitors.* The total number of visitors to a Facebook Page in a given time period; if someone visits three times in one day, she is counted three times.
- *Unique visitors.* The total number of unique visitors to a Facebook Page in a given time period; if someone visits three times in one day, he is counted only once.
- *Average Page views per visitor.* Page views divided by visitors in a given time period.
- *Interaction rate.* The number of people who interact with a Post ("like," make a comment, and so on) divided by the total number of people seeing the Post.
- *Click-through rate (CTR).* Percentage of recipients who have clicked on a link on the Page to visit a specific site.
- *Fan source.* Where a social network following comes from—with fans coming from a friend being more valuable than those coming from an ad.

Pinterest allows users to "pin" or share images of favorite interests on its site, which is useful for brand managers promoting their company's products.

© Lenscap/Alamy

Note that while sales revenues resulting from social media do not appear in these measures, as we move down the list, the measures are often more specific than comparable ones used in traditional media. This is because it is far simpler to electronically track the social media users who click on a website or ad than it is to track consumers who watch, listen to, or read traditional media.

Specialized Focus for Other Social Media   One of the advantages of social media is that communities can form around ideas and commonalities, regardless of the physical location of their members. While major social media such as Facebook or YouTube may garner the majority of the traffic, smaller media like Pinterest may be more successful for some products and services.

Pinterest, a virtual pinboard and content-sharing social network, allows people to "pin" or share images of their favorite things such as clothing, craft ideas, home décor, and recipes. Pinterest members create customized, themed "pinboards" to categorize their images such as "Odds & Ends," "Food," and "Knitting" shown on the Pinterest screen. These images are shared with other members of the Pinterest community. Members can also share their pinned images on Facebook and Twitter.[38]

Pinterest has over 72 million users, 85 percent of whom are women—with 75 percent of daily traffic coming through mobile applications.[39] So it has become a major sales driver for retailers and manufacturers that target women. In using Pinterest, brand managers can post images of their company's products on their Pinterest board and link them back to their websites.

Carmex Goes Viral with Luck and a LeBron James Bear Hug

Brand managers dream about their stars aligning—having their promotions go viral and reaping millions of dollars worth of free brand exposure. Carmex lip balm had this experience!

Achieving a brand manager's wildest dream! The text describes how the Carmex "shot seen 'round the world" achieved this dream—including 33 million YouTube viewers.

Credit: (all) Courtesy of Altus Business Development, Inc.

The Background   As noted earlier in the chapter, Carmex has a partnership with LeBronJames.com. It started when the firm found out that LeBron James of the NBA's Miami Heat professional basketball team uses Carmex in his pregame routine.

The Half-Court Hero Contest   As part of their partnership, Carmex created the "Carmex and LeBronJames.com Half-Court Hero" promotion. The promotion featured an online entry form and weekly prizes leading up to a grand prize drawing for one lucky winner to travel to Miami and have the chance to take a half-court shot worth $75,000. The "Hero" part meant that if the winner hit the shot—made the basket—Carmex would also donate $75,000 to the LeBron James Family Foundation and the Boys and Girls Clubs of America.

Between the third and fourth quarters of a Miami Heat vs. Detroit Pistons game at American Airlines Arena, Michael Drysch walked to center court in front of a sold-out

The Shot

Nothing but Net!

LeBron's Bear Hug

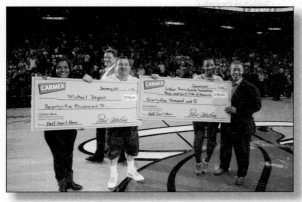

Michael Drysch receives his reward for sinking his unlikely hook shot in the "Carmex and LeBronJames.com 'Half-Court Hero'" promotion. Also benefiting were the LeBron James Family Foundation and the Boys and Girls Clubs of America!

Courtesy of Altus Business Development, Inc.

crowd of 20,000 fans. Michael carefully aligned himself just left of center court, took two steps, and launched a one-handed hook shot.

Nothing but net!! And $75,000 richer!

The crowd erupted as Michael turned and pumped his fist. But before he could celebrate any further, LeBron himself came running out of his Miami Heat huddle to bear hug Michael to the ground in a moment of pure jubilation.

The "Shot Seen 'Round the World" Goes Viral   Instantly, the footage of Half-Court Hero winner Michael Drysch's incredible hook shot and the celebratory bear hug from LeBron James went viral online. NBATV interviewed him side-by-side with James after the game. It was the #1 Play of the Day on ESPN's SportsCenter. The Carmex brand team immediately arranged a public relations tour for Michael Drysch that included a trip to New York City for appearances on *Good Morning America, Inside Edition, CNN Early Start,* and dozens of local radio shows.

Meanwhile, the Carmex marketing team kept Carmex's social media accounts and website updated throughout the weekend with Twitter and Facebook Posts from the public relations tour. Within three months, Carmex's Half-Court Hero shot had been seen by over 30 million YouTube viewers and became the most-watched video of all time on the National Basketball Association's YouTube page. In all, the promotion earned Carmex over 500 million media impressions across TV, print, online, and social media.[40]

Later, Michael and "The Shot" were featured in an ESPN commercial as part of their "I was on Sports Center" campaign. In addition, The Miami Heat visited President Barack Obama to celebrate its National Basketball Association Championship. President Obama, a big basketball fan himself, even referred to Michael and the Carmex Half-Court Hero shot by saying:

Now, one of the cool things about this job is welcoming championship sports teams from across the sporting world to the White House. And usually people enjoy coming to the White House. I have to say, I've never seen folks more excited than the Heat when they came last year. (Laughter.) I mean, LeBron was so pumped up I thought he was going to give me a hug and knock me over like the guy on SportsCenter who hit the half-court shot.[41]

Social Media Lessons for Brand Managers   "The lesson for brand managers is this: Watch for opportunities to manage luck," says Patrick Hudgdon, digital strategist who managed the promotion for Carmex. "Small, smart investments can pay off in big ways when your brand gets lucky. Find ways to use *both* social and traditional media—as we did for Carmex—to help the campaign go viral and to maximize the opportunity to achieve even greater success. Be ready!"

555

learning review »

19-7.   What is the difference between and marketing significance of a "passive receiver" for conventional media and an "active receiver" for social media?

19-8.   Stated simply, how can an advertiser on Facebook expect to generate sales?

19-9.   What did the Carmex team do to exploit its incredible good fortune after seeing Michael Drysch make his "Half-Court Hero" shot?

THE FUTURE: SOCIAL MEDIA + SMARTPHONES + EXOTIC APPS

LO 19-5 Identify the cause of the convergence of the real and digital worlds and how this will affect the future of social media.

Trends in marketing's use of social media reflect what scientists call "mirror worlds" or "smart systems" that are really the convergence of the real and digital worlds. A *smart system* is a computer-based network that triggers actions by sensing changes in the real or digital world. This section discusses: (1) the convergence of real and digital worlds; (2) how this convergence links social media to marketing actions; and (3) where all this *may* be headed in *your* future.

The Convergence of Real and Digital Worlds

Saying that our physical and virtual worlds are converging sounds like science fiction. This convergence of real and digital worlds is the result of a proliferation of interlinked smartphones, tablet devices, sensors, special identification tags, databases, algorithms, apps, and other elements. A look at several of these elements helps explain this real world–digital world convergence and what it means for marketing.

Smartphones   Seeing today's smartphones, users often forget how far they've come in 15 years and how they've changed marketing. In 1998, the RIM 950 revolutionized mobile e-mail. The device had a screen and a keyboard—but *no phone*. The revolution was completed in 2007 with Apple's legendary iPhone. It had all three basics—screen, multitouch keyboard, and phone. Today's GPS-enabled smartphones give mobile consumers access to online ads, local restaurant promotions, and time-sensitive discounts at retailers.[42]

Databases and Algorithms   As discussed in Chapters 8 and 9, finding prospective customers often involves market segmentation that requires databases searched with exotic algorithms—models used to query, organize, manipulate, and present data. The owners of these databases, among them Google and Facebook, must make them as useful as possible to potential advertisers in order to succeed.

Among databases, Google is the hands-down winner—indexing 30 trillion unique web pages across 230 million sites. Its search engine now gives results in answers to research queries in photos, facts, and "direct answers," and not just the "blue links" of website addresses. Google now offers its own social networking service, Google+, to obtain data about individuals by name, personal interests, and identities of friends.[43]

Facebook recently entered Google's territory by announcing Graph Search, its own search engine algorithm. Facebook users can conduct their own queries about people, places, photos, and interests. An example is "restaurants recommended by friends." This lets Facebook give advertisers real value in the "likes" found on its site. For example, a small chocolate retail shop in New York City can target young parents who buy lots of organic food products.[44] So it's not difficult to see how a casual "like" for a brand by a user in a database's "digital world" can converge into an actual "real-world" purchase by the user through a very targeted promotion planned by a brand manager.

Apps   The apps for smartphones are accelerating the convergence of the real and digital worlds. **Apps** (or *mobile apps* or *applications*) are small, downloadable software programs that run on smartphones and tablet devices. When Apple launched its iPhone, it didn't expect smartphone apps to be very important. Wrong! Apple's App Store currently offers 1.5 million apps either free or for sale, and Google Play offers 1.6 million apps for users of Android devices. With the wide array of apps to choose from, today's consumers typically spend two hours a day using about eight apps.[45]

Many apps are video games. Angry Birds, for example, has been downloaded more than 2 billion times since its 2009 release, which is one reason Angry Birds–themed products now range from mascara to toys and entertainment parks. The popularity of the game is declining though as it enters the decline stage of its product life cycle (PLC).[46]

The product life cycle of even very successful video game apps can reach the decline stage quickly—as shown by the Angry Birds game.

© Stock Experiment/Alamy

Video 19-4
Clash of Clans
kerin.tv/13e/v19-4

The text describes the strategy Candy Crush Saga uses to link the technical power of the *digital world* to the human psychology of its players in the *real world.*

© IanDagnall Computing/Alamy

The video games Farmville, Temple Run, QuizUp, 4Pics1Word, and Fruit Ninja also show the short PLC for these apps in today's tough competitive environment.

Enter Clash of Clans and Candy Crush Saga video games that exploit the real world–digital world convergence. Today's successful new video games (1) build on a huge personal-rewards psychology for players; (2) can be played on the small smartphone screens; (3) top the most-downloaded charts of Apple iOS, Google, Android, and Facebook; and (4) often use a "freemium strategy"—where the download is free but users pay for extra features, such as for ways to speed up the game.

Time magazine analyzes how designers of the Candy Crush video game use its key elements to link the *digital world* of Candy Crush to the personal *real-world* satisfactions and rewards of its players:[47]

- *It's better with friends.* Users can give—and get—extra lives using Facebook.
- *It never ends.* There are over 500 levels, and designers add more almost every week.
- *It makes the player feel special.* The game gives positive feedback for nearly every click and tap.
- *It lets a player—sort of—cheat.* Players can pay for power-ups to skip past wait times.
- *It's challenging.* Increasingly varied puzzles often take multiple attempts to complete.

The Candy Crush app has now been installed over 500 million times across Facebook, iOS, and Android devices.

Even Angry Birds has changed its strategy from charging a download cost to a freemium strategy with its recently launched "Angry Birds Go." Sound easy to build an app? Maybe. But hundreds of creative apps die a quiet death each year!

Mobile Marketing: Tightening Links to Marketing Actions

This convergence of the real and digital worlds has also contributed to the growth of *mobile marketing,* or the broad set of interactive messaging options that are used to communicate through personal mobile devices.[48] This continuous connection present in mobile marketing has led to important smartphone apps, such as:

- *Price-comparison searches.* Scan product bar codes or QR codes and research 500,000 stores, synchronizing searches between your computer and your smartphone.
- *Location-based promotions.* Use your GPS-enabled smartphone for location check-ins to receive discounts at stores such as JCPenney.
- *Loyalty programs.* Win loyalty points for walking into stores like Target or Macy's and receive discounts from them.

The number of smartphone shopping searches and purchases has exploded in recent years, causing huge challenges (such as showrooming) for conventional brick-and-mortar retailers.

The clear point of difference in mobile marketing is its unique ability to empower users by connecting with them individually and continuously—learning about their likes and personal characteristics and sharing this information with online friends and (often) marketers selling products. This socially networked world will lead to connected users having more direct interactions with sellers.

The convergence of social media, smartphones, tablet devices, and new apps will lead to companies having a more dynamic interaction with their customers. But is this an unqualified success for buyers? Consider the following perspectives.

A Consumer Purchase Where Sensors Have Some Control

A vending machine scans your face to identify your age and sex and changes its display and—in the future—may give you a quantity discount for buying two of your favorite candy bars (it knows about your Facebook "likes") while showing an electronic dinner coupon for a nearby restaurant if you appear between 7:00 and 9:00 P.M. this evening. The results of the candy and dinner offer are directly measurable for marketers. While it offers unusual convenience, does this buying situation start to interfere with your personal privacy?

A Consumer Purchase Where the Buyer Controls All
Some cities in South Korea and China are on the leading edge of virtual supermarket shopping. Tesco Home Plus, a supermarket chain, provides a quick spur-of-the-moment opportunity for grocery shopping. Shoppers use their smartphones to scan images on the wall of a subway station to buy Tesco's grocery products while waiting for their train. They use the smartphone app to pay for the groceries, which are delivered to their door right after they get home.[49] In this example, buyers achieve great convenience—probably an unqualified success.

Too busy to visit your grocery store this week? If you are in South Korea or China, you can shop on the wall of your subway station with your smartphone—and have your purchases delivered to your door!
© Imaginechina/Corbis

On Privacy: How Much "Convergence" Is Too Much?
Smart systems are fine up to a point. For example, most of us are comfortable letting convergence find us a timely deal at a local restaurant using a location-based app on our smartphone. It may even be all right if Google's latest database breakthrough automatically proposes an "ideal vacation plan" for us based on our normal preferences, weather conditions, and available hotel and airline prices.

But we may be concerned if retailers now place sensors in several hundred locations to track us following the signals emitted from our Wi-Fi-enabled smartphone. Here are some other numbers that may frighten you:

- 2,000-plus. Estimated number of times the online activity of an average Internet user is tracked every day.
- 3,000-plus. Number of "shopping tendencies" Acxiom says it can measure for nearly every U.S. household.
- 700 million. Approximate number of adult consumers in the global database of Acxiom Corp., a leading data broker.

About 68 percent of Internet users today feel that privacy laws don't protect them adequately. So 86 percent of them have used privacy technologies to take online steps to remove or mask their digital data.[50]

The future? Concerned about Internet privacy, the White House recently announced it would seek legislation to define the rights of consumers in the use of data involving their personal characteristics and activities.

19-10. What is an example of how the real (physical) and digital (virtual) worlds are converging?

19-11. What are apps and why are they important?

19-12. Can personal privacy become a problem as the real and digital worlds converge with smart systems?

LEARNING OBJECTIVES REVIEW

LO 19-1 *Define social media and describe how they differ from traditional advertising media.*

Social media are online media where users submit comments, photos, and videos, often accompanied by a feedback process to identify "popular" topics. Social media differ from traditional advertising media (newspapers, magazines, radio, and television) in that user-generated content (1) is relatively inexpensive to create, publish, and access, (2) requires little training to develop, (3) can deliver virtually instantaneous responses, (4) can quickly alter and repost, and (5) may not be as private or anonymous as users expect.

LO 19-2 *Identify the four major social media and how brand managers integrate them into marketing actions.*

Four major social media are Facebook, Twitter, LinkedIn, and YouTube. Facebook is a social network where users create a personal profile, add other users as "friends," and exchange comments, photos, videos, and "likes" with them. To increase traffic to a Facebook Page, brand managers can use paid ads and sponsored stories. Twitter enables users to send and receive "tweets," messages up to 140 characters long. For Twitter, brand managers can use monitoring programs to track what people are saying about their organization's brand. LinkedIn lets users post their personal profiles to a network of businesspeople. LinkedIn can be used to create a company profile to share brand information and career opportunities with LinkedIn users and to demonstrate the company's expertise and professionalism. YouTube is a video-sharing website where users can upload, view, and comment on videos. YouTube also allows marketers to create a brand channel to promote a product, show ads for it, and have viewers comment on it.

LO 19-3 *Describe the differing roles of those receiving messages through traditional versus social media and how brand managers select social media.*

With promotional messages received through traditional media, recipients are generally "passive receivers" and the communication ends with them. In contrast, recipients of social media messages are "active receivers," and the company sending them messages hopes they will become "evangelists" and send positive messages back to the company and to online friends. The factors a marketer uses to select specific social media involve assessing (1) the number of registered users and unique visitors to the company's website, (2) the characteristics (or profile) of those visitors, and (3) the focus of the website. Also, because each of the many social media alternatives has a unique focus (videos, short text messaging, and so on), marketers can modify their marketing programs to take advantage of these differences.

LO 19-4 *Compare the performance measures of social media linked to costs (inputs) versus revenues (outputs).*

Performance measures linked to costs (inputs) include (1) cost per thousand (similar to the CPM for a print ad), which is the number of times an ad is displayed to a user; (2) cost per click (CPC), which gives the rate the advertiser pays each time a visitor clicks on the ad and then jumps to the advertiser's web page; and (3) cost per action (CPA), which is the amount paid for every purchase that originates from an ad on a social media site. Examples of performance measures linked to revenues (outputs) include (1) users/members that have registered on social media websites; (2) the number of unique monthly users viewing the website at a given time; (3) page views, or the number of times a specific web page is loaded; and (4) visitors, or the total number of users viewing a particular web page during a specified time period.

LO 19-5 *Identify the cause of the convergence of the real and digital worlds and how this will affect the future of social media.*

The convergence of the real and digital worlds in social media is the result of the proliferation of interlinked smartphones, tablet devices, sensors, special identification tags, databases, algorithms, apps, and other elements. This convergence will allow consumers and marketers to increase the exchange of personal and product-related information with each other. For consumers, however, this could lead to a loss of privacy and possible exploitation by unscrupulous marketers.

19-1   What are social media?

Answer: Social media are online media where users submit comments, photos, and videos—often accompanied by a feedback process to identify "popular" topics. Business firms also refer to social media as "consumer-generated media." A single social media site with million of users interacting with each other, like Facebook, is a social network.

19-2   In classifying social media, what do we mean by (*a*) media richness and (*b*) self-disclosure?

Answer: Social media can be classified based on two factors: (*a*) Media richness involves the degree of acoustic, visual, and personal contact between two communication partners. (*b*) Self-disclosure involves the degree to which an individual shares his or her thoughts, feelings, likes, and dislikes when engaged in a social interaction.

19-3   Compare traditional media and social media in terms of time required to deliver the communication.

Answer: Traditional media can involve days or even months of continuing effort to deliver the communication, and time lags can be extensive. In contrast, individuals using social media can post virtually instantaneous content.

19-4   How is user-generated content presented by someone using Facebook?

Answer: User-generated content (UGC) refers to the various forms of online media content that are publicly available and created by end users. Facebook users create a personal profile, add other users as friends, and exchange comments, photos, videos, and "likes" with them. Additionally, users may chat with friends and create and join common-interest groups.

19-5   What are some ways brand managers use Facebook to converse with a brand's fans? How does Facebook facilitate mobile marketing activities?

Answer: A brand manager can create awareness for a product, service, or brand by creating a Facebook Page for it. To generate new customers and increase traffic to their Facebook Pages, brand managers can use paid ads and sponsored stories within the Facebook advertising platform. The marketing challenge for a Facebook Page is to post and create the content that will generate the best response. Facebook facilitates mobile marketing with new initiatives such as Instant Articles, Moments, and Custom Audiences, and by integrating its suite of mobile apps, which include Messenger, Instagram, and WhatsApp.

19-6   How can brand managers use YouTube to converse with customers? What is a new form of mobile marketing using online video?

Answer: YouTube allows brand managers to create an actual brand channel to host its advertisements and other video clips that can explain or demonstrate complex products. YouTube can also link to a brand's website. YouTube, because it is a visual medium, allows a brand manager to entertain as well as inform users about the brand. A new form of mobile marketing is the use of vbloggers to reach online audiences.

19-7   What is the difference between and marketing significance of a "passive receiver" for conventional media and an "active receiver" for social media?

Answer: Traditional media, like magazine or TV ads, generally use one-way communication from the sender to the receiver, whom the marketer hopes will buy the product advertised. A little word-of-mouth chatting may occur among

the consumer "passive receivers," but communications generally end with the receiver. Social media deliberately seek to ensure that the message does not end with an individual receiver. Instead, the goal is to reach "active receivers," those who will become "influentials" and be "delighted" with the brand advertised. These will then become "evangelists," who will send messages—user-generated content—to their online friends and then back to the advertiser about the joys of using the brand.

19-8   Stated simply, how can an advertiser on Facebook expect to generate sales?

Answer: The brand manager composes title, copy, and images or photos for an ad to be placed on Facebook. A website address links the ad to the brand's website or its Facebook Page. To encourage and produce new sales that can be tracked, the brand manager might also link the ad to a coupon code or some other promotional offer.

19-9   What did the Carmex team do to exploit its incredible good fortune after seeing Michael Drysch make his "Half-Court Hero" shot?

Answer: At a Miami Heat–Detroit Pistons game, Michael Drysch did the impossible and made Carmex's Half-Court Hero basketball shot. Instantly, the footage of Half-Court Hero winner Michael Drysch's incredible hook shot went viral online. The Carmex brand team immediately arranged a public relations tour for Drysch that included four Miami area news stations and a trip to New York City for appearances on several TV and radio shows. Meanwhile, the Carmex marketing team kept Carmex's social media accounts and website updated throughout the weekend with Twitter and Facebook posts from the public relations tour. Within three months, Carmex's Half-Court Hero shot had been seen by over 20 million YouTube viewers.

19-10   What is an example of how the real (physical) and digital (virtual) worlds are converging?

Answer: The convergence of real and digital worlds is the result of a proliferation of interlinked smartphones, tablet devices, sensors, special identification tags, databases, algorithms, apps, and other elements. In addition, apps for smartphones are accelerating the convergence of the real and digital worlds as they make the devices more productive and provide users with entertainment. Finally, marketers can tailor specific messages to targeted users by using their personal data and preferences so that they can order products and services as a result of receiving these offers.

19-11   What are apps and why are they important?

Answer: Apps are small, downloadable software programs that run on smartphones and tablet devices. They are speeding up the convergence of the real (physical) and digital (virtual) worlds. Many apps are related to social media, such as programs for (1) price-comparison searches; (2) loyalty programs; (3) location-based promotions; and (4) entertainment, such as video games, music, and others.

19-12   Can personal privacy become a problem as the real and digital worlds converge with smart systems?

Answer: The convergence of social media, smartphones, tablet devices, and new apps will lead to companies having a more dynamic interaction with their customers. This convergence allows for the collection of users' personal data, preferences, and behaviors, which allows marketers to tailor offerings based on these data. The issue is, do we want others to know all this information about us?

FOCUSING ON KEY TERMS

apps p. 556
blog p. 540
Facebook p. 544

LinkedIn p. 547
social media p. 540
Twitter p. 546

user-generated content
  (UGC) p. 540
YouTube p. 548

APPLYING MARKETING KNOWLEDGE

1   In your new job as a retail store manager you decide to add mobile marketing to your promotional campaign. Describe how a Bluetooth Low Energy (BLE) beacon could increase sales in your store.

2   You and three college friends have decided to launch an online business selling clothes college students wear—T-shirts, shorts, sweats, and so on. You plan to use Facebook ads. What "likes" or interests do (a) college men and (b) college women have that might help you in planning your Facebook strategy?

3   You are about to graduate from college and want a job in marketing research or sales. Go to the LinkedIn site, register, and determine what information you would put on your LinkedIn profile to help you find a new job.

4   What is the significance of user-generated content when contrasted with social media and traditional media?

5   You are a brand manager for a sneaker manufacturer like Nike or New Balance and are trying to use Facebook to reach (a) college-aged women and (b) men over 55 years of age. What three or four "likes" or interests would you expect each segment to have when you try to reach it with Facebook?

6   In measuring the results of social media, what are the (a) advantages and (b) disadvantages of performance measures linked directly to revenues versus costs?

BUILDING YOUR MARKETING PLAN

Remembering the target market segments you identified in Chapter 8 for your marketing plan:

1   (a) Identify which one of the four social media described in the chapter would be most useful and (b) give your reasons. Would you consider other social media like Pinterest? Why or why not?

2   Briefly describe (a) how you would use this website to try to increase sales of your products and (b) why you expect target market customers to respond to it.

561

VIDEO CASE 19   StuffDOT™, Inc.: Rewarding Users for Actively Shopping and Sharing!

"Coming from a rewards and loyalty background, I often wondered how to combine the best of rewards and commissions with the expanding universe of social media," says Jennifer Katz, founder and chief executive officer of StuffDOT, Inc.

Video 19-5
StuffDOT Video Case
kerin.tv/13e/v19-5

"Further, it seemed really unfair that only a few people were benefiting from all the content millions of people were providing for free online. I believe the individuals creating all this online content deserve to benefit from their efforts," says Katz.

"Thinking about this, one day our marketing director came into a meeting and explained how a really cute anchor bracelet that she posted on a social-sharing site went viral. But now she faced a six-week backlog to purchase it. So we all said, if she made a commission on every anchor bracelet that was sold because of that one post, she could have bought five. Right then and there, StuffDOT was born," explains Katz.

While the young social network is constantly changing, its beginnings offer a valuable case study.

STUFFDOT'S VISION, BRAND NAME, AND LOGO

StuffDot is designed to be the all-in-one site for online shopping and sharing. StuffDOT's vision is to reward users for what they are already doing online. Most other sites tend to keep all the affiliate fees and commissions for themselves. StuffDOT, however, enables users to benefit from all this online shopping and sharing. This is the first time, to StuffDOT's knowledge, that a firm has developed a platform where the people posting to social media are the same people who are rewarded for it. In addition, the StuffDOT team has added coupons, cash-back shopping from thousands of retailers, and a feature that allows users to create their own stores, called DOT shops.

"We chose the brand name StuffDOT because it was catchy and [we] felt we could really build on it," says Katz. "With the name StuffDOT, we could use Stuff, DOT, and StuffDOT, which also gives flexibility. The name also is great for campaigns like 'CareDot,' 'Spot the Dot,' or 'Stuff I Like.' The team tried other names, but they just didn't have that fun stickiness that the name StuffDOT does," says Jennifer Katz.

The StuffDOT team also tried and tested several different logos before coming up with the memorable, attention-getting logo shown above. People see the orange dot as friendly, familiar, and eye-catching and it has proven to be an easy logo to build on.

HOW STUFFDOT WORKS

Kelsey Fisher, StuffDOT's creative director, explains what a "Dot" is and the steps in "Dotting"—keys to understanding how StuffDOT users earn and redeem their resulting commissions.

What Is a "Dot"?

"Dots are posts ranging from products, to Do-It-Yourself projects, to recipes, to funny videos and random photos," Fisher explains. "A dot is something posted to view, to share, or to track for a future

Courtesy of StuffDOT, Inc.

Courtesy of StuffDOT, Inc.

purchase. A dot is simply a post of anything you want to display on the StuffDOT site," she says.

How to "Dot"

Kelsey Fisher explains the three steps to dot:

1. "Use the simple drag-and-drop process to add the 'Dot It' button to your toolbar in your web browser.
2. "Dot or post items you 'like' online by clicking on that button on your toolbar. For example, if you are browsing Macy's online store and see something you like, you can click on the 'Dot It' button in your toolbar and it will show up on your StuffDOT page.
3. "Watch your commissions grow as people share, buy, or click on the stuff you've 'dotted.' You can also earn commissions on your own purchases!" Fisher says.

Earning and Redeeming StuffDOT Commissions

So how does an online user actually earn commissions? When a user finds things they want to share or purchase online, they dot or post the item to StuffDOT. If the item appears with a sticker showing a commission percentage, this means it is from one of StuffDOT's retail partners and is commission-eligible.

When a dot leads to a purchase or a click-through view, or a share by the 'dotter' or someone else, the dotter will receive a commission. Users can also earn commissions by posting and purchasing their own items. Once a user's balance reaches $15, they can start redeeming gift cards from a variety of popular retailers."

ENHANCING STUFFDOT'S USER-FRIENDLINESS

A challenge for the StuffDOT team is keeping it simple, yet having features that make StuffDOT fun and rewarding.

"I work closely with the StuffDOT team to turn the concepts they create into user-friendly features on StuffDOT," says Sudipta Tripathy, StuffDOT's chief technology officer. "For example, we want to ensure that all new features have the same look and feel across all parts of the StuffDOT platform—website, Android app, or iOS app," he says.

Recent updates and features now enable StuffDOT users more ways to earn commissions. By moving many features to its mobile apps (photo), StuffDOT has added the flexibility to share, shop, and earn anywhere at any time. Some other examples of user-friendly features include:

- Retailer List. Adding a list of retailers and their commission percentages lets StuffDOT shoppers know the exact rewards from each store. Also, users can discover reward-eligible shops they did not even know about.
- Search Shops & Deals. Users now can search for products and deals from StuffDOT's retailers without leaving the site. StuffDOT members can then find, dot, and buy commission-eligible items in one easy-to-use platform.
- Commission Status. The redesigned commissions section shows users the values of their lifetime, current, and pending commissions. So they can track their purchase commissions and confirm their purchases are commission-eligible.

Courtesy of StuffDOT, Inc.

MARKETING STUFFDOT

StuffDOT has focused its initial marketing efforts on three areas: (1) partnerships, (2) the StuffDOT Internship and Campus Ambassador Program, and (3) social sharing.

StuffDOT's partnerships include online affiliate aggregators that give users access to over 20,000 online retailers that share affiliate fees and commissions.

In addition, StuffDOT has been working with select retailers to create unique promotional programs that benefit users and make the partner brand more prominent. For example, a recent promotion featured a free pair of running shoes for signing up, referring friends, and dotting. This not only built awareness for the brand of running shoes, but it also created a new user base for StuffDOT.

The StuffDOT internship and campus ambassador program (photo) not only gives students a rich experience working in new social media, but it has greatly enhanced the benefits of the StuffDOT platform. Student interns work both at the home office and on campus to create StuffDOT promotions. Depending on their interests, students may focus on organizing new-user workshops and street-team promotions or finding new partners and users through social networks. StuffDOT is looking continuously for new Campus Ambassadors.

Social-sharing features throughout the StuffDOT site make it very convenient for users to share items with friends or family. For example, a student who wants a new laptop for her birthday can share that item with friends on Facebook, and she can also e-mail that item with an embedded link to her parents as a reminder. That student can also earn a StuffDOT reward on the purchase—a "double" birthday present.[51]

Questions

1 What recent StuffDOT actions have added to its user-friendliness?
2 (a) Who are StuffDOT's major competitors and (b) what point(s) of difference should StuffDOT use to distinguish itself from them?
3 How should StuffDOT be marketed so that it becomes an integral part of everyday life?
4 How can the team create "buzz" for StuffDOT and grow its user base most effectively (a) using social media platforms (like Facebook and Twitter) and (b) using its own website?

Chapter Notes

1. "Connecting with the Cosmos: The Total Audience Media Universe," *Newswire,* Nielsen, March 19, 2015; Marc de Swaan Arons, Frank van den Driest, and Keith Weed, "The Ultimate Marketing Machine," *Harvard Business Review,* July–August 2014, pp. 55–63; Gian Fulgoni and Andrew Lipsman, "Digital Game Changers: How Social Media Will Help Usher in the Era of Mobile and Multi-Platform Campaign-Effectiveness Measurement," *Journal of Advertising Research,* March 2014, pp. 11–16; Tina Desai, "The Future of Mobile Marketing: Connecting the Physical with Digital," *Marketing Week,* November 26, 2014, p. 1; Peter Roesler, "Why Mobile Marketing Is Still the Next Big Thing," www.inc.com, August 18, 2014; Steven Tweedie, "The 10 Most Popular Apps of 2014," *Business Insider,* December 29, 2014; and Lauren Johnson, "This Year's 10 Biggest Shifts, Shake-Ups and Surprises in Mobile Marketing," *Adweek,* December 21, 2014, p. 1.

2. Dave Evans, *Social Media Marketing: An Hour a Day* (Indianapolis, IN: Wiley Publishing, Inc., 2009), pp. 57–59.

3. Andreas M. Kaplan and Michael Haenlein, "Users of the World, Unite! The Challenges and Opportunities of Social Media," *Business Horizons* 53, no. 1 (2010), pp. 59–68.

4. Guy Levy-Yurista, "Web 3.0 and Tomorrow's IoT: Human Identity Delivers the 'Internet of Me,'" http://insights.wired.com, December 16, 2015; and Sramana Mitra, "From E-Commerce to Web 3.0: Let the Bots Do the Shopping, www.wired.com, September 16, 2014.

5. Evans, *Social Media Marketing: An Hour a Day,* pp. 57–59; Jason Miletsky, *Principles of Internet Marketing* (Boston, MA: Course Technology, Cengage Learning, 2010), pp. 75–76; Kristin Tillotson, "Blogging's Getting Old These Days," *Star Tribune,* December 22, 2010, p. E1; and Soumitra Dutta and Matthew Fraser, "Web 2.0: The ROI Case," *CEO Magazine,* May/June 2009, pp. 42–44.

6. "Participative Web and User-Created Content: Web 2.0, Wikis, and Social Networking" (Paris: Organization for Economic Co-operation and Development, 2007); and Jason Daley, "Tearing Down the Walls," *Entrepreneur,* December 2010, pp. 57–60.

7. Kaplan and Haenlein, "Users of the World, Unite!" pp. 62–64.

8. Drake Bennett, "Ten Years of Inaccuracy and Remarkable Detail," *Bloomberg Businessweek,* January 10–January 16, 2011, pp. 57–61.

9. Michael Sebastian, "LinkedIn Sells Nearly Half a Billion Dollars in Ads Last Year," www.adage.com, February 5, 2015; and Jim Edwards, "This LinkedIn Deck Shows the ROI for 8 of Its Biggest Ad Clients," *Business Insider,* August 3, 2012.

10. Chiranjeev Kohli, Rajneesh Suri, and Anuj Kapoor, "Will Social Media Kill Branding?" Business Horizons, 58 (2015), pp. 35–44; and Starr Hall and Chadd Rosenberg, *Get Connected: The Social Networking Toolkit for Business* (Madison, WI: Entrepreneur Press, 2009), pp. 17–20.

11. Figure 16–2 is adapted from "The CMO's Guide to the 2014 Social Landscape." See http://visual.ly/cmos-guide-2014-social-landscape.

12. Aaron Smith, "6 New Facts about Facebook," www.pewresearch.org, Pew Research Center, February 3, 2014; "Announcing 2 Million Advertisers on Facebook," press release, Facebook website, http://newsroom.fb.com, February 24, 2015; Ashlee Vance, "Your Facebook Data Are Here," *Bloomberg Businessweek,* October 7–October 13, 2013, pp. 42–44; and Cooper Smith, "7 Statistics about Facebook Users That Reveal Why It's Such a Powerful Marketing Platform," *Business Insider,* November 16, 2013.

13. "Top 10 Ways to Engage Fans on Facebook," Buddy Media, Inc., 2010.

14. Ned Smith, "How Much Is a Facebook Friend Worth? $174.17," *BusinessNewsDaily,* April 26, 2013. See http://www.businessnewsdaily.com/4402-value-facebook-friend-marketing.html.

15. The discussion of StuffDOT was provided by Kelsey Fisher, Jenny Caffoe, Lexi Diderich, and Malyn Mueller of StuffDOT, Inc.

16. Deepa Seetharaman, "Facebook to Enhance Messenger App," *The Wall Street Journal,* March 26, 2015, p. B8.

17. Deepa Seetharaman, "Facebook Pushes Speedier News Publishing," *The Wall Street Journal,* May 14, 2015, p. B4.

18. Deepa Seetharaman, "Facebook' Facial Recognition Is Latest AI Step," *The Wall Street Journal,* June 24, 2015, p. B5; and Molly McHugh, "Facebook Moments Is a Smarter Photo App—Much Smarter," www.wired.com, June 15, 2015.

19. Rolfe Winkler and Jack Marshall, "Google Imitates Facebook with E-mail Marketing," *The Wall Street Journal,* April 15, 2015, p. B4; Vindu Goel, "Rise in Mobile Ads Pushes Up Facebook Results," *Star Tribune,* January 30, 2014, p. D3; and Evelyn M. Rusli, "For Mark Zuckerberg, Tumult and Turnaround," *The Wall Street Journal,* January 6, 2014, pp. A1,10.

20. Seetharaman, "Facebook to Enhance Messenger App."

21. Twitter website, https://about.twitter.com/company.

22. Thomas Lee, "Social-Media Bees Create Target Buzz," *Star Tribune,* April 13, 2013, pp. A1, A6; and Jeff Herring and Maritza Parra, "Make the Most of Tweeting," *Star Tribune,* January 6, 2011, p. E4.

23. Elizabeth Dwoskin and Yoree Koh, "Twitter Pushes Deeper into Data," *The Wall Street Journal,* April 16, 2014, p. B2.

24. LinkedIn website, https://press.linkedin.com/about-linkedin; and Craig Smith, "By the Numbers: 80 Amazing LinkedIn Statistics," *DMR Digital Marketing Ramblings,* February 9, 2014.

25. "LinkedIn Is Trying to Quicken Its Pulse," *Bloomberg Businessweek,* April 22–April 28, 2013, pp. 32–33; Emily Moltby and Shira Ovide, "Which Social Media Work?" *The Wall Street Journal,* January 31, 2013, p. B8; and Brandon Bailey, "Who Needs Friends? LinkedIn Has Success with Members," *Star Tribune,* April 25, 2013, pp. D1, D3.

26. Johnathon Podensky, "LinkedIn Search Just Got Smarter," LinkedIn Official Blog, March 25, 2103, http://blog.linkedin.com/2013/03/25/linkedin-search-just-got-smarter/.

27. "Building a Great Student Profile," LinkedIn for Students. See http://university.linkedin.com/linkedin-for-students.html.

28. Kolby Goodman, "Stand Above the Rest," *Diary of Alpha Kappa Psi,* Spring 2014, pp. 12–14.

29. YouTube website, https://www.youtube.com/yt/press/statistics.html; Craig Smith, "By the Numbers: 90+ Amazing YouTube Statistics," *DMR Digital Marketing Ramblings,* June 8, 2015; and Amanda Axvig, Vice President of Marketing, AOI Marketing, Inc.

30. Daisy Wyatt, "Most Viewed YouTube Videos of All Time: From 'Gangnam Style' to Katy Perry's 'Dark Horse,'" *The Independent,* June 26, 2015, http://www.independent.co.uk/artsentertainment/music/features/most-viewed-youtube-videos-from-gangnam-style-to-wreckingball-9607483.html; and YouTube website, https://www.youtube.com/results?search_query=most+viewed+video+on+youtube+of+all+time.

31. "Neal Mohan, "How to Win the Moments That Matter with Mobile Video," *Adweek,* April 3, 2015, p. 1; "Why Online Video Is a Must-Have for Your Mobile Marketing Strategy,"

www.thinkwithgoogle.com, April 2015; Alison Millington, "Snickers Seeking Global Reach with New Vlogger-Led Digital Campaign," *Marketing Week,* April 8, 2015; and Sarah Vizard, "YouTube at 10: How It Plans to Stay Ahead," *Marketing Week,* May 15, 2015.

32. Jonah Weiner, "Video Makes the Radio Star," *Bloomberg Businessweek,* April 1–April 7, 2013, pp. 75–77; and Amanda Axvig, Vice President of Marketing, AOI Marketing, Inc.

33. Lauren Drell, "Hashtags, and Infographics, and Videos! Oh My!" *Marketing Insights,* March/April 2014, pp. 40–47; Christa Toole, "Ten Tips for Those Who Still Aren't Using YouTube," *Advertising Age,* www.adage.com, October 19, 2010; and Felix Gillette, "On YouTube, Seven-Figure Views, Six-Figure Paychecks," *Bloomberg Businessweek,* September 27–October 3, 2010, pp. 35–36.

34. Suzanne Vranica, "YouTube to Offer Guarantees to Advertisers," *The Wall Street Journal,* March 31, 2014, p. B5.

35. "Most Popular Social Media Website in the United States in March 2015, Based on Share of Visits," *The Statistics Portal,* www.statista.com, 2015; and *DMR Digital Marketing Ramblings.*

36. This example and the section on measuring results were provided by Brian Stuckey and Amanda Axvig of StuffDOT, Inc.

37. The Jeff Gordon–Pepsi Max example was provided by Nancy Harrower, Concordia University–St. Paul; and Sheila Shayon, "Pepsi Continues to Bask in Branded Content Glory with Top YouTube Views," *Brand Channel,* April 8, 2013. See http://www.brandchannel.com/home/post/2013/04/08/Pepsi-Tops-YouTube-Leaderboard-040813.aspx.

38. Mae Anderson, "A Look at Why Social Media Site Pinterest Is Catnip to Retailers and Shoppers Alike," *Star Tribune,* April 25, 2014.

39. Craig Smith, "By the Numbers: 90+ Amazing Pinterest Statistics," *DMR Digital Marketing Ramblings,* May 23, 2015.

40. The Carmex "Half-Court Hero" example was written by Patrick Hodgdon, Manager of Digital Marketing, Bolin Marketing.

41. See https://www.whitehouse.gov/photos-and-video/video/2014/01/14/president-obama-honors-2013-nba-champion-miami-heat#transcript.

42. Sam Grobart, "Think Colossal," *Bloomberg Businessweek,* April 1, 2013, pp. 58–64.

43. Evelyn M. Rusli and Amir Efrati, "Facebook on Collision Course with Google on Web Searches," *The Wall Street Journal,* January 16, 2013, pp. A1, A10.

44. Evelyn M. Rusli, "Buy Signal: Facebook Widens Data Targeting," *The Wall Street Journal,* April 10, 2013, p. B4; and Hayley Tsukayama, "Facebook's Big Reveal: Social Search," *Star Tribune,* January 16, 2013, p. D6.

45. Jessi Hempel, "Smartphones: The War to Be No. 3," *Fortune,* February 4, 2013, pp. 35–36.

46. Juhana Rossi, "Angry Birds' Maker Perches for Global Growth Takeoff," *The Wall Street Journal,* April 4, 2013, p. B4; Spencer E. Ante, "Rovio Mines Video with 'Angry Birds Toons,'" *The Wall Street Journal,* March 12, 2013, p. B6; and John Gaudiosi, "Rovio Execs Explain What Angry Birds Toons Channel Opens Up to Its 1.7 Billion Gamers," *Forbes,* March 13, 2013. See http://www.forbes.com/sites/johngaudiosi/2013/03/11/rovio-execs-explain-what-angry-birdstoons-channel-opens-up-to-its-1-7-billion-gamers.

47. Telis Demos, "'Candy Crush' Maker Targets $7.6 Billion Value," *The Wall Street Journal,* March 13, 2014, p. B7; and "Tech, Mobile Games: Sweet! Delicious!" *Time,* December 2, 2013, pp. 51–54.

48. Andreas M. Kaplan, "If You Love Something, Let It Go Mobile: Mobile Marketing and Mobile Social Media 4x4," *Business Horizons* 55, no. 2 (2012), pp. 129–39.

49. Martin Petit D'Meurville, Kimberley Pham, and Courney Trin, "Shop on the Go," *Business Today,* February 15, 2015, pp. 113–16; and Kara McGuire, "Shoppers Hunt Bargains via Their Smart Phones," *Star Tribune,* November 28, 2010, pp. D1, D10.

50. Elizabeth Dwoskin, "Give Me Back My Privacy," *The Wall Street Journal,* March 24, 2014, pp. R1–2; Georgia Wells, "Real-Time Marketing in a Real-Time World," *The Wall Street Journal,* March 24, 2014, p. R3; and Elizabeth Dwoskin, "What Your Phone Is Sharing about Your Secrets," *The Wall Street Journal,* January 14, 2014, pp. B1, 4.

51. StuffDOT, Inc.: This case was written by Jennifer Katz, Amanda Axvig, and William Rudelius.

20

Personal Selling and Sales Management

LEARNING OBJECTIVES

After reading this chapter you should be able to:

 LO 20-1 Discuss the nature and scope of personal selling and sales management in marketing.

 LO 20-2 Identify the different types of personal selling.

 LO 20-3 Explain the stages in the personal selling process.

 LO 20-4 Describe the major functions of sales management.

Meet Today's Sales Professional

Have you been considering sales as a career opportunity? If so, then consider Lindsey Smith as a role model.

Lindsey Smith began her career representing Molecular Imaging Products within the Medical Diagnostics Division of GE Healthcare Americas. She joined the company eleven years ago right out of college with a BBA degree. The epitome of today's sales professional, she lists integrity, motivation, trust and relationship building, and a team orientation as just a few of the ingredients necessary for a successful sales career today.

As a sales professional, she recognizes the importance of constantly updating and refining her product knowledge, analytical and communication skills, and strategic thinking about opportunities to more fully satisfy each customer's clinical, economic, and technical requirements. And for good reason. Her customer contacts include physicians (radiologists, neurologists, and cardiologists), medical technologists, nurses, and health care provider CEOs, CFOs, and other administrators.

Lindsey Smith's selling orientation and customer relationship philosophy rest on four pillars:

1. *A commitment to creating value for clients.* Lindsey believes "every sales call and client interaction should create value for both the customer and the company."

2. *Seek to serve clients as a trusted consultant.* Lindsey emphasizes "being a resource for my customers by providing novel solutions for them."

3. *Reinforce the company's competitive advantage.* Lindsey continually reinforces GE Healthcare Americas' competitive advantage: "I emphasize my company's value proposition and showcase the company's product innovation, solutions, and service."

4. *Regard challenges as opportunities.* Lindsey says, "I consider challenges as opportunities to provide innovative solutions and resources to customers and to build client trust and long-term relationships."

Lindsey Smith's approach to selling and customer relationships has served her customers and her well. She is among the company's top revenue producers and has a long list of loyal customers. Not surprisingly, Ms. Smith has been a recipient of the company's Commercial Excellence Award in six of the last eight years.

© Hillsman Stuart Jackson

In 2014, Lindsey Smith was promoted to her current position as senior client director at GE Healthcare Americas. In this capacity, she represents and manages the entire GE Healthcare Americas company portfolio, including medical technology, health care consulting, information technology, service operations, and finance solutions for one of GE's largest strategic health care systems. She manages 75 commercial and operations personnel.[1]

This chapter describes the scope and significance of personal selling and sales management in marketing and creating value for customers. It first highlights the many forms of personal selling. Next, the major steps in the selling process are outlined with an emphasis on building buyer–seller relationships.

The chapter then focuses on salesforce management and its critical role in achieving a company's broader marketing objectives. Three major salesforce management functions are then detailed. They are sales plan formulation, sales plan implementation, and salesforce evaluation. Finally, technology's persuasive influence on how selling is done and how salespeople are managed is described.

SCOPE AND SIGNIFICANCE OF PERSONAL SELLING AND SALES MANAGEMENT

Chapter 17 described personal selling and management of the sales effort as being part of the firm's promotional mix. Although it is important to recognize that personal selling is a useful vehicle for communicating with present and potential buyers, it is much more. Take a moment to answer the questions in the personal selling and sales management quiz in Figure 20–1. As you read on, compare your answers with those in the text.

Nature of Personal Selling and Sales Management

> **LO 20-1** Discuss the nature and scope of personal selling and sales management in marketing.

Personal selling involves the two-way flow of communication between a buyer and seller, often in a face-to-face encounter, designed to influence a person's or group's purchase decision. However, personal selling also takes place over the telephone and through video teleconferencing and Internet-enabled links between buyers and sellers.

Personal selling remains a highly human-intensive activity despite the use of technology. Accordingly, the people involved must be managed. **Sales management** involves planning the selling program and implementing and evaluating the personal selling effort of the firm. The tasks involved in managing personal selling include setting objectives; organizing the salesforce; recruiting, selecting, training, and compensating salespeople; and evaluating the performance of individual salespeople.

Selling Happens Almost Everywhere

"Everyone lives by selling something," wrote author Robert Louis Stevenson a century ago. This is particularly true for manufacturing sales personnel, real estate brokers, stockbrokers, and salesclerks who work in retail stores. In reality, however, virtually every occupation that involves customer contact has an element of personal selling. For example, attorneys, accountants, bankers, and company personnel recruiters perform sales-related activities, whether or not they acknowledge it.

FIGURE 20–1

Personal selling and sales management quiz. Check your answers as you read the chapter.

1. What percentage of chief executive officers in the largest U.S. companies have significant sales experience in their work history? (check one)

   10% _____   30% _____   50% _____
   20% _____   40% _____   60% _____

2. About what percentage of an average field sales representative's time each work-week is spent actually selling to customers by phone or face-to-face? (check one)

   40% _____   50% _____   60% _____

3. "A salesperson's job is finished when a sale is made." True or false? (circle one)

   True   False

4. About what percentage of U.S. companies include customer satisfaction as a measure of salesperson performance? (check one)

   10% _____   30% _____   50% _____
   20% _____   40% _____   60% _____

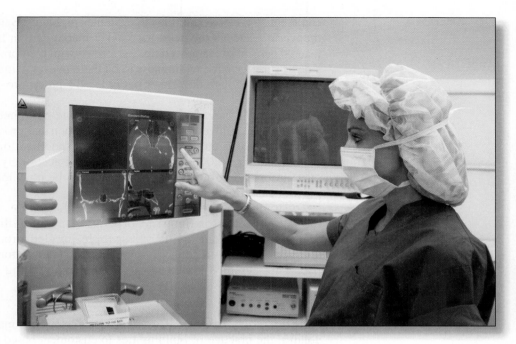

About 20 percent of chief executive officers in the largest U.S. corporations have significant sales experience in their work history.[2] (*What percentage did you check for question 1 in Figure 20–1?*) Thus, selling often serves as a stepping-stone to top management, as well as being a satisfying career path itself.

Personal Selling in Marketing and Entrepreneurship

Personal selling serves three major roles in a firm's overall marketing effort. First, salespeople are the critical link between the firm and its customers. This role requires that salespeople match company interests with customer needs to satisfy both parties in the exchange process. Second, salespeople *are* the company in a consumer's eyes. They represent what a company is or attempts to be and are often the only personal contact a customer has with the company. For example, as acknowledged by IBM's former chief executive officer, the company's 40,000-strong salesforce is "our face to the client."[3] Third, personal selling may play a dominant role in a firm's marketing program. This situation typically arises when a firm uses a push marketing strategy, described in Chapter 17. Avon, for example, pays almost 40 percent of its total sales dollars for selling expenses.

Personal selling has been also shown to be critical to successful entrepreneurial efforts for three reasons.[4] First, selling a business concept to potential investors is an entrepreneur's first sales effort. Second, selling the business concept to prospective employees necessary for the success of the venture is essential. Finally, the more traditional sales art of convincing customers to buy one's product or service, getting referrals, and building professional networks is necessary. In short, highly successful entrepreneurs have a great sales talent.

Creating Customer Solutions and Value through Salespeople: Relationship and Partnership Selling

As the critical link between the firm and its customers, salespeople can create customer value in many ways. For instance, by being close to the customer, salespeople can identify creative solutions to customer problems. Salespeople at Medtronic, Inc., the world leader in the heart pacemaker market, are in the operating room for more than 90 percent of the procedures performed with their product and are on call 24 hours a day. "It reflects the willingness to be there in every situation, just in case a problem arises—even though nine times out of ten the procedure goes just fine," notes a satisfied customer.[5]

Salespeople can create value by easing the customer buying process. This happened at TE Connectivity, a producer of electrical products. Salespeople and customers had a difficult time getting product specifications and performance data on the company's 70,000 products quickly and accurately. The company now has all of its information on its website, which can be downloaded instantly by salespeople and customers.

Customer value is also created by salespeople who follow through after the sale. At Jefferson Smurfit Corporation, a multibillion-dollar supplier of packaging products, one of its salespeople juggled production from three of the company's plants to satisfy an unexpected demand for boxes from General Electric. This person's action led to the company being given GE's Distinguished Supplier Award.

Relationship Selling Customer value creation is made possible by **relationship selling**, the practice of building ties to customers based on a salesperson's attention and commitment to customer needs over time. Relationship selling involves mutual respect and trust among buyers and sellers. It focuses on creating long-term customers, not a one-time sale. A survey of 300 senior sales executives revealed that 96 percent consider "building long-term relationships with customers" to be the most important activity affecting sales performance.[6]

Partnership Selling Some companies have taken relationship selling a step further and forged partnerships between buyer and seller organizations. With **partnership selling**, sometimes called *enterprise selling*, buyers and sellers combine their expertise and resources to create customized solutions; commit to joint planning; and share customer, competitive, and company information for their mutual benefit and, ultimately, the benefit of the customer.

As an approach to sales, partnership selling relies on cross-functional business specialists who apply their knowledge and expertise to achieve better customer solutions, lower cost, and greater customer value. Partnership selling complements the supply partnerships described in Chapter 6. This practice is embraced by General Electric, Honeywell, DuPont, and IBM.

Relationship and partnership selling represent another dimension of customer relationship management. Both emphasize the importance of first learning about customer needs and wants and then tailoring solutions to customer problems as a means to customer value creation. Recent research suggests that a salesperson may have a genetic predisposition to create customer value. See the Marketing Matters box for details.[7]

learning review »

20-1. What is personal selling?

20-2. What is involved in sales management?

Marketing Matters

Science and Selling: Is Customer Value Creation in Your Genes?

Is a predisposition to create customer value in your genes? Are you a born salesperson? Recent research by University of Michigan Marketing Professor Richard P. Bagozzi and his colleagues offers a novel insight into this question that may or may not surprise you.

Their research identifies a genetic marker, the 7R variant of the DRD_4 gene, that is correlated with a salesperson's predisposition or willingness to interact with customers and learn about their problems in order to meet their needs. The researchers also found that the presence of the A1 variant of the DRD_2 gene is correlated with predisposition or tendency to try to persuade customers to buy a given product rather than listen to their needs.

These two different genetic markers help explain the difference between a salesperson's customer orientation versus sales orientation. A customer orientation is guided by such ideas as, "I try to align customers who have problems with products that will help them solve their problems," where the aim is to satisfy mutual needs and the hope is to build a long-term relationship.

In contrast, a sales orientation is driven by notions such as, "I try to sell customers all I can convince them to buy, even if I think it is more than a wise customer should buy." In this case, the motivation is to satisfy one's own short-term interests and not necessarily the needs of the customer.

Faced with a selling situation, do you have a sales orientation or a customer orientation? Customer value creation may be in your genes!

© Dimitri Otis/Photographer's Choice/Getty Images

571

THE MANY FORMS OF PERSONAL SELLING

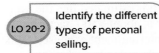

LO 20-2 Identify the different types of personal selling.

Personal selling assumes many forms based on the amount of selling done and the amount of creativity required to perform the sales task. Broadly speaking, three types of personal selling exist: order taking, order getting, and customer sales support activities. While some firms use only one of these types of personal selling, others use a combination of all three.

Order-Taking Salespeople

Typically, an **order taker** processes routine orders or reorders for products that were already sold by the company. The primary responsibility of order takers is to preserve an ongoing relationship with existing customers and maintain sales.

Two types of order takers exist. *Outside order takers* visit customers and replenish inventory stocks of resellers, such as retailers or wholesalers. For example, Frito-Lay salespeople call on supermarkets, convenience stores, and other establishments to ensure that the company's line of snack products (such as Lay's potato chips and Doritos and Tostitos tortilla chips) is in adequate supply. In addition, outside order takers often provide assistance in arranging displays.

Inside order takers, also called *order clerks* or *salesclerks,* typically answer simple questions, take orders, and complete transactions with customers. Many retail clerks are inside order takers. Inside order takers are often employed by companies that use *inbound telemarketing,* the use of toll-free telephone numbers that customers can call to obtain information about products or services and make purchases. In business-to-business settings, order taking arises in straight rebuy situations as described in Chapter 6.

Order takers generally do little selling in a conventional sense. They engage in modest problem solving with customers. They often represent products that have few options, such as magazine subscriptions and highly standardized industrial products. Inbound telemarketing is also an essential selling activity for more "customer service" driven firms, such as Dell. At these companies, order takers undergo extensive training so that they can better assist callers with their purchase decisions.

Order-Getting Salespeople

An **order getter** sells in a conventional sense and identifies prospective customers, provides customers with information, persuades customers to buy, closes sales, and follows up on customers' use of a product or service. Like order takers, order getters can be inside (an automobile salesperson) or outside (a Xerox salesperson).

Order getting involves a high degree of creativity and customer empathy and is typically required for selling complex or technical products with many options, so considerable product knowledge and sales training are necessary. In modified rebuy or new-buy purchase situations in business-to-business selling, an order getter acts as a problem solver who identifies how a particular product may satisfy a customer's need. Similarly, in the purchase of a service, such as insurance, an insurance agent can provide a mix of plans to satisfy a buyer's needs depending on income, stage of the family's life cycle, and investment objectives.

Order getting is not a 40-hour-per-week job. Industry research shows that outside order getters, or field service representatives, often work over 50 hours per week. As shown in Figure 20–2, 41 percent of an average field sales representative's time is actually spent selling by phone or face-to-face. (*What percentage did you check for question 2 in Figure 20–1?*) Another 24 percent is devoted to generating leads and researching customer accounts. The remainder of a sales representative's workweek is occupied by administrative tasks, meetings, service calls, travel, training, and customer follow-up.[8]

Order getting by outside salespeople is also expensive.[9] It is estimated that the average cost of a single field sales call on a business customer is about $500, factoring in the salesperson's compensation, benefits, and travel-and-entertainment expenses. This cost illustrates why outbound telemarketing is popular. *Outbound telemarketing* is the practice of using the telephone rather than personal visits to contact current and prospective customers. A much lower cost per sales call (from $20 to $25) and little or no field expense accounts for its widespread appeal.

Customer Sales Support Personnel

Customer sales support personnel augment the selling effort of order getters by performing a variety of services. For example, *missionary salespeople* do not directly solicit orders but rather concentrate on performing promotional activities and introducing new products. They are used in the pharmaceutical industry, where they encourage physicians to prescribe a firm's product. Actual sales are made through

Selling by phone or face-to-face

Generating leads and researching accounts

41%

24%

19%

16%

Service calls, travel, training, customer follow-up, etc.

Meeting and administrative tasks

FIGURE 20–2

How do outside order-getting salespeople spend their time each week? You might be surprised after reading the text.

Photos: Top left: © Asia Images/Getty Images; Top right: © Tetra Images/ Getty Images; Bottom right: © Susan Van Etten/ PhotoEdit, Inc; Bottom left: © Stanley Fellerman/Corbis

wholesalers or directly to pharmacists who fill prescriptions. *Sales engineers* specialize in identifying, analyzing, and solving customer problems. These salespeople bring know-how and technical expertise to the selling situation but often do not actually sell products and services. Sales engineers are popular in selling business products such as chemicals and heavy equipment.

Many firms engage in cross-functional **team selling**, the practice of using an entire team of professionals in selling to and servicing major customers.[10] Team selling is used when specialized knowledge is needed to satisfy the different interests of individuals in a customer's buying center. A selling team might consist of a salesperson, a sales engineer, a service representative, and a financial executive, each of whom would deal with a counterpart in the customer's firm.

Selling teams take different forms. In *conference selling,* a salesperson and other company resource people meet with buyers to discuss problems and opportunities. In *seminar selling,* a company team conducts an educational program for a customer's technical staff, describing state-of-the-art developments. IBM and Xerox pioneered cross-functional team selling in working with prospective buyers. Since then, other firms have embraced this practice to create and sustain value for their customers, as described in the Marketing Matters box.[11]

learning review   ≫

20-3. What is the principal difference between an order taker and an order getter?

20-4. What is team selling?

Creating and Sustaining Customer Value through Cross-Functional Team Selling

The day of the lone salesperson calling on a customer is rapidly becoming history. Today, 75 percent of companies employ cross-functional teams of professionals to work with customers to improve relationships, find better ways of doing things, and, of course, create and sustain value for their customers.

Xerox and IBM pioneered cross-functional team selling, but other firms have been quick to follow as they spotted the potential to create and sustain value for their customers. Recognizing that corn growers needed a herbicide they could apply less often, a DuPont team of chemists, sales and marketing executives, and regulatory specialists created just the right product that recorded sales of $57 million in its first year. Procter & Gamble uses teams of marketing, sales, advertising, computer systems, and supply chain personnel to work with its major retail-ers, such as Walmart, to identify ways to develop, promote, and deliver products. Pitney Bowes, Inc., which produces sophisticated computer systems that weigh, rate, and track packages for firms such as UPS and FedEx, also uses sales teams to meet customer needs. These teams consist of sales personnel, "carrier management specialists," and engineering and administrative executives who continually find ways to improve the technology of shipping goods across town and around the world.

Efforts to create and sustain customer value through cross-functional team selling have become a necessity as customers seek greater value for their money. According to the vice president for procurement of a *Fortune* 500 company, "Today, it's not just getting the best price but getting the best value—and there are a lot of pieces to value."

© blickwinkel/Alamy

THE PERSONAL SELLING PROCESS: BUILDING RELATIONSHIPS

LO 20-3 Explain the stages in the personal selling process.

Selling, and particularly order getting, is a complicated activity that involves building buyer–seller relationships. Although the salesperson–customer interaction is essential to personal selling, much of a salesperson's work occurs before this meeting and continues after the sale itself. The **personal selling process** consists of six stages: (1) prospecting, (2) preapproach, (3) approach, (4) presentation, (5) close, and (6) follow-up (see Figure 20–3).

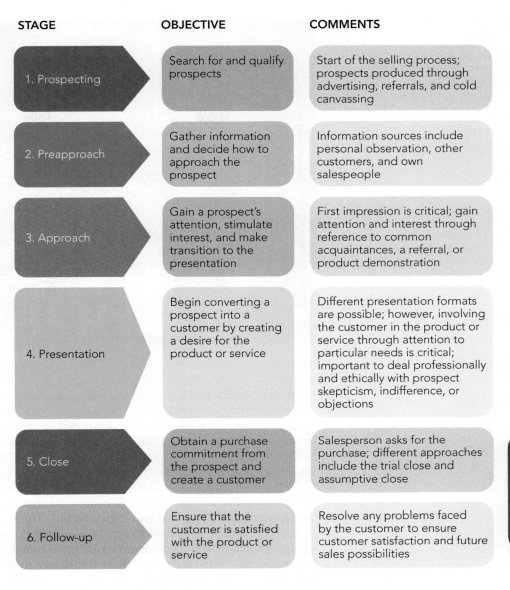

FIGURE 20–3

Stages and objectives of the personal selling process. Each stage is critical for successful selling and building a customer relationship.

STAGE	OBJECTIVE	COMMENTS
1. Prospecting	Search for and qualify prospects	Start of the selling process; prospects produced through advertising, referrals, and cold canvassing
2. Preapproach	Gather information and decide how to approach the prospect	Information sources include personal observation, other customers, and own salespeople
3. Approach	Gain a prospect's attention, stimulate interest, and make transition to the presentation	First impression is critical; gain attention and interest through reference to common acquaintances, a referral, or product demonstration
4. Presentation	Begin converting a prospect into a customer by creating a desire for the product or service	Different presentation formats are possible; however, involving the customer in the product or service through attention to particular needs is critical; important to deal professionally and ethically with prospect skepticism, indifference, or objections
5. Close	Obtain a purchase commitment from the prospect and create a customer	Salesperson asks for the purchase; different approaches include the trial close and assumptive close
6. Follow-up	Ensure that the customer is satisfied with the product or service	Resolve any problems faced by the customer to ensure customer satisfaction and future sales possibilities

Prospecting: Identifying and Qualifying Prospective Customers

Personal selling begins with the *prospecting* stage—the search for and qualification of potential customers. There are three types of prospects. A *lead* is the name of a person who may be a possible customer. A *prospect* is a customer who wants or needs the product. If an individual wants the product, can afford to buy it, and is the decision maker, this individual is a *qualified prospect*.

Leads and prospects are generated using several sources. For example, advertising may contain a coupon or a toll-free number to generate leads. Some companies use exhibits at trade shows, professional meetings, and conferences to generate leads or prospects. Staffed by salespeople, these exhibits are used to attract the attention of prospective buyers and share information. Others utilize the Internet for generating leads and prospects. Today, salespeople are using websites, e-mail, and social networks, such as LinkedIn, to connect to individuals and companies that may be interested in their products or services.

Another approach for generating leads is through *cold canvassing* or *cold calling,* either in person or by telephone. This approach simply means that a salesperson may open a directory, pick a name, and contact that individual or business. Despite its high refusal rate, cold canvassing can be successful.[12] However, cold canvassing is frowned upon in some cultures. For example, in most Asian and Latin American societies, personal visits, based on referrals, are expected.

Cold canvassing is often criticized by U.S. consumers and is now regulated. Research shows that 75 percent of U.S. consumers consider this practice an intrusion on their privacy, and 72 percent find it distasteful.[13] The *Telephone Consumer Protection Act* (1991) contains provisions to curb abuses such as early morning or late night calling. Additional federal regulations require more complete disclosure regarding solicitations, include provisions that allow consumers to avoid being called at any time through the Do Not Call Registry, and impose fines for violations. For example, satellite television provider DirecTV was fined $5.3 million for making thousands of calls to consumers who had put their telephone numbers on the Do Not Call Registry.[14]

Preapproach: Preparing for the Sales Call

Once a salesperson has identified a qualified prospect, preparation for the sale begins with the preapproach. The *preapproach* stage involves obtaining further information on the prospect and deciding on the best method of approach. Knowing how the prospect prefers to be approached and what the prospect is looking for in a product or service is essential, regardless of industry or cultural setting.

For instance, a Merrill Lynch stockbroker will need information on a prospect's discretionary income, investment objectives, and preference for discussing brokerage services over the telephone or in person. For business product companies such as Texas Instruments, the preapproach involves identifying the buying role of a prospect (for example, influencer or decision maker), important buying criteria, and the prospect's receptivity to a formal or informal presentation. Identifying the best time to contact a prospect is also important. Northwestern Mutual Life Insurance Company suggests that the following are the best times to call on people in different occupations:

dentists before 9:30 A.M., lawyers between 11:00 A.M. and 2:00 P.M., and college professors between 7:00 and 8:00 P.M.

The *preapproach* stage is especially important in international selling, where customs dictate appropriate protocol. In many South American countries, for example, buyers expect salespeople to be punctual for appointments. However, prospective buyers are routinely 30 minutes late. South Americans take negotiating seriously and prefer straightforward presentations, but a hard-sell approach will not work.[15]

Successful salespeople recognize that the preapproach stage should never be short-changed. Their experience coupled with research on customer complaints indicates that failure to learn as much as possible about the prospect is unprofessional and the ruin of a sales call.

Approach: Making the First Impression

The *approach* stage involves the initial meeting between the salesperson and the prospect, where the objectives are to gain the prospect's attention, stimulate interest, and build the foundation for the sales presentation itself and the basis for a working relationship. The first impression is critical at this stage, and it is common for salespeople to begin the conversation with a reference to common acquaintances, a referral, or even the product or service itself. Which tactic is taken will depend on the information obtained in the prospecting and preapproach stages.

How business cards are exchanged with Asian customers is very important. Read the text to learn the appropriate protocol in the approach stage of the personal selling process.

© *Phillip Jarrell/Taxi/Getty Images*

The approach stage is very important in international settings.[16] In many societies outside the United States, considerable time is devoted to nonbusiness talk designed to establish a rapport between buyers and sellers. For instance, it is common for two or three meetings to occur before business matters are discussed in the Middle East and Asia. Gestures are also very important. The initial meeting between a salesperson and a prospect in the United States customarily begins with a firm handshake. Handshakes also apply in France, but they are gentle, not firm. Forget the handshake in Japan. An appropriate bow is expected. What about business cards? Business cards should be printed in English on one side and the language of the prospective customer on the other. Knowledgeable U.S. salespeople know that their business cards should be handed to Asian customers using both hands, with the name facing the receiver. In Asia, anything involving a person's name demands respect.

Presentation: Tailoring a Solution for a Customer's Needs

The *presentation* stage is at the core of the order-getting selling process, and its objective is to convert a prospect into a customer by creating a desire for the product or service. Three major presentation formats exist: (1) stimulus-response format, (2) formula selling format, and (3) need-satisfaction format.

Stimulus-Response Format The **stimulus-response presentation** format assumes that given the appropriate stimulus by a salesperson, the prospect will buy. With this format the salesperson tries one appeal after another, hoping to hit the right button. A counter clerk at McDonald's is using this approach when he or she asks whether you'd like an order of french fries or a dessert with your meal. The counter clerk is engaging in what is called *suggestive selling*. Although useful in this setting, the stimulus-response format is not always appropriate, and for many products a more formalized format is necessary.

Formula Selling Format   The **formula selling presentation** format is based on the view that a presentation consists of information that must be provided in an accurate, thorough, and step-by-step manner to inform the prospect. A popular version of this format is the *canned sales presentation,* which is a memorized, standardized message conveyed to every prospect. Used frequently by firms in telephone and door-to-door selling of consumer products (for example, Kirby vacuum cleaners), this approach treats every prospect the same, regardless of differences in needs or preferences for certain kinds of information.

Canned sales presentations can be advantageous when the differences between prospects are unknown or with novice salespeople who are less knowledgeable about the product and selling process than experienced salespeople. Although it guarantees a thorough presentation, it often lacks flexibility and spontaneity. More important, it does not provide for feedback from the prospective buyer—a critical component in the communication process and the start of a relationship.

Need-Satisfaction Format   The stimulus-response and formula selling formats share a common characteristic: The salesperson dominates the conversation. By comparison, the **need-satisfaction presentation** format emphasizes probing and listening by the salesperson to identify the needs and interests of prospective buyers. Once these are identified, the salesperson tailors the presentation to the prospect and highlights product benefits that may be valued by the prospect. The need-satisfaction format, which emphasizes problem solving and customer solutions, is the most consistent with the marketing concept and relationship building.

Two selling styles are common with this format.[17] **Adaptive selling** involves adjusting the presentation to fit the selling situation, such as knowing when to offer solutions and when to ask for more information. Sales research and practice show that knowledge of the customer and sales situation are key ingredients for adaptive selling. Many consumer service firms such as brokerage and insurance firms and consumer product firms like Rockport, AT&T, and Gillette effectively apply this selling style.

Consultative selling focuses on problem identification, where the salesperson serves as an expert on problem recognition and resolution. With consultative selling, problem solution options are not simply a matter of choosing from an array of existing products or services. Rather, novel solutions often arise, thereby creating unique value for the customer.

Consultative selling is prominent in business-to-business marketing. Johnson Controls' Automotive Systems Group, IBM's Global Services, DHL Worldwide Express, GE Healthcare Americas, and Xerox offer customer solutions through their consultative selling style. According to a senior Xerox sales executive, "Our business is no longer about selling boxes. It's about selling digital, networked-based information management solutions, and this requires a highly customized and consultative selling process. So we look for consultative and business-savvy salespeople." But what does a customer solution really mean? The Marketing Matters box offers a unique answer.[18]

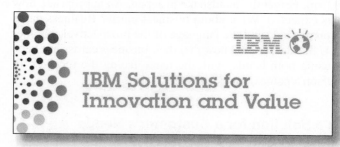

IBM is a leader in consultative selling with its focus on developing novel solutions that create customer value.
Source: International Business Machines Corp.

Handling Objections   A critical concern in the presentation stage is handling objections. *Objections* are excuses for not making a purchase commitment or decision. Some objections are valid and are based on the characteristics of the product or service or price. However, many objections reflect prospect skepticism or indifference. Whether valid or not, experienced salespeople know that objections do not put

Marketing Matters

Imagine This . . . Putting the Customer into Customer Solutions!

Solutions for problems are what companies are looking for from suppliers. At the same time, suppliers focus on customer solutions to differentiate themselves from competitors. So what is a customer solution and what does it have to do with selling?

Sellers view a solution as a customized and integrated combination of products and services for meeting a customer's business needs. But what do buyers think? From a buyer's perspective, a solution is one that (1) meets their requirements, (2) is designed to uniquely solve their problem, (3) can be implemented, and (4) ensures follow-up.

This insight arose from a field study conducted by three researchers at Emory University. Their in-depth study also yielded insight into what an effective

© Frank Herholdt/Stone/Getty Images

customer solution offers. According to one buyer interviewed in their study:

They (the supplier) make sure that their sales and marketing guys know what's going on. The sales and technical folks know what's going on, and the technical and support guys know what's going on with me. All these guys are in the loop, and it's not a puzzle for them.

So what does putting the customer into customer solutions have to do with selling? Three things stand out. First, considerable time and effort is necessary to fully understand a specific customer's requirements. Second, effective customer solutions are based on relationships among sellers and buyers. And finally, consultative selling is central to providing novel solutions for customers, thereby creating value for them.

579

an end to the presentation. Rather, techniques can be used to deal with objections in a courteous, ethical, and professional manner. The following six techniques are the most common:[19]

1. *Acknowledge and convert the objection.* This technique involves using the objection as a reason for buying. For example, a prospect might say, "The price is too high." The reply: "Yes, the price is high because we use the finest materials. Let me show you. . . ."

2. *Postpone.* The postpone technique is used when the objection will be dealt with later in the presentation: "I'm going to address that point shortly. I think my answer would make better sense then."

3. *Agree and neutralize.* Here a salesperson agrees with the objection, then shows that it is unimportant. A salesperson would say, "That's true. Others have said the same. But, they thought that issue was outweighed by other benefits."

4. *Accept the objection.* Sometimes the objection is valid. Let the prospect express such views, probe for the reason behind it, and attempt to stimulate further discussion on the objection.

5. *Denial.* When a prospect's objection is based on misinformation and clearly untrue, it is wise to meet the objection head on with a firm denial.

6. *Ignore the objection.* This technique is used when it appears that the objection is a stalling mechanism or is clearly not important to the prospect.

Each of these techniques requires a calm, professional interaction with the prospect and is most effective when objections are anticipated in the preapproach stage. Handling objections is a skill requiring a sense of timing, appreciation for the prospect's state of mind, and adeptness in communication. Objections also should be handled ethically. Lying or misrepresenting product or service features are grossly unethical practices.

The closing stage involves obtaining a purchase commitment from the prospect. Read the text to learn how the close itself can take several forms.

© Purestock/GettyImages

Close: Asking for the Customer's Order or Business

The *closing* stage in the selling process involves obtaining a purchase commitment from the prospect. This stage is the most important and the most difficult because the salesperson must determine when the prospect is ready to buy. Telltale signals indicating a readiness to buy include body language (prospect reexamines the product or contract closely), statements ("This equipment should reduce our maintenance costs"), and questions ("When could we expect delivery?").

The close itself can take several forms. Three closing techniques are used when a salesperson believes a buyer is about ready to make a purchase: (1) trial close, (2) assumptive close, and (3) urgency close. A *trial close* involves asking the prospect to make a decision on some aspect of the purchase: "Would you prefer the blue or gray model?" An *assumptive close* entails asking the prospect to consider choices concerning delivery, warranty, or financing terms under the assumption that a sale has been finalized. An *urgency close* is used to commit the prospect quickly by making reference to the timeliness of the purchase: "The low interest financing ends next week," or "That is the last model we have in stock." Of course, these statements should be used only if they accurately reflect the situation; otherwise, such claims would be unethical. When a prospect is clearly ready to buy, the final close is used, and a salesperson asks for the order.

Follow-up: Solidifying the Relationship

The selling process does not end with the closing of a sale; rather, professional selling requires customer follow-up. One marketing authority equated the follow-up with courtship and marriage by observing, "The sale merely consummates the courtship. Then the marriage begins. How good the marriage is depends on how well the relationship is managed."[20] The *follow-up* stage includes making certain the customer's purchase has been properly delivered and installed and addressing any difficulties experienced with the use of the item. Attention to this stage of the selling process solidifies the buyer–seller relationship. Research shows that the cost and effort to obtain repeat sales from a satisfied customer is roughly half of that necessary to gain a sale from a new customer.[21] In short, today's satisfied customers become tomorrow's qualified prospects or referrals. (*What was your answer to question 3 in the Figure 20–1 quiz?*)

learning review »

20-5. What are the six stages in the personal selling process?

20-6. What is the distinction between a lead and a qualified prospect?

20-7. Which presentation format is most consistent with the marketing concept? Why?

THE SALES MANAGEMENT PROCESS

LO 20-4 Describe the major functions of sales management.

Selling must be managed if it is going to contribute to a firm's marketing objectives. Although firms differ in the specifics of how salespeople and the selling effort are managed, the sales management process is similar across firms. Sales management consists of three interrelated functions: (1) sales plan formulation, (2) sales plan implementation, and (3) salesforce evaluation (see Figure 20–4).

Making **Responsible Decisions**

The Ethics of Asking Customers about Competitors

Salespeople are a valuable source of information about what is happening in the marketplace. By working closely with customers and asking good questions, salespeople often have firsthand knowledge of customer problems and wants. They also are able to spot the activities of competitors. However, should salespeople explicitly ask customers about competitor strategies such as pricing practices, product development efforts, and trade and promotion programs?

Gaining knowledge about competitors by asking customers

© Color Day Production/Getty Images

for information is a ticklish ethical issue. Research indicates that 25 percent of U.S. salespeople engaged in business-to-business selling consider this practice unethical, and their companies have explicit guidelines for this practice.

It is also noteworthy that Japanese salespeople consider this practice to be more unethical than do U.S. salespeople.

Do you believe that asking customers about competitor strategies and practices is unethical? Why or why not?

Sales Plan Formulation: Setting Direction

Formulating the sales plan is the most basic of the three sales management functions. According to the vice president of the Harris Corporation, a global communications company, "If a company hopes to implement its marketing strategy, it really needs a detailed sales planning process."[22] The **sales plan** is a statement describing what is to be achieved and where and how the selling effort of salespeople is to be deployed. Sales plan formulation involves three tasks: (1) setting objectives, (2) organizing the salesforce, and (3) developing account management policies.

Setting Objectives Setting objectives is central to sales management because this task specifies what is to be achieved. In practice, objectives are set for the total salesforce and for each salesperson.

Selling objectives can be output related and focus on dollar or unit sales volume, number of new customers added, or profit. Alternatively, they can be input related and emphasize the number of sales calls and selling expenses. Output- and input-related objectives are used for the salesforce as a whole and for each salesperson. A third type of objective that is behaviorally related is typically specific for each salesperson and includes his or her product knowledge, customer service satisfaction ratings, and selling and communication skills.

Increasingly, firms are also emphasizing knowledge of competition as an objective since salespeople are calling on customers and should see what competitors are doing. In fact, 89 percent of companies encourage their salespeople to gather competitive intelligence.[23] But should salespeople explicitly ask their customers for information about competitors? Read the Making Responsible Decisions box to see how salespeople view this practice.[24]

FIGURE 20–4

The sales management process involves sales plan formulation, sales plan implementation, and salesforce evaluation.

Sales plan formulation
- Setting objectives
- Organizing the salesforce
- Developing account management policies

Sales plan implementation
- Salesforce recruitment and selection
- Salesforce training
- Salesforce motivation and compensation

Salesforce evaluation
- Quantitative assessment
- Behavioral evaluation

Whatever objectives are set, they should be precise and measurable and specify the time period over which they are to be achieved. Once established, these objectives serve as performance standards for the evaluation of the salesforce, the third function of sales management.

Organizing the Salesforce   Organizing a selling organization is the second task in formulating the sales plan. Three questions are related to organization. First, should the company use its own salesforce, or should it use independent agents such as manufacturer's representatives? Second, if the decision is made to employ company salespeople, then should they be organized according to geography, customer type, or product or service? Third, how many company salespeople should be employed?

The decision to use company salespeople or independent agents is made infrequently. The decision itself is based on an analysis of economic and behavioral factors. An economic analysis examines the costs of using both types of salespeople and is a form of break-even analysis, which was discussed in Chapter 13.

Consider a situation in which independent agents would receive a 5 percent commission on sales, and company salespeople would receive a 3 percent commission, salaries, and benefits. In addition, with company salespeople, sales administration costs would be incurred for a total fixed cost of $500,000 per year. At what sales level would independent or company salespeople be less costly? This question can be answered by setting the costs of the two options equal to each other and solving for the sales level amount (using algebra!), as shown in the equation:

Total cost of company salespeople = Total cost of independent agents

$$[0.03(X) + \$500,000] = 0.05(X)$$

where X = sales volume. Solving for X, sales volume equals $25 million, indicating that below $25 million in sales independent agents would be cheaper, but above $25 million a company salesforce would be cheaper. This relationship is shown in Figure 20–5.

Economics alone does not answer this question. A behavioral analysis is also necessary and should focus on issues related to the control, flexibility, effort, and availability of independent and company salespeople.[25] A firm must weigh the pros and cons of the economic and behavioral factors before making this decision.

If a company elects to employ its own salespeople, then it must choose an organizational structure based on (1) geography, (2) customer, or (3) product (see Figure 20–6). A *geographical sales organization* is the simplest structure, where the

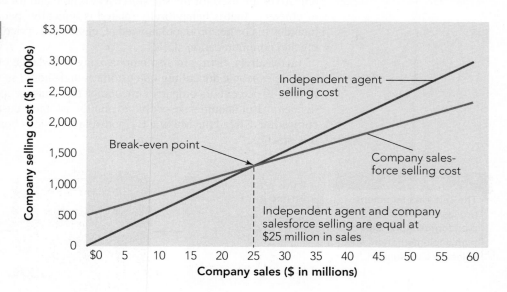

FIGURE 20–5

A break-even chart for comparing independent agents and a company salesforce includes an analysis of selling costs and sales. The break-even point occurs when company salesforce selling cost equals independent agent selling cost.

FIGURE 20–6
Different sales organizations.

Geographical sales organization

- General Sales Manager
  - Eastern Regional Sales Manager
  - Western Regional Sales Manager
    - District Sales Manager
    - District Sales Manager
      - Individual Salespeople

Customer sales organization

- General Sales Manager
  - Sales Manager Auto Industry
  - Sales Manager Farm and Construction Equipment
    - District Sales Manager
    - District Sales Manager
      - Individual Salespeople

Product sales organization

- General Sales Manager
  - Divisional Sales Manager Product A
  - Divisional Sales Manager Product B
    - Eastern Regional Sales Manager
    - Western Regional Sales Manager
      - District Sales Manager
      - District Sales Manager
        - Individual Salespeople

United States, or indeed the globe, is first divided into regions and each region is divided into districts or territories. Salespeople are assigned to each district with defined geographical boundaries and call on all customers and represent all products sold by the company. An advantage of this structure is that it can minimize travel time, expenses, and duplication of selling effort. However, if a firm's products or customers require specialized knowledge, then a geographical structure is unsuitable.

When different types of buyers have different needs, a *customer sales organization* is used. In practice this means that a different salesforce calls on each separate type of buyer or marketing channel. For example, Konica switched from a geographical to a marketing channel structure with different sales teams serving specific retail channels: mass merchandisers, photo specialty outlets, and food and drug stores. The rationale for this approach is that more effective, specialized customer support and knowledge are provided to buyers. However, this structure often leads to higher administrative costs and some duplication of selling effort, because several salesforces are used to represent the same products.

An important variation of the customer organizational structure is **key account management**—the practice of using team selling to focus on important customers so as to build mutually beneficial, long-term, cooperative relationships.[26] Key account management involves teams of sales, service, and often technical personnel who work with purchasing, manufacturing, engineering, logistics, and financial executives in customer organizations. This approach, which often assigns company personnel to a customer account, results in "customer specialists" who can provide exceptional service. Procter & Gamble uses this approach with Walmart, as does Black & Decker with Home Depot.

When specific knowledge is required to sell certain types of products, then a *product sales organization* is used. For example, Maxim Steel has a salesforce that sells drilling pipe to oil companies and another that sells specialty steel products to manufacturers. The advantage of this structure is that salespeople can develop expertise with technical characteristics, applications, and selling methods associated with a particular product or family of products. However, this structure produces high administrative costs and duplication of selling effort, because two company salespeople may call on the same customer.

In short, there is no one best sales organization for all companies in all situations.[27] Rather, the organization of the salesforce should reflect the marketing strategy of the firm. Each year about 10 percent of U.S. firms change their sales organizations to implement new marketing strategies.

The third question related to salesforce organization involves determining the size of the salesforce. For example, why do you think Frito-Lay has about 18,000 salespeople who call on supermarkets, convenience stores, and other establishments to sell snack foods? The answer lies in the number of accounts (customers) served, the frequency of calls on accounts, the length of an average call, and the amount of time a salesperson can devote to selling.

A common approach for determining the size of a salesforce is the **workload method**. This formula-based method integrates the number of customers served, call frequency, call length, and available selling time to arrive at a figure for the salesforce size. For example, Frito-Lay needs about 18,000 route salespeople according to the following workload method formula:

$$NS = \frac{NC \times CF \times CL}{AST}$$

Where,

NS = Number of salespeople
NC = Number of customers
CF = Call frequency necessary to service a customer each year
CL = Length of an average call
AST = Average amount of selling time available per year

How many route salespeople does Frito-Lay need to sell and service its retail accounts?

© David Goldman/AP Images for Frito Lay

Frito-Lay route salespeople sell and display products in 350,000 supermarkets, convenience stores, and other establishments. Salespeople should call on these accounts at least once a week, or 52 times a year. The average sales call lasts an average of 83 minutes (1.38 hour). An average salesperson works 2,000 hours a year (50 weeks × 40 hours a week), but 12 hours a week are devoted to nonselling activities such as travel and administration, leaving 1,400 hours a year. Using these guidelines, Frito-Lay needs

$$NS = \frac{350,000 \times 52 \times 1.38}{1,400} = 17,940 \text{ route salespeople}$$

The value of this formula is apparent in its flexibility; a change in any one of the variables will affect the number of salespeople needed. Changes are determined, in part, by the firm's account management policies.

Developing Account Management Policies The third task in formulating a sales plan involves developing **account management policies** specifying whom salespeople should contact, what kinds of selling and customer service activities should be engaged in, and how these activities should be carried out. These policies might state which individuals in a buying organization should be contacted, the amount of sales and service effort that different customers should receive, and the kinds of information salespeople should collect before or during a sales call.

An example of an account management policy in Figure 20–7 shows how different accounts or customers can be grouped according to level of opportunity and the firm's competitive sales position.[28] When specific account names are placed in each cell, salespeople clearly see which accounts should be contacted, with what kind of selling and service activity, and how to deal with them. Accounts in cells 1 and 2 might have high frequencies of personal sales calls and increased time spent on a call. Cell 3 accounts will have lower call frequencies, and cell 4 accounts might be contacted through telemarketing or direct mail rather than in person. For example, Union Pacific Railroad put its 20,000 smallest accounts on a telemarketing program. A subsequent survey of these accounts indicated that 84 percent rated Union Pacific's sales effort "very effective" compared with 67 percent before the switch.

Competitive position of sales organization

High — Low

Account opportunity level

High — Low

1

Attractiveness: Accounts offer a good opportunity because they have high potential and the sales organization has a strong position.

Account management policy: Accounts should receive a high level of sales calls and service to retain and possibly build accounts.

3

Attractiveness: Accounts may offer a good opportunity if the sales organization can overcome its weak position.

Account management policy: Emphasize a heavy sales organization position or shift resources to other accounts if a stronger sales organization position is impossible.

2

Attractiveness: Accounts are somewhat attractive because the sales organization has a strong position, but future opportunity is limited.

Account management policy: Accounts should receive a moderate level of sales and service to maintain the current position of the sales organization.

4

Attractiveness: Accounts offer little opportunity, and the sales organization position is weak.

Account management policy: Consider replacing personal calls with telephone sales or direct mail to service accounts. Consider dropping the account if unprofitable.

FIGURE 20–7

An account management policy grid grouping customers according to level of opportunity and the firm's competitive sales position.

Sales Plan Implementation: Putting the Plan into Action

The sales plan is put into practice through the tasks associated with sales plan implementation. Whereas sales plan formulation focuses on "doing the right things," implementation emphasizes "doing things right." The three major tasks involved in implementing a sales plan are (1) salesforce recruitment and selection, (2) salesforce training, and (3) salesforce motivation and compensation.

Salesforce Recruitment and Selection   Effective recruitment and selection of salespeople is one of the most crucial tasks of sales management. It entails finding people who match the type of sales position required by a firm. Recruitment and selection practices will differ greatly between order-taking and order-getting sales positions, given the differences in the demands of these two jobs. Therefore, recruitment and selection begin with a carefully crafted job analysis and job description followed by a statement of job qualifications.

A *job analysis* is a study of a particular sales position, including how the job is to be performed and the tasks that make up the job. Information from a job analysis is used to write a *job description,* a written document that describes job relationships and requirements that characterize each sales position. It explains (1) to whom a salesperson reports, (2) how a salesperson interacts with other company personnel, (3) the customers to be called on, (4) the specific activities to be carried out, (5) the physical and mental demands of the job, and (6) the types of products and services to be sold.

The job description is then translated into a statement of job qualifications, including the aptitudes, knowledge, skills, and a variety of behavioral characteristics considered necessary to perform the job successfully. Qualifications for order-getting sales positions often mirror the expectations of buyers: (1) imagination and problem-solving ability, (2) strong work ethic, (3) honesty, (4) intimate product knowledge, (5) effective communication and listening skills, and (6) attentiveness reflected in responsiveness to buyer needs and customer loyalty and follow-up. Firms use a variety of methods for evaluating prospective salespeople. Personal interviews, reference checks, and background information provided on application forms are the most frequently used methods.[29]

Successful selling also requires a high degree of emotional intelligence. **Emotional intelligence** is the ability to understand one's own emotions and the emotions of people with whom one interacts on a daily basis. These qualities are important for adaptive selling and often spell the difference between effective and ineffective order-getting salespeople.[30] Are you interested in what your emotional intelligence might be? Read the Marketing Insights About Me box and test yourself.

Salesforce Training   Whereas the recruitment and selection of salespeople is a one-time event, salesforce training is an ongoing process that affects both new and seasoned salespeople.[31] Sales training covers much more than selling practices. For example, IBM Global Services salespeople, who sell consulting and various information technology services, take at least two weeks of in-class and Internet-based training on both consultative selling and the technical aspects of business.

Training new salespeople is an expensive process. Salespeople in the United States receive employer-sponsored training annually at a cost of over $7 billion per year. On-the-job training is the most popular type of training, followed by individual instruction taught by experienced salespeople. Formal classes, seminars taught by professional sales trainers, and computer-based training are also popular.

Salesforce Motivation and Compensation   A sales plan cannot be successfully implemented without motivated salespeople. Research on salesperson motivation suggests that (1) a clear job description, (2) effective sales management practices, (3) a personal need for achievement, and (4) proper compensation, incentives, or rewards will produce a motivated salesperson.[32]

The importance of compensation as a motivating factor means that close attention must be given to how salespeople are financially rewarded for their efforts. Salespeople are paid using one of three plans: (1) straight salary, (2) straight commission, or (3) a combination of salary and commission. Under a *straight salary compensation plan,* a salesperson is paid a fixed fee per week, month, or year. With a *straight commission compensation plan,* a salesperson's earnings are directly tied to the sales or profit generated. For example, an insurance agent might receive a 2 percent commission of

Mary Kay, Inc. offers unique nonmonetary rewards to recognize its successful sales consultants, including cars. The color pink used by Mary Kay, Inc. on its cars is unique to the company.

Courtesy of Mary Kay, Inc.

Mary Kay Cosmetics, Inc.

www.marykay.com

$2,000 for selling a $100,000 life insurance policy. A *combination compensation plan* contains a specified salary plus a commission on sales or profit generated.

Each compensation plan has its advantages and disadvantages.[33] A straight salary plan is easy to administer and gives management a large measure of control over how salespeople allocate their efforts. However, it provides little incentive to expand sales volume. This plan is used when salespeople engage in many nonselling activities, such as account or customer servicing. A straight commission plan provides the maximum amount of selling incentive but can discourage salespeople from providing customer service. This plan is common when nonselling activities are minimal. Combination plans are most preferred by salespeople and attempt to build on the advantages of salary and commission plans while reducing the potential shortcomings of each. A majority of companies use combination plans today.

Nonmonetary rewards are also given to salespeople for meeting or exceeding objectives. These rewards include trips, honor societies, distinguished salesperson awards, and letters of commendation. Some unconventional rewards include the new pink Cadillacs, Buicks, BMWs, and jewelry given by Mary Kay Cosmetics to outstanding salespeople.[34]

Effective recruitment, selection, training, motivation, and compensation programs combine to create a productive salesforce. Ineffective practices often lead to costly salesforce turnover. The expense of replacing and training a new salesperson, including the cost of lost sales, can be high. Also, new recruits are often less productive than seasoned salespeople.[35]

Salesforce Evaluation: Measuring Results

The final function in the sales management process involves evaluating the salesforce. It is at this point that salespeople are assessed as to whether sales objectives were met and account management policies were followed. Both quantitative and behavioral measures are used to tap different selling dimensions.

Quantitative Assessments Quantitative assessments are based on input- and output-related objectives set forth in the sales plan. Input-related measures focus on the actual activities performed by salespeople such as those involving sales calls, selling expenses, and account management policies. The number of sales calls made, selling expense related to sales made, and the number of reports submitted to superiors are frequently used input measures.

Output measures often appear in a sales quota. A **sales quota** contains specific goals assigned to a salesperson, sales team, branch sales office, or sales district for a stated time period. Dollar or unit sales volume, last year/current year sales ratio, sales of specific products, new accounts generated, and profit achieved are typical goals. The time period can range from one month to one year.

Behavioral Evaluation Behavioral measures are also used to evaluate salespeople. These include assessments of a salesperson's attitude, attention to customers, product knowledge, selling and communication skills, appearance, and professional demeanor. Even though these assessments are sometimes subjective, they are frequently considered and, in fact, inevitable, in salesperson evaluation. Why? These factors are often important determinants of quantitative outcomes.

About 60 percent of U.S. companies now include customer satisfaction as a behavioral measure of salesperson performance. (*What percentage did you check for question 4 in Figure 20–1?*) The relentless focus on customer satisfaction by Eastman Chemical Company salespeople contributed to the company being named a recipient

Applying **Marketing Metrics**

Tracking Salesperson Performance at Moore Chemical & Sanitation Supply, Inc.

Moore Chemical & Sanitation Supply, Inc. (MooreChem) is a large midwestern supplier of cleaning chemicals and sanitary products. MooreChem sells to janitorial companies that clean corporate and professional office buildings.

MooreChem recently installed a sales and account management planning software package that included a dashboard for each of its sales representatives. Salespeople had access to their dashboards as well. These dashboards included seven metrics—sales revenue, gross margin, selling expense, profit, average order size, new customers, and customer satisfaction. Each metric was gauged to show actual salesperson performance relative to target goals.

Your Challenge

As a newly promoted district sales manager at MooreChem, your responsibilities include tracking each salesperson's performance in your district. You are also responsible for directing the sales activities and practices of district salespeople.

In anticipation of a performance review with one of your salespeople, Brady Boyle, you review his dashboard for the previous quarter. This information can be used to provide a constructive review of his performance.

Your Findings

Brady Boyle's quarterly performance is displayed below. Boyle has exceeded targeted goals for sales revenue, selling expenses, and customer satisfaction. All of these metrics show an upward trend. He has met his target for gaining new customers and average order size. But, Boyle's gross margin and profit are below targeted goals. These metrics evidence a downward trend as well. Brady Boyle's mixed performance requires a constructive and positive correction.

Your Action

Brady Boyle should already know how his performance compares with targeted goals. Remember, Boyle has access to his dashboard. Recall that he has exceeded his sales target, but is considerably under his profit target. Boyle's sales trend is up, but his profit trend is down.

You will need to focus attention on Boyle's gross margin and selling expense results and trend. Boyle, it seems, is spending time and money selling lower-margin products that produce a targeted average order size. It may very well be that Boyle is actually expending effort selling more products to his customers. Unfortunately, the product mix yields lower gross margins, resulting in a lower profit.

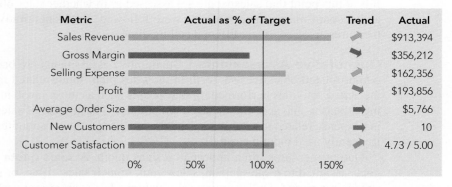

Metric	Actual as % of Target	Trend	Actual
Sales Revenue		↗	$913,394
Gross Margin		↘	$356,212
Selling Expense		↗	$162,356
Profit		↘	$193,856
Average Order Size		→	$5,766
New Customers		→	10
Customer Satisfaction		↗	4.73 / 5.00

of the prestigious Malcolm Baldrige National Quality Award.[36] Eastman surveys its customers with multiple versions of its customer satisfaction questionnaire delivered in nine languages. Some 25 performance items are studied, including on-time and correct delivery, product quality, pricing practice, and sharing of market information. Salespeople review the results with customers. Eastman salespeople know that "the second most important thing they have to do is get their customer satisfaction surveys out to and back from customers," says Eastman's sales training director. "Number one, of course, is getting orders."

Increasingly, companies are using marketing dashboards to track salesperson performance for evaluation purposes. An illustration appears in the Applying Marketing Metrics box.

Toshiba America Medical Systems salespeople have found computer technology to be an effective sales presentation tool and training device.

Source: Toshiba America Medical Systems

Toshiba America Medical Systems
www.toshiba.com

Salesforce Automation and Customer Relationship Management

Personal selling and sales management have undergone a technological revolution with the integration of salesforce automation into customer relationship management processes. In fact, the convergence of computer, information, communication, and Internet technologies has transformed the sales function in many companies and made the promise of customer relationship management a reality. **Salesforce automation (SFA)** is the use of these technologies to make the sales function more effective and efficient. SFA applies to a wide range of activities, including each stage in the personal selling process and management of the salesforce itself.[37]

Salesforce automation exists in many forms. Examples of SFA applications include computer hardware and software for account analysis, time management, order processing and follow-up, sales presentations, proposal generation, and product and sales training. Each application is designed to ease administrative tasks and free time for salespeople to be with customers building relationships, designing solutions, and providing service.

Salesforce Technology   Technology has become an integral part of field selling. Today, most companies supply their field salespeople with laptop computers. For example, salespeople for Godiva Chocolates use their laptop computers to process orders, plan time allocations, forecast sales, and communicate with Godiva personnel and customers. While in a department store candy buyer's office, such as Neiman Marcus, a salesperson can calculate the order cost (and discount), transmit the order, and obtain a delivery date within minutes from Godiva's order processing department.

Toshiba America Medical Systems salespeople use laptop computers with built-in DVD capabilities to provide interactive presentations for their computerized tomography (CT) and magnetic resonance imaging (MRI) scanners. The computer technology allows the customer to see elaborate three-dimensional animations, high-resolution scans, and video clips of the company's products in operation as well as narrated testimonials from satisfied customers. Toshiba has found this application to be effective both for sales presentations and for training its salespeople.

Salesforce Communication   Technology has changed the way salespeople communicate with customers, other salespeople and sales support personnel, and management. Facsimile, electronic mail, and voice mail are common communication technologies used by salespeople today. Mobile phone and tablet device technologies now allow salespeople to exchange data, text, and voice transmissions. Whether traveling or in a customer's office, these technologies provide information at the salesperson's fingertips to answer customer questions and solve problems.

Advances in communication and computer technologies have made possible the mobile and home sales office. Some salespeople now equip minivans with a fully functional desk, swivel chair, light, multifunctional printer, fax machine, mobile phone, and a satellite dish. Jeff Brown, an agent manager with U.S. Cellular, uses such a mobile office. He says, "If I arrive at a prospect's office and they can't see me right away, then I can go outside to work in my office until they're ready to see me."[38]

Home offices are now common. Hewlett-Packard is a case in point. The company shifted its U.S. salesforce into home offices, closed several regional sales offices, and saved millions of dollars in staff salaries and office rent. A fully equipped home office for each salesperson includes a notebook computer, fax/copier, cellular phone, two phone lines, and office furniture.

Perhaps the greatest impact on salesforce communication is the application of Internet technology. Today, salespeople are using their company's intranet for a variety of purposes. At HP Enterprise Services, a professional services firm, salespeople access its intranet to download client material, marketing content, account information, technical papers, and competitive profiles. In addition, HP Enterprise Services offers 7,000 training classes that salespeople can take anytime and anywhere.

Salesforce automation is clearly changing how selling is done and how salespeople are managed. Its numerous applications promise to boost selling productivity, improve customer relationships, and decrease selling cost.

learning review

20-8. What are the three types of selling objectives?

20-9. What three factors are used to structure sales organizations?

20-10. How does emotional intelligence tie to adaptive selling?

LEARNING OBJECTIVES REVIEW

LO 20-1 *Discuss the nature and scope of personal selling and sales management in marketing.*
Personal selling involves the two-way flow of communication between a buyer and seller, often in a face-to-face encounter, designed to influence a person's or group's purchase decision. Sales management involves planning the selling program and implementing and controlling the personal selling effort of the firm. The scope of selling and sales management is apparent in three ways. First, virtually every occupation that involves customer contact has an element of personal selling. Second, selling plays a significant role in a company's overall marketing effort. Salespeople occupy a boundary position between buyers and sellers; they *are* the company to many buyers and account for a major cost of marketing in a variety of industries; and they can create value for customers. Finally, through relationship and partnership selling, salespeople play a central role in tailoring solutions to customer problems as a means to customer value creation.

LO 20-2 *Identify the different types of personal selling.*
Three types of personal selling exist: (*a*) order taking, (*b*) order getting, and (*c*) customer sales support activities. Each type differs from the others in terms of actual selling done and the amount of creativity required to perform the sales task. Order takers process routine orders or reorders for products that were already sold by the company. They generally do little selling in a conventional

sense and engage in only modest problem solving with customers. Order getters sell in a conventional sense and identify prospective customers, provide customers with information, persuade customers to buy, close sales, and follow up on customers' use of a product or service. Order getting involves a high degree of creativity and customer empathy and is typically required for selling complex or technical products with many options. Customer sales support personnel augment the sales effort of order getters by performing a variety of services. Sales support personnel are prominent in cross-functional team selling, the practice of using an entire team of professionals in selling to and servicing major customers.

LO 20-3 *Explain the stages in the personal selling process.*
The personal selling process consists of six stages: (*a*) prospecting, (*b*) preapproach, (*c*) approach, (*d*) presentation, (*e*) close, and (*f*) follow-up. Prospecting involves the search for and qualification of potential customers. The preapproach stage involves obtaining further information on the prospect and deciding on the best method of approach. The approach stage involves the initial meeting between the salesperson and prospect. The presentation stage involves converting a prospect into a customer by creating a desire for the product or service. The close involves obtaining a purchase commitment from the prospect. The follow-up stage involves making certain that the customer's purchase

has been properly delivered and installed and addressing any difficulties experienced with the use of the item.

LO 20-4 *Describe the major functions of sales management.*
Sales management consists of three interrelated functions: (*a*) sales plan formulation, (*b*) sales plan implementation, and (*c*) salesforce evaluation. Sales plan formulation involves setting objectives, organizing the salesforce, and developing account management policies. Sales plan implementation involves salesforce recruitment, selection, training, motivation, and compensation. Finally, salesforce evaluation focuses on quantitative assessments of sales performance and behavioral measures such as customer satisfaction that are linked to selling objectives and account management policies.

LEARNING REVIEW ANSWERS

20-1 What is personal selling?
Answer: Personal selling involves the two-way flow of communication between a buyer and seller, often in a face-to-face encounter, designed to influence a person's or group's purchase decision.

20-2 What is involved in sales management?
Answer: Sales management involves planning the selling program and implementing and evaluating the personal selling effort of the firm. The tasks involved in managing personal selling include setting objectives; organizing the salesforce; recruiting, selecting, training, and compensating salespeople; and evaluating the performance of individual salespeople.

20-3 What is the principal difference between an order taker and an order getter?
Answer: An order taker processes routine orders or reorders for products that were already sold by the company. The primary responsibility of order takers is to preserve an ongoing relationship with existing customers and maintain sales. An order getter sells in a conventional sense and identifies prospective customers, provides customers with information, persuades customers to buy, closes sales, and follows up on customers' use of a product or service. Order getting involves a high degree of creativity, customer empathy, considerable product knowledge, and sales training.

20-4 What is team selling?
Answer: Team selling is the practice of using an entire team of professionals in selling to and servicing major customers. Team selling is used when specialized knowledge is needed to satisfy the different interests of individuals in a customer's buying center.

20-5 What are the six stages in the personal selling process?
Answer: The six stages in the personal selling process are: (1) prospecting—searching for qualified potential customers; (2) preapproach—obtaining further information on prospects and deciding on the best method of approach; (3) approach—setting up the first meeting between the salesperson and the prospect to gain his/her attention, stimulate interest, and establish a foundation for the relationship and eventual sales presentation; (4) presentation—converting a prospect into a customer by creating a desire for the offering; (5) close—obtaining a purchase commitment from the prospect; and (6) follow-up—delivering, installing, and/or resolving any difficulties with the purchase.

20-6 What is the distinction between a lead and a qualified prospect?
Answer: A lead is the name of a person who may be a possible customer whereas a qualified prospect is an individual who wants the product, can afford to buy it, and is the decision maker.

20-7 Which presentation format is most consistent with the marketing concept? Why?
Answer: The need-satisfaction presentation format emphasizes probing and listening by the salesperson to identify the needs and interests of prospective buyers and then tailors the presentation to the prospect and highlights product benefits, which is consistent with the marketing concept and its focus on relationship building.

20-8 What are the three types of selling objectives?
Answer: The three types of selling objectives are: (1) output-related (dollars or unit sales, number of new customers, profit); (2) input-related (number of sales calls, selling expenses); and (3) behaviorrelated (product and competitive knowledge, customer service satisfaction ratings, selling and communication skills).

20-9 What three factors are used to structure sales organizations?
Answer: Three questions need to be answered when structuring a sales organization: (1) Should the company use its own salesforce or independent agents such as manufacturer's representatives? (2) If the decision is made to employ company salespeople, then should they be organized according to geography, customer type, or product or service? (3) How many company salespeople should be employed?

20-10 How does emotional intelligence tie to adaptive selling?
Answer: Emotional intelligence is the ability to understand one's own emotions and the emotions of people with whom one interacts on a daily basis. Evidence suggests that emotional intelligence is two times more important in contributing to performance than intellect and expertise alone. Emotional intelligence has five dimensions: (1) self-motivation skills; (2) self-awareness, or knowing one's own emotions; (3) the ability to manage one's emotions and impulses; (4) empathy, or the ability to sense how others are feeling; and (5) social skills, or the ability to handle the emotions of other people. These qualities are important for adaptive selling.

FOCUSING ON KEY TERMS

account management policies p. 584
adaptive selling p. 578
consultative selling p. 578
emotional intelligence p. 586
formula selling presentation p. 578
key account management p. 583
need-satisfaction presentation p. 578

order getter p. 572
order taker p. 571
partnership selling p. 570
personal selling p. 568
personal selling process p. 574
relationship selling p. 570
sales management p. 568

sales plan p. 581
sales quota p. 587
salesforce automation (SFA) p. 589
stimulus-response presentation p. 577
team selling p. 573
workload method p. 584

1   Jane Dawson is a new sales representative for the Charles Schwab brokerage firm. In searching for clients, Jane purchased a mailing list of subscribers to *The Wall Street Journal* and called them all regarding their interest in discount brokerage services. She asked if they have any stocks and if they have a regular broker. Those people without a regular broker were asked their investment needs. Two days later, Jane called back with investment advice and asked if they would like to open an account. Identify each of Jane Dawson's actions in terms of the personal selling process.

2   For the first 50 years of business, the Johnson Carpet Company produced carpets for residential use. The salesforce was structured geographically. In the past five years, a large percentage of carpet sales have been to industrial users, hospitals, schools, and architects. The company also has broadened its product line to include area rugs, Oriental carpets, and wall-to-wall carpeting. Is the present salesforce structure appropriate, or would you recommend an alternative?

3   Where would you place each of the following sales jobs on the order-taker/order-getter continuum shown below? (*a*) Burger King counter clerk, (*b*) automobile insurance salesperson, (*c*) Hewlett-Packard computer salesperson, (*d*) life insurance salesperson, and (*e*) shoe salesperson.

Order taker	Order getter

4   Listed here are two different firms. Which compensation plan would you recommend for each firm, and what reasons would you give for your recommendations? (*a*) A newly formed company that sells lawn care equipment on a door-to-door basis directly to consumers; and (*b*) the Nabisco Company, which sells heavily advertised products in supermarkets by having the salesforce call on these stores and arrange shelves, set up displays, and make presentations to store buying committees.

5   Tyler Automotive, Inc. supplies 1,000 independent auto parts stores throughout the United States. Each store is called on 12 times a year, and the average sales call lasts 30 minutes. Assuming a salesperson works 40 hours a week, 50 weeks a year, and devotes 75 percent of the time to actual selling, how many salespeople does Tyler Automotive need?

6   A furniture manufacturer is currently using manufacturer's representatives to sell its line of living room furniture. These representatives receive an 8 percent commission. The company is considering hiring its own salespeople and has estimated that the fixed cost of managing and paying their salaries would be $1 million annually. The salespeople would also receive a 4 percent commission on sales. The company has sales of $25 million, and sales are expected to grow by 15 percent next year. Would you recommend that the company switch to its own salesforce? Why or why not?

7   Suppose someone said to you, "The only real measure of a salesperson is the amount of sales produced." How might you respond?

Does your marketing plan involve a personal selling activity? If the answer is "no," read no further and do not include a personal selling element in your plan. If the answer is "yes":

1   Identify the likely prospects for your product or service.

2   Determine what information you should obtain about the prospect.

3   Describe how you would approach the prospect.

4   Outline the presentation you would make to the prospect for your product or service.

5   Develop a sales plan, focusing on the organizational structure you would use for your salesforce (geographic, product, or customer).

"I'm like the quarterback of the team. I manage 250 accounts, and anything from billing issues, to service issues, to selling the products. I'm really the face to the customer," says Alison Capossela, a Washington, DC–based Xerox sales representative.

> **Video 20-2**
> **Xerox Video Case**
> kerin.tv/13e/v20-2

As the primary company contact for Xerox customers, Alison is responsible for developing and maintaining customer relationships. To accomplish this she uses a sophisticated selling process that requires many activities from making presentations, to attending training sessions, to managing a team of Xerox personnel, to monitoring competitors' activities. The face-to-face interactions with customers, however, are the most rewarding for Capossela. "It's an amazing feeling; the more they challenge me the more I fight back. It's fun!" she explains.

THE COMPANY

Xerox Corporation's mission is to "help people find better ways to do great work by constantly leading in document technologies, products, and services that improve customers' work processes and business results." To accomplish this mission Xerox employs 130,000 people in 160 countries. Xerox is the world's leading document management enterprise and a *Fortune* 500 company.

Xerox offers a wide range of products and services. These include printers, copiers and fax machines, multifunction and network devices, high-speed color presses, digital imaging and archiving products and services, and supplies such as toner, paper, and ink. The entire company is guided by customer-focused and employee-centered core values (e.g., "We succeed through satisfied customers") and a passion for innovation, speed, and adaptability.

THE SELLING PROCESS AT XEROX

In 2001, Xerox began a shift to a consultative selling model that focused on helping customers solve their business problems rather than just placing more equipment in their office. The shift meant that sales reps needed to be less product-oriented and more relationship- and value-oriented. Xerox wanted to be a provider of total solutions.

Today, Xerox has more than 8,000 sales professionals throughout the world who spend a large amount of their day developing customer relation-

ships. Capossela explains: "Fifty percent of my day is spent with my customers, 25 percent is following up with phone calls or e-mails, and another 25 percent involves preparing proposals." The approach has helped Xerox attract new customers and keep existing customers.

The sales process at Xerox typically follows the six stages of the personal selling process identified in Figure 20–3: (1) Xerox identifies potential clients through responses to advertising, referrals, and telephone calls; (2) the salesforce prepares for a presentation by familiarizing themselves with the potential client and its document needs; (3) a Xerox sales representative approaches the prospect and suggests a meeting and presentation; (4) as the presentation begins, the salesperson summarizes relevant information about potential solutions Xerox can offer, states what he or she hopes to get out of the meeting, explains how the products and services work, and reinforces the benefits of working with Xerox; (5) the salesperson engages in an action close (gets a signed document or a firm confirmation of the sale); and then (6) continues to meet and communicate with the client to provide assistance and monitor the effectiveness of the installed solution.

Xerox sales representatives also use the selling process to maintain relationships with existing customers. In today's competitive environment it is not unusual to have customers who have been approached by competitors or who are required to obtain more than one bid before renewing a contract. Xerox has teams of people who collect and analyze information about competitors and their products. The information is sent out to sales reps or offered to them through workshops and seminars. The most difficult competitors are the ones that have also invested in customer relationships. The selling process allows Xerox to continually react and respond to new information and take advantage of opportunities in the marketplace.

THE SALES MANAGEMENT PROCESS AT XEROX

The Xerox salesforce is divided into four geographic organizations: North America, which includes the United States and Canada; Europe, which includes 17 countries; Global Accounts, which manages large accounts that operate in multiple locations; and Developing Markets, which includes all other geographic territories that may require Xerox products and services. Within each geographic area, the majority of

Xerox products and services are typically sold through its direct salesforce. Xerox also utilizes a variety of other channels, including value-added resellers, independent agents, dealers, systems integrators, telephone, and Internet sales channels.

Motivation and compensation are important aspects of any salesforce. At Xerox there is a passion for winning that provides a key incentive for sales reps. Compensation also plays an important role. In addition, Xerox has a recognition program called the President's Club where the top performers are awarded a five-day trip to one of the top resorts in the world. The program has been a huge success and has now been offered for more than 30 years.

Perhaps the most well-known component of Xerox's sales management process is its sales representative recruitment and training program. "For recruitment, Xerox looks for seasoned businesspeople who can talk to customers," says Kevin Warren, president of United States customer operations at Xerox. "Our value proposition is that we take care of document management to help run your business," Warren explains. "So we look for consultative and business-savvy salespeople."

On the training front, Xerox developed the "Create and Win" program to help sales reps learn the consultative selling approach. The components of the program consist of interactive training sessions and distance-learning webinars. Every new sales representative at Xerox receives eight weeks of training development in the field and at the Xerox Corporate University in Virginia. "The training program is phenomenal!" according to Capossela. The training and its focus on the customer is part of the Xerox culture outside of the sales organization also.

Every senior executive at Xerox is responsible for working with at least one customer. They also spend a full day every month responding to incoming customer calls and inquiries.

WHAT IS IN THE FUTURE FOR THE XEROX SALESFORCE?

The recent growth and success at Xerox is creating many opportunities for the company and its sales representatives. For example, Xerox is accelerating the development of its top salespeople. Mentors are used to provide advice for day-to-day issues and long-term career planning. In addition, globalization has become such an important initiative at Xerox that experienced and successful sales representatives are quickly given opportunities to manage large global accounts.

Xerox is also moving toward an approach that empowers sales representatives to make decisions about how to handle accounts. The large number of Xerox customers means there are a variety of different corporate styles, and the sales reps are increasingly the best qualified to manage the relationship. This approach is just one more example of Xerox's commitment to customers and creating customer value.[39]

Questions

1 How does Xerox create customer value through its personal selling process?

2 How does Alison Capossela provide solutions for Xerox customers?

3 Why is the Xerox training program so important to the company's success?

Chapter Notes

1. Interview with Lindsey Smith, GE Healthcare Americas, June 6, 2015.
2. "The Path to Becoming a Fortune 500 CEO," *forbes.com,* December 5, 2011.
3. Jessi Hempel, "IBM's All-Star Salesman," www.cnnmoney.com, September 26, 2008.
4. Jim Clifton and Sangeeta Bharadwaj Badal, *Entrepreneural Strengths Finder* (New York: Gallup Press, 2014); and Meghan Casserly, "The Five Sales Tactics Every Entrepreneur Must Master," *forbes.com,* January 30, 2013.
5. "Surgical Visits," *Business 2.0,* April 2006, p. 94.
6. Mark W. Johnston and Greg W. Marshall, *Contemporary Selling: Building Relationships, Creating Value,* 4th ed. (Burr Ridge, IL: McGraw-Hill/Irwin, 2014).
7. Richard P. Bagozzi, et al., "Genetic and Neurological Foundations of Customer Orientation: Field and Experimental Evidence," *Journal of the Academy of Marketing Science,* September 2012, pp. 639–58; and "Does Your Salesperson Have the Right Genes?" *Harvard Business Review,* April 2013, p. 24.
8. Gerhard Gschwandtner, "How Much Time Do Your Salespeople Spend Selling?" *Selling Power,* March/April 2011, p. 8.
9. "The New Willy Loman Survives by Staying Home," *Bloomberg Businessweek,* January 14–January 20, 2013, pp. 16–17.
10. For an overview of team selling, see Eli Jones, Andrea Dickson, Lawrence B. Chonko, and Joseph P. Cannon, "Key Accounts and Team Selling: A Review, Framework, and Research Agenda," *Journal of Personal Selling & Sales Management,* Spring 2005, pp. 181–98.
11. "Team Selling Works!" www.sellingpower.com, March 24, 2013; "Group Dynamics," *Sales & Marketing Management,* January/February 2007, p. 8; and Steve Atlas and Elise Atlas, "Team Approach," *Selling Power,* May 2000, pp. 126–28.

12. Scott Sterns, "Cold Calls Have Yet to Breathe Their Last Gasp," *The Wall Street Journal,* December 14, 2006, p. D2.

13. Jim Edwards, "Dinner, Interrupted," *BrandWeek,* May 26, 2003, pp. 28–32.

14. Christopher Conkey, "Record Fine Levied for Telemarketing," *The Wall Street Journal,* December 14, 2005, pp. D1, D4.

15. Paul A. Herbing, *Handbook of Cross-Cultural Marketing* (New York: Haworth Press, 1998).

16. Philip R. Cateora, Mary C. Gilly, and John L. Graham, *International Marketing,* 16th ed. (Burr Ridge, IL: McGraw-Hill/Irwin, 2013).

17. This discussion is based on Johnston and Marshall, *Contemporary Selling;* and "In Transition—Xerox," www.sellingpower.com, June 15, 2011.

18. Kapil R. Tuli, Ajay K. Kohli, and Sundar G. Bharadwaj, "Rethinking Customer Solutions: From Product Bundles to Relational Processes," *Journal of Marketing,* July 2007, pp. 1–17.

19. For an extensive discussion of objections, see Charles M. Futrell, *Fundamentals of Selling,* 13th ed. (Burr Ridge, IL: McGraw-Hill/ Irwin, 2014), chapter 12.

20. Theodore Levitt, *The Marketing Imagination* (New York: Free Press, 1983), p. 111.

21. Stephen B. Castleberry, and John F. Tanner Jr., *Selling: Building Partnerships,* 9th ed. (Burr Ridge, IL: McGraw-Hill, 2014).

22. *Management Briefing: Sales and Marketing* (New York: Conference Board, October 1996), pp. 3–4.

23. Ellen Neuborne, "Know Thy Enemy," *Sales & Marketing Management,* January 2003, pp. 29–33.

24. Douglas E. Hughes, Joel LeBon, and Adam Rapp, "Gaining and Leveraging Customer-Based Competitive Intelligence: The Pivotal Role of Social Capital and Salesperson Adaptive Selling Skills," *Journal of the Academy of Marketing Science,* January 2013, pp. 91–110; Stephen Schultz, "Capturing CI through Your Sales Force," *Competitive Intelligence Magazine,* January–February 2002, pp. 15–17; Alan J. Dubinsky, Marvin A. Jolson, Ronald E. Michaels, Masaaki Katobe, and Chea Un Lim, "Ethical Perceptions of Field Sales Personnel: An Empirical Assessment," *Journal of Personal Selling & Sales Management,* Fall 1992, pp. 9–21; and Alan J. Dubinsky, Marvin A. Jolson, Masaaki Katobe, and Chae Un Lim, "A Cross-National Investigation of Industrial Sales People's Ethical Perceptions," *Journal of International Business Studies* (Fourth Quarter, 1991), pp. 651–70.

25. See Mark W. Johnston and Greg W. Marshall, *Sales Force Management,* 11th ed. (Burr Ridge, IL: McGraw-Hill/ Irwin, 2014), pp. 100–4; and William T. Ross Jr., Frederic Dalsace, and Erin Anderson, "Should You Set Up Your Own Sales Force or Should You Outsource It? Pitfalls in the Standard Analysis," *Business Horizons,* January–February 2005, pp. 23–36.

26. Eli Jones, et al., "Key Accounts and Team Selling." Also see, Arun Sharma, "Success Factors in Key Accounts," *Journal of Business & Industrial Marketing* 21, no. 3 (2006), pp. 141–50.

27. William L. Cron and David W. Cravens, "Sales Force Strategy," in Robert A. Peterson and Roger A. Kerin, eds., *Wiley International Encyclopedia of Marketing: Volume 1—Marketing Strategy* (West Sussex, UK: John Wiley & Sons, Ltd., 2011), pp. 197–207.

28. This discussion is based on William L. Cron and Thomas E. DeCarlo, *Dalrymple's Sales Management,* 10th ed. (Hoboken, NJ: John Wiley & Sons, Inc., 2009).

29. René Y. Darmon, *Leading the Sales Force* (New York: Cambridge University Press, 2007).

30. "Look for Employees with High EQ Over IQ," *forbes.com,* March 18, 2013; Blair Kidwell, David M. Hardesty, Brian R. Murtha, and Shibin Sheng, "Emotional Intelligence in Marketing Exchanges," *Journal of Marketing,* January 2011, pp. 78–93; and Elizabeth J. Rozell, Charles E. Pettijohn, and R. Stephen Parker, "Customer-Oriented Selling: Exploring the Roles of Emotional Intelligence and Organizational Commitment," *Psychology & Marketing,* June 2004, pp. 405–24.

31. Rosann L. Spiro, Gregory A. Rich, and William J. Stanton, *Management of a Sales Force,* 12th ed. (Burr Ridge, IL: McGraw-Hill/ Irwin, 2008), chapter 7; and Thomas L. Powers, Thomas E. DeCarlo, and Gouri Gupte, "An Update on the Status of Sales Management Training," *Journal of Personal Selling & Sales Management,* Fall 2010, pp. 319–26.

32. Thomas Steenburgh and Michael Ahearne, "Motivating Salespeople: What Really Works," *Harvard Business Review,* July–August 2012, pp. 71–75; Spiro et al., *Management of a Sales Force,* chapter 8. Also see Julia Chang, "Wholly Motivated," *Sales & Marketing Management,* March 2007, pp. 24ff.

33. This discussion is based on Johnston and Marshall, *Sales Force Management,* chapter 11; and Andris Zoltners, Prabhakant Sinha, and Sally E. Lorimer, *The Complete Guide to Sales Force Incentive Compensation* (New York: AMACOM, 2006).

34. www.MaryKay.com, downloaded June 5, 2015.

35. Jeffrey E. Lewin and Jeffrey K. Sager, "The Influence of Personal Characteristics and Coping Strategies on Salespersons' Turnover Intentions," *Journal of Personal Selling & Sales Management,* Fall 2010, pp. 355–70; and René Y. Darmon, "The Concept of Salesperson Replacement Value: A Sales Force Turnover Management Tool," *Journal of Personal Selling & Sales Management,* Summer 2008, pp. 211–32.

36. Gary Hallen and Robert Latino, "Eastman Chemical's Success Story," *Quality Progress,* June 2003, pp. 50–54.

37. Mark Cotteleer, Edward Inderrieden, and Felissa Lee, "Selling the Sales Force on Automation," *Harvard Business Review,* July–August 2006, pp. 18–22.

38. Darmon, *Leading the Sales Force.*

39. Xerox: This case was written by Steven Hartley and Roger Kerin. Sources: "In Transition—Xerox," www.sellingpower.com, June 15, 2011; Joseph Kornik, "Table Talk: A Sales Leaders Roundtable," *Sales & Marketing Management,* February 2007; Philip Chadwick, "Xerox Global Service," *Printweek,* October 11, 2007, p. 32; Sarah Campbell, "What It's Like Working for Xerox," *The Times,* September 14, 2006, p. 9; Simon Avery, "CEO's HR Skills Turn Xerox Fortunes," *The Globe and Mail,* June 2, 2006, p. B3; Julia Chang, "Ultimate Motivation Guide: Happy Sales Force, Happy Returns," *Sales & Marketing Management,* March 2006; and resources available on the Xerox website, www.xerox.com.

21

Implementing Interactive and Multichannel Marketing

Seven Cycles Delivers Just One Bike. Yours.

"One Bike. Yours." is the company tagline for Seven Cycles, Inc., located in Watertown, Massachusetts. And for good reason.

Seven Cycles is the world's largest custom bicycle frame builder. The company produces a broad range of road, mountain, cyclocross, tandem, touring, single-speed, and commuter bikes annually, and no two bikes are exactly alike.

At Seven Cycles, attention is focused on each customer's unique cycling experience through the optimum fit, function, performance, and comfort of his or her very own bike. According to one satisfied customer, "Getting a Seven is more of a creation than a purchase."

While Seven Cycles does offer stock frames in more than 200 sizes, each is still built-to-order and a full 95 percent of the bicycle frames that Seven ships are completely custom made. Customized elements include frame size, frame geometry, tubing diameters, and wall thickness, as well as countless options such as cable routing, water bottle mounts, paint color, and decal color. Every custom option is available at no additional charge and the number of combinations is virtually infinite.

The marketing success of Seven Cycles is due to its state-of-the-art bicycle frames. But as Rob Vandermark, company founder and president, says, "Part of our success is that we are tied to a business model that includes the Internet."

Seven uses its multilanguage (English, German, Chinese, Japanese, Korean, and Flemish) website (www.sevencycles.com) to let customers get deeply involved in the frame-building process and the selection of components to outfit their complete bike. It enables customers to collaborate on the design of their own bike using the company's Custom Kit fitting system, which considers the rider's size, aspirations, and riding habits. Then customers can monitor their bike's progress through the development and production process by clicking "Where's My Frame?" on the Seven Cycles website.

This customization process and continuous feedback make for a collaborative relationship between Seven Cycles, its nearly 200 authorized retailers in the United States, some 30 international distributors, and customers in 40 countries. "Our whole process is designed to keep the focus on the rider the bike is being built for, so it ends up being a very different and more interactive experience than most people are used to. That experience is a large part of the value we sell, above and beyond the bike," explains Jennifer Miller, operations manager at Seven Cycles.

seven ⑦ cycles

Both photos: Courtesy of Seven Cycles, Inc.

In addition to the order process, website visitors can peruse weekly news stories and learn about new product introductions to get a unique perspective on the business. They can read employee biographies online to learn more about the people who build the bikes. The website also offers a retailer-specific section as a 24/7 repository of updated information for the company's channel partners.

Beyond the website, current Seven owners can interact with the company on the Seven Cycles blog to learn about its activities and products. Seven Cycles also uses its company Facebook Page and Twitter account to post brief and timely updates and build a stronger sense of community around the brand.[1]

This chapter describes how companies design and implement interactive marketing programs. It begins by explaining how Internet technology can create customer value, build customer relationships, and produce customer experiences in novel ways. Next, it describes how Internet technology affects and is affected by consumer behavior and marketing practice. Finally, the chapter shows how marketers integrate and leverage their communication and delivery channels using Internet technology to implement multichannel marketing programs to better serve cross-channel consumers.

CREATING CUSTOMER VALUE, RELATIONSHIPS, AND EXPERIENCES IN MARKETSPACE

LO 21-1 **Describe what interactive marketing is and how it creates customer value, customer relationships, and customer experiences.**

Consumers and companies populate two market environments today. One is the traditional *marketplace.* Here buyers and sellers engage in face-to-face exchange relationships in a material environment characterized by physical facilities (stores and offices) and mostly tangible objects. The other is the *marketspace,* an Internet-enabled digital environment characterized by face-to-screen exchange relationships and electronic images and offerings.

Marketing in Two Environments

The existence of two market environments has been a boon for consumers. Today, consumers can shop for and purchase a wide variety of products and services in either market environment. Actually, most consumers now browse and buy in both market environments. More are expected to do so in the future as mobile devices, notably smartphones, expand their capabilities.

About 90 percent of Internet users ages 15 and older shop online in the United States. They are expected to buy $414 billion worth of products and services in 2018 (excluding travel, automobile, and prescription drugs). This figure represents about 11 percent of total U.S. retail sales.[2]

Marketing in two market environments poses significant challenges for companies. Companies with origins in the traditional marketplace, such as Procter & Gamble, Walmart, and General Motors, are continually challenged to define the nature and scope of their marketspace presence. These companies consistently refine the role of digital technology in attracting, retaining, and building consumer relationships to improve their competitive positions in the traditional marketplace while also bolstering their marketspace presence. Other companies with marketplace origins have chosen not to participate in the marketspace. Luxury fashion designs, for the most part, don't sell their products online. According to the founder of Prada, "We think that, for luxury, it's not right. Personally, I'm not interested."[3] Not surprisingly, over 90 percent of luxury fashion merchandise is sold exclusively through stores.

On the other hand, companies with marketspace origins, including Amazon.com, Google, eBay, E*TRADE, and others, are challenged to continually refine, broaden, and deepen their marketspace presence. At the same time, these companies, and other companies, must consider what role, if any, the traditional marketplace will play in their future. For example, eyeglass online retailer Warby Parker, clothing online retailer Bonobos, and jewelry online retailer Blue Nile have opened physical showrooms that give shoppers an opportunity to experience the company's products in person before purchasing them online. Regardless of origin, a company's success in achieving a meaningful marketspace presence hinges largely on its ability to design and execute a marketing program that capitalizes on the unique value-creation and relationship-building capabilities of digital technology in delivering a favorable customer experience.

Creating Customer Value in Marketspace

Why has the marketspace captured the eye and imagination of marketers worldwide? Recall from Chapter 1 that marketing creates time, place, form, and possession utilities, thereby providing value. Marketers believe that the possibilities for customer value creation are greater in the digital marketspace than in the physical marketplace.

Consider place and time utility. In marketspace, the provision of direct, on-demand information is possible from marketers *anywhere* to customers *anywhere, at any time,*

Why? Operating hours and geographical constraints do not exist in marketspace. For example, Recreational Equipment, Inc. (www.rei.com), an outdoor gear marketer, reports that 35 percent of its orders are placed between 10:00 P.M. and 7:00 A.M., long after and before retail stores are open for business. Similarly, a U.S. consumer from Chicago can access Marks & Spencer (www.marks-and-spencer.co.uk), the well-known British department store, to shop for clothing as easily as a person living near London's Piccadilly Square.

Possession utility—getting a product or service to consumers so they can own or use it—is accelerated. Airline, car rental, and lodging electronic reservation systems such as Orbitz (www.orbitz.com) allow comparison shopping for the lowest fares, rents, and rates and almost immediate access to and confirmation of travel arrangements and accommodations.

The greatest marketspace opportunity for marketers, however, lies in its potential for creating form utility. Interactive two-way Internet-enabled communication capabilities in marketspace invite consumers to tell marketers specifically what their requirements are, making customization of a product or service to fit their exact needs possible. Today, 35 percent of online consumers are interested in customizing product features or in purchasing build-to-order products that use their specifications.[4] At Seven Cycles, customers can arrange for a custom-made mountain bike to fit their specifications, as described in the chapter-opening example.

Seven Cycles offers form utility by creating customized bikes for customers in 40 countries.
Courtesy of Seven Cycles, Inc.

Seven Cycles, Inc.
www.sevencycles.com

Interactivity, Individuality, and Customer Relationships in Marketspace

Marketers benefit from two unique capabilities of Internet technology that promote and sustain customer relationships. One is *interactivity;* the other is *individuality.*[5]

Pavement. Dirt. **Whatever.**

No matter what form your two-wheeled passion takes. Whatever road, trail, or entirely improvised route you follow. There is a Seven for you. Expertly designed and handcrafted for who you are and the way you ride.

seven cycles

www.sevencycles.com   **telephone** 617.923.7774   **email** info@sevencycles.com   **One Bike. Yours.**

Mars, Inc. uses choiceboard technology to decorate M&M's® candies with personal photos and messages.

© Ira Roberts

Mars, Inc.

www.mymms.com

Video 21-1
My M&M's®
kerin.tv/13e/v21-1

Both capabilities are important building blocks for buyer–seller relationships. For these relationships to occur, companies need to interact with their customers by listening and responding to their needs. Marketers must also treat customers as individuals and empower them to (1) influence the timing and extent of the buyer–seller interaction and (2) have a say in the kind of products and services they buy, the information they receive, and in some cases, the prices they pay.

Internet technology allows for interaction, individualization, and customer relationship building to be carried out on a scale never before available and makes interactive marketing possible. **Interactive marketing** involves two-way buyer–seller electronic communication in which the buyer controls the kind and amount of information received from the seller. Interactive marketing is characterized by sophisticated choiceboard and personalization systems that transform information supplied by customers into customized responses to their individual needs.

Choiceboards A **choiceboard** is an interactive, Internet-enabled system that allows individual customers to design their own products and services by answering a few questions and choosing from a menu of product or service attributes (or components), prices, and delivery options. Customers today can design their own computers with Dell's online configurator, style their own athletic shoe at www.reebok.com, assemble their own investment portfolios with Schwab's mutual fund evaluator, build their own bicycle at www.sevencycles.com, create a diet and fitness program to fit their lifestyle at www.ediet.com, and decorate M&M's® with photos of themselves and unique messages at www.mymms.com. Because choiceboards collect precise information about the preferences and behavior of individual buyers, a company becomes more knowledgeable about a customer and better able to anticipate and fulfill that customer's needs.

Most choiceboards are essentially transaction devices. However, companies have expanded the functionality of choiceboards using collaborative filtering technology. **Collaborative filtering** is a process that automatically groups people with similar buying intentions, preferences, and behaviors and predicts future purchases. For example, say two people who have never met buy a few of the same DVDs over time. Collaborative filtering software is programmed to reason that these two buyers might have similar musical tastes: If one buyer likes a particular DVD, then the other will like it as well. The outcome? Collaborative filtering gives marketers the ability to make a dead-on sales recommendation to a buyer in *real time*. You see collaborative filtering applied each time you view a selection at Amazon.com and see "Customers who bought this (item) also bought. . . ."

Personalization Choiceboards and collaborative filtering are marketer-initiated efforts to provide customized responses to the needs of individual buyers. Personalization systems are typically buyer-initiated efforts. **Personalization** is the consumer-initiated practice of generating content on a marketer's website that is custom tailored to an individual's specific needs and preferences.

Today, one-half of the largest online retailers in the United States use personalization techniques.[6] For example, Yahoo! (www.yahoo.com) allows users to create personalized MyYahoo! pages. Users can add or delete a variety of types of information from their personal pages, including specific stock quotes, weather conditions in any city in the world, and local television schedules. In turn, Yahoo! uses the buyer profile data entered when users register at the site to tailor e-mail messages, advertising, and content to the individual—and post a happy birthday greeting on the user's special day.

Reebok uses choiceboard technology to create customized athletic shoes for its customers.

Courtesy of Reebok International Ltd.

Reebok

www.reebok.com

An important aspect of personalization is a buyer's willingness to have tailored communications brought to his or her attention. Obtaining this approval is called **permission marketing**—the solicitation of a consumer's consent (called *opt-in*) to receive e-mail and advertising based on personal data supplied by the consumer. Permission marketing is a proven vehicle for building and maintaining customer relationships, provided it is properly used.

Companies that successfully employ permission marketing adhere to three rules.[7] First, they make sure opt-in customers receive only information that is relevant and meaningful to them. Second, their customers are given the option to *opt-out,* or change the kind, amount, or timing of information sent to them. Finally, their customers are assured that their name or buyer profile data will not be sold or shared with others. This assurance is important because 76 percent of adult Internet users are concerned about the privacy of their personal information.[8]

Creating an Online Customer Experience

A continuing challenge for companies is the design and execution of marketing programs that capitalize on the unique customer value-creation capabilities of Internet technology. Companies realize that applying Internet technology to create time, place, form, and possession utility is just a starting point for creating a meaningful marketspace presence. Today, the quality of the customer experience produced by a company is the standard by which a meaningful marketspace presence is measured.

From an interactive marketing perspective, *customer experience* is defined as the sum total of the interactions that a customer has with a company's website, from the initial look at a home page through the entire purchase decision process.[9] Companies produce a customer experience through seven website design elements. These elements are context, content, community, customization, communication, connection,

Context
Site's layout and
visual design

Content
Text, pictures, sound,
and video that the
site contains

Commerce
Site's capabilities to
enable commercial
transactions

Community
The ways that the site
enables user-to-user
communication

Connection
Degree that site
is linked
to other sites

Communication
The ways the site
enables site-to-user,
user-to-site,
or two-way
communication

Customization
Site's ability to tailor
itself to different users
or to allow users to
personalize the site

FIGURE 21–1

Seven website design
elements that drive
customer experience.

Photo: © NetPhotos/Alamy

and commerce. Each is summarized in Figure 21–1. A closer look at these elements illustrates how each contributes to customer experience.

Context *Context* refers to a website's aesthetic appeal and the functional look and feel of the site's layout and visual design. A functionally oriented website focuses largely on the company's offering, be it products, services, or information. Deal-oriented travel websites, such as Priceline.com, tend to be functionally oriented with an emphasis on destinations, scheduling, and prices. In contrast, beauty websites, such as Revlon.com, are more aesthetically oriented. As these examples suggest, context attempts to convey the core consumer benefit provided by the company's offerings.

Content *Content* applies to all digital information on a website, including the presentation form—text, video, audio, and graphics. Content quality and presentation along with context dimensions combine to engage a website visitor and provide a platform for the five remaining design elements.

Customization Website *customization* is the ability of a site to modify itself to, or be modified by and for, each individual user. This design element is prominent in websites that offer personalized content, such as My eBay and MyYahoo!

Connection The *connection* element is the network of linkages between a company's site and other sites. These links are embedded in the website; appear as highlighted words, a picture, or graphic; and allow a user to effortlessly visit other sites with a mouse click. Connection is a major design element for informational websites such as *The New York Times*. Users of NYTimes.com can access the book review

Travelocity pays close attention to creating a favorable customer experience by employing all seven website design elements.
© Ira Roberts

Travelocity
www.travelocity.com

section and link to Barnes & Noble to order a book or browse related titles without ever visiting a store.

Communication *Communication* refers to the dialogue that unfolds between the website and its users. Consumers—particularly those who have registered at a site—now expect that communication to be interactive and individualized in real time much like a personal conversation. In fact, some websites now enable a user to talk directly with a customer representative while shopping the site. For instance, two-thirds of the sales through Dell.com involve human sales representatives.

Community In addition, many company websites encourage user-to-user communications hosted by the company to create virtual communities, or simply, *community*. This design element is popular because it has been shown to enhance customer experience and build favorable buyer–seller relationships. Examples of communities range from the Pampers Village hosted by Procter & Gamble (www.pampers.com) to the Harley Owners Group (HOG) sponsored by Harley-Davidson (www.harley-davidson.com).

Commerce The seventh design element is *commerce*—the website's ability to conduct sales transactions for products and services. Online transactions are quick and simple in well-designed websites.

Most websites do not include every design element. Although every website has context and content, they differ in the use of the remaining five elements. Why? Websites have different purposes. For example, only websites that emphasize the actual sale of products and services include the commerce element. Websites that are used primarily for advertising and promotion purposes emphasize the communication element. The difference between these two types of websites is discussed later in the chapter in the description of multichannel marketing.

Companies use a broad array of measures to assess website performance. For example, the amount of time per month visitors spend on their website, or "stickiness," is used to gauge customer experience.[10] Read the Applying Marketing Metrics box to learn how stickiness is measured and interpreted at one of the largest automobile dealerships in the United States.[11]

learning review

21-1. The consumer-initiated practice of generating content on a marketer's website that is custom tailored to an individual's specific needs and preferences is called _____.

21-2. What are the seven website design elements that companies use to produce a customer experience?

ONLINE CONSUMER BEHAVIOR AND MARKETING PRACTICE IN MARKETSPACE

Who are online consumers, and what do they buy? Why do they choose to shop and purchase products and services in the digital marketspace rather than (or in addition to) the traditional marketplace? Answers to these questions have a direct bearing on marketspace marketing practices.

Who Is the Online Consumer?

Online consumers are the subsegment of all Internet users who employ this technology to research products and services and make purchases. As a group, online consumers are equally likely to be women and men, and they tend to be better educated, younger, and more affluent than the general U.S. population. This makes them an attractive market. Even though online shopping and buying is popular, a

Marketing **Insights About Me**

Am I Addicted to the Internet? Answer 20 Questions to Find Out

Online shopping has become commonplace in the United States. For some consumers, however, online shopping has become an Internet shopping addiction. If you exhibit the following symptoms, you may be addicted:

1. You spend more time than you should shopping online.
2. You promise to stop ordering so much online, but are unable to resist.
3. Your frequent purchases and spending causes financial problems and relationship troubles.
4. When you are not shopping online, you are planning your next online shopping spree.

5. Internet shopping has a negative impact on other parts of your life, such as work, school, friendships, and family.

© Alex Slobodkin/iStock/Getty Images

Internet shopping addiction is considered part of a broader condition known as Internet addiction. PsychCentral has an online, interactive quiz to test whether your Internet behavior is, or is becoming, an addiction. Visit the PsychCentral website at www.psychcentral.com/netaddiction/quiz/, answer 20 questions, and get your Internet addiction score.

small percentage of online consumers still account for a disproportionate share of online retail sales in the United States. It is estimated that 20 percent of online consumers account for 69 percent of total consumer online sales. Also, women tend to purchase more products and services online than men.[12]

The prevalence of online shopping and buying has sparked interest in how the Internet has contributed to compulsive shopping and buying among online consumers. Read the Marketing Insights About Me box to spot the symptoms of Internet shopping addiction, one form of Internet addiction. Click the link shown in the box, answer 20 questions, and see how you score on the Internet Addiction Quiz.

What Online Consumers Buy

LO 21-2 Explain why certain types of products and services are particularly suited for interactive marketing.

Much still needs to be learned about online consumer purchase behavior. Although research has documented the most frequently purchased products and services bought online, marketers also need to know *why* these items are popular in the digital marketspace.

Six general product and service categories account for about 70 percent of online consumer buying today and for the foreseeable future, as shown in Figure 21–2.[13] One category consists of items for which product information is an important part of the purchase decision, but prepurchase trial is not necessarily critical. Items such as computers, computer accessories, and consumer electronics fall into this category.

A second category contains items that can be delivered digitally, including computer software, books, music, and video.

Unique items, such as specialty products, foods, beverages, and gifts, represent a third category. A fourth category includes items that are regularly purchased and where convenience is very important. Many consumer packaged goods, such as grocery products, health care and personal care items, and home office products, fall into this category. A final category of items consists of highly standardized products and services for which information about price is important. Certain kinds of home furnishings, automotive products, and casual apparel make up this category.

Why Consumers Shop and Buy Online

LO 21-3 Describe why consumers shop and buy online and how marketers influence online purchasing behavior.

Why do consumers shop and buy online? Marketers emphasize the customer value-creation possibilities, the importance of interactivity, individuality, and relationship building, and their ability to produce a positive customer experience in the new

2015: Percent of Online Retail Sales	Product Category	2018: Percent of Online Sales
21.9%	Computer & consumer electronics	22.0%
17.2%	Apparel & accessories	17.5%
10.4%	Automobile & auto parts	10.5%
9.1%	Books, music, and video	9.4%
6.4%	Furniture & home furnishings	6.7%
5.6%	Health & personal care	5.6%

NOTE: Online retail sales exclude airline travel, event tickets, and prescription drugs.

FIGURE 21–2

Five product categories account for about 70 percent of online retail sales today—a trend that is projected to continue in the future.

marketspace. However, consumers typically refer to six reasons they shop and buy online: convenience, choice, customization, communication, cost, and control (Figure 21–3).

Convenience   Online shopping and buying is *convenient*. Consumers can visit Walmart at www.walmart.com to scan and order from among thousands of displayed products without fighting traffic, finding a parking space, walking through long aisles, and standing in store checkout lines. Alternatively, online consumers can use **bots**, electronic shopping agents or robots that search websites to compare prices and product or service features. In either instance, an online consumer has never ventured into a store. However, for convenience to remain a source of customer value creation, websites must be easy to locate and navigate, and image downloads must be fast.

A commonly held view among online marketers is the **eight-second rule**: Customers will abandon their efforts to enter and navigate a website if download time exceeds eight seconds. Furthermore, the more clicks and pauses between clicks required to access information or make a purchase, the more likely it is a customer will exit a website.

Choice   *Choice,* the second reason consumers shop and buy online, has two dimensions. First, choice exists in the product or service selection offered to consumers.

FIGURE 21–3

Why do consumers shop and buy online? Read the text to learn how convenience, choice, customization, communication, cost, and control result in a favorable customer experience.

Photo: © Fuse/Getty Images

Zappos.com is successful because it meets all the requirements necessary for consumers to shop and buy online. In less than 10 years, the company has posted significant annual sales of shoes, apparel, bags, accessories, housewares, and jewelry.

© Ira Roberts

Zappos.com

www.zappos.com

Buyers desiring selection can avail themselves of numerous websites for almost anything they want. For instance, online buyers of consumer electronics can shop individual manufacturers such as Bose (www.bose.com) and QVC.com, a general merchant that offers more than 100,000 products.

Choice assistance is the second dimension. Here, the interactive capabilities of Internet-enabled technologies invite customers to engage in an electronic dialogue with marketers for the purpose of making informed choices. Choice assistance is one of the reasons for the continued success of Zappos.com. The company offers an online chat room that enables prospective buyers to ask questions and receive answers in real time. In addition, carefully designed search capabilities permit consumers to review products by brand and particular items.

Customization   Even with a broad selection and choice assistance, some customers prefer one-of-a-kind items that fit their specific needs. *Customization* arises from Internet-enabled capabilities that make possible a highly interactive and individualized information and exchange environment for shoppers and buyers. Remember the earlier Reebok, Schwab, Dell, and Seven Cycles examples? To varying degrees, online consumers also benefit from **customerization**—the practice of not only customizing a product or service but also personalizing the marketing and overall shopping and buying interaction for each customer.[14]

Customerization seeks to do more than offer consumers the right product, at the right time, and at the right price. It combines choiceboard and personalization systems to expand the exchange environment beyond a transaction and makes shopping and buying an enjoyable, personal experience.

Communication   Online consumers particularly welcome the *communication* capabilities of Internet-enabled technologies. This communication can take three forms: (1) marketer-to-consumer e-mail notification, (2) consumer-to-marketer buying and

Staffers in Gatorade's "Mission Control" room in Chicago, Illinois, monitor Internet and social media outlets, such as Facebook and Twitter, 24 hours a day. Whenever someone uses Twitter to say they are drinking a Gatorade or mentions the brand on Facebook or in a blog, it pops up on-screen at Mission Control. In this way, conversations featuring Gatorade provide useful consumer insights into how the brand is viewed and used.
© *Clayton Hauck Photography*

Gatorade
www.gatorade.com

service requests, and (3) consumer-to-consumer chat rooms and instant messaging, in addition to social networking websites such as Twitter and Facebook.

Communication has proven to be a double-edged sword for online consumers. On the one hand, the interactive communication capabilities of Internet-enabled technologies increase consumer convenience, reduce information search costs, and make choice assistance and customization possible. Communication also promotes the development of company-hosted and independent **web communities**—websites that allow people to congregate online and exchange views on topics of common interest. For instance, Coca-Cola hosts MyCoke.com, and iVillage.com is an independent web community for women and includes topics such as career management, personal finances, parenting, relationships, beauty, and health.

Web logs, or blogs, are another form of communication. A *blog* is a web page that serves as a publicly accessible personal journal for an individual or organization. Blogs are popular because they provide online forums on a wide variety of subjects ranging from politics to car repair. Companies such as Hewlett-Packard, PepsiCo, and Harley-Davidson routinely monitor blogs and social media posts to gather customer insights.[15]

On the other hand, communications can take the form of electronic junk mail or unsolicited e-mail, called **spam**. In fact, 67 percent of e-mail messages in the world are spam.[16] The prevalence of spam has prompted many online services to institute policies and procedures to prevent spammers from spamming their subscribers, and several states have antispamming laws. The 2004 *CAN-SPAM (Controlling the Assault of Non-Solicited Pornography and Marketing) Act* restricts information collection and unsolicited e-mail promotions on the Internet.

Internet-enabled communication capabilities also make possible *buzz,* a popular term for word-of-mouth behavior in marketspace. Chapter 5 described the importance

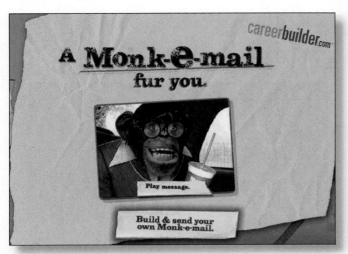

Careerbuilder.com, an online career placement company, has produced a great viral marketing success with its Monk-e-mail featuring talking monkeys. People can stylize their monkeys by choosing headgear, clothes, glasses, backgrounds, and other features. They can also record a message using one of four monkey voices, or their own voice. Monk-e-mail can be sent to friends or posted on Twitter.
© Ira Roberts

CareerBuilder
www.careerbuilder.com

Video 21-2
Frito-Lay
kerin.tv/13e/v21-2

of word of mouth in consumer behavior. Internet technology has magnified its significance. According to Jeff Bezos, president of Amazon.com, "If you have an unhappy customer on the Internet, he doesn't tell his six friends, he tells his 6,000 friends!"[17] Buzz is particularly influential for toys, cars, sporting goods, motion pictures, apparel, consumer electronics, pharmaceuticals, health and beauty products, and health care services. Some marketers have capitalized on this phenomenon by creating buzz through viral marketing.

Viral marketing is an Internet-enabled promotional strategy that encourages individuals to forward marketer-initiated messages to others via e-mail, social networking websites, and blogs. There are three approaches to viral marketing. First, marketers can embed a message in the product or service so that customers hardly realize they are passing it along. The classic example is Hotmail, which was one of the first companies to provide free, Internet-based e-mail. Each outgoing e-mail message had the tagline: "Get Your Private, Free Email from MSN Hotmail." This effort produced more than 350 million users.

Second, marketers can make the website content so compelling that viewers want to share it with others. Careerbuilder.com has done this with its Monk-e-mail site, which allows users to send personalized, private-themed e-cards for all occasions. More than 100 million Monk-e-mails have been sent since 2006. Finally, marketers can offer incentives (discounts, sweepstakes, or free merchandise). For example, Burger King asked, "What do you love more, your friend or the Whopper?" in its Whopper Sacrifice campaign. Facebook users were asked to "unfriend" 10 people from their Facebook friends list in exchange for a free burger.[18]

Cost Consumer *cost* is a fifth reason for online shopping and buying. Many popular items bought online can be purchased at the same price or cheaper than in retail stores.[19] Lower prices also result from sophisticated software that permits **dynamic pricing**, the practice of changing prices for products and services in real time in response to supply and demand conditions. As described in Chapter 14, dynamic pricing is a form of flexible pricing and can often result in lower prices. It is typically used for pricing time-sensitive items such as airline seats, scarce items found at art or collectible auctions, and out-of-date items such as last year's models of computer equipment and accessories. Ticketmaster has recently experimented with dynamic pricing to adjust the price of sports and concert tickets in response to demand.

A consumer's cost of external information search, including time spent and often the hassle of shopping, is also reduced. Greater shopping convenience and lower external search costs are two major reasons for the popularity of online shopping and buying among women—particularly those who work outside the home.

Control The sixth reason consumers prefer to buy online is the *control* it gives them over their shopping and purchase decision process. Online shoppers and buyers are empowered consumers. They deftly use Internet technology to seek information, evaluate alternatives, and make purchase decisions on their own time, terms, and conditions. For example, studies show that automobile shoppers spend an average of eleven hours researching cars online before setting foot in a showroom.[20] The result of these activities is a more informed and discerning shopper.

Even though consumers have many reasons for shopping and buying online, a segment of Internet users refrains from making purchases for privacy and security reasons. These consumers are concerned about a rarely mentioned seventh C—cookies.

609

Cookies are computer files that a marketer can download onto the computer and mobile phone of an online shopper who visits the marketer's website. Cookies allow the marketer's website to record a user's visit, track visits to other websites, and store and retrieve this information in the future. Cookies also contain visitor information such as expressed product preferences, personal data, passwords, and credit card numbers.

Cookies make possible customized and personal content for online shoppers. They also make possible the practice of behavioral targeting for marketers. **Behavioral targeting** uses information provided by cookies for directing online advertising from marketers to those online shoppers whose behavioral profiles suggest they would be interested in such advertising. A controversy surrounding cookies is summed up by an authority on the technology: "At best cookies make for a user-friendly web world: like a salesclerk who knows who you are. At worst, cookies represent a potential loss of privacy."[21] Read the Making Responsible Decisions box to learn more about privacy and security issues in the digital marketspace.[22]

When and Where Online Consumers Shop and Buy

Shopping and buying also happen at different times in marketspace than in the traditional marketplace.[23] About 80 percent of online retail sales occur Monday through Friday. The busiest shopping day is Wednesday. By comparison, 35 percent of retail store sales are registered on the weekend. Saturday is the most popular shopping day. Monday through Friday online shopping and buying often occur during normal work hours—some 30 percent of online consumers say they visit websites from their place of work, which partially accounts for the sales level during the workweek.

Favorite websites for workday shopping and buying include those featuring event tickets, auctions, online periodical subscriptions, flowers and gifts, consumer electronics, and travel. Websites offering health and beauty items, apparel and accessories, and music and video tend to be browsed and bought from a consumer's home.

learning review »

21-3. What are the six reasons consumers prefer to shop and buy online?

21-4. What is the eight-second rule?

CROSS-CHANNEL CONSUMERS AND MULTICHANNEL MARKETING

LO 21-4 Define cross-channel consumers and the role of transactional and promotional websites in reaching these consumers.

Consumers often shop and buy in both online and offline environments. Individuals who move effortlessly between these environments have given rise to the cross-channel consumer and the importance of multichannel marketing.

Who Is the Cross-Channel Consumer?

A **cross-channel consumer** is an online consumer who shops online but buys offline, or shops offline but buys online. They differ from exclusive online consumers and exclusive offline consumers (see Figure 21–4). These distinctions will vary by the products or services shopped and bought.[24] For example, e-books are shopped and purchased by exclusive online consumers. Expensive, custom-made furniture and home furnishings are typically shopped and purchased by an exclusive offline consumer.

Showrooming Cross-channel consumers who shop offline but buy online engage in **showrooming**—the practice of examining products in a store and then buying them online for a cheaper price. While obtaining a lower price is the primary motivation for showrooming, showroomers often gather additional merchandise information, look for online promotions or deals, and check merchandise reviews and rating. About three-fourths of online consumers have engaged in showrooming for one or more products. Consumer electronics and home appliances are the most popular showrooming product categories.

Webrooming Cross-channel consumers who shop online but buy offline engage in **webrooming**—the practice of examining products online and then buying them in a store. While lower price is a significant motivator for webrooming, webroomers cite other factors as well: avoid shipping costs, gain immediate possession of a product, and allow for easier returns. About 80 percent of online consumers have engaged in

FIGURE 21–4

Cross-channel consumers engage in "showrooming" and "webrooming" depending on how they shop and buy online and offline.

webrooming for one or more products. Automobiles and auto parts, apparel (including shoes), and home office equipment are popular webrooming product categories.

Recent research indicates that 6 in 10 webroomers have showroomed while 9 in 10 showroomers have webroomed. Cross-channel consumers overall account for a significant amount of online activity and sales. Retail sales from cross-channel consumers is estimated to be about five times greater than from online-only retail sales.

Implementing Multichannel Marketing

The prominence of cross-channel consumers has focused increased attention on multichannel marketing. Recall from Chapter 15 that *multichannel marketing* is the blending of different communication and delivery channels that are mutually reinforcing in attracting, retaining, and building relationships with consumers who shop and buy in the traditional marketplace and marketspace—the cross-channel consumer.

The shopping and buying path for cross-channel consumers indicates that company websites should be different. And they are. Websites play a multifaceted role in multichannel marketing because they can serve as either a communication or delivery channel. Two general applications of websites exist based on their intended purpose: (1) transactional websites and (2) promotional websites.

Multichannel Marketing with Transactional Websites   *Transactional websites* are essentially electronic storefronts. They focus principally on converting an online browser into an online, catalog, or in-store buyer using the website design elements described earlier. Transactional websites are most common among store and catalog retailers and direct selling companies, such as Tupperware. Retailers and direct selling firms have found that their websites, while cannibalizing sales volume from stores, catalogs, and sales representatives, attract new customers and influence sales. Consider Victoria's Secret, the well-known specialty retailer of intimate apparel for women ages 18 to 45. It reports that almost 60 percent of its website customers are men, most of whom generate new sales volume for the company.[25]

Promotional websites seek to engage the visitor in an interactive experience involving games, contests, and quizzes with electronic coupons and other gifts as prizes.

© Maridav/iStock/Getty Images

Transactional websites are used less frequently by manufacturers of consumer products. A recurring issue for manufacturers is the threat of *channel conflict,* described in Chapter 15, and the potential harm to trade relationships with their retailing intermediaries. Still, manufacturers do use transactional websites, often cooperating with retailers. For example, Callaway Golf Company markets its golf merchandise at www.callawaygolf.com but relies on a retailer close to the buyer to fill the order. The retailer ships the order to the buyer within 24 hours and is credited with the sale. The majority of retailers that sell Callaway merchandise participate in this relationship, including retail chains Golf Galaxy and Dick's Sporting Goods. According to Callaway's chief executive officer, "This arrangement allows us to satisfy the consumer but to do so in a way that didn't violate our relationship with our loyal trade partners—those 15,000 outlets that sell Callaway products."[26]

Multichannel Marketing with Promotional Websites   *Promotional websites* have a very different purpose than transactional sites. They advertise and promote a company's products and services and provide information on how items can be used and where they can be purchased. They often engage the visitor in an interactive experience involving games, contests, and quizzes with electronic coupons and other gifts as prizes. Procter & Gamble maintains separate websites for many of its leading brands, including Scope

FIGURE 21–5

Implementing multichannel marketing with promotional websites is common today. Two successes are found at Hyundai Motor America and the Clinique Division of Estée Lauder, Inc.

- 70% of Hyundai leads come from its website.
- 80% of people visiting a Hyundai dealer first visited its website.

- 80% of current Clinique buyers who visit its website later purchase a Clinique product at a store.
- 37% of non-Clinique buyers make a Clinique purchase after visiting its website.

Video 21-3

Pampers

kerin.tv/13e/v21-3

mouthwash (www.getclose.com) and Pampers diapers (www.pampers.com). Promotional sites are effective in generating interest in and trial of a company's products (see Figure 21–5).[27] Hyundai Motor America reports that 80 percent of the people visiting a Hyundai store first visited the brand's website (www.hyundaiusa.com) and 70 percent of Hyundai leads come from its website.

Promotional websites also can be used to support a company's traditional marketing channel and build customer relationships. This is the objective of the Clinique Division of Estée Lauder, Inc., which markets cosmetics through department stores. Clinique reports that 80 percent of current customers who visit its website (www.clinique.com) later purchase a Clinique product at a department store, while 37 percent of non-Clinique buyers make a Clinique purchase after visiting the company's website.

The popularity of multichannel marketing is apparent in its growing impact on online retail sales.[28] Fully 70 percent of U.S. online retail sales are made by companies that practice multichannel marketing. Multichannel marketers are expected to register about 90 percent of U.S. online retail sales in 2018.

learning review »

21-5. A cross-channel consumer is _____.

21-6. Channel conflict between manufacturers and retailers is likely to arise when manufacturers use _____ websites.

613

LEARNING OBJECTIVES REVIEW

LO 21-1 *Describe what interactive marketing is and how it creates customer value, customer relationships, and customer experiences.*

Interactive marketing involves two-way buyer–seller electronic communication in a computer-mediated environment in which the buyer controls the kind and amount of information received from the seller. It creates customer value by providing time, place, form, and possession utility for consumers. Customer relationships are created and sustained through two unique capabilities of Internet technology: interactivity and individuality. From an interactive marketing perspective, customer experience represents the sum total of the interactions that a customer has with a company's website, from the initial look at a home page through the entire purchase decision process. Companies produce a customer experience through seven website design elements. These elements are context, content, community, customization, communication, connection, and commerce.

LO 21-2 *Explain why certain types of products and services are particularly suited for interactive marketing.*
Certain types of products and services seem to be particularly suited for interactive marketing. One category consists of items for which product information is an important part of the purchase decision, but prepurchase trial is not necessarily critical. A second category contains items that can be digitally delivered. Unique items represent a third category. A fourth category includes items that are regularly purchased and where convenience is very important. A fifth category consists of highly standardized items for which information about price is important.

LO 21-3 *Describe why consumers shop and buy online and how marketers influence online purchasing behavior.*
There are six reasons consumers shop and buy online. They are convenience, choice, customization, communication, cost, and control. Marketers have capitalized on these reasons through a variety of means. For example, they provide choice assistance using choiceboard and collaborative filtering technology, which also provides opportunities for customization. Company-hosted web communities and viral marketing practices capitalize on the communications dimensions of digital technologies. Dynamic pricing provides real-time responses to supply and demand conditions, often resulting in lower prices for consumers. Permission marketing is popular given consumer interest in control.

LO 21-4 *Define cross-channel consumers and the role of transactional and promotional websites in reaching these consumers.*
A cross-channel consumer is an online consumer who shops online, but buys offline or shops offline, but buys online. These shoppers are reached through multichannel marketing. Websites play a multifaceted role in multichannel marketing because they can serve as either a delivery or communication channel. In this regard, transactional websites are essentially electronic storefronts. They focus principally on converting an online browser into an online, catalog, or in-store buyer using the website design elements described earlier. On the other hand, promotional websites serve to advertise and promote a company's products and services and provide information on how items can be used and where they can be purchased.

LEARNING REVIEW ANSWERS

21-1 **The consumer-initiated practice of generating content on a marketer's website that is custom tailored to an individual's specific needs and preferences is called _____.**
Answer: personalization

21-2 **What are the seven website design elements that companies use to produce a customer experience?**
Answer: From an interactive marketing perspective, customer experience is defined as the sum total of the interactions that a customer has with a company's website, from the initial look at a home page through the entire purchase decision process. Companies produce a customer experience through seven website design elements, which are: (1) context—a website's aesthetic appeal and functional look and feel reflected in site layout and visual design; (2) content—all digital information on a website, including the text, video, audio, and graphics; (3) community—the user-to-user communications hosted by the company to create virtual communities; (4) customization—the ability of a site to modify itself to, or be modified by, each individual user; (5) communication—the dialogue that unfolds between the website and its users; (6) connection—the network of linkages between a company's site and other sites; and (7) commerce—the website's ability to conduct sales transactions for products and services. Most websites do not include every design element. Although every website has context and content, they differ in the use of the remaining five elements. See Figure 21–1.

21-3 **What are the six reasons consumers prefer to shop and buy online?**
Answer: The six reasons consumers prefer to shop and buy online are: convenience, choice, customization, communication, cost, and control. See Figure 21–3. A potential seventh reason is cookies.

21-4 **What is the eight-second rule?**
Answer: The eight-second rule is a view that customers will abandon their efforts to enter and navigate a website if download time exceeds eight seconds.

21-5 **A cross-channel consumer is _____.**
Answer: A cross-channel consumer is an online consumer who shops online, but buys offline, or shops offline, but buys online.

21-6 **Channel conflict between manufacturers and retailers is likely to arise when manufacturers use _____ websites.**
Answer: transactional

FOCUSING ON KEY TERMS

behavorial targeting p. 610
bots p. 606
choiceboard p. 600
collaborative filtering p. 600
cookies p. 610
cross-channel consumer p. 611

customerization p. 607
dynamic pricing p. 609
eight-second rule p. 606
interactive marketing p. 600
online consumers p. 604
permission marketing p. 601

personalization p. 600
showrooming p. 611
spam p. 608
viral marketing p. 609
web communities p. 608
webrooming p. 611

1 Have you made an online purchase? If so, why do you think so many people who have access to the Internet are not also online buyers? If not, why are you reluctant to do so? Do you think that electronic commerce benefits consumers even if they don't make a purchase?

2 Like the traditional marketplace, the digital marketspace offers marketers opportunities to create time, place, form, and possession utility. How do you think Internet-enabled technology rates in terms of creating these values? Take a shopping trip at a virtual retailer of your choice (don't buy anything unless you really want to). Then compare the time, place, form, and possession utility provided by the virtual retailer to that provided by a traditional retailer in the same product category.

3 Visit Amazon.com (www.amazon.com) or Barnes & Noble (www.barnesandnoble.com).

As you tour the website, think about how shopping for books online compares with a trip to your university bookstore to buy books. Specifically, compare and contrast your shopping experiences with respect to convenience, choice, customization, communication, cost, and control.

4 You are planning to buy a new car so you visit www.edmunds.com. Based on your experience visiting that site, do you think you will enjoy more or less control in negotiating with the dealer when you actually purchase your vehicle?

5 Visit the website for your university or college. Based on your visit, would you conclude that the site is a transactional site or a promotional site? Why? How would you rate the site in terms of the six website design elements that affect customer experience?

BUILDING YOUR MARKETING PLAN

Does your marketing plan involve a marketspace presence for your product or service? If the answer is "no," read no further and do not include this element in your plan. If the answer is "yes," then attention must be given to developing a website in your marketing plan. A useful starting point is to:

1 Describe how each website element—context, content, community, customization, communication, connection, and commerce—will be used to create a customer experience.

2 Identify a company's website that best reflects your website conceptualization.

■ connect

VIDEO CASE 21   Pizza Hut and imc^2: Becoming a Multichannel Marketer

It's no surprise that Pizza Hut is the world's largest pizza chain with more than 10,000 restaurants in 100 countries. But did you know that Pizza Hut became one of the top 35 U.S. Internet retailers in 2009?

> **Video 21-4**
> **Pizza Hut**
> **Video Case**
> kerin.tv/13e/v21-4

According to Brian Niccol, Pizza Hut's chief marketing officer (CMO), "We've done what many would say is impossible. We successfully built an online business in three years that produces hundreds of millions of dollars in annual revenue. Today, Pizza Hut is a category leader in the interactive and emerging marketplace." So how did they do it? Pizza Hut simply revolutionized the quick serve restaurant (QSR) world through a multichannel marketing approach that created a

Source: Pizza Hut, Inc.

customer experience and a customer engagement platform that was second to none.

THE RETAIL PIZZA BUSINESS

With three national competitors dominating the marketplace, the pizza business is very competitive. Even customers who could be considered heavy users of a particular brand regularly purchase from competitors on the basis of timing, pricing, and convenience.

In general, Pizza Hut's most frequent customers (and likely those of the other two major competitors) divide into two categories: (1) families, primarily time-starved mothers, looking for a quick and simple mealtime solution; and (2) young adult males who fuel their active lifestyle with one of the world's most versatile and convenient foods (no cooking, no utensils, no cleanup, and left-overs are perfect for breakfast). While these two groups could not be more dissimilar on the surface, value and convenience are important for both groups. Cost-conscious mothers look for a good quality product and a hassle-free eating experience. Deal-seeking young adult males seek more of the food they love with less time and cash invested in the process.

The importance of the take-home and delivery segment of the U.S. pizza market is illustrated by the fact that Pizza Hut's principal national competitors focus exclusively on this aspect of the business. Most take-home and delivery sales are ordered before a customer enters the restaurant. By 2006, a growing number of retail pizza customers had become comfortable ordering pizza online. Pizza ordering, as it turned out, was an ideal product for the digital world. People understood the basic menu, generally knew that they could customize their order in a variety of ways, and were accustomed to not being in the store when ordering. Brand retail presence and established customer delivery networks also made the shift to online ordering easier for national pizza chains than other national quick serve restaurants. But, as Pizza Hut understood, there is still an incredible level of complexity in making something truly sophisticated simple and easy for the customer.

CREATING A PLAN OF ACTION

For the most part, the intent of online ordering for the pizza business was to make transactions with the customer easier and cheaper for the brand. Pizza Hut recognized the opportunity to engage people with its brand and with other people directly and do something special; namely, build sustainable relationships with its customers and enable Pizza Hut to engage people in a more meaningful and profitable way. In short, Pizza Hut set about to reinvent the retail pizza business by breaking away from a transactional platform to an efficient and powerful customer engagement platform by reaching out to customers' kitchens and couches to offer a better mealtime ordering, delivery, and dining experience.

Pizza Hut selected imc^2 as one of its lead agencies to plan a comprehensive interactive strategy that focused first on the redesign of the Pizza Hut corporate website (including redefining the customer experience online and across all of the brand's touchpoints) and then on a series of progressively sophisticated and industry-leading customer engagement strategies. imc^2 brought 15 years of experience in interactive marketing and brand engagement to the assignment. Its clients have included Coca-Cola, Johnson & Johnson, Pfizer, Omni Hotels, Hasbro, Procter & Gamble, and Samsung, among a host of other companies, large and small.

Source: Pizza Hut, Inc.

PIZZAHUT.COM, CUSTOMER EXPERIENCE, AND BRAND ENGAGEMENT

Pizza Hut and imc[2] executives agreed that the strategy for reinventing the retail pizza business would involve developing opportunities for customers to engage with the brand by using the right technologies to enable and encourage interaction. A new website was necessary to better address all major design elements. How Pizza Hut and imc[2] executed these design elements not only created value for its customers, but also served as a basis for differentiation in the retail pizza business. Let's look at these design elements and PizzaHut.com's performance.

The Pizza Hut website was completely redesigned to support nationwide online ordering in 2007 (including all franchise locations for the first time) and is updated frequently to keep up with the company's fast-paced marketing strategy and ambitious product innovation rollout schedule. Since promotions are an important expectation in pizza purchasing and speak to the brand's consumers in a language that clearly connects with their desire for value, the website *context* and *content* balance the ability to shop for a deal with quick and easy ordering access for people who arrive at PizzaHut.com ready to purchase. The site presents a number of Pizza Hut's current offers in the central viewing window as well as through the rolling navigation directly underneath the main content. Primary navigation for information, such as the menu, locations, and nutrition facts, are displayed horizontally across the top of the rotating content.

Website *customization* is achieved in several ways, but the primary utility is to simplify ordering. For customers who have already registered, there are several personalization options, including rapid ordering called *Express Checkout*—a feature that's based on saved preferences similar to a "playlist." For example, if you have a group of friends that likes to watch movies together, you might create an order named *Movie Night* that has your group's favorite pizzas. Using the *Express Checkout* option accessible directly on the home page, you can select *Movie Night*, quickly review the order, click the "submit" button, and the pizzas are on their way, relying on saved delivery and payment options through a stored *cookie* (a piece of digital code that is used to identify previous visitors) to speed the transaction. With this type of functionality, you can think of convenience as an investment that creates loyalty and somewhat insulates the brand against switching down the line when customers would have to register with and learn a competitor's system, and where access to their favorite features might not be available.

Source: Pizza Hut, Inc.

Website *content* and *communications* are integrated with the company's overall communications programs—including traditional media—with product innovations, promotions, and special events shared across platforms. True to the brand, communications are fun and energetic, matching bold images and vibrant color with a smart, clever, and lighthearted voice. One noteworthy example includes the 2008 April Fools' Day rebranding of the company as "Pasta Hut" to coincide with the launch of the brand's innovative line of Tuscani Pastas. This campaign included online support in the form of display media (banner ads) and the temporary rebranding of PizzaHut.com as PastaHut.com with special imagery and copy supporting the name change. Not only did the brand get plenty of coverage in the press, but it deepened the connection with customers by showing their willingness to be spontaneous and fun, inviting people to play along with the joke.

Pizza Hut's integrated marketing communications approach enables the company to easily test and incorporate other items and brands under the larger corporate umbrella, such as the WingStreet operation and the pasta extension. This demonstrates the brand's ability to stretch the QSR concept way beyond its pizza roots and suggests the kind of direction the company may pursue in the future.

PizzaHut.com and the brand's other online assets are all about getting the world's favorite pizza and signature products into the hands and stomachs of customers. Since *commerce* is a huge consideration on the site, there are multiple pathways for ordering, including several onsite methods, a Facebook app (the first national pizza chain to produce an ordering application for the world's leading social networking site), a branded desktop widget, mobile ordering (also known as Total Mobile Access, added in 2008, that includes both a WAP [wireless application protocol] site and text ordering), and a sophisticated and simple iPhone app released in 2009 that lets customers build and submit their order visually. Additional revenue streams can also be quickly built online, as demonstrated by the eGift Card program conceived and implemented by imc[2] over a weekend during the 2008 holiday season.

Realizing that it did not make sense for the company or its customers to create a *community* on the site, Pizza Hut tapped into Facebook to achieve results in a very cost-effective manner. With approximately 1 million fans and the first of its kind Facebook ordering application, the brand can efficiently engage a huge group of people in a very natural way without disrupting their daily routine. Again, the brand understands that if you make something convenient, you can increase trust while securing greater transactional loyalty. Pizza Hut's 2009 program to identify a summer intern, or *Twintern*, responsible for monitoring and encouraging dialogue on Twitter and other social media networks is another example of how the brand is building on existing platforms and making effective use of the massive social marketing infrastructure.

PizzaHut.com connects mobile, desktop, social networks, and other digital gateways to complement traditional media and its retail presence. So when Pizza Hut thinks about the *connection* design element, it includes more than just linking to other websites online. Rather, it provides a comprehensive approach to creating a seamless customer experience wherever and whenever people want to engage with the brand.

PERFORMANCE MEASUREMENT AND OUTCOMES

Pizza Hut diligently measures the performance of Pizza Hut.com. The company created a customized marketing dashboard that allows the Pizza Hut management team to monitor various aspects of the brand's marketing program and provides an almost constant stream of fresh information that it can use to optimize engagement with people or tweak various aspects of performance.

The results have been remarkable, but understand that due to the highly competitive nature of the industry, they are fluid and only represent a moment in time. Consider, for example:

1 PizzaHut.com dominates the pizza category with number one rankings in website traffic and search volume. According to comScore, a global leader in digital analytics and measurement, the Pizza Hut site achieves the most traffic per online dollars spent in the pizza category.
2 PizzaHut.com became one of the top 35 Internet retailers in the United States in 2009, up from 45th in 2008.
3 Pizza Hut's iPhone app had more than 100,000 downloads in the first two weeks after release.

WHAT'S NEXT

So what's next for PizzaHut.com? While the brand has made huge gains in a very short time period, staying on top in the rapidly evolving digital marketplace requires constant attention. Pizza Hut envisions that its online business will surpass the $1 billion mark within the next five years, and that digital transactions will lead all revenue within a decade.

While understandably protective of the company's future strategy, Pizza Hut CMO Niccol has ambitious goals and he's not joking when he deadpans, "I want Pizza Hut to become the Amazon of food service and be pioneers for the digital space. I do not want us to be a brick-and-mortar company that just dabbles in the space." The transition to something along the lines of the Amazon model suggests that the brand might further evolve its identity as a pizza business and stretch or completely redefine the QSR model.

Most brands that want to grow in the evolving economy will have to think and plan long-term and be able to act swiftly as marketplace conditions change. imc² Chief Marketing Officer Ian Wolfman, when assessing the future of marketing, sums up the opportunity neatly. "Our agency believes that marketing's current transformation will result in a complete reorientation of how brands and companies engage with their consumers and other stakeholders. Brands that thrive will be those, like Pizza Hut, that can efficiently build sustainable relationships with people—relationships that have both high trust and high transactions" (see Figure 1). He goes on to explain that "brands taking a longer view have an unexpected

FIGURE 1

imc² Brand Sustainability Map

advantage over traditional models that often focus too tightly on hitting near-term quarterly targets." Referring to research his agency has done on the subject, Wolfman points out that the most successful brands in the future will likely be those that resonate with people on a deeply emotional level and operate with a clearly defined sense of purpose.

Pizza Hut, with its focus on digitally enabled customer convenience and category innovation, is ideally positioned to connect with people on a level that builds trust and increases transactions. Referring to the initial time investment, however modest, that customers have to make in registering with the system and enabling various devices, Niccol sees the landscape as very promising for brands that put their customers' interests and preferences first. "If we do our job right—creating authentic engagement and making it convenient and valuable for people to interact with the brand—the numbers follow."[29]

Questions

1 What kind of website is PizzaHut.com?
2 How does PizzaHut.com incorporate the seven website design elements?
3 How are choiceboard and personalization systems used in the PizzaHut.com website?

Chapter Notes

1. Interview with John Lewis, account executive at Seven Cycles, Inc., April 19, 2013; and www.sevencycles.com, April 20, 2013.
2. "U.S. Online Retail Forecast: 2013–2018," www.forrester.com, June 2, 2015.
3. "Transaction Denied," *Bloomberg Businessweek,* July 13, 2014, p. 90.
4. Rupal Parekh, "Personalized Products Please but Can They Create Profit?" *Advertising Age,* May, 21, 2013, p. 4.
5. Rafi A. Mohammed, Robert J. Fisher, Bernard J. Jaworski, and Gordon J. Paddison, *Internet Marketing: Building Advantage in a Networked Economy,* 2nd ed. (Burr Ridge, IL: McGraw-Hill/Irwin, 2004).
6. Natasha Singer, "E-Tailer Customization: Convenient or Creepy?" www.nytimes.com, June 23, 2012.
7. Judy Strauss, and Raymond Frost, *E-Marketing,* 7th ed. (Upper Saddle River, NJ: Prentice Hall, 2014).
8. Piet Levy, "The Data Dilemma," *Marketing News,* January 30, 2011, pp. 20–21.
9. This discussion is drawn from Jeffrey F. Rayport and Bernard J. Jaworski, *e-Commerce,* 2nd ed. (Burr Ridge, IL: McGraw-Hill/Irwin, 2004); and *The Essential Guide to Best Practices in eCommerce* (Portland, OR: Webtrends, Inc., 2006).
10. Mylene Mangalindan, "Web Sites Want You to Stick Around," *The Wall Street Journal,* April 15, 2008, p. B5.
11. This example and data provided courtesy of The Sewell Automotive Companies.
12. "State of the U.S. Online Retail Economy," www.comscore.com June 10, 2015.
13. "U.S. Retail Ecommerce Sales by Product Category, 2012–2018," www.emarketer.com, April 11, 2015.
14. Jerry Wind and Arvind Ranaswamy, "Customerization: The Next Wave in Mass Customization," *Journal of Interactive Marketing,* Winter 2001, pp. 13–32.
15. Valerie Bauerkin, "Gatorade's Mission: Sell More Drinks," *The Wall Street Journal,* September 14, 2010, p. B6; Tom Hayes and Michael S. Malone, "Marketing in the World of the Web," *The Wall Street Journal,* November 29–30, 2008, p. A13. Also see Kate Fitzgerald, "Blogs Fascinate, Frighten Marketers Eager to Tap Loyalists," *Advertising Age,* March 5, 2007, p. S-4.
16. "Read This and Win Million$!!!" *The Economist,* January 26, 2013, p. 60.
17. Quoted in Strauss and Frost, *E-Marketing,* p. 357.
18. Victoria Taylor, "The Best-Ever Social Media Campaigns," www.forbes.com, August 17, 2010.
19. "Showrooming Hits Luxury Fashion," *The Wall Street Journal,* April 10, 2014, pp. B1, B2.
20. "Say Goodbye to the Car Salesman," *The Wall Street Journal,* November 21, 2013, pp. B1, B2; and "Death of a Car Salesman," *The Economist,* August 22, 2015, pp. 52–53.
21. "Cookies Cause Bitter Backlash," *The Wall Street Journal,* September 20, 2010, pp. B1, B2.
22. "Terms and Conditions," *Marketing News,* November 2014, pp. 35–41; "Consumers Want Consent in Data Mining of Personal Info," *Dallas Morning News,* June 5, 2015, pp. D1, D6; Joseph Turow, "Behavior Aside, Consumers Do Want Control of Their Privacy," *Advertising Age,* January 28, 2013, p. 32; "Are Digital Foxes Guarding the Web's Privacy Hen House?" *The Wall Street Journal,* December 14, 2012, p. B1; 2014 *Internet Crime Report,* www.ic3.gov.
23. Kathleen Kim, "More Employers Letting Employees Shop Online at Work," www.inc.com, November 14, 2012; and "Survey: Many Admit to Online Shopping at Work," www.moneycentral.msn.com, December 2, 2008.
24. This discussion is based on the following sources: "Webrooming and Showrooming in 2015," *multichannelmerchant.com,* January 19, 2015; "Study Shows Prevalence of Consumer Webrooming," *adweek.com,* May 9, 2014; "Total Retail: Retailers and the Age of Disruption," *pwc.com,* February 2015.
25. "Retailers' Panty Raid on Victoria's Secret," *The Wall Street Journal,* June 20, 2007, pp. B1, B12.
26. Stephanie Kang, "Callaway Will Use Retailers to Sell Goods Directly to Consumers Online," *The Wall Street Journal,* November 6, 2006, p. B5.
27. Erik Hauser and Max Lenderman, "Experiential Marketing," *Brandweek,* September 20, 2008.
28. "Attention Shoppers: Online Product Research," www.pewresearch.org, September 29, 2010.
29. Pizza Hut: This case was prepared by Pizza Hut and imc[2] executives for exclusive use in this text.

22

Pulling It All Together: The Strategic Marketing Process

LEARNING OBJECTIVES

After reading this chapter you should be able to:

LO 22-1 Explain how marketing managers allocate resources.

LO 22-2 Describe Porter's generic business strategies and synergy analysis planning frameworks.

LO 22-3 Explain what makes an effective marketing plan.

LO 22-4 Use a time-based agenda and an action item list to conduct a meeting.

LO 22-5 Describe an organization's marketing department and the role of a product manager.

LO 22-6 Explain the use of marketing ROI, metrics, and dashboards in evaluating marketing programs.

Strategic Marketing Helps General Mills Adapt to New Tastes!

Consumer tastes are changing and so are consumer expectations for new products. This is particularly true in the supermarket where consumers are increasingly demanding convenient, healthy, and good-tasting food. At consumer foods manufacturer General Mills that means Vivian Milroy Callaway faces exciting challenges as she helps the company adapt to the changes.

As vice president of the Center for Learning and Experimentation at General Mills, Callaway is responsible for helping uncover and introduce new-product ideas for the company. The strategic marketing process—planning, implementation, and evaluation—is essential to her job and recently played an important role in the development of a new dessert concept called Warm Delights.

To start the process Callaway did not look at the new dessert concept alone—but in relation to all the other sweet treats people were eating. "One of my challenges," she says, "is that consumers often say one thing in marketing research studies and then do something else when facing a supermarket shelf." To overcome this problem, Callaway and her team ran marketing experiments that involved putting a prototype dessert in a store, measuring the results, improving the prototype, and then repeating the process.

The research helped better understand many aspects of the product that were important to consumers. For example, the research revealed that extending the black microwavable bowl outside the edges of the Warm Delights package would better communicate its cooking convenience to prospective buyers. So the unique packaging with the bowl edges exposed was adopted. After many additional experiments, the result was a successful nationwide launch of Warm Delights microwavable desserts, followed quickly by a product line extension, Warm Delights Minis. Growth of both products suggests that the process provided a good match with consumer tastes![1]

Planning for Even More Change

General Mills' U.S. retail sales now exceed $10 billion from several divisions including baking products, snacks, frozen foods, yogurt, and cereal. While consumer tastes in each category are changing, a quick environmental scan of the largest division, cereal, shows how important a good strategic marketing process is for the company. Consider the following:

• *Expense.* The launch of a new cereal typically costs up to $30 million and usually involves replacing one of more than 300 competing breakfast cereals already sitting on retailers' shelves.

© McGraw-Hill Education/Editorial Image, LLC, photographer

Video 22-1
General Mills
kerin.tv/13e/v22-1

Changes in consumers' tastes led General Mills to replace the artificial colors and tastes in its Trix cereal.

Source: General Mills

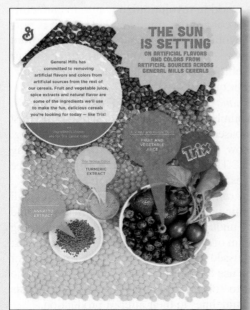

- *Success rate.* Only one out of four brands "succeeds," which is defined as maintaining distribution for three to four years in the $9.5 billion-a-year U.S. ready-to-eat (RTE) cereal market. Adding to the challenge: Retail food industry sales did not grow while costs increased.

- *Market trends:* The lack of growth in the RTE cereal market is being caused by several factors including (1) consumers are moving away from products with too much sugar, genetically modified ingredients, or artificial food dyes, and toward products perceived as healthy or labeled organic; and (2) consumers are avoiding higher shelf prices, which are the result of rising costs.[2]

Creative Initiatives at General Mills

General Mills introduces more than 300 new food products each year in response to consumers' changing tastes. In fact, the company website emphasizes the perspective that drives them to continually offer what consumers are asking for: "We serve the world by making food people love." In light of these consumer trends and the intense competition it faces in the consumer foods industry, General Mills is offering a variety of new products, among them:

Fiber One snack bars
Chex gluten-free mix
Nature Valley Protein granola
Trix with four colors (instead of six to eliminate artificial colors and flavors)[3]

The success or failure of these and other products is related to the planning, implementation, and evaluation phases of the strategic marketing process General Mills uses. This chapter elaborates on some of the issues and techniques presented in Chapter 2 and introduces additional tools and strategies to help marketing, product, and brand managers succeed in the ever-changing, competitive marketplace. Marketing strategies now emerging at General Mills and other firms provide examples.

621

MARKETING BASICS: DOING WHAT WORKS AND ALLOCATING RESOURCES

LO 22-1 Explain how marketing managers allocate resources.

As noted in Chapter 2, corporate and marketing executives search continuously to find a competitive advantage—a unique strength relative to what competitors are doing now and likely to do in the future.[4] Having identified this competitive advantage, they then must figure out how to exploit it.[5] This involves (1) finding and using what works for their organization and industry and (2) allocating resources effectively.

Finding and Using What Really Works

In a five-year study, researchers conducted an in-depth analysis of 160 companies and more than 200 management tools and techniques, such as supply chain management or use of an intranet. Their findings? Individual management tools and techniques had no direct relationship to superior business performance in the companies.[6]

What *does* matter? The researchers concluded that four basic business and management practices are what matter—"what really works," to use their phrase. These are (1) strategy, (2) execution, (3) culture, and (4) structure. Firms with excellence in all four of these areas are likely to achieve superior business performance. The researchers concluded that which of these basic practices a firm chooses to use is less important than flawless execution of the ones it does use.

Industry leaders such as Home Depot do all four of the basic practices extremely well, not just two or three, and are vigilant about continuing to do them well when conditions change. In contrast, Lululemon, Blackberry, and Groupon are struggling today to get these basics right and regain their past success. Let's look at companies that stand out today in each of the four key business practices:

Costco and Toyota achieve excellence with two key business practices—a clear, focused strategy (Costco) and a performance-oriented culture (Toyota).

Costco: © incamerastock/Alamy; Toyota: © Peter Probst/Alamy

- *Strategy: Devise and maintain a clearly stated, focused strategy.* While Walmart may be the unstoppable force in mass-merchandise retailing, its Sam's Club comes up short in warehouse club retailing. The winner: Costco Wholesale, the largest membership warehouse club chain in the United States. A key reason is its focused strategy based on the knowledge that of all U.S. retail channels, warehouse clubs attract the largest proportion of affluent shoppers. Costco's strategy: Sell a limited selection of branded high-end merchandise at low prices.[7]

- *Execution: Develop and maintain flawless operational execution.* Toyota is generally acknowledged as the best in the world in revolutionizing auto manufacturing. It created the doctrine of *kaizen,* or continuous improvement, which is now used throughout the auto industry. Toyota has also launched a new program called "bundled development" that allows suppliers to develop parts three or four years in advance, independent of a vehicle's design, to create "better performance, easier manufacturing, and higher quality."[8]

- *Culture: Develop and maintain a performance-oriented culture.* For the sixth time in seven years Google was recently ranked number one on *Fortune's* list of the 100 Best Companies to Work For. Its culture is based on several key principles including: "Focus on the user and all else will follow," "You can make money without doing evil," and "Great just isn't good enough." The performance result? High employee job satisfaction, 17 percent growth in sales, and 11 percent growth in profits.[9]

- *Structure: Build and maintain a fast, flexible, flat organization.* Successful small organizations often grow into bureaucratic large ones with layers of managers and red tape that slow decision making. The unquestioned all-time leader in delivering world-class aircraft with only a small team of engineers, designers, and machinists: Lockheed Martin's Skunk Works. Discussed later in the chapter, its first director set key organizational guidelines, like "use a small number of good people who can talk to anyone in the organization to solve a problem."[10] France and Russia have attempted to apply Skunk Works guidelines to their aircraft production.

Video 22-2
Skunk Works
kerin.tv/13e/v22-2

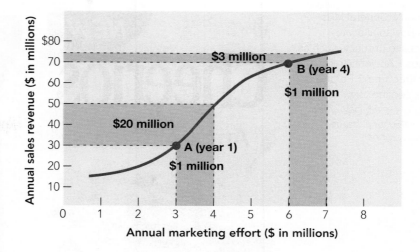

Of course, in practice a firm cannot allocate unlimited resources to achieving each of these business basics. It must make choices based on where its resources can produce the greatest return, the topic of the next section.

Allocating Marketing Resources Using Sales Response Functions

A **sales response function** relates the expense of the marketing effort to the marketing results obtained.[11] To simplify the examples that follow, only the effects of annual marketing effort on annual sales revenue will be analyzed, but keep in mind that the concept applies to other measures of marketing success—such as profit or units sold.

Maximizing Incremental Revenue Minus Incremental Cost Economists give managers a specific guideline for optimal resource allocation: Allocate the firm's marketing, production, and financial resources to the markets and products where the excess of incremental revenues over incremental costs is greatest. This parallels the marginal revenue–marginal cost analysis discussed in Chapter 13.

Figure 22–1 on the next page illustrates the resource allocation principle that is inherent in the sales response function. The firm's annual marketing effort, such as advertising, personal sales, sales promotion, direct marketing, and public relations expenses, is plotted on the horizontal axis. As the annual marketing effort increases, so does the resulting annual sales revenue, which is plotted on the vertical axis. The relationship is assumed to be S-shaped, showing that an additional $1 million of marketing effort, from $3 million to $4 million at Point A, results in far greater increases of sales revenue in the midrange ($20 million) of the curve than at either end. This is because at the left end of the S-curve, the cost of the marketing effort to gain new customers is high for they must be made aware of the product. In contrast, at the right end of the S-curve, the easy-to-get customers are already buying the product and gaining new customers is again very costly—as illustrated by Point B at the right end.

An Example of Resource Allocation Suppose Figure 22–1 shows the situation for a new General Mills product such as Cheerios + Ancient Grains, the first mainstream cereal featuring Kamut, spelt, and quinoa grains. It is targeted at health-conscious consumers who want a great-tasting cereal. Cheerios + Ancient Grains is an extension of Cheerios, the best-selling cereal brand in the United States.[12]

Also assume that the sales response function in Figure 22–1 doesn't change through time as a result of changing consumer tastes and incomes. Point A shows the position of the firm in year 1, whereas Point B shows it three years later in year 4. Now suppose General Mills decides to launch new advertising and sales promotions that increase its marketing effort for the brand from $3 million to $6 million a year. If the relationship in Figure 22–1 holds true and is a good picture of consumer purchasing behavior, the sales revenues of Cheerios + Ancient Grains should increase from $30 million to $70 million a year.

Let's look at the major resource allocation question: What are the probable increases in sales revenue for Cheerios + Ancient Grains in year 1 and year 4 if General Mills spends an additional $1 million in marketing effort? As Figure 22–1 reveals,

Year 1

Increase in marketing effort from $3 million to $4 million = $1 million.

Increase in sales revenue from $30 million to $50 million = $20 million.

Ratio of incremental sales revenue to effort = $20 million:$1 million = 20:1.

Year 4

Increase in marketing effort from $6 million to $7 million = $1 million.

Increase in sales revenue from $70 million to $73 million = $3 million.

Ratio of incremental sales revenue to effort = $3 million:$1 million = 3:1.

Thus, in year 1 a dollar of extra marketing effort returned $20 in sales revenue, whereas in year 4 it returned only $3. If no other expenses are incurred, it might make sense to spend $1 million in year 4 to gain $3 million in incremental sales revenue. However, it may be far wiser for General Mills to invest the money in one of its other brands, such as its new line of gluten-free Chex granola mix.

The essence of resource allocation is simple: Put incremental resources where the incremental returns are greatest over the foreseeable future. For General Mills, this means that it must allocate its available resources (talent and dollars) more efficiently when developing its broad portfolio of products and brands and creating the marketing actions required to reach their respective target market segments. Harvard professors Clayton Christensen and Derek van Bever have observed, however, that since the recession some companies have preferred to retain capital rather than invest in new products—a circumstance they call *the capitalist's dilemma.*[13]

Allocating Marketing Resources in Practice General Mills, like many firms in the consumer packaged foods industry, does extensive analysis using **share points**, or percentage points of market share, as the common basis of comparison to allocate marketing resources effectively for different product lines within the same firm. This

FIGURE 22–2

The actions in the strategic marketing process are supported and directed by detailed reports, studies, and memos.

practice allows the company to explore questions like, "How much is it worth to us to try to increase our market share by another 1 (or 2, or 5, or 10) percentage point(s)?"

This analysis enables higher-level managers to make resource allocation trade-offs among different kinds of strategic business units owned by the company. To make these resource allocation decisions, marketing managers must estimate: (1) the market share for the product; (2) the revenues associated with each point of market share (a share point in breakfast cereals may be five times what it is in cake mixes); (3) the contribution to overhead and profit (or gross margin) of each share point; and (4) possible cannibalization effects on other products in the line (for example, sales of new Cheerios + Ancient Grains might reduce sales of regular Cheerios).

Resource Allocation and the Strategic Marketing Process   Company resources are allocated effectively in the strategic marketing process by converting marketing information into marketing actions. Figure 22–2 summarizes the strategic marketing process introduced in Chapter 2, along with the pertinent marketing actions and information. Figure 22–2 is really a simplification of the actual strategic marketing process. In practice, marketing actions and the information needed to develop them overlap throughout the three phases of the strategic marketing process.

The upper half of each box in Figure 22–2 highlights the actions involved in that part of the strategic marketing process, and the lower half summarizes the information and reports used. Note that each phase has an output report, as shown below:

Phase	Output Report
Planning	Marketing plans (or programs) that define goals (with pertinent marketing metrics) and the marketing mix strategies to achieve them
Implementation	Action memos that tell (1) *who* is (2) to do *what* (3) by *when*
Evaluation	Corrective action memos, triggered by comparing results with goals, often using the firm's marketing metrics and displayed in marketing dashboards

The corrective action memos become feedback loops in Figure 22–2 that help improve decisions and actions in earlier phases of the strategic marketing process.

22-1. What are the four basic practices "that really work" that characterize industry-leading firms?

22-2. What is the significance of the S-shape of the sales response function in Figure 22–1?

THE PLANNING PHASE OF THE STRATEGIC MARKETING PROCESS

Four aspects of the strategic marketing process deserve special mention: (1) the vital importance of marketing metrics in marketing planning; (2) the variety of marketing plans; (3) marketing planning frameworks that have proven useful; and (4) some key marketing planning and strategy lessons.

The Use of Marketing Metrics in Marketing Planning

Planners have a tongue-in-cheek truism: "If you don't know where you're going, any road will get you there." In making marketing plans, the "road" chosen is really the quantitative goal *plus* the quantitative metric used to measure whether the goal is being achieved.

Today, measuring the results of marketing actions has become a central focus in many organizations. This boils down to defining "where the organization is going"—the quantitative goals—and "whether it is really getting there"—the quantitative marketing metrics used to measure actual performance. This emphasizes the need for data-driven decision making (mentioned in Chapter 2) and the importance of choosing and displaying the right marketing metrics in marketing dashboards so managers can quickly view the results.[14]

Most firms stress innovation to help achieve growth. Marketing departments work closely with R&D and operations departments to complete successful innovation projects.[15] So what metrics might they use to measure their innovation performance?

A survey of 800 executives led several researchers to suggest that "a company undertaking a major strategic initiative to enhance its innovation and product-development capabilities" should use two kinds of metrics:[16] *output metrics,* which measure results, and *input metrics,* which measure efforts going into developing new products. Areas of performance most often measured using these metrics are:

- Revenue growth due to new products or services and customer satisfaction with new products or services (*output metrics*).
- Number of ideas or concepts in the new-product pipeline and R&D spending as a percentage of sales (*input metrics*).

A careful look at these innovation metrics reveals that it is generally far easier to measure marketing inputs rather than marketing outputs. For example, measuring "the number of ideas or concepts in the new-product pipeline" (an input) is far easier than measuring "customer satisfaction with new products or services" (an output). But the evaluation phase of the strategic marketing process seeks to compare actual results—an output metric—with the goals set. So where possible, marketing managers prefer to use effective output metrics if they are available.

The Variety of Marketing Plans

The planning phase of the strategic marketing process usually results in a marketing plan that sets the direction for the marketing activities of an organization. As noted earlier in Appendix A, a marketing plan is the heart of a business plan. Like business plans, marketing plans aren't all from the same mold; they vary with the length of the planning period, their purpose, and their audience. Let's look briefly at two kinds: long-range and annual marketing plans.

Long-Range Marketing Plans Typically, long-range marketing plans cover marketing activities from two to five years into the future. Except for firms in industries such as automobiles, steel, or forest products, marketing plans rarely go beyond five years into the future because the tremendous number of uncertainties makes the benefits of planning less than the effort expended. Such plans are often directed at senior-level executives and the board of directors.

Annual Marketing Plans Annual marketing plans are usually developed by a marketing or product manager (discussed later in the chapter) in a consumer products firm such as Campbell Soup Company. These plans detail marketing goals and strategies for a product, product line, or entire firm for a single year. Suppose Campbell's annual planning cycle starts with a detailed marketing research study of current users and ends after 42 weeks with the approval of the plan by the division general manager, 10 weeks before the fiscal year starts. Between these points there are continuing efforts to uncover new ideas through key-issues sessions with specialists both inside and outside the firm. The plan is fine-tuned through a series of often excruciating reviews by several levels of management, which leaves few surprises and little to chance.

Marketing Planning Frameworks: The Search for Growth

Marketing planning for a firm with many products competing in many markets is a complex process. Yet in a business firm, all these planning efforts are directed at finding the means for increased growth in sales and profits. Two marketing planning frameworks that help executives make important resource allocation decisions are (1) Porter's generic business strategies and (2) synergy analysis. Both frameworks relate to elements introduced in earlier chapters.

Porter's Generic Business Strategies As shown in Figure 22–3, Michael E. Porter has developed a framework in which he identifies four basic, or "generic,"

Consumer packaged goods firms like Campbell Soup Company create detailed annual marketing plans to focus their strategies.
© McGraw-Hill Education/ Editorial Image, LLC, photographer

LO 22-2   Describe Porter's generic business strategies and synergy analysis planning frameworks.

FIGURE 22–3

Porter's four generic business strategies involve combinations of (1) competitive scope, or the breadth of the target markets, and (2) a stress on lower cost versus product differentiation.

SOURCE OF COMPETITIVE ADVANTAGE

Competitive scope	Lower cost	Differentiation
Broad target	1. Cost leadership strategy: Campbell Soup	2. Differentiation strategy: General Mills
Narrow target	3. Cost focus strategy: IKEA	4. Differentiation focus strategy: Chobani

business strategies.[17] A **generic business strategy** is one that can be adopted by any firm, regardless of the product or industry involved, to achieve a competitive advantage.

Although all the techniques discussed here involve generic strategies, the phrase is most often associated with Porter's framework. In this framework, the columns identify the two fundamental alternatives a firm can use in seeking a competitive advantage: (1) It can become the low-cost producer within the markets in which it competes or (2) it can differentiate itself from competitors by developing points of difference in its product offerings or marketing programs. In contrast, the rows identify the competitive scope: Choosing a broad target means the firm will be competing in many market segments, whereas choosing a narrow target means the firm will be competing in only a few segments or even a single segment. The columns and rows result in four generic business strategies, which can provide a competitive advantage among similar strategic business units in the same industry. These four strategies are as follows:

Which of Porter's generic strategies is IKEA using? For the answer and a discussion of these strategies, see the text and Figure 22–3.

Source: IKEA

1. A **cost leadership strategy** (cell 1) focuses on reducing expenses and, in turn, lowers product prices while targeting a broad array of market segments. This may be done by securing less expensive raw materials from lower-cost suppliers or investing in new production equipment to reduce unit costs and improve quality. Campbell Soup's sophisticated product development and supply chain systems have led to huge cost savings. So its cost leadership strategy has resulted in lower prices for customers—causing its market share to increase to approximately 60 percent of the soup market.

2. A **differentiation strategy** (cell 2) requires products to have significant points of difference in product offerings, brand image, higher quality, advanced technology, or superior service to charge a higher price while targeting a broad array of market segments. This strategy allows the firm to charge a price premium. General Mills uses this strategy in stressing its nutritious, high-quality brands in reaching a diverse array of customer segments.

3. A **cost focus strategy** (cell 3) involves controlling expenses and, in turn, lowering product prices targeted at a narrow range of market segments. Retail chains targeting only a few market segments in a restricted group of products often use a cost focus strategy successfully. IKEA has become the world's largest furniture retailer by selling flat-pack, self-assembly furniture, accessories, and bathroom and kitchen items to cost-conscious consumers.

4. Finally, a **differentiation focus strategy** (cell 4) requires products to have significant points of difference in order to target one or only a few market segments. Chobani Greek Yogurt, discussed in Chapter 1, uses a differentiation focus strategy. Its 2007 launch of a healthy, high-quality, great-tasting yogurt using natural ingredients successfully reached the small but now exploding segment of consumers who favor Greek-style yogurt.

These four generic business strategies are the basis for Michael Porter's theory about what makes a nation's industries successful, as discussed in Chapter 7.

Synergy Analysis **Synergy analysis** seeks market-product opportunities by finding the optimum balance between marketing efficiencies versus R&D–manufacturing efficiencies. Using diversification analysis from Chapter 2 and the market-product grid framework from Chapter 9, we can see two kinds of synergy that are critical in developing corporate and marketing strategies: (1) marketing synergy and (2) R&D–manufacturing synergy.

Marketing **Matters**

A Test of Your Skills: Where Are the Synergies?

To try your hand at this multibillion-dollar synergy game, assume you are the vice president of marketing for Great States Corp., which markets a line of nonpowered, powered walking, and powered riding lawn mowers throughout North America. A market-product grid for your business is shown to the right. You distribute your nonpowered mowers in all three market segments, but you offer your walking powered mowers only in suburban markets. Your powered riding mowers are not offered in any of the three market segments.
Here are your strategy dilemmas:

1. Where are the marketing synergies (efficiencies)?
2. Where are the R&D–manufacturing synergies (efficiencies)?
3. What would a market-product grid look like for an ideal company that Great States could merge with to

achieve both marketing and R&D–manufacturing synergies (efficiencies)?

To consider these questions, read the text and study Figure 22–4 and the figure below.

While the search for synergies starts within the organization itself, marketing and manufacturing synergies can also come about through mergers and acquisitions that perform organizational functions more efficiently. For example, as noted in the Marketing Matters box, assume you are the vice president of marketing for Great States Corp.'s line of nonpowered lawn mowers and powered walking mowers sold to the consumer market. You are looking for new product and new market opportunities to increase your revenues and profits.

You conduct a market segmentation study and develop a market-product grid to analyze future opportunities. You identify three major segments in the consumer market based on geography: (1) city, (2) suburban, and (3) rural households. These market segments relate to the size of lawn a consumer must mow. The product groupings are (1) nonpowered, (2) powered walking, and (3) powered riding mowers.

Five alternative marketing strategies are shown in the market-product grids in Figure 22–4.[18] As mentioned in Chapter 9, the important marketing synergies, or efficiencies, run horizontally across the rows in Figure 22–4. Conversely, the important

FIGURE 22–4

Market-product grids show alternative strategies for a lawn mower manufacturer. Try to find synergies in each strategy—if any exist.

How might you segment the lawn mower market? What marketing synergies might result? For the answers, see the text.

© VStock/Alamy

R&D–manufacturing synergies, or efficiencies, run vertically down the columns. Let's look at the synergy effects for the five combinations in Figure 22–4.

A. *Market-product concentration.* The firm benefits from its focus on a single product line and market segment, but it loses opportunities for significant synergies in both marketing and R&D–manufacturing.

B. *Market specialization.* The firm gains marketing synergy through providing a complete product line for the city market segment, but R&D–manufacturing has the difficulty of developing and producing three different products.

C. *Product specialization.* The firm gains R&D–manufacturing synergy through producing only a nonpowered lawn mower, but gaining market distribution in the three different geographic areas will be costly.

D. *Selective specialization.* The firm doesn't gain either marketing or R&D–manufacturing synergies because of the uniqueness of the market-product combinations.

E. *Full coverage.* The firm receives the maximum potential synergies in both marketing and R&D–manufacturing. The critical question to be answered: Is the firm spread too thin because of the resource requirements needed to reach all market-product combinations?

The Marketing Matters box poses the question of what the ideal partner for Great States would be if it merged with another firm, given the market-product combinations shown. If you want to follow a full-coverage strategy, then the ideal merger partner is shown in Figure 22–5. This partnership would give the maximum potential synergies—if you are not spreading the resources of your merged companies too thin. Marketing gains by having a complete product line in all regions, and R&D–manufacturing gains by achieving production efficiencies through the firm's access to new markets and its ability to produce larger volumes of its existing products.

FIGURE 22–5

This is the ideal merger for Great States to obtain full market-product coverage. The ideal partner offers lawn mower products to the exact segments of customers not being served by Great States.

Great States' market-product offerings *before* the merger

$+$

The market-product offerings of an *ideal* partner before the merger

$=$

Market-product offerings of the resulting merged firm *after* the merger

learning review »

22-3. What is the difference between an input metric and an output metric?

22-4. Describe Porter's four generic business strategies.

22-5. Where do (*a*) marketing synergies and (*b*) R&D–manufacturing synergies appear when using the synergy analysis framework?

Some Marketing Planning and Strategy Lessons

LO 22-3 | Explain what makes an effective marketing plan.

Applying marketing planning frameworks is not automatic; in fact, it requires a great deal of managerial judgment. Commonsense requirements of an effective marketing plan are discussed next, followed by problems that can arise.

Guidelines for an Effective Marketing Plan   President Dwight D. Eisenhower, when he commanded Allied armies in World War II, made his classic observation, "Plans are nothing; planning is everything." It is the process of careful planning that focuses an organization's efforts and leads to success. The plans themselves, which change with events, are often secondary. Effective planning and plans are inevitably characterized by identifiable objectives, specific strategies or courses of action, and the means to execute them. Here are some guidelines for developing effective marketing plans:[19]

- *Set measurable, achievable goals.* Ideally, goals should be quantified and measurable in terms of what is to be accomplished and by when. So, "Increase market share from 18 percent to 22 percent by December 31, 2016," is preferable to "Maximize market share given our available resources." Also, to motivate people, the goals must be achievable.
- *Use a base of facts and valid assumptions.* The more a marketing plan is based on facts and valid assumptions, rather than guesses, the less uncertainty and risk are associated with executing it. Good marketing research helps.
- *Use simple, but clear and specific, plans.* Effective execution of plans requires that people at all levels in the firm understand what, when, and how they are to accomplish their tasks. Involve people with the right skills and experience in the planning effort.
- *Have complete and feasible plans.* Marketing plans must incorporate all the key marketing mix factors and be supported by adequate resources.
- *Make plans controllable and flexible.* Marketing plans must enable results to be compared with planned targets, often using precise marketing metrics. This allows replanning—the flexibility to alter the original plans based on recent results.
- *Find the right person to implement the plans.* But make sure that person is heavily involved in making the plans.
- *Work toward consensus-building.* "Ownership" of the plan by team members and stakeholders increases the chances for its success.

Problems in Marketing Planning and Strategy   An all-too-frequent problem in marketing planning and strategy is that bad news is filtered out as information goes up each organizational level (see Chapter 2), giving top management a very rosy picture. J.D. Power III did marketing research at Ford four decades ago. "There was no interest in finding out what customers really thought," he says. "Instead, we were constantly asked to 'torture the data until it confessed,' giving us the answers the execs wanted."[20]

So he founded J.D. Power & Associates to do customer satisfaction studies. One of his first marketing research clients was Toyota, which listened and has used hundreds of J.D. Power studies over the years. Today, J.D. Power & Associates is one of the world's best-known marketing information companies and now serves not only the auto industry but also the health care, telecommunications, insurance, financial services, and other industries. Other key problems that emerge from a firm engaging in the strategic marketing process include the following:

1. *Plans may be based on very poor assumptions about environmental forces,* especially changing economic conditions and competitors' actions. A Western Union plan failed because it didn't reflect the impact of deregulation and competitors' actions on business.
2. *Planners and their plans may have lost sight of their customers' needs.* But not at the Papa John's pizza chain. The "better ingredients, better pizza" slogan makes the hair stand up on the back of the necks of competing Pizza Hut executives. The reason is that this Papa John's slogan reflects the firm's obsessive attention to detail, which is stealing market share from the much-bigger Pizza Hut. Sample detail: If the cheese on the pizza shows a single air

Video 22-3
Papa John's
kerin.tv/13e/v22-3

bubble or the crust is not golden brown, the offending pizza is not served to the customer.

3. *Too much time and effort may be spent on data collection and writing plans that are too complex to implement.* One firm cut its planning instructions "that looked like an auto repair manual" to five or six pages for operating units.

4. *Line operating managers often feel no sense of ownership in implementing the plans.* Andy Grove, when he was CEO of Intel, observed, "We had the very ridiculous system . . . of delegating strategic planning to strategic planners. The strategies these [planners] prepared had no bearing on anything we actually did."[21] The solution is to assign more planning activities to line operating managers—the people who actually carry them out.

General Mills: Global Strategies to Find Synergies, Segments, and Partners

General Mills' successful introduction of French-developed Yoplait yogurt to U.S. consumers . . .

© McGraw-Hill Education/Editorial Image, LLC, photographer

. . . led the way to its global search for new products today, such as Wanchai Ferry dinner kits from Hong Kong.

© McGraw-Hill Education/Mike Hruby, photographer

Competing in today's global marketplace, General Mills is concerned with *both* selling its products and brands in countries around the world *and* obtaining ideas for new products from anyone, anywhere, who has a great product or technology. The company's joint venture with Swiss-based Nestlé in Cereal Partners Worldwide provides General Mills access to European, Latin American, and Asian consumers—offering everything from cereals to ice cream bars.

General Mills now conducts a global search for new ideas, products, and technologies. The success of Yoplait yogurt ("The Yogurt of France") has led the firm to broaden its yogurt offerings—including the recently introduced Yoplait Greek 100 Whips!, a 100-calorie Greek-style yogurt available in eight flavors. General Mills also has brought other products developed outside the United States to our shores. Wanchai Ferry brand dinners are an adaptation of frozen dumplings developed by Madame Kin Wo Chong, a Hong Kong entrepreneur who started by selling her dumplings in 1977 from a cart on the city's Wanchai Ferry pier. General Mills first introduced Wanchai Ferry as a dry dinner kit to which one added meat. And surprise! The brand is now one of General Mills' new stars in China and is sold in about 100 Chinese cities.[22]

Have a great idea for a new technology or product General Mills might use? Under the General Mills Worldwide Innovation Network (G-WIN), the company wants your idea to help accelerate its innovation efforts. You can contact General Mills online at www.generalmills.com/Company/Innovation/G-Win.aspx to submit your idea. But the new product or technology must uniquely meet a large unmet consumer need, be technically feasible, fit within General Mills' product categories or brands, and be a "game-changer"![23]

Balancing Value and Values in Strategic Marketing Plans

Two important trends are likely to influence the strategic marketing process in the future. The first, *value-based planning,* combines marketing planning ideas and financial planning techniques to assess how much a division or strategic business unit (SBU) contributes to the price of a company's stock (or shareholder wealth). Value is created when the financial return of a strategic activity exceeds the cost of the resources allocated to the activity.

The second trend is the increasing interest in *value-driven strategies,* which incorporate concerns for ethics, integrity, employee health and safety, and environmental safeguards with more common corporate values

Ask Disruptive Questions to Achieve Disruptive Innovations

The glamour of successfully launching a Google, Apple, or Facebook hides one blatant fact: Launching a revolutionary new product or service is incredibly difficult! Research on disruptive innovations suggests that precise, focused questions can be used in developing new products or reaching key market segments. This involves invoking powerful questions "to help see beneath the surface of everyday action and discover what's never been."

"Disruptive innovators" often start by exploring *what currently is* and then moving to a powerful search for *what might be.* Rather than simply ask for "any questions" or "any suggestions" in a meeting, disruptive innovators often:

Google logo: © Justin Sullivan/Getty Images; Apple logo: grzegorz knec/Alamy; Facebook logo: © Ingvar Björk/Alamy

1. Ask "what is" questions. This helps reveal *what is happening* here and now.
2. Ask "what caused" questions. This helps explain *why things are the way they are.*
3. Ask "why" and "why not" questions. This helps reveal changes to reach *what might be.*
4. Ask "what if" questions. This helps suggest and *get reactions to new actions*—perhaps a new-product concept.

Using these questions effectively can reveal solutions to a variety of problems, not just new-product innovations. Try asking these questions in your next group-project meeting.

---

such as growth, profitability, customer service, and quality. Some experts have observed that although many corporations cite broad corporate values in advertisements, press releases, and company newsletters, they have not yet changed their strategic plans to reflect these stated values. U.S. firms, like those around the world, are increasingly called on to be good global citizens and to support sustainable development.

Disruptive Innovations and Long-Range Marketing Plans *Disruptive innovations* create a new market by initially reaching new customers through displacing an existing market's low-end product. The innovation eventually displaces the original product or technology, creating havoc for organizations that operate in the old, displaced market and disrupting their long-range marketing plans.

However, these disruptive innovations don't replace an existing product or technology overnight. Instead, established firms in the industry initially conclude the disruptive innovation isn't worth pursuing because the new market is too small and takes scarce resources away from improving their existing products. Eventually, the disruptive innovation becomes pervasive enough to invade the large, traditional markets, often driving the original firms out of business. Examples include Wikipedia, which caused *Encyclopedia Britannica* to stop print production in 2012 after 244 years, and liquid-crystal displays (LCDs), which replaced cathode ray tubes (CRTs) in TVs in the 2000s, and digital media, which replaced CDs and DVDs.[24]

How can marketing managers recognize and incorporate disruptive innovations in their long-range plans? While no perfect answer exists, the Marketing Matters box shows the first giant step toward an answer: Ask tough, focused, disruptive questions. Research shows that (1) disruptive innovators ask more questions than they get answers to and (2) good questions provide greater value than good answers![25]

THE IMPLEMENTATION PHASE OF THE STRATEGIC MARKETING PROCESS

The postgame summary provided by a losing football coach often runs something like, "We had an excellent game plan; we just didn't execute it." The planning-versus-execution issue applies to the strategic marketing process as well: When a marketing plan fails, it's difficult to determine whether the failure is due to a poor plan or poor implementation.

Is Planning or Implementation the Problem?

Effective managers tracking progress on a struggling plan first try to identify whether the problems involve (1) the plan and strategy, (2) its implementation, or (3) both, and then they try to correct the problems. But as discussed earlier in the chapter, research on what really works shows that successful firms have excellence on both the planning and strategy side and the implementation and execution side.

At the other extreme, most of the hundreds of dot-com firms like Pets.com that failed in the late 1990s had both planning *and* implementation problems. Their bad planning often resulted from their focus on getting start-up money from investors rather than providing real value to customers. Bad implementation by some of these dot-coms led to their spending huge sums on wasteful Super Bowl television ads to try to promote their failing websites. Also, many of these Internet firms didn't understand key implementation issues that involved inventories, warehouses, and physical distribution.

Increasing Emphasis on Marketing Implementation

Today, the implementation phase of the strategic marketing process often involves moving many planning activities from planners to the line managers responsible for implementing the plans. General Electric's legendary CEO Jack Welch is credited with making GE more efficient and far better at implementation. When Welch became CEO, GE was bogged down with 25,000 managers and close to a dozen layers between him and the factory floor.

In his "delayering strategy," Welch sought to cut GE's levels in half and to speed up decision making and implementation by building an atmosphere of trust and autonomy among his managers and employees. Where possible, he made the people planning the project responsible for carrying it out. Today, businesses around the world use GE's focus on implementation as a benchmark.[26]

Open communications at Lockheed Martin's Skunk Works have led to state-of-the-art aircraft like this F-35 Lightning II Joint Strike Fighter. *U.S. Navy photo courtesy Lockheed Martin/Released*

Improving Implementation of Marketing Programs

No magic formula exists to guarantee the effective implementation of marketing plans. In fact, the answer seems to be a balance between good management skills and good practices, from which have come some guidelines for improving program implementation.

Take Action and Avoid Paralysis by Analysis
Management experts warn against "paralysis by analysis," the tendency to excessively analyze a problem instead of taking action. To overcome this pitfall, they call for a "bias for action" and recommend a "do it, fix it, try it" approach.[27] Their conclusion: Perfectionists finish last, so getting it

90 percent perfect and letting the marketplace help in the fine-tuning makes good sense in implementation.

Lockheed Martin's Skunk Works got its name from the comic strip *L'il Abner*. Led by Kelly Johnson, Skunk Works developed its legendary reputation for achieving superhuman technical feats by stressing teamwork and working within the constraints of small budgets and tight deadlines. Under Johnson, the Skunk Works turned out a series of world-class aircraft, such as the F-35 Lightning II Joint Strike Fighter. Two of Kelly Johnson's basic tenets: (1) Make decisions promptly, and (2) Avoid paralysis by analysis. One U.S. Air Force audit showed that Johnson's Skunk Works could carry out a program on schedule with 126 people, whereas a competitor in a comparable program was behind schedule with 3,750 people.[28]

Video 22-4
F-35
kerin.tv/13e/v22-4

Surface Problems with Open Communications Two more Kelly Johnson axioms from Lockheed Martin's Skunk Works apply here: (1) When trouble develops, surface the problem immediately, and (2) Get help—don't keep the problem to yourself. Success often lies in fostering a work setting that is open enough so employees are willing to speak out when they see problems, without fear of punishment. The focus is placed on trying to solve the problem as a group rather than finding someone to blame. In this "open communications" environment, solutions are solicited from anyone who has a creative idea to suggest—from the janitor to the president.

Toyota's new service center uses the *genchi genbutsu*— "go and see"—principle to train its new mechanics.
Source: Toyota Motor Sales

Communicate Goals and the Means of Achieving Them Those called on to implement plans need to understand both the goals sought and how they are to be accomplished. Historically, Toyota's growth has been built on a foundation of QDR—quality, dependability, and reliability. Besides emphasizing "always better cars" under new CEO Akio Toyoda, the Toyota design team encourages a more "emotional" link between buyers and Toyota vehicles. And it continues to stress *genchi genbutsu*—"go and see"—a principle that suggests that to truly understand a situation one needs to go to the source and see it for yourself. For example, Toyota engineers observe production on the factory floor and drive vehicles in real-use situations. The *genchi genbutsu* principle was the driving force behind the construction of Toyota's new Tajimi Service Center, which simulates 13 driving conditions to train 4,800 mechanics each year.[29]

Have a Responsible Program Champion Willing to Act Successful programs almost always have a **program champion**, a person who is willing and able to "cut the red tape" to move the program forward. Such a person often has the uncanny ability to move back and forth between the "big picture" and the specific details as the situation warrants. Program champions can be notoriously brash in overcoming organizational hurdles. The U.S. Navy's Admiral Grace Murray Hopper gave the world not only an early computer language but also her famous advice for cutting through an organization's red tape: "Better to ask forgiveness than permission."

Reward Success but Don't Punish Failure Sara Blakely, founder and 100 percent owner of Spanx, has a simple mantra: "Failure just leads you to the next great thing"—so learn takeaway lessons from your failures. Her vision for her start-up was to eliminate "visible panty lines" when women dressed in stylish outfits. So she cut the feet off her control-top pantyhose, wrote her own patent application, and made all her initial sales calls. Blakely sent a basket of her prototypes to

Learning from Mistakes and Avoiding Traps on the Way to Blue Oceans

In their best-selling book *Blue Ocean Strategy*, W. Chan Kim and Renée Mauborgne suggest that value innovation is most likely in the "blue oceans" of uncontested market spaces where new demand can be developed. Some companies make mistakes in their efforts to grow, however; Southwest Airlines, for example, bought Muse Air; Intel tried to sell RAMBUS technology; and BMW developed a premium-end two-wheeled scooter, the C1. All these initiatives failed.

Authors Jim Collins and Morten T. Hansen acknowledge that good companies sometimes make big mistakes. But they view mistakes as "expensive tuition." "Better get something out of it, learn everything you can, apply the learning, and don't repeat," they say.

What are the circumstances that may lead to mistakes? Consider these "traps" identified by Kim and

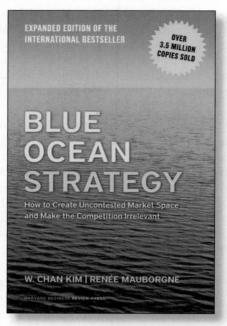

© McGraw-Hill Education/Editorial Image, LLC, photographer

Mauborgne: (1) information from customers and noncustomers will lead to different conclusions, (2) some market niches are too small to be sustainable, (3) new technology may not lead to new demand, (4) new innovation doesn't have to mean destruction of existing markets, and (5) differentiation and low-cost strategies are viewed as mutually exclusive options, but they shouldn't be.

So in spite of mistakes and an environment full of traps how can a company thrive? Collins and Hansen believe three behaviors are key: *fanatic discipline,* or a consistency of action, *empirical creativity,* or using evidence rather than opinions, and *productive paranoia,* or always considering competitive vulnerabilities.

You might recognize the names of some of the companies that do this well. They include Amgen, Intel, Microsoft, and Southwest Airlines!

Founder Sara Blakely launched Spanx with a simple mantra: "Failure just leads you to the next great thing."

© ZUMA Press, Inc./Alamy

LO 22-4 Use a time-based agenda and an action item list to conduct a meeting.

Oprah Winfrey, who selected Spanx as her Product of the Year. Today, Spanx has 200 products, including a men's line of undershirts, underwear, and socks.[30]

When an individual or a team is rewarded for achieving an organization's goal, they have maximum incentive to see a program implemented successfully because they have personal ownership and a stake in that success. At the same time, many firms owe their success to learning important lessons from their failures. See the Marketing Matters box to learn about traps companies should avoid as they pursue uncontested market spaces often called "blue oceans."[31]

Schedule Precise Tasks, Responsibilities, and Deadlines Successful implementation requires that members of the program team understand its goals, the tasks they are responsible for to help reach those goals, and the deadlines for completing them. To implement the thousands of tasks for a new aircraft design, Lockheed Martin typically holds weekly program meetings.

In most organizations, the meeting chairperson calls the meeting to order and hands out an agenda with the topics listed sequentially. The difficulty with this is that if the critical topic is an agenda item near the end of the list, meeting members don't know this, and they waste a lot of the meeting time on earlier agenda items. A better approach is a **time-based agenda**, a meeting agenda that shows the running time allocated to each agenda item. In a time-based agenda, time is shown as *running time* (2:00, 2:03, etc.) and not *target time* (3 minutes, 10 minutes, etc.), which lets participants know better how the meeting is progressing. A sample time-based agenda for a marketing department meeting is shown below:

Running Time	Topic	Who Leads	Objective Info	Objective Action
2:00	1. Review meeting objectives	Gina	×	
2:03	2. Check status of past action items	Gina	×	
2:13	3. Analyze client's marketing needs	Gina		×
2:25	4. Assess client's promotion options	Roger		×
2:30	5. Agree on client's promotion goals, media	Steve		×
2:57	6. Summarize action items	Gina	×	
3:00	7. Adjourn meeting	Gina		×

In the time-based agenda above, everyone knows topic #5—Steve's leading the discussion to agree on the client's promotion goals and media to use—is especially critical and is allocated the most time. They also know if a topic is for "info" (information), they are to listen and not spend valuable time discussing it. Sharing ideas is only for items with an "×" in the "Action" column.

The outcome of each of these program meetings is an **action item list**, an aid to implementing a plan that consists of four columns: (1) the task; (2) the person responsible for completing that task; (3) the date to finish the task; and (4) what is to be delivered. Note that topic #6 in the time-based agenda is "Summarize action items," so that everyone in the meeting knows the actions for which they are responsible. A sample action item list is shown below:

Action/Task	Who Does	By When	Deliverable
1. Write Client A proposal	Lisa	March 3	Draft proposal
2. Identify new clients	Kris	March 6	Draft client call list
3. Develop Client B print ad	Mike	March 10	Submit final ad

It is clear from this example that Kris knows she is responsible for providing a list of new clients by March 6. Within hours of completing a program meeting, the action item list is circulated to those attending. This then serves as a starting point for the next meeting, shown as topic #2 in the time-based agenda on the previous page. Meeting minutes are viewed as secondary and backward-looking. Action item lists are forward-looking, clarify the targets, and put strong pressure on people to achieve their designated tasks by the specified deadlines.

Related to the action item lists are formal *program schedules,* which show the relationships through time of the various program tasks. Scheduling an action program involves: (1) identifying the main tasks; (2) determining the time required to complete each task; (3) arranging the activities to meet the deadline; and (4) assigning responsibility for completing each task. The most widely used program schedule is the Gantt chart, described in Chapter 2 (see Figure 2–10, which illustrates the use of a Gantt chart to schedule tasks and complete a team project on time).

learning review »

22-6. What is the meaning and importance of a program champion?

22-7. Describe one or two lessons from Lockheed Martin's Skunk Works that can be applied to implementing marketing programs.

22-8. How are (a) a time-based agenda and (b) an action item list used in a marketing program meeting?

Organizing for Marketing

LO 22-5 Describe an organization's marketing department and the role of a product manager.

A marketing organization is needed to implement the firm's marketing plans. Today's marketing organizations understand: (1) the evolving role of the chief marketing officer; (2) how line versus staff positions and divisional groupings interrelate to form a cohesive marketing organization; and (3) the role of the product manager.

The Evolving Role of the Chief Marketing Officer The senior executive responsible for a firm's marketing activities shown in Figure 22–6 is increasingly given the title of chief marketing officer (CMO) rather than vice president of marketing. This reflects the broadening of the CMO's role as the inside-the-company "voice of the consumer." So today, it is critical that CMOs understand (1) the changing characteristics of domestic and global consumers, (2) the role of digital media and mobile marketing in integrated marketing efforts, and (3) the benefits of the

FIGURE 22–6

This organization of a strategic business unit in a typical consumer packaged goods firm shows two product or brand groups— biscuit mixes and refrigerated biscuits.

many new multichannel data streams in decision making and marketing effectiveness assessment. These broadened responsibilities have led to increasing influence also. Recent surveys indicate that 60 percent of CMOs report directly to the CEO or COO, and that they are retained in their positions for more than five years.[32]

Line versus Staff and Divisional Groupings Although simplified, Figure 22–6 shows the organization of a typical strategic business unit in a consumer packaged goods firm like Procter & Gamble, Kraft, or General Mills. It consists of the Dinner Products, Baked Goods, and Desserts groups and highlights the distinction between line and staff positions. Managers in **line positions**, such as the senior marketing manager for Biscuits, have the authority and responsibility to issue orders to people who report to them, such as the two product managers shown in Figure 22–6. In this organizational chart, line positions are connected with solid lines. People in **staff positions** (connected by dotted lines) have the authority and responsibility to advise people in line positions but cannot issue direct orders to them.

Most marketing organizations use divisional groupings—such as product line, functional, geographical, and market-based—to implement plans and achieve objectives. Only the first of these appears in the organizational chart in Figure 22–6. The top of the chart shows organization by **product line groupings** in which a unit is responsible for specific product offerings, such as Dinner Products or Desserts.

At higher levels than what is shown in Figure 22–6, grocery products firms are organized by **functional groupings**—such as manufacturing, marketing, and finance—that represent the different departments or business activities within a firm.

Most grocery products firms use **geographical groupings**, in which sales territories are subdivided according to geographical location. Each director of sales has several regional sales managers reporting to him or her, such as western, southern, and so on. These, in turn, have district managers reporting to them, with the field sales representatives operating at the lowest level.

A fourth method of organizing a company is to use **market-based groupings**, which utilize specific customer segments, such as the banking, health care, or manufacturing segments. When this method of organizing is combined with product groupings, the result is a *matrix organization.*

A relatively new position in consumer products firms is the *category manager* (the senior marketing manager in Figure 22–6), who is responsible for an entire product line—all biscuit brands, for example. These marketers attempt to reduce the possibility of one brand's actions hurting another brand in the same category. Procter & Gamble uses category managers to organize by "global business units," such as baby care and beauty care. Cutting across country boundaries, these global business units implement standardized worldwide pricing, promotion, and distribution.

Role of the Product Manager The key person in the product or brand group is the manager who heads it. As mentioned in Chapter 11, this person is often called the *product manager* or *brand manager*. This person and his or her assistants comprise the *product group* or *brand group,* enclosed by the dashed red line in Figure 22–6. These product or brand groups are the basic building blocks in the marketing department of most consumer and business product firms. The function of a product manager is to plan, implement, and evaluate the annual and long-range plans for the products for which he or she is responsible.

There are both benefits and dangers to the product manager system. On the positive side, product managers become strong advocates for the assigned products, cut red tape to work with people in various functions both inside and outside the organization, and assume profit-and-loss responsibility for the product line. On the negative side, even though product managers have major responsibilities, they have relatively little direct authority, so they must use persuasion rather than issue direct orders to implement their marketing plans.

THE EVALUATION PHASE OF THE STRATEGIC MARKETING PROCESS

LO 22-6 Explain the use of marketing ROI, metrics, and dashboards in evaluating marketing programs.

Evaluation, the final phase of the strategic marketing process, involves (1) the marketing evaluation process itself and (2) the use of marketing ROI, metrics, and dashboards. We conclude this section with a look at how General Mills uses marketing metrics and dashboards.

The Marketing Evaluation Process

The essence of marketing evaluation involves (1) comparing results with planned goals to identify deviations and then (2) taking corrective actions.

Identifying Deviations from Goals Figure 22–7 on the next page shows that marketing plans made in the planning phase have both quantified goals and a specific marketing metric used to measure whether the goal is actually achieved. Marketing actions are taken in the implementation phase to attempt to achieve the goals set in the planning phase. In the evaluation phase, as Figure 22–7 shows, the quantitative results are measured using the marketing metrics and compared with the actual results of the marketing actions. For speed and efficiency, the results are compared with goals and often shown to marketing managers on marketing dashboards to enable them to take timely actions.

Acting on Deviations from Goals A marketing manager interprets the marketing dashboard information using *management by exception,* which involves identifying results that deviate from plans to diagnose their causes and take new actions. The marketing manager looks for two kinds of deviations, each triggering a different kind of action:

- *Actual results exceed goals.* In this case, marketing must act quickly to exploit unforeseen opportunities. In the past year Starbucks has added six new Frappuccino flavors, opened "Tasting Room" and "Express" stores, and introduced a partnership with streaming music service Spotify. It also upgraded its Mobile Order and Pay app to allow faster service and to link with the My Starbucks Reward Program and Prepaid Starbucks cards. The result: at its annual meeting of shareholders Starbucks reported sales grew to more than $16 billion and that its baristas now serve 7,000 beverages "every minute of every day." Having exceeded its goals, Starbucks announced plans to add 8,000 new stores over the next five years; double its food sales through breakfast, lunch, and snack offerings; and expand sales of its Teavana brand by selling the tea in all of its stores in China and Japan.[33]

FIGURE 22–7

The evaluation phase of the strategic marketing process ties results and actions to goals, often using marketing metrics and dashboards.

With 22,000 stores in 66 countries Starbucks is still growing and plans to open another 8,000 stores—including many express stores like this one.

© McGraw-Hill Education/Editorial Image, LLC, photographer

For how the Detroit Institute of Arts uses direct observation and interviews to measure the results of its marketing actions, see the text.

© Fabrizio Costantini

- *Actual results fall short of goals.* This requires a corrective action. One of America's favorite snacks, Hostess Twinkies, was first produced in 1930 and eventually generated $1 billion in sales from 14 plants and 9,000 employees. As consumers became more health-conscious, however, sales began to decline. Dean Metropoulos, who has made a career of saving distressed brands, bought Hostess, modernized the manufacturing, doubled the product's shelf life, and capitalized on the pop culture status of the Twinkie. Today, Twinkies are available in all Walmart stores, 100,000 convenience stores, and vending machines, and sales have exceeded the goals in the business plan.[34]

"Hiring a Milkshake" and Digging Beneath the Numbers

The "goals" used in marketing metrics are almost always *quantitative* goals. But sometimes the numbers can hide what is really happening and digging beneath the surface is needed to reveal the insights that lead to better marketing actions. A product and service example illustrate this issue.

A fast-food chain asked a team of consultants to beef up sales of its milkshakes. The chain had huge files about the likes of loyal milkshake customers. Changing the milkshakes based on those likes had no impact on sales. So consultants tried a different approach and asked: "What job is a customer trying to do when he hires a milkshake?" After looking at the results, the consultants found that (1) half the milkshakes were bought by men in the early morning; (2) it was the only thing they bought; and (3) they then drove off in their car with it.

Research on why these customers "hired the milkshake" revealed they (1) all had a similar job (2) with a long, boring drive to work and (3) needed something to do while driving.

One hand had to be on the wheel, but, jeez, somebody gave me another hand and there isn't anything in it. And I'm not hungry yet but I know I'll be hungry by ten o'clock. So what do I hire? If you promise not to tell my wife, I hire doughnuts a lot, but they crumb all over my clothes and they're gone too fast. . . . But, let me tell you, this milkshake is so viscous that it takes twenty-five minutes to suck it up that little straw. And you can turn it sideways and it doesn't fall out![35]

The Meeting of David and Abigail by Peter Paul Rubens. It is one of the gallery's big draws.

Matt Sikora, the museum's director of evaluation, with his hand-held computer. ▼

After noticing that visitors overlooked the gallery summary panel, the museum moved it next to this Rubens.

Museum visitor from ▶ Youngstown, OH.

By understanding what job the customers were trying to get done, how to improve the milkshake product became clear: You make the milkshake more viscous and put chunks of fruit into it to make sucking through a straw on the commute more unpredictable, interesting, and rewarding!

With services, measuring results that lead to actions becomes even more intangible. As shown in the photo, the Detroit Institute of Arts observes and interviews visitors to make its galleries more appealing. It discovered that visitors were often confused by the museum's panels—the written descriptions next to the art. So it made the panels more user-friendly by:

- Moving them closer to the art.
- Reducing the maximum word count from 250 to 150.
- Increasing readability by breaking up blocks of text with bullet points, subheadings, color, and graphics.

The result: These changes have significantly increased the "readership" of these descriptive panels, some of which in the past were read by only 2 percent of gallery visitors.[36]

Marketing ROI, Metrics, and Dashboards

In the past decade, measuring the performance of marketing activities has become a central focus in many organizations. This boils down to some form of the question, "What measure can I use to determine if my company's marketing is effective?"

No single measure exists to determine if a company's marketing is effective. In finance, the return on investment (ROI) metric relates the total investment made to the total return generated from the investment. The concept has been extended to measuring the effectiveness of marketing expenditures with **marketing ROI**, the application of modern measurement technologies to understand, quantify, and optimize marketing spending.[37]

The strategic marketing process tries to improve marketing ROI through the effective use of marketing metrics and dashboards:

- *Marketing metrics.* Depending on the specific goal or objective sought, one or a few key marketing metrics are chosen, such as market share, marketing ROI, cost per sales lead, cost per click, sales per square foot, and so on.[38] This is step 2 (set market and product goals) of the planning phase shown in Figure 22–2.
- *Marketing dashboards.* Ideally, the marketing metrics are displayed—often daily or weekly—on the marketing dashboard on the manager's computer. With today's syndicated scanner data, website hits, and TV viewership tracking, the typical manager faces information overload. So an effective marketing dashboard highlights actual results that vary significantly from plans. This alerts the manager to potential problems.[39]

These highlighted exceptions or deviations from the marketing plan (shown in the evaluation phase in Figure 22–2) are the immediate focus of the marketing manager, who then tries to improve the firm's marketing ROI.

Evaluation Using Marketing Metrics and Marketing Dashboards at General Mills

Let's assume it is mid-January and you are part of Vivian Callaway's Warm Delights team at General Mills. Your team is using the marketing data and metrics shown in the marketing dashboard in Figure 22–8. We can summarize the evaluation step of the strategic marketing process using this

You've eaten healthy all day and now you want something quick and tasty to satisfy your sweet tooth. Try Warm Delights Minis—the 150-calorie, microwavable dessert! Just add water in the container and cook for 1 minute. Then, enjoy!

© McGraw-Hill Education/ Editorial Image, LLC, photographer

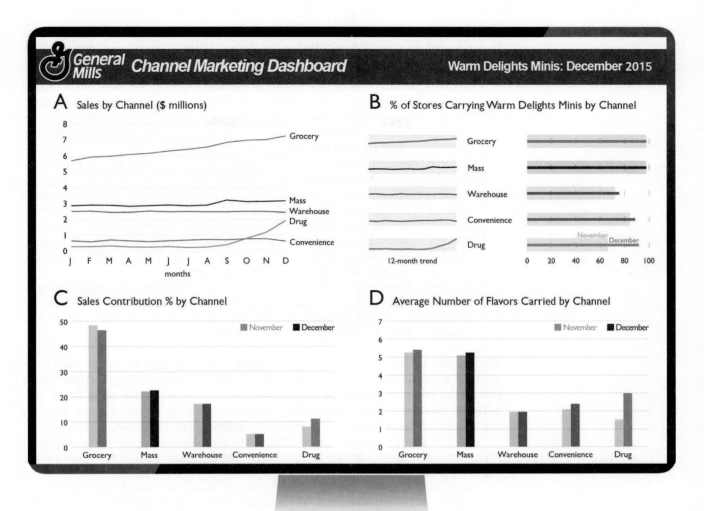

FIGURE 22–8

As a member of the Warm Delights team at General Mills, here is the marketing dashboard you see on your computer screen. You can use this dashboard to update the distribution channels strategy for the recently introduced line of Warm Delights Minis.

Source: Nelson Ng, Data Visualization Advisor, Dundas Data Visualization, Inc.

dashboard and the three-step Challenge-Findings-Actions format used in the Applying Marketing Metrics boxes in the book.

The Distribution Challenge for Warm Delights Minis   You've been asked to analyze the channel of distribution strategy of the Warm Delights Minis product. This hypothetical example is based on the type of scanner data that might appear in a computer display used by General Mills. However, details have been modified to simplify the data and analysis.

The marketing dashboard in Figure 22–8 focuses on the distribution of the existing Warm Delights Minis flavors—Molten Caramel Cake and Molten Chocolate Cake.[40] As with all new grocery products, the challenge is to gain distribution on retailers' shelves. So the marketing metrics in Figure 22–8 show the distribution of Warm Delights Minis in the five main channels of distribution used by General Mills. These five channels and their shortened names in Figure 22–8 are:

- Grocery stores/supermarkets—Grocery
- Mass merchandisers—Mass
- Warehouse/club stores—Warehouse
- Convenience stores—Convenience
- Drugstores/pharmacies—Drug

The Findings for Warm Delights Minis   The Figure 22–8 marketing dashboard describing the 2015 performance of Warm Delights Minis is divided into four charts, each with different marketing metrics:

- *Chart A: Monthly Sales by Channel ($ millions).* This shows the sales revenues for warehouse and convenience stores are flat or trending downward while those for mass merchandisers and grocery are up slightly. The grocery channel is clearly the most important. But the really encouraging news is the jump in sales in the drugstore channel from September to December.
- *Chart B: Percentage of Stores Carrying Warm Delights Minis by Channel.* The horizontal bar chart—a narrow December bar within the wider November bar—explains much of the major increase in September to December drugstore dollar sales seen in Chart A. Chart B shows that from November to December the percentage of drugstores carrying the Warm Delights Minis jumped from about 64 percent to 91 percent.
- *Chart C: Sales Contribution % by Channel.* The monthly bars total 100 percent. While the chart shows the importance of the grocery channel, it also shows the increased monthly sales revenue in the drug channel.
- *Chart D: Average Number of Flavors Carried by Channel.* This paints the picture more clearly. An important reason for the increased dollar sales from the drug channel is due to increasing the average number of flavors carried in a drugstore from 1.4 to 3.0 from November to December.

The Actions for Warm Delights Minis   Further analysis of the marketing dashboard showing the sales by channel of individual flavors of Warm Delights Minis reveals the jump in sales in the drugstore channel is because (1) a major chain (like Walgreens) added the line and (2) drugstores are embracing the new flavors, which is very important because they are now actively selling many food lines.

Your investigation also reveals a different situation for the four channels other than drugstores. The minor changes in sales there are due to the two new flavors simply replacing older, slower-moving ones.

Hot desserts normally experience an increased seasonal demand in winter. So because sales and distribution are growing, you decide to invest in the brand and schedule additional national TV advertising in late January and throughout February to exploit both the seasonal demand and recent sales trends. Seeing the jump in sales from adding a major drugstore chain, you research ways to attract other potential chains in all the five main channels Warm Delights Minis uses.

learning review

> 22-9. What are four groupings used within a typical marketing organization?
>
> 22-10. How do marketing metrics tie the goal-setting element of the planning phase of the strategic marketing process to the evaluation phase?

LEARNING OBJECTIVES REVIEW

LO 22-1 *Explain how marketing managers allocate resources.*
Marketing managers use the strategic marketing process and marketing information, such as marketing plans, sales reports, and action memos, to effectively allocate their scarce resources to exploit the competitive advantages of their products. Marketers may use techniques like sales response functions or market share (share point) analysis to help them assess what the market's response will be to additional marketing efforts.

LO 22-2 *Describe Porter's generic business strategies and synergy analysis planning frameworks.*
Porter identifies four generic business strategies that firms can adopt: (1) a cost leadership strategy, which

focuses on reducing expenses to lower product prices while targeting many market segments; (2) a differentiation strategy, which requires products to have significant points of difference to charge a premium price while targeting many market segments; (3) a cost focus strategy, which involves controlling costs to lower prices of products targeting only a few market segments; and (4) a differentiation focus strategy, which requires products to have significant points of difference to reach one or only a few market segments.

The synergy analysis framework focuses on two kinds of synergies: marketing synergies (efficiencies), which run horizontally across the row of the various products offered by the firm to a single market segment; and R&D–manufacturing synergies (efficiencies), which run vertically down a column of the various market segments targeted for a given product or product class. This results in five alternative combinations: market-product concentration, market specialization, product specialization, selective specialization, and full coverage.

LO 22-3 *Explain what makes an effective marketing plan.*
An effective marketing plan has measurable, achievable goals; uses facts and valid assumptions; is simple, clear, and specific; is complete and feasible; and is controllable and flexible.

LO 22-4 *Use a time-based agenda and an action item list to conduct a meeting.*
Successful implementation of a marketing program requires that meetings be run efficiently and that team members know what they are to do. A time-based agenda for a meeting shows the running time allocated to each agenda item, thereby reducing irrelevant discussion. An action item list helps program implementation and consists of four columns: (1) the task; (2) the person responsible for completing the task; (3) the date to finish the task; and (4) what is to be delivered—such as a draft proposal or a client call list.

LO 22-5 *Describe an organization's marketing department and the role of a product manager.*
First, marketing departments must distinguish between line positions, those individuals who have the authority and responsibility to issue orders to people who report to them, and staff positions, those individuals who have the authority and responsibility to advise but cannot directly order people in line positions to do something.

Second, marketing organizations use one of four divisional groupings to implement marketing plans: product line groupings, which are responsible for specific product offerings; functional groupings, which represent the different departments and business activities within a firm; geographical groupings, in which sales territories are subdivided on a geographical basis; and market-based groupings, which utilize specific customer segments.

Product managers interact with many people and groups both inside and outside the firm to coordinate the planning, implementation, and evaluation of the marketing plan and its budget on an annual and long-term basis for the products for which they are responsible.

LO 22-6 *Explain the use of marketing ROI, metrics, and dashboards in evaluating marketing programs.*
The evaluation phase of the strategic marketing process involves measuring the results of the marketing actions from the implementation phase and comparing them with goals set in the planning phase. Marketing metrics, used to help quantify the goals in the planning stage, are of two kinds: input metrics and output metrics. The marketing manager then takes action to exploit positive deviations from the plan and to correct negative ones. Today, managers want an answer to the question, "Are my marketing activities effective?" One answer is in using marketing ROI, which is the application of modern measurement technologies to understand, quantify, and optimize marketing spending. Quantifying a marketing goal with a carefully defined output metric and tracking this metric on a marketing dashboard can improve marketing ROI.

LEARNING REVIEW ANSWERS

22-1 What are the four basic practices "that really work" that characterize industry-leading firms?

Answer: The four basic business and management practices that matter are: (1) strategy—devise and maintain a clearly stated, focused strategy; (2) execution—develop and maintain flawless operational execution; (3) culture—develop and maintain a performance-oriented culture; and (4) structure—build and maintain a fast, flexible, flat organization.

22-2 What is the significance of the S-shape of the sales response function in Figure 22–1?

Answer: The sales response function relates the expense of marketing effort to the marketing results obtained. Different levels of marketing effort will cause different rates of sales revenue growth. In Figure 22–1, an additional $1 million of marketing effort results in far greater increases of sales revenue in the midrange of the curve than at either end. At the left end of

the S-curve, the cost of the marketing effort to gain new customers is high for they must be made aware of the product. In contrast, at the right end of the S-curve, the easy-to-get customers are already buying the product and getting every new one is again very costly.

22-3 What is the difference between an input metric and an output metric?

Answer: Marketing metrics are used to measure actual organizational performance—whether its goals have been achieved. An output metric is a measure of actual results, such as sales revenues due to new offerings and customer satisfaction with new offerings during a specified time period. An input metric measures the efforts that go into developing new offerings, such as the number of ideas or concepts in the new-product pipeline and R&D spending as a percentage of sales.

22-4 Describe Porter's four generic business strategies.

Answer: Porter's four generic business strategies are: (1) Cost leadership strategy, which focuses on reducing expenses and, in turn, lowers product prices while targeting a broad array of market segments. (2) Differentiation strategy, which requires products to have significant points of difference to charge a higher price while targeting a broad array of market segments. (3) Cost focus strategy, which involves controlling expenses and, in turn, lowering product prices targeted at a narrow range of market segments. (4) Differentiation focus strategy, which requires products to have significant points of difference to target one or only a few market segments.

22-5 Where do (a) marketing synergies and (b) R&D–manufacturing synergies appear when using the synergy analysis framework?

Answer: Synergy analysis seeks market-product opportunities by finding the optimum balance between marketing efficiencies versus R&D–manufacturing efficiencies. This can be accomplished by using both diversification analysis and the market-product grid framework. (a) Marketing synergies run horizontally across the rows. As a result, a firm may experience the market specialization effect if it provides a complete product line for a given market segment. (b) R&D–manufacturing synergies run vertically down the columns. As a result, a firm may experience the product specialization effect if it provides a product item for all market segments. A firm can experience both marketing and R&D–manufacturing efficiencies if it offers full coverage: a complete product line targeted at all market segments.

22-6 What is the meaning and importance of a program champion?

Answer: A program champion is able and willing to cut red tape and move the program forward to get it implemented. Such a person often has the uncanny ability to move back and forth between the "big picture" and the specific details as the situation warrants. Program champions can be notoriously brash in overcoming organizational hurdles. An adage voiced by a program champion: "Better to ask forgiveness than permission."

22-7 Describe one or two lessons from Lockheed Martin's Skunk Works that can be applied to implementing marketing programs.

Answer: Examples of lessons from Lockheed's Skunk Works are: (1) make decisions promptly; (2) avoid "paralysis by analysis," which is the tendency to excessively analyze a problem instead of taking action; (3) when trouble develops, surface the problem immediately; (4) get help—don't keep the problem to yourself; (5) hold weekly meetings using a time-based agenda, which is one that shows the running time allocated to each agenda item; and (6) create an action item list.

22-8 How are (a) a time-based agenda and (b) an action item list used in a marketing program meeting?

Answer: Successful implementation requires that members of the program team understand its goals, the tasks they are responsible for to help reach those goals, and the deadlines for completing them. Time-based agendas and action item lists are two tools to assist program champions and others on the project to manage meetings and deadlines. A time-based agenda shows the running time allocated to each agenda item. It sets the agenda for the next meeting and its minutes become secondary and backward-looking. An action item list is the outcome of these meetings. It is an aid that consists of four columns: (a) the task, (b) the person responsible for completing that task, (c) the date to finish the task, and (d) what is to be delivered. Action item lists are forward-looking, clarify the targets, and put strong pressure on people to achieve their designated tasks by the specified deadlines.

22-9 What are four groupings used within a typical marketing organization?

Answer: The four marketing organizational groupings are: (1) product line, in which a unit is responsible for specific product offerings; (2) functional, where different departments or business activities within a firm are represented, such as manufacturing, marketing, and finance; (3) geographical, in which sales territories are subdivided according to geographical location; and (4) market-based, which uses specific customer segments. When this method of organizing is combined with product groupings, the result is a matrix organization.

22-10 How do marketing metrics tie the goal-setting element of the planning phase of the strategic marketing process to the evaluation phase?

Answer: For each marketing plan goal developed in the planning phase for an organization's offering, a marketing metric is created to measure whether the goal actually has been achieved. Marketing actions are then taken in the implementation phase with these goals in mind. In the evaluation phase, actual results are measured using this marketing metric to compare the established goal with the results to identify any deviations that need to be either exploited or corrected when revising the marketing plans for the next period.

FOCUSING ON KEY TERMS

action item list p. 637
cost focus strategy p. 628
cost leadership strategy p. 628
differentiation focus strategy p. 628
differentiation strategy p. 628
functional groupings p. 639

generic business strategy p. 628
geographical groupings p. 639
line positions p. 639
market-based groupings p. 639
marketing ROI p. 642
product line groupings p. 639

program champion p. 635
sales response function p. 623
share points p. 624
staff positions p. 639
synergy analysis p. 628
time-based agenda p. 637

APPLYING MARKETING KNOWLEDGE

1   Assume a firm faces an S-shaped sales response function. What happens to the ratio of incremental sales revenue to incremental marketing effort at the (*a*) bottom, (*b*) middle, and (*c*) top of this curve?

2   What happens to the ratio of incremental sales revenue to incremental marketing effort when the sales response function is an upward-sloping straight line?

3   Assume General Mills has to decide how to invest millions of dollars to try to expand its dessert and yogurt businesses. To allocate this money between these two businesses, what information would General Mills like to have?

4   Suppose your Great States lawn mower company has the market-product concentration situation shown in Figure 22–4A. What are both the synergies and potential pitfalls of following expansion strategies of (*a*) market specialization and (*b*) product specialization?

5   The first Domino's Pizza restaurant was near a college campus. What implementation problems are (*a*) similar and (*b*) different for restaurants near a college campus versus a military base?

6   A common theme among managers who succeed repeatedly in program implementation is fostering open communication. Why is this so important?

7   In regard to implementing a marketing program, what are the advantages of (*a*) a time-based agenda over a traditional agenda and (*b*) an action item list over traditional meeting minutes?

8   In the organizational chart for the consumer packaged goods firm in Figure 22–6, where do product line, functional, and geographical groupings occur?

9   Why are quantified goals in the planning phase of the strategic marketing process important for the evaluation phase?

BUILDING YOUR MARKETING PLAN

Do the following activities to complete your marketing plan:

1   Draw a simple organizational chart for your organization.

2   Develop a Gantt chart (see Chapter 2) to schedule the key activities required to implement your marketing plan.

3   In terms of the evaluation, list (*a*) the four or five critical factors (such as revenues, number of customers, variable costs) and (*b*) how frequently (monthly, quarterly) you will monitor them to determine if special actions are needed to exploit opportunities or correct deviations.

4   Finalize your marketing plan based on the outline presented in Appendix A.

VIDEO CASE 22   General Mills Warm Delights: Indulgent, Delicious, and Gooey!

Vivian Milroy Callaway, vice president for the Center for Learning and Experimentation at General Mills, retells the story for the "indulgent, delicious, and gooey" Warm Delights product. She summarizes, "When you want something that is truly innovative, you have to look at the rules you have been assuming in your category and break them all!"

Video 22-5
Warm Delights Video Case
kerin.tv/13e/v22-5

When a new business achieves a breakthrough, it looks easy to outsiders. The creators of Betty Crocker Warm Delights stress that if the marketing decisions had been based on the traditions and history of the cake category, a smaller, struggling business would have resulted. The team chose to challenge the assumptions and expectations of accumulated cake category business experience. The team took personal and business risks, and Warm Delights became a roaring success.

PLANNING PHASE: INNOVATION, BUT A SHRINKING MARKET

"In the typical grocery store, the baking mix aisle is a quiet place," says Callaway. Shelves sigh with flavors, types, and brands. Prices are low, but there is little consumer traffic. Cake continues to be a tradition for birthdays and social occasions. But, consumer demand has declined. The percentage of U.S. households that bought at least one baking mix in 2000 was 80 percent. Fifteen years later the percentage was about 62 percent, a very significant decline.

Today, a promoted price of 89 cents to make a 9 × 12 inch cake is common. Many choices, but little differentiation, gradually falling sales, and low uniform prices are the hallmarks of a mature category. But it's not that consumers don't buy cake-like treats. In fact, indulgent treats are growing. The premium prices for ice cream ($3.00 a pint) and chocolate ($3.00 a bar) are not slowing consumer purchases.

The Betty Crocker marketing team challenged the food scientists at General Mills to create a great-tasting, easy-to-prepare, single-serve cake treat. The goal: Make it indulgent, delicious, and gooey. The team focused the scientists on a product that would have:

- Consistent great taste.
- Quick preparation.
- A single portion.
- No cleanup.

The food scientists delivered the prototype! Now, the marketing team began hammering out the four Ps. They started with a descriptive name "Betty Crocker Dessert Bowls" (see photo) and a plan to shelve it in the "quiet" cake aisle. This practical approach would meet the consumer need for a "small, fast, microwave cake" for dessert. Several marketing challenges emerged:

- *The comparison problem.* The easy shelf price comparison to 9 × 12 inch cakes selling for 89 cents would make it harder to price Dessert Bowls at $2.00.
- *The communication problem.* The product message "a small, faster-to-make cake" wasn't compelling. For example, after-school snacks should be fast and small, but "dessert" sounds too indulgent.
- *The quiet aisle problem.* The cake-aisle shopper is probably not browsing for a cake innovation.
- *The dessert problem.* Consumers' on-the-go, calorie-conscious meal plans don't generally include a planned dessert.
- *The microwave problem.* Consumers might not believe it tastes good.

In sum, the small, fast-cake product didn't resonate with a compelling consumer need. But it would be a safe bet because the Dessert Bowl positioning fit nicely with the family-friendly Betty Crocker brand.

IMPLEMENTATION PHASE: LEAVING BEHIND THE SECURITY OF FAMILY

The consumer insights team really enjoyed the hot, gooey cake product. But they feared it would languish in the cake aisle under the "Dessert Bowl" name since this didn't capture the essence of what the food delivered. They explored who the indulgent treat customers really are. The data revealed that the heaviest buyers of premium treats are women without children. This focused the team on a target consumer: "What does she want?" They enlisted an ad agency and consultants to come up with a name that would appeal to "her." Several independently suggested the "Warm Delights" name, which became the brand name.

An interesting postscript to the team's brand name research: A competitor apparently liked not only the idea of a quick, gooey, microwavable dessert but also the "Dessert Bowls" name! You may now see its competitive product on your supermarket's shelves.

Targeting on-the-go women who want a small, personal treat had marketing advantages:

- The $2.00 Warm Delights price compared favorably to the price of many single-serve indulgent treats.
- The product food message "warm, convenient, delightful" is compelling.
- On-the-go women's meal plans do include the occasional delicious treat.

One significant problem remained: The cake-aisle shopper is probably not browsing for an indulgent, single-serve treat.

The marketing team solved this shelving issue by using advertising and product point-of-purchase displays outside the cake aisle. This would raise women's awareness of Warm Delights. Television advertising and in-store display programs are costly, so Warm Delights sales would have to be strong to pay back the investment.

Vivian Callaway and the team turned to market research to fine-tune the plan. The research put Warm Delights (and Dessert Bowls) on the shelf in real grocery stores. A few key findings emerged. First, the name "Warm Delights" beat "Dessert Bowls." Second, the Warm Delights with nuts simply wasn't easy to prepare, so nuts were removed. Third, the packaging with a disposable bowl beat the typical cake-mix packaging involving using your own bowl. Finally, by putting the actual product on supermarket shelves and in displays in these stores, sales volumes could be analyzed.

EVALUATION PHASE: TURNING THE PLAN INTO ACTION!

The marketing plan isn't action. Sales for Warm Delights required the marketing team to (1) get the retailers to stock the product, preferably somewhere other than the cake aisle, and (2) appeal to consumers enough to have them purchase, like, and repurchase the product.

The initial acceptance of a product by retailers is important. But each store manager must experience good sales of Warm Delights to be motivated to keep its shelves stocked with the product. Also, the Warm Delights team must monitor the display activity in the store. Are the displays placed in the locations as expected? Do the sales increase when a display is present? Watching distribution and display execution on a new product is very important so that sales shortfalls can be addressed proactively.

Did the customer buy one or two Warm Delights? Did the customer return for a second purchase a few days later? The syndicated services that sell household panel purchase data can provide these answers. The Warm Delights team evaluates these reports to see if the number of people who tried the product matches with expectations and how the repeat purchases occur. Often, the "80/20 rule" applies. So, in the early months, is there a group of consumers who buy repeatedly and will fill this role?

For ongoing feedback, calls by Warm Delights consumers to the toll-free consumer information line are monitored. This is a great source of real-time feedback. If a pattern emerges and these calls are mostly about the same problem, that is bad. However, when consumers call to say "thank you" or "it's great," that is good. This is an informal quick way to identify if the product is on track or further investigation is warranted.

GOOD MARKETING MAKES A DIFFERENCE

The team took personal and business risks by choosing the Warm Delights plan over the more conservative Dessert Bowls plan. Today, General Mills has loyal Warm Delights consumers who are open to trying new flavors, new sizes, and new forms. If you were a consultant to the Warm Delights team, what would you do to grow this brand in terms of product line and brand extensions?[41]

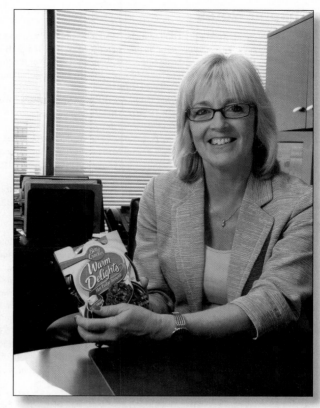

© Daniel Hundley/Token Media

Questions

1 What is the competitive set of desserts in which Warm Delights is located?

2 (*a*) Who is the target market? (*b*) What is the point of difference on the positioning for Warm Delights? (*c*) What are the potential opportunities and hindrances of the target market and positioning?

3 (*a*) What marketing research did Vivian Callaway execute? (*b*) What were the critical questions that led her to conduct research and seek expert advice? (*c*) How did this affect the product's marketing mix price, promotion, packaging, and distribution decisions?

4 (*a*) What initial promotional plan directed to consumers in the target market did Callaway use? (*b*) Why did this make sense to Callaway and her team when Warm Delights was launched?

5 If you were a consultant to Vivian Callaway, what product changes would you recommend to increase sales of Warm Delights?

Chapter Notes

1. Scott Stoddard, "Top Dividend Stock General Mills Adapts to New Tastes," *Investors Business Daily,* May 28, 2015, p. B9; Lucy Maher and Susie Stulz, "Millennials Take Over the Store Aisle," *Adweek,* June 22, 2105, pp. S1–15; and Personal interviews with Vivian Milroy Callaway.

2. Sarah Nassauer, "What If We All Bought Organic?" *The Wall Street Journal,* March 18, 2015, p. D1; "Annie Gasparro, "General Mills to Cut Costs—Company Announces New Initiatives Amid Slow U.S. Sales," *The Wall Street Journal,* June 26, 2104, p. B4; "General Mills Overview," and "General Mills 2014 Annual Report," see General Mills website, http://www.generalmills.com/en/Company/Overview.

3. Lisa Belfuss, "Why Trix Cereal Will Soon Have Four Colors Instead of Six," *The Wall Street Journal,* June 23, 2105, p. B2; and "Betty's Must-Have New Products," see http://www.bettycrocker.com/products/new-products.

4. Hugh Courtney, John T. Horn, and Jayanti Kar, "Getting into Your Competitor's Head," *The McKinsey Quarterly,* February 2009.

5. Roger A. Kerin, P. Rajan Varadarajan, and Robert A. Peterson, "First-Mover Advantage: A Synthesis, Conceptual Framework, and Research Proposition," *Journal of Marketing,* October 1992, pp. 33–52; and Pankaj Ghemawat, "Sustainable Advantage," *Harvard Business Review,* September–October 1986, pp. 53–58.

6. Nitin Nohria, William Joyce, and Bruce Roberson, "What Really Works," *Harvard Business Review,* July 2003, pp. 42–52; and "Who Gets Eaten and Who Gets to Eat," *The Economist,* July 12, 2003, pp. 61–63.

7. "Costco Brand of Retailing Continues to Resonate," *MMR,* May 25, 2015, p. 56; and Armin Harris et al., "The Directors: Costco Wholesale," *Fortune,* May 4, 2009, pp. 100–1.

8. David Sedgwick, "Toyota's New Plan: Design Parts, Then Cars," *Automotive News,* June 15, 2015, p. 33; Geoff Colvin, "How It Works," *Fortune,* February 27, 2012, pp. 71–79; and Kathleen Kerwin and Paul Magnusson, "Can Anything Stop Toyota?" *BusinessWeek,* November 17, 2003, pp. 114–22.

9. Milton Moskowitz and Robert Levering, "The 100 Best Companies to Work For," *Fortune,* March 15, 2015, pp. 143–144; and "The 500 Largest U.S. Corporations," *Fortune,* June 15, 2015, p. F4.

10. Ben R. Rich and Leo Janos, *Skunk Works* (Boston: Little, Brown and Company, 1994).

11. Murali K. Mantrala, Probhakant Sirha, and Andris A. Zoltners, "Impact of Resource Allocation Rules on Marketing Investment-Level Decisions and Profitability," *Journal of Marketing Research,* May 1992, pp. 162–75.

12. Mike Hughlett, "General Mills Adds New Cereals to Take On Trends," www.startribune.com, December 14, 2014; and Bridget Christenson, "New Products Deliver on Taste," Taste of General Mills, www.blog.generalmills.com, December 16, 2014.

13. Clayton M. Christensen and Derek van Bever, "The Capitalist's Dilemma," *Harvard Business Review,* June 2014, pp. 60–68.

14. Steve Lohr, "When There's No Such Thing as Too Much Information," *The New York Times,* April 24, 2011, p. BU3; and Mark Jeffery, *Data-Driven Marketing* (Hoboken, NJ: John Wiley & Sons, 2010), chapters 1 and 2.

15. Lisa C. Troy, Tanawat Hirunyawipada, and Audhesh K. Paswan, "Cross-Functional Integration and New Product Success: An Empirical Investigation of the Findings," *Journal of Marketing,* November 2008, pp. 132–46.

16. Renee Dye and Olivier Sibony, "How to Improve Strategic Planning," *The McKinsey Quarterly,* August 2007; and Jacques Bughin, Amy Guggenheim Shenkan, and Marc Singer, "How Poor Metrics Undermine Digital Marketing," *The McKinsey Quarterly,* October 2008.

17. Michael E. Porter, *Competitive Advantage: Creating and Sustaining Superior Performance* (New York: The Free Press, a Division of Simon & Schuster, 1985), adapted with permission.

18. Adapted from Philip Kotler and Kevin Lane Keller, *Marketing Management,* 13th ed. (Upper Saddle River, NJ: Prentice Hall, 2009), pp. 228–229.

19. Several of the items in the list are adapted from Massimo Garbuio, Dan Lovallo, and Patrick Viguerie, "How Companies Make Good Decisions," *The McKinsey Quarterly,* December 2008; Renee Dye and Olivier Sibony, "How to Improve Strategic Planning," *The McKinsey Quarterly,* August 2007; and Jungkiu Choi, Dan Lovallo, and Anna Tarasova, "Better Strategy for Business Units," *The McKinsey Quarterly,* June 2007.

20. University of Pennsylvania Wharton Alumni Emeritus Society, *Spring 2009 Newsletter,* p. 2.

21. Stratford Sherman, "How Intel Makes Spending Pay Off," *Fortune,* February 22, 1993, pp. 57–61.

22. Bridget Christenson, "New Products Deliver on Taste," General Mills website, December 16, 2014, http://blog.generalmills.com/2014/12/new-products-deliver-on-taste/?_ga=1.226301978.1452213074.1435594206; Mike Hughlett, "From Pushcart to Grocery Cart," *Star Tribune,* February 7, 2011, pp. D1, D2.

23. "G-WIN," General Mills website, https://generalmills.com/Company/Innovation/G-WIN .

24. Anirban Sen, "Disruptive Innovation Is a Strategy, Not Just the Technology," *Business Today,* January 4, 2015, pp. 150–58; and Clayton M. Christensen, *The Innovator's Dilemma: When New Technologies Cause Great Firms to Fail* (Boston, MA: Harvard Business School Press, 1997).

25. Hal B. Gregerson, Jeff Dyer, and Clayton M. Christensen, "Why Ask Why?" *Chief Executive.Net,* January/February 2012, pp. 40–43.

26. Brendan Walsh, "Winning, Jack Welch," *Director,* June 2015, p. 18; and Jack Welch and Suzy Welch, *Winning* (New York: Harper Collins, 2005).

27. Stuart Crainer, "In Search of Excellence: 30 Years On," *Business Strategy Review,* Fall 2012, pp. 78–80; Thomas J. Peters and Robert H. Waterman Jr., *In Search of Excellence: Lessons from America's Best-Run Companies* (New York: Harper & Row, 1982).

28. Tom Peters, "Winners Do Hundreds of Percent over Norm," *StarTribune,* January 8, 1985, p. 5B; and Rich and Leo Janos, *Skunk Works,* pp. 51–53.

29. "Genchi-genbutsu Renewed," *Industrial Engineer,* September 2013, p. 11; and Geoff Colvin, "How It Works," *Fortune,* February 27, 2012, p. 75.

30. Clare O'Connor, "Spanx Inventor Sara Blakely on Hustling Her Way to a Billion-Dollar Business,' forbes.com, October 21, 2014, p. 21; "The Best Advice I Ever Got: Sara Blakely," *Fortune,* November 12, 2012, p. 124; and the Spanx website, www.spanx.com.

31. W. Chan Kim and Renée Mauborgne, "Red Ocean Traps," *Harvard Business Review,* March 2015, pp. 68–73; Jim Collins and Morten T. Hansen, *Great By Choice* (New York: HarperCollins, 2011); and W. Chan Kim and Renée Mauborgne, *Blue Ocean Strategy* (Boston: Harvard Business School Press, 2005).

32. *CMO Survey Report: Highlights and Insights, cmosurvey.org,* February 2015; "Survey Finds CMOs Who Report to CEO Earn More," *Report On Salary Surveys,* The Bureau of National

Affairs, September 2014, pp. 7–8; "Big Data Rewrites the CMO's Role," *Marketing Week,* September 13, 2013, p. 50; David Court, "The Evolving Role of the CMO," *The McKinsey Quarterly,* August 2007; and Alexander Krasnikov and Satish Jayachandran, "The Relative Impact of Marketing, Research-and-Development, and Operations Capabilities on Firm Performance," *Journal of Marketing,* July 2008, pp. 1–11.

33. "Complete Recap of Starbucks 2015 Annual Meeting of Share-holders," Starbucks website, https://news.starbucks.com/news/starbucks-2015-annual-meeting-of-shareholders, March 18, 2015; Samantha Sharf, "Starbucks Sales Swell In 'Christmas Blend' Quarter, *Forbes.com,* January 22, 2015, p. 22; Lauren Johnson, "Starbucks and Spotify Link Up to Bring Digital Music into Stores," *Adweek,* April 22, 2015, p. 1; Denver Nicks, "Starbucks Plans New Tasting Rooms and Ex-press Stores, *Time.com,* September 8, 2014, p.1; and Daniel Wolfe, "Starbucks' Mobile Pay Updates Win Over New Audi-ences," *American Banker,* April 27, 2015.

34. Steven Bertoni, "The Twinkie Miracle," *Forbes,* May 4, 2015, pp. 74–82.

35. Larissa MacFarquhar, "When Giants Fail," *The New Yorker,* May 14, 2012, pp. 81–95.

36. Isaac Arnsdorf, "The Museum Is Watching You," *The Wall Street Journal,* August 18, 2010, pp. D1, D2.

37. James D. Lenskold, *Marketing ROI* (New York: McGraw-Hill, 2003).

38. "More Companies Require Revenue-Focused Marketing ROI Measures, Study Finds," *Marketing News,* April 2015, p. 4; Michael Krauss, "Balance Attention to Metrics with Intuition," *Marketing News,* June 1, 2007, pp. 6–8; John Davis, *Measuring Marketing: 103 Key Metrics Every Marketer Needs* (Singapore: Wiley and Sons, 2007); and Paul W. Farris, Neil T. Bendle, Phillip E. Pfeifer, and David J. Reibstein, *Marketing Metrics* (Upper Saddle River, NJ: Wharton School Publishing, 2006).

39. Malcolm Craig, *Thinking Visually: Business Applications of 14 Core Diagrams* (New York and London: Continuum, 2000).

40. The illustrative example of using a marketing dashboard at General Mills was developed by David Ford and Vivian Milroy Callaway.

41. Warm Delights: This case was prepared by Roger Kerin, Steven Hartley, and William Rudelius.

C

APPENDIX

PLANNING A CAREER IN MARKETING

GETTING A JOB: THE PROCESS OF MARKETING YOURSELF

Getting a job is usually a lengthy process, and it is exactly that—a *process* that involves careful planning, implementation, and evaluation. You may have everything going for you: a respectable grade point average (GPA), relevant work experience, several extracurricular activities, superior communication skills, and demonstrated leadership qualities. Despite these, you still need to market yourself systematically and aggressively; after all, even the best products lie dormant on retailers' shelves unless marketed effectively.

The process of getting a job involves the same activities marketing managers use to develop and introduce products and brands into the marketplace.[1] The only difference is that you are marketing yourself, not a product. You need to conduct marketing research by analyzing your personal qualities (performing a self-audit) and by identifying job opportunities.

© Rafal Olechowski/Alamy

Based on your research results, select a target market— those job opportunities that are compatible with your interests, goals, skills, and abilities—and design a marketing mix around that target market. *You* are the "product"; you must decide how to "position" and "brand" yourself in the job market.[2]

The price component of the marketing mix is the salary range and job benefits (such as health and life insurance, vacation time, and retirement benefits) that you hope to receive. Promotion involves communicating with prospective employers through written and electronic correspondence (advertising) and job interviews (personal selling). The place element focuses on how to reach prospective employers—at the career services office, job fairs, or online, for example.

This appendix will assist you in career planning by (1) providing information about careers in marketing and (2) outlining a job search process.

CAREERS IN MARKETING

The diversity of marketing opportunities is reflected in the many types of marketing jobs, including product management, marketing research, and public relations. While many of these jobs are found at traditional employers such as manufacturers, retailers, and advertising agencies, there are also many opportunities in a variety of other types of organizations.

Professional services such as law, accounting, and consulting firms, for example, have a growing need for marketing expertise. Similarly, nonprofit organizations such as universities, the performing arts, museums, and government agencies are developing marketing functions. Event organizations such as athletic teams, golf and tennis tournaments, and the Olympics are also new and visible sources of marketing jobs.

The diversity of marketing jobs is also changing because of changes in the marketing discipline. The growth of digital marketing, mobile marketing, and social media has created a variety of new jobs including data analysts, content marketing specialists, and social media managers. The growth of multichannel and omnichannel marketing has led to the need for channel integration specialists. The increasing involvement and engagement of consumers have required public relations personnel to become social networking experts and consumer-generated content managers. Other specialties in demand now include customer relations management (CRM), multicultural marketing, and viral marketing.[3]

Examples of companies that have opportunities for graduates with degrees in marketing include Accenture, American Express, AT&T, Forever 21, Google, Kroger, Macy's, MetLife, Microsoft, PricewaterhouseCoopers, Procter & Gamble Co., Saks Fifth Avenue, The Nielsen Company, United Airlines, and Wal-Mart.[4] Most of these career opportunities offer a chance to work with interesting people on stimulating and rewarding problems. One product manager comments, "I love marketing as a career because there are different challenges every day."[5]

Recent studies of career paths and salaries suggest that marketing careers can also provide excellent opportunities for advancement and substantial pay. For example, one of every eight chief executive officers (CEOs) of the nation's 500 most valuable publicly held companies held positions in marketing before becoming CEO.[6] Similarly, reports of average starting salaries of college graduates indicate that salaries in marketing compare favorably with those in many other fields. The average starting salary of new marketing undergraduates in 2014 was $43,123, compared with $32,454 for journalism majors and $37,557 for advertising majors.[7] The future is likely to be even better. The U.S. Department of Labor reports that employment of advertising, promotion, and marketing managers is expected to grow at a rate of 12 percent through 2022. This growth is being spurred by the introduction of new products to the marketplace and the growing need to "manage digital media campaigns, which often target customers through the use of websites, social media, and live chats."[8]

Figure C–1 describes marketing occupations in seven major categories: product management and physical distribution, advertising and promotion, retailing, sales, marketing research, global marketing, and nonprofit marketing. One of these may be right for you. Additional sources of marketing career information are provided at the end of this appendix.

Video C-1

Careers

kerin.tv/13e/vC-1

Product Management and Physical Distribution

Many organizations assign one manager the responsibility for a particular product. For example, Procter & Gamble (P&G) has separate managers for Tide, Cheer, Gain, and Bold. Product or brand managers are involved in all aspects of a product's marketing program, such as marketing research, sales, sales promotion, advertising, and pricing, as well as manufacturing. Managers of similar products typically report to a category manager, or marketing director, and may be part of a *product management team* to encourage interbrand cooperation.[9]

College graduates with bachelor's and master's degrees—often in marketing and business—enter P&G as assistant brand managers, the only starting position in its product or brand groups. As assistant brand managers, their responsibilities include developing a detailed marketing plan for a specific brand and learning consumer, shopper, and customer insights. With good performance and demonstrated leadership, after three to six years the assistant brand manager is promoted to brand manager, then after four to eight years to associate marketing director, and after three to eight years to marketing director. These promotions often involve several brand groups. For example, a new employee might start as assistant brand manager for Folger's coffee, be promoted to brand manager for Crest toothpaste, become an associate marketing director for P&G's soap products, and finally a marketing director for a different brand group. Other positions important at P&G include launch leader, account manager, and market manager.[10]

Several other jobs related to product management (see Figure C–1) deal with physical distribution issues such as storing the manufactured product (inventory), moving the product from the firm to the customers (transportation), and engaging in many other aspects of the manufacture and sale of goods. Prospects for these jobs are likely to increase as a wider range of products and technologies lead to increased demand. In addition, as manufacturers cut costs, they are increasingly shifting more responsibilities to wholesalers.[11]

Product or brand managers are involved in all aspects of a product's marketing program.
© Dibyangshu Sarkar/AFP/Getty Images

PRODUCT MANAGEMENT AND PHYSICAL DISTRIBUTION

Product development manager creates a road map for new products by working with customers to determine their needs and with designers to create the product.

Product or brand manager is responsible for integrating all aspects of a product's marketing program including research, sales, sales promotion, advertising, and pricing.

Supply chain manager oversees the part of a company that transports products to consumers and handles customer service.

Operations manager supervises warehousing and other physical distribution functions and often is directly involved in moving products on the warehouse floor.

Inventory control manager forecasts demand for products, coordinates production with plant managers, and tracks shipments to keep customers supplied.

Physical distribution specialist is an expert in the transportation and distribution of products and also evaluates the costs and benefits of different types of transportation.

SALES

Direct or retail salesperson sells directly to consumers in the salesperson's office, the consumer's home, or a retailer's store.

Trade salesperson calls on retailers or wholesalers to sell products for manufacturers.

Industrial or semitechnical salesperson sells supplies and services to businesses.

Complex or professional salesperson sells complicated or custom-designed products to businesses. This requires understanding of the product technology.

Customer service manager maintains good relations with customers by coordinating the sales staff, marketing management, and physical distribution management.

NONPROFIT MARKETING

Marketing manager develops and directs marketing campaigns, fund-raising, and public relations.

GLOBAL MARKETING

Global marketing manager is an expert in world-trade agreements, international competition, cross-cultural analysis, and global market-entry strategies.

ADVERTISING AND PROMOTION

Account executive maintains contact with clients while coordinating the creative work among artists and copywriters. Account executives work as partners with the client to develop marketing strategy.

Media buyer deals with media sales representatives in selecting advertising media and analyzes the value of media being purchased.

Copywriter works with art director in conceptualizing advertisements and writes the text of print or radio ads or the storyboards of television ads.

Art director handles the visual component of advertisements.

Sales promotion manager designs promotions for consumer products and works at an ad agency or a sales promotion agency.

Public relations manager develops written or video messages for the public and handles contacts with the press.

Digital marketing manager develops and executes the e-business marketing plan and manages all aspects of the advertising, promotion, and content for the online business.

Social media marketing manager plans and manages the delivery of marketing messages through all social media and monitors and responds to the feedback received.

RETAILING

Buyer selects products a store sells, surveys consumer trends, and evaluates the past performance of products and suppliers.

Store manager oversees the staff and services at a store.

MARKETING RESEARCH

Project manager coordinates and oversees market studies for a client.

Account executive serves as a liaison between client and market research firm, like an advertising agency account executive.

Marketing research analyst analyzes consumer data to identify preferences, behavior patterns, and user profiles to create and evaluate marketing programs.

Competitive intelligence researcher uses new information technologies to monitor the competitive environment.

Marketing database manager is responsible for collection and maintenance of data and information, support of the data analytics and decision support systems, and timely and accurate report generation.

Source: Adapted from Lila B. Stair and Leslie Stair, *Careers in Marketing* (New York: McGraw-Hill, 2008); and David W. Rosenthal and Michael A. Powell, *Careers in Marketing,* © 1984, pp. 352–54.

FIGURE C–1

Seven major categories of marketing occupations.

Advertising and Promotion

Although we may see hundreds of advertisements in a day, what we can't see easily is the fascinating and complex advertising profession. The entry-level advertising positions filled every year include jobs with a variety of firms. Advertising professionals often remark that they find their jobs appealing because the days are not routine and they involve creative activities with many interesting people.

Advertising positions are available in three kinds of organizations: advertisers, media companies, and agencies. Advertisers include manufacturers, retail stores, service firms, and many other types of companies. Often they have an advertising department responsible for preparing and placing their own ads. Advertising careers are also possible with the media: television, radio stations, magazines, and newspapers. Finally, advertising agencies offer job opportunities through their use of account management, research, media, and creative services.

Starting positions with advertisers and advertising agencies are often as assistants to employees with several years of experience. An assistant copywriter facilitates the development of the message, or copy, in an advertisement. An assistant art director participates in the design of visual components of advertisements. Entry-level media positions involve buying the media that will carry the ad or selling airtime on radio or television or page space in print media. Some agencies are encouraging employees to develop skills in multiple roles. Advancement to supervisory positions requires planning skills, a broad vision, and an affinity for spotting an effective advertising idea. Students interested in advertising should develop good communication skills and try to gain advertising experience through summer employment opportunities or internships.[12]

Growing interest in integrated marketing programs has increased opportunities for sales promotion managers, public relations managers, and Internet marketing managers. These positions require an understanding of the potential synergy of all promotional tools. Responsibilities include the design and implementation of sweepstakes, sampling programs, events and partnerships, newsletters, press releases and conferences, e-mail promotions, web-content management, and permission marketing campaigns. In addition, as advertisers increase search marketing budgets, the number of search marketing positions is increasing. Finally, many companies have decided that they need social media managers to ensure that messages can be sent to and received from the millions of people now on Facebook, Twitter, and other social media websites.[13]

Retailing

There are two separate career paths in retailing: merchandise management and store management (see Figure C–2). The key position in merchandising is that of a buyer, who is responsible for selecting merchandise, guiding the promotion of the merchandise, setting prices, bargaining with wholesalers, training the salesforce, and monitoring the competitive environment. The buyer must also be able to organize and coordinate many critical activities under severe time constraints. In contrast, store management involves the supervision of personnel in all departments and the general management of all facilities, equipment, and merchandise displays. In addition, store managers are responsible for the financial performance of each department and for the store as a whole. Typical positions beyond the store manager level include district manager, regional manager, and divisional vice president.[14]

Most starting jobs in retailing are trainee positions. A trainee is usually placed in a management training program and then given a position as an assistant buyer or

Retailers such as Macy's and Bloomingdale's offer careers in merchandise management and store management.
© Francis Dean/Deanphotos/Newscom

FIGURE C–2

Two common retailing career paths include merchandise management and store management.

Merchandise management

Buyer trainee → Assistant buyer → Buyer → Merchandise division manager

Store management

Management trainee → Assistant department manager → Department manager → Store (branch) manager

FIGURE C–3

Employment opportunities in selected sales occupations (2012–2022).

Occupation	2012 Employment	2022 Employment	Percentage Change 2012–2022	Growth
Insurance sales agents	443,400	489,300	10%	45,900
Real estate brokers and sales agents	422,000	468,600	11%	46,600
Retail salespersons	4,668,300	5,118,500	10%	450,200
Wholesale and manufacturing sales representatives	1,863,000	2,032,300	9%	169,300
Securities, commodities, and financial services sales agents	354,600	394,300	11%	39,700

Source: *Occupational Outlook Handbook, 2014–15 Edition* (Washington, DC: U.S. Department of Labor, Bureau of Labor Statistics).

assistant department manager. Advancement and responsibility can be achieved quickly because there is a shortage of qualified personnel in retailing and because superior performance of an individual is quickly reflected in sales and profits—two visible measures of success. In addition, the growth of multichannel retailing has created new opportunities such as website management and online merchandise procurement.[15]

Sales

College graduates from many disciplines are attracted to sales positions because of the increasingly professional nature of selling jobs and the many opportunities they can provide. A selling career offers benefits that are hard to match in any other field: (1) the opportunity for rapid advancement (into management or to new territories and accounts); (2) the potential for extremely attractive compensation; (3) the development of personal satisfaction, feelings of accomplishment, and increased self-confidence; and (4) independence—salespeople often have almost complete control over their time and activities.

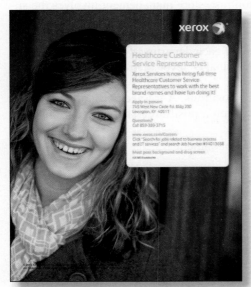

Xerox is well known for its sales career opportunities.

Employment opportunities in sales occupations are found in a wide variety of organizations, including insurance agencies, retailers, and financial service firms (see Figure C–3). In addition, many salespeople work as manufacturers' representatives for organizations that have selling responsibilities for several manufacturers.[16] Activities in sales jobs include *selling duties*, such as prospecting for customers, demonstrating the product, or quoting prices; *sales-support duties*, such as handling complaints and helping solve technical problems; and *nonselling duties*, such as preparing reports, attending sales meetings, and monitoring competitive activities. Salespeople who can deal with these varying activities and have empathy for customers are critical to a company's success. According to *Bloomberg Businessweek*, "Great salespeople feel for their customers. They understand their needs and pressures; they get the challenges of their business. They see every deal through the customer's eyes."[17]

One of the fastest areas of growth in sales is in the direct marketing industry. Interest in information technology, customer relationship management (CRM), and integrated marketing has increased the demand for

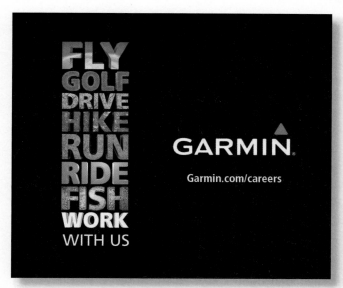

Garmin is an example of a company that encourages students to think about a career and the culture of the company.
Source: Garmin

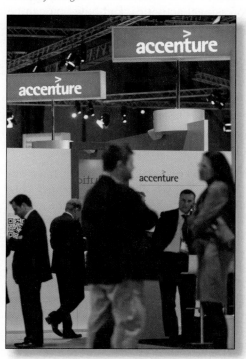

Accenture places thousands of consultants throughout the world.
© Angel Navarrete/Bloomberg via Getty Images

contact with customers. For many firms this means increasing the amount of time salespeople spend with clients; for other firms it means increased use of web conferencing technology; for still others it means sophisticated e-mail marketing. *Sales & Marketing Management* magazine's recent issue on sales technology describes the many new data analysis, social collaboration, and virtual meeting solutions that provide better relationships between salespeople and customers. Consultant Susan Aldrich observes that customers always say, "I want you to know about me and offer me things that are relevant to me."[18]

Marketing Research

Marketing researchers play important roles in many organizations today. In fact, *U.S. News & World Report* suggests that market research analyst positions are the number one job in business. They are responsible for obtaining, analyzing, and interpreting data to facilitate making marketing decisions. This means marketing researchers are basically problem solvers. Success in the area requires not only an understanding of statistical analysis, research methods, and programming, but also a broad base of marketing knowledge, writing and verbal presentation skills, and an ability to communicate with colleagues and clients. According to Stan Sthanunathan, vice president of marketing strategy and insights at Coca-Cola, a researcher's job "is to bring out opportunities."[19] Individuals who are inquisitive, methodical, analytical, and solution-oriented find the field particularly rewarding.

The responsibilities of the men and women currently working in the market research industry include defining the marketing problem, designing the questions, selecting the sample, collecting and analyzing the data, and, finally, reporting the results of the research. These jobs are available in three kinds of organizations. *Marketing research consulting firms* contract with large companies to provide research about their products or services.[20] *Advertising agencies* may provide research services to help clients with questions related to advertising and promotional problems. Finally, some companies have an *in-house research staff* to design and execute their research projects. Online marketing research, which is likely to become the most common form of marketing research in the near future, requires an understanding of new tools such as dynamic scripting, response validation, intercept sampling, instant messaging surveys, and online consumer panels.[21]

Although marketing researchers may start as assistants performing routine tasks, they quickly advance to broader responsibilities. Survey design, interviewing, report writing, and all aspects of the research process create a challenging career. In addition, research projects typically deal with such diverse problems as consumer motivation, pricing, forecasting, and competition in domestic and international markets. Successful candidates "like what they're doing and get excited over their work, whether it be listening to a focus group or running a complex data mining model," according to Carolyn Marconi, director of marketing research for the Vanguard Group, Inc.[22]

International Careers

Many of the careers just described can be found in international settings—in large multinational U.S. corporations, small- to medium-size firms with export business, and franchises. The international consulting firm Accenture, for example, has thousands of consultants around the world. Similarly, many franchises such as 7-Eleven, which has 47,621 foreign locations, are rapidly expanding outside the United States.[23] The changes in the European Union, Brazil, Russia, India, China, and other growing markets are likely to provide many opportunities for international careers.

Several methods of gaining international experience are possible. For example, some companies may alternate periods of work at domestic locations with assignments outside the United States. In addition, working for a firm with headquarters outside the United States at one of its local offices may be appealing. In many organizations, international experience has become a necessity for promotion and career advancement. "If you are going to succeed, an expatriate assignment is essential," says Eric Kraus of Gillette Co. in Boston.[24]

Applicants for international positions need language skills and an ability to adapt to different business models, management styles, and local practices. In addition, as multinational firms use worldwide communication technologies to build global teams of people who have never met, collaboration skills become increasingly important. Accenture uses instant messaging, voice, video and online meetings, and telepresence technology to help its 336,000 employees serve clients in more than 120 countries. Similarly, IBM helps thousands of its employees be a part of "innovation jams" with a team home page on the company intranet.[25]

THE JOB SEARCH PROCESS

Activities you should consider during your job search process include assessing yourself, identifying job opportunities, preparing your résumé and related correspondence, and going on job interviews.

Assessing Yourself

You must know your product—you—so that you can market yourself effectively to prospective employers. Consequently, a critical first step in your job search is conducting a self-inquiry or self-assessment. This activity involves understanding your interests, abilities, personality, preferences, and individual style. You must be confident that you know what work environment is best for you, what makes you happy, the balance you seek between personal and professional activities, and how you can be most effective at reaching your goals. This process helps ensure that you are matching your profile to the right job, or as business consultant and author Jim Collins explains, "Finding the right seat on the bus."[26]

Asking Key Questions   A self-analysis, in part, entails asking yourself some very important and difficult questions (see Figure C–4). It is critical that you respond to the questions honestly, because your answers ultimately will be used as a guide in your job selection.[27] A less-than-candid appraisal of yourself might result in a job mismatch.

Identifying Strengths and Weaknesses   After you have addressed the questions posed in Figure C–4, you are ready to identify your strengths and weaknesses. To do so, draw a vertical line down the middle of a sheet of paper and label one side of the paper "strengths" and the other side "weaknesses." Based on your answers to the questions, record your strong and weak points in their respective columns. Ideally, this cataloging should be done over a few days to give you adequate time to reflect on your attributes. In addition, you might seek input from others who know you well (such as parents, close relatives, friends, professors, or employers) and can offer more objective viewpoints. They might even evaluate you on the questions in Figure C–4, and you can compare the results with your own evaluation. Finally, to help identify additional

INTERESTS

- How do I like to spend my time?
- Do I enjoy working with people?
- Do I like working with tangible things?
- Do I enjoy working with data?
- Am I a member of many organizations?
- Do I enjoy physical activities?
- Do I like to read?

ABILITIES

- Am I adept at analysis?
- What are my hardware, software, and operating system skills?
- Do I have good verbal and written communication skills?
- What special talents do I have?
- At which abilities do I wish I were more adept?

EDUCATION

- How have my courses and extracurricular activities prepared me for a specific job?
- Which were my best subjects? My worst?
- Is my GPA a good indication of my academic ability? Why?
- Do I aspire to a graduate degree? Is this something I want to pursue before beginning my job? Or after?
- Why did I choose my major?

PERSONAL GOALS

- What are my short-term and long-term goals? Why?
- Am I career oriented, or do I have broader interests?
- What are my career goals?
- What jobs are likely to help me achieve my goals?
- What do I hope to be doing in 5 years? In 10 years?
- What do I want out of life?
- What work–life balance do I prefer?

PERSONALITY

- What are my good and bad traits?
- Am I competitive?
- Do I work well with others?
- Am I outspoken?
- Am I a leader or a follower?
- Do I work well under pressure?
- Do I work quickly, or am I methodical?
- Do I get along well with others?
- Am I ambitious?
- Do I work well independently of others?

DESIRED JOB ENVIRONMENT

- Am I willing to relocate? Why?
- Do I have a geographical preference? Why?
- Would I mind traveling in my job?
- Do I have to work for a large or nationally known firm to be satisfied?
- Must my job offer rapid promotion opportunities?
- If I could design my own job, what characteristics would it have?
- How important is high initial salary to me?

EXPERIENCE

- What previous jobs have I held? What were my responsibilities in each job?
- What internships or co-op positions have I held? What were my responsibilities?
- What volunteer positions have I held? What were my responsibilities?
- Were any of my jobs or positions applicable to positions I may be seeking? How?
- What did I like the most about my previous jobs? What did I like the least?
- If I had it to do over again, would I work in these jobs? Why?

FIGURE C–4

Questions to ask in your self-analysis.

strengths, you might purchase a copy of the very popular book *StrengthsFinder 2.0* by Tom Rath. A hypothetical list of strengths and weaknesses is shown in Figure C–5.

What skills are most important? The answer, of course, varies by occupation and employer. Recent studies, however, suggest that problem-solving skills, communication skills, interpersonal skills, analytical and computer skills, and leadership skills are all valued by employers. Personal characteristics employers seek in a job candidate include honesty, integrity, motivation, initiative, self-confidence, flexibility, and enthusiasm. Finally, most employers also look for work experience, internship experience, or co-op experience. Internships "give you hands-on experience and make you a stronger job candidate," explains Arlene Hill, director of career development at American University's Kogod School of Business. Candidates who are pursuing digital marketing positions must have skills related to search engine optimization (SEO), search engine marketing (SEM), mobile marketing, social media, and content management.[28]

Taking Job-Related Tests   Personality and vocational interest tests, provided by many colleges and universities, can give you other ideas about yourself. After tests have been administered and scored, test takers meet with testing service counselors to

FIGURE C–5

Hypothetical list of a job candidate's strengths and weaknesses.

Strengths	Weaknesses
I enjoy being with people.	I am very demanding of team members.
I am an avid reader.	I have minimal work experience.
I have good communication skills.	I have a mediocre GPA.
I am involved in many extracurricular. activities	I am sometimes impatient.
I work well with others.	I resent close supervision.
I work well independently.	I work methodically (slowly).
I am honest and dependable.	I will not relocate.
I am willing to travel in the job.	I procrastinate unless there is a deadline.
I am a good problem solver.	I lack a customer orientation.
I have a good sense of humor.	I have poor technical skills.

discuss the results. Test results generally suggest jobs for which students have an inclination. The most common tests at the college level are the Strong Interest Inventory and the Campbell Interest and Skill Survey. Some counseling centers and career coaches also use the Myers-Briggs® Type Indicator personality inventory and the Peoplemap™ assessments to help identify professions you may enjoy.[29] If you have not already done so, you may wish to see whether your school offers such testing services.

Campus career centers are excellent sources of job information.
© GIPhotoStock Z/Alamy

Identifying Your Job Opportunities

To identify and analyze the job market, you must conduct some marketing research to determine what industries *and* companies offer promising job opportunities that relate to the results of your self-analysis. Several sources that can help in your search are discussed next.

Career Services Office   Your campus career services office is an excellent source of job information. Personnel in that office can (1) inform you about which companies will be recruiting on campus; (2) alert you to unexpected job openings; (3) advise you about short-term and long-term career prospects; (4) offer advice on résumé construction; (5) assess your interviewing strengths and weaknesses; and (6) help you evaluate a job offer. Career services offices are also expanding to help students connect with companies that might not recruit on campus.[30] In addition, the office usually contains a variety of written materials focusing on different industries and companies and tips on job hunting.

Monster.com is a popular employment website where students can match their skills and interests with job openings.
Source: Monster.com

Online Career and Employment Services   Many companies no longer make frequent on-campus visits. Instead, they may use the many online services available to advertise an employment opportunity or to search for candidate information. The National Association of Colleges and Employers, for example, maintains a site called NACElink Network (www.nacelink.com). Similarly, Monster.com and Careerbuilder.com are online databases of employment ads, candidate résumés, and other career-related information. Some of the information resources include career guidance, a cover letter library, occupational profiles, résumé templates, and networking services.[31] Employers may contact students directly when the candidate's qualifications meet their specific job requirements. The advantage of this system for students is that regardless of the size or location of the campus they are attending, many companies have access to their résumé. Some job boards even allow applicants to post audio and video clips of themselves. One advantage for recruiters is that some of the job boards utilize software for performing background verification.[32] Your school's career center may also have a home page that offers online job search information and links to other Internet sites.

Library   The public or college library can provide you with reference material that, among other things, describes successful firms and their operations, defines the content of various jobs, and forecasts job opportunities. For example, *Fortune* publishes a list of the 1,000 largest U.S. and global companies and their respective sales and profits, and Dun & Bradstreet publishes directories of more than 26 million companies in the United States. The *Occupational Outlook Handbook* is an annual publication of the U.S. Department of Labor that provides projections for specific job prospects, as well as information pertaining to those jobs. A librarian can indicate reference materials that will be most pertinent to *your* job search.

Advertisements   Help-wanted advertisements provide an overview of what is happening in the job market. Local (particularly Sunday editions) and college newspapers, trade press (such as *Marketing News* or *Advertising Age*), and business magazines contain classified advertisement sections that generally have job opening announcements, often for entry-level positions. Reviewing the want ads can help you identify what kinds of positions are available and their requirements and job titles, which firms offer certain kinds of jobs, and levels of compensation.

Employment Agencies   An employment agency can make you aware of several job opportunities very quickly because of its large number of job listings available through computer databases. Many agencies specialize in a particular field (such as sales and marketing). The advantages of using an agency include that it (1) reduces the cost of a job search by bringing applicants and employers together, (2) often has exclusive job listings available only by working through the agency, (3) performs much of the job search for you, and (4) tries to find a job that is compatible with your qualifications and interests.[33] In the past, some employment agencies have engaged in questionable business practices, so check with the Better Business Bureau (www.bbb.org) or your business contacts to determine the quality of the various agencies.

Personal Contacts and Networking   An important source of job information that students often overlook is their personal contacts. People you know often may know of job opportunities, so you should advise them that you're looking for a job. Relatives and friends might aid your job search. Instructors you know well and business contacts can provide a wealth of information about potential jobs and even help arrange an interview with a prospective employer. They may also help arrange *informational interviews* with employers that do not have immediate openings. These interviews allow you to collect information about an industry or an employer and give you an advantage if a position does become available. It is a good idea to leave your résumé with all your personal contacts so they can pass it along to those who might be in need of your services.

Student organizations (such as the student chapter of the American Marketing Association and Pi Sigma Epsilon, the professional sales fraternity) may be sources of job opportunities, particularly if they are involved with the business community. Local chapters of professional business organizations (such as the American Marketing Association and Sales and Marketing Executives International) also can provide job information; contacting their chapter president is a first step in seeking assistance from these organizations. Creating and maintaining a network of professional contacts is one of the most important career-building activities you can undertake.[34]

There are many popular social networking sites available to job seekers. LinkedIn, for example, has 300 million users, including recruiters. Other sites include Plaxo, Twitter, Jobster, Facebook, Craigslist, MyWorkster, VisualCV, and JobFox. Some of the sites allow users to create and post a traditional résumé while others facilitate personalized web pages with video, audio, images, and even work samples. BranchOut.com can link to Facebook and pull education and work history from pages to help identify a network of friends who have worked for a specific company. Even Pinterest has job-related and personal-brand pinboards. Using all or many of these sites provides greater exposure. Remember, however, to be consistent in the image and information presented online.[35]

State Employment Office State employment offices have listings of job opportunities in their state and counselors to help arrange a job interview for you. Although state employment offices perform functions similar to employment agencies, they differ in listing only job opportunities in their state and providing their services free of charge.

Direct Contact Another means of obtaining job information is direct contact—personally communicating to prospective employers (either by mail, e-mail, or in person) that you would be interested in pursuing job opportunities with them. Often you may not even know whether jobs are available in these firms. If you correspond with the companies in writing, a letter of introduction and an attached résumé should serve as your initial form of communication. One way to make direct contact with companies is to attend a career or job fair. These events allow many employers, recruiters, and prospective job seekers to meet in one location.[36] Your goals in direct contact are to create a positive impression and, ultimately, to arrange a job interview.

Writing Your Résumé

A résumé is a document that communicates to prospective employers who you are. An employer reading a résumé is looking for a snapshot of your qualifications to decide if you should be invited to a job interview. It is imperative that you design a résumé that presents you in a favorable light and allows you to get to that next important step.[37] Personnel in your career services office can provide assistance in designing résumés.

The Résumé Itself A well-constructed résumé generally contains up to nine major sections: (1) identification (name, address, telephone number, and e-mail address); (2) job or career objective; (3) educational background; (4) honors and awards; (5) work experience or history; (6) skills or capabilities (that pertain to a particular kind of job for which you may be interviewing); (7) extracurricular activities; (8) personal interests; and (9) personal references.[38]

There is no universally accepted format for a résumé, but three are more frequently used: chronological, functional, and targeted. A *chronological* format presents your work experience and education according to the time sequence in which they occurred (i.e., in chronological order). If you have had several jobs or attended several schools, this approach is useful to highlight what you have done. With a *functional* format, you group your experience into skill categories that emphasize your strengths. This option is particularly appropriate if you have no experience or only minimal experience related to your chosen field. A *targeted* format focuses on the capabilities you have for a specific job. This alternative is desirable if you know what job you want and are qualified for it.

In any of the formats, if possible, you should include quantitative information about your accomplishments and experience, such as "increased sales revenue by 20 percent" for the year you managed a retail clothing store. A résumé that illustrates the chronological format is shown in Figure C–6.[39]

There are several other important considerations as you prepare your résumé. First, remember that your résumé is a marketing tool and its purpose is to present you for a particular job or role. Therefore, anticipate that you will have more than one version of your résumé, or more likely, a customized résumé for each job opportunity you are considering. Second, although traditional printed versions of résumés can be created with visually appealing fonts and graphics, a simpler, digital version of your résumé is also a necessity. A digital résumé should use a popular font (e.g., Times New Roman) and relatively large

FIGURE C–6

A chronological résumé presents your education and work experience in the sequence in which they occurred.

Sally Winter

Campus address (until 6/1/2016):	Home address:
Elm Street Apartments #2B	123 Front Street
College Town, Ohio 44042	Teaneck, NJ 07666
Mobile phone: (555) 424-1648	Phone: (555) 836-4995
Email: swinter@osu.stu.edu	
LinkedIn: www.linkedin.com/in/sallywinter	

Education

B.S. in Business Administration, Ohio State University, 2016, cum laude
3.3 overall GPA—3.6 GPA in major

Work Experience

Paid for 70 percent of my college expenses through the following part-time and summer jobs:

Summer 2015 Legal Secretary, Smith, Lee & Jones, Attorneys at Law, New York, NY
- Took dictation and transcribed tapes of legal proceedings
- Typed contracts and other legal documents
- Reorganized client files for easier access
- Answered the phone and screened calls for the partners

2013–2015 Academic Years Salesclerk, College Varsity Shop, College Town, Ohio
- Helped customers with buying decisions
- Arranged stock and helped with window displays
- Assisted with website design and content management
- Took over responsibilities of store manager when she was on vacation or ill

2010–2013 Assistant Manager, Treasure Place Gift Shop, Teaneck, NJ
- Supervised two salesclerks
- Helped select merchandise at trade shows
- Handled daily accounting
- Worked comfortably under pressure during busy seasons

Campus Activities

- Elected captain of the women's varsity tennis team for two years
- Worked as a reporter and night editor on campus newspaper for two years
- Elected historian for Mortar Board chapter, a senior women's honorary society

Computer Skills

- Microsoft Office, Google Drive, Wordpress, basic HTML5

Personal Interests

- Collecting antique clocks, listening to jazz, swimming

References Available on Request

font size (e.g., 10–14 pt.) and avoid italic text, shading, or underlining. Finally, your résumé should accommodate employers who use applicant tracking software (ATS) to search for keywords. You should identify potential keywords for each job posting and include them within your experience, accomplishments, and education descriptions.[40]

Related to the use of technology, video résumés are becoming increasingly popular as a means for job seekers to communicate their personality to employers with job opportunities in customer-facing roles such as sales and public relations. In addition, don't forget that many employers may visit social networking sites such as Facebook, or may simply "Google" your name, to see what comes up. Review your online profiles before you start your job search to provide a positive and accurate image![41]

Letter Accompanying a Résumé   The letter accompanying a résumé, or cover letter, serves as the job candidate's introduction. As a result, it must gain the attention

FIGURE C–7

A sample letter
accompanying a
résumé provides
the job candidate's
introduction.

Sally Winter
Elm Street Apartments, #2B
College Town, Ohio 44042
January 31, 2016

Mr. J. B. Jones
Sales Manager
Hilltop Manufacturing Company
Minneapolis, MN 55406

Dear Mr. Jones:

Dr. William Johnson, Professor of Business Administration at the Ohio State University, recently suggested that I write to you concerning your opening and my interest in a sales position. With a B.S. degree in business administration and courses in personal selling and sales management, I am confident that I could make a positive contribution to your firm.

During the past four years, I have been a salesclerk in a clothing store and an assistant manager in a gift shop. These two positions required my performing a variety of duties including selling, purchasing, stocking, and supervising. As a result, I have developed an appreciation for the viewpoints of the customer, salesperson, and management. Given my background and high energy level, I feel that I am particularly well qualified to assume a sales position in your company.

My enclosed résumé better highlights my education and experience. My extracurricular activities should strengthen and support my abilities to serve as a sales representative.

I am eager to talk with you because I feel I can demonstrate to you why I am a strong candidate for the position. I have friends in Minneapolis with whom I could stay on weekends, so Fridays or Mondays would be ideal for an appointment. I will call you in a week to see if we can arrange a mutually convenient time for a meeting. I am hopeful that your schedule will allow this.

Thank you for your kind consideration. If you would like some additional information, please feel free to contact me at (555) 424-1648. I look forward to talking with you.

Sincerely,

Sally Winter

enclosure

and interest of the reader or it will fail to give the incentive to examine the résumé carefully. In designing a letter to accompany your résumé, address the following issues:[42]

- Address the letter to a specific person.
- Identify the position for which you are applying and how you heard of it.
- Indicate why you are applying for the position.
- Summarize your most significant credentials and qualifications.
- Refer the reader to the enclosed résumé.
- Request a personal interview, and advise the reader when and where you can be reached.

A sample letter comprising these six factors is presented in Figure C–7.

Interviewing for Your Job

The job interview is a conversation between a prospective employer and a job candidate that focuses on determining whether the employer's needs can be satisfied by the candidate's qualifications. The interview is a "make or break" situation: If the interview goes well, you have increased your chances of receiving a job offer; if it goes poorly, you probably will be eliminated from further consideration.

Preparing for a Job Interview To be successful in a job interview, you must prepare for it so you can exhibit professionalism and indicate to a prospective employer that you are serious about the job. When preparing for the interview, several critical activities need to be performed.

Before the interview, gather facts about the industry, the prospective employer, and the job. Relevant information might include the general description for the occupation; the firm's products or services; the firm's size, number of employees, and financial and competitive position; the requirements of the position; and the name and personality of the interviewer. Obtaining this information will provide you with additional insight into the firm and help you formulate questions to ask the interviewer. This information might be gleaned, for example, from corporate annual reports, *The Wall Street Journal,* Moody's manuals, Standard & Poor's *Register of Corporations, Directors, and Executives, The Directory of Corporate Affiliations,* selected issues of *Bloomberg Businessweek,* or trade publications. You should also study the LinkedIn profiles, Twitter feeds, and blogs of the people you'll be meeting. If information is not readily available, you could call the company and indicate that you wish to obtain some information about the firm before your interview.[43]

Preparation for the job interview should also involve role playing or pretending that you are in the "hot seat" being interviewed. Before role playing, anticipate questions interviewers may pose and how you might address them (see Figure C–8). Do not memorize your answers, though, because you want to appear spontaneous, yet logical

FIGURE C–8

Anticipate questions frequently asked by interviewers and practice how you might respond.

Interviewer Questions

1. How would you describe yourself?
2. What do you consider to be your greatest strengths and weaknesses?
3. Describe your most rewarding college experiences.
4. What do you see yourself doing in 5 years? In 10 years?
5. What are three important leadership qualities that you have demonstrated?
6. What do you really want out of life?
7. What are your long-range and short-range career goals?
8. Why did you choose your college major?
9. In which extracurricular activities did you participate? Why?
10. What jobs have you enjoyed the most? The least? Why?
11. How has your previous work experience prepared you for a marketing career?
12. Why do you want to work for our company?
13. What qualifications do you think a person needs to be successful in a company like ours?
14. Describe a creative idea you produced that led to the success of a project.
15. What criteria are you using to evaluate the company for which you hope to work?
16. Describe a project where you worked as part of a team.
17. What can I tell you about our company?
18. Are you willing to relocate?
19. Are you willing to spend at least six months as a trainee?
20. Why should we hire you?

FIGURE C–9

Interviewees should develop questions about topics that are important to them.

Interviewer Questions
1. Why would a job candidate want to work for your firm?
2. What makes your firm different from its competitors?
3. What is the company's promotion policy?
4. Describe the typical first-year assignment for this job.
5. How is an employee evaluated?
6. What are the opportunities for personal growth?
7. Do you have a training program?
8. What are the company's plans for future growth?
9. What is the retention rate of people in the position for which I am interviewing?
10. How can you use my skills?
11. Why is this position vacant?
12. How would you describe the ideal candidate?
13. Why do you enjoy working for your firm?
14. How much responsibility would I have in this job?
15. What is the corporate culture in your firm?

and intelligent. Nonetheless, it is helpful to practice how you might respond to the questions. In addition, develop questions you might ask the interviewer that are important and of concern to you (see Figure C–9). "It's an opportunity to show the recruiter how smart you are," comments one recruiter.[44]

When role playing, you and someone with whom you feel comfortable should engage in a mock interview. Afterward, ask the stand-in interviewer to candidly appraise your interview content and style. You may wish to make a video of the mock interview.

Before the job interview you should attend to several details. Know the exact time and place of the interview; write them down—do not rely on your memory. If your initial interview is a video interview, test your Internet connection, software (e.g., skype), camera, and lighting.[45] Get the full company name straight. Find out what the interviewer's name is and how to pronounce it. Have a notepad and a pen at the interview in case you need to record anything. Make certain that your appearance is clean, neat, professional, and conservative. And be punctual; arriving tardy to a job interview gives you an appearance of being unreliable.

View the interview as a conversation between the prospective employer and you.

© White Packert/The Image Bank/Getty Images

Succeeding in Your Job Interview You have done your homework, and at last the moment arrives and it is time for the interview. Although you may experience some apprehension, view the interview as a conversation between the prospective employer and you. Both of you are in the interview to look over the other party, to see whether there might be a good match. When you meet the interviewer, greet him or her by name, be cheerful, smile, and maintain good eye contact (in the case of a video interview, look at the camera!). Take your lead from the interviewer at the outset. Sit down after the interviewer has offered you a seat. Sit up straight in your chair, and look alert and interested at all times. Appear relaxed, not tense. Be enthusiastic.

During the interview, be yourself. If you try to behave in a manner that is different from the real you, your attempt may be transparent to the interviewer or you may ultimately get the job but discover that you aren't suited for it. However, remember that the interview is not the time to tweet, text, or take a telephone call.[46] In addition to

© Jeff Shesol

assessing how well your skills match those of the job, the interviewer will probably try to assess your long-term interest in the firm.

As the interview comes to a close, leave it on a positive note. Thank the interviewer for his or her time and the opportunity to discuss employment opportunities. If you are still interested in the job, express this to the interviewer. The interviewer will normally tell you what the employer's next step is—probably a visit to the company.[47] Rarely will a job offer be made at the end of the initial interview. If it is and you want the job, accept the offer; if there is any doubt in your mind about the job, however, ask for time to consider the offer.

Following Up on Your Job Interview After your interview, send a thank-you note to the interviewer and indicate whether you are still interested in the job. If you want to continue pursuing the job, polite persistence may help you get it. The thank-you note is a gesture of appreciation and a way of maintaining visibility with the interviewer. (Remember the adage, "Out of sight, out of mind.") Even if the interview did not go well, the thank-you note may impress the interviewer so much that his or her opinion of you changes.

After you have sent your thank-you note, you may wish to call the prospective employer to determine the status of the hiring decision. If the interviewer told you when you would hear from the employer, make your telephone call *after* this date (assuming, of course, that you have not yet heard from the employer); if the interviewer did not tell you when you would be contacted, make your telephone call a week or so after you have sent your thank-you note. While e-mail is a common form of communication today, it is often viewed as less personal than a letter or telephone call, so be confident that e-mail is preferred before using it to correspond with the interviewer.[48]

As you conduct your follow-up, be persistent but polite. If you are too eager, one of two things could happen to prevent you from getting the job: The employer might feel that you are a nuisance and would exhibit such behavior on the job, or the employer may perceive that you are desperate for the job and thus are not a viable candidate.

Handling Rejection You have put your best efforts into your job search. You developed a well-designed résumé and prepared carefully for the job interview. Even the interview appears to have gone well. Nevertheless, a prospective employer may send you a rejection letter. ("We are sorry that our needs and your superb qualifications don't match.") Although you will probably be disappointed, not all interviews lead to a job offer because there normally are more candidates than there are positions available.

If you receive a rejection letter, you should think back through the interview. What appeared to go right? What went wrong? Perhaps personnel from your career services office can shed light on the problem, particularly if they are accustomed to having interviewers rate each interviewee. Try to learn lessons to apply in future interviews. Keep interviewing and gaining interview experience; your persistence will eventually pay off.

SELECTED SOURCES OF MARKETING CAREER INFORMATION

The following is a selected list of marketing information sources that you should find useful during your academic studies and professional career.

Business and Marketing Publications

Paul Farris, Neil Bendle, Phillip Pfeifer, and David J. Reibstein, *Marketing Metrics: The Manager's Guide to Measuring Marketing Performance,* 3rd ed. (New Jersey: Pearson, Inc., 2015). This book provides readers with a system for organizing marketing metrics into models and dashboards that translate numbers into management insight.

Eric J. Forte, Cassandra J. Hartnett, and Andrea L. Sevetson, *Fundamentals of Government Information: Mining, Finding, Evaluating, and Using Government Resources* (New York, NY: Neal-Schuman Publishers, Inc., 2011). This manual provides the background knowledge and tools needed to access online and print government information resources. Key topics include consumer information, census data, and summaries from the *Statistical Abstract of the United States.*

Paul Hague, Nick Hague, and Carol-Ann Morgan, *Market Research in Practice: How to Get Greater Insight from Your Market* (Sterling, VA: Kogan Publishers, 2013). This book offers a practical guide to the basics of marketing research. Filled with real-world applications and important details, the book presents a step-by-step approach to conducting primary research, from planning a project through execution, analysis, and presentation of findings.

Linda D. Hall, *Encyclopedia of Business Information Sources,* 32nd ed. (Detroit: Gale Group, 2015). A bibliographic guide to over 25,000 citations covering more than 1,100 primary subjects of interest to business personnel.

Hoover's Handbook of World Business (Austin, TX: Mergent, Inc. 2015). A detailed source of information about companies outside the United States, including firms from Canada, Europe, Japan, China, India, and Taiwan.

Marketing Dictionary (American Marketing Association). This online resource contains definitions of marketing phrases and terms and is continually adding new terms to keep marketers up to date. See https://www.ama.org/resources/Pages/Dictionary.aspx.

Jadish Sheth and Naresh Malhotra, eds., *International Encyclopedia of Marketing* (West Sussex: John Wiley & Sons Ltd., 2011). This six-volume reference contains 360 entries from over 500 global experts. Entries are arranged alphabetically within each subject volume, and each volume carries an index.

Kirk Tyson, *The Complete Guide to Competitive Intelligence* (Lees Summit, MO: Leading Edge Publications, 2010). This book provides detailed instructions on how to establish networks, conduct interviews, and gather and analyze intelligence to create a comprehensive competitive intelligence process.

Career Planning Publications

© Studio Works/Alamy

Paul Bailo. *The Essential Digital Interview Handbook: Lights, Camera, Skype* (Pompton Plains, NJ: Career Press, 2014).

Richard N. Bolles, *What Color Is Your Parachute? 2016: A Practical Manual for Job-Hunters and Career-Changers* (Berkeley, CA: Ten Speed Press, 2015). A companion workbook is also available. See www.jobhuntersbible.com.

Reid Hoffman and Ben Casnocha, *The Start-Up of You: Adapt to the Future, Invest in Yourself, and Transform Your Career* (New York: Crown Publishing Group, 2012).

Miriam Salpeter, *Social Networking for Career Success* (New York, NY: Learning Express, 2013).

Louis R. VanArsdale and Jessica Li, *Government Jobs in America 2015* (New York: Community Publications, and Government Job News, 2014).

Martin Yate, *Knock 'em Dead 2015: The Ultimate Job Search Guide* (Holbrook, MA: Adams Media Corporation, 2014).

Websites: Resources on job searches, résumé writing, interviewing, and U.S. and international job postings:

www.accessalesjobs.com	www.usajobs.gov
www.jobbankinfo.org	www.simplyhired.com
www.truecareers.com	www.monster.com
www.careerXroads.com	www.jobbankusa.com
www.careers.org	www.studentcentral.com
www.careerbuilder.com	www.vault.com
www.careers-in-marketing.com	www.wetfeet.com
www.idealist.org	www.indeed.com

Selected Periodicals

© Mike Hruby

Ad Week, Nielsen Business Media, Inc. (weekly). See www.adweek.com. (subscription rates: $99 per year, print and iPad; $79 iPad edition)

Advertising Age, Crain Communications, Inc. (weekly). See www.adage.com. (subscription rate: $109 per year)

Barron's, Dow Jones & Co., Inc. (weekly). See http://online.barrons.com/home-page. (subscription rate: $12.49/month)

Bloomberg Businessweek, McGraw-Hill Companies (weekly). See www.businessweek.com. (subscription rate: $39.97)

Business Horizons, Indiana University c/o Elsevier Science Publishing (bimonthly). See www.elsevier.com. (subscription rate: $120/year)

Chain Store Age, Lebhar-Friedman, Inc. (monthly). See www.chainstoreage.com. (subscription rate: $150)

eCommerce Times, ECT News Network, Inc. (daily). See www.ecommercetimes.com.

Forbes, Forbes Inc. See www.forbes.com. (subscription rate: $20/year)

Harvard Business Review, Harvard University (monthly). See www.hbr.org. (subscription rates: $89 online and print; $99 print, online, and tablet)

Industrial Marketing Management, Elsevier Science publishing (8 issues). See www.elsevier.com. (subscription rate: $167)

International Journal of Electronic Commerce, M. E. Sharpe Publishing (quarterly). See http://www.ijec-web.org/. (subscription rate: $99)

Journal of Consumer Marketing, Emerald Group Publishing, Ltd. (7 issues). See www.emeraldinsight.com. (subscription rates: $3,549; $32 for 30-day access)

Journal of Consumer Research, University of Chicago Press (quarterly). See www.journals.uchicago.edu. (subscription rates: $152 online; $172 print and online; student $25 print and online)

Journal of Interactive Marketing, Direct Marketing Educational Foundation (quarterly). See www.elsevier.com. (subscription rate: $313)

Journal of International Marketing, American Marketing Association (quarterly). See www.marketingpower.com. (subscription rates: $120 print; $145 print and online)

© Mike Hruby

Journal of Marketing, American Marketing Association (quarterly). See www.marketingpower.com. (subscription rates: $135 print; $162 print and online)

Journal of Marketing Communications, Routledge Publishing (five times per year). See www.tandfonline.com. (subscription rate: $184)

Journal of Marketing Education, Sage Publications (three times per year). See www.sagepub.com. (subscription rate: $109)

Journal of Marketing Research, American Marketing Association (bimonthly). See www.marketingpower.com. (subscription rates: $135 print; $162 print and online)

Journal of Personal Selling and Sales Management, American Marketing Association (quarterly). See www.jpssm.org. (subscription rate: $79)

Journal of Public Policy and Marketing, American Marketing Association (semiannually). See www.marketingpower.com. (subscription rates: $90 print; $115 print and online)

Journal of Retailing, Elsevier Science Publishing (quarterly). See www.elsevier.com. (subscription rate: $173)

Journal of the Academy of Marketing Science, Springer Science and Business Media LLC (six issues). See www.springer.com/jams. (subscription rate: $193)

Marketing Education Review, CTC Press (three times per year). See www.marketingeducationreview.com. (subscription rate: $60)

Marketing Health Services, American Marketing Association (quarterly). See www.marketingpower.com. (subscription rate: $100)

© Mike Hruby

Marketing Insights, American Marketing Association (quarterly). See www.marketingpower.com. (subscription rate: $100)

Marketing News, American Marketing Association (biweekly). See www.marketingpower.com. (subscription rates: $85 nonmembers; $53 members; $65 students)

Media Week, Quantum Business Media (weekly). See www.mediaweek.co.uk. (subscription rate: $200)

PR Week, Haymarket Media (weekly). See www.prweek.com/us. (subscription rate: $298)

Sales and Marketing Management, Lakewood Media Group, LLC. See www.salesandmarketing.com. (subscription rate: free)

Stores, National Retail Federation (weekly). See www.nrf.com or www.stores.org. (subscription rates: $120 for nonmembers; free for members)

The Wall Street Journal Interactive, Dow Jones & Company, Inc. (weekly). See www.wsj.com. (subscription rates: $103 online; $119 print; $140 online and print)

Professional and Trade Associations

American Advertising Federation
1101 Vermont Ave. N.W., Suite 500
Washington, DC 20005-6306
(202) 898-0089
www.aaf.org

American Association of Advertising Agencies
1065 Avenue of the Americas
New York, NY 10018
(212) 682-2500
www.aaaa.org

American e-Commerce Association
2346 Camp St.
New Orleans, LA 70130
(504) 495-1748
www.aeaus.com

Courtesy of American Marketing Association

American Marketing Association
645 N. Michigan Ave., Suite 800
Chicago, IL 60611
(800) AMA-1150
www.marketingpower.com

American Society of Transportation and Logistics
P.O. Box 3363
Warrenton, VA 20188
(202) 580-7270
www.astl.org

Business Marketing Association
1445 N. North Park Ave.
Chicago, IL 60610
(630) 544-5054
www.marketing.org

Direct Marketing Association
1120 Avenue of the Americas
New York, NY 10036-6700
(212) 768-7277
www.the-dma.org

Direct Selling Association
1667 K Street N.W., Suite 1100
Washington, DC 20006
(202) 452-8866
www.dmachoice.org

International Franchise Association
1501 K Street N.W., Suite 350
Washington, DC 20005
(202) 628-8000
www.franchise.org

International Newspaper Marketing Association
1200 Main St. #2611
Dallas, TX 75202
(214) 373-9111
www.inma.org

Internet Marketing Association
10 Mar Del Rey
San Clemente, CA 92673
(949) 443-9300
www.imanetwork.org

Marketing Research Association
110 National Dr.
Glastonbury, CT 06033-1212
(860) 682-1000
www.mra-net.org

Marketing Science Institute
1000 Massachusetts Ave.
Cambridge, MA 02138-5396
(617) 491-2060
www.msi.org

Mobile Marketing Association
41 E. 11th St
11th floor
New York, NY 10003
(646) 257-4515
www.mmaglobal.com/

National Retail Federation
325 7th St. N.W., Suite 1100
Washington, DC 20004
(800) NRF-HOW2
www.nrf.com

Product Development and Management Association
15000 Commerce Parkway, Suite C
Mount Laurel, NJ 08054
(800) 232-5241
www.pdma.org
Professional Association of Customer Engagement
8500 Keystone Crossing, Suite 480
Indianapolis, IN 46240
(317) 816-9336
http://www.paceassociation.com/
Public Relations Society of America
33 Maiden Lane
New York, NY 10038-5150
(212) 460-1400
www.prsa.org

Sales and Marketing Executive International
P.O. Box 1390
Suma, WA 98295-1390
(312) 893-0751
www.smei.org
Society for Marketing Professional Services
44 Canal Center Plaza, Suite 444
Alexandria, VA 22314
(800) 292-7667
www.smps.org
Society of Competitive Intelligence Professionals
7550 IH 10 W., Suite 400
San Antonio, TX 78229
(703) 739-0696
https://www.scip.org/

Appendix Notes

1. Joann S. Lublin, "The Year Ahead: Your 'Personal Brand' May Need Some Work," *The Wall Street Journal,* January 2, 2014, p. B4; Catherine Kaputa, *You Are a Brand! How Smart People Brand Themselves for Business Success* (Boston, MA: Nicholas Brealey Publishing, 2010); Diane Brady, "Creating Brand You," *Bloomberg Businessweek,* August 22, 2007, pp. 72–73; and Denny E. McCorkle, Joe F. Alexander, and Memo F. Diriker, "Developing Self-Marketing Skills for Student Career Success," *Journal of Marketing Education,* Spring 1992, pp. 57–67.

2. Debra Wheatman, "Seven Tips for Conducting a Targeted Career Campaign," *Marketing News,* January 2015, p. 62; Morag Cuddeford-Jones, "Managing a Marketing Career Is Academic," *Marketing Week,* January 16, 2013; Linda J. Popky, *Marketing Your Career: Positioning, Packaging and Promoting Yourself for Success* (Woodside Business Press, 2009); Marianne E. Green, "Marketing Yourself: From Student to Professional," *Job Choices for Business & Liberal Arts Students,* 50th ed., 2007, pp. 30–31; and Joanne Cleaver, "Find a Job through Self-Promotion," *Marketing News,* January 31, 2000, pp. 12, 16.

3. Michelle Boggs, "Hiring Trends for the Year Ahead," *Marketing News,* April 2015, p. 63; Kevin Cochrane, "The 21st Century Marketer," *Marketing News,* March 30, 2011, p. 22; and John N. Frank, "Stand Out from the Crowd, Landing a Marketing Job Today Means Touting Your Specialty and Staying Positive," *Marketing News,* January 30, 2009, p. 22.

4. *Job Outlook 2015* (Bethlehem, PA: National Association of Colleges and Employers, November 2014); www.Monster.com, accessed July 12, 2015; and Milton Moskowitz and Robert Levering, "100 Best Companies to Work For," *Fortune,* March 15, 2015, pp. 141–54.

5. Nicholas Basta, "The Wide World of Marketing," *BW's Guide to Careers,* February–March 1984, pp. 70–72.

6. Anjali Bansal, David S. Daniel, John T. Mitchell, and Patrick B. Walsh, "The CEO Today: Sharing Leadership at the Top," *Research & Insight,* SpencerStuart, March 2013, http://www.spencerstuart.com/research/articles/1642/; Jonathan Harper and Frank Birkel, "From CMO to CEO: The Route to the Top," *Research & Insight,* SpencerStuart, December 2009, http://www.spencerstuart.com/research/articles/1329/; and "Leading CEOs: A Statistical Snapshot of S&P 500 Leaders," *Research & Insight,* SpencerStuart, December 2008, http://www.spencerstuart.com/research/ceo/975/.

7. Salary Survey (Bethlehem, PA: National Association of Colleges and Employers, Spring 2015), pp. 6, 14.

8. "Advertising, Promotions, and Marketing Managers," *Occupational Outlook Handbook,* 2014–15 Edition (Washington, DC: U.S. Department of Labor), http://www.bls.gov/ooh/management/advertising-promotions-and-marketing-managers.htm, accessed July 14, 2015.

9. Matthew Creamer, "P&G Primes Its Pinpoint Marketing," *Advertising Age,* May 7, 2007.

10. "P&G Profiles," P&G website, http://www.experiencepg.com/our-people/profiles.aspx, accessed June 3, 2013.

11. "Wholesale and Manufacturing Sales Representatives," *Occupational Outlook Handbook,* 2014–15 Edition (Washington, DC: U.S. Department of Labor), http://www.bls.gov/ooh/sales/wholesale-and-manufacturing-sales-representatives.htm#tab-6, accessed July 14, 2015.

12. "Freedom to Explore Different Career Paths Makes for a More Well-Rounded, Dedicated Staff," *Advertising Age,* March 26, 2012, p. 14; S. William Pattis, *Careers in Advertising* (New York: McGraw-Hill, 2004).

13. "13 Professional Skills for a Rewarding Career in Digital Marketing," *Business2Community.com,* January 9, 2013; Sarah Lundy, "Job Opportunities Multiply in Social Media: With More People Connecting Online, Businesses Rush to Join the Party," *Buffalo News,* January 10, 2011, p. C1; Duane Forrester, "Search Can Offer Jobs, Decent Salaries," *Advertising Age,* May 26, 2008, p. 28; and Tanya Lewis, "Talent in Demand," *PR Week Career Guide,* 2006, pp. 4–6.

14. Ellen Davis, "The Increasing Scope of Retail Careers" *Stores Magazine,* July 31, 2014, p. 73; and Roslyn Dolber, *Opportunities in Retailing Careers* (New York: McGraw-Hill, 2008).

15. Peter Coy, "Help Wanted," *Bloomberg Businessweek,* May 11, 2009, pp. 40–46; and "The Way We'll Work," *Time,* May 25, 2009, pp. 39–50.

16. "Wholesale and Manufacturing Sales Representatives," *Occupational Outlook Handbook,* 2014–15 Edition (Washington, DC: U.S. Department of Labor), http://www.bls.gov/ooh/sales/wholesale-and-manufacturing-sales-representatives.htm, accessed July 14, 2015.

17. Jack and Suzy Welch, "Dear Graduate . . . To Stand Out among Your Peers, You Have to Overdeliver," *Bloomberg Businessweek,* June 19, 2006, p. 100.

18. "The Tech Effect," *Sales and Marketing Management,* July/August 2015, pp. 40–41; and Elisabeth A. Sullivan, "One-to-One," *Marketing News,* June 15, 2009, pp. 10–13.

19. Carol Shea, "Career Advice for New Marketing Researchers," *Marketing News,* July 2015, p. 61; Piet Levy, "10 Minutes with Stan Sthanunathan, Vice President of Marketing Strategy and Insights, The Coca-Cola Co.," *Marketing News,* February 28, 2011, p. 34; and Edmund Hershberger and Madhav N. Segal,

"Ads for MR Positions Reveal Desired Skills," *Marketing News,* February 1, 2007, p. 28.

20. "Market Research Analyst," in Les Krantz, ed., *Jobs Rated Almanac,* 6th ed. (New York: St. Martin's Press, 2002).

21. Deborah L. Vence, "In an Instant, More Researchers Use IM for Fast, Reliable Results," *Marketing News,* March 1, 2006, p. 53; and Joshua Grossnickle and Oliver Raskin, "What's Ahead on the Internet," *Marketing Research,* Summer 2001, pp. 9–13.

22. Matt Valle, "Eight Reasons to Choose Market Research as a Career," *Marketing Insights,* April 2014, pp. 12–13; and Carolyn D. Marconi, "Desperately Looking for New Talent Is a Recurring Theme," *Marketing Research,* Spring 2000, pp. 4–6.

23. "2015 Franchise 500," *Entrepreneur* website, www.entrepreneur. com, accessed July 14, 2015.

24. Lisa Bertagnoli, "Marketing Overseas Excellent for Career," *Marketing News,* June 4, 2001, p. 4.

25. "Accenture Broadcast Services: A Global Communications Capability," Accenture website, https://www.accenture. com/us-en/success-accenture-broadcast-services-global-communications-capability, July 14, 2015; "Global Consulting Firm Accenture Opens Office in Calgary," *Postmedia Breaking News,* February 6, 2013; and "Managing Collaborators No Matter Where They Sit," *The Huffington Post,* April 17, 2013.

26. Barbara Flood, "Turbo Charge Your Job Search, Job Searching and Career Development Tips," *Information Outlook,* May 1, 2007, p. 40.

27. Robin T. Peterson and J. Stuart Devlin, "Perspectives on Entry-Level Positions by Graduating Marketing Seniors," *Marketing Education Review,* Summer 1994, pp. 2–5.

28. Avi Levine, "Seven Skill You Need to Land a High-Paying Digital Marketing Job," *Marketing News,* May 2015, p. 58; Louis Lavelle, "Business Schools Embrace the Liberal Arts," *Bloomberg Businessweek,* April 10, 2013; Regina Pefanis Schlee and Katrin R. Harich, "Knowledge and Skill Requirements for Marketing Jobs in the 21st Century," *Journal of Marketing Education,* December 2010, pp. 341–52; and "10 Job Hunting Tips," *Marketing News,* November 15, 2010, p. 19.

29. Flood, "Turbo Charge Your Job Search."

30. "More MBA Grads Take the Road Less Traveled," *Bloomberg Businessweek,* April 18–24, 2011, p. 53.

31. Susan Adams, "Secrets of Making the Most of Job Search Websites," *Forbes.com,* January 15, 2014, p. 13; and Francine Russo, "The New Online Job Hunt," *Time,* October 3, 2011, pp. B14–B16.

32. Peter Cappelli, "Making the Most of On-Line Recruiting," *Harvard Business Review,* March 2001, pp. 139–46.

33. Ronald B. Marks, *Personal Selling: A Relationship Approach,* 6th ed. (New York: Pearson, 1996).

34. Chris Farrell, "It's Not What Grads Know, It's Who They Know," *Bloomberg Businessweek,* June 18, 2012, pp. 9–10; Sima Dahl, "A New Job Is No Excuse to Ease Up on Networking," *Marketing News,* February 28, 2011, p. 4; Leonard Felson, "Undergrad Marketers Must Get Jump on Networking Skills," *Marketing News,* April 8, 2001, p. 14; Wayne E. Baker, *Networking Smart* (New York: McGraw-Hill, 1994); and Piet Levy, "AMA Chapters across the Country Are Increasingly Using Job Boards, Networking Events and Other Techniques to Help Members in This Economy," *Marketing News,* March 15, 2009, p. 14.

35. "Careers in Marketing: Utilizing Social Networking to Improve Your Job Prospects," *CareerAlley,* July 22, 2012; "Finding Job Candidates Who Aren't Looking," *Bloomberg Businessweek,* December 17, 2012, pp. 41–42; Sima Dahl, "Pinning Your Career Hopes on Pinterest," *Marketing News,* May 15, 2012, p. 5; Tim Post, "New Graduates Use Social Media to Look for Jobs," *St. Paul Pioneer Press,* June 3, 2011; Susan Berfield, "Dueling Your Facebook Friends for a New Job," *Bloomberg Businessweek,* March 7, 2011, p. 35; and Dan Schawbel, "Top 10 Social Sites for Finding a Job," *Mashable,* February 24, 2009.

36. Stacie Garlieb, "How to Fare Well at a Job Fair," *Marketing News,* May 2014, p. 60; and "Stand Out at the Career Fair," *Job Choices for Business & Liberal Arts Students: 2009,* 52nd ed. (Bethlehem, PA: National Association of Colleges and Employers, 2008), pp. 22–23.

37. Amy Diepenbrock, "Will Your Resume Open the Door to an Interview?" *Job Choices for Business & Liberal Arts Students, 2011,* National Association of Colleges and Employers, p. 31; and Marianne E. Green, "Marketing Yourself: From Student to Professional," *Job Choices for Business & Liberal Arts Students: 2009* (Bethlehem, PA: National Association of Colleges and Employers, 2008), pp. 28–29.

38. Marianne E. Green, "Resume Writing: Sell Your Skills to Get the Interview!" *Job Choices for Business & Liberal Arts Students,* 50th ed., 2007, pp. 39–47.

39. C. Randall Powell, "Secrets of Selling a Résumé," in Peggy Schmidt, ed., *The Honda How to Get a Job Guide* (New York: McGraw-Hill, 1984), pp. 4–9.

40. Debra Wheatman, "Resume Trends Worth Following," *Marketing News,* July 2014, p. 63; Karla Ahern and Naomi Keller, "Expert Advice: Your Resume Questions Answered," *Marketing News,* September 2014, p. 61; Sima Dahl, "Social Media and Your Job Search: How the Age of the Referral May Impact Your Career," *Marketing News,* September 30, 2012, p. 6.

41. Lydia Stockdale, "How to Make a Great Video CV," *The Guardian,* February 27, 2014; Robert Klara, "These Guys Want to Clean Up Your Reputation," *Adweek,* March 3, 2014, p. 22–23; "Post with Caution: Your Online Profile and Our Job Search," *Job Choices for Business & Liberal Arts Students: 2009* (Bethlehem, PA: National Association of Colleges and Employers, 2008), p. 30; "If I 'Google' You, What Will I Find?" *Job Choices for Business and Liberal Arts Students,* 50th ed., 2007, p. 16.

42. William J. Banis, "The Art of Writing Job-Search Letters," *Job Choices for Business and Liberal Arts Students,* 50th ed., 2007, pp. 32–38; and Arthur G. Sharp, "The Art of the Cover Letter," *Career Futures* 4, no. 1 (1992): pp. 50–51.

43. Lindsey Pollak, "The 10 Commandments of Social Media Job Seeking," *Job Choices for Business & Liberal Arts Students, 2011,* National Association of Colleges and Employers, p. 20; Alison Damast, "Recruiters' Top 10 Complaints," *Bloomberg Businessweek,* April 26, 2007; and Marilyn Moats Kennedy, "'Don't List' Offers Important Tips for Job Interviews," *Marketing News,* March 15, 2007, p. 26.

44. Sima Dahl, "Where Do You See Yourself in Five Years?" *Marketing News,* November 15, 2010, p. 4; and Dana James, "A Day in the Life of a Corporate Recruiter," *Marketing News,* April 10, 2000, pp. 1, 11.

45. Meghan Casserly, "'You Look like a Convict' and the Most Common Pitfalls of Interviewing over Skype," *Forbes.com,* October 3, 2012.

46. Paul Davidson, "Managers to Millennials: Job Interview No Time to Text," *USA Today,* April 29, 2013.

47. Robert M. Greenberg, "The Company Visit—Revisited," *NACE Journal,* Winter 2003, pp. 21–27.

48. Mary E. Scott, "High-Touch vs. High-Tech Recruitment," *NACE Journal,* Fall 2002, pp. 33–39.

GLOSSARY

above-, at-, or below-market pricing Setting a market price for a product or product class based on a subjective feel for the competitors' price or market price as the benchmark. p. 379

account management policies Policies that specify who salespeople should contact, what kinds of selling and customer service activities should be engaged in, and how these activities should be carried out. p. 584

action item list An aid to implementing a plan that consists of four columns: (1) the task; (2) the person responsible for completing that task; (3) the date to finish the task; and (4) what is to be delivered. p. 637

adaptive selling A need-satisfaction presentation format that involves adjusting the presentation to fit the selling situation, such as knowing when to offer solutions and when to ask for more information. p. 578

advertising Any paid form of nonpersonal communication about an organization, product, service, or idea by an identified sponsor. pp. 472, 500

all-you-can-afford budgeting Allocating funds to promotion only after all other budget items are covered. p. 484

apps Small, downloadable software programs that can run on smartphones and tablet devices. p. 556

attitude A learned predisposition to respond to an object or class of objects in a consistently favorable or unfavorable way. p. 134

baby boomers Includes the generation of 76 million children born between 1946 and 1964. p. 75

back translation The practice where a translated word or phrase is retranslated into the original language by a different interpreter to catch errors. p. 187

balance of trade The difference between the monetary value of a nation's exports and imports. p. 177

barriers to entry Business practices or conditions that make it difficult for new firms to enter the market. p. 87

barter The practice of exchanging products and services for other products and services rather than for money. p. 350

basing-point pricing Selecting one or more geographical locations (basing point) from which the list price for products plus freight expenses are charged to the buyer. p. 389

behavioral targeting Uses information provided by cookies for directing online advertising from marketers to those online shoppers whose behavioral profiles suggest they would be interested in such advertising. p. 610

beliefs A consumer's subjective perception of how a product or brand performs on different attributes based on personal experience, advertising, and discussions with other people. p. 134

blended family A family formed by merging two previously separated units into a single household. p. 77

blog A contraction of "web log," a web page that serves as a publicly accessible personal journal and online forum for an individual or organization. p. 540

bots Electronic shopping agents or robots that search websites to compare prices and product or service features. p. 606

brand community A specialized group of consumers with a structured set of relationships involving a particular brand, fellow customers of that brand, and the product in use. p. 139

brand equity The added value a brand name gives to a product beyond the functional benefits provided. p. 305

brand licensing A contractual agreement whereby one company (licensor) allows its brand name(s) or trademark(s) to be used with products or services offered by another company (licensee) for a royalty or fee. p. 306

brand loyalty A favorable attitude toward and consistent purchase of a single brand over time. p. 134

brand name Any word, device (design, sound, shape, or color), or combination of these used to distinguish a seller's products or services. p. 303

brand personality A set of human characteristics associated with a brand name. p. 305

branding A marketing decision in which an organization uses a name, phrase, design, symbols, or combination of these to identify its products and distinguish them from those of competitors. p. 304

breadth of product line The variety of different product items a store carries. p. 441

break-even analysis A technique that analyzes the relationship between total revenue and total cost to determine profitability at various levels of output. p. 362

break-even chart A graphic presentation of the break-even analysis that shows when total revenue and total cost intersect to identify profit or loss for a given quantity sold. p. 363

break-even point (BEP) The quantity at which total revenue and total cost are equal. p. 362

brokers Independent firms or individuals whose principal function is to bring buyers and sellers together to make sales. p. 458

bundle pricing The marketing of two or more products in a single package price. p. 375

business The clear, broad, underlying industry or market sector of an organization's offering. p. 32

business analysis The stage of the new-product development process that specifies the features of the product and the marketing strategy needed to bring it to market and make financial projections. p. 279

business plan A road map for the entire organization for a specified future period of time, such as one year or five years. p. 54

business portfolio analysis A technique that managers use to quantify performance measures and growth targets to analyze their firms' strategic business units (SBUs) as though they were a collection of separate investments. p. 36

business products Products organizations buy that assist in providing other products for resale. Also called *B2B products* or *industrial products*. p. 266

business-to-business marketing The marketing of products and services to companies, governments, or not-for-profit organizations for use in the creation of products and services that they can produce and market to others. p. 154

buy classes Consist of three types of organizational buying situations: straight rebuy, new buy, and modified rebuy. p. 163

buying center The group of people in an organization who participate in the buying process and share common goals, risks, and knowledge important to a purchase decision. p. 162

capacity management Integrating the service component of the marketing mix with efforts to influence consumer demand. p. 336

category management An approach to managing the assortment of merchandise in which a manager is assigned the responsibility for selecting all products that consumers in a market segment might view as substitutes for each other, with the objective of maximizing sales and profits in the category. p. 453

cause marketing Occurs when the charitable contributions of a firm are tied directly to the customer revenues produced through the promotion of one of its products. p. 112

caveat emptor The legal concept of "let the buyer beware" that was pervasive in the American business culture prior to the 1960s. p. 104

central business district The oldest retail setting, usually located in the community's downtown area. p. 452

channel conflict Arises when one channel member believes another channel member is engaged in behavior that prevents it from achieving its goals. p. 419

channel of communication The means (e.g., a salesperson, advertising media, or public relations tools) of conveying a message to a receiver during the communication process. p. 470

choiceboard An interactive, Internet-enabled system that allows individual customers to design their own products and services by answering a few questions and choosing from a menu of product or service attributes (or components), prices, and delivery options. p. 600

code of ethics A formal statement of ethical principles and rules of conduct. p. 106

collaborative filtering A process that automatically groups people with similar buying intentions, preferences, and behaviors and predicts future purchases. p. 600

commercialization The stage of the new-product development process that positions and launches a new product in full-scale production and sales. p. 281

communication The process of conveying a message to others that requires six elements: a source, a message, a channel of communication, a receiver, and the processes of encoding and decoding. p. 470

community shopping center A retail location that typically has one primary store (usually a department store branch) and often 20 to 40 smaller outlets, serving a population of consumers who are within a 10- to 20-minute drive. p. 452

competition The alternative firms that could provide a product to satisfy a specific market's needs. p. 86

competitive parity budgeting Allocating funds to promotion by matching the competitor's absolute level of spending or the proportion per point of market share. Also called *matching competitors* or *share of market*. p. 483

constraints In a decision, the restrictions placed on potential solutions to a problem. p. 208

consultative selling A need-satisfaction presentation format that focuses on problem identification, where the salesperson serves as an expert on problem recognition and resolution. p. 578

consumer behavior The actions a person takes in purchasing and using products and services, including the mental and social processes that come before and after these actions. p. 123

Consumer Bill of Rights (1962) An outline presented by President John F. Kennedy in 1962 that codified the ethics of exchange between buyers and sellers, including the rights to safety, to be informed, to choose, and to be heard. p. 104

consumer ethnocentrism The tendency to believe that it is inappropriate, indeed immoral, to purchase foreign-made products. p. 188

consumer products Products purchased by the ultimate consumer. p. 266

consumerism A grassroots movement started in the 1960s to increase the influence, power, and rights of consumers in dealing with institutions. p. 89

consumer-oriented sales promotion Sales tools used to support a company's advertising and personal selling directed to ultimate consumers. Also called *consumer promotions*. p. 519

convenience products Items that the consumer purchases frequently, conveniently, and with a minimum of shopping effort. p. 266

cookies Computer files that a marketer can download onto the computer and mobile phone of an online shopper who visits the marketer's website. p. 610

cooperative advertising Advertising programs whereby a manufacturer pays a percentage of the retailer's local advertising expense for advertising the manufacturer's products. p. 525

core values The fundamental, passionate, and enduring principles of an organization that guide its conduct over time. p. 31

cost focus strategy One of Porter's generic business strategies that involves controlling expenses and, in turn, lowering product prices targeted at a narrow range of market segments. p. 628

cost leadership strategy One of Porter's generic business strategies that focuses on reducing expenses and, in turn, lowers product prices while targeting a broad array of market segments. p. 628

cost per thousand (CPM) The cost of reaching 1,000 individuals or households with the advertising message in a given medium (M is the Roman numeral for 1,000). p. 508

cost-plus pricing Summing the total unit cost of providing a product or service and adding a specific amount to the cost to arrive at a price. p. 376

countertrade The practice of using barter rather than money for making global sales. p. 176

cross tabulation A method of presenting and analyzing data involving two or more variables to discover relationships in the data. Also known as *cross tab*. p. 222

cross-channel consumer An online consumer who shops online but buys offline, or shops offline but buys online. p. 611

cross-cultural analysis The study of similarities and differences among consumers in two or more nations or societies. p. 185

cultural symbols Things that represent ideas and concepts. p. 186

culture The set of values, ideas, and attitudes that are learned and shared among the members of a group. p. 80

currency exchange rate The price of one country's currency expressed in terms of another country's currency. p. 190

customary pricing Setting a price that is dictated by tradition, a standardized channel of distribution, or other competitive factors. p. 379

customer contact audit A flowchart of the points of interaction or "service encounters" between consumers and a service provider. p. 330

customer experience The internal response that customers have to all aspects of an organization and its offering. p. 15

customer experience management (CEM) The process of managing the entire customer experience with the company. p. 335

customer relationship management (CRM) The process of identifying prospective buyers, understanding them intimately, and developing favorable long-term perceptions of the organization and its offerings so that buyers will choose them in the marketplace. p. 15

customer service The ability of logistics management to satisfy users in terms of time, dependability, communication, and convenience. p. 425

customer value The unique combination of benefits received by targeted buyers that includes quality, convenience, on-time delivery, and both before-sale and after-sale service at a specific price. p. 11

customer value proposition The cluster of benefits that an organization promises customers to satisfy their needs. p. 10

customerization The growing practice of not only customizing a product or service but also personalizing the marketing and overall shopping and buying interaction for each customer. p. 607

customs What is considered normal and expected about the way people do things in a specific country. p. 186

data The facts and figures related to the project that are divided into two main parts: secondary data and primary data. p. 210

decoding The process of having the receiver take a set of symbols, the message, and transform them back to an idea during the communication process. p. 471

demand curve A graph that relates the quantity sold and price, showing the maximum number of units that will be sold at a given price. p. 358

demand factors Factors that determine consumers' willingness and ability to pay for products and services. p. 359

demographics Describing a population according to selected characteristics such as age, gender, ethnicity, income, and occupation. p. 74

depth of product line The store carries a large assortment of each product item. p. 441

derived demand The demand for industrial products and services that is driven by, or derived from, the demand for consumer products and services. p. 156

development The stage of the new-product development process that turns the idea on paper into a prototype. p. 279

differentiation focus strategy One of Porter's generic business strategies that requires products to have significant points of difference to target one or only a few market segments. p. 628

differentiation strategy One of Porter's generic business strategies that requires products to have significant points of difference to charge a higher price while targeting a broad array of market segments. p. 628

direct marketing A promotional alternative that uses direct communication with consumers to generate a response in the form of an order, a request for further information, or a visit to a retail outlet. p. 475

direct orders The result of direct marketing offers that contain all the information necessary for a prospective buyer to make a decision to purchase and complete the transaction. p. 489

discretionary income The money that remains after paying for taxes and necessities. p. 83

disintermediation Channel conflict that arises when a channel member bypasses another member and sells or buys products direct. p. 419

disposable income The money a consumer has left after paying taxes to use for necessities such as food, housing, clothing, and transportation. p. 83

diversification analysis A technique that helps a firm search for growth opportunities from among current and new markets as well as current and new products. p. 39

dual distribution An arrangement whereby a firm reaches different buyers by employing two or more different types of channels for the same basic product. p. 413

dynamic pricing The practice of changing prices for products and services in real time in response to supply and demand conditions. p. 609

dynamic pricing policy Setting different prices for products and services in real time in response to supply and demand conditions. Also called a *flexible-price policy*. p. 382

economic espionage The clandestine collection of trade secrets or proprietary information about a company's competitors. pp. 105, 185

economy Pertains to the income, expenditures, and resources that affect the cost of running a business and household. p. 82

eight-second rule A view that customers will abandon their efforts to enter and navigate a website if download time exceeds eight seconds. p. 606

80/20 rule A concept that suggests 80 percent of a firm's sales are obtained from 20 percent of its customers. p. 631

electronic commerce Any activity that uses some form of electronic communication in the inventory, exchange, advertisement, distribution, and payment of products and services. p. 86

e-marketplaces Online trading communities that bring together buyers and supplier organizations to make possible the real time exchange of information, money, products, and services. Also called *B2B exchanges* or *e-hubs*. p. 165

emotional intelligence The ability to understand one's own emotions and the emotions of people with whom one interacts on a daily basis. p. 586

encoding The process of having the sender transform an idea into a set of symbols during the communication process. p. 471

environmental forces The uncontrollable forces that affect a marketing decision and consist of social, economic, technological, competitive, and regulatory forces. p. 10

environmental scanning The process of continually acquiring information on events occurring outside the organization to identify and interpret potential trends. p. 72

ethics The moral principles and values that govern the actions and decisions of an individual or group. p. 102

everyday low pricing (EDLP) The practice of replacing promotional allowances with lower manufacturer list prices. p. 387

exchange The trade of things of value between buyer and seller so that each is better off after the trade. p. 5

exclusive distribution A level of distribution density whereby only one retailer in a specific geographical area carries the firm's products. p. 416

experience curve pricing A method of pricing based on the learning effect, which holds that the unit cost of many products and services declines by 10 percent to 30 percent each time a firm's experience at producing and selling them doubles. p. 376

exporting A global market-entry strategy in which a company produces products in one country and sells them in another country. p. 192

Facebook A website where users may create a personal profile, add other users as friends, and exchange comments, photos, videos, and "likes" with them. p. 544

family life cycle The distinct phases that a family progresses through from formation to retirement, each phase bringing with it identifiable purchasing behaviors. p. 140

feedback In the feedback loop, the sender's interpretation of the response, which indicates whether a message was decoded and understood as intended during the communication process. p. 472

field of experience A mutually shared understanding and knowledge that the sender and receiver apply to the message so that it can be communicated effectively during the communication process. p. 471

fixed cost (FC) The sum of the expenses of the firm that are stable and do not change with the quantity of a product that is produced and sold. p. 362

fixed-price policy Setting one price for all buyers of a product or service. Also called a *one-price policy*. p. 381

FOB origin pricing The "free on board" (FOB) price the seller quotes that includes only the cost of loading the product onto the vehicle and specifies the name of the location where the loading is to occur (seller's factory or warehouse). p. 388

Foreign Corrupt Practices Act (1977) A law, amended by the International Anti-Dumping and Fair Competition Act (1998), that makes it a crime for U.S. corporations to bribe an official of a foreign government or political party to obtain or retain business in a foreign country. p. 186

form of ownership Distinguishes retail outlets based on whether independent retailers, corporate chains, or contractual systems own the outlet. p. 438

formula selling presentation A sales presentation format that consists of information that must be provided in an accurate, thorough, and step-by-step manner to inform the prospect. p. 578

four I's of services The four unique elements to services: intangibility, inconsistency, inseparability, and inventory. p. 323

frequency The average number of times a person in the target audience is exposed to a message or an advertisement. p. 508

full-service agency An advertising agency that provides the most complete range of services, including market research, media selection, copy development, artwork, and production. p. 517

functional groupings Organizational groupings that represent the different departments or business activities within a firm. p. 639

gap analysis A type of analysis that compares the differences between the consumer's expectations about and experiences with a service based on dimensions of service quality. p. 330

Generation X Includes the 50 million people born between 1965 and 1976. Also called the *baby bust*. p. 75

Generation Y Includes the 72 million Americans born between 1977 and 1994. Also called the *echo-boom* or the *baby boomlet*. p. 76

generic business strategy A strategy that can be adopted by any firm, regardless of the product or industry involved, to achieve a competitive advantage. p. 628

geographical groupings Organizational groupings in which sales territories are subdivided according to geographical location. p. 639

global brand A brand marketed under the same name in multiple countries with similar and centrally coordinated marketing programs. p. 183

global competition Exists when firms originate, produce, and market their products and services worldwide. p. 181

global consumers Consumer groups living in many countries or regions of the world who have similar needs or seek similar features and benefits from products or services. p. 183

global marketing strategy A strategy used by transnational firms that employ the practice of standardizing marketing activities when there are cultural similarities and adapting them when cultures differ. p. 182

goals Statements of an accomplishment of a task to be achieved, often by a specific time. Also called *objectives*. p. 32

green marketing Marketing efforts to produce, promote, and reclaim environmentally sensitive products. p. 111

gross income The total amount of money made in one year by a person, household, or family unit. Also known as *money income* at the Census Bureau. p. 83

gross rating points (GRPs) A reference number used by advertisers that is obtained by multiplying reach (expressed as a percentage of the total market) by frequency. p. 508

hierarchy of effects The sequence of stages a prospective buyer goes through from initial awareness of a product to eventual action that includes awareness, interest, evaluation, trial, and adoption of the product. p. 482

hypermarket A form of scrambled merchandising, which consists of a large store (more than 200,000 square feet) that offers everything in a single outlet, eliminating the need for consumers to shop at more than one location. p. 442

idea generation The stage of the new-product development process that develops a pool of concepts to serve as candidates for new products, building upon the previous stage's results. p. 275

idle production capacity Occurs when the service provider is available but there is no demand for the service. p. 324

infomercials Program-length (30-minute) advertisements that take an educational approach to communication with potential customers. p. 510

information technology Includes all of the computing resources that collect, store, and analyze data. p. 221

in-house agencies Consist of the company's own advertising staff, who may provide full services or a limited range of services. p. 518

institutional advertisements Advertisements designed to build goodwill or an image for an organization rather than promote a specific product or service. p. 501

integrated marketing communications (IMC) The concept of designing marketing communications programs that coordinate all promotional activities—advertising, personal selling, sales promotion, public relations, and direct marketing—to provide a consistent message across all audiences. p. 470

intensive distribution A level of distribution density whereby a firm tries to place its products and services in as many outlets as possible. p. 416

interactive marketing Two-way buyer–seller electronic communication in which the buyer controls the kind and amount of information received from the seller. p. 600

internal marketing The notion that a service organization must focus on its employees, or internal market, before successful programs can be directed at customers. p. 335

Internet of Things (IoT) The network of products embedded with connectivity-enabled electronics. p. 86

intertype competition Competition between very dissimilar types of retail outlets that results from a scrambled merchandising policy. p. 442

involvement The personal, social, and economic significance of the purchase to the consumer. p. 27

joint venture A global market-entry strategy in which a foreign company and a local firm invest together to create a local business in order to share ownership, control, and profits of the new company. p. 194

key account management The practice of using team selling to focus on important customers so as to build mutually beneficial, long-term, cooperative relationships. p. 583

label An integral part of the package that typically identifies the product or brand, who made it, where and when it was made, how it is to be used, and package contents and ingredients. p. 310

laws Society's values and standards that are enforceable in the courts. p. 102

lead generation The result of a direct marketing offer designed to generate interest in a product or service and a request for additional information. p. 489

learning Those behaviors that result from (1) repeated experience and (2) reasoning. p. 133

level of service Describes the degree of service provided to the customer from three types of retailers: self-, limited-, and full-service. p. 438

limited-service agencies Advertising agencies that specialize in one aspect of the advertising process, such as providing creative services to develop the advertising copy, buying previously unpurchased media space, or providing Internet services. p. 517

line positions Managers who have the authority and responsibility to issue orders to the people who report to them. p. 639

LinkedIn A business-oriented website that lets users post their professional profiles to connect to a network of businesspeople. p. 547

logistics Those activities that focus on getting the right amount of the right products to the right place at the right time at the lowest possible cost. p. 421

loss-leader pricing Deliberately selling a product below its customary price, not to increase sales, but to attract customers' attention to it in hopes that they will buy other products with large markups as well. p. 380

manufacturers' agents Agents who work for several producers and carry noncompetitive, complementary merchandise in an exclusive territory. Also called *manufacturers' representatives*. p. 458

market People with both the desire and the ability to buy a specific offering. p. 9

market-based groupings Organizational groupings that use specific customer segments. p. 639

market modification Strategies by which a company tries to find new customers, increase a product's use among existing customers, or create new use situations. p. 300

market orientation An organization with a market orientation focuses its efforts on (1) continuously collecting information

about customers' needs, (2) sharing this information across departments, and (3) using it to create customer value. p. 15

market-product grid A framework to relate the market segments of potential buyers to products offered or potential marketing actions. p. 239

market segmentation Involves aggregating prospective buyers into groups, or segments, that (1) have common needs and (2) will respond similarly to a marketing action. pp. 42, 238

market segments The relatively homogeneous groups of prospective buyers that (1) have common needs and (2) will respond similarly to a marketing action. p. 12

market share The ratio of sales revenue of the firm to the total sales revenue of all firms in the industry, including the firm itself. p. 32

market testing The stage of the new-product development process that exposes actual products to prospective consumers under realistic purchase conditions to see if they will buy. p. 280

marketing The activity, set of instructions, and processes for creating, communicating, delivering, and exchanging offerings that have value for customers, clients, partners, and society at large. p. 5

marketing channel Consists of individuals and firms involved in the process of making a product or service available for use or consumption by consumers or industrial users. p. 408

marketing concept The idea that an organization should (1) strive to satisfy the needs of consumers while also (2) trying to achieve the organization's goals. p. 14

marketing dashboard The visual display of the essential information related to achieving a marketing objective. p. 33

marketing metric A measure of the quantitative value or trend of a marketing action or result. p. 34

marketing mix The controllable factors—product, price, promotion, and place—that can be used by the marketing manager to solve a marketing problem. p. 10

marketing plan A road map for the marketing actions of an organization for a specified future time period, such as one year or five years. pp. 33, 54

marketing program A plan that integrates the marketing mix to provide a good, service, or idea to prospective buyers. p. 12

marketing research The process of defining a marketing problem and opportunity, systematically collecting and analyzing information, and recommending actions. p. 206

marketing ROI The application of modern measurement technologies to understand, quantify, and optimize marketing spending. p. 642

marketing strategy The means by which a marketing goal is to be achieved, usually characterized by a specified target market and a marketing program to reach it. p. 44

marketing tactics The detailed day-to-day operational marketing actions for each element of the marketing mix that contribute to the overall success of marketing strategies. p. 45

marketspace An information- and communication-based electronic exchange environment mostly occupied by sophisticated computer and telecommunication technologies and digital offerings. p. 86

measures of success Criteria or standards used in evaluating proposed solutions to the problem. p. 208

merchandise line Describes how many different types of products a store carries and in what assortment. p. 438

merchant wholesalers Independently owned firms that take title to the merchandise they handle. p. 457

message The information sent by a source to a receiver during the communication process. p. 470

mission A statement of the organization's function in society that often identifies its customers, markets, products, and technologies. Often used interchangeably with *vision*. p. 31

mixed branding A branding strategy where a firm markets products under its own name(s) and that of a reseller because the segment attracted to the reseller is different from its own market. p. 310

mobile marketing The broad set of interactive messaging options that enable organizations to communicate and engage with consumers through any mobile device. p. 513

moral idealism A personal moral philosophy that considers certain individual rights or duties as universal, regardless of the outcome. p. 107

motivation The energizing force that stimulates behavior to satisfy a need. p. 130

multibranding A branding strategy that involves giving each product a distinct name when each brand is intended for a different market segment. p. 308

multichannel marketing The blending of different communication and delivery channels that are mutually reinforcing in attracting, retaining, and building relationships with consumers who shop and buy in traditional intermediaries and online. p. 413

multichannel retailers Retailers that utilize and integrate a combination of traditional store formats and nonstore formats such as catalogs, television home shopping, and online retailing. p. 456

multicultural marketing Combinations of the marketing mix that reflect the unique attitudes, ancestry, communication preferences, and lifestyles of different races. p. 79

multidomestic marketing strategy A strategy used by multinational firms that have as many different product variations, brand names, and advertising programs as countries in which they do business. p. 182

multiproduct branding A branding strategy in which a company uses one name for all its products in a product class. p. 308

need-satisfaction presentation A sales presentation format that emphasizes probing and listening by the salesperson to identify the needs and interests of prospective buyers. p. 578

new-product development process The seven stages an organization goes through to identify opportunities and convert them into salable products or services. p. 274

new-product strategy development The stage of the new-product development process that defines the role for a new product in terms of the firm's overall objectives. p. 274

noise Extraneous factors that can work against effective communication by distorting a message or the feedback received during the communication process. p. 472

North American Industry Classification System (NAICS) Provides common industry definitions for Canada, Mexico, and the United States, which makes it easier to measure economic activity in the three member countries of the North American Free Trade Agreement (NAFTA). p. 155

objective and task budgeting Allocating funds to promotion whereby the company: (1) determines its promotion objectives; (2) outlines the tasks to accomplish those objectives; and (3) determines the promotion cost of performing those tasks. p. 484

objectives Statements of an accomplishment of a task to be achieved, often by a specific time. Also called *goals*. p. 32

observational data Facts and figures obtained by watching how people actually behave, using mechanical, personal, or neuromarketing data collection methods. p. 212

odd-even pricing Setting prices a few dollars or cents under an even number. p. 374

off-peak pricing Charging different prices during different times of the day or during different days of the week to reflect variations in demand for the service. p. 334

off-price retailing Selling brand-name merchandise at lower than regular prices. p. 450

online consumers The subsegment of all Internet users who employ this technology to research products and services and make purchases. p. 604

open innovation Practices and processes that encourage the use of external as well as internal ideas as well as internal and external collaboration when conceiving, producing, and marketing new products and services. p. 273

opinion leaders Individuals who exert direct or indirect social influence over others. p. 137

order getter Sells in a conventional sense and identifies prospective customers, provides customers with information, persuades customers to buy, closes sales, and follows up on customers' use of a product or service. p. 572

order taker Processes routine orders or reorders for products that were already sold by the company. p. 571

organizational buyers Those manufacturers, wholesalers, retailers, service companies, not-for-profit organizations, and government agencies that buy products and services for their own use or for resale. pp. 18, 154

organizational buying behavior The decision-making process that organizations use to establish the need for products and services and identify, evaluate, and choose among alternative brands and suppliers. p. 161

organizational culture The set of values, ideas, attitudes, and norms of behavior that is learned and shared among the members of an organization. p. 31

packaging A component of a product that refers to any container in which it is offered for sale and on which label information is conveyed. p. 310

partnership selling The practice whereby buyers and sellers combine their expertise and resources to create customized solutions, commit to joint planning, and share customer, competitive, and company information for their mutual benefit and, ultimately, the benefit of the customer. Also called *enterprise selling*. p. 570

penetration pricing Setting a low initial price on a new product to appeal immediately to the mass market. p. 373

perceived risk The anxiety felt because the consumer cannot anticipate the outcomes of a purchase but believes there may be negative consequences. p. 133

percentage of sales budgeting Allocating funds to promotion as a percentage of past or anticipated sales, in terms of either dollars or units sold. p. 483

perception The process by which an individual selects, organizes, and interprets information to create a meaningful picture of the world. p. 131

perceptual map A means of displaying in two dimensions the location of products or brands in the minds of consumers to enable a manager to see how they perceive competing products or brands, as well as the firm's own product or brand. p. 257

permission marketing The solicitation of a consumer's consent (called "opt-in") to receive e-mail and advertising based on personal data supplied by the consumer. p. 601

personal selling The two-way flow of communication between a buyer and seller, often in a face-to-face encounter, designed to influence a person's or group's purchase decision. pp. 473, 568

personal selling process Sales activities occurring before, during, and after the sale itself, consisting of six stages: (1) prospecting, (2) preapproach, (3) approach, (4) presentation, (5) close, and (6) follow-up. p. 574

personality A person's consistent behaviors or responses to recurring situations. p. 131

personalization The consumer-initiated practice of generating content on a marketer's website that is custom tailored to an individual's specific needs and preferences. p. 600

points of difference Those characteristics of a product that make it superior to competitive substitutes. p. 42

posttests Tests conducted after an advertisement has been shown to the target audience to determine whether it accomplished its intended purpose. p. 518

power center A retail location consisting of a huge shopping strip with multiple anchor (or national) stores. p. 451

predatory pricing The practice of charging a very low price for a product with the intent of driving competitors out of business. p. 391

prestige pricing Setting a high price so that quality- or status-conscious consumers will be attracted to the product and buy it. p. 373

pretests Tests conducted before an advertisement is placed in any medium to determine whether it communicates the intended message or to select among alternative versions of the advertisement. p. 516

price (P) The money or other considerations (including other products and services) exchanged for the ownership or use of a product or service. p. 350

price discrimination The practice of charging different prices to different buyers for products of like grade and quality. p. 390

price elasticity of demand The percentage change in quantity demanded relative to a percentage change in price. p. 360

price fixing A conspiracy among firms to set prices for a product. p. 389

price lining Setting the price of a line of products at a number of different specific pricing points. p. 374

price war Successive price cutting by competitors to increase or maintain their unit sales or market share. p. 384

pricing constraints Factors that limit the range of prices a firm may set. p. 355

pricing objectives Specifying the role of price in an organization's marketing and strategic plans. p. 353

primary data Facts and figures that are newly collected for the project. p. 210

private branding A branding strategy used when a company manufactures products but sells them under the brand name of a wholesaler or retailer. Also called *private labeling* or *reseller branding*. p. 309

product A good, service, or idea consisting of a bundle of tangible and intangible attributes that satisfies consumers' needs and is received in exchange for money or something else of value. pp. 17, 266

product advertisements Advertisements that focus on selling a product or service and which take three forms: (1) pioneering (or informational), (2) competitive (or persuasive), and (3) reminder. p. 500

product class Refers to the entire product category or industry. p. 298

product differentiation A marketing strategy that involves a firm using different marketing mix actions to help consumers perceive the product as being different and better than competing products. p. 238

product form Pertains to variations of a product within the product class. p. 298

product item A specific product that has a unique brand, size, or price. p. 268

product life cycle Describes the stages a new product goes through in the marketplace: introduction, growth, maturity, and decline. p. 292

product line A group of product or service items that are closely related because they satisfy a class of needs, are used together, are sold to the same customer group, are distributed through the same outlets, or fall within a given price range. p. 268

product line groupings Organizational groupings in which a unit is responsible for specific product offerings. p. 639

product mix Consists of all of the product lines offered by an organization. p. 268

product modification Involves altering one or more of a product's characteristics, such as its quality, performance, or appearance, to increase the product's value to customers and increase sales. p. 300

product placement A consumer sales promotion tool that uses a brand-name product in a movie, television show, video game, or a commercial for another product. p. 523

product positioning The place a product occupies in consumers' minds based on important attributes relative to competitive products. p. 256

product repositioning Changing the place a product occupies in a consumer's mind relative to competitive products. p. 256

product-line pricing The setting of prices for all items in a product line to cover the total cost and produce a profit for the complete line, not necessarily for each item. p. 382

profit The money left after a for-profit organization subtracts its total expenses from its total revenues and is the reward for the risk it undertakes in marketing its offerings. p. 28

profit equation Profit = Total revenue − Total cost; or Profit = (Unit price × Quantity sold) − (Fixed cost + Variable cost). p. 352

program champion A person who is willing and able to "cut the red tape" to move the program forward. p. 635

promotional allowances Cash payments or an extra amount of "free goods" awarded sellers in the marketing channel for undertaking certain advertising or selling activities to promote a product. p. 387

promotional mix The combination of one or more communication tools used to: (1) inform prospective buyers about the benefits of the product, (2) persuade them to try it, and (3) remind them later about the benefits they enjoyed by using the product. p. 470

protectionism The practice of shielding one or more industries within a country's economy from foreign competition through the use of tariffs or quotas. p. 178

protocol A statement that, before product development begins, identifies: (1) a well-defined target market; (2) specific customers' needs, wants, and preferences; and (3) what the product will be and do to satisfy consumers. p. 271

public relations A form of communication management that seeks to influence the feelings, opinions, or beliefs held by customers, prospective customers, stockholders, suppliers, employees, and other publics about a company and its products or services. p. 474

publicity A nonpersonal, indirectly paid presentation of an organization, product, or service. p. 474

publicity tools Methods of obtaining nonpersonal presentation of an organization, product, or service without direct cost, such as news releases, news conferences, and public service announcements (PSAs). p. 526

pull strategy Directing the promotional mix at ultimate consumers to encourage them to ask the retailer for a product. p. 481

purchase decision process The five stages a buyer passes through in making choices about which products and services to buy: (1) problem recognition, (2) information search, (3) alternative evaluation, (4) purchase decision, and (5) postpurchase behavior. p. 124

push strategy Directing the promotional mix to channel members to gain their cooperation in ordering and stocking the product. p. 480

quantity discounts Reductions in unit costs for a larger order. p. 385

questionnaire data Facts and figures obtained by asking people about their attitudes, awareness, intentions, and behaviors. p. 215

quota A restriction placed on the amount of a product allowed to enter or leave a country. p. 178

rating The percentage of households in a market that are tuned to a particular TV show or radio station. p. 508

reach The number of different people or households exposed to an advertisement. p. 507

receivers Consumers who read, hear, or see the message sent by a source during the communication process. p. 470

reference groups People to whom an individual looks as a basis for self-appraisal or as a source of personal standards. p. 138

regional shopping centers A retail location consisting of 50 to 150 stores that typically attract customers who live or work within a 5- to 10-mile range, often containing two or three anchor stores. p. 451

regulation Restrictions state and federal laws place on a business with regard to the conduct of its activities. p. 88

relationship marketing Links the organization to its individual customers, employees, suppliers, and other partners for their mutual long-term benefit. p. 12

relationship selling The practice of building ties to customers based on a salesperson's attention and commitment to customer needs over time. p. 570

response In the feedback loop, the impact the message had on the receiver's knowledge, attitudes, or behaviors during the communication process. p. 471

retail life cycle The process of growth and decline that retail outlets, like products, experience, consisting of the early growth, accelerated development, maturity, and decline stages. p. 454

retail positioning matrix A matrix that positions retail outlets on two dimensions: breadth of product line and value added, such as location, product reliability, or prestige. p. 447

retailing All activities involved in selling, renting, and providing products and services to ultimate consumers for personal, family, or household use. p. 436

retailing mix The activities related to managing the store and the merchandise in the store, which include retail pricing, store location, retail communication, and merchandise. p. 449

reverse auction In an e-marketplace, an online auction in which a buyer communicates a need for a product or service and would-be suppliers are invited to bid in competition with each other. p. 167

reverse logistics A process of reclaiming recyclable and reusable materials, returns, and reworks from the point of consumption or use for repair, remanufacturing, redistribution, or disposal. p. 426

sales forecast The total sales of a product that a firm expects to sell during a specified time period under specified environmental conditions and its own marketing efforts. p. 227

sales management Planning the selling program and implementing and evaluating the personal selling effort of the firm. p. 568

sales plan A statement describing what is to be achieved and where and how the selling effort of salespeople is to be deployed. p. 581

sales promotion A short-term inducement of value offered to arouse interest in buying a product or service. p. 475

sales quota Specific goals assigned to a salesperson, sales team, branch sales office, or sales district for a stated time period. p. 587

sales response function Relates the expense of the marketing effort to the marketing results obtained. p. 623

salesforce automation (SFA) The use of computer, information, communication, and Internet technologies to make the sales function more effective and efficient. p. 589

scrambled merchandising Offering several unrelated product lines in a single store. p. 442

screening and evaluation The stage of the new-product development process that internally and externally evaluates new-product ideas to eliminate those that warrant no further effort. p. 277

secondary data Facts and figures that have already been recorded prior to the project at hand. p. 210

selective distribution A level of distribution density whereby a firm selects a few retailers in a specific geographical area to carry its products. p. 417

self-regulation An alternative to government control whereby an industry attempts to police itself. p. 92

service continuum The range of offerings companies bring to the market, from the tangible to the intangible or the product-dominant to the service-dominant. p. 325

services Intangible activities or benefits that an organization provides to satisfy consumers' needs in exchange for money or something else of value. pp. 266, 322

seven Ps of services marketing An expanded marketing mix concept for services that includes the four Ps (product, price, promotion, and place or distribution) as well as people, physical environment, and process. p. 333

share points An analysis that uses percentage points of market share as the common basis of comparison to allocate marketing resources effectively for different product lines within the same firm. p. 624

shopper marketing The use of displays, coupons, product samples, and other brand communications to influence shopping behavior in a store. p. 451

shopping products Items for which the consumer compares several alternatives on criteria such as price, quality, or style. p. 266

showrooming The practice of examining products in a store and then buying them online for a cheaper price. p. 611

situation analysis Taking stock of where the firm or product has been recently, where it is now, and where it is headed in terms of the organization's marketing plans and the external forces and trends affecting it. p. 40

skimming pricing Setting the highest initial price that customers really desiring the product are willing to pay when introducing a new or innovative product. p. 372

social audit A systematic assessment of a firm's objectives, strategies, and performance in terms of social responsibility. p. 113

social class The relatively permanent, homogeneous divisions in a society into which people sharing similar values, interests, and behaviors can be grouped. p. 142

social forces The demographic characteristics of the population and its culture. p. 74

social media Online media where users submit comments, photos, and videos—often accompanied by a feedback process to identify "popular" topics. p. 540

social responsibility The idea that organizations are part of a larger society and are accountable to that society for their actions. p. 110

societal marketing concept The view that organizations should satisfy the needs of consumers in a way that provides for society's well-being. p. 17

source A company or person who has information to convey during the communication process. p. 470

spam Communications that take the form of electronic junk mail or unsolicited e-mail. p. 608

specialty products Items that the consumer makes a special effort to search out and buy. p. 266

staff positions People who have the authority and responsibility to advise people in line positions but cannot issue direct orders to them. p. 639

standard markup pricing Adding a fixed percentage to the cost of all items in a specific product class. p. 375

stimulus-response presentation A sales presentation format that assumes that given the appropriate stimulus by a salesperson, the prospect will buy. p. 577

strategic marketing process The approach whereby an organization allocates its marketing mix resources to reach its target markets. p. 40

strategy An organization's long-term course of action designed to deliver a unique customer experience while achieving its goals. p. 428

strip mall A retail location consisting of a cluster of neighborhood stores to serve people who are within a 5- to 10-minute drive. p. 451

subcultures Subgroups within the larger, or national, culture with unique values, ideas, and attitudes. p. 142

supply chain The various firms involved in performing the activities required to create and deliver a product or service to ultimate consumers or industrial users. p. 421

sustainable development Conducting business in a way that protects the natural environment while making economic progress. p. 113

sustainable marketing The effort to meet today's (global) economic, environmental, and social needs without compromising the opportunity for future generations to meet theirs. p. 111

SWOT analysis An acronym describing an organization's appraisal of its internal **S**trengths and **W**eaknesses and its external **O**pportunities and **T**hreats. p. 41

synergy analysis Seeks market-product growth opportunities by finding the optimum balance between marketing efficiencies versus R&D–manufacturing efficiencies. p. 628

target market One or more specific groups of potential consumers toward which an organization directs its marketing program. p. 9

target pricing Consists of (1) estimating the price that ultimate consumers would be willing to pay for a product, (2) working backward through markups taken by retailers and wholesalers to determine what price to charge wholesalers, and then (3) deliberately adjusting the composition and features of the product to achieve the target price to consumers. p. 375

target profit pricing Setting an annual target of a specific dollar volume of profit. p. 377

target return-on-investment pricing Setting a price to achieve an annual target return on investment (ROI). p. 378

target return-on-sales pricing Setting a price to achieve a profit that is a specified percentage of the sales volume. p. 377

tariffs Government taxes on products or services entering a country that primarily serve to raise prices on imports. p. 178

team selling The practice of using an entire team of professionals in selling to and servicing major customers. p. 573

technology Inventions or innovations from applied science or engineering research. p. 84

telemarketing Using the telephone to interact with and sell directly to consumers. p. 446

time-based agenda A meeting agenda that shows the running time allocated to each agenda item. p. 637

total cost (TC) The total expense incurred by a firm in producing and marketing a product. Total cost is the sum of fixed cost and variable cost. p. 362

total logistics cost The expenses associated with transportation, materials handling and warehousing, inventory, stockouts (being out of inventory), order processing, and return products handling. p. 425

total revenue (TR) The total money received from the sale of a product. p. 361

trade name A commercial, legal name under which a company does business. p. 303

trademark Identifies that a firm has legally registered its brand name or trade name so the firm has its exclusive use, thereby preventing others from using it. p. 303

trade-oriented sales promotions Sales tools used to support a company's advertising and personal selling directed to wholesalers, distributors, or retailers. Also called *trade promotions*. p. 524

trading down Reducing a product's number of features, quality, or price. p. 302

trading up Adding value to the product (or line) through additional features or higher-quality materials. p. 302

traditional auction In an e-marketplace, an online auction in which a seller puts an item up for sale and would-be buyers are invited to bid in competition with each other. p. 166

traffic generation The outcome of a direct marketing offer designed to motivate people to visit a business. p. 489

triple-bottom line The recognition of the need for organizations to improve the state of people, the planet, and profit simultaneously if they are to achieve sustainable, long-term growth. p. 111

Twitter A website that enables users to send and receive "tweets," messages up to 140 characters long. p. 546

ultimate consumers The people who use the products and services purchased for a household. Also called *consumers, buyers,* or *customers.* p. 18

uniform delivered pricing The price the seller quotes that includes all transportation costs. p. 388

unit variable cost (UVC) Variable cost expressed on a per unit basis for a product. p. 362

unsought products Items that the consumer does not know about or knows about but does not initially want. p. 266

usage rate The quantity consumed or patronage (store visits) during a specific period. Also called *frequency marketing.* p. 244

user-generated content (UGC) The various forms of online media content that are publicly available and created by end users. Also called *consumer-generated content.* p. 540

utilitarianism A personal moral philosophy that focuses on "the greatest good for the greatest number" by assessing the costs and benefits of the consequences of ethical behavior. p. 108

utility The benefits or customer value received by users of the product. p. 18

value The ratio of perceived benefits to price; or Value = (Perceived benefits ÷ Price). p. 351

value consciousness The concern for obtaining the best quality, features, and performance of a product or service for a given price that drives consumption behavior. p. 81

value pricing The practice of simultaneously increasing product and service benefits while maintaining or decreasing price. p. 352

values A society's personally or socially preferable modes of conduct or states of existence that tend to persist over time. p. 185

variable cost (VC) The sum of the expenses of the firm that vary directly with the quantity of a product that is produced and sold. p. 362

vendor-managed inventory (VMI) An inventory management system whereby the supplier determines the product amount and assortment a customer (such as a retailer) needs and automatically delivers the appropriate items. p. 426

vertical marketing systems Professionally managed and centrally coordinated marketing channels designed to achieve channel economies and maximum marketing impact. p. 414

viral marketing An Internet-enabled promotional strategy that encourages individuals to forward marketer-initiated messages to others via e-mail, social networking websites, and blogs. p. 609

warranty A statement indicating the liability of the manufacturer for product deficiencies. p. 312

web communities Websites that allow people to congregate online and exchange views on topics of common interest. p. 608

webrooming The practice of examining products online and then buying them in a store. p. 611

wheel of retailing A concept that describes how new forms of retail outlets enter the market. p. 453

whistle-blowers Employees who report unethical or illegal actions of their employers. p. 107

word of mouth The influencing of people during conversations. p. 138

workload method A formula-based method for determining the size of a salesforce that integrates the number of customers served, call frequency, call length, and available selling time to arrive at a figure for the salesforce size. p. 584

World Trade Organization (WTO) A permanent institution that sets rules governing trade between its members through panels of trade experts who decide on trade disputes between members and issue binding decisions. p. 179

yield management pricing The charging of different prices to maximize revenue for a set amount of capacity at any given time. p. 375

YouTube A video-sharing website in which users can upload, view, and comment on videos. p. 548

NAME INDEX

A

Aaker, David A., 235, 533, 536
Abel, Bill, 366
Abela, Andrew V., 52
Abell, Derek F., 53
Abernathy, Avery M., 537
Abraham, Magid M., 536
Abrams, Rhonda, 55, 68
Achenreinver, Gwen Bachman, 150
Adams, Joe, 346
Adams, Susan, 671
Adamy, Janet, 235
Adkins-Green, Sheryl, 199, 200, 202
Advincula, Dorothy, 496
Agarwal, Manoj K., 318
Agnihutri, Raj, 52
Ahearne, Michael, 595
Ahern, Karla, 671
Ailawadi, Kusum L., 495
Aizen, I., 150
Alba, Joseph W., 149
Aldrich, Susan, 657
Alexander, Joe F., 670
Allen, Alisa, 395, 396
Allman, Greg, 367
Alsughayir, A., 203
Alva, Marilyn, 97
Ambler, Tim, 52, 533
Anderson, Eric, 465
Anderson, Erin, 172, 595
Anderson, James C., 24
Anderson, Mae, 533, 565
Andrus, Paula, 346
Angwin, Julia, 99
Ansoff, H. Igor, 53
Ante, Spencer E., 52, 565
Anthony, Scott, 235
Arens, Christian, 536
Arens, William F., 536
Armstrong, J. Scott, 53
Armstrong, Lance, 506
Arnsdorf, Isaac, 651
Arons, Marc de Swaan, 564
Arora, Neeraj, 465
Ash, John, 121
Ash, Mary Kay, 199, 200
Atlas, Elise, 594
Atlas, Steve, 594
Austin, Manila S., 496
Avery, Jill, 346
Avery, Simon, 595
Avery, Susan, 173
Axvig, Amanda, 564, 565
Aydelott, Erin, 536

B

Baack, Daniel W., 535
Bacon, Jonathan, 97

Badal, Sangeeta Bharadwaj, 594
Badaracco, Joseph L., Jr., 120
Badenhausen, Kurt, 53
Baek, Tae Hyun, 497
Bagozzi, Richard P., 24, 571, 594
Bahrami, B., 150
Baig, Edward C., 99
Bailey, Brandon, 564
Bailey, Jeffrey J., 533
Bailo, Paul, 668
Baker, Julie, 465, 466
Baker, Wayne F., 671
Balasubramanian, Sridhar, 466
Ball, A. Dwayne, 347
Balter, David, 139
Banerjee, Syagnik, 99
Banis, William J., 671
Banks, Tom, 466
Bansal, Anjah, 670
Barczak, Goria, 288
Barich, Howard, 465
Barnes, Brooks, 235
Barnes, Jimmy D., 496
Barnes, John, 466
Barone, Emily, 98
Barrett, Paul, 99
Bartholomew, Doug, 433
Bartiromo, Maria, 537
Bartz, Bianca, 495
Bashford, Suzy, 97
Bass, Stephen J., 466
Basta, Nicholas, 670
Bates, Albert D., 466
Bates, Douglas D., 235
Batra, Rajeev, 535
Bauerkin, Valerie, 619
Bawa, Kapil, 536
Baxter, Kevin, 347
Baxter, Tom, 535
Bay, Willow, 235
Beaty, Sharon E., 150
Becker, Jill, 464
Behravesh, Nariman, 98
Belfuss, Lisa, 649
Belk, Russell, 150
Bell, Glen, 493, 494
Bellizzi, Joseph A., 346
Bellman, Lawrence M., 466
Belson, Ken, 369
Belton, Gabrie, 534
Ben-Akiva, Moshe, 150
Bendapudi, Neeli, 345, 347
Bendle, Neil T., 52, 466, 651, 668
Bennett, Drake, 564
Bennett, Greg, 285
Bennett, Laura, 285
Bennett, P. D., 346
Berfield, Susan, 671
Berg, Madeline, 533
Bergen, Mark E., 369, 534
Berger, Arthur Asa, 318

Berkowitz, Eric N., 262
Berman, Barry, 345
Bernard, Lisa A., 465
Berner, Robert, 467
Berry, Jeff, 536
Berry, Jon, 150
Berry, Leonard L., 345, 346, 465
Bertagnoli, Lisa, 671
Bertoni, Steven, 651
Best, Michael L., 97
Best, Roger, 150
Bettencourt, Lance A., 344, 346
Bettencourt, Nuno, 367
Beyoncé, 506
Bezos, Jeff, 430, 431, 432, 609
Bharadwaj, Sundar G., 203, 346, 595
Bianco, Anthony, 262
Bieber, Justin, 549
Bigne, J. Enrique, 496
Bilger, Birkhard, 369
Binkley, Christina, 369
Birkel, Frank, 670
Birkner, Christine, 151, 345
Biswas, Neelanjan, 235
Bitner, Mary Jo, 344, 345, 346, 347, 466
Blackwell, Roger D., 149
Blackwood, Amy S., 344
Blakely, Sara, 635–636
Blanchard, Dave, 433
Blasko, Vincent, 496
Bloch, Thomas, 346
Block, Martin P., 496
Block, Terry, 498
Blocker, Christopher P., 346
Bloom, Paul N., 120
Boboltz, Sara, 495
Boccara, Brur, 150
Boddy, Clive R., 235
Bodur, Onur H., 465
Boehrer, Katherine, 464
Boenigk, Michael, 496
Boerman, Sophie C., 536
Boggs, Michele, 670
Bohlen, Betsy, 98
Bolles, Richard N., 668
Bon Jovi, Jon, 367
Bonoma, Thomas V., 172
Booen, Brett, 433
Boone, Jana, 319
Boring, Christopher, 450
Born, Pete, 345
Boulding, William, 24
Bower, David E., 345
Bowie, Norman E., 120
Boyd, Harper W., Jr., 263
Boyle, Brady, 588
Bozman, Carl S., 533
Brady, Diane, 670

Brady, Michael K., 347
Brady, Tom, 80
Brandau, Mark, 497
Branson, Richard, 526
Brat, Ilan, 235, 464
Breugelmans, Els, 466
Bridges, Virginia, 465
Brin, Sergey, 530, 531
Brinkley, Christie, 510
Briseno, Terri, 99
Brodie, Roderick J., 53
Brosnan, Pierce, 327, 506
Brown, Bruce, 235
Brown, Charlie, 536
Brown, Jeff, 590
Brown, Shari, 465
Brown, Stephen W., 344, 345, 346, 347, 466
Brown, Tom J., 235, 289
Bruell, Alexandra, 497, 535
Brunel, Frederic, 150
Brunt, Jonathan, 497
Brusco, Michael J., 347
Brynjolfsson, Erik, 52
Bucchioni, Paul, 464
Buchanan, Bruce, 533
Buck, Claudia, 536
Bughin, Jacques, 52, 650
Bulik, Beth Snyder, 496
Bullock, August, 132, 150
Burdett, Dan, 549
Burdick, Richard K., 172
Burin, Norm, 466
Burke, Richard, 169
Burritt, Chris, 98
Burrow, Peter, 537
Burrows, David, 52
Burton, Scot, 534
Bush, Michael, 345, 495
Bush, Robert P., 235
Buss, Dale, 288
Bustillo, Miguel, 464
Butterworth, Siobhain, 497
Buzzell, Robert D., 536
Bylykbashi, Katrina, 466
Byron, Ellen, 97, 262, 369

C

Caffoe, Jenny, 564
Cai, Jane Zhen, 465
Callaway, Vivian Milroy, 620, 642, 647, 648, 649, 651
Cameron, James, 206
Cammarano, Roy F., 344
Campbell, Sarah, 595
Campo, Katia, 466
Cannon, Joseph P., 120, 594
Capossela, Alison, 593, 594
Cappelli, Peter, 671

Cardona, Mercedes, 464
Carducci, Bernardo J., 150
Carlotti, Steve, 98
Carneiro, Bianca, 464
Carpenter, Gregory S., 25
Carr, Austin, 97
Carral, Teré, 225, 226–227, 235
Carrillat, Francois A., 534
Carter, Franklin, 496
Carter, Jim, 466
Casnocha, Ben, 668
Cass, Ronald A., 396
Casserly, Meghan, 594, 671
Cassidy, Tom, 152, 153
Castillo, Michelle, 533, 536
Castleberry, Stephen B., 595
Cateora, Philip K., 203, 595
Chafwick, Philip, 595
Chahal, Mindi, 97
Chan, Kimmy Wa, 345
Chandler, David, 121
Chandra, Shobhana, 97
Chang, Chingching, 533
Chang, Julia, 595
Chang, Kenneth, 235
Chapuy, Cyril, 506
Chase, Lisa, 25
Cheng, Andria, 464
Cheong, Yunjae, 497
Chesky, Brian, 320
Chevalier, Michael, 537
Chiagouris, Larry, 121
Chiang, Alexander, 52
Chin-Shih Tsai, 345
Choi, Jungkiu, 650
Chonko, Lawrence B., 594
Chopra, Sunil, 432, 433
Christensen, Clayton M., 288, 624, 650
Christenson, Bridget, 650
Chu, Wujin, 172
Chua, K. K., 200
Churchill, Gilbert A., Jr., 235, 289
Clancy, Rebecca, 534
Clark, Bruce H., 52
Clark, Dave, 431
Clark, Don, 24
Clark, Moira, 465
Claus, J., 150
Cleaver, Joanne, 670
Cleeren, Kathleen, 537
Clifford, Stephanie, 235, 369, 465
Clift, Vicki, 345
Clifton, Jim, 594
Cline, Thomas W., 534
Cochrane, Kevin, 670
Cockrill, Antje, 496
Coffey, Brendan, 151
Cohen, Ben, 26
Cohen, Dorothy, 99, 533
Cohen, Noam, 235
Cohen, William A., 68
Cohn, D'Vera, 150
Colby, Charles L., 346
Colby, Sandra L., 97
Coleman-Lochner, Lauren, 24

Coleman, Barbara Carrick, 495
Colford, Steven W., 537
Collins, Jim, 52, 636, 650, 658
Collis, David J., 24
Colvin, Geoff, 262, 650
Compeau, Larry D., 533
Conant, Jeffrey S., 346
Conkey, Christopher, 595
Conklin, J. C., 369
Conlin, Michelle, 99
Conniff, Megan, 464
Connor, Michael, 121
Cook, James, 262
Cook, Tim, 36, 37, 39, 265, 356
Cooper, E., 495
Cooper, Martha, 432
Cooper, Robert G., 288
Cooper, Scott W., 68
Coopersmith, Jonathan, 318
Corbin, Lori, 496
Cordeiro, Anjali, 369
Corfman, Kim, 150
Corliss, Richard, 235
Corson, J. J., 121
Corstjens, Marcel, 464
Costner, Kevin, 204
Cotteleer, Mark, 595
Coughlin, Natalie, 285
Court, David, 650
Courtney, Hugh, 650
Courtney, Martin, 497
Covel, Simona, 288
Covello, Joseph A., 68
Cowles, Deborah L., 262
Coy, Peter, 97, 369, 670
Coyne, Kevin P., 396
Craig, Malcolm, 651
Craig, Nick, 51
Crain, Rance, 535
Crainer, Stuart, 650
Crane, Frederick G., 262, 346
Cravens, David W., 595
Crawford, Merle, 288
Creamer, Matthew, 537, 670
Croce, Maria, 465
Crockett, Roger O., 120, 121
Cron, William L., 595
Cronin, J. Joseph, Jr., 345
Crosby, Jackie, 464
Crosby, Lawrence A., 346, 347, 466
Cross, James, 536
Cruise, Tom, 523
Cuddeford-Jones, Morag, 670
Cunningham, Lawrence F., 344
Cunningham, Todd, 496
Curhan, Ronald C., 537
Curtis, Jacqueline, 465
Cyrus, Miley, 327
Czinkota, Michael, 202

D

D'Astous, Alain, 534
D'Innocenzio, Ann, 262

D'Meurville, Martin Petit, 565
Dahl, Sima, 671
Dahlhoff, Denise, 318
Daley, Jason, 564
Daley, Shawn P., 173
Dalrymple, Jim, 466
Dalsace, Frederic, 595
Dalton, Catherine M., 52
Damast, Alison, 671
Daniel, David S., 670
Daniels, Chris, 464
Dant, Rajiv P., 24
Darden, William, 345
Darmon, René Y., 595
David, Bob, 464
Davidson, Adam, 98
Davidson, Paul, 671
Davidson, William R., 466
Davis-Blake, Alison, 97
Davis, Ellen, 670
Davis, James E., 536
Davis, John, 52, 466, 651
Dawes, Philip l., 172
Dawley, Jacqueline, 262
Day, George S., 25, 52, 235
De Meulenaer, Sarah, 534
De Pelsmacker, Patrick, 534, 536
Dean, Joshua, 23
DeCarlo, Thomas E., 595
Deighton, John, 318
Dekimpe, Marnik G., 537
Dell, Lauren, 496
Dell, Michael, 174, 417
Delo, Cotton, 99, 497
Delong, Thomas J., 344
Demos, Telis, 565
DeNavas-Walt, Carmen, 98
Dens, Nathalia, 534, 536
Desai, Tina, 538, 564
Devlin, J. Stuart, 671
Dhar, Sanjay K., 396
Di Benedetto, Anthony, 288
Di Mascio, Rita, 346
Diaz, Ann-Christine, 533
Diaz, Cameron, 526
Dichter, Ernest, 536
Dickey, Jack, 263
Dickson, Andrea, 594
Dickson, Peter R., 150
Diderich, Levi, 564
Diepenbrock, Amy, 671
Dilworth, Dianna, 464
Diorio, Carl, 235
Diriker, Memo F., 670
Dirksing, Peter, 286
Dobscha, Susan, 24, 346
Dockterman, Eliana, 533
Dodd, Mike, 369
Dodds, William D., 369, 465
Dodes, Rachel, 235
Dogan, Mustafa, 21
Doherty, Anne Marie, 466
Dolan, Robert J., 173
Dolber, Roslyn, 670
Donaldson, Thomas, 120
Donegan, Dan, 367

Dong, Beibei, 345
Donlon, J. P., 262
Donnelly, James H., 345
Donovan, Doug, 345
Donovan, Landon, 341
Donovan, Robert J., 150
Donthu, Naveen, 172
Dorsch, Michael J., 345
Dos Santos, Giovani, 342
Dowling, Grahame R., 172
Drell, Lauren, 565
Drew, Christopher, 289
Dreze, Xavier, 465
Driest, Frank van den, 564
Drysch, Michael, 554–555
Du, Rex Y., 150
Dubinsky, Alan J., 595
Dudlicek, Jim, 235
Duncan, Ewan, 25
Duncan, Tom, 497
Dupre, Elyse, 344
Dutta, Soumitra, 564
Dwoskin, Elizabeth, 564, 565
Dwyer, F. Robert, 172
Dye, Renee, 650
Dyer, Jeff, 650
Dylan, Bob, 367

E

Eakin, Tim, 497
Earnhardt, Dale, Jr., 502
Eaton, Leslie, 464
Ebenkam, Becky, 99
Edelman, Benjamin, 535
Edwards, Jim, 564, 595
Efrati, Amir, 565
Ehret, Michael, 24
Einwiller, Sabine A., 496
Eisend, Martin, 495
Eisenhower, Dwight D., 631
El-Ansary, Adel I., 432
Elledge, Josh, 536
Ellin, Abby, 346
Elliott, Stuart, 496, 537
Ellison, Sarah, 288
Eng, Dinah, 262, 288
Engardio, Pete, 121
Engel, James F., 149
Enman, Charles, 345
Eppright, David R., 534
Erenberg, Grigori, 536
Erickson, Peter, 288
Esty, Daniel C., 347
Etgar, Michael, 533
Ethans, Arno J., 172
Evans, Dave, 564
Evans, Kenneth R., 24
Evans, Phillip, 52
Ewoldt, John, 464

F

Fahey, Liam, 25
Fahy, John, 346

Fajen, Stdphen, 535
Falcone, John, 99
Fan, Ming, 396
Farrell, Chris, 671
Farris, Paul W., 52, 533, 651
Fay, Brad, 150
Felice, Steve, 174
Felson, Leonard, 671
Feng Zhu, 465
Fera, Rae Ann, 533
Fernandez, Karen V., 533
Fetscherin, Marc, 319
Few, Stephen, 52
Fiedler, Lars, 467
Fine, Leslie M., 345
Finn, Ryan, 235
Fishbein, Martin, 150
Fisher, Kelsey, 562, 564
Fisher, Marshall L., 466, 467
Fisher, Robert J., 432, 619
Fisher, Stacy, 522
Fitch, Stephane, 98
Fitzgerald, Kate, 537, 619
Fleming, Anne, 123
Flood, Barbara, 671
Folkens, Dave, 495
Folse, Judith Anne Garretson, 534
Forbes, Thom, 24, 288
Ford, David, 235, 651
Fornier, Susan, 24, 318, 346
Forrester, Duane, 670
Forster, Julie, 288
Forte, Eric J., 668
Foster, Thomas A., 433
Foust, Dean, 99
Fowler, Geoffrey A., 235
Fox, Justin, 263
Frank, John N., 670
Frank, Zac, 288
Franks, Judy, 487
Fraser, Cynthia, 346
Fraser, Matthew, 564
Fredrix, Emily, 534
Freedman, Alix M., 120
Freeman, Sholnn, 150
Friars, Eileen M., 465
Friedman, Milton, 110–111, 116
Frier, Sarah, 97
Frizell, Sam, 98
Frost, Raymond, 619
Fry, Erika, 467
Fry, Richard, 97
Fujimoto, Takahiro, 432
Fulgoni, Gian, 564
Fusaro, Dave, 24
Futrell, Charles M., 595

G

Gaida, Kathleen A., 346
Galbraith, J. K., 99
Gantt, Henry L., 44
Garbuio, Massimo, 650
Gardyn, Rebecca, 98
Garino, Jason, 466

Garlieb, Stacie, 671
Garner, Jennifer, 506
Gasparro, Annie, 24, 68
Gaudiosi, John, 533, 565
Gauri, Dinesh Kumar, 465
Gebbia, Joe, 320
Gebhardt, Gary F., 25
Gedenk, Karen, 495
Geewax, Marilyn, 466
Geier, Ben, 97
Gelb, Gabriel M., 346
George, William R., 345, 346
Gerlach, James, 344
Gerlach, Jerry, 467
Germann, Frank, 467
Geron, Tomio, 344
Gerrard, Steven, 342
Gerst, Jeff, 232, 233, 235
Gery, Nurit, 466
Ghemawat, Pankaj, 650
Ghermezian family, 461
Ghosh, Pulak, 235
Gianelloni, J. L., 347
Gibson, Lawrence D., 235, 535
Gillette, Felix, 565
Gilly, March C., 346
Gilly, Mary C., 203, 595
Gilmore, James H., 345
Glassel, Linda, 260, 262, 263
Glazer, Emily, 288
Gloeckler, Geoff, 97
Goel, Vindu, 564
Gogoi, Pallavi, 99
Gold, Laurence N., 536
Goldberg, Marvin E., 496, 534
Golden, Linda L., 466
Goldman, Doron, 533
Goldmark, Alex, 345
Goldstein, Linda A., 97
Gonul, Fusun F., 496
Goode, Mark M., 496
Goodman, Kolby, 564
Goodman, Peter S., 537
Goodwin, Stephen A., 533
Gordon, Jeff, 552, 565
Gotlieb, Jerry, 533
Gottfried, Miriam, 235
Gould, Michael, 450
Graber, Donald R., 203
Graham, John L., 203, 595
Graiko, Stacy, 496
Grama, Ananth, 235
Grannis, Kathy, 465
Grant, Kate, 327
Grant, Kelli B., 98
Green, Marianne E., 670, 671
Green, Mark C., 202, 203
Greenberg, Karl, 347
Greenberg, Robert M., 671
Greenfield, Jerry, 26
Greengard, Samuel, 467
Greenleaf, Eric A., 150
Greenspan, Robyn, 173
Gregerson, Hal B., 650
Gregor, William T., 465
Gremler, Dwayne D., 346, 347

Grewal, Dhruv, 24, 346, 369, 465,
    466, 533
Greyersen, Hal B., 288
Griffin, Abbie, 288
Griffith, Eric, 98
Grimm, Julie Ann, 99
Grobart, Sam, 565
Groene, Nicole, 535
Groenke, Michelle, 98
Gronroos, Christian, 344, 346
Gronstedt, Anders, 496
Groom, Alyssa S., 495
Grossman, Lev, 24
Grossnickle, Joshua, 671
Groth, Markus, 346
Grove, Andy, 632
Grove, Ronald, 235
Grove, Stephen J., 345
Gruca, Thomas S., 346
Gryta, Thomas, 98
Gschwandtner, Gerhard, 594
Gulati, Ranjay, 466
Gumbel, Peter, 25
Gundlach, Gregory T., 24, 120
Gupta, Sunil, 150
Gupte, Gouri, 595
Gustafsson, Katarina, 24
Gwinner, Kevin P., 346

H

Ha, Anthony, 534
Haas, Edward, III, 303
Haenlein, Michael, 541, 564
Hagey, Keach, 319
Hague, Nick, 668
Hague, Paul, 668
Hahn, Minhi, 535
Hair, Joseph F., Jr., 235
Hair, Neil, 465
Hall, James, 53
Hall, Joseph M., 466
Hall, Julie, 288
Hall, Linda D., 668
Hall, Starr, 564
Hallen, Gary, 595
Hamilton, Laird, 285
Hamilton, Rebecca W., 288
Hammond, John S., 53
Hammond, Michele, 97
Hampp, Andrew, 535, 537
Han, Angie, 536
Handler, Doug, 98
Hanford, Desiree J., 99
Hang, Haiming, 537
Hanifin, Bill, 466
Hansen, Morten T., 52, 636, 650
Hanssens, Dominique M., 533
Hao, Lin, 396
Hardesty, David M., 595
Harich, Katrin R., 671
Harper, Jonathan, 670
Harris, Armin, 650
Harris, Frederick H. dB., 347
Harris, Lloyd C., 465

Harris, Paul, 668
Harrison-Walker, L. Jean, 345
Harrison, George, 367
Harrower, Nancy, 565
Hartley, Robert F., 121
Hartley, Steven W., 53, 99,
    151, 173, 262, 289, 347,
    369, 396, 467, 536, 537,
    595, 651
Hartline, Jana, 117
Hartman, Cathy L., 98, 464
Hartnett, Cassandra J., 668
Hartzell, Dane, 232
Hastie, Reid, 288
Hathcote, Jan M., 533
Haughney, Christine, 535
Hauser, Erik, 619
Hawkins, Delbert I., 150
Hayes, Tom, 619
Hazelgren, Brian J., 68
Heibing, Roman G., Jr., 68
Heine, Christopher, 533, 535
Heinzinger, David, 434
Helm, Burt, 344
Helsen, Kristiaan, 202
Hempel, Jessi, 53, 151, 344, 433,
    565, 594
Hemphill, Thomas A., 99
Henderson, Verne E., 120
Henn, Jamie, 328
Hennig-Thurau, Thorsten, 345, 346
Henry, David, 99
Heppelmann, James E., 24
Herbing, Paul A., 203, 595
Herring, Jeff, 564
Herring, Tyler, 260, 263
Herrmann, Andreas, 466
Hershberger, Edmund, 670
Hesseldahl, Arik, 369
Hiebing, Roman G., Jr., 68
Higgins, Michelle, 99
Higgins, Tim, 121
Hill, Arlene, 659
Hilton, Kyle, 235
Himich, Matthew, 99
Hipp, Jonathan, 262
Hirsh, Jerry, 149
Hirunyawipada, Tanawat, 650
Hite, Robert E., 346
Hlavinka, Kelly, 536
Hobbs, Thomas, 24
Hochman, Kevin, 315, 316,
    317, 318
Hochman, Sarah, 77
Hodgdon, Kirk, 394, 396
Hodgdon, Patrick, 555, 565
Hof, Robert D., 53, 537
Hoffman, Reid, 668
Hoffman, Tom, 536
Hogg, Bevill, 169
Holden, Richard, 530, 532
Holland, Frank, 52
Holmes, Elizabeth, 150, 464
Honebein, Peter C., 344
Honigman, Daniel B., 346
Hooley, Graham J., 496

Hope, Chris, 121
Hopewell, Nikki, 495
Hopkins, Michael S., 235
Hopper, Grace Murray, 635
Horn, John, 235, 396
Horowitz, Bruce, 318
Houston, Mark B., 346
Howard, Charley, 497
Howard, Daniel L., 369, 466
Howard, John A., 150
Howard, Ron, 486
Howard, Theresa, 497
Hoyer, Wayne D., 121, 150
Hsiao-Wen Hsiung, 345
Hsieh, Tony, 24, 236, 262
Hsu, Tiffany, 263
Huddelston, Tom, Jr., 99
Hudson, Kris, 98
Hughes, Douglas E., 595
Hughlett, Mike, 650
Humphrey, Katie, 98
Humphreys, Jeffrey M., 68, 150
Hunt, Helen, 204
Hunt, James B., 534
Hunt, Kenneth A., 465
Hurd, Bo, 148
Hutchinson, Wesley, 149
Hutt, Michael D., 172
Hyman, H., 495

I

Iacobucci, Dawn, 345
Ian, Scott, 367
Idelson, Karen, 537
Idena, Matthew, 97
Inderrieden, Edward, 595
Iqbal, Azhar, 98
Isidore, Chris, 534
Ive, Jonathan, 276
Ives, Nat, 464

J

Jackson, Donald W., 172
Jackson, Samuel L., 506
Jacobs, Bert, 275
Jacobs, John, 275
Jacobs, Paul, 496
Jacobson, Don, 263
Jacoby, Jacob, 369
Jahoda, M., 495
Jain, Ambuj, 369, 466
James, Dana, 671
James, Harvey S., 121
James, LeBron, 394, 506, 554–555
James, Meg, 235
Janke, James, 467
Janos, Leo, 650
Janos, Rich, 650
Jap, Sandy D., 172, 173
Jargon, Julie, 263
Jarvis, Jeff, 537
Jasper, Dan, 461, 463
Jaworski, Bernard J., 432, 619

Jayachandran, Satish, 650
Jefferson, Elana Ashanti, 536
Jeffrey, Mark, 52, 235, 650
Jenner, Kendall, 303
Jenner, Kylie, 303
Jesperson, Frederick F., 99
Jie Wei, 466
Jobs, Steve, 8, 38, 254, 264, 265
Johannes, Amy, 536, 537
Johansson, Johnny K., 202, 203
John, Deborah Roedder, 150
Johns, Chris, 97
Johnson, Eugene M., 346
Johnson, Gavin, 235
Johnson, Gerry, 52
Johnson, Kelly, 635
Johnson, Lauren, 564, 650
Johnson, Lisa, 463
Johnson, Lynne D., 495
Johnson, Sharna, 465
Johnson, Sheree L., 346
Johnston, Mark W., 594, 595
Johnston, Wesley J., 24, 172
Jolson, Marvin A., 536, 595
Jones, Cobi, 341
Jones, Conor, 25
Jones, D. G. Brian, 24
Jones, Eli, 594, 595
Jones, John Philip, 496
Jordan, Michael, 506
Joshi, Amit, 533
Joslyn, Mark, 169, 170, 172
Jun Pang, 346

K

Ka-Man Cheung, 495
Kador, John, 52
Kaepernick, Colin, 506
Kahn, Barbara E., 396
Kahn, Kenneth B., 288
Kallayil, Gopip, 531
Kamakura, Wagner A., 150
Kambatla, Karthik, 235
Kambil, Ajit, 173
Kaminsky, Philip, 432
Kane, Colleen, 97
Kane, Hukari, 120
Kane, Rich, 52
Kane, Yukari Iwatani, 24
Kang, Stephanie, 432, 619
Kanter, James, 99
Kapferer, Jean-Noel, 396
Kaplan, Andreas M., 564, 565
Kaplan, Andrew M., 541
Kaplan, David, 464
Kaplan, Don, 496
Kapoor, Anuj, 564
Kaputa, Catherine, 670
Kardashian, Khloe, 445
Kardashian, Kim, 445
Kardashian, Kourtney, 445
Karim, Sohel, 25
Karlgaard, Rich, 24
Karniouchina, Ekaterina V., 536

Karremans, J., 150
Katobe, Masaaki, 595
Katz, Jennifer, 561, 562, 565
Kaye, Kate, 99
Keane, Robbie, 342
Keaveney, Susan M., 465
Kedmey, Dan, 347, 533
Keegan, Warren J., 202, 203
Keh, Hean Tat, 346
Keith, Janey E., 172
Keith, Robert F., 25
Kellaris, James J., 534
Keller, Ed, 150
Keller, Kevin Lane, 202, 318, 319, 650
Keller, Naomi, 671
Kelly, David, 99
Kennedy, John, 50
Kennedy, John F., 104
Kennedy, Marilyn Moats, 671
Kennerty, Mike, 367
Kent, Robert, 534
Kepczyk, Roman H., 99
Kerin, Roger A., 24, 52, 53, 203, 262, 263, 318, 369, 466, 496, 595, 650, 651
Kerwin, Ann Marie, 345
Kerwin, Kathleen, 650
Khadder, Tania, 288
Kher, Unmesh, 121
Khermouch, Gerry, 537
Kidd, Patricia, 99
Kidwell, Blair, 595
Kim Wo Chong, 632
Kim, Hyeong Min, 465
Kim, Ilchul, 495
Kim, Jooyoung, 495
Kim, Kathleen, 619
Kim, Peter, 53
Kim, W. Chan, 52, 636, 650
Kisiel, Ryan, 534
Kitchen, Philip J., 495
Klaassen, Abbey, 535, 537
Klapper, J. T., 495
Klara, Robert, 671
Klein, Chris, 341, 344
Klein, Noreen M., 465
Klein, Thomas A., 120
Klie, Leonard, 97
Kloberdanz, Kristin, 98
Klum, Heidi, 327, 445
Knapp, Don, 344
Kobe, Kathryn, 99
Koh, Yoree, 564
Kohli, Ajay K., 172, 595
Kohli, Chiranjeev, 564
Kohls, L. Robert, 98
Kollias, Giorgis, 235
Konus, Umut, 466
Kopale, Praveen K., 466
Kopp, Wendy, 29
Kornik, Joseph, 595
Koselka, Rita, 465
Kotabe, Masaaki, 202
Kothari, Ashish, 24
Kotler, Philip, 25, 465, 466, 537, 650

Kowitt, Beth, 25
Krantz, Les, 671
Krasnikov, Alexander, 650
Krattenmaker, Tom, 52
Kraus, Eric, 658
Kraus, Matthias, 467
Krauss, Michael, 52, 651
Kreider, Rose M., 97
Krishna, Aradhna, 214, 235, 466
Krishnan, R., 466
Kroc, Ray, 453
Krugel, David, 536
Kruschwitz, Nina, 235
Krush, Michael T., 52
Kuan-Ying Chen, 345
Kuchihar, Rakesh, 97
Kumar, Vipin, 24, 235
Kuster, Franziska, 495
Kydd, Arthur R., 54, 68

L

LaBelle, Patti, 327
Lackner, Joseph, 24
Lade, Diane C., 345
Laezniak, Gene R., 120
Lafley, A. G., 276
Lahiri, Rangin, 235
Lakhan, Dave, 150
Lal, Rajiv, 464
Lam, Simon S. K., 345
Lane, Vicki R., 534
Lang, Brent, 496
Langert, Bob, 475
LaReau, Jamie, 496
Larocca, Tracee, 494
Laroche, Michel, 345
LaRocque, Ed, 118
Lashinsky, Adam, 288
Last, Richard, 467
Latino, Robert, 595
Latson, Jennifer, 467
LaValle, Steve, 235
Lavelle, Louis, 671
Lavidge, Robert J., 496
Lavie, N., 150
Lavigne, Melissa, 86
Law, Stella Wai-Art, 25
Lazure, Josianne, 534
Learmonth, Michael, 497
LeBon, Joe, 595
Leckenby, John D., 497
Lee, Don Y., 172
Lee, Edmund, 99
Lee, Felissa, 595
Lee, Hau L., 432
Lee, Kyoochin, 465
Lee, Kyung Ah, 346
Lee, Myung-Soo, 149
Lee, Sun Young, 495
Lee, Thomas, 99, 564
Lee, Yih Hwai, 534
Lee, Yong-Ki, 346
Lefkofsky, Eric, 149

Lehmann, Donald R., 150, 318
Leigh, Thomas W., 172
Leighton, Michael, 169, 171
Lello, Kevin, 367
Lemon, Katherine N., 346
Lemos, Robert, 535
Lencioni, Patrick M., 52
Lenderman, Max, 619
Lenskold, James D., 651
Leo, Pamela, 236
Leon, Robert P., 465
Leonard, Devin, 98
Leone, Robert P., 235
Leppanen, Casey, 342, 343
Lesser, Eric, 235
Levere, Jane L., 344
Levering, Robert, 650, 670
Levey, Richard H., 464
Levine, Avi, 671
Levitt, Theodore, 32, 52, 595
Levy-Yurista, Guy, 564
Levy, Keith, 517
Levy, Michael, 396, 496
Levy, Piet, 97, 466, 495, 619,
    670, 671
Levy, Sidney J., 25
Lewin, Jeffrey E., 172, 595
Lewis, Carol, 465
Lewis, Ioni, 534
Lewis, Jamie M., 97
Lewis, John, 619
Lewis, Tanya, 670
Li, Jessica, 668
Li, Mei, 345
Li, Zhan G., 466
Lieber, Ronald B., 466
Lilien, Gary L., 172, 467
Lim, Chea Un, 595
Lim, Elison Ai Ching, 534
Lin, Lynn Y. S., 496
Lindstrom, Martin, 150, 214, 235
Linshi, Jack, 53, 97
Liodice, Bob, 495
Liovio, Louis, 534
Lipsman, Andrew, 564
Lirtsman, Alex, 498
Liu, Xijian, 464
LL Cool J, 327
Lletget, Sebastian, 342
Lloyd, Mary Ellen, 99
Lock, Tony, 497
Loda, Marsha D., 495
Lodish, Leonard M., 536
Lohr, Steve, 466, 650
Lorimer, Sally F., 595
Lovallo, Dan, 650
Lovelock, Christopher, 344,
    346, 347
Low, George S., 496
Lowenhar, Jeffrey A., 496
Lowry, Tom, 537
Lubin, David A., 347
Lublin, Joan S., 670
Luckerson, Victor, 263
Lumpkin, James R., 432
Lundy, Sarah, 670

Lunte, Kathryn, 235
Lusch, Robert F., 344
Lutz, Richard J., 150
Lynch, James E., 496
Lynch, John, 150

M

MacArthur, Kate, 318
MacDuffie, John Paul, 432
MacFarquhar, Larissa, 651
MacInnis, Deborah J., 121, 150
MacMillan, Douglas, 151
Macoolyn, Gillian, 150
Magid, Larry, 53
Magnusson, Paul, 650
Mahajan, Vijay, 53
Maher, Lucy, 649
Maheswari, Sapna, 497
Makarem, Suzanne C., 344
Malaviya, Prashant, 536
Malcolm, Robert, 52
Malhotra, Naresh, 466, 668
Malone, Michael S., 619
Malphurs, Aubrey, 52
Mandel, Michael, 99
Mangalindan, Mylene, 619
Manning, Eli, 138
Manning, Peyton, 327
Mantrala, Murali K., 650
Marconi, Carolyn D., 657, 671
Marie-Odile, Richard, 345
Marken, G. A., 537
Markham, Stephen K., 24
Markides, Costas, 52
Marks, Ronald B., 671
Marlin, Brenda, 496
Marlin, Brenda, 496
Marshall, Greg W., 594, 595
Marshall, Jack, 564
Martin, Andrew, 120
Martin, Dick, 495
Martineau, Pierre, 451, 465
Masidlover, Nadya, 464
Maslow, Abraham H., 150
Mason, Andrew, 146, 147, 149
Massante, Lou, 173
Masterson, Peggy, 535
Mathur, Anil, 345
Mathwick, Charla, 466
Matson, Holly, 233
Matthews, Chris, 97
Mattila, Anna S., 345
Mattioli, Dana, 464
Mauborgne, Renée, 52, 636, 650
Maxham, James G., III, 345
May, Eleanor, 466
Mazaheri, Ebrahim, 345
McAfee, Andrew, 52
McAlister, Leigh, 396
McCarthy, E. Jerome, 10, 24
McCartney, Scott, 396
McClelland, Anna Sheen, 466
McColgan, Ellyn A., 344
McColl-Kennedy, Janet R., 344
McConaughey, Matthew, 506

McCorvey, J. J., 24
McCracken, Harry, 235
McCullough, Jim, 346
McDonald brothers, 493–494
McDonald, Hugh, 367
McGuire, Kara, 536, 565
McHugh, Molly, 564
McKeever, John M., 346
McKeever, Mike, 68
McMath, Robert M., 7, 24, 288
McNair, Malcolm P., 466
McRae, Matt, 348
Meichtry, Stacy, 396
Meindl, Peter, 432, 433
Mendelsohn, Bruce, 235
Menon, Anil, 121
Mercer, Dick, 99
Metropoulos, Dean, 641
Metz, Cade, 99
Meuter, Matthew L., 344
Meyer, Christopher, 25
Mezrich, Ben, 24
Michaels, Daniel, 289
Michaels, Ronald E., 595
Michiels, Ian, 263
Mick, David Glen, 24, 346
Mickelson, Phil, 406
Mihas, Liz, 98
Milk, Chris, 498
Miller, Jennifer, 596
Miller, Rich, 97
Miller, Steve, 433
Millington, Alison, 565
Milliot, Jim, 52
Mindlin, Alex, 535
Miniard, Paul W., 149
Minor, Michael S., 466
Minsker, Maria, 533
Mishra, Dita, 495
Mitchell, Dan, 97, 263
Mitchell, John T., 670
Mitra, Sramana, 564
Mittal, Banwari, 150, 318
Mohammed, Rafi A., 432, 619
Mohan, Neal, 564
Mohr, Jakki J., 172, 496
Moin, David, 536
Moltby, Emily, 564
Monfils, Gael, 262
Monroe, Kent B., 346, 368, 369,
    396, 465
Montgomery, Alexandra, 98
Monts, Michael A., 120
Moon, Youngme, 173
Moore, Elizabeth S., 25, 150
Moorman, Christine, 52
Moorthy, Janakiraman, 235
Moran, Charlotte, 77
Morash, Edward, 345
Morgan, Carol-Ann, 668
Morgan, Felicia N., 345
Morimoto, Mariko, 497
Morin, Rich, 150
Morinoto, Risako, 121
Morrison, Maureen, 263,
    289, 497

Mortimer, Kathleen, 346
Moscaritolo, Angel, 347
Moskowitz, Milton, 650, 670
Mossler, Julie, 148, 149
Mothersbaugh, David L., 150
Mudambi, Susan M., 344
Mueller, Malyn, 564
Mueller, Samuel, 463
Mulhern, Francis J., 465
Mullins, John W., 263, 318
Mullman, Jeremy, 535
Muralie, Sushma, 495
Muris, Timothy, 120
Murphy, Jean, 433
Murphy, Patrick E., 24, 120
Murphy, Richard, 52
Murray, Keith B., 345
Murtha, Brian R., 595
Murthy, Archana K., 496
Muscove, Brenda J., 496

N

Nadarajah, Murali, 467
Nagarajan, Hina, 201
Nagele, Kim, 152, 153, 163, 172
Nakata, Cheryl, 344
Nam, Jung-Heon, 346
Nanath, Krishnadas, 235
Narius, James A., 24
Narver, John C., 25
Nasheri, Hedich, 120
Nassauer, Sarah, 649
Nath, Prithwiraz, 173
Navarro-Bailon, Maria Angeles,
    497
Naylor, Karen, 97
Nedungadi, Prakesh, 150
Neeson, Liam, 506
Neff, Jack, 121, 235, 288, 319,
    466, 497, 535
Nelson, Katherine A., 120
Nesdale, Andrew, 150
Neslin, Scott A., 466, 495
Netemeyer, Richard G., 345, 534
Neuborne, Ellen, 595
Newman, Andrew Adam, 466, 533
Newsome, Laynie, 348
Newstead, Kate, 534
Newton, Jeff, 432
Niccol, Brian, 615, 618, 619
Nichols, Michele, 345
Nickerson, Mary, 119, 121
Niejens, Peter C., 536
Nohr, Marc, 497
Nohrin, Nitin, 650
Norris, Chuck, 510
Norris, Donald, 533
Norton, Rob, 535
Nowlin, Edward L., 52

O

O'Brien, Jeffrey M., 53, 262
O'Brien, Keith, 263

O'Brien, Kyle, 21, 22
O'Connell, Vanessa, 369
O'Connor, Clare, 463, 650
O'Malley, Kathy L., 533
O'Marah, Kevin, 433
O'Reilly, Lara, 497
Obama, Barack, 555
Odell, Patricia, 98, 263
Ohnsman, Alan, 98
Oja, Dan, 120
Olenski, Steve, 150
Oliver, Jason, 345
Olsen, Jerry C., 369
Olsen, R. Paul, 345
Olson, Jerry C., 150, 151, 346
Olson, Parmy, 53, 235
Omoto, Yukihiro, 464
Opdyke, Jeff D., 369
Ordonez, Jennifer, 289
Orlik, Tom, 464
Ortinau, David J., 235
Ortman, Jennifer M., 97
Ortmeyer, Gwen, 465
Ostrom, Amy, 345
Ostrom, Amy L., 344
Ostrower, Jon, 289
Ovide, Shira, 564
Owens, Jan P., 262
Ozment, John, 345

P

Paddison, Gordon J., 432, 619
Page, Larry, 530, 531
Palenchar, Joseph, 53
Palmatier, Robert W., 24, 432
Palmer, Adrian, 346
Palmer, Alex, 497
Palmeri, Christopher, 262
Palmisano, Samuel J., 50, 51, 53, 424
Parasuraman, A., 345, 346, 465
Pardee, Thomas, 496
Parekh, Rupal, 151, 534, 535, 619
Park, Dae-Hwan, 346
Park, Schoon, 535
Parker, R. Stephen, 595
Parment, Anders, 496
Parra, Maritza, 564
Parsons, June Jamich, 120
Parsons, Patrick R., 537
Parton, Dolly, 367, 445
Parvatiyar, Atul, 203
Passariello, Christina, 433
Paswan, Ajudesh K., 650
Pasztor, Andy, 289
Patel, Kunur, 151
Patnaik, Sandeep, 533
Patterson, Paul G., 345
Patti, Charles H., 496
Pattis, William, 670
Paul, Michael, 346
Pauwels, Koen, 52, 98, 466
Peacock, Peter, 347
Pease, Heather, 343, 344

Pechman, Cornelia, 496, 533, 534
Pelton, Lou, 432
Perdue, Stephanie, 493
Pereira, Joseph, 396
Perkins, Olivera, 465
Perlman, David, 148
Peros, Vasilos, 99
Perry, Kate, 564
Peter, J. Paul, 150, 151
Peters, Kevin, 466
Peters, Leah E., 56, 57, 68
Peters, Randall F., 56, 57, 68
Peters, Thomas J., 650
Peterson, David, 98
Peterson, Robert A., 24, 52, 53, 263, 318, 369, 466, 595, 650
Peterson, Robin T., 671
Peterson, Tim, 497, 534
Petrof, John Y., 346
Petrova, Elina, 496
Pettijohn, Charles E., 595
Pettijohn, Sarah L., 344
Pfeifer, Phillip E., 52, 466, 651, 668
Pham, Kimberley, 565
Phelps, Michael, 285
Phillips, Wendy, 172
Pieters, Rik, 121, 150, 495, 535
Pine, Joseph, 345
Podensky, Johnathan, 564
Podoshen, Jeffrey S., 344
Poetsch, Rob, 494
Poggi, Jeanine, 235, 533
Pohl, Mike, 462
Pollak, Lindsey, 671
Pooley, Eric, 98
Poon, T. Y., 536
Pope, Pat, 97
Popeil, Ron, 510
Popky, Linda J., 670
Porras, Jerry I., 52
Port, David, 97
Porter, Michael E., 24, 52, 99, 627–628, 650
Portillo, Ernesto, 465
Post, Tim, 671
Postrel, Richard, 536
Powell, C. Randall, 671
Powell, Michael A., 654
Power, J. D., III, 631
Powers, Blake, 534
Powers, Kemp, 396
Powers, Thomas L., 595
Powers, Todd, 496
Prasongsukarn, Kriengsin, 345
Pratt, Chris, 486
Prendergast, Gerard P., 495, 536
Pressel, Morgan, 406
Prins, Remco, 496
Proctor, Bernadette D., 98
Psy, 549
Pthak, Shareen, 533
Pullen, John Patrick, 262
Purnawirawan, Nathalia, 536
Purvis, Scott C., 533
Putrevu, Sanjay, 534

Q

Quelch, John A., 465, 536, 537
Quinn, Jane Bryant, 120

R

Radelat, Ana, 99
Raju, Jagmohan S., 396
Raman, Ananth, 466, 467
Raman, Kaylin, 496
Ramaswamy, Arvind, 619
Randall, Donna, 346
Randas, Kamalini, 347
Rangan, Kasturi, 25
Ranjan, Jayanthi, 235
Rao, Akshay R., 369, 396
Rao, Leona, 263
Rao, Vithala R., 120, 318
Rapp, Adam, 595
Raskin, Oliver, 671
Rassekh, Farhad, 121
Rassouli, Javad, 496
Ratchford, Brian T., 149
Rath, Tom, 659
Rawson, Alex, 25
Ray, Ipshita, 121
Rayport, Jeffrey F., 619
Rea-Holloway, Melinda, 235
Rechtin, Mark, 121
Rees, G., 150
Refermat, Emily, 464
Regan, Helen, 496
Reibling, Ellen Thomas, 496, 534
Reibstein, David J., 52, 466, 651, 668
Reichheld, Frederick F., 344
Reid, Mike, 497
Rein, Irving, 537
Reinhold, Jennifer, 173
Reinold, T., 497
Reis, Al, 263
Reisinger, Don, 53
Rendon, Jim, 25
Renslow, Jill, 461, 462, 463
Retsky, Maxine L., 99
Ricadela, Aaron, 344
Rich, Ben R., 650
Rich, Gillian, 98
Rich, Gregory A., 595
Rich, Motoko, 262
Richerson, Steve, 99
Rigby, Darrell K., 52, 466
Rigdon, Edward, 466
Ritson, Mark, 319
Robinot, E., 347
Robinson, David, 495
Rockwood, Kate, 24
Rodriguez, Juan, 98
Roeger, Katie L., 344
Roesler, Peter, 564
Rogers, Bruce, 98
Rogers, Everett M., 318
Rogers, Richard, 199
Romaniuk, Jenni, 495, 534

Rometty, Virginia, 50
Ronkainen, Ilkka A., 202
Rose, Charlie, 288
Rose, Susan, 465
Rosecky, Richard B., 536
Rosen, Dennis L., 533
Rosen, Emanuel, 150
Rosen, Judith, 466
Rosenberg, Chadd, 564
Rosenthal, David W., 654
Ross, Ashley, 533
Ross, William T., Jr., 595
Rossi, Juhana, 565
Rossiter, John R., 150
Rotfeld, Herbert J., 537
Roundtree, Robert I., 344
Rovell, Darren, 318
Roy, Susanna, 289
Rozell, Elizabeth J., 595
Rubens, Peter Paul, 641
Rubin, Ann, 49, 51
Ruddock, Graham, 496
Rudelius, William, 68, 262, 263, 565, 651
Rueter, Thad, 464
Rukstad, Michael G., 24
Rusli, Evelyn M., 564, 565
Russo, Francine, 671
Rust, Ronald T., 288
Ryals, Lynette, 346
Ryan, Joe, 345
Rylander, Don, 235

S

Sachs, Denielle, 52
Sager, Jeffrey K., 595
Salmon, Walter J., 536
Salmon, Warner, 465
Salpeter, Miriam, 668
Samli, A. Coskun, 203
Samouel, Phillip, 465
Sanburn, Josh, 263
Sanchez, Joan M., 97
Sandberg, Sheryl, 544
Santos, Neymar da Silva, 506
Sanyal, Dipyaman, 235
Saporito, Bill, 24, 262, 263, 396, 466
Saran, Cliff, 99
Sarel, Dan, 533
Sasser, W. Earl, Jr., 344, 345
Sauer, Abe, 536
Savage, Rick, 367
Savitz, Andrew W., 121
Sayre, Kate, 149
Schawbel, Dan, 671
Scheuing, Eberhard E., 345, 346
Schindler, Robert M., 396
Schlee, Regina Pefanis, 671
Schmidt, Peggy, 671
Schmidt, Sarah, 463
Schmitt, Bernd H., 346
Schmitt, Genevieve, 300
Schneider, Joan, 288

Scholes, Kevan, 52
Schramm, Wilbur, 495
Schultz, Don E., 495, 496, 497
Schultz, E. J., 533, 534
Schultz, Stephen, 595
Schumann, David W., 533
Schumann, Jan H., 535
Schwager, Andre, 25
Schwartz, Alvin, 536
Schwartzberg, Gary, 277
Scott, Mary E., 671
Sebastian, Michael, 98, 564
Sedgwick, David, 650
Seetharaman, Deepa, 564
Segal, Madhav N., 670
Seiders, Kathleen, 346
Seligman, Daniel, 496
Selwitz, Robert, 533
Semuels, Alana, 344
Sen, Anirban, 650
Sethuraman, Raj, 396
Sevetson, Andrea L., 668
Shaeffer, Leland D., 288
Shanborn, Jessica, 52
Sharapova, Maria, 262
Sharf, Samantha, 650
Sharma, Arun, 595
Sharp, Arthur G., 671
Shasteen, Rhonda, 201
Shaw, Eric H., 24
Shayon, Sheila, 565
Shea, Carol, 670
Sheatsley, P., 495
Shedlock, Michael, 464
Sheehan, Norman, 466
Sheehy, Gail, 98
Shen, Anyam, 347
Sheng, Shibin, 595
Sheng, Yuan, 496
Shenkan, Amy Guggenheim, 52, 650
Sherman, Strafford, 650
Sherry, John F., Jr., 25
Shervani, Tasadduq A., 25
Sheth, Jagdish N., 150, 203, 318, 346, 668
Shih, Clara, 98
Shocker, Allan D., 150
Shockley, Rebecca, 235
Shoemaker, Robert W., 536
Shroer, James A., 496
Shulman, Lawrence E., 52
Sibony, Olivier, 650
Siegel, Lee, 151
Sifferlin, Alexandra, 97
Sightings, Tom, 97
Sikora, Matt, 641
Silver-Greenberg, Jessica, 99
Silverstein, Michael J., 149
Simchi-Levi, David, 432
Simchi-Levi, Edith, 432
Simester, Duncan, 465
Singer-Vine, Jeremy, 369
Singer, Marc, 52, 650
Singer, Natasha, 619
Sirha, Probhakant, 650

Sirianni, Nancy J., 344
Sivakumar, K., 344, 345
Skally, Nick, 260, 261, 263
Slater, Stanley F., 25
Sloane, Garett, 24
Smith, A. B., 466
Smith, Aaron, 564
Smith, Chris Silver, 535
Smith, Cooper, 564
Smith, Craig, 564, 565
Smith, Katie, 533
Smith, Lindsey, 566, 567, 594
Smith, Ned, 564
Smith, Scott M., 150
Smith, Shane, 52
Smith, Shaun, 346
Smith, Tim J., 396
Snider, Mike, 99
Snook, Scott, 51
Snyder, Benjamin, 263
Snyder, Jasper, 496
Solheim, Jostein, 27
Solis, Brian, 346
Solomon, Michael R., 150
Soltani, Ashkan, 369
Somers, Suzanne, 510
Sonne, Ann Pail, 262
Spangenberg, Eric R., 466
Speh, Thomas W., 172
Spencer, Jane, 150
Spethmann, Betsy, 537
Spiegel, Alison, 536
Spielberg, Steven, 523
Spiro, Rosann L., 595
Spotts, Harlan E., 533
Sprott, David E., 466
Srinivasan, Kannan, 496
Srinivasan, R., 496
Srivastava, Rajendra K., 25
Staelin, Richard, 24
Stafford, Edwin R., 98, 464
Stair, Leslie, 654
Stair, Lisa B., 654
Stalk, George, 52
Stanley, Paul, 367
Stanton, John L., 496
Stanton, William J., 595
Stayman, Douglas M., 536
Steel, Emily, 24, 235
Steenburgh, Thomas, 595
Steenkamp, Jans-Benedict, 466
Stein, Joel, 223, 235
Steinberg, Brian, 534
Steiner, Christopher, 151
Steiner, Gary A., 121, 496
Stelter, Brian, 235
Stephens, Robert, 95, 96, 269, 288
Stern, Louis W., 432
Sterns, Scott, 595
Stevens, Laura, 52
Stevenson, Robert Louis, 568
Stewart, David, 533
Stewart, Joan, 495
Sthanunathan, Stan, 657, 670
Stiving, Mark, 396
Stockdale, Lydia, 671

Stoddard, Scott, 649
Stoller, Martin, 537
Stone, Brad, 97, 99, 151, 289
Stone, John, 262
Strang, Robert A., 536
Strauss, Judy, 619
Stroebe, W., 150
Strom, Andrea, 268
Strom, Brian, 268
Strunk, William, 68
Strutton, David, 432
Stuckey, Brian, 565
Sudhir, K., 120
Sullivan, Anthony, 510
Sullivan, Elizabeth A., 288, 346, 670
Sunnoo, Dunn, 496
Sunstein, Cass, 288
Suri, Rajneesh, 465, 564
Suter, Tracy A., 235, 289
Swaminathan, Srinivasan, 534
Swanson, Dana, 287, 288
Swartz, Teresa, 345
Sweet, Elizabeth, 98
Swift, Taylor, 461, 549
Swinmurn, Nick, 236
Swire, Donald, 53
Szymanski, D., 203

Talukdar, Debabrata, 149
Tan, Chong Leng, 533
Tanner, John F., Jr., 172, 534, 595
Tansuhaj, Patriya, 346
Tarasova, Anna, 650
Tay, Richard, 534
Taylor, Steven A., 345
Taylor, Victoria, 619
Teal, Derrick, 464
Team, Trefis, 97, 263
Teinowitz, Ira, 464, 533
Teisberg, Elizabeth, 347
Teixeira, Thales, 535
Tellefsen, Thomas, 172
Tetreault, Mary Stanfield, 345
Thakor, Mrugank V., 465
Thomas, Carl, 285, 286
Thomas, Dan R. E., 346
Thomas, Dave, 216, 248
Thomas, John F. Hogan, 396
Thompson, Debora V., 536
Thompson, Debora Viana, 288
Tietje, Brian, 25
Till, Brian D., 535
Tilley, Aaron, 97
Tillotson, Kristin, 288, 564
Timiraos, Nick, 98
Tobin, Lucy, 121
Tomkovick, Chuck, 534
Toole, Christa, 565
Townsend, Matt, 497
Toyoda, Akio, 635
Toyoda, Kiichiro, 117
Trachtenberg, Jeffrey A., 52, 262

Traczyk, Patty, 534
Trainor, Kevin J., 52
Treacy, Michael, 24, 537
Trevino, Linda K., 120
Trin, Courtney, 565
Tripathy, Sudipta, 563
Trivedi, Minakshi, 465
Tropp, J., 497
Troy, Lisa C., 650
Tsang, Alex S. L., 536
Tsukayma, Hayley, 565
Tucker, Amy L., 347
Tufte, Edward R., 52
Tuli, Kapil R., 595
Turner, Daniel, 288
Turner, Neil, 321
Turow, Joseph, 619
Twain, Mark, 224
Tweedie, Steven, 564
Tyson, Kirk, 668

U

Ulukaya, Hamdi, 2, 3, 21, 22
Upah, G. D., 346
Upbin, Bruce, 53
Upton, Nicholas, 97
Urbany, Joel E., 150
Useem, Jerry, 466
Uslay, Can, 536
Usunier, Jean Claude, 203

V

Vakratsas, Demetrios, 533
Valentino-DeVries, Jennifer, 99, 369
Vallaeys, Frederick, 532
Valle, Matt, 671
Van Bever, Derek, 624, 650
Van Brussel, Joe, 51
Van den Bulte, Christophe, 24
Van Heck, Eric, 173
Van Heerde, Harald J., 537
Van Hyning, Chuck, 68
Van Reijmersdal, Eva, 536
Van Rossum, Wouter, 24
Van Waterschool, Walter, 24
VanArsdale, Louis R., 668
Vance, Ashlee, 344, 564
Vandermark., Rob, 596
Vanhuele, Marc, 465
Varadarajan, P. Rajan, 53, 121, 346, 650
Varadarajan, R., 203
Vargo, Stephen L., 344
Vascellaro, Jessica E., 99, 537
Veblen, T. B., 99
Vekatesh, R., 172
Velsaco, Schuyler, 536
Vence, Deborah L., 671
Veres, Rob, 369
Vergara, Sofia, 506
Verhoef, Peter C., 466, 496
Vespa, Jonathan, 97

Viguerie, Patrick, 650
Vijayaraghavan, Vinceta, 344
Vitner, Mark, 98
Viveiros, Beth Negus, 497
Vizard, Sarah, 97, 565
Von Wangenheim, Florian, 535
Voorhees, Clay M., 347
Voss, Glenn B., 465
Vranica, Suzanne, 565
Vriens, Marco, 99

W

Wagner, Kurt, 318
Wahba, Phil, 263, 464, 465, 466
Wakabayashi, Daisuke, 98
Walker, Helen, 172
Walker, Kristen L., 262
Walker, Orville C., Jr., 263, 318
Walsh, Brendan, 650
Walsh, Meghan, 24
Walsh, Patrick B., 670
Wanamaker, John, 516
Wang, William, 348
Ward, James C., 466
Ward, Ronald W., 536
Warren, Kevin, 594
Waterman, Robert H., Jr., 650
Watson, Berry, 534
Watts, Naomi, 506
Waxer, Cindy, 497
Waxman, Olivia, 97
Webb, Tom, 466
Weber, Karl, 121
Webster, Frederick E., Jr.,
    24, 172
Webster, John, 496
Wedel, Michel, 466, 495, 535

Weed, Keith, 564
Weeks, Max, 98
Weidenhamer, Deanna, 464
Weigold, Michael F., 536
Weinberger, Hannah, 98
Weiner, Jonah, 565
Weinstein, Art, 52
Weisal, Kimberly, 262
Weisbaum, Herb, 534
Weiss, Allen, 98
Weiss, Bari, 151
Weitz, Barton A., 24, 25,
    172, 396
Welch, David, 98, 319
Welch, Jack, 634, 650, 670
Welch, Suzy, 650, 670
Wells, Georgia, 565
Wensley, Robin, 24, 25
Wentz, Laurel, 98
Werner, Ray O., 120
Wernle, Bradford, 496
Werther, William B., Jr., 121
West, Maureen, 345
West, Susan, 533
Westerlund, Jane, 397, 399,
    400–401, 402, 403,
    404–405
Wheatman, Debra, 670, 671
Wheeler, Joe, 346
White, Amy, 496
White, E. B., 68
White, Katherine M., 534
White, Tiffany Barnett, 346
White, Tina, 344
Wiener, Joshua L., 536
Wiersema, Fred, 537
Wiersema, Fred D., 24
Wiertz, Caroline, 346
Wiles, Michael A., 464

Wilkie, William L., 25,
    150, 533
Williams, Kiah, 29
Williams, Robin M., Jr., 98
Wilson, James Q., 120
Wilson, Rick T., 535
Wind, Jerry, 619
Wind, Yoram, 53
Windorski, David, 12–14
Winer, Russell S., 318,
    346, 396
Winfrey, Oprah, 14, 636
Winkler, Rolfe, 564
Winslow, George, 235
Winslow, Ron, 369
Winter, Rebecca, 263
Winters, Lewis C., 533
Wirtz, Jochen, 344, 346, 347
Wittenbraker, John, 346
Wittington, Richard, 52
Woelbing, Alfred, 394
Woelbing, Don, 394
Woelbing, Eric, 394
Woelbing, Paul, 394, 395
Woellert, Lorraine, 433
Wolfe, Daniel, 651
Wolfinbarger, Mary, 235, 346
Wolfman, Ian, 316,
    618–619
Wong, Anthony, 172
Wong, Vanessa, 497
Woods, Tiger, 506
Woodside, A. G., 346
Woodside, Arch G., 535
Wouters, Marijke, 536
Wozniak, Steve, 254
Wyatt, Daisy, 564
Wyckoff, D. Daryl, 345
Wyner, Gordon, 24, 52

Y

Yalch, Richard, 150
Yang, Nu, 52
Yate, Martin, 668
Yi-Zheng Shi, 495
Yikur, Rama, 534
Yim, Chi Kin (Bennett), 345
Yin, Sara, 535
Yong Jian Wang, 466
Yong Zhang, 534
Yoon, Hye Jin, 495
Young, Clifford E., 344
Young, Katy, 534
Yu-Chi Wu, 345

Z

Zakarin, Jordan, 464
Zaltman, Gerald, 172
Zamiska, Nicholas, 263
Zate, Joseph, 396
Zeithaml, Valerie A., 150, 345,
    346, 347, 369
Zhang, Xiaoquan (Michael), 465
Zhao, Guangzhi, 496, 534
Zhen Zhu, 344
Zidansek, Manja, 466
Zimmer, Mary R., 466
Zimmerman, Amy, 396
Zimmerman, Ann, 369
Zimoch, Rebecca, 68
Zinkham, Geoege M., 534
Zirkle, Michael, 288
Zmuda, Natalie, 99, 262, 495, 533
Zoltners, Andris A., 650
Zuckerberg, Mark, 4, 70, 71,
    544, 546

COMPANY/PRODUCT INDEX

A

AA Direct Connect, 419
Abbott Laboratories, 166
ABC, 343
Abercrombie & Fitch, 139–140
Aberdeen Group, 244
Accenture, 326, 334, 335, 506,
  563, 657, 658
Accutron, 307
Ace Concierge, 322
Ace Hardware, 415
ACES Flight Simulator, 462
ACH Food Companies, Inc., 143
ACNielsen, 165
Acxiom Corporation, 558
Adidas, 183, 184, 302, 333, 441
adverCAR, 321
Aeon, 437
AFLAC, 506, 544
Airbedandbreakfast.com, 320
Airbnb, 511
  redefining services, 320–321
Airbus, 181, 354, 357
Alamo.com, 412
Alaska Airlines, 343
Allbookstores.com, 446
Alliance Data, 223
Allstate, 324
Alma, 79
Amazon, 8, 85, 86, 148, 236, 357,
  371, 373, 374, 381, 382,
  408, 412, 413, 419, 442,
  444, 456, 545, 598, 618
  marketing channels, 430–432
Amazon Cloud Drive, 430
Amazon.com, 446, 456
Amazon Fire TV, 430
Amazon Fresh, 432
Amazon Kaizen, 432
Amazon Kindle, 32, 39, 430, 470
Amazon Kindle Fire, 373
Ambassador brand cards, 413
American Airlines, 76, 323, 375,
  419, 523
American Express, 308, 323, 333,
  483, 653
  cause marketing, 112
American Express Centurian
  Card, 131
American FactFinder, 83
American Girl, 462
American Hospital Supply, 420
American Lung Association, 119
American Red Cross, 31, 33, 154,
  326–437, 328, 501, 526
Amgen, 636
Anacin, 307
Android, 277, 306, 356, 430, 556,
  557, 563

Android TV, 338, 527
Angel City Brigade, 342
Angry Birds, 556–557
Angry Birds Go, 557
Anheuser–Busch, 144, 504, 517
  corporate social responsibility,
  100–101
ANN INC.'s Loft chain, 241
Ann Taylor, 241, 455
Anytime Fitness, 440
AOL's Shop@AOL, 430
Apple App Store, 556
Apple I, 254
Apple II, 269, 281
Apple III, 264
Apple iMac, 254, 255, 266, 276
Apple Inc., 4, 8, 10, 32, 36, 45, 54,
  77, 92, 142, 183, 184, 195,
  241, 272, 295, 303, 306,
  356, 371, 413, 414, 417,
  500, 523, 556, 633
  major strategic business units, 37
  new-product development,
  264–265
  and planning gap, 46
  segmentation strategy, 255
Apple Industrial Design Group, 276
Apple Lisa, 265
Apple Macintosh, 254, 264
Apple Newton, 8, 264
Apple Pay, 85, 434, 539
Apple Stores, 453, 462, 524
  effectiveness, 452
Apple TV, 510
Apple Watch, 10, 37, 38, 39, 46,
  265, 266, 276, 434
Arctic Cat, 160
Arm & Hammer, 308
Associated Grocers, 415, 439
AT&T, 87, 126, 157, 187, 194,
  338, 483, 506, 512, 515,
  578, 653
Audi, 523
Aurora Foods, 306
Autobytel.com, 412
Avert Virucidal, 281
Aviator glasses, 523
Avis, 256, 416
Avis Budget Group, 321
Avon Products, Inc., 18, 112,
  447, 569
Axe, 306
Axe deodorant, 307

B

Bagel-fuls, 277
Baked Doritos, 383
Baked Tostitos, 382

Banana Republic, 241, 462
Barbie dolls, 190, 191, 355
Barnes & Noble, 32, 112, 371, 441,
  456, 603
Barnesandnoble.com, 446, 456
Barnes & Noble Nook, 470
Bass Shoe Outlet, 450
Bausch and Lomb, 523
Bayer, 501
BBDO, 326
Beats by Dre, 506, 523
bebe, 505
Bebo, 260
Bed Bath & Beyond, 519
Bell's Burgers, 493
Ben and Jerry's, 30, 31, 33, 36,
  39, 522
  diversification analysis, 40
  marketing dashboard, 35
  social mission, 26–27
  SWOT analysis, 41–42
Benetton, 183, 455
Ben Franklin, 415
Bertie Bott's Flavour Beans, 524
Best Buy, 95, 96, 166, 269,
  270, 294, 348, 357, 381,
  417, 441–442, 443, 451,
  452, 522
Be Tough, 291
Betty Crocker, 227–228, 647, 648
Bic pens, 307
Bic perfume, 306
Bio-Energy Recovery Systems, 101
BJ's Wholesale Club, 348, 450
Black & Decker, 180, 195, 196,
  308, 309, 583
Blackberry, 622
Blistex, 219, 394, 395
Bloomingdale's, 420, 438, 448,
  450, 451
Bloomspot, 148
BlueKai, 223
Bluemercury, 438
Blue Nile, 598
Bluetooth Low Energy beacon, 538
BMW, 12, 117, 282, 333, 446,
  587, 636
BMW Cruise bikes, 333
Boeing Company, 87, 157, 165,
  181, 192, 228, 354, 357
Boeing 787 Dreamliner, 157, 281
Bold detergent, 307, 653
Bolin Marketing, 232, 394, 395
Bonobos, 598
Booz Allen Hamilton, 326
Bose, 305, 607
Boston Consulting Group, business
  protfolio analysis, 36–39
Boston Market, 454
Boucheron, 416

Boys and Girls Clubs of America,
  112, 554
BP, 526
Brainstorm Bakery, 268
BranchOut.com, 662
Brand Central, 327
Brawny paper towels, 303
Breakers, The, 322
Brickmania, 462
Bridgestone, 302
BrightHouse, 316
Bring It, 291
Brinks, 326
British Airways, 126
Brooks Brothers Clothiers, 131, 448
Brother, 295
Bubba Gump Shrimp Company, 524
Budweiser, 101, 504
Budweiser Light, 133
Buffalo Wild Wings, 343
Bufferin, 307
Bugatti Chiron, 350–351, 355
Buick, 127, 587
Bumble Bee tuna, 388
Burger Chef, 455
Burger King, 106, 246–247, 251,
  253, 254, 256, 609
  commercialization, 281–282
Burlington Coat Factory, 450
Burt's Bees, 395
Business Talk Radio, 510
Buzzfeed, 546
BzzAgent, 138
  business model, 139

C

Cadbury Schweppes, 306
Cadillac, 419, 422, 587
CallawayGolf.com, 406
Callaway Golf Company, 612
  marketing channels, 406–407
Calvin Klein, 80
Camay, 308
Campbell Soup Company, 91, 143,
  166, 214, 243, 301, 308,
  310, 359, 426, 627, 628
Campbell V8, 129
Campus Ambassadors, 546, 563
Candy Crush Saga, 557
Capital One, 506
Caplow Company
  operating statement, 397–400
  operations, 397
  ratios
    to analyze operations, 400–401
    to set and evaluate price,
    401–405
CareerBuilder, 609, 660

Caress soap, 307
Carma Laboratories, Inc., 219
  pricing strategy, 394–396
  social media use, 547
CarMax, 381–382, 436, 437
Carmex, 219, 394–396, 547, 550,
  554, 555
  Facebook and, 232–234
  social media programs, 220
Carmex Healing Cream, 394
Carmex Hydrating Lotion, 394
Carmex-LeBronJames.com, 550
Carmex Moisture Plus, 233, 395
Carnation Company, 109
Carnival Cruises, 504, 526
CarPlay, 264
Carrefour, 437, 442
Cartier, 305, 373
Catalyst Paper, Inc., 152
Caterpillar, 160, 411, 412, 427
Cause Marketing Forum, 112
CC Cream Sunscreen, 181
Celestial Seasonings, 408
Cerdelga, 111
Cereal Partners Worldwide,
  414, 632
CGCT, 194
Chanel, 184, 197, 373, 417
Chaps, 306
ChapStick, 219, 220, 394, 395
Charlesburg Furniture, 418
Chase Ultimate Rewards, 523
Checkers Drive-In Restaurants, 454
Cheer, 653
Cheerios, 217, 333, 414, 623, 626
Cheerios + Ancient Grains,
  623–624, 626
Cheerios Protein Oats & Honey
  cereal, 85
Cheese Nips, 310
Cheetos, 194
Chevrolet, 343, 422
Chevrolet Bolt, 276–277
Chevrolet Spark, 307
Chevron, 409, 501, 541
Chevy Volt, 81
Chex gluten-free mix, 621, 624
Chex granola mix, 624
Chicken of the Sea, 310
Chipotle Mexican Grill, 253
Chips Ahoy!, 312
Chobani, Inc.
  growth opportunity, 23
  idea, 21
  innovation and social
    change, 22–23
  marketing strategy, 2–3
  place strategy, 22
  price strategy, 21–22
  product strategy, 21
  promotion strategy, 22
Chobani Flip Creations, 3, 23
Chobani Food Incubator, 3
Chobani Greek Yogurt, 9, 628
Chobani Greek Yogurt Oats, 3
Chobani Kids, 3

Chobani Kids Pouches, 23
Chobani Kitchen, 22
Chobani Simply 100, 23
Chobani SoHo, 3, 23
Chobani Tots Greek, 3
Christian Dior, 379
Christie's, 184
Church & Dwight, 308
Cisco Systems, 177
Citibank, 522
Citigroup, 541
Citizen watches, 138
CityDeal, 149
CK One, 80
Clairol, 133
Clash of Clans, 557
Cling-Free, 307
Clinique, 613
Clorox, 307
CNBC, 212
CNN, 281, 328
Coca-Cola Company, 8, 81, 90,
  106, 126, 181, 183, 184,
  187, 189, 195, 296, 303,
  305, 310, 312, 409, 416,
  439, 484, 504, 521, 523,
  608, 616, 657
  cola wars, 106
Coca-Cola Life, 8
Colgate-Palmolive Company, 133,
  134, 180, 281
Colgate's Kitchen Entrees, 281
Colgate toothpaste, 360
Colgate Total Advanced Gum
  Defense, 269
Comcast, 483
comScore, 514
ConAgra Foods, 149, 309
C1 scooter, 636
Converse sneakers, 441
Cool Mint Chocolate Clif Bar, 8
Cool Ranch Doritos Locos Tacos,
  468, 469
Coors, 157
Corning, Inc., 154, 163
Corona Extra, 138
Costco Warehouse Club, 166, 309,
  348, 437, 440, 450
Costco Wholesale, 622
Cost Cutters Family Hair
  Salon, 334
Coupon Information
  Corporation, 520
Courtyard hotels, 309
Cover Girl, 143, 183
Covergirl.com, 299
Craftsman radial saw, 374
Craftsman tools, 140, 307
Craigslist, 512, 513, 661
Crapola, 268
Crapola Granola, 268
Crate and Barrel, 444
Cray Inc., 268
Creative Labs, 71
Cree LED light bulb, 28
Crest Neat Squeeze toothpaste, 276

Crest toothpaste, 268, 419, 653
Croma, 174
Crowdrise, 328
Cub Foods, 440
Cunard Cruise Line, 84

D

Daimler AG, 177
Dance Central 3 video game, 357
Danon, 2, 3, 22
Darberry, 149
DeBeers, 184
Deere & Company, 158–159
Deli Creations, 214
Dell.com, 412, 446, 603
Dell Inc., 86, 96, 105, 167, 197,
  276, 382, 412, 417, 444,
  445, 486, 572, 600, 607
  international marketing,
    174–175
  supply chain, 423–424
Del Monte, 310
Delta Air Lines, 375
Destiny USA, 439
Detroit Pistons, 554–555
DeWalt, 308, 309
Dew Tour, 498
Dex Media, 512
DHL Worldwide Express, 327, 578
Dial Company, 310
Dial soap, 498
Dick's Sporting Goods, Inc., 406, 612
DieHard batteries, 307
Diesel, 81
Diet Mountain Dew, 502
Dillard's, 442
DirecTV, 375, 576
Discman, 286
Diversityinc.com, 157
  organizational buying, 158
DKNY, 426
DogVacay, 320
Dollar General, 81, 241, 450
Dollar Rent A Car, 256
Dollar Tree, 450
Dollar Value Stores, 382
Domino's bubble gum, 306
Domino's Handmade Pan Pizza, 6
Domino's Pizza, 331, 358, 359
Don Miguel, 62
Donna Karan, 426
Doritos, 127, 194, 303, 309, 382,
  504, 521, 572
Doritos Locos Tacos, 468, 469,
  494, 522
DoubleClick, 532
Dove hair care products, 138
Downy fabric softener, 268
Dr Pepper, 305
Dun & Bradstreet, 401, 661
Dunder Mifflin office supplies, 524
DuPont, 177, 570, 574
Duracell, 305, 307, 374
Dyson Air Multiplier, 85

E

Eastern Mountain Sports, 287
Eastman Chemical, 587–588
Easy Off, 307
eBay, 86, 166, 306, 355, 357,
  444, 598
  and small business, 165
eBay Marketplace, 165
Eddie Bauer, 413, 456
eHarmony, 131
Ektelon, 260
Electric Drive Transportation
  Association, 119
Electrolux, 447
Elegant Medleys, 270
Encyclopaedia Britannica, 275, 633
Energizer, 373, 506
Energizer Advanced Formula, 374
Energizer e^2 AA alkaline
  batteries, 374
Environmental Media
  Association, 119
Epicurious, 434
Epson, 307
Ericsson, 194
Ernst & Young, 21, 334
ESPN, 338, 343, 510, 555
Essex restaurant, NY, 148
Estée Lauder, Inc., 218, 613
Etch-A-Sketch, 523
E*Trade, 275, 598
Euphrates, 21
Eveready, 307
Excedrin, 307
eXelate, 223
EXO, 260
Expedia, 419
Experian Simmons, 245, 246
Exxon, 196, 307
eZone, 174

F

Facebook, 2, 4, 15, 22, 34, 62, 73,
  80, 81, 101, 137, 148, 149,
  206, 218, 219, 220, 223,
  253, 260, 261, 287, 316,
  320, 328, 343, 446, 468,
  474, 475, 477, 488, 489,
  494, 498, 501, 502, 521,
  532, 538, 540, 541, 547,
  548, 551, 553, 554, 557,
  558, 597, 608, 609, 617,
  618, 633, 661, 662
  and brand manager's
    strategy, 544
  and Carmex, 232–234
  compared to other social
    media, 543
  description, 543–544
  and environmental forces, 70–71
  launching new social networks,
    545–546
  mobile marketing, 546

Facebook Messenger, 538
Fairfield Inn, 309
Fairmont Hotels, 333
Family Dollar Stores, 382, 450
Family Life Network, 510
Fancy Feast, 270
Farm Radio Network, 510
Farmville, 557
Fashionmall.com, 446
Fatburger, 455
FedEx, 156, 194, 327, 386, 409, 427, 515, 574
Festival Series guitars, 367
Fiat Chrysler, 483
Fiber One snack bars, 621
Fingos, 281
Fistula Foundation, 327
Fitbit, 38
Five Guys Burgers and Fries, 253
FlexBall, 85
Flickr, 328, 343, 486
Florida Gators, 290
Florida Orange Growers, 301
Florsheim, 441
Fodor's travel guide, 474
Folger's coffee, 310, 653
Foot Locker, 419
Ford CMAX, 81
Ford Firebird, 307
Ford Focus, 96, 309
Ford Fusion, 309
Ford Motor Company, 4, 119, 127, 180, 240, 267, 307, 309, 422, 480–482, 483, 631
Ford Mustang, 307, 309
Ford Pinto, 307
Ford Taurus, 309
Ford Thunderbird, 240
Forest Stewardship Council, 152
Forever 21, 653
4pic1 Word, 557
Four Seasons Hotel, Beverly Hills, 445
Four Seasons Hotels and Resorts, 489
Foursquare, 22, 343
Fox Business, 212
Fox network, 343
Fox News, 338
Fox Sports, 499
Fran Wilson Creative Cosmetics, 192
in Japan, 193
Fresh Foam Zente, 228
Fresh Step cat litter, 133
Friendster, 223
Frigidaire, 441
Frito-Lay, Inc., 75, 127, 189, 194, 195, 218, 296, 303, 309, 382, 383, 540, 571–572, 584
Fritos corn chips, 127
Fruit Ninja, 557

F 35 Lightning I Joint Strike Fighter, 634, 635
Fuller Brush, 447

G

Gain, 653
Galaxians, 342
Galaxy smartphone, 498, 500
Games by James, 462
Gap, Inc., 147, 241, 455
Gap.com, 446
Gap Factory Store, 450
Garlic Cake, 272
Garmin, 657
Gatorade, 292, 303, 305, 306
brand extensions, 290–291
Gatorade Endurance Carb Energy chews, 292
Gatorade Endurance Formula, 290
Gatorade Energy Bar, 290
Gatorade Energy Drink, 290
Gatorade Fierce, 290, 291
Gatorade Frost, 290
Gatorade Mission Control, 608
Gatorade Nutritional Shake, 290
Gatorade Performance Series, 290
Gatorade Rain, 291
Gatorade Thirst Quencher, 291
Gatorade X-Factor, 290, 291
Gatorade Xtremo, 290
Geek Squad, 269, 270
in changing environment, 95–96
company history, 95
future of, 96–97
Geico, 504, 506, 515
General Electric, 12, 14, 15, 126, 165, 274, 308, 355, 381, 413, 441, 570, 634
General Electric Healthcare Americas, 566–567, 578
General Electric Medical Systems, 166
General Mills, 4, 193, 215, 218, 275, 277, 281, 300, 623, 628, 639, 640
evaluation, 649
evaluation at, 642–644
implementation, 648
Nestlé partnership, 414, 632
planning, 648
strategic marketing, 620–621
Warm Delights, 647–649
General Mills BehaviorScan, 280
General Mills Worldwide Innovation Network, 632
General Motors, 119, 194, 276–277, 295, 321, 419, 422, 483, 598
Genzyme, 111
Georgia Pacific, 303
Gerber, 195, 308, 354
Getaround, 320
Ghostbuster ambulance, 7
Ghostery, 223

Gillette Company, 183, 196, 292, 301, 306, 578, 658
Gillette for Women, 196
Gillette Fusion razor, 292, 294, 295, 297, 372
Gillette razors, 268, 305
Gilt, 148, 502
Gilt.com, 446
Gino's Hamburgers, 455
Girl Scouts, 326
Glass Plus, 307
Gliden, 306
Global Healthcare Exchange, 166
Gmail, 538
Godiva Chocolates, 589
Go-Gurt Fizzix, 277
Golden Beauty, 196
Golden Gate Bridge Foundation, 119
Goldman Sachs, 526
Golf Galaxy, Inc., 406, 612
Good Start, 109
Goodyear Tire Company, 79, 157, 302, 414, 419
Google, Inc., 70, 86, 87, 92, 129, 211, 212, 331, 356, 489, 490, 513, 549, 557, 558, 598, 604, 622, 633, 653
business model, 530–531
corporate culture, 531
future strategy, 532–533
online advertising, 531–532
Google Ad Preferences, 223
Google AdSense, 532, 553
Google AdWords, 531–532, 553
Google Catalogs, 445
Google driverless cars, 279
Google Glass, 278, 434
Google Maps, 538
Google Offers, 148, 446
Google Play, 538
Google +, 343, 538, 556
Google's Bigtables, 221
Google Search, 538
Google Wallet, 434
Goya Foods, 143
Graph Search, 556
Grease Monkey, 336
Great Atlantic & Pacific Tea Company, 89
Greenpeace, 326
Grey Poupon, 214
Grip, 547
Group Danone, 194
Groupon, 446, 519, 622
challenges, 148–149
company and concept, 147–148
and consumer behavior, 148
mission, 146
Groupon Getaways, 147
Groupon Goods, 147
GrouponLive, 147
Groupon Mobile, 148
Gucci, 131, 184, 416, 417

Gulfstream Aerospace Corporation, 157, 478–479
Gunderson & Rosario, Inc., 272

H

H. J. Heinz Company, 17
Häagen-Dazs, 112, 303
Hachette Book Group, 419
Hallmark Cards, Inc., 77, 327, 413
Hamburger Helper, 215
Hampton Hotels, 440
H&R Block, 232, 334, 416, 440
Hanes Brands, Inc., 311
Harkman Electric, 411, 412
Harley-Davidson, Inc., 139, 159, 195, 300, 305, 306, 603, 608
and Milson Manufacturing, 160
Harris Corporation, 581
Hart Schaffner & Marx, 379
Hasbro, 616
Hautelook.com, 446
Hawaiian Punch, 300, 301
Healthy Choice, 149
Healthy Young Vending, 443–444
H-E-B supermarkets, 214
Heinz Ketchup, 310
Helena Rubenstein, 196
Hellmann's, 134
Henredon, 306
Herbalife, 343, 447
Hershey Foods, 379
Hershey's Reese's Pieces, 523
Hertz Corporation, 256, 332
Hewlett-Packard, 159, 190, 282, 295, 325, 379, 426, 540, 590, 608
reverse logistics, 427
Hewlett-Packard Enterprise Services, 590
Hey! There's A Monster In My Room spray, 271
HGTV "Dream Home Giveaway," 521
Hibu, 512
Hidden Valley Ranch Low-Fat Salad Dressing, 307
Hidden Valley Ranch Take Heart Salad Dressing, 307
Hi5, 260
Hilton Hotels, 333, 338
History channel, 510
Hockey Puck Mouse, 265
Holiday Barbie, 190
Holiday Inn, 416, 448
HoloLens, 498
Home Depot, 158, 321, 326, 410, 436, 439, 449, 451, 489, 583, 622
Home Shopping Network, 413, 445
Honda, 119, 308
Honda Civic, 387
Honey Nut Cheerios, 414
Honeywell, 570

HootSuite, 547
HospitalNetwork.com, 165
Hostess Twinkies, 641
Hotmail, 609
Hot Wheels, 355
House of Comedy, 462
Howlin' Coyote Chili, 57–67
HTC, 498
HTC One, 125
H20 Audio, 285, 287
Huggies, 181
Hulu, 320, 510
Hyundai Motor America,
    313, 613

I

iAd Network, 17
Ibanez, 367
IBM, 17, 18, 86, 154, 187, 307,
    411, 423, 427, 501, 569,
    570, 573, 574, 578, 658
  integrated supply chain, 424
  Smarter Planet strategy, 49–51
  vision, mission, and strategy, 50
IBM Global Services, 578, 586
IBM Sequoia, 159
IBM's Watson computer, 411
Ichiro Suzuki, 355
IDEO, 276
IKEA, 184, 212, 444, 498, 628
Illumination Entertainment, 521
iMacs, 46
imc^2, 316, 615, 616–617
Independent Grocers Alliance
    (IGA), 415, 439
IndieGoGo, 328
Infomercial Monitoring Service
    Inc., 510
InMarket, 434
In-N-Out Burger, 455
Instagram, 2, 22, 233, 287,
    468, 477, 494, 538, 539,
    546, 548
Intel Corporation, 300, 632, 636
Intellidyn, 223
Intelligent Quisine, 359
Interbrand, 38
iPad, 17, 32, 37, 38, 39, 46,
    264, 268, 276, 281,
    306, 356, 511
iPhone, 37, 38–39, 46, 125, 183,
    264, 265, 276, 277, 286,
    317, 356, 500, 556
iPhone mini, 356
iPhone 6, 266
iPhone 6 Plus, 266
iPod, 37, 38, 39, 264, 272,
    281, 317
iPod Classic, 286
iPod Shuffle, 286
iPod Touch, 286
IRI, 280
IRT's InfoScan, 211
iVillage.com, 608

J

J. D. Power & Associates, 211,
    349, 631
Jack in the Box, 440, 455
Jaguar, 241, 446
Jamba Juice, 253
Jawbone fitness tracker, 38
JCPenney, 142, 152, 153, 157, 451,
    456, 488, 515, 557
JCPMedia, Inc., 163
  organizational buyer, 152–153
Jefferson Smurfit Corporation, 570
Jello, 90
JetBlue Airways, 336
  load factor, 337
Jiffy Lube, 417
Jif peanut butter, 357
JobFox, 661
Jobster, 661
Joffrey Ballet, 147
John Deere equipment,
    159, 160
Johnson & Johnson, 30, 126, 142,
    166, 302, 357, 616
Johnson Controls' Automotive
    Systems Group, 578
José Olé, 62
Joy perfume, 307
JW Marriott, 462

K

Kanebo, 193
Kellogg, 142, 157, 306
Kellogg's Heartwise, 307
Kellogg's Special K, 216
Kellogg's Fiberwise, 307
Kenmore appliances, 307
Kentucky Fried Chicken,
    471, 494
Keurig Green Mountain, 72
Kia Motors, 133
Kickstarter.com, 54, 277
Kimberly-Clark, 127, 181,
    281, 308
Kindle Fire tablets, 430
Kirby vacuum cleaners, 578
Kit Kat bars, 187
Kleenex, 4, 11, 127, 290, 305,
    306, 312
Klondike, 472, 474
Kmart, 138, 419, 441, 442
Kmart Supercenters, 442
Kodak, 275
Kohler, 352
Kohl's, 408, 434
Konica, 583
Kraft American cheese, 302
Kraft Crystal Light Liquid, 502
Kraft Foods, 21, 79, 214, 277, 312,
    519, 639
Kraft Miracle Whip, 310
Kroger, 214, 309, 375, 395, 414,
    519, 653

L

L.L.Bean, 355, 413, 444, 445
Lacoste, 430
LA Galaxy, sports marketing,
    341–344
Lalique, 373
Land Rover, 241
Lands' End, 36
Landsend.com, 489
Lay's Kettle Cooked potato
    chips, 75
Lay's potato chips, 127, 189, 296,
    408, 572
Lay's snack chips, 303
LeBronJames.com, 547
LeBron James Family
    Foundation, 554
Lee's blue jeans, 183
L'eggs, 311
LEGO Group, 7, 183, 207–209, 300
Legos, 462
Lender's Bagels, 306
Lenovo, 131
Leo Burnett Company, 316
Let Her Jump, 316–317
Levi's jeans, 408, 500, 523
Levi Strauss & Company, 111,
    113, 184, 190
Lexmark, 295
Lexus, 117, 422, 504
Lexus RX 450h, 279
LG, 377
LG 55-inch Smart TV, 355
LG G4, 125, 126
LG 77-inch 4K Ultra HD OLED
    TV, 4
Life Is Good T-shirt, 275
LifeLock, 510
Life Savers, 273
Lifetime channel, 510
Limited, The, 455
Lincoln, 422
LinkedIn, 223, 540, 541, 543, 551,
    575, 661, 665
  in brand manager's strategy, 548
  compared to other social
    media, 543
  for job search, 548
  overview, 547
Liquid Paper, 296
List Ease app, 434
LivingSocial, 148, 446, 519
Liz Claiborne, 36, 113
Lockheed Martin, 43, 87, 155,
    376, 636
Lockheed Martin's Skunk Works,
    622, 634, 635
Loctite, 504
Loehmann's, 440
Long John Silver, 494
L'Oréal, 183, 196, 306, 483, 506
Louis Vuitton, 177, 304, 305, 306
Lowe's, 158, 413
Luggage Club, 322

Lululemon, 80, 622
Luvs, 303
Luxottica Group, S.p.A., 306
Lyft, 320, 382
  surge pricing, 383

M

MacBook Air, 46, 255
MacBook Pro, 46, 255
MAC Group, Inc., 448
Macintosh Portable, 264
Mac mini, 255
Mac Pro, 255
Macy's, Inc., 324, 409, 438,
    442, 462, 522, 557, 562,
    653, 655
Magic Bullet, 510
Major League Baseball, 290, 341
Major League Soccer, 290, 341
Mall of America
  concept, 461–462
  management of, 462
  as market, 462–463
  and social media, 463
M&M's, 9, 385, 474, 475,
    521, 600
Mansar Products, Ltd., 410, 411
March of Dimes, 327, 328
Marina Maher Communications, 316
Marketing Group, 406
Marks & Spencer, 430, 599
Marlboro Light Kings, 361
Marriott EDITION Hotels and
    Vacation Clubs, 309
Marriott hotels, 15, 17, 498
Marriott International, 308–309
Mars, Inc., 410, 411, 600
Marsh Supermarkets, 434
Mars rover Curiosity, 7
Mary Kay, India, 200–202
  building a brand, 201
  sales force, 201
  supply chain, 201–202
Mary Kay Cosmetics, Inc., 133,
    181, 447, 587
  in Asian-Pacific markets, 200
  business model, 199–200
MasterCard International,
    112, 186
Match.com, 29, 131
Mattel, 113, 183, 190, 191
Maxim Steel, 583
Maybelline, 195
Mayo Clinic, 268, 329
Mazda, 489
Mazola Corn Oil, 143
McDonald's, 79, 113, 132, 144,
    183, 185–186, 193, 194,
    246–247, 251, 253, 254,
    256, 375, 416, 439, 440,
    448, 453–454, 455, 475,
    493, 504, 521, 527, 577
McDonald's Monopoly, 521
McKesson Corporation, 166, 419

Mean Stinks, 317
MediaCom, 486
Medtronic USA, 36, 166, 357, 569, 570
MEplusYOU, 316
Mercedes-Benz, 117, 194, 197, 446, 523
Mercury, 422
MergeVR, 498
Merrill Lynch, 324, 576
Messenger, 546
Meth Project, 505
MetLife, 653
MetLife.com, 412
Metro Group, 437
Metropolitan Life Insurance, 143, 144
MGA Entertainment, 140
Miami Heat, 79, 554–555
Michelin, 10, 131, 180, 302, 305, 307
MicroFridge, 244
Microsoft Bing, 129, 211, 532
Microsoft Corporation, 87, 92, 308, 420, 498, 513, 531, 541, 636, 653
Microsoft Project, 44
Microsoft Xbox, 268, 357, 431
Microsoft Zune, 272, 281
Milson Manufacturing, marketing philosophy, 160
MindMeld, 85
Mindstorms kit, 207–209
Minecraft video game, 7
Mini Cooper, 188, 350–351
Mintel, 7
Mission Foods, 62
Mobile, 522
Mobile TV, 338
Molecular Imaging Products, 566
Moments, 546
MoneyGram, 87
Monk-e-mail, 609
Monster.com, 660
Monster Energy, 380
Moodmatcher lipstick, 193
Moore Chemical & Sanitation Supply, Inc., 588
Mophie, 504
Moschino, 80
Motorola, 38, 265, 427
Motorola Droid Turbo, 125, 126–127
Mountain Dew, 494, 498
Mozilla, 92
MSN Hotmail, 609
MSN Money, 532
MTV, 510
Muse Air, 636
MyBestSegments, 245
MyCoke.com, 608
MyeBay, 602
My first Craftsman, 140
MySpace, 223
MyWorkster, 661
MyYahoo!, 600, 602

N

N. Peal, 523
Nabisco, 310, 458
NACElink Network, 660
NASCAR, 290, 327, 499, 502, 532
National Association for PET Container Resources, 86
National Basketball Association, 79, 290, 341, 494, 555
National Celebrity Cabinet, 327
National Football League, 275, 290, 341
National Geographic, 546
National Hockey League, 290, 341
NationofResponsibleDrinkers.com, 100
Nationwide, 504
Nature Conservancy, 17
Nature Valley granola, 275
Nature Valley Protein granola, 621
NBC, 343
Neiman Marcus, 379, 420, 440, 441, 442, 452, 589
NeoGrid, 166
Nescafé, 196
Nestlé Food Corporation, 109, 184, 187, 196, 312, 343, 413, 519
    General Mills partnership, 414, 632
Netflix, 86, 281
Netmarket.com, 446
New Balance, Inc., 228, 302
Newegg.com, 413
Newsfeed, 546
Newton MessagePad, 8
New York Mets, 355
New York's Metropolitan Opera, 323
New York Times, 546, 602
New York Yankees, 355
Next Issue Apple, 85
Nexus Player, 338
Nickelodeon Universe, 462
Nielsen Company, 211, 212, 439, 506, 509, 513–514, 538, 653
Nielsen PRIZM, 243
Nielsen Television Index Ranking Report, 213
Nike, 28, 113, 114, 142, 183, 184, 195, 302, 305, 419, 441, 502, 506
Nike Shox NZ, 419
99 Cents Only Stores, 382
Nine West, 390
Nintendo, 357
Nintendo Wii U, 268
Nissan Motor Company, 157, 190, 194, 521
Nokia, 427
Nordstrom, 11, 420, 441, 462, 498
Nordstrom Bank, 441
Nordstrom Rack, 450

Norske Skog, 152
Northrup Grumman, 87
Northwestern Mutual Life Insurance Company, 576
NPD Group, 60, 219
Nuprin, 307
NutraSweet, 90
NutriBullet, 510
NYTimes.com, 602

O

Obsession perfume, 307
Oculus Rift, 498
Oculus VR, 71
Off 5th, 450
Office Depot, 96, 294, 456
OK Go, 549
Olay, 75
Old Navy, 241
Old Spice, 318, 505, 506
Omni Hotels, 616
One Concierge, 322
Open Table, 148
Opium, 416
Oral-B toothbrushes, 85
Orbitz, 412, 419, 599
Oreos, 310
Orkut, 260
Oscar Mayer, 142, 214
OUT! International, 272
Outward Bound, 326
Owens-Corning Fiberglass Corporation, 90
OxiClean, 510
Oxygen channel, 510

P

Pampered Chef, 447
Pampers, 112, 181, 268, 303, 419
Pampers Village, 603
Panasonic, 441
Pandora, 223, 320, 510
Panera Bread, 253
Pantene, 300
Papa John's International, 440, 631
Paradise Kitchens marketing plan, 56–67
Paragon Trade Brands, 309
Parker Guitar, 368
Parking Panda, 320
Payless ShoeSource, 448, 449
Peace Corps, 17, 18, 327
Peapod.com, 446
Pebble smartwatch, 277
Penske Logistics, 427
Pepperidge Farm, 479
Pepsi, 343
PepsiCo, 3, 4, 8, 22, 105, 134, 157, 177, 181, 189, 194, 290, 300, 303, 305, 311, 312, 409, 415, 484, 506, 551–552, 608
    cola wars, 106

Pepsi MAX, 532
Pepsi True, 8
Pepsi XL, 8
Performance Racing Network, 510
Perrier, 111
Pert shampoo, 187
Petco, 417
Pets.com, 634
PetSmart, 417
Pew Internet & American Life Project, 610
Pez Candy, Inc., 310
    customer value in packaging, 311
Pfizer, 501, 616
PGA, 406
PGA Tour Sportstores, 406
Philadelphia cream cheese, 277
Philadelphia Phillies, 323
Piece Brewery & Pizzeria, 148
Pillsbury Company, 61
Pinterest, 22, 80, 343, 554, 662
Pitney Bowes, 157
Pittsburgh Pirates, 355
Pizza Hut, 176, 494, 631
    action plan, 616
    customer experience, 617–618
    performance measures and outcomes, 618
    retail business, 615–616
PizzaHut.com, 617–618
PKG, 653
Planters peanuts, 458
PlasticsNet, 165
Plaxo, 661
Playboy, 306
Plum District, 148
Polo, 306
Porsche, 308, 488
Porsche Boxter, 308
Porsche Carrera, 308
Post Cereals, 128, 129
Post-it Flag, 12
Post-it Flag Highlighters, 10, 13, 14
Post-it Flag Pen, 13, 14
Post-it line, 12
Post-it Note, 12, 13
Prada, 30, 417, 598
Pret shampoo, 187
Priceline.com, 489, 602
Price Sports, Inc., segmentation strategy, 260–262
PricewaterhouseCoopers, 653
Pringles, 311
Procter & Gamble, 112, 142, 159, 160, 163, 181, 190, 194, 211, 213, 214, 239, 268, 270, 276, 300, 303, 308, 309, 312, 360, 387, 416, 419, 421, 483, 519, 574, 583, 598, 603, 612–613, 616, 639
    brand-building, 315–318
    product line, 307
ProGlide, 295
Programme for the Endorsement of Forest Certification, 152

Progresso Light soups, 277
Promise Me, 328
Propel Fitness Water, 290
PRS Group, 191
Prudential, 75
PsychCentral, 605
Publishers Clearing House, 522
Publix, 214
Purina, 478
Purina Elegant Medleys, 270

Q

Qpod, 149
Qtips, 90
Quaker Oats Company, 290,
    302, 306
Quill.com, 524
QuizUp, 557
QVC, 445
QVC.com, 607

R

Race for the Cure, 17
RadioShack, 354
Ralph Lauren Company, 306, 414,
    420, 436, 437
Ralston Purina, 302
RAMBUS, 636
Range Rover, 523
Ray-Ban, 523
Rayovac, 309, 374
ReadySetRocket, 498
Recreational Equipment, Inc.,
    287, 599
Red Baron, 225, 358–360, 361, 387
Redbox, 440, 544
Red Bull, 306, 379
    pricing strategy, 380
RedLaser, 357
Red Lobster, 130
Reebok, 113, 194, 601, 607
Reebok.com, 599
Reebok Russia, 194
Regal Entertainment, 376
REI; see Recreational
    Equipment, Inc.
RelayRides, 320, 321
RELPAX, 480, 481
Renaissance Hotels, 309
Rentoid, 320
Revitalift Filler, 506
Revlon, 79, 486
R/GA ad agency, 506
RIM (Research in Motion), 556
Riot Squad, 342
Rite Aid, 522
Ritz-Carlton, 322, 323, 336
Rock and Roll Hall of Fame and
    Museum, 376
Rockport, 306, 578
Rockstar, 380
Rolex, 184, 373, 379
Rolls-Royce, 184, 373

Ronald McDonald Houses, 113
Ross Stores, 450
Ruffles potato chips, 127
Ruiz Foods, 62

S

Safeway, 162, 166, 375, 410, 498
St. Joseph aspirin, 302
Saks Fifth Avenue, 426, 438, 441,
    448, 450, 451, 653
Saks Inc., 417
Salvation Army, 326
Sam's Club, 348, 417, 419, 425,
    450, 622
Samsung Electronics, 38, 76, 177,
    295, 308, 377, 500
Samsung Galaxy, 39, 125
Samsung's Gear VR, 498
San Diego Padres, 487
Sanford Corporation, 296
Santitas tortillas, 309
Scandinavian Airlines, 355
Schwab, 326, 600, 607
Schwab.com, 412
Schwan Food Company, 225, 410
SciFi Channel, 486
Scion, 117
Scope, 612–613
Scotch-Brite Greener Clean
    pads, 4, 17
Scotchgard, 106, 108
Scoutmob, 148
Scripto, 312
Sea Life Minnesota, 462
Sears, 307, 309, 326, 381, 419,
    451, 462
Secret deodorant, 315–318
Seiko, 197
Sergio Rossi, 416
Seven Cycles, Inc., 599, 607
    interactive marketing,
    596–597
Sevencycles.com, 599
7-Eleven, 157, 162, 253, 408, 410,
    417, 439, 657
7UP, 307
Sewell Automotive Companies, 604
Sharp, 307
Shasta, 343
Shaw's, 500
Shell Oil, 486
Sheraton hotels, 333
Sherwin-Williams, 414
Shiseido, 183, 193
ShopNBC, 445
Shop24, 441
Shredded Wheat, 128
Siemens AG, 157, 186
Singapore Airlines, 76
Sirius XM Satellite Radio, 510,
    511, 527
SIRUM, 28, 29
Skippy peanut butter, 222,
    357, 379

Skippy Squeez It, 310
Skittles, 504
Skype, 498
Sling TV, 85
SMG, 316
S'mores Frappuccino, 72
Snake Light flexible flashlight, 195
Snapchat, 70, 494, 539
Snapple, 306
Snelling and Snelling, Inc., 416
Snickers, 138, 503, 549
Snow Master, 132
Snow Pup, 132
Sodima, 193
Sonatica, 34
Sony Corporation, 142, 183, 190,
    282, 308, 348, 357, 377,
    523
Sony Energy Devices Corporation,
    105
Sony PlayStation, 431, 498
Sony PlayStation 4, 268, 382
Sony PlayStation 3, 268
Sony's Project Morpheus, 498
Sotheby's, 184
Source Perrier S.A., 111
Southwest Airlines, 31, 33, 326,
    336, 636
Space Adventures, 334, 335
Spanx, 635–636
Sperry boat shoes, 441
Spic and Span, 312
Spinlister, 320
Spirit Airlines value pricing, 352
Sports Authority, 436, 437, 441
Sports Chalet, 287
Sprint, 87, 126, 515
Stake Fastener Company, 411, 412
Staples, 96, 413, 417, 441, 442
Starbucks, 11, 72, 194, 253, 336,
    477, 523, 640, 641
    sustainable procurement, 161
Starkist, 303
Star Wars lightsabers, 355
Stokely-Van Camp, Inc., 290
Storenvy, 446
Strategic Business Insights, 135,
    136
Strauss Group, 194
StuffDOT, Inc., 8
    and Facebook, 545–546
    marketing, 563
    rewarding users, 561–563
    user-friendliness, 562–563
    uses, 545
    vision, brand name, and logo,
    562
StumbleUpon, 223, 521
Subway, 439, 440, 486
Supercuts, 440
Survey Monkey, 216
Susan G. Komen for the Cure, 327,
    328
Sustainable Forestry Initiative, 152
Swatch watches, 379
Swiffer WetJet, 270

T

T.J. Maxx, 450
Tab, 296
Taco Bell, 138, 454, 522
    integrated marketing
        communications, 468–469,
        493–495
Taco Bell Cantina, 495
Taco Bell Express, 494
TAG Heuer, 373
Target.com, 8
Target stores, 11, 18, 28, 162, 166,
    194, 302, 348, 395, 410, 419,
    434, 437, 438, 439, 441, 442,
    452, 519, 545, 557
Task Rabbit, 320
Teach for America, 28, 29
TeamLeBron, 547
Teavana, 640
TE Connectivity, 570
Telemundo, 486
Telepresence Robots, 85
Temple Run, 557
Tesco, 166, 334, 437, 442
Tesco Home Plus, 558
Tesla Motors, 85, 276–277
Texaco, 501
Texas Instruments, 576
TextileWeb, 165
ThePoint.org, 147
ThighMaster, 510
Thirsty Cat, 272
Thirsty Dog, 272
3D Printing Store, 85
3M Corporation, 17, 106, 108, 111,
    274, 277–278, 282, 292
    marketing program, 12–14
Ticketmaster, 609
Tide, 212, 268, 419, 653
Tide Naturals, 212, 214
Tide Pods, 276
Tidy Bowl, 307
Tiffany & Company, 187, 414,
    448, 449, 452
Time, Inc., 140, 143
Time Warner, 87
Time Warner Cable Sports, 343
Tippr, 148
T-Mobile, 87, 523
Tombstone Pizza, 359
Tommy Hilfiger, 183
Tomra Systems, 85, 86
Tony's Pizza, marketing research,
    225–227
Toro, 132, 160, 383, 384, 386
    product line, 307
Toshiba America Medical Systems,
    589
Tostitos, 309, 382, 383, 572
Total Gym, 510
Total Toothpaste, 134
Tower.com, 446
TownePlace Suites, 309
Toyopet, 117

Toyota Camry, 355, 387
Toyota Corolla, 117
Toyota Motor Corporation, 111,
        157, 160, 410, 422, 521,
        622, 631, 635
    business philosophy, 117–118
    company history, 117
    environmental vision, 118–119
    future, 119–120
    strategic partnerships, 119
Toyota Prius, 81, 118–119, 279
Toyota Tundra, 117
Toyota USA Foundation, 118
Toy perfume, 80
Toys "R" Us, 522
Trader Joe's, 17
    relationship marketing, 15–16
Transamerica, 76
Travelocity, 446, 506, 603
Trek Bicycle Corporation
    company background, 169–170
    eco buying, 171–172
    organizational buying, 170–171
Trek Wear, 169
Trend Hunter, 215
Triarc Companies, 306
Trix, 621
Tropicana, 303
True Religion, 462
TRUSTe, 610
TSCentral, 576
Tumblr, 206
Tupperware, 612
Twentieth Century Fox, 206
Twitter, 2, 15, 22, 70, 73, 206, 218,
        220, 223, 260, 261, 287,
        328, 331, 343, 446, 468,
        474, 475, 477, 489, 494,
        502, 504, 512, 532, 539,
        540, 541, 543, 548, 551,
        597, 608, 661, 665
    in brand manager's strategy, 457
    compared to other social
        media, 543
    overview, 546–547
Tylenol, 133
Tylenol Cold & Flu, 133
Tylenol Cold P.M., 133
Tylenol 8-Hour, 134

U

Uber, 320, 382, 511
    surge pricing, 383
Ubitus Game Cloud, 323

UGG, 80
Ultra Downy, 268
Uncle Ben's Calcium Plus rice, 302
Under Armour, 80, 502, 523
Unilever, 27, 77, 302, 303
Union Pacific Railroad, 584
United Airlines, 323, 653
United Parcel Service, 32, 103,
        194, 327, 407, 427, 574
United Parcel Service Supply
        Chain Services, 427
United States Postal Service, 327,
        338, 432, 444–445
United Technologies, 106, 167
United Way, 326
Universal Pictures, 486
Univision, 486
UPM-Kymmene, Inc., 152
U.S. Cellular, 590
U.S. Rice Millers' Association, 178

V

Valpac, 434
Valve, 498
Vanguard Group, Inc., 657
Van Heusen Factory Store, 450
Vans skate shoes, 441
Velocity fragrance, 133
Verizon, 87, 266, 483
Verso Paper, 152
Vicks, 187
Victoria's Secret, 441
Vidal Sassoon, 379
Viking, 260
Vine, 468, 494
Virgin Galactic, 322–323
Virgin Group, 526
Visa, 186, 416
VisualCV, 661
VIZIO, Inc., 377
    value pricing, 348–349
VIZIO HDTVs, 348
Volkswagen, 117, 143, 190, 477,
        486, 541
Volkswagen Beetle, 95
Volvo, 241, 256
VR Skate, 498

W

W. W. Grainger, 165
Walgreens, 166, 233, 395, 439
Walkman, 286
Walmart, 10, 96, 111, 149, 160,

        180, 197, 219, 242, 290,
        302, 309, 312, 348, 395,
        416, 417, 419, 420, 423,
        437, 438–439, 441, 442,
        445, 448, 449, 450, 519,
        574, 583, 598, 606, 622,
        641, 653
    supply chain, 424–425
Walmart.com, 606
Walmart Neighborhood Markets,
        241, 425, 442
Walmart Smart Network, 523
Walmart Stores, Inc., 81
Walmart Supercenters, 425, 442
Walt Disney Company, 240, 306,
        332, 336, 338, 483, 485
Wanamaker's Department
        Store, 516
Wanchai Ferry brand, 632
Warby Parker, 598
Warm Delights, 620, 647–649
Warm Delights Minis, 642–644
Washburn Guitars pricing
        decisions, 367–368
Washburn Maya Pro, 368
Web 2.0, 540
Web 3.0, 540
Weight Watchers, 277
Welch's grape jelly, 222
Wells Fargo Bank, 436
Wendy's, 242, 246–247, 254,
        256, 455
    customer information survey,
        216–218
    customer satisfaction survey,
        222–224
    market segmentation, 248–253
West Edmonton Mall, 451, 461
Western Union, 87, 631
Westin hotels, 333
Weyerhaeuser, 156
WhatsApp, 546
Wheaties, 217
Whirlpool Corporation, 156, 180,
        184, 190, 196, 276, 310,
        417, 441
Whole Foods Market, 77, 501
Whopper, 90
Wicks, 187
Wilkinson Sword, 350
Williams-Sonoma, 445
Wilson Cirrus One BLX tennis
        racquet, 381
Windows Vista, 272
Windows XP, 272
WingStreet, 494

Winnie the Pooh, 306
Wolf gas ranges, 385
Womendrivers.com, 123
Women's National Basketball
        Association, 290
Woot, 148
World Book, 447
World Wildlife Fund, 119
Wrigley's gum, 195

X

Xerox Color WorkCentre, 248
Xerox Corporate University, 594
Xerox Corporation, 9, 90, 228–229,
        247–248, 293, 427, 572,
        573, 574, 578, 656
    future of salesforce, 594
    mission, 593
    sales management, 593–594
    selling process, 593
X-1, new-product development,
        285–288

Y

Yahoo!, 148, 223, 513, 531,
        532, 600
Yahoo! Finance, 532
Yahoo's Hadoop, 221
Yamaha, 160, 367
Yipit, 446
Yoplait, 2, 3, 22, 193, 632
Yoplait Greek 100 Whips!, 632
YouTube, 2, 15, 206, 215, 328,
        331, 343, 468, 477, 486,
        487, 502, 506, 532, 538,
        541, 543, 548, 549, 550,
        551, 554, 555
    in brand manager's strategy,
        549–550
    compared to other social
        media, 543
    overview, 548–659
Yum! Brands, 494, 495
Yves Saint Laurent, 131, 416

Z

Zappos.com, 11, 12, 336, 444, 607
    market segmentation, 236–237,
        238–239
Zipcar, 321, 441
Zip the Cat Beanie Baby, 355

SUBJECT INDEX

A

AARP The Magazine, 511
**Above-, at,- or below-market
    pricing, 379**
  and Red Bull, 380
Academy of Motion Picture Arts
    and Sciences, 521
Accept objections, 579
Accessory equipment, 267
Account executive
  in advertising, 654
  in marketing research, 654
**Account management
    policies, 584**
  grid for, 585
Accredited Business Seal
    Program, 92
Achievement-motivated groups, 136
Achievers, 136, 137
Acknowledge and convert
    objections, 579
Action item list, 44, 637
Action plan, Pizza Hut, 616
Adaptive selling, 578
Administered vertical marketing
    systems, 416
Administrative expenses, 400
Adoption, 483
Advertisements
  conditional content, 515
  designing
    message content, 505–506
    message creation, 506–507
  institutional, 501–502
  product, 500
Advertising, 472, 500
  advantages, 472–473
  to business buyers, 476
  careers in, 654–655
  cooperative, 525
  corrective, 91
  costs, 473
  deceptive, 91
  Google, Inc., 530–533
  institutional ads, 501–502
  in introduction stage, 291
  misuse of cultural symbols, 187
  nonpersonal component, 472
  and online tracking, 92
  paid aspect, 472
  posttesting, 518
  pretesting, 516–517
  product ads, 500
  scheduling
    and buyer turnover, 515
    forgetting rate, 516
    and purchase frequency, 515
    types of, 516
  strengths and weaknesses, 473

teaser, 138
and TV ratings, 213
unintended word meanings, 187
use of mass selling, 472
with virtual reality, 498–499
Advertising Age, 79, 494, 661
Advertising agencies, 506–507
  Alma, 79
  full-service, 517
  imc², 616–618
  in-house, 518
  limited-service, 517–518
  marketing research by, 567
Advertising budget
  competitive parity budgeting, 504
  and super Bowl ads, 503–504
Advertising campaign
  Dell Inc., 175
  nonprofit organizations,
    326–327
Advertising expenditures
  by media type, 507
  in multibranding, 309
  on social media, 538
  Super Bowl ads, 503–504
  top ten companies, 483
  TV ads, 507
Advertising media
  basic terms
    cost per thousand, 508
    frequency, 508
    gross rating points, 508
    rating, 508
    reach, 507–508
  Internet, 512–514
  magazines, 511
  newspapers, 511–512
  outdoor, 514–515
  place-based media, 515
  radio, 510–511
  selection criteria, 515
  television, 509–510
  vehicle within each
    medium, 407
  Yellow Pages, 512
Advertising program
  assessing
    carrying out, 517–518
    making needed changes,
      518–519
    posttests, 518
    pretests, 516–517
  developing
    designing ads, 504–507
    identifying target audience, 503
    media alternatives, 509–515
    media selection, 507–508
    scheduling, 515–516
    setting budget, 503–504
    specifying objectives, 502–503

Advertising-related legislation, 91
Advertising Research
    Foundation, 503
Advocacy advertisements, 501
Ad Week, 506
African Americans
  buying patterns, 143–144
  buying power, 142
  differences among, 143
  motivated by quality and
    choice, 144
  size of population, 79
  spending by, 79
Agents
  definition, 408
  types of, 458
Aggregators, 446
Agree and neutralize, 579
Aided recall, 518
Airline industry
  frequency marketing, 244
  load factor, 336–337
  yield management pricing, 375
Alcohol responsibility, 100–101
Algorithms, 556
Alliance for Audited Media, 512
Allowances
  Caplow Company, 397
  case, 525
  finance, 525
  floor stock protection
    program, 525
  free goods, 525
  freight, 525
  merchandise, 524–525
  promotional, 387
  trade-in, 387
All-you-can-afford budgeting, 484
Alternative evaluation,
    124–125
  consideration set, 125
  consumer smartphone
    purchase, 162
  evaluative criteria, 125
  in organizational buying, 162
  women car buyers, 122
American Association of
    Advertising Agencies,
    506–507
American Community Survey,
    83, 211
American Enterprise
    Institute, 165
American households, 76–77
American Marketing Association,
    209, 661
  definition of marketing, 5
  Statement of Ethics, 107,
    108–109
America's Funniest Videos, 510

America's Got Talent, 469
Anchor stores, 451
Ancillary services, 479
Annual marketing plan, 627
Antitrust laws
  Clayton Act, 89, 420, 421
  Federal Trade Commission
    Act, 90
  Germany, 197
  Lanham Act, 90
  and marketing channels,
    420–421
  per se illegal concept, 90
  Robinson-Patman Act, 89, 92
  rule of reason, 421
  Sherman Act, 88–89, 90,
    420, 421
App enhancement, 546
Approach stage
  cultural differences, 577
  definition, 577
  in international selling, 577
  objectives, 575
Apps, 556
  most popular, 538
Art director, 654
Asian Americans
  assimilated, 144
  buying patterns, 144
  buying power, 142
  characteristics, 144
  makeup of subculture, 144
  nonassimilated, 144
  size of population, 79
  spending by, 79
Aspiration groups, 139
Association of Magazine
    Media, 503
Association of National
    Advertisers, 517
Associative reference groups, 139
Assumptive close, 580
Assurance of services, 330
At-market pricing, 379, 380
Attitude change, 134
Attitudes, 134, 142
  changing by men and
    women, 80–81
  societal, 104
Attitude tests, 518
Auctions
  online, 166–167
  reverse, 166, 167
  traditional, 166–167
Automatic vending, 443–444
Automobile industry
  brand names, 307
  divestments by Ford, 241
  electric cars, 298–299
  logistics management, 423

product differentiation, 240–241
supply chain, 422–423
Toyota, 117–120
women car buyers, 122–123
women working in, 122
Auto Trader, 511
Avatar, 204, 206
Avengers: Age of Ultron, 523
Average page views per visitor, social media, 553
Awareness, 482

B

Baby boomers, 75
Baby boomlet, 76
Baby bust, 75
Back translation, 187
Bad timing, 272
Bait and switch, 391
Balance of trade, 177
Banner blindness, 513
Bargains conditional on other purchases, 391
Barriers to entry, 87
Barter, 350
in world trade, 176–177
Basing-point pricing, 389
legality of, 390
B-Corp Certification, 26
Beginning inventories, 400
Behavioral evaluation is salesforce evaluation, 587–588
Behavioral learning, 133
Behavioral segmentation
consumer markets
by product features, 244
by usage rate, 244
organizational markets, 248
Behavioral targeting, 482, 610
Beliefs, 134, 142
Believers, 136
Below-market pricing, 379, 380
Benchmark items, 449
Benefit Corporation movement, 26
Benefits of marketing, 18
Best Global Brand survey, 38
Better Business Bureau, 92
Better Homes and Gardens, 85
Big data, 221–222
used to curb smoking, 361
Billboards, 514
Black Friday, 446
Black-ish, 79
Blacklist, 212
Blended family, 77
Blog, 540, 541
Bloomberg Businessweek, 656, 665
Blue ocean strategy, 636
Boston Consulting Group, 46
business portfolio analysis, 36–39

Bots, 606
Brand awareness, 305
Brand-building
Gatorade, 290
Mary Kay, Inc., 201
Brand community, 139
Brand development index, 300, 301
Brand equity, 305
financial advantages, 306
steps in creating, 305–306
valuing, 306
Brand extension, 270–271
definition and risks, 308
Gatorade, 290
Brand group, 639
Branding, 303
consumer benefits, 304
Branding strategies
brand extension, 308
diagram, 307
mixed branding, 310
multibranding, 308–309
multiproduct, 308
private branding, 309
subbranding, 308
Brand licensing, 306
Brand loyalty, 134, 527
Brand management
benefits to consumers, 304
brand equity, 305–306
branding strategies, 307–310
brand personality, 305
and counterfeit products, 303–304
picking brand names, 306–307
Procter & Gamble, 315–318
terminology, 303
trademark protection, 303
Brand managers, 43, 654
Carmex and social media, 554–555
Facebook strategy, 544
LinkedIn strategy, 548
role of, 639
roles of, 300
social media role, 551–552
Twitter strategy, 547
YouTube strategy, 549–550
Brand names, 303
complexity of choosing, 304
favorable phonetic association, 307
fit with company image, 307
importance to companies, 305
meanings in other languages, 307
no legal restrictions, 307
product benefits, 306–307
simple, 307
StuffDOT, 562
Brand personality, 305
Brands
and attitude change, 134
consideration set, 125
creating, 290–291
eliciting proper responses, 305
establishing meaning of, 305
evaluative criteria, 125

global, 183
new forms of engagement, 468–469
usage rate surveys, 245
Brand sustainability map, 618
Breadth of product line, 441
in retail positioning matrix, 448
Break-even analysis, 362
break-even chart, 363–364
calculating break-even point, 362–363
Break-even chart, 363, 582
Break-even point (BEP), 362
calculating, 363–364
to make pricing decisions, 367–368
Bribe Payers Index, 106, 107
Bribery, 105–106, 186
Brigham Young University, 277
Brokers, 458
as intermediary, 408
Build-to-order system, 241
Bullet graphs, 34
Bundle pricing, 375
Bureau of Labor Statistics, on savings rate, 84
Business, 32
Business analysis, 279
at X-1, 286–287
Business cards, 577
Business culture
composition of, 104
ethics of competition, 105–106
ethics of exchange, 104–105
Business firms, 28; *see also* Companies
criticism of ethics of, 103
goals of, 32
reasons for segmentation, 238
Business-format franchises, 439–440
Business model
and global competition, 32
Google Inc., 147–148
Mary Kay, Inc., 199–200
Milsco Corporation, 160
Business plan, 54
compared to marketing plan, 54–55
elements of, 55
most-asked questions, 55
writing style suggestions, 55–56
Business portfolio analysis, 36, 46
for Apple Inc., 38–39
growth-share matrix, 37–38
primary strengths, 39
Business practices, Toyota, 117–118
Business products and services, **266;** *see also* Organizational buying
cost-plus pricing, 376
marketing channels, 411–412
types of, 267
Business publications, 668

Business-to-business exchanges, 165
Business-to-business marketing, 154
consultative selling, 578
online buying in, 164–167
Business-to-business products, 266
Business 2.0, 511
Buy classes, 163
Buyers
in buying centers, 163
channel choice requirements
convenience, 417
information, 417
pre- or postsale services, 417
variety, 417
competitive bids, 157
nature of solutions, 579
no economical access to, 272
organizational, 18
potential number of, 157
power of, 88
in retailing, 654
Buyer turnover, 515
Buying center, 162
buy classes in
modified rebuy, 164
new buy, 163
straight rebuy, 164
composition of, 163
roles in
buyers, 163
deciders, 163
gatekeepers, 163
influencers, 163
users, 163
Trek Bicycle Corporation, 171
Buying committee, 162
Buying decision
in organizational buying, 156
postpurchase stage, 480
prepurchase stage, 479
purchase stage, 479–480
Buying function, 161
Buyology (Lindstrom), 215
Buy one, get one free, 387
Buzz, 138, 608–609
Buzz experience, 139

C

Cable TV, 510
CAFTA-DR, 181
Campbell Interest and Skill survey, 660
Campus career service office, 660
Canned sales presentation, 578
Cannibalization, 241
CAN-SPAM Act of 2004, 91, 608
Capacity management, 336
load factor, 336, 337
pricing differences, 336–337
Capitalist's dilemma, 624
Career planning publications, 668
Careers and marketing, 4

Careers in marketing
  advertising, 654–655
  and changes in marketing
    discipline, 652
  diversity of opportunities,
    652–653
  identifying job opportunities
    campus career service
      office, 660
    direct contact, 662
    employment agencies, 661
    help-wanted ads, 661
    library reference sources, 661
    networking, 662
    online career services,
      660–661
    personal contact, 662
    state employment
      agencies, 662
  information sources, 668–670
  international careers, 654,
    657–658
  job interviews, 664–667
  job search process
    job-related tests, 659–660
    self-assessment, 658–660
  marketing research, 654, 657
  as opportunity for
    advancement, 653
  physical distribution, 653, 654
  process of getting a job, 652
  product management, 653, 654
  promotion, 654–655
  résumé preparation, 662–664
  retailing, 654, 655–656
  sales, 654, 656–657
  starting salaries, 653
Car rental agency activities,
  331, 332
Carrying costs, 324
Case allowance, 524, 525
Cash and carry wholesalers, 457
Cash cows, 37, 45
Cash discounts, 387
Catalogs, 444–445
Category development index,
  300, 301
Category killers, 441–442
Category management, 453
Caucasians, 79
Causal research, 208
Cause marketing, 112
  American Express, 112
Caveat emptor, 104
Cease and desist orders, 91
Celebrity endorsements,
  445, 506
Census 2010, 211
Census Bureau, 75
Central business district, 451
Cents-off coupons, 65
CEOs, 29
  marketing experience, 653
  sales experience, 569
Certified Professional in Supply
  Management, 152

Channel captain
  definition, 420
  sources of influence, 419–420
    economic influence, 420
    identification, 420
    legitimate right, 420
Channel conflict, 419
  and disintermediation, 419
  horizontal, 419
  in multichannel marketing, 612
  vertical, 419
Channel of communication, 470
Channel strategies
  pull strategy, 481
  push strategy, 480–481
Charges, 333
Charitable contributions, 112
Chicago Sun-Times, 512
Chief marketing officer, 30, 43
  role of, 638–639
Child Protection Act, 89
Children, consumer
  socialization, 140
Children's Online Privacy
  Protection Act, 91, 105
China
  Mary Kay, Inc. in, 200
  merchandise trade, 176
  tobacco production and use,
    102–103
Choice, reason for online shopping,
  606–607
Choiceboards, 600
  collaborative filtering, 600
Chuck, 96
Clayton Act, 89, 390
Click fraud, 514
Clickstream, 382
Click-through rate, 553
Clinton Foundation, 29
Clinton Global Initiative, 89
Closed-end questions, 218
Closing stage, 580
CNBC, 212
CNN Early Start, 555
Co-create value, 324
Code of Business Practices
  (BBB), 92
Code of ethics, 106
  American Marketing
    Association, 107, 108–109
  United Technologies, 107
Coffee industry, trends in, 72–73
Cognitive dissonance, 126–127
Cognitive learning, 134
Cohabitation, 77
Cola wars, 106
Cold calling, 576
Cold canvassing, 576
Collaborative filtering, 600
Collaborative projects, 542
College Board, 82
College students
  digital natives, 477
  illegal downloading by, 103
  job search, 548

target audience, 477
  and 3M strategy, 12–14
College tuition increases, 82
Combination compensation
  plans, 587
Combined statistical areas, 78
Commerce, 618
  website element, 603
Commercialization, 281
  Boeing 787 Dreamliner, 281
  Burger King's french fries,
    281–282
  risks with grocery products, 282
  time to market, 282
Commission, 350
Communication, 470
  with college students, 477
  decoding, 471
  elements of, 470
  encoding, 471
  errors in, 471
  feedback, 471–472
  in marketing, 6
  in marketing program, 635
  noise, 472
  in online shopping
    blogs, 608
    buzz, 608–609
    forms of, 607–608
    spam, 608
    viral marketing, 609
    web communities, 608
  salesforce, 589–590
  in supply chain management, 426
  website element, 603
Communication adaptation
  strategy, 196
Communication infrastructure, 189
Community
  Pizza Hut, 618
  website element, 603
Community shopping centers, 451
Companies; see also Business firms
  analysis by Paradise Kitchens, 61
  challenge of marketing in two
    environments, 598
  consumer base, 80
  environmental awareness, 81
  fewer gender distinctions, 80–81
  image and brand name, 307
  profit equation, 352
  strategies to reduce perceived
    risk, 133
  use of social media, 142
Company effects on pricing, 382–383
Comparable value comparisons, 391
Comparative advertisements, 500
Comparisons with suggested
  prices, 391
Compensation
  of salesforce
    combination plan, 587
    commission plan, 586–587
    straight salary, 586
  starting salaries in marketing, 653
  Xerox salesforce, 594

Competencies, 35–36
Competition, 86
  created by Internet, 357
  ethics of, 105–106
  forms of, 87
  global, 32
  in global markets, 36
  for Groupon, 149
  laws protecting, 88–89
  in market segments, 253
Competition-oriented pricing
  approaches
  above-, at-, or below-market
    pricing, 379–380
  customary pricing, 379
  loss leader pricing, 380
Competitive advantage
  from core competencies, 36
  finding and exploiting, 622
  from packaging and labeling,
    310–312
Competitive advertising, 500
Competitive bids, 157
Competitive effects on pricing, 384
Competitive forces
  components
    entry, 87
    existing competitors, 88
    power of buyers and
      suppliers, 88
    substitutes, 88
  for Facebook, 70
  forms of competition, 86–88
  identified by environmental
    scanning, 73
  small businesses, 88
  types of, 72
Competitive institutional
  advertisements, 502
Competitive intelligence
  researcher, 654
Competitive market
  monopolistic competition,
    356–357
  monopoly, 356–357
  oligopoly, 356–357
  as pricing constraint, 356–357
  pure competition, 356–357
Competitive parity budgeting,
  483–484, 504
Competitive position, in target
  market selection, 251
Competitor analysis, Paradise
  Kitchens, 60–61
Competitors
  blurred distinctions among, 36
  existing, 88
  for Geek Squad, 96
  new-product ideas, 276–277
  prices of, as constraint, 357
  reacting to position of, 303
  salespeople's knowledge of, 581
Complexity of products, 478–479
Complex professional
  salesperson, 654
Components, 267

Computer Weekly, 511
Concepts, 209
Concept tests, 204–206, 278
Conditional content, 515
Conference Board, 82
Conference selling, 573
Connected glasses, 434
Connection, website element, 602–603
Connections (businesspeople), 546
Connectivity, 84
Consensus-building, 631
Consideration set, 125
Constraints, 208
Consultative selling, 578
Consumer behavior, 123; *see also* Online consumer behavior
African Americans, 143–144
aided by Groupon, 146–147
Asian Americans, 144
flawed, 114–115
Hispanics, 143
and product life cycle
and diffusion of innovation, 298
from early adopters to laggards, 298
means of overcoming barriers, 299
psychological barriers, 298
risk barriers, 298
slow adoption of electric cars, 298–299
usage barriers, 298
value barriers, 298
profiles of product adopters, 299
psychological influences
learning, 133–134
lifestyle analysis, 135–137
motivation, 130–131
perception, 131–133
personality, 131
values, beliefs, and attitudes, 134
purchase decision process
alternative evaluation, 124–125
information search, 124
level of involvement, 127–129
postpurchase behavior, 126–127
problem recognition, 124
purchase decision, 125–126
situational influences, 129
in services purchases
at car rental agencies, 332
customer contact audit, 330–332
process, 329
quality assessment, 329–330
relationship marketing, 332
smartphone purchase, 162
sociocultural influences
culture and subculture, 142–144
family, 140–142
personal, 137–138

reference groups, 138–140
social class, 142
stages of buying decision, 479–480
using coupons to influence, 148
women car buyers, 122–123
Consumer Bill of Rights, 104, 107
Consumer Confidence Index, 82
Consumer-driven pricing actions, 357
Consumer Electronics Association, 96
Consumer Electronics Show, 85
Consumer ethnocentrism, 188
Consumer expectations
about economy, 82
gap analysis, 330
and postpurchase behavior, 126
Consumer Expenditure Survey, 84
Consumer-generated media, 540
Consumer Goods Pricing Act, 389, 390
Consumer income
demand factor, 359
discretionary income, 83–84
disposable income, 83
and global marketing, 189–190
gross income, 83
Consumer involvement; *see* Involvement
Consumerism, 89
Consumer learning, 133
Consumer lifestyle; *see* Lifestyle
Consumer markets
means of segmenting
behavioral by product features, 244
behavioral by usage rate, 244
demographic, 23
geographic, 23
psychographic, 243–244
patronage of fast-food restaurants, 245–247
PRIZM segmentation system, 245
segmentation bases, 244–245
Consumer needs
discovering, 7
met with new products, 7–8
new product not satisfying, 271–272
satisfying, 9–10
unsatisfied, 6
versus wants, 8–9
Consumer-oriented sales promotions, 519
contests, 520
coupons, 519–521
deals, 521
loyalty programs, 522–523
point-of-sale displays, 523
premiums, 520
product placements, 523–524
rebates, 523
samples, 522
sweepstakes, 520–522

Consumer perception
perceived risk, 133
selective, 131–132
Consumer products
convenience, 266–267
shopping, 266–267
specialty, 266–267
unsought, 266–267
Consumer Product Safety Act, 89
Consumer Product Safety Commission, 89, 104
Consumer products and services, **266**
marketing channels, 410–411
Consumer protection, 8–9
Consumer Reports, 61, 124, 162
Consumers
awareness of competitors' prices, 357
baby boomers, 75
benefits from branding, 304
benefits from intermediaries, 408–409
brand connection, 306
change in consumption orientation, 81
cross-channel, 611–612
environmental awareness, 80
Generation X, 75–76
Generation Y, 76
global, 183–184
and hierarchy of effects, 482–483
organizational buyers, 18
selection criteria, 124–125
ultimate, 18
understanding food values, 2
use of social media, 538–539
utilities from retailing, 436–437
value conscious, 81
Consumer socialization, 140
Consumer spending
by African Americans, 79
by Asian Americans, 79
by Hispanics, 79
survey on, 84
Consumer tastes
changing, 253–254, 621
changing for food, 2
demand factor, 358–359
Consumer wants, 8–9
Consumption orientation, changes in, 81
Content, website element, 602
Content communication, 542
Contests
advantages and disadvantages, 520
growth of, 521
objectives, 520
Context, website element, 602
Continuous improvement, 622
at Amazon, 432
Continuous innovation, 269–270
Continuous (steady) schedule, 516

Contractual vertical marketing systems
franchising, 415–416
retailer-sponsored cooperatives, 415
in retailing
franchise systems, 439–440
retailer-sponsored cooperatives, 439
wholesaler-sponsored voluntary chains, 439
wholesaler-sponsored voluntary chains, 415
Control, reason for online shopping, 609–610
Controlled test markets, 280
Controlling the Assault of Non-Solicited Pornography and Marketing Act, 91, 608
Convenience
for buyers, 417
reason for online shopping, 606
in supply chain management, 426
Convenience products, 266
bases of comparison, 267
Convergence of real and digital worlds
apps, 556–557
databases and algorithms, 556–557
mobile marketing, 557–558
smartphones, 556
Conversation velocity, 219
Cookies, 610
Cooperation in marketing channels, 419–420
Cooperative advertising, 525
Copyright, 89
Copyright infringement, 104
Copywriter, 654
Core competencies, 35–36
Paradise Kitchens, 57
Core values, 31
IBM, 50
Mary Kay, Inc., 200
Corporate branding, 308
Corporate culture
and code of ethics, 106–107
co-worker behavior, 107
definition, 106
top management behavior, 107
Corporate level, 28–30, 33
Corporate philanthropy, Google, Inc., 531
Corporate retail chains, 438–439
Corporate social responsibility, Anheuser–Busch, 100–101
Corporate vertical marketing systems
backward integration, 414–415
forward integration, 414–415
Corrective advertising, 91
Cosmo Girl, 511
Cost barriers, 298
Cost control
break-even analysis, 362–364
importance of, 362

Cost-effectiveness, criterion for market segments, 243
Cost elements of operating statement
    costs of goods sold, 398–399
    expenses, 400
Cost focus strategy, 628
Cost justification defense, 390
Cost leadership strategy, 628
Cost of goods sold, 397–398
    terms related to, 399
Cost-oriented pricing approaches
    cost-plus pricing, 376
    experience curve pricing, 376–377
    standard markup pricing, 375–376
Cost per thousand (CPM), 508
Cost-plus fixed-fee pricing, 376
Cost-plus percentage-of-cost pricing, 376
Cost-plus pricing, 376
Cost reduction in packaging, 312
Costs
    of changing prices, 355
    disadvantage for TV advertising, 510
    of economic espionage, 185
    incremental, 384–385, 623
    logistics, 425
    magazine advertising, 511
    of order getters, 572
    of promotion programs, 486
    reason for online shopping, 609
    social media performance measure, 552–553
    in target market selection, 251
    of training salesforce, 586
    of TV ads, 507
    types of, 362
Costs of production and marketing, as pricing constraint, 355
Counterfeit products, 303–304
Countertrade, 176
    popular locations for, 177
Coupon fraud, 520–521
Coupons
    advantages and disadvantages, 520
    as aid to sales, 520
    costs, 520
    monetary value, 519
    objectives, 520
    online, 519
    Paradise Kitchens, 65
Co-workers, ethical behavior, 107
Credibility of media, 542
CROPing, 22
Cross-channel consumer, 611–612
Cross-cultural analysis, 80, 185
Cross-docking, 424
Cross-functional business specialists, 570
Cross-functional group, 163
Cross-functional teams, 30

Cross-functional team selling, 573, 574
Cross tab, 222
Cross-tabulation, 222
    developing, 222–224
    disadvantages, 224
    example, 223
    interpreting, 224
Crowdfunding, 277
Crowdsourcing, 7, 276
Cultural diversity
    in approach stage, 577
    cross-cultural analysis, 185
    cultural symbols, 186–187
    customs, 186
    ethnocentrism, 187–188
    language, 187
    values, 185–186
Cultural ethnocentrism, 187–188
Cultural symbols, 186
    misuse in advertising, 187
Cultural values, 185–186
Culture, 80
    changing attitudes, 80–81
    changing values, 81
    influence on purchase decision, 142–144
    as socializing force, 103
Cumulative quantity discounts, 386
Currency exchange rate, 190
Customary pricing, 379
Customer analysis, Paradise Kitchens
    demographics, 61
    health and nutrition concerns, 62
Customer contact audit, 330
    car rental agencies, 331, 332
    service blueprint, 332
    and service delivery, 336
Customer effects on pricing, 383–384
Customer experience, 15
    definition, 601
    online, 601–603
    Pizza Hut, 618
    Seven Cycles, Inc., 596
Customer experience management (CEM), 278, 335–336
Customerization, 607
Customer loyalty, Trader Joe's, 16
Customer relationship management (CRM), 15, 570
    and customer experience, 15–16
Customer relationship philosophy, General Electric Healthcare Americas, 566
Customer relationships, 15
    in marketspace, 600–601
    Xerox, 593–594
Customers, 18; *see also* Consumer *entries*
    connecting packaging and labeling to, 312
    current, 36
    in customer solutions, 579

new-product ideas, 276
    reaching, 2
Customer sales organization, 583
Customer sales support personnel, 572–573
Customer satisfaction, 126, 127
    goal of business, 32
    is salesforce evaluation, 587–588
    value to companies, 127
Customer service, 425
    in logistics management, 425–426
    Zappos.com, 236
Customer service manager, 654
Customer value, 10–11
    impact of technology, 85–86
    from intermediaries, 408–409
    from marketspace, 598–599
    from packaging and labeling, 310–312
    from personal selling, 570, 571
    from team selling, 574
Customer value proposition, 10
Customization, 607
    Seven Cycles, Inc., 596
    website element, 602
    of websites, 617
Customized interaction, 472
Customs, 186
Cyber Monday, 446

D

Dancing with the Stars, 469
Data, 210
    needed for marketing actions, 209
    types of, 210
Data analysis, 225
Data analytics, 12, 86, 221–222, 456–457
    elements of, 221
Databases, 12, 212, 556
    in direct marketing, 489
Data collection
    concepts, 209
    methods, 209
    primary data, 212–224
    secondary data, 210–211
Data mining, 222
    downside, 223
Data Protection Directive (EU), 490
Data services, 211
Data visualization, 34, 221
Deadlines
    defining, 43–44
    scheduling, 636–638
Dealers, 408
Deals
    advantages and disadvantages, 520
    definition, 521
    objectives, 520
Deceptive advertising, 91
Deceptive Mail Prevention and Enforcement Act, 91

Deceptive pricing
    definition, 390
    types of, 391
Deciders, in buying centers, 163
Decision making, 207
    evaluation of, 227
Decisions
    characteristics, 207
    constraints in, 208
    evaluation of, 227
Decline stage; *see* Product life cycle; Retail life cycle
Decoding, 471
Deletion; *see* Product deletion
Demand
    derived, 156
    elastic, 360
    estimating, 358–360
    inelastic, 360
    as pricing constraint, 355
    primary, 292
    selective, 292
Demand curve, 358
    factors influencing demand, 358–359
    movement along *vs.* shift of, 359–360
    for prestige pricing, 373
    and total revenue, 361
Demand factors, 359
    consumer income, 359
    consumer tastes, 358–359
    price and availability of similar products, 359
Demand-oriented pricing approaches
    bundle pricing, 375
    odd-even pricing, 374
    penetration pricing, 373
    prestige pricing, 373–374
    price lining, 374
    skimming pricing, 372–373
    target pricing, 374–375
    yield management pricing, 375
Demographics, 74
    American households, 76–77
    baby bust, 75
    customers of Paradise Kitchens, 61
    generational cohorts, 75–76
    of Hispanic population, 143
    population shifts, 77–78
    racial and ethnic diversity, 78–80
    U.S. population, 75
    world population, 74–75
Demographic segmentation
    consumer markets, 243, 244
    organizational markets, 247–248
Denial, 579
Department, 30
Department of Commerce, 28
Department of Energy, 51
Department of Justice, 87, 159
    and marketing channels, 420

Department of Labor
  Consumer Expenditure
    Survey, 84
  on jobs in marketing, 653
  *Occupational Outlook
    Handbook,* 661
Department of Transportation, 352
Department stores, 450–451
Dependability in supply chain
  management, 426
Dependent variable, 220
Depth interviews, 215
Depth of product line, 441
Derived demand, 156
  for business products, 267
Descriptive research, 208
Desk jobbers, 458
Detroit Institute of Arts, 640–641
Developing countries, 189–190
Development, 279
  at X-1, 287
Deviations
  acting on, 46
    example, 641–642
    results exceed goals, 640
    results fall short, 640–641
  identifying, 45, 640
  positive or negative, 46
Dex One, 512
**Differentiation focus
  strategy, 628**
Differentiation positioning, 256
Differentiation strategy, 628
Diffusion of innovation, 298
Digital marketing manager, 654
Digital Millennium Copyright
  Act, 89
Digital natives, 477
Digital photography, 275
Direct channels
  business products, 411
  consumer products, 410
Direct contact, for job search, 662
Direct exporting, 192
Direct forecast, 228
Direct investing, 194
Direct labor cost, 399
Direct mail, 444–445
  expenditures, 507
Direct Mail Association
  (UK), 490
Direct-mail coupons, 65
Direct marketing, 475
  costs, 473
  customer information
    databases, 488
  databases, 489
  disadvantages, 475–476
  expenditures, 488
  forms of, 487–488
  in global marketing, 489–490
  growth of, 488
  information technology, 489
  privacy issue, 490
  of services, 335
  strengths and weaknesses, 473

value of
  for consumers, 489
  for sellers, 489
Direct Marketing Association, 444,
  446, 447, 489
Direct marketing channels, 413
Direct orders, 489
Direct or retail salesperson, 654
Direct selling
  examples, 447
  reasons for growth, 447
Direct-to-consumer
  advertising, 481
Discontinuous innovation, 270
Discounts
  cash, 387
  definition, 385
  quantity, 385–386
  seasonal, 386
  trade/functional, 386
Discount stores *vs.* off-price
  retailing, 450
Discretionary income, 83–84
Disintermediation, 419
Disposable income, 83
Disruptive innovation, 275, 633
Dissociative reference groups,
  139–140
Distribution
  exclusive, 416–417
  in growth stage, 294
  intensive, 416
  in introduction stage, 292
  regular, 270
  selective, 417
  of services, 335
Distribution-related
  legislation, 91
Distribution strategy
  in global marketing, 196–197
  Prince Sports, Inc., 261–262
Distributors, 408
Diversification, 40
Diversification analysis, 39
  market development, 39
  market penetration, 39
  product development, 39–40
  strategy, 40
Diversity, supplier, 157, 158
Divestments by Ford Motor
  Company, 241
Divorce, 77
DMAchoice, 490
Dogs, 38
Dogster magazine, 477
Downloading, illegal, 104
Downsizing
  definition, 302
  economics of, 303
Drives, 133
Drop shippers, 458
Dual adaptation strategy, 196
Dual distribution, 413
  legality of, 420
Dues, 350
Dumping, 197

Durable goods, 266
Dynamically continuous
  innovation, 270
Dynamic pricing, 609
Dynamic pricing policy, 382

E

E.T. the Extra Terrestrial, 523
Early adopters, 299
Early majority, 299
E-books, 370–371
Echo-boom, 76
E-commerce, 89, 184
Economic Census, 211
Economic espionage, 105, 185
  and cola wars, 106
Economic Espionage Act of
  1996, 185
Economic forces
  consumer income, 83–84
  for Facebook, 70
  identified by environmental
    scanning, 73
  macroeconomic conditions,
    82–83
  types of, 72
Economic infrastructure,
  188–189
Economic integration
  CAFTA-DR, 181
  European Union, 179–180
  North American Free Trade
    Agreement, 180
Economic mission, 26
Economics of surge pricing, 383
Economies of scale, 241
Economy, 82
  consumer expectations
    about, 82
Effective consumer response
  delivery system, 426
E-hubs, 165
Eight-second rule, 417, 606
80/20 rule, 246
Elastic demand, 360
Electronic commerce, 86
Electronic intermediaries, 412
Electronic junk mail, 608
E-marketplace, 165
  examples, 165–166
  online auctions, 166
  private exchanges, 166
Emory University, 579
Emotional intelligence, 586
Empathy of services, 330
Empire, 79
Employees
  and demographic
    segmentation, 248
  new-product ideas, 275
Employee welfare, 32
Employment agencies, 661
Encoding, 471
Ending inventories, 400

Endorsements, 133
Enterprise selling, 570
Entertainment industry as
  oligopoly, 87
Entertainment Weekly, 486
Entrepreneur, 440
Entrepreneurship, personal selling
  in, 569
Entry, 87; *see also* Barriers
  to entry
Environmental awareness
  of companies, 81
  and consumer behavior,
    114–115
  of consumers, 80
  millennials, 77
  Toyota, 117–120
  Trek Bicycle Corporation,
    171–172
Environmental forces, 5–6, 10
  competitive forces, 86–88
  economic forces, 82–84
  for Facebook, 70
  regulatory forces, 88–92
  social forces, 74–81
  technological forces, 84–86
  types of, 72
Environmental issues
  leadership in, 119
  in packaging, 312
  in retailing, 439
Environmental preservation, 101
Environmental scanning, 72
  American FactFinder, 83
  on consumer spending, 82
  today's marketplace, 73
  tracking trends, 72–73
  trends identified by, 73
Environmental sustainability
  initiatives, 158
Environmental trends, 72–73
E-Privacy Directive (EU), 490
Equipment-based services, 326
Esquire Sportsman, 511
Ethical behavior, critical
  perceptions, 103
Ethical dilemma, whistle-
  blowers, 107
Ethical duties, 108
Ethical/legal framework,
  102–103
Ethical marketing behavior, factors
  affecting
  business culture, 104–106
  corporate culture, 106–107
  co-worker behavior, 107
  cultural norms, 103–104
  industry practices, 104–106
  personal moral philosophy,
    107–109
  top management behavior, 107
Ethics, 16, 102
  of asking about competitors, 581
  of consumers, 114–115
  of subliminal messages, 132
  of surge pricing, 383

Ethics of competition
  bribery and kickbacks, 105–106
  economic espionage, 105
  Economic Espionage Act, 106
  Foreign Corrupt Practices
    Act, 106
Ethics of exchange
  caveat emptor concept, 104
  right to be heard, 105
  right to be informed, 105
  right to choose, 105
  right to safety, 104–105
Ethnic diversity, 78–80
Ethnocentric consumers, 188
Ethnographic research, 214
European Union
  Data Protection Act, 91
  Data Protection Directive, 490
  E-Privacy Directive, 490
  General Data Protection
    Regulation, 490
  hypermarkets, 442
  map, 180
  marketing opportunities, 179–180
  membership, 179
  and Microsoft, 87
  and protectionism, 178
  tariffs, 178
Evaluation, 482
Evaluative criteria, 125
**Everyday low pricing (EDLP),
  387,** 449
  at supermarkets, 388
Evidence management, 336
Examiner.com, 512
Exchange, 5
  by barter, 350
  ethics of, 104–105
  in marketing, 6
Exchange rate fluctuations, 190
Exclusive dealing, 91, 421
Exclusive distribution, 416–417
Exclusive territorial
  distributorships, 91
Expense
  of media, 542
  of product launch, 620
  types of, 400
Expense-to-sales ratio, 400
Experience curve pricing, 376
Experiencers, 136, 137
Experiments, 219–221
Expertise of channel systems, 420
Exploratory research, 208
Exporting, 192
  direct or indirect, 192
  by small and medium
    enterprises, 192–193
Exports, 176–177
Express warranty, 313
Extended problem solving, 128
External data, 210
External search, 124
External target audience, 54, 55
Extranets, 86
Extreme value retailers, 450

F

Facebook, 544
  in brand manager's strategy, 544
  compared to other social
    media, 543
  launching new social networks,
    545–546
  mobile marketing at, 546
  number of users, 544, 551
  overview, 544
Facilitating function, 409
Failure fees, 282
Fair Packaging and Labeling
  Act, 89
Fairtrade, 26
Family branding, 308
Family decision making
  preteens and teens, 141
  roles in purchase process,
    141–142
  wives and husbands, 141
Family influence, 141–142
Family life cycle, 140
  diagram, 140
  middle-aged married
    couples, 141
  older married or unmarried, 141
  single parents, 141
  traditional family, 140
  young married couples, 141
  young singles, 141
*Family Talking About
  Drinking,* 100
Fans, social media, 553
Fan source, 553
Fares, 333, 350
Fast and the Furious, The, 204
Fast-food restaurant patronage,
  245–247
Fast prototyping, 282
Fax machine product life cycle,
  293–295
Fear appeals, 505
Feature bloat, 269
Federal Bureau of Investigation,
  106, 114
Federal Communications
  Commission
  on advertising, 502
  and online tracking, 92
  on product placements, 524
  on subliminal messages, 132
Federal Trade Commission,
  31, 87
  on buy one, get one free, 387
  cease and desist orders, 91
  Do Not Call Registry, 105
  environmental guidelines, 115
  *Guides against Deceptive
    Pricing,* 390
  and marketing channels, 420
  National Do Not Call Registry,
    446–447, 490
  on newness of products, 270
  and online fraud, 610

  on personal information
    collection, 105
  on privacy, 490
  on promotions, 527
  on sweepstakes, 521
  on warranties, 313
Federal Trade Commission Act,
  91, 389, 390, 391
Federal Trademark Dilution Act, 90
Federation of European Direct
  Marketing, 490
FedStats, 212
Feedback, 472
  on social media, 540
Feedback loop, 471–472
Fees, 333, 350
Feminism, 80
Field of Dreams, 204
Field of experience, 471
Fighting brands, 309
Final price, 372
  calculating, 351
Finance allowance, 524, 525
Financial aspects of marketing
  operating statement, 397–400
  ratios for analyzing operations,
    400–401
  ratios for setting and evaluating
    price, 401–405
Financial data, Paradise Kitchens,
  65–66
Financial systems, 189
Firms, 28
Fitness, 288
Fixed alternative questions, 218
Fixed cost (FC), 362
  Washburn Guitar, 368
Fixed-price policy, 381–382
Flexible pricing policy, 382
Flighting (intermittent)
  schedule, 516
Floor stock protection
  program, 525
FOB origin pricing, 388, 390
FOB with freight-allowed pricing,
  389, 390
Focused strategy, 622
Focus groups, 215
Follow-up stage, 580
Food and Drug Administration,
  109, 307
Food brokers, 458
Forbes, 29, 320
Foreign Corrupt Practices Act,
  106, **186**
Forgetting rate, 516
Former price comparisons, 391
Form of ownership, 438
  contractual systems, 439–440
  corporate chains, 438–439
  independent retailers, 438
Formula selling presentation, 578
Form utility, 409, 436–437
  definition, 18
  from marketspace, 599
For-profit organizations, 28, 326

Forrest Gump, 524
Fortune, 622, 661
Four I's of services, 322–325, **323**
Four Ps of marketing, 9–10
  in marketing program, 43
Fox News, 288
Franchising, 193–194
  manufacturer-sponsored retail
    franchise systems, 415
  manufacturer-sponsored
    wholesale franchise
    systems, 415
  in retailing
    attractiveness, 440
    business-format, 439–440
    fees to franchisors, 440
    product-distribution, 439–440
    top five in U.S., 440
  service-sponsored franchise
    systems, 416
  service-sponsored retail
    franchise systems, 415–416
Free goods allowance, 525
Free trials, 133
Freight absorption pricing, 389
Freight allowances, 525
Frequency, 508
Frequency marketing, 244
Fresh off the Boat, 79
Full coverage, 630
Full-line forcing, 421
Full-line wholesalers, 457
Full-service agency, 517
Full service retailers, 441
Full warranty, 313
Functional discounts, 386
Functional groupings, 639
Functional level, 30, 33
Fuzzy front end methods, 215

G

Game of Thrones, 498
GamePro, 511
Gantt chart, 44, 45, 637–638
Gap analysis, 330
Garden Design, 511
Gasoline prices, 83
Gatekeepers, 163
Genchi genbutsu principle, 635
General Data Protection Regulation
  (EU), 490
General expenses, 400
Generalized life cycle, 297
General merchandise
  wholesalers, 457
Generational cohorts
  baby boomers, 75
  Generation X, 75–76
  Generation Y, 76
Generational marketing, 76
Generation X, 75
  males, 502
Generation Y, 76
  income of, 80

Generic, 90
Generic business strategy,
   627–**628**
   cost focus strategy, 628
   cost leadership strategy, 628
   differentiation focus
     strategy, 628
   differentiation strategy, 628
Geographical groupings, 639
Geographical price adjustments
   basing-point pricing, 389
   FOB origin pricing, 388
   FOB with freight-allowed
     pricing, 389
   multiple-zone pricing, 389
   single-zone pricing, 388–389
   uniform delivered pricing,
     388–389
Geographic sales organization,
   582–583
Geographic segmentation
   consumer markets, 243, 244
   organizational markets,
     247–248
GeoVALS, 137
Germany, antitrust laws, 197
Global companies
   global brands, 183
   strategies, 182–183
   types of, 181–182
Global competition, 32, 181
Global consumers, 183
Global environmental scan
   cultural diversity, 185–188
   economic considerations
     currency exchange rates, 190
     income and purchasing power,
       189–190
     infrastructure, 188–189
     political stability, 191
     trade regulations, 191
Global impact of retailing, 437
Global marketing
   in borderless economic world
     decline of protectionism,
       178–179
     economic espionage, 185
     economic integration,
       179–181
     global competition, 181–184
     networked global
       marketspace, 184
   direct marketing in, 489–490
   entry strategies
     Dell Inc., 174–175
     direct investment, 194
     exporting, 193–194
     franchising, 193–194
     joint ventures, 194
     licensing, 193–194
     Mary Kay, Inc., 199–200
Global marketing manager, 654
Global marketing strategy, 182
   examples, 182–183
Global marketplace, competition
   in, 36

Goals, 32
   acting on deviations from,
     640–641
   of business firms, 32
   communicating, 635
   identifying deviations from, 640
   measurable and achievable, 631
   of nonprofits, 33
   Paradise Kitchens, 58
   quantitative, 641
Goal setting, 42
Good Housekeeping Seal, 133, 310
Good Morning America, 502, 555
Goods
   durable, 266
   marketing of, 17
   nondurable, 266
Gourmet, 511
Government agencies, 28
Government-sponsored
   services, 327
Government units, 155
Gray divorce, 77
Gray market, 197
Green businesses, 338
Green jobs, 77
Green machines, 444
Green marketing, 111
Green technologies, 85
Green vehicles, 119
Grocery Headquarters, 60
Grocery products
   commercialization problems, 282
   regional rollouts, 282
Gross domestic product, 82
   services percentage of, 322
   small business percentage
     of, 88
   U.S. percentage of trade, 177
Gross income, 83
Gross margin, 399
Gross profit, 399
Gross rating points (GRPs), 508
Gross sales, 397
Groupthink, and new-product
   failures, 272–273
Growth, and target market
   selection, 251
Growth share matrix
   definition, 37
   quadrants, 37–38
Growth stage; *see* Product life cycle
Growth strategies
   business portfolio analysis,
     36–39
   diversification analysis, 39–40
Guarantees, 133
Guides against Deceptive Pricing
   (FTC), 390

H

Habits, and brand loyalty, 134
Harley Owners Group, 139
*Harry Potte*r books, 240

Harvesting strategy, 296
   marketing objectives, 293
Head-to-head positioning, 256
Health, and packaging, 312
Help-wanted ads, 661
Hierarchy of effects, 482
   adoption, 483
   awareness, 482
   evaluation, 482
   interest, 482
   trial, 483
High-involvement purchase,
   127, 128
High-learning products, 297
High-resource achievers, 136
High-resource experiencers, 136
High-resource groups, 137
High-resource innovators, 137
High-resource thinkers, 136
Hispanics
   buying patterns, 143
   buying power, 142
   demographics of, 143
   diversity of, 143
   expected growth of, 79
   makeup of, 78
   and multicultural marketing, 79
   purchasing power, 60
   spending by, 79
Home offices, 590
Horatio Alger American Citizen
   Award, 200
Horizontal channel conflict, 419
Horizontal price fixing, 389
Hotels at Home, 333
Households
   American, 76–77
   gross income, 83
   TV ratings, 213
   with TV sets, 509
Huffington Post, 512
Humorous appeals, 506
Hunger Games, 204–206, 240
Hypermarket, 442

I

Idea generation, 275
   from competitors' products,
     276–277
   from customers, 276
   from employees and friends, 275
   from inventors, 277
   research and development
     labs, 276
   from small businesses, 277
   from suppliers, 276
   from universities, 277
   at X-1, 286
Ideals-motivated groups, 136
Ideas, 266
   at Chobani, Inc., 21
   marketing of, 17
Idle production capacity, 324
Ignore objections, 579

Image of retail outlets, 451
IMC audit, 486–487
Implied warranty, 313
Imports, 176–177
Impression management, 336
Inbound telemarketing, 572
Inc. magazine, 320
Income
   of consumers, 83–84
   global levels, 74–75
Income statement, 397
Inconsistency, 323
Incremental costs and revenues,
   384–385, 623
Independent agents, 582
Independent retailers, 348
Independent variable, 220
Index of Consumer Sentiment
   1963-2015, 82–83
India
   Dell Inc. in, 174–175
   Mary Kay in, 200–202
Indirect channels
   business products, 411–412
   consumer products, 410–411
Indirect exporting, 192
Individual interviews, 215
Individuality in marketspace,
   599–600
Industrial firms
   North American Industry
     Classification System, 155
   types of, 154
Industrial products, 266
Industrial salesperson, 654
Industrial services, 267
Industry, 28
   and marketing plan, 54
Industry analysis, Paradise
   Kitchens, 60
Industry practices
   ethics of competition, 105–106
   ethics of exchange, 104–105
Inelastic demand, 360
Infant Formula Act, 89
Influencers, 163
Infomercials, 510
Information
   for buyers, 417
   negative word of mouth, 138
   for women car buyers, 122
Informational advertisements, 500
Information search
   consumer smartphone
     purchase, 162
   for extended problem
     solving, 128
   inadequate, 125
   on Internet, 126
   for limited problem solving, 128
   in online shopping, 610
   in organizational buying, 162
   and perceived risk, 133
   primary sources, 124
   for routine problem
     solving, 128

Information sources for marketing
  careers
  business publications, 668
  career planning publications, 668
  marketing publications, 668
  periodicals, 668–669
  professional and trade
    associations, 669–670
Information technology, 221
  in direct marketing, 489
  and dynamic pricing, 382
  and relationship marketing, 12
  in supply chain management,
    425
In-house agencies, 518
In-house research staff, 567
Innovation
  Chobani, Inc., 22–23
  continuous, 269–270
  diffusion of, 298
  discontinuous, 270
  disruptive, 275, 633
  dynamically continuous, 270
  open, 273
  radical, 271
Innovators, 137
  profile of, 299
In-pack coupons, 65
Input measures
  in salesforce evaluation, 587
  social media performance,
    552–553
Input metrics, 626–627
Input-related sales objectives, 581
Inquiry tests, 518
Inseparability, 323–324
Inside Edition, 555
Inside order takers, 572
Installations, 267
Institutional advertisements, 501
  advocacy, 501
  competitive, 502
  pioneering, 501
  reminder, 502
In-store demonstrations, 65
Insurgent, 523
Intangibility, 323
**Integrated marketing
  communications
  (IMC), 470**
  communication process, 470–472
  executing and assessing
    audit, 486–487
    costs, 486
    media agencies, 486
    pretests and posttests, 487
    test-results database, 487
  program development
    designing promotion, 485
    identifying target
      audience, 482
    scheduling, 485–486
    selecting tools, 485
    setting budget, 483–485
    specifying objectives,
      482–483

promotional elements
  advertising, 472–473
  direct marketing, 475–476
  personal selling, 473–474
  public relations, 474–475
  sales promotion, 475
promotional mix development
  buyer decision stages,
    479–480
  channel strategies, 480–481
  product characteristics,
    478–479
  product life cycle, 477–478
  target audience, 476–477
  Taco Bell, 468–469, 493–495
Integrated supply chain, 424
Intellectual property, worldwide
  theft of, 104
Intelligent enterprise, 221
Intelligent marketing enterprise
  platform, 221
Intensive distribution, 416
Interaction rate, social media, 553
Interactive Advertising Bureau, 513
Interactive marketing, 600
  creating customer value, 589–599
  customer relationships, 599–601
  individuality, 599–600
  online consumer behavior, 604–
    610, 604–611
  online customer experience,
    601–603
  Seven Cycles, Inc., 596–597
Interactivity in marketspace,
  599–600
Interest, 350, 482
Intermediaries
  communication with buyers, 417
  consumer benefits, 408–409
  electronic, 412
  focus of promotion, 476
  functions
    facilitating, 409
    logistics, 409
    transactional, 408–409
  in online retailing, 446
  pre- and postsale service, 417
  types of, 408
  variety carried by, 417
Internal data, 219
Internal marketing, 335
Internal search, 124
Internal target audience, 54, 55
International Anti-Dumping and
  Fair Competition Act, 186
International firms, 182
International Franchise
  Association, 440
International marketing careers,
  654, 657–658
International selling
  and approach stage, 577
  and preapproach stage, 577
International Standards
  Organization, 112, 338
International trade; *see* World trade

Internet; *see also* Online shopping
  addiction to, 605
  creating competition, 357
  eight-second rule, 417
  online tracking, 92
  pop-up blockers, 216
  for primary data, 216
  and purchase decision, 126
  salesforce communication, 590
  spam blocker, 216
  and word of mouth, 138
Internet advertising
  advantages and disadvantages, 509
  appeal of, 512–513
  classified ads, 513
  click fraud, 514
  current disadvantages, 513–514
  expenditures, 507
  going viral, 513
  Google, Inc., 531–532
  mobile marketing, 513
  smart-pricing, 514
  variety of options, 513
Internet marketing channels, 412
Internet of Things (IoT), 84, 86
Internet Tax Freedom Act, 91
Intertype competition, 442
Intranets, 86
Introduction stage; *see* Product
  life cycle
Inventors, 277
Inventory
  beginning and ending, 400
  carrying costs, 324
  definition, 399
  low at Walmart, 424
  in services, 324–325
  vendor-managed, 426
Inventory control manager, 654
Involvement, 127
  extended problem solving, 128
  high-involvement purchase, 127
  limited problem solving, 128
  low-involvement purchases,
    127, 128
  and marketing strategy, 128–129
  routine problem solving, 128
ISO 14000 standards, 112

J

Japan, tariffs, 178
Job analysis, 585
Job description, 585
Job interview, 664–667
  follow-up, 667
  handling rejections, 667
  preparing for, 665–666
  questions asked at, 665, 666
  succeeding in, 666–667
Job-related tests, 659–660
Job search process, 548, 652
  identifying opportunities, 660–662
  job-related tests, 659–660
  self-assessment, 658–t659

Joint ventures, 194
Journal of Marketing, 209
Journal of Marketing Research, 209
Jurassic World, 486, 523
Jury tests, 517

K

Kaizen, 622
Kelley Blue Book, 351, 504
Key account management, 583
Key business practices, 622
Key traits of personality, 131
Kickbacks, 105–106, 186
Kogod School of Business, 659

L

Label, 310
Labeling
  communication benefits, 310
  competitive advantage from,
    310–312
  connecting with customers, 312
  cost reduction, 312
  customer value from, 310–312
  functional benefits, 310–311
  open dating, 311
  perceptual benefits, 311–312
  private, 309
Laggards, 29
Language(s)
  back translation, 187
  meanings of brand names, 307
  misinterpretations, 471
  official, 187
  used by Seven Cycles, Inc., 596
Lanham Act, 89–90, 303
Late majority, 299
Lawrence Livermore National
  Laboratory, 159
Laws, 102
Leadership in Energy and
  Environmental Design,
  77, 439
Lead generation, 489, 575–576
Learning, 133
  behavioral, 133
  and brand loyalty, 134
  cognitive, 134
  and product newness, 270
Learning effect, 378
LEED; *see* Leadership in Energy
  and Environmental Design
Legal and regulatory forces; *see*
  Regulatory forces
Legal systems, 189
Legitimate right, 420
Level of service, 438
  full service, 441
  limited service, 441
  self-service, 440–441
Lexis/NexisAcademic, 212
Library, for job opportunities, 661
Licensing, 193–194

Life-cycle curve, 297
Lifestyle
    definition, 135
    and psychographics, 135
    and social class, 142
    VALS framework, 135–137
Lifestyle segmentation, 243–244
Likert scale, 218
L'il Abner, 635
Limited-coverage warranty, 313
Limited-line wholesalers, 457–458
Limited problem solving, 128
**Limited-service agencies,
    517**–518
Limited service retailers, 441
Linear trend extrapolation,
    228–229
Line positions, 639
Line *vs.* staff divisional
    groupings, 639
LinkedIn, 547
    in brand manager's strategy, 548
    compared to other social
        media, 543
    for job search, 548
    number of users, 551
    overview, 547
Linked prosperity, 26
List or quoted price
    balance incremental costs and
        revenues, 384–385
    company effects, 382
    competitive effects, 384
    customer effects, 383–384
    price policy choice, 381–382
    special adjustments
        allowances, 387
        discounts, 386–387
        geographical, 388–389
Load factor, 336–337
Local Search Association, 512
Logistical function, 409
Logistics, 421
    third-party providers, 427
Logistics management
    at Amazon, 431
    in auto industry, 423
    elements of, 421
    and reverse logistics, 425–427
    and supply chain, 422
    in supply chain
        customer service concept,
            425–426
        total cost concept, 425
Logo, 303
    StuffDOT, 562
Logotype, 303
Long-range marketing plan, 627
Long-term relationships, 526–527
Loss-leader pricing, 380
Lost-horse forecast, 228
Louvre, Paris, 17–18
Lower class, 142
Low-involvement purchases,
    127, 128
Low-learning products, 297

Low-resource believers, 136
Low-resource groups, 137
Low-resource makers, 136
Low-resource strivers, 136
Low-resource survivors, 137
Loyalty card apps, 434
Loyalty programs
    advantages and disadvantages, 520
    in mobile marketing, 557
    Nordstrom Rewards, 441
    objectives, 520
    recent trends, 522–523
Luxury goods
    exclusive distribution, 416–417
    prestige pricing, 373
    as store purchases, 598

M

Macroeconomic conditions, 82–83
Madrid Protocol, 90
Magazine advertising
    advantages and
        disadvantages, 509
    cost disadvantage, 511
    expenditures, 507
    infrequency, 511
    marketing advantage, 511
    specialized medium, 511
Magazines
    failures, 511
    market segments, 240
Magnuson-Moss Warranty/FTC
    Improvement Act, 313
Mail surveys, 215
Maintained markup, 449
Makers, 136, 137
Malcolm Baldrige National Quality
    Award, 588
Mall intercept interviews, 218
Management by exception, 640
Managers
    key business practices, 622
    of services, 333
Managing for long-run profits, 354
Manufacturers
    and channel conflict, 419
    performance contracts, 524–525
    pricing by, 383–384
    recycling products, 86
    trade discounts, 386
    training salesforces of
        distributors, 525
Manufacturers' agents, 458
Manufacturers' Agents National
    Association, 458
Manufacturer's branch office, 458
Manufacturer-sponsored retail
    franchise systems, 415
Manufacturer-sponsored wholesale
    franchise systems, 415
Manufacturers' representatives, 458
Manufacturer's sales office, 458
Manufacturer's suggested retail
    price, 390

Maricopa County, Arizona, 102
Markdown, 402–403
    timing of, 449
Market, 9
    Mall of America as, 462–463
    in organizational buying, 156
Market attractiveness, too
    little, 272
Market-based groupings, 639
Market development, 39
Market-dominated information
    sources, 124
Market drivers, 220
Market Force Information, 16
Marketing, 5; *see also* Ethical
        marketing behavior;
        Financial aspects of
        marketing; Global
        marketing
    beneficiaries, 18
    and career, 4
    changes in discipline, 652
    changes with social media,
        538–539
    and consumer protection, 8–9
    controllable forces, 9–10
    discovering consumer needs, 7
    diversity of opportunities in, 652
    effect of technological advances,
        85–86
    effects of price elasticity of
        demand, 360–361
    ethical/legal framework, 102–103
    ethics, 16
    evolution of
        customer relationship era, 15
        marketing concept era, 14
        production era, 14
        sales era, 14
    factors required for
        communication, 6
        something to exchange, 6
        unsatisfied needs, 6
    focus on customer relationship
        management, 15–16
    and forms of utility, 18
    generational, 76
    goals, 5
    Mall of America, 463
    meeting needs with new
        products, 7–8
    methods related to
        sampling, 209
        statistical inference, 209
    multichannel, 413
    multicultural, 79
    objectives in product life
        cycle, 293
    objectives of Paradise Kitchens,
        61–62
    to organizational buyers, 18
    organizing
        line *vs.* staff groupings, 639
        role of chief marketing
            officer, 638–639
        role of product managers, 639

    personal selling in, 569
    role of price, 350
    social responsibility, 16–17
    StuffDOT, 563
    two environments of
        marketplace, 598
        marketspace, 598
    to ultimate consumers, 18
    uncontrollable forces, 10
    what is marketed, 17–18
    who markets, 17
Marketing action data, 210
Marketing actions, 5–6
    criterion for market segments,
        243
    data needed for, 209
    evaluation of results, 227
    findings for, 225–226
    implementation, 227
    from market segmentation, 238
    possible, 208
    to reach segments
        changing consumer tastes and,
            253–254
        eye on competitors, 253
        immediate strategy, 252–253
    recommendations, 226–227
    from SWOT analysis, 41
Marketing analytics to track
    performance
    marketing dashboards, 33–35
    marketing metrics, 34–35
Marketing channels, 408; *see also*
        Logistics; Supply chain
    at Amazon, 430–432
    Callaway Golf, 406–407
    conflict and cooperation in,
        418–421
    costs of, 417–418
    customer value from, 408–409
    direct and multichannel
        marketing, 413
    dual distribution, 413
    factors in choice and
        management
        buyer requirements, 417
        profitability, 417–418
        target market coverage,
            416–417
    General Mills, 643
    intermediaries, 408–409
    Internet, 412
    legal and ethical considerations
        dual distribution, 420
        exclusive dealing, 420
        full-line forcing, 421
        refusal to deal, 421
        resale restrictions, 421
        tying arrangements, 420–421
        vertical integration, 420
    strategic alliances, 414
    structure and organization
        for business products and
            services, 411–412
        for consumer products and
            services, 410–411

Marketing channels—*Cont.*
  types of intermediaries, 408
  and utility for consumers, 409
  vertical
    administered systems, 416
    contractual systems, 415–416
    corporate systems, 414–415
Marketing concept, 14
Marketing concept era, 14
Marketing dashboards, 33
  General Mills, 642–644
  to improve marketing ROI, 642
  Sonatica, 34
Marketing database manager, 654
Marketing department, 5
  key role of, 30
  structure, 9
Marketing impact data, 210
Marketing implementation, 634
Marketing information, 210
Marketing manager, nonprofit
  organizations, 654
Marketing metrics, 34
  advertising media selection, 507
  Apple Stores, 452
  Ben and Jerry's, 35
  brand development index, 301
  Carmex social media
    programs, 220
  category development index, 301
  Charlesburg Furniture, 418
  effectiveness of store format, 453
  General Mills, 642–644
  to improve marketing ROI, 642
  integrated marketing
    communications
    spending, 484
  JetBlue Airways, 337
  for marketing planning
    input metrics, 626–627
    output metrics, 626–627
    quantitative metrics, 626
  new-product performance,
    273–274
  Red Bull prices, 380
  salesperson performance, 588
  underperforming states, 273
  website performance, 604
Marketing mix, 10
  controllable factors, 9–10
  customer value proposition, 10
  in introduction stage, 292
  in marketing program, 43
  in organizational buying, 156
  poor execution of, 272
  prices in, 352–353
  promotion in, 470
  at 3M Corporation, 13
Marketing News, 661
Marketing organization design, 43
Marketing plan, 33, 54
  annual, 627
  clear and specific, 631
  compared to business
    plan, 54–55
  complete and feasible, 631

elements of, 55
format
  complexity of organizations, 54
  industry type, 54
  target audience and purpose, 54
guidelines, 631
IBM Smarter Planet strategy, 51
long-range, 627
most-asked questions, 55
Paradise Kitchens
  core competencies, 58
  distribution strategy, 65
  financial data and projections,
    65–66
  implementation plan, 67
  interpreting, 56
  marketing program, 64–65
  mission and goals, 57
  organizational structure,
    66–67
  performance evaluation, 67
  points of difference, 63
  positioning, 63
  price strategy, 64
  product strategy, 64
  promotion strategy, 64–65
  situation analysis, 59–62
  strategic focus and
    plan, 57–58
  sustainable competitive
    advantage, 58
  target market, 63
problems
  balancing value and values,
    632–633
  data collection time, 632
  effect of disruptive
    innovations, 633
  line manager attitude, 632
  lost sight of customer needs,
    631–632
  poor assumptions about
    environmental forces, 631
  writing style suggestions, 55–56
Marketing planning framework
  generic business strategies,
    627–628
  planning strategy lessons
    balancing value and values,
      632–633
    effect of disruptive
      innovations, 633
    guidelines, 631
    potential problems, 631–632
  synergy analysis, 628–630
Marketing program, 12, 42
  elements of, 43
  execution of
    marketing strategy, 44–45
    marketing tactics, 45
  improving implementation
    avoiding paralysis by analysis,
      634–635
    communicate goals, 635
    don't punish failure, 635–636
    open communication, 635

precise tasks, responsibilities,
  and deadlines, 636–638
program champion, 635
reward success, 635–636
and market segments, 12
Paradise Kitchens
  place strategy, 65
  price strategy, 64
  product strategy, 64
  promotion strategy, 64–65
reach of, 13
relationship marketing, 10–12
at 3M Corporation, 12–14
worldwide
  distribution strategy, 196–197
  pricing strategy, 197
  product and promotion
    strategies, 195–196
Marketing publications, 668
Marketing research, 206
  careers in, 654, 657
  Carmex, 233–234
  causal, 208
  challenges, 206–207
  collecting relevant information
    primary data, 212–224
    secondary data, 210–211
  descriptive, 208
  exploratory, 208
  findings
    data analysis, 225
    developing, 224–226
    present findings, 225–226
  five-step approach, 207
  forms of, 7
  at General Mills, 620
  marketing actions from,
    226–227
  measures of success, 208
  in movie industry, 204–206
  problem definition
    identify marketing
      actions, 208
    set objectives, 207–208
  research plan development
    determine data collection, 209
    identify needed data, 209
    specify constraints, 208
  sales forecasting techniques,
    227–229
Marketing research analyst, 654
Marketing research consulting
  firms, 567
Marketing ROI, 642
  marketing dashboards, 642
  marketing metrics, 642
Marketing strategy, 44–45
  Ben and Jerry's, 26–27
  blue ocean strategy, 636
  Choubani, Inc., 2–3
  integrating social media
    measuring results, 552–554
    producing sales, 551–552
    selecting media, 551
    strategic marketing
      process, 550

and involvement, 128–129
product differentiation, 238
and supply chain management
  alignment, 423
  Dell Inc., 424
  Walmart, 424–425
  Tiffany/Walmart, 241, 242
  X-1, 287–288
Marketing synergies, 245–255, 629
Marketing tactics, 45
Market modification, 300
  finding new customers, 300
  increasing product use, 301
  new use situation, 301
Market orientation, 14–15
Market penetration, 39
Marketplace
  definition, 598
  environmental scanning, 73
  in online retailing, 446
Market-product concentration, 630
Market-product focus, Paradise
  Kitchens
  marketing/product objectives,
    62–63
  points of difference, 63
  positioning, 63
  target market, 63
Market-product grid, 239
  developing, 251
  for synergy analysis, 629
Market segmentation, 42, 238
  consumer markets, 243–247
  criteria for forming segments, 243
  grouping buyers into segments,
    242–248
  grouping products into
    categories, 248–250
  marketing actions from, 238
  marketing actions to reach target
    markets, 252–254
  market-product grid, 250
  market-product synergies,
    254–255
  market size estimation, 250
  organizational markets, 247–248
  Prince Sports, Inc., 260–262
  PRIZM system, 245
  and product positioning,
    256–257
  reasons for, 238
  strategy at Apple Inc., 254–255
  target market selection, 251
  timing means of, 240–242
  variables for consumer markets,
    244, 247
  variables for organizational
    markets, 248
  Zappos.com, 236–237, 238–239
Market segments, 12, 629
  build-to-order system, 241
  of buyers, 242–243
  criteria for forming, 243
  definition, 238
  in market-product grid, 239
  mass customization, 241

multiple products and multiple segments, 240–241
one product with multiple segments, 240
Prince Sports, Inc., 261
synergies *vs.* cannibalization, 241–242
Washburn Guitar, 367
X-1, 287
Market share, 32
auto insurance companies, 504
battle for, 455
and coupons, 520
in maturity stage, 295
objective of pricing, 354
relative, 37
Market size
estimation, 250
and target market selection, 251
Marketspace, 86
blue ocean strategy, 636
choiceboards, 600
collaborative filtering, 600
creating customer value, 589–599
customer relationships, 599–600
individuality, 599–600
as marketing environment, 598
online consumer behavior, 604–611
permission marketing, 601
personalization, 600–601
utilities from, 589–599
Market specialization, 630
Market testing, 280
controlled test markets, 280
simulated test markets, 280
standard test markets, 280
when not feasible, 381
Market trends, 621
Markup, 375–376, 401–402, 449
Maslow's hierarchy of needs, 130–131
Massachusetts Institute of Technology, 86
Media Lab, 207
Mass customization, 241
Mass selling, 472
Matching competitors budgeting, 484
Matrix organization, 639
Maturity stage; *see* Product life cycle; Retail life cycle
Maximizing current profit, 354
Measures of success, 208
Media; *see also* Advertising media
ability to reach audiences, 542
credibility, 542
expense and access, 542
permanence, 542
social *vs.* traditional, 542, 550
time to delivery, 542
training for, 542
Media agencies, 486
Media buyer, 654
Media Ratings Council, 514

Media richness, 540
Meet-the-competition defense, 390
Men
as car buyers, 122–123
changing attitudes, 80–81
as consumer base, 80
percent of world population, 74
Men's Vogue, 511
Merchandise
category management, 453
in retailing mix, 452–453
Merchandise allowance, 524–525
Merchandise line, 438
breadth of, 442
depth of, 441–442
scrambled merchandising, 442
Merchandise management, 655
Merchant wholesalers, 457
cash and carry wholesalers, 457–458
desk jobbers, 458
drop shippers, 458
general merchandise wholesalers, 457
rack jobbers, 457
specialty merchandise wholesalers, 457
truck jobbers, 458
Message, 470
subliminal, 132
Message content
fear appeals, 505
humorous appeals, 506
informational and persuasive, 505
sex appeals, 505
Message creation
advertising agencies, 506
celebrity endorsements, 506
translating ideas into ads, 506–507
Message problems, 471
Methods, 209
Metro, 512
Metropolitan division areas, 78
Metropolitan statistical areas, 78
Micropolitan statistical areas, 78
Middle-aged married couples, 141
Middle class, 142
Middlemen, 408
Millennials; *see also* Generation Y
as business leaders, 77
and smartphones, 549
and suburban growth, 77
Million Dollar Baby, 204
Minions, 521
Minority, 75
Mission, 31
examples, 11
IBM, 50
Paradise Kitchens, 57
Xerox, 593
Missionary salespeople, 572–573
Mission statement
Ben and Jerry's, 26
examples, 31
social element, 31

Mixed branding, 310
Mobile apps; *see* Apps
Mobile marketing, 513, 538–539
definition, 557
empowering users, 558
on Facebook
e-mail marketing, 546
faster news publishing, 546
integration of app enhancement, 546
photo-sharing, 546
location-based promotions, 557
loyalty programs, 557
price-comparison search, 557
privacy issues, 558
and video bloggers, 549
Modern Family, 524
Modified rebuy, 163, 164
Trek Bicycle Corporation, 171
Momentum, 511
Monopolistic competition, 87
definition, 356, 357
Monopoly, 87
definition, 356, 357
Moody's Investors Services, 665
Moral idealism, 107
Moral philosophy
definition, 107
moral idealism, 107–108
utilitarianism, 108–109
Moral standards, 103
Motivation, 130
in hierarchy of needs, 130–131
of salesforce, 586–587
Xerox salesforce, 594
Movement along a demand curve, 359–360
Movie industry
concept testing, 204–206
marketing research, 204–206
market segments, 240
product placements in, 523
revenues, 204
test screenings, 206
MSN News, 288
Multibranding, 308
advertising and promotion costs, 309
application of, 308–309
fighting brands, 309
market segments, 309
Multichannel marketing, 413; *see also* Interactive marketing; Marketspace
for Callaway Golf, 406
cross-channel consumers, 612–613
implementing
with promotional websites, 612–613
with transactional websites, 612
Pizza Hut, 615–619
popularity of, 613

Multichannel retailers, 456
Multichannel retailing
examples, 455–456
synergies, 456
Multicultural Agency of the Year, 79
Multicultural marketing, 79
Multicultural population, 79
Multidomestic marketing strategy, 182
Multinational firms, 182
Multiple-zone pricing, 389
Multiproduct branding, 308
Myers-Briggs Type Indicator, 660
Mystery shoppers, 213–214

N

NAICS; *see* North American Industry Classification System
National Aeronautics and Space Administration, 155, 376
National Business Hall of Fame, 200
National Cable and Telecommunication Association, 510
National Do Not Call Registry, 92, 105, 446–447, 490, 576
National Highway Traffic Safety Administration, 111
National Retail Federation, 449
National Weather Service, 515
NCIS, 213
Near field communication products, 434
Needs, 8–9
criterion for market segments, 243
hierarchy of, 130–131
perceived, 124
unsatisfied, 6
Need-satisfaction presentation, 578
Negative deviations, 46
Negative word of mouth, 138
Net sales, 397
Networked global marketspace, 184
Networking, for job search, 661–662
Neuromarketing, 214
New buy, 163
Trek Bicycle Corporation, 171
New car buying decisions, 122
Newness
compared to existing products, 269
from consumer's perspective, 269–270
in legal terms, 270
from organizational perspective, 271–272
as pricing constraint, 355
New-product concept, 209

New-product development process, 274
at Apple Inc., 264
business analysis, 279
commercialization, 281–282
development stage, 279–280
disruptive innovation, 275
early-stage financing, 277
fast prototyping, 282
General Mills, 620
in global marketing, 195–196
idea generation, 275–277
market testing, 280–281
new-product strategy
development, 274–275
open innovation, 273
parallel development, 282
screening and evaluation,
277–278
speed as factor in, 282
Stage-Gate process, 274
from technology, 85
at X-1, 285–288
New-product failures
at Apple Inc., 264–265
marketing reasons
bad timing, 272
incomplete protocol, 271
insignificant points of
difference, 271
no access to buyers, 272
not satisfying customer needs,
271–272
poor marketing mix
execution, 272
poor quality, 272
too little marketing
attractiveness, 272
organizational inertia reasons
groupthink, 272–273
not-invented-here
problem, 273
New-product launch
expense of, 620
Milsco Corporation, 160
success rate, 621
New products
business fit, 279
degree of learning required of
consumers, 269–270
meeting needs with, 7–8
number introduced by General
Mills, 621
number introduced each month, 7
perspectives on newness, 269–271
positioning, 256–257
problem of defining, 268–269
showstoppers, 89
from wheel of retailing, 453–454
**New-product strategy
development, 274–275**
at X-1, 286
News conference, 526
Newspaper advertising
advantages and disadvantages, 509
expenditures, 507

local medium, 511
national campaigns, 512
online newspapers, 512
trends influencing, 512
Newspapers
circulation decline, 512
revenue decline, 512
News releases, 526
Newsweek, 439
New Yorker, 142
New York Times, 512, 542
Noise, 472
Noncumulative quantity
discounts, 386
Nondurable goods, 266
Nonmonetary rewards, 587
Nonprofit organizations, 28
examples, 326–327
goals, 33
market segmentation, 238
promotional activities, 327
public service
announcements, 526
social marketing, 328
Nonselling duties, 656
Nonstore retailing
automatic vending, 443–444
catalogs, 444–445
direct mail, 444–445
direct selling, 447
online retailing, 445–446
telemarketing, 446–447
TV home shopping, 445
Norms, 103–104
North American Free Trade
Agreement, 155
and protectionism, 178
**North American Industry
Classification System
(NAICS), 156,** 211, 247
Not-invented-here problem, 273
Nutritional Labeling and Education
Act, 89

O

Objections
techniques for handling, 579
types of, 578–579
**Objective and task budgeting,
484–485**
Objectives, 32
of advertising program, 502–503
of consumer-oriented sales
promotions, 520
in marketing research, 207–208
in organizational buying, 157
of pricing, 353–354
of promotion, 482–483
of sales plan, 581–582
in target market selection, 251
Observational data, 210, 212
ethnographic research, 214
mechanical methods, 212–213
from mystery shoppers, 213–214

neuromarketing methods, 214
personal methods, 213–214
Occupational Outlook Handbook
(Dept. of Labor), 661
Odd-even pricing, 374
Offerings, 28
Office, The, 524
Off-peak pricing, 334
Off-price retailing, 450
versus discount stores, 450
outlet stores, 450
single-price retailers, 450
warehouse clubs, 450
Older married or unmarried, 141
Oligopoly, 87
definition, 356, 357
Olympic Games, 485
Olympic Teams, 2, 22
Omnichannel marketing, 413
Omnichannel retailing, 456
One-price policy, 381
Online advertising, Google, Inc.,
531–532
Online auctions
reverse auctions, 167
versus traditional auctions,
166–167
Online behavioral advertising, 490
Online buying
auctions, 166–167
in business-to-business markets,
164–167
prominence of, 164–165
vertical organizational markets,
165–166
Online career and employment
services, 660–661
Online consumer behavior
consumer characteristics, 604–605
eight-second rule, 606
purchase behavior, 605
reasons for shopping, 605–610
choice, 606–607
communication, 607–609
control, 609–610
cost, 609
customization, 607
times and places for shopping,
610–611
Online consumers, 604
Online coupons, 519
Online customer experience
commerce, 603
communication, 603
community, 603
connection, 602–603
content, 602
context, 602
customization, 602
definition, 601
Online databases, 212
Online marketing research, 567
Online newspapers, 512
Online retailing
catalogs, 444
Cyber Monday, 446

failure to check out, 446
melding with traditional
retailing, 445–446
price comparisons, 446
shipping options, 446
StuffDOT, 562–563
varying approaches, 446
Online shopping
behavioral targeting, 610
bots, 606
cookies, 610
eight-second rule, 606
privacy and security, 610
projected sales by 2018, 598
showrooming, 611
webrooming, 611–612
Online surveys, 215
Online tracking, 92
On-the-job training, 586
Open dating, 311
Open-ended questions, 218
Open innovation, 273
Operating statement
cost elements, 398–400
definition, 397
illustration, 398
sales elements, 397
Operations manager, 654
Opinion leaders, 137
percentage of adults, 137–138
Opportunities; *see* SWOT analysis
Opt-in requirement, 490, 601
Opt-out, 601
Order, size of, 157
Order clerks, 572
Order cycle, 426
Order getter, 572
Order taker, 571
Organizational buyers, 18, 154
and reverse auctions, 167
Organizational buying
buyer–seller relationships
complex negotiations, 159
long-term contracts, 159
reciprocity, 159
supply partnerships, 159–160
sustainable procurement,
160–161
characteristics and
dimensions, 156
competitive bids, 157
derived demand in, 156
JCPMedia, Inc., 152–153
marketing channels, 411–412
number of potential buyers, 157
objectives, 157–158
size of order or purchase, 157
supplier capabilities, 152
supplier diversity, 157–158
trade promotions, 524–525
Trek Bicycle Corporation,
170–172
**Organizational buying
behavior, 161**
buying centers, 162–164
buying function, 161

buying process stages, 161–162
compared to consumer behavior, 161, 162
Organizational buying criteria
commonly used, 158
supplier development, 157–158
Organizational chart, 5, 29
Organizational culture, 31
Mary Kay, Inc., 200
performance-oriented, 622
Organizational foundation
core values, 31
definition, 30
direction, 32
goals and objectives, 32–33
mission, 31
organizational culture, 31
Organizational markets
government units, 155
industrial, 154
means of segmenting, 247–248
North American Industry Classification System, 155
online auctions, 166–167
online buying, 164–165
resellers, 154
virtual, 165–166
Organizational structure
divisional groupings, 639
fast, flexible, and flat, 622
matrix organization, 639
Paradise Kitchens, 66–67
and sales management
customer, 583
geographic, 582–583
product, 583
Organizational synergy, 241
Organizations
buying function, 161
definition, 28
for-profit, 326–327
forward-looking, 30
influence on marketing, 5
intelligent enterprise, 221
newness from perspective of, 270–271
new-product failures
groupthink, 272–273
not-invented-here problem, 273
nonprofit, 326–327
social entrepreneurs, 29
strategic direction
current status analysis, 35–36
growth strategies, 36–40
strategic marketing process, 40–46
strategies
at corporate level, 28–30
at functional level, 30
at strategic business units level, 30
variation by level, 33
variation by product, 33
types and complexity of, 54
types of, 28

Outbound telemarketing, 572
Outdoor advertising
advantages and disadvantages, 509
billboards, 514
conditional content, 515
expenditures, 507
public service announcements, 515
recent growth, 515
transit advertising, 514
Outdoor Advertising Association of America, 515
Outlet stores, 450
Output measures
in salesforce evaluation, 587
social media performance, 552–553
Output metrics, 626–627
Output-related sales objectives, 581
Outside order takers, 571–572

P

Packaging, 310
communication benefits, 310
competitive advantage from, 310–312
connecting with customers, 312
cost reduction, 312
customer value from, 310–312
environmental concerns, 312
functional benefits, 310–311
health, safety, and security concerns, 312
perceptual benefits, 311–312
Page views, social media, 553
Paid search, 513
Panels, 219
Parallel development, 282
Parallel importing, 197
Paralympic Teams, 2
Paralysis by analysis, 634–635
Parks and Recreation, 212
Partnership Program, 27
Partnership selling, 570
Patents, 104
PC Magazine, 85, 511
Peer-to-peer sharing services, 320–321
Penetration pricing, 373
in introduction stage, 292
People, 142
People-based services, 326
People en Español, 143
Peoplemap assessments, 660
People meter, 212
Per capita income, international variations, 189
Perceived risk, 133
Percentage of sales budgeting, 483
Perception, 131
selective, 131–132

Perceptual map, 257
for positioning, 256–257
for repositioning, 257
Performance contracts, 524–525
Performance evaluation
Paradise Kitchens, 67
of salesforce, 587–588
strategic marketing process
acting on deviations, 46, 640–641
compare results, 45
identifying deviations, 45, 640
management by exception, 640
marketing dashboards, 642–644
marketing metrics, 642–644
marketing ROI, 640
Performance measures
linked to inputs and costs, 552–553
linked to outputs or revenues, 553–554
Pizza Hut, 618
return on investment, 404–405
for social media
cost per action, 553
cost per click, 552–553
cost per thousand, 552–553
Performance-oriented culture, 622
Periodicals for marketing careers, 668–669
Permanence, of media, 542
Permission marketing, 601
Per se illegal concept, 90, 389
Personal contact, for job search, 661
Personal influence
opinion leaders, 137–138
word of mouth, 138
Personal information sources, 124
Personal interview surveys, 215
Personality, 131
key traits, 131
self-concept, 131
Personality tests, 659–660
Personalization, 600
permission marketing, 601
by Yahoo!, 600
Personalized URLs, 445
Personal needs, 131
Personal selling, 473, 568
advantages, 474
costs, 473
creating customer value, 569–570
partnership selling, 570
relationship selling, 570
customized interaction, 472
disadvantage of flexibility, 474
in entrepreneurship, 569
forms of
customer sales support personnel, 572–573
order getters, 572
order takers, 571–572

General Electric Healthcare Americas, 566–567
in marketing, 569
of services, 335
strengths and weaknesses, 473
team selling, 573
at Xerox, 593–594
Personal selling process, 574
close, 580
follow-up, 580
objectives, 575
preapproach, 576–577
presentation formats, 577–579
prospecting, 575–576
stages, 574
Pharmacy Times, 394
Physical distribution, 653
specialist, 654
types of careers in, 654
Physical environment, 336
Physiological needs, 130
Pineapple, 511
Pinterest, 554
Pioneering advertisements, 500
Pioneering institutional advertisements, 501
Pi Sigma Epsilon, 661
Place, in marketing mix, 10
Place-based media, 515
Place strategy; *see also* Marketing channels
Chobani, Inc., 22
in marketing program, 43
Paradise Kitchens, 65
at 3M Corporation, 13
Place utility, 409, 436–437
definition, 18
from marketspace, 598–599
Planning
versus implementation, 634
value-based, 632–633
Planning gap, 45
Point-of-sale displays
advantages and disadvantages, 520
buying decisions, 523
objectives, 520
Points of difference, 42
insignificant, 271
Paradise Kitchens, 63
Political-regulatory climate
political stability, 191
trade regulations, 191
Political risk rating, 191
Political stability, 191
Popular Mechanics, 137
Population
trend toward older, 75
United States, 75
world, 74–75
Population explosion, 74
Population Reference Bureau, 74
Population shifts
within states, 77
state-to-state, 77
statistical areas, 78

Portfolio tests, 516–517
Positioning statement, 256
Positive deviations, 46
Possession utility, 409, 436–437
    definition, 18
    from marketspace, 599
Postpone technique, 579
Postpurchase behavior
    cognitive dissonance, 126–127
    consumer smartphone
        purchase, 162
    and customer satisfaction, 126
    and expectations, 126
    in organizational buying, 162
Postsale services, 417
Posttests, 487, 518
    aided recall, 518
    attitude tests, 518
    inquiry tests, 518
    sales tests, 518
    Starch test, 518
    unaided recall, 518
Power center, 451
Power of buyers and suppliers, 88
Preapproach stage
    definition, 576–577
    in international selling, 577
    objectives, 575
Precycling, 86
Predatory pricing, 391
Premium, 350
Premium price, 379
Premiums
    advantages and
        disadvantages, 520
    objectives, 520
    self-liquidating, 521
Presale services, 417
Presentation stage
    formula selling format, 578
    handling objections, 578–579
    need-satisfaction format, 578
    objectives, 575, 577
    stimulus-response format,
        577–578
Prestige pricing, 373
Pretests, 487, 516
    jury tests, 517
    portfolio tests, 516–517
    theater tests, 517
Pretty Woman, 204
Price(s)
    effect of exchange rate
        fluctuations, 190
    final, 351, 372
    indicator of value, 351
    in marketing mix, 10, 352–353
    role in marketing, 350
    terms for, 333, 350
Price comparison smartphone
    apps, 126
Price differentials, 383
    changing market conditions, 390
    cost justification defense, 390
    meet-the-competition
        defense, 390

Price discounting, 90
Price discrimination, 390
Price elasticity of demand, 360
    for cigarettes, 361
    effect on marketing decisions,
        360–361
    effect on public policy, 360–361
    equation, 360
    and price lining, 374
Price equation, 350–351
Price fixing, 90, 389
    horizontal, 389
    and rule of reason, 390
    vertical, 390
Price level, appropriate, 372–380
Price lining, 374
Price matching, 442
Price policy
    dynamic, 382
    flexible, 381–382
Price premium, 379
Price setting
    markdown, 402–403
    markup, 401–402
    and stockturn rate, 403
Price strategy, 353
    Carmex products, 394–395
    Chobani, Inc., 21–22
    in global marketing, 197
    in marketing program, 43
    Paradise Kitchens, 64
    at 3M Corporation, 13
Price war, 384
Pricing
    competition-oriented
        approaches, 379–380
    cost-oriented approaches,
        375–377
    demand-oriented approaches,
        372–375
    differing structures, 336–337
    dynamic, 609
    e-books, 370–371
    estimating demand, 358–360
    estimating revenue, 361
    legal and regulatory aspects
        deceptive pricing, 390, 391
        geographical pricing, 390
        predatory pricing, 391
        price discrimination, 390
        price fixing, 389–390
    price elasticity of demand,
        360–361
    printed books, 390
    profit-oriented approaches,
        377–379
    in retailing
        everyday low prices, 449
        maintained markup, 449
        off-price retailing, 450
        shrinkage problem,
            449–450
        single-price retailers, 450
        timing of markdowns, 449
    of services, 333–334
    Washburn Guitar, 367–368

Pricing actions
    consumer-driven, 357
    seller/retailer-driven, 357
Pricing constraints, 355
    competitors' prices, 357
    cost of changing prices, 355
    costs of production and
        marketing, 355
    demand, 355
    legal and ethical
        considerations, 358
    newness, 355
    single product *vs.* product
        line, 356
    type of competitive market,
        356–357
Pricing objectives, 353–354
    market share, 354
    profit, 354
    sales revenue, 354
    social responsibility, 354
    survival, 354
    unit volume, 354
Pricing-related legislation, 90
Primary data, 210
    advantages and
        disadvantages, 212
    big data, 221–222
    cross-tabulations, 222–224
    data analytics, 221–222
    data mining, 212
    observational data, 212–214
    panels and experiments,
        219–221
    questionnaire data, 213–218
    from social media, 218–219
    types of, 210
Primary demand, 292
Privacy
    and data mining, 223
    in direct marketing, 490
    and Federal Trade
        Commission, 105
    in online shopping, 610
    and online tracking, 92
Private branding, 309
Private labeling, 309
PRIZM segmentation system, 245
Problem definition in marketing
    research, 207–208
Problem recognition, 124
    consumer smartphone
        purchase, 162
    in organizational buying, 162
Problem solving, 128
Process in services marketing, 336
Product(s), 17, 266
    benchmark items, 449
    build-to-order, 241
    changed by technology, 86
    classifying
        business products, 266, 267
        consumer products, 266–267
    counterfeit, 303–304
    embedded with microchips, 86
    fads, 297

fashion, 297
feature bloat, 269
grouped into categories, 248–250
high-learning, 297
increase use of, 301
low-learning, 297
in marketing mix, 10
mass customization, 241
multiple, with multiple
    segments, 240–241
new use situation, 301
one, with multiple segments, 240
in organizational buying, 156
purchased online, 605, 606
shelf life, 310
synergies *vs.* cannibalization,
    241–242
usage rate surveys, 245
variation by, 33
Product adaptation, 195
Product advertisements, 500
Product attributes/features
    behavioral segmentation, 244
    new, 134
    perceived importance, 134
Product bundling, 30
Product characteristics
    ancillary services, 479
    complexity, 478–479
    risk for buyer, 479
Product class, 268, 298
    primary demand for, 292
Product deletion, 296
    marketing objectives, 293
Product development, 39–40
Product development manager, 654
Product differentiation, 238
    in auto industry, 240–241
    in growth stage, 294
Product-distribution franchises,
    439–440
Product extension, 195
Product form, 268, 298
Product group, 639
Product invention, 195–196
Production era, 14
Product item, 268
Product liability claims, 313
Product life cycle, 292
    and consumer behavior, 298–299
    decline stage
        drop in sales, 295
        harvesting strategy, 296
        product deletion, 296
    fax machines, 294
    growth stage
        broadened distribution, 294
        marketing objectives, 293
        more competition, 294
        product differentiation, 294
        repeat purchasers, 294
        sales increase, 294
    introduction stage
        advertising and
            promotion, 292
        fax machines sales, 293

gaining distribution, 292
marketing objectives, 293
penetration pricing, 292
primary demand, 292
reasons for resisting
products, 298
selective demand, 292
skimming strategy, 292
trials, 292
length of, 296
managing
market modification, 300–301
product/brand managers, 300
product modification,
300–301
repositioning, 302
marketing objectives, 293
maturity stage
holding market share, 294
marketing objectives, 293
slowing sales, 294
product advertisements, 500
product class and form, 298
in promotional mix, 477–478
shape of curve, 297
stage in, as pricing
constraint, 355
Product line, 268
Apple Inc., 38–39, 264
Carmex, 232–233
and price lining, 374
Xerox, 593
Product line extension, 270
brand strategies, 308
Gatorade, 290
at 3M Corporation, 14
Product line groupings, 639
Product-line pricing, 382
Product management, 653
types of careers in, 654
Product management teams, 653
Product managers, 43, 654
role of, 300, 639
Product-market focus, 42
Product mission, 26
Product mix, 268
Product modification, 300
Product objectives, Paradise
Kitchens, 61–62
Product placement, 523
advantages and
disadvantages, 520
annual value, 524
in movies, 523
new forms of, 524
objectives, 520
reverse, 524
in TV shows, 524
in video games, 523
Product positioning, 256
differentiation, 256
head-to-head, 256
Paradise Kitchens, 63
using perceptual maps,
256–257
Product-related legislation, 89–90

Product repositioning, 256
to catch rising trend, 302
changing value offered, 302
downsizing, 302–303
effects, 303
reaching new markets, 302
reacting to competitors, 302
Product sales organization, 583
Product specialization, 630
Product strategy
Chobani, Inc., 21
in global marketing, 195–196
in marketing program, 43
Paradise Kitchens, 64
at 3M Corporation, 13
Product synergies, 255
Product warranty, 312–313
Professional associations,
669–670
Profit, 28
effect of exchange rate
fluctuations, 190
goal of business, 32
objective of pricing, 354
Profitability
e-books, 371
in marketing channels, 417–418
Profit-and-loss statement, 397
Profit before taxes, 400
Profit equation, 352
Profit-oriented pricing
approaches
target profit pricing, 377
target return-on-investment
pricing, 377–378
target return-on-sales pricing,
378–379
Profit potential criterion for market
segments, 243
Profit responsibility, 110–111
Program champion, 635
Program meetings, 636–638
action item list, 637
program schedule, 637–638
time-based agenda, 637
Program schedule, 637–638
Project manager, 654
Promotion(s)
building long-term relationships,
526–527
careers in, 654–655
communication in, 470
costs in multibranding, 309
deceptive, 527
design of, 485
executing and assessing
audit, 486–487
costs, 486
media agencies, 486
test-results database, 487
expenditures of top ten
companies, 483
in introduction stage, 291
in marketing mix, 10, 470
scheduling, 485–486
self-regulations, 527

of services, 335
specifying objectives, 482–483
viral marketing, 609
Promotional allowances, 90, **387**
legislation on, 390
Promotional elements
advertising, 472–473
in buying decision stages,
479–480
and channel strategies, 480–481
comparisons of, 473
direct marketing, 475–476
personal selling, 473–474
and product characteristics,
478–479
in product life cycle, 477–478
public relations, 474–475
sales promotion, 475
selecting right tools, 485
Promotional mix, 470
developing
balance of elements, 476
buying decision stages, 479–480
channel strategies, 480–481
product characteristics,
478–479
target audience, 476–477
product life cycle and, 477–478
Promotional Products Association
International, 521
Promotional websites, 612–613
Promotion budget
all-you-can-afford
budgeting, 484
competitive parity budgeting,
483–484
objective and task budgeting,
484–485
percentage of sales
budgeting, 483
Promotion decision process, 482
Promotion-related legislation, 91
Promotion strategy
Chobani, Inc., 22
in global marketing, 195–196
communication adaptation, 196
dual adaptation, 196
in marketing program, 43
Paradise Kitchens, 64–65
Prince Sports, Inc., 261–262
at 3M Corporation, 13
Prospect, 575
information on, 576
Prospecting
cold canvassing, 576
definition, 575
lead generation, 575–576
objectives, 575
Protectionism, 178
beer import tariffs, 178
costs to customers, 178
decline of, 178–179
quotas, 178–179
sugar and textile import quotas,
178, 179
tariffs, 178

Protocol, 271
incomplete, 271
Prototypes, 279
at X-1, 287
Psychographics, 135; *see also*
VALS framework
Psychographic segmentation,
consumer markets, 243–244
Psychological barriers, 298
Psychological influences
motivation, 130–131
perception, 131–132
personality, 131
Public information sources, 124
Publicity, 474
credibility, 474
disadvantages, 475
Publicity tools, 526
to create visibility, 526
news conference, 526
news release, 526
public service
announcements, 526
Public policy, effects of price
elasticity of demand,
360–361
Public relations, 474
costs, 473
publicity tools, 526
strengths and weaknesses, 473
use of mass selling, 472
Public relations manager, 654
Public service announcements,
335, 526
in outdoor advertising, 515
Pull strategy, 481
Pulse (burst) schedule, 516
Purchase
online shopping behavior, 605
size of, 157
Purchase decision process, 124
alternative evaluation, 124–125
buying value, 125–126
characteristics, 128
consumer smartphone
purchase, 162
criteria for, 124–125
information search, 124
level of involvement, 127–129
need perception, 124
new car buyers, 122
in organizational buying, 162
postpurchase behavior, 126–127
situational influences, 129
when to buy, 126
from whom to buy, 125–126
Purchase discounts, 399
Purchase frequency, 515
Purchasing power
and global marketing, 189–190
Hispanics, 60
Pure competition, 87
definition, 356, 357
Pure monopoly, 87
definition, 356, 357
Push strategy, 480

Q

Qualified prospect, 575
Quality
    goal of business, 32
    poor, 272
    of services, 329–330
Quantitative assessments, 587
Quantitative goals, 641
Quantitative metrics, 626
Quantity discounts, 90, **385**
Question marks, 37
Questionnaire data, 210,
        214–218, **215**
    closed-end questions, 218
    depth interviews, 215
    dichotomous questions, 218
    fixed alternative questions, 218
    focus groups, 215
    fuzzy front end methods, 215
    idea evaluation method,
        215–218
    idea generation methods, 215
    individual interviews, 215
    mail surveys, 216
    mall intercept interviews, 218
    online surveys, 216
    open-ended questions, 218
    personal interview surveys, 216
    precise questions, 216–218
    telephone interviews, 216
    Wendy's consumer survey,
        216–217
Quick response, 426
Quotas, 178–179
Quoted price; *see* List or
        quoted price

R

Rack jobbers, 457
Radio advertising
    advantages and disadvantages,
        509
    expenditures, 507
    listening times, 510–511
    number of stations, 510
    segmented medium, 510
Radio frequency identification
        tags, 222, 439
Rating, 508
Ratios
    to analyze operations, 400–401
    for setting and evaluating price
        markdown, 402–403
        markup, 401–402
        return on investment,
            404–405
        stockturn rate, 404
Raw Bike, 511
RD-manufacturing synergies, 630
Reach, 507
    of media, 542
Reader's Digest, 522
Real Yellow Pages, 512

Rebates
    advantages and disadvantages,
        520
    definition, 523
    objectives, 520
Receivers, 470
    field of experience, 471
Recessions, 82
Recipes, 65
Reciprocity, 159
Recycling, 312
    of products, 86
    and reverse logistics, 426–427
Reference groups, 138–139
    aspiration, 139
    associative, 139
    dissociative, 139–140
    effect on purchase decision,
        138–139
Refusal to deal, 421
Regional rollouts, 282
Regional shopping centers, 451
*Register of Corporations, Directors,
        and Executives,* 665
Regular distribution, 270
Regulation, 88
Regulatory forces
    advertising-related
        legislation, 91
    brand names, 307
    distribution-related
        legislation, 91
    for Facebook, 70
    identified by environmental
        scanning, 73
    and marketing channels
        dual distribution, 420
        exclusive dealing, 420
        full-line forcing, 421
        refusal to deal, 421
        resale restrictions, 421
        tying arrangements, 420–421
        vertical integration, 420
    on pricing, 90
        deceptive pricing, 390–391
        geographical pricing, 390
        predatory pricing, 391
        price discrimination, 390
        price fixing, 389–390
    product-related legislation,
        89–90
    on promotions, 91, 527
    protecting competition, 88–89
    and self-regulation, 92
    on sweepstakes, 521–522
    types of, 72
Reinforcement, 133
Reinforcement advertising, 500
Relationship marketing, 12
    in purchase of services, 332
Relationship selling, 570
Relative market share, 37
Reliability of services, 330
Reminder institutional
        advertisements, 502
Reminder product advertising, 500

Rent, 350
Repeat purchasers, 294
Replenishment, 426
Requirement contracts, 91
Resale price maintenance, 390
Resale restrictions, 421
Research and development
        labs, 276
Research plan; *see* Marketing
        research
Reseller branding, 309
Resource allocation
    essence of, 624
    General Mills, 623–624
    maximizing incremental
        revenues, 623
    share points analysis, 624–625
    and strategic marketing process,
        625–626
    using sales response
        function, 623
Resources, obtaining, 43
Response, 133, **471–472**
Response Magazine, 510
Responsibilities
    defining, 43–44
    scheduling, 636–638
Responsiveness of services, 330
Restaurant Business, 476
Résumés
    accompanying letter, 663–664
    chronological format, 662, 663
    functional format, 662
    printed or digital versions,
        662–663
    sections of, 662
    targeted format, 662
    video résumé, 663–664
Retailers; *see also* Retail outlets
    for Callaway Golf, 406
    definition, 408
    measures of success
        sales growth, 453
        sales per square foot, 453
    number of, 154
    preference for exclusive
        distribution, 417
    smart systems, 51
Retailer/seller-driven pricing
        actions, 357
Retailer-sponsored cooperatives,
        415–416
Retailing, 436
    careers in, 654, 655–656
    changing nature of
        from new technologies,
            434–435
        retail life cycle, 454–455
        wheel of retailing, 454–455
    consumer utilities offered by,
        436–437
    environmental issues, 439
    future changes
        data analytics, 456–457
        multichannel retailing,
            455–456

    global economic impact, 437
    intertype competition, 442
    levels of retailer involvement, 443
    in Mall of America, 462–463
    nonstore, 443–447
    Pizza Hut, 615–616
    types of merchandise line,
        441–442
Retailing mix, 449
    communication, 451–453
    merchandise offerings, 452–453
    pricing, 449–450
    store location, 450–451
Retailing strategy
    retailing mix, 449–453
    retail positioning matrix,
        449–450
Retail life cycle, 454–455
    accelerated growth, 455
    decline stage, 455
    early growth, 454–455
    maturity stage, 455
Retail outlets
    Apple Stores, 452
    benefits of data analytics, 457
    Black Friday, 446
    category killers, 441–442
    different types of, 437
    forms of ownership, 438–440
    in hypermarkets, 442
    level of service
        full service, 441
        limited service, 441
        self-service, 440–441
    locations, 450–451
        central business district, 451
        community shopping
            centers, 451
        power centers, 451
        regional shopping centers, 451
        strip malls, 451
    new forms of
        discount stores, 454
        factory outlets, 454
    positioning, 447–449
    specialty outlets, 441
    in supercenters, 442
    use of sensors, 558
Retail Planning Associates,
        Ohio, 450
**Retail positioning matrix,
        447–448**
    breadth of line, 448
    possible positions, 448–449
    value added, 448
Retain communication, 451–452
Retirement of baby boomers, 75
Return on assets, 354
Return on investment, 354, 378
    calculating, 404–405
Return on investment metric, 642
Returns, 397
    fraudulent, 450
Revenues
    estimating, 361
    incremental, 384–385, 623

objective of pricing, 354
Paradise Kitchens, 65–66
social media performance
measure, 552–553
Reverse auction, 167
Reverse logistics, 427
Reverse product placements, 524
Reverse vending machines, 86
Rich media, 513
Rich site summary, 513
Right to be heard, 105
Right to be informed, 105
Right to choose, 105
Right to safety, 104–105
Risk
perceived, 133
in product purchase, 479
Risk reduction, with brand
loyalty, 134
Risky Business, 523
Robinson-Patman Act, 89, 92,
389, 390
Rolling Stone, 511
Routine problem solving, 128
Rube Goldberg machine, 549
Rule of reason, 390, 421
Runner's World, 511
Running time, 637

S

Safety
and packaging, 312
substance of, 122
Safety needs, 130–131
Sales
Callaway Golf, 406
in decline stage, 295
effect of exchange rate
fluctuations, 190
General Mills, 620
goal of business, 32
increase in growth stage, 294
in maturity stage, 295
from multichannel marketing, 613
related to coupons, 520
Sales and Marketing Management,
657, 661
Sales clerks, 572
Sales elements of operating
statement
allowances, 397
gross sales, 397
net sales, 397
returns, 397
Sales engineers, 573
Sales era, 14
Salesforce
determining size of, 584
manufacturer training
of, 525
Mary Kay, Inc., 201
motivation and compensation,
586–587
organizing, 582–583

recruitment and selection
emotional intelligence, 586
job analysis, 585
job description, 585
at Xerox, 593–594
Salesforce automation (SFA), 589
communication, 589–590
examples, 589
technology, 589
Salesforce evaluation
behavioral evaluation, 587–588
quantitative assessments, 587
Salesforce survey forecast, 228
Salesforce technology, 589–590
Sales forecast, 217
direct, 228
lost-horse, 228
salesforce survey, 228
survey of buyers' intentions, 228
Sales forecasting techniques
judgments of decision makers,
228
statistical, 228–229
survey of knowledgeable
groups, 228
Sales growth, 453
Sales jobs
customer relationship
management, 656–657
nonselling duties, 656
sales support duties, 656
selling duties, 656
types of careers in, 654,
655–657
Sales management, 568
account management
policies, 584
customer relationship
management, 589–590
functions, 580
and organizational structure,
582–583
organizing salesforce, 582–584
salesforce automation, 589–590
salesforce evaluation, 587–588
salesforce motivation and
compensation, 586–587
salesforce recruitment and
selection, 585–586
salesforce training, 586
sales plan formulation, 581–584
sales plan implementation,
585–587
setting objectives, 581–582
at Xerox, 593–594
Sales organizations, types of,
582–583
Salespeople, knowledge of
competitors, 581
Sales per square foot, 453
Sales plan, 581
formulation
account management policies,
584, 585
organizing salesforce, 582–583
setting objectives, 581–582

implementation
motivation and compensation,
586–587
recruitment and selection,
585–586
training, 586
Sales promotion, 475
advantages, 475
advertising support, 475
consumer-oriented, 519–524
costs, 473
of services, 335
strengths and weaknesses, 473
trade-oriented, 524–525
use of mass selling, 472
Sales promotion manager, 654
Sales quota, 587
Sales response function, 623
Sales support duties, 656
Sales tests, 518
Samples
advantages and disadvantages, 520
new products, 522
objectives, 520
Sampling, 209
San Francisco Chronicle, 512
Saturday Night Football, 510
Savings rate, 84
Scheduling, 44
Scrambled merchandising, 442
Screening and evaluation, 277
external approach, 278
internal approach, 277–278
at X-1, 286–287
Seals of approval, 133
Seasonal discounts, 386
Secondary data, 210
advantages and disadvantages, 211
external, 211
internal, 210
online databases, 212
Secret Sales Pitch (Bullock), 132
Security
in online shopping, 610
and packaging, 312
Selective comprehension, 132
Selective demand, 292
Selective distribution, 417
Selective exposure, 131–132
Selective perception, 131–132
Selective retention, 132
Selective specialization, 630
Self-actualization needs, 131
Self-assessment, 658–659
Self-concept, 131
Self-disclosure, 541
Self-expression motivated
groups, 136
Self-liquidating premiums, 521
Self-regulation, 92
of promotion, 527
Self-service retailers, 440–441
Self-service technologies, 324
Selling, 568–569
management of, 580
at Xerox, 593

Selling agents, 458
Selling duties, 656
Selling expenses, 400
Semantic differential scale, 218
Seminar selling, 573
Semiotics, 187
Semitechnical salesperson, 654
Sensors, 558
Sentiment, 219
Service blueprint, 332
Service companies, 154
Service continuum, 325
Service failures, 331
Service quality
assessment of, 329–330
dimensions of, 330
Services, 266
classifying, 267
for-profit *vs.* nonprofit
organizations, 326–327
government-sponsored, 327
people *vs.* equipment-based, 326
component of global
economy, 322
cost-plus pricing, 376
credence properties, 329
experience properties, 329
exporting, 322
four I's of
inconsistency, 323
inseparability, 323–324
intangibility, 323
inventory, 324–325
future of, 338
green businesses, 338
increased demand for, 322
industrial, 267
managers of, 333
off-peak pricing, 335
in organizational buying, 156
peer-to-peer sharing,
320–321
percentage of gross domestic
product, 322
purchased online, 605, 606
purchase of
at car rental agencies, 332
customer contact audit,
330–332
process, 329
quality assessment, 329–330
relationship marketing, 332
Services marketing, 17
capacity management, 336
LA Galaxy, 341–344
managing
customer experience
management, 335–336
distribution, 334
internal marketing, 335
pricing, 333–334
product components, 333
promotion, 335
physical environment, 336
process, 336
redefined, 320–321

Service-sponsored franchise systems, 416
Service-sponsored retail franchise systems, 415–416
Services sweethearting, 338
Seven P's of service marketing, 333
Sex appeals, 505
Share of market budgeting, 484
Share of voice, 219
  social media, 553
Share points, 624–625
Shelf life, 311
Sherman Antitrust Act, 88–89, 102, 389, 390, 391
Shift of a demand curve, 359–360
Shopper marketing, 451–452
Shopping experience, 122
Shopping products, 266
  bases of comparison, 267
Showrooming, 611
Showstoppers, 89
Shrinkage, 449–450
Signpost items, 449
Simulated test markets, 280
Single parents, 141
Single-price retailers, 449
Single product *vs.* product line, 356
Single-zone pricing, 388–389
Situational influences, 129
Situation analysis, 40–41
  Paradise Kitchens, 59–62
60 Minutes, 213
Skateboarder, 511
Skimming pricing, 372
  in introduction stage, 292
  versus penetration pricing, 373
Slotting fees, 282
Small and medium enterprises
  as competition, 88
  exporting by, 192–193
  marketing careers in, 4
  new-product ideas, 277
  number of, 88
Small Business Administration, 2
Smart contact lenses, 435
Smartphones, 538
  apps for, 556–557
  changes over time, 556
  evaluative criteria, 125
  in future of retailing, 434
  privacy issues, 558
  video games, 556–557
Smart Planet strategy, IBM, 49–51
Smart-pricing, 513
Smart watches, 434
Smoking-related illnesses, 102–103
Sneaker News, 511
Soccer, 341–344
Social audit, 113
Social authority, of media, 542
Social class, 142
Social entrepreneurs, 29

Social forces, 74
  culture, 86–87
  demographics, 74–80
  for Facebook, 70
  identified by environmental scanning, 73
  types of, 72
Social marketing, 328
Social media, 540
  aspect of promotion, 468
  bases of comparison, 543
  blogs, 540, 541
  Carmex use of, 554–555
  classifying
    collaborative projects, 541
    content communities, 541
    media richness, 541
    self-disclosure, 541
    social networking sites, 541
    virtual game worlds, 541
    virtual social worlds, 541
  compared to traditional media, 542
  convergence of real and digital worlds, 556–557
  defining, 540
  Facebook, 543–546
  for job search, 661–662
  LinkedIn, 547–548
  and Mall of America, 463
  mobile marketing, 557–558
  multicultural audiences, 80
  number of users, 551, 554
  origin of, 540
  performance measures
    linked to inputs or costs, 552–553
    linked to outputs or revenues, 553–554
  for primary data, 218–219
  sales production, 552–553
  selection options
    audience data available, 551
    recent activity, 551
    specialized focus, 554
  and strategic marketing process, 550–551
  StuffDOT, 545–546, 561–563
  versus traditional media, 550
  Twitter, 546–547
  use by Taco Bell, 494
  user-generated content, 540
  YouTube, 548–550
Social media marketing manager, 654
Social media metrics, 219
Social mission, 26
Social needs, 131
Social networking sites, 542
Social responsibility, 16–17, **110**
  Anheuser–Busch, 100–101
  concepts of
    profit responsibility, 110–111
    societal responsibility, 111–112
    stakeholder responsibility, 111

and consumer ethics, 114–115
  goal of business, 32
  objective of pricing, 354
  social audit, 113
  sustainable development, 113–114
  Toyota, 117–120
Societal culture, 103–104
Societal marketing concept, 17
Societal responsibility
  cause marketing, 112
  definition, 111
  green marketing, 111–112
  sustainable marketing, 111
  triple-bottom line, 111
Sociocultural influences
  culture, 142–144
  family, 140–142
  personal, 137–138
  reference groups, 138–140
  social class, 142
  subcultures, 142–144
Source, 470
Spam, 608
Spark lines, 34
Special fees, 350
Specialty merchandise wholesalers, 457–458
Specialty outlets, 442
Specialty products, 266
  bases of comparison, 267
  exclusive distribution, 416–417
Speed
  factor in new-product success, 282
  need for, 122
Sponsored videos, 539
Sporting Goods Manufacturers Association, 260
Sporting News Baseball Yearbook, 240
Sports Illustrated for Kids, 140, 511
Sports marketing, 341–344
Spreadsheets, 378–379
Staff positions, 639
Stage-Gate process, 274
Stakeholder responsibility, 111
Stakeholders, 31
Standard & Poor's *Register of Corporations, Directors, and Executives,* 665
Standard markup pricing, 375
Standard test markets, 280
Starch test, 518
Stars, 37, 45
Star Wars, 205
State employment agencies, 662
State Hermitage Museum, Russia, 17, 18
Statistical areas, 78
Statistical inference, 209
Stimulus discrimination, 133
Stimulus generalization, 133
Stimulus-response presentation, 577

Stock keeping units, 268
  number of, in supermarkets, 272
Stockturn rate, 404
Stop Counterfeiting in Manufactured Goods Act, 304
Store atmosphere, 451–452
Store loyalty, 527
Store management, 655
Store manager, 654
Straight commission compensation plan, 586–587
Straight rebuy, 163, 164
  Trek Bicycle Corporation, 171
Straight salary compensation plan, 586
Strategic business unit level, 30
Strategic business units, 30, 632
  in business portfolio analysis, 36–39
  quadrants, 37–38
  sales performance, 34
Strategic channel alliances, 414
Strategic direction
  business portfolio analysis, 36–39
  current status analysis
    competencies, 35–36
    competitors, 36
    customers, 36
  diversification analysis, 39–40
Strategic marketing process, 40
  diagram of, 625
  evaluation phase
    act on deviations, 47, 640–641
    comparing results, 45
    identifying deviations, 45, 640
    marketing dashboards, 642–644
    marketing metrics, 642–644
    marketing ROI, 642
  General Mills, 620–621
    evaluation phase, 649
    implementation phase, 648
    planning phase, 648
  implementation phase
    action item list, 44
    defining tasks, responsibilities, & deadlines, 43–44
    design of marketing organization, 43
    emphasis on implementation, 634
    execution of program, 44–45
    Gantt chart, 44–45
    marketing program improvements, 634–636
    obtaining resources, 43
    organizing marketing, 638–639
    planning *vs.* execution issue, 634
    scheduling, 44
  key business practices, 622–623
  output report, 625
  planning gap, 45

planning phase
  goal setting, 42
  marketing planning
    framework, 627–630
  marketing program, 42
  market-product focus, 42
  situation analysis, 40–41
  strategic lessons, 630–633
  SWOT analysis, 40–41
  use of marketing metrics,
    626–627
  variety of marketing plans, 627
resource allocation, 623–626
and social media, 550
trends influencing
  value-based planning, 632
  value-driven strategies,
    632–633
Strategic partnerships, 119
Strategic performance, tracking
  with marketing dashboards,
    33–35
  with marketing metrics, 34–35
Strategy, 28
  at IBM, 49–51
  at 3M Corporation, 12–14
  and types of competitive market,
    356
  value-driven, 632–633
  in visionary organizations, 30–33
Strengths; *see* SWOT analysis
Strip mall, 451
Strivers, 136
Strong Interest Inventory, 660
Styling, source of, 122
Subbranding, 308
Subcultures, 142
  African Americans, 142, 143–144
  Asian Americans, 142, 144
  Hispanics, 142, 143
  largest in U.S., 142
Subliminal perception, 132
Substitutes, 88
  demand factor, 359
Success rate, 621
Suggestion selling, 577–578
Super Bowl, 138
  advertising during, 503–504
Supercenters, 442
Supermarkets
  everyday low prices, 388
  failure fees, 282
  number of stock keeping
    units, 272
  slotting fees, 282
Superpages, 512
Supplier capabilities, 152
Supplier development, 157–158
Suppliers
  and customer solutions, 579
  to JCPMedia, Inc., 152
  new-product ideas, 276
  power of, 88
  and reverse auctions, 167
  vendor-managed inventory, 426
Supplies, 267

Supply chain, 427–422
  flow and output, 425
  integrated, 424
  versus marketing channels,
    421–422
  Mary Kay, Inc., 201–202
  order cycle time, 426
Supply chain management
  at Amazon, 431
  in auto industry, 422–423
  cross-docking, 424
  customer service factors,
    425–426
  definition, 422
  information technology, 425
  and logistics management, 422
  and marketing strategy
    alignment, 423
    Dell Inc., 424
    Walmart, 424–425
Supply chain manager, 654
Supply partnership
  characteristics, 159–160
  Milsco Corporation, 160
Support products, 267
Surcharges, 350
Surge pricing, 382–383
Survey of buyers' intentions, 228
Survey Research Center, University
  of Michigan, 82
Survival, objective of pricing, 354
Survivors, 137
Sustainability, 338
Sustainable competitive advantage,
  Paradise Kitchens, 57, 58
Sustainable development, 113
  benefits for consumers, 114
  recent initiatives, 113–114
Sustainable marketing, 111
Sustainable procurement, 160
Sweepstakes
  advantages and disadvantages, 520
  fraudulent, 527
  and legislation, 521–522
  objectives, 520
  types of, 521
SWOT analysis, 40–41, 41
  basis of, 41
  Ben and Jerry's, 41–342
  marketing actions from, 41
  Paradise Kitchens, 59–60
Syndicated panel data, 211
Synergies
  versus cannibalization, 241–242
  organizational, 241
Synergy analysis, 628
  marketing synergies, 629
  RD-manufacturing synergies, 630

T

Tangibility of services, 330
Target audience, 54, 55
  for advertising, 502
  behavioral targeting, 482

business buyers, 476
college students, 477
identifying, 482
intermediaries, 476
Target market(s), 9
  criteria for selecting
    compatibility with
      organizational objectives, 251
    cost of reaching segments, 251
    expected growth, 251
    market size, 251
  Paradise Kitchens, 63
Target market coverage
  exclusive distribution, 416–417
  intensive distribution, 416
  selective distribution, 417
Target pricing, 374–375
Target profit pricing, 377
**Target return-on-investment
  pricing, 378**
**Target return-on-sales pricing,
  377–378**
Target return pricing objective, 354
Target time, 637
Tasks
  defining, 43–44
  scheduling, 636–638
Team selling, 573
  conference selling, 573
  customer value from, 574
  seminar selling, 573
Teaser advertising, 138
Technological advances/change
  benefit of product life cycle, 296
  and business models, 32
  effect on marketing, 85–86
  in service industry, 338
  in television, 510
Technological forces
  and data analytics, 86
  for Facebook, 70
  and Geek Squad, 95–96
  identified by environmental
    scanning, 73
  impact on consumer value,
    85–86
  technology of tomorrow, 74–75
  types of, 72
Technology, 84
  changes in retailing from,
    434–435
  salesforce automation, 589
  salesforce communication,
    589–590
  of tomorrow, 84–85
  vending machines, 444
Teen People, 511
Telemarketing, 446
  inbound, 572
  National Do Not Call Registry,
    105, 446–447, 490, 576
  outbound, 572
  sales, 446
Telephone Consumer Protection
  Act of 1991, 91, 576
Telephone interviews, 215

Television
  ethnic diversity on, 79
  product placements in, 524
  self-regulation, 92
Television advertising
  advantages and disadvantages,
    509
  cost disadvantage, 510
  costs of, 507
  expenditures, 507
  households with TV, 509
  infomercials, 510
  Super Bowl ads, 503–504
  viewing habit changes, 509–510
  wasted coverage, 510
Television home shopping, 445
Television ratings, 212
Test marketing, 280
Test markets, 220
Test-results databases, 487
Test screenings, 206
Theater tests, 517
Thinkers, 136, 137
Third-party logistics providers, 427
Threats; *see* SWOT analysis
3D technology, 85
Tiffany/Walmart strategy, 242, 243
Time, 472, 511, 557
Time, in supply chain
  management, 426
Time-based agenda, 637
Time to delivery, 542
Time to market, 282
Time utility, 409, 436–437
  definition, 18
  from marketspace, 598–599
Together Green, 119
Top Gun, 523
Top management, 28–29
  ethical behavior, 107
Total cost (TC), 362
Total Guitar, 368
Total logistics cost, 425
Total revenue (TR), 361
Toy Story, 523
Tracking studies, 206
Trade associations, 669–670
Trade discounts, 386
Trade feedback effect, 176
Trade-in allowances, 387
Trademark, 303
Trademark Law Revision Act, 90
Trademark protection, 303
Trademarks, 89, 104
  becoming generic, 90
  court ruling on, 90
Trade name, 303
**Trade-oriented sales
  promotions, 524**
  allowances, 524–525
  cooperative advertising, 525
  discounts, 524–525
  salesforce training, 525
Trade promotions, 524
Trade regulations, 191
Trade salesperson, 654

Trading down, 302
Trading up, 302
Traditional auction, 166
Traditional family, 140
Traditional media *vs.* social
    media, 542
Traffic generation, 489
Training
    of distributors' salesforces, 525
    for media, 542
    for retailing careers, 655–656
    of salesforce, 586
    Xerox salesforce, 594
Transactional function, 408–409
Transactional websites, 612
Transit advertising, 514
Transnational firms, 182
Transparency International, 106, 107
Travel Weekly, 288
Trend analysis, 72–73
Trend extrapolation, 228–229
Trends, rising, 302
Trial, 291, 483
Trial close, 580
Triple-bottom line, 111
Truck jobbers, 458
Tuition, 333, 350
Twilight Saga, 240
Twitter, 546–547
    in brand manager's strategy, 547
    compared to other social
        media, 543
    number of users, 546, 551
    overview, 543
Tying arrangements, 91, 420–421

U

Ultimate consumers, 18
Unaided recall, 518
Unethical behavior
    bribes and kickbacks, 105–106,
        107, 186
    by consumers, 114–115
    economic espionage, 105, 106
Uniform delivered pricing, 388
Unique visitors, social media, 553
United Kingdom, Direct Mail
    Association, 490
United Nations, 74
United States
    changing values, 81
    costs of economic espionage, 185
    cultural changes, 80–81
    Hispanic population, 60
    household income, 83
    households, 76–77
    Index of Consumer Sentiment
        1963-2015, 82
    merchandise trade, 176
    National Parks, 119
    number of companies, 154
    number of government units, 155
    number of retailers, 154
    number of small businesses, 88

number of wholesalers, 154
perspective on world trade, 177
population, 75
population shifts, 77–78
racial and ethnic diversity, 78–80
recessions 1973-2009, 82
revenues of nonprofits, 326
services percentage of Gross
    domestic product, 322
statistical areas, 78
subcultures, 142–144
supercenters, 442
survey on cigarette prices, 361
top five franchises, 440
United States Air Force, 635
United States Army recruiting
    program, 131
United States Supreme Court
    on price setting, 102
    on trademarks, 90
Unit variable cost (UVC), 362
Unit volume, 354
Universities, 277
University of Florida, 290
University of Virginia Health
    System, 338
Unsought products, 266
    bases of comparison, 267
Upper class, 142
Urgency close, 580
U.S. Census Bureau, 28, 74, 75,
    76, 83, 211
U.S. Green Retail Association, 439
U.S. News & World Report, 511, 657
U.S. Patent and Trademark Office,
    303, 304
Usage barriers, 298
Usage instructions, 133
Usage rate, 244
    and behavioral segmentation, 248
    80/20 rule, 246
USA Today, 511, 512
USA Today Ad Meter, 504
User-generated content (UGC),
    540
Users, 163
    social media, 553
Utilitarianism, 108
Utility, 18
    from marketspace, 598–599
    types of, 409, 436–437

V

Valid assumptions, 631
VALS framework
    achievement-motivated
        groups, 136
    diagram, 135
    high- and low-resource
        groups, 137
    ideals-motivated groups, 136
    motivation, 135–136
    resources, 136
    self-expression motivated
        groups, 136

Value, 351
    assessing, 124–125
    buying, 125–126
    changing
        downsizing, 302–303
        trading down, 302
        trading up, 302
    co-create, 324
    created by personal selling, 570
    creation of, 632
    customer perception of, 11
    perception and price, 374
    realizing, 126–127
    seeking, 124
Value added, 448
Value barriers, 298
Value-based planning, 632
Value consciousness, 81
Value-driven strategies, 632–633
Value pricing, 352
    Spirit Airlines, 352
    Vizio, Inc., 348–349
Values, 142, 185
    changes in, 81
    corporate, 632–633
    examples, 11
    IBM, 50
    societal, 104
    varying, 134
Variable cost (VC), 362
    Washburn Guitar, 368
Variety
    buyers' interest in, 417
    of marketing plans, 627
Vending machines, 443–444
    reverse, 86
Vendor-managed inventory
    (VMI), 426
Vendors
    definition, 161
    minority-owned, 157–158
    women-owned, 157–158
Venture capital firms, 277
Vertical channel conflict, 419
Vertical integration, legality
    of, 420
Vertical marketing systems
    administered systems, 416
    contractual systems, 415–416
    corporate systems, 414–415
Vertical marketing systems, 414
Vertical organizational markets,
    165–166
Vertical price fixing, 390
Video bloggers, 549
Video games, product placements
    in, 523
Viral marketing, 609
Virtual game worlds, 541
Virtual reality in advertising, 498–499
Virtual social worlds, 542
Vision
    examples, 11
    Facebook, 70
    StuffDOT, 562
Visionary organizations, 30–33

Vocational interest tests, 659–660
Voice, The, 521
VR headsets, 498

W

Wages, 350
Wall Street Journal, 212, 288,
    512, 665
Wants, 8–9
Warehouse clubs, 450
Warranty, 133, 312
    legislation on, 313
    types of, 313
Wasted coverage, 510
Weaknesses; *see* SWOT analysis
Wearable technology, 434–435
Web communities, 608
Webrooming, 611
Websites
    blogs, 608
    customization, 617
    design elements, 602–603
    eight-second rule, 606
    favorites for workday
        shopping, 611
    marketing metrics, 604
    performance measures, 603–604
    Pizza Hut, 617
    promotional, 612–613
    transactional, 612
Wheel of retailing, 453
    new forms of outlets, 454
    new products from, 453–454
Whistle-blowers, 107
Wholesalers
    and channel conflict, 419
    definition, 408
    number of, 154
    pricing by, 383–384
Wholesaler-sponsored voluntary
    chains, 415, 439
Wholesaling
    agents, 458
    brokers, 458
    manufacturer's branch
        office, 458
    manufacturer's sales office, 458
    merchant wholesalers, 457–458
Wiki, 540
Wikipedia, 275, 541, 633
Winter Olympics of 2016, 485
Wired magazine, 471
Wireless technology, 444
Wireless telephone industry as
    oligopoly, 87
Women
    as car buyers, 122–123
    changing attitudes, 80–81
    as consumer base, 80
    percent of world population, 74
    working in auto industry, 122
Women-owned vendors,
    157–158
Women's Running, 288

Word of mouth, 138
buzz, 138
and BzzAgent, 139
magnified by Internet, 138
negative, 138
online shopping, 609
Workload method, 584
Workplace diversity, 158
World population, 74–75
World trade
barter in, 176–177
countertrade, 176–177
decline of protectionism, 178–179

and economic integration,
179–181
global perspective,
176–177
and income growth, 190
International Anti-Dumping
and Fair Competition
Act, 186
leaders in merchandise trade,
176
trade feedback effect, 176
trade regulations, 191
U.S. perspective, 177

**World Trade Organization
(WTO), 179,** 322
Worldwide marketing program; *see*
Marketing program

Y

Yachting, 511
Yellow Book, 512
Yellow Pages
advantages and disadvantages, 509
high level of use, 512
number of, 512

**Yield management
pricing, 375**
form of dynamic
pricing, 382
Young married couples, 141
Young singles, 141
YouTube, 548
in brand manager's strategy,
549–550
compared to other social media,
543
number of users, 551
overview, 548–549